MICHAEL PALIN established his reputation with *Monty Python's Flying Circus* and *Ripping Yarns*. His work also includes several films with Monty Python, as well as *The Missionary*, *A Private Function*, an award-winning performance as the hapless Ken in *A Fish Called Wanda*, *American Friends* and *Fierce Creatures*. His television credits include two films for the BBC's *Great Railway Journeys*, the plays *East of Ipswich* and *Number 27*, and Alan Bleasdale's *GBH*. He has written seven bestselling travel books to accompany his series *Around the World in 80 Days*, *Pole to Pole*, *Full Circle*, *Hemingway Adventure*, *Sahara*, *Himalaya* and *New Europe*. He is also the author of a number of children's stories, the play *The Weekend* and the novel *Hemingway's Chair*. In 2006 the first volume of his diaries, *1969–1979: The Python Years*, spent many weeks on the bestseller lists. In 2008 an updated special edition of *Around the World in 80 Days* was published to coincide with his BBC documentary *Around the World in 20 Years*. Visit his website at www.palinstravels.co.uk.

BASIL PAO began his photographic career in 1980 on his return to Hong Kong after ten years in the United States, where he was an art director for Atlantic, Polygram and Warner Bros. He first worked with Michael Palin on the design for book accompanying Monty Python's *Life of Brian*. They have since collaborated on the books based on his seven travel series. In 2007 he wrote and photographed *China Revealed: A Portrait of the Rising Dragon*.

SAHARA

MICHAEL PALIN

Photographs by Basil Pao

PHOENIX

A PHOENIX PAPERBACK

First published in Great Britain in 2002
by Weidenfeld & Nicolson
This paperback edition published in 2003
by Phoenix,
an imprint of Orion Books Ltd,
Orion House, 5 Upper St Martin's Lane,
London WC2H 9EA

An Hachette UK company

3 5 7 9 10 8 6 4

A CIP catalogue record for this book
is available from the British Library.

ISBN 978-0-7538-1739-1

Printed and bound in Great Britain by Clays Ltd, St Ives plc

The Orion Publishing Group's policy is to use papers that
are natural, renewable and recyclable products and
made from wood grown in sustainable forests. The logging
and manufacturing processes are expected to conform to
the environmental regulations of the country of origin.

www.orionbooks.co.uk

For Helen, Tom, Will and Rachel

INTRODUCTION

My father was in charge of the Export Department of a steelworks and every Christmas he received an enormous box of dates from their agent in Algeria, addressed to a Mr E. M. Palm. I remember wondering if he should tell them, but he never bothered. Perhaps he thought the supply of dates might dry up if they discovered his name wasn't Palm.

I didn't want them to stop coming either, not because of the dates, but because of the box they came in. The illustration on the packet fuelled powerfully romantic fantasies of somewhere hotter, drier and even more exotic than south Yorkshire; a place where men with turbans, baggy velvet pants and wicked moustaches reclined under palm trees with veiled and sequinned ladies, whilst their faithful camels stood in picturesque silhouette against the setting sun.

The first 'proper' book I was ever given was *Tales from the Arabian Nights*. Its seductive illustrations, by A. E. Jackson, combined with the date boxes to fan a precocious fascination for things of the desert. Curved swords, soft silks, tassels and see-through skirts. Mirages and genies, huge jellies and lubricious oils and unguents. The desert world seemed, apart from the odd beheading, to be a place of complete sensual fulfilment. Even delight itself was Turkish.

Almost fifty years later there came a chance to expose my childhood fantasies to the harsh glare of reality.

In the first spring of the new millennium I met up with Roger Mills, director of many of the travel programmes I've done, at a pub opposite Notting Hill police station. Over a pint or two he suggested a journey through Francophone Africa, those huge and empty countries from Cameroon northwards, once loosely federated as part of the French empire. Rarely visited by British television, they might provide fresh pickings and new discoveries.

I got home, unfolded a map, and saw one word spread across most of these countries. Sahara.

The French empire was interesting, but it had come and gone. The Sahara is a potent, evocative reality. It is one of the world's great brands. No one name so completely epitomises an environment. Oceans can be Atlantic or Pacific or Indian, mountains can be Himalayas or Andes or Alps, but if you want to convey desert, you only have to say 'Sahara'.

It embodies scale and mystery, the thin line between survival and destruction, the power to take life or to transform it. A self-contained, homogenous, identifiable world, uncompromising and irreducible.

In other words, a challenge. And by no means an easy one.

As big as the United States, with a population the size of Norfolk, the Sahara is only 15 per cent sand, and though the great ergs, the sand seas, are among the most exquisitely beautiful landscapes I've ever seen, there is a dark side. The Sahara is also a killer, scorching the life out of crops, people, and all but the most tenacious living creatures. It's growing larger every year as drought turns pasture back into sand, which the remorseless desert wind carries into towns and villages until they die of suffocation. It has its share of war and conflict. Many areas we wanted to see were inaccessible because of minefields and military activity.

Yet how close it is to us. The Sahara lies just beyond the borders of Europe. The heart of the desert is three hours' flying time from Paris, four hours from London. This proximity is not lost on the many thousands of sub-Saharan Africans who cross the desert to escape what they see as poor, unstable and oppressive regimes back home.

Today, the Sahara, far from being a cosy date-box illusion, has become a bridge from Africa into Europe, and a bridge that is increasingly well used by those prepared to risk their lives for a better life on the other side of the Mediterranean. If the Sahara was my fantasy, Europe is theirs. Perhaps they will learn from their journey, as I did from mine, that fantasy and experience never quite match up.

Michael Palin, London, 2002
www.palinstravels.co.uk

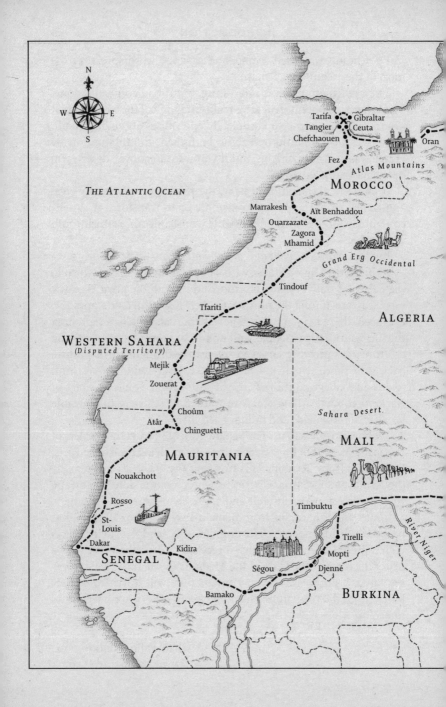

N
W · E
S

THE ATLANTIC OCEAN

Tarifa · Gibraltar
Tangier · Ceuta
Chefchaouen
Oran

Fez
Atlas Mountains
MOROCCO

Marrakesh · Aït Benhaddou
Ouarzazate
Zagora
Mhamid
Grand Erg Occidental

Tindouf
ALGERIA

Tfariti

WESTERN SAHARA
(Disputed Territory)

Mejik
Zouerat

Choûm
Atâr · Chinguetti
MAURITANIA

Sahara Desert

MALI

Nouakchott

Rosso
Timbuktu

St-Louis
Tirelli
Dakar · Kidira
Mopti
SENEGAL
Ségou · Djenné
Bamako
BURKINA

River Niger

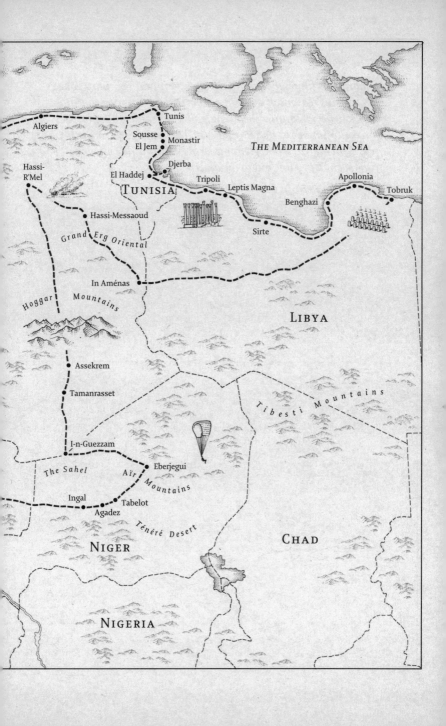

Sahara was filmed between February 2001 and February 2002. For various reasons, it was impossible to shoot it as one continuous journey. Summer heat and all-year-round bureaucracy forced a number of breaks upon us. The diary days in the text represent days at work, give or take the very rare day off, and not time spent travelling out to the desert.

CONTENTS

GIBRALTAR

Day One

═══════════⌐═══════════

GIBRALTAR

Only 300 miles from the Sahara Desert there is a place where brass bands play, warm beer is served and a blue lamp marks the police station. Where people shop at Marks & Spencer and twenty-one gun salutes sound on royal birthdays. Where Noël Coward played cabaret and John Lennon got married.

This corner of a foreign land that seems forever England is a gnarled limestone rock, nearly 4 miles long and 1400 feet high, tucked into Spain's lower regions like a prostate, dominating the dozen miles of ocean that separate Europe from Africa.

For the Berber chief Tariq Ibn Ziyad, who first settled on the Rock thirteen centuries ago, it held the promise of escape from the hostile Sahara and a stepping stone to the rich underbelly of Europe. It became known as Jebel el Tariq, Tariq's mountain, which, eroded down to the single word Gibraltar, it has remained ever since.

The Britishness of Gibraltar, which began with Admiral Rooke's invasion in 1704, is well entrenched. Contemplating my map of North Africa outside Pickwick's Pub, I order a coffee. No messing with *latte* or *machiato* here.

'Coop or Moog?' I'm asked in a thick Geordie accent.

I choose cup.

Cars are squeezed into a pleasant shady square beside me. Buildings are squeezed around the cars: an attractive colonial house with deep balconies and freshly painted wrought-iron railings on one side, the handsome Georgian façade of the garrison library on the other and, next to it, the offices of the *Gibraltar Chronicle*, the veteran local newspaper, which broke the news of Nelson's victory at Trafalgar.

For me, a first-timer in Gibraltar, there have already been surprises.

First of all, that there are buildings of quality which are not just selling duty-free booze or fish and chips, and secondly, that Gibraltar's Britishness is one layer of a deceptively international cake. The balconied, green-shuttered cottages that stretch up the steep alleyways leading off Main Street were largely built by Portuguese and Genoese, and the Catholic cathedral was converted from a mosque by the Spanish. There are, I'm told, more working synagogues on Gibraltar than in the whole of Spain. The Alameda gardens reflect Andalusian taste. The uncharitable view is that Gibraltar is an ordnance depot reinventing itself as a tax haven, but the reality is more complicated and a lot more attractive.

Nevertheless, it is Britishness that holds this polyglot community together. Sitting on the terrace of the Rock Hotel as the day fades, it is quite possible to believe that the sun will never set on this tenacious shred of Empire. Sipping a cocktail, surrounded by comfortable, chintzy, Home Counties decor and the soft sound of *Daily Telegraph*s slipping from snoozing laps, I imagine the Rock of Gibraltar as a liner, loosing its moorings and sailing slowly off, bearing inside its crumbling white flanks the last traces of the old order. This, I must admit, is after a couple of quite generous whiskies, of the sort I am unlikely to find elsewhere on this trip, together with marmalade, eggs and bacon, cups of tea, pints of beer, *Match of the Day* and all those things that I miss idiotically when I'm in foreign parts – and parts don't come much more foreign than the Sahara Desert.

Later, I settle into bed and with one long, last, loving glance at the Corby trouser press, turn out the light.

Day Two

ACROSS THE STRAIT

At the highest point of the Rock of Gibraltar, where a sheer cliff face plunges 1400 feet into the Mediterranean, there is a gun emplacement called O'Hara's Battery capable of lobbing artillery shells from Europe into Africa. I'm assured it's never been used in anger and, indeed, as I climb the last few steps on this idyllic Mediterranean morning, the only signs of anger are from seagulls swooping at my head to warn me off their nests.

From up here, the confrontation of the continents is quite a sight to behold. The two land masses don't just meet, they rise to the occasion. The white cliffs of Gibraltar facing up to the serrated black crest of Jebel Musa on the Moroccan shore. The Greeks and Romans were aware of the symmetry and called the twin peaks the Pillars of Hercules, the end of the known world, beyond which lay outer darkness.

Gibraltar remains protective to the last, as if testing my resolve to take on something as bleak and inimical as the Sahara. Since the beginning of human history people have been trying to leave the desert behind, from Tariq Ibn Ziyad and the Islamic armies who crossed the Strait in the eighth century, to the African migrants trying to cross it today. On the morning news there is a report of a boat-load of immigrants capsizing in the Strait last night. Amongst them were three pregnant women. They were only saved from drowning because one of them carried a mobile telephone. I try to find a Spanish newspaper for more details, but no Spanish dailies are sold anywhere in Gibraltar. I sense a glimmer of paranoia here, as if the natural siege mentality that seems to hold Gibraltarians together might be threatened by too much information.

So I'm not persuaded to linger, not by the fine books and leather armchairs of the garrison library, nor by the sound of the British Grenadiers, nor even by the sight of the midday flight back to London roaring across the airport runway, which also happens to be the main road out of Gibraltar.

Once the plane has raced past us and soared out over the Atlantic, the barrier opens and it's a short walk to the frontier. This is not a happy place, for either side. Spain has never concealed its irritation over what it considers British occupation of Spanish territory, and the referendum of 1967 in which Gibraltarians voted overwhelmingly to remain British was followed by closure of the frontier for sixteen years.

Now things are less confrontational but just as niggly. The Spanish examine drivers' papers with elaborate care, causing huge traffic jams, and the Gibraltarians reply with a large sign pointing out who's to blame: 'Gibraltar regrets the inconvenience caused to you due to frontier restrictions imposed by the Spanish authorities contrary to your European rights to free movement'.

The next sign we encounter reads 'Policía', and after a perfunctory going over we're out the back door of a long, low, anonymous customs shed and into Spain, where a huge welcoming billboard directs us to the nearest McDonald's.

The ferries that cross the Strait of Gibraltar leave from Algeciras, 3 miles from the frontier. We board a solid, ponderous old vessel called *City Of Algeciras*, which will take one and a half hours to cover the dozen nautical miles between here and Africa. As the new generation of lightweight ferries has clipped the crossing time to thirty-five minutes, I'm not surprised to hear that this is her final voyage.

I'm puzzled, though, by the lack of any ceremony. If this had been, say, the last journey of an Isle of Wight ferry, it would surely be full of people in anoraks pointing cameras and tape-recording the last blasts of the ship's horn. Instead, it's like a ghost ship. In the saloon the television screens beam American basketball to rows of empty seats. In the main lounge 'Don't Let the Sun Go Down on Me' thuds out to a few thin Moors with wispy beards and close-cropped black hair.

A vigorous westerly rips in as we reach the open sea, where the bottle-neck entrance to the Mediterranean shrinks to a mere 9 miles. This is dangerous water, a tide race of accelerating currents and a thousand ship movements a day, a difficult stretch to navigate at the best of times, but in a tiny boat, at the dead of night, potentially suicidal.

The bonus of this urgent west wind is a panorama of dramatic clarity. The fingers of Europe and Africa almost touching and between them, dead centre, the sun merging slowly with the horizon. I feel for a moment a jubilant sense of freedom, of being in limbo, beyond tribal loyalties, national boundaries, anthems, flags, customs, papers, permissions and prejudices, free from all restraints except the elements themselves. I feel positively Homeric. Then a particularly fierce gust picks me up and hurls me, bodily, into the bar.

MOROCCO

Day Three

═══════◈═══════

TANGIER

'When I meet fellow Americans travelling about here in North Africa, I ask them, "What did you expect to find here?" Almost without exception, regardless of the way they express it, the answer reduced to its simplest terms is a sense of mystery.'

Thus wrote Paul Bowles, the American writer who adopted Tangier, in the book that lies where it fell from my bed last night.

Earlier in the evening, a group of elderly Moroccan musicians had played a thin, tinkling version of 'Happy Birthday' for me in the hotel restaurant. It was such an uncompromisingly Arab sound that it was only halfway through that I realised it was 'Happy Birthday' at all, and for that reason alone I shall treasure the memory of it.

It's six o'clock now and I'm trying to shake off the first hangover of my fifty-ninth year. The new day glows cruelly bright behind the curtains and I can't ignore it. I swing myself out of bed, surprised by the cool touch of a marble floor, and throw open the curtains. But the smarter the hotel the less easy it is these days to throw open the curtains, and by the time I've found the right cord to pull and disentangled the net from the main drape I'm seriously irritated and irreversibly awake.

The view is less spectacular and much friendlier than I'd expected. It's a painter's view. Below me is a small verdant garden, dominated by the luxurious crown of a palm tree and a solitary Norfolk pine standing with its branches out like a cake stand. Running roughly in line from west to east are a harbour wall, with a ferry boat alongside, a distant beach already covered with tiny figures and, rising gently behind the curving bay, the headland, beyond which a pipeline dives beneath the Strait, carrying 10,000 million cubic metres of Algerian natural gas into Europe every year.

The town is compact. Narrow streets rise and fall around low hills and their damp cobbles catch the morning sun. The buildings look more French than Spanish, with red roofs and white-plastered walls, sooty and streaked by the rain, from which sprouts a canopy of television aerials and satellite dishes. The sharp clarity of the light is softened by the drowsy mix of early-morning sounds – dogs barking, doves cooing, a fishing-boat engine springing to life.

I'm excited. I know there's a way to go before we reach the Sahara but I'm on the starting grid. Tangier, where Europe clings onto Africa and Africa clings onto Europe, has a fine record for great departures. Among my birthday presents from the crew, piled up beside a bottle of duty-free champagne (empty), are two books about Ibn Battuta, one of the greatest travellers of all time and a Tangerine, born in this town in 1304. At the age of twenty-one, he set out on the first stage of a 75,000-mile adventure through most of the known world, across the Sahara to Timbuktu, up to Spain and through Europe to Persia, Arabia, Sumatra, India and China, returning home thirty years later to write a book about it.

Not a bad role model.

The El Minzah Hotel opens onto a busy street leading up from the port and the market. There are cars, but they're well outnumbered by human traffic. Berber women, tough, pugnacious and wide, plod up the hill as if wearing all the clothes they own at the same time. Their low centres of gravity allow them to carry virtually anything. I wouldn't be surprised to see one of them with a small car on her back. The men, by contrast, don't carry, they push. Covered from head to foot in thick woollen burnouses (the wind that's keeping the clouds away is brisk and chilly), they steer rubber-wheeled handcarts full of bits of this and that up the centre of the road. Amongst the crowd are men in sharp suits doing nothing but standing and looking around. The admirable Alan, our fixer, tells me they're probably policemen. At dinner last night a local man went out of his way to deny that Morocco was a police state.

'Not at all,' he insisted, 'it is a *well-policed* state.'

There's an Anglican church near by which was painted by Matisse, one of a number of artists, from Delacroix to Francis Bacon, drawn to Tangier by the quality of light and the tolerant hedonistic atmosphere, which also attracted writers like Bowles and Joe Orton and William Burroughs. Putting thoughts of hedonism aside for an hour or two, I fish out my only tie and walk over there for Sunday Service. My parents would have been proud of me.

Walking to church in Sheffield was never like this. The entrance to St Andrew's, Tangier is virtually obscured this morning by a Berber street market. Doughty ladies from the mountains have taken over the pavement, spreading in front of them a fragrant assortment of fresh cheeses, onions, carrots, thick sheaves of mint, coriander, sage and rosemary.

Somewhere behind the piles of food I locate two white gateposts, which mark the way into the churchyard. Once inside, I feel like Alice in Wonderland. Nothing is quite what you expect it to be.

Down by the gatepost, squeezed into a corner of the wall, is a makeshift wooden construction that I take to be a kennel, but which, on closer examination, proves to contain a bearded old man, who glares back at me. A moment later an attractive Arab woman pops in through the gate, squats down and begins to dictate a letter to him.

Leaving the boxed scribe behind, I walk up the shaded path. On either side of me is a thick, entangled, but artfully managed secret garden of cypress, gum and false pepper trees, jacaranda and creepers and assorted thick bushes, in the recesses of which I can dimly make out graves and headstones. On closer inspection most of these bear the names of people from the Scottish Highlands. Curiouser and curiouser.

Then there is the church itself. It emerges from all this greenery looking like something out of the Cotswolds, except that the tower from which the blue cross of St Andrew flies is decorated with Moorish tiles. The church porch has an Islamic horseshoe arch and inside is a chancel arch, around which the Lord's Prayer is picked out in Arabic.

I'm warmly welcomed by a manic garrulous Moroccan, in white *djellaba* and black astrakhan hat, given to fits of giggling, lunging kisses and a curious staccato English punctuated regularly by the phrase 'thank you very much'. He introduces himself as Mustapha Chergui, the church caretaker. Thank you very much. For thirty-eight years, thank you very much. In between pointing out such features as the coffered chancel ceiling, carved from cedar wood by master craftsmen from Fez, and the display of arum lilies, which he fetches every Sunday from the market, he has to rush away to help Mary Evans, one of the churchwardens, prepare the hymn books.

Mustapha Chergui and Mary Evans are not really off the same menu. She is quintessentially English, pronounces lost 'lorst' and, very much in the tradition of Tangier travellers, is just back from Syria and Jordan.

The congregation begins to assemble. Only a smattering of the 150-strong British community comes to church, one of them being an engaging Australian-born journalist called Jonathan Dawson.

Thanks to him, I soon know all the dramatis personae, that Mrs Evans, the churchwarden, married 'one of the few straight chaplains the church ever had' and that by far the greater proportion of the congregation are Nigerians involved in getting themselves and others across the Strait of Gibraltar.

So here we all are: the British upper-class ladies, the Nigerian migrants, Mustapha the sexton and myself, all leafing through our books to find Hymn Number One Hundred and Forty-Four and in our own ways, and often our own keys, giving voice to 'Glorious Things Of Thee Are Spoken'.

The Nigerians treat the service as a moveable feast, coming and going according to the demands of their mobile phones, which go off frequently, often in the middle of prayers. (Jonathan tells me that the Christmas service was constantly interrupted by mobiles playing 'Jingle Bells'.) No-one seems to mind them nipping out to do business during Matins. Their attendance rate today is impressive, if variable, rising from eight before the collection to twenty-five afterwards.

At the end, when we've filed out and the chaplain has shaken hands with everyone, I ask him about the Nigerians. He says life is precarious for them here. The Moroccans arrest them and then dump them back at the Algerian border. The chaplain introduces me to a young man called Regis, a Catholic with a plastic rosary around his neck. He has just walked back from the border by foot. It took him four days, but he didn't dare take public transport in case he was arrested again. Once again, I find myself wondering what it is about their own country that makes these young men risk arrest, beatings, drownings and the Sahara Desert.

Then something reminds me I'm still in Wonderland.

Hobbling out behind Regis is a tiny Englishwoman with a fierce stare. Her name is Lady Baird. She must be well into her eighties and yet has come to live here relatively recently. When I ask her what brought her to Tangier, she replies crisply, 'A garden! The most beautiful garden in Morocco.'

I'm about to ask her whether this wasn't a lot to take on at such a late age, when, on seeing Jonathan Dawson pass by, Lady Baird indignantly indicates her right leg.

'You see that?' she cries. 'Birdie did that!'

'Birdie?'

'His bird. Bit me on the leg.'

Birdie, it transpires, is a cockerel who lives in Jonathan's apartment.

He doesn't attempt to deny it.

'Bit a great hole in her leg,' he confirms.

I said he was lucky not to be sued. Jonathan looks uncharacteristically sheepish.

'Well, he did bite a very distinguished American woman and she thought it was rather funny, but after three courses of antibiotics and massive doctor's bills, I'm afraid it was a bit of a strain on the friendship.'

We walk down the path away from the church. Through the trees, across the road, I can see a façade with the faded lettering, 'Grand Hôtel Villa De France'. Green louvered shutters swing in the wind. It was from one of those rooms, Room 35, that Matisse looked out and painted this unique Anglo-Arab church and the trees and the sea beyond, as it all looked ninety years ago.

'He is a misogynist, I'm afraid,' says Jonathan, by way of explanation. 'Only ever bites women.'

I don't think he meant Matisse. But who knows.

The day ends on twin notes of anticlimax, both football related. Roger wants to film activity on the town beach, the public playing fields of Tangier. To integrate me in this happy recreational scene he has persuaded a local team to let me have a kick around with them. Considering their average age is about sixteen and there are distinct language problems, they do everything to make it easy for the elderly Englishman thrust into their midst, and I'm eager to show that, despite being two years short of sixty, I still know a few tricks.

One of these is the sliding tackle, which, together with the hefty up-field boot, was the basic essential of football as I was taught it. I win the ball, but, this being sand and not the Wembley turf I'm used to, I'm unable to move it, and as one of my legs sprints off the other one stays firmly beneath the ball. As my groin is prised apart I have no option but to fall flat on my back. I see the camera crew chuckling away on the touchline. Good old Michael, really entering into the spirit. This gives me fatal encouragement to get up and race off after the action. One more kick and something goes twang internally, and I hobble around, cursing. More laughter from the camera crew, and it's several minutes before they realise that this is not an Equity performance, but for real.

To have so recklessly disabled myself so early in the journey could pose all sorts of problems, but at least I satisfied the first rule of filming – if you're going to get hurt, get hurt on camera.

Day Four

TANGIER TO CHEFCHAOUEN

Woken again by the intensity of the fresh-risen sun, a glare so fierce I think there might be a blaze outside my window. But it's bright rather than hot, and in the shaded street outside the hotel I can understand why the men are wearing thick jackets and have the hoods of their burnouses pulled up.

'Morocco is a cold country with a hot sun.' Jonathan Dawson squints into the light. 'That's what someone told me when I came here. If you're sitting in the shade over there you might be freezing your tits off, but when you're sitting out here it's hot, you know.'

We're on the terrace of the Café Tingis in the Petit Socco, a square once renowned for all sorts of naughtiness. Jonathan, with his piercing blue eyes, swept-back silvery hair and air of languid amusement, seems to thrive on Tangier. He came here in 1992 to do a piece for the *Evening Standard* and stayed.

He sighs a little regretfully as his *café au lait* arrives.

'They used to sell booze, all these caffs.' In 1956, after Morocco won independence, liquor was banned from the medina and the party, if not over, at least went underground.

'So Tangier is a shadow of its former racy self?'

Jonathan rakes the square with a half-smile. 'Everything is here if you want it. You can have boys, girls, cockerels or anything you want . . .'

'Drugs?'

'It's not, er . . . legal, but it's sort of slightly not illegal. I don't encourage it,' he says, before adding cheerfully, 'I've got a great friend coming to stay. She's a dope-smoking grandmother. You should be interviewing her.'

For Jonathan, Tangier remains a tolerant place, where you can be what you want to be. He likes the sea and the beaches and the fresh-ness of the food, the fact that it can get cold enough for open fires and, of course, the prices.

'You can buy a villa here for less than the cost of a London base-ment.'

We finish our coffees. The noise levels in the square are rising. Laughter, argument, the booming of a television set from the dark-ened interior of a café opposite. It's time for us to move on south, but Jonathan won't let us go just yet.

'I've got some lovely wine. Come back for a quick gargle.'

Jonathan lives not in a villa but in a top-floor apartment crowded with books, paintings and fine furniture. Across this fine furniture struts Birdie, the confident comb-tossing, lady-pecking cockerel with whom Jonathan lives.

Jonathan shouts at him frequently, but Birdie takes very little notice.

'He's not an egg-laying bird. He's not house-trained. He's a lia-bility.'

'So why do you keep him?'

'Oh well, I'm alone and he's alone and we keep each other company, I suppose. He likes a bit of telly actually. He likes a cup of tea and a bit of telly.'

'Does he like a gargle?'

'Well, he used to have a bit of wine with porridge, but I stopped that. He got a bit fond of it.'

At this point Jonathan notices my empty glass and shouts towards the kitchen.

'Mr Lassan!'

Mr Lassan, the third member of this ménage, is Jonathan's manservant and a compulsive kleptomaniac.

'I had a remote control bell for Mr Lassan, but he sold it when I was in Marrakesh.'

Mr Lassan turns out to be a middle-aged Moroccan with a curious lopsided leer, which Jonathan puts down to the fact that he has a new set of teeth.

'He can't stop smiling because they won't close.'

Apparently, Mr Lassan keeps losing his teeth. He says they go missing when he takes them out in the hammam, the public baths, but Jonathan suspects him of selling them. 'I mean what sort of man takes his teeth out at the hammam?'

Mr Lassan tops up our glasses, turns on his heel and leaves with a slow, insolent swagger. Jonathan looks after his retreating figure and sighs heavily.

'He's a terrible tosser, but I'm afraid I'm fond of him.'

He pauses and breaks into a smile.

'He's like Tangier. He's an addiction.'

Heading south and east out of the city, on the road to Tétouan, my guidebook notes what could be a good omen for the journey. Outside the football stadium we shall pass the only memorial to the great traveller, Ibn Battuta, which stands on a plinth beside it. The plinth is there but unfortunately the statue is gone. Our driver thinks it was stolen some time ago.

He doesn't know why.

Skirting the city of Tétouan, we follow the road up a broad rising valley. The green and wooded landscape with flocks of sheep and cattle could be Wales or Scotland save for the red-capped French kilometre posts by the side of the road and the occasional vivid glimpse of Berber shepherdesses in scarlet hats, white tops, boots and bright-red knickerbocker leggings.

Late in the day we come to a town spread dramatically across the steep sides of a jagged limestone ridge. It's called Chefchaouen. As in Tangier, there is an old and new town. The French never attempted to fuse the two together, so the old town, the medina, remains pretty much as it must have been when it was founded at the end of the fifteenth century as a mountain retreat for those Moors and Jews expelled from Spain by the Catholic Monarchs.

It is said that up until 1920 only three Christians had ever found their way into Chefchaouen, and until 1937 slaves were openly traded in its market.

Now it's on the tourist trail as a picturesque mountain town and the hippie trail as a fine place to enjoy the much sought-after local marijuana, known as *kif*. Or as the rock and roll bands used to call it, Moroccan Red.

Around the long rectangular central space, the Plaza Uta El Hammam, are grouped an elegantly harmonious cluster of old buildings: the mosque with its delicately beautiful six-sided minaret of brick and plaster, the low white walls and fine doorway of the *medersa*, the Koranic school, and the crumbly, toffee-coloured walls of the casbah, the old castle, from whose gardens rise palms and cypress trees.

At one end of the square is a *funduq*, or caravanserai. These were originally intended to be stopovers for those coming into the town to buy and sell goods. Around a whitewashed courtyard two arcaded storeys provide room for unloading and quartering of the animals, with sleeping accommodation for their masters above. This *funduq* has not yet been tarted up for the tourists. A bed frame, painted silver, sits in the middle of the yard, mangy cats slope around bales of straw, a chicken, one leg tied by a string, is at the end of its tether, pecking at the ground. Robed men from out of town recline on plastic chairs, arms behind their heads, doing nothing much. The place smells, not unappealingly, of skins and leather and horse dung.

We are not allowed to film anything in Chefchaouen until we have a police escort, so we kill time in the Plaza eating minced lamb and sipping non-alcoholic drinks. The mint tea is good but danger-ous, as it immediately attracts a crowd of bees. These are apparently a serious nuisance, especially in the warmer months, when special covers are provided for the tea, but the honey they make up here is

much sought after. General Franco had his private supply of it air-
lifted to Spain.

A man in wrap-around dark glasses, straight-line moustache
and a black suit approaches. The sort of man who could only be one
of two things, a policeman or a pimp. He turns out to be our official
escort. Throwing himself into the job with gusto, he shoos away
anyone within a hundred-yard radius of the camera, creating the
impression that the town has been hurriedly evacuated.

Despite protestations that my hamstring is getting better, Roger
is keen for me to attend the public baths tomorrow and have it massaged. I have to buy something to wear. My guidebook advises
shorts for men, knickers for women. Walk into the souk, down
whitewashed alleyways, past buildings painted an almost fluorescent, swimming-pool blue, an effect created by mixing lime and
water with the paint. Blue, in many striking variations, is the predominant colour of old Chefchaouen. Apparently it's good for
keeping evil spirits at bay.

Find a shop with a comprehensive display of shorts. The shopkeeper is obliging, and I pass a complimentary remark on the
popularity of the place.

'Many people here. Many people in your town.'

He smiles thinly.

'Too many,' he says.

Before turning in, I walk into the Plaza. By night, the great space
is very different; more mysterious, but more personal. Irregular
stabs of light pierce half-closed doors and shuttered windows.
There is subdued chatter, some music, faces at upper windows,
figures silhouetted on back-lit balconies. If this had been a town in
Britain the noise would surely have been growing by now; there
would be laughter, fights, shouting and raucousness. Then a familiar smell drifts across from the half-lit balconies, spicing the cold
night air with a sweet aroma and bringing on a flush of nostalgia.

Now I understand why it's so quiet. Everyone's stoned.

Day Five

CHEFCHAOUEN TO FEZ

Wake feeling distinctly queasy in the digestion department. Bowel control will be essential this morning as the prospect of being washed and scrubbed and massaged before the cameras looms. Am tempted to take a tab of Immodium, but this turns intestines into Elgin Marbles and I'm not ready for that. I'll have to rely on mind over matter, never one of my strong points.

It turns out I'm not the only one affected this morning. Anyone who had the minced lamb in the main square last night is feeling similarly delicate.

The hammam is neither health club nor massage parlour. Its function is primarily religious; to provide ritual cleansing and purification. Before attending prayers in the mosque, every good Muslim must wash hands, lower arms, nose, mouth, ears, feet and ankles. If he or she has had sexual intercourse that day, a complete body wash is expected.

The abundant amounts of hot water required for such ablutions were, and often still are, beyond the means of most households, hence the importance of the public facility.

I'm not surprised to hear that there appears to be difficulty in obtaining permission to film. In fact, I feel slight relief.

But our police escort manages to talk them into it, provided we film before the baths open for men at eleven. Women's hours are in the afternoon.

This raises the question of who will be there if it's closed to the public. Our drivers and our police escort sportingly agree to be extras, though, to my deep concern, they assure me that I will be stretched by a professional.

The baths are located in an old building at the bottom of a steep, cobbled street. You wouldn't know they were there, except for a blackened hole high on the outer wall, from which a telltale plume of steam issues from the boiler.

The door is low, studded and painted pale blue. It gives onto a cool stone-flagged passageway, at the end of which is an open changing area, laid with coloured raffia mats and lit by daylight from above.

My Chefchaouen shorts, though long and suitably modest, are a trifle narrow at the waist, not helping an already delicate digestive situation. I put my clothes in a locker and heave open a hulking metal door. A concrete counterweight on a rope slams it shut behind me. I find myself in the first of three chambers graded by heat. Gentle in the first, stronger in the second and in the third and final room, where the action takes place, powerful enough to send the sweat surging. The rooms are dimly lit, with vaulted ceilings and white tiles halfway up the walls. There are alcoves in the first two rooms, for resting and cooling down, and in the hot room a series of partitioned stalls where the intimate parts may be washed in some privacy.

As the heat pumps up through the floor the washing begins. You can wash yourself or be washed. In my case Ali, my driver, round as a Buddha, takes on the task of cleaning me up, first with extensive lathering and shampooing, then by rubbing me with a viciously abrasive mitt, which reduces my outer skin to thin rolls of dirt.

Meanwhile, the masseur, thin and wiry, with a villainous slash of a moustache, is at work on one of our other drivers. By rocking him backwards and forwards, with legs and arms interlocked, he seems intent on elongating Youssef even beyond the 6 foot 5 he already is.

Then it's my turn on the human rack. As I slither into his clutches it occurs to me that this could be dangerous. My Arabic is of no help. 'Good morning', 'Thank you' and 'Tea, please' are the only three phrases I can remember, and none of these is going to help me here. Anything useful, like 'pulled hamstring', 'food poisoning' or 'I confess!' will require a dictionary, which I don't have.

He indicates to me to lie flat and works thoroughly but compassionately, body on body, stretching, bending and using a lot of what the late great Charles Atlas used to call 'dynamic tension'. His manipulations remain this side of agonising but our intricate couplings leave me feeling pleasantly loose-limbed.

After the massage, Ali dumps several buckets of warm water over me. He aims each one at the crown of my head and the force of the water leaves me gasping. But as I sit and recover in a marble-tiled alcove in one of the cooler outer chambers, head back, staring up at the peeling plaster, it occurs to me that not only have I survived what could have been a dreadful embarrassment, but also my stomach feels much better. I mean, much better.

Our drivers go back to being drivers, but there's a sort of cama-raderie amongst us that didn't exist before the hammam. I'm quite blasé, especially about the massage. It was nothing. Just a scratch. They grin knowingly, and it's only when we're on the road again that I hear they had specially asked the masseur to go easy on me. Roger, very amused, tells me the exact words they used translate roughly as 'treat him like a virgin'.

The mountains of Morocco were formed millions of years ago by the collision of the land masses of Africa and Europe, which created a series of folds, running southwest to northeast and pro-viding a spectacular roller-coaster landscape. The road we take to Fez crosses the first of these great ranges, the Rif. Rising over 8000 feet, the mountains are creased and cracked into an often inaccess-ible network of valleys and peaks, providing cover for local warlords, who have always been more powerful here than central government. Though we pass cork forest and olive groves and flocks of goats along the way, the mountain soil is not fertile. The only crop that grows anywhere is *Cannabis indica*, kif.

It is illegal to possess, deal in or move kif within Morocco, yet somehow it's always available, and there's a big demand for it abroad (the chaplain at St Andrew's in Tangier told me that part of his responsibilities were to administer to the dozen or more English and Americans currently in prison on smuggling charges).

All of which makes these mountains potentially dangerous and lawless places, and we are warned not to stop under any circum-stances. Any accident or breakdown will usually have been arranged as a trap.

Occasionally I see young men loitering, but mostly the road is empty, curling round dark and craggy outcrops, high enough at one moment to see eagles wheeling below, then falling steeply down through pine and cedar forest to meadows and verges thick with oleander.

As we emerge from the Rif the land ahead of us opens out into a panorama of rolling hills and fields, a wide Moroccan prairie. From this, in turn, emerges one of the great cities of the Arab world.

Five hours after leaving Chefchaouen, the city of Fez appears due south on the horizon. Low, treeless and compact.

Day Six

FEZ

To an ear disoriented by deep sleep it sounds like bagpipes warming up or a very ancient siren being cranked into life. Then, after a moment of struggling wakefulness, it coalesces into a rough approximation of a voice, albeit weirdly stretched and distorted. Just as it seems to grow clear and explicable another voice chimes in, at a different pitch and much further away, then another, close by, hard, hooting and metallic, then another and another, until waves of overlapping, over-amplified exhortation burst from the darkened city. If I knew Arabic I would know they were saying, 'God is Great. There is No God But God. Prayer is Better than Sleep.'

I check my watch. It's 4 a.m.

Soobh Fegr, the dawn summons, is one of five calls to prayer that mark the Muslim day. I have heard it many times, but never anything as spectacular or prolific as the prayer calls of Fez, a rolling wall of sound rising from over fifty mosques, cradled in a bowl of hills.

Infidel that I am, I fall to sleep rather than prayer, and by the time I wake sunlight is thumping against the window and the only sound is the trilling of birds.

I step out on my fifth-floor balcony. All the trees in Fez seem to be clustered in the hotel gardens below me. Three enormous jacarandas, wispy casuarinas, orange and lemon trees, fat, spreading palms and amongst them a great congregation of birds, rushing from one tree to another, perching, pecking, preening and darting away. It occurs to me that they may well be birds from Lincolnshire or the Wirral down here for the winter. They recently tagged an osprey that had flown from Rutland Water to Senegal, over 3000 miles, in twenty-one days. Which is a lot quicker than we're going.

Like Chefchaouen, old Fez was a security-conscious city. Until 1912 and the arrival of the French, no-one could enter without a pass, and even then they would be expected to conduct their business and leave within forty-eight hours. The city gates were locked at sunset and those who failed to abide by the rules would likely as not end up, along with others who fell foul of the law, with their heads on spikes outside. And all this well into my own father's lifetime.

As was their wont, the French built their own separate new town and left the medina alone. Thanks to this enlightened, if crafty, policy, it remains, according to my Cadogan guidebook, 'the most complete Islamic mediaeval city in the world'. It's also a mysterious, labyrinthine place, enclosed and secretive. I need an interpreter. To interpret not just the language but the city itself.

Which is how I meet Abdelfettah Saffar, known to his English wife as Fats and to his friends as Fettah.

'Like the cheese,' he says with a well-worn smile.

He has a house in the old town, which he's been restoring for three years, speaks impressively good English, once lived on a houseboat on the Thames and at one time designed a Moroccan-style bathroom for Mick Jagger's house in Richmond.

He's shorter than me and about twenty years younger, with a neatly trimmed black beard, white *djellaba*, bare feet tucked into a pair of *babouches*, backless yellow slippers, and an efficient black briefcase.

Twenty-first-century Fez may look mediaeval, but it's a working town. Thousands live, shop, worship and do business without ever having to leave the medina. The streets are narrow, and though all motor traffic is forbidden, you're quite likely to be run down by a mule or squashed against the wall by an overladen donkey. In the Arab fashion, domestic life is discreet and hidden away, but commerce is open, visible and upfront. It's also organised traditionally, into guilds of craftsmen. Each guild area announces itself with a distinctive scent, what Fettah calls 'a geography of smell'. The acrid whiff of pigment in Dyeing Street, cedar wood shavings in Carpenters Street, leather in Tanners Street, the fragrance of fresh-made sweets and nuts in Nougat Street, the seductive sizzle of grilling meat along Butchers Row.

A traffic jam in old Fez can be a treat for the nostrils. At one point on Talaa Kebira (Main Street) I'm thrust to one side by a man with a tray of freshly-baked bread on his head, who is trying to avoid a woman carrying a basket of fresh vervain, who, like him, is trying to avoid a mule laden with fresh oranges.

We pass along an alleyway of open-fronted stalls, which rings with the sound of metal beating. The din is cacophonous and comforting, and through the smoke from their fires I can see men and boys, forging, beating and shaping copper and brass into an inexhaustible supply of low-tech utensils. There are huge bowls, some 3 or 4 feet wide, in which meat, dried with salt and spices, will be preserved through the winter (a throwback, says Fettah, to the siege days, when the city gates sometimes remained shut for months). There are tall fluted instruments for distilling perfumes like rosewater, crescent moon and star fixtures for cemeteries and mosques, and stacks of teapots. Down the street a young boy and an old man with thick gold-rimmed glasses are stooped over a low table, stitching together pointy-toed leather slippers like the ones Fettah is wearing, and a little further on a man is turning table legs on a spindle, using one foot to drive it and the other to guide a chisel tucked between his toes.

An arched gateway, sandwiched between two small shops, gives onto a courtyard where lime is being daubed on animal hides to strip them clean. This *funduq* is a monochrome world, full of ghostly surfaces so thickly coated with white lime and plaster that it's difficult to see where the layers of paint end and the buildings begin. A tall black African stirs a vat of fresh lime with a wooden pole, as stocks of fleeces sway through the archway on the backs of donkeys.

There is not a single piece of machinery here. It is a glimpse of a pre-industrial age.

Fettah says he has something special to show me. It doesn't look promising. We squeeze up narrow stairs covered in threadbare red carpet into a shop packed tight with leather goods of all kinds. We pass through ever smaller and more claustrophobic rooms, until, without warning, we're at the back of the building and light is spilling onto a wide terrace.

With a dramatic flourish, this tight, concealed old city, is thrown wide open. Below us, like a giant paintbox, is a honeycomb of fifty or sixty stone vats, each one around 4 feet across, filled with pools of richly coloured liquid ranging from snow white through grey, milky brown and pale pink to garnet red, metallic blue and saffron yellow. It is a complete and immaculately preserved mediaeval tannery.

Water, heaved up out of the Fès river by a massive wheel, is distributed amongst the vats, in which the tanners mix the heavy combination of water, hides and dye using only prehensile feet and the pressure of the muscles in their legs. This is a young man's game. The tanners have no protection from the sun, and temperatures can rise above 50°C/122°F in high summer. For a day's work in these conditions Fettah reckons they take home 100 deram. Around six pounds.

And it's not only the heat they have to endure. A sharp acidic stench rises from the kaleidoscope of colours below, a combination of the sheep's urine and pigeon shit used in the dyeing process. The tanners have had to get used to it. A tour group watching them from an adjacent balcony are offered sprigs of mint as nosegays.

Apart from the slow, rumbling creak of the water wheel, there is no sound other than voices, splashes and the sound of wet hides slapping on the side of the kilns. If I close my eyes I could be in a great open-air bathhouse.

Fettah reminds me that the Fez of 600 years ago would have had 200 such tanneries, as well as 467 *funduqs*, 93 public baths and 785 mosques.

There is a minor jam along one of the passageways on our way out of the medina, caused by a donkey shedding a load of mattresses. No-one seems impatient to pass, nor to pass comment on the Laurel and Hardy-like attempts at reloading. It's the way life is in this extraordinary city. The walls of Fez have kept the modern world at bay. What I have sensed today is little different from the impressions of two French travellers, the Tharaud brothers, who came through here in the 1930s.

'In Fez there is only one age and one style, that of yesterday. It is the site of a miracle. The suppression of the passage of time.'

FEZ

Today Fettah has asked me round to his house.

The entrance gives nothing away. A discreet little doorway set into the high walls of one of the warren of passageways in the medina. This gives onto another much narrower passage, dimly lit and smelling of cool, damp plaster, another modest doorway and then, a revelation. A covered courtyard, its walls decorated with intricate arabesque patterns and glazed *zellij* tiles, rises 60 feet to the roof of the house. This soaring space opens onto a blue and white-tiled terrace, almost as broad as the courtyard is tall, with a garden beyond, full of flowers, shrubs and various fertile trees, which are pointed out to me in detail by Narjiss, one of Fettah's two young daughters, with occasional promptings from her mother.

'We've got lemon, we've got orange . . . we've got, er . . .'

'Pomegranate . . .'

'Yes . . . we've got pomegranate . . .'

'Olives . . .'

'Yes, we've got olives.'

'Kumquat . . .'

'I know! I know!'

As at the tanneries yesterday, the contrast between the close-packed streets outside and the airy spaciousness inside is more than remarkable; it's almost an optical illusion.

'Doors within doors within doors,' is how Fettah describes the phenomenon of public and private Fez. 'The more you get into it, the more you're lured into it.'

His property has a floor space of 22,000 square feet, but it's by no means the largest private house in the medina. Many of them are in poor condition, and it is only over the last three years that there has been much interest in restoring them. In London, such a mansion would be worth many millions. It cost Fettah £60,000.

Abdelfettah is proud of his city. As the craftsman son of a crafts-man father, he believes passionately in the preservation of the medina and the traditional styles and skills of the craftsmen within it. He does not see his enthusiasm as narrow or nationalist. Since he and his wife returned here after seven years in England they have welcomed people from twenty-eight different countries to a house which they see as a meeting place for musicians, writers, film-makers and, of course, artists from all over the world.

Off to one side of the property, through small rooms where lunch is being prepared by smiling relatives, is another spacious courtyard with workshops set around it. Amongst them is Fettah's studio, where he works on elaborate and complex plaster-work decorations.

I ask him why Islamic art has to be abstract. Is representation of nature and the human body really forbidden?

Fettah thinks there is no express ban in Islam but that creating the likeness of man and nature is, as he puts it, stepping into God's field.

'Islamic art,' he says, 'is the story of the line . . . the Muslim artist just exploits it to the maximum.'

His own work is painstakingly and meticulously carved by hand. He starts with a blank space and fills it up as the ideas come to him.

'I'm interested in the accident,' he says. 'I find English people plan too much. The accidental is not there.'

He should know, for he married an English girl, Naomi. Slim, angular and a head taller than her husband, she's articulate and down-to-earth, as befits a Suffolk farmer's daughter. Besides Narjiss they have another daughter, called Emily, and a cat called Compost, who lies in the garden bed where he's not meant to. I ask her why they decided, after seven years together in England, to come and live in Fez.

'Fettah's a Moroccan man,' she says, as if explaining something she's had to explain to herself often enough. 'He didn't take on some of the roles that Englishmen take. When he realised what child-rearing was, he's going, "Where's your mum? Where are your sisters? Where are your friends?" I was going, "No, no, you've got to do it, you've got to do it."'

Figures flit by in doorways behind her.

'Life here's very much a community thing. You're never on your own, you're always surrounded by family and friends. And they all help and there's a real teamwork going on. So, in that respect, life's easier.'

Fettah is one of seventeen brothers and sisters. His father had three wives, and for a while, siblings were arriving at the rate of two a year.

Naomi smiles and loops a rogue strand of hair back over her ear.

'The two younger wives are still alive. They live together in one house and they're both called Fatima and they get on fine.'

This must account for all the smiling ladies in the kitchen, preparing food, playing with the children, helping here and there. It must account for why Fettah can find time for work, teaching, restoring the house and running music festivals, and why sometimes Naomi misses privacy and space of her own.

'Fez is quite a traditional city and people are fairly conservative. If you go out in the street you have to have a reason for going out, for shopping and visiting . . . you don't just sort of amble. Women are at home, cooking, cleaning, looking after children, that's their role.'

This is said with a touch of regret but no malice. Anyway, Naomi thinks that attitudes have changed in the three years she's lived in Morocco. People are less frightened of expressing themselves, of talking about politics.

'Holding hands and kissing in doorways. That's all changed since I've been here.'

This day of peace and quiet, walking around Fettah and Naomi's garden, eating a vast couscous around the table on the terrace, hearing of their plans for the house and their affection for these unique surroundings, has lulled me into a dangerous sense of contentment. I haven't thought of the Sahara all day.

It's all about to change. This time tomorrow, *inshallah*, we'll be in the city of Marrakesh, beyond which sand and mountains merge into the edge of the void.

Ring Jonathan Dawson in Tangier to thank him for his hospitality, only to hear that Birdie has broken his beak. Apparently he pecked at some phantom delicacy on the terrace and bit hard on a floor tile. His beak has gone black at one end and may have to be removed.

Day Eight

FEZ TO MARRAKESH

Fez and Marrakesh, the two most important cities of old Morocco, lie in the centre of the country, built to guard ancient trade routes through the Atlas Mountains. Modern Morocco has moved to the coast, around the capital Rabat, and Casablanca, the country's biggest city, with a population twice that of the old towns – Tangier, Fez and Marrakesh – put together.

This is why we find ourselves accelerating south by heading west, using the fast motorway system around Meknès, Rabat and Casablanca as the quickest way to get to Marrakesh.

South of Casablanca the main road slims down to a poorly sur-faced single carriageway, choked with trucks and buses. Quite suddenly, some 80 miles north of Marrakesh, the landscape under-goes a transformation. Maybe I was asleep and just woke up, but as we pull up out of a dip beneath a railway bridge I notice Morocco has changed colour. The greens and golds of the fertile northern plain have been reduced to a line of pale yellow wattle trees running beside the road. Beyond them, the land is brick-red and bare.

The walls of Marrakesh reflect this red land with a beguiling rosy glow which deepens as the afternoon light fades. Running unbro-ken for over 6 miles, their towers and battlements throw a spectacular cloak around the city. But if Fez was enclosed, almost hidden away behind its walls, Marrakesh is bursting out of them. The new town pushes right up close. It's colourful and expansive, with broad avenues and a Las Vegas-like dazzle and swagger. Slab-like resort hotels, with names like Sahara Inn, jostle alongside a brand-new opera house. This is an old city desperate to accommo-date the modern world.

I'm disappointed. I'd expected something exotic and unpre-dictable. After all Marrakesh has the most romantic connotations of any city in this romantic country. Perhaps it's because the snow-capped range of mountains that frames the city in every tourist brochure is virtually invisible in the haze. Perhaps it's because almost everyone I've seen so far is white and European like me, or perhaps it's because I feel, on these tidy tree-lined streets, that I could be anywhere.

Then someone suggests the Djemaa el-Fna.

To get to it I have to leave the wide streets and bland resort hotels of the New Town and pass inside the peach-red city walls through the twin arched gates of Bab er Rob and Bab Agnaou.

Once inside the gates the atmosphere is transformed. Tourist buses prowl, but they have to move at the pace of a largely African throng. The tallest building is not an international hotel but the elegant and decorative minaret of the Koutoubia mosque, rising to a majestic height of 230 feet, from which it has witnessed goings on in the Djemaa el-Fna for over 800 years. There is an entirely unsubstantiated story that because the minaret directly overlooked a harem only blind muezzins were allowed up it.

The Djemaa el-Fna is not a beautiful space. It's a distended rectangle, surrounded by an undistinguished clutter of buildings and lines of parked taxis. Its name translates as 'Assembly of the Dead', which is believed to refer to the practice of executing criminals here.

It's bewildering. There's so much noise that they could still be executing criminals, for all I know. There seems no focal point to the commotion – no psychic centre. At one end, where gates lead into the souk, tourists take tea on café balconies and overlook the action from a safe distance. The locals favour the food stalls, which are drawn up in a circle at the centre of the Djemaa, like Western wagons waiting for an Indian attack. They are well lit, and the people serving the food have clean white coats and matching hats. This concession to First-World hygiene is deceptive. The rest of the Djemaa el-Fna is a realm way beyond protective clothing.

A troupe of snake charmers with wild hair and staring eyes tries to provoke old and tired cobras into displays of aggression, playing pipes at them with ferocious intensity. A squad of lethargic transvestites dances lazily, clicking finger cymbals without much conviction. Not that they need to do much more than that. Judging by the size of the crowds around them, the very fact of a man dressed as a woman is deeply fascinating to Moroccans. There are fortune-tellers, fire-eaters and boxers prepared to take on all-comers. Performing monkeys, chained and skinny, will be thrust on you for photographs. Berber acrobats hurl each other around while their colleagues work the crowd with equal agility. There are self-taught dentists, astrologers and men who let scorpions loose across their faces.

Women do not seem to take much part in these entertainments, but they form the majority of the beggars, moving silently through the crowd, sleeping children on their shoulders, palms outstretched.

The Djemaa el-Fna is part fairground, part theatre, part zoo, underscored with a frisson of mysticism and primitive ritual.

Despite my appetite for all things strange and wonderful, I feel more and more of an outsider as the evening wears on and the hysteria mounts, stoked by the constant thudding of drums, squealing of pipes and blasts from brass horns. Repetitive, remorseless rhythms shred away the layers of consciousness until you either give in or, as I did, flee the whole madness and retreat to the wonderful world of bland resort hotels.

Day Ten

MARRAKESH

The grandest hotel in Marrakesh, and one of the most famous in the world, is the Mamounia, named after the exotic gardens around it, which were laid out by Pasha Mamoun, a governor of Fez, in the eighteenth century. It was once the official residence of the crown prince, until the French turned it into a hotel of great style, sophistication and expense.

The shopping arcades of the Mamounia do not deal in take-home gifts, unless there's someone you know who might want a 6-foot silver lion sinking its claws into a 5-foot silver antelope, and the shopkeepers are not the sort who will fish out a box of matches and an evening paper from under the counter for you. In fact, they would not dream of calling themselves shopkeepers. They are dealers in and connoisseurs of fine things. Determined not to be intimidated, I enter one of these emporia hoping to find something useful, like a leopard-skin satellite dish or a lapis lazuli shoe-horn, and end up making the acquaintance of an exquisitely jewelled Spaniard called Adolpho de Velasco. He is not even a dealer, he is a designer.

'A big designer,' he corrects me. 'I launch the oriental look in the whole world,' he claims, before adding, endearingly, 'I'm not modest. When I do something that I like, I like people to appreciate it.'

He sees no contradiction between the jet-set playground Marrakesh has now become and the spartan fortress founded nine centuries ago by Abu Bakr and his holy warriors, fresh out of the southern desert.

Marrakesh, he says, has always benefited from a trade in fine things from across the Sahara. 'An enormously rich trade – glass, jewellery, precious stones, spices, silks.'

I ask him if he has spent much time in the desert himself. He rolls his eyes theatrically.

'Yes.' He pauses. 'And it's terrifying.'

Beneath a shock of carefully coiffured hair Adolpho's lean, leathery face takes on the aspect of an early Christian martyr, racked by some distant anguish.

'It's something that takes you, as it were, into another dimension.'

Cheered by this, I bid Adolpho goodbye, only to receive an expansive invitation to come to his home for a drink at the end of the day. He gives me an address.

'Next to Yves Saint Laurent.'

And he's not referring to the shop.

I visit the souk, the old market in the medina, for a dose of reality, but even here the modern world seems to have won the day. I'm drawn with dreadful inevitability into a carpet emporium, an attractive vaulted interior off a muddy back street. The salesman has lived in London for many years.

'Marloes Court.'

Then, as if I don't believe him, he adds, in quick succession, 'Andy Williams was my best friend. Do you know the Sombrero Night Club?'

His name is Michael.

'Same as yours,' he adds, warmly if unnecessarily.

I hover over an undoubtedly tempting Berber rug, bearing a Star of David motif, a reminder that it was not just Moors but the Jews as well who were thrown out of Spain by the Catholic Monarchs.

'I'm going south, across the desert. I can't take things like that with me.'

He shrugs, as if to say how could anyone who knows the Sombrero Club be going south across the desert.

There are some bewitching sights. Lengths of freshly dyed cotton are hung to dry across one alley, forming a swirling indigo canopy above us, and in the yard that leads off it I catch a glimpse of the men who dye the cloth, bent to their task, arms and torsos stained deep blue.

By the time I leave the souk the sun's going down, and so are my energies. Then I remember that I have to find Yves Saint Laurent.

Yves, as I like to call him, lives in and owns the Majorelle Garden, a botanical garden in the New Town, and Adolpho de Velasco lives in a house surrounded by tall trees just over the wall from the great man. Adolpho is more than a neighbour; he is one of Yves' forty 'favourites', which, amongst other things, means being privileged to receive one of his specially painted Christmas cards. Adolpho has a set of them, all framed, of which he is very proud. He's proud too of how he has expanded his cottage by converting a loggia into a conservatory, with an open fire crackling at one end and the stout trunk of a false pepper tree rearing up and through the roof as if an elephant's foot had just come through the building.

Immaculate in a gold-trimmed *djellaba* and stroking a very large citrine medallion around his neck, Adolpho smokes imperiously, talks flamboyantly and orders his servant to replenish my glass of pink champagne with such frequency that almost every sentence of my interview ends with the words 'don't mind if I do'.

Adolpho is a hot-blooded, passionate Mediterranean of the sort our fathers warned us about. He does not like things, he loves things. Himself, Morocco, his neighbour, emeralds, whatever. In fact, the only thing he doesn't love appears to be tourists from Birmingham, one of whom had complained of having her bottom pinched while walking in the souk. Adolpho was indignant.

'"What she look like?" I ask my friend. "Well, she was like this, she was like that."

'I say, "Bill, was she ugly?" "Yes," he say. "Yes. Very." I say how lucky girl she was. Never in England, in Birmingham, will ever, ever, her bottom be pinched.'

His eyes swell with pride for his adopted land.

'Lucky country. Lucky country.'

Day Eleven

MARRAKESH

I meet Amina Agueznay at a scrubby patch of wasteground outside the city walls, where taxis, donkeys and minibuses have worn the grass bare as they come and go touting for business. Names of destinations are shouted out and horns blasted to announce the imminent departure of buses, which everyone knows will not leave according to any timetable but only when they're full to bursting.

Amina is very much a modern Moroccan, a jewellery designer in her mid-thirties, unmarried and independent. She's short, bespectacled, articulate and possessed of an attractive self-confidence. She has lived and worked in New York and her English accent is more Mafia than Moroccan.

When we met yesterday I put it to her that the Atlas Mountains, the world-renowned backdrop to Marrakesh, are a computer-generated image to fool the tourists, for strain my eyes as I have these past forty-eight hours, I have seen nothing more than a dim grey blur in the hazy skies to the south.

According to Amina, the mountains not only exist, but they're less than two hours away, and she will show me villages more breathtakingly beautiful than anything else I've seen in Morocco.

She picks her way coolly through this frenzied transport market until she finds a *grand taxi*, an old Mercedes of the sort I remember in Munich in the 1970s, which she judges to be safe and sound. As we make to get in, an old man deftly intercepts us and stretches out a hand for some money. Amina gives him a coin. Very important, she says. Moroccans are very superstitious, especially about jour-neys, and a coin to a beggar will help ward off the evil eye.

We head south, passing low, flat-roofed houses with rough-textured, dried-mud walls. Storks circle above them, carrying food to nests high on chimneys or tall trees. Our taxi driver has perfected a technique of roaring up to the vehicle in front, hugging its slipstream, but not overtaking until he can clearly see an oncoming vehicle.

Around 30 miles from Marrakesh we stop, to my relief, at a large village called Asni. Outside the cafés, tagines simmer on charcoal braziers, salesmen offer us an assortment of knives, rings, fossils and crystalline rocks, and Berber women, wearing long green cloaks and white headscarves with lacy fringes, pass by with loads of undergrowth on their backs.

I learn from Amina that the Berbers (the word comes from the Greek for barbarians) were the original inhabitants of Morocco. Some say they came from the Caucasus Mountains but no-one dis-agrees that they moved into Morocco long before the Arabs. Ibn Khaldun, the great fourteenth-century chronicler of Arab history wrote of the Berbers: 'the men who belong to these family of peoples have inhabited the Maghreb since the beginning'. The Arab word Maghreb means 'the lands of the west' or 'the lands of the setting sun'.

Despite the fact that over seventy-five per cent of all present-day Moroccans are of Berber descent, the Berbers have been tradition-ally repressed by their Arab conquerors and largely confined to rural mountain areas like the High Atlas. Amina says that things are different now. There are Berbers in the cities. They're hard-working, ambitious and creative. She seems uncomfortable with direct questions about Arab–Berber relations. Maybe it's because Morocco is anxious to avoid any equivalent of the recent violent protests by Algeria's Berbers over the suppression of their culture. Maybe it's because Amina, it transpires, is a Berber herself, from the south on her mother's side and from the Rif Mountains on her father's side.

Beyond Asni the road rises so steeply that we have to exchange our Mercedes for a pick-up truck, squeezed into the back with a group of villagers.

The road coils along a gorge beside a riverbed, bone-dry today but bearing the scars of fierce torrents of the past. In two places the concrete highway has collapsed and been washed away, and they have been waiting since 1975 to have it repaired. We pass a precipitous village called Imbil, which sells postcards and has a government centre for hikers. From here a dirt track climbs steeply through a landscape of dry stone-walled terraces, which support sturdy vegetable plots and cherry orchards. The air cools and bubbling streams race down the mountain.

The dusty white hairpin bends are becoming so tight that the hard-worked pick-up, unable to make them in one, negotiates a series of death-defying three-point turns, leaving us at times backed up to the very edge of a precipice, with only a handbrake between us and a 1000-foot drop.

At last we pull up onto a flat saddle of land offering temporary relief and a breathtaking view down the valley. To the south, a dizzy succession of interlocking spurs, and to the north, a spread of horizontal terraces and rooftops. This is the village of Aremd, 8000 feet high, overlooked by jagged raking ridges and wedged in a fold of the mountains, with this narrow, gravelled track as its only lifeline.

The silence of the mountains amplifies any sound that breaks it. The cracking of a twig for a fire, a dog's bark, a child's shout identify the village long before we reach it. A picnic is laid for us on carpets and cushions set on a terrace shaded by walnut trees. After washing our hands in water from a silver salver, a meal of couscous and tagine, the name of the food and also the conical earthenware pot it comes in, is served, with Amina and myself as guests of honour. This brings its own problems. There are no knives, forks or spoons and I have to learn to eat Berber-style, using my right hand only – the left being traditionally reserved for ablutions. This is not without its own very strict etiquette. One does not stick one's hand in and pick out what one wants. Oh dear me, no. One uses one's thumb and two fingers, the thumb squeezing the food into a ball solid enough to dip carefully into the sauces and return to one's mouth. All this from ground level.

I find it hard enough even to reach the rice without swaying most ungracefully off balance, and the rolling of it into a ball using only three digits is a damn sight harder than it sounds. Especially as the rice is hot.

Mercifully, a small band starts up, creating a diversion and enabling me to use an extra digit to grab some of the wonderfully tender chunks of lamb soaked in the juice of olives.

Oranges, mint tea and a rosewater finger bowl are brought round and our *déjeuner sur l'herbe* continues with the performance of a courtship dance. Men and women form up in two lines facing each other. The men, all in white *djellabas*, chant, yodel and beat out a rhythm with hand-held drums, whilst the women clap their hands and respond with their own chant. One from each side dances in the middle. The man struts and shakes his shoulders in passable imitation of an animal ruffling its feathers and scratching the ground. The dancers never touch each other, yet it's performed with a flash of the eyes and a boldness of movement that makes it highly charged. Something chaste and wild at the same time.

Day Twelve

Marrakesh to Ouarzazate

Marrakesh bus station, romantically known as the Gare de Voyageurs, is not the sort of place to arrive at the last minute.

The details on the departures board are predominantly in Arabic, and in the busy central hall mine is one of the few heads moving from left to right as I try to decipher the scant French translation.

The depot is modern, concrete and functional, and beside the '*Horaires de Départ*' a large portrait of the old king, Hassan II, looks down on the confusion from a veneered wooden frame. The king is the supreme civil and religious leader of his country, and remembering Amina's words yesterday about the superstition attached to any journey, I suppose it is reassuring to have the Commander of the Faithful gazing down on you as you look for the right destination, even if he has been dead for two years.

I must have forgotten to add '*Inshallah*' (God willing) when I bought my ticket, for once through the gate, I narrowly avoid being mown down by two departing coaches before I locate the Express

Nahda service for Ouarzazate, Zagora and the south.

The last few seats fill up in an atmosphere of increasing anxiety amongst the squad of young men who appear to run the bus company. Lists are checked, cross-checked and checked again, with deepening frowns.

Eventually, with a valedictory fart of thick black smoke, our elderly Daf pulls out of the yard and begins a slow crawl round the outskirts of Marrakesh in heavy morning traffic.

At one stop I watch a man in a *djellaba* and straw hat scraping up donkey droppings from the middle of the road with two boards. I can't work out if he's from the council or just an opportunist. When I was growing up in Sheffield the police horses used to pass our house on some sort of exercise, and if any dung was left behind I had to watch in profound embarrassment as my father and our next door neighbour, both keen rose-growers, raced out with shovels and fought over it.

When we're finally clear of the city the driver shoves a dusty cassette into a slot on the dashboard and the bus fills with the sound of chanting. It's a tape of the Koran, played to invoke Allah's protection on our journey and recited, I'm told, by an Egyptian who is considered such a star that he intones the Holy Book at Mecca itself.

The driver seems a placid, reliable sort, rarely using his horn in anger and seemingly undistracted by a plastic vine which trails up one side of the windscreen, dangling its faded black grapes over a photograph of a woman, veiled in white, hands raised in devotional gesture, which is stuck on the windscreen above his head.

The mountains begin to close in, and, as the driver hauls the coach round a dizzying succession of hairpins, the prevailing colour of the countryside changes from rufous maroon to brown and grey. Convoys of four-wheel drive vehicles, carrying their affluent tourist cargoes towards the Desert Experience, hover impatiently behind us.

Some four hours after leaving Marrakesh the coach pulls in to the small, noisy town of Taddert, the last truck stop before the Tichka pass. The smoky aroma of fresh-grilled kebabs is irresistible, though obtaining one isn't quite so simple. Helpful locals point me to a roadside butcher, from whom I buy the meat, before taking it over to the fire, where I pay again to have it cooked. As I tuck into it, a truck, on its way down from the pass, air brakes hissing, comes to rest opposite me. It carries a load of cattle and one little old man, gripping the sides and peering impassively from a long line of bovine backsides.

After Taddert it isn't long before we run clear of the last agricultural terraces and climb slowly and steadily upwards between bare, fractured rock until we reach a plateau covered in short spongy grass and pools of standing water, where a few sheep graze. This is harsh inhospitable land, watershed country, whose melting snows feed rivers that will run either north to the plains of Marrakesh or south to die out in the desert.

We're at the pass (*tizi* in Berber) moments later. A bristle of communications masts and a sign, around which some European boys are draped for a photograph, announce that we are at the top of the Tizi n'Tichka, at 7500 feet, the highest pass over the Atlas Mountains.

An hour or so later, I leave the coach near the town of Aït Benhaddou. We're still on the flanks of the Atlas Mountains, but for the first time on the edge of real desert. The landscape reminds me of Arizona, flat-topped mesas turning red, gold and purple as the sunlight moves over them. Yet this small town we've come to, some 15 miles off the main road, is one of the most familiar on the planet. Anyone who has seen *Gladiator* will have seen it. Anyone who has seen *Lawrence of Arabia* or *Romancing the Stone* or *The Four Feathers* will have seen it.

Almost the only time I went to the cinema with both my parents was to see biblical epics. The last one I remember us enjoying was called *Sodom and Gomorrah*, which, with lines like 'Beware the Sodomite patrols', was perfect for a young adolescent about to go away to an all-male boarding school. Only today do I find out that the Sodom that so impressed me in Sheffield forty-five years ago is the village I'm in today.

Like so many settlements on the old trade routes south, Aït Benhaddou was fortified by the warlords who controlled the High Atlas, the most famous of whom was T'hami El Glaoui, who ran southern Morocco as his own fiefdom right up until independence from the French in 1956. A multitude of picturesque towers rises from a rocky bluff overlooking a wide dry riverbed, at the top of which are the prominent ruins of an *agadir*, a fortified granary, its bastions now so eroded by the rain they look like melted candles.

This was a wealthy town, renowned for the beauty of its women as well as the splendour of its buildings, and when the clear sunlight catches the elegant tapered towers with the richly decorated patterns on their upper walls and archways I can understand why the tourists, and the film-makers, keep coming back.

I enter past the recently demolished arena from *Gladiator* and up into the streets, tapping walls every now and then to make sure they're real. The hardened clay pathways are narrow and picturesque and eerily tidy. There are no motor vehicles and, it seems, very few residents. The only shops are selling souvenirs and gifts for tourists. Aït Benhaddou is a sort of Sleeping Beauty – pretty, well preserved and oddly sterile, waiting for the next movie to bring it back to life.

It is late in the afternoon, and as we near Ouarzazate the landscape is spectacular in the declining sunshine. Rock faces twisted like muscles in spasm are scoured by a low sunlight that picks out every nuance of colour until they glow like smouldering coal.

And all at once I see my first mirage. It's an ancient and glittering citadel rearing up out of nowhere, part fortress, part palace. On closer inspection it proves to be the city of Jerusalem, and on even closer inspection it proves to be held up by scaffolding.

Shouts of 'Dino!' and the smell of fresh paint fill the desert air as an Italian construction crew go about their business putting the finishing touches to marble urns, copper braziers and plasterboard loggias.

'Jesus and Judas,' reads the windscreen sticker on one of their vans.

At the Berber Palace Hotel in Ouarzazate this evening a young Englishman introduces himself. He's an actor, playing John the Disciple in an ABC television version of the New Testament currently being shot in the Moroccan Jerusalem. A short curly haired American, naked save for a towel around his waist, passes through the lobby exclaiming loudly, 'Boy, that hammam has knocked me out! Wow!'

My friend calls him over.

'Michael, meet Jesus.'

Arched doorway at Chefchaouen, Morocco.

GIBRALTAR

Top: On the road in Gibraltar. *Left to right*: Peter Meakin, Nigel Meakin, Aaton Super 16 XTR Prod (aka 'The Baby'), MP, Roger Mills, Gloria Macedo, Natalia Fernandez, John Pritchard.

Centre: Africa, seen from O'Hara's Battery and seagull toilet. The distant peak of Jebel Musa (2761 feet) breaks the clouds on the other side of the Strait of Gibraltar.

Below: The Royal Gibraltar Regiment is the Rock's own army. Here they put on a ceremonial parade in Casemates Square.

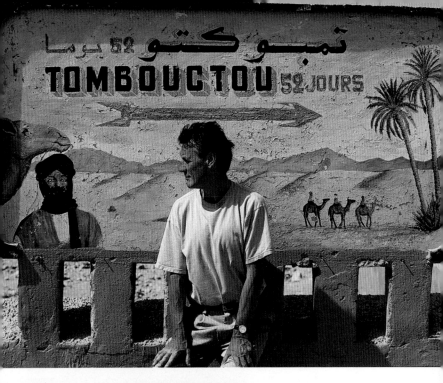

MOROCCO

Above: Timbuktu sign, Zagora, Morocco.

Left: Catching up with the diary in the corner of a café in the casbah, Tangier.

Top: Backstage at St Andrew's Church, Tangier. Mustapha Chergui, sexton for the last thirty-eight years, introduces me to Fatima, his wife of forty years, and their son (framed).

Above: Jonathan and Birdie enjoy a quiet moment.

Man of the mountains in the square at Chefchaouen.

Top: Trio of fine buildings in the Plaza Uta El Hammam, Chefchaouen: (*left to right*) casbah, *medersa* (Koranic school) and mosque.

Above: Lounging around in the *funduq.* Out-of-town traders mull over marketing strategy.

Left: The calm before the storm. On my way to the hammam clutching my new shorts.

Below: Hands up those who've had enough. My masseur and I get to grips at the hammam at Chefchaouen.

Street life in Fez. The low-tech medina is an intricate network of small businesses that has remained largely unchanged for the last 1000 years.

Left: Hides on their way to the tannery.

Centre: Donkey bearing radishes. No motor vehicles are allowed in.

Below: The nearest thing to a supermarket.

Right: Abdelfettah in his workshop, carving designs in white plaster.

Below: Worshippers wash before prayer at the Kairouyine Mosque in Fez. Founded in 859, it is one of the largest and finest mosques in North Africa, accommodating 20,000 people. Alongside it is one of the oldest universities in the world (founded in 850), and the incomparably rich Kairouyine Library.

Paintbox effect at the medieval tanneries in Fez. Skins are treated and dyed in stone vats, as they have been for hundreds of years, by individual human effort. There were once 200 tanneries like this.

Right: Aït Benhaddou. Impressive and elegant towers below, thanks to Hollywood and UNESCO, but the neglected old fortification at the top of the hill is half reduced to ruin by rain and wind.

Below: Southern Morocco. Bedouin tribesmen secure their camels in the teeth of a gale. Many now depend for their livelihood on the demand for camel safaris from increasingly adventurous tourists.

Top: Man strikes oil in the main square. Other attractions include acrobats, transvestites, snake charmers and dentists.

Above: Haggling for a pair of backless slippers they call 'babouches'. The sign of quality is the number of stitches round each one. The yellow pair had 350 on each slipper.

ALGERIA

Top: Smara Camp, Algeria. For the last twenty-five years it has been home to 40,000 Saharawi refugees, who left their Western Saharan homeland rather than accept Moroccan domination.

Above: Saharawi women outside a weaving school. Women virtually run the camps. They cook, build, administrate and run the children, whilst many of the men are in the army.

Top left: Metou, the partly Welsh-educated woman who showed me round the camp, sporting her traditional *melepha* and less traditional jeans and Doc Martens.

Top right: Abstract patterns are important, as Islam discourages figurative art. Here just a glimpse on a *melepha* and tent covering behind.

Above: Bachir, Krikiba and the children.

Top left: Sweet tea is the national drink of the Sahara. Everything stops for its preparation, which must never be hurried.

Above: In Western Sahara: camel stew with the drivers.

Top right: Tyremarks on the surface of a typical *reg*, the flat gravel or coarse sand plains which are a driver's delight.

This is a historic moment, but all I'm worried about is that if he shakes hands his towel will fall off.

So we just say 'Hi!', and Jesus hurries away to change.

'There's a whole lot of us here,' says my friend. 'We're all disciples.'

Sure enough I notice them later in the restaurant, all with identical beards. At a table for twelve.

Day Thirteen

OUARZAZATE TO TINFOU

Ouarzazate recedes into the distance. A town of substance, a regional capital, a centre for the increasing trade in tourists who want the Desert Experience without having to go too far into the desert. It has an airport and some big hotels and a military garrison but not much else to hold us up.

The mountains are not quite done with us yet. We may have crossed the High and Middle Atlas but there's still the Anti-Atlas ahead of us. As the road climbs towards yet another pass the Land Rover coughs and splutters and we pull in to the side. Our driver opens the bonnet and releases a hissing cloud of steam. Like a priest wielding a censer, he scatters a couple of bottles of Sidi Mansour mineral water over the radiator and we set off again. A few miles later the knocking from the engine becomes so insistent that I wonder if there might not be someone trapped inside. Our driver tries manfully to ignore it, but you might as well ignore a broken leg, and reluctantly he brings us to another, and I suspect more permanent, halt.

As we're staring into the engine, two very sleek Toyotas, coming fast out of the desert, bowl down the hill towards us. Seeing our plight, the occupants stop, offer greetings in the Arab fashion, right hand lightly touching the heart, and a man in a cotton robe, face shrouded in a blue veil, comes across to us. His skin is dark and tight across his cheekbones. He appraises us with a fierce unblinking eye before reaching into his robes.

'I am a nomad. Here is my card.'

It's a kind offer, and reminds me of the Monty Python sketch of a cliff-side full of hermits, chatting, gossiping and offering to do each other's shopping.

Squeezed into one vehicle, we toil without further incident up to the pass, the unforgettably named named Tizi n'Tinififft, 5500 feet above sea level. To the north, east and west the crests of a half-dozen mountain ranges extend to the horizon. A gorge splits the earth and we follow the curving walls and rock-stacks of the canyon down towards the incongruous green ribbon of palm trees and cultivated land that marks the course of the River Drâa.

The Drâa was once one of the great rivers of North Africa, mentioned by Ptolemy as running from the Atlas Mountains to the Atlantic Ocean. As the desert has spread the river has shrivelled and, in this last hot decade, has disappeared into the sand without even reaching the sea.

Here, beyond the town of Agdz, the Drâa is fresh off the slopes and shows how barren desert can be transformed if there's water around. A carpet of palm trees extends for up to a mile across the valley floor, providing a livelihood for a string of towns and villages along its route. It is, in effect, one long oasis, with glimpses of silver-green water amongst the trees, and brightly coloured clothes drying on bushes, through which flocks of black goats pick their way. The valley provides the best dates in the world, so they say, and we stop to buy some from a boy of nine or ten who stands by the side of the road holding a basket in outstretched hand.

Within seconds a crowd of competitors, none older than fourteen or fifteen, engulfs me.

It seems fun, but the force with which they fight to get near me, the intense clamour for a sale and the almost studied indifference of my driver to these skinny jostling boys give me the feeling that this is as much about survival as free enterprise. Perhaps all is not as well as it looks in the picturesque villages of the Drâa valley.

It's early afternoon when we drive into Zagora through a horseshoe-arched gateway and down Avenue Mohamed V, which, with its arcades and long line of shaded shop-fronts, has the atmosphere of a Wild West frontier town. Children walking back from school hold exercise books up to their faces to keep the sun off.

There is a scuffed, crudely painted, concrete road sign here, a child's-eye view of desert sands, camels and gleaming-eyed Touareg grouped around a grubby arrow and the words '*Tombouctou 52 Jours*'. It's a reminder that Zagora is the largest town we shall see for another 1000 miles and that its tourist hotels and hard-topped roads may seem like rare luxuries in the days ahead.

After Zagora the palm groves thin out and the casbahs become fewer and farther between. The Drâa reduces to a trickle, then ceases to flow altogether. A fierce gusty wind springs up from nowhere, gathering the sand and dust into clouds that cover the sun and plunge this dazzling landscape into anonymous greyness.

Progress slows and we rest up for the night at Tinfou, 20 miles south of Zagora and a few miles short of the end of the road at Mhamid.

The Auberge du Repos de Sables has great character, if limited comforts. The building is a small casbah, complete with four clay-brick towers at its corners, at the top of one of which is my room. The *auberge* is family owned and run in very laid-back style by the El Faraj family, painters and potters whose work covers the walls. The rooms are small, whitewashed and simply furnished with bamboo and beam ceilings.

I open out my Michelin map, 'Africa North and West', until it covers most of the bed. I look at the route we've taken so far – blue sea, then red and white roads that have carried us across the green and brown of mountain and valley. From here on there is only one colour: golden yellow, stretching 1000 miles, south, east and west. The size of many Moroccos.

Except for the single word Sahara in bold black type, there is hardly any print across this emptiness apart from a number of faint blue inscriptions: '*Mejaouda, Peu d'Eau à 4m*', '*Hassi Tartrat, Potable*', '*Oglat Mohammed, Eau Bonne*'. I realise that not only is this the first map I've used which has sources of water specifically marked, but that their names are often hundreds of miles apart.

In the night a fierce wind bursts open the shutters behind my bed and I'm aware how much cooler I feel. By morning I'm reaching for a sweater.

Day Fourteen

TINFOU TO TINDOUF

Wake at six as a muezzin's cry rends the stillness. Fortunately, I can control this one, as the voice comes from a pink alarm clock bought in the bazaar at Marrakesh. Click it off and lie there idly speculating whether any Muslims have ever been woken by the sound of the Bishop of Bath and Wells.

Examine the day. It looks perfect. Clear skies, translucent desert light. I climb down the ladder from my turreted refuge and take in the beauty of the morning. Just outside the main gate, three camels sway their heads towards me before resuming their chewing. I watch a couple of sparrows perching on swaying palm fronds and can't help noticing how chubby they are for birds on the edge of a desert. The road is empty, save for a slowly advancing figure on a moped.

The only shadow in this sub-Saharan Eden is a dry cough that I picked up yesterday.

A persistent, gritty, welcome-to-the-desert cough.

By the time we're packed and ready to go the wind has started to rise. The last Moroccan road quickly runs out and we're off piste, swerving and twisting as the drivers search out the hard surfaces. A screaming wind is scything sand off the dunes and hurling it across our windscreen. As we enter the Sahara, it's as if we're entering a storm at sea.

Beyond Mhamid the desert stretches away into Algeria, the second-largest country in Africa. It is not best friends with neighbouring Morocco, and one of the reasons lies beside the solitary tarmac road that runs across this flat and rubble-strewn landscape. Above a walled compound on the outskirts of Tindouf, a flag slaps and cracks in the wind. The flag – a chevron, three horizontal bands and the moon and star of Islam – belongs to none of the countries whose frontiers meet in this desolate spot. Not Algeria, Morocco nor Mauritania. It is the flag of the Saharawi Arab Democratic Republic, and you will scour the atlas in vain for its name, for officially it doesn't exist.

Inside the compound there is an almost cloistered hush. The wind has dropped and the stillness of the surrounding desert deadens noise like a fresh snowfall. In the middle of a quadrangle of sand and stones people are meeting and talking softly in the shade offered by an open-sided thatch-roofed shelter. Around the walls of the compound runs a single-storey block of rooms providing accommodation and other facilities. The writing on the walls provides a clue to the mystery of the Saharawis. '*Tienda*' above the shop, '*Comedores*' above the refectory. Another clue is in the faces of those talking. Over half are clearly not African. They're light-skinned, with chunky moustaches and round, earnest faces.

There's a WC prominently indicated, one of a row of privies in an ablution block. As I push open the door I'm hit by a sharp whiff of uric acid rising from the damp sides of a hole in the mud floor. We who are used to having our body waste disposed of instantly forget that in the desert flushing lavatories appear only in mirages.

Our host for the next few days is a short, wiry man of middling age, eyes creased and narrowed. With his hands sunk deep in the pockets of a thick quilted jacket and his body angled forward as if braced for the next sandstorm, everything about him suggests stoic defiance.

His name is Bachir Mehdi Bhaya and Algeria is not his home. He was born and brought up in the contentious territory of Western Sahara, a land of long coastline and hostile desert, larger than the United Kingdom, which once comprised the Spanish colonies of Río de Oro and Saguia el Hamra. When the Spanish abruptly left in 1975 taking everything including the bodies in their cemeteries, they offered what was left to Morocco and Mauritania.

The Polisario Front (Frente Popular para la Liberación de Saguia el Hamra y de Río de Oro), acting on behalf of the half million inhabitants, known as Saharawis, who wanted to be neither Mauritanian nor Moroccan, began a guerrilla offensive. They were encouraged by the judgement of an International Court of Justice, which upheld the right of the locals to self-determination and scored early guerrilla successes against the Mauritanians, who have now abandoned claims to Western Sahara. The Moroccans are less amenable. They regard Western Sahara as having pre-colonial ties with the rest of Morocco. Its acquisition would almost double the size of their country, and the exploitation of valuable phosphate deposits would be a huge boost to their economy. To this end they encouraged 350,000 settlers to move in to Western Sahara during the 1970s.

Rather than accept this 'invasion', almost half the Saharawis fled to Algeria, who offered them land on this bleak military exercise area to set up temporary camps.

But, as the saying goes, 'there is nothing more permanent than the temporary', and, twenty-five years later, this compound near Tindouf remains the first port of call for anyone wanting to do business with the Saharawis. This includes many NGOs from all over Europe, but predominantly Spain, which explains the sallow men with moon faces and chunky moustaches, drawn here by the old colonial connection.

They are anxious to offer what help they can until the United Nations, which has monitored a ceasefire between the Moroccans and the Polisario for ten years, can come up with some permanent solution to the problem.

Bachir, who has lived as a refugee for nearly half his life, is the personification of the embattled exile. He will not compromise. He and his people will not rest until things are done the way they want them done. I recognise the syndrome. It's like being a Yorkshireman. As it turns out he has spent time in Leeds and learnt his English there, so he takes this as a compliment.

'I like them,' he says, grinning.

'We're very stubborn,' I remind him.

He nods approvingly.

'I like stubborn people. I'm one of them. Even if I'm wrong, I'm right.'

He won't hear of us staying here with the other foreign visitors.

'You will all stay at my house,' he insists.

And I know there's no point in arguing.

ALGERIA

Day Fifteen

Smara Refugee Camp

The extraordinary thing about Bachir's house is that we all fit in. How many of us would be able to accommodate seven extra people and forty-five pieces of luggage and equipment when you've already got a wife, four children and a constant influx of relatives? It's not as if his home is that much larger than any of the others in Smara. Exile means equality. Within its low, mud-brick walls are the standard small courtyard, kitchen, single squat toilet, two rooms and a tent.

The tents are of traditional design, with tall peaks and wide rectangular bases. According to Bachir, they are not only practical but also symbolic, a reminder to the Saharawis of their nomadic inheritance, and a reminder too that this cheerless landscape is only a temporary resting place on the journey back to their homeland.

The sun's up around eight. Two of us have slept in the tent and the other five, including myself, are squeezed into a room at the opposite end of the courtyard with the equipment strewn around us like the spoils of a pirate raid. Three of Bachir's children, including the two five-year-old twins, stand at the door, eyes wide, watching us folding up sleeping bags, cleaning teeth, combing hair, taking this, that and the other pill, and washing ourselves as best we can in small bowls of water, filled from the communal can.

Smara, a dozen miles into the desert from Tindouf, is, like the three other refugee camps, named after a town in Western Sahara. Though the camp has roughly the same population as the city of Winchester, it has neither mains water nor electricity. The communal water can for drinking, cooking, washing and sanitation is filled from metal cisterns half a mile away, which are in turn filled by old Volvo tankers, supplied by the UN, which shuttle between the camp and its nearest water source, an artesian well 16 miles away.

No-one in their right mind would choose to live in this sun-bleached, rubble-strewn wilderness, which makes the self-belief of the Saharawis seem all the more impressive. Despite the fact that they have few influential friends, 170,000 of them are content to remain in someone else's desert waiting for a breakthrough.

Bachir is proud of this solidarity, but aware too that it will not last for ever. He clutches at any straws to raise morale. The recent decision of the Spanish government to honour the pensions of those Saharawis who served in the Spanish army is seen as a major benefit, putting a little money into the pockets of those who have too often relied on UN hand-outs, and creating a small but growing private market in the camp.

We walk down the main street, where the shops are little more than makeshift stalls, fashioned from branches hung with whatever coverings can be found. This results in some bizarre combinations: a shack entirely covered by an ancient German wall map of South East Asia, another dominated by a poster of a Cuban beach resort. Out front are small amounts of oranges and onions, car tyres, clothes, a few plastic buckets. A butcher's shop has a dismembered camel carcass on the floor and, outside, on the ground in front of the shop, is its head, complete and looking strangely serene.

This evening, as a fat full moon rises over the camp, Bachir's wife Krikiba produces a meal for all of us and her family, cooked, as far as I can see, on one primus stove on the mud floor of a tiny kitchen.

We slip our shoes off and enter the tent. A white strip light, powered by electricity from a solar panel, casts a harsh glare. There are no chairs, and, unable to lounge and eat with nomadic nimbleness, we contort ourselves awkwardly on the mats, carpets and cushions, providing a continuing source of entertainment for family, relatives and neighbours as we tuck into camel casserole and rice. This is the first time I've knowingly eaten camel. The meat has a slightly sweet flavour, more like mutton than beef, and I can't stop myself wondering if any of this was ever attached to the head I saw in the market, with its inscrutable Mona Lisa smile.

Day Sixteen

SMARA CAMP

The children are getting bolder now, especially Sidi, the more hyperactive of the five-year-old twins. In between fetching water and preparing breakfast, Bachir tries to call him to order, but the lure of thirty pieces of film equipment is too much and he spends most of his time in our room shrieking with excitement at each new discovery.

Though I hear the muezzin's call in the morning, religion does not seem a big issue here. Education and political discipline are more important. Bachir and Krikiba's children are educated at the primary school near by, after which they will go to one of the two big boarding schools that serve the camps. The literacy rate amongst the Saharawis is now 90 per cent, far higher than in Morocco or Algeria. The Hispanic connection is strong and many of the teachers are from Cuba. Some of the brighter pupils go over there to complete their education.

Bachir introduces me to a young woman called Metou. She is in her early twenties, was born in the camps and has never seen her homeland. She's bright, well educated, lively and attractive, a modern girl. She wears a light, but all-encompassing, purple sari called a *melepha*, which doesn't attempt to hide the imitation leather jacket, jeans and Doc Marten boots beneath. Metou is a cosmopolitan Saharawi. She has travelled in Europe, speaks fluent Spanish, French and English and spent time at university in Wales. Beneath the blazing Saharan sun we discuss the knotty problem of getting from Machynlleth to Aberystwyth by public transport.

She takes me to a workshop in a collection of mud buildings called the 27th February Village, which cumbersome title commemorates the day on which the landless Saharawi Democratic Republic was founded, in 1976.

Thirty women are weaving brightly patterned rugs and carpets on the simplest of hand-looms. The carpets are made of thick, coarse sheep's wool, in bright, strong colours and improvised designs, and I'd buy a couple if we weren't on our way to Timbuktu.

The women run the camps, says Metou. They cook, build, administrate and raise the children. The young men leave at eighteen for military training.

I ask her if keeping a conscripted army isn't just a romantic gesture, bearing in mind there has been no fighting for years. Her response is quick and unapologetic.

'My people are tired of being ignored. If force has to be used to gain our birthright of independence, then that's the way it must be.'

Smara camp is so well run that it really doesn't resemble a camp at all. As I look out from a low hill, which is now the cemetery, the pale brown mud houses blending in with the desert around them could have been there for ever. The considerable size of the cemetery, a scattering of rocks and boulders just outside the town, suggests that life expectancy is low. Bachir shakes his head vigorously.

'It is seventy, eighty years.'

Sanitation is basic, he concedes, but the air is dry and there have been no epidemics here.

He smiles at my nannyish concern. 'People don't die in the desert, you know.'

In that case, the size of the cemetery merely emphasises how long the Saharawis have been away from home.

That night in the camp we tuck into camel kebab and pasta cooked with carrots and turnips, served, as ever, with tea. Tea is central to the nomadic life. In a land where alcohol is forbidden and most bottled drinks are beyond people's means, it offers welcome, gives comfort, stimulates conversation and provides a focus for social intercourse. Being a rare indulgence in a land of extreme scarcity, its preparation is taken very seriously. The water we splash on our faces in the morning is not good enough for the tea.

'Too salty,' says Bachir. 'The best water for tea comes from 50 miles away.'

Water this prized should not be heated on a gas ring, but on a brazier with charcoal from acacia wood, which heats the water more slowly and provides better flavour. Once heated, the tea is poured from one vessel to another before being tipped into small glass tumblers from ever-increasing height. Then it's tipped from tumbler to tumbler, until the required alchemy is deemed to have taken place, whereupon it is poured with one last grand flourish that leaves a foaming head on each individual glass. These are offered around on a tray and drunk swiftly. Then the glasses are washed and a second serving is prepared, tasting delicately different as the sharpness of leaf and sweetness of sugar continue to blend. The process is repeated a third time and that's it. I'm told that if you're offered a fourth glass it's a polite way of saying you've over-stayed your welcome.

Tonight Bachir's brother-in-law and two other men are sat around the brazier taking tea with us. Their eyes sparkle and their faces crease easily into laughter. It seems a good time to ask Bachir about the future for the Polisario.

He plays down the military solution.

'We still have many friends,' he argues, reminding me that only a year ago the UN Secretary General, Kofi Annan, and US Secretary of State, James Baker, had been staying in this same camp. The Moroccans might be supported by other Arab monarchies, like Saudi Arabia and Jordan, but the Polisario have powerful European allies, especially the Spanish, their old colonial masters, who now seem to be falling over themselves to help. Assuaging guilt? Annoying the French? Whatever the reason, Bachir is a grateful man.

'Five . . . six thousand Saharawi children go to stay with Spanish families every summer, and the families come back to see us.' His eyes shine in the lamplight. 'Two thousand came last year to the camps – doctors, nurses, teachers.'

He pauses as if aware I'm not convinced.

'We are small, but sometimes the small guys win. Look at Kuwait . . .'

But he and I both know that the Saharawis are, in world terms, much smaller small guys than the oil-rich monarchies of the Gulf.

Day Seventeen

Smara Camp

My request for a bin for the rubbish rapidly accumulating in our cramped quarters is met with a blank stare. Rubbish is a Western concept. What I wanted to throw away – paper, a spent packet of film, a mineral-water bottle – certainly wasn't rubbish to them, and as Krikiba and the children rifled through my pile of rejects, I felt embarrassingly over-stocked. What we see as basic necessities they see as complicated over-indulgences. Take toothpaste, for instance. Sidi and Khalia, the terrible twins, are fascinated by our teeth-cleaning rituals. Not just that we prefer to foam at the mouth rather than use acacia sticks like everyone else, but that once we've foamed we seem to have such trouble getting rid of it. At first light the streets of Smara are dotted with frothing Westerners looking for somewhere to spit out and little heads peering out of doorways to observe this quaint ritual.

Nor is toothpaste the only problem. There's a toilet paper crisis looming. All of us, family and crew, evacuate into the same hole in the ground. It's situated in a mud enclosure in the corner of the yard and is about the size and shape of a small slice of Hovis. There is a plastic jug of water beside it, which is considered sufficient for washing and cleaning. Those of us brought up to regard toilet paper as one of the essentials of civilised society are rapidly bunging up this delicate system and waste levels are rising alarmingly. There are reports that Krikiba has been seen coming out of the hut with a rubber glove on up to her elbow. I'm sure it's as well for everybody that we are moving on tomorrow.

Day Eighteen

Smara Camp to Tfariti

The wind is rising. As it gusts it hisses against the tent and there's a grittier than usual texture to the freshly-baked bread this morning. We've eaten most of the camel by now, but it appears at breakfast today in one last manifestation. Along with the usual offering of tea, coffee, bread and oranges is a dish of beans and diced camel liver. Out of a confusion of politeness, greed and a misplaced desire to experience all life has to offer, I pop a couple of cubes into my mouth. I know immediately that this is a mistake. The liver has a high, slightly gamey piquancy. But it's too late. One has already gone before I can retrieve it. I put up my hand to palm the other, only to meet Krikiba's eye. She beams at me expectantly. What can I do but grin and swallow.

In bright sun, sharp shadow and a cold wind the drivers Bachir has organised to take us several hundred miles down the West Saharan borderlands to the Mauritanian frontier are loading up. Our overnight bags are being squeezed into any available space left around the 200-litre fuel drums, which weigh down two small pick-up trucks. Ourselves and the rest of the baggage, as well as a cook, food and cooking materials, are divided between three four-wheel drive vehicles, which stand as tall as the house we're about to leave.

The children are going to miss us. We've been like a travelling funfair for them, and the extended family presses things upon us at the last moment, including a cassette of Saharawi music and a near-impregnable can of Spanish ham, which none of them is allowed to eat. As a parting gesture, eighteen-year-old Hadi, Bachir's pretty, coy niece, introduces me to her boyfriend. He's a young soldier and doesn't smile. The long-suffering Krikiba is persuaded into a hug and even, for Vanessa, a kiss.

Finally, away we go, up the hill from the house, sliding and swerving on the fine sand until we have a grip on the stony rubble at the top.

My last images of Smara camp are the small plots on the edge of town, fenced with anything from rice sacks to beaten-out oil cans, where people keep their livestock – goats, sheep, even camels. Two young girls are dragging a length of chicken wire across the sand to build another enclosure. That life goes on like this in these most straitened of circumstances is extraordinary. Smara is becoming less like a camp and more like a proper town every day. For everyone under twenty-five this is their only home. And that's not good news for the Polisario.

All morning we rumble across the *hammada*, stony, gravel-strewn desert, which appears featureless and forbidding, but is constantly changing. At one moment we'll be on the flat, at another cutting down a ravine or passing a small hill, both of which seem to come from out of nowhere. A scattering of acacia trees suddenly evaporates, leaving no cover at all. At moments like this, when there is no single piece of shade as far as the eye can see, the desert becomes quite frightening, and our vehicles seem small and pathetically vulnerable. It's like being on a rowing boat in the middle of the ocean.

Fifty-five miles later we stop at a Polisario checkpoint. A rough barrier made from lengths of piping, a few outbuildings, goats sheltering beneath the skeleton of a jacked-up, wheel-less lorry. A couple of Toyota pick-up trucks stand side by side with a couple of anti-aircraft guns in the back. The Saharawi army, Bachir points out.

The only exception to the general air of lethargy is the presence of a single swallow, darting and swooping above us.

I assume this is the border between Algeria and Western Sahara, but no-one seems quite sure. Bachir, squinting into the wind and dust, says we must move on, we've many hours driving still ahead. Najim, who's driving me and Basil, has wandered off and ambles back as the engines are being re-started, bringing wild dates for everybody, straight off the tree.

There is no surfaced road of any kind, but we follow the piste, as they call it, and every now and then pass a black tyre half sunk into the sand. The sight of these markers, sometimes at 5- or 10-mile intervals, becomes immensely reassuring.

At least someone has been here before us.

For a while, the terrain turns viciously stony, as if all the sand cover had been sifted through, leaving only this underlay of sharp grey points, jabbing at our tyres and sabotaging our progress. Ironically, it's on a much less hostile surface of soft white shells that we have our first puncture. Bachir kneels, scrabbles in the dust and picks out a handful of stones. He straightens up.

'Look, you see. Shells, little fish. This was all sea bed once.'

The desert as ocean again.

A half-hour later we're hurtling across a hard-baked gritty plain, flat as an ironing board, with nary a bush or a boulder breaking the surface as far as the eye can see. The drivers can at last put their feet down, and we fly across the desert, each vehicle swathed in its own dust, a string of small clouds chasing each other.

It's well into the afternoon before we find anywhere suitable to stop for lunch. A scattering of smoothly rounded boulders offers shade and there are a few dry and whitened trees for firewood. As the drivers gather wood, the cook, a middle-aged man with a broad, guileless face, thick moustache and greying hair, walks a little way off and falls to his knees in prayer. He picks up a handful of dust and rubs it up and down his forearms and on his brow, mimicking, I suppose, the act of purification in a waterless world.

The meal is, surprise, surprise, camel stew, cooked in a pot over the fire, and accompanied by good sticky rice and washed down with Coca-Cola, our main treat in this world without alcohol and wistfully referred to as Coke du Rhône. Now we are indisputably in Western Sahara, Bachir is a changed man. He looks around at the rocks and the desiccated trees with proprietorial satisfaction.

'Ours is the best desert!'

I laugh. But he doesn't.

'It is known to be the greenest, Michael.'

Greenest? I look around at the tawny undergrowth. This is chauvinism gone mad.

'All the great desert poets come from this part of Western Sahara.'

A woman laden down with possessions appears amongst the rocks, going apparently from nowhere to nowhere. When she comes closer the drivers shout a greeting. She nods amiably, comes over for a chat and carries on. It's certainly a friendly desert.

Hours later, the vehicles have stopped again. The sun has set and the horizon is a sand-stained yellowish rim. Our drivers have got out and are kneeling in a line in this desolate place, bowing to Mecca. Bachir, hands sunk deep in coat pockets, looks out ahead. He doesn't join them.

'I am not devout,' he says matter-of-factly.

An hour later, more mundane thoughts. Where are we going to eat and where are we going to sleep? We've been on the road twelve hours and Bachir has stopped the vehicles and is consulting with his driver. No-one appears to have a map, but there's much pointing into the darkness.

Then we're all urged to get in again. They've missed a turning.

Half an hour further on and out of the pitch blackness appears the outline of a long, low, grimly unwelcoming building on the crest of a hill. Built by the Spanish military, this decommissioned barracks is to be our home for the night. We're billeted in two rooms with seriously dodgy wiring. Turning the light off involves physically pulling apart two wires to deactivate the current. No-one dares turn it on again.

The cook is the only one who seems unconditionally happy to be here. With a real kitchen to work in, he sets to work on a vegetable stew, with just a little camel in it.

WESTERN SAHARA

Day Nineteen

TFARITI

Revenge of the camel. Plucked from deepest sleep, I just have time to stumble up from my mattress, grab torch and toilet paper, pull open the jarring metal door of our dormitory and race to the nearest lavatory. A strong wind has got up and I'm aware of how Gothic a scene this must be – white-T-shirted figure with disordered shock of hair, sprinting along concrete passageways open to the sky, as the wind howls after him, setting doors and windows banging.

I know things are bad as I have to do this twice more, on each occasion reaching the hole in the ground only just in time and holding my breath against the stench emanating from it.

Five o'clock. Woken by the chimes of a grandfather clock. For a moment I believe myself to be safe and well in some ivy-covered country-house hotel, and then I remember that the sound is coming from John Pritchard's alarm clock and I'm actually recovering from diarrhoea in a barracks in Western Sahara.

Roger and Bachir try to cajole the reluctant, slumbering drivers into a six o'clock start, but they won't move until they've lit a fire and brewed some tea. It's nearer seven when we bounce and sway off down the hill, heading north and east for a privileged glimpse of the front line between Moroccans and Saharawis, one of the world's best-kept secrets.

In 1982, in an attempt to consolidate their military superiority over the Polisario, the Moroccan government began work on a system of fortifications stretching for over 1000 miles along the edge of occupied Western Sahara.

This mighty Moroccan wall, longer than the Great Wall Of China, reportedly costs $2 million a day to maintain. As we brake, turn, twist and sway for mile after mile across a carpet of fractured stone slabs I should be feeling intrepid and privileged, but to someone suffering from camel poisoning the ride is slow torture. By gulping mouthfuls of air and staring fixedly at the horizon, I manage to hold out for three hours before the desire to shed last night's stew becomes uncontrollable and I have to ask Najim to pull up.

I retch violently, spewing potatoes and carrots on the desert floor (probably the most moisture to have fallen in that spot for years). When it's over I feel a soothing hand on my brow. It's Khalihena, tall, grave, the oldest and quietest of the drivers, who gazes down at me with wise concern through a pair of thick tortoiseshell-rimmed glasses. He holds out a bottle of water and motions me to wash my face.

I feel too ill to be embarrassed, and ridiculously touched that he should be the one to take care of me like this.

Though the Moroccans and the Polisario have observed a cease-fire for the last eleven years, they have not become friends, and as both sides have troops in positions near to the wall, we have to approach with the utmost caution, accompanied now by two armed pick-up trucks. Then it's a scramble up a slope dazzlingly rich in fossilised fish, plants and other evidence of the old once-fertile Sahara. From a ridge at the top we look down over a mile-wide no-man's-land that separates the two sides. There's no question of going any further, as the Moroccans have mined the border.

I realise that this wall, an abomination to the Polisario, keeping them, as it does, from their own land, also defines them and inspires them and, in their eyes, legitimises their struggle. There can be no question of a contest between equals. The Polisario army numbers around 20,000 men, but despite the ceasefire it's kept in readiness. To see them at work we are driven from the wall to the HQ of the Second Army District, in a cleverly camouflaged position protected by monumental rocks, strangely weathered and smoothed, like a hillside of Henry Moores.

In the lee of these boulders are mud-brick huts, with corrugated metal roofs, and the occasional Russian-built tank pulled in close for safety. On a parade ground, marked by small stones laid out in neat rows and painted white, the flag of the Saharawi Arab Democratic Republic flutters above three more tanks and four pick-ups fitted with anti-aircraft guns. A massive curved rock, resembling the head of a whale, juts out on a rise overlooking the parade ground, and beneath it a narrow entrance leads into the belly of the whale, a deep cave lined with carpets and cushions which is the nerve centre of this particular army post.

I'm still in the grip of whatever microbe is ravaging my system, so I retreat to the coolest corner of the cave and sit out a lunch of salad, goat and oranges, thinking of the only two things that appeal in these circumstances, sleep and death.

Unfortunately, neither is an option, as the commander of the Second Army District has made himself available for interview. He's a man of dignified composure and stern, hawk-like eye, who gives nothing much away. How does he keep up morale when there has been no war to fight for thirteen years? No problem, he claims. They are all committed to the struggle for free expression for the Saharawi people. And they have sophisticated weaponry. When I press him for more details this seems to mean the ageing tanks from Eastern Europe and the fortified Toyota pick-ups drawn up below.

Later, he and I walk out to inspect the troops. They are a ragged band, small in number, an assortment of ages wearing an assortment of uniforms. One has green espadrilles instead of army boots. Unless the Polisario is hiding some crack force from us, their military potential, even for guerrilla fighting, seems negligible.

The heat rises and my system continues to reject whatever is in there that it doesn't like. Once outside the cave, there is no escape or comfort. The skies are cloudless. The heat and the constant dusty wind scour my skin and turn my throat to sandpaper. There is no toilet but the desert, and as I crouch behind boulders feeling utterly miserable I am filled with desperate admiration for the soldiers who have endured conditions like these for years and a formless anger at those who make it necessary for them to do it.

It's a two-hour drive back to the barracks in Tfariti. I have to ask them to stop once again but this time I'm bent double with nothing to show for it. Everyone else turns their back, but Khalihena comes over to me once again, pours me some water, motions to his mouth and repeats in his soft French, 'Mange, mange'.

When I get back to the barracks, I take his advice, and thanks to a combination of Pepto Bismol, acupressure recommended by Basil and fresh bread and cheese, I steady the system and fall into a long deep sleep.

Day Twenty

Tfariti to Mejik

Though in my memory the fort on the hill will always be a sick room, I leave Tfariti with the optimism that always attends a departure and the prospect of a new destination.

Bachir aims to travel another 200 miles to the southwest, setting up camp for the night before moving on tomorrow to the rendezvous with our Mauritanian team at a place called Mejik.

Through the cracked glass of our windscreen we can see the relatively green landscape around Tfariti revert rapidly to stony desert. Despite the lack of cover, there always seems to be something out there, a solitary tree, a trotting herd of wild donkeys, even a skeletally thin dog that sniffs at us as we go by. And always the wind, sweeping across, sifting the sand, smoothing the rocks, leaching the rough ground and exposing the fossilised remains of a previous, very different Sahara, which, as recently as 10,000 years ago, was a grassland full of wild animals.

We stop for lunch in the shade and cover of a fallen acacia tree. Bachir rubs some resin off the bark and tells me to taste it. A sharp, cleansing, minty freshness.

'Arabic gum. Very good for all kinds of intoxication.'

I know the name well. Over the centuries, fortunes have been made from gum arabic, and it's still high on any list of West African exports. A preservative for food, it's also used for pharmaceuticals and making inks. It's rather satisfying to find something so precious in the wood the chef is gathering to make our fire.

The fire is started by rubbing twigs together, then larger branches are laid on. Mohammed Salim, one of the drivers, face old and weathered, cheekbones cantilevered out, skin pulled tight as a drum, is sifting through the sand for camel droppings. So good is the camel at absorbing and re-using what it eats that these come out as small, regular-sized, dark brown pellets, referred to by the experts as nuggets. Quickly hardened by the sun, they make ideal pieces for a board game. Mohammed marks out a grid of squares in the sand and lays the pellets out like draughts. Najim, who he's challenged to a game, breaks twigs to use as his men. So the game of *dhaemon*, a sort of desert draughts, begins. As it warms up, Mohammed Salim becomes more and more excited, emitting a string of cries, shrieks, theatrical screams, imprecations and histrionic submissions to Allah, occasionally catching our eye and cracking a conspiratorial smile. Najim plays the straight man, not that he has much option, and wins the game.

Lunch is far behind us when, amongst swirling dust, tussocky grass and severely decreasing visibility, Bachir brings his lead vehicle to a halt and consults, rather anxiously, with Haboub, the most dashing of the drivers. There's much kneeling and peering off into the soupy dust clouds. Are we lost? Bachir's reply, intended to be reassuring, rapidly becomes one of our favourite sayings, to be used often in times of deep crisis.

'No we are not lost. We just cannot find the place.'

He suggests that we drive on after dark and try to reach Mejik. No-one complains, but there is an unspoken anxiety amongst us. Given the combination of dust clouds, pitch darkness and lack of any identifiable road or track, how good is our chance of finding Mejik?

Haboub shrugs, flashes a big white-toothed grin, flicks open a leather pouch and fills his pipe.

We reach Mejik a little before nine. Though there is a well-lit UN compound near by, we are booked once again into a barracks, set in a crumbling concrete-walled enclosure. Someone has at least made a stab at brightening up the place. The narrow, unroofed strip of passageway outside our rooms has been laid with crazy paving, and along it runs a dried-up garden bed decorated with Russian shell-cases. The accommodation, consisting of two large unfurnished dormitories, a lavatory and washroom, is much the same as at Tfariti, except that, instead of a plastic jug, this lavatory has a luxury attachment, a flush.

I pull it. Nothing happens.

Day Twenty-One

Mejik to Zouérat

Slept soundly and am now packing to make ready for the crossing into Mauritania.

The border is only 15 miles away. Bachir says that we will be the first foreigners ever to cross it at this point, after negotiations made possible because of the currently cordial relations between Mauritania and the Polisario.

Over a last meal of bread and coffee he expands on this.

'We have nothing in common with the Moroccans. We have everything in common with the Mauritanians – culture, language, songs, dance.'

The UN mission here, frustrated by both sides in its attempt to organise a referendum on the future of Western Sahara, has run up costs of $250 million and may well lose patience. Doesn't he think there will come a time when they will have to reach a compromise?

Bachir doesn't hesitate.

'There can be no compromise. We will be like a camel's thorn to the Moroccans.'

He is smiling, a little grimly perhaps, but not without some relish.

'The more a camel tries to get a thorn out of its foot, the deeper it goes in, and the harder it is to get rid of it.'

At eleven, a line of vehicles emerges from the swirling sand to the south and soon we're shaking hands with a new set of escorts. Compared with the Saharawis, the Mauritanians, marked out by their billowing pale blue robes, which they call *boubous*, carry with them a worldliness, a touch of confidence and panache, which comes, I suppose, from having a country of your own.

Cassa is dark, attractive, in his thirties, I should imagine, and seems to be in charge of the operation, alongside an Englishman, Bob Watt. Abdallahi, pale-skinned, more Arab than Berber, is our official helper from the Mauritanian Ministry of Communications. Rumour has it that he's the Minister himself.

Mohammed Salim, so ebullient at desert draughts yesterday, is subdued. He has some problem with his eye and we've left him medicine from our filming kit. Nevertheless, he hugs me with surprising force as we begin our long farewells.

The fort at Mejik and the waving Saharawis are quickly obscured by a violent sandstorm. I still have my dry desert cough, which the sand hissing against the windows and squeezing in through the floor isn't doing anything to improve. Visibility drops to a hundred yards. It feels as if we are in limbo, and the lack of any point of reference increases the unreality of anything we glimpse outside. Did we really pass a new-born camel, still wet from its mother, lying on the sand? Or a UN border patrol in four immaculate white Land Cruisers, their aerials swinging and bending in the wind like fishing rods?

Then, three short, sharp shocks in rapid succession – a line of concrete houses, a railway line and a hard-top road. Never mind water in the desert; after days of being thumped and jolted and flung about, it's tarmac in the desert that sends the spirits soaring.

The controversial Mauritanian border is not marked, and there is nothing to indicate a change of country until we reach a checkpoint, a metal rondavel, clanging violently in the wind. Two tall, loose-limbed guards peruse our passports, with more bewilderment than suspicion, and then we are free to enter the town, nay veritable metropolis, of Zouérat, where there are bicycles and motorbikes and cars and garages and shops and sports grounds and, at last, a hotel, the Oasian. The Polisario camps were much cleaner than Zouérat, and young boys there did not flock round, hands out for money or presents, as they do here.

But, for now, the promise of cold beer and a hot shower makes up for everything.

There is no hot water, owing to a problem with the boiler, but the beer is awfully good and I'm able to get through to Helen on the satellite phone and tell her I was dying but survived. She tells me that last night she dreamt I was in bed beside her, sent back home by the BBC for being physically not up to it. I'm quite touched by the fact that we should be having the same anxiety dreams.

MAURITANIA

Day Twenty-Two

Zouérat

One significant change since we crossed the border is the appearance of baguettes and croissants at the breakfast table. For the first sixty years of the twentieth century, first as a protectorate and later as a colony, Mauritania, land of the Moors, was a neglected part of the French empire in Africa. La Mauritanie, as big as France and Spain put together, with a population barely that of Paris, became a place of exile, a dustbin for troublemakers, sidelined from the real French interests in Senegal and Morocco. But the French brought their *boulangeries* and the Mauritanians kept them when they became an independent Islamic republic in 1960.

It's interesting to see what survives of the colonial presence in these countries. In Western Sahara the Spanish legacy lives on in the Polisario, in their education and their political allegiances, and yes, I did have some *chorizo* with my camel one evening, but that's about it. Here in Zouérat, the French influence seems superficially stronger, extending beyond baguettes to *lycées* and *gendarmeries*, pastis in the bar and French news on the television.

After breakfast I walk outside to take a look at the town. Seeing me coming, a gauntlet of salesmen rise effortlessly from their haunches to enjoin me to buy this or that ornament, scarf, ring, necklace, leather pouch. I smile widely and appreciatively and do not stop. When I reach the gate, I pause for a split second, which is long enough for a young man to enquire solicitously about my health before showing me some postcards. I make for the street. Before I can reach it two young boys leap off a donkey cart stacked with charcoal and race towards me, all big smiles and outstretched hands.

'*Donnez-moi un cadeau. Donnez-moi un Bic!*'

When I decline they scamper off and leap back onto their cart, aiming a couple of wild blows at the donkey.

Zouérat is a frontier town, with all the mess and brutality that goes with the sniff of money. In the cluster of jagged peaks to the south of the town is enough iron ore to last 200 years, a resource that has transformed this corner of the desert into a multi-million-dollar asset, supplying 40 per cent of Mauritania's foreign earnings.

All the jobs, houses, public transport and associated support trades are in the domain of SNIM, Société Nationale Industrielle et Minière, the once French, now Mauritanian-owned company that mines the ore. Without SNIM Zouérat would be no more than a collection of tents.

Which, in the poorer parts, it already is.

The backstreets of Zouérat are open rubbish tips, lined with low, shabby buildings, but when the doors are open, business spills out everywhere, like the desert after rain. Barbers, garages, telephone points and lots of *quincailleries* (ironmongers). Cutting, fabricating and panel beating seems to be going on in every corner. I watch a middle-aged, red-robed man, using only an axe, hammer and his own sandaled foot for purchase, transform a BP oil drum into a 6-foot length of fencing in less than five minutes.

The reason why ironmongery should be the growth industry here is all tied in with desertification and the influx of nomads. Three years of drought have brought thousands in from the desert, desperately in need of shelter. We go to meet a family living in 'tin city'. Their home is a tent within a compound fenced with recycled metal. The outside of the tent still bears the manufacturer's imprint, 'Mining Explosive. Product Of South Africa'. Inside, the sacks are lined with strips of patterned cloth, and the woman who has invited me in indicates a rug. Her mother fiddles nervously with a row of beads. I slip off my shoes and squat down. Both of the women are in black. Others of the family, all women or children, gather around and regard me curiously. Tea is prepared, as in Western Sahara, with much ritual. They speak in Arabic and Cassa translates their story.

They came in from the desert five years ago and still have no mains water, relying on the irregular visits of the water cart. Nor do they have electricity, though a neighbour has recently let them have a lead off their supply. She proudly points out an uncovered cable snaking across the sand from the fence next door. They have a goat and live mainly off rice and couscous. A younger sister makes some money clearing sand from the railway line. One of her boys goes to school; the other doesn't, because he is mentally handicapped and there is no provision for him. There is, in all this, not a trace of self-pity. They simply hope the rains will come and turn the desert green again and enable them to return to the life they know best. Meanwhile, home is a tent of explosive sacks behind a fence made of oil drums.

'What makes you happy?' I ask.

Even mother, nervously twisting her beads, smiles as this is translated to them. They don't even have to think of the answer.

'Whatever God gives, makes us happy.'

Outside in the street, the gang of children following us down through the rubbish in which the goats graze doesn't look as if much makes them happy. In too many of their eyes is the flat, unresponsive blankness of poverty. In the livelier ones there is something more, a sullen resentment looking for an outlet.

An interesting incident on our way back to the hotel. Despite the present government's desire to keep it quiet, it's well known that Mauritania was one of Saddam Hussein's staunch allies, so much so that Saddam sent his wife and children to the town of Atâr, 100 miles south of here, for safekeeping during the Gulf War. Roger has noticed a painted sign portraying Saddam, looking dapper and suave in suit and tie, above a tyre shop. When he asks if we can film it, not only is the answer no, but Abdallahi, our man from the ministry, makes a personal visit to the shop and demands that the sign be taken down instantly.

Day Twenty-Three

ZOUÉRAT TO AZOUGUI

The iron ore that is the bedrock of the Mauritanian economy is shifted from the desert to the coast on a single-track railway line, which is as important to the country as the iron itself. The Polisario knew this, and their repeated attacks on the line are what eventually forced the Mauritanians to abandon plans to occupy Western Sahara back in 1979.

It's not surprising therefore that we have to negotiate two or three increasingly serious roadblocks as we drive 9 miles south and east from Zouérat to the Guelb mine.

With the storm still howling across the desert, sand-ploughs are out keeping the road clear, and our first sight of the boxy super-structure of the mine buildings is through a spectral cloud of rasping stinging dust.

At Guelb, the desert has been transformed into a dark satanic world of noise and movement. Caterpillar trucks grind up and down, bringing freshly mined material to the crushers. From there, conveyor belts carry the pulverised rock to a hopper, which fills railway wagons at the rate of 100 tonnes a minute. Today, the wind is catching the iron ore dust between hopper and wagon and sweeping most of it out across the desert in billowing black clouds. Through this mad screaming tempest of wind and dust, yellow and blue diesel locomotives, bells sounding dolefully, keep the wagons moving slowly forward.

Groups of maintenance workers pass by, faces muffled against the blackened sand, dark glasses covering their eyes, looking like mummified escapees from some experimental hospital. Everything about them is threadbare apart from their gleaming new shovels.

Three iron ore trains run every day, seven days a week, between the mines and the Atlantic port of Nouâdhibou. The good news for us is that one train a day also carries passengers.

Just after midday I find myself at a platform-less halt known cryptically as 'Arrêt TFM'. There must be a couple of hundred people gathered here as the monster of a train shuffles slowly towards us. For what seems an eternity, 163 wagons, piled high with rock and black dust, roll past before the two passenger coaches at the back reach the station.

When they do, and the train has shuddered to a halt, there is pandemonium. Passengers don't mount the train, they storm it, scrambling up the steep embankment aiming for two narrow doors, both of which are manned by railway officials whose sole duty seems to be to repel them. They shriek at the crowds and the crowds shriek back. Enormous women with huge bundles leap onto the ladders and force their way past. A pair of arms emerges from a window and a baby is tossed up into them. A man with a roll of carpet on his shoulder turns, Laurel and Hardy-like, one way and then the other, thwacking people on either side. Human buttresses are formed, leading from the embankment to the train doors.

Casting all human decency aside, I elbow my way past old women, children and blind men and grasp the rail, shouting above the noise that I have a Première Classe ticket. The guard shakes his head and bars my way. I'm about to lose what little control I still have when I realise the guard is directing me to the last car on the train, a box-like wagon with circular holes in its side that looks suspiciously like a recycling container. This, it turns out, *is* Première Classe.

Once inside the container its appearance begins to make sense. It's essentially a guard's van, with a central raised section like a ship's bridge, from where company operatives can survey the length of the train, which today is roughly a mile. From up here I can see that those who were not able to get aboard the coaches have scrambled onto the goods wagons and are settling in on top of the iron ore. One wagon is entirely occupied by a herd of goats.

This ship of fools moves off southwards at a steady 25 miles per hour. Alongside us the tarmac road falters and merges with the sand. This line is now the only man-made route across the desert.

It is not pretty desert. Grey dust blows over a scruffy plain of rocks and rubble, enlivened occasionally by the detritus of a derailed train or the bleached corpse of an abandoned pick-up truck. I lie down and try to read, but it's not easy, as the slightest change in speed convulses the train.

After several hours of extremely slow progress the train rumbles to a halt at a small town called Choûm. Scarcely has it done so than Choûm station is transformed into the scene of a major disaster. Passengers getting off the train claw at half-open doors as passengers getting on the train hurl themselves at the same half-open doors like soldiers entering a besieged city. Babies are thrown about, the carpet man is cutting his own swathe through the crowds and the low hum of diesel engines mingles with the pathetic falsetto of ore-stained goats.

This is where we get off. If we can.

From Choûm the train turns west to reach the Atlantic coast sometime tomorrow. We pick up the vehicles and head south and east, into the interior of Mauritania, away from the long arcing border of Western Sahara, which has held us like a magnet these past ten days.

As if reflecting the change of direction the landscape changes too. A long escarpment wall has risen up from nowhere and dominates the eastern horizon until the light goes down and it blends into the general darkness. Our convoy rattles on, twisting and turning until the track tackles the escarpment head-on. For the first time since crossing the Atlas Mountains we are climbing, steadily, if not spectacularly, following the thin dusty plume of the vehicle ahead.

We level out on a plateau of splintered rocks. It's a bare, dispiriting place.

Night falls, and with it comes that vague anxiousness I've felt many times since we left Morocco. A feeling that we could go on like this for days and nothing would ever change.

I wake from a bumpy back-seat slumber to find we've stopped. Ahead of us figures in veils flit away from our headlights into a large, crisply flapping tent. Cassa has got out and is striding off into a grove of trees. We disembark. Stretch legs, yawn, drink some water. It's nine o'clock by my watch when Cassa returns with furrowed brow and motions us into the vehicles.

Apparently, a friend of his, who was to put us all up tonight in his 'Typical Nomadic Tent', has disappeared into the desert, as nomads do, and not come back.

So, off we go again. Back into the night.

Half an hour later, dots of light flicker in the distance. They prove to belong to a small encampment outside the little town of Azougui, which bears unlikely signs of tourist facilities. As we turn into the compound our headlights pick out a painted board, the name of an *auberge* and the reassuring words beneath it, '*Près de la Ville. Loin du Son Stress*'.

It's not where we were meant to be, but no-one's complaining.

Day Twenty-Four

AZOUGUI TO ATÂR

Pass the night in a thatched hut, shared with Basil, with barely room to stand up straight. Woken in the small hours by the sounds of a ferocious cat fight. The ensuing trip to the loo is quite tricky. The door of the hut is tiny. I crawl out like a bee leaving a hive, to be rewarded with a massive and magnificent night sky. In the absence of moonlight the definition and abundance of the heavens is overwhelming, and I find myself praising my Maker for giving me such a weak bladder.

The morning reveals a number of similar straw huts, shaped like igloos and set around a large tent, over 30 feet square, and two whitewashed stone buildings with gabled roofs which look incongruously like Welsh chapels. Looking beyond the camp, I see a much less inimical landscape than the rest of the western Sahara. Palm trees and long grass fill in the empty spaces between the acacia trees and dry-stone walls border the tracks that lead up to the quiet, laid-back little town. Over a breakfast of fresh-baked bread and bananas, Cassa tells me that Azougui was once a trading post on the edge of the desert, where gold and salt and slaves changed hands. It was from here that a particularly aggressive dynasty of Berber peoples known as the Almoravids set out on a quest for more land, which led them north, to found Marrakesh, before moving across the Strait of Gibraltar and into Europe.

Cassa, a youngish man, elegant and rather aristocratic, runs tours into this part of Mauritania, and I would not dream of questioning the validity of anything he says were it not for his playful but confusing habit of hopping from intense seriousness to hooting laughter in the same breath.

On our way south and east we pass through a remarkable landscape, where the constant, unblinking process of disintegration and decay that characterises the Sahara takes rich and varied forms, from spectacular, Rio Grande-like mesas to soft sand dunes, crumbling escarpments and moon-like rubble-strewn plains. In the midst of this austere beauty is the small town of Atâr, neither austere nor beautiful. But today and tomorrow Atâr will be in a world spotlight. The Paris–Dakar Rally is coming to town.

The Paris–Dakar arouses mixed emotions. For the organisers, it is the most gruelling event on the motorsport calendar, pitching man and machine against one of the harshest environments on the planet. For opponents, like the French Green party, it is 'colonialism that needs to be eradicated', costing sums 'equal to the annual health budget of some of the countries the race crosses'.

In 1999 it was held up by bandits whilst crossing Mauritania. In 2000 threats from Algerian fundamentalists forced the contestants into an air-lifted leapfrog over the country, and last year the driver of a back-up vehicle lost a leg after hitting a land mine near the Moroccan wall.

But the Paris–Dakar, now commonly known as The Dakar, as Paris is no longer its obligatory starting point, has, since its inception in 1978, survived wars and rumours of wars, fatalities and serious accidents, to grow and flourish, carried on by its own obstinate momentum and man's insatiable urge to do things the hard way.

Somewhat ironically for a town surrounded by desert, Atâr suffered from catastrophic floods in the 1980s and all buildings of character seemed to have been washed away and replaced with nondescript concrete and breeze-block. One exception to the overall dusty brown of the narrow streets are the Total gas stations, which are a riot of liberally applied red and white paint. Total, it turns out, are the sponsors of the Dakar Rally.

We find accommodation, albeit modest, at the Auberge El Medina, on a corner where four sandy streets meet. An unattended donkey trots past as we push open the heavy metal doors into a courtyard bordered with pink oleander and yellow hibiscus. Mats are laid out for communal eating and two large tents stand at one end of the yard. Privacy is not a characteristic of desert life. The idea of a room of your own is alien to a country whose traditions are nomadic and gregarious, but the proprietors of the Auberge El Medina have judiciously spread their cultural options. On the other three sides of the courtyard are five rooms with locks on the doors. However, each room has at least six beds in it.

Walking outside after we'd settled in, I had expected to see a town gripped by Rally fever, with banners, bunting and bars open all day. There are, of course, no bars in the non-alcoholic Islamic Republic of Mauritania, and the lack of bunting and banners is explained later in the afternoon when the Rally finally hits town.

It comes, not along the road, but down from the sky. A series of distant rumbles heralds a steady flow of cargo planes, amongst them a Hercules and three or four high-winged Russian Antonovs, descending to the south of the town. They bring in the Rally, keeping it as exclusive as any travelling circus, a self-sufficient unit effectively isolated from any reliance on, or interaction with, the local people.

Atâr airport is in very good condition. The Rally organisers have seen to that. It stands on the outskirts of town, an immaculate collection of domed and arcaded buildings standing out from the surrounding half-built houses and empty walled compounds like a Christmas present on a rubbish tip. A small city has sprung up on the tarmac, huddled around a dozen planes and half a dozen helicopters, all of which, apart from an elderly cream Dakota belonging to the Mauritanian air force, are only here for the Rally.

One Antonov freighter is fitted out as a hospital, another as a catering store. Still others belong to the big works teams, whose riders bivouac in matching tents pitched in the protective shade of the wings. Striped marquees have been erected for the administration and the press, lap-tops cover trestle tables, mobiles are constantly in use (though it's impossible to get a mobile signal anywhere else in Mauritania), fridges full of cold drinks hum away in the desert sun.

But the plane that really matters is the Hercules. Without the Hercules, Atâr would not have got its gleaming new airport and freshly laid tarmac, for inside its ample flanks are the 22 tonnes of editing equipment, which provide the television coverage on whose revenue the Rally's survival depends.

Wires and cables spill like entrails from its belly, connecting up satellite dishes and generators and even a makeshift studio, complete with potted plants, set up on the tarmac for live interviews with the drivers, which will be pumped out to the four corners of the world.

Way beyond the bustling, hi-tech centre of this instant city, a suburban sprawl of less privileged competitors stretches to the far corners of the airstrip. At its shadeless limits, where the tarmac runs out and the rubble begins, a tent, a Union Jack and an old Range Rover, with a row of white socks drying on its bonnet, mark the headquarters of the only British interest left in the Rally. The tent is shared by Dave Hammond, a short and amiable motorbike rider, and his two mechanics. Dave is what's known as a privateer, someone who has entered the race 'for the romance of the event', without the backing of any of the big teams. Not for him the Mitsubishi millions. His fuel tank bears the name of Webb's Garages of Cirencester.

And bears it proudly. Fifty-two bikes have already dropped out and Dave is lying twenty-first of the 115 still left. He's optimistic. At this stage of the rally the pressure is on the big boys and they begin to make mistakes. Dave reckons that if he doesn't do anything silly he'll pick up places at the expense of those being forced to take risks.

I ask him if he has any sense of where he is. He shakes his head and laughs.

'I just know we're going south, because it's getting hotter and hotter.'

The Dakar Rally, it seems, is really nothing to do with seeing the world. It's about machines and drivers. Where you are is less important than how fast you got there and whether you still have a vehicle that can get you out. Someone tells me of a first-time American competitor, thrown off his bike five days ago in Morocco, who'd asked plaintively, 'Is there much more sand out there?'

Day Twenty-Five

ATÂR

You have to be up at sparrow-fart to catch the Rally. The first riders on this time-trial stage, a loop starting and ending in Atâr, have left the airport by eight o'clock, and it's been a long and tricky drive to find a position along the course ahead of them. Once again, the first sign of activity is aerial. A muttering and thudding fills the valley and seconds later a silver helicopter streaks in over sand and stone tracks it has taken us an hour to negotiate. It circles gracefully, picks a spot and swoops to earth, disgorging a camera crew at the point where the piste is marked by a low but nasty run of bumps. A few locals have gathered to watch. They crouch on their haunches, arms resting on knees, looking more bemused than expectant. A donkey watches impassively from a nearby clump of tamarisk trees. A few yards further on, a group of village women are standing up against a flimsy fence, holding a sign on which is written 'Go, Johnny Go!', believed to be a reference to the presence of the veteran Gallic rocker Johnny Hallyday in one of the cars.

More helicopters appear. Some land in a scatter of sand, others hover briefly before sweeping away in search of the next good vantage point. Then the first of the bikes comes into sight around the base of a sand dune, swaying and skidding past at speeds of around 60 miles per hour, sending up a fine plume of red sand as its rider, standing, arms and legs braced, works furiously at throttle and brake to get a grip on this treacherous surface.

One of the bikes hits a submerged stone and careers off course, flinging its rider to the ground. He remounts and roars by. We check the number. Somehow it had to be. 126. Dave Hammond, Great Britain.

Before the cars come through we move on to a better vantage point overlooking the village of Tougadh. Because it's up in the hills, the buildings of Tougadh are sturdier than most I've seen in the Mauritanian Sahara, a mix of rectangular houses and circular huts, most of them resting on a skilfully cut dry-stone base and topped with mud and thatch. The village lies across a rising slope, with the head of the valley at one end and a thick grove of date palms at the other. There is no movement amongst the huts. A figure lies asleep outside one of the houses, head resting in the crook of an arm.

Then comes a distant hum, like the sound of a swarm of bees. Moments later the sound changes from swarming bee to angry hornet and a thin line of dust can be seen snaking through the palms. Swinging wildly on the sandy track, the lead car bursts out of the trees and into the village. Compared with the motorbikes, whose riders could at least be seen grappling with their machines, it's disappointingly anonymous. A red box driven by two Lego men. Compelled by Rally regulations to observe a speed limit whilst passing through a village, it croaks and barks through the gears with rather bad grace as it climbs between the houses and over the hill. A young man from the village clambers up, waving vigorously at us. For a moment I think this must be the first Mauritanian to show any excitement about the race, but it turns out he wants to sell us some of his dates.

For the next two hours the sixty-five cars left in the race snarl by, hauling the message of McDonald's and Microsoft, PlayStation and Gauloises through the sleepy, unappreciative village. After the cars come the trucks and an armada of support vehicles, until all that's left is a Toyota Land Cruiser containing three journalists covering the rally. They seem in no great hurry and are opening up the daily ration kits issued to them by the organisers. David Park, from the *New York Times*, is impressed.

'What have we got today? *Pâté de volaille.* There's sausage, cheese, two biscuits, one for the pâté, one for the cheese. *Petit Napoléon.*' He shakes his head in awe and admiration. 'It's so . . . French!'

A line of village children stand watching Park and his friends as if they've come from Mars. They might as well have done. In almost every material respect they are different from the inhabitants of Tougadh. Well-fed, prosperous, highly mobile, technologically sophisticated, multinational. Everything this part of Africa is not. Park hands out most of the content of his ration bag to the children. His smile is broad, theirs are tentative. Then his Toyota fires into life, the palm thatch fence sways in the slipstream and the last of the Rally is gone, possibly until next year, probably for ever. A little way up the hill, a man still lies asleep with his head in the crook of an arm.

All the competitors, apart from a few stragglers, are back at the airport by mid-afternoon. Minor injuries are nursed, positions checked. Stories and rumours spread through the camp. One car somersaulted over a dune, but when the co-driver managed to struggle back to lay a helmet on the dune as a warning sign the next car flew right over him. Alfie Cox, one of the top bikers, won the stage, despite riding the last 200 miles without water after a fall had severed his supply. Leading the six trucks left in the race is the Russian team, admired by one English journalist less for their driving than their spectacular devotion to the hard stuff.

'Anything'll do. They finished off the windscreen washer fluid last night.'

And Dave Hammond is still in the race. Despite two falls, he completed the 250-mile course in just over four hours and has moved up to eighteenth place. He and his mechanics are cleaning the bike meticulously.

After they've finished they'll gather with other riders to watch video footage of their day's performance.

There's a strong family feeling at work here. At heart, the Dakar Rally is about fraternity – bands of brothers united by common language, enthusiasms and ambitions. I admire their mad bravery, but we don't have much in common. Mauritania excites me much more than motorsport.

Day Twenty-Six

ATÂR TO CHINGUETTI

It's still dark when I wake at the Auberge. It takes a while to work out why the room appears to be shaking. Then the dull reverberation focusses into a familiar sound. The planes are leaving. The circus is moving on. The Dakar Rally is taking to the skies again.

Sure enough, as we pass out of Atâr later in the morning, the airport is empty, the tarmac cleared. Soldiers are no longer in position. The corrugated metal sheets of a '*Toilette Publique*' are being dismantled. A line of damaged bikes waits to be collected and flown home. A goat sniffs around the leftovers of the bivouac and somewhere out in the desert the strike force heads south. They'll be in Dakar long before us, that's for sure. But we'll have seen a lot more.

It's a good day to be on the move. Skies bright and clear, mellow winter temperatures peaking at around 30°C/86°F. We're climbing up between the sheer, brick-red walls of the Adrar Massif in scenery that could have come straight out of a John Ford Western. What's more, we're on that luxury of luxuries – a freshly tarmacked road, paid for and constructed by the Chinese in return for fishing concessions off Mauritania's Atlantic coast.

Having done its basic job of taking us through the pass and onto the escarpment, the tarmac ends abruptly. The road reverts to dirt track but soon the rubble gives way to softer, sandier terrain, and by the time we reach the outskirts of Chinguetti we are on the edge of a sand sea, classic date-box desert, for which the Arab word *erg* sounds awfully inadequate.

The fine golden sand looks soft and seductive, but it is the most difficult and dangerous surface and dune-driving requires great skills. Despite clever use of the four-wheel drive, we have to make three attempts to climb one towering dune. My heart is in my mouth each time, for we seem so close to tumbling over and crashing down the slope.

Once at the top I'm left gasping, not so much at the perilousness of the ascent, as by the revelation of the sand sea, stretching to the horizon. The sinuous outlines of the dunes, formed by the wind into hundreds of thousands of peaks and crests and troughs, is mesmerisingly beautiful. Though the sand is constantly in motion, being smoothed and reshaped by the wind, there is an illusion of complete stillness, the sculpted contours of the sandscape smooth as marble, not a grain out of place, everything in perfect equilibrium.

John studies it more philosophically.

'I suppose you could say it's the ultimate wasteland,' he observes. 'The world's surface reduced to fine dust.'

He's right of course.

Day Twenty-Seven

CHINGUETTI

Looking over the battlements at Fort Saganne, our French Legion lookalike hotel, as another hot day gets underway, I can see below me a network of lanes and low stone and plaster houses that could have been there for months or years, it's hard to tell. Their walls are uneven, often broken and collapsed into piles of rubble. A woman who has been peeing unselfconsciously in the sand goes back into her house. The front door is of corrugated metal, hanging from one hinge. Beyond is an area of wide sandy spaces with shops and long, low, concrete civic buildings. To one side stands the tall shell of the electricity generating station, its walls punctured by Polisario mortars twenty-three years ago and still unrepaired. But a half-mile or so beyond all that, stretched across a low hill and bordered by palm trees, old Chinguetti, with its assortment of towers and red-gold stone walls, stands out handsomely, like a mediaeval hill town.

From the battlements of Fort Saganne, Chinguetti, seventh holiest city of Islam, looks a place of substance and civility.

When we drive into the old town, across the bone-dry football pitch that occupies the flat plain between old and new Chinguetti, the reality is rather different. For a start, the taller and more spectacular of the two minarets turns out to be a water tower.

Though the old mosque has been beautifully restored, the warren of streets around it is like a ghost town. Discarded sardine tins, batteries, padlocks, Pepsi cans and electric cables lie half-buried in the sand. Birds dart through the ruined houses, and occasionally a veiled figure will call out from a doorway, indicating that their house is not abandoned and pointing out the word '*boutique*' scrawled beside it on the wall and the small collection of local artefacts dimly visible inside. In other streets the stone walls are all that remains. Behind solid carved doorways, once prosperous houses lie open to the sky and the sand.

The desert is taking over Chinguetti.

There are surprises. I'm trudging up a side street when I hear the sound of voices chanting. It comes from the other side of a low wall, in which a green door stands ajar. I peer round it and find myself in a white-walled courtyard. A dozen children, all clutching wooden boards covered with Arabic writing, are sat in a row facing the wall, reciting texts in high sing-song voices. Standing above them, occasionally stooping to correct some misreading is a tall, elderly man, veiled in black and white, with hollow cheeks and a straggly grey beard, as long and pointed as his face. He is the imam of the mosque whose minaret, shaped like a Gothic church tower, we passed earlier. This is his house and also the *medersa*, the Koranic school, where the children learn the holy texts, and where some of the better students will be able, one day, to recite the entire Koran from memory. They don't seem to be learning anything else.

He shakes hands with Cassa but not with any of us, I notice, but when he answers our questions his fierce countenance cracks easily into a twinkling smile, revealing two prominent, immaculately white teeth.

Beckoning us into the shade, he orders two of the senior boys, clearly his favourites, to offer round a wooden bowl of *zrig*, a thick mixture of goat milk, water, millet and sugar.

In a voice thin and husky from a lifetime of summoning the faithful he tells us that the minaret is the second oldest in continuous use anywhere in the Muslim world. Until very recently, he says, he used to climb up and make the call to prayer from the top of the tower; now he's not strong enough and has to rely on a microphone down below.

Along a side street nearby, the word '*Bibliothèque*' is scrawled in white paint on the stone lintel of an otherwise inconspicuous doorway. Stepping inside, I find myself in a room, no more than 15 feet square, with bamboo mats on the floor and rough-plastered walls. An old man rises to greet me.

Behind him, stacked on shelves, are bundles of papers wrapped in leather bindings or manila folders. They are books and documents of extraordinary beauty, many of them six or seven hundred years old. In some cases the pages have come loose from their bindings, but in all of them the quality of the work is exquisite. They have been in his family for centuries and he treats the texts like old friends, moving his finger from right to left, as the Chinese and Japanese do, across the delicate, spidery calligraphy.

There is a commentary on the Koran, with notes around the margins, and a book of Islamic law, still clearly readable, detailing legal procedures – numbers of witnesses, rights of the accused – all dating back to the golden days when Chinguetti was one of the great centres of Islamic scholarship.

'This land,' he says, head inclined towards mine but eyes fixed somewhere in the distance, 'was called Chinguetti before it was called Mauritania.'

I ask him if there might be a price at which he'd part with a book like this, but he shakes his head. These are his life, and part of the life of his fathers and forefathers. He cannot let them down by selling them.

In the main square of Old Chinguetti is a more organised collection of the city's treasures. The Bibliothèque Al Halott can be found off the courtyard of a fine old house, behind ancient acacia wood doors. Beneath weathered black beams are bulky modern filing cabinets containing 1400 manuscripts. A father-and-son team looks after them, and so valuable are the works that they only allow visitors in one or two at a time. Their pride and joy – '*le plus ancien ouvrage*' – is a Koran, brought here from Mecca in AD 1000. They have a book on astronomy dating from the fourteenth century, clearly showing the planets of our solar system circling the sun, proving that Arab scholars knew something that the authorities in Europe refused to acknowledge for a further 200 years.

Six o'clock. The best time of day. People are out in the streets again, shops are open, children, rolling old tyres, race after each other. The big heat is off, the setting sun turns the desert a rosy purple and the sounds of the city soften to a murmur.

Walking in the new town, I find myself first watching, then participating in a game of *dhaemon*, as taught me by Mohammed Salim of the Polisario. An erect, bare-headed man, who clearly fancies himself as the local Grand Master, is taking on all comers and thrashing them. He barely raises his eyes from the sand as I'm sat down opposite him and given my quota of *crottes de chameau*, camel droppings. Then something goes wrong with his strategy. Soon I have at least a dozen friends and advisers ready to manage my every move, shouting, debating and arguing with increasing hysteria as they scent a rare victory in the air.

Sure enough the sticks are uprooted with increasing regularity and the all-conquering camel turds are sweeping across the sand, until, with sharp cries of delight, the foreigner steals a victory.

I seem to have had all Chinguetti on my side, for as I walk back to the hotel later I keep getting waves of acknowledgement, broad grins and cheery shouts of '*Champion!*'

My stock with the owners of the Hôtel Fort Saganne is already pretty high.

'*Vous êtes le deuxième star ici!*' they enthuse, '*le premier star*' being Gerard Depardieu, who stayed and worked here whilst making what was by all accounts a very bad film called *Fort Saganne* in 1984. I only wish their facilities matched their view of my status. Though I am in Depardieu's room, the generator provides light and electricity only fitfully, the bedside light is operated from a switch 20 feet away from the bed, the pillow is made from some form of granite and the painting and decoration seem to have been completed by someone with a serious grudge against society.

It all becomes a bit clearer when they reveal that Depardieu didn't stay in this room at all, but in a Winnebago parked outside. They even show me the spot.

'It was parked over there!'

My room was the one used in the film itself.

As Fort Saganne was all about the terrible privations endured by members of the French Foreign Legion, this explains a lot.

Day Twenty-Eight

CHINGUETTI TO NOUAKCHOTT

Around a quarter to seven the generator coughs into life, which means electricity and hot water will be available until half past nine, when they turn it off again. Up onto the battlements for a last reminder of the panorama of Chinguetti, this quintessential image of the desert. It requires a vivid imagination to evoke the glory days of the thirteenth and fourteenth centuries, when Ibn Battuta came down here from Tangiers, when there were seventy-six libraries in the town and when the constant coming and going of camel trains between Morocco and the fabulous kingdom of Mali made Chinguetti one of the centres of the civilised world.

Now the desert is quiet. The trade has gone elsewhere, by ship around the coast, on overland trucks that can't cope with the fine sand seas that enclose Chinguetti.

But, splendidly isolated as it may feel, Chinguetti is only 1200 miles from the coast of Europe, and if not trucks and boats, then aeroplanes may yet be its saviour. There is a growing curiosity about the desert, and as more tourists brave the Sahara south of Morocco this particular combination of landscape and history could well bring some money back to this historic city.

These tourist-board thoughts come to me as I wait at the small airstrip outside Chinguetti. I'm cadging a ride to Nouakchott, the Mauritanian capital, aboard a Cessna, from which Nigel has been filming the desert sands.

We peel off the baking tarmac and into the air, spreading panic amongst the camels careering below us. Soon the ancient crust of the old Saharan plateau pushes through the desert sands, exposing fault lines that reveal shiny, fractured, black rock and reminding me more than anything of the world's second largest desert, Antarctica.

After two hours in the air the colours begin to change. The charred blacks and browns of the escarpment give way to a green and white landscape as we slowly descend towards Nouakchott. The green is from stands of trees and fields of crops, a reminder of what irrigation can do in the fiercest of deserts, but it's the white that predominates, a great spreading undercloth of limestone and salt, as if the desert had been bleached as it reached the sea.

Our plane banks and turns and as it begins its final approach to the Mauritanian capital I can just about make out the Atlantic Ocean, away to the west.

Below us, streets and cars and palaces and office blocks and other visions of a way of life I'd half forgotten race up towards the plane. After where we've been, the thought of descending into the midst of a million people seems a great anticlimax, and the more I look forward to the creature comforts of a big city hotel the more I feel that I'm betraying the desert.

Day Twenty-Nine

NOUAKCHOTT

After one night at the Monotel Bar-El-Barka I realise that my appreciation of the simple life is a cracked and broken vessel. Maybe it's a question of age, but the delight I have taken in switching the air-con on and off, flushing and re-flushing the lavatory, caressing the bedside light and reading the laundry list from start to finish, including the women's section, suggests to me that I am not cut out for deprivation.

If twelve days of desert travel can reduce me to gibbering delight at the sight of one of the world's shortest room-service menus, what is to become of me when we turn east again, back to the sands?

There is water outside my room that is just for swimming in. It's surprisingly cold and refreshing. The only other occupants are two Mauritanian children, who seem amazed by the whiteness of my body, which, fresh from a long English winter, is very white indeed. They stare open-mouthed, as if seeing a ghost.

Thirteen years ago, whilst filming *Around the World in 80 Days*, I was stuck on a Yugoslav freighter moving agonisingly slowly across the Bay of Bengal. The tiny mess room was dominated by a map of the world. To help pass the time, my cameraman, Nigel Meakin, and I competed with each other to memorise every African country and, for extra points, the name of its capital. Mauritania was a tough one, but Nouakchott was a match winner. Nouakchott was the Holy Grail of obscurity.

Which is why I experienced more than the usual frisson of first-timer's excitement when I saw the name on the airport building, and why I immediately bought up all three postcards in the hotel shop. And why I'm rather ashamed to learn that this city we could never remember is the biggest in the Sahara.

I take some comfort from the fact that this is a recent development. Nouakchott, whose name, my guidebook tells me helpfully, may mean 'Place of Wind' or 'Place of Floating Seashells', was only created in the late 1950s, and even by 1980 had less than 150,000 inhabitants. Then came fourteen years of drought and an influx of refugees, which has pushed the population beyond the million mark.

Located at the collision point of Sahara Desert and Atlantic Ocean, the city of Nouakchott feels a bit like a lifeboat, tossed between two seas – one sand, one salt – with new people scrambling on board all the time. It has had neither the time nor the resources to create an identity or shape a character. It is just a place full of people.

There are some grandiose government buildings and a quarter where diplomats and foreign businessmen live in well-fenced comfort, but the heart of the city, down by the Grand Marché is a steaming, jostling mass of on-street commerce. The buildings that line the Avenue Abdul El Nasser lack any distinction, but in a sense that's not the point. They are just spaces to be filled, emptied, leaned against and sheltered beneath by the throng of buyers, sellers, hawkers, beggars and all the other players on this congested stage: smooth young men in dark glasses, exuding unspecified threat, blind old men being led about by young companions, venerable, bearded figures swathed in veils, and poised young girls in deep-blue robes balancing on their heads trays of soft drinks the colour of dentist's mouthwash. Around them a ragged army of street sweepers, with faces wrapped like mummies, carry out the Sisyphean task of keeping the capital clean.

The crowd is fed by a cruising stream of green and yellow minibuses, setting down and picking up constantly. Weaving amongst them are all shades of the transport spectrum, from donkey-drawn carts to Mercedes 200s, with missing fenders, sightless headlamps and window-cracks like spider's webs.

The children beg blatantly and cheerfully.

'*Donnez-moi quelque chose!*'

I see no-one buying, selling or reading a newspaper.

The Atlantic shore, a mile or so from the centre of the city, offers the prospect of space and sea breezes, somewhere to cool off away from the clamour. I make for it at sunset, following the road across a desolate wasteland of broken shells and crusted sand dunes (the white blanket I'd seen from the air yesterday). The road does not, in fact, lead to a place of peace and quiet contemplation (they don't build roads in Africa for that sort of thing); it leads to a great heaving fish market, the Plage des Pêcheurs, Fishermen's Beach.

Dominated at one end by the curved concrete roof of the market building and at the other by the ghostly hulks of two wrecked freighters, this half-mile stretch of beach seethes with human activity. Donkeys pull carts through the sand, exhorted with sharp blows from their drivers. A man passes through the crowd with a plank on his head, carrying a dozen loaves of fresh-baked bread. Salesmen offer football shirts and trainers, combs, brushes, even a set of gleaming new spanners. Women in bold patterned veils or turbans gossip together, breaking off every now and then to call to their children. It's a family affair, part Billingsgate, part Blackpool, part B&Q. The majority of those here are black Africans. The Arabs, with their nomadic traditions, don't eat much fish, preferring the desert staples of camel, mutton or goat meat.

Long low boats with crescent-shaped hulls painted bright primary colours are everywhere, some drawn up on the beach, others out on the viscous Atlantic swell, bringing in their catch from the cool and fertile offshore currents. When full, the boats come to within a few yards of the shore and a score of porters plunge into the water. Mostly teenage boys, they compete with each other, racing with trays of swordfish, barracuda, sea bass and red mullet balanced on their heads, up through the crowds to the market. Their sense of urgency and the accompanying din of shouts, protests, yelps and laughter indicate the sense of elation that such an abundant food source can bring to a small country, but one of the market traders puts it in perspective. Many of the boats here, he says, are from neighbouring Senegal, and what does come in is only what has been rejected by the Japanese, Korean and Chinese factory ships lurking out beyond the horizon.

Day Thirty

NOUAKCHOTT

Strange weather. A warm wind blows from a brooding, hazy sky. The air is heavy, as if it might rain, which in a city that receives only

4 inches a year (London has nearer 30) would be quite an occasion.
I feel a little disoriented by Mauritania. Having passed through an
enormous country, I find myself in this wide, flat, shapeless capital
feeling that I could be anywhere. I remember my colleague Graham
Chapman on a Python tour of Canada being asked by a local tourist
guide what he thought of Regina, Saskatchewan. Graham looked
around at the flat expanse of prairie stretching away in every direction and then enquired, with winning politeness, 'Why didn't they
put it over there?'

Guidebook information is scarce, only fifty pages in my *Rough
Guide*, half that for neighbouring and much smaller Senegal, so for
on-the-spot information I seek out the honorary British consul,
Nancy Abeiderrahmane MBE, or Nancy Jones from Essex, as she
was before she married a Mauritanian in the late 1960s. I found her
at work in a spotlessly clean compound off an unmade, sand-
strewn road, from which she runs the highly successful Tiviski
dairy business. Beneath the shade of two spreading neem trees and
between an unloading tanker and a refrigerated delivery van, I'm
welcomed by a small, vivacious, middle-aged woman in a white
sari, obviously treated with respect by her workforce. The yard and
the unloading bays, where milk is brought in from farms and from
hundreds of small producers, many of them desert nomads, is constantly being hosed down. '*Portez Le Turban SVP*' (Please Wear a
Turban), says the sign on the door of the plant, and Nancy calls
someone over to help me tie a length of black cotton into a *howli*,
the Moorish head-wrap. It isn't easy. My nose keeps getting in the
way. The man is dismissed and another more senior member of
Nancy's 180-strong workforce takes over. He doesn't fare much
better. It's a bit like tying a bow tie, easier to do for yourself than
someone else. Nancy notices I have some hair showing, which is
hygienically impermissible, and yet another man, who for all I
know could be the chairman of the board, is summonsed. He does
the trick, and, looking like a passable imitation of Lawrence of
Arabia, I step, not into the desert, but into the bottling plant. It's the
coldest place in Africa; a gleaming world of stainless steel and
streamlined automation. Milk from cows, goats and camels is
poured into cartons at the rate of 2000 an hour. The plant works
seven days a week and sells product to over 2000 shops. The water

they use is recycled to irrigate a garden on a nearby roundabout.

In the office, flanked by computers and a sign on the wall, 'Don't EVER Give Up', I'm treated to a tasting of Tiviski's products, including conventional cow's milk, sweeter than its English counterpart, and less conventional but quite delicious ranges like date yoghurt, camel cheese and, the pride of her production, camel milk. Camel milk, Nancy assures me, is the answer to all our prayers.

'It has half the fat of cow's milk, and less sugar, so good for diabetics. It has a lot of vitamin C. It's good for vascular problems, women take it to have a clear complexion and they say it's a tonic for men.' Nancy smiles, and takes a breather before adding, unconvincingly, 'Whatever that means.'

'One protein in it is similar to human insulin, and as camels are pretty close to humans in the evolutionary tree, so the proteins are closer to humans, and it's less allergenic than cow's milk, she explains.

I want it and I want it every day from now on. But I can't, because I live in Europe, and the European regulations don't cover camel products. The EU won't even acknowledge that camels have products.

'But we're getting there,' says Nancy, and I believe her. She's not the sort of person to start out unless she intends getting there.

I ask her about Mauritania.

Life is hard for most people here – 'Everybody makes do with very little' – but she points to rapid change. Forty years ago there was not one mile of tarred road in the entire country. Now there is water and electricity supply to most homes in the city. It is a tolerant country; women do not have to cover their faces or accept polygamy. If a man wants a new wife he must divorce the old one first. This makes divorced women much sought after in Mauritania. They do not have any ties and they generally will have benefited from a divorce settlement. She feels quite comfortable as a female entrepreneur in a country that has women in the cabinet, law, medicine and even in the army. 'People,' she says with a touch of a smile, 'are very nice to women.'

She nimbly sidesteps the knotty question of slavery, which was only formally abolished here in 1981, but acknowledges that the Moorish social system is complex and tribal, with warrior and scholar tribes.

WESTERN SAHARA

Above: Inspecting Polisario troops near the wall. Their problem is partly lack of equipment, partly motivation after an eleven-year ceasefire. The flag of the Saharawi Arab Democratic Republic flies at the right.

Left: Nothing is wasted in the desert. Empty ammunition cans help solve the housing shortage.

Above: The team that brought us safely through our first test in tough desert travel. Mohammed Salim is on my right, and next to him is the gentle Khalihena, who looked after me at my lowest ebb.

Centre: Street art in Zouérat. The bold telephone sign not only looks good, but is also vital in a place where many cannot read.

Below: The portrait of Saddam that we're not allowed to film.

MAURITANIA

Top: Worker at the iron ore mines, wrapped up against the howling wind. The world's longest train is loading in the background.

Above left: The reason why ironmongery is Zouérat's growth industry. Drought has brought great demand for shelter as nomads come in from the desert.

Top left: Rush hour at Arrêt TFM. Fight for seats on one of the Sahara's only trains. Those in Iron Ore class are already in position.

Centre left: Englishman makes the mistake of saying 'After you'.

Left: Jumping the queue, Mauritanian-style.

Breaking the silence. The first of 115 motorbikes slides and slithers through the sand dunes south of Atar.

Top: The First World flies in for the day. Atar airport becomes media city as the Dakar Rally hits town.

Above, left and right: Tougadh village. Western wealth makes little impression on the locals. The adverts are all for the television coverage.

Top: With the owner of a one-room library in Chinguetti. In his case the family silver is the written word.

Above: Writing was a work of art for Islamic scholars. The calligraphy in the books in Chinguetti's libraries is up to 1000 years old.

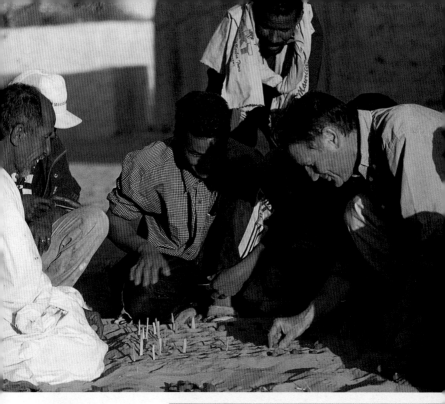

Top: With a little help from my friends, I'm never short of advice in my struggle against the Grand Master of Chinguetti.

Above: Three of my champion *crottes.*

Right: Yes! The turds have it! England 1, Mauritania 0.

Top: Nouakchott beach, where the Sahara meets the Atlantic. A mile of fish market with a backdrop of wrecked freighters.

Above: Never a shortage of helpers to bring the boats in. A boy waits with his plastic tray to carry fish up to be weighed. But the best of the catch is trawled by foreign factory ships out beyond the horizon.

The southern Saharan look. A woman, more Negro than Arab, chews on an acacia stick, the Saharan equivalent of toothbrush and toothpaste combined.

Fabrics for sale in Nouakchott market. Bold colours and patterns are one of the great delights of the southern Sahara.

SENEGAL

Left: At the end of the island on which St-Louis, first French foothold in Africa, was founded, a museum and cultural centre rises beside the waters of the Sénégal.

Main picture: Fishwives in St-Louis. The fires burn all day long at this massive smokery on the banks of the River Sénégal.

Life in St-Louis.

Right: Outside a shop with a tall, dashing salesman and short plaster figures of the *colon*, the caricature of the French colonialist in Africa.

Centre: Women return from the market, heads full.

Below: At lunch with artist Jacob Yakouba and his soap-star wife, Marie-Madeleine.

Left: All needs catered for on the streets of Dakar.

Below right: Pre-*Tabaski* sheep-fattening grips Dakar.

Wrestling is the second biggest sport in Senegal.

Above left: At a local contest in a Dakar suburb, the boys show how it should be done.

Above right and below, left and right: My failed attempt to leave without the cheerleader noticing.

Top: A sweet potato changes hands at Kayes station. The mud-stained coach bears the logo of Chemins de Fer de Mali.

Above: At Mehani in Mali, the local train we've waited two hours for pulls in, and becomes an instant shopping mall.

There are two national sports. One is *dhaemon*, the desert draughts I played in Chinguetti, and the other poetry.

'In a decent gathering like a wedding party the young men are expected to improvise four verses of poetry and others to compose a reply. Everybody can recite lots and lots of poetry.'

She sees similarities between Mauritanians and the British.

'They love wit and they're always ready to say something funny. And you'll have noticed the country runs on tea. The cooking is, likewise, not terribly noteworthy.'

Day Thirty-One

NOUAKCHOTT TO ST-LOUIS

It's 127 miles from the capital of Mauritania to the border with Senegal. Both countries were once part of Afrique Occidentale Française, a huge slab of the French colonial empire. As we drive out of Nouakchott this morning, we are reminded of the new world order.

The American embassy is a fortress, bristling with razor wire, sprung with alarms and guarded by armed men. The Presidential Palace, a drab grey mass, of considerable size and very little beauty, was built by the Chinese.

However, the French influence lives on. As we pull up in the town of Tiguent we're ambushed by half a dozen children, heavily armed with baguettes, who crowd around the doors, shouting and jabbing loaves through the window until we submit and reach in our pockets for our last few *ouguiya*. The bread tastes good; a richer, stickier consistency than French baguette and with the added ingredient that marks it out as fresh – Saharan sand.

The French language remains the lingua franca and the one in which we're interrogated at a series of army roadblocks.

At one of these enforced halts, a tall, thin, young soldier in camouflaged fatigues approaches our vehicle and examines the contents carefully. His eyes flick towards us.

'*Parti à Rosso*?' he asks.

Yes, we reply cautiously. We are going to Rosso.

He looks us up and down, slowly, then appears to come to a decision. We hold our breath.

'*Vous avez une place?*'

He wants a lift.

As we near the River Sénégal, the bleached white shell-fields of Nouakchott give way to terracotta dunes dotted with spiky grass scrub and acacia trees just tall enough to provide shelter for the Fulani herders. As the sands of the Sahara blow in from the north and east, they're forced progressively closer to the River Sénégal. Only ten years earlier, the issue of land ownership along the border brought Mauritania and Senegal to the brink of war. Senegal kicked out Mauritanian traders and Mauritania allowed equally violent reprisals against 'southerners'. Today relations are better, but the security presence is strong enough to make filming a delicate task.

By midday we are passing a network of irrigation ditches and the first glimpse of grassland for two and a half weeks. The fields contain sugar cane, rice and grazing land, grown under a scheme which I see from a billboard is financed by the government of the Emirates, 3000 miles across the other side of the desert. An example of pan-Islamic co-operation, which could prove a much bigger influence on West Africa than anything French, American or Chinese.

At Rosso we reach the river and the next frontier, and take our place in a shuffling line of vehicles, most of which look like survivors of a stock car race, weighed down to the floor with goods, wires hanging out of empty headlamp sockets. We're a captive audience and vendors gather at the windows. It's very hot and hard to be patient in the face of endless demands for *cadeaux* and *bonbons*. We are not allowed to film and the ferry gates are shut.

Repair to the Pâtisserie El Belediya, which serves food on metal tables beneath walls of peeling paint. We are the only Westerners. A television set high on the wall is showing women being interviewed in houses reduced to rubble. It's hard to tell if it's the West Bank or the suburbs of Baghdad, recently hit by air strikes ordered by America's new president, George W. Bush, but none of those watching shows any hostility towards us.

After eating a skeletal chicken in casserole, I buy a carton of

Nancy's Tiviski brand camel's milk from the freezer behind the counter and drink it outside on a porch where there is, at least, some breeze. Basil is doing his flowing t'ai chi routine, which a couple of locals watch with amused curiosity.

'Kung fu?' asks one of them.

I nod. 'Sort of.'

After three journeys round the world with him, I'm used to Basil being mistaken for Bruce Lee.

Three hours later we are aboard the 80-foot floating platform that will take us into Senegal. It runs on African time, leaving only when it is full to bursting point.

The river, about a half-mile wide, curves languidly towards us through what might almost pass for meadows, which dip down to tall reed beds. Occasionally, the slim, wooden canoes they call pirogues will put out from either shore, precariously packed with foot passengers, all standing.

On the far side are low buildings, a single palm tree, a water tower and a small crowd watching us as keenly as we're watching them. The fact that the town on both sides is called Rosso seems to misleadingly minimise the difference between the two banks. In fact, the River Sénégal, rising over 1000 miles away in the mountains of Guinea, is an important boundary. It separates not only Mauritania from Senegal, but also Sahara from Sahel, the transitional land, half desert and half savannah, whose name means 'shore' in Arabic. More significantly, the River Sénégal divides Arab Africa to the north from Black Africa to the south.

The last few passengers hurry aboard, urged into a sprint by the long-awaited rumble of the diesel engine. We move stiffly out into the stream. I want to stare into the dark brown tide and think romantic thoughts of Saharan rivers, but it's impossible. I've been trapped by a cheerfully persistent ten-year-old boy called Lallala who wants something, anything, from me.

I try to shut him up by giving him a tin of Smith and Kendon travel sweets I have with me. It doesn't work. He wants me to translate all the words on the lid.

'Ken-don? What is Ken-don?'

On Senegalese soil just before four o'clock. Our minders engage in a long negotiation over equipment and visas at the handsome customs shed, built like a small French town hall. It bears not only the inscription '*Directeur Général des Douanes de Republique de Sénégal*', but also a motto, '*Devenir Meilleur Pour Mieux Servir*' (Become Better to Serve Better). Very un-African.

Another long wait. Buses and trucks squeeze out of the narrow car park. Currency changers move amongst the recently arrived, offering deals on the Mauritanian *ouguiya*, which, on account of the foreign aid propping up Mauritania, is stronger than the CFA franc used by Senegal.

A tall man in a white robe wanders around calling out 'Me bank!' and waving a wad of notes.

To begin with, the roads this side of the border are much rougher. Tarred but severely pot-holed, they ensure a jolting, punishing ride towards St-Louis. Then, quite suddenly, we appear to have time-travelled to provincial France. The road surface becomes smooth and white-lined. Every village leading into St-Louis has speed restrictions and signs warning us to belt up, back and front. And there are cyclists everywhere, turning out of leafy lanes and emerging from the university campus on drop-handlebar bikes, wearing Tour de France T-shirts. I can't remember seeing bicycles at all in Mauritania. Basil agrees.

'Beat-up old cars and donkey carts and nothing in between.'

Shortly before six we cross a wide estuary onto a narrow island with a cathedral and cinemas and draw up beside the clipped hedges, shady balconies and colourful awnings of the Hôtel De La Poste, where a long line of Monsieur Hulots is waiting to sign in ahead of us. I can even use my mobile to phone home. This is more than culture shock. It's cultural convulsion.

SENEGAL

Day Thirty-Three

St-Louis

I've spent the last twenty-four hours in France. It was unadventurous, but it was easy, pottering around the hotel from bar to restaurant to the Piscine Jardin with its wrought-iron flamingos, or just sitting on my hibiscus-clad balcony watching the majestic River Sénégal sweep beneath the majestic seven-span girder bridge built by Louis Faidherbe, Governor of Senegal, in the 1860s. After a bit, the Frenchness became almost suffocating, from the check tablecloths to the endless pictures and models of the *colon*, the caricature of the Frenchman in Africa, complete with pipe and pith helmet.

The overriding obsession of the Hôtel de la Poste is with the 1920s, when St-Louis was the most important town in French colonial Africa and a company called Aeropostale launched a regular mail service from Toulouse to Dakar. The pilots flew their fragile planes alone, often through the night, without radio or radar, in all weathers. They became national heroes, with one of them, Antoine de Saint-Exupéry, writing bestselling books about his experiences. On 12 May 1930, a young man called Jean Mermoz took off from St-Louis and headed out across the Atlantic Ocean to make the first successful airmail connection with South America. The sky was no limit. Soon they were flying as far as Buenos Aires and even over the Andes to Santiago, Chile. Then, in December 1936, Mermoz left St-Louis in his sea-plane 'Croix du Sud' to make his twenty-fourth crossing of the Atlantic. He was never seen again.

Mermoz-mania still grips the hotel. Paintings of the planes and the epic route they covered are spread across the walls and even on the ceiling of the restaurant. In reception there are framed press clippings and evocative posters, and in a mural halfway up the stairs the head and shoulders of Mermoz rise from the cold grey waters of the Atlantic, as if gasping for one last breath.

Before flying he always stayed at the Hôtel de la Poste, and always in room 219, on the corner, with the river on one side and the Art Deco post office on the other. It's the room I'm in now.

Today I venture out of this tempting haven and take a longer look at St-Louis. No sooner have I stepped out into the street than a score of voices compete for my attention, crutches and wheelchairs race towards me and arms beckon me towards the pony and traps that wait listlessly by. I hire one for the morning and we set out across Faidherbe's bridge, which clangs and rumbles beneath a constant stream of foot, car, bicycle and hoof traffic.

One book I'm reading describes its builder as 'a visionary', a man who more than anyone embodied the ideal of a West African empire built upon the virtues of French culture and the French way of life. Faidherbe believed unquestioningly that *la mission civil-isatrice*, if decisively and compassionately applied, would benefit the indigenous people, enabling them to set aside their ancient superstitions and divisive tribal loyalties and share in the Gallic enlightenment. They would become *les évolués*, the evolved.

It was already too late. The mixing of French and African cultures had been going on long before Faidherbe. Soldiers and traders from Bordeaux settled the town in the mid-seventeenth century and many married the local Fula women, creating an aristocratic class of mulattos, or *métis*, as the French called them. Many of these women became powerful and successful matriarchs, known as *signares*, and they wielded great influence in St-Louis.

My thin and straining horse, his coat worn black by the harness, seems happier when we are off the bridge, on which he slithered awkwardly. As we explore the quieter backside of the island, along by the wharves where the warehouses for the rich trade in gum arabic were located, it becomes clear that the French dream of urban orderliness is not shared by the majority of the Senegalese. The roofs of the old, red-tiled, balconied colonial buildings are full of holes. Their once neat shutters are missing and the rutted dirt streets beneath are full of people, talk, small-scale enterprise, food and rubbish.

Another, shorter bridge takes us onto a long thin finger of land between the river and the ocean. Having water around is such an unfamiliar experience that I hire a pirogue to take me back to the hotel. On the way, we pass an extraordinary Dickensian scene. Stretching along the banks of the river is a great concourse of fish smokeries. Long racks of darkening fish stretch across a fuggy landscape of makeshift ovens, tended by fierce and grimy women. They scream abuse and wave their arms at us when the camera turns towards them.

Eat a late lunch at the house of Jacob Yakouba, one of the best-known Senegalese artists. His house is surrounded by a pink-washed wall covered in bougainvillea and there is a large tent in the garden, where friends, fellow artists, writers and politicians can hang out. Here Jacob, like a cultural Godfather, dispenses advice, encouragement and artistic protection to a considerably extended family.

He's a stocky bear of a man, a Senegalese Picasso, with a massive head and thick calves emerging from capacious navy-blue shorts. He's been painting since he was seven. Despite his bull-like size, his gaze is gentle and his speech unexpectedly soft. I watch him working in his studio on a disappointingly conventional portrait of a pretty, loosely clad woman. The walls of the studio are thick with similar paintings, all quite joyfully sexy.

'I prefer to paint women, first because of my mother, who helped me to become an artist. Then, because of my wife Marie-Madeleine. When I meet her it give me strength to focus my work on women.'

He admits that painting women so explicitly in a Muslim country could be a problem, but he has an international reputation and, anyway, fanaticism doesn't exist so much in Senegal.

'In St-Louis all the big families are Catholic or Muslim. We have always lived side by side. At Christmas the Muslims celebrate with the Catholics and during *Tabaski*, the sheep festival, the Catholics celebrate with the Muslims.'

He completes a last, long brush-stroke, caressing the outline of neck and shoulder, and stands back, head cocked.

'Anyway, women are beautiful. I was born from a woman so I don't see why there should be any taboos.'

At that moment there is a swirl of pink at the door and the afore-mentioned Marie-Madeleine makes a modestly grand entrance, to see if we are ready to eat. I realise that not only is she a formidable presence, but also her formidable figure is the subject of many of the paintings.

We sit round the table and all dip into a single dish containing a powerfully delicious concoction called *domoda*. Fish balls, made with green onions, parsley, garlic and spices, are served in a rich stew with sweet potatoes. When I ask how long it must have taken someone to prepare all this Jacob beams at the womenfolk.

'They did it all,' he says generously, before adding, 'in the Moulinex.'

Much laughter.

Marie-Madeleine is probably better known in Senegal than Jacob, as she appears regularly in a TV soap opera, in which she plays a tough woman refusing to be traded between husbands. All of which makes for an interesting insight into marriage *à la Sénégal*.

Jacob explains that Islam gives the man the right to have up to four wives, but legally, under the Family Code, he must choose monogamy or polygamy. Once chosen the option cannot be reversed.

Marie-Madeleine remembers the day she and Jacob went to the tribunal to get married.

'They asked Jacob, "Do you want to be monogamous or polygamous?"'

Jacob goes on. 'When I said monogamy, the judge just looked at me and said, "Hold on. Are you crazy, man?" I said why. He said, "You're a man, you'll regret this."'

Marie-Madeleine heaves with laughter.

'And how long have you been married?' I ask.

'Thirty years.'

As I leave I tell them we have to be in Dakar next morning. Jacob grimaces.

Has he ever thought of moving to the capital?

He shakes his head dismissively.

'Never!'

'Why is that?'

'Dakar has no soul, no life! *Pas d'âme!*'

Day Thirty-Four

DAKAR

I peer desperately through the window of our vehicle looking for the soul of Dakar, but all I can see is a 30-foot-high Coca-Cola bottle and a lot of sheep. Then we plunge down beneath a flyover and onto a thickly clogged four-lane highway leading to the centre of the city.

Six hours after leaving St-Louis, we're picking our way slowly through suburban neighbourhoods sporting parking meters, traffic lights, health clubs, even a cyber café, and more sheep.

I'm bewildered by all this ovine activity, until I learn that we are a week away from *Tabaski*, the day on which Muslims commemorate the story they share with Jews and Christians of Abraham being commanded by God to sacrifice his son Isaac, only to spare him at the last minute and allow a sheep to be substituted. At *Tabaski* the head of every Muslim household must kill a sheep and cook it for his family. The deed must be done personally and the sheep must be alive on *Tabaski* morning, so a frozen supermarket sheep will not do. Which must account for the enormous number of fluffy white creatures massed in the city of Dakar this afternoon. Wherever a few blades of grass can be found they're nibbling away – on traffic islands, motorway verges and football pitches. Jarga, a sheep-fattening product, is advertised on billboards, and a banner spread across the street proclaims '*Promotion Tabaski! Gagnez des Moutons!*' – 'Win A Sheep!'

It's not only sheep they're selling. Every traffic jam is a retail opportunity in Dakar. Salesmen come tapping at the glass, offering up a formidable array of carved heads, sunglasses, hi-fi equipment, shirts, cutlery sets and carving knives (presumably for doing the deed on *Tabaski* morning). So slow is our progress that at one point salesman's enthusiasm successfully coincides with occupant's boredom, and Peter, our camera assistant, purchases some irresistible electronic bargain. The goods are handed over and Peter is sifting uncertainly through his CFAs when the lights change and we move unexpectedly rapidly across a busy intersection. The salesman plunges into the traffic and races suicidally after us. Just as he catches up, another bottleneck clears and we accelerate down a main road. All of us inside are now rooting for the waving figure behind, who, with total disregard for personal safety, leaps, vaults, twists and turns his way through the traffic to reach us just as the lights flick to green. Like a relay runner stretching for the baton, he grasps the money, and a great cheer goes up as we pull away.

Evening at our hotel overlooking the sea. Yellow weaver birds are busy in the trees, which swing and bend in a pushy westerly breeze. A couple of miles offshore is the low rocky outline of Goree Island, dark as its history. Goree was a trading depot for the rich produce of the African interior, gold, skins, gum arabic, but above all the several million slaves bought from Arab and African traders and shipped to the plantations of America by Portuguese, English, Dutch and French. Not that it was a business for which Westerners were originally responsible, for it had been going on long before they arrived. It's estimated that between ten and fourteen million slaves were transported across the desert between 650 and 1900. Goree has become the symbol of this most cruel of all Saharan trades, and is now a World Heritage Site, with many black Americans coming over to remember ancestors for whom Goree Island had been their last view of Africa.

I order a Gazelle beer and open up my map. I'm at the most westerly point of the African continent. However, there is a train that leaves this city twice a week for Bamako, the capital of Mali. It will take us back into the interior and to within striking distance of Timbuktu. That, I remind myself, is why we are here.

Dakar has a reputation as a lively, liberal, cosmopolitan town with a thriving music scene, which is why we find ourselves, late on this first evening, in a thatched shed down by the Fish Market. One side is open to the sea and the Atlantic slurps gently against a jetty, causing soft breezes to waft in and aerate the sticky atmosphere inside. Unfortunately, these cooling breezes also carry a pungent aroma of sewage and rotting fish. This seems to make absolutely no difference to the enthusiasm with which everyone throws themselves into dancing, foot-tapping and drinking to a six-man band called Nakodje. The sound is a fusion of Western and West African, with saxophone, clarinet and guitar lining up alongside Fula flute from Guinea and a *balaphon* (like a xylophone) from Mali. The audience embraces white and black, men and women in equal numbers. I find myself sitting next to a group of staid-looking Senegalese men in suits. They show a surprising interest in our filming and are keen to know if my programmes sell in Senegal. When I shake my head apologetically their eyes light up with relief, and they explain that they are Muslim and if it had been on Senegalese TV their wives would have seen them drinking beer.

The manager, a rangy black man with rubbery legs and red eyes, has taken a shine to me and announces my presence here to a bemused audience.

Towards the end of the evening, I'm at the bar drinking a last Flag beer and talking to Malek, the young Senegalese bass guitarist, who's halfway through a business management course, and Tom Vahle, an American member of the band, who has taught himself to play the Fula flute.

'It only has three holes in it. It's a combination of singing and blowing at the same time.'

An arm snakes round my shoulder and the face of the club manager looms close to mine. He's seriously unsteady now and I'm not altogether sure what he's on about.

'I'm Lebou,' he says with a flourish. 'We are fishermen, right. Dakar belongs to us.'

He's also an ex-basketball player, now sixty years old. I'm impressed and ask him how he stays in shape. He leers, wobbles, grabs my head and whispers loudly in my ear.

'Making love. Every single night.'

This boast completely convulses him and induces a brief coughing fit. My recollections of the ensuing conversation are hazy, to say the least, but I do remember a nicely surreal exchange when he was expanding on his previous experience.

'Is this different from the other clubs you've managed?'

'Oh . . . yeah.'

'Why?'

'The other clubs were,' he pauses for quite a while, searching for the right word, 'rectangular.'

Day Thrity-Five

DAKAR

The national sport of Senegal is *la lutte*, wrestling, and there is a competition tonight out in Pikine, one of the poorer suburbs of Dakar, which will be attended by Mor Fadan Wade, the great hero of Senegalese fighting, and one of the president's bodyguards. Though we have an early start to catch the Bamako train tomorrow, this sounds like an unmissable opportunity.

It's a long drive across town and the paved roads have turned to sand by the time we pull up beside a collection of low, dimly lit buildings. We're warned to watch our belongings, but the young men who crowd around the bus offering to carry our gear are exuberant rather than threatening, and I feel more secure out here than in the centre of town.

A circle of white plastic chairs marks the ring where the wrestling will take place. The sandy arena is illuminated by floodlights on tall poles and a PA system is already in operation blasting out exhortations to the slowly gathering crowd.

I'm taken through an entrance behind the floodlights to meet the man himself. A passageway opens onto a small courtyard, which resembles a scene from my first illustrated Bible. Mor Fadan, a huge man with shaved head and wearing a light blue robe, dominates the space, and around him are gathered, in various attitudes of deference, men, women, children and, of course, sheep. A steady stream of people come in to shake his mighty hand. Someone calls me over and the fawners and grovellers are pushed to one side as I'm led before him.

His sheer bulk could bring out the fawner and groveller in anyone, but it's the only thing about him that's intimidating. His handshake is soft as putty and his voice is deep and measured. He answers my damn fool questions with extraordinary patience. Yes, this is his house. Yes, he has two wives, but bashfully adds that he can't remember how many children, and, yes, he is the African Olympic Wrestling Champion.

He talks of the popularity of the sport, which is second only to football in Senegal, and it's clear that this man who can fill stadiums is only here tonight to encourage the young local boys. The entourage closes in again, someone finds me a Coke and I escape outside for a breather.

The ringside is filling up and the ring is full of leaping, strutting, chasing and grappling children mimicking their heroes. The night-time chill reminds me of the desert. It must have been around 35°C/95°F on the streets of Dakar this afternoon. Now it's cool enough to pull on a sweater.

Mor Fadan asks me to sit beside him during the fights. This is quite a moment for a shy boy from Sheffield, entering the ring and being introduced to the local mafia as Mor's new bosom buddy, but there's still no sign of any serious grappling taking place.

The contestants are parading around the ring in a rhythmic dance, all linked together and kicking their feet out in a sort of macho hokey-kokey. Then, one after the other, they approach the thudding drums and dance up against them, rhythm fighting rhythm, as they strut their aggressive poses, kicking the sand like angry elephants. The drummers, stripped to the waist and glistening like contestants themselves, keep up a relentless, brain-scouring beat.

A couple of compères work the crowd, screaming themselves hoarse, urging, exhorting, praising, joking. It's after midnight when the local politicians, bigwigs and worthies make their appearance, all anxious to clutch, and be seen to be clutching, the champion's hand.

By now, the contestants, uniformly lean, wiry and young, are stripped down to single elaborately tied loincloths, like underfed sumo wrestlers, raising the level of excitement amongst the women in the crowd. (There is none of the public segregation we saw in the Arab countries). Their cries and shouts of encouragement merge with the throbbing of the drums and the relentless yelling of the compères as the bouts, at last, begin.

Starting with a curiously fey stance, like cats on their back legs, the wrestlers flap at each other's hands, before grasping each other in a shoulder lock. A flick of the legs from this position can send an opponent off balance and onto the floor, and once a shoulder hits the sand the bout is over. Some contests last a few seconds and others can go on for minutes, as bodies freeze in perfect equilibrium, each one waiting for a moment of weakness to send his opponent tumbling. It lacks the theatrical flamboyance of Western wrestling but makes up for it in a fascinating contest of balance, coordination and sheer physical strength.

By one o'clock the crowd has grown to several thousand and I'm told this will last long into the night. Mindful of the fact that we start a thirty-six-hour train journey tomorrow, I'm going to have to go. A discreet exit is not possible. As I get up to leave one of the compères spars up to me and draws me into the ring, dancing before me and grasping me in mock combat until he releases me with an enormous beam on his face. The crowd laughs and applauds. As we drive out of the dusty run-down suburbs and head for the sea, I'll not easily forget my night in Pikine.

Day Thirty-Six

DAKAR TO BAMAKO

The railway line that runs for 760 miles from Dakar on the Atlantic Ocean to Bamako on the River Niger was built long before the countries it connects came into being. When work began in Bamako in 1907, Mali was called French Sudan, and when the railway reached Dakar in 1923, Senegal was an anonymous part of French West Africa.

Not surprisingly, the station from which we are due to leave at ten o'clock this morning is a confident example of the colonial style. It consists of three arched bays, framed by red and brown brickwork, with wrought-iron canopies, pilasters supporting decorated tile friezes, separate entrances marked '*Départ*' and '*Arrivée*', and a big working clock in the central tower. On either side of the central façade are louvered galleries, which look to be occupied. Laundry lines swing in the breeze and I think I can see sheep up there.

We've been warned that Dakar is the pickpocket capital of the world, and exploratory arms have already stretched through the minibus windows. An opportunist salesman tries to interest us in a range of 'Titanic' sports bags, which, as the volume of our luggage is already proving a problem for the porters, is an act of mindless optimism.

As the Bamako express only runs twice a week, there's a certain amount of nervous tension as we walk ourselves and our procession of porters through '*Départ*' to the platform where our train, twelve coaches and four freight wagons long, sits waiting in the sun. The coaches, old French railway stock painted light and dark green with a red stripe, bear the barely legible name Chemins de Fer de Mali. A General Motors diesel is panting heavily at the front.

We pull out of Dakar twenty-one minutes late and run for a while past red-brick, red-tiled sheds. These soon give way to a depressing run of goat-attended rubbish dumps and people squatting down beneath fading signs that read '*Défense d'Uriner et Déposer ses Ordures*' (No Urinating or Dumping of Rubbish).

The train is a huge consumer unit, a small town on wheels, and wherever we stop we attract crowds of suppliers. As we crawl through the suburbs of Dakar it's like taking a train through the middle of a department store. On both sides of us are piles of handbags, underwear, men's fashion, ladies' fashion, shoes, scarves, robes and hats. All within inches of our rumbling steel wheels.

The restaurant car is going to be a vital part of our survival strategy. First signs are encouraging. It's comfortable enough, with a mural painted at one end, and not too busy, as most of the passengers bring their own food or buy at the window.

An American woman and her companion, a man from Guinea, are at one of the tables. She's a New Yorker living in Dakar. She has silver earrings and a thick pair of Ray-Bans. I ask her what she misses about Dakar when she goes back to the States.

'Oh, just about everything,' she says, drawing out the words with relish. 'The way people say hello to each other, take time to greet each other.'

Greeting is important in Africa. I've noticed that. It's not something that should ever be hurried.

We fall to talking about countries and boundaries. Her friend Barik regrets the failure of an attempt to set up a West African federation after independence.

'The countries shouldn't have been isolated. Historically, there were huge states that covered large portions of the Sahara.'

The Mali Empire and the Ghana Empire were two such states. Rich and sophisticated civilisations of the fifteenth and sixteenth centuries when, according to Barik, people travelled ·in perfect safety across vast areas. The modern states, he thinks, have created arbitrary and unworkable boundaries. He cites the River Sénégal border between Mauritania and Senegal.

'The same people live on both sides of the river, but they can no longer cross freely.'

We're now away from the crowded Dakar corridor and passing through flat countryside studded with the curious battleship-grey baobab trees. With their thick metallic trunks and stubby branches, they look like some prehistoric arboreal throw-back, gnarled and twisted like old prize-fighters.

The baobab is not like other trees. It gets smaller as it grows older. It stores copious amounts of water in its trunk and can survive for hundreds of years, because it won't burn. Its bark provides rope and packing material, its sweet-smelling flowers provide food and decoration and a medicine called *alo*, its pulp is good for blood circulation and its seeds for fertiliser. Scarcely surprising, therefore, that this ugly duckling is a source of considerable superstition, revered in every community and often used as a burial place. Looking at them as they pass by the window, they look friendless and faintly absurd, and it isn't hard to see why people believe the story that the devil planted them upside down.

In a nearby couchette is an English teacher, an impressive Fulani woman in a pale purple robe and headdress and a striking silver necklace. With her confident English and her forthright, expressive delivery, she seems to epitomise the strength and presence that I've seen in many black West African women. Rather disconcertingly, for such an embodiment of the matriarchal virtues, her name is Daddy. Well, that's how it's pronounced. It's spelt D-h-a-d-i.

I ask her about the role of women in West Africa.

'She is the protector, you know, the keeper of, let's say, a culture, a civilisation. It's the role of a woman to take care of children, you know. She can give advice, she retains a lot of secrets.'

When I ask her what sort of secrets, she uses the example of female circumcision, or excision, which is still carried out here when girls are ten or eleven.

'It is said that a girl must be excised. If she's not excised she's like a male.'

I've heard this justification for circumcision before. The belief that the foreskin is something female in the male and the clitoris something male in the female.

'There is a woman who is going to be in charge of their education during that time of excision. She's going to teach them how to take care of their husband when they get married. She's going to teach them to be submissive to their in-laws, their husband, for a good wife is the one who is submissive. So, that's why I was telling you that the woman holds the secret of African society.'

'Is it changing? I mean all this being taught to be submissive.'

She spreads her hands helplessly.

'This is something crazy. I'm not going to be submissive to my husband, you know. Maybe to respect my husband, but he's going to respect me too.'

As for female circumcision, she thinks it will begin to die out. The National Assembly in Senegal has brought in a law against it, but the women who were practising it, the ones who held the secrets, are having to be given financial incentives to end their vested interest in this particular ritual.

Dhadi is a Muslim, but stoutly against the prevailing custom of polygamy.

'First of all, I'm jealous. I don't want to share my husband. And then second,' she wags her finger to formidable effect, 'in every polygamist house there is trouble. Because co-wives, you know, are jealous. Sometimes one of the wives will go to the marabout . . .'

'The marabout?'

'Well, he's the kind of priest . . . he's a seer. He can see into the future and also he can, you know, make some juju. And for example, if one of the kids fails his exam, she says to the marabout, "It's my co-wife. She's a witch. That's why my kid can't succeed."'

She doesn't hold out much hope that polygamy will go the way of circumcision. She reckons only 3 or 4 per cent of Senegalese feel as she does.

'These are hard times. I believe it will change, but it will be hard, very hard.'

It's not just what she says but how she says it that makes Dhadi exceptional. Or maybe not. Maybe African women are by nature more direct, more open, more honest and considerably less submissive than their menfolk expect them to be.

Night falls and we are still some way short of the Malian border. To the bar, where three or four customers are gathered in the gloom, drinking Cokes from the bottle. I'm the only one ordering beer, until the crew finish filming of course. The barman is a big man with a tartan cap and shades. A radio is crackling out. Highlights of a football game. Last night Senegal were playing a vital World Cup qualifying match with Morocco. I ask the result. It was a draw. Senegal are through to the finals.

Chicken for supper. It's fine, but the bench I sit on collapses.

Day Thirty-Seven

DAKAR TO BAMAKO

After a night of slow jolting progress, during which I dreamt of baobab trees and disorder, we've reached Kidira, on the Senegal–Mali border. It's been daylight for almost an hour and the train has been firmly stationary since then.

This is up-country rural Africa, with none of the shouting and hysteria of the city we left twenty-one hours ago. Because of the great heat, people move slowly, if they move at all. Employees of the railway unload packages without urgency, breaking off at the slightest excuse to slap hands, exchange jovial greetings and embark on long, animated conversations punctuated by inexplicably hysterical laughter.

When we finally depart Kidira at half past nine, we've slipped four hours behind schedule. Five minutes later we cross the Falémé, a tributary of the Sénégal, cutting north to south with a red earth escarpment rising on its eastern bank. We're now in Mali. By midday we're alongside the Sénégal itself, flowing strong and substantial, through the arid bush country, known by its French name, *la brousse.*

A long halt at Kayes, which has the reputation of being the hottest town in Africa, set in a bowl surrounded by hills full of iron-bearing rock. Check my thermometer. It's 39°C in the shade, 102°F, not bad for February. The barman and restaurant car staff are out on the platform, seeking relief beneath an umbrageous mimosa. Opposite is a big handsome run-down colonial building, an uncommon mix of Franco-Moorish styles, red brick combined with horseshoe arches and elaborate balconies. It appears to be occupied by dozens of families. By the side of the railway track the words '*Défense d'Uriner, 3000 Fr.*' are fading slowly from the wall.

Just when it seems we might be destined to spend the rest of our lives in Kayes, a shudder runs through the train and we jerk into motion. Our endlessly cheery guard reckons we'll be in Bamako at ten o'clock tonight and slaps his hand in mine to seal the prediction.

The scenery changes now, as we cross the land of the Malinke people, from whom Mali took its name. This is more like the heat-cracked plateau of Mauritania than the flat bush country of Senegal. Escarpments and weirdly sculpted rocks rise around us. We stop at stations without platforms, surrounded by thatch-roofed rondavels and mud huts, where women with charcoal braziers in one hand and corn-cobs in the other ply the train, selling bananas, roast goat, loaves of bread, tea, smoked fish, yams, bags of nuts.

At a place called Mehani we are becalmed again, waiting for a train from Bamako to come through on the single-track line ahead of us.

I feel tired, unwashed and greasy, but I keep my spirits up by reading Sanche de Gramont's *The Strong Brown God*, and imagining how immeasurably more awful it was for the British explorer Mungo Park, as he made his way through this same territory in 1796, intent on becoming the first Westerner to set eyes on the fabled River Niger.

Dusk is falling as the Bamako–Kayes train comes in. It pulls up opposite us, each window crammed with faces.

The last sight I remember before night falls is crossing the

Sénégal for the very last time, at the point where, fed by the Bafing and Bakoye rivers, it is a majestic half-mile wide, its banks turning a deep ruddy brown in the dying light.

It's ten o'clock and we are still so far from Bamako that I cannot even make light of it with our friendly guard. Faced with the realisation that we shall have to spend another night on the train, the spirit seems to have gone out of everyone. They just want to be home, not on this hot and sticky train, full of people but empty of almost everything else. There is an air of resigned listlessness as we swing once more into the darkness.

MALI

Day Thirty-Eight

BAMAKO

As if this second, unscheduled night is not wretched enough, my bowels, so well-disciplined since Western Sahara, suddenly demand attention. It's as if they know that it's hot, the train is unstable, there's no water left in any of the lavatories and there's someone sleeping in the corridor who I have to step over each time.

As my internal convulsions match those of the train, I look in vain for any sign of city lights, but it's not until five o'clock that I hear J-P outside my door.

'Breakfast in Bamako,' he announces cheerfully.

Forty-three hours after leaving Dakar, eight hours later than schedule, having covered the distance at an average speed of 28 miles per hour, we creak to a halt at Bamako station at five-forty on a Monday morning. For a moment all is quiet. The first streaks of dawn light pierce the clouds in the eastern sky, the smell of a new day edges out the smell of an over-used train, and though we can see only the darkened outlines of station buildings, there is an air of expectation.

Then the doors swing open and for the first time I realise just how many people have been aboard the Dakar–Bamako express. And how much they've brought with them. The narrow platform is soon submerged beneath people and their stuff. Chairs, sofas, lengths of carpet, great bulging sacks, cooking stoves, lengths of piping. All become weapons in the fight for the exit.

We are trying our best to film this, which only adds to the chaos. Two men offering us taxis and cheap hotels follow us everywhere. Somewhere further up the platform there are cries and shouts and people fall back as a scuffle begins. A man suspected of stealing has been dragged off the train and is being savagely beaten by his fellow passengers.

I make a scrawled note in my diary: 'Bamako Station, five-forty a.m. The Heart of Darkness'.

Breakfast in Bamako. Part Two. A couple of hours ago I felt like a piece of litter ready to be swept up and thrown away. Now I'm sitting by the banks of the River Niger with a cup of coffee and a plate of bacon and eggs in front of me. I'm washed and freshly dressed and have just seen a sunrise as beautiful as any since this journey began. Deepest gloom has given way, suspiciously quickly, to pure, uncritical ecstasy, as we sit on this terrace on stilts built out over the river that will lead us to Timbuktu. A golden sun grows in confidence. There is a swimming pool, fresh fruit, and a day off to rest, relax and generally wallow in the delights of not having to move.

Day Forty

BAMAKO

At first light this morning the surface of the River Niger shone like silver, and as I watched, a boy in a dug-out canoe slowly poled himself through the water hyacinth, a slim black silhouette against the lightening sky, as spare and sharp as a character in Chinese calligraphy.

An hour later the sun is up and the banks of the river are lined with children bathing and men and women washing. This is where the hotel laundry is done and it's deeply satisfying to watch my travel-worn jeans being pounded against the rock whilst I drink a cup of coffee on the terrace.

We drive into Bamako. The road surface is like a Mohican haircut. A thin strip of tarmac, worn down to hard-baked earth on either side. Like Nouakchott in Mauritania, Bamako is a city that has grown fast since independence, and for the same reasons – drought and the southward march of the Sahara Desert. Forty years ago, 160,000 people lived here; now there are more than a million, one tenth of the population of this huge country, and enough of them have old, poorly maintained cars to fill the air with a pervasive soup of pollution.

We pass buildings that date Bamako's history like rings on a tree trunk. First, and nearest the hotel, the gorgeously named Bobolibougou market, a forest of stalls stretching way back from the roadside and disappearing into Stygian gloom. Their knobbly wood frames and thatched roofs cannot have changed much since Mungo Park came here. Further into town, the road leads us past the heart-sinking bulk of the Hôtel l'Amitié, ten storeys of grey concrete with grass sprouting from the cracks. This unlovely landmark is a reminder of the days after independence, when Mali took the hardline socialist route, bankrolled by China and the Soviet Union. A later stage of development is represented by the Saudi-financed road bridge across the Niger, and one later still by the unmissable BCEAO tower, a bank headquarters which looks from a distance like a skyscraper made of mud. This could be said to represent the latest phase of Mali's development – African capitalism.

The everyday commercial life of Bamako is not to be found in air-conditioned office blocks, but out in the open, on the hot, busy streets. This is where we find the fetish stalls, stocked with animal skins, shrunken monkey heads, dried ears and hearts, bird's feet, crocodile parts and all the other charms and potions for the *gri-gri* – black magic or traditional healing – which is still such a powerful force in the country.

This is where we find the windowless huts of businesses with names like 'Coiffure, Harrods style' and 'M. Yattara, Boutique', the latter, consisting of a table, a bench and a kettle, located outside the gates of the station we arrived at two mornings ago. So low were my spirits then that I hardly noticed the station itself, which is another French colonial gem, faced in local red sandstone, roofed in terracotta tiles and dominated by a clock tower with the proud inscription 'Chemin de Fer de Dakar en Niger' picked out in gold leaf. Sadly, the original clock has gone missing and been inadequately replaced by one out of somebody's kitchen. Less grand, but equally purposeful inscriptions adorn the walls of the forecourt, including two '*Défense d'Uriner*' signs and a third which warns: '*Défense Absolut d'Uriner*', under pain of arrest by Special Police. The mind boggles at what sort of highly honed skills these special police must require.

Order a coffee, which is made in a tall glass with about eight grains of Nescafé and half a tin of evaporated milk. It tastes disgusting. Mr Yatarra is a character though. He speaks good English and eyes us with lofty amusement. When J-P asks him if he is happy for us to film, he pats the side of his voluminous *djellaba*.

'I am happy in my pocket,' he says beadily, demonstrating a shrewd feel for First-World guilt.

'This is Africa. You must give me something. We are many.'

A beggar approaches, holding his tin with the stump of a severed arm. Mr Yatarra ignores him.

Watching people coming and going, I'm impressed once again by how much in Africa travels by head. A woman strides by, carrying a riot of carrots that seem to sprout from her like orange dreadlocks, another bears two large clay pots, each at least a foot across, one on top of the other and both on top of her head. A very lean, tall man in a 'Giggs 11' T-shirt, a pile of sports bags on his head, reluctantly breaks step to avoid an older man, head bent beneath the weight of two double mattresses.

In an attempt to make sense of such an exhilarating but unfamiliar world, I hope to meet up with Toumani Diabate, one of a group of local poets and musicians which is building a growing following for Malian music in Europe and America, and whose album, *Djelika*, I've been listening to constantly for the last three months.

Everyone seems to know Toumani. As soon as I mention his name Mr Yatarra nods and points out the way to his house.

'Another coffee?'

'Not right now, thanks.'

It turns out that Toumani has seven houses and no-one is quite sure which one he's in. We're told to await him at the most likely, a tall rambling complex off a baked-earth street. It's a modest enough area, but lines of broken glass and razor wire on top of the 15-foot walls of the courtyard are a bit of a giveaway. The rock star-style elusiveness and eventual arrival in dazzling white open-topped Mercedes lead me to suspect ego trouble. I could not have been more wrong.

Toumani is, I would guess, around forty. He wears a wide white robe, like a Pierrot at the circus, and walks awkwardly, the result of childhood polio. But he's co-operation personified, happy to climb to the top of his three-storey house, where the light is better for our filming, to give me a masterclass in the kora and an insider's view of the problems and pleasures of living in Mali.

He talks softly and seriously. I learn about the *griots*, the poets and musicians of which he is one, who can trace themselves back to the Malian Empire of the thirteenth century, when they were employed to sing the praises of their leaders and in turn became the keepers of the oral tradition. Which is how he learnt to play the kora, a Mandinke instrument played in Guinea and Benin before being introduced to Mali.

'I come from seventy-one generations of kora players,' he says matter-of-factly.

The kora has twenty-one strings and a long neck rising from a cowhide-covered base.

'Is it made by your family?'

'Of course. This is my family history. It's not like a piano or a guitar that we have to go to the shop to buy.'

Toumani's father, Sidiki Diabate, was, he says, king of the kora, but his son took it in a very different direction.

'I was listening to James Brown's music, to Otis Redding's, to Jimi Hendrix, to Salif Keita (the most famous of all Malian musicians), to jazz from Guinea. And I said, I have to open a new door for the kora. Everybody can join the kora music now, not only listen to it, but to come and play with the kora.'

And they have. Toumani mentions Peter Gabriel, Taj Mahal and the Spanish flamenco group Ketama amongst those he has worked with.

Toumani's gentle manner disguises a prodigious energy. He travels the world, then comes back to Bamako to teach (there is an American student with him today), write and record new material, both for himself and for the young Malian musicians he encourages. He becomes most animated as he talks about his latest discoveries, two rappers who call themselves called *Les Escrocs*, The Crooks. Though American in style, Toumani encourages them to write lyrics that are positive rather than aggressive. So, their first single, which he has produced, is an attempt to spread the message that kids should get an education. This is something that weighs heavily on Toumani.

'If you don't go to school, the poor will always be poor and the rich will always be rich. A country with young people who don't go to school is like a car without an engine.'

He is not hopeful of rapid change, but he is proud of his country. Mali, he says, may be one of the poorest countries in the world, but in its culture and the hospitality of its people it's one of the richest.

Then he plays the kora for me. It's set in a frame support in front of him. He plays, legs astride the base, using only the thumb and forefinger of both hands. A magical sound comes out, midway between that of a harp and a lute. A complex of themes so skilfully interwoven that the music seems to be carrying you effortlessly through a labyrinth of stories and memories. It's soothing and strong at the same time, and hits heart and head with equal power.

Day Forty-One

BAMAKO TO DJENNÉ

Rested and refreshed beside the banks of the Niger, it's now time to follow the river up into the Sahara. Rivers and Sahara sound a distinct contradiction in terms and it's not surprising that the Niger has always fascinated writers and travellers. For a long time it was one of the great geographical riddles. Herodotus and Pliny believed it was joined to the Nile, possibly flowing underground through central Africa. The Romans added little information, as they baulked at crossing the Sahara, and for almost 1500 years the generally accepted authority for the river's course was the Egyptian geographer Ptolemy, whose map, drawn up in the first century AD, showed the Niger flowing from central Africa *westwards* into the Atlantic. This was confirmed by a twelfth-century scholar, al-Idrisi, from Ceuta, who called it 'the Nile of the Negroes'.

The problem is that neither of these learned gentlemen had ever seen the river. Nor was it easy for travellers from Europe or Islamic North Africa to check their assumptions. The Sahara was a formidable barrier and the Atlantic was much feared. The currents took sailors south, but they had no means of navigating their way back. Cape Bojador, on the coast of what is now Western Sahara, was considered the safe southern sailing limit. Beyond that was *terra incognita* and a sea full of dragons and sea monsters.

Arab traders were eventually lured across the forbidding Sahara Desert by the promise of gold in the lands to the south. So successful were they, that by the end of the Middle Ages two-thirds of all the world's gold came from West Africa. This created an Islamic cultural and commercial hegemony from which Christians were largely excluded. Leo Africanus, an Arab from Fez, who converted to Catholicism and worked for the Pope, became the first to give an eyewitness account of the mysterious River Niger. Published in Italian in 1600, Africanus' book described sailing the Niger from Timbuktu to Guinea, which makes it scarcely believable that he should have confirmed the conventional error that the river flowed west. But he did. The only one who dared to suggest the Niger flowed *east* was the man from Tangier, Ibn Battuta. But no-one had listened to him.

The expedition that finally solved the riddle was inspired not so much by religion or commerce as scientific curiosity. The African Association, founded in London in 1788, charged the young Scotsman Mungo Park with the task of discovering, once and for all, 'the rise, the course, and the termination of the Niger'.

Park and his expedition started inland from Gambia in June 1795. After extraordinary misadventures, terrible hardships and considerable dangers, they reached the town of Ségou over a year later.

Mid-afternoon, 204 years later, *I*'ve reached Ségou, after a four-hour drive from Bamako, and I'm standing on a soft sand beach with a copy of Mungo Park's journal, *Travels into the Interior of Africa*, open at his entry for 20 July 1796.

'As I was anxiously looking around for the river, one of them called out, *geo affili* (see the water), and looking forwards, I saw with infinite pleasure the great object of my mission – the long-sought-for, majestic Niger, glittering to the morning sun, as broad as the Thames at Westminster, and flowing *slowly to the eastward*.'

With this single observation, Mungo Park saw off 2000 years of error. It was one of the great geographical discoveries. Encouraged, Park set himself the greater task of tracing the course of the entire river. He was brave, but also obtuse and severely inept at man management, and ten years later he died in a hail of spears and arrows as his boat raced through a gorge at Jebba, in what is now Nigeria. He never succeeded in following the river to the sea.

Looking out now across a broad, placid, unexpectedly blue stream, with kingfishers hovering and sweeping down into the reed-beds, it's hard to believe that this river could have been the cause of so much pain and grief before the riddle of its course was finally solved, forty years after Mungo Park stood here. We now know it to be the third longest river in Africa, flowing for 2600 miles from the mountain rainforests of Guinea, making a long slow horseshoe bend through the Sahara, then turning south to reach the sea in a wide marshy delta near Port Harcourt in Nigeria.

Ségou is one of a string of towns sustained by the Niger, and despite having busy streets and one or two company headquarters, its mood seems to reflect the pace of the river, calm and pleasantly unruffled. Lorries rumble ponderously up from the riverbank, laden with freshly made mud bricks that have been hardening in the sun. Out on the stream, fishermen in pirogues as slender as driftwood pole themselves in and out of a lazy current, so sluggish that, to be honest, I wouldn't be able to tell which way it was flowing. A sandy road has become a temporary football pitch and misdirected passes bounce off cars without anybody seeming to care very much.

Between the high walls of old colonial villas, a track leads through to a riverside street, on which is a haven called L'Auberge. A small terrace with white tables and red chairs leads into a cool dark room with a long polished wood bar, which doubles as reception. The only occupant is a tall, ascetic, white man with an untended beard and a backpack that rises above his head like some portable throne. The walls are decorated with masks, drums, necklaces of cowrie shells and some richly carved wooden doors, which, I'm told, are made by the Dogon people who live, almost hidden away, in the mountains north and east of the river. The special of the day is chalked up on a board. Rabbit with baked apple. The prospect of anything without chicken in it reduces me to near-slobbering hysteria.

The owner appears from behind the bar. He's soft-spoken and welcoming and his name is Abi Haila. He's Lebanese. His countrymen, he says, are like the Irish, scattered all over the world. His father's family came here in 1914 on a boat full of emigrants, who got off in Dakar thinking it was Brazil, or so he says. Anyway they stayed and prospered and now run a number of hotels and businesses. This appealing, hospitable, unpretentious place seems a tempting alternative to the drive to Djenné, but it's fatal to blur the distinction between holiday and filming, and after a couple of chilled Castel beers it's back to the schedule.

We eat on the move. Goat roasted at a stall on the outskirts of Ségou and served in brown paper. Once past the aromatic taste of the charcoal, it's a long, long chew. I'm still finding bits of it in my teeth when we turn off the main road and into Djenné five hours later. The overhead lights of a gas station illuminate an enigmatic scene; a donkey and cart drawn up beside a petrol pump.

Djenné is surrounded by the waters of the Bani river for most of the year, and even now, when the river is low, we have to wait for a ferry to take us across. Alongside us is a pick-up, whose cargo seems to defy all the laws of physics. Boxes, bags, plastic sacks, rolls of carpet and car tyres rise above it, layer perched on swaying layer, and on top of it all are a half dozen trussed sheep.

Day Forty-Two

DJENNÉ

Of all the cities on the edge of the Sahara Djenné is the one I'm most excited about. Ever since I first saw pictures of the mud-made Great Mosque with its distinctive conical towers, pierced by wooden beams which jut out of the walls as if the building were undergoing acupuncture, I've had it marked down as somewhere unique and exotic.

Obviously others have too, for my night's sleep at the tourist *campement* is constantly interrupted by sounds of flushing, washing, coughing, farting and footsteps. This journey has been so far off the beaten track that I'd forgotten about tour groups. These are the first we've come across since Marrakesh. One group is

British. I know I shouldn't feel this way, but when I'm asked if I've ever been to Stoke-on-Trent all my romantic illusions of desert travel begin to wilt.

Watch brilliantly coloured geckoes darting about the garden until our guide arrives. He's an energetic, eloquent, persuasive local man called Amadou Cissé but known to all as Pigmy, because by Malian standards he is compact. I instinctively feel I shall be all right with Pigmy. He's steeped in local life and has a twitchily restless urge to show me the town. He wears a loose brown robe, one of the wide-brimmed, triangular Fulani hats with a bobble on top that remind me of Moroccan tagines, dark glasses and a big silver Rolex. It's going to be hot he says (what's new?), so we should get out early. It's also market day, so the town will be full, and what's more, it's the market day before the festival of *Tabaski*, so it will be full of sheep. As head of a household he is expected to make a sacrifice and a decent-looking ram is top of his shopping list. We launch into the crowd, most of whom Pigmy seems to know intimately. Barely breaking his stride, he networks his way forward, grabbing hands, kissing cheeks (of men only) and tossing tantalising morsels of information over his shoulder.

'That's my cousin, he's crazy! . . . Her brother knows my sister . . . He is my friend, he owes me money.'

There is no sheep shop as such. Pigmy merely pushes through until he finds a man standing on a corner with a few animals around him. He is a lot older than Pigmy with a pinched face, shrewd moustache and white skullcap. After handshakes and banter he indicates his best beast and Pigmy squats down and begins to feel around.

'It should be a really good and complete sheep, you see.' His voice drifts up from somewhere down by its backside. 'Not with one eye or one leg.' He examines its balls closely. 'Should be like a very nice sheep.'

Pigmy straightens up and turns to the sheep merchant, pointing out a tiny contusion on its nose. 'You have some problem here.' He shakes his head and ostentatiously starts to look elsewhere.

The sheep seller knows that with less than twenty-four hours to go before *Tabaski* he may well get left with surplus animals. Numbers are discussed. Pigmy haggles him down from 40,000 to

37,500 francs, about £37.50. A lot of money, but as Pigmy says it is an important festival and a man in his position is expected to buy the best he can. Two boys are summonsed and sent to deliver the beast to Pigmy's house. We plough on into the crowd.

Many of these people are not from Djenné, but from surrounding villages, too small to have markets of their own. The men fish and herd the animals, the women prepare them for market, making yoghurt, smoking fish. He shows me the different sections of the market: the Bambara people with their millet and rice, the Fulani with their milk and butter, and the smoked and cured produce of the Niger fishermen, disconcertingly called Bozos.

He gives me advice on how to tell Fulani women. Swiftly raking the crowd, he picks out a strikingly tall woman in a dress and headscarf of busy matching patterns.

'She is one.'

Pigmy points at her face.

'You see the tattooing here, round her mouth and this here,' he says, indicating a small mark below her right eye. 'This shows the family she is from.'

I'm impressed by his diagnosis, until he rather spoils it by adding, 'I know her. She is my sister's cousin.'

After the two of them have exchanged a brief and apparently contentious piece of family gossip, we move on.

'They are the most beautiful women in Africa,' he enthuses, breaking off to draw my attention to someone who looks more gorgeous than any we've seen today.

'She is not Fulani,' he says dismissively, 'she is Songhai.'

He comes up to a girl with a round face, doe-like eyes and large breasts.

'She is Fulani,' says Pigmy with a big smile. 'This is Aya. My family wanted me to marry her.'

I think I'm beginning to get the hang of this. If Pigmy fancies them, they're Fulani.

Making the most of the shade, we walk through a low building onto a factory floor of women at sewing machines, maybe forty or fifty of them, every one clacking away at full tilt to satisfy the crowd waiting to collect repaired clothes, re-stitched sheets, finished dresses, robes, headdresses. Then we're out of this dark and

tumultuously noisy room and into a light and tumultuously noisy
square, at the far end of which, bathed in dusty sunlight, is the
building I feel I know so well, the Grande Mosquée, the largest
mud-built structure in Africa.

'In the world,' Pigmy corrects me.

To Western steel, glass and concrete tastes, the mud-walled
mosque seems to obey none of the normal rules of construction.
It's organic, fairy-tale architecture, the ultimate winner of any
beach building competition. Instead of the columns, capitals and
cornices we've been brought up to think of as architectural basics, it
features tall conical shapes reminiscent of termite mounds. Three
40-foot towers, each one crowned with an ostrich egg, face onto the
square, linked by a wall of slim, pointed buttresses.

The mud walls are renewed every year in one great communal
enterprise. Women carry the water to mix the mortar, which the
men then carry and apply to the walls, using the projecting beams
like scaffolding. During the work, anyone who needs refreshment is
invited in and given tea by the old ladies of the town, but anyone
seen to be avoiding work is hooted at by the women.

Pigmy waxes lyrical about the hundred pillars inside and the
hundred windows in the roof, but when I ask if I can go and see
them he is apologetic. Apparently, some Americans recently used
the interior for a fashion shoot and so offended local sensibilities
that non-Muslims are no longer allowed in.

We walk back together to Pigmy's house, through quieter streets,
where all the houses seem miniatures of the mosque, walls modelled with plaster laid over mud brick, one organic outer-skin,
buttressed and rounded off. Outside one house, a group of children
are mixing fresh mortar with their feet, imitating the tradition of
the *barey*, the master masons of Djenné. The mortar looks grey and
lifeless until it dries on the walls and soaks up the sunlight and
turns a soft brown. At sunrise and sunset it is golden.

At Pigmy's house I meet his wife of eight months. She sits in a
doorway of the courtyard, having her ankles hennaed for the big
day tomorrow. She's placid and pretty, with an aura of quiet ease
that contrasts sharply with Pigmy's restless energy. I ask how they
met. Apparently, she sold milkshakes in the market and Pigmy
flirted with her (as I'd seen him do with cousins and sisters of

friends that he encountered earlier today). Milkshakes, however, grew into true love. His parents were not keen, because she was a country girl and he was a relatively affluent city boy. Pigmy is strong-willed and insisted on marrying her, even though the price he paid for not having a wife found for him by the family was to forfeit gifts from his parents' friends.

He speaks earnestly of her many virtues, but she says nothing, just turns her big brown eyes towards him. The woman who is preparing her feet for the henna is, by contrast, an older woman, with a canniness that reflects a much deeper knowledge of life. Occasionally she will break into Pigmy's romantic banter with muttered asides that send him into fits of laughter. He turns to me.

'She is like a *griot*,' he explains. 'She is free to say anything she wants.'

This sounds interesting.

'Can you ask her to tell me the real story, Pigmy?'

He translates. She replies with a wicked smile. He rocks back with laughter.

'She say, if she were English, she would tell you a lot of things, but she don't speak English.'

He throws a sidelong glance at his adoring wife.

'I think it's good she don't speak English.'

Day Forty-Three

DJENNÉ

Tabaski morning in Djenné. The dust is rising in the streets. Pigmy, resplendent in a billowing robe of crisp white cotton trimmed with silver and grey embroidery, is walking with me and many hundreds of others to hear the imam's address and witness the ritual sacrifice that will be the signal for the day's festivities to begin. I feel conspicuously dull in my chinos and Gap Oxford, for all around me people are in their traditional finery. Malians dress splendidly anyway, but today they pull the stops out. No two people in this vast throng seem to be dressed alike.

This celebration of the sparing of Abraham's son from sacrifice is one of the most important days in the Muslim calendar. It's not so much the sparing itself they celebrate, but Abraham's act of obedience, his willingness to sacrifice his own son if that was what his God ordered him to do. Submission to the will of Allah is the cornerstone of Islam. It is what the word Islam means.

There are so many people expected at these special prayers that the mosque is too small to hold them, so the ceremony takes place in an open area at the edge of town. Getting there is like being in a football crowd on its way to the stadium. We're swept along by a generally good-natured, expectant, ever-growing tide. It's going to be a very hot day, and many are carrying prayer mats in one hand and big, colourful umbrellas in the other. At the site, worshippers assemble in long rows, those with the biggest umbrellas and the finest prayer mats in the front and the least privileged in an overspill yard with only strips of paper to kneel on.

Women are conspicuous by their absence. When I ask where they are Pigmy shifts a little uncomfortably.

'The women will be at the back,' he says vaguely.

The truth of which I can't check, as the back of the crowd is now so far away.

Pigmy estimates today's attendance at around 8000. All over the Arab world there will be similar gatherings, and by the end of the day several million sheep will have disappeared off the face of the earth.

The imam steps up to a microphone set up beneath the sort of garish orange umbrella you might find at a beach bar. A few feet away, tethered in the shade of a neem tree, is the beast he will soon slaughter. It paces about, bleating every now and then and eyeing the growing crowd nervously, like an actor on opening night.

At half past nine silence falls over this vast congregation and prayers begin. A light breeze stirs the young trees. The long rows of worshippers chant their prayers and kneel and rise, kneel and rise, in unison. I check my thermometer. It's 35°C/95°F in the shade.

After the prayers, a collection is taken and the impressive discipline of the worshippers breaks up. Some of the older men are helped away, the younger ones are allowed to move up to get a better view of the proceedings and everyone starts chattering, even though the imam is still delivering benedictions and demanding responses.

I hear Pigmy mutter 'Enough benedictions', but it's another five minutes before the imam concludes the blessing and two of his assistants move forward and release the sheep from the tree.

This is accompanied by a great surge forward to the area where the sacrifice will take place, completely obscuring the view of Nigel and Basil, who have been at carefully chosen camera positions for an hour or more. Everyone is turning to each other and shaking hands and exchanging greetings. My hand is pumped as enthusiastically as anyone else's.

'*Sambe, sambe. Amina*,' Pygmy teaches me to say. I presume it's the equivalent of 'Happy Tabaski'.

Somewhere in all this mass of humanity, the first sheep of the day dies in Djenné.

Pigmy now has to emulate the imam's sacrifice and he is unusually preoccupied as we trudge back through the winding streets of the town. A cloud of dust raised by the feet of 8000 celebrants hangs thick and unavoidable in the hot and motionless air. By the time we reach his house I feel as if I've swallowed a small desert.

Pigmy makes a traditional round of the neighbours, briskly darting in and out of doorways exchanging greetings.

'*Sambe, sambe. Amina.*'

Trickles of blood, running out of waste pipes and into the open drains that run down the centre of the streets, indicate that for some houses, the sacrifices have already begun. At Pigmy's house, grand by Djenné standards, with upstairs rooms for relatives, we are welcomed by his father, who sits in half-darkness by the door, greeting everyone with a handshake and a broad smile. Through in the courtyard, Pigmy's wife, together with his mother and aunts, all gorgeously attired, sit on upturned plastic buckets, slicing vegetables.

They remain profoundly unimpressed, as a knife is put into Pigmy's quivering hand and he and the £37.50 sheep make their fateful tryst in a corner of the yard. Pigmy, not yet an expert, is, thankfully, assisted by a butcher, who instructs him in the art of swift throat-cutting. The deed is done in accordance with the ancient law, and the sheep is lifted over a drain. The blood pumps from its neck and runs away beneath the wall and into the street.

Pigmy looks much relieved as the knife is taken from him. It's carefully washed by the butchers, who immediately set to work skinning the carcass. With temperatures in Djenné creeping up to 40°C/104°F, their speed and skill is, as they say, of the essence.

Should you ever have to do this at home, here's a hot tip from the professionals. Slit the skin around one leg, then blow through the incision until the skin inflates and breaks clear of the flesh beneath. It takes time and considerable lung-power, but if all goes well the hide should slip off like a banana skin.

Half an hour later the sheep is reduced to the sort of anonymous chunks we Westerners are more comfortable with and Pigmy's majestic mother is dropping them one by one into the pot. All that remains of yesterday's purchase is the head and a pile of feet stacked neatly in one corner of the yard.

Nothing, I'm told, is wasted. The head will be boiled for soup, which Pigmy raves about, and the testicles will be distributed to the young boys of the neighbourhood.

'It helps to make them clever,' explains Pigmy. A theory which, if proven, could change school dinner menus forever.

The festive meal, to which I'm invited, is a considerable anticlimax. It's cooked beautifully but consumed rapidly and in silence, apart from a few laughs when I commit the dreadful faux pas of using my left, or washing, hand to scoop up the food. We squat or sit cross-legged round one large dish, men separate from the women, who eat in the corner where they cook. Family and friends arrive and dig in, as if they've been on hunger strike. I could do with a much more leisurely, discursive pace, if only because I still have great trouble rolling rice into balls with three fingers of one hand, then dipping this into the fresh bubbling stew without scalding myself.

I find my gaze straying over to the women. Pigmy's mother, dressed in vibrant red like a pillar box, chews away on a huge bone whilst his wife, a freshly hennaed vision in lilac gown and hat, munches contentedly, and doesn't catch my eye.

Then all at once it's over, and the traditional three glasses of powerful mint tea are prepared.

'Always drink after the meal, not before. It is too strong for the taste,' counsels Pigmy.

Then fond farewells. They seem genuinely sorry to see us go, but I can't help feeling there'll be much more fun when the camera's gone.

We work our way back to the *campement* along streets stained with blood and strewn with sheep's feet, dodging across the cracked and broken remains of a covered French drainage system. It seems a shame that this attractive and ancient city, older than Timbuktu, once proud possessor of great libraries and over sixty Koranic schools, should have left such a system to rot.

From my conversations with Pigmy, the decline seems to have set in many years ago. In 1591 to be precise, when the glorious Songhai Empire, which succeeded the equally rich and civilised Mali Empire, unsuccessfully faced an invasion from Morocco. Though numerically superior, the Songhai army's bows and arrows were of little use against Moroccan muskets. A dark age followed. The Empire collapsed, the gold trade passed out of their hands and the Touareg nomads moved in to control the trade routes.

The French tried to improve public services and more recently UNESCO has raised funds to preserve the old mud buildings, but Djenné, like Chinguetti in Mauritania, remains a casualty of history, a shadow of what it must once have been.

Still, *Tabaski* has brought the town to life. No longer confined to courtyards and back-rooms, the women who have prepared the feasts are now out on the streets, meeting, strolling and confidently flaunting their freshly plaited hair and freshly hennaed heels and exultantly extrovert outfits.

I borrow a *mobylette* and drive into the centre of town for one last look at the biggest mud building in the world. In front of the mosque, children are prodding charcoal fires on which they will cook the sheep's head soup. A trio of schoolboys, giggling with delight, show me the ancient art of making whoopee cushions out of sheep's scrotums.

We leave Djenné through the brick archway with its pointed oval battlements, down to the ferry where Brahmin cattle graze, seemingly oblivious to the white egrets on their heads. It's sunset by the time we board the ferry and the flies are out.

Day Forty-Four

MOPTI TO DOGON COUNTRY

Whereas Djenné felt trapped by the river, Mopti, only 65 miles northeast, thrives on it. Its natural advantages are obvious. A hundred yards from the hotel's Soudan-style mud portals, the Bani flows in close parallel with the wider and grander Niger. These two great rivers come together less than a mile away.

Not surprisingly, Mopti has become the riverine trading centre Djenné once was, and if we want a boat to take us to Timbuktu this is the place to find it.

But it's the day after *Tabaski*, and this normally busy port seems to be suffering from a hangover. Not an alcohol hangover, obviously; more of a sheep hangover. As they used to be everywhere, in courtyards and on street corners, on lorries and boats and motorbikes, on the tops of buses and the back of pick-up trucks, their disappearance leaves a bit of a gap, physically and perhaps psychologically as well.

The normal babble of commerce is stilled and though the occasional pirogue slips out across the Bani, white sail raised to catch the breeze, Mopti seems gripped by torpor.

It's not difficult to find the Niger ferry boats. They look like floating apartment blocks. Three blue and white, triple-decked, steel-hulled monsters drawn up alongside one another. There's no way to get to them that doesn't involve slithering down the effluent-strewn bank of the river, and I have to pick my way over discarded tins, dismembered animals, twisted clothing, motor car parts, a petrified cat with rictus grin and string pulled tight around its neck, and other things I dare not even look at. I reach a wooden gangplank, which leads onto a barge, from which it's a step over the deck-rail and onto the ferry.

Silence, broken only by the hollow ring of my footsteps on sheet-steel plates. The Niger ferries seem completely abandoned. Then I become aware that on the next ferry, moored up against this one and sporting the name 'Tombouctou', there is a small group of people, lounging in chairs around a charcoal brazier, from which a wisp of smoke rises.

I make my way across, half expecting to be ordered off, but instead I'm met with smiles and offered a cup of tea by a trimly bearded man in a violent orange and blue floral robe and green headdress. He turns out to be the captain of the *Tombouctou*. His wife is scrubbing down a whiskered fish, which normally lives in the river mud. It wriggles angrily and appears to continue to do so until, and a little bit after, she slits it down the middle. She slices it deftly and lays the fillets on the fire. Another man sits on a plastic strip chair, one leg drawn up, picking at his toes. There are two others, one in T-shirt and trousers, the other in a bulbous pale blue robe. I ask if they're passengers. The captain laughs and shakes his head. They're his brothers come for tea.

The *Tombouctou* is clearly not going anywhere. The captain points at the stinking mud banks I've just crossed.

'The water is too low.'

We could wait a day or two. I ask him when he will be operating again.

'July.'

'*July?*'

Now that's another matter. July is over three months away. The fish begins to sizzle nicely and one of the captain's brothers has made some tea.

I knock back the first glass and stare out at the river. I'm feeling rather foolish, but the captain could not be more understanding as I explain the purpose of our journey, and he nods with wide-eyed interest when I tell him where we've already been. He's a travelling man. I learn from him that for big ferries like his the Niger is only navigable for six months of the year, and with the river this low our best bet is to try the smaller local boats down in the port.

Thanking him for his help and his tea I retrace my steps back across the foul-smelling ooze. I'm rewarded by a chance encounter with a man who knows a man who knows a man who has a *pinasse*, a stouter, bigger version of a pirogue, which, if we make it worth his while, could be encouraged to take us up river. Because of the *Tabaski* holiday, this would not be for a few days.

He indicates the boat, a gawky, gaudily painted vessel, drawn up on the mud and leaning slightly to one side. An upper deck and engine house, bearing the words 'Pagou Manpagu' and decorated with playing-card symbols and the crescent moon of Islam, have been grafted, ruthlessly, onto a long, curved hull.

The delay is frustrating. We were all subconsciously prepared for a return to the heart of the Sahara. Decide to apply the boy scout motto 'adopt, adapt and improve' and head out to the Bandiagara escarpment to spend the next few days camping amongst the Dogon, a unique tribe, neither Muslim nor Christian, who, for 600 years, have virtually cut themselves off from the rest of the world.

Late afternoon. It's becoming abundantly clear that, as far as the Dogon are concerned, their 600 years of privacy are up. A new highway is being built between Mopti and Bandiagara. Graders and rollers are at work and dust clouds hang in the air. Occasionally, a minibus emerges from the haze and rattles past us, carrying an exhausted tour group back from what they call Dogon Country.

Then the new road curves away to the south and I realise that it's not a conveyor belt for tourists after all, but the first stage of a trunk road across the border to Ouagadougou, the thriving capital of neighbouring Burkina Faso. This leaves us stuck at a barrier on the outskirts of Bandiagara, arguing with two or three surly men who, with no apparent authority, are demanding 500 CFAs per person and 250 per vehicle before we can proceed.

Having settled for 250 francs from each vehicle and nothing extra for the occupants, these self-appointed toll collectors roll a red and white striped oil drum out of our path with bad grace. Maybe they put a curse on us. After a mile or so, the springs crack on one of the vehicles.

We refresh ourselves with slices of mango bought from children on the street, whilst our drivers bind up the fractured leaf springs with an inner tube from a bicycle tyre. This piece of improvisation is immediately and searchingly put to the test as we proceed on progressively stonier, more unstable tracks up onto the escarpment. We seem to go on for ever. Dusk falls. I begin to see things in the half-light. Ghostly figures with enormous gleaming foreheads turn out to be women with aluminium water pots on their heads, and giant likenesses of Edward Scissorhands turn out to be baobab trees racing towards our headlights.

The road begins to drop down in a series of hairpin bends, bouncing us up and down and side to side at the same time. Despite this, I fall into a brief doze as we reach the valley floor.

I'm woken by a ferocious revving of engines. Our four-wheel drive is sliding about, out of control, rushing forwards then slipping back. Our driver brakes, reverses, revs up again and charges forward. By the light of our crazily swinging headlights I can see what the problem is. We're halfway up a sand dune and the wheels are unable to grip.

A voice shouts out of the darkness. One of the other vehicles has come back to lead us up. This time we make it, up over the rise, and our driver sweeps alongside his colleagues as if he'd just won a Grand Prix rather than nearly killed us.

In a shallow bowl of sand, ringed with low bushes, stands a semi-circle of small tents. To one side, beneath one of the few trees of any size, a fire is burning. I've lost count of the hours since we left the banks of the Bani river, but it doesn't matter now. We're in Dogon Country, and this is our new home.

Day Forty-Five

TIRELLI

The Sahara is officially said to begin north of latitude 16. The Pays de Dogon (it sounds so much better in French) is around 14 degrees north, but the cool night, which had me scrambling into my sleeping bag around 4 a.m., and the sand that has already found its way into the most private parts of me and my luggage, take me right back to our days in Western Sahara. As if the insidious sand isn't enough, there is the added refinement of *krim-krim*, thorny burrs camouflaged in sand, which attach themselves to skin and clothing like fishhooks. Those of us who have already used the bushes as our bathroom have been particularly affected, and in quite sensitive places too.

There are bonuses of course, one of which is the spectacular sight of the escarpment wall, rising about a mile to the west of the camp, its long straight brow glowing red and gold in the early sunlight.

Little is known about the first people to inhabit the 125-mile escarpment other than that they were little and were called the Tellem. They fled to safety here 1000 years ago. They were planters and crop growers and no match for the Dogon hunters, originally believed to have come from the Nile Valley, who took over their land 400 years later, in their turn fleeing, this time from the spread of Islam.

The Tellem built houses in and amongst the caves halfway up the cliff wall, some of which can still be seen. The Dogon use them as burial grounds, often hauling bodies up on the end of ropes.

I learn all this from Amadou, an urbane English-speaking Dogon, who lives in Bandiagara. There is no shortage of esoteric information about the Dogon. In fact, there is a joke that runs 'how many people are there in a Dogon family?', the answer to which is five. Two parents, two children and one French anthropologist.

With Amadou as my guide, we drive over the ridge and down through scattered trees to Tirelli, one of a string of villages set at intervals into the base of the cliff. At first it's hard to tell if there's a village there at all. In the morning shadow its sandy-grey stone buildings merge with the rock in perfect camouflage. The effect is clearly intended.

The houses that rise steeply up the cliff side are skilfully integrated with the massive boulders around them. They are built of dry-stone walls, capped with a smooth, chamfered layer of the clay, rice husks and straw mix known as *banco*. Water spouts project from the corners. Amongst the houses are the eye-catching granaries, with *banco* walls and pointed, overlapping mops of thatch, like witches' hats. There are men's and women's granaries. The women's are divided into four compartments: north, east, south and west. A representation of the world. Each one contains a different food: peanuts, millet, beans, rice. But in the middle of all these is a small circular hole, the centre of the world, and it is here that the women keep their most valuable belongings, money, jewellery, precious stones, gold and silver. There are no such fripperies in the men's granaries, which are used purely as stores for the staple diet of millet.

We wind our way up to the village, which is crisscrossed by narrow tracks. There is no room for vehicles here, and the heaviest loads, in particular water from the well below, are carried up in calabash gourds on the women's heads.

Amadou leads. He's wearing a Dogon hat, white and pointed, with tassels (to keep the flies off when eating), and a cool, loose, white cotton jacket over a black T-shirt, a combination which occasionally makes him look like a mad vicar. Almost everything he tells me about the Dogon confirms that, though modern influences are creeping in, this ancient inbred way of life bears no relation to any of the other cultures and religions that have shaped this part of Africa. The Dogon world is a one-off.

He introduces me to the headman of the village, Dogolu Say, a tall, impressive, serious man, in a pointed hat and an indigo robe. (This he casts aside in the heat of the day to reveal a Copacabana Beach T-shirt.) He, in turn, takes me first to see the *forgeron*, the blacksmith, a formidably powerful man in the Dogon world, taught by God (who they call Ama) how to bring fire up from the earth.

Progress round the village is slow, partly because of the heat and partly because of the endless greetings. African greeting is fulsome at the best of times, but a Dogon 'Good Morning' can last several minutes. Dogolu cannot pass anyone without initiating a ritual of questions and responses, delivered in sing-song rhythm and designed to ascertain the health of not just wife, sons, brothers, sisters, daughters, cousins, in-laws and anyone else you might have met in your life, but also house, onion patch, rice supplies, bicycle, dog, donkey and so on. Try it, with rhythm.

aga po (How are you?)
sèwa (Fine)
oumana sèwa (How's the family?)
sèwa (Fine)
ounou sèwa (How are the kids?)
sèwa (Fine)
yahana go sèwa (How's the wife?)
sèwa (Fine)
deh sèwa (How's your father?)
sèwa (Fine)

nah sèwa (How's your mother?)

sèwa (Fine)

And so on, and on. Once the list is completed the roles are reversed and the whole process starts again. It's a happy sound, with a style and bounce to it like good rap.

For the most important man in the Dogon cosmology, the blacksmith looks like any other short, harassed, middle-aged tradesman as he goes about his business in a low-roofed forge built up against the side of a great boulder, whose cracks and crevices provide shelf space for his tools. The fire is kept alive by his daughter, a girl of seven or eight, who sits at the fire busily working a pair of bellows made from goatskin and date-palm wood.

Apart from making things like clasps and locks for the granaries, the blacksmith makes knives for, and performs, male circumcision. His wife, and presumably one day the apprentice daughter who is working the bellows, performs the female circumcision. The explanation for this procedure in Dogon mythology is that Ama, who created the universe, made Earth to be his mate. Earth had male and female organs, characterised by ant hills and termite mounds. When Ama attempted congress with his beloved Earth, his entry was barred by the termite mound, which he had to remove before copulation could begin. So the termite mound represented the clitoris, and the world could not have been created until it was removed. Which is why, to this day, all the women in Tirelli will be, or have been, circumcised.

On the way back through the village we come across the hunter, another important figure in Dogon tradition. He's a slight, nervous man with a fur hat and a flintlock rifle, which may look quaint but is an important status symbol for the Dogon. I ask what there is to hunt in this hot, stony landscape. He talks of wild rats and monkeys, and produces a shrunken monkey head to prove it. The flintlock looks so ancient that I can't see it being a serious threat to life. We run the camera expectantly, but the first time the hunter fills his rifle with powder and demonstrates, nothing happens. He refills, fires again. Another click. Amadou and others offer advice, and the third time he virtually empties an entire goat-horn full of saltpetre into the breech.

This time there is a loud report. Ignited powder flies out of the side of the gun and I feel a series of sharp stings across my face. The hunter looks exultant. Amadou and the headman rush up to me. There are specks of blood across my forehead, some only millimetres away from my eyes, and sharp stabs in my forehead.

A happy side of the whole experience is that the hunter and I become firm friends. I accuse him of trying to kill me and make elaborate hiding movements whenever I see him. Whenever he sees me, he dissolves into helpless laughter.

By midday we surrender to the ferocious heat burning off the rocks and take a break on the terrace that acts as the village's reception area. Beneath a palm-thatch roof is a table, benches, a couple of hammocks and an array of carved artefacts. There are single figures, women with prominent eyes, long stylised faces and breasts projecting forward like rockets, and doors and panels with the ancestors kneeling in long rows, interwoven with lizards, tortoises and the most important creature in Dogon tradition, the serpent, credited with leading the Dogon people to the escarpment.

I'm drowsing fitfully when I become aware of other white faces on the terrace. A tall Dutchman is poking around amongst the carvings. He introduces himself as a former guide now looking for African art to sell to galleries in Europe. He doesn't think much of the collection here. The problem, he says, is that 95 per cent of the stuff is made for tourists. What he's looking for is the 5 per cent of original work that makes it all worthwhile.

He's friendly and knowledgeable and I find myself nodding sympathetically, but when he's gone I'm left with a considerable feeling of indignation. Africa is being looted once again, this time by someone of impeccable taste, who should know better. And it's pretty much defenceless, lacking the resources and the organisation to prevent its treasures ending up, like its animals once did, on rich men's walls, thousands of miles away.

Later, back at camp, our resourceful director, Mr Davidson has investigated the culinary situation and decided that the licence-payers' money is best spent on a freshly roasted goat. We're also working on a theory that wine can be chilled by burying the bottle in the sand an hour or so before drinking.

Despite the threat of *krim-krim*, most of the evening is spent crawling around in the darkness, trying to find where we've put it.

Day Forty-Six

TIRELLI

This morning I'm invited to lunch with Dogolu, the headman. He lives, with two wives and thirty dependents, in a labyrinth of buildings surrounding a precipitous, rocky courtyard. Such is the verticality of Tirelli that one side of their house is about 20 feet higher than the other. Dogolu squats on a rock and talks as the women prepare the meal. Life is not as confined here as it appears to be. Of his nine children, some are studying in Bamako, while others are married and living separately.

The ingredients for lunch are certainly fresh. Most of them are still running around the yard when we arrive. Calabashes full of water are being brought up from the well and millet is being pounded by three girls working pestles taller than themselves. It can take an hour or more of backbreaking work before the millet grain is sufficiently pulverised and the girls ease the laborious process by working in time to a soft, rhythmic chant.

Because the shadow cast by the midday sun is so deep, and because my dinner with Dogolu is to be filmed, J-P asks if the meal can be served on the sunny side of the courtyard. The headman looks at us pityingly, and I soon know why.

What follows is the hottest, and one of the least comfortable, sequences I've ever filmed. John Pritchard clocks the temperature in the unshaded overhead sun at 55°C/131°F. Dogolu has managed to coerce an assortment of male relatives to crouch round the communal bowl with me. Fortunately, there's only one course. It's a millet porridge, in the centre of which is a bright green sauce made from the baobab leaf, and, mixed in with this, a mutton, aubergine and onion stew. They urge me to eat but every time I pick up a glob of the millet paste it is so hot that I have to release it almost immediately. Desperate not to offend my hosts' hospitality, I try transferring smaller amounts, but it's still an ordeal. Passing the food from fingers to lips to tongue to throat is like walking over hot coals.

Amadou grins broadly at my discomfort and points out that amongst the Dogon the ability to eat hot food is a sign of manly prowess. Giggles from the circle around the pot. I laugh too, slightly hysterically.

Later, at siesta, my dreams are a heady mix of fire and flame and vaguely erotic termite mounds.

In late afternoon, when the day is beginning to cool from its earlier rock-cracking heat, the men of Tirelli assemble on the only flat area in the village for a ceremonial dance that is to herald a week of funeral celebrations. Amadou says that celebrations on this scale only follow animist funerals. Animism, which attributes a living soul to all natural objects – trees, boulders, clouds, thunderstorms – remains the religion of the vast majority of Dogon.

Before proceedings begin, men with fly-whisks clear children from the dancing ground. Women can watch, but only from a distance. The masked dancers enter. Two drummers start the beat. Then others join in, striking curved hand-bells, and a piper adds the sound of a whistle to set up a persistent, repetitive rhythm. A chorus, of whom Amadou is one, urges on the dancers, who leap into the ring, dressed in raffia headdresses and skirts in bright yellow, pink and orange over baggy Dogon trousers. The most spectacular dance is performed by half a dozen men on painted stilts, wearing girl masks decorated with cowrie shells and false breasts made of baobab fruit. All the other dancers have elaborately decorated headdresses, which vary from horned antelope heads to likenesses of birds and the huge wooden mask called *tiu* that can be up to 18 feet long.

It is dazzling in its colour and energy, but I'm frustrated at not being able to comprehend more than the surface of this complex, expressive ritual.

The end of the dance does not mean the end of celebrations in Tirelli. The dancers are rewarded with a special brew of *kojo*, millet beer, and things really get going after we've gone.

As I lie in my tent, exhausted, as we all are, by another hot day of hard labour, the sound of partying carries across on the night air and, not for the first time in West Africa, I'm lulled to sleep by the distant sound of people having a much better time than me. And they're at a funeral.

Day Forty-Seven

Tirelli

Made my own minor anthropological discovery this morning. I was behind a bush having a pee in the usual way when I noticed two of the Malian cooks also relieving themselves close by. I was standing. They were kneeling, rendering themselves at once less conspicuous and less affected by the brisk morning breeze. Is this just a desert thing, I wonder? Answers on a postcard please.

Today we strike camp and return to Mopti. Which is probably just as well, as food and water are both running out. I'd been getting quite skilful at washing my entire body in one mug of water, but that's the trouble with camping. Just as you're getting used to it, it's time to go home.

We drive down to Tirelli for the last time. Life goes on and there seems to be no evidence of a wild night. A man is stripping the bark of a baobab tree and slicing it into strips for binding thatch and tying wood. Others are at work on the onion field, vivid green in this bleached landscape. As the village's only cash crop, it's allowed precious supplies of extra water. A small market is set up amongst the trees.

Above these Thomas Hardyesque scenes rise the red-brown walls of the escarpment, protective and uncompromising at the same time.

As we clamber up into the village one last time I'm reminded of the severe beauty of the place. The proportions of the houses, the materials that match the surrounding rocks, the harmony of the village with its environment. The cliff is still, as it has been for 1000 years, a sanctuary, lacking cars and satellite dishes and overhead wires and things that seem to be everywhere in the world but here.

But it's no use getting sentimental. As we load our gear, women climb slowly past us, carrying the never-ending shuttle of water up to the village. They ignore our awkward smiles. As our car finally pulls away, I reach for the outstretched hand of a boy who rushes up to the window. But he doesn't want to shake my hand. He just wants a pen or a sweet or a coin.

We remain us. They remain them. For how long, I'm not sure.

One of the small pleasures of hard travel is the way basics can be transformed into luxuries. Tonight, back at the Kanaga Hotel in Mopti, the finest champagne in the world would be no match for the forbidden delights of running water.

The heat and dust of the Pays de Dogon have taken their toll. The plastic cap on my tube of travel wash has melted, my urine is the colour of mustard and it takes so long to strip away the layers of dust that I feel as if my body might have turned to mud.

Tomorrow we face the Niger, so it's an early night. Lean over to switch off my light when a power cut kills it for me.

Day Forty-Eight

ON THE NIGER

Mopti is a changed place this morning as we head down to the waterfront in search of our transport to Timbuktu. The river is busy again. Slender pirogues, so weighed down with people that the boats themselves are hardly visible, are punted to and from the network of fuzzy green islands that lie revealed between the Bani and the Niger. The river bank heaves with activity. A group of women in scarves and long saris are bent over vegetable beds hastily planted to take advantage of the newly exposed mud, and nearer the port itself rows of earthenware pots wait to be loaded. Beside them, to my surprise, for I thought such things never existed outside of Bible stories, are tablets of salt. They're slim, rectangular blocks, like large paving stones, bound with lengths of cloth, their grey crystalline surfaces glittering in the sunlight.

Salt was once so valuable to the people who lived south of the Sahara that it was traded weight for weight with gold. The forty or fifty tablets stacked here show that the Sahara's chief export is still in demand. I try to lift one and it's not easy. I'm told they weigh 40 kilograms each.

In the midst of all this organised confusion is the brightly coloured hull of our *pinasse*, but getting to it is not so easy. The market is in full swing and every salesman in Mopti seems determined to give us a send-off. Sunglasses, batteries, water, hats, fruit and fish are pressed on us from one side, and *bics, cadeaux, bonbons* are demanded on the other. A gauntlet of commerce. Death by a thousand offers. I suppose I should be used to it by now, but, today, the combination of heat, smell, weight of my bags and the scramble through the sewerish sediments is truly nightmarish.

Throwing my bags ahead of me, I reach for the helping hand of a crew member, who pulls me away from the nightmare and onto the deck of the *Pagou Manpagu*.

It takes me only a moment to realise that the *Pagou Manpagu* has no deck. One moment I'm poised on the side of the hull and the next I'm down in the bilges with everyone else. Squeeze myself into a corner beside one of the bridge supports and take stock. Makeshift bamboo-strip floorboards run along the line of the keel and already most of the space is occupied, mainly by women and children. Fires are being lit and food prepared. There is a shout from a boat alongside and I look up just in time to see a goat suspended in mid-air. It disappears heavenwards to be followed by another three, wriggling and squirming as they're hauled past me onto the roof.

A few last arrivals jump aboard as the heat, trapped by the river bank above us, grows from intense to suffocating. Then, with a long, sucking sigh, the hand-hauled anchor pulls free of the mud and we move slowly out into the stream. My feet slip momentarily and I look down to see that I've dislodged a floorboard and sent a line of cockroaches scuttling for cover. With flies fussing at my face, cockroaches retreating back to the dark recesses beneath my feet and a small circle of children staring curiously, I realise I've stepped out of a nightmare and into some Dantesque punishment.

And what's worse, I know it's going to look so damn picturesque on camera.

The babble of Mopti slips away on our port side and we make our way gingerly through the maze of small islands, not much more than sandbanks really, which lie at the confluence of the Niger and the Bani. Some are barren, others are covered with a thin frizz of green grass, on which ewes and lambs, goats and cattle graze.

Navigation is tricky. The pilot stands astride the bows like an Old Testament prophet, his pole rising and falling as he shouts soundings up to the helmsman, cross-legged at the wheel on the bridge above me.

Once out onto the main stream of the Niger, we run into a brisk, refreshing headwind, and, with navigation a little easier, the crew busy themselves with other problems, chief of which is stemming a number of leaks that appear to have sprung in the gnarled cedar timbers of the hull.

Young boys are despatched to scour the hold for pieces of old rag, which are then prodded into the leaks with sticks and nails. With the wind whipping up sizeable waves, it looks like a losing battle, but the crew seems unfazed, assuring me that now we're out on the open water the timbers will soon expand and close the gaps.

Later. I've made myself a nest in the bows, found some boxes on which to perch and watch the world go by. Above my head I hear the squeak of the greasy chain cable, which snakes its way, quite unprotected, along the length of the ship, between wheel and rudder. I've thought of travelling up on top, but though the upper deck is marginally cleaner, it's more exposed and, anyway, it's busy. The covered area is occupied by the crew, who lounge around and drink tea, and the rest of it is occupied by goats.

In the confusion of departure I've failed to register quite where we are. As often happens in the world's iconic places (viz. North and South Poles) the romantic loses out to the practical. Survival comes before reflection. Here I am on the Niger, a river whose exploration cost so many lives and whose exact course was not known to any European 150 years ago, and all I can worry about is a cockroach or two. I stare out across the choppy grey waters and try to think important thoughts.

To be honest, the scenery doesn't help. The river is about a quarter of a mile wide at this point and flows through an arid, sandy landscape, broken by occasional stands of mango and euca-lyptus, planted I assume as windbreaks. There is a surprisingly abundant bird life along the riverbank – egrets and herons, waders, kingfishers, even an eagle – but the scattered villages of the Bozo fishermen are dispiriting skylines of low mud huts and flat, straw-thatch roofs.

The one delightful surprise comes as we round one of the few bends in the river. I spy something over on the southern shore which I first take to be a mirage. Indistinct in the dusty haze and rising out of nowhere is the pinnacled outline of a building of shimmering beauty, as if King's College Chapel at Cambridge had been transported from the banks of the Cam to the banks of the Niger. It's a mosque to rival that of Djenné, with a pale gold minaret, four-tiered like a pagoda, rising above a cluster of orange-tipped towers. Amongst these drab villages it is sensationally incongruous, as well as light, majestic and timeless.

It passes out of sight behind a grove of trees and we see nothing like it again.

Late lunch of couscous and vegetables specially prepared for the film crew. We watch with some envy as the rest of the steerage class passengers prepare themselves a goat stew, flames crackling away on the floor of the hold, only a couple of feet from where people are bailing out water. Soon afterwards, we put in at a small town. Amongst the newly embarking passengers is a white woman. Very white, in fact. The paleness of her skin is emphasised by a simple long black dress with red and gold trim around the neckline. She's as incongruous as the mosque we've just passed. A Viking on the Niger. She does, indeed, turn out to be Norwegian, and though she looks as if she had stepped off the plane from Oslo this morning, she has lived in Mali for six years as a Christian missionary, learning the Fulani language and writing a book on Fulani women. Her name is Kristin.

We sit and talk up in the bows, making the most of the cooling headwinds.

To understand Mali, she thinks, you have first to understand the differences between its peoples. There are the Bozos, who are the river people, and the Bobos, who live up in the inland Delta and have dogs and whose villages are not recommended for overnight stays. There are the ungovernable Touareg nomads of the north, who were in open rebellion against Bamako until four years ago and who remain very much a law unto themselves, with less than one per cent of their children in school. At the other extreme are the Bambara, more progressive and urbanised, and the Fulani, who see themselves as the aristocrats of Mali, with a sharply defined moral code which Kristin says is best described by the English word 'chivalry'.

I ask her what she makes of the apparent segregation of men and women in almost every area of African social life. Kristin thinks this is all about ways of seeing.

'Publicly they live a very separate life, but in private they're very attentive to each other.'

She thinks the image of the marginalised, oppressed African woman is wrong.

'They're very strong, very proud of who they are.'

Then how does she account for the continuing practice of female circumcision?

'What is sexual pleasure here and in Europe is quite different. We have a tendency of thinking that sexual pleasure is impossible for a woman that has been circumcised. I don't share that opinion.'

The waves are hitting hard now, rocking the boat and slapping at the hull as they ripple beneath us.

Kristin is adamant that Western solutions cannot be applied to African relationships. 'What men find attractive in Africa doesn't necessarily correspond to what is attracting a man in Europe. You know, in Europe a woman should be skinny, but here a woman should be fat. And the women are very concerned how to be attractive and how to attract a man . . .'

At this vital moment we're suddenly thrown forward. With a shuddering rumble the *Pagou Manpagu* lurches to a halt. We've run aground. Kristin seems unperturbed.

'Isn't it serious?'

She shakes her head. 'I travel the river a lot.'

At that moment the pilot grabs his pole and leaps into the river, which seems a suicidal thing to do, until I see him stride off into the middle of the Niger with the water barely above his knees. He's joined by others, until the whole river is full of men walking about. After much discussion they assemble at the back and push, but to no avail. The *Pagou Manpagu* is stuck fast.

As darkness falls we're all taken off in a small boat and put ashore on a wide sandy beach not far from the town of Konna. Kristin has had enough by now and decides to carry on by road.

The rest of us make camp as best we can and settle down to another night under the stars. The good news is that we don't have to sleep on board the *Pagou Manpagu*. The bad news is that after this positively Homeric journey we have advanced precisely thirty-four and a half miles towards Timbuktu.

Day Forty-Nine

ON THE NIGER

Out of the tent just after six. We are in a very bleak spot, a flat coverless expanse of mud and sand with a cordon of local Bozos, or possibly Bobos, already gathered and regarding us with unemotional interest.

Flat, coverless expanses present problems for the morning toilet. A nonchalant reconnaissance turns into a quarter of a mile hike, before I find anything resembling a dip in the ground.

Back at the camp I find a bowl of warm water outside the tent and coffee, tea, bread and fruit laid out on a table. Our little knot of spectators – old women, children, a couple of lean and mean dogs and an old man with prayer beads – waits patiently. They are not trying to sell us anything, for they have nothing to sell. They're waiting for anything we don't want. Mineral water bottles and film cartons are popular. Nigel donates a pair of his shorts, which, after a day in the bowels of the *Pagou Manpagu*, look beyond redemption to me, but are eagerly accepted.

Most of us are now convinced that the boat we were on yesterday was actually for carrying goods rather than people, which would account for the lack of most of the basics, including a deck.

Our spirits are immeasurably lifted, therefore, by the news that the crew of the *Pagou Manpagu* are refusing to take their boat any higher up the river, and if we want to get to Timbuktu we shall have to make alternative plans. With a huge sigh of relief we transfer to a local pirogue. It's 25 feet long, with a curved rattan canopy offering protection from the sun, and an upright rattan screen marked 'WC' offering privacy and a hole in the stern. The boat is lighter and much more agile than the *pinasse* and its shallow draught should see us safely over the sandbanks. And it has that rare and almost unimaginable luxury, seats.

The surface of the river is a mill pond this morning. A stand of tamarind trees is reflected serenely in the water. A line of cows, silhouetted against the eastern horizon, and the occasional sight of low, wood-hulled barges under sail add to the cosy impression that this corner of the Niger could be a seventeenth-century Dutch landscape.

As the day wears on, the alternation of trees, pasture and small fishing villages on one side of the river and exposed and featureless stretches of sand on the other becomes relentlessly monotonous. Occasionally, there will be something to divert the attention; the plunge of a kingfisher or a shiny orange-eyed hippo head breaking the surface, spluttering indignantly. 'Dear Sir, I wish to complain in the strongest possible terms . . .'

We put ashore every now and then at sad, impoverished little villages, where flies gather round the running noses of little children and their mothers' eyes look blankly back at us.

Then the river course widens out into a series of small lakes and there is nothing to see but water and sky. To keep moving is essential, not just to get us there, but also because it is the only way to alleviate the great heat of the day in this vast and shelterless landscape.

Day Fifty-One

TIMBUKTU

In 1806, Mungo Park, ten years after becoming the first white man to see the River Niger, was within a whisker of adding to his reputation by reaching the legendary, remote and fabulous city of Timbuktu.

Unfortunately, the tranquil approach we're making tonight is markedly different from the conditions in which he came here. Everything had gone wrong for Park on his second visit to Africa, and Sanche de Gramont, in *The Strong Brown God*, sums up his problem succinctly: 'He was taking a makeshift boat pieced together from two rotten Bambara canoes down an uncharted river whose banks were occupied by Christian-hating Tuaregs and rapacious blacks.'

Not surprisingly, Park didn't stop to look around, and it was another twenty years before a fellow Scot, Alexander Gordon Laing, approaching from the desert to the north, became the first European to reach Timbuktu for nearly 300 years.

Neither survived to tell their tales.

Timbuktu remains well off any beaten track. There is an airstrip from which tourists are flown in and out, but it remains a city at the end of the road, centre of an administrative region but not much else. Yet its appeal remains almost as potent as it was for Laing and those who risked their lives to follow him. To the almost certain puzzlement of the locals, Westerners remain drawn to Timbuktu like moths to a candle. No other city remains as synonymous with the fabulous, the lonely and the remote. Timbuktu, *la mystérieuse*, they call it in the tourist brochures – a Holy Grail for the adventurous traveller.

It's hard to remain unexcited as we glide slowly into the little inlet at Kabara, the port for Timbuktu itself.

Our arrival coincides with one of the very finest African sunsets, perhaps the best I've witnessed on this journey. In a huge sky, day and night are for a moment perfectly balanced. The sun going down on one side, as a full moon rises on the other. Colours change slowly and majestically. Light blue becomes pink-tinged grey and minutes later, as we grate against the gravel bank, half the sky is lemon and the other half is violet.

A hippo burps in the distance and above us a stream of bats swerves out across the sky. This is why I leave home. Moonlight bathes the groves of trees beside the good metalled road that runs the 14 miles from Kabara into Timbuktu. At the city limits the tarmac gives out and leaves us to the sand. I crane my head around to see if I can see anything fabulous, but all I see is a roundabout with a lumpy concrete monument and battered sign welcoming us to 'Timbuktu, City of Three Hundred and Thirty-Three Saints'.

First impressions – interiors lit by bare bulbs, donkeys swaying down the street with bales of hay ballooning around them, tall figures in indigo robes caught in the glare of our headlights.

Our hotel, the Relais Azalai, is on a low rise on the western edge of town, overlooking what until recently was a river. We unload and carry our bags in through a now familiar line of salesmen, only this time they are Touareg, lean, olive-skinned faces swathed in black and indigo headdresses. And they're not just outside the hotel; the staff at reception are also swathed in black or blue headdresses. This is the first sign that Timbuktu is not like other places. Up to now, nomads have always been on the fringes of urban life. In Timbuktu they run the place.

Enjoy a few luxuries – a shower, cold beers, a hot meal and a bed. My air-conditioning sounds like an overladen truck on a very steep hill. But what the hell, I'm in Timbuktu.

Day Fifty-Two

TIMBUKTU

Walk out of the hotel to look around, but it's quite impossible. The only reason a foreigner would walk out of his hotel unescorted is clearly to buy something, and the Touareg know nothing of the soft sell.

By the time I'm driven back in by the rattling of silver rings and the cries of 'I give you good price', I have time to take in a pretty depressing landscape. The walls of Timbuktu look fine, but in front of them is another Timbuktu, a city of semicircular huts set in thorn bush stockades and covered in sheeting of rattan or plastic. Its trees and bushes are hung with plastic bags and children and animals share the sand.

It seems the Touareg, who founded Timbuktu 900 years ago, are still coming in from the desert.

My spirits rise when we're driven into town. A city that seems almost determined to be decrepit still has some beautiful buildings. One of the finest is the catchily named Djingareiber Mosque. It's also one of the very few buildings that would have been here in the golden age of the fifteenth and sixteenth centuries, when Leo Africanus described Timbuktu as a city where the king 'kept a magnificent and well-furnished court', with 'a great store of doctors, judges, priests and other learned men, that are bountifully maintained at the king's expense'. Irregular walls run round the mosque, curved and crenellated with rounded Sudanese outlines and supported with well-cut buttresses. The *banco* plaster that covers the walls is so recent that it's patterned with the handprints of those who applied it.

We are allowed inside. At the main door two boys offer their help.

'We will guard your shoes,' they promise solemnly, laying my travel-stained sneakers one beside the other with great tenderness, as if they were new-born children.

What strikes me immediately is how cool it is inside the walls, and how dark. Narrow arcades run through a forest of rough-plastered columns, 130 of them, receding into the gloom.

It has an ancient, unostentatious feel to it, enclosed and protective, intimate and impressive at the same time. There is little decoration. Long timber beams, said to be cut from Dom palms 60 miles away from the city, support the ceiling. The walls and columns are a mixture of local limestone, mud bricks and plaster. The extra strength of the stonework probably accounts for why this mosque has proved more durable than its counterpart in Djenné. It has stood here since 1327, when it was built by a man called El Saheli, credited as the inventor of the process by which mud bricks are made to this day.

I stroll amongst the columns, savouring the silence. Every now and then a shaft of sunlight breaks through, piercing the darkness like a silver blade, or a door opens, briefly silhouetting a figure against a shining wall of heat.

The imam of the Djingareiber Mosque is coolness itself. He arrives for Friday prayers decked out in a swirl of airy, white, cotton robes and a matching turban. A neatly trimmed white beard contrasts sharply with the deep ebony of his skin. After prayers he invites us to his house nearby. It's odd to walk in off the street and find yourself in a house carpeted with sand, albeit of much finer quality than the public sand outside. Also odd that in such a substantial property the interior doors should be faced with corrugated tin.

We sit in the sand and take tea together, whilst in clear and careful French he explains the history of Timbuktu. He's at great pains to emphasise the intellectual and scholarly achievements of the Middle Ages and the sharp and sudden decline that followed the Moroccan invasion at the end of the sixteenth century. Scholars were deported and killed he says, with grave concern, as if it had happened yesterday.

Talking to this wise and educated man, it's difficult to avoid the conclusion that Timbuktu has been in steady decline since the time of William Shakespeare.

Even when Europeans finally braved the hostility of the desert to reach it, there was a definite hint of anticlimax. René Caillié, who came here in 1828, found 'this capital of the Soudan, which had for so long been the goal of all my ambitions' to be little more than 'a jumble of badly built houses, ruled over by a heavy silence'. On the other hand, Alexander Laing, the Scot who beat him to it by two years, wrote that 'in every respect except in size . . . it has completely met my expectations'.

Laing's achievement in reaching Timbuktu at all becomes the more admirable, or insanely foolhardy, when you consider that in the 250 years following the Moroccan invasion, forty-three Europeans set out to reach the city and only four succeeded, of which he was the first. He crossed the Sahara from Tripoli in Libya, a 2000-mile journey during which he was brutally attacked and severely wounded by tribesmen on the way and murdered by them, for refusing to renounce his Christianity, on the way back. He was thirty-three.

During his five-week stay in the city, though, Laing was well looked after by the trading community and the house in which he stayed still stands.

On the wall above the door is a plaque to his memory, whilst in front of the house, stuck in the sand, a less discreet signboard announces in loud stencil that this is 'Mission Culturelle, Site No. 2. Gordon Laing'.

By the standard of the time, this slim two-storey corner house must have been quite substantial. Inside, the rooms are clean and empty. I'm told it's up for rent and consider putting down a deposit for the address alone.

An 8- by 5-foot downstairs room with yellow washed walls leads, via a flight of narrow stairs, up to another low room with delicately carved arabesque shutters, and from there onto a flat roof.

I stand out here for as long as I can bear the scorching midday heat, taking in the view.

Stretched out beneath me is a pale, dusty city with the colour bleached out of it. There are few modern buildings, and, apart from the pyramid-shaped minarets of the mosques, the overall feel is of flat roofs and iron-grilled windows, broken up by the occasional colonial touch: a stone arch, an attempted balustrade. There are satellite dishes on the walls but open sewers down the centre of the streets. Many buildings are either crumbling or derelict and the tents, families and livestock of the nomads have taken over the corpses of abandoned houses.

I shade my eyes and stare out beyond the walls to the desert, which has the city in an ever-tightening grip. Due north, the direction that both Laing and Caillié took when they left Timbuktu, there is no accommodation for the traveller before the town of Taoudenni, more than 400 miles into the desert. And you would not be welcome there. Taoudenni is a Saharan Siberia, an unimaginably hostile place, where Mali sends her criminals and troublemakers to work the salt mines, out of the sight of foreigners.

Back down amongst its narrow streets, Timbuktu feels tired, as if the effort of just being here at all is using up all her energies. There is none of the brash bounce of Mopti or the fragile charm of Djenné. The shops have little to sell, and though the Mission Culturelle does its best to direct you to interesting places, it does so without much conviction.

The best time to wander comes later, when the great disabling heat of the day is over. Then I happily potter in a warren of back streets, stepping over an open latrine to look more closely at a plaque announcing the house of one of the greatest Saharan explorers of all. 'Heinrich Barth 1853–1854'. Barth travelled thousands of miles across the desert and *did* live to tell the tale, becoming professor of geography at Berlin University. I buy bread straight out of one of the cone-like ovens that dot the city. The bread is good – light, and with just a hint of that familiar gritty texture which tells you, as if you didn't know by now, that you are back in the Sahara.

The local people are not the extroverts of Dakar or Bamako, but though they're wary of us, they're curious at the same time. I fall to wondering if I've been too hard on the city. Maybe, after eight weeks on the road, it's me that's knackered, not Timbuktu.

Day Fifty-Three

TIMBUKTU

Up at seven. In the courtyard of the Relais Azalai a little bird, crown and breast dusted red, skitters amongst the lacework of bougainvillea bushes, tired and dry in the already intense heat. A boy is watering the mottled garden, valiantly but hopelessly, with a thin, trickling hose.

Reception is quiet. The beady-eyed salesmen who patrolled it last night, robes full of unmissable bargains, are gone. A solitary figure in crumpled blue and white robe lies curled up on one of the chairs, eyes shut, breathing deeply. Suddenly, without warning, his hands shoot out and with a resounding crack he clamps them either side of a mosquito. He examines his victim briefly and settles back to sleep.

It turns out that this is Mohammed, a camel owner who is taking us out into the desert to meet a caravan returning from the north and to help us find one with whom we can travel on from here.

He pulls himself wearily off the chair and greets us all with a handshake, though he says nothing.

It's only later, when I hear him talking with a friend, that I realise his voice has almost gone. The words squeeze out in a husky croak, and I wonder if this is a price he's paying for a life lived in the scouring sands of the Sahara.

A few miles out of town, past the nomad encampments, where the sand is dark with sheep and goat droppings, I climb to the top of a dune for my first sight of a camel train. A long, elegant procession breaks the perfect symmetry of blue sky and brown sand as it picks its way towards us. There are thirty or forty animals, all single-humped Arabian camels, properly called dromedaries, roped together in single file. I try to imagine what a sight it would have been in the heyday of trans-Saharan caravans, when 20,000 camels crossed the desert at a time. Today's modest column is led by a wiry Touareg with his black headdress unwound and draped around his neck. A sprawling herd of goats crosses their path. Industrious dung beetles scuttle about in the sand beneath my feet. A man in a vivid yellow robe appears on the crest of a nearby dune, accompanied by a young boy. He watches us watching him, and yawns. This must be the nearest the Sahara gets to a rush hour.

The camels draw closer, moving with a careful gait, noses upturned, as if finding the whole thing intensely distasteful. On every one of their backs are slung two glittering silver-grey slabs of salt. I half expect to find commandments written on their sides. In fact, the only inscription on the tablets is the name of the owner, marked in red dye.

Mohammed greets the leader of the caravan, and whilst they talk the camels fold themselves gratefully down onto the sand, like collapsible tables, front legs first, back legs folded in neatly beneath their behinds. In motion and in repose these are graceful animals; it's just the bit in between that's a mess.

The blocks of salt they carry each weigh around 50 kilograms, over 100 pounds, so those camels with four on their backs would have been hauling almost a quarter of a ton of salt across the desert, fourteen hours a day, for the past three weeks. No wonder they are so happily sighing, gurgling, chomping and farting their appreciation at having arrived in Timbuktu. I wonder if they instinctively knew that the end was in sight, could perhaps sniff the waters of the Niger, onto which their burdens would soon be transferred and shipped downstream to the markets of sub-Saharan Africa.

The bad news is that, after talking to the leader of the caravan, Mohammed establishes that, with high summer and infernal temperatures just beginning, no more salt caravans will be entering or leaving Timbuktu for several months. If we really want to travel with a camel train, we will do better to head east, where there is still a regular salt run across the Ténéré Desert between Agadez and Bilma. I have read about the Ténéré. Set almost at the centre of the Sahara, it has a reputation for stark beauty and fierce heat.

Back at the hotel, my resolve falters. No-one, I'm firmly assured, will be in the heart of the desert in high summer. The nomads move south and will not return until after the rains, which will render much of the route impassable until they end in August and September.

So we decide to follow the ancient desert ritual of migration and return home. We shall use an English summer to cool off until the Saharan summer has burnt itself out.

NIGER

NEAR INGAL

There are, at a rough estimate, one and three-quarter million nomads in the Sahara, of whom about a million are Arab and half a million are descended from pre-Arab inhabitants, like the Berbers of Algeria and Morocco and the Touareg, Toubou and Fulani of the central and southern Sahara. Every year a substantial number of these transient populations converge on the town of Ingal, 70 miles west of Agadez, in the Republic of Niger, for a grand get-together called *Cure Salée*. It means, literally, 'salt cure', a celebration of the fattening of the cattle after the summer migration.

It's the beginning of September when we return to the Sahara and though the sun is still powerful, something is different. The desert air is humid. The hard brown earth is covered in a thin fuzz of green grass. The rains have come and transformed a desert that is always ready to blossom. Where there was only sand a few weeks ago there are now small ponds and trees waist high in standing water. And the Sahara is no longer a bug-free zone. At dawn and dusk the mosquitoes are out, malarial and dangerous.

The bush is busy with people, moving, like us, towards Ingal; but unlike us they are walking and have walked several hundred miles with their families and their animals to the summer grazing in the south and back again. We fall in with a group of Wodaabe, a pastoral and nomadic branch of the Fulani people, who are found right across the southern Sahara from Senegal to Chad.

They carry their goods on donkeys or on their backs. Most of them are barefoot or wearing flip-flop sandals. Their legs and feet must be immune to the sharp burrs that lurk in the tussocky grass, attaching themselves to skin and clothing, stabbing and pricking and defying all but the most delicate attempts to remove them.

Mothers carry the smallest children on their backs, but any child above the age of six or seven is at work, leading a donkey, carrying a lamb or keeping an eye on the sheep and goats. The older boys and the men are preoccupied with the cattle, the wealth of these families and virtually their only tradeable asset. Survival of the cattle is the reason they have made this long march and, now, when their beasts are fattening and their assets are so close to being realised, their protection has never been as important.

There are anxious faces. The group is heading towards a creek, where there is water and a place to spend the night, but as soon as the cattle smell the water they stampede forward and have to be restrained with shouts and sticks.

The donkeys have little option but to trudge doggedly through the bush, weighed down as they are with baskets, blankets, bed-rolls, braziers, babies, cooking pots and goatskin water bags.

Standing out from the tall, dark Africans is a short, ruddy European. Her name is Céline, and she's from Montauban in southwest France. For the last few weeks she's been travelling with the Wodaabe. Doulla Makao, her friend, is one of the leaders of this group. He's tall and slim and looks inconsolably sad, though I sense that much of this is down to sheer physical exhaustion. His manner is gentle and unhurried. He speaks English and French and has travelled to Europe. He seems an unlikely figure to be tramping across the bush, but when I suggest this he doesn't seem to understand what I mean. These are his people, where else would he be?

His people consist of a group of families, his own and those of four or five blood relatives. Given that Doulla alone has three wives and, as he puts it, 'another on the way', as well as six children, the total adds up to that of a small village. They're on their way to *Cure Salée* but have decided against setting up camp too close to Ingal, as there is a rumour that the water there is tainted. Water seems to be the only thing these people fight over.

'Arabs control most of the wells,' says Doulla, 'and sometimes they don't want anyone else to have them.'

I ask him what they fight with. Knives, guns?

He smiles, indeed almost laughs out loud at the thought.

'No, no, with these,' he says, raising his fists like a boxer.

The thought of this frail ascetic figure trading blows with anyone defies the imagination.

They are trying to raise money to buy a well of their own, which, as Doulla says, would change their lives. They could leave some of their people here throughout the summer, especially the old and infirm, and the children, who remain uneducated because they're never in one place long enough.

They make camp close to a line of trees which rise above the scrubby bushes, denoting the presence of a water course. I ask Doulla how long they will stay here.

It depends on the amount of grazing land, he says.

'When there's enough, we stay for four to seven days.'

They have no huts or tents, but they do have impressively large beds, which the women raise up on four funnel-shaped supports, a foot or so off the ground. They spread them with rugs and kilims in vivid, showy colours. Sticks are cut and stuck in the ground at the corners of the bed and thin cotton cloth slung over them to create some privacy. The sun goes down over a huddle of four-posters, making the bush look like a bedding department.

We pitch our more modest collection of lightweight, bed-less tents on a patch of bare sand nearby.

Night falls. As we sit down to a bowl of soup and a plate of something and rice, the sound of celebrations carries across from the Wodaabe camp, and soon Doulla emerges from the gloom, along with Perri, the head of the well-buying association who, at all times of day or night, wears a huge pair of Austrian dark glasses.

Doulla invites me to join their dance. It is the Wodaabe way of welcoming us into their group. I'm pretty exhausted, and was looking forward to climbing into my tent and crashing out, but to refuse would clearly be a serious breach of etiquette.

I'm led into the centre of a circle of Wodaabe men, clapping and chanting responses and moving round in a slow, rhythmic shuffle. Then the circle closes in, moving tight around me. I can smell sweat and the sweet earth smell of their clothes, but the smiles and the sound of the voices are reassuring. It may look like a war dance, but it's more like a ritual embrace, a binding together against a hostile world. Not for the first time, I sense that the Wodaabe are decent, tolerant people, inclined to peacefulness and probably easily exploited. Doulla translates their song for me:

'Oh lovely girl with eyes like gazelle,
White teeth and face like the moon,
Which shines like the sun,
You are as beautiful as milk.'

They're not the only ones out dancing tonight. Nigel has rigged up a powerful lamp to shoot the sequence and in its beam is a huge swarm of insects, turning, twisting, cavorting and careering around each other. Decide against sleeping under the stars.

Day Fifty-Five

NEAR INGAL

Because of the great heat of the day, the comparatively cool hours around dawn are valuable and much gets done. We are up at first light, just before six, but the Wodaabe women have been at work for an hour or more. The thorn bushes are hung with washing. The children are up and dressed and their mothers are out finding wood for the fire. After this they still have to prepare the food, milk the cows and fetch water from the creek.

As the bed forms the centrepiece of each family's living area, it doesn't surprise me to hear that the Wodaabe can't marry until they can afford one of their own. If they had mortgages, young Wodaabe couples would put them down on a bed. Another much-respected sign of wealth and status is the number and quality of your calabashes, the hollowed-out pumpkins, often painted and decorated, which are indispensable for cooking and eating.

Breakfast, and indeed every other meal, consists basically of milk and millet. The long, repetitive process of pounding the millet, usually entrusted to the young girls, is already underway, producing the soft, thudding rhythm that is the heartbeat of so many West African communities. After an hour, sometimes longer, the millet is ready to be mixed with water into the unappetising grey paste that will provide their nourishment for the day.

Céline, who for one summer, at least, has left the lush farmlands of Aquitaine to live with the Wodaabe, tells me that on occasions there is not even enough millet to go round.

'Sometimes they eat only milk.'

She has much admiration for their resilience and her insights into the character of the Wodaabe strike a chord with my own.

'They will not ask anything about you, or take anything from you.'

They have, she says, a free and open attitude to relationships – which can cause problems – but they are not afraid to express shame and regret and accept that life requires patience and tolerance.

This stoic attitude doesn't always do them much good. One of the women has had her fingers broken when a cow stepped on her hand. By the time Pete, who has been on the BBC medical course, gets to examine her, it's clear that the wound is two or three days old and in imminent danger of turning gangrenous. He cleans and binds it as best he can, but it's obvious she needs stronger antibiotics and possibly surgery. We offer to take her to a doctor in Ingal, but she shakes her head very definitely. She will wait until she can walk in with the others. Though she may lose her hand, there is no changing her mind.

Despite hard lives and harsh conditions, the Wodaabe are by no means grey or ground down. Celebration, dance and the pursuit of beauty are important parts of their everyday life and all three come together in the *Gerewol*, an extraordinary Fulani ritual that will be part of their *Cure Salée* celebrations. The young, unmarried men spend hours making themselves look beautiful, painting their faces red, highlighting their eyes with white lines and their lips with black powder. The effect is to make them look feminine and prematurely aged at the same time. The display is combined with a formal dance, at which these richly adorned men vie with each other for the favours of the young girls. The girls make the choice. It's free and open, and whilst it does not have to end in marriage, it does have to end in a night together.

Doulla takes me by the hand and leads me through the bush to a clearing, where a *Gerewol* is in progress. Young men, pouring sweat under aniseed-red make-up, are rising slowly up and down on their toes to the accompaniment of a long, droning chant. Their arms come forward, raising the long decorated sticks that each man carries and which I'm told are symbols of the warrior, whilst their faces perform a pantomime of grinning, eye-rolling and lip-pursing.

The girls are brought forward, also dressed and made up, one hand shielding the face in a show of shyness and modesty.

The girls turn to face the row of dancing men, bringing the grimacing and eye-rolling to grotesquely bizarre heights, before coming forward, one by one, and choosing their man by a single touch.

What makes this whole surreal performance rather appealing is the similarity to a lot of things we do ourselves. It is basically a ritualised high-school hop or coming-out dance, the difference here being that the sexual motive is not only acknowledged and accepted but actively encouraged.

Later, in my tent, sweltering my way to sleep, I can hear the *Gerewol* still going on, and the insistent thrum of the voices gives way to dreams of tall thin pouting men, their make-up running onto sweet, shy girls. More bromide in the tea for me.

Day Fifty-Six

INGAL

Woken early by the sound of donkeys having nightmares and cattle chomping grass inches away from my head. Used to the constant hum of city life, I find these sporadic rural noises quite disconcerting.

Never one of life's natural campers, I'm still getting used to the absence of personal space. My territory extends as far as the flap of my tent, which is about a foot away; beyond that I share Africa with everyone else. I'm pungently reminded of this when, just before dawn, easing myself out of the tent, clutching a trowel and paper for my morning toilet, I step straight onto a freshly laid cowpat.

(The trowel, by the way, is to enable me to dig my own latrine and cover it up afterwards. If I'm really serious about protecting the Sahara I should also take matches to burn the paper, for nothing much biodegrades out here.)

After everyone has eaten, the camp is dismantled and the families set out to walk the last 45 miles through the bush to Ingal. All they ask from us in return for their hospitality is medicine. Eye disease, malaria and chronic stomach pain from tainted water are endemic complaints. As we turn out our medical bags, it's sobering to realise just how much pain they must take for granted.

We squeeze Doulla and Perri and a dozen others into our filming vehicles so that they can go ahead and find accommodation. There isn't much room, so Doulla volunteers to travel on the roof rack. He seems to have all the makings of a saint, but he shrugs off any credit and reminds me that in Africa no vehicle goes anywhere until it's full, and that means on top as well. This doesn't prevent me thinking of him being flung around above me as we pitch and toss along the rutted un-made track. I comfort myself with the thought that we're reducing his journey time from two days to two hours.

There is relief all round when Ingal's soaring communications mast looms up on the horizon, and a few minutes later we bounce out of the bush and along increasingly busy streets until we emerge onto a huge open area.

At first I can hardly believe my eyes. In the middle of deeply impoverished rural Africa there is a neon-lit showground, screeching distorted announcements, a car park full of gleaming Mercedes, a double-decker tourist bus, women dressed to the nines in sequinned finery, racing camels showing their paces, Touareg chieftains trailing entourages, police and soldiers mingling with ticket-sellers and sharp-eyed boys pushing Coca-Cola sales carts through the crowd. The air is thick with dust and the reek of fuel from humming generators.

'CURE SALÉE 2001,' announces a billboard. 'Our Three Themes – SIDA (AIDS), PALU (Malaria), Polio.' It seems much more than a gathering of nomads – a combination of county show and trade fair, school sports day and political rally, Royal Tournament and Boy Scout Jamboree.

The wind tugs at the white, green and orange horizontals of the national flag, unfurled above a group of government-sponsored stalls offering family planning and veterinary advice. The crowd passes them by, intent on celebration rather than self-improvement. Walking through the throng, their ostrich feather headdresses rising above the crowd, are groups of young Wodaabe men, made up like models on a catwalk, preening and effeminate, white rings around their eyes, blackened lips, slashes of yellow across foreheads and down noses, off to dance their own grimacing, eye-rolling *Gerewol*, dressed like girls to attract the girls.

Our little Wodaabe group has fallen silent. They look around with quick nervous glances. The natural ebullience of last night seems to have faded, and as they move off to look for somewhere to stay they seem uneasy and out of place.

As the heat of the day declines the energy levels rise. More and more people mill around, seeing and being seen, greeting and parading. I find myself introduced to an impressive man in white robes, the mayor of Tamanrasset in Algeria, who shouts over the noise that he is hoping we will come and see him on our way north. A moment later someone grasps my hand, a Frenchman who is trying to save the ostrich population of the nearby Aïr Mountains, which is now down to two. He's trying to get them to mate. I don't hear how, as a red-capped policeman on a camel, ghetto-blaster strapped to his thigh, rides between us.

We set up camp at the far end of the flat, gritty strip, but even here, half a mile from the celebrations, I'm kept awake at night by the sounds of amplified announcements, music and the stabbing beams of fast cars roaring away. Where they're going to I've absolutely no idea.

It's all part of the bracing confusion of *Cure Salée*, the party in the middle of nowhere.

Day Fifty-Seven

INGAL

Doulla, Perri and the advance guard of Wodaabe have found some accommodation in town. They've rented two houses with interlocking walled compounds from some Hausa boys. The Hausa, from the south of the country, make up over half the population. Urbanised and opportunistic, they largely control the commercial life of Niger.

Two of them lounge in the shade of the doorway, eyes following us with self-assured curiosity. They're dressed in T-shirts and jeans and wear big watches, and I have the feeling that they can't understand why we should be so interested in a bunch of nomads.

I recall Céline telling me back at the camp that the Hausa-led central government does not have much time for the Wodaabe, being suspicious and hostile, as governments often are, towards those who have no fixed address. So it's not a great surprise to find Doulla and Perri somewhat subdued. They don't like renting and they don't like houses.

Not that this one impresses with its permanence. The mud that binds the building together looks to have been mixed from the contents of a rubbish tip. Shreds of plastic bag, silver paper, bottle caps, glass, fabric and even leather shoe straps protrude from the walls. On the other hand, I can see it's Turner Prize potential. A house made of everyday life.

Accompany Doulla and Perri to buy provisions. In the market, shopkeepers sit cross-legged beneath grass-thatch awnings. Beside them are bowls of sugar, blocks of salt, sacks of tobacco and dried chillies and boxes of green china tea. Staples like millet and kola nuts lie out in the open, piled high on plastic sheeting. After buying the basics, Doulla and Perri get down to what they really enjoy, looking at clothes. They show me the intricate differences in the thread of the indigo-blue turban material and the finer points to look out for when buying the loose robe and leggings that form the basic nomad's outfit.

Later, bearing bags of millet, sugar and mint, but with no money left over for new outfits, Doulla and Perri return to their lodgings to prepare for the big night, the first public performance of their *Gerewol*.

We return to our camp site, passing the various shops and stalls on the edge of the showground. One is run by the Niger Post Office, which proves to be boldly internationalist, with colour-soaked special issues devoted to such typically African heroes as Raphael, Rembrandt and Princess Di. Another booth boasts a pair of skis and a snowboard. A dashingly elegant Touareg appreciates my curiosity and tries to sell me a course of sand-skiing lessons. On some of the higher dunes, he says, when the sand is cold and crisp, it can be just like the Alps. He may be right, but the name on his card doesn't exactly fill me with confidence.

'Danger,' it reads. 'Abdul Khadir Danger.'

It's late in the afternoon when we return to the Wodaabe compound. Hairdressing and make-up is already underway as they prepare themselves for their first night at *Cure Salée*. Doulla is having his hair dressed by one of the women. Almost unrecognisable without his headcloth, he has, like most of the Wodaabe, and unlike the Hausa, a surprisingly luxuriant growth, which is being carefully plaited until tresses hang down by his ears like those of a Hasidic Jew.

Other young men sit in a line, holding up plastic-framed vanity mirrors, which no self-respecting Wodaabe youth would be seen without. Each one has a sandal on the ground in front of him, which he uses as a palette for the colours. The predominantly yellow base is powder from a stone called *macara*, which they find out in the bush. The black lipstick is from another mineral, called stibnite.

Those already made up are scrambling into leather leggings and exchanging their everyday sandals for elaborate, decorated versions, which they slip on lovingly. Then they tie each other's white turbans, onto which are fixed headdresses of cowrie shells, precious stones and, to cap it all, ostrich feathers.

Once this long and painstaking process is complete, they leave their temporary home and walk the mile or so to the showground. Despite the confidence of their display, they still seem pitifully self-conscious. Country cousins in the big city.

The thudding music grows louder and the red and white Coca-Cola umbrellas draw closer. Our friends sing, not very convincingly, more to keep their spirits up, as their eyes search the crowd for fellow Wodaabe, like new arrivals at an old school reunion. Suddenly I feel that our presence is superfluous. The best way we can repay their hospitality is probably to stay out of the way. It's their show now.

AGADEZ

I'm standing on the small roof terrace of the Pensione Tellit in Agadez. A hot and hazy sunset is over and night is wrapping itself around the mud-brown walls of this old trading town. Orange lights mark out the network of narrow streets that connect a spread of rounded walls and flat, rectangular roofs. There's only one tall building in town and that's the minaret of the Grande Mosquée, a pyramid of mud, stones and projecting wood beams which rises high above the surrounding town. Anywhere else in the world it might barely be noticed, but this one is the tallest building for a thousand miles and, along with the mosques at Djenné and Timbuktu, it has almost mythic status in Islamic Sahara. I'm staring at it now, as my wife, on the other end of a satellite phone, is describing the almost unbelievable destruction of two other iconic towers, 6000 miles away, in New York.

The news that greeted us all on our arrival at this modest comfortable little whitewashed hotel seems incomprehensibly unreal, but friends and family, contacted by satellite phone, confirm that the attacks not only happened but were seen to happen and are being replayed constantly to those who might have missed them.

They appear to have taken place right across the northeastern United States. The President is in hiding and the country has virtually shut down. Though nobody has claimed responsibility, the finger of blame is being pointed at Arab terrorists and reprisals are said to be imminent.

We eat later, under the stars, beneath a sky which, even out here, seems less friendly than it did last night. All of us are shell-shocked, turning over what we have heard, flailing around for explanations, repeating the facts and trying to fit them into theories, wondering what on earth might happen next.

Day Fifty-Nine

AGADEZ TO TABELOT

A night of raucous air-con and bad dreams. When I come to write the day's date in my notebook I pause. Yesterday I wrote 'Tuesday, September 11th' without noticing.

Today I write 'Wednesday, September 12th' without conviction. According to radio reports, casualties in New York alone are said to be in their thousands. *Thousands.* Thousands of people, in a city which, apart from Sheffield and London, I probably know better than any other. I flick back the page of my notebook and look at what I scribbled before climbing into bed last night: 'I can think of no parallel act of destructive violence in my lifetime aside from Hiroshima and Nagasaki.'

Out on the tiny courtyard breakfast is laid out. The sky is clear blue, the morning sunlight will soon be tipping over the wall and spilling onto us. I eat bread, two eggs, honey and tea, with which I swallow my malaria pill. The others begin to emerge from their rooms. John has heard the latest news on BBC World Service. Details it's hard to deal with – mobile phone calls from those who knew they were going to die, people jumping eighty floors from the blazing Trade Center. Things you don't want to hear.

But our waiter is the same and the manager is the same and outside in the small square the same cast of characters rise to their feet as we appear, not to talk about terror attacks or the likelihood of a world war, but to sell, cajole and wheedle, exactly as they did when we arrived from Ingal yesterday. The short thick-set man with the rings and silver Touareg crosses: 'I am good friend of the English. I have jewellery. You have come to Niger, you must buy something.' The tall, imposing man with a craggy face and thin grey beard, who stalks me, repeating over and over again, 'You must talk with me. I know Ginger Baker.' A blind woman, hand outstretched, led around by a little girl. Two men on crutches, fleet and persistent. The children, as ever, wanting a gift or some money.

Here in Agadez the world hasn't changed. And why should it?

Niger is not a player. It is one of the poorest countries on the planet. Its gross national product works out at $850 per person per year. There are no banks of television screens here pumping out the apocalyptic scenes they're seeing back home. In Niger the literacy rate is barely 15 per cent, and I have not seen a single newspaper or magazine on the streets of Agadez. Life goes on.

We have heard that there is a possibility of joining a camel caravan at Tabelot, a town 50 miles to the northeast as the crow flies, though more like six hours in a vehicle, as it lies deep in the Aïr (pronounced 'eye-eer') Mountains.

I'm excited at the prospect, not just of joining a camel train, but of entering, for the first time, one of the three legendary mountain ranges of the Sahara, the others being the Tibesti in Chad and the Hoggar in southern Algeria.

I'm not disappointed. This is a tortured, twisted, dramatic landscape, created by immense volcanic forces, which have swung the bedrock of the Sahara from the horizontal to the vertical, rolled it over and left it to shatter and splinter in the heat. Rock-fields stretch away into the distance, charred like the rakings from a furnace. Across this untamed surface runs a roughly cleared track. As we shake and sway along, the goatskin in which the water supply is kept, lashed to the side of the car to keep cool, occasionally swings round and taps ghoulishly at the window, as if the goat had come back to life and was asking to be let in.

After five hours we run into Tabelot. It's not much more than a large village, but significantly different from the villages on the plain. The mud walls of the compound are stout affairs, with stone foundations. The tents inside them are more substantial too, with heavy flanks hanging from a strong rattan spine. It all makes sense as soon as I step down from the four-wheel drive and feel the pleasant sensation of a fresh, almost cooling edge to the air. We're in the mountains, 2000 feet higher than Agadez, looking across to a mountain peak that's 3000 feet higher still.

Our accompanying team, led by the imperious Mohammed Ixa, a tall, straight-backed Touareg swathed in a yellow robe, slings a plastic cover between acacia trees and vehicles to provide us with some shade. A groundsheet is laid, and as soon as the sponge rubber mattresses are arranged on top of it Mohammed selects one, lies down, closes his eyes beatifically and proceeds to listen to his radio through an earpiece for the next couple of hours. Meanwhile, his minions prepare a late lunch of all the things the guidebooks advise you not to eat – hand-prepared salad (but *whose* hands?), watermelon (who knows where the water's come from?) – that sort of thing. Apart from French bread and hard-boiled eggs, it's all there is, so we eat it anyway. A fierce gusting wind snatches at the plastic awning above us, which snaps and crackles but holds fast. This is the *harmattan*, someone says, the wind from the heart of the desert, hot and dry enough to split tree trunks.

Around four the wind begins to drop, and I'm taken to meet Omar, who will be leading the camel train to Bilma. He is a Touareg, around forty years old. Square and almost stocky, he has a wide, friendly face, deep black skin and a thin black beard. He smiles readily, with a shy lowering of the head as he does so.

He's proud of his village and takes us a mile or so away to see the oasis on which Tabelot's survival depends. The water table is close to the surface here and two or three wells feed prolific fields of onions, carrots, maize, millet, and orchards of orange, lemon, fig and pomegranate. In a shady clearing a young boy leads a docile white camel up and down a 30-foot pathway. The camel is harnessed to a rope, which is wound round a wooden pulley and drops down into a 50-foot well, from which it draws water in a glistening black goatskin bag. A funnel attached to the bag flops out like a great tongue, regurgitating the water down a wooden pipe into an elaborate system of mud-walled channels and conduits that carries it eventually into the fields. Every few trips the boy rewards the camel with a mouthful of maize leaves, which it despatches noisily, like a paper-shredder.

As we walk back past freshly tilled onion fields, it's easy to forget we're anywhere near the Sahara. Doves are cooing, streams are gurgling and a balmy and benevolent humidity seems to seep up through the ground.

Omar insists I try dates straight from the tree, which is not as easy as it sounds, for he has to find someone more athletically built than himself to shin up and get them. They appear to grow in white plastic bags. I'm reassured that this is not another GM food trial but a precaution to stop the birds getting at them. And there are birds everywhere: large black birds with white caps, small, noisy, bouncy wagtails, red-dusted firefinches darting in and out of the trees. We move on, munching the dates, which are disappointingly leathery, passing red peppers spread out to dry in groves of grapefruit, grenadine and mango.

We end up at Omar's house back in the village. He lives in a modest collection of straw huts and stone and mud buildings with his four wives and fifteen children, ranging in age from one month to eighteen years. I ask him if he's rich.

'No,' he replies gracefully, 'but in terms of children, yes.'

When I enquire if there are problems with such a large family, he nods. Shortage of food, medicine, clothing. Wouldn't it be better to have fewer of them, I ask, impertinently.

He shrugs, head on one side. No, he says, with a coy half-smile, he likes a lot of children.

And the wives, do they get on well?

Before he can reply there is a loud guffaw from the youngest and prettiest of them. Judging by the blank looks of the others, she is the only one who understands French.

Omar, who doesn't look like a ladies' man, smiles bashfully and mutters something about '*jalousie*'.

Tonight we are entertained, as is the custom when strangers arrive, by an evening of dancing. In the moonlight, the young women sit together beneath a tree, singing and chanting, while the men form a line opposite them and either singly or in pairs approach the women to dazzle them with their dancing. The beat gradually increases, the movements become wild and flamboyant and inventive, the foot-stomping harder and faster, as each man tries to outdo the other, dancing themselves to the point of hysteria, arms and legs flying, robes stuck to their backs with sweat. The women remain sitting, chanting repetitively and gradually becoming obscured by the cloud of dust raised by their suitors. My eyes sting and a dry, rasping cough catches in my throat, but it's impossible not to be drawn in.

To grunts of approval I'm led forward hand in hand with the man who is going to introduce me to the dance. He watches apprehensively as I improvise a routine that owes less to classical dancing and more to the Ministry Of Silly Walks. Not only am I asked to reprise it, but later I'm paid a high compliment by my sponsor.

'All the forty-year-old women say they have never seen a non-Touareg dance so well.'

TABELOT

Uneasy lies the head that wears the crown. Despite accolades from forty-year-old Touareg women, my dreams are more Sunday morning indigestion than Saturday Night Fever, and, waking before dawn, I reach for my head-torch, toilet paper, garden trowel and matches and extricate myself as swiftly as I can from the tent. This is never as easy as it should be, and as I corkscrew my way out into the surrounding darkness I imagine this is what it must be like being born. The sky is clear and dense with stars and the temperature has plunged 20 degrees. It's a good walk to the nearest patch of cover, and as I crouch over my excavations it occurs to me that these are the only times when I'm truly alone in the desert and should be savoured. By the time I'm home and dry, as it were, I have to pull on a sweater to keep warm.

An hour later, the deep lilting cry of Tabelot's muezzin calls the faithful to prayer. Check my clock. It's five. Soon there are sounds of life, soft footsteps passing my tent, grunts of goats and bleats of sheep. There's no such thing as a lie-in in the desert.

Some thirty camels are assembled on a stony stretch of ground surrounded by low houses. Mohammed Ixa, glass of tea in hand, points with languid admiration at the white camels, peculiar to this part of the Sahara.

'*Le chameau d'élégance*,' he purrs, in a Maurice Chevalier sort of way.

For some reason, I've been allotted the most non-white of them. Indeed, his name, Ekawik, evidently means Blackie. There is much laughter from the camel team as I try to pronounce the name, so I'm probably saying something rude by mistake.

Meanwhile, Omar moves quietly amongst them, inspecting a

MALI

Architectural star of the Sahara. The Great Mosque at Djenné, the largest mud-brick building in the world. The projecting wooden posts are for the masons to stand on during the yearly re-mudding of the mosque.

Top left: Bamako, Mali. First sight of the River Niger. The terrace of the Hotel Mande, on which I eat the best breakfast of the entire trip, pokes into view from behind the bougainvillea.

Top right: Laundry on the Niger. Dominating the Bamako skyline in the background is the bridge over the Niger and the 'mud skyscraper', actually a bank headquarters.

Above: Kora masterclass with Toumani Diabate.

Top: With Amadou (Pigmy to his friends) outside one of Djenné's unique mud mansions.

Above: Thousands at prayer on *Tabaski* morning, in their best outfits. Dress code: be different from the person next to you.

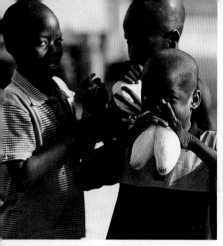

Top: Tabaski snapshots.

Top left: Young boys, given the sheep's testicles after *Tabaski*, use the scrotums as whoopee cushions.

Top right: The first sacrifices stain the streets of Djenné.

Above: Carpet salesmen at the Mopti dockside, picking their way through indescribable things left behind by the receding river.

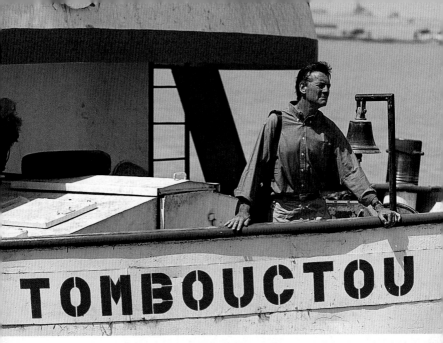

Top: Going nowhere. One of the big Niger ferry boats becalmed at Mopti.

Above: Mural of Dogon Country. A sneak preview of my next destination on a hotel wall.

Top: Baobab Avenue, Tirelli. The lower bark of the tree is stripped to provide fibre for rope, whilst the leaves are crushed to make a sauce to liven up the unvarying diet of millet.

Above: With Amadou, my guide, and assorted family members in the headman's compound. Thatched-roofed granaries in the background.

Above: The hottest meal of my life. Temperatures of 55°C / 131° F roast my head, whilst my fingers are scalded by a red-hot mixture of millet and baobab sauce. The tasselled hats are typically Dogon; the straw and leather wide-brim, worn by the headman, is Fulani.

Left: Watching the *tingetange*, stilt dancers, at a celebration of the dead. Four or five feet off the ground, with masks, cowrie-shell bodices and horsetails, the dancers require exceptional skills and long training.

Right: A Dogon boy's drawing of a dancer's mask, which can be anything up to 18 feet long.

Top: Children wave as we pass the small town of Quadagga, proud possessor of a gem of a mosque, which I first thought was a mirage of King's College Chapel, Cambridge.

Above: The newly restored walls of the 680-year-old Djingareiber Mosque in Timbuktu – the oldest mosque in continuous use in West Africa. It was built by El Saheli, the man credited with inventing this style of mud-brick architecture.

Getting in some camel practice. I make my first acquaintance with the Touareg, the 'veiled men' of the desert who founded Timbuktu 800 years ago.

Above: Fresh bread from the street ovens is one of the pleasures of Timbuktu.

Below: A Touareg cross. One thing I *did* buy outside the hotel.

Right: Looking out of the upstairs window of the house which gave brief protection to Alexander Gordon Laing, the Scottish explorer who rediscovered Timbuktu in 1826 and was killed on his way home, aged thirty-three.

NIGER

Top left: The yellow base used on the faces of these Gerewol is made from a local stone. Cowrie shells and ostrich feathers are essential ingredients in the art of seduction.

Top right: Camel-driven irrigation system at the oasis of Tabelot.

Above: Tabelot. At home with Omar (centre), his four wives and some of their fifteen children.

For the young Wodaabe, eye-rolling means sex appeal. The lips and eyes are accentuated with kohl, made from ground stibnite.

Life with the camels. Lunchtime.

Top: In the foreground, they graze the acacia trees, their heavy-duty tongues stripping thorns as sharp as nails to get to the leaves.

Above: A loosening of the turban to get some air to the brain.

Top: A trans-Saharan *camion* carries workers and all their worldly goods, from Libya back south.

Above left: Another Tamahaq language class with Izambar.

A baby gazelle, deserted by its mother, was found near the camp one morning. Gazelles are able to survive in the desert as they never need water, drawing all the moisture they require from plants.

Top: Divided loyalties. Izambar, in indigo robe at far right of picture, and Omar, next to him, watch as I try to tear myself away from the team. A sad and happy leave-taking, after almost a week together.

Above: Which way is Algeria?

harness here and there and helping one of his eight-strong team to heave baggage, bedding, food and water aboard. The camels endure all this with permanent expressions of weary disdain, as if the whole of the rest of the world is a bad smell they have to endure.

The salt pans of Bilma lie 350 miles to the east and the journey will take almost two weeks.

Omar's plan is to set off this morning and get ahead of us. The first two days will be along mountain trails so narrow and precarious that we shall be unable to get our filming equipment anywhere near. He will rendezvous with us at the point where they emerge from the mountains into the desert proper.

To the accompaniment of rumbling groans and one or two angry roars, the camels are brought to their feet and the tethering ropes removed from their front legs. As Omar hands me the guide rope I'm reminded how big these creatures are. Ekawik's head rises several feet above mine and he observes me through the luxuriant lashes of his heavy-lidded eyes. I smile back with what I hope will convey both friendliness and confidence and pat his flanks, which he doesn't like at all.

As far as camel trains go, ours is modest. In 1922 a Captain Angus Buchanan saw a caravan leave Tabelot with 7000 camels and 1100 men. The train stretched 6 miles from front to back. We have twenty-eight camels, nine men and stretch about 200 yards.

There are no emotional leave-takings and, as far as I can see, none of Omar's four wives or fifteen children turns up to say goodbye. Gingerly attached to Ekawik, I accompany the caravan out of the village and over the first hill. There I hand over the reins and watch them snaking their way off through the rocks, nodding and swaying as if in slow motion.

The Aïr Mountains form such an impenetrable barrier to the north and east that to link up with the camel train we must retrace our steps back to Agadez and take the Bilma road, which skirts the high ground and heads straight across the desert. Mohammed and the drivers are anxious to be on the move, as the clouds grow thicker and greyer above us. In the rainy season one downpour can easily turn roads into rivers. They pack up the camp at speed and we set off at the faster end of safe, stones spinning off the track behind us.

Though the rain holds off, Mohammed keeps an anxious eye on the clouds massing around the 3500-foot summit of Mount Taghouaji, halfway between us and Agadez.

He becomes increasingly concerned when we come across evidence of a recent deluge, and progress is reduced to a snail's pace as our drivers feel their way through flooded ruts and potholes. We narrowly avoid a dried-up riverbed that has turned into a fast flowing stream, 50 yards wide and rising all the time. The sudden power of a desert flood is an awesome sight and Mohammed is persuaded to stop and let us take some film. Then we're back into the cars and racing the last few miles to Agadez, which is, amazingly, dry as a bone.

Back at the friendly little Pensione Tellit, I run into its owner and founder Vittorio, a sixty-five-year-old ex-bank employee from Rome, who first came to Agadez in 1970, fell in love with the place, married a Touareg girl and set up the only Italian ice-cream parlour in the Sahara. He's quietly spoken and looks not unlike an expatriate Roman emperor, with close-cropped white hair and a toga-like African robe. Besides this tiny hotel he has a restaurant called Le Pilier on the main road to Algeria. It's beautifully designed in the Soudan style and serves a very fine spinach and ricotta ravioli.

It's not a great time to be in the tourist business. The economy of Niger is in a parlous state. Income from uranium found in the Aïr Mountains has dried up and the area is only just beginning to recover from the Touareg rebellion of the 1990s. Though the uprising is over, the situation remains volatile. Only two years ago the president was assassinated and most Western governments still warn travellers against going anywhere north of Tahoua, 200 miles south of where we are right now.

When I ring home tonight, however, it sounds as if the rest of the world is much more dangerous than Niger. American airports are still closed. There is talk of war and warnings of further attacks, perhaps on London and Paris as well. Now that the terrorists are known to be Muslim, people back home are worrying that we must be especially vulnerable, here amongst the mosques and muezzins.

In fact, we are, right now, in probably one of the safest places on earth.

Day Sixty-One

INTO THE TÉNÉRÉ DESERT

'How are you, Britisher? I show you something.'

'I must talk with you. I know Ginger Baker!'

'*Donnez-moi un cadeau!*'

As we appear at the door of the Pensione the usual suspects waiting in the shade of the Hôtel de l'Aïr across the street leap to their feet. Today I do not totally ignore the street cries of Agadez. Mindful of what is to come – prolonged exposure to the hottest part of the desert – I negotiate for a turban and am now the proud owner of a 15-foot length of indigo cotton. It seems an awful lot to wrap round a size six and seven-eighths head, but they tell me some turbans are 20 feet long.

As we shall be camping for the foreseeable future, our departure from Agadez is delayed to enable everyone to repack, reducing bags and baggage to the minimum, and to spoil ourselves with an early lunch of *penne arrabiata* with aubergine and a glass of wine or three at Le Pilier.

A couple of hours later, the memory of the meal and the cool, airy courtyard of the restaurant is a distant dream. The Bilma road is a bleak and uncompromising strip of desert dust, defined only by the imprint of vehicles that have passed this way before. The rains have not reached this far south, nor does it look as if they have done so for many years. The ground is hard and hot. Fine green lines, the only hint of decoration in a landscape of sombre browns and blacks, follow cracks in the rocks where a residue of moisture has been trapped. Unbelievably, there are people living here, on the very edge of survival. A thin straw hut bends with the wind. Outside it, children with wild hair and torn blue smocks watch us pass, standing barefoot on the stones, a donkey stock-still beside them.

There are army checkpoints. Whilst Mohammed presents our papers I get out for a breather, only to be hit by a wall of heat unlike anything I've yet experienced. Whatever is the opposite of wind chill, this is it. Air stoked up to 55°C/131°F and driven on by the *harmattan* rakes the desert like a blast from a flame-thrower.

I'm told that in desert as hot as the Ténéré, the human body loses 2 gallons of water a day, which is 9 litres, and 4 gallons if you're on the move, so one should really keep drinking constantly. We have bottles of water with us but they heat up quickly and warm water is so much more difficult to gulp down. J-P has come up with an ingenious answer. He drops a couple of mint tea bags into a plastic bottle, which he wedges on top of the dashboard. The head-on sunlight heats it, the bounce of the vehicle stirs it and the near boiling infusion that results is a lot more palatable than lukewarm mineral water.

The vehicles judder and shudder over a surface that changes with frightening suddenness from hard earth to corrugated rocky ridges. A few miles back we passed a donkey rolling on its back, enjoying a dust bath. Just now we saw another donkey, stretched out by the side of the road, skin drawn back on its jaw, dead of thirst.

Mohammed Ixa points out four fluted columns, apparently of golden sandstone, 3 or 4 feet high, arranged in the shape of a square. The stones are actually petrified wood and mark a pre-Islamic grave. Which means someone was laid to rest here at least fourteen centuries ago.

As the sun is beginning to sink, we see, coming towards us, what looks like a huge upturned ship, with dozens of people clinging to the wreckage. As it comes closer it's revealed to be a Mercedes truck, groaning beneath the weight of fifty or sixty people, close-packed on top of a cargo of rugs, carpets, blankets and bedding which swells out way beyond the sides of the vehicle. Bags of food, water and provisions hang down its flanks like fenders.

Initially friendly shouts from the occupants turn to angry gesticulations as soon as we attempt to film them.

These are trans-Saharan *camions*, carrying an illegal labour force across the very heart of the desert from the poorer black African countries of the south to the oil-rich countries of Libya and Algeria. The workers generally have no papers or passports, so the *camions* move at night and take considerable detours to avoid checkpoints.

We put the cameras away and watch them recede slowly and ponderously on the twisting track towards Agadez, a fat, swaying silhouette against the setting sun.

Day Sixty-Two

THE TÉNÉRÉ DESERT

We camped last night in complete isolation. Or so I thought until this morning, when, out of nowhere, figures appeared, moving slowly towards us: a group of three women, one with a babe in arms, and a young boy. They were terribly thin and frail. Against the early morning light they seemed almost insubstantial, like wraiths. They didn't speak, just stood and watched us, passive and expressionless. The oldest of the women, who looked seventy but was probably no more than forty, touched her eye and then her leg.

Our drivers looked embarrassed. She was asking for medicine and they didn't have any. If they had, they'd be using it themselves.

We gave them whatever we could, along with some water, and Amadou the cook found some scraps of food. They were still standing there when we drove away.

Most mornings we're quite jolly when we hit the road, but today the mood is muted. It was as if we were all thinking the same thing. That the people who had visited us were starving and there was nothing we could do.

There is more sand about now. Pale, almost white, it gathers at the base of huge black basalt rocks making them look as if they are not rooted in the earth but floating a few feet above it. It blows up against camel skeletons that lie by the road, making graceful streamlined shapes out of bleached corpses.

El Haj, who's driving Basil, J-P and me, is tall, quiet and, I should imagine, quite badly paid. He is a Toubou from the Bilma region and J-P speaks good enough French to get him talking. He's not complimentary about anyone apart from the Toubou, finding the Touareg arrogant and the Fulani, of whom the Wodaabe are a subdivision, too submissive. He cheers up visibly when talking of the

Hausa. They're the people everyone detests, he says confidently.

'After all, they're the bosses.'

By mid-morning the mountain range has receded and we turn off the track not far from the site of the celebrated Arbre du Ténéré. Long renowned for being the only tree standing in hundreds of square miles of surrounding desert, the Arbre du Ténéré became even more famous when, in 1973, a truck knocked it over. The bits and pieces have been stuck together and it now resides in a place of honour at the national museum in Niamey.

We turn north now, across country, to the spot where we hope to find Omar and the camel train. The Ténéré, considered by those who know these things to be the most beautiful part of the Sahara, does not make things easy for us. After following a long and ultimately impassable wadi (dried-up river bed), we're forced to turn back and look for a way through the sand dunes. The first few are low and relatively uncomplicated, but eventually we reach a big one, 100 feet or more and steep. The first two vehicles of our convoy make it, but El Haj doesn't. Revving the engine is fatal, as it just digs the wheels in deeper, so he has no option but to roll rather shamefacedly backwards until he finds level ground.

He lets down the front tyres to increase grip and we put our shoulders to the back of the vehicle as he tries again. Despite all our combined efforts, the wheels spin helplessly, we're covered in flying sand and the attempt is abandoned. El Haj wipes his brow and reluctantly climbs up onto the roof to get down the sand ladders which he probably should have used in the first place. Two of these, placed in front of the back wheels, provide the resistance he needs. But once moving he mustn't stop, and with shouts of encouragement we watch our means of transport hurtle up the dune, pause agonisingly briefly on the crest and disappear over the other side. Our cheers die quite quickly as we realise we have to retrieve the ladders and climb up after him. John Pritchard checks the temperature. It's 56°C/133°F.

After another hour's abortive searching of spectacular but camel-less desert, Mohammed, at the wheel of the first vehicle, suddenly yelps, points and roars off towards a clump of rangy acacias marking a shallow dip in the ground. I don't immediately see the caravan, as it blends so seamlessly into the background, but there they are, Ekawik and his colleagues, fearlessly stripping acacia branches, masticating 2-inch-long thorns to get to the tiny green leaves. Lying in thin shade nearby is Omar and his team.

We make camp in the lee of a 30-foot sand dune and pick our way through another salad, augmented with tuna this time. Before we go out to begin work, I give my increasingly burnt British skin a good coating of sun oil, forgetting as I do so that the wind has peppered my face with fine grains of sand. It's momentarily agonising, like giving myself a facial with an emery board. To avoid any further damage, Omar insists I wear my new turban. He helps tie it for me. I would never have imagined that 15 feet of coiled cotton could make such a difference to my life. Quite apart from protection against the sand, it also keeps me much cooler than a hat. And I look like Lawrence of Arabia. Well, his father, anyway.

Day Sixty-Three

THE TÉNÉRÉ DESERT

The pace of desert life is almost exactly the opposite of the life I'm used to back home. Because of the ferocity of the climate, even the most simple activities must be taken slowly. There is no need to hurry and no benefit in doing so.

For the cameleers, the day follows a timeless, preordained pattern. Prayer, then breakfast cooked over a fire of sticks and branches, then the thick woollen blankets, under which they sleep at night (they don't have tents), are rolled up, secured with twine and laid beside each camel. The camels are brought to their knees and loaded up. Guide ropes are reinserted in mouths stained yellowy-green from cud-chewing, and they are brought to their feet. This provokes a tumult of braying and grunting. I wish I knew what they were saying, for it sounds important to them. Is it passionate protest or is it merely an assertion of team spirit at the start of a new day? Is it 'how many more times do I have to tell you, I'm *not* a beast of burden, right', or is it 'Good morning everyone. Another scorcher by the looks of things'?

Ekawik doesn't speak to me at all. In fact, he doesn't seem the slightest bit interested in making friends with me, despite my syco-phantic patting of his flanks and complimentary remarks about the two silver good luck charms hanging from a chain around his neck.

He does, however, honk savagely when asked to carry me. This doesn't help, as I've never felt very comfortable on a ship of the desert. Once perched on Ekawik's hump, I feel about as steady as I would on a surfboard. I've also been provided with a lethal, though aesthetically pleasing, ceremonial saddle with high, spiky prongs and pommels back and front. I may look like some visiting poten-tate when I'm up there, but when it comes to dismounting, I find it impossible to get my leg over, as it were, and I have to be dragged from the saddle like someone being pulled from a car wreck. Much giggling from the cameleers.

The rhythm of the journey is set by the camels. Normally, they would be on the move at four in the morning, walking for fourteen or fifteen hours a day with two breaks, at midday and late after-noon. Omar tells me that when he's on the road he only has three or four hours sleep a night.

Ekawik and his friends are happiest when performing some-thing steady, simple and repetitive, like walking or chewing the cud. They are superbly adapted to this climate and terrain. Long legs raise them clear of the hot sand, a layer of fat on their backs protects them from the blazing sun. Heat escapes from their big, reassur-ingly rounded flanks, so they appear not to perspire, and even in this frightening heat they can go for days without any water at all. And their metabolism, as I've learnt from playing with their nuggets, is extraordinarily economical.

Izambar Mohammed, one of the nine-strong team of cameleers, is the *chanteur*, the one who sings and chants and makes up songs to pass the time as we go. He warns me about staying too close to the camels, especially their rear ends. Using fluent mime, he points out the ones that are the worst kickers. Somehow it doesn't surprise me that they include Ekawik.

Day Sixty-Four

The Ténéré Desert

Things are better today. I've been taken off Ekawik and allotted a white camel of extraordinary docility whose name I'm told is Ashid. Instead of the VIP saddle, which threatened to castrate me every time I tried to dismount, I now sit astride a less glamorous but much more comfortable roll of bedding.

We have left the mountains behind but are still in a landscape studded with volcanic remains. Fields of cracked basalt rock occasionally break through the stony cover, providing streaks of vivid colour, jet black against the pale straw of the sand. The low ridges make for difficult going. The camels are not happy on slopes, especially if they are covered in soft sand, and Omar has to lead them down with great care, moving forwards at a slow shuffle, testing the ground, as if picking his way through a minefield. The camels slip and slide unhappily in his wake, back legs stiff, straight and awkward, as if this is the first time they've ever been asked to walk downhill.

I'm beginning to get to know the cameleers, though none of them speaks anything but Tamahaq. Harouna is the oldest and is frequently consulted by Omar. Elias and Akide Osman are the youngest, affable but detached. I get the impression that a career in cameleering is not all they want out of life. Izambar's chanting is becoming a bit of a bore, but that could be because I'm not getting the full benefit of his improvised lyrics, which occasionally crack up the entire camel train, probably at my expense. Omar is a good-natured and thoughtful man, unquestionably respected by the others. I've never seen him on a camel. He's always walking, keeping an eye out for loose loads, checking the route ahead. He speaks good French and I like to walk and talk with him, as it takes the mind off the monotony. We talk about the recent war between the Touareg and the government in Niamey. The Touareg, rather optimistically, demanded more funds and less interference. The north of the country virtually closed down for six years, Omar had friends killed and arrested and most of the foreign visitors were frightened away. As he was taking tourists on desert safaris for ten times the money he made from salt caravans, this seriously affected his livelihood. But he never considered giving up and doesn't expect he ever will. He likes walking with the camels. He says it gives him time to think.

By midday he has brought us to a spreading acacia, where we are to lunch and rest up in the heat of the day.

The sight of this single tree, which only survives out here because of root systems which search out water 100 feet or more below the surface, gives an extraordinary lift to the spirits. It's like coming across a house or even a small village.

Everyone gets to work. The camels suddenly become talkative, making their usual sounds of complaint or joy as their burdens are removed. Their front legs are hobbled, but this doesn't stop them shuffling nimbly off to a particularly tempting goblet-shaped bush. Soon they're squeezed around it, feeding, with heads lowered in concentration, like men at the urinals when the half-time whistle has gone.

Those camels that can't find a place at the bush, nibble away at the acacia, impervious to thorns as hard and sharp as small nails.

Today we have a special treat, the Saharan equivalent of a Sunday lunch. And it will be fresh. Omar is sharpening his knife and the two sheep and small black goat which have been brought along from Tabelot are eyeing him beadily. Harouna and Izambar drag one of the sheep over. His companions, far from shying away, follow curiously and have to be chased off.

Whilst Harouna and Izambar hold it down, Omar deftly cuts the sheep's throat. It gasps and shudders as the blood drains from its body. The goat approaches again and this time Izambar throws sand at it to keep it away. Moussa takes over now, skinning and disembowelling the sheep, hanging the carcass from a stout branch and carefully cutting it up. The valuable hide, meanwhile, is laid out and rubbed over with sand to clean it.

Wood has been gathered and a fire lit. Akide Osman is making bread, kneading the dough into a flat disc. Once the embers of the fire are hot enough, he rakes them to one side and lays the bread on the hot sand, first one side, then the other, after which he piles sand

and glowing embers on top, creating an instant oven. Omar, meanwhile, slices an onion using a broken razor blade, and Moussa prises open a tin of tomatoes with his knife (memo to enterprising businessman – tin openers for the Touareg), drops them into a blackened cooking pot and mixes them with couscous.

Twenty minutes later, the roundel of bread is exhumed, and, after the charcoal and sand have been dusted off, it's passed down the line. It's not quite what I expected, being much harder, stickier and sweeter than bread.

'*Galette,*' explains Omar, helpfully.

Izambar, who is keen to teach me Tamahaq, the language of the Touareg, points to it.

'*Tagella,*' he says.

'Tagella,' I say, exactly as he's said it, only this time everyone falls about.

'*Tagella,*' he repeats.

'Tagel-la,' I reply, this time with extra care. Everyone falls about again.

This pantomime goes on until we're all laughing hysterically. Clearly my pronunciation does not mean bread. It probably means the private parts of a goat, or personal attributes of my mother, but whatever it is, it proves that there's nothing like a bit of incomprehension to bring people together.

I am honoured to be the first to taste the mutton stew. The meat is a little tired, but it had been walking in the sun for four days. Thankfully, the Touareg do not insist on my rolling the food up into a ball with two fingers of my right hand before popping it into my mouth. Out here in the desert they know how to live. I'm handed a wooden spoon, one of four that we share between us.

Izambar teaches me '*isan*', meaning meat, and '*izot*', which I think means 'this is very good', but induces more mirth when I say it.

There is some laughter too when I take off my turban, or *tagelmoust* in Tamahaq.

'You have a blue head,' says Omar, and I laugh indulgently. It's not until someone holds up a mirror that I realise I do indeed have a blue head, a stripe of indigo following a perspiration line right across my forehead.

Day Sixty-Five

THE TÉNÉRÉ DESERT

Omar tells me that camels only need two hours' sleep a night, and having got up to commune with nature in the early hours I can confirm that the majority were up and grazing in the moonlight. Two were lying flat out on their sides and three or four others were kneeling, with their long necks bowed and heads resting on the floor like wilted plants.

Breakfast this morning is the remains of the mutton, reinforced with rice and macaroni. Heavy and almost indigestible, but as the next meal may not be for ten hours there's no question of not eating it.

By mid-morning, having completed shots of departure from camp, the crew and gear are taken on in vehicles to the next stopping place. I could go with them, but I've not walked much with the camels in the heat of the day and I feel I must try it. I fill my water bottle, and take another litre, which Omar insists on carrying for me. We set off, twenty-eight camels, eight cameleers, me, Omar, one sheep and a small black goat. No-one is striding out. The overriding consideration in this climate is to conserve energy, and I fall happily into the steady even pace. The only sound, apart from the soft rustle of moving camels and the flip-flopping of Omar's sandals on the ground, is an occasional burst of song from Izambar, which rises, hangs in the air and blows away into silence. All that matters is the present. The past and future cease to exist.

Omar and I fall to talking about the health of camels and what threats they face out here. He says parasites, insects and particularly spines in their feet can easily cause infection (which is ironic, having seen them crunch 2-inch thorns in their mouths without blinking). One esoteric piece of information is that if a camel eats a praying mantis it will die. The camel, that is, not the praying mantis.

I stop to jot down this little gem, and by the time I've put my notebook back in my bag, Omar has moved ahead, his well-worn light blue robe billowing out to reveal deep-blue cotton leggings beneath. Several camels have passed me. I've lost Ashid and am alongside a camel I don't recognise. I look up to see Akide lying flat out on top of it. He grins down at me. I hope he's impressed that I've opted to walk with them, but I'm pretty sure he thinks I'm completely mad.

A tiny lizard, shockingly naked and white, pops its head out from a stunted clump of grass, takes one look at us and darts back in again.

The wind changes direction and starts to blow grains of sand directly towards me. I glance sideways up at the camels, but they seem completely unaffected, long lashes down, protecting their eyes from whatever is thrown at them.

I take a swig of water, trying not to break step as I do so. Omar is even further away now, and I'm almost halfway down the camel train, alongside Izambar, who returns my smile but, for once, says nothing.

I look down. The desert floor has changed yet again and is now covered in a series of crusty flakes, like fragments of eggshell. Like dew, dried and hardened.

I look back at my footprints. They're quite deep, much deeper than the camel prints beside them. Their broad feet work like snowshoes, distributing their weight and leaving barely a mark.

The classic description of a camel is a horse designed by committee, but it's not quite fair. I see it more as a horse designed by rival universities, all of whom got a grant for different parts. Technologically, it is far more interesting than a horse; it's just that the whole lot could do with some co-ordinating hand.

Time for some more water. I've almost drained my water bottle, but I notice none of the cameleers has taken a drop. We're walking along a wadi and Omar is up on top of a low dune, scanning the land ahead. As we draw level I raise my bottle and he comes down towards me and fills it up again.

Then he leads us out of the wadi and onto the dune, beautiful to look at but murderous underfoot. My feet slip down into the sand and for the first time on the walk I feel faint alarm. By the time we're at the top of the dune I can hear my heart thudding. I slither down the other side and find myself in a long curving bowl between two ridges, dotted with tussocks of *krim-krim* grass and the bleached white branches of dead trees.

Elias Abrokas, swathed in a multicoloured scarf, draws water from a green plastic container into a stainless-steel bowl and walks up the line with it. No-one seems to take more than a couple of gulps, and the camels don't stop.

The sight makes me thirsty and I take out my bottle. It's nearly empty again, and by now I'm level with the last three camels. Tuck my bottle back in my bag, put my head down and concentrate on catching up. Mercifully, there is harder sand down here and my boots can get some grip.

After a few minutes of concentrated effort I look up and see Omar as far ahead as ever. I redouble my efforts, setting myself a target to pass three camels in five minutes, but make no headway at all. I've lost the rhythm, the beat, whatever it is that moves camels so easily across the sand. If I pause for a breather I know I shall only slip further back. To shout for help seems pathetic. I look ahead of me. The camel train moves on remorselessly. Akide is still lying peacefully across his camel's back; Izambar has nodded off. Omar is taking the same small, regular paces as when we started. So how have I got down here?

The last camel comes level and passes me. My mouth is dry but I've no more water. The stories I've heard around the campfire spring, unwelcome, into my mind. Of vehicles breaking down and guides dying of thirst as they went for help; of the stranded French couple who gave their six-month-old baby their own blood to drink and still perished.

In only two hours, the joy of solitariness and contemplation has become the fear of isolation and abandonment. Marine metaphors come constantly to mind. I'm out of my depth.

Like a man overboard shouting after a receding ship.

Then Omar turns and motions that there is something up ahead. I wave my bottle as high as I can, neck downwards. He doesn't move but watches the camels pass until I reach him. He hands me what's left of the water and enquires, wordlessly, how I am.

'*Très bon, merci, Omar,*' I lie.

There, in the distance, is a tree, and, below it, a ring of four-wheel drives and Pete cleaning the camera and, almost certainly, Mohammed Ixa lying on his back, listening to the radio.

THE TÉNÉRÉ DESERT

A new arrival at the camp this morning. A baby gazelle, no more than a day old, has been found abandoned by its mother, possibly frightened by the arrival of the camel train. It is a tiny, spindly, shivering thing, with its coat all mussed up; confused, lost and breathing hard. Its legs are as thin as matchsticks, its eyes big, black and searching, its ears as long as a rabbit's. The news that Amadou is to take care of it worries me initially. He is, after all, our chef. But I'm assured that this delicate little beauty will not end up in the pot like the two sheep and the goat, now *one* sheep and a goat, which accompany the caravan. Later, I see the gazelle being held in the massive hands of El Haj, whilst Amadou tries to get her to take milk from the end of his finger.

The camel train moves into spectacular desert today. '*Désert absolu*', as my *Guide Bleu* describes it. The *krim-krim* grass, acacia scrub, even the ubiquitous desert melon bushes, whose fruit is tempting but inedible, have all disappeared. This is landscape reduced to its barest essentials, a rippling, rolling, shadeless surface purged of every living thing.

The immense emptiness quietens everyone. Progress is slow and steady, although such is the lack of distinctive landmarks it sometimes feels as if we're walking on the spot.

In the middle of the morning, several hours out from the camp, there's a sudden commotion up front, voices raised, a quite un-desert-like sense of urgency and emergency. The camels have come to a halt, so it must be serious. I hurry up the line to find Moussa and Amadou skipping round, shouting and pointing down at the sand, as Izambar runs in with a stone and proceeds to beat at something in the sand. There's great excitement, halfway between fear and fun. Eventually, to gasps of mock horror, Izambar raises above his head a small, white, and, by now, entirely lifeless snake, about 18 inches long. He moves it sharply towards me and I duck back involuntarily. Encouraged by the response, he pretends to eat it, provoking howls of delighted disgust.

Omar, who has been watching all this clowning with the mildly indulgent smile of a teacher on a school outing, tells me that this is the much-feared *vipère du sable*, the sand viper, whose bite, relatively harmless for humans, can cripple a camel. The desert is clearly not as empty as it looks.

As if to rub this in, Mohammed, normally so languid and laid-back, gives a sharp cry as we lie on the mats after lunch. He's been bitten by a scorpion. I'm lying next to him and move pretty smartly out of the way, as someone grabs my boot and deals the scorpion a fatal blow. Like the snake earlier, the scorpion looks a pale defence-less little creature, the last thing in the world to cause trouble, but even after the poison is sucked out and sedatives administered Mohammed is clearly in serious pain, and says he will be for another four hours.

The excitements of the day are not yet over. Shortly after darkness has fallen, distant headlights stab the gloom and soon we hear a rapidly approaching vehicle and, at the same time, a high-pitched drone in the sky above us. There is some nervous speculation that we have been mistaken for Osama Bin Laden and American Special Services have come to deal with us, but the reality proves to be a pair of French paragliders. First the ground support arrives and minutes later, once signal lights have been set up and vehicle head-lights switched on to pick out the landing strip, an Icarus appears, strapped to a motor attached to a wheel-like frame and swinging on the end of a yellow mattress parachute. After two or three low passes over the camp this surreal figure hits the ground to a burst of spontaneous applause.

Renaud Van De Meeren is the flyer and François Lagarde the ground crew. As they join us around the single lamp it's hard to distinguish features, but François is clearly the older man. Wiry, tall, with a boyish flop of fair hair, he has flown his machine all over the world but still regards the Sahara as his favourite desert.

'It's still alive, you know. There is authentic life, here.'

He talks about the paraglider like a boy with a new toy. The whole kit folds down into two bags and can be carried with them as accompanying baggage. Yesterday they were in Paris. And the experience of flying it? Smooth and solid.

'Like swimming in oil.'

Their theatrical arrival is upstaged by the clutch of Western newspapers and magazines that they have brought with them. These contain the first pictures we have seen of the attacks on America eight days ago. Since then we have all carried our own separate mental pictures of the destruction, made up of descriptions from families and friends at home, BBC World Service reports and individual imaginings. Now, by the light of a flickering lamp in the heart of the Sahara, we share with the rest of the world, for the first time, the classic images that will come to define the tragedy; bodies falling through the air, black smoke blotting out Lower Manhattan, dust clouds racing down the streets.

By the time I climb into my tent it's nearly eleven. This is very late for the desert, where darkness rules and we're usually in bed by half past nine, yet for once I can't get to sleep. The arrival of the paragliders, with their papers and their magazines reminding us of where we came from and what we shall soon have to go back to, has broken the spell, compromised our isolation, drawn us back into the wider world just as it was becoming soothingly irrelevant. Much as we might want it otherwise, life in the desert is a diversion and the blazing skyline of New York is the reality.

And that's not all that's keeping me awake. There are persistent scratchings on the side of my tent, as if the wind is blowing something against it. But there is no wind.

Heart beating a little faster, I pull the zip open and peer out, but there's nothing there, and indeed what could be there, in the middle of the Ténéré? Apart from camels. Oh, and snakes. And scorpions. And gazelles. And paragliders.

The Ténéré Desert

The noises in the night prove to have been the work of little black beetles, and judging by the network of tracks around my tent they had put in a full night's work. There are over 350 species of black beetle in the Sahara, but I haven't seen so many in one place since we watched the camel train come into Timbuktu. They bustle around as I pack, full of curiosity, wanting to get into everything, as they had presumably wanted to get into my tent last night. Nor was I the only one to have been kept awake by them. J-P, dark-eyed and dishevelled, became convinced that hyenas were prowling around and has barely slept a wink. I can understand it. In such a soundless environment the slightest noise can become weirdly amplified. And he had had a brandy or two.

Renaud, whose speciality is aerial photography, is also up early to take advantage of the light at sunrise. Lashed to the wheel of his paraglider like some mediaeval penitent, he runs into the wind, but there isn't enough to fill his parachute, and he has to keep on running, trying to find the elusive lifting breeze. He disappears behind a dune, engine revving away. There's a pregnant pause, and a moment later the sound of an engine cutting out, followed by a short splintering crash.

Renaud is fine, but his machine is a write-off. Later, François manages to get his craft airborne and the morning's travelling is enlivened by his appearances over the dunes, sweeping down across the camel train, filming with one hand, steering with the other.

To get the right pictures the camels have to be led backwards and forwards over the same ground, which emphasises how, in a way, things have changed. Omar and his team are following us instead of us following them. Whatever relationship I might have assumed I was forging with the Touareg has been subsumed by Western technology.

In the evening I have one last meal with the cameleers. In a recklessly generous act of hospitality they cook the remaining sheep, preceded by a tasty mix of crusty-topped goat's cheese and dates. We sit round the fire and go through my Touareg vocabulary for the last time.

'*Tagel-la.*' (Roars of laughter.) '*Izot!*' '*Issan!*'

As we raise our glasses of mint tea I teach Izambar some useful English in return.

I advise him that the English say 'Bottoms Up' when they raise a glass.

Izambar is a very quick learner, though his first faltering attempts – 'Bott-erm erp' – give me a chance to get back for all the *Tagel-la*s.

The main thing is that we laugh a lot. Almost like old friends.

Day Sixty-Eight

OUT OF THE TÉNÉRÉ DESERT

Breakfast on the side of a long stony slope with no cover other than a few boulders. Ekawik, perhaps sensing my imminent departure, is very frisky and when Elias has finished loading him he breaks away, scattering his cargo and skipping about with joyful abandon. For his pains he gets a ticking off and a very severe kick up the bottom (not an easy thing to do to a camel).

'*Méchant. Très méchant*,' mutters Omar, but he can't help smiling.

I want to give Omar something for his help and good company, but all he will take is my bottle of eye-drops. Eye problems are the most common complaint in his village and he will keep these till he gets back. It feels a pathetically inadequate thanks, but I think he has enjoyed himself. We have been on the move with the camel train for five days. They have adapted their movement to our own and would normally, by now, be over halfway to Bilma. As it is, we have moved only about 100 miles from the mountains. We must leave them to go on at their own pace and I must strike off, north, to the Algerian border.

ALGERIA

I-n-Guezzam

I approach Algeria with a certain amount of trepidation. The second largest country in Africa, and the tenth largest in the world, has, since 1992, been sidelined to the fringes of the international community, a nation synonymous with trouble. Information is hard to find. My Lonely Planet guide apologetically devotes only ten pages to it. 'Due to its continuing problems,' they explain, 'Algeria was the one African nation we were unable to visit.'

The BBC advised against operating there, and the Foreign Office insisted that if we go we should take armed bodyguards. Even the artesian well at the border, marked so hopefully in blue on my Michelin map, has the word *'sulfureuse'* alongside it.

The country that fought a bloody civil war to win its independence from France in 1962 is currently involved in another, just as bloody, which began in 1992, when the military-dominated, socialist regime cancelled an election which they feared was going to be won by an Islamist opposition party. The opposition militarised itself as the GIA (Armed Islamic Group), and it is estimated that in less than ten years more than 100,000 people have died on both sides.

Everyone tells me, however, that the worst of the trouble is confined to the north, where 85 per cent of the population lives. Everyone, that is, but the driver who is at this very moment carrying me across a swathe of flat, gritty desert (*reg* as opposed to *erg*) towards the border town of I-n-Guezzam.

His small talk features mouth-drying accounts of the extreme lawlessness of the Sahara. Smuggling is a way of life. Mostly cigarettes, made illegally in Nigeria and brought north by the truckload. Governments have little influence in isolated areas still controlled by local warlords.

Had I not heard of Mokhtar ben Mokhtar, alias Louar, the One-Eyed One?

I shake my head, '*Qu'est-ce qu'il fait?*'

My driver can't believe his luck. '*Qu'est-ce qu'il fait!*'

He's stockpiled thousands of illegal weapons, stolen several hundred four-wheel drives and shot down an aircraft. He has a fleet of vehicles equipped with satellite navigation, armed with AK-47s and refuelled from dumps deep in the sand. An entire Dakar Rally had once been diverted to avoid going through his territory.

'Which is where, exactly?'

My driver gestures, a circular motion of the right hand that leaves little room for doubt. Wherever it was that Mokhtar ben Mokhtar operated, we're in the middle of it.

'I was told it was Islamic fundamentalists that stopped the Rally.'

He shakes his head. 'Mokhtar works for himself. And for the freedom of the South.'

'South?'

'Of Algeria.'

The car slides to a halt.

'There it is!'

My driver points to two metal posts stuck in the sand.

There always seems something faintly absurd about borders. One stone belonging to one government and the stone next to it belonging to another. In the immense void of the desert, marks of sovereignty seem gloriously irrelevant. Yet here they are, confirmed in a plinth at the base of a 6-foot-high oval steel tube.

'*F. Algéro–Nigérienne 27/11/1981*'

The clipped inscription has been crudely applied, picked out by a finger whilst the concrete was still wet.

Next to it is a shorter triangular steel post, which my driver tells me is an upright for the *palissade*, a fence which the authorities hope will one day make this a serious border and stop the likes of Mokhtar ben Mokhtar treating Algeria's desert like his own private fiefdom. This could be the fencing contract of all time. Algeria's Saharan border is nearly 2000 miles long.

There is one other marker at this desolate spot. It's a small concrete trig point left behind by the French. Detailed measurements and the words '*Nivellement Général*' are inscribed in a clear, legible and ornate inscription. This was the work of people who intended to stay in Algeria for a long time.

Near by, the shells of two abandoned cars lie in the sand, as if, like marathon runners breasting the tape, the effort of getting to the line was all they could manage. Jettisoned tyres, a carburettor and an un-rusted cylinder head are scattered about.

Across the border our Algerian hosts wait to greet us. Said Chitour is a journalist from Algiers who has worked tirelessly for this day. He's a stocky, busy man in his early forties, anxious and exuberant at the same time. With him is our security man, Eamonn O'Brien, with a broad smile and the reassuring physique of Action Man, and an assortment of uniformed attendants. Gendarmes in green, border police in black. All are armed. Said reminds us that no walkie-talkies or satellite phones are to be used while we are in Algeria. Security, he says, with a quick shrug and a smile, before turning to the drivers.

'Come! We go!' he shouts, a touch manically. Engines rumble into life and, accompanied by our substantial entourage, we head across the two or three miles of no-man's-land that separates the end of Niger from the first town in Algeria.

The crescent moon and green and white verticals of the national flag flutter above the sub-prefect's office in the main street of I-n-Guezzam. Construction is going on to turn this dirt strip into a dual carriageway, but work seems desultory. Two rake-thin guards, rifles slung over their shoulders, stand outside the office where our papers are being checked. As we wait, Said confides to me that I-n-Guezzam is considered the end of the earth, and a posting here is usually a penalty for past mistakes. I like Said. He is clearly proud of his country and impatient with it at the same time, like a father with a delinquent son.

He apologises that there are no hotels of sufficient quality in I-n-Guezzam. We have been invited instead to spend the night on the roof of the mayor's house. This is a two-storey brick and plaster building with a small garden tucked away behind high walls. The downstairs rooms are full of people, mostly family I assume. The mayor, a tall slim Touareg, wears a yellow turban, matching *gandoura* (an Arab kaftan), leggings in cream and red check and a pair of thin scholarly glasses. Our presence is clearly something unprecedented in I-n-Guezzam and he is forever bringing people up to the roof to meet us. The commissar, a short stocky man in T-shirt and Umbro training pants, shakes hands all round, followed shortly by someone introduced to us as the Surgeon of Police. I think they're all quite keen to hang around and party, but we cross-Saharan travellers are by now desperately in need of food and sleep.

Day Seventy

I-n-Guezzam to Tamanrasset

I should be used to the gripping chill of the desert nights by now, but I still find myself reaching for a sweater in the small hours. I find I've laid my sleeping bag beside a small drainage hole in the wall, through which a blast of gritty wind is blowing straight into my face. Stuff my towel into the hole, wrap my turban round my head and settle myself back to sleep. It doesn't come easily. There is a constant subdued roar coming from somewhere, as if planes are warming up for take-off (I'm later told it's the town generator). I can't wait for the dawn.

It is a beauty. The sun rises as a pulsing red ball, glowing like a hot coal before softening into a peachy glow which fills the sky with benevolent promise. (I keep making a mental note to myself not to describe any more sunrises, but some are majestic and, jaded travellers though we are, we never ignore them. They raise the spirits like nothing else. Apart from a cold beer.)

The mayor and the commissar and the surgeon of police all gather around as we load up. They're candid about the problems down here at the frontier. There is no oasis and no water for crops, so all their food must be brought in from Tamanrasset, 250 miles away.

The mayor unpicks a stick from his teeth and gestures at a row of new houses across the street.

'The people are poor, but very conservative. We build new houses, with floors, and they still want to sleep on the sand.'

As Said puts it, they mistrust the 'chair culture'. They remain nomads at heart, so everything expendable is dumped in the street for the goats to sift through.

'And the women,' the mayor shakes his head, 'you don't see them. Some of them never leave their houses.'

As the time comes for yet another goodbye, the mayor and his friends are warm and courteous, but I sense they are already switching off, preparing to return to the reality of their isolation. They know that almost anywhere else is better than here and yet it is their home. To survive it must require a particularly indomitable spirit.

The road to Tamanrasset follows one of the oldest trade routes across the Sahara, from Nigeria to Algeria, across the very heart of the desert. It is still a sand piste. There are signs of a hard-top being laid north of I-n-Guezzam, but it runs beside us, tantalisingly unfinished. The surface, by no means free of rocks and boulders, is generally firm, but there are softer patches where wheels cease to grip and the cars begin to swing.

This is a main road without garages or tow-trucks, so virtually everything that breaks down is left to the mercy of the sands. It was between I-n-Guezzam and Tamanrasset that Margaret Thatcher's son went missing in the 1980s. He and his girlfriend were rescued after a long and expensive search. Not everyone was so lucky. A few miles off the main piste is an undulating area of fine sand and basalt boulders so strewn with old car bodies that it's known as the Cemetery. Quite what happened to all these wrecks is difficult to tell. Some are twisted out of recognition, others seem just to have been abandoned, one door swung open, as if someone had decided to get out and walk. Anything that could be removed from them has been removed. The wind, a constant companion in the desert, catches at their metal skeletons, making them twitch and vibrate as if not quite dead. An old Deux Chevaux, painted all the colours of the rainbow and half filled with sand, adds a touch of colour to the wreckage, a reminder of the part deserts played in the hippie dream. There is no shelter here and not a cloud in the way of a sun which is sending temperatures beyond 38°C/100°F.

The wonder is that any of these cars got this far.

Seven hours after setting out, we arrive in the well-kept streets of Tamanrasset. The town feels as if it has just had a makeover. Kerb-stoned sidewalks, concrete arcades, lines of shade-giving trees, walls and buildings decorated in what seems to be a regulation shade of blood-brown. Even the razor wire has been painted in Tamanrasset.

Day Seventy-One

TAMANRASSET TO ASSEKREM

Around 10.30 the four rusty flagpoles on the forecourt of the Hotel Tahat recede into the distance as we take to Tamanrasset's gloriously smooth and comfortable roads. Within a mile we throw an abrupt right onto a track so ferociously jagged that for a moment I fear we might have been hijacked.

It does not get much better. Every now and then we come to a stretch that is merely rutted earth, but these are few and far between. Generally, it is a bed of broken and solidified lava, over which the vehicle judders and shudders as if possessed. A puncture offers some brief respite, then the whole painful process begins again. But it is a price almost worth paying for magnificently dramatic scenery. We are in the Hoggar Mountains, which, with peaks rising to 10,000 feet, are amongst the highest in the Sahara. They're formed by the hard cores of ancient volcanoes, eroded into a series of weird and wonderfully shaped towers, plugs and pinnacles.

Some have incised vertical surfaces, as if they've been clawed, others are so deeply scored that their sides look like organ pipes or massive petrified tree roots. On one the scarring runs in all directions like a starburst captured in stone. There are knobs, spires, needles, arcs and bluffs, rocks standing four square on plinths of rubble, resembling mediaeval castles. Tenacious tufts of grass cling to the defiles and gullies; otherwise, this is a land of rock and stone. The Touareg know it by the suitably Tolkien-ish name of Atakor.

Just as I'm constructing romantic notions of mythological lands, a squat white Mercedes jeep bounces down the track towards us. Not unbelievable in itself, but quite a shock when I see it has British number plates. It pulls up and out gets a bony, angular man of late middle age, with a flick of fair hair and a quick, elfin-like energy. With mutual exclamations of surprise we introduce ourselves. His name is Tom Sheppard, a well-known traveller with books to his name.

Like many twentieth-century Englishmen, from T. E. Lawrence to Wilfred Thesiger, he has a passion for desert, and particularly this part of the Algerian desert. He's been coming here for forty years, following tracks marked on the old French maps.

'The Hoggar's very special.'

He likes the compactness of the area, and that there is, within 1000 square miles, such an extraordinary combination of mountain and dune.

'Pristine dunes, quite untrodden by anyone at all.'

He hasn't seen another human being for eight days, one of which was his sixty-eighth birthday. He describes it with almost military relish.

'I had a really special meal on that one. Meat and two veg. Chilled grapefruit for goodness' sake. Damp kitchen towel, wrapped around the tin, the dryness of the air makes evaporation and you get cooled grapefruit segments. What more could you ask for a birthday?'

Life has been made much safer for him since the advent of satellites.

'God bless the Americans for putting them up there.'

He enthuses about something called EPRB, Electronic Precision Recording Beacon – basically a distress signal, which bounces off a satellite to centres all over the world. He's had to use it in Libya recently.

'And they were onto it, just like that, eleven minutes after starting transmission.'

I'd like to talk a lot more, but Tom politely turns down our offer of lunch. Though he exudes conviviality, his pleasure is in going solo, and as his dust-covered Mercedes, as compact and self-contained as its owner, crunches off down the track, I find myself distinctly envious of the man.

Having covered the next 50 miles in a painful four and a half hours, we catch sight of a tiny hut silhouetted on a ridge high above us, a refuge built by the ascetic French missionary Charles de

Foucauld ninety years ago. After a few more agonisingly slow hair-pins we pull up at the gates of a compound below the hut, where there is a hostel maintained by the town of Tamanrasset.

The accommodation is basic mountain stuff: an uncompromising stone-walled building, with two outside lavatories (quite far outside), three dormitories and a communal meeting room, with rugs and cushions, chairs, tables and an open fire. After our meal we sit in here with Arouj, the administrator, a heavily turbaned, moustachioed Touareg, probably a devastatingly handsome man in his youth, now a little fleshed out. Business doesn't look good. There's room here for 150, but apart from ourselves there are only four other visitors tonight. One is a young German biker, who set out to cross the Sahara with two friends, both of whom have had to return home after arguments with sand dunes. Arouj orders some mint tea for us all. He's pleased to see us. Very few British ever come here, he says. Germans, yes, Italians (for the rock climbing) and Spanish.

French?

He wobbles his hand. *Some* French.

I feel for him. The locals have put a lot into this place. There is an airstrip at Tamanrasset, and the Hoggar mountain area is a national park, protected by UNESCO. But as long as Algeria remains better known for its civil war, places like Assekrem will remain a well-kept secret.

I make my apologies and get off to bed. We're to be up at five tomorrow to walk up to the refuge. Arouj hands me his card. It has his website marked.

Day Seventy-Two

═══════◯═══════

ASSEKREM TO HASSI-MESSAOUD

An alarm sounds in our dormitory, followed by total silence. Then a rustling of sleeping bags, a muffled curse, a cough, a variety of yawns and silence again. We've all been very well behaved in the night. No raucous snoring, farting or too many trips to the toilet. I know, because I've been awake most of the time. I never sleep comfortably if there's an unusually early start in the offing. My body

knows it's in for a shock and stays on red alert for most of the night.
A torch is switched on, the first light of the morning.

Pull myself reluctantly from my sleeping bag, which has had
more use in the Sahara than on all my previous journeys put
together. I keep thinking I won't need it any more, then up comes a
night like this. Middle of the Sahara and cold as a Scottish winter.

Bleary, grunted greetings. Queue for the lavatory, faces washed
with a splash of bottled water. Tea has been made by someone, God
bless them. Then out onto the mountainside. The mass of bright
stars, normally such a delight, seems to be almost hostile this
morning, the cold already intensified by a wicked little wind. The
top of the hill is a few hundred feet away, up a steep zigzag footpath.
Nigel and Pete set the pace, weaving up it like mountain goats,
despite carrying more than anyone else. Maybe Nigel, a well-estab-
lished quinquagenarian like myself, felt an urge to prove himself
after yesterday's encounter with the boyish sixty-eight-year-old
Tom Sheppard.

By the time we've reached the top of the path and the broad flat
plateau on which Père de Foucauld built his refuge, we're above
9000 feet and gulping gratefully at the chilly air.

There is still three-quarters of an hour to go before sunrise, but
the stars are fading slowly and a faint lemon-magenta glow is
shading the eastern horizon. Up here the mountains are all below
us. Only one summit, that of Tahat, away to the north, is superior,
and that by a few hundred feet. Even before the sun comes up the
view is breathtaking. The misty pre-dawn light compresses the
spaces between the mountains, giving the appearance of a solid
range to what we know to be a collection of eccentric individuals.

Said whispers in my ear.

'This is third best sunrise in the world, after Fiji and Ceylon.'

He pauses a moment for me to take this in.

'The purity of the air here is recorded by the meteorological
station and sent back to the United States. To measure carbon and
ozone in the atmosphere.'

(I'm not altogether sure about this purity of the air bit; it brings
to mind something less reassuring that I recently read in Jeremy
Keenan's book *Sahara Man*. At In Ecker, less than 60 miles north-
west of here, the French tested their first nuclear weapon.

According to Keenan, there is anecdotal evidence of poisonous emissions and mysterious deaths immediately afterwards.)

A bitter north wind drives me to take shelter in the refuge. Above the doorway of this plain stone construction is a white marble panel. It reads '*Charles de Foucauld, juillet–décembre 1911*'. Inside, a narrow passage leads to a small chapel, where there is a picture of a lean Frenchman with a well-trimmed beard dressed in a white monk's habit, and, above it, the emblem of a red heart with a cross rising from it.

Fifty-three years before he built this refuge de Foucauld was born in Strasbourg, a *vicomte* from a privileged and wealthy background. He joined the French army and was posted to Algeria, where he lived a playboy life, doing little but splash his money around on parties and mistresses. Then, suddenly and quite drastically turning his back on the easy life, he travelled North Africa disguised as a Jewish rabbi, joined a Trappist order at the age of thirty-one and, twelve years later, entered the priesthood. His work brought him to the Touareg of the Hoggar Mountains, amongst whom he gained considerable respect, not only learning their language but also producing the first French–Tamahaq dictionary.

He accepted, indeed revelled in, the isolation of the desert. There is a shelf beside the chapel on which a book of his writings lies open at the place where de Foucauld gives his own account of what has brought us here: 'The beauty of the view defies description or even imagination . . . it is marvellous.'

There's not much I can add to this as I watch the sun rise over the Hoggar Mountains, giving each peak form and colour and revealing the spectacular proportions of this strange and unforgettable landscape.

The Sahara's fearsome reputation for ending people's lives prematurely was enhanced by the murder of de Foucauld, who was shot and killed in Tamanrasset five years after building this refuge. The order he founded, the Little Brothers of Jesus, continues his work, supported by Algeria's Muslim government. The current incumbent, Brother Edward, offers tea to ourselves and two other tourists who've struggled up to the sunrise. He tells us that Père de Foucauld, far from being forgotten, is in the preparatory stages of canonisation and will very soon be made a saint.

He also asks if we wouldn't mind taking down to Tamanrasset a Korean acolyte, who has just spent forty days and nights on his own up here. We pick him up later in the car park, an incessantly smiling, patient man, jauntily dressed in fishing hat, windcheater and jeans. It looks more like he's spent four hours in Banana Republic than forty days in solitary.

We're back in Tamanrasset by midday. Snatched rudely from the sublime to the ridiculous, we find ourselves struggling to negotiate forty-odd bags through an overcrowded airport with 'Feelings' playing over the Tannoy. Nor does the culture shock end there. We are soon aboard a 737 bound for Hassi-Messaoud. It has taken us four hours to drive the 40 miles from Assekrem; the next 700 miles of our journey will take less than ninety minutes.

As we take to the air I can't take my eyes off the panorama of peaks spread out below me like tombstones, and even when the Hoggar Mountains slip away to the south, the desert landscape remains hypnotically beautiful. A series of round black circles, the traces of spent volcanoes, cover the surface like blisters, before giving way to a wide flat tableland eroded into a series of long twisting terraces. This in turn gives way to the glorious salmon pink of the Grand Erg Oriental, part of the sand sea that swirls across the centre of Algeria in long languid curves.

As we begin our descent the unbroken stretch of virgin sand becomes increasingly tarnished. Straight black lines cross the landscape below, connecting up a series of tiny installations, making the surface of the desert look more like a printed circuit board. The lower we get the more depressing it becomes. The sand sea is riddled with roads, pipelines, clusters of low huts surrounded by smeared black pits, at the centre of which, like the totems of some ancient religion, are towers spouting flame. This is Algeria's Aladdin's Cave. Within a 300-mile radius of the rapidly approaching oasis of Hassi-Messaoud are sufficient reserves of oil and gas to make this embattled country the third richest (after Libya and Tunisia) in the Sahara.

In an already security-obsessed country the oil and gas production facilities are fortresses in themselves. No vehicles are allowed up to the airport buildings, and we have to carry all our equipment 300 yards down the road, through a narrow checkpoint and across into a car park surrounded by a 10-foot-high razor-wired steel fence. Behind the bars of the car park are more white faces than I've seen on our entire journey. They stare out from minibuses and four-wheel drives, company coaches and private saloons, their gazes neutral and incurious as they wait to be driven away. These are not the faces of people glad to be here; they're the faces of people who have to be here. They're the oil men.

We are in turn collected and driven to our accommodation in *bâtiments durs*, long low huts, like grey steel tents, put up by the French in the 1950s. A television is on in a small communal area just inside the door of the hut and a rugby match between Ireland and England is playing.

The crew, lured by beds and bathrooms, crash out in their rooms, and I'm the only one to witness England's defeat and Eamonn O'Brien's unconfined joy.

Day Seventy-Three

HASSI-MESSAOUD

I feel thoroughly disorientated. I saw with my own eyes last night that we were in the middle of the desert, but this morning I step out of our hut to find it surrounded by tall swaying trees. Green lawns and flower beds border the road to the communal dining block. Hassi-Messaoud means 'the well of the man called Messaoud', and I can't imagine he would recognise his watering hole since the oil men got here. A network of electric pumps works round the clock to bring water up from hundreds of feet below the surface, enough to support 15,000 trees and 40,000 people. This tiny postage stamp of greenery, this blip in the wastes of the Sahara, has flocks of ducks and herds of goats, palm trees producing the very finest *deglet noir* dates, cows producing four barrels of milk a day, tennis courts, schools, swimming pools, fountains and a cinema.

This eerie similarity to a piece of provincial France is not accidental.

When oil was first discovered in the desert in the 1950s, Algeria was an integral part of France, not a colony, but a series of *départe-ments*, as much a part of the mother country as Aveyron or Vaucluse. The French purred with pleasure at the news of this first-ever discovery of oil on its territory and immediately put in the investment needed to retrieve it, creating, amongst other things, the man-made oasis of Hassi-Messaoud.

At almost the same time, however, the Algerian uprising began and by 1962 France was forced to grant full independence to its most obstinately defended African possession. The French dream of a Saharan equivalent of North Sea oil finally died in 1971, when the Algerian oil industry was nationalised, without a cent of com-pensation to the French government.

Nevertheless, French influence still clings to the place. The VIP dining room is called the Salle Bleue and is decorated with a nice touch of Gallic surrealism, featuring nets, fish tanks, underwater grottoes and other watery themes. At lunch, to which I'm enter-tained by the executives of Sonatrach, the Algerian state oil and gas company, French is spoken and there are many courses: salad, hard-boiled eggs with caviar, carrots, lettuce and tomato, grilled swordfish, lamb chops, omelette, lemon tart with cream, fruit and coffee.

'We eat well before Ramadan,' jokes one of my hosts.

The only thing missing is a bottle of Beaujolais, but the ban on alcohol is, I'm assured, a general rule in all drilling areas, anywhere in the world.

The Algerian executives seem comfortably westernised. The head of the base refers to his countrymen as 'Mediterranean people' and dinner-table conversation revolves around such bour-geois topics as children's education, keeping fit, summer holidays and life in Algiers, to which most of them return for three weeks' leave, every four weeks. I ask them the reasons for the high level of security at Hassi-Messaoud, the massive fences, the armed guards, the watchtowers. Do terrorists strike this far south?

A few swift glances are exchanged around the table, a wordless debate as to how much I should be told. Oil workers were killed in 1992 but since then it's been safe. The boss man leans back, dabbing his mouth with a napkin. Apart, that is, from 'Glass Eye'.

Glass Eye? Some nasty infection carried by blowing sand?

No, Glass Eye is a bandit who steals vehicles and reads Islamic tracts to his captives.

Ah, this is beginning to sound familiar. Does he ride around at the head of a fleet of Land Cruisers full of armed men?

General nodding. That's the man.

Also known as Louar, the One-Eyed One?

They seem awfully impressed with my information. I'm awfully impressed by Glass Eye's range. We're 800 miles from the border, where I first heard of him.

To be honest, they're happier talking about hydrocarbons than one-eyed bandits. This doesn't make for jolly banter, but it's interesting to learn that the oil which has paid for Hassi-Messaoud, the Salle Bleue and this six-course dinner is no longer the biggest money-spinner for Algeria. They currently produce less than Britain's North Sea fields. Natural gas reserves, I'm told, put her fourth in the world league after Russia, the USA and Canada.

Our hosts are determined that, before we move on, we should visit the gas production plant, 200 miles northwest. There is a plane that leaves every morning, at half past six.

Irresistible.

Day Seventy-Four

═══════⌒═══════

Hassi-R'mel

One advantage of being up at five is to witness the industrialisation of the Sahara in its most dramatic form. Dozens of flares blaze away in the desert, creating the eerie illusion of a false sunrise. The rigs, hung with arc lights for round the clock production, are dotted about in the sand, buzzing with the might and menace of rockets at their launch pads. This, you feel, is the work of the gods.

Barely visible in the glare from the working lights are the dim, huddled Bedouin encampments outside the security fence, a reminder of what it must have been like here before oil was discovered, when the nomads and their families came to find water at Messaoud's well. The only way they can get close to it now is to take on some menial work inside the base, but they're removed from its green and pleasant avenues at the end of the day.

Hassi-R'Mel is cooler and fresher than Hassi-Messaoud, and its airport cleaner and less frenetic. We're given a VIP welcome, which means tea and biscuits on arrival at the airport and a turnout of executives, including my host for the morning, the impressively titled Head of Quality and Quantity Control. His name is Salah Benyoub, an amiable and unassuming middle-aged man, dressed in striped shirt and wearing a baseball cap over a hairless scalp, which, he readily tells me, is the result of recent chemotherapy. He has worked here for thirty years and speaks good English, which, he says, is the lingua franca of the oil and gas business. It's an international business too. Salah has been to Texas and vacationed in Vegas.

'Did you lose any money?'

'Of course. That's what you're meant to do isn't it?'

Once tea and polite introductions are over, we're driven over to the heart of the operation, the CNDG, the National Centre For Despatching Gas. This proves to be a huge and rambling complex of multicoloured pipes (yellow for natural gas, brown for liquid nitrogen, green for composite), looking more like some computer-generated model than the real thing. Gas from far below the surface comes up in molten form, is treated and eventually chilled to minus 170 degrees, at which temperature it is sent through one of two pipelines, either west to Spain, under the Strait of Gibraltar, or east to Italy, under the Mediterranean. When it reaches the other end of the pipeline it is warmed and expands to 600 times its volume. Every cubic foot that leaves Hassi-R'Mel turns into 600 cubic feet at the receiving terminal.

It's all a bit much for me to take in, but I do like the thought that the yellow paint on the pipe at the back of my cooker matches the yellow paint of the 4-foot thick pipes rearing above my head in the middle of the Algerian desert.

One thing I will remember from this froth of facts and figures is that by 2005, at the cost of $5 billion, there will be another route across the Sahara. It will be laid at a minimum of 6 feet below ground and will connect Europe to the gas fields of northern Nigeria. This will mean a lot more yellow pipes at Hassi-R'Mel and add a new name to the long and not always illustrious list of cross-Saharan trade. Gold, salt, slaves and, now, natural gas.

Day Seventy-Six

═══════ ⌒ ═══════

In Aménas

It's ironic that, given the mighty size of Algeria, the first trace of the oil that transformed the country was found within strolling distance of Libya, near the village of In Aménas. Since then, natural gas has been discovered too, and there are four big fields running along the border, being jointly developed by Sonatrach and BP-Amoco. In Aménas now has an airport, maintenance depots, storage yards and a lot of Brits.

I'm driven out to a drill site at the base of one of the steep, flat-topped, sandstone escarpments south of the town, accompanied by an Algerian from the BP/Sonatrach partnership. His name is Tobba, a geologist by profession, who came out here in 1983. He's a genial man, small and wearing a BP cap.

He's the first Algerian I've met, apart from Said, who's been to England and I ask him for his impressions. He was struck, he said, by the contrast between the beauty of the countryside and the ugliness of public behaviour. He was with his wife and children and found the sight of embracing and kissing in the street very hard to deal with. The same with drinking. He didn't mind bars but was embarrassed by people drunk on streets where he was walking with his children. As Tobba is clearly an educated, decent man, neither severe nor prudish, these criticisms hurt. Arabs generally behave with dignity in public, and in a society which takes no alcohol, there is a marked lack of that unreasoned, aggressive posturing that flares up so easily back home.

The drill site is a square patch of ground, fortified by an 8-foot-high sand wall, known as a berm, and heavy security paraphernalia, including a wall of lights outside, a chicane at the entrance, guard towers and a protection force of gendarmes. I later learn there are fifty of them. This is how important the gas is to Algeria.

A board at the entrance lists the personnel on site, along with their job titles. It reads like a cast list in a theatre programme. There's Tool Pusher, Company Man, Chief Mechanic, Driller,

Assistant Driller, Derrick Man and (very Shakespearian this) Roughnecks and Roustabouts.

We seem to have arrived at a bad time. The site is being dismantled and the 180-foot-high derrick lies on its side awaiting collection. A small group of British workers is supervising an Algerian workforce of loaders and drivers in blue boiler suits and turbans. Willy Wallace, a roly-poly Scot with a Viva Zapata moustache, fingers the stiff creases of a tight and suspiciously pristine outfit.

'They made us wear these. Must have known you were coming.'

Willy's life seesaws between down-to-earth domesticity and the almost recklessly exotic. He's been on rigs in the North Sea, Colombia, the Congo, China and Kazakhstan. Colombia was 'scary'. He was shot at and, as he put it, 'had to hide under the desk a few times'. Kazakhstan was the only place in the last nine years where he didn't need any guards with him. The other half of his life is back home in Scotland, with his wife, a son at Stirling University and a different set of drinking buddies, for whom Coca-Cola is no longer the strongest thing on offer.

He waves vigorously as a 50-tonne truck toils slowly by, the driver waving back from a cab high above our heads.

They've been on this site for sixty-two days. Working round the clock, it took them thirty-two of these days to drill over 8000 feet down into the desert. Gas was found but not at sufficient pressure to make production worthwhile. They're moving on to another site, identified for them by the geologists after a three-day seismic test in which 600 miles of the Sahara was wired up and an artificial earthquake created.

According to Willy, expenditure on the ultimately fruitless work has been augmented by certain below-the-line items.

'We had a visit from Glass Eye. Took 60,000 dollars worth of surveying equipment.'

We drive back into In Aménas. A few huts and palm trees linger on the outskirts, a dusty hint of what the village must have been like before it was engulfed by the oil industry. Now it's dominated by compounds full of storage tanks and drilling equipment, watchtowered and double-fenced. The wind scythes across the desert, tearing at a foliage of plastic bags caught on the razor wire. A filthy sign welcomes us: 'Throw Your Litter Away For A Clean and Beautiful Village.'

Tonight the Brits working here have laid on a party for us. As Mike Batley, our portly, solicitous host, cooks sausages on the patio of a bungalow, we could almost be back in Maidenhead. Except that we are on the equivalent of an industrial estate, with the steel walls of a maintenance shed rearing up behind us.

Mike has worked abroad for much of his life and makes me feel like a novice at this travel thing. He, on the other hand, envies our freedom to move about Algeria. Oil workers are virtual prisoners in their camps, and he bemoans the fact that we have seen more of the country in seven days than he's seen in seven years.

Beers appear from the fridge, and a bottle or two of Algerian wine loosen tongues around the table. Everyone seems to like the desert. Mike notices how it sharpens the senses.

'We're spoilt for smell,' he says. 'Smell a rose in the desert and it's much more acute and intense.'

Sue, a drilling engineer from Aberdeen, finds the desert different, unusual, exotic, whilst John, a geologist from Holmfirth, is passionate about sand dunes. South of the site we visited today there are some of the biggest he's seen. Five hundred feet high.

When the conversation turns to the wider picture, the geopolitics of oil, the subject becomes murkier. Someone makes the point that the USA has vast petrochemical reserves, but it knows that the longer it can keep them in the ground the better, so American foreign policy is led by the need to find cheap energy sources beyond its boundaries.

It all seems academic here, full of sausages and red wine, under a huge sky in the serene silence of the Sahara, but a few thousand miles away, in Afghanistan, another desert is being blasted by B-52s, and no-one knows what fury this might provoke.

Day Seventy-Seven

ON THE LIBYAN BORDER

Roads are rare in the Sahara. They are usually built to exploit resources of some sort, and once they reach those resources they stop.

So it doesn't surprise me that the road to Libya, after winding its way across a grubby oilscape of grit and shale, littered with pipes, empty cable spindles and rusting Portakabins, comes to an abrupt halt at the top of a cliff. The debris also comes to an abrupt halt. Instead, there is a magnificent view of towering, shining dunes, soothed by the wind into graceful, sensuous contours and stretching out to the east as far as the eye can see. This is Libya.

Between the dunes and the edge of the cliff is a flat and sandy valley floor, about a mile wide, and in the middle of this is a single acacia tree. This marks the border.

There is no fence or wall or guard-post or flagpole or barrier to be seen. Just the tree and, beneath it, an indistinct cluster of white dots. I'm told by one of our tireless escorts that the tree is a famous meeting place, where people on both sides of the border, Libyans and Algerians, get together to take tea and exchange news and gossip.

We drive down off the *falaise* and I join a group of them for local dates and strong mint tea. The sun slowly declines, turning the colour of Libya from gold to russet. It is a grand, remote, spectacular spot and for once a border lives up to its romantic expectations.

LIBYA

Day Seventy-Nine

TOBRUK

It's a warm, clammy evening on the north coast of Libya. A coach has disgorged a number of elderly Britons at the door of the blandly modern Al-Masera hotel. Once in their rooms, they will be able to push aside the net curtains and look out over the sea, where a sharp curve of the coastline has created a perfect harbour. It will mean more to them than the average tourist, for sixty years ago they nearly died defending it.

At Tobruk, the Sahara meets the Mediterranean Sea and we are less than 250 miles from the Greek mainland, closer to Europe than at any time since leaving Gibraltar. A hundred and fifty miles the other way, to the south, is the Great Sand Sea, a massive wilderness of parallel sand ridges, hundreds of feet high, rolling across the desert like waves in a hurricane. In the Second World War, the battle for control of Egypt and the Suez Canal was confined to the area between these two seas, a thin strip of land, whose only outlet was the port of Tobruk. The fighting was fierce and Tobruk itself changed hands five times between 1940 and 1942. But for eight crucial months, between April and December 1941, despite being surrounded by the enemy and bombed from the air, Allied troops clung onto Tobruk and kept open a vital supply line. The siege cost many lives, and the men filing into the hotel, some shuffling in on the arms of others, some with sticks and some in wheelchairs, are returning, one last time, to the place where they lost so many friends.

Considering theirs is an eight-day trip and they've already done the battle site of El Alamein earlier today, the veterans are holding up well at the supper that's been laid on for them. It could be something to do with Avril, Lady Randell, a vivacious woman with short-cropped blonde hair and unquenchable enthusiasm, who has organised many of these reunions. It could also be something to do with the fact that being together again reminds them of happy as well as hellish times.

I find myself sitting next to a smart, tweed-jacketed man called Ray Ellis, with thick white hair and a ruddy face. His regiment, the South Nottinghamshire Hussars, were trapped by the Germans in a corner of bleak desert known, ironically, as the Knightsbridge Box. They had already been in the desert for a year, without a day's leave, when, under heavy attack, they were given orders 'to fight until the last drop of ammo'. Ray it was who fired the last shot, before being captured, taken to Tripoli and put aboard a coal-carrying cargo ship bound for Italy. This journey, which he spent crammed together with all the other prisoners in a sealed hold, with one meal a day and the constant fear of being blown up by British air and sea patrols, was, he admits, more terrifying than anything he'd endured at the siege of Tobruk. On arrival, he and his colleagues, filthy and emaciated, were paraded through the streets of a small town near Naples. He was at his lowest ebb, when, out of the jeering crowd, came a young girl, who ran up to him and pressed a peach into his hand. He pauses here, not for breath but to let the emotion register, as if the peach had just that moment been handed to him. He nods gently at the memory, and goes on.

He escaped and was on the run for nine months, hidden by Italian families. He still sees them and has written a book about his experiences, which will soon be published in Italy, though not, it seems, in the UK. Ray has a bit of a double act with another South Notts man, Harry Day. Harry was a medical orderly – 'Never a proper soldier,' Ray chips in – who has given me a booklet issued by the Ministry of Information in 1941 called *Destruction of an Army*. It's full of wonderful sepia photos of the Libyan campaign, as fought by decent chaps who smoked pipes a lot.

Ray nods sagely. 'It's a hundred per cent propaganda from start to finish.'

He's not the only one who's written about his experiences. Frank Harrison, once of the Royal Signals, is a painter and a poet as well as an author. Partly disabled after a recent stroke, he's here with his wife. He talks almost lyrically about the appalling conditions they endured. Any guidebook I've ever read about desert survival emphasises the vital importance of drinking several litres of water a day. Frank and 25,000 others like him were expected to live, work, and, if necessary, fight on one cupful.

'And that was for everything.'

Far from complaining, Frank suggests they developed a sort of evolutionary adaptation to the conditions.

'The surprising thing was, none of us grew beards. I don't know why, but it's true. I don't think I had a day's illness in the nine months I was in Tobruk. We were fit. We were terribly fit.'

They didn't have tents and mostly lived in holes, like shallow graves, that they'd managed to dig out of the compacted mud.

'We loved our holes,' says Frank, eyes wandering briefly into the middle distance. 'That's why we won the name rats. Desert Rats.'

The Desert Rats have more stamina than I. Leaving them burning the midnight oil, I retire to my eccentric room. The bathroom is like a Laurel and Hardy set, with a shower that sends out spray from every point apart from the head and a lavatory flush that requires both hands and one foot against the wall to operate. Over many years of travelling I have acquired the habit, though I often regret it, of checking the state of the bed sheets. I'm pleasantly surprised to find my sheet at the Al-Masera is as clean as a whistle, but as soon as I climb in my foot goes right through it. This is not the time to have a go at hard-working attempts to improve tourist facilities, but there are certain basics, like non-splitting sheets, that someone ought to have noticed. Tourist brochures are another. If you really want to bring in the visitors it is surely not too much to employ a translator who knows their language. The leaflet in my room invites me to visit 'scenes of the Second World Ear', and has a lot of trouble with the word 'snacks'.

'Lunch is mainly takeaway snakes. Dinner is the major meal. It is a full one consisting of different Slacks . . .' It concludes with a wonderfully loopy passage about Libyan beaches that could have been written by the late, great Stanley Unwin: 'You may enjoy the moonlighted nights and sleep smoothly on the sea waves songs in your tent.'

Clutching the two halves of the sheet around me, I at least drift off to sleep with a smile.

Day Eighty

TOBRUK

A busy day ahead for the vets. Already, groups are gathering in the lobby. In one of them is a Maori woman who lost her brother at Tobruk. Twenty Maoris were killed here, she says.

'For what?' She spreads her arms. 'Senseless. We've tried to come to terms with it. We cry, then we laugh.'

Martyn, a New Zealander a little younger than myself, is here to try to find the grave of his uncle, Owen Gatman of the New Zealand Division. He and eleven others were killed when the Panzers overran their position. Their grave has never been found. Martyn has now moved on from searching files and archives to searching the desert with a pick and a sledgehammer. Though he says he found 'a couple of promising mounds', the hard ground has yielded no secrets so far. But he won't give up.

Stephen Dawson of The Royal Horse Artillery, who served throughout the siege, is eighty-nine, tall and thin, with sunken El Greco cheeks. Part of the agreement with the Libyans is that uniforms should not be worn at the reunion, so Stephen is dressed for the day ahead in a bobble hat, a windcheater and trousers a little too short. Slung across his chest is an old bag, webbing blancoed and frayed, which he carried throughout the war.

'I was completely technically incompetent,' he observes cheerfully, 'so I was put on signals.'

The desert held no terrors for him.

'I'm an agoraphiliac. I loved it.'

A bagpiper, kilted and sporranned, walks behind him, causing Libyan heads to turn, and the young bugler, a boy from the Royal Green Jackets and the only one here who's actually still in the army, looks around, pursing his lips nervously. I reckon he's at least sixty-five years younger than the rest of the soldiers.

The Acroma-Knightsbridge Cemetery is a few miles outside Tobruk, in an area of stony ground and occasional fields, in which small birds dart and dive amongst resilient cornstalks.

It is looked after, on behalf of the War Graves Commission, by a Libyan, Mohamed Haneish, and his wife. He's a soft-spoken, courteous man with short-cropped grey hair, who calls the dead his 'boys'. Mohamed has worked here for eighteen years and his father tended the graves for thirty years before that. He complains about the salinity of the water and the difficulty he has making things grow, but you wouldn't know it. The place is immaculate. Enclosed within a well-built sandstone wall, with an arched gate-house entrance, are 3649 graves, every one of identical size, set in neat rows on perfectly tilled ground, interspersed with trees and enough flowers to bring butterflies dancing around the head-stones.

I wander down the lines. On closer examination, these apparently identical stones reveal rich diversity: Jewish stars, New Zealand ferns, inscriptions in Afrikaans and Urdu, French, Yugoslav, Polish and Arabic. Mohamed points out two VCs, one of whom, we learn from his inscription, was a chartered accountant, and only one woman, Janie Beryl Wright of the Nursing Reserve. The dedications range from the affecting 'Good Night Little Brother' to the conscience-tweaking 'Fight to build as we have fought to destroy'. The effect of these ranks of white stones, set in the pale red sand, is terribly moving.

The service of remembrance gets underway as the weather deteriorates. It's cool and feels like rain. The vets process in, led by Douglas Waller, wearing a beret and gripping the Rats of Tobruk standard for all he's worth in the strengthening wind. As the trees swing about above the headstones, which seem to stand out more vividly now the sky has darkened, the words of Laurence Binyon's poem, 'For the Fallen', are quietly but firmly recited by the living on behalf of the dead.

'They shall grow not old as we that are left grow old:
Age shall not weary them, nor the years condemn.
At the going down of the sun and in the morning
We will remember them.'

Then the piper plays, and, after prayers have been read, thanks given and wreaths laid, Paul, the bugler, sounds the Last Post.

There are, I notice, four Libyans buried in the Commonwealth cemetery at Acroma.

On their graves, instead of 'Rest in Peace', is an Arabic inscription. Translated, it reads 'He is forgiven'.

On the way back into Tobruk, we pass the sombre bulk of the German war memorial. It is a replica of a Teutonic castle, on whose dark protective walls the names of the dead are inscribed, unaccompanied by details of rank or regiment. It is simple, powerful and completely different from the cemeteries we saw earlier. The contrast reveals a lot about national character and the myth and legend by which it is expressed. The Allied dead lie in gardens, as if in a state of Eden-like, prelapsarian innocence, as far away as could be imagined from war and suffering. The Germans lie in a different kind of sanctuary. A castle, a bastion, a place where warriors who have fought the good fight sleep with the gods. Both sorts of memorial show, sadly, that our ability to create order and dignity for the dead greatly exceeds our ability to do the same for the living.

The afternoon programme includes a reception at the hotel laid on by the Libyan government. Before the reception there are speeches by a group of distinguished figures. One is introduced as Brigadier Suleiman, 'commander of all the forces in Eastern Libya'.

'Strong Gaddafi man,' Stephen Dawson whispers in my ear.

He is impressive in a suit, with a droopy grey moustache and a confidently authoritative manner, much of which is lost in translation. The interpreter is the complete opposite of the brigadier. He's a sullen civilian in a suit two sizes too big for him. He's also completely useless, and there are long periods of silence between his halting translations. At one stage he turns to the audience and shrugs his shoulders sulkily.

'It's just too many words.'

Finally, the brigadier's patience snaps and he fixes the translator with a terrible eye.

'Do not have breakfast with my language!' he roars, before going on to deliver the rest of his speech in perfectly good English.

This knockabout disguises quite serious material. The gist of the brigadier's message is that Libyans are still being killed and maimed by mines left over from the Second World War and he and his government want maps of the minefields handed over and a big international effort made to clear them.

At the side of the stage are display boards, which are so universally ignored that I feel duty bound to have a look. They don't make comfortable viewing. Alongside photos of mines being laid by Germans and Allies alike are photographs of Libyans mutilated by them sixty years later.

A ceremony was to be held down at the waterfront, at the point where the defenders of Tobruk were finally relieved, but Lady Randell had found that this was now a sewage outlet, so it's relocated to a small patch of open ground with the harbour on one side and a building site on the other. There is something about the banality of the surroundings that makes this last little piece of drama all the more affecting. As the blustery wind flicks at the yellow standard of the Tobruk Desert Rats, a message from the Queen is read out, and a wreath is tossed into the harbour. As it drifts away the eighteen octogenarians are brought to attention and marched off, one last time, in the direction of Tobruk.

'Eyes left!' Heads turn towards the British ambassador, who takes the salute, standing in the grounds of a half-finished house.

Day Eighty-One

TOBRUK TO BENGHAZI

This morning we part company with the Rats of Tobruk. They are going east, to Egypt, and we are turning west, across the northern edge of the Sahara, all the way to Tripoli and the Tunisian frontier, 1200 miles away.

Our coach is big and pink and accommodates not only ourselves but also a half-dozen Libyan escorts, including two government minders and a video cameraman whose job it is to record our every move. The staff from Apollonia Tours are attentive, regularly plying us with refreshments, coffee, tea, water, biscuits and sweeties, when really the only thing we want them to do is to turn off the Richard Clayderman tape.

Once we're past the port of Darnah, the immaculately surfaced, virtually empty road rises and falls and snakes around pretty bays, as we run along the knuckle of land that brings Libya to within 250 miles of mainland Europe. Almost at the apex of this chunky headland are the remains of Apollonia, once the port for the Roman city of Cyrene, high up on the hills behind it. I'm not a great one for archaeological sites – I think I lack the patience required to imagine so much from so little – but Apollonia is enchanting. A strong offshore wind has swept away the murky humidity of Tobruk and turned the Mediterranean a glamorous, white-flecked blue. Beside it, along a mile of coastline, rise a series of graceful ruins. One of them, the Eastern Basilica, is especially elegant. A grove of slender columns made from green and white cipolin marble outlined against an azure sky. Between them are traces of a superb mosaic floor, with images of Africa, wild animals and palm trees. Such treasures would be dazzling enough in a museum, but to find them, intact and largely unspoiled, where they were laid 2000 years ago is almost unbelievable, and has me worrying immediately that they are not sufficiently protected. Not that there are any crowds here. A scattering of Italians, a few Dutch, otherwise we have it to ourselves.

Further on, looking out over the sea, is one of the most perfectly located theatres I have ever seen, and in excellent condition too. Time seems frozen as I climb on the stage, waves thumping against the rocks a hundred yards behind me, the steep stone tiers rising and curving around in front of me. Test the acoustics with a few lines from Julius Caesar, not long dead when this was built, but am booed off by the crew.

As the road winds up the hill behind Apollonia, it passes a complex of ancient tombs and catacombs extending right across the hillside, most of them fallen into a romantic state of disrepair. Those classical carvings, vaults, decorated lintels and bits of sarcophagi that haven't already been looted lie around in staggering profusion, visited mainly by flocks of sheep and herds of goats picking away at the scrubby grass that covers them.

The extent of this burial ground gives some idea of the importance of the city of Cyrene, much of which still stands, built into the folds of the hills. Two mighty propylaea, a colonnade and several headless deities with exquisitely sculpted robes adorn the old Greek

ALGERIA

Top: Back of beyond. The Niger–Algeria border posts.

Centre: On the road to Tamanrasset we pass what's known as the 'Cemetery', a graveyard of hopes that driving across the Sahara was easy.

Below: Whatever happened here? One probably turned without indicating.

Top: Sahara sunset on the way north through Algeria.

Above: With Tom Sheppard, doyen of the desert.

Top: In the heart of the Hoggar Mountains. The peaks are the cores of old volcanoes.

Above: With Brother Edward of Les Petits Frères de Jésus, successor of Charles de Foucauld at the remote refuge at Assakrem, over 9000 feet above the Sahara.

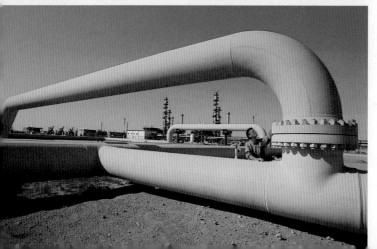

Top left: Algeria's Aladdin's Cave. Oil pipes and flares foul the desert near Hassi-Messaoud but, along with natural gas, the fields provide 90 per cent of the country's foreign earnings.

Centre left: Salah Benyoub at the CNDG at Hassi-R'Mel. Natural gas that will cook lunches from Milan to Mannheim to Madrid is prepared here and despatched along sub-Mediterranean pipelines.

Below left: The scale of Hassi-R'Mel shows the hidden potential of the Sahara. Soon the first ever trans-Saharan pipeline will bring natural gas here from northern Nigeria.

Main picture: The Libyan frontier near In Aménas is marked by a single tree. This spare, un-cluttered, beautiful spot was one of my favourite places in the Sahara.

LIBYA

Top: With Ray Ellis in the cemetery – all ranks and nationalities have exactly the same size gravestones.

Above left: Preparing for the last ceremony of the day: the floating of a wreath on the waters of the harbour that the Rats defended for so long.

Above right: With the Australian memorial rising behind them, Lady Randell comforts relatives of Australian and Maori war dead.

Top: The Rats of Tobruk, sixty years on. 'Lord Haw-Haw' in the Second World War taunted in his propaganda broadcasts: 'Come out of your holes you rats!' And they did. *Left to right*: Francis Cload, Douglas Waller, Leslie Meek, Frank Plant, Peter Vaux, Frank Harrison, Harry Day, James Pearce, Stephen Dawson, Ray Ellis.

Above: At Acroma-Knightsbridge Cemetery, Mohamed Haneish and his wife keep the place immaculate, working wonders with limited resources. Water is scarce and, because they're close to the sea, it's brackish and salty. Mohamed, whose father taught him the job, calls the dead 'my boys'.

Top: Apollonia. Remains of a 2000-year-old mosaic flooring, showing palm trees and wild animals.

Above: Abdul Gerawi, our chief Libyan guide (in the well-cut Western-style clothes worn by most professional Libyans), watches filming in the magical Roman theatre at Apollonia, rediscovered only forty years ago.

Left: Sweeping gaze. Plenty of brushes, but where are all the people?

Centre: Benghazi schoolchildren stop to watch the filming.

Below: Inside the Great Manmade River Project. This is the size of the pipes, of which 1000 miles are already laid, as part of Colonel Gaddafi's ambitious plan to water his country by tapping underground reservoirs deep in the desert.

Top: Camel delivery service stops to offer assistance.

Above: More old ruins at Leptis Magna. Well, I had been filming for three months.

TUNISIA

Right: Like rows of open oyster shells, sunbathers flank the pool of one of the big hotels on the lotus-eating Isle of Djerba. In Tunisia, tourist revenue makes up for the lack of oil earnings with which neighbours Libya and Algeria have been blessed. Or cursed.

Centre: Greek amphorae stacked on the harbourside at Houmt Souk. They're not for sale; they're for catching octopuses.

Below: There Must Be Easier Ways to Make A Living, Number 24: wrestling freshly caught octopus.

Top: Return to the crucifixion scene. Walking round a troglodyte home in El Haddej. Both *Life of Brian* and *Star Wars* were filmed in this unique, moon-like landscape.

Above: Taking tea with Bilgessou and his wife and daughter. Refusing to move from the cave he's lived in all his life, he makes money by providing accommodation for curious travellers.

Right: The Roman amphitheatre at El Jem was the third biggest they ever built; I walk the underground chambers where both the gladiators and the lions were kept before a fight. They still have a deeply unsettling atmosphere.

Centre and below: Nostalgic return to the Ribat at Monastir, a ninth-century Arab fortress, in which the tolerant Tunisians let us film *Life of Brian*, twenty-four years ago. Aficionados will recognise the tower from which Brian leapt only to be rescued by a flying saucer.

ALGERIA

Top: Every home a balcony, decreed Napoleon III. The apartment blocks of Algiers, with louvered shutters and neo-classical details, are a reminder that for more than 100 years, until independence in 1962, Algiers was as much a part of France as the Lyons or Marseilles it resembles.

Above: On the roof of the Villa Suzini. Behind me, sunlight across the city explains why the French called it Alger La Blanche, the White City. In the cellars of this pretty Moorish villa Algerians who resisted French rule were beaten, tortured and often killed during the independence struggle in the 1950s.

Right: On the road to Djerba, Tunisia. *Standing left to right:* Basil Pao, John Paul Davidson, Peter Meakin, Claire Houdret. *Sitting:* Pritchard, Meakin, Mohammed (driver), Man With Grin.

Centre: A wall in Belcourt is covered with football slogans. The English contribution, though misspelt, is not forgotten.

Below: In the casbah, Algiers. This is the oldest part of town and dates from long before the French arrived. It's also the heart of anti-government feeling. The houses are squeezed tight along narrow alleyways, making it easy to defend and very difficult to attack.

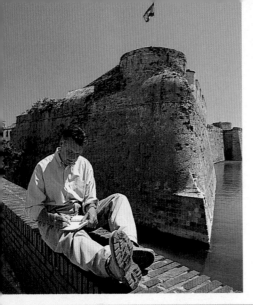

The Portuguese-built bastions of what is now a piece of Spanish territory in Africa, the city of Ceuta.

settlement, erected in the seventh century BC. A cluster of elegant baths and fountains show the preoccupations of the Romans, who grafted their own architecture onto the Greek original. I'm poking around them when I find a goat in the hypocaust. Quite a shock, but a good name for a volume of archaeological memoirs. A Goat in the Hypocaust.

Following the railway tracks laid by the Italians in the 1920s to help them excavate and restore the site I come across the eye-catching Fountain of The Nymph Cyrene. With its carved statue of a young girl gracefully ripping open a lion's mouth, it's an ingenious way of telling a story and creating a water outlet at the same time. In Greek mythology, Cyrene so attracted Apollo with her animal wrestling skills that he sent a chariot to pick her up and take her across the water to the fertile highlands of northern Libya, in which green and pleasant land they consummated their relationship and she bore him a son.

The land that Apollo chose for his tryst with Cyrene is known nowadays as Jebel Akhdar, the Green Mountain, and it is quite an extensive upland area, its scenery not a lot different from Provence or even at times, where the roads narrow and the limestone walls crowd in, from Dorset. Annual rainfall up here is about the same as London's and wide and fertile cornfields stretch away on either side of the road. It was grain that brought the Romans to Africa, and vast quantities were shipped across the Mediterranean, earning Libya the title of 'the breadbasket of Rome'.

Cyrene was continuously occupied for over 1200 years, until the Arab invaders of the seventh century, not much interested in classical cities, let it fall back gradually into oblivion.

The Italians returned to the province of Cyrenaica in the 1920s but met spirited resistance to their colonising from a local leader called Umar al-Mukhtar. In 1930 General Graziani was sent out from Rome to deal with the opposition. Al-Mukhtar was captured and hanged, and those who resisted Graziani's policies were rounded up into concentration camps.

So hated did the Italians make themselves in this short period that there is now almost no indication they were ever here on the Green Mountain. Al-Mukhtar, on the other hand, is still remembered as a hero and received the ultimate accolade of being portrayed on screen by Anthony Quinn.

As we descend from the plateau towards Benghazi, the olive groves, junipers and stands of cypress and Aleppo pine grow fewer and the number of roadblocks increases.

Like Tobruk, Benghazi is a city of infrastructure, girdled by a network of underpasses, ring roads and flyovers, all largely free of traffic, and as the road signs are only in Arabic it's impossible to tell where they're going. The woods and fields of Jebel Akhdar seem like a dream as we cruise slowly through a bare and featureless cityscape, coming eventually to rest before the concrete and glass terraces of the Hotel Tibesti. I would have said at the doors of the Hotel Tibesti, or even at the portals of the Hotel Tibesti, but the architects of this magnificent late 1970s pile miscalculated the height of the concrete roof above the entrance and all tourist buses have to park and unload in a nearby road, making it a good walk to the hotel lobby through a taxi rank, a small garden, past ornamental fountains and up a substantial flight of steps.

Day Eighty-Two

BENGHAZI

In the lobby of the Hotel Tibesti hang neat placards with quotes from Colonel Gaddafi's *Green Book*. To us sophisticated Westerners, for whom talking about political theory is about as uncomfortable as talking about piles, it seems pretty odd to have 'Committees Everywhere' hanging up in a place of hospitality and entertainment, not to mention the even less catchy 'The Social i.e. National Factor is the Driving Force Of Human History'. But that's how it is here in the Jamahiriya, the 'state of the masses', where Muammar Gaddafi has run the show for the last thirty-one years. After he and fellow army officers got rid of a monarchy backed by America and Britain, Gaddafi made sweeping changes. Private enterprise was banned, foreign influence discouraged and the country reorganised around people's committees and congresses. Alcohol was banned.

Bankrolling the revolution was not a problem, Libya being in the enviable position of having the world's third largest oil earnings and a population less than that of Greater London.

Gaddafi's survival owes much to his ability to reinvent himself. He's been at various times scourge of the West and leader of the Arab world; currently he is the great Pan-African. The change can be charted on the billboards.

It's not quite the old communist-style cult of personality, but there is a lot of him about. The standard image is full face, aviator shades, pillbox-style *chechia* perched on thick black curly hair, skin creased by deep, but reassuring, Jagger-style grooves. None of the Soviet-style hard man here. He looks every inch the entertainer (and is almost the same age as Mick). On one rapidly fading bill-board I saw, above the words 'American aggression', Gaddafi, fist raised, defying the bolts and arrows of missile attack (fifteen years ago his adopted daughter was killed in the American air attacks on Benghazi and Tripoli). Around this centrepiece were depictions of the caring Colonel, visiting children in schools and hospitals. On more recent posters he's likely to be seen emerging from a map of Africa, shedding a halo of golden rays across the continent. The parallel that comes irresistibly to mind is with Cecil Rhodes and his dream of spreading the red of the British Empire from Cape to Cairo.

The redirection of Gaddafi's foreign policy towards Saharan Africa should not perhaps be a surprise. He has always identified with the nomads and still prefers to live in a tent rather than a palace. There are few leaders these days who care much about the Sahara and I would very much have liked to have met and talked to him about his policy.

So far our advances have met with no success. The Libyan authorities remain deeply mistrustful of Western media and today we have to content ourselves with another closely guided tour.

Abdul and Mohammed collect me in their car. Abdul is our chief minder from the Government Media Department, while Mohammed, slimmer, younger and already a father of five, is an air-traffic controller in Benghazi. This, apparently, is not a full-time job; he's also a plumber and a painter.

'One thousand, nine hundred kilometre beach begin here,'

announces Abdul, waving his arm at a flat milky-green wasteland studded with cones of freshly tipped rubbish. I'm taken to meet a friend of theirs who runs a tourist village. Photographs are taken. Along another meaningless swirl of motorway into the centre of the city. A number of Italian colonial buildings remain, including a Venetian-style governor's residence, now the headquarters of the local committee. It's a Friday and there aren't many people in the streets. Those that are about seem to favour Western dress. There are more sharp, Italian-style suits than there are *tarbooshes* and *djellabas.*

Lunch is long and formal. The tables are big enough for a peace conference, and conversation is in the polite international style, with bursts of animated misunderstanding punctuated by longer periods of silence. Afterwards we prowl around two good-looking mosques, and a small square dominated by a classical copper-domed cathedral, now also a mosque. I climb the wide stone steps that lead to the portico, only to find the massive west door bricked up. Perhaps anxious to correct any bad impression we might have got from the boarded-up cathedral, Abdul takes us to a Catholic church and mission run by Franciscans, closed in the early years of the revolution and reopened in 1976 after a Catholic–Islamic pact was signed in Tripoli. Seven priests and thirty-five nuns keep it open all week, and offer mass in five languages: Arabic, English, Italian, Polish and Korean.

The bishop of Cyrenaica, a short, genial Maltese, explained this eclectic mix. Poles work on a lot of the urban construction projects and the Koreans on the Great Manmade River Project, Gaddafi's epic scheme to bring fresh water from underground aquifers thousands of feet below the desert to irrigate the coast. At one time the project used Filipinos, very good Catholics.

'There were thousands of them,' sighed the bishop, wistfully.

Our day in Benghazi may have lacked sparkle, but the night is memorable for one of the most dangerous journeys I've ever undertaken. Our hosts had organised a trip to a local restaurant, not by car or pink coach, but in horse-drawn buggies. Though a battle-hardened film crew are perhaps not the best people to take advantage of such romantic transport, it all started well enough, until we turned off the quiet street, up a slip road and onto an eight-lane motorway. At one point it seemed as if our driver, who obviously thought his place was in heaven, had panicked. The horse certainly had. He swung his head from side to side, eyeballs staring manically skywards, nostrils pumping away like pistons as the traffic roared by.

Eventually, we found sanctuary in the crawler lane, and remained there for what seemed like hours, before we found our exit. The food was as good as anything we've had in Libya, but I did miss the alcohol that had been my only hope of surviving the journey home.

Day Eighty-Three

BENGHAZI TO SIRTE

No sign of the horses this morning, which is a relief, as we have the best part of 400 miles to cover. The pink coach is once more at our disposal and Farsi, the video cameraman, is back in action, recording our walk from the lobby to the door and the door to the coach, whilst Abdul photographs him photographing us.

In the middle of a roundabout on the outskirts of Benghazi is a huge installation commemorating the Great Manmade River Project. Its centrepiece is a circular stack of pipes embedded in concrete looking like a giant metal cake. Around it, the cardinal points of the compass are marked by 30-foot-long pipe sections. I climb inside one of them.

About 13 feet in diameter, it feels more like a small Underground station than a water pipe. A quarter of a million of these sections were used in the first phase of the project alone, and apparently the number laid now would stretch from the southern tip of Italy to the Orkney Islands. There have been unforeseen problems, however, one of which is the high saline content of the underground water, which is causing corrosion and leakage that is either very serious or little more than expected, according to who you talk to. Abdul, not surprisingly, is of the latter opinion. A group of passing schoolboys sees us filming and pandemonium and excitement break out. They point, shout, laugh, until their enthusiasm is cut short by our driver, Faraj, who climbs down and gives them a terrific scolding. Their faces fall and I can see momentary fear in their eyes. It's a pity, as this is the first time we've seen any reaction from Libyans on the street and I was rather enjoying it. We're herded back onto the pink coach, sedated with Richard Clayderman and driven south, into increasingly dry, hot, stony desert.

Instead of trees, there are electricity pylons and instead of wheat fields, there is scrub grass interspersed with pipeline, the occasional flaming head of an oil well, trailing a dirty black slick along the horizon. Near Brayqah, concrete holding-tanks, into which the Manmade River disgorges, nestle in the gritty sand, each one as big as two football pitches. A little further on, a metal arch with Gaddafi's likeness painted on it marks the entrance to a massive dusty white complex, where the giant pipes are made. By now the Clayderman tape has reached 'Tulips From Amsterdam' for the fifth time, and cries for a lunch stop, or even an engine failure, are increasing. Thirty miles later, Abdul and Faraj spot three trees, close enough together to qualify as a picnic spot.

The picnic lunch is a big disappointment. And I mean big. Jumbo-sized white boxes reveal salad, chicken and cold chips. And it looks as if we might be here for some time. Whilst attempting a tricky and not strictly necessary three-point turn, Faraj has run the back wheels into soft sand and the coach is spread across half the carriageway like a beached whale. Various passing vehicles are flagged down to help, including a lorry with twenty kneeling camels in the back, all nodding away gently like toys on the back shelf of a car, but none has any towing equipment. The police arrive with a chain. It snaps. By now we have an expectant audience of fourteen people, twenty camels and a small car park of vehicles. Faraj looks as whipped and chastened as the little boys he screamed at this morning.

Eventually, a low-loader with a bulldozer on board, heaves us out and we carry on our way.

Mile after mile of salt scrub numbs the senses, but Mohammed has a treat in store for us. An in-coach movie. It turns out to be *Lion Of The Desert*, a Hollywood biopic of the great national hero, Umar al-Mukhtar. The irony of the Libyan national hero being celebrated by the Great Satan doesn't seem to worry them, and we settle back to a truly blood-drenched couple of hours. If the Libyans are happy to have Anthony Quinn portray their hero, then presumably the Italians would have been relieved that the villain of the piece, Colonel Graziani, is played by Oliver Reed, and Mussolini by a stratospherically over-the-top Rod Steiger.

By these standards, the casting of Sir John Gielgud as a Bedouin was pretty obvious. *The Lion Of The Desert* brings us safely to the birthplace of The Guide Of The Revolution. Besides being Gaddafi's birthplace, Sirte is a potential new capital of the Great Socialist People's Libyan Arab Republic. Modest outskirts of low mud and brick houses give way to a complex of hotels and government offices. Landscaped towers of white stone and black glass could be a corporate HQ in California, until you get inside and find the decorative style is pure Arabian Nights, festooned with spangly curtains, brass lamps and throne-size chairs which take three people to move. A Pan-African conference is to be held here soon, but at the moment, as with so much of 'official' Libya, this grand and expensive campus is deserted. Abdul finds us some food, though once more it's Western rather than local, but at least there is a bowl of *harissa*, the hot pepper paste, to breathe life into our hamburger and chips.

Day Eighty-Four

SIRTE TO TRIPOLI

As we set off for another long day's drive up the coast I ask Abdul if there's any serious alternative to driving or taking a camel. Wouldn't a railway help? Indeed, he says, and Colonel Gaddafi is very keen on railways, but there aren't any in Libya. The national airline has been badly hit by the continuing American embargo on aircraft spares. Motor car spares are equally hard to find, causing many unnecessary road deaths. The Colonel has tried to deal with this by 'inspiring' a new design of five-seater vehicle. With glare-free headlights, non-exploding tyres, high-impact bumpers and all round air-bag protection, it would be the world's safest car. It's to be called The Rocket of the Libyan Jamahiriya. Now that's a proper name for a car. Well, better than Cherry anyway.

Nigel is losing his patience with the camera. Not his, but the Libyan government's. I actually heard him this morning going on about how he hates being followed by a camera. Well now he knows what it's like. I ask Farsi, the cameraman, what they are going to do with all this footage of us entering and leaving hotels. He seems quite aggrieved by my question.

'There's only six hours.'

A few miles short of Tripoli is Leptis Magna, the richest and most magnificent of all the Roman cities in Africa. We pile out and take the tour. It is indeed wonderful, much more grand than Cyrene and much bigger too. A paved street, the Via Colonnata, runs for almost half a mile, and to walk its well-worn slabs is to feel yourself in the heart of a great city. The smaller details stick in my mind, like the beautifully carved dolphins standing on their heads in the market, probably the sign of a Roman fishmongers' stall, but the massive interior of the new Basilica at Leptis is hugely impressive.

It was used as a law court and to stand in it, dwarfed by the mighty Aswan granite columns, is to experience an almost palpable sense of the brute force of Rome.

Next to it, the 300-foot-long, 200-foot-wide Imperial Forum is like a vast mad monumental mason's yard. Columns, capitals, decorated friezes, plinths, pendentives, bas-reliefs and massive heads with curls like eighteenth-century wigs lie around as if an earthquake had just struck.

The sumptuousness of Leptis Magna may look very European, but it would not have been built without Saharan money. The bread which Libya so copiously supplied to Rome could not in itself have provided sufficient revenue for excess of this scale. The difference was made up of the wealth of gold, ivory and slaves, brought here on caravans from across the Sahara Desert.

There is a parallel here with the wealth of present-day Libya, which also comes from the desert. Gaddafi's oil, which is not only copious but also of very good quality, keeps the West going, the same way Libyan grain kept Rome going. Who needs who most?

TRIPOLI

Our last day in Libya. From the balcony of a monstrous hotel I look out over the harbour. A ferry is loading, one of six or seven ships in port. It's a hazy, warm day, and the wind that sends the green flags fluttering carries a faint tang of sulphur from the chain of chemical works and refineries that dot the coast. Below me is a green and white-domed mosque, squeezed in by the side of the surging highway that leads towards the skyscrapers of the city. The centre of Tripoli, a wide, open meeting place called Green Square, lies beside the castle, at the place where the old medina and the newer, largely Italian streets meet. The green louvered shutters of the houses remind me of Gibraltar. I still feel frustrated. Abdul, Mohammed and the others have treated us well, but I feel we've also been strong-boxed. It's been hard to meet people beyond the pink coach.

So I'm surprised when a youngish Libyan man approaches me in Green Square. He extends a hand and asks, in good English, what I think of the country. I murmur the usual praise and we shake.

'I won't tell you what I think,' he says bitterly, and is gone.

TUNISIA

DJERBA

Seventy-five miles across the Tunisian border is the island of Djerba. It claims to be the Land of the Lotus-Eaters, celebrated in Homer's *Odyssey*. In one of history's most famous examples of R and R, Odysseus and his crew put in here for a while and surrendered themselves to the soothingly narcotic fruits of the lotus.

These days it's hard to find the lotus or its fruit, but there is a heady local preparation called *boukha,* made from fermented dates or figs, which seems to have pretty much the same effect. After Libya, where fermented anything was forbidden, the sudden proliferation of hotels offering every sort of inebriant from Baileys to Bloody Marys is a profound shock to us all and a lot of surrendering goes on.

Nor is this the only shock. The sheer numbers of lotus-seekers thronging the north coast of Djerba is in bewildering contrast to where we've just been, and indeed with almost anywhere else on this journey. German, Dutch and Swedish seem to be the native languages here.

This sudden return to a world of wine lists and multi-channel television produces an odd sinking feeling and an unexpected upsurge of nostalgia for those trips into the desert in the wee small hours, armed only with trowel and toilet roll.

DJERBA

The design of our hotel, a huge U-shaped wall facing out to sea, tries hard to create a feeling of all-embracing exclusiveness, an ample concrete bosom of pleasure, where all your needs will be attended to, where food, drink, recorded music and thalasso-therapy are always at hand.

Try and get away from this fortress of fun and you will find twenty or thirty others, right next door, all offering similar versions of what you've got, and before long you realise that wherever you are is just like where you've come from.

Somewhere outside the fortress walls is Djerba itself, an offshore island, 18 by 16 miles, flat, dry and agricultural. Compared with the desert we've come through, it looks almost lush, but the reality is that rainfall is low, only 8 inches a year, and the water saline. The dates from Djerba's palm trees are only suitable for animal feed and the olive groves yield low returns. The island's most productive pastures are the shallow waters that surround it. Fishing here is a traditional industry, carried on by traditional methods.

On the dockside at Houmt Souk are stacked rows of turnip-shaped, terracotta pots. These elegant little amphorae, about 18 inches high, are not for tourists to take home; they're for catching octopus. Each one has a rim at the top, around which a string is tied, attaching it to a long line of pots which are then dropped into the sea a few miles offshore. For some reason, octopuses are irre-sistibly drawn to the pots, curling up inside them and presenting a perfect gift for fishermen. It's a technique that's been used since the Phoenicians came this way 3000 years ago, and the octopuses still haven't caught on.

We've wangled ourselves aboard one of the brightly painted, low-tech fishing boats, which is setting out to check its lines.

Once out of the harbour, we run into a lively sea, licked up by a freshening wind. The stubby, wooden-hulled boat bounces all over the place as we search for the line they put down a couple of days ago. So competitive is the fishing out here that they mark the line as discreetly as possible, and it's only after a half-hour search that they detect the green plastic bottle to which the line is attached. By now the boats are bucking all over the place as the pots are hauled up from the sea bed no more than 12 feet below us. I'm hanging on for dear life as we hurtle up and plunge down the waves, but the fisher-men are balanced only by knees against the rail as they inspect the pots. There are fifty on this line. One after another contains only sand and seaweed and is tossed back into the water. Not an octopus to be seen. It's early in the season, they say.

We head for another line. The wind is strengthening and the boat tossing ever more violently, but the third pot they pull out produces a great cry and the pink rubbery mass inside is tipped out unceremoniously onto the deck.

Then another and another. All hands are at the pots and I'm given the job of keeping the catch in a large blue plastic tray. This isn't easy. The octopuses are not at all keen to stay on the tray and once they get a leg outside it their suckers clamp onto the wooden deck. By the time I've loosened one leg, the other seven are stuck fast. Clinging to the octopuses with one hand and a piece of superstructure with the other, I succeed in wrenching them off, only to be flung across the boat, octopus in hand and fast latching onto my arm.

Keeping the octopuses in the tray becomes like a routine invented for a Japanese game show, but it seems to cheer the fishermen up no end. Meanwhile, I've become quite an admirer of these tenacious creatures and am thinking of starting an Octopus Protection League.

Knowing the British, there probably already is one.

In the late afternoon, as the shops are opening, I walk through the souk, which seems well stocked with goods, mostly aimed at the tourist market. Rugs, tiles, lamps, hands of Fatima, pieces of Rose du Sable (natural sculptures of crystallised gypsum found in the desert), hubble-bubble pipes and the like. There are some superior items in a shop owned by a man known as 'El Haj', including a Turkish carpet woven with a million knots per square metre. El Haj (an abbreviation earned by anyone who has been on the haj, the pilgrimage to Mecca) is a short, scholarly man with a neat moustache and thick glasses, wearing a cream *gandoura* over a tartan shirt. He speaks English well, and five other languages too, but almost apologetically, looking down as he does so.

Though tourism supplies 70 or 80 per cent of his trade, he is not entirely happy with its impact on the island. Local families won't walk on the beach any more because of the number of naked and semi-naked tourists, a phenomenon which he thinks is encouraging some Muslim youths to drink alcohol and sell themselves for casual sexual encounters.

Sex tourism, in Djerba?

He nods. 'When he sees a nude lady on the beach, he thinks it means she is looking for adventure. They should respect our culture, our religion. They can come for the sun but they don't have to take all their clothes off and walk.'

When he was a boy, the north coast was wild and deserted. Now there are a hundred hotels there. They attract a large workforce from outside the island, which has to be absorbed. Thankfully, he says, Djerbans are traditionally tolerant.

'I think this is the only place where you find Jewish and Muslims living together.'

Peacefully, he must mean.

'We have the oldest synagogue in North Africa. I think 586 before Christ it was built.'

Many of the Djerban Jews have gone to France, often running corner shops known simply as '*le djerbain*', but many come back to marry. There are 2000 of them in Houmt Souk.

'I take my car to a Jewish man, I buy my jewellery from a Jew, a number of my neighbours are Jewish and I'm a Hajan practising Islam, and there's no problem with it.'

On our way back, between the outskirts of Houmt Souk and the first hotel, there is a surprisingly tranquil stretch of national park. The air is now so still that sky and sea merge seamlessly, one reflecting the other like a continuous sheet of glass. In front of which, as if in a mirage, oystercatchers, herons and flocks of flamingos are feeding. But the hotels are getting awfully close.

Day Eighty-Nine

DJERBA TO EL HADDEJ

Before I set out on this Saharan journey southern Tunisia was the closest I'd ever been to the desert. That was in 1978 and I came here to be crucified. Security problems in Israel and an appetite for biblical epics had created a lucrative role for Tunisia as a stand-in for the Holy Land. Not only did Tunisia look right, it was also both friendly and stable, and when the producers of Monty Python's *Life of Brian* approached the local authorities they agreed to let us use locations in Monastir and Sousse for urban Jerusalem, whilst the scenes set outside the city were to be shot in the bleaker, more desolate south, around Matmata on the edge of the Jebel Dahar mountains.

A wide bend in the road and a hill with a long flat-topped ridge spreading out below it has a curiously familiar feel, and as the bus climbs I remember, with a shock of recognition, that this is where we filmed the Sermon on the Mount. That day in November 1978, very similar buses, in which several hundred of our extras had been brought up earlier, appeared on this road halfway through the afternoon's filming. The extras, who had been forced to stand around watching Englishmen do silly things all day, saw this as a sign that it was all over and began to stampede off the Mount and down to their buses. Terry Jones, our director, raced after them, urging them to come back. Unfortunately, he was dressed as the virgin Mandy at the time, and the memory of this black-clad old crone screaming at 500 joyful Arabs is an image of the Matmata hills which will give me pleasure on many a cold day.

So it is that, soon after lunch, in a flat hazy light, I find myself standing above the village of El Haddej, almost twenty-three years, to the day, since I hung on one of two dozen crosses, tapping my feet and singing 'Always Look on the Bright Side of Life'.

El Haddej looks much as I remember it. It's set in a landscape of low, yellowing hills scored by deep gullies, as if it had just dried out after a mighty flood. In fact, it has not rained here for three years, and the land is bone dry. There are the usual hardy bushes, a few palms, their lower fronds discoloured by drought, and on the side of a hill an old man is watering a single young olive tree, which won't give fruit in his lifetime.

These hills were settled by Berbers over 2000 years ago. Finding little cover above ground, they took to the caves below, and to this day their descendants still live as troglodytes.

From up here their homes look like a series of lunar craters, some with cars or pick-ups parked on the rim, others barely visible in the folds of soft, friable rock around them.

The troglodytes of the Matmata hills are experiencing rapid

change. The combination of a well-organised tourist industry and the choice of one of the caves as Luke Skywalker's birthplace has, as in Djerba, brought lucrative tourist business to a poor area. Some caves have been turned into hotels, but when these proved too small to accommodate tour groups, hotels were built to look like caves.

I start to walk down the hill, passing a small dog, which barks ferociously at a line of sheep but rushes away in terror at the approach of a black plastic bag slowly twisting in the wind. I look down into two or three dwellings which appear to have been abandoned. Holes some 60 feet across and 30 feet deep have collapsed in on themselves. To add a final indignity, rubbish has been dumped inside them.

There is one cave which is still occupied and rents out rooms, or cavities, perhaps.

The only entrance is through a dimly lit tunnel. It's some 30 yards long, and smells of fur and dung. At its darkest point I run slap into a donkey, which is quietly munching away at some straw. Emerging into the soft grey light of a courtyard, I see an elderly man and two women waiting to welcome me. The man's name is Bilgessou. He stands straight-backed, wearing a fine red skullcap and a knee-length brown overcoat, his bearing matching a military-style silver moustache. Next to him, in brightly coloured Berber stripes, are his wife Manoubia and their daughter Jemila. They stand almost motionless, like a tableau waiting to be photographed.

After we have introduced ourselves, they pull aside a palm wood door and usher me into a side room off the courtyard. The roof is a low, smoke-stained vault, lit by a single bulb (there is electricity here, but water has to be fetched from the well). Bilgessou sets to work making tea on a calor gas stove, Jemila sits down, revealing a bright and well-holed pair of yellow stockings, and she and her mother set to work rubbing the skins off peanuts and dropping them into a bowl. A rangy black and white cat appears from the depths of the cave, is shooed away but holds its ground, eyeing the preparations.

Once the tea has been made and poured, as it is throughout the Sahara, with a flourish from as far above the glass as possible,

Bilgessou takes the bowl of nuts and scatters them onto a roasting tray, which he lays on the fire. Most of this is done in silence, as none of them speak French and I don't speak Arabic, but Jemila has a sweet understanding smile and somehow it doesn't feel wrong to be silent.

However, once the first glass of tea has been taken, Bilgessou begins to talk, in a powerful voice, with a lot of barking, back-of-the-throat sounds.

The young don't want to live in the caves any more, he says. They're moving above ground, tempted away by ready-made houses in New Matmata. The authorities don't understand. They've shown little interest in preserving the troglodyte way of life, except for the tourists. He extends an arm towards his wife. She has never left El Haddej in her life. She can't be expected to change just like that.

I'm handed a biscuit and a cotton cloth to put on my knee to catch the crumbs.

Anyway, he goes on, these troglodyte houses make sense. They're safe and secure, warm in winter and cool in summer. The soft rock is easy to excavate, and, unlike the timber round here, there's plenty of it.

When he stops, the silence returns, thick and heavy, deadened by the weight of the earth around us.

They show me my room. It's across the courtyard and up a flight of irregular stone steps, cut from the clay. The coffin-shaped entrance has decorated stone dressings and inside is a vaulted space, some 20 feet deep, with just enough room to stand straight at its centre. The walls have been plastered and painted white at some time, but that's faded now. A mattress is laid along one side where the wall slopes down quite sharply. Dangerous if you wake suddenly in the night.

Not far from here is a tantalising example of the old way of life that Bilgessou fears is disappearing for ever – an underground olive oil press, set into the side of a hill. Inside the cave is a circular chamber, consisting of a platform, around which is just enough room for a donkey to walk. The oil-maker tips a basket of olives – stalks, leaves and all – onto the platform. Then the donkey, harnessed to a pole, and wearing a pair of pointed woven blinkers that look like a large wicker brassiere, starts to plod round. The pole turns a spindle, which rolls a cylindrical stone block over the olives, reducing them to an inky mulch.

The mulch is then stuffed inside pancake-sized rattan discs, which are stacked one on top of the other, fourteen at a time, and squeezed in a wooden press. Every 100 kilograms of olives produces 35 litres of oil.

The reek of olives is quite heady and every inch of this dark, cramped, glistening chamber is thick and sticky with accretions, like the inside of an immensely ancient cooking pot.

Walk back to Bilgessou's cave. What's the address I wonder? What would I ask for if I were lost? Number 43, The Mountain? The family are in the courtyard, in exactly the same positions, Bilgessou standing like an old soldier, Jemila and Manoubia sitting on stones. Their life encompassed by this pit of crumbling red rock.

And later, as darkness falls, I find myself doing exactly the same thing, just sitting there, on the steps outside my room, looking up at the stars. It's not that there's nowhere to go, or anyone's stopping me taking a walk out of the tunnel to see some other folks on the hill, it's just that once you're in here the outside world ceases to mean very much. There is no view but upwards.

Before I go to sleep I get out my portable DVD player, watch myself being crucified and feel better.

Day Ninety

El Haddej to Sousse

As we pick our way through the spare and stony cover of the Matmata hills I realise that this is the last I shall see of the desert for a while. The final leg of my journey will take me north and west to see the other side of the great desert countries like Tunisia and Algeria. The side where people live, where capital cities lie, where the great trans-Saharan trade routes began and ended, where the Sahara was talked about, its wealth evaluated, its various conquests planned.

It's no coincidence that Libya, Tunisia and Algeria, the three richest countries of the Sahara, share a Mediterranean coastline. Their capitals are all much closer to the markets of Europe than those of Africa. The remains of so many Greek and Roman cities show how close the historical links have been. Yet all three are firmly Arab and Muslim countries. Together with Morocco and Mauritania they're collectively known by the Arabic word Maghreb, the land of the West, and their political alliances are currently with each other, through the Maghreb Union Treaty of 1989, rather than with Europe. Libya, it seems, doesn't mind this too much. It's looking back into the desert. The conferences that were being prepared in Sirte and Tripoli are, some consider, the first step to Colonel Gaddafi's goal of a United States of the Sahara. Will Tunisia and Algeria go along with this or might they be ready to look north again?

The last sand seas may be behind me, but the intellectual, cultural and political heart of some powerful Saharan countries lies ahead.

From Gabès the main road north follows the coastline, running between the sea and the railway, along avenues of eucalyptus with enormous olive plantations stretching away in long straight lines on either side of the road.

The industrial port of Sfax is signalled by a plume of black smoke trailing out across the Mediterranean, and for several miles we pass through a wasteland of spoil heaps and phosphate factories. I couldn't help noticing the name of the road: Boulevard de l'Environment.

By lunchtime we have reached El Jem and are able to eat beside one of the finest sights in Tunisia, the honey-coloured walls of the third biggest amphitheatre the Romans ever built.

It's a powerful presence. Fourteen hundred feet in circumference, it could accommodate over 30,000 spectators.

Gazing unhurriedly at it over a lamb kebab, I'm struck by the boldness of the design. The massive blocks of stone not only had to be hauled in from quarries 20 miles away, they also had to be stacked in an elliptical wall 100 feet high, supported entirely by its arches. No buttressing, no concrete, just a precisely calculated balancing act.

El Jem itself is a modest market town, whose entire population could fit in one end of the colosseum, and, like flies round an elephant, the locals get on with life apparently oblivious to the monster in their midst.

Unless, of course, they're in the tourist business, which is not looking too bright at the moment. The shadow of September 11th means horses and carts go by unoccupied and there are plenty of spare tables to be had. Guides saunter about, but no-one looks desperate, or in any way resentful of our being here. One man in a striped robe, skullcap and dark glasses spies us and breaks into a broad grin.

'Allô, allô, my friend, 'ow are you? We are the Taliban. Only joking.'

Tunisia is the smallest and most compact of all the Saharan countries, and as we've been used to driving two or three hours between trees, let alone towns, our surroundings seem to be changing with indecent haste. Within half a day we've been from troglodytes to amphitheatres, and an hour later we're at the gates of one of the largest and best-preserved Arab fortresses in North Africa, the Ribat of Harthouma in Monastir. Its towers, turrets and battlements stand proudly beside the sea, rich cream against azure blue. It may lack the majesty of El Jem, but it has a more subtle appeal, the quiet dignity of a fortress that has survived 1200 years of conflict. How, then, were we ever allowed to shoot *Life Of Brian* here? A party of schoolchildren is listening dutifully to an account of the history of this venerable building. I find myself longing to take them on an alternative history tour, to show them where John Cleese had a boulder dropped on top of him, where Brian leapt from a tower only to be rescued by a flying saucer, and where 500 Tunisian extras laughed at Biggus Dickus.

The truth is that the Ribat is now so squeaky clean that it's lost a bit of character. Lew Grade's Jesus of Nazareth set, which once loomed up beside it, has long gone, replaced by ornamental gardens, and where we lounged around between takes, being rude about each other's beards, is now paved and swept clean as a whistle.

Our art department and the current restorers were both in the same game, trying to bring an ancient, partly ruined fortress to life, and to be honest I think we did a better job. The Ribat is still a good place to visit, with high walls and battlements completely, indeed recklessly accessible, but I preferred it with the market stalls, ex-lepers and writing on the wall.

We spend the night in nearby Sousse at another big, comfortable holiday factory by the sea. Though business is down by 50 per cent since September 11th, it's still as busy as a railway station, and what it must be like at full capacity is terrible to contemplate.

I meet up in a local café with a group of Tunisians all involved in the tourist industry. Around us are tables full of men playing cards. Some football game flickers away, largely ignored, on a wall-mounted television. El Mejid, a pale-skinned, squarely built Tunisian, who looks more Irish than Arab, runs Berber evenings six days a week out at an old olive oil factory. Belly-dancing, bareback riders, waiters with bottles on their heads, a meal and all the wine you can drink for 13 dinars a head, roughly £6.75. One of his friends puffs on a *chicha*, a hubble-bubble pipe; another, wearing a tracksuit, arrives late after a work-out. He looks tired and his back is giving him trouble. He's the only one who breaks ranks and expresses any doubts about the benefits of tourism. He worries about the growth of the cities, with a corresponding break-up of family life and threat to traditions.

'The wedding,' he says, 'the traditional wedding used to be about one week. Now it's only one day or two days.'

His colleagues shake their heads. They seem willing to pay almost any price to bring in the visitors. I ask if they see any point in limiting the new developments.

'No limit, I think. We used to receive three millions and now about five millions. Maybe in ten years ten millions.'

Ten millions. On current figures that's more than the entire population.

Day Ninety-One

SIDI BOU SAID

Sidi Bou Said is next door to Carthage and both are salubrious suburbs of the capital, Tunis. The town is up on a hill, and our hotel looks out over the green and swaying trees of the coastal plain, towards the Gulf of Tunis and the 2000-foot mountains of the Cap Bon peninsula. It's a grand and comfortable view, full of colour and pleasant rambling houses dotted about. The only similarity with the bald slopes of the south are the small white-domed marabouts, tombs of holy men, which are scattered through the country. Sidi Bou Said was himself a holy man ('*sidi*' in Arabic is equivalent to 'saint' or 'master'), who, after a trip to Mecca at the end of the twelfth century, settled on this hill and lived a much respected ascetic life.

Several centuries later, Sidi Bou Said's fine location seduced a quite un-ascetic set of Europeans, led by a rich Frenchman, Baron Rodolphe d'Erlanger, who built an Anglo-Oriental mansion which is still here today. He created an international appetite for these picturesque cobbled streets on the hill and, rather like Tangier, Sidi Bou Said was near enough to Europe for writers and artists to pick up the scent, Paul Klee, August Macke and André Gide amongst them.

It's still a highly fashionable, moderately bohemian enclave and its centre is the celebrated Café des Nattes.

It stands in a dominant position at the top of Sidi Bou Said High Street, and even when you've climbed up the hill there's still a score of steep steps between you and the door, so you're guaranteed to enter breathless. The wide, but intimate, rectangular room was once part of a mosque and dates back to the fourteenth century. There is a well-used feel to it, a definite sense of layers of history, behind the black and white horseshoe arch of the doorway. It's a bit self-consciously traditional – very woody, with striped pillars and roof beams painted red, white and green, song birds in filigree cages, old wireless sets, black and white archive photos of Sidi Bou Said on the wall and a man behind the counter with a sprig of jasmine behind his ear. Wise old waiters in green and black striped jackets serve a largely young, international clientele sitting cross-legged on woven straw mats, the *nattes* that gave the place its name.

I order a thick, rich Turkish coffee and a glass of *thé aux pignons*, tea with pine nuts, for my companion Moez, a Tunisian film producer and director. Several people are puffing contentedly at bubbling *chichas*, so we order one to share. Moez says there's an extra intensity to the smoking, since Ramadan began two days ago, forbidding the taking of anything by mouth during the hours of daylight. Not that this produces a drastically slimmed-down nation. Apparently, the month of fasting results in such indulgence during the hours of darkness that people come out of it having put on weight.

The *chicha* is brought over by the waiter and set with courteous formality on a green baize table beside me. It's the size of a small vacuum cleaner, and comes with various accessories, like a silver tray of fresh charcoal and a pair of tongs. My breath draws the smoke from the coal down through the tobacco and it cools as it passes the water chamber. It gurgles pleasantly and is completely legal. According to Moez, the sound is an important part of the relaxing process. The other is breath control. An accomplished smoker can keep the pipe going for an hour or more.

'It's not easy,' Moez cautions, as I start puffing away like a steam engine. 'Both of us would burn the tobacco in ten minutes.'

We talk about his work. He's making a film about the Tunisians who died in the Second World War. From the war movies I remember, you'd be forgiven for thinking any Tunisians were involved at all.

Plenty of big foreign epics have been made in the country, including *Star Wars*, *The English Patient* and *Raiders of the Lost Ark*, but Moez prefers to work on local subjects.

'We need to see our images, you know. The audiences here like to see Tunisian faces, Tunisian stories, Tunisian jokes.'

Day Ninety-Two

SIDI BOU SAID

Out early. Sidi Bou Said is very walkable. It's spotlessly clean with almost every wall and house and building painted white and cerulean blue. Bougainvillea and morning-glory burst out of tight, green gardens and spill over into the streets. The national flag is everywhere, red and white crescent and stars wrapped round lamp-posts and on bunting hung across the street. Tomorrow is the fourteenth anniversary of what the Tunisians celebrate as '*Le Changement*', the day in 1987 when the great founding president, Habib Bourguiba, was declared senile and unfit to rule and power was painlessly transferred to his deputy, Ben Ali.

Ben Ali's likeness is everywhere. A fleshy, pleasant-looking man staring glassily down from the posters and wearing a purple sash. He is almost as popular as Bourguiba and credited with bringing in young well-educated technocrats to modernise industry and busi-ness. Ben Ali and the Technocrats may sound like a 1960s rock band but they are hailed here as the new saviours of Tunisia.

One of those Tunisians who has benefited from all this lives nearby, in a sprawling 100-year-old mansion next to a golf course in Carthage. Three seriously impressive satellite dishes sprout from the roof. Leaves blow across a tennis court and gather in the swim-ming pool. Over the hedges there's a glimpse of orange orchard, and at least a dozen oddly assorted dogs caper about beneath palms, pines and cypress trees at the top of a long drive. All it needs is a shooting party and a crowd of Tunisian country gentlemen to complete the picture. In fact, one small middle-aged woman emerges from the front door to welcome us. She's short and compact with thick dark hair and a strong broad face. Her name is Hyett Alouami. She's fifty and has two children. Her husband died of an aneurysm at the age of forty-six.

From the moment she greets us it's clear that this is the sort of formidable woman who doesn't do things by halves. She has not one but twelve dogs, all of them from a shelter which she herself started. She also has three cats and four transport companies.

She introduces us to the dogs, which have names like Café, Choco-lat and Vodka. One she's particularly fond of is just called Back.

'Because he keeps coming back,' she explains.

She gives instructions to an elderly manservant in a fez and green wellies, slipping her hand through his arm as they walk together through the garden. Then we repair to the waterfront to talk, for most of her life has been spent in the shipping business.

She was born on a farm near Sousse, but began work in the port of Bizerte, not as a clerk in an office, but actually on the dockside, in the resolutely male world of stevedores.

'It was hard for the first five or six years, sure. There were always little things. I always had to open the gates for myself in the morning.'

She speaks effusively of her country's debt to President Bourguiba. Without his insistence on a secular state, free universal education and equal opportunity for women, she would never have had the chance to go into business, let alone run companies. She is not alone. She reckons there are at least 1000 women of her generation who are entrepreneurs. All of which makes Tunisia quite exceptional in the Arab world. I ask her quite why this should be. The Tunisians, she points out, are a mixture of many races, including Romans, Phoenicians, Turks, Greeks; even the Normans came down here.

'It's a melting pot and that makes the nation a little bit different from other Arab countries.'

How different?

She nods, then stares out across the bay for a moment, before delivering a trenchant, if heretical judgement on the Tunisian male.

'They are educated, they are sweet.' She watches me for a moment. 'But he's quiet, he's not a fighter.' She breaks into a smile. 'We say the Tunisian men are women.'

The smile becomes a surprisingly deep throaty chuckle.

'I mean, I prefer that they are women rather than be men and kill each other.'

I ask her if Tunisia itself feels threatened, a slip of a country sandwiched between the oil- and gas-rich giants of Libya and Algeria. Again, her reaction is not quite what I'd expected. Her eyes seem positively to shine at the prospect of not having oil.

'We are lucky. We are lucky to be in a small country without oil. Oil . . . is a malediction. God continued not to give us oil so we have to work hard to survive. In a way we feel a little bit more proud than the Libyan and the Algerian. We, not we, I mean Bourguiba, has invested a lot in education, health care and women. And women are leading the country, actually.'

Day Ninety-Three

TUNIS TO ALGIERS

The electric train service into Tunis is clean, efficient, regular and stops at Carthage, which may have been laid waste by the Romans 2000 years ago but is now the smartest place to live in Tunisia. A sign of its significance is that there are no less than five Carthage stations listed between here and Tunis. I get on at Carthage Hannibal, partly because station names don't come much better than that, and partly because I've always had a fondness for anyone who stood up to the Romans. Hannibal's dramatic invasion of Europe and his spectacular feat of transporting an entire army over the Alps made him their enemy number one and resulted in the eventual destruction of the Carthaginian empire. As a symbolic gesture of this destruction the Romans ploughed up the fields and sowed them with salt.

At Tunis Marine we disembark and take the tram a short way through the city to the main station in Place Barcelone, from where the Trans-Maghreb express leaves for Algiers.

We pull out, on time, at 1.10 p.m. Six blue and white coaches run by SNCFT, Société Nationale de Chemins de Fer Tunisienne, the name itself an indication of how comfortably Tunisia has dealt with its French colonial past. A hundred and twelve miles, and three hours away is the border with Algeria, where things are tragically different.

Jamina, the girl sitting opposite me, is studying in Tunis and going back to see her family at the weekend. She speaks English well, but with the over-deliberate emphasis of someone who has taken the learning of it very seriously. Jamina gets off the train at Ghardimaou, less than a mile from the Algerian border. I watch her go, confident and self-possessed, on her way to see her mother, who was illiterate but whom she and her sisters have taught to read and write.

She has a spring in her step, a belief in herself and her country, which is a sharp and poignant contrast to the apathy and resignation I've seen in so much of the Sahara.

ALGERIA

ALGIERS

Eamonn O'Brien is walking me through the lush gardens of the Hotel El Djazair, Algiers, formerly the St George, known to the Victorians as 'The Leading Hotel of North Africa'. An elaborate network of paths winds past beds in which hibiscus, rose and flowering cacti seem to grow in profusion, undaunted by prolific fronds of banana and palm trees. The paths, together with occasional colonnades, pergolas and ornate ironwork screens, show that this bosky little Eden has not grown wild. It was laid out by the British, who built the hotel in the 1880s, when the warm Mediterranean air, sheltered by the mountains from the harsh dry winds of the interior, made Algiers a favoured destination.

The hotel, with its rambling mix of European and Moorish styles, looks much the same as it does in the century-old black and white photos on its walls. But one thing has changed. There is no equivalent now of the crowd of smiling, heavily dressed foreigners photographed taking cocktails under wide umbrellas. Neither the British, nor anyone else for that matter, come to Algiers these days to enjoy the balmy warmth of a Mediterranean winter. It is, as Eamonn is telling me, just too dangerous.

Sitting together on a bench between two ornamental columns, like characters out of a John Le Carré novel, Eamonn tells me the grim reality of present-day Algeria. An estimated 100,000 people have lost their lives in the civil war, which began ten years ago when the government cancelled an election that a radical Islamic party was poised to win. Since 1993, all foreigners have been under a fatwah, a sentence of death, and over 100 have been killed. As the aim of the rebels is to cause maximum embarrassment to the government, those with a high public profile are particularly at risk.

I'm not exactly Tom Cruise, but I appreciate Eamonn paying me the compliment of scaring me stiff.

Four members of the SPS, the Service de Protection Spéciale, will be with me every time I leave the hotel. With Eamonn, that's five, so we've almost doubled our crew already. And that's not all. In certain high-risk areas like the casbah, another six members of the SPS will be drafted and men from the Commissionaire de Police of the casbah, the Casbah Cops as Eamonn calls them, will throw a *cordon sanitaire* around us.

Having never had a *cordon sanitaire* thrown anywhere near me before, I suppose I should feel faintly flattered, but I feel bound to ask Eamonn if it's all absolutely necessary.

His reply is terse and to the point.

'You're a public figure. You're a guest of the Algerian government. And frankly, if I lose you, I lose my job.'

Pure James Bond.

My immediate security team, four lean young men in suits with two-way radios, are affable and approachable. I learn from them that the French for walkie-talkie is *talkie-walkie*. That cheers me up a bit.

I'm also reunited with Said Chitour, who takes me first to the Villa Suzini, a handsome Moorish house from whose roof there is a fine panorama of the city, laid out across wide, sometimes steep slopes curving round a generous bay. The French called it Alger La Blanche, and it is still a brilliantly white city, laid out like Lyon or Marseille, with tiers of imposing terraces, breaking down into the less regular outlines of the old town, the casbah, on the western arm of the bay.

To the east, the skyline is dominated by a towering monument of 300-foot palm leaves, built of reinforced concrete, and dedicated to the martyrs of the revolution. Martyrs are very important to the Algerians, though there have been so many claimed by different sides that the word has become almost meaningless.

Unlike other countries of the French empire, such as Tunisia, Senegal, Mauritania and Mali, Algeria's independence was won at considerable cost. Hundreds of thousands of French settlers had made their lives here, and, rather than accommodate the demands for self-determination that swept through Saharan Africa in the

1950s and 1960s, they decided to make a fight of it. Their battle to turn back the tide of history ended in ignominious failure in 1962, when General de Gaulle, heavily influenced by world opinion, finally handed over the country to the nationalist FLN (National Liberation Front).

The elegant old Villa Suzini played a particularly sinister part in all this. Down in the cellars, below the Carrara marble floor and the mosaic tiles and coloured glass of the central courtyard, are rooms into which the sun never shines. Plaster peels off the walls and there is a sour smell of damp. It was down here that the French paras interrogated their suspects. Torture was routinely used. Electric shocks were administered to various parts of the body through serrated pincers known as 'crocodiles'. Some of those who died of their beatings were buried in the garden or thrown down a well at the back of the house. The Villa Suzini was, until two or three years ago, used as an office, but now, apart from a sallow-complexioned caretaker and two or three dogs, it is deserted. No-one will work here.

'Too many ghosts,' explains Said.

Near the villa there is a funicular railway, and we take a car down the hill into the working-class district of Belcourt, where Albert Camus, winner of the Nobel Prize for Literature, was brought up, and about which he wrote in an unfinished autobiographical novel, *Le Premier Homme* (The First Man).

He made much in his book of the different levels in Algiers, both literal and metaphorical, with the poor crowded down by the port and the big houses with gardens higher up the hill. It's like that still. In one short ride in a bruised and dented cable car, the atmosphere of the city changes, from villas to tenements, from well-swept streets to open ground strewn with drifting rubbish. Though the streets are meaner, they're full of life and bustling activity. One of them borders a cemetery, whose outer wall is an open-air clothing store, hung with dresses, nighties, headscarves, coats, trousers and huge brassieres, with one section entirely devoted to football strips. One of the young boys wears a Manchester United shirt, but the strips on sale are mainly those of the big Algiers club, CRB Belcourt. Various international team names have been painted on the wall, including one which just reads '*Holygans*'.

The Camus family apartment at 93, Rue Mohammed Belouizdad

(formerly the Rue de Lyon) is still there, above a photographer's shop. There is nothing to commemorate the fact that a Nobel prize-winner lived here, but then Camus was a French Algerian, one of the European settlers they called the *pieds noirs*, and he was as critical of the Marxist revolutionaries of the FLN as he was of the French colonialists. But it does mean that the room in which he worked is very little changed, apart from a sticker in Arabic on the door, which reads 'In the name of God and Mohammed his messenger'. It's small, maybe 15 by 18 feet, with grey-blue French windows opening onto the street with its neatly clipped shady trees. It faces west and even now, in November, I can feel the force of a midday sun that must have made life unbearable in the long hot summers.

The modest two-storey house may be unheralded, but it's certainly not unused. It's owned by an old but sprightly Algerian, who lives there with his wife, three sons and their wives and children. Eighteen people altogether.

One of the sons says that we are the first people to visit since 1998. I'm quite moved to be here and linger by the window for a while, looking out at the children's wear shop opposite, the milling crowd, the line at a bus stop, the ordinary everyday life of the city which Camus observed so carefully.

Day Ninety-Five

ALGIERS

Judging by the headline in *Liberté*, this might not be the best day for our visit to the casbah. *'Algérie en Colère!'* it screams – 'Algeria in Anger!' – but for once it isn't a massacre or another killing that's responsible. The anger this time is directed at the inadequacy of public services, and especially the water supply, which has remained unchanged since the French left. After another long dry summer, water in some areas is now rationed to one day in five, and there are reports of a typhoid outbreak in the poorer parts of the city. We're told on no account to drink tap water.

Before entering the casbah we rendezvous with the local police outside the white walls of the Barberousse prison, named after the Barbarossa brothers, two Turkish corsairs brought in by the ruler of Algiers to fight off Spanish invaders in the sixteenth century. It stands at the top of the hill looking balefully out over the narrow, crowded roofs of the casbah. Because of the heightened security and the momentousness of our visit (the first foreign film crew to be allowed in for several years), we're all a touch jumpy, and when, with a sudden blaring of horns, a convoy of cars bursts round the corner, we instinctively rush for cover. Much mirth on the part of the security men, as it turns out to be nothing more than a wedding procession, in the middle of which is a portable band – six musicians in fezzes, white cotton tunics and red waistcoats, sitting in the back of a pick-up truck. With a salvo of car horns they move past down the road.

So thorough have the security forces been that when Said and I at last cross the road and enter the network of descending alleyways, the casbah is like a ghost town. Five hundred years of human traffic may have worn down the old stone steps and cobbled passageways, but there are no traffic jams today. I catch glimpses of faces at black-grilled windows, set high in the walls above us. Doors scrape into place just before we reach them, and I can hear the hum of voices behind them. I have the feeling that the casbah is only holding its breath until we've gone.

It doesn't surprise me that UNESCO has named the casbah a World Heritage Site. It is undeniably atmospheric. The buildings crowd in on one another. Some of them, judging by their elaborately detailed stone doorways and patches of decorative tiling embedded in cracked white plaster, must be substantial inside. Many houses have upper storeys cantilevered out over the alley and supported by rows of wooden poles, so they almost touch at the top. They have mains water and electricity now, but some houses still rely on the old system of collecting rainwater on the rooftops. Litter drifts about and there is a pungent smell of wet plaster and drains. Said confirms my suspicion that everything is going on the other side of the walls.

'It's overpopulated. Sometimes you find six families in the same house. It's too much people.'

'How many?'

'Sixty people sometimes.'

The house where Ali La Pointe and three other resistance heroes chose to be blown apart by the paras rather than surrender (a story powerfully told in the film *The Battle of Algiers*) has been rebuilt. On the wall an Arabic inscription details the circumstances of their deaths on 8 October 1957.

I can understand now what made the casbah such a superb defensive position and why the resistance, the 'freedom fighters' as Said always calls them, were able to hold out for so long against crack French paratroops. Sophisticated weapons and modern vehicles are useless in streets the width of a loaded donkey, or on roofs which act as another thoroughfare for those who know their way around them.

As we near the main road at the lower end of the casbah there is a milling throng. Eamonn walks beside me, casting wary looks, but everyone seems to be either friendly or preoccupied.

I feel that we have barely touched the real world of the casbah, which, as in all Arab communities, is private and inward-looking, so Said takes me round to the shrine of Sidi Abderrahmane, a holy man of great powers who lived here in the sixteenth century. The sound of female voices rises from inside as we approach the domed building surmounted by a tall balconied minaret.

This is traditionally a place for the women to come and invoke the help of the saint in childbirth or with problems of infertility, but the imam is happy for us to join them. Remove my shoes and enter in reverent silence. I needn't have bothered. The small chamber is less like an English parish church than a kindergarten at collection time. Small children sit and play as their mothers worship in their own way. Nothing is formal. One woman hugs the side of the tomb, singing plaintively, another bows to Mecca, another has brought her new-born baby to touch the wooden casket that contains the saint's remains. It's the first place, she declares proudly, that he's ever been taken to. Brightly coloured texts run round the walls, heavy cut-glass lamps hang, undusted, from the ceiling, and in one corner is a heavy-duty industrial safe, with a slit for offerings. Said tells me that the poorer women sometimes stuff chewing gum in the slit and come back later to collect money that hasn't gone down.

By now I've completely forgotten that I might be a target. The *cordon sanitaire* has been discreet to the point of invisibility and the people of Algiers as cordial and curious as anywhere in the Sahara.

Day Ninety-Six

ALGIERS TO ORAN

A peerless morning. The only cloud in the sky is caused by an enormous flock of small birds, which plunges us into shadow as we wait in the hotel courtyard for transport to the station. More and more birds seem to join all the time, crying and calling, until their numbers reach a critical mass and, as if on a given signal, they execute a dizzyingly precise banking turn and disappear southwards. Our coach driver tells me they're swallows, migrating from Europe to winter in the Sahara. They regroup here on the mountainous shoreline before starting the final leg of their journey.

We who are migrating the other way, out of the Sahara and into Europe, are also on the last leg of a journey. Today we catch the train to Oran, second city of Algeria, which is less than 300 miles from where we set out all those months ago.

Eamonn is anxious. Travelling from Algiers to Oran by train is, in security terms, an out of the frying pan into the fire situation. He has trawled his dictionary of doom this morning. Over the last ten years this has been the most bombed railway line in the world; it passes through an area known as the Triangle of Death (not mentioned in the timetable) and terrorists have been known to board the train and kill people 'in awful circumstances'.

It all sounds theatrically exaggerated on this brilliant, life-enhancing morning, as we drive down through the city for the last time, past the grand arcades, the long straight thoroughfares, the great domed Post Office – built by the French in 1913, but so Moorish in its inspiration that it looks like a mosque – and the long white walls of the apartment blocks, flecked with the bright colours of a thousand sun blinds.

Our train was once the romantically named Algiers–Casablanca

Express, but the land border with Morocco has been closed since 1995, after disagreements over security, and it's now terminated at Oran, 300 miles and five hours away. The silver-ribbed aluminium shell of our coach is studded with small holes, and I'm just about to bring these to Eamonn's attention when a group from Algerian Railways arrives to welcome us aboard and generally look after all our filming needs. One of them is a dark-haired lady with long, lustrous hair and a brisk, efficient manner which barely conceals a palpable nervousness.

She dismisses any current problems on the line.

'It's all much better now,' she assures me confidently, rather spoiling the effect by adding, '*touche bois*'. Touch wood. *Inshallah* would have been more appropriate.

The train rolls out on time and I push aside the flimsy green curtain to take a last look at Alger La Blanche, which I doubt I shall see again for a long, long time. The morning sun catches the roofs of the casbah and the city finally slips away behind a succession of tunnels and flyovers.

The railway runs through a poor area consisting of cheap new housing blocks, separated from the line by a corridor of concrete walls and steel fences which rise on either side of the train. This grim barricade continues into open countryside, where fields, apple orchards and vineyards stretch away towards the grey-green foothills of the Atlas Mountains. The fields around Blida were once renowned for their roses; now the town is part of the aforementioned 'Triangle of Death', which is marked by Blida in the west, Bouira in the east and Algiers in the north. It was in this deceptively benign landscape that the GIA used to stop trains by putting an accomplice on board to pull the communication cord. As the train came to a halt they would board and either kill their victims there and then or take them away and murder them. There are no communication cords on the trains any more. Even the nice friendly PR team from the railway cannot disguise the problems here. The woman with the lustrous hair lost her voice for three years after seeing some soldiers, who were guarding one of her stations, murdered. Like many other victims of the GIA their throats had been cut.

Once beyond Blida, the continuous protective wall stops, but heavy security remains in place, with block-houses and pillboxes at strategic points like bridges or tunnel entrances.

The worst of the attacks peaked around 1995 and recently the government has experimented with an amnesty, which seems to have reduced the levels of violence.

The damage nowadays is more likely to be inflicted by bored teenagers throwing stones, which happens all the time and explains not only the number of Plexiglas window panes but also the scattering of dents on the bodywork which caught my eye as I was boarding.

We're climbing now, through a long tunnel and into a station called Ain Torki. The only people on the platform are soldiers wearing camouflage, but in the distance, my eye is caught by a procession of women leaving a graveyard, scarves and veils streaming behind them, plumes of colour in a hard brown landscape.

At Chlef, two and a quarter hours into the journey, our guard is changed and no less than eighteen black-clad members of the Gendarmerie Nationale, wearing body armour, squeeze aboard. Eamonn casts a professional eye over them and notes that one or two have Simonov precision rifles.

'*They're* serious.'

The soldiers settle down behind us, but when Nigel raises the camera they all move away and hide.

The last few miles into Oran are particularly sad. An arid landscape of stony ploughed fields is covered with blowing rubbish and drifting plastic bags. The stations, once trim symbols of French civic pride, are falling apart, with gaping holes in pantiled roofs, windows smashed, red-brick walls stained and grafittied. It pains me to say so, because our Algerian hosts are charming, co-operative, friendly and above all desperate to please, but this is a vision of callous decay.

And, perhaps, a perfect metaphor for post-colonial Sahara. The old owners have been thrown out and the new ones still haven't decided what to do with the property.

Oran Station emphasises the point. It is a magnificently stylish example of the Mauresque style, full of height and light and space, set off by ornate wood mouldings and iron-work screens. It's been kept in very good condition, but not so the Hôtel Terminus next door. Beneath the layers of dust, the broken lighting and the holes in the ceiling, the grand vision of the French railway builders is unmistakable. Solid Moorish arches rise from the mosaic floor, a fireplace in massive blocks of grey marble is incised with the initials P. L. M., the Paris, Lyon and Marseille Railway. Above it is a mirror 9 feet high. Everything is intended to elevate and inspire, but this purpose has sadly been forgotten. No pastis here now, no freshly opened bottles of wine, no aproned waiters bustling amongst tables buzzing with gossip from Paris and Algiers. Instead, there's Coke or Fanta and a handwritten sign above a lifeless bar: '*La maison ne fait pas du crédit.*'

We are eating later at the Comet, a plain old-fashioned restaurant, whose wine list and entrecôtes go a long way to making up for the Hôtel Terminus, when the flow of conversation is interrupted by the chanting of a crowd outside. It sounds like football supporters celebrating, and Said, who goes outside to check, confirms that this is the case, Kabilya JSK having defeated AC Africa from Côte d'Ivoire, to win the African club soccer championship.

The hooting and shouting grows louder and more vociferous and seems no longer entirely to do with football. I'm sure I hear the word '*Assassins!*' repeated over and over. The proprietor pushes his windows shut, which doesn't do much good, and, if anything, urges the crowd on. There seem to be only two words they're chanting now.

'*Pou-voir! Assa-ssins! Pou-voir! Assa-ssins!*'

Said goes to the door, but peers out a lot more warily. For the first time I begin to wonder where my *cordon sanitaire* has gone. Probably been given the night off for getting us to Oran safely.

After a few more minutes, during which the stamping and shouting rises to a frightening intensity, the crowd moves on.

I ask Said what it was all about.

Don't worry, he reassures me, it wasn't directed at us. Kabilya, where the winning team comes from, is a mountainous region of eastern Algeria, not Arab but Berber. They are a strong-willed, proud and enterprising people (the actress Isabelle Adjani is Kabilyan) and have their own quarrel with the government over suppression of their language and culture. After a recent protest march in Algiers, forty young men disappeared, and the word is that they were taken away on police wagons. The military-backed government is known by its opponents as *Le Pouvoir*, The Power, hence the shouts of '*Pouvoir*' and '*Assassins*'.

In Algeria it's quite common for football teams to be used for political protest.

'Were you as worried as I was?' I ask Said.

'If this had been in Algiers, yes.'

Day Ninety-Seven

ORAN

The good news is that my hotel overlooks the sea. The less good news is that between me and the sea is a warehouse, a grain silo, two fuel storage tanks, a stack of containers and a chimney. The positively bad news is that at six o'clock this morning I was bent double with stomach cramps. Since my emetic experiences in Western Sahara I've kept a bottle of Pepto-Bismol nearby and am gulping the thick chalky fluid every hour on the hour.

I don't think I'm the only one with problems. The hotel itself looks distinctly off colour. My bathroom ceiling has been partly removed to provide access to a water pipe, and every now and then strange, animal-like cries issue from the gaping hole. The tap on my basin coughs and splutters in a horrible parody of my own lurchings and strainings, and I can find no taps on the bath tub at all.

I make my way gingerly to breakfast. I'm on the tenth floor but I haven't used the lift since I saw the owner banging the control panel to make the light come on, so it's a long walk down. As I pass the third floor I have to step over a stream of water, which is running down the corridor from beneath the door of Room 306.

As if things aren't delicate already, my first walk through Oran reminds me that this is the city immortalised by Camus in his novel *La Peste* (*The Plague*).

In it one of the characters actually keels over and dies of the plague on the stage of the Opera House. This splendidly florid edifice still stands at one side of the Place du 1ᵉʳ Novembre 1954, formerly the Place d'Armes. It makes for an interesting culture clash. Brazenly bare-breasted women loom large at the top of the Opera House, whilst a statue in the middle of the square bears a quotation from the Koran: 'And Victory is from God and God is merciful.'

This then is the end of the road. It looks as if the only way from here to Morocco might be by sea, and, given the current state of relations between Morocco and Algeria, even that could be tricky.

Back to the hotel. Get talking to a tall, rather striking Algerian with a family in Stockholm. He is curious to know what I think of the bombing of Afghanistan. Something in his manner rubs me up the wrong way and instead of expressing my doubts I dither indecisively. He thinks it will only strengthen the hand of the Islamists. I shift the discussion to something that has worried me ever since I came to Algeria. What happened after the glorious armed struggle against the French? How come the freedom fighters of the FLN became the oppressors? How did the anti-colonial legacy of the 1960s become today's 'Pouvoir', a military state almost wholly dependent on oil and gas exports to the West?

He looks witheringly at me.

'A hundred and forty years of colonialism cannot be destroyed right away.'

He shrugs and reaches for his briefcase.

'Mistakes will be made.'

Day Ninety-Eight

CEUTA

There is an alternative to Morocco. Two hundred and sixty miles west of Oran, tucked in at the foot of the mountains at the point where two continents almost meet, is a low-slung town occupying a narrow isthmus between two peaks. Neither part of Morocco nor Algeria, it belongs to one of the less well-known African countries – Spain.

The heavily fortified town of Ceuta has been Spanish sovereign territory since 1580. It's one of two Spanish towns barnacled onto the coast of Morocco, ensuring that the transition from Africa to Europe is not as clean as one might romantically like it to be. It's reachable by a combination of ferries, and I duly find myself spending my last night in the Dark Continent at a Parador hotel drinking Rioja and eating *jamón serrano*. Very confusing.

Day Ninety-Nine

CEUTA TO GIBRALTA

In my experience, hotel brochures, especially of the aspiringly glossy variety, always feature a room spectacularly better than the one you're in and a swimming pool you can never find. In the case of the Hotel La Muralla, Ceuta, I do find the pool, which is similar in every respect to its photo except that the one in the photo has water in it. The brochure is gushingly enthusiastic about Ceuta's history. In fact, I can't imagine why I've never heard of the place.

'Phoenicians, Romans, Arabs, Visigoths, Portuguese and Spanish successively took control of the ancient city.'

Good harbours, like the one I entered last night, so close to the Mediterranean gateway, meant trade, security and wealth. Under its Arab rulers Ceuta had all three, but couldn't hold onto them against the determined and expansionist Portuguese. In 1415 they conquered Ceuta and took their prize seriously enough to build a powerful fortification, La Muralla (City Wall). It remains in place, solid and imperturbable, and I enjoy a good walk around the sturdy, elegantly angled walls, crenellated and studded with barbican towers, which slide down into the clear green waters of a moat. Felipe II united Portugal and Spain and in 1580 Ceuta became a possession of the Spanish crown, and has remained so ever since. Though it has the look and feel of a European city, the central square is nevertheless called the Plaza de Africa. It contains a small church dedicated to Our Lady of Africa and a monument commemorating the Spanish invasion of Morocco in 1859.

In the gardens of this quiet square, sitting on the grass or pacing the neat hedge-lined paths that radiate from the monument, are a number of young men. All Africans, they range from tall loose-limbed Blacks to paler Arabs, some in Western dress and others in flowing robes. They look like me; a little awkward, strangers in a foreign land.

I ask one of them where he's from. His English is not so good, and he prefers to talk in French. He's from Mali, on the other side of the Sahara, and has made his way here to try to find work in Spain and once in Spain, any of the European Union countries. He points out an Algerian, a group of Mauritanians. They're here to pick up scraps of information, about who's going where and how, about deals, about boats crossing the Strait, about how they can take the final step on their long journeys. They've come to the Plaza de Africa because they want to get out of Africa.

I ask how they survive in Ceuta. Most of them, it turns out, are in a holding centre run by the Spanish authorities on behalf of the European Union, where they are given food and accommodation until they can be found work in Europe.

Later in the day we visit the centre, a bright, freshly painted, concrete encampment up in the hills, surrounded by a grove of mournfully swaying eucalyptus trees. Here in the Centro de Estancia Temporal de Imigrantes are gathered 335 men, 42 women and 13 children, waiting for permits and, in some cases, asylum papers to enable them to get work 'up in the Peninsula', as they call Spain and Portugal.

The place is newly opened and is clean, orderly and antiseptic; an institution in which no-one has anything wrong with them, like a hospital in which all the patients are well or a jail in which everyone is free. It's full of Africans but unlike any African village I've ever seen.

Despite an educational programme, offering language tuition and some job training, most of the inmates stand around or pace the compound with an air of displaced restlessness.

The director is a decent man, who takes some pride in the fact that fifty-nine of them have been found work in the previous six months, but most of those I talk to dispute that. A Nigerian in a Cardinals baseball shirt has been here five months. His journey sounds like ours in reverse. Up through Mali and Senegal and Western Sahara to Morocco. As Moroccan government policy is to send all immigrants back, I ask him how he got through.

'On a Zodiac (a small rubber dinghy) across the sea.' He adds bitterly, 'I thought they were taking me to Europe.'

Another Nigerian has come across the desert, 1000 miles or more. He nods bleakly and repeats the word 'desert' as if at some infinitely painful memory.

He made it to Ceuta as a stowaway on a ship from Morocco. It cost money, though not as much as the $1500 a Mauritanian paid to make the same journey. The stories tumble out, and the resentment too.

'Ten months! Ten months we have been here!' shouts a woman with hair in braids. She has left her children behind in Sierra Leone.

'Help us! Tell the world!' shouts a young man as we leave.

On a clear day the hopeful immigrants in Ceuta could see the green hills of Spain with the naked eye. They could certainly see the man-made forest of wind turbines running over the crest of the hills, propellers spinning on top of giant white stalks. If they had a strong enough telescope they could see telescopes looking back at them from the hills above the town of Tarifa. Tourists come here to be thrilled by the prospect of the sheer rock walls of Morocco, and the sight of the Strait of Gibraltar, no wider than a Swiss lake. They buy postcards and take photographs of the 9-mile distance between them and Africa.

For some it might jog memories of unsettling newspaper photographs of couples sunbathing on a Spanish beach beside the huddled body of someone who drowned trying to get to Europe. What the tourists will not know is that some evenings, hundreds of Africans will set out to cross the Strait and land a half-mile away from where they're standing. They will have paid a lot of money to risk their lives, travelling in unlit boats, without lifejackets or maps of any kind, across one of the busiest and most unpredictable stretches of water in the world. Some will never make it. Over 3000 have died attempting the crossing in the last three years.

There is heat still left in the afternoon as I reach the Spanish mainland and walk along the beach at Tarifa with Belinda Whaley-Braithwaite, a traveller herself, who rode from here to Paris on a horse called Dragon and wrote a book about it. Now she and her husband live most of the year in a pretty house with six guest rooms a mile or so across the fields.

The beaches are long and full of fine white sand, and in the creamy blue-black breakers kite-flyers, surfers, swimmers and fishermen try to stay out of each other's way.

Then we come across a red and blue striped fishing boat, no more than 20 feet long, broken and embedded in the sand. It looks quite picturesque, until you realise why it is here and who it has brought.

'Sometimes they can be up to 700 in a night, and the police may only catch 200, so the rest are in the countryside. If they're Moroccan there's an agreement, so they'll be sent back, but the people who've come from Chad or Senegal . . .'

'From Black Africa?'

'Black Africa, yes, there isn't the same agreement, so they're quite happy to be caught.'

Belinda, perhaps being something of an adventurer herself, talks with a sort of shocked admiration for what they go through. Boats the size of the one we're looking at may have forty bodies in them, including pregnant women who want their children to be born in Europe. Other boats never make it to the shore, leaving their charges to swim in over the reef. Unscrupulous skippers lie to them, telling them they're a hundred yards from land when in fact they're still half a mile out.

The lucky ones who do get ashore bring waterproof bags with a change of clothes.

Some speak only Arabic and clutch pieces of paper with contact names and numbers. One came to Belinda's door and asked her if she might help her contact a Spanish Internet address. The name she had been given, but didn't understand, was a very sick joke. It was two Spanish words, 'puerto muertos', literally 'the port of the dead'.

As we walk back to her house, through dunes littered with cast-off clothes that may well have protected people on mighty journeys across the Sahara, Belinda explains why she thinks the best way to deal with the immigrants is to allow them a short-term visa.

'Then at least they could come and try it out. I think a lot of them actually come over here and don't like what they see. It's more expensive to live here, they can't get a job, so they're actually happy to go back to their families.'

She pauses and looks out the way we've come.

'But you know, when all your family and friends have clubbed together to get this ticket for you to Paradise . . . How do you go back?'

It's dark by the time we reach Gibraltar. There's a queue to get in. Our driver grumbles about the usual Spanish prevarication. But there's a lot more for him to grumble about since we left here all those months ago. The British and Spanish governments have been doing the unthinkable – talking joint sovereignty. Though they've been assured that nothing will be decided without a referendum, the folks who live on the Rock are very angry. Joint sovereignty may mean the end of this bickering at the border, but the very sugges-tion of a Spanish flag flying on Gibraltar, even alongside the Union Jack, is seen by some here as the first rumbling of betrayal, the beginning of the end.

For me, for all of us, this *is* the end. After nine countries and some 10,000 miles of travel we've made it back to the reassuring armchairs of the Rock Hotel. By tomorrow we'll all be back home, worrying about the price of car insurance and why the plumber hasn't called.

I've had a few beers of celebration and I'm a little light-headed as I stumble out onto my balcony at midnight. I look out over the star-lit Strait towards Africa and try to think big thoughts about what I've learnt from all this, other than that nowhere is Paradise.

AFTERWORD

I'm glad to be home, but in the all-moving, all-talking mayhem of modern life, my restless thoughts go back to that great place of silence and apparently infinite space. I need to be reminded of its special qualities, but, like keeping up with an old friend, that can be hard work.

Even checking the weather (sad person that I am) isn't easy. The likes of Nouakchott and Bamako rarely show up on a list of world cities.

A few scraps of news have come out of the desert since we finished our journey. A United Nations report blames high-tech foreign fleets for destroying Mauritania's fishing industry. The Polisario has released 115 Moroccan soldiers, held in their desert jails for twenty-five years (they never told me about them), but Saharawi independence looks as far away as ever as the UN discusses an American-backed compromise proposal for Western Sahara. Nancy Abeiderrahmane has had her attempt to sell camel cheese in Europe turned down, because the camels are not mechanically milked, and the drought in Algeria ended savagely and dramatically soon after we left, with hundreds drowned by floodwater in the capital. Dave Hammond, the British motorcycling hope in the Dakar Rally, was in twentieth place with only two stages left when he fell into a hidden chasm on the blind side of a sand dune. He spent many weeks in a Paris hospital but is now back home and recovering. As I write, the British and Spanish prime ministers are meeting to discuss plans for the Rock, whilst the government of Gibraltar is putting ads in British newspapers to ask for support.

Otherwise, the mystery of the Sahara remains largely intact. Except in my dreams, where it still springs vividly to life.

Michael Palin, May 2002

BACKGROUND READING

I gratefully acknowledge a number of other people's efforts, including the *Rough Guide to West Africa*, Lonely Planet's *Africa on a Shoestring*, the Footprint guides to Morocco, Libya and Tunisia, Barnaby Rogerson's *Cadogan Guide to Morocco* and *A Traveller's History of North Africa*, Ross Velton's *Bradt Guide to Mali*, Kim Naylor's *Discovery Guide to West Africa* and James Wellard's *The Great Sahara*. Hollyman and Van Beek's beautiful book on the Dogon is one of the best on a difficult subject. Sanche de Gramont's *The Strong Brown God* and T. Coraghessan Boyle's *Water Music* were essential River Niger reading. I found the Eland edition of Mungo Park's *Travels into the Interior of Africa* indispensable and Quentin Crewe's *In Search of the Sahara*, Jeremy Keenan's *Sahara Man*, Richard Trench's *Forbidden Sands* and Martin Buckley's *Grains of Sand* informative and inspiring. Hachette's *Guide de Sahara*, Chris Scott's *Sahara Overland* and Simon Glen's *Sahara Handbook* are all good chunky guides that get right to the heart of desert travel.

ACKNOWLEDGEMENTS

The filming of Sahara lasted a little over four months and covered nearly 10,000 miles. The preparation for the journey and the process of welding it into a series took the best part of a year. No-one had an easy job.

At our home base in London, Anne James steered the boat through choppy waters, from launch to final anchorage, with diligence, energy and enthusiasm. Natalia Fernandez dealt with every detail of our travel plans, which, considering the bureaucratic complications in this part of the world, deserves more than your average respect. Janina Stamps, who set us on the road, and Gina Hobson, who brought us back and saw the programmes to their conclusion, applied skill and experience to some nightmare situations, and Lyn Dougherty rode expertly through the minefields of cash flow.

Paul Bird and Alison Davies at the office helped preserve my sanity, without apparently losing their own, and Alison tucked and tidied the manuscript.

Elizabeth Parker wrote music for the series and Bernard Heyes designed our maps and titles. George Foulgham and all the team at VideoLondon made it sound wonderful and the amazing Alex Richardson took on the task of editing all four hours. Though he and his family may be regretting it, I, quite selfishly, am delighted. Nicola Moody at the BBC gave us generous encouragement and great support.

It's impossible to thank everyone who helped us out on the road.

Many of those to whom I owe my thanks are mentioned in the text. Of those who are not, but without whom we could never have made such a journey, I must not forget Marie Gloria Macedo, Richard Stanforth, Alan Keohane, Bob Watt, Djadje Ba, Violet Diallo, Barry Halton, Mike Lord and Stirling Security Services, Mr Ahmed Faci, Kahlifa Airways, Simon Khoury at Arab Tours, Judith and Fanta and Tidene Expeditions in Niger.

Our core filming team, whose average age, we were shocked to find, is well into the mid-fifties, were nevertheless a credit to Saga Filming. Nigel Meakin on camera and John Pritchard on sound (and putting anything back together again within five minutes) took to the desert with cool authority. Peter Meakin, apart from bringing the average age of the crew down by a good ten years, loaded, unloaded and shot film in quite horrendous conditions, without ever once complaining. Except when his father wasn't looking.

John Paul Davidson ('J-P') led our motley group through Senegal, Mali and Niger and always had a bit of goat ready for us at the end of a long day, and, even more miraculously, a bottle of very warm red wine to wash it down. His enthusiasm was wonderful to behold and his investments in the local economy were much appreciated.

Roger Mills directed my first steps out of the Reform Club fourteen years ago, when *Around the World in 80 Days* was a new and nervous departure for me. The fact that we still travel together shows not only how unadventurous we are, but how much we trust each other and how much we still enjoy it. The fact that Roger took on the extra responsibility of Series Producer this time shows a fine streak of masochism.

Vanessa Courtney, another veteran of previous travels, scoured remote parts of Africa on a gruelling recce with Roger and saw us safely through Morocco. Dudu Douglas-Hamilton in Mali, Jane Chablani in Niger and Claire Houdret in Tunisia buttered up the locals and generally made wheels run smoothly in often difficult situations. Simon Neatham provided me with a tent.

My thanks to Bobby Birchall at DW Design for all the time he put in to make the hardback edition of the book look so good. At Weidenfeld & Nicolson Claire Marsden has been the most sympathetic and conscientious of copy editors, and Michael Dover the most generous, supportive and hospitable of editors. Thanks too to David Rowley and to Angela Martin for all her work in ensuring that someone actually read the book.

Finally, thanks to my good friend, gastronomic adviser and stills photographer Basil Pao for bringing back as fine a set of holiday snaps as you could wish for. What the world doesn't know is that the secret of his success is a constant supply of certain throat sweets to which the whole crew became addicted. These Valda Pastilles, or Green Jobs, as he called them, became essential morale boosters on an adventure low on luxuries.

MICHAEL PALIN established his reputation with *Monty Python's Flying Circus* and *Ripping Yarns*. His work also includes several films with Monty Python, as well as *The Missionary*, *A Private Function*, an award-winning performance as the hapless Ken in *A Fish Called Wanda*, *American Friends* and *Fierce Creatures*. His television credits include two films for the BBC's *Great Railway Journeys*, the plays *East of Ipswich* and *Number 27*, and Alan Bleasdale's *GBH*. He has written seven bestselling travel books to accompany his series *Around the World in 80 Days*, *Pole to Pole*, *Full Circle*, *Hemingway Adventure*, *Sahara*, *Himalaya* and *New Europe*. He is also the author of a number of children's stories, the play *The Weekend* and the novel *Hemingway's Chair*. In 2006 the first volume of his diaries, *1969–1979: The Python Years*, spent many weeks on the bestseller lists. In 2008 an updated special edition of *Around the World in 80 Days* was published to coincide with his BBC documentary *Around the World in 20 Years*. Visit his website at www.palinstravels.co.uk.

BASIL PAO began his photographic career in 1980 on his return to Hong Kong after ten years in the United States, where he was an art director for Atlantic, Polygram and Warner Bros. He first worked with Michael Palin on the design for book accompanying Monty Python's *Life of Brian*. They have since collaborated on the books based on his seven travel series. In 2007 he wrote and photographed *China Revealed: A Portrait of the Rising Dragon*.

HIMALAYA

MICHAEL PALIN
Photographs by Basil Pao

A PHOENIX PAPERBACK

First published in Great Britain in 2004
by Weidenfeld & Nicolson
This paperback edition published in 2005
by Phoenix,
an imprint of Orion Books Ltd,
Orion House, 5 Upper St Martin's Lane,
London WC2H 9EA

An Hachette UK company

3

Reissued 2009

A CIP catalogue record for this book is
available from the British Library.

ISBN 978-0-7538-1990-6

Printed and bound in Great Britain by Clays Ltd, St Ives plc

The Orion Publishing Group's policy is to use papers that
are natural, renewable and recyclable products and
made from wood grown in sustainable forests. The logging
and manufacturing processes are expected to conform to
the environmental regulations of the country of origin.

www.orionbooks.co.uk

Contents

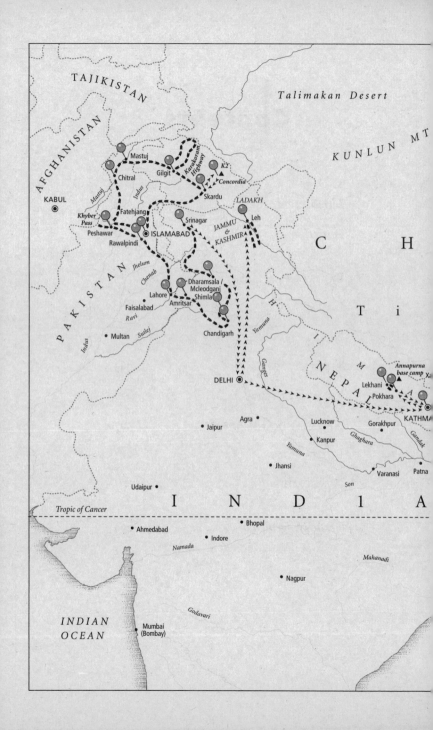

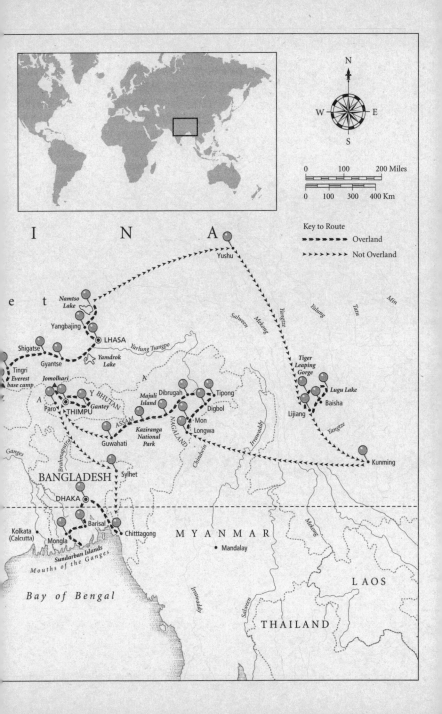

Introduction

I've always had a soft spot for my *Penguin Encyclopaedia of Places.* On a dull day when I should be talking to someone about tax returns I like to open it at random and set off a few quiet fantasies. Initial disappointment that you've opened it at Norwich and Nottingham can turn quickly to a frisson of excitement as, lower down the page, your eye alights on Noumea, Nova Lisboa and Novara, all places I'd leave for tomorrow if someone said I had to.

At the end of 2002, with *Sahara* still warm, as it were, Roger Mills came up with the idea of following it with a series on the Silk Route. When I looked at the map I saw an awful lot of desert along the way, and I was looking for something that would take me away from desert sands for a while. I was about to close the atlas regretfully when my eye drifted south and east to where the Silk Route becomes entangled with that long, white-tipped mass of mountains, hanging like a raised eyebrow above India, and connected by the single word: Himalaya.

Something began to tingle. I reached for the *Encyclopaedia of Places* and found the page I was looking for. '*Hillingdon*, Greater London Borough', '*Hinckley*, Urban District in Leicestershire' and there, snugly between the two, '*Himalaya*. In Sanskrit, "Abode Of Snow". Vast mountain system in central Asia lying along the S edge of the Plateau of Tibet, enclosed by the Indus and the Brahmaputra Rivers. It extends generally ESE in an immense curve about 1500 miles long.' There wasn't a word in that brief description that didn't thrill me, and by the time I shut the book I knew what the next two years were going to be about. (No, not Hillingdon in 12 one-hour episodes.)

What the Sahara is to desert, the Himalaya is to mountains. Both share the same contradictory attractions, appealing and appalling, tempting and terrifying in equal, and ultimately irresistible, measure.

By rights I should have followed up *Sahara* with something easier. Perhaps I should have taken more seriously our sound recordist John Pritchard's suggestion of a series called 'Death By Luxury'. But it's the mind as well as the body you have to look after, and that's where the Himalaya seemed to have the edge.

All the elements that appeal to me most about travel were on offer. The stimulus, mental and physical, of working at extremes, the breaking of new ground (I had never been to any of the places on our route), and the chance to go in by the back door, as it were, and see how lives are lived in a fascinatingly mixed bag of countries: superpowers of the future like India and China; countries like Pakistan, recently pushed to the centre of international politics; secretive, unconquered mountain kingdoms like Nepal and Bhutan; and remote lands on the margin of the world's consciousness like Nagaland and Ladakh.

The idea seemed to appeal to my team as instantly as it did to me, and setting aside advancing ages and hopes for quieter lives, we committed to a Himalayan journey at the beginning of 2003.

From the outset problems loomed as large as the mountains themselves. Pakistan was, though I'm glad to say no longer is, the subject of a Foreign Office advisory against all but essential travel. The whole Kashmir region was highly volatile, and the Maoists in Nepal were engaged in an increasingly threatening guerrilla war with the government. The Chinese were highly sensitive about allowing television crews into Tibet, and the Indian government was wary of our safety in Assam.

To their enormous credit, our production team soothed troubled brows successfully and we were able to leave for the Khyber Pass in May 2003.

There were crisis points, including a brush with the Maoists in Nepal, a nasty bout of illness halfway up Annapurna, and the loss, and subsequent recovery, of one of our crew to altitude sickness as we pushed up to Everest Base Camp. There were problems that could have been much worse, like the SARS epidemic in China, snowstorms in Bhutan and strikes in Bangladesh, but we were more or less intact by the time our tired little band emerged triumphant from a circuitous progress through six countries and 3000 miles of Himalaya at the beginning of April 2004.

The schedule was very tight, and I'm aware that these diaries are stronger on spontaneity than sober reflection.

What I feel we have achieved, none the less, is to put the Himalaya in a human perspective. We found people living at altitudes higher than the highest mountains in Europe; ancient civilizations surviving on arid, wind-scoured plateaux; gorges two and a half miles deep, through which traders have found their way for thousands of years and, everywhere, religion, vibrant and colourful, and thriving in adversity. In short, we found a Himalaya not reticent and forbidding, but permeated by every sort of human activity.

A battleground of immense geological forces that is a centre of human tectonics as well, with sacred and secular, tribal identity and national aspiration, tradition and technology, all pushing up against each other.

The scope of our journey means that this is not a mountaineer's account of the Himalaya, it's a traveller's account. This is Himalaya, not from top to bottom, but from one end to the other; from the Khyber Pass where in a tight knuckle of mountains the great ranges of the Hindu Kush, the Karakoram and the Himalaya are born, to Bangladesh, where the Himalaya, reduced to dust and sand, is swept out into the waters of the Bay of Bengal.

Great journeys tend to bring me out in a rash of over-used superlatives, so all I will say this time is that Himalaya was a wonderfully, magically, brilliant journey, with more gasps of astonishment per square mile than any other in my entire life. And for once, I think I might be right.

Michael Palin, London, June 2004

A word about dates

We began our journey on 12 May 2003 and due to vagaries of the climate, timing of religious festivals and other key events like polo matches and Horse Fairs, returned to the region at various times before our final arrival home on 7 April 2004. We filmed for a total of six months. This account is based on notebooks and tape recordings kept at the time. Apart from missing out some rest days and days at airports, I've presented the journey as a continuous narrative, because that, in effect, is exactly what it was.

Postscript

Since I put these diaries together there have been significant changes in the region, mainly affecting India and Pakistan, and by and large hopeful. Even before the defeat of the BJP in the Indian elections in May 2004 cross-border relations with Pakistan had been improving, and both sides were pledged to a peaceful outcome in Kashmir, the most troubled area we went through. With the advent of India's first non-Hindu Prime Minister, Manmohan Singh, this process is expected to continue.

Indians are playing cricket in Pakistan again and the British Foreign Office has lifted its advice against non-essential travel to the country. On 22 May 2004 Pakistan was re-admitted to the Commonwealth after five years, a decision which India supported.

The day after that decision a bomb killed 33 people in Kashmir. Change clearly won't happen overnight, but there is cause for cautious optimism. Less so in Nepal where the Maoists and the monarchy seem unable to sink their differences. There are sinister rumours that Tiger Leaping Gorge in Yunnan might disappear beneath the waters of a reservoir, but better news for Bangladesh's cricket team who have won their first Test Match and a one-day series too.

MP, February 2005

Pakistan

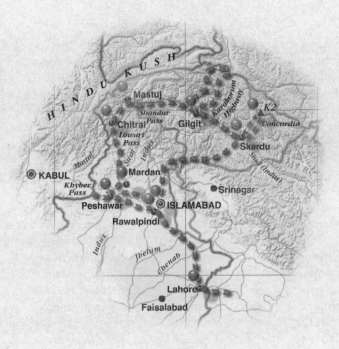

Day One : Up the Khyber

Below the walls of the fort that guards the Khyber Pass there is a viewing platform on which rows of chairs are set out, facing Afghanistan, like circle seats at the theatre. They convey an air of expectation, of something about to happen, of a curtain about to rise on great events.

Casts of thousands have at one time or another filled the plains below, as greedy armies, seeking the great prize of India, gathered at this narrow western gateway. Darius I, King of Persia, led his soldiers through the pass nearly 500 years before the birth of Christ. He was followed, nearly two centuries later, by Alexander the Great. Six hundred years ago I would have seen Tamburlaine's army, down from Samarkand, toiling up the hill towards me, and 400 years after that, the lone, exhausted figure of Army Surgeon Brydon bringing news of the annihilation of 17,000 of his colleagues who had set out to conquer Afghanistan for the British.

Despite the bloody nose of that terrible defeat in 1842, the British returned to Khyber almost 50 years later. Recognizing that the Afghans could not be subdued by war, they sought to keep them in their place by peaceful treaty. Having made a deal with Kabul, they instructed Mortimer Durand to invent a border between Afghanistan and Queen Victoria's India.

To make things easier for everybody Durand marked the borderline with giant numerals engraved on the foothills, and they can still be seen on the Afghan side of the pass. '1', '2', '3', '4'. The limits of the British Empire.

The Durand Line made no sense, then or now, to the Pathans who live on either side of it, nor does it appear to have made much sense to the generations of British squaddies sent to guard it, who accorded this bleak spot a memorable place in Cockney rhyming slang. Khyber Pass, Arse. (Khyber is locally pronounced with a soft 'K', so 'Carry On Up the Khyber' would, with Pashto inflection, become 'Harry On Up the Hyber'.)

But the Pakistan army of today takes the border very seriously, and they have provided an ambitious plaster model that mirrors the terrain ahead of me: the dark shadows of the mountains, the low brown hills, and the long and winding road that twists and turns between them.

'Such a river of life as nowhere else exists in the world', is how Kipling described the road that crosses the Khyber Pass. It was first laid nearly 500 years ago by the Afghan Emperor Sher Shah Suri to connect the extremes of his territory, Kabul in Afghanistan and Dacca in Bengal. In those days it was said that an unaccompanied woman could travel its 1500-mile (2400 km) length without fear or hindrance.

The British later paved it and christened it the Grand Trunk Road. Abbreviated to the colloquial 'GT Road', it remains to this day one of the most important transport arteries on the subcontinent.

Railways, rather than roads, were the status symbols of Britain's empire, and it was inevitable that there would eventually have to be a railway up to the Khyber. Construction began in the 1920s, amply fulfilling the criteria for a colonial railway, being both expensive and difficult to build.

At the cost of some £100,000 a mile, a line was squeezed for 27 miles through the rocky foothills between Peshawar and the Afghan border, an impressive burrowing job requiring 34 tunnels and 92 bridges and cuttings.

Though the last mile or two is now a spectacular no-man's land of abandoned viaducts and fallen arches, the line from Peshawar to Landi Khotal has been kept open for its tourist value.

Recent business has been badly hit by post 9/11 security scares and, for a while, the British Foreign Office was advising travellers not to come to Pakistan at all, so it's not surprising that Landi Khotal station is quiet as the breeze this morning as I wait for the train, which, I'm reliably informed, is the first to have left Peshawar for three months.

A group of teenage boys is fascinated by our presence. They form a circle around me, curious, unthreatening and very close.

'D'you live round here?' I ask their ringleader.

He replies in English with a toss of the head, confidently, if eccentrically.

'Why not?'

'D'you see many people from England here?'

'From England? Why not?'

I ask him if he's working.

'I have finished school. I have no job. There are no jobs here.'

'Have you brothers and sisters?'

'Why not?'

'How many?'

'We are 30 in our family.'

We're interrupted by a distant wheezing hiss and the whoop of a train whistle and as we turn, there, breasting the incline into the station, is a surreal snapshot of Empire.

Despite the silver-painted crescent moon and star of Islam on their noses, the breathless pair of geriatric locomotives that gasp to a halt beside me were built in Britain, in 1916. They draw two tankers of fuel and two coaches, from which descends a well-behaved group: workers from a bank in Islamabad, an imposing white-haired Welshman who is headmaster of an exclusive private school in Peshawar, prosperous-looking businessmen with cameras and binoculars and their unveiled wives. A band, immaculately turned out in plumed hats, tartan scarves and white gaiters, dismounts from the train. With a flourish of the bandmaster's silver-topped baton, the sound of drum and bagpipe mingles with the sighing of steam engines and the polite chatter of disembarked passengers. Only the presence of black-clad Pathan policemen with rifles spoils the powerful impression of having been transported back to an Edwardian house party.

A short, harassed man, carefully turned out in polo shirt and slacks, seeks me out and introduces himself as Zahoor Durrani, the man whose travel company keeps the Khyber Railway alive. He has organized today's outing. Included in the price of the ticket is a lunch and, there being no facilities of any kind at the station, Zahoor buses us to the Khyber Rifles Officers' Mess, where this nor-mally arid landscape of rock and scree is cloaked with green lawns, rose-beds and ancient maple and walnut trees. A buffet lunch is served from a tent, after which we're entertained by military dancers in local costume. The dance seems a little camp at first, with much tossing of heads and raising of knees, when, quite suddenly, from among scarves and voluminous tunics the dancers produce rifles, which they loose off in time to the music. This, I'm assured, is how they celebrate in the Tribal Areas, and I'm just relieved that there are no US warplanes within range.

Back aboard the train, we pull out of Landi Khotal as the track cuts through successive outcrops of bare rock, amplifying the shriek of the bogies into ear-splitting howls. Then the walls of a longer gorge begin to close in, and the heat of the day and the stench of the furnace become almost unbearable.

We grind to a halt in one of the tunnels, trapped like bread in a toaster, and are only saved from suffocation at the very last minute, when the cow that was blocking the tunnel is persuaded to move.

The last miles of the journey are less fraught, a slow glide into the wide Vale of Peshawar, with time to indulge the voyeuristic pleasures of railway travel: surreptitious views over high walls into courtyards and back gardens, glimpses of life backstage, where mothers and wives prepare food and hang out the washing, and children carry bundles of wood and bring the cows and goats home. As the train passes it gives a look-at-me whistle. The animals run away from it, the children run towards it, and the women stare with a frank curiosity they'd never allow themselves if their men folk were about.

On the outskirts of Peshawar we pass one of the newest cities in Pakistan, the Kachi Gahi refugee camp, thought to be the largest in the world. It grew up in 1982 to deal with the displacement of Afghans after the Soviet invasion. Because the Afghans are great entrepreneurs, trade has thrived here and almost anything from guns to drugs to washing machines is available in Smuggler's Bazaar, the heart of this warren of sheds and shacks. Since the fall of the Taliban the trickle of overladen trucks returning to Afghanistan has become a flood, yet 1.5 million refugees remain in this camp alone. And this is a fraction of the 18 million displaced people for whom Pakistan is their temporary home.

Zahoor Duranni tells me all this without any emotion, other than some quiet pride that his country has dealt with this enormous burden without complaint.

He gestures down towards the sprawling camp.

'We're all the same people.'

Day Two : Peshawar

It's 7.30 in the morning and the throng of humanity I saw at the refugee camps last night is reproduced on the streets of Peshawar. Beside the Grand Trunk Road is the Bala Hisar, a huge and sprawling pink brick fortress that seems to have squeezed civilian life into a crush of nearby side streets.

Zahoor tells me that most of the people here are small farmers in town for the day to buy and sell. This is peasant capitalism, with no co-operatives or supermarket chains getting in the way as individuals set up stalls or simply open bundles of whatever they have, wherever they want.

There is a loose sort of organization. Chargan Mandi is the chicken market, Sabzi Mandi is the vegetable market and Chour Bazaar is basically Things Fallen Off The Back Of A Lorry market.

Zahoor advises us to remove all BBC stickers from our vehicles.

'Just to be safe,' he says, apologetically. There are plenty of Taliban sympathizers among these milling crowds, and with the highly unpopular Iraq war only recently over, our presence here in the conservative North-West Frontier Province makes us, though he never actually uses the word, targets. Hence our police escort and the armed guard deputed to stay by my side at all times.

I understand their concern, but emphasizing our separateness seems only to serve the purpose of those who want to keep people apart. It saddens me that extremists, on both sides, should have pre-empted the natural act of communication.

We drink some green tea at a smoky café with a dark and cheerful interior, and carry on regardless. There is so much to take in. The profusion of stuff. Mangoes from the Punjab piled up alongside bananas from Sind Province to the south, onions, squash, pears, peaches, a wheelbarrow of apricots being heaved through the crowd by a tiny old man, two young boys carrying nets to catch pigeons, which they will later sell. Beside a pick-up, a group of men are squatting down. One of them scoops up a half-dozen live chicks, stuffing them into a small cloth bag and pulling the drawstring tight. At a shop-front behind them a man sits cross-legged stirring rice and meat in a pan the size of a small pond.

There is a sudden flurry of movement. Traders pick up their

wares and abandon their pitches, as, preceded by a lugubrious wail, a diesel locomotive looms up from nowhere, towering above the crowds and heading for the very heart of the market. At the very last minute, and with considerable reluctance, the throng parts to allow the nine o'clock to Karachi to continue its 1100-mile cross-country journey.

No sooner has the last coach rumbled through than the market reassembles, with little more than a vague irritation on the part of the traders that they should have to share *their* railway track with trains.

Peshawar, whose name means 'The Place at the Frontier', is the first big city on the Pakistan side of the Khyber Pass and was once encircled by a stout protective wall, with 16 gates to allow travellers and merchants through. One of the first places they gathered was Qissa Khwani Bazaar, which means Storyteller Street, for it was here that voyagers to and from the west would swap tales of the outside world.

Today, Storyteller Street has become Dental Alley. In between the photocopiers, money-changers and electric fan shops is a profusion of premises hung with painted signs depicting gleaming gnashers clamped tight between wholesomely pink gums.

I enter a tiny, hexagonal room at the base of one of the remaining stone towers of the Kabuli Gate. Most of the space is taken up by the impressive bulk of Abdul Wahid, proprietor of the Khyber Dentist Clinic.

Stone walls keep the clinic pleasantly cool, but it's impossible to keep out the roar of Peshawar's mighty traffic. An unbroken succession of private buses, turning out of the junction with Hospital Street, hoot furiously at each other while their conductors shout for business, yelling their destinations, selling tickets on the move and, when full, slapping the sides of their vehicles with cacophonous panache.

I've spent a lifetime in dental treatment of one kind or another, so I'm quite interested to see how Mr Wahid works. I squeeze into his chair, taking care not to dislodge the ominously placed green plastic bucket beside it. As I settle back I find myself staring at a wall decorated with a pair of dentures and a copy of the Koran.

The side walls are hung with various examples of gnasher-related art work: a collage of glamorous lady film stars with big toothy

grins, a framed set of photos of drills at work in diseased mouths
(fortunately in black and white) and a faded chart depicting 'The
Four Steps Of Dental Decay'.

I avert my eyes, only to catch sight of an ancient rusty drill,
standing to one side of the chair like a withered arm.

With fingers the size of small trees, Abdul Wahid stretches my
mouth into a rictal grin and feels around inside, squeezing each
tooth in a vice-like grip. He doesn't seem impressed by my Disney-
land of caps and bridges, and suggests I give up using toothpaste
and use powder and my finger instead.

His charges are reasonable: 100–300 rupees (£1–£3) for an extrac-
tion, fillings from as little as 50p and a full set of acrylic dentures
from £15, though these look as though they may have been enjoyed
by more than one previous owner.

If artistic self-expression has an outlet in Peshawar it seems to be
in transport. Taxis, buses, auto-rickshaws and trucks are rampantly
customized, bedecked with lurid colours, gleaming attachments,
chrome strips, mirrors, glittering lights, prods, protuberances and
general ornamentation that would have them instantly pulled over
by the police in any Western city.

Zahoor takes me to a grimy yard on the outskirts of the city,
where a half-dozen trucks are being beautified by teams of painters
and mechanics, welders and artists, working side by side in Ruskin-
ian harmony. They're assisted by a number of young boys, helping
out fathers, uncles and cousins, and learning how to strip down
gear-boxes long before their voices break.

Decoration is ubiquitous and uninhibited. No inch of the
vehicle, apart from the windscreen and the tyres, remains
unadorned. Everywhere else is covered in whatever the owner and
artist agree on, from abstract shapes to animals, birds, flowers,
vignettes of mountain scenery, roadside views, Koranic verses,
names and Roman numerals.

A fringe of painted chains hangs down from the bumpers like
beads on a flapper's dress. Multicoloured hubcaps protrude from
the wheels, a combination of Damien Hirst and Boadicea.

We're offered tea in grubby enamel cups as one of the master
painters begins work on the tailgate of a truck. A green base has
already been applied (green being the colour of Islam) and he is
now, with extraordinary speed and confidence, sketching the

outline of a partridge, a bird held in high regard by the Pathans, who believe it has many powers including the exorcism of devils.

Less than an hour later the partridge is six feet high and standing proudly on top of a pile of stones in a romantic alpine landscape of lakes, snow-capped mountains, and houses set on tree-lined river banks, above which a name has been delicately picked out in Pashto. 'The Flower of Durband', a reference to the owner's home village.

The head and his team of seven take a week to decorate a truck from start to finish, for which they charge 15,000 rupees (£150).

By the time we get back to the hotel, exhausted but exhilarated by the intensity of life here, I'm ready for a beer at the Gulbar, about the only place in Peshawar where alcohol can legally be sold, to non-Muslims only of course. But the doors are firmly closed, bound together with adhesive tape. A sticker announces that the bar has been 'sealed off' until further notice, by order of the local authorities.

I learn later that this has nothing to do with hygiene or any trading malpractice. It's to do with moves by the MMA, the conservative Islamist majority in the local assembly, to introduce Sharia law on the North-West Frontier.

The Sharia law would not only ban alcohol for foreigners (hardly a nightmare) but close cinemas, ban non-religious music, forbid male doctors to examine women, forbid male tailors to make garments for women, and make failure to pray punishable by law.

Eat at the hotel's Chinese restaurant and, with only tea to linger over, am back in my room by nine. A small sticker is attached to the desktop in my bedroom. On it is an arrow indicating the direction of Mecca, and a card, which reads 'For Prayer Mat Dial 47'.

Day Three : South to Darra Adam Khel

Islam has been dominant in this part of the world since AD 711, when Muhammad Bin Qasim of Damascus conquered the Indus valley, which had been Buddhist for hundreds of years. Islam was once at the forefront of cultural and political progress but now, it seems, up here on the North-West Frontier, it's being taken in the opposite direction.

Certainly the belligerence of the Iraq war and the incompetence of the peace has given the Islamists great new material as they pursue their goal of oppressive obedience.

The world is, fortunately, never clear and simple, and as we ride south to Darra Adam Khel, a town devoted almost entirely to the production of guns, I find myself confused by Zahoor's defence of such a place. Weapons, he says, have always been important to the proud, unconquered people who live on the North-West Frontier.

'For them,' he explains, 'a gun is a social necessity. Pathans carry guns the way Londoners carry umbrellas.'

What's more, he claims that the existence of and respect for the gun has reduced crime and kept order.

'Charlton Heston would be proud of them,' I suggest.

Zahoor nods seriously.

'He was in Peshawar.'

Why should I not be surprised that Charlton Heston was in Peshawar? The common ground is, of course, the West. The Wild West and the North-West Frontier have so much in common: proud, patriarchal societies with a marked dislike of outside interference, and strict moral codes of their own.

One of the twin pillars of Pathan tribal society is the concept of *melmastia* – hospitality. Unfortunately, the other is *badal* – revenge – which can be swift and violent and provoked by as little as a glance at someone else's wife.

A few miles due south of Peshawar, we're halted at a barrier marking the transition between what are called the Settled Areas and the Tribal Areas. Beyond this our Peshawar police escort has no jurisdiction, so they are replaced by thinner, less well-equipped Tribal police who seem delighted to see us. We pull out behind them onto a busy road full of toiling over-loaded trucks heading south in the direction of Karachi.

In the fields veiled women bend in rows, cutting sheaves of corn, and beside the road schoolboys are playing cricket in their uniform blue *shalwar-kameez*, the combination of long shirt over loose baggy trousers that is Pakistan's national dress.

Darra High Street, described by Geoffrey Moorhouse as 'the noisiest street in the world', runs for almost a mile and is filled with the roar of horn-blaring, gear-changing trucks punctuated by the crackle of gun-fire.

You never quite know where the shots are coming from. As I cross the street a preoccupied figure in a white robe pops out of a shop behind me, raises an AK-47, blasts a few rounds into the air, shakes his head and disappears inside again to make adjustments.

Seeking relief from the din, I walk into a small arcade running at right angles off the main street. It is, to all intents and purposes, an arms mall, consisting of everything from workshops to carpeted rooms where you can select the weapon of your choice while taking tea with the management. In one establishment an earnest, bespectacled young man sits cross-legged, fashioning a trigger for a mini-Kalashnikov using pliers and a small hammer. Next door to him an older, bearded man scrutinizes a freshly made Mauser like a scholar bent over sacred texts.

The equipment may be low-tech but the standard of plagiarism is extremely high. Originally confined to making copies of the British Army's great standby, the Lee Enfield .303, Darra's retailers now offer brand-name pump-action rifles, revolvers, automatics and quite probably rocket-launchers. One man proudly shows me a James Bond pen that can fire real bullets (he proves this to me by stepping out into the street and loosing it off).

'Very popular with the tourists,' he assures me, adding regretfully, 'Until two years ago.'

Everything in Darra is faintly bizarre, so I'm not entirely surprised when, out of the corner of my eye, I spot an elderly man with a long white beard apparently climbing into a litter bin. Once inside he bobs down out of sight, and the crew think I've made the whole thing up until his face reappears over the top of the bin and, rearranging his robe, he steps out and proceeds on his way.

The grey, serrated steel tub that would in Britain be either a bin or a council flower bed turns out to be one of the smallest public lavatories I've ever seen. Barely three feet high, it sits astride a narrow concrete culvert along which water flows, though not, I notice, today.

A young man approaches and asks me where I'm from. Yesterday in Peshawar he would have been moved on pretty quickly, but today my police escort is nowhere to be seen. I later learn they're down the main street having their photo taken by Basil.

The young man speaks English well, but claims he's the exception. There is a lack of money for education and most men of his age have little option but to leave school early and go straight into the gun-making business. When he hears I'm from the BBC he is complimentary. Everyone listens to their Pashto service in the evenings. They are trusted, but less so after the Iraq war.

I bridle a little. Would he rather Saddam Hussein had remained in power?

He shakes his head vehemently. He hated Saddam Hussein. He hated him because he accepted American help to fight a fellow Islamic country, Iran.

I'm embarrassingly aware how much longer his memory is than mine.

Day Four : Fateh jang

We've already had to postpone our trip to see Prince Malik Ata. Mysterious objections from the government seem to centre around a security problem. Something vaguely to do with bombs and the military. As the Prince lives in the middle of agricultural country-side no-one can understand what all the fuss is about, least of all him.

After a volley of phone calls the objections have been withdrawn and he has promised to lay on a special welcome to make up for any inconvenience.

So we find ourselves heading east along the GT Road, crossing the great River Indus, which, along with the Tigris and Euphrates, nourished the first urban civilizations in the world. When Alexander the Great reached this point he ordered a half-mile bridge of boats to be built to carry his 50,000-strong army across. Today, much of the flow has been diverted for irrigation, but the sight of one of the world's great rivers rolling below the battlements of the old fort at Attock makes the heart beat a little faster.

Once off the Trunk Road we meander along country lanes. Brick kilns are the only signs of industry; otherwise it's quietly rural. At one point we pass a funeral. A small procession, led by a group of men dressed head to foot in white is carrying the body through the bush. They all appear to be hurrying.

The entrance to Prince Malik's country estate consists of modest cast-iron gates set between concrete posts. Once through them we follow a long, secretive track through acacia thickets, which, after almost half a mile, opens out onto a rather grand avenue of maples, beneath which a small crowd struggles to control a number of stocky, short-legged bulls wearing scarlet pom-pom hats and garlands round their necks. An open, four-wheeled carriage with a plumed and turbanned rider at the reins stands waiting behind two chestnut palominos. Fifteen elderly men in white *shalwars* and black-trimmed gold waistcoats are drawn to attention. One or two of them carry rifles. All are having orders barked at them by a figure in a brilliant white cotton *shalwar* and tight black sleeveless tunic sitting astride a black stallion. Beneath a bulbous turban, a magnificently curled moustache dominates a fleshy face. A pair of watery, aristocratic eyes turns towards us.

'We must go soon, I cannot hold the bulls much longer.'

Roger steps down from the vehicle, exchanges greetings and begins to explain how he intends to shoot the sequence. But Malik Ata Muhammed Khan, Prince of the Awans, is not the slightest bit interested.

'You will put Michael in the coach over there!' he decides. 'Then I will tell them to begin the procession, and your camera will get a good shot from here.'

There is clearly no point in arguing, and I hurry back down the drive to the waiting carriage.

'Michael!' he bawls after me. 'Walk round the side! Those bulls are dangerous!'

As if to prove his point, one of them breaks free of its restraining rope, snorts, lowers its head and kicks out (maybe in protest at having to wear a scarlet pom-pom hat). Someone goes down.

'Right! Start now!'

It doesn't seem to matter that no-one really knows what they're doing. It all looks absurdly colourful and manically vibrant, like the opening scene of a musical. The bulls are led forward, the veteran guard of honour present whatever arms they can lay their hands on, and my two glorious palominos, who seem to be quietly giggling to each other throughout, set off at a canter that turns into an unstoppable gallop.

Cries of 'That's far enough!' fade into the distance as we hurtle through a set of grand gates, and up garden paths, eventually pulling to a halt at the front of a large white mansion with wide, presidential steps leading up to a towering columned portico.

I'm told it's modelled on the Royal Military College, Sandhurst, though it reminds me more of a plantation house in Louisiana.

Now that he's orchestrated the grand welcome the Prince is off his charger and visibly relaxed. He organizes drinks for us. Retainers (probably not the right word, but they behave exactly like retainers) carry trays of Pepsi Cola out into the garden. I suggest to him that a place of this size must be an awful burden to keep up.

'It is only one,' Prince Malik replies breezily, 'I have four others.'

I ask him about the episode with the bulls earlier.

'Was anyone hurt?'

'Yes,' he says, rather dismissively, as if it happened all the time. 'One old fellow had his arm broken. I've sent him to the hospital.'

The Prince calls forward one of the faithful fifteen who had mounted the guard of honour for my arrival.

'Here is a chap you must meet, Michael.'

A slightly stooped, handsome old man with lively eyes and a fine white beard steps out of the line.

'He fought in the First World War, you know. He's 104. He was a very big man.'

He turns a little towards me, lowering his voice.

'Much smaller now of course.'

The Prince seems to have a thing about height. He talks proudly of his great-grandfather, of whom he has a photograph taken at George V's coronation.

'He was a big man. Seven foot two.'

He has ordered lunch to be prepared for us. As we go inside he chides Vanessa about the problems we have had getting permission to come here.

'Always ask the army. It's the only discipline there is in this country. Did you not get my email?'

Vanessa shakes her head.

'Then your computer is wrong. Burn it.'

There seems to be almost too much space inside the house. Even without seeing any of the 28 bedrooms, I feel it in the dining room, with its high empty walls and giant table on which the eight places set out for us barely make an impression.

'D'you eat here even when you're on your own?' I ask the Prince.

'My father told me never to dine alone,' he replies briskly. 'If I have no-one to dine with, I go outside and find someone.'

At one end of the gloomy room, tall green electric fans are

clustered together, heads bowed like dormant sunflowers. At the other, there is a marble mantelpiece on which is framed a front page of *The Times* with a photo of Prince Malik tent-pegging in Hyde Park.

'I was the champion tent-pegger in Pakistan. It is a very difficult thing to do you know.'

With some relish he describes the origins of the sport.

'When attacking a camp the first wave of horsemen would go in early in the morning and uproot the tent by its pegs, revealing the dazed occupants doing…' he pauses, 'whatever they might be doing. Then the next wave of slightly less skilful troops comes in and cuts off their heads.'

At this he rocks with laughter. A man in a turban, with all the aplomb of a *maître de vin*, tops up my glass of Pepsi-Cola from a plastic bottle.

As the food is brought round Prince Malik enlarges on his life and reveals a keenly felt regret for the passing of the old ways. He is a countryman, not at all happy in the city. He loves country sports and rides at least twice a day for several hours.

'I am the last of the dinosaurs, who live like this. Who organize entertainments for the people. The new generation are only interested in becoming technocrats.'

More food issues forth from the Stygian gloom of the kitchen, ending up with a particularly delicious concoction of almond, egg and honey.

'The honey is off my land. It is very good. Have some more.' He pushes a bottle of Côtes du Rhône towards me. It's full of honey, not wine.

In the afternoon, despite the great heat, he insists that we visit the fort in Fatehjang. This is where the local *jerga*, or council of elders, meets. Recently they dealt with a vendetta that had gone on so long between two families that 13 had been killed on both sides. At the *jerga* they agreed that there would be no more killings, and, having forsworn further violence on the Holy Koran, the feud was declared to be at an end, with none of the murderers facing trial. Prince Malik shrugs.

'That is the way it works in the country.'

He insists that, if we are really interested in the rural life, we must come along as his guests to a bull-race in nearby Taxila tomorrow. Of course we can't say no. He wouldn't let us.

Day Five: Taxila

Taxila, at the axis of routes connecting Central Asia with Persia and the south, is one of the oldest continuously populated cities on earth. A university was thriving here 2500 years ago and remains of Buddhist temples, monasteries and stupas indicate its importance long before Islam or Christianity were born.

Following a narrow road through olive groves and fields of peanuts, we pull up a low hill until we reach an encampment where the animals are being unloaded from the back of trucks. Stalls selling food and soft drinks have been erected.

To get to the course means negotiating various ridges and ditches, behind, and sometimes alongside, swaying pairs of bulls, led out by owners and supporters to a relentless squealing of pipes and thumping of drums, each group trying to make more noise than their rivals.

There's such a squeeze that it's impossible to avoid bull contact. To my relief, they're smaller than the bulls I had a close encounter with in Pamplona. Of a breed called Dhanni, they have short legs, a distinctive fatty crest curling out from their shoulders and are mostly white with splodgy black markings that look as if someone has thrown a pot of paint at them. Today, each one is turned out in their party best, their ferocity compromised by brightly coloured medallions and favours, ribbons and rosettes, gaudy horn-dressings and fluffy pom-poms. One wretched beast, with a tasselled, silver-trimmed, see-through muslin coat thrown over him, looks as if he's just stampeded through a lingerie department.

Ahead of the melee I can see the course, a wide stretch of open field, 600 yards long, marked by red flags on tall poles. Beside it and about halfway down the course a truck and trailer have been decked out with red chairs protected by a huge and ornate sun awning. Beneath it sits the unmistakable figure of the Prince.

He's in ebullient mood, which could be something to do with the presence of two tall, slim, European girls among his guests. He's already been out riding with them this morning.

With the racing about to begin, we ask if we can film up at the start, where a big crowd is milling around.

The Prince looks doubtful for a moment then barks an order and a man rushes over.

'He will go with you. He has a gun and speaks English.'

The bulls race in pairs, yoked together with heavy wooden frames called *joots*, from which the reins run back to a rider, who stands, as best he can, on a small board with a metal base, little more than a glorified tin-lid.

While dozens of people grapple to get the *joot* onto the two sets of shoulders, the bulls are kicking up the dust as they duck and weave and back up in a desperate attempt to avoid being involved in the racing in any way. Once harnessed, the animals are dragged unceremoniously to the starting line. Outriders heave them into position while the jockey, nervously clutching a flag on a stick, readies himself to spring onto the board the moment the bulls are released. This is where the race is won or lost. The bulls' desire to get away must be timed exactly with the attachment of the rider to his board. With luck the jockey retains his balance, and the bulls race off with the outriders running alongside to keep them in a straight line, before letting go, slapping the bulls' hides with a valedictory shout, and leaving the crouched figure to scud across the bumpy, uneven surface like a terrestrial water-skier, hanging on for dear life.

As if this isn't perilous enough, some enthusiastic teams throw firecrackers to 'panic' their bull into even greater speeds.

One team loses control at the start and the bulls make a 90-degree turn and plunge headfirst into the crowd. Two more hurtle off towards a flagpole that Basil has chosen as a photo-position, taking out the flag and almost Basil as well as they race off the course to the freedom of the fresh-cut wheat fields beyond.

Prince Malik says this only confirms that bulls aren't stupid. They know that their best interest lies in getting rid of their handlers as soon as possible, by any means possible. As he's explaining this a pair that seemed to be going well take an inexplicable left turn and head straight towards us. Nigel and Pete, filming with their backs to the course, are the last to notice. Grabbing the camera and tripod they dive for cover as Prince Malik roars helpfully.

'Under the truck! Always under the truck!'

At the end of the day, as the racing is drawing to a close and the heat haze fades to reveal the low, reassuring contours of the Margalla Hills to the north, we're treated to a meal at a nearby village. It's laid out in suitably princely style, with dishes of tikkas and masalas in silver salvers on long tables and local specialities of partridge and quail.

'Now, quail racing,' the Prince enthuses, 'that is where the big money goes. You know, small fortunes are won or lost on quail races.'

As ever, I'm not entirely sure where fact and fiction merge in Prince Malik's stories, but before we can question him further, he shakes hands and apologizes that he must return to the course for the prize-giving.

'And those quails, Michael. They are not from a farm. They are shot in the forest.'

A countryman to the last.

Day Seven: Peshawar to the Kalash Valleys

It's a few minutes after five and just getting light as our convoy negotiates the suburbs of Peshawar. By the end of today, all being well, we should be off the plain and experiencing our first taste of big mountain scenery in the heart of the Hindu Kush range.

In the soft morning light pony and traps loaded with produce head for the city markets, boys cross a river on a gently undulating wooden bridge, a thin strip of black smoke drifts from a brick kiln, and in the fields figures are already at work bringing in the harvest.

We rumble across the wide and powerful waters of the River Kabul, swelled with snowmelt and curling back against the stanchions of a long steel bridge. It's joined in turn by the River Swat, creating a green and fertile plain, with fields of sugar cane and tobacco interspersed with orchards of plums, apricots and pears.

We pull off the road for something to eat at a hotel of very few stars but quite a lot of what the guides call charm. Along a wide verandah, tables with wonky legs are set out on a mud floor. Instead of chairs there are the ubiquitous charpoys, bedsteads with rope bases that are quite uncomfortable to sit on, but as soon as you pull your legs up and stretch out, make absolute sense.

Bleary staff appear from dark rooms and I realize that, although we've been on the road for more than two hours, it's still only half-past seven.

After a breakfast of bananas, hard-boiled eggs, green tea, fresh chapattis and malaria tablets I'm back in the jeep and climbing out of the plain and up to the Malakand Pass.

Here, on the endemically war-like North-West Frontier, almost any pass or prominence bears a fortification of some kind, ranging from fully-fledged fortresses to barricaded look-out points they call picquets or pickets. The best known of these is still called Churchill's Picket, where the great man, then a reporter for the *Daily Telegraph*, was holed up in 1897. A force of 1000 British and Sikh soldiers was defying an army of 10,000 Pathans, led by one Hajji Shaib Balee, whom the British press quickly, if predictably, christened the Mad Mullah. Young Winston sent back a blood-curdling account of the dangers they faced. 'Death by inches and hideous mutilation are the invariable measure of all who fall in battle into the hands of the Pathan tribesmen.'

I can hear him saying it.

The sun is well up now, but the roads badly kept and progress increasingly slow. My feeling of good fortune in being here at all is tempered by constant bumping and jarring and an enveloping cloud of dust and exhaust fumes from the vehicle in front.

Maqsood Ul-Mulk, who has organized our journey today, is a comfortably built man in his early forties with an amused air of quiet contentment, which may well come from being a member of the family who've ruled the Chitral Valley for several generations. He points across at the far bank of the River Panjkora, which runs beside us at a fast, muddy grey lick. The road is better over there, because it used to be a big poppy growing area. The central government, under a new policy headlined Poppy-Free Pakistan, offered new roads and houses if the locals agreed to change from opium to less controversial crops. They accepted the offer.

'What do they grow now?' I ask.

Maqsood gives the hint of a smile.

'Onions.'

A bad road becomes atrocious as we wind up to the 10,000-foot Lowari Pass. Closed by snow for six months of the year, this lifeline to the Chitral Valley has only just reopened and the soft-top track has wilted badly under the weight of over-loaded trucks struggling to restock the valley after the long winter.

The rapidly decomposing track climbs tortuously up above the snow line, slicing through sheer ice walls at the end of dirty brown glaciers, negotiating fast flowing streams of melt-water that tumble across the road before being flung into waterfalls below. The sun is blotted out by drifting grey clouds and hailstones scatter across the windscreen. With much blasting of horns and squeezing past trucks stalled on perilous precipices, we eventually obtain the top of the pass, marked by a small stone hut and a low wall of plastic-wrapped soft drinks.

Our drivers can't celebrate yet, for the road on the other side is even worse, a sheer plunge, which we ease down with the help of 47 sweaty-palmed hairpin bends. Tree trunks stripped bare by avalanche dot the route like tombstones.

Thirteen and a half hours after leaving Peshawar, we are down into the valley and gliding onto tarmacked road again.

By now it's dark and though it's frustratingly hard to see what's out there, I have a sense of being somewhere special. The stars are white as pearls and homes are lit by single lamps and the flicker of wood-fires.

A further three hours later one of the most spectacularly beautiful and consistently uncomfortable journeys I can remember draws to an end as we reach our home for the night, a plain and simple guesthouse above the tumbling waters of a young mountain river. And I was right. It is somewhere special. There are women without veils and wine to drink and villagers with clear blue eyes. This is a very unusual part of Pakistan.

Day Eight : The Kalash Valleys

All night long the river keeps up a light roar, which, in my semi-sleep, becomes transmogrified into the rumble of an ancient air-conditioner. Finally woken by sunlight as hard and bright as Excalibur, I take in the simple tongue and groove walls, flimsy curtains and bare floor of the cabin I'm sharing with Basil, and conclude that this is not air-con territory. Through the window I have my first glimpse of a narrow twisting valley and an extended village of stone-walled houses squeezed along it.

The village of Rumbur takes its name from the river that runs through it, one of a number of steep and vigorous torrents cutting down through the mountains that separate the Chitral Valley from Afghanistan, chiselling out well-concealed canyons that have for centuries been the refuge of a tribe quite distinct from the rest of

Pakistan. They have their own language, dress, customs and religion and because they are non-Muslim they have been historically known as Kafirs (Infidels), and this tight little land of theirs as Kafiristan.

Today they are better known as the Kalash ('black') after the colour of their clothes, despite the incidence of light skin, fair hair and blue eyes, which some say marks them out as descendants of Alexander the Great's soldiers.

Pale faces look curiously at us over the dry-stone wall that divides our compound from the lane outside. The fact that some of them are women is a great contrast with the rest of the North-West Frontier, where the rule of purdah is so strictly observed that no woman will look you in the face in public.

The Kalash ladies who peer so frankly at us, often dissolving into giggles at what they see, wear wide black dresses, tied with woollen scarves with multicoloured threads attached and strips of coloured ribbon on hems and cuffs. Their hair, which they never cut, is braided or plaited tight against the scalp and a long headdress, decorated with beads and cowrie shells, runs down from their crown to below their waist.

Saifullah Khan, a man of around 40 with grey threads in his thick dark hair and a face broad and olive-skinned as a Spanish farmer, is proprietor of the guesthouse and spokesman for the community. He's the only one of the Kalash to have received an education outside the village and after a breakfast of walnut bread he takes us on a walk around, pointing out this and that and constantly hitching up the pants of a grubby brown *shalwar-kameez* as he does so.

We're at 6500 feet (1980 m) and as the Kalash live in a largely pre-industrial state, with almost no modern gadgetry of any kind, the air is clear and fresh. Two small hydroelectric generators provide what electricity is needed; otherwise, life is entirely based around agriculture. The women till the fields in traditional costume while the men look after the livestock. The houses, stout and stone-walled, are tiered up on top of each other to save space, with one person's roof another's front porch. They have neither gabled roofs nor chimneys and the smoke from the open fires has to find its way out of a hole in the ceiling.

It's picturesque and soothingly quiet, but as we walk through the village there are signs that all is not well. Children have runny noses and dirty faces, their clothes are grubby and their eyes often red and watery from the wood smoke that fills the houses. Faces show the effects of in-breeding and for each smile we get there will be another dull, dejected, vacant glance. Though Saifullah is proud and protective of his community, he can't disguise the problems. The Kalash, infidels, squeezed to the very edge of their country, are neither powerful nor numerous. Rumbur consists of 50 families, about 300 people, and the combined population of the Kalash villages is around 4000.

Their best hope of survival is tourism. Aware of the potential, the government has given them better roads and schools that teach Urdu and English, but of the money charged for permits to visit the Kalash valleys Saifullah reckons only 5 per cent finds its way through to the community.

In a stone hut with an irrigation channel running through it, an old man on his haunches watches barley being ground between two stones turned by the force of water. A few yards further on there is a handsome new suspension bridge that allows vehicles right up into the village. The road passes a long, low building with a high wall snaking around it. This is the menstruating hut. Kalash theology has very strong notions of purity and impurity. Menstruation is confirmation of women's impurity, and when their periods begin they must leave their homes and enter a communal house.

Mothers must give birth in the hut and remain there for 20 days afterwards. Only after undergoing a purification ceremony can they return home and rejoin village life.

We climb a hill above the village through glades of juniper and mulberry. Halfway up, I catch the sharp, sweet smell of something rotten. Ahead of me are small piles of wood and glass and I realize we're picking our way through a graveyard. Saifullah seems unconcerned as he points out decomposing coffins on top of the ground. That's the Kalash way of death, he says. The bodies are never buried and the tops of the coffins are often left open to let the souls escape. I fear souls must have escaped quite recently.

At the top of the hill the modern world intrudes again in the shape of a long, open-sided building that looks like a bus shelter. This is another government perk, provided for the village as a permanent arena for the music and dancing for which the Kalash are renowned. Every year there is a music festival here that pulls in the tourists, many of whom come to see something unheard of in Pakistan: women dancing together in public. The emancipation of Kalash women has brought them the unwelcome attention of men from outside, seeking a sexual freedom denied to them in the rest of Pakistan.

Supper is very jolly. Saifullah's cooked some locally caught trout for us and produces a bottle of his home-brew, grape juice from last summer, which is still fermenting and tastes like fortified sherry.

Day Nine : To Chitral

Wake to the sound of water and the smell of wood smoke. After a couple of nights here I no longer feel cut off from the world, but protected from it, and not particularly anxious to move away. I can understand why Saifullah values the isolation that has shaped and strengthened this tight-knit community, and why he loves visitors so long as they don't want to change anything.

As our jeep rolls over the bridge and down the hill, the Rumbur valley narrows behind us until the village and the thin strips of green fields that sustain it disappear altogether, and we find ourselves descending through a tight, treeless gorge onto whose steep sides the track hangs by its fingernails. Nadir Begh, my driver, anxious at the best of times, never unfurrows his brow. He's less concerned by the precipice below than the rock wall above. Recently descended loose grey shale lies scattered across the road and he peers up in the air, accelerating forward at the slightest trickle of dust.

We're all relieved as the valley widens and reveals a perspective of broad mountain slopes that lead the eye remorselessly upwards to the solitary bulk of Tirich Mir, 25,228 feet (7708 m), the highest mountain in the Hindu Kush and, I realize, the highest mountain I've ever seen.

As we near Chitral, orchards and tranquil stretches of woodland cluster beside the road. We pass groups of men shaking mulberries from the trees with long sticks, and a line of very small children coming out of school, all dressed in vivid green *shalwar-kameezes* and looking like a procession of parrots.

The Hindu Kush Heights Hotel is set on the side of a hill with a fine view of the valley and Chitral town. Recently built, the emphasis is firmly on local design and craftsmanship at the expense of tel-evisions and mini-bars. In the garden the heat smells of rosemary and jasmine.

The owners and creators of this remarkable hotel are both of that great Chitral dynasty, the Ul-Mulk family. Siraj, a man of my own age and a one-time Pakistan Airlines pilot, is one of several sons of the last ruler or Mehtar (Persian for prince) of Chitral. His father was married to Siraj's mother for 80 years.

'They were two and four when they got married.'

Clean-shaven and soft-spoken, and wearing a Western shirt and trousers, Siraj is pale enough to pass for a suntanned Suffolk farmer, except for the flat, felt Pashtun cap, the *pakol*, which perches on top of the head in summer and rolls down for extra protection in the winter.

Though the Mehtar surrendered all his political powers to the Pakistani state in 1972, Siraj is still technically a prince and his wife Ghazala, with the piercing, dark eyes and intense good looks of the Pathan, a princess.

Three pet dogs help complete a sense of sharing a family house, rather than an impersonal hotel, and their guest book shows that they are by no means cut off up here in the valley. A framed photo shows the staff posing next to General Musharraf and on the wall by the door hangs a signed photo of thanks from Robert De Niro.

Ghazala is much amused that when De Niro came to stay, Siraj asked him what line of work he was in.

Despite their international clientele they observe the local custom. Ghazala, for instance, has elected to observe purdah and cannot walk into the town uncovered.

I join her and Siraj as they walk the dogs on the hillside behind the hotel. She enjoys this walk because she doesn't feel trapped by having to wear the veil. As we pick our way through artemisia scrub we talk about the two standards of behaviour. Though Pakistan's constitution makes no discrimination on grounds of gender, for traditional reasons most women choose to remain behind the veil. This cannot but result in some inequality, however self-inflicted, and it shows up in national literacy figures. For men literacy in Paki-stan is around 60 per cent; for women, 35 per cent.

Day Ten : Chitral

Chitral, a compact riverside town and centre of a close-knit valley community, has grown and prospered in recent years with the influx of Afghans, who came over the mountain passes during the Taliban years. Siraj reminds me that the border is less than 50 miles (80 km) to the west.

'You see, in winter we're cut off from the rest of Pakistan, but we're not cut off from Afghanistan.'

He's complimentary about the Afghan influence. They rejuvenated the sleepy town, bringing new cafés and restaurants, improving the choice of food in the shops, opening butchers, greengrocers, carpet-weaving and other businesses and generally demonstrating their talent as entrepreneurs. Now many of them are returning home and Chitral is once again reverting to its natural sleepiness.

There was a time, a hundred-odd years ago, when it was the British who were the new arrivals in Chitral. Seeing Chitral's western passes as potentially vulnerable back doors through which the expansionist Russians might steal into their Indian empire, they installed a garrison at the fort. The Great Game, as the rivalry between the two 19th-century superpowers came to be known, saw one of its more dramatic moves played out in Chitral in 1895.

The Ul-Mulk family were at the centre of events. Siraj's great-grandfather Aman died in 1892 after a 35-year reign, instigating a vicious war of succession in which his various sons quarrelled with, plotted against and killed each other, until one decided his best hope of survival was to create a local alliance aimed at throwing the British out of their kingdom.

The siege of Chitral may not be as well known as those of Khartoum or Mafeking, but it was pretty heroic stuff, as the defenders, mainly Sikh troops under British officers, forced to eat their horses to survive, held out for 48 days before being relieved by a force of men, mules and cannons that had marched over the high passes of the Hindu Kush in the middle of winter.

The fort where the horse-eaters held out is still there, sitting low on a promontory round which the muddy grey river swirls. Its 25-foot-high, 240-foot-long walls still stand, but they look a little sad, with plaster cracked and fallen away, revealing the bare bones underneath. Groves of tall trees loom over the bedraggled ramparts and beneath them contented cows chomp their way through fields of wild cannabis.

Chitral's ageing fort is upstaged by its neighbour, an exuberantly decorated mosque in a central Asian style with onion domes and white stucco, paid for by Siraj's grandfather in the 1920s.

I ask him if it was common for ruling families to sponsor mosques.

He laughs.

'Well, I suppose, like in England, they wanted God on their side.'

The sound of chanting comes from a long, columned chamber off the courtyard. We step inside. Sixty young boys are learning the Koran by heart. They kneel before copies of the Book, rocking backwards and forwards on their haunches as they recite.

A mullah sits at a small table, peering myopically at a text as he listens to a boy sitting in front of him.

'These boys are being forced to learn the Koran in Arabic, a language quite foreign to them,' whispers Siraj, as we watch.

'It's like reading prayers in Latin.'

Many of the boys watch us back, clearly much more interested in what we're doing than what they're learning.

Repetition of the Koran, at the expense of other subjects like science and maths, has become the main discipline of these *madrassas*, religious schools, which have increased in number since the Taliban was thrown out of Afghanistan and fled across the border.

'It won't last,' says Siraj. 'They have nothing much to offer the people.'

Polo, on the other hand, seems to have a lot to offer. Chitral's polo ground is a long, green rectangle behind the Mountain Inn, sloping up quite markedly at both ends.

An early evening training game is in progress, and even this draws a crowd of several hundred. As Siraj explains:

'Over here you don't have to be a rich man to play polo. You could be the most important person in Chitral, but if you happen to be playing on the field here you could be written off by your barber or your shoemaker.'

Polo thrived here on the border country after being introduced from Persia, and was known to be played on occasions with enemies' heads and sheep carcasses.

Unlike the international game, invented by the British, which is broken into seven-minute segments, at the end of which horses can be substituted, they play what they call 'free-style' polo, with no referee and no rules. Each chukka lasts 25 minutes, with no change of horses, unless one is injured.

At half-time, Siraj introduces me to the captain of the Chitral team, his brother Sikander, ten years his junior. He's hot and sweating after a first half in which he's been evaluating his new horse, Bucephalus. (Another example of the resonance of Alexander the Great, Sikander being a derivation of Alexander, whose favourite horse was Bucephalus.)

This is one of the last trial games before selection of the team to take on arch-rivals Gilgit in the biggest free-style polo match in the world.

It's to be played on the top of the 12,000-foot (3660 m) Shandur Pass, the highest point of the mountain road that connects the two competing communities. At least 5000 Chitral fans will make the journey up to the pass to support their team.

Sikander grins broadly, and grips my hand in a firm Ul-Mulk handshake.

'See you there!'

Day Twelve : Chitral

Therapeutic recovery time at Hindu Kush Heights. The food is good and varied here, cooked with a light touch and the emphasis on home-grown vegetables and treats like mushrooms off the mountains, quite a relief from the heavy curries of Peshawar. The scenery is magnificent without being overpowering, mountains with a human face, and our last night in Chitral is to be marked by a visit to a *baipash*, an old Chitrali house where local music and dancing will be laid on. My heart sinks as the dreaded spectre of a 'folklorique' evening looms. Siraj is enthusiastic, though, and describes what we shall see and hear as the last of its kind, a style of music and poetry that is 'locked in the mountains'.

We drive out, crossing the river over a sturdy suspension bridge built by the British in the 1920s at the personal request of Siraj's grandfather. He'd been so excited by hearing of the invention of the car that he ordered a fleet of Baby Austins to be delivered to him in Chitral, without realizing that cars couldn't cross rivers. The bridge was obligingly completed by sappers from the garrison in two months.

His grandfather's ignorance of cars sounds pretty comprehensive. Apparently, when the tyres wore out, he just sold the cars. A lucky dealer from Karachi bought the whole lot, changed the tyres and sold the fleet in mint condition.

The *baipash* is a carefully preserved 300-year-old house, approached through a large garden with tall and immaculate drystone walls, reinforced with horizontal timbers to protect against earthquakes. The layout inside is the traditional single chamber with a central hearth and opening in the roof above for smoke to escape. Around the walls are darkened wooden stalls where cattle would once have been kept. The columns that support the roof are also wooden and carved with plant and flower motifs. It's dark, stuffy, cosy and presided over by a tall, gaunt man with white beard and thick, sprouting eyebrows. With a strong and piercing gaze, he reminds me of a manic Scots preacher.

He's 77 years old, with a wicked sense of humour. At some length, he expounds on the abundance of hallucinatory substances in the sylvan glades of Chitral.

'Did you ever try any of these drugs?' I ask him.

He shakes his head.

'Oh no. But I've been smoking hash for 40 years.'

Once the music begins I can't take my eyes off him. Like the venerable leader of a jazz band, he's at the very heart of the action, sometimes plucking skilfully at a sitar, sometimes singing, but always urging others on, holding out long thin arms and flicking his bony wrists in time to the beat of sitars, tambourines and a pink jerrycan that does for percussion.

The pattern is the same each time. The music starts slowly, then one of the audience gets up and begins to move with delicate shuffles of the feet and upraised arms, gradually becoming more animated. As the tempo of the music accelerates, so does the speed and intensity of the movement, until both merge into a stomping, exultant crescendo, which leaves everyone exhausted, ecstatic and applauding wildly.

There is a sense of real joy as the music and dancing goes on. The songs and the style of playing are improvisations on music that has been part of this isolated culture for centuries. Once small groups like these forget, it may disappear altogether.

Which explains the intensity of Siraj's pleasure as he listens, his description of the songs and the music as being 'locked in the mountains', and the infectious magical warmth that banishes my worst memories of things folklorique.

Day Thirteen: Chitral to Mastuj

On the road again. I have a different jeep, and a different driver. Raza Khan is younger and less earnest than Nadir Begh. Whereas Nadir used to comb his hair every time we did a shot, even if we were a tiny speck on a mountain panorama, Raza is a little more relaxed and wears a baseball cap, reversed. He's a Chitrali and everyone we meet on the road seems to be either an intimate friend of his or a member of his family.

Long before they were Chitralis, the inhabitants of these mountain areas were collectively known as the Kho, and I've acquired a modest, locally printed guide book that has a glossary of words in the language they still speak here, known as Khowar. It's pleasingly phonetic and in between gasping with awe at the scenery I try out a few words on Raza. Father is *tut*, mother is *nun*, grandfather is *bap*, grandmother is *wow* and foot is *pong*. This is the sort of language I like.

There is a page of Miscellaneous Phrases, which is short but has an interesting theme. 'Have you a wife?', 'Do you love your wife?', 'Is it late?', 'At what time shall we start?', 'Well done', 'Thank you', 'Don't go naked', 'There is a pain in my leg' and 'When will you come back?' It conjures up images of a lusty life in the mountains.

We climb slowly up the valley, the river rushing past us at great speed, huffing and puffing and occasionally leaping ostentatiously into the air as if trying to attract our attention.

As the road deteriorates the mountains grow more spectacular and quite suddenly we turn onto a flat saddle of land to be confronted by the dazzling white bulk of a massif called Buni Zum, 21,000 feet (6400 m) high, trailing glaciers and massive hanging slabs of snow. It provides a backdrop for a huge cricket match being played among the rocks, with dozens of boys fielding over a vast area.

We spend the night in the grounds of a crumbling, but still dignified fort, which commands the confluence of two rivers at the town
of Mastuj. Another Ul-Mulk family house, given to them by the
British in 1913 as thanks for their loyalty, it's currently run by Siraj's
father Khushwaqt, a dapper, bright-eyed man who has just celebrated his 90th birthday, and who everyone knows as the Colonel.
Hoping to attract tourists, they have built some handsome wood
cabins around the perimeter of a luxurious greensward beside the
fort, the sort of flat open ground where you can imagine tourna-
ments taking place. Unfortunately, the builders have done a runner
and all that's working are the bathroom fittings. So we sleep outside
in tents and clamber into the empty buildings for a shower. Very
odd.

I'm kept from deep sleep by an unlikely combination of cold
wind and apricots. The window panel flaps of my tent don't zip up
and the night breeze freshens to a chilly blow that provokes a gentle
deluge of apricots dropping off the trees, bouncing onto the tin
roofs of the unfinished chalets, rolling down the corrugated iron in
interesting ways and plopping onto the roof of my tent.

Day Fifteen: From Mastuj Fort to the
Shandur Pass

Three hours of dogged mountain driving out of Mastuj, our convoy
is climbing out of the last cultivated valley, which now lies far below
us, tucked into the massive rubble-strewn flanks of mountainside
like a fig leaf on a grey marble statue. With a last heave of the gears
we push through 12,000 feet (3650 m) and soon level out onto a
grassy plateau with a blue lake spread along its length and saw-tooth
mountains surrounding it. We've reached the Shandur Pass, the
watershed between the valleys of Chitral in the Hindu Kush and
Gilgit in the Karakoram.

Although the three-day festival doesn't begin till tomorrow, this
normally desolate and lonely place is beginning to resemble a small
town. Vehicles raise clouds of dust as they arrive on the plateau
laden with people, food, bedding and tents. As many as 10,000 are
expected for the big polo game and shops and businesses from the

surrounding villages have moved up here to supply them.

Cafés are opening, offering the obligatory karaoke, stalls are selling rugs and blankets, generators are coughing into life, and special prayer areas are being marked out with stones.

A yak has just been slaughtered at an improvised butcher's shop, its throat cut with a foot-long curved knife. The severed head lies in a nearby stream, creamy-white innards spread out on a boulder. Customers are already queuing up to buy the cuts of meat, hanging from a horizontal wooden pole, a washing-line of flesh.

Our accommodation is in a small encampment conveniently close to the polo ground and next door to the Chitral team quarters, where I meet up again with Sikander Ul-Mulk.

The word is not good. One of the best horses they have has been hurt in training and another is lame after being hit by a ball in a practice game. News from the Gilgit team is of ominous confidence.

It might be something to do with altitude but by ten o'clock I'm blissfully tired and ready for bed. No sooner have I wriggled into the foetal warmth of my sleeping bag than the whole site explodes with noise. A thumping of drums, a squeaking of pipes, clapping, cheering and general encouragement fills the night air. When the party ends I'm aware of how bitterly cold it is. As the night goes on my tent seems to attract an icy chill and I have a short but powerful nightmare based on the scene in *The Long Good Friday* where recalcitrant gang members are strung from hooks in a cold store.

Day Sixteen : The Shandur Pass

A beautiful morning. The clear skies that made the night so cold are china blue and an unblinking sun shines down, mocking my night's misery.

There are three big polo games over the next three days. The two villages nearest the pass, Laspur on the Chitral side and Ghiza on the Gilgit side, play each other today. Tomorrow is the turn of the Chitral and Gilgit 'B' teams, and the final day is the big match between the 'A' sides.

The Laspur team is camped, modestly, a mile or so back towards the pass. With only an hour to go before the game, supporters are still arriving, many of them walking up the long steep road from the village. Before they leave for the ground each player seeks the blessing of the elders of the village. Meanwhile, their supporters sit around listening to music. Various men (there are no women to be seen) are moved to dance. One of them moves particularly gracefully. My guide whispers in my ear.

'He is Taliban.'

During a break in the dancing there is an address from a man in a dirty *shalwar-kameez*, with a stick, a pack and leathery, sun-scorched features. Whether he intends to look like the classic yokel or not I don't know, but it's clear from the way the audience listens that he is a star, and a comedy star at that. My guide tries to translate but the laughs come so thick and fast that he has trouble keeping up.

It's all good anti-government stuff. According to my guide, it's a popular grouse on both sides of the pass that the government praises the spirit of the mountain communities but fails to put any money their way.

Like any good comedian his eyes flick round the audience, and pretty soon alight on me. To gales of laughter he tells me that his people pray constantly for the restoration of British rule and he asks me to tell the Queen that if she gives them each a thousand rupees she can have their village back.

Meanwhile, the players are emerging from a team talk and are getting ready to mount their horses. In their red jerseys, white *pakol* hats, red knee pads and black boots they stand out like mediaeval knights among the rough and ready dress of the villagers. The captain, a wiry middle-aged man wearing dark glasses, caresses his horse's head and talks soothingly into its ear.

A fiercely fought game sees Laspur coming in to win an 8-7 victory. The crowd pour onto the pitch and no-one tries to stop them. The quiet, rather studious figure I saw whispering soothing confidences to his horse two hours ago is the hero of the day, flung up onto the shoulders of rapturous supporters. First blood to the Chitral Valley. Hopefully, it will be a good omen.

Day Seventeen : The Shandur Pass

I've acquired a thick Chinese blanket from the temporary shopping mall up here on the pass and though my tent remains an ice-box, I actually slept last night, after an unpromising start when I was kept awake, not by drums and pipes but by someone being very funny near my tent. I couldn't tell whether it was Urdu or Pashto they were speaking, but it didn't really matter. His total control of the audience was wonderfully infectious and I lay curled up in my many layers of thermals, shirts, sweaters and fleeces, giggling away, without understanding a word.

More people have arrived overnight and our encampment is now part of a growing community. Figures are scattered among the grassy boulders, cleaning teeth, scrubbing feet and washing faces in bowls of water heated on a brushwood fire, which Maboub, who is in charge of these matters, has to keep continually tended, as thinner air at this height make things harder to burn. In the kitchen tent, where a violent gas fire looks like an accident waiting to happen, Zahoor, the chef, produces scrambled eggs, fried potatoes and even porridge for our breakfast.

At the far end of the valley, away from the hustle and bustle of the ever-expanding encampment, the 'A' teams are out beside the lake practising shots, gallops, passes and tight-reined turns. Both sides exercise together in the cool of early morning, then return to their separate camps.

Gilgit's team is drawn entirely from the ranks of police and army. They're well-drilled, organized, efficient but institutional. Their captain, Bulbul Jan, is a tall middle-aged man with neat, short hair and the modest, kindly manner of an avuncular schoolmaster. Hard to believe as he talks softly to us that he is one half of the most successful combination in free-style polo. The other is his tall, black Punjabi stallion, Truc.

Bulbul is 55 and his horse is 21. Together they have played in 15 of these matches and have led Gilgit to victory for the last two years, proving that despite the Herculean efforts required of them up here on the plateau, guile and experience still count as much as youth and strength. Bulbul claims that Truc can tell him, within 24 hours of a game, just how things will work out.

'So what about your chances tomorrow?'

Truc bares his teeth and rears his head away, clearly impatient to end the interview.

'Truc is in a very good mood,' pronounces Bulbul Jan.

Chitral come across as the gentlemen amateurs, with an altogether more happy-go-lucky approach to their polo, but the mood at the camp today is subdued. Gilgit won the 'B' game this morning, though one of their horses collapsed and died of a heart attack at the end of the first chukka. Neither side wants this to happen, and Sikander admits that this is only one of several such deaths over the last few years, grim reminders of the demands of such a physical game at such a high altitude.

He concedes that Gilgit's 'A' team are the favourites. They are unchanged from last year, and unlike Chitral's series of misfortunes, have had no casualties among their horses. I ask about the rumours I've heard about black magic and spells being put on the teams.

He shrugs.

'I never used to believe it, but now since everyone does, I've also started believing it.'

'You think it's more than just coincidence?'

He nods.

'More, yes, more than coincidence.'

He thinks the only possible advantage for Chitral is that they have Afghan horses, tough and strong after apprenticeships carrying men and goods over the high border passes.

I ask what it will be like if they should lose tomorrow.

'Terrible. Terrible.'

He laughs, a little desperately.

'We try to go back in the dark. We pack up, get ready and leave at night.'

'Do they forgive quickly in Chitral?'

Sikander Ul-Mulk pauses, then shakes his head philosophically.

'It takes about a month or two.'

Day Eighteen : The Shandur Pass

The weather is perfect.

A crowd, estimated at around 15,000, has gathered at the ground well in advance of the game. Apart from a VIP area on top of the main stand, the accommodation is basic, ranging from purpose-built concrete terraces to standing room on the various low mounds of glacial debris that enclose the playing area. One of these, with perhaps the least good view, is reserved for women.

The six players of each side parade onto the pitch, Chitral in scarlet, Gilgit in blue and white. Protection is optional. None of the Gilgit side wears protective headgear, whereas three of the Chitralis have helmets and one wears a *pakul*.

I'm squeezed into one of the terraces. There are no seats and we just settle ourselves as best we can on mud and stones. My eyes meet those of a policeman with riot helmet, night stick and dark glasses, sitting at the end of our row. He pulls on a cigarette and turns away. Above us is a line of brightly coloured kites, strung together, stretching right across the ground. (I later learn that there are 105 of them, thus winning, for a Doctor Ejazul Haq of Islamabad, the world record for the number of kites 'aired on a single thread'.)

Silence falls as a prayer is read out from the Koran. The horses canter forwards to the centre-line to receive the ball. Bulbul Jan, bareheaded, looks every bit the midfield general, effortlessly in control at the centre of his team. Truc, less effortlessly in control, is the first to fertilize the pitch.

I don't blame him. If I was facing 50 minutes of constant running, sudden sprints, balls flying about and full-speed charges towards two-foot-high stone walls, I'd have probably done the same. In free-style polo the player is as much fair game as the ball and deliberate obstruction with either horse or mallet is a great skill. Nor are the horses and players the only ones taking risks. Mallets are dropped or broken with considerable frequency and stable boys take terrible risks rushing into the fray with replacements.

The game is non-stop, fast and even.

Predictably, Gilgit score first with Bulbul pushing in an easy goal after a furious build-up. He now gets to restart the game with a *tapokh*, which is very good to watch. The goal scorer races up the field at full gallop, holding both the ball and the mallet in the same hand, then, still with one hand only, releases the ball and strikes it ahead of him. It's often missed or half hit, but the apricot-wood hammer of Bulbul's stick meets the ball head on. It soars up the other end, bounces past the goal and is thrown back into play by a spectator, this keeping any interruption to the flow of play to a minimum. Maqbool pulls a goal back for Chitral and they go into the break unexpectedly level.

After a long interval display of ceremonial dancing, all hands and arms turning and twisting gracefully, the players are back on the pitch and a repeat of the first half is played out in the first few minutes. A Gilgit goal, then a Chitral equalizer. As a well-informed spectator next to me says it's now all about the stamina of the horses.

Gilgit's powerful ponies begin to outrun Chitral, racing after the long ball with breathtaking speed. Two more Gilgit goals, then Bulbul Jan and the ageing Truc first set up a superb through pass for the fifth goal before running in the next one themselves. 6-2.

The Chitral supporters simply disappear at this point, streaming off the mounds and emptying the stands. Their departing cars send up columns of dust that blow over the ground as if bringing down a final curtain over their team's efforts.

The departure of these fair-weather supporters seems, perversely, to spur on the Chitral team and they pull back two goals in an unexpectedly nail-biting finish.

Gilgit have made it a hat trick of wins and won best player award. For Chitral there is the consolation of Best Horse, won by a tireless grey called Computer, and not much else but a night-time skulk back down the mountain.

I'm sure someone somewhere will claim it's been a victory for black magic.

Day Nineteen : The Karakoram Highway

The view from my hotel window in Gilgit is an exercise in contrasts. Immediately outside is a carefully tended rose garden, of the sort you might see in a Best Kept Village in the Cotswolds. A half mile further away, this tidy view swells into a stupendous wall of mountain scenery, rising from the muddy cliffs carved out by the River Gilgit.

Soon we're running north, deeper into these mountains, along the road that bears their name – the Karakoram Highway, also known as the Eighth Wonder of the World.

A collaboration between the Chinese and the Pakistanis, the road winds 800 formidable and majestic miles, from Kashgar in western China almost to the Pakistan capital, Islamabad. It first took traffic in 1978 after 20 years of construction. Considering the obstacles in its course – some of the highest and least stable mountains in the world, fierce winds, temperature extremes ranging from icy cold to blazing summer heat – 20 years is pretty quick, but the human price paid was considerable. Between 500 and 800 Pakistanis and untold Chinese died in its construction, roughly one life for every kilometre.

Before there was the KKH there was the Silk Road, a network of trails and passes that led from Persia and Turkey through Afghanistan and into China, a commercial conduit following and enriching the precious routes through the mountains.

Apart from the increased prosperity brought by the road itself, many projects round here bear the name of the Aga Khan, spiritual head of the Ismaili Muslims, a Shiite sect who believe their leader to be a direct descendant of the Prophet's son-in-law. The Aga Khan Foundation provides money for education (especially girls' schools), healthcare and agricultural schemes. The results can be seen in the communities through which we pass. The settlements are tidy, with solid communal buildings and ingenious irrigation systems flowing between immaculately built dry-stone walls.

In the Hunza valley, believed to be the model for many Shangri-las and the inspiration for James Hilton's book *Lost Horizon*, the Karakoram Highway is quiet as a country lane, running beside neatly planted fields of spinach, potatoes and cabbage and sun-dappled orchards of apricot, apple, peach, pear and plum. Yet this is one of the geomorphic hot spots of the world. This tranquil countryside lies above the epicentre of a titanic geological upheaval. Around 50 million years ago India collided with the rest of Asia, or rather the great mass called the Indian plate drifted north and ran into the much larger mass of the Eurasian plate. The force of the impact pushed one over the other and thrust them both skywards, creating a momentum that is still at work, carrying India deeper into Asia at the rate of two inches a year. The Hindu Kush, the Karakoram, the Pamirs and the Himalaya are all, in a sense, wreckage from one of the great head-on collisions in the history of the planet.

A sign outside a modest little town reads simply, 'Chalt. Where Continents Collide'. Which certainly puts 'Artichoke Capital of the World' in its place.

There are few spots where the consequences of tectonic trauma are more dramatically visible than at the Rakaposhi View Restaurant in Ghulmet. Rakaposhi is one of the most imposing peaks of the Karakoram, rising to 25,500 feet (7772 m). As we sit at a table beneath a willow tree eating fresh-picked cherries we are looking at the highest unbroken mountainside on earth. From the River Hunza, just below us, to the summit of its western face far above us, a single slope rises 18,000 feet (5486 m). Three and a quarter miles of rock, glacier and gravity-defying terraces of snow and ice.

And the lavatory's spotless.

The KKH, like an earlier engineering marvel, the Forth Railway Bridge, needs constant attention as the road climbs higher and the ice cracks the rock and the snowmelt sends the rubble slithering down onto the highway. So it's no great surprise to hear that a landslide has blocked the road between here and the 16,000-foot (4877 m) Khunjerab Pass which leads into China. Even if we got there we couldn't go further, as the frontier has been closed due to the SARS epidemic. We detour up to the village of Altit.

The Altit road is not one for faint hearts; it's just an unfenced track of flattened debris dug across the middle of a 3000-foot spill of scree. Halfway along it someone tells me that the word Karakoram means 'crumbling rock' in Turkish.

I'm much relieved when we drop slowly down through the tree line, but just as I'm feeling secure we have to cross a slatted bridge of warped and bent timbers, between which I can see a lot more of the raging waters of the Hunza than I'd like to. Under the weight of each vehicle it bounces up and down as if it were made of elastic. Never have I been so happy to reach the other side of a bridge.

On the way back to Gilgit, the sun hits the eastern spires and ridges of the mountains and turns their tips the colour of molten metal. I only hope the Himalaya can live up to the magic of the Karakoram.

Day Twenty : Gilgit to Skardu

We have been given the go-ahead by the Pakistan military to join one of their helicopters on a service flight from Skardu in Baltistan, to Concordia, close to the Chinese border, where ten of the world's top 30 peaks are clustered, including K2 (Karakoram 2), the second highest mountain in the world.

It's mountaineering made easy but not to be sniffed at for all that. Last night I called my friend Hamish MacInnes in Scotland for the reactions of a world-class climber. He gave me various words of encouragement, among them the fact that the road to Skardu is known as 'the road that eats jeeps'.

Skardu is only 99 miles (160 km) from Gilgit, but we're told it will take most of the day. Progress is slowed down by rock falls and land-slips at roughly one-mile intervals. Some bring us to a halt, some have to be negotiated with infinite care. Road gangs, muffled like mummies against the dust and heat, stop to watch us pass, then resume the Sisyphean task of fighting landslides with spades, shovels and wheelbarrows.

We turn off the KKH and stop for refreshment. Across the road a large man sprawls across the threshold of a very small shop. He's sunk deep in an armchair and has one leg up against the door-post. A sign above him announces 'Ahmad, Gems and Minerals. We Deals In Precious Stones'. Up here, mineral seams are routinely exposed by the massive geological upheavals. As they bring our tea they tell us we've had one big piece of luck. The road that eats jeeps reopened only two days earlier after unusually heavy spring rain closed it at 126 separate places.

As we set off along yet another gorge I'm aware that this is a significant moment for us. Dominating the mountains on the far side of the Indus is the westernmost bastion of the Himalaya. Nanga Parbat, an uncompromising, irregular giant of a mountain, rises to 26,650 feet (8125 m). It has wide flanks and a bad reputation. It's known as Killer Mountain, claiming 50 lives before it was first scaled by an Austrian, Hermann Buhl, in 1953. According to Hamish, Buhl was a very hard nut indeed. Those who came on his expeditions were issued with one-way tickets only.

Progress seems positively jaunty for a few miles. Then the walls of the gorge close in and the eating of the jeeps begins as we grind along, clinging to the roller-coaster track above the Indus, at one moment rising so high above the river that we can no longer hear its roar, at the next plunging to within range of its wind-tossed spray, and all the time bumping and juddering over half-cleared piles of rubble that fling me from side to side like someone in the terminal throes of fever.

The existence of a road at all in this desperately confined space is something of a miracle. It seems to be maintained by the army, and the different companies of engineers have their names engraved on a rock at the end of each section. A camouflaged vehicle comes at us round a tight bend and as we go through the elaborate ritual of manoeuvring past each other I notice the slogan on the side of its cab. 'Pakistan Army. Men At Their Best.'

At Skardu, the hyperactive River Indus, which has been leaping and writhing past us for most of the day, flattens out into a wide alluvial lagoon.

We find ourselves in a very singular hotel where the lights don't always work but the waiters wear white gloves to serve dinner.

It's called Shangri La.

Day Twenty One : Skardu to Concordia

There's a crashed DC-3 just outside my room. Apparently, it came down after take-off at Skardu 49 years ago and, spotting an opportunity, the owner of the Shangri La Resort bought it, rolled it into the gardens, took off the wings, fitted some tables and turned it into a café.

Contradictions are apparent again this morning. The gardens are tended with obsessive efficiency, each blade of grass individually manicured by a dedicated, well-equipped team, yet the breakfast is a very sad affair, with toast so pale and limp that we re-christen the wicker container it comes in the laundry basket.

Such trivial preoccupations are soon behind us as we assemble at the air base for a briefing on today's flight up into the high mountains. The message here is macho, and our two pilots are from a team called 'The Fearless Five, M-17 pilots'.

I should imagine fearlessness is an asset if you have to fly M-17s. They're heavy-duty Russian supply helicopters, the very embodiment of brawn before beauty. We fan out along bench seats running around the side of the cabin. It's unpressurized and, as we're going up beyond 15,000 feet (4570 m), we've been warned that for the first time since we've been in Pakistan we may get really cold.

The helicopter roars into the air, and once in the air the roar is augmented by various rattles and groans. Communication is only possible by shouting into the ear from point blank range.

Below us, the green fields become sparse and scattered and eventually disappear altogether as we enter the valleys that lead to Concordia. What is for us a 90-minute flight would be an eight-day trek on the ground.

The mountains close in. Steep slopes and jagged summits rise above us, the clatter of the engines echoes back off the rocks and the M-17 that looked so bulky and secure on the ground seems suddenly small and vulnerable. At 11,000 feet (3350 m) the pen I'm making notes with explodes, spattering ink around like a nosebleed.

We're now over the imperceptibly moving tongue of the Baltoro glacier, not romantically blue and white but covered with a grey patina of dust and debris and dotted with lurid green pools where the snow and ice crust has collapsed.

Then all at once we're flying clear of the grey constraints of the canyons and out into crystal clear sunshine and over an ice plateau of staggering beauty, with razor-sharp peaks surrounding the confluence of the Baltoro and Godwin-Austen glaciers. A tricky landing. The crew are put off first, as they need to be on the ground to shoot me emerging. We pirouette up into the air and once again circle this astonishingly beautiful coming together of ice, snow and mighty mountain peaks. As they attempt the landing a second time no-one bothers to lower the steps, so I spill out of the plane with as much dignity as I can muster and run, fast and low, away from the rotors and towards the camera. My feet strike a soft patch and I plunge forward, headfirst into snow alarmingly deeper than anything I expected.

We know we have only a few minutes to shoot before the helicopter returns and yet the best full frontal view of K2 is almost half a mile away. Led by two army guides, who are actually stationed up here, we make our way through the snow. We try to hurry but it's hopeless, as the surface is melting in the sun. Every now and then people ahead of me drop down to their waist as if a trap door had opened beneath them.

I can't quite believe that all this is really happening. That I'm struggling in slapstick fashion through six feet of snow in a country where the average daytime temperatures have been around 40°C (104°F). That, only five hours after drinking a cup of coffee in a crashed DC-3, I should be a mere five miles from the second highest peak on earth, half a dozen miles from the Chinese border and 13 miles from where heavily armed Pakistani and Indian troops are eye-balling each other on the Line of Control.

The reward for all our efforts is an uninterrupted view of K2, standing with symmetrical grandeur to the northwest, straddling the Chinese border. Not a wisp of cloud obscures the summit, which I know has tempted many to risk, and in some cases give their lives on a mountain much harder and crueller than Everest.

I feel hugely lucky to be here at Concordia, even if we have done it the easy way. And the helicopter doesn't return for almost an hour, giving us time to take it all in, and, very slightly, to panic.

Day Twenty Three : Islamabad

The mountains where we've spent the last two weeks seem a distant memory. Everything is so different down here on the plain. And Islamabad is different again. Nothing stood here 45 years ago, when it was chosen to be Pakistan's new capital, replacing the original capital Karachi, which, 1550 miles (2480 km) away to the south, was considered to be too remote from the heart of the country. Now nearly a million people live here.

The crowds and turbulence we experienced in Peshawar's densely packed bazaars are absent. Islamabad is formal, with long wide avenues and comfortable residential houses laid out in numbered sectors. Instead of Storyteller Street, a typical address in Islamabad might be House 3, Street 18, H-8.

This experiment in New World orderliness has been remarkably successful. Its position certainly helps, on the border between the North-West Frontier and the Punjab, as does the presence of the ministries. Each with their competing landmark buildings, the grandiose Prime Minister's Secretariat in Neo-Mughal style, the Revenue Buildings in American Modern, and the Supreme Court in a mixture of both, they give Islamabad a sort of official liveliness.

It isn't a city to tempt you out for a stroll. That's not how it works. If you're staying in the Marriot the city comes to you, and our lobby is full of delegations, advisers, journalists, educationalists, air-con salesmen, arms dealers and anyone else wanting the ear of the government.

Islamabad is also home to one of Pakistan's national heroes, a cricketer who led his side to a never-to-be forgotten World Cup victory, founded a cancer hospital in memory of his mother, but failed to work his magic in the world of politics. His name is Imran Khan and his PTI, anti-corruption party has only one seat in the National Assembly, his own. It's said that the reasons why he picked up so few votes were that those he attracted were below the voting age of 21, and those he alienated, like the landowners, remain very powerful.

In today's morning paper, however, a disillusioned former colleague of Imran is more severe. He blames Imran's dictatorial tendencies. 'This is not cricket, this is politics. And Imran has never understood that fact.'

We turned up at an unostentatious detached house in a leafy street whose name I forget, but it might have been 14.

Imran is in a meeting but three amiable dogs rise to greet us, tails wagging vigorously, until that becomes too much of an effort and they collapse, bellies flat against warm stones or on their backs in the shade of the verandah, legs spread-eagled in abandon.

After a half-hour or so, Imran, unheralded by minders, secretaries or advisers, slips quietly onto the verandah, wearing a light blue *shalwar-kameez*. His complexion is clear and unlined and his long face has a few interesting angles, which makes him more than conventionally handsome. When we ask him if he minds us filming the house he waves his arm agreeably. He'll only be here another three months, and his wife Jemima is back in their house in London.

Tea and soft drinks are brought out. When I tell him of our visit to Skardu, his face lights up.

'The most beautiful country,' he says with feeling. 'The Baltis are friendly and decent folk.'

Imran scratches the luxuriating Labrador with his foot. He talks carefully, as economical with words as he was with runs, seldom raising his voice, but relying more on expressively graceful hands to emphasize or illustrate a point. His soft-voiced, unemotional delivery masks bracing views.

On matters of religion he feels the clergy, rather than the scholars, are the big problem. The Koran, he maintains, quoting from it with confidence, is an example for life, but the mullahs seek to reduce its message to fit their own interpretations.

'And some of them are decadent, you know,' he says with a real touch of anger.

He feels the Taliban began as a genuine people's movement, a reaction against the summary justice and tyranny of the warlords.

'But they were taken over by extremists.'

We talk about the British influence. He thinks it not only strong, but fundamental. India and Pakistan were created by the British, who saw the plethora of tribes, small rulers, languages and customs as unwieldy and difficult. By playing them off against each other they created a centralized administration that India had never known before. It was a classic case of divide and rule.

I ask him if many of the old institutions aren't still in place, or in the case of his alma mater, Aitcheson's College, the Eton of Pakistan, positively thriving.

'For the elite we had what's called the "English medium education" and for the masses the "Urdu medium education", so the elite became quite Westernized and the rest of society was not that much touched by Westernization, as you've seen as you travel around.'

'Are you tolerant of these schools still existing?'

'No, I think it's terrible this educational apartheid.'

I press him on whether a bright lad from the bazaars would ever make it to the top in Pakistan, and he shakes his head quite vigorously.

'Highly unlikely.'

He says he made the transition from cricket to politics because he felt that, with the way things were going, his country faced a bleak future. The population growth was the highest in the world, people weren't being educated and governments were corrupt and unconcerned with investment in human beings.

'It was pretty tough because I had to stand up to the status quo, which is very strong in this country.'

He doesn't mince words. 'Money in Pakistan is in the hands of crooks. The majority of people who go into politics make money through illegal means.'

Our government minder is listening in to all this and I fear the worst, but at the end of the interview all he asks of us is that we take a photograph of him with his hero.

Unlike the locked and barred Gulbar at the hotel in Peshawar, there is a place in the bowels of the Marriott where non-Muslims can enjoy an alcoholic beverage. It's called The Bassment, which may or may not be a spelling mistake, and we agree to meet down there after work. I'm the first to arrive. Disapproval, in the forbidding shape of an unsmiling hotel bouncer in a suit, begins at the top of the stairs. He stands, arms folded, legs apart, resolutely avoiding eye contact, guarding the heavy door that opens onto a dank stairwell whose walls give off a pervasive odour of tobacco smoke, long since exhaled. At the bottom two swing doors open onto a long, apparently empty chamber sunk in Stygian gloom, pierced only by tiny disco lights sunk into the ceiling. Concrete walls increase the atmosphere of being in a bunker. At the bar is a Norwegian. We exchange a wary grunt of greeting, like two people who've come together to commit the same crime.

I order a beer. They have no international brands, only beer brewed in Pakistan.

Which is how I begin my acquaintance with the life-saving products of the Murree Brewery.

Day Twenty Four : Rawalpindi

Islamabad, its critics say, is 12 miles outside Pakistan, and this morning, as we drive out past the well-fenced government buildings and onto the wide, landscaped, highly under-used modern highway that surrounds the city I know what they mean. Everything is discreet, tidy, straight and planned, and it's not until we reach the outskirts of Islamabad's twin city, Rawalpindi, affectionately abbreviated to Pindi, that Pakistan comes back to life.

Not far from the airport, we're diverted off the main road by hundreds of police. After some time a convoy of outriders, some in open cars with gloriously conspicuous scarlet berets, races by on either side of three blacked-out Mercedes, any one of which, or possibly none, contains President Musharraf. Significantly, he doesn't live with the civil servants in Islamabad but in Rawalpindi, where the army is based, and this whole extravagant process, an entire six-lane highway closed for a half-hour, is a reminder of where the power lies in Pakistan.

At Independence in 1947, Mohammed Ali Jinnah, known to all as the Quaid-e-Azam, Father of the Nation, wanted Pakistan to remain a secular state but, divided as the country was into West Pakistan and East Pakistan (later to secede and become Bangladesh), the only real bond that held the disparate tribal groups together was religion. In 1956 the Constitution accepted this and declared Pakistan an Islamic Republic. The army, seeing power drifting away from them, staged their first coup two years after that and, despite various attempts to hand power to democratically elected leaders, Pakistan still is a military state, and one of the most hotly debated issues is whether or not Musharraf should give up his uniform and run for democratically elected office.

Turning off the Grand Trunk Road we pass the high, blotchy walls of the old barracks behind which one of Pakistan's experiments with democracy came to a grim end, when Zulfikhar Ali Bhutto, a populist, secular prime minister, was hanged on the orders of General Zia, leaving Zia free to accelerate the process of Islamization.

At the heart of this nerve centre of the Islamic Republic, sandwiched between the barracks and the military headquarters, is the Murree Brewery, Pakistan's largest purveyor of alcoholic beverages.

Originally established in 1861, up in the Murree Hills, north of Islamabad, by Henry Whymper, brother of the first man to climb the Matterhorn, it's a place steeped in irony. Ninety-five per cent of the brewery's 450-strong workforce is Muslim and officially not allowed to touch the product their lives depend on. The owner, Minoo Bhandara, is a scholarly Parsee who writes regular newspaper columns and his business card notes that he was 'adviser to the President 1982–1985' (that same President who hanged Bhutto). His office, dominated by a 150-year-old mahogany table, feels as if it would be more at home in an Oxbridge college than a brewery.

Minoo would make a good don. He is slightly stooped, and a large pair of glasses with thick lenses gives him an owlish air. He's soft-voiced, courteous, a touch pedantic and very much at home in a well-worn rattan chair.

His Muslim brew master, Muhammed Javed, has been here 17 years. More in the mould of the modern executive, he's a genial, youthful-looking man with degrees from universities in the Punjab and America.

His enthusiasm for the production of alcohol is abundant. He walks me past the beer production line, enthusing over the current output of 10,000 bottles an hour ranging from high strength Millennium at 7.5 per cent alcohol, through the popular and medal-winning Murree Classic at 5.5 to a Pils Light at 3.5.

This selfless Muslim workforce also produces 20 brands of spirit including gin and vodka.

Despite draconian laws on the possession of alcohol – a prison sentence of three to four years, un-bailable, and quite possibly a caning as well – it's pretty clear that the Murree Brewery wouldn't be in business if its customers were only non-Muslims.

Minoo argues that it's foolish to suppose there is no demand for alcohol in Pakistan and if he doesn't supply it then someone else will. Either the bootleggers smuggle foreign whisky in on dhows from places like Dubai, or for those who can't afford bootleg, there is moonshine liquor, often made from what he calls 'denatured alcohol'.

He looks over his glasses at me, rather severely.

'"Denature" is an old English word for poison.'

One of the outlets where non-Muslims can legally acquire Murree's output is at Flashman's Hotel in Rawalpindi. A run-down collection of white bungalows, looking a bit like a 1940s film studio, it stands just off the Grand Trunk Road and next to a handsome Victorian church with everything but the spire painted deep pink.

Round the back of Flashman's, if you know who to ask, you'll find two well-scuffed shutters, bordered with a patina of black grease from thousands of hands. A sign, in Urdu, announces that opening time is three o'clock. A line, looking suspiciously Muslim, has already formed. About 3.15 the shutters are opened and I soon find myself peering through a barred window into a gloomy little room full of storage boxes and men drinking tea.

Before I buy I have to fill in a permit, which requires me, among other things, to give my father's name and my religion.

'Agnostic?' I suggest, trying to be completely honest.

The man at the counter looks blankly back.

'Agnostic with doubts,' I write down, and hand back the form. This entitles me to six units of alcohol a month, a unit being one bottle of spirits or 20 bottles of beer. I buy a bottle of Vat No.1 Rawalpindi whisky at a cost of 350 rupees (about £3.50), which the attendant wraps in brown paper and hands through the bars to me.

'Drink only in room,' he cautions. 'Not in public.'

I nod, grateful for the advice. He must have got the measure of me, for as I turn away he shouts hopefully.

'I do gin!'

Day Twenty Five : Rawalpindi to Lahore

For a military state Pakistan has a remarkably free press. Or so it seems as I read an editorial this morning addressing what it calls the Military-Mullah alliance. The writer's argument is that since General Zia's time the military and the Islamists have sought each other's support against secular democracy.

The only difference between them, it argues, is that the clerics have beards and the army have moustaches.

A front page headline warns of the heatwave that waits for us tonight in Lahore. '50 Die As Punjab Boils.'

On our way to the station in Rawalpindi, there is reassuring evidence of the hopefully inextinguishable richness of Pakistani life. Run-down streets dotted with foreign language schools and computer shops, and looming above them hand-painted billboard ads for the latest movie adventures of Shaan Shahid, Pakistan's screen heart-throb, glowering menacingly, as blood courses from a head wound, or grinning, equally menacingly, as he brandishes a Kalashnikov. He seems to be the star of every film they make.

Stopping to buy provisions in the Rajah Bazaar, I'm approached by a heavily bearded man offering to sell me a CD of Mullah Omar and Osama Bin Laden praying together at a mosque in Idris. Never seen before, he says.

Another seems pleased that we represent the BBC. 'Everyone in Pakistan believe BBC, but not CNN,' he assures me, readjusting his New York Yankees baseball cap.

It's heating up as promised – 44°C (111°F) by the time we reach Rawalpindi Station, a huge conflation of Scottish baronial turrets and cupolas with a bland modern extension tacked on. Porters cluster around us and a thin-faced ascetic old man with a Gandalf-like white beard grabs one of my cases, hoists the other onto his head and, a little disappointed that I choose to carry my own shoulder bag, marches off through the crowds.

Our driver nods approvingly. This old man is a great character, he says. He was carrying bags for British officers before independence. That was 55 years ago.

There are three classes on the train, two with air-con and one without. We're in air-con, 2nd class and are made comfortable by an army of solicitous attendants marshalled by a man in a white suit, green peaked hat and a crimson arm band, grandly embroidered with the words Conductor Guard. A rich cast of characters, all with titles clearly inscribed on jackets or lapels, come through offering refreshment of various kinds. My favourite is the Iceman, a stocky, embattled figure in a frayed white jacket, whose bulbous eyes and droopy moustache remind me of a small-time crook in a French gangster movie. He hauls a huge bucket in which is a block of ice with bottles squeezed around it. There is a tired, emaciated Sweet Seller and various perkier, smartly turned-out young men described on their lapel badges as either Buttlers (sic) or Waiters. Waiter No. 14 brings chai, sweet milky tea, and Buttler No. 7 collects the money.

The name Punjab is an elision of Paan, five, and Aab, waters, and refers to the five rivers on which the prosperity of the province depends. Connected up, under the British occupation, by a network of branch canals and distribution channels, the flows of the Indus, Chenab, Ravi, Sutlej and Jhelum support 70 million people, almost half the population of Pakistan. Seventy miles south of Pindi a mile-long railway bridge crosses the river into the town of Jhelum. Walking out on the station there I fall into conversation with a tall, irrepressibly cheery young man with wide, expressive eyes. His name is Asim and he's on his way to Lahore with his brother, Azam, an accountant who is having a weekend-long engagement party. They buy me pakoras, savoury fritters, from a stall on the platforms and we munch away in mutual enthusiasm. I will love Lahore, he promises.

'They are not fundamentalists there. Lahore is a city of very loving people, very wide-hearted, very loving.'

He puts away another pakora.

'Lahori people are very fond of eating,' confirms Asim.

'And is there a lot of night life?'

He nods animatedly.

'Oh yes, two, three, four o'clock in the morning, people are eating different dishes at different places.'

South of Jhelum the scenery changes from scrubby bush plateau to the freshly shorn fields of the Punjab plain.

Back on the train the Iceman is coming. I talk with a pale German girl who converted to Islam a year ago and two young, articulate computer programmers in shirts and trousers travelling with their father. He is shy, speaks no English, wears an embroidered skull cap and *shalwar-kameez* and looks steadily forward.

The light is softening and the day is cooling and people are out beside the railway; leading dusty-flanked water buffaloes to be fed, carrying goods home on the back of bicycles and playing cricket with breeze blocks for stumps.

It's dark when we reach Lahore. Outside the station, a colossal brick and stone fortified folly, I pick up an auto-rickshaw to the hotel. We grind off onto wide roads and through careless traffic, adding our own little cloud of pollution to a thick, hot, suffocating fug, tight as a strait-jacket.

Day Twenty Six: Lahore

Up at 5.45 to beat the heat. We make our way to the low hill that dominates the heart of this flat city and on which stand two of the most beautiful buildings in the subcontinent, Lahore Fort and the Badshahi Mosque. Both were built by the Mughal (the word derives from Mongol) emperors who came out of south central Asia and through Afghanistan around the time that Henry VIII was planning the Reformation. Using rifles, mortars and gunpowder, previously unheard of in India, they seized Lahore in 1524 and subdued Delhi two years later.

These two cities became the twin jewels of an empire that lasted almost 200 years and was characterized by blood, death, romantic tragedy and some of the most exquisite buildings, gardens, books and paintings in the world.

The Mughals were not the first to fortify Lahore. Some 13 or 14 strongholds have succeeded each other on this hill, but today's fort, completed by the Emperor Akbar, has stood solidly behind its mighty brick walls for 450 years.

It is a huge complex, but we find ourselves caught for some time in a small office, with a beamed roof and lots of tasteful antique furnishings, making the acquaintance of the curator, who has a bad cold.

I have the feeling the last thing he wants to do is to go outside. Two days ago Lahore had its highest temperature for 75 years, he tells us, reaching for a tissue. 'Forty-Nine Centigrade!'

Fortunately, it will be cooler today he prophesies. Perhaps 47 at most.

The appeal of the Lahore fort is a successful combination of intimacy and grandeur. Power with a human face. There is the massive Elephant Path, a wide flight of steps with long, shallow stairs designed to enable rich courtiers to bring their elephants into the heart of the fort without having to dismount. There are courtyards of immense size, criss-crossed with cooling water channels (sadly dry today), and audience chambers supported by forests of sandstone columns, and in among them, exquisite architectural miniatures.

The Shish Mahal, the Palace of Mirrors, is a series of cool, serene rooms open at one side and enclosed at the other by an exquisitely carved screen through which the breeze is drawn by a 17th-century carved marble air-con system. Narrow apertures on the outside widen out on the inside to draw the cool air in. And it does work. The walls are picked out with glass mosaics, paintings of gardens and countryside and complex mirrored panels.

It was in one of these, so the story goes, that Emperor Akbar noticed his son Jahangir exchange flirtatious glances with the Emperor's favourite courtesan, Anarkarli, aka Pomegranate Blossom. As a punishment Akbar ordered her to be walled-up, alive. When Jahangir became Emperor he built a grand tomb at the place where she died, on which were written the words:

'Ah, could I behold the face of my beloved once again, I would give thanks until the day of resurrection.'

The curator sniffs and sighs. Not because he's moved by the story, but because he says it never happened. True or false, Anarkali has become a folk hero for many Lahoreans and the main market of the city is named after her.

Another gem, the Naulaka Pavilion, has less gruesome romantic attachments. Its canopied roof, an exquisitely carved blanket of marble, said to be modelled on a Bengali hut, covers walls and pillars intricately decorated with tiny carved panels filled with stones of agate, lapis lazuli, gold, jade and cornelian. It was built by Emperor Shah Jahan for his wife Mumtaz, of whom he must have been pretty fond. When she died he built the Taj Mahal for her.

The view from this cool pavilion out towards the Badshahi Mosque is a reminder of what makes Mughal architecture so fine. It's all about balance and symmetry. Towers, domes, minarets, columns and cupolas, some in red stone, some in white marble, are all gracefully harmonized. The Mughal emperors set out to balance power and pleasure, and no-one ever achieved this more successfully.

It's midday and in the mosque the sandstone slabs are so hot that a thin strip of carpet has been laid out, which is continually being hosed down. This requires a lot of water, as the 500 feet (160 m) square courtyard is one of the largest of any mosque in the world, and can hold upwards of 60,000 worshippers.

Today most of them are inside the shade of the tall Prayer Chamber, ten bays deep and topped by three white marble domes. The imam is giving his address but there seems to be little of the formality of worship in an English church. Some stand to listen, some kneel. People come and go, others talk to each other, some attend to their own devotions while young children run around at the back. Only when it comes to the holy prayer do they all come together to stand in line, barefoot, heads lowered. Then, moving as one, they bow to the waist, stand upright, kneel, press foreheads on the ground twice, then stand up and begin the process over again. There's something simple and powerful about such a communal act of humility in such splendid surroundings.

This evening we meet for a meal at the house of the well-connected Yusuf Salahuddin, who, hearing of our curiosity about Shaan Shahid, the actor on all the posters, is to take us to see him filming at the studios on the Multan Road, heart of Lahore's film industry, or Lollywood as it's known.

Yusuf's house is a warren of tastefully decorated rooms and courtyards in the Old Town. On antique tables stand photos of himself with Imran Khan, Jimmy Goldsmith and others. In the courtyard we eat the most delicious mangoes I've ever tasted and talk about what we've seen in Pakistan. His views on the trigger-happy North-West Frontier are far from reverential.

'They'll shoot you if they feel like it. Any excuse. If they don't like the food, or the way you smile, or farting. Farting, that's very bad. Farting is a crime on the North-West Frontier. And the older you are when you fart the worse it is.'

He insists we come back here for the Basant festival in April. Everyone in Lahore flies their kites for a day.

'It must be a beautiful sight.'

'Beautiful?' He shakes his head in mock horror. 'It's war!'

Apparently it gets seriously competitive, with rooftop rivals attaching knives and glass to their string to cut each other's kites adrift. (I've since heard that the mayor of Lahore has banned next year's kite festival because of risk of injury.)

It's late by the time we head down to the studios but Yusuf assures us that there is no point in getting there earlier. Because of the heat, all the shooting is done at night.

He explains that someone like Shaan will have several films on the go at once.

'What sort of films?'

'All the same,' he says. 'All Punjabi films have the same ingredients. One boy, two girls, one boy, one girl, two girls, one boy. We are a very emotional people, we like to cry our heart and soul out.'

Shaan arrives. A trim figure, early to mid-thirties, with black trousers and tunic and dyed blond hair. A good face, strong features, heavily muscled arms. Not unlike the young Brando.

A big wedding scene, in which Shahid plays an angry lover, is about to go before the cameras. There's the usual scrum of activity around the set. Turbanned figures on lighting gantries re-direct the lamps, extras wait nervously in a back room, a leading lady is applying the heavy and elaborate layers of make-up that seem to be obligatory for any heroine, while the director, Sangeeta, a big, fair-skinned, bespectacled woman, prowls around like the headmistress of a particularly troublesome comprehensive, cajoling, exhorting, upbraiding and generally trying to hurry the process along.

The set is all fairy lights and soft furnishings and fussy white balconies.

'This is what Punjabis want,' says Shaan, in quiet, fluent English. 'This is their fantasy of success.'

As he waits for his moment to be shot by the bride's father, he seems calm and quite happy to talk. He says he's been in the business 14 years and I ask him how many films he's made.

'223, I think, or is it 4?' He considers for a moment. 'And two of those years I spent in New York, so, yes, that's 224 in 12 years'.

His father was a director, producer and writer, his mother the leading actress in Pakistan, so Shaan has no illusions about the business, or his success. He's a family man. Loves to be woken by his daughter, he says.

'I wake up by 12.30, I go to my gym, I have breakfast, then I come to work. I do about nine projects a day.' He reckons he finishes a film every 28 days.

'Are you allowed to kiss on screen?'

'Not on the lips. On the hand or the forehead, or you know on the side cheek or something, but not on the lips. My wife's not going to agree to that, so forget it.'

'Does that seem unnatural to you?'

'No, that's very natural.'

I wonder if he fears any backlash from resurgent, conservative, Islamist elements in the country, who've made no secret of their dislike for the cinema.

'There's a bunch of people that need to be taught that this is something that has nothing to do with religion; it's a form of expression, it's a form of art and that's it.'

There are shouts from the set. The bride's father has been handed his gun and had his moustache reapplied, and pink spray is erupting from the fountain at the bottom of the stairs at the back. To my surprise Shaan calls me onto the set to have my photo taken with the actors.

'They are all big fans.'

I shake hands with the bridegroom, who beams with excitement.

'This is very exciting for us. We love British comedy.'

I shrug modestly.

'Oh yes. Mr Bean, Benny Hill. We love it!'

I think it's time for me to go to bed.

Day Twenty Seven : Lahore

A short night. Spend the morning at what has been described as the 'Versailles of the Punjab', the Shalimar Gardens, created 360 years ago by that prodigious creator of fine monuments Emperor Shah

Jahan, the tasteful tyrant who gave the world, among other things, the Taj Mahal.

Long, metre-thick pink and cream sandstone walls protect the gardens from the commotion outside, and a great and soothing sense of space and tranquillity envelops you as you enter.

In a city bulging at the seams it is both gratifying and surprising that these 40 acres of royal pleasure gardens survive at all, even though it's clearly a struggle to maintain them to Shah Jahan's specifications.

The layout is formal, based on descriptions in the Koran, with three descending terraces and the ultimate in water features – streams, pools, cascades and waterfalls – all set in precise geometric harmony. In the days when the Emperor and Empress looked out at each other from their own personal pavilions, separated by shaded walkways and water channels, 400 fountains played in the gardens, kept at constant pressure by water from huge storage tanks continually topped up from a canal by a conveyor belt of wheels and buckets.

But that was the 17th century and modern technology just hasn't been able to keep up. The 20th-century pumps are far less effective and water springs from the calcified fountains in dribbles rather than jets. An old man is wading around in the water tank unclogging non-performing fountains by hammering a wooden peg into their sclerotic spouts.

There is, sadly, no sign of the 128 gardeners recorded in an early description of the Shalimar Gardens. Instead there is a man cutting the grass with a small domestic lawnmower hauled by a water buffalo. Every now and then he brings the buffalo to a halt and empties the grass cuttings into the nearest ornamental lake, where they're devoured by large and slothful fish.

Eating being one of the preoccupations of Lahoris, I end the day in Food Street, on the recommendation of Asim and Azam, my friends from the train. I think they've slightly oversold the place. It's picturesque enough, with fresh-painted wooden verandahs and shiny, stuccoed balconies, but it's obviously designed for tourists and has that cheerful soulless glow of civic improvement. The food, especially the house speciality of Mutton Karahi, served in the wok it's cooked in, is good, strong and filling, but how I long for a beer to wash it down. The soda I'm allowed is just not the same.

The alcohol ban brings the conversation around to religion, and my assumption that because Asim and Azam are young 'modern' Pakistanis they would be less interested in matters of faith than their elders proves to be wrong.

Azam, the accountant, maintains that being a Muslim means that the Koran orders everything for him, offering guidance and instruction in every area of life.

He picks a glass up from the table.

'Even a simple thing like this glass. How I hold it. In my right hand, never my left. I should always drink sitting down, never standing up. I should look into the glass as I drink.'

He puts the glass down and looks across the table at me, almost defiantly.

'I do all these things not just because it says so in the Koran, but also because I know they are good for me.'

Tomorrow Azam will become engaged and they will have a big party. He doesn't know when they'll marry. It could be a year, two, or even three years.

'Will you live together until then?'

Both he and Asim shake their heads vehemently.

'Oh, no. No. Sex before marriage is out of the question.'

Day Twenty Eight : Lahore to Amritsar

On the front page of the newspaper there is a photograph of a man on a ladder painting black stripes over an advert that shows an unveiled woman holding an apple drink. He is described as a member of the Shabab-I-Milli Islamist Activist group. Lower down the page are pictures of two sisters, their faces disfigured by acid thrown by the husband of one of them. 'Acid attacks,' notes the report, 'are among the worst of the huge numbers of crimes against women committed in Pakistan.'

There could hardly be two more graphic reminders of the problems that loom ahead for the country as it tries to reconcile progress with deeply entrenched tradition.

As I pack for the last time before crossing the border to India, I have to say that Pakistan has been a revelation. Simplistic post 9/11 propaganda sought to equate it with terrorism, as if you could equate a population greater than that of France and Germany combined with any single thought or idea. I have found Pakistan to be infinitely more complex and diverse than I had been prepared for. Wilder and more beautiful too. Never once did I feel threatened. Give or take a few cold beers, I leave it with regret.

The Indian border is only 18 miles (30 km) from Lahore, an accident of politics that brought terrible suffering to the city when Pakistan was created in 1947. The exact details of where the frontier would run were not revealed by the British until a few hours before independence was declared. When it became clear that one of India's oldest and most prestigious cities was to become part of Pakistan an hysterical panic broke out. As half a million Hindus and Sikhs fled east and even more Muslims fled west, reprisals on both sides were swift and bloody.

Cross-border trains arrived at Lahore station full of massacred corpses. Men, women and children on both sides were attacked and killed. Law and order were paralysed as the communal violence took its course. The British refused to bring their army out onto the streets to help. Across the subcontinent as a whole it is estimated that partition resulted in over a million deaths.

The legacy of hatred still smoulders. The border post at Wagah is the only official land crossing between Pakistan and India, and even then Pakistanis and Indians are only allowed to cross in specially secure trains between Lahore and Amritsar. Foreigners, if they have the time and patience, can walk through from Pakistan to India, and this is what we intend to do.

The thermometer has fallen to a mere 41°C (106°F), but the humidity has risen. There was quite a storm across these plains last night and a combination of dust and moisture makes the air thick and sticky. It's what Roger calls a three-shirt day.

The canals that run along the side of the road to Wagah are thronged with people cooling off. Families picnicking on the banks watch children splashing in the mud, men wash rickshaws and bicycles in the water, women, veiled and sari-ed, take tentative dips. Hot-headed teenage boys fling their shirts off and leap from bridges. There seems to be a heightened devil-may-care mood along the roadside today. As the traffic grinds to a standstill boys who would not normally have dared approach us dance like scarecrows in front of our minibus and bang the sides as we move on. It's nice to have one last image of Pakistan with its hair down.

At the border the road peters out in an open assembly area, full of trucks. Beyond this rises a modern red brick arch decorated with faux-Mughal columns and cupolas and flanked by terraced seating. Through the arch can be glimpsed two pairs of heavy metal gates, with a white line between them, which is the border itself. Beyond them rises another arched gateway inscribed with the single word 'India', the grandness of the gesture somewhat compromised by a row of threadbare potted plants arranged along its parapet.

This is the arena for a nightly display of nationalist feather ruffling, as both sides lower their flags in a ceremony deliberately designed to provoke unabashed jingoism in the assembled crowds.

Loudspeakers blare out. The terraces are filling up and a heavily perspiring man wearing a T-shirt in green and white national colours is warming up an already damp crowd.

'Pa-ki-stan!' he shouts.

'PA-KI-STAN!' they roar back.

Two very small children carrying flags are sent out by their mothers to join him. They're greeted with tumultuous applause.

We can hear the same sort of thing happening on the Indian side, the only noticeable difference being that they have music playing from their loudspeakers, while the Pakistanis have prayers and readings from the Koran.

At 6.05 precisely (this is, after all, a military ceremony) a bugle sounds, and, to resounding cheers, two of the tallest people I've seen in Pakistan march out towards the border gates. These are Punjabi Rangers and to say they march is an understatement. Every movement is executed with barely suppressed fury. Arms are snapped out like freshly drawn swords, legs fly into the air, high enough to brush the nose with the knee, before thudding into the ground with the force of a steam-hammer. This study in bellicosity is emphasized by uniforms as black as their smouldering eyes. Fan-shaped headdresses rise like hackles from their turbans.

They are followed by a squad of 12 more Rangers, who emerge with a splendid mixture of panache, aggression and bad acting that has the crowd roaring.

Speeding, slowing, high kicking, strutting, stamping, grimacing, leering and hissing with a finely honed ferocity, they create the impression of caged beasts ready at any moment to bite their opponents' heads off.

The Indian guard, in light khaki with red and gold turban plumes and white gaiters, march out to meet them. They try hard to be as theatrically aggressive as their Pakistani counterparts but somehow you don't feel their hearts are really in it.

Nevertheless, the show must go on and both sides, now eyeball to eyeball, contrive to present a quite surreal display of precision nastiness, raising their forearms like weapons, pawing the ground, baring their teeth and snarling at one another like turkey-cocks.

Even the lowering of the flag is conducted with a tight-lipped, carefully choreographed, competitive swagger, the final flourish of which is the controlled slamming of the gates between the two countries.

Applause and cheers follow the two flag parties as they march rabidly back towards their respective arches.

After this the whole thing degenerates into a PR exercise as the men who have terrified us for the last 30 minutes reappear to mingle with the crowd and have their photograph taken with kiddies and members of Parliament.

This pantomime at the border sends out confusing signals. Beyond the arches and the terraces where this carefully calculated piece of theatre has taken place is the reality of the Indo-Pakistan border: a mile-wide strip of no-man's land, guarded and patrolled as far as the eye can see by troops armed with more than high kicks and grimaces. Follow this line north into Kashmir and you will find several hundred thousand heavily armed men facing each other, not for entertainment, but because 56 years after independence, the line of partition remains a deep, unhealed wound.

India

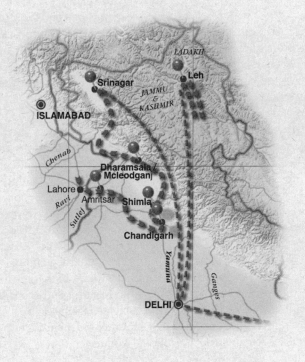

Day Thirty : Amritsar

A sign greets the traveller who makes the long walk across no-man's land and through the easternmost archway. 'India, the Largest Democracy in the World, Welcomes You'. As if to emphasize what a difference a half-mile makes, cold beer salesmen assail you and you are liable to be overtaken on the road by women on motorbikes. But the difference between the severity and discipline of Islamic Pakistan and the liberalism of secular India seems nowhere better demonstrated than in the border city of Amritsar.

Muslim and Hindu live reasonably happily together here (indeed, it's a fact that, despite Partition, there are more Muslims in India than in Pakistan), but the predominant religion in the first big city on the Indian side of the border is neither Muslim nor Hindu. Amritsar is a Sikh town.

Sikhism, professed by 65 per cent of the population here, is one of the world's newer faiths. It was founded by one Guru Nanak, in the early years of the 16th century. After a lifetime of travel, he concluded from what he saw that 'God is to be found neither in the Koran or the Puranas' (the sacred Hindu texts). Unable to accept the Hindu caste system, or what he saw as the intolerance of Islam, Guru Nanak came up with an admirably pragmatic solution. One God for all, rich or poor, with no human hierarchies or priesthoods, idols or icons coming in between.

In a nod towards another religion, the Sikh gurus chose a pool visited by Lord Buddha around which to build their first temple. It was called Amrit Sovar (The Nectar Pool) and though the name was elided to Amritsar, the pool, much extended, still exists and the temple built around it is now one of the most famous shrines in the world.

To get to the Golden Temple I take a motorcycle rickshaw into the centre of the city. The bracing, or exhausting, anarchy of Indian streets begins as soon as we leave the hotel. Cars veer out of side roads without stopping, lame dogs hop gamely across your bows, bicycles and buses appear from nowhere and blasts of the horn mingle with blasts from exhausts. At a roundabout we are forced into the middle of the road to avoid not just a cow, but a cow feeding its calf. As we pull out, a scooter with three small children concertinaed in between their mother and father hoots indignantly at us before disappearing in a cloud of fumes from the back of a passing truck.

Road safety signs with slogans like 'Hell or Helmet!' and 'Stay Married! Divorce Speed!' are partially obscured and universally ignored.

An additional discomfort for an Englishman driving into Amritsar is a series of very public reminders of how much we were once disliked.

On one roundabout is a statue of a dashing figure in a theatrical moustache, a *puja* garland around his neck, running forward pointing a gun. This celebrates the assassin Udham Singh, who shot and killed Sir Michael O'Dwyer, a hated governor of the Punjab, in London in 1940.

Around the next corner is a statue to S. C. Bose, who felt so strongly about getting the British out of India that he tried to ally his Indian National Army with the Germans and Japanese in the Second World War. A half-mile further on is the alleyway leading to the Jallianwala Bagh, where 400 peacefully but illegally protesting Indians were massacred on the orders of Brigadier-General Reginald Dyer in April 1919, an outrage considered by many to mark the beginning of the end of British rule. Today the site is a park where a sacred flame burns, sponsored by Indian Oil.

The complex of buildings that contains the Golden Temple is called a Gurudwara (Gateway to the Gurus), the name given to all places of worship of the 20 million or so Sikhs in India. This, the holiest and grandest of them all, dominates the centre of Amritsar, its balconied, white stucco facade and flamboyantly domed roof rising exotically above a clutter of stalls, billboards, shops and crowded pavements where groups of Dalits ('the oppressed') squat inches from the traffic.

There is a strict dress code for the Golden Temple. First of all the head must be covered at all times. Scarves of various colours are readily available for non-Sikhs, either from any one of the 17 young lads who converge on you as soon as you pull up outside, or more cheaply from one of the stalls inside the forecourt. Shoes and socks must be removed. By the time we have deposited them at special lockers (a lady takes mine, something that would never have happened in Pakistan), we look like a line of pantomime pirates. Hands must then be washed at marble-lined public basins and bare feet passed through a trough of water at the bottom of the steps.

The combination of the heat of the day, the constant crowd moving in and out and the carrying of film gear makes all these preliminaries rather a trial, but the sight that greets us when we finally reach the gateway arch banishes thoughts of discomfort, at least for a minute or two.

The Golden Temple itself, called by Sikhs the Hari Mandir (God's Temple) sits, like a great glittering barge, in the centre of a huge tank of water, with one narrow causeway (jammed with people throughout the day) connecting it with the promenade and the dazzling white ancillary buildings that enclose it on all four sides.

Four gates, one on each side, symbolize the inclusivity of Sikhism, the temple's openness to all, irrespective of religion, caste, creed or sex. The four equal entrances are not all that distinguish it from other religious buildings. Instead of climbing to an altar, the stairs to the Golden Temple lead downwards to the holy place, an encouragement to approach with humility.

Once down the steps to the waterside, there isn't much encouragement to sit around. Most of the pilgrims are moving, in a remorseless clockwise flow, around the marble-flagged promenade, some strolling, some bustling purposefully, some dodging the mops and buckets of the cleaners, most squeezed onto coconut matting to avoid burning their feet, while hymns from the Holy Book are sung over booming loudspeakers. Some men are stripped down, bathing in the holy water, which seems to be largely full of fat carp with gulping, Jagger-like mouths. Very few visitors, apart from a one-legged man lying asleep, head resting on his crutches, are doing nothing.

I notice how much more openly curious people are here than in Pakistan.

'What is the country in which you are residing?' they ask. 'For what purpose have you come?'

Occasionally, a passing family group will quite unapologetically insert themselves alongside us and get a friend to take a photo, as if we too are part of the tourist attractions. Helpful explanations of what's going on are given, whether solicited or not.

An elderly gentleman with a long beard points in the direction of the Hari Mandir.

'Whatever you require from God he is giving you. That is what they are singing about.'

There is a brisk, businesslike pragmatism about the Sikhs. They don't seem over-concerned with the mysteries of belief.

Philanthropy, along with business enterprise and physical bravery, is a vital part of Sikhism and all their temples have a *langar*, a kitchen preparing free meals around the clock, financed through the one-tenth of their income that all Sikhs are expected to give to good works. It's a huge operation, with an estimated 50,000 meals prepared each weekday and twice that at weekends. The work is all done by volunteers, and any Sikh, whether surgeon or street cleaner, is expected to come and help chop onions or wash dishes. In the words of one of the ten holy Gurus on whose teachings Sikhism is based: 'If you want to understand me, come into my kitchen.' This we do.

The kitchen is spread through several buildings. One is entirely devoted to a chapatti production line. A rat skips nimbly out of the way as fresh sacks of flour are cut open and fed into the bowels of a slowly turning machine, which regurgitates the flour as dough. One group of helpers rolls the dough into balls, another flattens each ball out into a pancake, and another lays them out on hotplates the size of double beds, made from cast-iron sheets laid on bricks with gas fires underneath, and capable of taking a couple of hundred chapattis at a time. When one side is done the chapattis are flipped over in quick, dexterous movements of a long thin implement with a half-moon end. When the flipper is satisfied both sides are right he gives an extra strong flick, which sends the chapatti flying off the hotplate to land neatly on a pile on the floor. The piles are then removed and carried out to the refectory.

The chapatti production line shares a tall barn-like space with dal cauldrons, the largest cooking vessels I've ever seen. Vats like giant tympana are set above gas jets and stirred with mighty ladles.

I pick my way through the kitchens, across a terrace where 30 or 40 people sit slicing onions and garlic, green peppers and ginger, and up the stairs to take a meal in one of the spartan communal dining rooms. Each floor is the size of a warehouse and can accommodate 3000 covers at any one time. I join a line of people who file in and sit cross-legged at a long coir mat, soggy from periodic washing. Volunteers pass through, giving out segmented stainless steel trays, which others then fill up with chapatti, dollops of pickle and dal ladled out of steel buckets. Water is poured into our mugs from another bucket.

As a helpful man next to me says, this whole process embodies the Sikh teaching that we are all equal and we must learn to serve each other.

This high-volume soup kitchen is not the only service; there are also free dormitories here providing accommodation for 25,000 people a night.

It looks and sounds like a fine and good thing but there have been abuses of the system. I notice a sign advising 'Pilgrims must not accept eatables from strangers', which refers to a recent spate of cases of people being drugged and their belongings stolen.

Twenty years ago this altruistic environment saw dreadful violence when a group of Sikhs demanding their own state barricaded themselves in the Akhal Takht, the second most sacred building on the site.

The siege was lifted in the infamous Operation Bluestar, when the Indian army brought tanks into the temple and pulverized the building. It's estimated that several thousand died in the fighting. Such was the strength of feeling that a few months later Prime Minister Indira Gandhi, who authorized the attack, was assassinated by Sikh members of her own bodyguards.

Such trauma seems almost inconceivable tonight as a setting sun burnishes the 500 kilograms of gold that sheathe the marble walls of the Hari Mandir, hymns echo around the arcades and turbanned and bearded Sikh men and their families move slowly in through its doors to pay homage to the Holy Book, the most precious object in a religion that rejects idolatry.

Day Thirty One : Amritsar to Chandigarh

India is much concerned these days with behavioural improvement. Yesterday I noticed the road safety campaign (though I seemed to be the only one who did) and this morning I see that the government is tackling the vexed subject of 'night soil', or open-air defecation, which is such a feature of life here. A series of adverts in the morning papers appeals to people to stop 'easing themselves' in public places. 'Easing oneself' is a new euphemism to me, but I rather like it and will use it whenever possible.

Heading south from Amritsar on the main road to Chandigarh we pass an horrific accident. Two trucks have collided head-on with such force that one of them has burst, oozing a load of gravel from its ruptured sides. My driver says that truck-drivers not only don't have to take a test, they don't even have to be able to read.

The road we're on is a four-lane intercity highway, yet it's also a country road with farm vehicles, and indeed farm animals, crossing it whenever they feel like it.

At any given time we're sharing the NH-1 with cars, trucks, battered Tata buses (driven like the wind), auto-rickshaws, pedal rickshaws, scooters, horse-drawn carts, buffalo-drawn carts, tractors, dogs, bicycles, motorbikes, pedestrians and unattended cows, sheep and goats.

A roadside billboard cheers me up. 'Youghal and Sons. Where Fashion Ends.'

We take a short cut off the main road along an avenue of eucalyptus trees, which leads promisingly quietly through a green and pleasant countryside of rice and barley fields dotted with elegant white cattle egrets. Quite out of the blue we're brought to a halt by a traffic jam ahead of us. I ask my driver what's going on and he shakes his head in exasperation. It's a police check.

When we finally pull up alongside the policeman he swaggers slowly over to our driver. He looks like the corrupt cop out of central casting. Overweight, ponderous and self-important. He sniffs loudly as he examines our driver's papers, but when he sees us in the back he becomes a little more animated. After a couple more questions he hands the papers back and waves us quickly on.

My driver chuckles.

'He's fleecing people. Taking their money to drive along his road. I told him we were making a film for BBC Television. That's why we got through so fast!'

Arrive on the leafy ring roads of Chandigarh about six. And, miraculously, in one piece.

Day Thirty Two: Chandigarh to Shimla

Chandigarh seems to consist entirely of roundabouts. Beautiful, well-kept, florally abundant roundabouts, sending the traffic spinning from one to another like some endless Scottish reel.

Verdant avenues of peepul, ashoka and mango trees connect this gently swirling system, leading, presumably, to a city of some substance, for Chandigarh is the capital of two states, Punjab and Haryana. I say presumably, because in our short stay here it is difficult to see much beyond the roundabouts and dead-straight, repetitive avenues.

What I do see reminds me of Islamabad. Both are post-Independence cities, built in a self-consciously modern style to replace the architecture of the Raj with something new and fresh, and more in keeping with what Nehru called 'the nation's faith in the future'. Both are discreet, tidy and a little cheerless.

At least Chandigarh secured the services of the top man. Swiss architect Le Corbusier designed the grid-plan layout and the boxy, modular buildings in concrete and red brick that can be glimpsed every now and then between the trees.

When I enquire what sort of person lives in this mecca of modernism I'm told that it's mostly wealthy Punjabi farmers approaching retirement.

My local informant summed up Chandigarh as 'a town of white beards and green hedges'. And sadly I'm not here long enough to disprove it.

It's time to return to the mountains, and we begin the journey dramatically, aboard the Himalayan Queen railway service to Shimla, a town high in the Shiwalik foothills, from where the British Empire in India was run during the hot summer months and which is now the capital of Himachal Pradesh (Himalaya Province).

The 2'6" narrow-gauge railway to Shimla climbs 7000 feet (2130 m) in 57 miles (92 km) and there is barely a level stretch of track on the entire route.

Midday at Kalka station. Ten minutes before the Queen leaves, the express from Delhi arrives, disgorging yet more passengers for the Shimla train. Half-term holidays have just begun and sturdy schoolgirls with backpacks and walking sticks are fighting with harassed family groups for a place in one of the seven small coaches.

The stationmaster, a stout man with a shiny bald head, ignores the helpless cries of his staff as he rolls out a liturgy of statistics.

'Indian Railways is the biggest employer in the world, you know. We move ten million people a day, over 6000 kilometres of track.' He dabs a handkerchief at his forehead, then tucks it in his pocket and produces a small scrapbook.

'You want to film the viaduct?' he asks. 'You can do that.'

He opens the book to reveal a grainy photograph of the railway line running over a multi-storey stone bridge, and holds it up to the camera.

'There,' he smooths down the page, 'you film that.'

'We'd rather film the real thing,' says Nigel with a trace of irritation. The stationmaster, undeterred, riffles through the pages.

'Look at that!' he holds the book up again. A wintry scene of the same viaduct. 'That is *snow*!'

Somehow, everyone squeezes aboard and, on time at 12.10, the Himalayan Queen pulls out past Kalka signal box, rounds a curve and heads for the hills, passing by a mix of factories and rust-stained housing blocks surrounded by lush sub-tropical vegetation. A line-side tree sways beneath the weight of a family of monkeys the size of small Labradors.

'Langurs,' says the woman opposite me. 'They're the biggest monkeys of all.'

I offer some sweets to her and her family and we start talking. She's a large very jolly lady and her name is Deepti. She works for the ministry of defence in Delhi and is on a week's holiday with her husband and two boys. I ask her if the Britishness of Shimla is still an attraction for Indian tourists.

She frowns and shakes her head.

'They're not so interested in all that, no.'

She reminds me that vital conferences between Gandhi, Nehru and Jinnah aimed at getting the British out of India also took place in Shimla.

We rattle into a tunnel. One of 103 on the line, their entrances all numbered and marked with the exact length.

Deepti opens plastic containers and gets out lunch for the family. She was up at four this morning, she says, preparing *pooris* and *aloo* for the journey, and she insists on sharing them with me.

The deep-fried fluffy *pooris* mix deliciously with the curried potato. There are four more hours of the journey to go and I feel in no hurry at all, which is just as well, for the progress of the Himalayan Queen is dogged rather than dashing. We rarely make much more than 20 miles an hour, which is all you want with good food, good company and a good view.

I stand at the open door and let the gradually cooling air blow over me as we snake round corners and in and out of trim stone tunnels dug into the hillside like rabbit holes. As we climb, the date palms, rubber trees and bougainvillea give way to grassy meadows, oak scrub and then spindly deciduous woodland.

I have a knowledgeable companion in Raaja Bhasin, a neat, theatrical, young man who has written books on Shimla. The British, he tells me, had discovered the spot in the 1820s, and it was so much to their liking that in 1864 it was declared their summer capital.

'At that time one-fifth of the human race was administered from Shimla.'

As the railway was not opened for another 39 years, the entire apparatus of government had to be moved up from Calcutta on bullock carts.

When it was eventually decided to go ahead with a railway they moved fast. The line was built in little more than two years, and the basic structures remain in good order a hundred years later. The high standards expected took their toll. Raaja tells the story of a Colonel Barog who supervised the construction of one of the tunnels working from each end simultaneously. Unfortunately, they failed to meet in the middle and Barog, distraught at the miscalculation, shot himself.

Half an hour out of Shimla we're into alpine forest and there is a cool, refreshing scent of pine in the air. The railway runs between tall rhododendron trees and the big cedars they call deodars, until all at once we're among the half-timbered villas and cottages with verandahs and cast-iron canopies that comfortably conform to my image of Shimla. But as we pull away clear of the trees and get our first glimpse of the town itself I realize I've got it very wrong.

Modern Shimla is no cosy retreat in the mountains but a city of considerable scale, home to 150,000, spread out over five hills and liberally sprinkled with concrete apartment blocks.

On the steep street outside the station there is a chaos of drivers, passengers and vehicles manoeuvring in an impossibly small space. Once away from this bottleneck our taxi crawls slowly round the side of the hill and along the Mall until we reach the Cecil Hotel.

This famous Shimla landmark has been extensively and, I should imagine, expensively, restored.

The room is lovely and, as darkness falls, I just want to throw open the balcony doors and taste the freshest air since we left the mountain valleys of the Karakoram.

As soon as I do so my telephone rings and I'm politely but firmly requested not to, as monkeys will get into my room. Monkeys are a big problem, they assure me. Big enough to install sensors in my tall, tempting balcony doors to sound an alarm whenever I open them.

Day Thirty Four : Shimla

Wake to grey skies and rain. Filming delayed till the weather clears. Retire to the best bed on the journey so far and read the Dalai Lama's book *The Art of Happiness*. We have been granted an audience with him in a few days' time and I began the book a little out of duty. Now I find I'm getting a lot out of it. There is something infectious about his optimism, an optimism which comes from confronting rather than avoiding the unacceptable and acknowledging, understanding and demystifying it.

An hour later the clouds have passed over and I can see a crystal clear sky beyond my monkey-besieged windows.

I can see the enemy clearly. They move in family groups along the wall opposite, scratching themselves and ambling rather cockily along, until some commotion breaks out and they race in all directions, shrieking and snarling.

I gaze out in frustration, feeling an unlikely empathy with those mega popstars, besieged in hotel rooms by their fans.

From being just a summer hideaway, Shimla grew to become the nerve centre of Britain's Indian empire for eight months of the year and in 1888 a building considered appropriate for this role was completed. The Vice-Regal Lodge is an extraordinary edifice. Built at the top of a hill and the peak of Victorian self-confidence, it is authority made manifest, superiority set in stone. The British relationship with India changed in the 1860s, after the bloodshed of the Indian

Mutiny, or the first War of Independence, as most Indians call it. What had been a loosely commercial enterprise, a sort of mercantile laissez-faire, began to be seen as a moral obligation. Previously relaxed relations between British and Indians were discouraged. Better communications meant that wives and families could come out to India, ending inter-marriage with locals. The army was strengthened and concentrated in well-armed cantonments.

'Keeping India at bay', is how my friend Raaja sums up this new imperial vision, as we walk in the gardens of the Lodge this morning. In his view, the sombre grey walls that rise above us repre-sented a deliberate attempt by the British to recreate the island mentality in India. The Vice-Regal Lodge stood not just for power, but for permanence.

Permanence lasted less than 60 years and to add insult to injury many of the most important talks that led to the departure of the British took place behind these grandiose faux-baronial walls. All the founders and future leaders of India and Pakistan at one time trooped in below the lions rampant that stand guard above the carved stone portals.

'Gandhi disliked it,' says Raaja. 'While everybody else came in rickshaws, two men pushing and two men pulling, Gandhi walked.'

Mountbatten, the man charged with giving India its independ-ence, met the leaders of the Princely States here, reminding himself of who the most important ones were by using the mnemonic 'Hot kippers make good breakfast'. Hyderabad, Kashmir, Mysore, Gwalior and Baroda.

The fact that the monumental Vice-Regal Lodge still stands is hardly surprising. It would probably need some controlled nuclear device to take down these massive walls, but the fact that it is so well maintained, with gardeners sweeping immaculate lawns and care-fully raking the gravel on the forecourt, says a lot about the attitude of the Indians after independence.

'There was no wholesale desecration of imperial buildings in Shimla,' says Raaja. 'Everything was left pretty much as it was.'

The Vice-Regal Lodge has been reborn as an Institute for South-East Asian Affairs. The Ballroom is now a library. Functional shelf stacks fill a floor that in its heyday had hundreds of dancers swirling across it, themed perhaps in Chinese or Regency fancy dress. Though chandeliers still hang from its ceiling, the spot where the orchestra played is now marked by a large sign that reads 'Silence'.

An index board showing where books can be located still uses vice-regal descriptions like State Lounge and Fan Room. Social Sciences can be found in the Ballroom, the Tibetan Collection in the Pantry, and copies of *The Muslim World* and *American Scientist* sit side by side in the Dining Hall.

Modesty and earnestness has replaced display and grandeur. Entertainment has given way to enlightenment. This bastion of British certainty has become a place of enquiry, curiosity and debate. Three very Indian preoccupations.

The imposing site on which Shimla is built can best be seen from the Ridge, a long, thin, open area that stands at the narrowest point of the bluff. It's a watershed, with rivers on one side running east to the Bay of Bengal, and on the other, west into the Arabian Sea.

This afternoon it's thronged with holiday strollers eating pizza and ice cream. Though the milling tourists are almost entirely Indian, the centre of the town still lives up to its description as 'a little bit of Cheltenham in India'. Statues of Mahatma and Indira Gandhi are overshadowed by the tall Gothic Revival tower of Christ Church dominating one end of the Ridge, looking yellow, blotchy and feverish with plants pushing up out of holes in its red, corrugated-iron roof. A little way down the hill is the Arts and Crafts Style Town Hall, about the only building in town with a slate roof (Raaja tells me that corrugated iron is preferred because monkeys pull the tiles out).

A flight of steps leads down from the Ridge to another Cheltenham-ish landmark, the Gaiety Theatre. It was built about the same time as the Vice-Regal Lodge, as a home for a thriving amateur dramatic club in Shimla, which gave its first performance in 1838. With few women around at that time, the female roles had to be taken by army officers, one of whom refused to shave his moustache off for a love scene.

A heavy stone exterior gives little indication of the little gem of an auditorium inside. Horseshoe shaped and decorated with carved wood and plaster of Paris stucco, it has a dress circle supported by slender columns with gold-leaf capitals. The stage, spacious for a theatre that only seats 200, has been graced by Kipling, Baden-Powell, who later founded the Boy Scouts, and more recently Felicity Kendall and legendary Indian stars like the singer K. L. Saighal and the Bollywood actor Anupam Kher.

Our visit has coincided with a performance of an early play by Michael Frayn, called *Chinamen*. With huge successes running currently on Broadway and in the West End, I imagine this is quite a coup for them, and have taken the trouble to ring Michael and solicit a message of support for the cast.

The director, Mrs Neelam Dewan, thanks me profusely for this, as she had been given a copy of the play without a front page and didn't know who the author was.

She seems a little harassed. Last night's performance had been spoiled by mass amnesia on the part of the actors.

Had they not had time to learn their lines, I asked her.

Oh yes, they had time, but they are all in the army and very busy.

So I stumbled on the truth. This pretty little theatre survives as a sort of social club for the military. The activities of the Green Room bar and lounge upstairs subsidize the thespian activities below, the quid pro quo being that the army are offered the best parts, and the best seats.

As curtain up approaches, men trained to lead hundreds into battle are pacing about backstage, like schoolboys about to go before the headmaster, repeating the same lines over and over again. It's a full house tonight with the local commander in chief attending. This only seems to ratchet up the tension.

I have been asked to give a short address before the play begins.

'What is your name again, please?' asks the young captain who's been asked to introduce me. 'Palin…Palin.' He tries it out a few times before giving me an apologetic smile.

'I'm the entertainments officer. I do bingo, mainly.'

At 7.30 precisely he pushes aside the decaying velvet curtain, tells a few nervous jokes and then I hear my moment of glory approach.

'Ladies and Gentlemen, may I ask you to give a very warm welcome for our special celebrity guest, Mr Michael Plain!'

This sort of sets the tone for the evening. Despite the best efforts of Mrs Neelam Dewan, both as director and leading actress, some of the colonels and majors in the cast do have recollection problems, and I understand now why the two prompters are given such prominent mention in the programme and why, when they come on stage at the end, Mrs Punam Gupta and Mrs Vijaylaksmi Sood receive thunderous applause and garlands of flowers.

Afterwards we all repair to the Green Room and tell each other how wonderful we were and the Commanding Officer, Lt-General Singh, a Sikh in a handsome rose-pink turban, insists that we return to his house for a drink. It's a short walk from the hotel and Roger is much impressed that the guards on the gate snap to attention and present arms as we enter. It's after midnight when we leave, and they totally ignore us.

Day Thirty Five : Shimla to Dharamsala

Pack up. Take a last look out of the French windows I'm not supposed to open. Expect the monkeys to at least look up, but they're all gathered around a rubbish skip, picking around in the contents as if it were the first day of Harrods' sale.

Or perhaps they've heard what's happening to their brothers and sisters in Delhi. *The Times of India* reports that the authorities there have decided to start rounding up some of the monkeys that roam the city and deport them. More controversially, they're to take 2000 cows out of circulation as well. Not, I notice, to improve road safety, but, so they say, to curb the illegal milk trade.

We leave the bow windows, pebble-dash walls and wrought-iron balconies behind and continue north by car to another hill station, Dharamsala, best known for being the headquarters of the Dalai Lama and the Tibetan government in exile.

Our driver, like many middle-aged men in India and Pakistan, has coloured his greying hair with henna, in his case so generously that it's almost bright scarlet and a tell-tale contrast with his grey moustache. Basil has christened him 'Red'.

Outside the village of Ghumarwin Red gives an agonized cry and swings the wheel frantically.

'That is very bad,' he says, in genuine distress. 'That was a snake on the road.'

Basil is unsympathetic.

'You swerved to avoid a snake?'

'It is Monday. Shiva's day. It is very bad luck.'

'No, it's not, it's Tuesday.'

A great weight seems to fall from Red's shoulder.

'Ah, yes, that's good. That is Hanuman's day. He is the monkey god.'

'So you've got to watch out for monkeys.'

'Oh yes.'

Basil, proud owner of a lovely wheaten terrier called Ed, asks which day he should avoid dogs.

'Dogs?' Red laughs dismissively. 'No. Always killing dogs.'

The country road is undulating and undramatic, rising and falling as we cross the valleys of modest rivers running down from the mountains into the Punjab. Reminders of worship are never far away, from brightly painted roadside shrines daubed in mauve, bright pink or orange, to busloads of pilgrims in yellow robes with red and gold sashes. They're causing traffic jams as they converge on the temple at a place called Jawalamukhi. The attraction here is that natural gas issues from the cliff in the form of an 'eternal' blue flame and feeds a constantly boiling pool of water. This is considered magical proof of the power of the local gods.

By evening we've reached our hotel, once a tea-planter's bungalow, with fine views over the green Kangra valley below and the Dhauladar Mountains above, on whose wooded slopes Dharamsala and its sister McLeodganj are set like Tuscan hill villages.

No monkeys to besiege us down here but caged dogs bark all night long.

Read *The Art of Happiness* and try to avoid feeling murderous.

Day Thirty Six: Dharamsala and McLeodganj

It's six o'clock in the morning and the first streaks of light are in the sky as we drive along the narrow streets of Dharamsala and continue up the road that climbs through pine, oak and rhododendron woods to the less mellifluous-sounding village of McLeodganj. ('Ganj' means market and McLeod, presumably, was a Scotsman.) To complicate matters, this place with a Hindu-Scots name is filled with Tibetans.

The reason they're here is that the Chinese, having invaded Tibet in 1949, began to consolidate their political power by eliminating any opposition. In 1959 this resulted in an uprising in Lhasa, which was put down with such force that, fearing for his life, the Dalai

Lama, leader of Tibetan Buddhism and Head of State, decided to flee his country.

He crossed the Himalaya into India and in a brave gesture of generosity, Prime Minister Nehru gave him sanctuary and later a more permanent home in Dharamsala. (Many other countries would have had misgivings about what this would do to their relations with China.) Chinese oppression of Buddhists is less virulent now than it was at the height of the Cultural Revolution, but they have tightened their economic and political hold on Tibet and 44 years after his flight, the Dalai Lama, and the Tibetan government, remain in exile.

We're up this early to catch a dawn ceremony at the Lhagyal Ri Temple, just a short walk down the hill from the monastery where the Dalai Lama now lives.

On a terrace of land with tall pines falling away to one side are a series of stupas, the dome-shaped shrines in which are kept scriptures or remains or clay likenesses of the gods. A great wall of prayer flags forms a backdrop behind them. There's a residual night-time chill in the air but already a line of devotees are quietly moving along a line of brightly painted prayer wheels, which culminates in one huge wheel about eight feet high. They spin them and murmur prayers as they go. They then feed sprigs of juniper branch into small open ovens and leave gifts by the fire, a flask of tea or a bottle of barley wine. The aromatic, spicy smell of the wood smoke mingles with the pines to give a strong heady flavour to the dawn.

As the sun rises its rays hit the columns of smoke and turn them into long diagonal shafts of light. At that moment four monks, cross-legged on the floor before a microphone, begin to recite prayers.

Dogs sniff around. A herd of cows plods slowly across the front of the temple past the prayer wheels and on into the woods. No-one seems to bat an eyelid. It's part of life and all life is sacred to the Buddhist.

The only organized part of what seems to me a delightfully laid-back, unstructured ceremony is a ritual throwing of *tsampa*, barley flour. I'm encouraged to join in and, picking up a handful of the flour, I take my place in line facing the stupas. Prayers are recited, hands are raised three times and then, altogether, we toss the flour forwards, an offering to the gods, and a wake-up call to their protectors.

On the way back up the hill a driveway turns sharply right, up to the Namgyal monastery, or Little Lhasa, as it's known, where the Dalai Lama is currently in residence. An inveterate traveller, he's just returned from a five-city tour of the US. Our appointment to see him is in two days' time, but there is a flurry of activity around the buildings and word comes through that he is leading prayers in the temple and if we're lucky we might be able to get in and film the ceremony. From then on everything happens very quickly. We're introduced to one of the Dalai Lama's private secretaries, a tall young man in immaculate grey suit, with a Tibetan waistcoat to match, who ushers us through a side entrance, up a flight of steps and through a metal detector. We're then body-searched quite thoroughly and led up into a light, airy courtyard, half covered with a corrugated plastic sun-roof. The floor is packed with people, many of them robed and beaded Westerners, but we are led on past them to the edge of an inner area, where, surrounded by a sea of shaven-headed, saffron-robed monks, the familiar bespectacled figure of the best known Buddhist in the world, the incarnation of Aval-okiteshvara, the Bodhisattva of Love and Great Compassion, sits on a cushioned platform leading the prayers. Every eye and ear is concentrated on him and yet he seems a modest figure, swaying slowly as he speaks and sounding profoundly weary. Occasionally he leans forward to shake a small bell.

We watch all this from a side door, not 20 feet away from him, which gives onto a stage, dominated by a statue of the Buddha and stacked with piles of sweets, biscuits and fruit such as you might find in a church at Harvest Festival. When we have finished filming we're moved smartly away, as the prayers come to an end and the assembled throng rises to its feet and begins to move forward for a glimpse of the great man as he leaves, preceded, I notice, by a guard with a sub-machine gun.

In the crush, I lose sight of the crew and find myself at the bottom of a wide flight of stairs, with everything apparently going on above me. Then, out of the melee, the Dalai Lama appears, descending the stairs on the arms of two assistants. I step back out of the way but my retreat is blocked by a crash barrier, so I just bow my head and try to look invisible.

As he comes down off the steps I notice that the set gaze with which he intoned the prayers earlier has gone and he's looking around him with an animated smile, seemingly delighted to make eye contact. A few feet away from me he stops, looks over in my direction and waves. I cast a quick look behind me, but there's no-one there. I look back and he's waving again, almost as if he'd seen an old friend. I take one last quick look round then walk forward and shake his hand. I seem to have done the right thing, as he beams at me and, behind heavy dark spectacle frames, his eyes sparkle.

I mutter something about looking forward to talking to him later in the week. He nods, squeezes my hand and looks at me again in that pleased-to-see-you sort of way before moving on. The crowd, temporarily halted, passes by after him and I reassume my role as man at the crash barrier.

'He probably did recognize you,' says someone as we eat breakfast on the terrace of a pretty guesthouse overlooking the monastery. 'He loves showbiz folk.'

This barbed compliment comes with little evidence other than his wearily over-quoted association with Richard Gere, who has stayed at this guesthouse and whose name appears, interestingly, among a list of sponsors of the Sulabh Public Toilets, Baths and Sanitary Complex by the temple car park. Among the other dozen or so donors listed I couldn't help noticing the name of Mae Loo.

Public relations are important to the Tibetans, for McLeodganj is more than just temples and the Dalai Lama's residence. It is home to a flourishing number of enterprises, political, religious and commercial, all of which are designed to demonstrate the seriousness and competence of the government in exile. Everywhere we go we are handed well-produced information sheets by well-dressed, knowledgeable and patient young men, who do a thoroughly professional job of marketing the mysteries of Tibet. I discover a perfect example of old traditions and modern delivery when I visit the Tibetan Medical and Astrology Centre. Though there are beggars at the door, inside all is clean, whitewashed and businesslike. The ground floor is more like a warehouse, with sacks of herbs coming in and boxes of medicine going out. Upstairs the astrologers work away on quietly humming computers surrounded by the intricate Buddhist paintings on cloth that they call *thangkas* (pronounced 'tankers').

Outside the window prayer flags are tied to nests of satellite dishes. One sending out messages, the other receiving them.

Knowing I was coming here, I sent details of my place and time of birth to the Astrology Centre so that they could prepare a chart for me. The service costs around £50 a time and is available to anyone, as are the protective amulets that I notice they sell here (with instructions to wrap in yellow cloth and wear around the neck).

A young man, with curly dark hair, introduces himself as Phurbu Tsering, the astrologer in charge of my case. He is, like most of the young men here, neatly turned out in Western style, with sports jacket, jeans and Gap shirt.

He it is who has calculated my incarnation prospects. As reincarnation is one of the basic beliefs of Buddhism (the Dalai Lama is a reincarnation of the last Dalai Lama, who was a reincarnation of the Dalai Lama before that, and so on), it helps to know what your chances are. There are six realms in which you can end up. God, Demi-God and Human Being are all good and Animal, Hell and Bad Spirits all less good.

With a certain amount of apprehension I open my chart, which is headed with my Tibetan birthdate, the 1st day of the 3rd month of Water-Sheep year. With mixed feelings (mainly of relief) I read on. 'You were likely to be an elephant in your previous life, but you are going to be born as a daughter of a rich family in the West.'

Basil finds this particularly funny and is convinced that I'll be reincarnated as one of John Cleese's grandchildren.

The rest of the chart has mixed news. I'm told I 'believe in honesty and logic feeling, not emotion' and 'never indulge in meaningless gossips and talks'. That doesn't sound right.

Blue, red and white are my lucky colours (which presumably means I can support Sheffield Wednesday and Sheffield United at the same time). Thursday is my worst day, Fridays and Mondays my best and my marriage has been 'disheartening'. How can I tell Helen this after 38 years?

Phurbu Tsering is sincere, friendly and speaks excellent English, and clearly believes in the truth of what he's found in my chart. He takes me to one side as we leave and urges me to be particularly careful this year. He sees change and a crisis ahead. As I'm about to spend the next two months crossing the highest mountain range on earth, this is not exactly what I need to hear.

I ask Phurbu if he has had his own astrological chart made. He shakes his head. There is no record of his date or time of birth. All this information, and everything else his family owned, was left behind when his parents fled Tibet.

He smiles gravely.

'I was born on the roadside.'

Perhaps the crown jewel of the exiles' achievement is the Norbulingka Institute, named after the Dalai Lama's summer palace in Lhasa, and dedicated to the preservation of Tibetan craft and culture. Once through the gates we're in lush, beautifully ordered gardens rising gently in a series of terraces to the gold-tipped temple at the top of the hill. The paths are paved with slate slabs, and soft, gently swaying stands of bamboo are both protective and mysterious. Flowers trail round columns and arches and water flows artfully down, bubbling from gargoyle mouths into a series of fishponds. The air is charged with the constant high-pitched trill of insects.

It's described to me as 'a campus' but with cell-phone beeps and a constant quiet coming and going between departments, another description comes to mind.

This is a highly motivated Garden of Eden.

It nevertheless retains a typically Buddhist character. There is an amiable sense of tranquillity, people don't shout and everyone works with seraphic concentration, whether in the *thangka* workshop, painting fine detail on a banner of beasts, angry gods and flying horses, or in the metal shop, hammering out the base of a sitting Buddha from a sheet of copper, or in an inscription room, sitting beneath a framed picture of the Dalai Lama and copying onto long, thin, rectangular plates the text of Buddhist scriptures picked out in gold, coral and silver.

Everywhere we go we are received with quiet cordiality and politely but persistently followed by a video camera recording our every move.

It's impressive, if a little tiring, all this courtesy and hospitality, and I'm not quite sure where it will all lead. The Tibetans in exile are skilful operators and I admire the tenacity and persistence with which they court world opinion, but as time goes by the Chinese are strengthening their hold on Tibet, while adopting more liberal policies towards the Buddhists and better relations with the rest of the world. It's hard to see where the leverage might be applied to get them to change their policy and allow a meaningful Tibetan government to work from Lhasa rather than McLeodganj.

Another problem is that over the last 44 years increasing numbers of the people who are running the government in exile have been born and bred in India and have never seen the country they represent.

As we saw at Norbulingka this afternoon, life is comfortable for the cultural executives and it would surely not be easy to uproot themselves from this congenial corner and relocate to a cold plateau on the far side of the Himalayan wall.

Day Thirty Eight : Dharamsala and McLeodganj

Our audience with the Dalai Lama is at 2.15 this afternoon. We arrive early and film in the streets of McLeodganj. It's Gandhi's birthday and a public holiday, but no day off for the desperate figures in vests and cotton trousers trying to mend roads as cars continue to drive along them, or for the limbless beggars squatting beneath a Western Union sign, or the bundles of rags with hands protruding outside the cyber café. I've never seen so many mutilated and deformed people in one place, and there's not much you can do but walk on and try to avoid eye contact. Their own people, I notice, ignore them completely.

I stop to make some notes leaning up against a metal post crowned with a thick mesh of unprotected electric cabling. A boy, not more than five or six, holds out his hand.

'Hello.' He repeats softly, 'Hello.'

An older man with a stick simply stands there with a small pail, whimpering soundlessly. Passing these wraith-like figures are the substantial, muscular, Western backpackers who home in on these places, looking for cheap accommodation while sporting designer shades that would cost a street mender six months' wages.

Poverty is corrosive, but it's always worse when it is found side by side with wealth. Occupants of shanty towns in the Philippines or South America are as poor as this but they have their own, fierce, communal pride, and (apart from BBC film crews) they don't have rich foreigners walking their streets every day.

We're at the Tsechokling Temple in good time. The Dalai Lama is giving a public audience before he speaks to us and security is tight. A beagle sniffer-dog is led along the line by a Sikh policeman. In the outer office leading to the Dalai Lama's private quarters we're politely asked to sit and wait while our papers are checked. A poster on the opposite wall makes depressing reading. 'China's Record in Tibet' is blazoned across the top. 'More than a Million Killed, More than 6000 Monasteries Destroyed, Thousands in Prison, Hundreds Still Missing', and in big red letters at the bottom, 'China Get Out of Tibet'.

The Dalai Lama's bungalow is spacious but not ostentatious. A room full of the various medals, awards and citations he's been given from all over the world gives onto a long, cool, marble-tiled verandah, from which a few steps lead down to a driveway that snakes around an oval garden bed full of conventional roses and marigolds. A desk has been set up at the bottom of these steps, beneath the protective shade of bushy bougainvillea. A long line of visitors is being led in, at its head an Indian Catholic priest in white robe with a prominent crucifix around his neck.

Monks line the drive, a most benevolent form of crowd control.

At 12.40, dead on time, the man they've been waiting for appears and without fuss or bother he begins to greet them, going through all 700, showing interest in every individual, catching the eye, trying to avoid identical responses. Whereas a lot of the Westerners pass by quite briskly, like students collecting passing-out degrees, the Tibetan monks approach slowly, utterly awed, some bent double in their supplication. Though I have the impression that the Dalai Lama is not comfortable with too much respect, he listens earnestly and at length to their requests and has a nice way of rubbing his hand across their shaven heads and, occasionally, bending forward to brush his lips against their foreheads.

By two o'clock the last of the line has gone through, and he is escorted away by his efficient, ever so slightly severe minders, only to reappear on the verandah minutes later to address a group of 60 new arrivals from Tibet, refugees who have just made the difficult and dangerous crossing through the mountains as he did 45 years ago. One of his private secretaries translates his remarks for me. Very interesting they are too. He begins in a folksy way, sitting, hands on hips, trying to draw these cowed and respectful new

Partridge and mountain peaks. A romantic image of home comes to life in a truck painter's yard in Peshawar.

Above: At the Khyber Pass. The Grand Trunk Road (*to the right*) winds into Afghanistan.
Below: Gunsmith, Darra, North-West Frontier.

OPPOSITE PAGE Dental Alley, *aka* Qissa Khwani Bazaar, Peshawar. Abdul Wahid (*bottom*) thinks the whole head might have to come off.

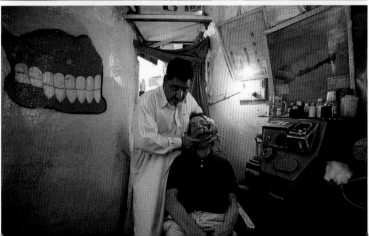

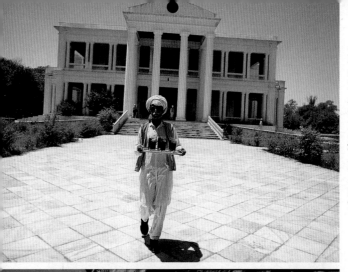

Left: Palatial hospitality at Chateau Fatehjang. *Middle:* At Prince Malik's travelling pavilion I meet an ex-jockey, on the left. The sport cost him an arm. *Bottom:* Bull-racing near Taxila.

OPPOSITE PAGE *Top:* At Rumbur. Kalash girls, barley field, dry-stone wall, traditional costume, modern foot. *Bottom:* Threading our way through the Hindu Kush. The rugged route out of the Kalash valleys.

Above: Chitral. With Siraj Ul-Mulk at a *madrassa* (a religious school) in the mosque his grandfather built. *Left:* A boy recites the Koran, which he must learn by heart.

OPPOSITE PAGE *Top:* No lie-in when the band's around. Early-morning music heralds the start of the Polo Festival at the Shandur Pass. *Middle:* Winning combination. Truc and Bulbul Jan. *Bottom:* Pakistanis are cricket mad, even at 10,000 feet (3050 m).

My first taste of the high life. Dropping off at Concordia, where great glaciers meet K2 at three miles above sea level.

OPPOSITE PAGE *Top:* Solving the world's problems with Imran Khan. His dog's heard it all before. *Bottom:* At Rawalpindi, crossing the most famous road in the subcontinent. First laid across north India some five hundred years ago.

Top: My night with the stars. Shaan Shahid (*left*), and other top Pakistani thesps, on set at the Bari Studios, Lahore. *Above:* Who is the fairest of them all? Last-minute checks at Bari Studios.

OPPOSITE PAGE *Top:* Street cleaners in Rawalpindi take a photo break. In the background, Shaan Shahid, Lollywood heart-throb, dominates the billboards. *Bottom:* Prayers at the 330-year-old Badshahi Mosque, Lahore.

Top: Unblocking the fountains. Shalimar Gardens, Lahore. *Above:* Buffalo-assisted lawn-mower, Shalimar Gardens.

OPPOSITE PAGE *Top:* Wagah border crossing. A red-letter day for the local porters as the BBC leaves Pakistan. *Middle:* Pakistan's Punjabi Rangers strut their stuff at the border. *Bottom:* With their Indian counterparts, they prepare for competitive flag-lowering.

Top: Kalka, Himachal Pradesh (Himalaya Province). The public pump still has a vital role in Indian life. And the railways are the biggest single employer in the world. *Above:* First glimpse of the scale of Shimla, 7260 feet (2213 m) above sea level. Provincial capital of Himachal Pradesh.

OPPOSITE PAGE *Top:* Ablutions in the Amrit Sarover, the 'pool of nectar', at the Golden Temple, Amritsar. *Bottom:* With two guardians of the temple. Their robes and spears symbolize the dual nature of the Sikhs: service and defence.

Aboard the Himalayan Queen on the 57-mile run from Kalka to Shimla.

arrivals out. He starts by asking if any of them had been caught by the border police, or lost money and valuables on the way. He asks about the current state of the hospitals and schools. Do they teach Tibetan? How many lumberjacks are there in Tibet these days (a reference to the massive deforestation since the Chinese arrived)? Then he talks to them quietly but with authority. He tells them that since September last year the government in exile has renewed official contact with the Chinese. Though he hears that the Chinese occupation is even more repressive than the year before, he notes that more Chinese are visiting Tibet, both as tourists and pilgrims, and that there is a growing interest in things Tibetan around the world, which is putting pressure on the Chinese.

It is important that they retain their Tibetan culture and language but Buddhism is far from being an irrelevant, unchanging religion. Buddhists and scientists have much in common, while in the field of psychology the Buddhists are well ahead. He grins. By 2000 years.

We will win, he assures them, because we have truth and truth will ultimately prevail. Don't worry. Educate yourselves. Learn Chinese. Learn about the world outside Tibet, because if he ever returns to Lhasa he will not go back to a feudal society. Go back, he says to the ones who plan to return home, and tell them that.

It's a sober, realistic, pragmatic message, implying, quite clearly, that the past is past. He has accepted the fact, if not all the practices, of the Chinese occupation. It echoes the mix of Buddhist spirituality and 21st-century savvy that characterizes the operation here in McLeodganj.

Meanwhile we have set up our cameras and lights in the audience room, hung with *thangkas* with a finely modelled shrine to the Buddha at one end, but as our time comes round, the secretary appears, eyebrows raised apologetically, to tell us that a group of local worthies have to be accommodated, but his Holiness hopes to get them through in five minutes. It sounds as if he'll be exhausted.

At 2.25 we are advised that he will be coming. I arm myself with a *katag*, a thin white scarf, which is a mark of greeting and respect among Tibetans. Try not to dwell on the fact that I am about to embark on a 40-minute talk with the spiritual leader of one of the great religions and can't remember a single one of the questions I rehearsed in my room last night. The only warning I am given is to avoid asking specific questions about his current relations with the Chinese. Two of his closest advisers will sit in on the interview, to help translate, they say, but I know they're there to keep an eye on us.

The 14th Dalai Lama, born Llamo Thondup, the son of peasant farmers, confirmed as the incarnation of the 13th Dalai Lama when only two years old, arrives without fuss or fanfare, entering the room unescorted and looking pretty good for a 68-year-old who must have shaken a thousand hands already today. His presence is powerful, but in no way intimidating.

He pauses in the doorway, bringing his hands together and bowing his head towards me in traditional Buddhist greeting. His skin is clear and healthy, his complexion barely lined. He holds his head slightly forward, giving the impression of someone who likes to listen as much as command. Pushing his maroon and yellow robes back up onto his left shoulder, he comes towards me. His arms, like those of any Buddhist monk, are bare, save for a chunky watch on his right wrist, and noticeably hairless. Almost brushing aside my offer of the *katag*, he gives me a firm Western handshake. His grip is strong and his palms cool. He sets me at ease straight-away, grinning broadly.

'Your face very familiar because of TV.'

Well, what can I say to the man who has stared at me from his book cover this past week.

'You watch the BBC then?'

'Practically every day.'

I'm genuinely surprised. This is a monk I'm talking to.

'Because I have more trust.'

'Yes?'

'And...some beautiful documentaries on film, including your own sort of film.'

My head is swimming. This is turning into some fantasy com-mercial, and there seems to be no stopping him.

'And sometimes...I wish to journey with you,' says the Dalai Lama. 'I could see many places, and meet different people.'

I can't remember the exact details of the fact sheet I was given earlier, but I think that, since he first travelled outside India in 1973, the Dalai Lama has been to 50 countries or more.

'From my childhood I always have curiosity...to know more

about different people, different culture, and as a Buddhist monk I also, you see, have an interest to learn more about different religious traditions.'

I tell him we're going to Tibet next.

'But I don't think you'd want to come with us.'

He laughs very hard at this, then says quietly and seriously, 'Although I'm here outside Tibet, not inside Tibet, as a Tibetan I want to extend my welcome to you to visit my old country.'

There's pathos in this remark. A reminder that he speaks for 120,000 Tibetans living in exile.

I ask what we will find there, what may have changed most.

He cites Chinese immigration. Tibetans are a minority in Lhasa now.

'These people find it very, very difficult to preserve their own cultural heritage. So that's on the negative side.'

Unexpectedly, he picks out the modern buildings in Lhasa as a positive, but is worried that the big new blocks are being filled up by Chinese, not Tibetan workers. The unskilled Chinese make money more easily.

Another positive is, he says, the growing interest in spirituality in China. There is great interest in Buddhism in 'China proper', as he calls it. Especially, he notes, among the richer Chinese.

He's engagingly happy to talk about everyday life.

'One week ago I return from United States. Sleep not much problem, but my stomach still on American time.'

He pats his midriff.

'Toilet usually morning, but nowadays it's evening.'

He beams mischievously.

'That can't change through prayer.'

I learn that he gets up at 3.30 every morning, but goes to bed around 8.30, and that he recently lost his temper, in a dream.

I ask him if he ever loses his temper in real life.

'Sometimes yes, but not remain long.'

For his relatively robust health he thanks his parents for giving him a good body and his general peace of mind.

'Sleep without sleeping pill, happy without tranquillizer.'

For a world leader he seems extraordinarily well-balanced, natural and unaffected. His emotions are spontaneous, his judgements carefully pragmatic. He would justify the violence of a

Second World War or a Korean War on the grounds of just causes, but not Vietnam, nor I sense Iraq.

He feels that not enough was done to negotiate a peaceful solution with Iraq. He suggests that some council of wise men should perhaps have gone to Saddam Hussein. Those he admires and would have included, along with Muslim leaders, are Vaclav Havel, Bishop Tutu, Nelson Mandela and Jimmy Carter.

He believes it is very important to enlist with everyone, high or low, on a personal level. To communicate the positive.

Does he worry about his own safety when he travels?

'Generally no. Friendly atmosphere should immediately happen. When I'm passing through a street I always smile, when I look at another...nice smile. But then sometimes you see the other side, no smile.'

It all begins to sound a bit Mary Poppins when I write this down, but there is nothing remotely weak or woolly about the man himself. He just doesn't do cynicism.

We talk on well over our allotted 40 minutes, and even when an hour's up he is happy to pose for a photograph. (I have it on the wall beside me as I write up these notes. The Dalai Lama is in the middle, clasping Nigel's hand on one side and mine on the other. The crew are spread out on either side and I don't think I've ever seen this hard-worked unit looking so happy.)

The only sign of any tension is after he's gone, when both the Dalai Lama's private secretaries lay aside their two-way radios and pitch in to help us de-rig our lamps, wires and cables. The next interview (with an Israeli crew) is already 20 minutes late.

Day Forty : Srinagar, Kashmir

An hour and a half after the azan (the Muslim call to prayer) has woken me, replacing the barking of dog packs as the sound of the night, I'm reclining like a maharajah's mistress on the soft cushions of a long flat-bottomed boat with a canopy above my head. Behind me a small, tightly built figure is propelling me slowly forward with a single paddle.

A heron perches elegantly on a thin pole, ignoring us as we slip slowly through lotus beds towards a robust stone bridge beyond which I can dimly see and hear a clutter of canoes and the distant sound of voices.

My hooded skiff, known as a *shikara*, has an English name board fitted above the bows. 'Stranger In Paradise', it reads, and it's very suitable.

Stranger I certainly am and Dal Lake in Srinagar, long, wide and lazy, with high mountains protecting its northeasterly shore, would give many paradises a run for their money. Except that this one is in Kashmir, where, nowadays, heaven and hell come pretty close.

To get to this idyllic place we have had to undergo tighter security checks than anywhere else on the journey. Police and army posts, baggage and permit checks dot the road to Srinagar with increasing frequency.

It's not cosmetic, either. Within a couple of miles of this aqueous paradise 16 people have been killed by bomb and bullet in this last month alone, and to that figure can be added another 60,000 who have died in Kashmir since the conflict began.

Why?

In 1947, when India and Pakistan became independent, Kashmir was a Princely State of India, ruled by Maharajah Hari Singh. All 565 Princely States, comprising 100 million people, were required to sign instruments of accession to the newly formed country. What made Kashmir different was that 80 per cent of its population was Muslim.

Hari Singh hummed and hawed and eventually decided, two months after independence (and not without some heavy pressure from Nehru), that his state would stay a part of India.

The outrage of the new Pakistan government was predictable. After all, their country was set up as a homeland for Muslims and indeed the letter 'K' in its name stands for Kashmir. (The 'P' is for Punjab, the 'A' for Afghania (a romantic synonym for the North-West Frontier), the 'S' for Sind and the 'Stan' is an abbreviation of Baluchistan.)

Some Pathans took the law into their own hands and moved into Kashmir, taking over an area which has since become known as Azad (Free) Kashmir. Indian troops moved in to counter them and the long cycle of violence began.

In 1949 a ceasefire came into force, one of whose conditions was that a plebiscite should be held for the inhabitants of all Kashmir to decide on their future. It's never happened. Instead, this spectacularly lovely land has become the arena in which all the fear and loathing between Pakistan and India has come to a head. Thousands of soldiers face one another across a Line of Control. By the late 1990s the potential of the Kashmir dispute escalated from destructive to catastrophic as the Pakistanis confirmed that, like India, they now had the power to wage a nuclear conflict.

The houseboats that can still be found clinging to the shores of the lake are symbols of the days when Kashmir was not the problem, but a hideaway from all the problems elsewhere. If you can forget the roadblocks and the army patrols, the magic spell remains.

Among reasons to be thankful for being on Dal Lake this morning is the ban on outboard motors, which keeps the mood of the place as reflective as its still waters. There's time to take in the passing scene, admire majestic chinnar trees on the shoreline, the white walls and domes of an impressive waterside mosque and, alongside it, a run of multi-windowed three- or four-storey wood and brick houses that would not be out of place in a Baltic seaport.

For hundreds of years the lake has been farmed by the Mihrbari people, market gardeners living on islands only accessible by boat. Thirty-five thousand of them still live on the water, farming lotus beds for food, cattle feed and the famed Kashmiri honey that comes from their pink flowers. Willow and poplar trees on the islands are cut for thatching and building materials, vegetables are cultivated in hydroponic gardens set among compressed bulrushes and all commerce is conducted from boat to boat in a floating market that starts at daybreak every morning. Suppliers from the city bring their barges down and bargain for turnips, potatoes, spinach, pumpkins, shallots, big fat radishes, aubergines, mint and okra.

We're here within an hour of dawn and the market is in full swing. Several boatloads of flower sellers, pushing through the jam make a beeline for us (we are, apart from an Israeli couple, the only people resembling tourists here today). It doesn't stop at buying flowers. This merely spurs them on to sell you seeds as well. The more you resist the more they like it.

'I have blue sunflower seeds.'

'No, thank you.'

'I have lotus seeds.'

'I've bought some already.'

'What lotus seeds you have bought?'

'Blue.'

'I have six-colour lotus seeds. And wild orchid and wild tulip.'

'I have no money.'

'You buy and send me the money.'

At this point one would normally wind up the window and roar off as fast as possible, but as we're both in paddle boats there is no prospect of a quick getaway and either you drift along together for several miles or, as I did, you buy six-colour lotus seeds for all your friends. These disappeared mysteriously into a hotel wastepaper basket about a week later.

It's still only breakfast time as I get back to the houseboat moored on the western shore of the lake, which will be our home for the next couple of days. Mr Butt, the owner of Butt's Clermont Houseboats, is worrying away at a table laid out in what was an old Mughal garden, believed to have been built by the Emperor Akbar and called the Garden of the Morning Breeze. Soon we're chomping on eggs, pancakes, thick toasted bread, honey and Kashmiri tea, a fragrant alternative to the straight cuppa, made with saffron and almonds.

Mr Butt circles nervously. He is a man of immense enthusiasm, very responsive to compliments and given to hugging the bearer of them with delight. On the other hand, the slightest thing that goes wrong produces intense anguish and much shouting at the staff. There seems to be no middle ground between euphoric happiness and utter despair.

This makes him an anxious but attentive host and even before I'd checked in he was proudly showing off the signed photographs of previous guests that adorn the walls of his office. They range from Lord Louis Mountbatten, the man who partitioned India and Pakistan, to George Harrison, who stayed here in 1966 to learn the sitar from his friend and guru Ravi Shankar. I ask which boat George had stayed in and a small cloud passes over Mr Butt's beaming features.

Later I could see why. It lies in a side channel, half submerged with water. Mr Butt couldn't afford to keep it afloat.

Newspaper cuttings are displayed alongside the photos: recommendations from the *Washington Post* and the *New York Times* and a flattering inclusion, together with such high-tone places as the Regent in Hong Kong and the Lowell, New York, in Charles Michener's 'Hotels You Won't Want to Leave'. These clippings are now yellowing and curled at the edges and there is none much later than the early 90s. When the troubles in Kashmir escalated, the press reviews turned to scare stories and the only foreign visitors were journalists covering the conflict.

Mr Butt admits there were times when he was near to tears. Staff he'd known all his working life had to be laid off, and at the nadir of his fortunes the army commandeered his property and set up camp in the Garden of the Morning Breeze. Things improved briefly from 1995 to 1999 but any hope of a steady recovery is stymied by every fresh atrocity, every fresh confrontation.

I can only feel grateful to this cheerful, distracted man for keeping going, for his boats are neither functional nor cheap to run. Mine is very splendid, with elaborately carved woodwork inside and out, a carpeted sitting room with very fine crewel-work embroidery and a grand dining room with cedar panelling, chandeliers, cut glass and an oval rosewood dining table.

This evening the skies darken, the lake empties of boats and after a brief and eerie period of silence and total calm the heavens open and there's nothing to do but sit tight and watch the rain splashing in great glassy drops on the water lily beds that surround the boats.

If anything, Dal Lake is even more beautiful in the rain.

Day Forty One : Srinagar

The storm rumbles on through the night and as the growls of retreating thunder merge with the cries of the muezzin I reach for my torch (there has been no mains power since the rain began). It's five o'clock, but I feel wide awake. I dreamt very vividly last night. Super-charged dreams, as if the electricity in the air had given them an extra intensity. I saw my father very clearly and I rushed up and hugged him, something I never did when he was alive, and heard myself say 'Hello Dad!' except it wasn't my voice at all but the voice of my son.

An hour later dawn is breaking and we're driving out onto the wet and windswept streets of Srinagar. The night-time curfew has only just ended and the streets are empty save for foot patrols and packs of stray dogs. Srinagar must have been a handsome city once. There are still many tall, steeply gabled, half-timber, half-brick buildings, a few onion domes and a magnificent mosque with roofs, turrets and spires with echoes of Russia and lands to the north.

The Indian government has 600,000 army and security forces in Kashmir and their ubiquitous presence has coarsened the city and compromised whatever beauty it might have had. Apart from bunkers and armoured patrol cars, there are barbwired and sand-bagged surveillance posts, sports pitches that have been turned into army camps, and I'm told there's not a single cinema operating in Kashmir's capital now. All have been requisitioned for military accommodation.

On the corner of the busy main street, Lal Chowk, and opposite the heavily fortified Telegraph Office stands the Greenway Hotel. Two weeks ago two suspected Islamic militants holed up here and withstood a siege for 20 hours before police blew the building apart with mortar fire. Ten people were killed and 40 wounded and the Greenway now consists of little more than half a roof, scorched black walls and a crumpled framework of charred and blistered timbers. Around the time this happened six more people were killed when a car blew up in the vegetable market.

On the edge of the old town is a patch of green grass and a stagnant rubbish-filled pond. Horses graze and dogs chase, snarl, fight and mate amongst the filth. Next door to this soiled little field is a small cemetery, neatly walled and fenced. Inside, gravestones fringed in green and topped with sturdy metal pennants mark the resting place of those who have died in the struggle. An arch over the entrance announces it as the Kashmir Martyrs' Graveyard. Most of the graves are inscribed in Urdu, but beneath a cypress a neglected metal sign in English reads:

'Master Shaheed Yawar Says
Do Not Shun The Gun
My Dear Younger Ones
The War For Freedom
Is Yet To Be Won.'

It's rusty and fading and must have been there for some time, unlike two freshly dug mounds, crudely decorated with a border of pebbles, containing a mother and a three-month-old baby killed in crossfire outside the Greenway Hotel. There are some 400 graves here and many more lie in similar plots throughout Kashmir. Flowers have been planted around the place, perhaps to represent on earth the gardens the martyrs are promised in heaven. Though governments may see the Kashmir struggle as the troubles, most of those who lie here saw it as a war.

This is brought forcibly and uncomfortably home to me by the bizarre conflation of our own patriotic rhetoric that is inscribed above the arched gateway of the Kashmir Martyrs' Graveyard: 'Lest You Forget We Have Given Our Today for Tomorrow of Yours'.

The only place where the violence seems not to have made a mark is on the water, and along one arm of the lake 60 or 70 house-boats, with jolly names like 'King of Kashmir', 'Himalayan Fantasies' and 'Buckingham Palace', still court the tourists. They're moored up cheek by jowl, end on to the bank, cabins tweely curtained, fenced sundecks ringed with pot plants, waiting for the next boom. Their design is cosy and old-fashioned and can't have changed much since the houseboat era began in the 1880s, when the British got around laws preventing outsiders from buying lakeside property by build-ing their mansions on the water instead.

A white-crested kingfisher studies the limpid surface of the lake. Our presence on the bank has already attracted a flotilla of water taxis and eager salesmen flaunting jewellery, papier-mâché and various ethnic trinkets.

'Where are you from?' shouts one man.

When we tell him he shouts manically back.

'England! Fish and Chips! Bangers and Mash! Marmite Sand-wiches! Good Heavens!'

August, they say, had been a good month for Indian tourists. Then came the September violence and 30 per cent of the bookings were cancelled immediately.

I go out again on the lake at dusk. The rain has cleared the air and the water is a mirror, reflecting a huge golden sunset. It's ironic that of all the places I've been on my journey so far, this should be the closest I've come to perfect peace.

Day Forty Two : Ladakh

The looming presence of the mountains around two sides of Dal Lake reminded me that, after almost two weeks, we were once again getting close to the high Himalaya. This morning, as we land at Leh after a complicated flight from Srinagar via Delhi, the change from foothills to mountains is complete. Nature is not generous up here. The air is powder dry and the rocky slopes all round us are bare and deeply gullied. For the first time in a long while I feel my lungs working, pumping a little harder to pull in the oxygen, for we are at 11,650 feet (3550 m), nearly two and a quarter miles above sea level.

Sonia Gandhi, daughter-in-law of one premier and wife of another, is visiting this remote province and her convoy of chunky white Ambassador cars, honest but unglamorous, winds its way through the security chicane and out of the airport, while we are still waiting for our bags.

Nothing is quite as I expected. The porters and baggage handlers are stocky thick-set women wrapped in red cardigans, headscarves and baggy blue pantaloons and they jostle with each other for the heaviest bags. Their features are more Mongolian than Indo-Aryan, with darker, berry-brown complexions and broad cheeks.

The only similarity with where we've come from is the heavy military presence: jet fighters in revetments at the airport, a sprawling barracks on the way into Leh. Once again there is a sensitive border nearby, only this time it's not Pakistan they're worried about, but China.

Ladakh, meaning 'many passes', is a part of Jammu and Kashmir but has little in common with the rest of India, nor indeed with the rest of the state. Over half the population is Buddhist and its strategic position on the old Silk Road means it shares more with Tibet and Central Asia.

The architecture, too, is different from anything I've seen so far: stone walls and rugged houses with flat roofs that seem to have bushy undergrowth piled on top of them. (I never worked out if these rooftop toupees were fuel stores or a form of insulation.) The run-down palace that dominates the centre of Leh is on a grand scale and has the same upwardly tapering walls that I've seen in pictures of the Potala Palace in Lhasa.

The streets of Leh are busy, in a low-tech way. A row of men, some holding prayer wheels, sit cross-legged on the pavements behind sacks rolled back to show off various nuts and spices and fruits. I buy rather a lot of apricot kernels, because someone said they make you live longer, and am tempted by the piles of shawls, scarves and rugs made from *pashm*, the fine underfleece of goat's wool that is the speciality of this part of India. The pashmina sales-men look particularly doleful, as their trade, like everyone else's in Kashmir, is heavily affected by the troubles. They seem to face the situation with remarkable stoicism. I'm back among mountain people – patient, taciturn and politely wary of outsiders. Masters of survival.

There is evidence that their independence is being compromised by various life-improvement campaigns, from tidiness to road safety. At a busy road junction a prominent and colourful display board advises the locals to 'Learn and Repeat, Signs and Traffic Signals'.

As I'm reading it a black cow, followed by her calf, emerges from behind the board and, without signals of any kind, saunters off into the rush-hour traffic.

I think we should use cows for traffic calming at home. They're much more effective than sleeping policemen. And they give milk.

The road safety campaign extends beyond Leh. As we drive across the desert, following the slim green band of cultivation along the River Indus, we're treated to an assortment of useful warnings: 'Peep Peep, Don't Sleep', 'Drive Like Hell – You'll Be There' and 'Be Mr Late Rather Than the Late Mr', which is marginally our favourite. The road surface is good, better than you'd expect in such a remote place. The reason, of course, is that the highway is built and maintained by the army, or 'The Mountain Tamers', as they like to call themselves.

It's not road safety they're worried about up here, it's invasion.

The scenery has a spare and minimal beauty and the buildings along the way, though few and far between, are very dramatic. Some ten miles along the highway to Manali, the walls of the old palace of the kings of Leh rear up along a prominent ridge to the north of the road. A king hasn't lived there for 400 years, but the evidence of power and wealth still clings to the place, both in the scale of the ruins and, on a nearby hillside, row upon row of crumbling white monuments. From a distance they resemble lines of half-melted snowmen, with the outlines of once square bases, conical middles and pointed tops now soft and imprecise. These stupas, or *chortens*, as they're called in Tibetan, contain the remains of lamas and monks from the monastery attached to the palace as well as members of the royal family and their possessions.

They vary in size, the highest being almost 20 feet tall. Usually situated in favourable geomantic locations, their design represents steps to enlightenment. They are constructed on five levels, with the square base symbolizing the earth and the tapering tops the sky and stars. As I wander among them I can see that few are intact. Most are leaning or cracked down the sides and all look as if they may have been opened up at some time. Intriguingly, many seem to have been freshly whitewashed, suggesting someone is still looking after them.

I have the feeling, as I stand in the middle of this field of whited sepulchres with little more than a stand of poplars growing in the valley below, that there was a time when these bare hills on the banks of the Indus must have supported a small empire. What was so different then? More water perhaps, a wider flood plain or perhaps just the power and influence that came from living on the Silk Route.

As we head east more stunning monasteries and temples appear out of nowhere. Thikse straddles an outcrop of rock with the smaller outbuildings that are the monks' quarters wrapped around the steep sides below it. This has been a working monastery (or *gompa*, in Tibetan) for nearly 1000 years and 60 lamas still live here.

The richest and most striking of the great Indus valley *gompas* is Hemis, another half-hour's drive along the main road and then by a side track up into a narrow gorge squeezed between walls of striped granite, folded and thrust upwards at 45 degrees to the plain below.

The last part of the climb to the monastery is up a long stone staircase. By the time I reach the top my breathing is shallow and my legs feel like lead, but the dramatic entrance makes me glad I persevered.

Despite the narrow site, the courtyard that opens out beyond the main gateway gives a heady sense of space. High stone walls rise on three sides while the fourth is open to the bare rock slopes beyond. The walls are covered in paintings and a line of prayer wheels runs along one side. Another mighty flight of steps leads to the prayer hall, whose entrance is flanked by wooden pillars with carved figure-heads and richly coloured paintings of dragons and gods. A wooden gallery runs around the walls and an arcade below has what look like very ancient wall paintings of the Buddha. Among the treasures of Hemis is a *thangka* so precious and huge that it is only displayed in public every 12 years. 2004 is the next time it will be exhibited. We've missed it by a matter of months.

We drive on as far as Chemrey Gompa, another monastery topping a carefully selected crag. Can't help but marvel at the careful painting of these monastery walls and the way the white, brown and maroon, and the timber and stone construction, harmonize so elegantly with the dry and tawny landscape around.

By now, all of us are feeling the press of altitude and by the time we've returned to Leh and eaten *momos* (Tibetan stuffed dumplings) and noodles, none of us has much energy left. There only remains one thing to do before bed and that's to raise a glass of beer to Roger and Nigel, who were both with me exactly 15 years ago today, filming my departure from the Reform Club and the start of *Around the World in Eighty Days*.

Nepal

Day Forty Four: Kathmandu

We arrived here last night from Delhi on the penultimate night of Dasain, a big Nepali festival, and though badly in need of some rest and recuperation after our Indian adventure, the final day's celebrations cannot be missed.

To start the day we've been asked by Pratima Pande, a formidable, energetic, Gordonstoun-educated Nepali, to watch a *puja*, a ritual act of worship, at the home of one of her in-laws. This being the first time I've ever been to Nepal, I'm craning my head out of the car window as we drive there. I have a sense of streets that are less hectic and a city much easier on the eye than those we've seen these past few weeks. Buildings look like buildings rather than structures for supporting billboards.

The house is comfortable but not opulent. As we arrive a group of musicians are parading around the garden before taking up a position on the far side of a small swimming pool. It's a bit of a squeeze, as two of them are wielding large, curved horns.

I'm told that this is Bijaya Dasami, the 'victorious tenth day' of the Dasain festival and Pratima and her husband, mother-in-law, brothers-in-law, nephews, nieces and cousins are here to celebrate King Rama's victory over the demon Ravana, helped by Shiva's consort, Durga.

I'm desperately trying to get all this down in my notebook when the music starts and the family priest, an unassuming, modestly dressed figure, who looks as if he might have come to fix the plumbing, steps forward. The exact timing of the *puja* is very auspicious and it cannot be delayed for foreign film crews. He sets the ball rolling by applying a dab of yellow to the forehead of the oldest member of the family, Pratima's 82-year-old mother-in-law. Today, Pratima tells me, everyone in Nepal, from the King downwards, will wear this mark, the *tika*.

After some light family argument over the exact order of things, the ceremony continues, in strictly hierarchical fashion, with the five brothers, and then the children, kissing the feet of their elders and giving each other the male *tika*, made from a preparation of curd, rice and vermilion powder. *Jamara*, shoots of barley, are placed on the head or in a garland around the neck as a symbol of fertility and longevity.

As an outsider I'm struck by how seriously all this is taken. Pratima's brothers-in-law are hard-nosed, professional people, one a doctor, one a banker, two others in the army. They're dressed in the *labada salwar*, a knee-length tunic, with tight leggings and black leather shoes, but over it they wear a Western-style sports jacket.

Many of them have been educated in Britain or America, their children speak fluent English and go to private schools. Yet here they are taking part in an ancient and rural ritual with a thoroughness that one can't imagine among their counterparts in the West.

The first thing to remember, says Pratima, is that not only is Hinduism the religion of 90 per cent of Nepal, the Nepalis take pride in being more scrupulous in their observance of festivals. The Indians, she says, have shortened their ceremonies.

'We take three days to get married. They do it in a day!'

She herself is off to a private audience at which she will be given *tika* and blessed by the King, who is some sort of relative (they're both from the Rana family). This afternoon, he will be doing the same for the public in the grounds of the palace. Would I like to come along?

The prospect of meeting the king of a country I've only been in for 12 hours appeals in a surreal sort of way, and I scurry back to the Yak and Yeti Hotel to find a tie and get my only jacket pressed.

There is a certain amount of morbid curiosity here, for the Nepali monarchy was very nearly wiped out in June 2001, when the King and Queen and seven other members of the family were murdered by the Crown Prince, who then turned a gun on himself. Rumours abound as to what really happened but it seems he was a heavy drinker, loved guns and flew into an hysterical rage when his father refused him permission to marry the girl he wanted.

At three o'clock I'm with Pratima in the grounds of the Royal Palace, blinking a little wearily in the bright sunshine as King Gyanendra Bir Bikram Shah Dev, the late Crown Prince's uncle and incarnation of Vishnu the preserver, descends his front steps between statues of guardian animals – dragons, horses, peacocks, dolphins and elephants – to the strains, and in this case strains is the right word, of a Scottish-sounding dirge weirdly played by a pipe band in red and white plaid scarves and white gaiters.

The palace, with its Potala-like central tower, Hindu temple shapes, Tibetan loggias, red-brick skin and clusters of concrete columns that hang down without touching the ground, seems to have been built in a style that might best be described as Himalayan Fantasy. Which might also apply to the rest of the day.

The King takes his place behind a red, padded leather desk, which makes him look a bit like a hotel receptionist. At a given signal his subjects begin to move forward and he sets to work applying *tika* to the nation's foreheads. Having so recently seen the Dalai Lama work a line, I know that it's possible to combine gravitas and jollity, but King Gyanendra maintains one expression throughout, and that is a sort of jowly glumness, as if being ruler of Nepal is absolutely the worst job in the world.

The line is slowed down ahead of me by a succession of middle-brass army officers whose huge, peaked caps have to be pushed back before the *tika* can be applied, then repositioned to enable them to salute. It all takes time and the King looks even more bored by the time my turn comes. Pratima moves forward to introduce me. I don't know what's said, but a flicker of animation crosses the royal features and after applying the royal *tika* to my deeply incised brow, the King extends a hand (his own) for me to shake and, leaning forward, wishes me a happy stay in Nepal.

'It could be the highlight of his afternoon,' says a Brit, working in the country. 'He needs all the friends he can get.'

Whatever his personal popularity, the institution of monarchy seems strong enough to attract a queue of people that extends all the way back to the heavy iron gates and for a few hundred yards out along the road, and those at the end of the line must be among the poorest in the kingdom.

No sooner are we back in the Yak and Yeti looking at laundry lists for the first time in a week than word comes through that a special ceremony, happening only once every 12 years, will be taking place in the heart of the old city later tonight. It's being kept very secret because it involves the King, who, because of the fear of attacks from the Maoist guerrillas, rarely goes out in public within the city.

It sounds a long-shot but we follow it up and make our way to Hanuman Dhoka, the Old Royal Palace. Although it is dimly lit and hard to distinguish individual buildings, the complex of streets and squares has an extraordinary atmosphere. I'm reminded of walking at night in St Petersburg or Rome. There is a theatrical unreality to the place. Astonishing buildings, unlike anything I've seen before, are silhouetted against the night sky. Towering pagodas with long wide-eaved roofs, stacked one above the other, are topped with Hapsburg-like spires. Deep balconies cantilever out on long poles, the lintels and sills of the windows are thick timber beams. A fairy-tale kind of architecture, the more magical for being first encountered at night.

The general public seems conspicuously absent. We walk through empty squares until we come upon a small crowd that seems to consist mainly of flak-jacketed military, armed police and press photographers in dark suits.

The authorities look nervous, their eyes constantly scanning us and each other. Nigel grabs a camera position a few feet off the ground beneath a lamppost, and defends it against all comers as we wait for the production to begin.

After some time a procession can be heard approaching. Led by women with lamps and incense sticks and musicians playing cymbals and drums, a group of masked figures enters the square. The masks are big, elaborate and brightly coloured and their arrival provokes a mad rush as the press photographers, closely ringed by police, scoot across towards them like a squad of black beetles, thrusting people aside with their cameras as they try to get close. The masked dancers, some of them with towering headdresses and wearing animal skins like African witch doctors, seem to have been at it some time, and they twist and turn to the music as if in a trance.

There is still no sign of the King. The photographers have taken their pictures, the dancers have made their spectacular entrance and by the time the royal motorcade looms out of the darkness, the energy and spontaneity have all but evaporated. Army, police and plain-clothes security men with fingers at their ears move in around the King and escort him forwards. The most impressive of the masked figures, a representation of the goddess Bhadrakali, with a blue face, staring eyes and scarlet lips, moves up close to the King. She blesses him with divine powers, hands over a sword, flashbulbs erupt and moments later it's all over.

The press pack close in; the King, tiny and insignificant beside the great blue head of the goddess, gives a brief and nervous smile, before being rushed back to his Mercedes and away.

This combined display of paranoia and celebration puzzles me greatly. Why was it so important to take such a risk with the King's safety? If it was so important why weren't the public invited? What is it that frightens King Gyanendra so much?

Perhaps I shall learn more as we go along. If this is the overture, my stay in Nepal promises to be a very rich piece indeed.

Day Forty Six : Kathmandu to Lekhani

Kathmandu airport is busy. Next door to the long, modern, red-brick sweep of the international terminal, domestic flights are checking in at a functional, concrete building with yellow-stained walls. The slip-slap of sandals mingles with the ring of discordant announcements as tiny Nepali porters carry in the bags of strapping Western hikers bound for the mountains. We're travelling to nearby Pokhara on Buddha Air, one of a string of local carriers with vaguely unconvincing names, like Cosmic Air, Shangri-La Air and Yeti Air-lines. The crowds here this morning, indeed the existence of the airport itself, are still a relatively new thing for Nepal, which was only opened to foreigners in the 1950s.

A twin-prop Beech 1900 carries us out over the Kathmandu Valley, the widest valley in the Himalaya. Over a third of Nepal's urban population lives here and more are moving all the time; from the air the buildings expand along the main roads like concrete ten-tacles squeezing the green out of the rice paddies.

On our starboard side the peaks of the high Himalaya drift tanta-lizingly in and out of cloud cover, and by the time we begin our descent the cover is burnt off and the long, irregular, snow-capped ramparts of the Annapurna Ridge define the northern horizon.

In the days to come we shall be walking up there but today, as we skim down over the glittering lake, which, combined with the mountains, lures the tourists to Pokhara, we have only time to transfer our bags to vehicles and move on.

We are heading away from the tourist trails into the mountains west of Pokhara to the rural heartlands, where one of Nepal's most famous exports comes from. Described variously as 'tough', 'hardy' and 'indomitable', the Gurkhas have long punched above their weight in the British Army. Since the first battalions were formed in 1815, these Nepali mercenaries have been fierce and faithful servants of the Crown, with a reputation for unwavering loyalty and unquestioning ruthlessness.

There are 3500 Gurkhas in the British Army at the moment (and 50,000 in the Indian army) and they have served all over the world, including recently in the Falklands and Iraq. The Nepali government allows a certain number to be recruited each year and Lt-Colonel Adrian Griffith, the Gurkha Chief of Staff in Nepal, has suggested we accompany him to the village of Lekhani to see how the recruiting process works. Adrian, slim, straight-backed and a couple of decades older than he looks, is the epitome of the decent Englishman abroad. At the age of eight, he first read the Johnny Gurkha stories in *Victor* magazine and the fascination that developed led him to join the regiment 15 years later.

Until recently there were no roads west of Pokhara and among the predominantly poor farmers in this inaccessible network of valleys and foothills one of the world's few surviving Communist parties is alive and well.

Succoured by poverty and feeble administration, the Communist Party of Nepal (Maoist) demands the removal of the monarchy, the setting up of a constituent assembly and the re-writing of the constitution. Since 1996 they have chosen to pursue the class struggle through guerrilla warfare. Over 7000 people have been killed, 10,000 injured and many more forced out of their homes as they took on the police and the army. No-one seems quite sure what their leadership is up to at the moment. Prachandra, leader of the insurgents, has sounded more conciliatory recently and they have observed a ceasefire for the Dasain festival. But that, as I know, ended the day before yesterday.

It's a soft, warmish morning. We stop at a police checkpoint. Beside the road a group of women in saris are breaking rocks. (Female road gangs were quite common in north India, but this is the first I've seen here.) At Baglung the good road runs out, and we have to pull over for a moment while our Gurkha escort checks out reports that a bomb has been found on the track ahead. We order a cup of chai from a roadside shack. A woman with a jewel in her nose sloshes milk from a kettle into a saucepan thick with ancient deposits, adding spoonfuls of sugar from what looks like an old tin of black paint. This is all boiled up with a touch of cardamom and, I presume, some tea inserted at some stage. It tastes rather good.

West of Baglung the road becomes a slow, muddy, rutted track. In the absence of drains or culverts, water runs off the paddy fields and onto the road. At one stage my driver refuses point blank to take his nice, clean four-wheel drive through a lake of unspecified depth.

One of the Gurkha officers has a quiet word with him, then a slightly louder word, after which he drops all his objections and drives through the lake.

After two hours of painfully slow progress the track runs out. Everything is unloaded and re-packed in cone-shaped wicker baskets, *dokos*, which are then loaded onto the backs of porters and, looking like something out of the archives of the Royal Geographical Society, our 44-man, and one woman, procession, complete with everything, including the kitchen sink, sets off across the hills to find Lekhani. Worryingly, its name doesn't appear on any of the maps I have and the Sherpas who are organizing our transport are from a completely different part of Nepal. Local enquiries have to be made, which usually means chatting up someone half-buried in a paddy field.

Eventually, winding down across slippery, vertiginous rocks, between terraced fields of sorghum and millet, we come to our village, with attractive stone houses, some thatched, some tiled, spread along the hill, between spurs of rock running down to a valley far below. On the northern horizon a spectacular panorama of Annapurna, Machhapuchhre with its distinctive twin summits and the 26,750-foot (8150 m) Dhaulagiri massif looks sublime in the late afternoon sunlight.

The only disadvantage of this precipitous location is that there are only two unoccupied flat places in Lekhani. One is a sports ground, where the recruiting will take place tomorrow, and the other is an old cow patch, corrugated with dried mud. This is where we pitch our tents.

Day Forty Seven : Lekhani

It's not just dried mud I was sleeping on last night. As I made my way to the makeshift toilet, my torch picked out evidence that a menagerie of beasts had been easing themselves on our campsite for quite some time. When it also picked out a trail of bones and an abandoned flip-flop I decided to switch it off.

Up at six. Nawang Dorjee, who I think may be the nicest person in the world, brings me tea and a little while later a small bowl of hot water for washing. Check the view. Yes, everything's still there. The Himalayas, the rocky slopes, the wooded spurs, the village without roads or streets. Poinsettia, oleander, frangipani and dry-stone walls. Farmhouses, simple and solid, as beautiful as any Italian hill village. When you look more closely, though, you can see that none of them has glass in the windows, only wooden shutters to keep out the winter cold, and the living space, though picturesque, is squeezed on one level, with space below reserved for stores of grain, firewood, animal feed and the animals themselves. A number of the houses have water buffaloes in the basement, big and black, like old vintage cars.

As I clean my teeth I look up the hill. A buffalo, being milked by an old woman, her head resting against its wide grey flanks, gazes impassively back. Prayer flags move lazily on their poles (there must be a Tibetan influence here), smoke drifts from the rooftops below and a pair of young women, with long dark hair, coming slowly up the hill, stop for a moment to adjust the headbands that carry the full weight of their baskets and to give us a good looking over.

At breakfast Adrian tells me about Long Noses and Flat Noses, something I've heard our Sherpas talking about. Nepal, he says, has a fundamental ethnic division between the Indo-Aryan with origins in the south and the Mongolian who originates from the north. Sherpas think of themselves as Flat Noses and superior to the Long Noses, who in turn think of themselves as more urban and intellectual than the Flat Noses.

'Traditionally, but not exclusively, it's been the Mongolian hill men who we've recruited,' Adrian explains.

'The hill farmer lives a very hard existence, and he comes from a hierarchical society and if you superimpose military discipline and military training you've got the makings of a very good soldier.'

He reckons there will be 100, maybe 150 potential recruits today, many of whom will have walked as much as eight or ten hours to get here. There seem to be many more than that already, clustered in groups lower down the hillside, around the old volleyball pitch, which has been adapted for the recruiting, with gallows-like structures put up for the exercises and schoolroom desks brought out for the officials.

The whole event is organized by the local recruiting officer, the *galla-wallah*. He is a local man who will have been given instructions as to how many recruits are needed and scoured the villages to find likely candidates. The most that can be selected today will be 44. The *galla* is paid a small basic salary and a bounty for every successful recruit.

The Gurkha regiment has to walk a delicate tightrope between offending the Nepali army and provoking the Maoists, so the *galla* deliberately keeps the procedure informal and unmilitary. There are no weapons or uniforms in evidence. Sporting a baseball cap and a blue and red striped rugby shirt he gives an introductory talk, which, despite general squeaks, laughs and shouts from the local children, meanders on for some 25 minutes. He's followed by the village headman and then Adrian.

Adrian's much shorter speech, in fluent Nepali, is greeted with loud applause. He's garlanded by the local women and then cuts a red ribbon to mark the start of proceedings.

After the young men are registered and their height measured, they have to perform a series of physical tests. The first are heaves up onto a bar (the British Army requirement is six, the Gurkhas demand 12), after which they have to show that they can expand their chests by two inches. According to Adrian, this is a rule of thumb way of anticipating possible tuberculosis problems later on. The disease is prevalent here.

The boys puff their chests out to bursting point, and those who fail the first time are allowed to take strenuous exercise and try again. One of them completes a frenetic routine of 40 or 50 push-ups before leaping up, panting like a racehorse, and rejoining the queue.

He scrapes through the two-inch test next time, but his chances of being among the final 44 are still slim and, even if he gets through, this is only the first phase of the process. Successful applicants here go for a gruelling Hill Selection later in the year and only the best of those will go through to Central Selection in Pokhara after that. Some five months from now, the 24,000 original applicants will be reduced to a lucky 230, who will then leave Nepal for induction training in Singapore or at Catterick in North Yorkshire.

'It's a big culture shock,' Adrian admits, before adding, a trifle ruefully, 'But the army's a culture shock anyway.'

The rewards are substantial. As a serving soldier, the Gurkha gets the same pay as a British soldier, around £1000 a month. By comparison, a captain in the Royal Nepal Army is paid around £100 a month. On retirement many Gurkhas come back to Nepal and make a good living in the tourist business, buying hotels and guest-houses.

Adrian brushes off any suggestion that there might be local resentment at having these elite fighters poached by a foreign power. Adding up pensions, welfare schemes, direct expenditure, as well as the return of money earned abroad, he reckons the Gurkhas are worth £68 million a year to the Nepali economy.

Because the turnout out has been much higher than expected, with 251 applicants registered, they are only halfway through the programme by the end of the day. The *galla* seems pleased as he brings the results up to date. Twenty-three failed in the heaves, 40 in the sit-ups (in which one boy managed 98 in less than 2 minutes), 13 failed the eye-test and 7 were deemed too short. This leaves 168 still in the running for 44 places.

It's been a long hot day for everyone, so we discreetly open a bottle of whisky to celebrate with Adrian and the organizers up in our dining tent.

After a while the *galla* comes in to join us. He looks decidedly uncomfortable and, mopping his brow with a handkerchief, he talks rapidly to the others in Nepali. I can see expressions change.

Adrian translates for us. Some 'visitors from the forest' have approached the *galla*. They now want to talk to the rest of us. He nods, anticipating my question. They're Maoists.

A delegation, including our director J-P, follows two young men who look like students, one with a colourful embroidered shoulder bag, the other carrying documents of some sort in plastic folders. They look quite harmless, as if they might be on their way to a tutorial, but the submissiveness of everyone concerned suggests they have something more than moral authority.

They lead our people out of earshot, off behind a small temple, beside which a gnarled old bo tree grows. After half an hour they're back. J-P reports they met with four of them, all young, the same sort of age as the recruits, two of whom were polite and reasonable and two 'a bit nasty'.

They have asked the *galla*, Adrian and two other Gurkha officers, to go with them to meet what they call their high command, two hours' walk away into the forest. While we are taking all this in, three of the Maoists appear at the door of our tent. One, in a white shirt, is short and chunky and wears glasses reminiscent of Piggy in *Lord of the Flies*. He has a row of pens clipped in his top pocket. Another holds a radio. We mask the whisky bottle as they peer round the tent. Once they've gone another boy appears. He wears a baseball cap and speaks to the Sherpa Nawang, expecting him to translate. Nawang's eyes simply grow wide and he seems transfixed, speechless with anxiety. The boy's tone seems apologetic. Cradling a silver torch, he puts his hands together in the traditional greeting.

'Namaste.'

At that moment the stocky accomplice appears once again. He is less charming and, having scrutinized us all one last time, he makes a remark and goes.

Nawang eventually recovers enough to translate.

'He said he has the tape measure.'

The *galla*, together with all his records and the tape he used to measure the chests, has gone, along with Adrian and his two fellow officers. Though there appeared to be no physical threat, there seemed no question of their not going, nor of who they were going with. I walk outside. The sun has set and the distant peaks of the Himalaya, a moment ago blood-red and magnificent, are now cold, grey and remote. I find myself scanning the faces of the villagers. Everything seems very different from this morning. Perhaps they all hate us, stirred to anger by the Maoists, who've portrayed us as friends of a corrupt and oppressive government?

I realize, rather pathetically, how easily I project my own feelings onto others. If I'm happy, they must be happy. Now I'm suspicious, they must be too. Their expressions give nothing back. They get on with their work and I get on with my insecurities.

To complete a rotten end to the day, our cooks serve us goat in batter with tuna sauce.

Day Forty Eight : Lekhani to Pokhara

Adrian and his companions have not returned. Wongchu, our experienced Sherpa leader, doesn't want to stay here a moment longer than we have to, and in truth, there's nothing much we can do.

We wait until nine, then strike camp and head off down to the valley. As we leave the village we pass groups of young men standing around. Faces that were so eager yesterday, are either blank or confused as they wait to be told what they probably know already, that all their efforts were wasted.

I feel we've let them down and try to avoid catching their eye.

Soon Lekhani passes out of sight, and we pick our way down steep and precarious clay tracks through tiny settlements where we are the objects of considerable curiosity. The sticky heat of the valley replaces the cool of Lekhani, and I'm pouring sweat by the time we step carefully along the knife-edge rim of a rice paddy and out onto a level but half-finished highway, which in happier circumstances might have prompted mass whistling of the River Kwai march.

The road-head, over two hours' walk from Lekhani, is at a pretty village called Dopali, surrounded by silent, wooded slopes and a clean, fast-rushing stream. Life seems utterly restful here. An old lady cradles a cat, a family sit on the steps of a beautifully carved timber-frame house whose long doors are folded open to reveal slanting rays of sun spilling onto a cool, clay floor. Dopali is like something in a dream, a vision of delicious drowsiness and lethargy sent to subvert the purposeful and debilitate the dedicated.

We pick up vehicles here and, once away from the villages, J-P calls Adrian's superiors in Kathmandu to tell them the bad news. Absurdly, whoever he gets through to is not helpful. It's a Sunday, the commanding officer is having lunch and can't be disturbed. As J-P won't disclose details of what's happened, they seem to presume he hasn't any, and the harder he tries to convince them, the harder they stonewall.

It is a credit to J-P's persistence that eventually the word gets through.

By the time we're back in Pokhara all hell is let loose. At least three separate calls from the British Embassy ask us not to breathe a word of what has happened at Lekhani to anyone. This is the first time the Maoists have abducted a serving British officer, and may mark a significant change in policy. We eat, but, for once, no-one's terribly hungry.

By evening there is still no word of Adrian and the others.

Day Forty Nine : Pokhara to Chomrung

Early morning microlite flight over the lake and up towards the mountains. Myself in one tiny craft, Nigel filming me from another. Feel terrifyingly unsafe. Tucked in behind a Russian pilot with a big seventies moustache who speaks only in thumbs-up signs, with thin air on either side. Cavorting at 10,000 feet above the ground, secured only by a car seat-belt across my lap, I experience pure terror for the first half-hour, and for the next, as we come down low over the shining lake and wooded hills, pure joy.

When I get back to breakfast, someone shows me the front page of the *Kathmandu Times*. So much for secrecy. 'Maoists abduct British Army Officers', reads the headline. Below is a jumbled report, which not only includes our director among the abducted, but has promoted him as well. He appears in the story as 'Brigadier General John Paul', which I hope won't go to his head.

And still no word on their whereabouts.

While we're in Pokhara a good opportunity arises to try and glean a little more insight into just what's going on in the country. John Cross, born in London and at various times in his life a soldier, diplomat and author of eleven books, including *Whatabouts and Wherabouts in Asia*, is an ex-Gurkha and expert in jungle warfare. He lives in a comfortable house in the quieter part of Pokhara with his adopted Nepali family.

We talk beside a small Hindu temple in his garden. It's an esoteric affair, containing a Buddha, a picture of the Blarney Stone, and a figure of St Jerome, the patron saint of languages.

'Cover all our options,' he grins.

John is a wiry, sharp-eyed 78-year-old. He still looks and sounds military, with a clipped delivery, straight back, green shorts and socks pulled up to the knee, but his replies are never predictable. He speaks ten Asian languages.

'I learnt one in seven days. Mind you, I wasn't eating.'

He sees an historical pattern in what's happening here.

'This is my third revolution,' he tells me. 'The first one was in Malaya, the second was in Laos. The first one the government won, one-zero, the second the Communists won, one-all, and this is my third. Third time lucky for who?'

He sees it as something that's been bubbling for a long time.

'The poor have been marginalized.'

Law and order and a strong political base are prerequisites for defeating the rebels, but understanding the poor, as he has tried to do by travelling up and down the country, is also vital.

Wearing thick, dark glasses for his fading eyesight, John brushes off my query as to whether he's been tempted to try and help the Nepali government sort this one out.

'I've got to keep a low profile here.' He smiles. 'The doctor said get hit on the head, you're blind for life.'

We leave Pokhara this morning for our first serious assault on the mountains. Brigadier General John Paul, mindful of the fact that we will soon be crossing into Tibet and operating for several days above 16,400 feet (5000 m), has scheduled a five-day, altitude-training trek to Annapurna Base Camp.

The one sop is that, because of time constraints, we shall be taken by helicopter to our start point at Chomrung. A 20-minute flight instead of what would be a two-day walk.

Once the helicopter has delivered us we're left in deep and almost sensuous silence, hemmed in by the steep and thickly wooded walls of a valley, one side in brilliant sunshine, the other in deep, impenetrable shade.

At this height – we're at just over 7000 feet (2130 m) – even the most precipitous slopes are cultivated. Across the valley, I can see a farmhouse with 40 terraces, descending the hillside below, one after the other. Rising high in the distance, the summits of Annapurna and Machhapuchhre (Fish Tail Mountain) mark the parameters of our adventure; our constant companions on the trail, the objects of our pilgrimage.

For now, the atmosphere is relaxed. We sit outside the hotel in warm sunshine surrounded by all the trappings of an English country garden: thickets of marigold, chrysanthemum and nasturtium, butterflies fluttering round hydrangea bushes. The trail up to Annapurna runs through the hotel and a steady stream of walkers comes by. Three Israeli students tell us they have been approached by Maoists and asked for 1000 rupees (about £7) each. They pleaded student poverty but the Maoists were insistent, and, as one was armed, they thought it best not to argue. They were dealt with very courteously and issued with receipts. An English hiker we talk to later said that he and his party were asked for 2000 each. The Maoists justified the price hike because the British, and the American, government supplies arms to Nepal (the very arms which the Maoists are probably using).

The guerrillas don't like the Annapurna Conservation Area, presumably because it's a government initiative, and recently forced six of the checkpoints on the trail to close. The 1000 rupee fee that was levied to pay for conservation work they now take for themselves.

Nevertheless, Wongchu, so nervy yesterday, doesn't think we'll have trouble with the Maoists, who he refers to, dismissively, as 'Jungle Army' and, even more derisively, Long Noses.

There seem to be plenty of other things to worry about, if a large sign just outside the hotel is to be believed.

We are, apparently, in an Avalanche Risk Area. 'Cross the Risk Area before 10 am', the sign warns. If you avoid the avalanche, you could still fall victim to Acute Mountain Sickness.

Symptoms are divided into 'Early', which include, 'Headache, Loss of Appetite, Dizziness, Fatigue on Minimal Exertion' (I had three of these four in Ladakh), and 'Worsening', characterized by 'Increasing Tiredness, Severe Headache, Walking Like Drunk and Vomitting' (sic).

'What To Do?' asks the big metal signboard. The answer is unequivocal.

'Descend! Descend! Descend!'

The accommodation, on two floors, is clean and basic, with a bed and pillow and a lavatory and washroom at the end of the block. There is electricity but it only manifests itself in one dim bulb per room. As a result of strict anti-litter controls, all drinking water is boiled, instead of bottled. The chicken at supper is, well, muscular.

Day Fifty : Chonrung to Dovan

We set off about eight. Our 35 porters, though expertly marshalled by our 13 Sherpas, are not used to the stop-start interruptions of filming, and by 9.30 we have reached only as far as the Chomrung General Store. More worryingly, our progress up to Annapurna has been entirely downhill. We'll surely have to pay for this.

The store, crowded with schoolchildren buying sweets before climbing up to their school in Chomrung, is our last chance to buy what J-P calls 'sophisticated provisions'.

The range of goods on the shelves gives a foretaste of the weapons we might need should we ever have to touch the void: Pringles, porridge oats, toilet paper, vodka, 'Man's Briefs', chocolate, 'Bandage for Knee Caps', nail clippers, Chinese playing cards and rum.

Once outside the village we continue down on paths occasionally stepped with wide stone slabs (mostly laid by women of the local Gurung tribe) until we cross the Modi Khola (the River Modi) and at last the ascent begins. The porters bend to their work. As I watch their rubber sandals nimbly negotiate the rocks ahead of me I'm ashamed to think how long I spent deciding which kind of boots to wear. And some of them are carrying 40 kilograms in their wicker backpacks.

For a while it's idyllic. Prayer flags festoon the trees at intervals, fat bees feed off the cornflowers, lizards sprint across the mica-sparkling rock.

'Namaste,' I say cheerfully to everyone we pass.

On one particularly steep section we're overtaken by a mule train, the animals sashaying nimbly past and shoving me sideways into the bushes with their panniers.

'Namaste!'

Wongchu sticks fairly close to me. He's been given the impression that I'm someone of consequence, though he's not absolutely sure why. He's in his late thirties, solidly built with the broad features and high cheekbones of a northern Nepali or a Red Indian chief. He's horrendously over-qualified for this sort of work, having twice summitted Everest. On one of those occasions he arrived at the top at 5.30 in the morning, so far ahead of the rest of the party that he lay down on top of Everest and fell asleep until they arrived. Now that is cool.

He talks in staccato bursts of heavily compressed English, a lot of which I miss.

'Bondo. They call me Bondo.'

Above: The Vice-Regal Lodge at Shimla. *Below:* Keeping out of the sun or keeping out of the book? Shy ladies on the Ridge at Shimla.

Top: On the road to Dharamsala. Our well-hennaed driver, 'Red', and a lunch bristling with green chillies. *Bottom:* Country life in Himachal Pradesh. Rich land, poor farmers.

Top: Bulrush fields hide the river south of Dharamsala. *Above:* Tibet in India. Hanging prayer flags out near the Lhagyal Ri temple at McLeodganj.

At the Tibet Medical and Astrology Centre. I learn from Phurbu Tsering that I was an elephant in my previous life.

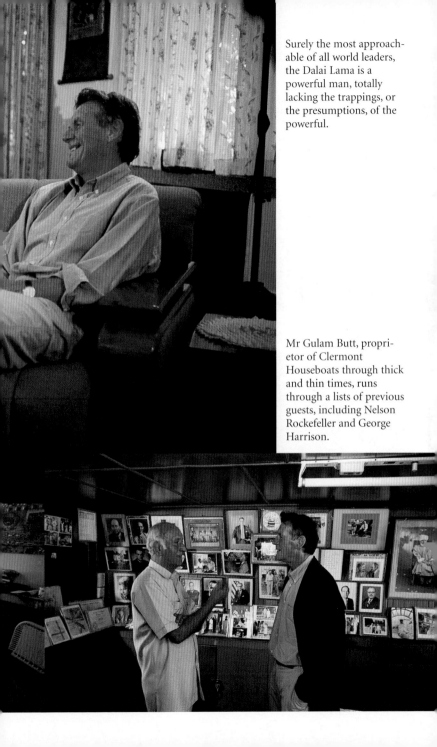

Surely the most approachable of all world leaders, the Dalai Lama is a powerful man, totally lacking the trappings, or the presumptions, of the powerful.

Mr Gulam Butt, proprietor of Clermont Houseboats through thick and thin times, runs through a lists of previous guests, including Nelson Rockefeller and George Harrison.

Top: The Kashmir Martyrs' Graveyard, one of many for those Muslims who've died fighting, or because of fighting, for freedom from India. *Above:* The remains of the Greenway Hotel, Srinagar, destroyed by the Indian army after Islamic militants holed up there. OPPOSITE PAGE A selection of the famous and once much sought-after house-boats of Srinagar.

Left: Hindu Nepal. In Patan's Durbar Square stone elephants, carved 380 years ago, guard the entrance to Shiva's temple. *Below:* Kathmandu. In the grounds of the Royal Palace, the great and good of Nepal stand in line for the royal *tika*.

Top: Before it all went wrong. Adrian Griffith talks to the *galla*, the recruiting officer, prior to addressing the village in fluent Nepali. *Above:* Some of the 251 would-be Gurkhas start stretching the sinews. Only 44 will get to the next stage of testing.

Crossing the cable bridge at Dopali, having been forced to abandon Gurkha recruiting after Maoist guerrillas abducted Adrian and other senior officers.

The steep, stone steps out of Chomrung. They look helpful, but became slow torture.

Above: Machhapuchhre, 'Fish Tail Mountain', is looking in much better shape than I am, as Wongchu (who has twice climbed Everest) hangs patiently behind me. *Below:* A mug of garlic soup as the afternoon mist comes down over Machhapuchhre, the sacred mountain they say has never been climbed.

Right: A doorway in Patan shows the fine design and craftsmanship of the Newari people. *Middle and bottom:* Durbar Square, Patan. Kunder Dixit, urbane, resourceful editor of the *Nepali Times.* A man does *puja*, a ritual offering to the gods at Krishna Mandir.

The view that makes it all worthwhile. The Annapurna Sanctuary, a 360-degree panorama with nine summits reaching 23,000 feet (7000 m).

Above: With Pratima on a bridge over the Bagmati River at Pashupatinath, the most important Hindu temple complex in Nepal. *Below:* Male members of the family lay a deceased relative on the funeral pyre at the cremation ghats at Pashupatinath.

Above: Sadhus, itinerants who have renounced all worldly possessions and dedicated their life to lord Shiva, at Pashupatinath. *Below:* The world's most sociable hermits. These sadhus will do anything for you, including their Roy Wood and Wizzard impersonation.

Prayer flags flutter from the huge stupa at Boudhanath, the most important Buddhist site in Kathmandu and heart of the city's Tibetan community.

I nod and smile, vaguely.

'Bondo,' he repeats, smiling broadly. 'The Gun.'

'Ah, yes.'

'Ask anyone on Everest for Wongchu, they may be confused. Bondo Wongchu everybody know.'

He drops bits of information at regular intervals, as if I need food for the mind as well as the body. Did I know that the tip of Everest is limestone, a seabed pushed five and a half miles into the sky.

I ask him what he thinks about the situation in Nepal.

He looks around with a shrug and an expansive sweep of the arm.

'Nobody in charge of the country any more.'

We climb over a spur and begin moving down through thick rhododendron and then bamboo forest. The way becomes increasingly dark, overgrown and claustrophobic. The sun has disappeared behind the mountains and a white mist is descending over the forest as we reach our overnight stop at Dovan. There are three of the long, grey, stone buildings with their blue, painted, tin roofs to choose from: The Dovan Guest House, the Annapurna Approach Lodge and Restaurant Hotel Tip Top. All are identical and all are full. In the courtyards a largely Western crowd of trekkers is resting, washing, snacking, lolling and generally looking knackered.

'Tourism,' mutters Wongchu, contemptuously. Though of course he makes his living from it.

The Sherpas set up camp. We've had a long, hard day's walk and only about 1000 feet (300 m) to show for it.

Basil is in a bad way. He doesn't like trekking – 'the longest walk I do is from the bar to the table' – and seems to have been cursed with a cold and a knife-like sore throat.

The talk at supper is not uplifting, turning mainly around the choice of our next camping spot, bearing in mind the risk of avalanche further up the mountain.

As we sit at the table after supper, Wongchu, unbidden, comes round and massages shoulders, arms, heads. A good massage too. He has fingers like steel.

'Sleep well, now,' he assures me.

How wrong he was.

Day Fifty One : Dovan to Derali

Temperatures fell sharply in the night and when I push back the flap of my tent it's ice cold with condensation. As we approach the toughest part of the trek, I can no longer ignore the inconvenient fact that I am feeling pretty lousy, and, if I'm about to get what Basil is already suffering from, things could get a lot worse.

He sits at breakfast with a pile of tissues beside him, dressed all in black and looking like death warmed up. In between painful coughs and raucous nose-blowings he delivers sharp and pithy observations on the joys of trekking, most of which seem to be eluding him.

French toast and boiled eggs are barely digested before the Sherpas set about striking camp with military precision. They like to keep moving. Or do they know something about avalanches we don't?

I stubbornly resist offers from Nawang and Wongchu to carry my backpack for me. It's become a matter of pride for me to carry it, a defiant attempt to show that there is still something I can do for myself.

We set out at half-past seven, climbing up steep stone staircases through a tangle of semi-tropical woodland, with wispy lengths of Spanish moss trailing from the branches of the trees like a trail of feather boas. When we emerge from the trees the sunshine is still way up in the mountain tops but the air is cool and fresh.

I feel a sudden surge of joie de vivre and ask Wongchu if he thought I could climb Everest. Flattered that he says yes with barely a pause I ask how long it would take.

'You must do training. Get used to altitude. Climb other mountains first.' He looks me up and down. 'I get you up there in maybe 75, maybe 100 days.'

I was thinking about a week.

'No time on this schedule, then.'

He grins and indicates my backpack.

'You want me take that?'

The distance between us and the tantalizing ceiling of sunlight high above us is gradually decreasing, but it's not until 10.15 that it tips over the rim of the mountains and spills into the valley. The temperature change is instant and dramatic. Off with fleece and on with 35 factor sun cream.

The scenery change is equally dramatic. After 24 hours of some-times oppressive forest, the valley now opens and widens out and for the first time I have a sense of the monumental scale of what we are heading into. The 40-mile-long wall that stretches from Anna-purna I in the west to Annapurna II in the east has no fewer than nine summits above 23,000 feet (7010 m). Even closer to us are Annapurna South at 23,678 feet (7200 m), Hiunchuli, over 21,000 feet (6400 m) and, barely five miles due east, the mesmerically eye-catching Machhapuchhre, the highest of its two pinnacles rising just short of 23,000 feet (7010 m).

This is sublime mountain scenery. Only Concordia in Pakistan, on the threshold of K2, reduced me to the same sense of inarticulate wonder.

Not much time for wonder, inarticulate or otherwise, as we have to keep moving, stopping, filming, moving and eventual stopping for a more substantial breather beneath a soaring overhang called the Hinko Rocks.

Animism preceded and has survived the religions that came to Nepal and it doesn't surprise me to hear that this conspicuous rocky cave is a sacred place. Talking of myths and legends, I ask Wongchu about the yeti.

He says that like everyone else round here he believes it exists.

'I saw some yeti in the mountain.'

'What did it look like?'

'Look like monkey, it look like people like us.'

Wongchu rolls off a list of unlikely but intriguing facts. The best way to catch a yeti is to get him drunk. He likes tea and he likes alcohol, and people used to trap yetis by putting out a dead dog full of alcohol. It's the people who have hunted the creatures down.

'And now, one only left yeti.'

Beyond Hinko a sheer rock face rises to one side of the path, steep, smooth and sheer. A thin, white plume of a waterfall drops from way above, glancing off the rock and ricocheting down towards us in slow motion, it seems.

When the snow comes these rocks turn lethal. This is the high-risk avalanche area and Wongchu has seen people killed here. The only possible chance you have to avoid a fall is to have a sense of hearing acute enough to pick up the very first sound. The avalanche sound, Wongchu calls it. Then, as he puts it, 'Quick run.'

We reach the Sangri-La (sic) guesthouse at lunchtime and decide to go no further today. It turns out to be a good decision. By 2.30 swirling, vaporous cloud has descended, bringing the temperature down with it. Out of T-shirts and shorts and into scarves, hats, gloves and eventually thermals. We have a grandstand view of Machhapuchhre, revealing itself in tantalizing Garboesque glimpses between the drifting cloud.

It's a holy mountain. It is forbidden to slaughter any animal within its sacred valley, and Wongchu says his attempts to obtain permission to climb it have always been refused.

As the conditions become increasingly cold and inhospitable, the only members of our expedition who look at all cheerful are the porters. Released from their loads half a day early, they spend the afternoon noisily gambling away their take-home pay. A coin is thrown on the ground and where it lands it's replaced with a stone. Players then have to hit the stone with their coins. If you hit the stone, you pocket all the coins that have missed. It's a game that has apparently come down from Mongolia and is played throughout the Himalaya.

It's very much a participation game and the porters come alive, greeting every move with raucous shouts, jeers, groans and laughter. I've rarely seen so many people having such a good time for so long. It's quite depressing really, and brings on a prolonged bout of coughing.

We eat early, sitting on wool-covered benches round a rectangular table that is usually heated from beneath by a kerosene stove, but it isn't working tonight. Freshly made Gurung bread, thick, yet light and filling, then anodyne vegetable noodle soup and fried rice. The staple diet of the mountains is *dal baht*, lentils and rice, but our cooks seem unwilling to offer us this and instead try manfully to provide us with what they think Westerners want.

The night is cold. I take Nurofen and hope that it will help me sleep. It knocks me out for two-hour periods, tames the coughing but provides little relief from an increasingly angry, sore throat. One word repeats itself in my disordered dreams. Descend! Descend! Descend!

Day Fifty Two: Derali to Machhapuchhre Base Camp

At breakfast Wongchu asks me how I am. I give him quite a detailed progress report on cold, cough, sandpaper-like throat and general collapse of system.

He ponders this in a Harley Street sort of way, before narrowing his eyes like Sherlock Holmes confronted with a new and unexpected clue.

'You have beer last night?'

I try to cast my mind back.

'A little.'

Wongchu nods gravely.

'No beer.'

The sun is still out of reach, setting fire to the crests of the mountains, but still a long way from delivering us from this bitter morning chill. We fall to reminiscing about the good old days in the heart of the Sahara desert.

The porters, so ebulliently happy yesterday afternoon, are quiet and subdued. They crouch, huddled together for warmth, waiting to be called out, helped on with their baskets and sent on their way. They're Tamang people from Loswa district close to Kathmandu, all of them slight and wiry, as if honed down to the lowest body weight for the work they have to do. They will be paid $8 for each day on the mountain.

Though we have only about 1000 feet (300 m) to climb today, the path rises and falls in a frustrating switchback.

I've given up saying 'Namaste' to everyone who passes, but I'm momentarily cheered when I plod up to the top of yet another stone staircase and come level with two middle-aged American ladies. I see a look of recognition on one of their faces and hear a gasp of excitement as I pass.

'Oh, my God!'

I nod appreciatively, straighten my back and move on.

'It's *Eric Idle*!'

This precipitates serious psychological collapse. A half-hour later, exhausted by the pain of swallowing and the increasing effort required to pull in oxygen at this height, I finally yield my backpack to Wongchu. He takes it with a quiet smile, as if accepting the surrender of a garrison after a long siege.

Shedding the weight doesn't make things any better. Whereas I was out in front with the leaders yesterday, I can only watch the gap between us widen as they disappear ahead and leave me leaning on my climbing pole, heaving for breath, Nawang and Wongchu standing solicitously by.

Stagger into Machhapuchhre Base Camp around lunchtime. It's a much more open, jollier place than last night's guesthouse, full of infuriatingly happy campers sitting outside their tents, spraying each other with a water hose, hanging clothes on washing lines and generally having the time of their lives.

Even the majestic scenery — shapely Fish Tail and chunky Annapurna — fails to lift my spirits. I feel completely busted. The merest movement, to take food, to peel off a coat, to unpack an overnight bag, requires major physical effort. After a cup of garlic soup I decide there is nothing to do but take to my bed. Because of my condition, I'm upgraded from tent to room. It's standard mountain lodge accommodation, a stone-walled cell, eight foot by ten foot, with a flagged floor that traps the cold and damp like a cheese store, and a wooden bed frame on which is a thin mattress and a pillow. There is not much else to do but turn my back on one of the finest mountain panoramas in the world and climb, fully dressed, into my sleeping bag until whatever it is passes.

'You eat,' orders Wongchu when I surface a few hours later. 'Need food.'

No-one else says anything. I think I must frighten the crew a bit. They've never seen me quite like this: glum and unresponsive.

Force down some garlic soup, enlivened with shards of spring onion and green pepper. My neck and forehead are feverishly hot, and once I've finished, all I want to do is to go back to bed. Wongchu and Nawang deal with me most tenderly. Despite all my protestations, they prepare a bowl of steaming inhalant and insist I use it. Nawang gets fresh hot water from the cooks and helps me bathe my feet. Then they guide me into my sleeping bag, with Wongchu applying massage as I go. I feel rather as if I'm being laid out, and I must say at this moment the Grim Reaper would not be an unwelcome visitor.

Wongchu wants one of the Sherpas to come and sit with me through the night, but I dissuade him, and, watched over by an inanimate but impressive array of tablets, tissues, ointments, creams and sprays, I close my eyes and wait.

Day Fifty Three: to Annapurna Base Camp

I wake up, wrenched from sleep by some chest-wracking cough, and am seized by near panic. Everything is pitch black, silent and cold as ice. I have no sensation of where I am. Perhaps Nawang and Wongchu have found me a flotation tank. I scrabble around for my head-torch, sending a bottle of pills clattering across the hard stone floor. For a few minutes I simply lie there, staring up at a circle of slatted, paint-peeling board above me and waiting for my heart to slow down.

All sorts of things go through my mind. The one thing I can't dismiss is that I might have to think the unthinkable. That, for the first time in any of my journeys, I may have to face the possibility of failure. I'm 60, after all, and there has to be a point at which the body puts its foot down, as it were.

For a depressing hour or so I can't escape this profound feeling of being defeated, physically and mentally, by the Himalaya.

When I next wake, though there is absolutely no physical sign of time passing, I know, even before I search for my torch, that I've been out for a while. And in that time some sea change has taken place. I'm no longer hot and feverish, and the sense of survival seems stronger than the sense of doom.

With some effort I pull myself up and take sips of hot water from the thermos Nawang insisted I keep beside me. It's four o'clock in the morning and as sure as I was three hours ago that I wouldn't make it, I know now that there can be no question of turning back.

This morning, I feel I'm emerging from hibernation. Last night was winter and this is spring.

I leave the camp, with Nawang and Wongchu, climbing due west. The snowfields of the Annapurna Himal lie dead ahead, shining and brilliant in the rising sun. It's an adventurous morning's filming too, off the main track and clambering very slowly through the thick grass, with the camera catching our silhouettes against the hard glare of the mountains.

Nawang stays beside me all the way, making sure I take regular slugs of water. Wongchu, who, reassuringly, seems to think I no longer need his personal supervision, walks ahead, looking like Geronimo and pausing occasionally to chat to some descending female trekker, preferably Swiss or Austrian. These encounters really seem to cheer him up, as well as making up for my dawdling.

So it is a tired but unrecognizably happier band that pulls itself up the last, agonizingly long and steep flight of steps to Annapurna Base Camp.

Appropriately enough for Annapurna, the Hindu goddess of fertility, a *dal baht* lunch is waiting, and on the sun-filled terrace I can sit and enjoy a combination of relief and release. For the time being, at least, I don't need to go any higher.

There's quite a crowd of trekkers already at the camp and, with a captive audience, Wongchu is in his element. Like many climbers I know, he has an inexhaustible supply of disaster stories. He points out a small Buddhist shrine just outside the camp, which marks the spot where Anatoly Boukreev, a Russian climber, was killed by an avalanche. Annapurna I has taken the lives of some 15 people. Some, he adds mysteriously, have died because they offended the mountain gods.

'By eating meat?'

'Eating meat, yes. But also having sex.'

'Having sex?'

He nods knowingly. It happened to a climber he knew on one of his Everest expeditions.

'He had sex with many different kind of women in the Himalaya.'

He pauses until all heads are turned in his direction.

'He was the one who died on that expedition.'

As there has been absolutely no question of my having sex on Annapurna, the gods seem to be positively smiling. For once the sunset is not lost in the mist, and at six o'clock, 40 or 50 people from all over the world gather to watch the light show on the peaks of Machhapuchhre. A small act of homage to the Himalaya.

Day Fifty Four: Annapurna Base Camp to Pokhara

Last night my chest and lungs were better behaved but I was kept from deep sleep by an avalanche of images that roared through my brain, unbidden and unstoppable, for most of the night, making it feel like a video stuck on fast forward. At least I had no recurrence of the sensory deprivations of the night before. My room has two windows and I can see the cold mountainside in the moonlight. I can hear my neighbour through the wall. It's Basil, with a cough so fierce and bronchial that it sounds dangerous.

We're due to be taken off by helicopter some time this morning. I must be honest and say that, for me, it's not a moment too soon.

I think back to the enthralled group silent in the face of the majestic beauty of Machhapuchhre last night and I wonder if we aren't all in danger of falling into the romantic delusion that by staring at these great massifs of rock and ice we achieve some form of communication with them, as if something so forbiddingly colossal must somehow be friendly.

The mountains are far more likely to be enemies than friends. We take them on at our peril and, despite all nature's warnings, long to go higher. And the higher we go the more the mountains tighten their grip, squeezing the life out of most people, gently in some cases, more severely in others. The locals who see the mountains as gods to be appeased are only translating pragmatic experience. Human beings are not meant to live at these heights and they should expect trouble if they do.

If there is a reward for reaching this height (13,400 feet (4080 m)) it is the exhilaration of the immense. Because we're that much closer to the top of the peaks, the sunlight reaches us earlier than it did below and the dazzling clarity of the light sharpens and intensifies every detail of this mighty bowl of mountains. My scepticism thaws a little with the sun and as we walk beyond the camp and look out over the monumental sweep of the glacier that unwinds from the Annapurna Ridge, gouging a valley from the sheer rock, I realize how extraordinarily lucky I am to have seen all this.

And how much luckier to have a helicopter to take me away from it.

Our magic carpet arrives on time and, anxious not to hang around in these unpredictable conditions, takes off as soon as we've strapped ourselves in. Below us, in the slipstream, our porters spread-eagle themselves on their tents to stop them blowing away. I feel embarrassed and a little ashamed. We could have got down without a helicopter, but we certainly couldn't have made it up the Annapurna trek without our porters.

After circling the massif, we turn due south, following coiling glaciers, until they melt into streams that cross the spiky grassland and grow into small rivers, which disappear first into coniferous then tropical rain forest, re-emerging where the trees have been cut back to make room for cultivated clearings. Then the first isolated settlements appear and the clearings grow into terraces and the settlements grow into mountain villages with marked tracks, and the terraces become rice paddies in all shades of green and yellow and the marked tracks become paved roads, with power lines running beside them through the tin-shack slums around the airport. And the rivers become a lake.

The evolution of human settlement in 22 minutes. At Pokhara, the joys of hot water, shower, bed and the excellent news that Adrian Griffith and his fellow Gurkha officers were released, unharmed, after 48 hours in the forest.

Day Fifty Six : Kathmandu

Post-Annapurna elation will be short-lived. Higher mountains and tougher conditions are forecast for the crossing into Tibet, but for now we have breathing space in one of the most intriguing cities of the Himalaya.

My guide to the Nepali capital is Kunda Dixit, editor of the *Nepali Times*, an English weekly with a circulation of 8000. It's crisply laid out and well designed and has a sharp, well-informed, provocative style. The most recent edition carries the latest World Terrorism Index, which shows that, despite the Maoists, Nepal still comes below the UK.

So I'm not entirely surprised to find that Kunda Dixit is an urbane, elegant figure with a shock of prematurely silver hair, dressed immaculately in a pale grey *labada* and knitted tunic. I am surprised to hear that his real love is flying and his fantasy is that, with a pilot suddenly taken ill, Kunda takes control, lands the plane perfectly and is asked to take over the national airline.

We meet up in Patan, once one of three independent kingdoms in the valley, and now almost a suburb of Kathmandu.

The jewel at the heart of Patan (pronounced Parton, as in Dolly) is Durbar Square, a dazzling collection of buildings dating back 350 to 500 years, to the days before Prithvi Naryan Shah, king of Ghorka, unified the kingdoms of the valley in 1768 and created modern Nepal. There are temples, palaces with golden gates, a huge bell suspended between two pillars and a lion on a column. Nepal was never colonized, so the architecture has no Western derivative and its distinctive fusion of Indian and Tibetan influences was created by the Newars, the people of the valley, and craftsmen of the highest order.

As we wander through the colonnades of the Krishna Mandir, a stone-built Hindu temple topped with a *shikhara*, the characteristically Indian, curvilinear spire, we can look across to the Royal Palace, in a completely different style, refined by the Newari architect Arniko in the 14th century. It has powerful horizontals of brick and timber with deep, overhanging eaves, projecting balconies cantilevered out over finely carved, timber supports, and, inside, an elegantly proportioned *chowk*, or courtyard.

Kunda tells me that the Kathmandu Valley, once a lake, is rich in fertile, alluvial soil. The kingdoms, grown fat from consistently good harvests, ploughed their surpluses into religion, festivals and fine buildings, competing with each other for the tallest tower or the biggest bell.

'They used to say there were more temples in Kathmandu than houses and more gods than people.'

The buildings are not purely for show. A family arrives to do a *puja* at Krishna Mandir, unsettling a flock of pigeons, who create a sharp gust of wind as they take off, circle and descend en masse a few feet away.

The most dramatic building in the square is the five-storeyed pagoda of the Taleju Mandir, with a bronze stupa at its apex. The pagoda, a tapering succession of roofs symbolizing the various stages of enlightenment, was perfected here in Nepal, and it was Arniko who took the design to the Ming court at Peking.

One of the pleasures of meandering round Durbar Square is the immense amount of carved and sculpted detail. In the Royal Palace there are stone slabs called *shildayras* that carry historical records from the Lichavi period, 1800 years ago. On the beams in the *chowks* are intricately worked and painted lotus flowers, dragons and swastikas, and the stone walls of Krishna's temple are adorned with athletic, erotic couplings.

'Krishna is the god of love,' explains Kunda. 'He's a young guy with a flute and girlfriends all over the world.'

I'm rather envious.

'Our gods don't tend to have girlfriends. It's something we've rather missed out on.'

The smallest of the old kingdoms was centred on Bhaktapur, seven miles east of Kathmandu. On our way out there we're waved past a police checkpoint set up since the Maoists recently brought their attacks to Kathmandu itself. They're searching all the buses that run out to the country areas in the east. According to Kunda, journeys that took 12 hours can now take 48.

Kunda's view is that the Maoists' recent change of tactics, targeting civilians in the capital, has lost them support.

'It's not that the Maoists are terribly brilliant or strong, just that successive governments have been weak and fractious and corrupt, and they (the Maoists) have tapped into that bedrock of neglect and apathy and frustration in the people. They've grown so fast precisely because everything else has been in such disarray.'

With an estimated 10,000 to 15,000 rebels, with looted arms from the police and the army, how does he see the future?

There can, he is sure, be no military solution. There has to be compromise. The institution of monarchy is quite strong and Nepalis identify their country with it, but the King can no longer be an absolute ruler. He must be firm but fair. (Which seems to suggest he's neither.)

He points to achievements brought about by strong policies resolutely applied.

Forestry conservation has been a big success since local people were given their own areas of forest to administer, the hydroelectric programme, building of roads, water improvement projects. All give him hope.

'And,' he concludes, 'Nepal's press has never been freer.'

We're turning into the bus park below the walls of Bhaktapur.

'The Prime Minister has been sacked, parliament is in limbo, but the press is free.'

The day that started promisingly is growing grey and gloomy as, having paid our $10 fee to enter the city, we climb up the steps and in through a narrow, rose-brick gateway.

For Basil it's a nostalgic return. Much of Bertolucci's *Little Buddha*, on which he worked as both actor and stills photographer, was shot in Bhaktapur. Though smaller than Kathmandu or Patan, Bhaktapur, whose name means 'city of devotees', once boasted 99 separate *chowks*. A powerful earthquake in 1934 did serious damage and now only five of these grand courtyards are left. That they are here at all is largely due to a German-sponsored reconstruction programme. The connection with Nepal seems a curious one, but it goes back a long way. A German Jesuit sent one of the Malla kings of Nepal a telescope as early as 1655. Hitler sent a later king a Mercedes.

As in Patan and, indeed, old Kathmandu itself, there is some glorious work in Bhaktapur. The Sun Dhoka (Golden Gateway) is an arched entrance surrounded by richly ornamented deities covered in gilded, embossed copper. The figures of the gods are still worshipped and I see young Nepalis touching them and then their foreheads as they pass. All over the temple area there are statues and carvings worn shiny by touch. We clamber up into a small, octagonal, carved timber gem called Chyasin Mandap, the Pavilion of the Eight Corners, an 18th-century original, meticulously restored around an earthquake-proof, steel shell. A much grander building stands nearby: Nyatapola, the tallest pagoda in Nepal. Five-tiered and standing 100 feet high, it somehow survived the 1934 earthquake quite unscathed. One might imagine this would increase its attraction for devotees, but when I climb up the long, steep staircase past sculpted ranks of temple guardians – wrestlers, elephants, lions, griffins – I find only dust and a group of street children. Apparently, this magnificent building is dedicated to an obscure Tantric goddess, Siddhi Lakshmi, who very few people have heard of, let alone worship. As the temples rely on rich patrons for their upkeep, Nyatapola remains neglected.

There is hope. Kunda is generally optimistic about the way the old city centres are looked after (all three are UNESCO sites). He's much less happy about the way modern development is going. The urban sprawl around Kathmandu is, he feels, destroying the identities of the three cities. They are becoming part of a Kathmandu conurbation, which is bad for Nepal. It increases the centralization of wealth and government in the valley, further alienating the country areas, and puts great pressure on limited resources. Water supply is becoming a major problem. The latest proposal is to bring water in direct from a glacier, 15 miles away. It will be the biggest engineering project in Nepal's history, and if it works it will only bring more people and more money to the central valley, further dividing the country. And it would not go unopposed. Only yesterday, Kunda reminds me, the Maoists destroyed a hydroelectric plant.

On our way back, the insalubrious suburbs, and the congested roads that take us through them, seem to bear out Kunda's darker prophecies, but life is not all gloom.

He tells the story of sitting next to Prince Charles (of whom he has a very high opinion) at a Nepali banquet. Halfway through the meal Charles upended a full portion of rice wine into his lap.

'Great embarrassment all round?'

'No, everything was fine.' Kunda smiles at the recollection. 'I told him that was the way we do our dry cleaning here.'

Day Fifty Seven : Kathmandu

To a high-walled, heavily gated, but otherwise reassuringly normal home near the Gurkha headquarters for a reunion with Adrian Griffith, the British Gurkha officer sent to look after us who ended up being abducted himself.

A relief to find him in good health and good spirits. We drink tea in his garden with his admirably phlegmatic wife, who claims never to have worried that he wouldn't come back. Adrian, whilst refusing to answer what he calls 'operational questions', gives us a little more background to what happened that evening when the Maoists called him away from his whisky.

They were taken to an empty house an hour from Lekhani and about five hours later, about midnight, were led deeper into the forest. His escort were not angry but they were insistent, and they had weapons concealed in their shoulder bags.

'Pistols?'

'Yes, pistols.'

'I went to sleep in a very filthy bed from which I received a lot of flea bites.' (His only injuries, fortunately.)

All the next day was spent talking, or rather, being talked at, by his abductors. On the second day of their captivity, by which time the story was all across the world's newspapers, word came down from the Maoist high command that Adrian and the others should be released. He feels pretty sure that the local commanders had been reprimanded by their superiors for taking him in the first place.

I asked if he ever felt in real danger. He said his two worries were of the danger of being caught in crossfire if the security forces mounted an operation to free him and the knowledge that a Nepali member of the Gurkha staff, abducted a year before, had been held for seven weeks.

'I think we were an opportunity target. They came down in order to disrupt the recruiting, realized there was someone more senior from the British Gurkhas there and saw it as a chance to publicize their cause.'

What of the recruits who'd sweated and strained their way through a day of tests?

Well, they would be given the chance to try again. This was the only time Adrian sounded less than convincing.

Before we leave Kathmandu, I meet up once again with the redoubtable Pratima Pande, who insists that I should see one of the great sights of Kathmandu, the temple complex at Pashupatinath, the holiest Hindu site outside India. Pashupati is one of the many names (around a thousand in all) of Shiva, the most revered god in the Hindu pantheon. So sacred is this site that non-Hindus are not allowed inside the temple at the heart of it. If they were, they would be able to see one of its great attractions, a ten-foot-high male member, or *linga*, which, and I rely on my *Rough Guide* for this, refers to a myth whereby 'Shiva transformed his phallus into an infinite pillar of light and challenged Brahma and Vishnu – the other members of the Hindu trinity – to find the ends of it. Both were forced to abandon the search.'

Below the temple and flanked by the burning ghats runs the River Bagmati, which, despite carrying the effluent of 1.5 million people, is a holy river, and eventually joins the Ganges. Monkeys scuttle along the parapet ahead of us as we pause on one of two stone and brick bridges and look down on a sight I've heard about but never witnessed. A number of platforms, sort of jetties for the soul, are built on the riverbank and on these the dead are cremated on wood pyres. One or two have bodies burning on them already, others are being cleared after a cremation. Attendants, brisk and businesslike in white aprons and cotton vests, are brushing the platforms clean, sending burning embers flying into the river, where they hit the water with a hiss and bob off down the Bagmati, trailing plumes of smoke like so many miniature steamships.

As we watch, a corpse is carried down past the temple and onto the bridge. Six members of the family are in attendance. They turn off and lay the body down beside a pyre already decorated with garlands of marigold.

Pratima explains that in Hindu culture it is very important that people do not die in their house, or that on death they are removed as soon as possible, so that the spirits captured there can be released. Indeed, there are those who, thinking their time is up, ask to be brought down to this holy place to die, only to recover and get up and go home at the end of the day.

The family we were watching have taken up their litter and moved across to the other side of the bridge, having strayed inadvertently onto the ghats reserved for upper-class Brahmins. This, Pratima tells me, is where the various members of the Nepali royal family were brought after the massacre two and a half years ago. Five of them, including the King and Queen, their younger son, and two princesses were cremated the same day they were murdered.

The family have now found the pyre reserved for them. To aid combustion, an attendant inserts slices of ghee (clarified butter) between the split logs. The mourners, all men (no women mourners are allowed to attend a cremation), are preparing themselves. The eldest son is sitting on the steps of the ghat having his head shaved by a priest, a *pandit*, with a cut-throat razor. He wears a plain white robe, white being the Hindu colour of mourning. There is something quite affecting about seeing the way he submits to this very simple, very public act of obsequy, in full view of any who happen to be passing.

The priest then talks to the family, presumably instructing them as to how it's all done, and they then lift the body from its bamboo stretcher, carry it, a little awkwardly, three times round the pyre, before laying it down, the head exposed. It's the body of a woman, younger than I expected, maybe not his mother or grandmother but his wife.

Basil leaves and water are placed in the dead woman's mouth as *prasad*, food consecrated and blessed by the gods.

Ghee is then placed on her body, with sandalwood to add a sweet-smelling incense, and the oldest male heir then walks around the pyre three times more. Then it is he who applies a lighted taper to the body, always near the mouth.

Shaking with emotion, he then bows, walks to the end of the pyre and buries his head on her feet. I feel I should look away, but I can't. I know nothing about these people yet, in this brief ceremony, I feel a wave of empathy, not just for them, but for loss, for the end of a life. I come from somewhere where death is kept private, almost as if it's an embarrassment. We send our loved ones away hidden in a box, into a hidden fire. We don't even press the button that sends the coffin sliding into that fire. It's all at arm's length. Here in Pashupatinath it's very much hands on. The reality of death, the fact of death, is confronted, not avoided.

We walk on across the bridge, to the east bank of the river. Everything here is odd and unfamiliar. There are animals everywhere: dogs, cows and some of the 400 monkeys who scamper over roofs and walls, eyes and little pink hands out for any offering left unattended. Along the side of the hill is a series of small, stone shrines, each one containing a stone phallus, dedicated to Shiva. They were built to commemorate those women who came here to commit *sati*, to be burned alive beside their husbands, as was the custom before the British made it illegal. Among the temples and terraces higher up we come upon an enclosure where sadhus, flamboyant ascetics as I suppose you might describe them, gather. The holy men, who call themselves *babas*, are not at all averse to posing for the tourists. I rather like the idea of exhibitionist hermits and particularly enjoy the milk *baba*, who lives solely on milk, and an 87-year-old with six-foot-long tresses, who obligingly puts his leg behind his head for me.

Bearing in mind that I shall be in Tibet tomorrow night, it seems suitable that we end the day at the biggest Buddhist temple in Kathmandu, built for those who for thousands of years have come through here on the road to and from the lands to the north.

Boudhanath stupa is immense, some 130 feet (38 m) high, and it squats like some great white spaceship, surrounded by shops, hotels and houses, off one of the busiest streets of the city. A pair of painted eyes looks down from the wall, serenely surveying the flock of birds, spread across the dome like stubble on a huge bald head, the shopkeepers and the crowd of pilgrims walking round and round in a clockwise direction, gaining more merit for each circuit they make. A web of colourful flags flaps from the highest point of the stupa, sending their prayers out to the gods. To my classically conditioned mind, all this display seems excessive and garish, like wrapping St Paul's Cathedral in Christmas paper.

Pratima invites us to a very smart party this evening. Lots of important foreign diplomats being introduced. I'm tired and just want to go to bed, but I do treasure one bit of polite conversation.

I'm introduced to an immaculately dressed man who takes a slightly pained glance at my appearance. I don't catch his name and grabbing a passing glass of wine, I hear myself asking, 'I'm sorry, ambassador of where?'

'France.'

It's time to move on.

Day Fifty Eight : Kathmandu to the Chinese Border

The road that winds its way northeast from Kathmandu is called the Arniko Highway. It's appropriately named, for Arniko was the Nepali architect credited with introducing the pagoda to China and the road that bears his name leads to the only crossing point between the two countries.

It is quite likely that there was more contact between Nepal and China 600 years ago than there is today. The road route from Kathmandu to Lhasa has only been open since the 1980s.

The landscape at first is unsensational, the highway rising and falling over undulating, terraced foothills. A string of tourist hotels with names like Snow View Resort and Himalaya Lookout carry the promise of great things to come, but sadly fail to deliver. The mountains ahead of us remain undetectable behind a layer of sluggish low cloud.

This concentrates the eye on more intimate views: villages of brick and thatch houses and tiny plots of land, ploughed by hand, with nothing much to suggest anything has changed in the last few hundred years. Verdant, fertile country, but rural life is still on an intimate scale. At the bend of a river a mixed team of cows and donkeys is being turned in tight circles to thresh the freshly cut wheat. Milk churns are carried on bent backs.

The only significant modern intrusions are regular police checkpoints (not a purely Nepali phenomenon, we've learnt to expect men with guns everywhere in the Himalaya) and the bizarrely large number of whisky adverts on the side of the houses. Names like Matador, Pied Paper and Bond are so ubiquitous they give the impression that much of rural Nepal must be on the bottle.

The only other product that is so obviously trumpeted is education. They're proud of their schools here and it's common to see crocodiles of young children, in matching uniforms, ties and backpacks, emerging from establishments like The Golden Future High School or The Wisdom Academy.

After lunch at Barabhise in the valley of the fast-flowing Bhote Koshi (Tibet River), the countryside narrows into a deep, forested gorge. A bridge with a bungee jump incongruously attached rises high above us and a little further on we pass a heavily guarded hydroelectric power station. Just as everything seems to be getting steep and claustrophobic, the walls of the gorge widen, quite abruptly, to reveal, high above us across the end of the valley, the white-stacked rectangles of a mountain city. My first glimpse of Tibet.

Nepali immigration is in a large bare room decorated with three framed pictures of King Gyanendra, his queen and Ganesh, the elephant god. Having had our names laboriously entered on a Departure Record, we walk up a dirty muddy road towards the border crossing on Friendship Bridge.

As we have all our gear to transfer, we cautiously back our vehicles into the middle of the 200-foot bridge to the exact point where Nepal ends and China begins. I don't think anyone's ever done this before, and there is much shouting from both ends. In the mayhem we say our farewells to Wongchu and Nawang and Mingmar, the trio of Sherpas who have looked after us so magnificently, while at the same time keeping an eye out for our Chinese escort.

He turns out to be a slim, young man in a sky-blue fleece, holding some papers and looking extremely anxious. So preoccupied is he with this unorthodox crossing that he doesn't introduce himself for another two hours. Only then do I learn he's a Tibetan, by the name of Migmar.

Anything in the Himalaya with the word 'friendship' attached is bound to be Chinese, and, sure enough, they built Friendship Bridge across this gorge in 1985. It's a grim and deeply confusing place to be and we are pretty soon ordered to stop filming. As Wongchu and Nawang wave one last time before disappearing into the crowd behind a 'Welcome to the Kingdom of Nepal' sign, I experience an emotion not dissimilar to that of seeing my mother wave goodbye to me on my first day at school.

We're now in the hands of unsmiling Chinese border guards in uniforms that seem to have been specifically designed to be too big. With the SARS epidemic so recently over, I first have to fill in a Quarantine Form. I then take it to a booth where a man in a white coat checks it, produces a gun, points it right between my eyes and pulls the trigger. He then peers at the gun, notes down my temperature and motions me into China.

The disorientation continues. Not only does the traffic drive halfway across the bridge on the left (Nepal) and the other half on the right (China) but, because of time changes, one end of Friendship Bridge (China) is two hours and fifteen minutes ahead of the other (Nepal). Propelled suddenly from mid-afternoon to early evening, we load up and drive as fast as we can, which means extremely slowly, up the six miles of slippery, winding track between the bridge and the Chinese immigration and customs post. Across the valley I can see Kodari, the last town in Nepal, receding below us. The gorge is steep and very beautiful but scarred with piles of rubbish, regurgitated from the backs of the buildings and spilling down to form scummy, foaming pools at the water's edge. In every country we've been so far private cleanliness and public squalor seem to quite happily co-exist and I've never really been able to work out why.

We arrive at Chinese immigration as it is about to close, and it's only pressure from our local hosts that stops us having to spend the night in the vehicles. We're allowed to take an overnight bag and walk up to the hotel, but everything else must be locked in the cars overnight.

Later: Room 505 of the Bai Ma Hotel, Xangmu. TV but no heating. Communal lavatory and bathroom down the passage. Single strip light, thin, inadequate curtains that are no match for the street lamps outside, and windows that seem specifically designed to funnel jets of cold air into the room.

This basic hotel, which we're assured is the best in town, is saved by its small, warm and cheerful dining room. Over *momos* (traditional Tibetan shell-shaped dumplings), stir-fry and Budweiser brewed in Wuhan, we meet up with Nina Huang Fan, our Chinese production assistant from Beijing, Mr Yang, the man the Chinese have sent to keep an eye on us, and Migmar, the soft-spoken young Tibetan, who still seems traumatized by the events on Friendship Bridge.

We're joined by Mr Tse Xiu, who is someone high up in the Foreign Relations Ministry of the Tibetan Autonomous Region. He speaks with quiet authority, but not in English, unfortunately. When his message is relayed to us it's not exactly heartening. Everest Base Camp, which we are scheduled to reach in 48 hours, is presently suffering from strong winds and temperatures down to -25°C (-13°F) at night. He advises us to make the best of a hot shower tonight, as there will be no more creature comforts for a while.

Have showered in a trickle of tepid water and am writing this with a blanket around me and wondering just how much colder it's going to get.

Tibet

Day Fifty Nine : Xangmu to Tingri

Xangmu high street, quiet as the grave when we arrived, erupts into life at night. Sounds of shouting, drilling, thumping and banging drift, unhampered, through tightly closed windows and into my head. I pull all the blankets off the unoccupied bed next to me, curl up in a foetal ball and hope it will all just go away. It doesn't. It gets worse. The hissing, clunking, industrial sounds seem to be augmented by flashes and crackles. Can someone really be spot-welding out there at 12.15? The prospect of how exhausted I'll feel in the morning keeps me awake for at least another hour.

Wake at eight, but it's still pitch dark. In fact, it doesn't begin to get light for another half-hour. The government of China, in their wisdom, decreed that the whole country, wider than the United States, should have only one time zone. The further west you are the later daybreak comes.

The street outside, apart from the frequent clearing of throats and whistling of spittle, is quiet again this morning. I can find no satisfactory explanation for the nocturnal activity other than that Xangmu is a frontier town and frontier towns have a life of their own. We walk down the hill to resume the customs procedures.

A truck marked 'Four Friends Transport. Live Long Friendship Nepal, India, China, Bhutan' is at the head of a long queue of vehicles heading towards Nepal. There isn't much room at the customs, and trucks, individuals, a bewildered-looking tour group and a flock of sheep are all trying to get through at the same time. Young, officious border guards in slack uniforms either push people around or ignore them completely. High up on the wall, and conveniently inaccessible, is a small box marked 'Complaints about Immigration'.

By the time all the formalities have been completed – and to be fair, a British film crew is a very rare sight in Tibet – it's early afternoon. Our final departure is marked by a small ceremony at which the manager of the Bai Ma Hotel gives us each a white scarf to bring us good luck on our journey. He seems a decent man, doing his best, though I notice he doesn't have a complaints box.

As we drive out of Xangmu (with few regrets, in my case) the squash of white-tiled buildings eases and we can see the wooded gorge we climbed yesterday, plunging picturesquely down to Nepal. The road to Lhasa (now, inevitably, re-christened the Friendship Highway) continues to climb steeply, through forested slopes and past tumbling waterfalls, until it brings us at last to the edge of the Tibetan plateau. The Roof of the World was once a seabed. What lay beneath the ancient Sea of Tethys was heaved up onto the top of the world by the same collision of the Indian and Eurasian plates that built the Himalaya. It now rests at an average height of 13,100 feet (4000 m) and from its steep sides stream some of the world's greatest rivers: the Indus, Salween, Yangtze, Irrawaddy, Yellow River and Brahmaputra.

In the relatively short distance from Xangmu, we've made dramatic progress, vertically, if not horizontally. We're only 20 miles from the Bai Ma Hotel, but 5000 feet (1520 m) above it. Apart from a few poplar groves, the tree cover has gone and on the mountainsides bare rock shows through tight, tussocky cover. At a cold, exposed little town called Nyalam we stop to have papers checked before entering a new administrative zone. Women in masks sweep the street, outside a modern building a prosperous-looking man makes two of his employees unroll a length of carpet, which he proceeds to examine with great care. Recently completed terraced housing runs along the side of the road, an early indication of Beijing's plans to make Tibet a new frontier. This is a cheerless place, though J-P, never daunted, manages to find a shop selling wine and we roll across the River Matsang two bottles of Dynasty Red to the better.

The road continues upwards, over long, undulating, brown hills, until we reach the prayer flag-bedecked pass of Tong La, over 17,000 feet (5180 m) above sea level and the highest place I've ever been on earth (coming in well ahead of my previous record, the hot springs in San Pedro de Atacama in Chile at 14,700 feet (4480 m)).

Everything is bewildering, strange and wonderful. Running the length of the southern horizon is a chain of towering, white peaks and on the grassland below us a herd of yak, short-legged creatures, bodies close to the ground, their thick, black hair standing out against greeny-brown hills behind them.

We stop and walk a little way from the car, every step feeling like 20 at this altitude.

But that doesn't dampen the exhilaration.

It's dark when we reach the town of Tingri and, after some initial confusion, find our way off the highway and into a capacious courtyard, which looks like that of a monastery, but in fact belongs to the Snow Leopard Hotel. Life centres around a big, low, woody room with painted beams and a brick parqueted floor, largely lit by the glow from a stove of burning yak dung in the centre of the room. This is what was lacking in those inhospitable Annapurna cabins: a fire, so simple and so intensely welcoming. We cluster round it and a lady with braided hair and rubicund, muddied face offers us yak butter tea. Nigel describes the taste as 'liquid gorgonzola', which is absolutely spot on. The rancid smell of the tea and the sharp aroma of yak dung smoke is not as horrible as it sounds. I find it odd, yes, but interestingly strange and unfamiliar, quintessentially Tibetan and proof that north of the Himalaya everything is very different.

In the dim recesses of the room we're served a very good meal of noodles with mushroom, pork, green peppers and lumps of soft, white, doughy Tibetan bread.

We're advised to break out the sleeping bags tonight. It will be below zero in our un-heated rooms.

Leaving the fire is the hardest thing, but once across the yard, beneath a bracingly clear night sky, I'm into a pretty little room, so different from last night. Proper curtains, a colourful wall with a frieze of painted flowers. Beside the bed I have a wooden cabinet, also very charmingly painted. By the light of a very dim bulb I can make out leering gods, dragons, clouds, waves and what look very much like flying teeth.

The only setback tonight is that the bottles of wine from Nyalam proved undrinkable.

Day Sixty : Tingri to Rongbuk

Though perfectly comfortable in my congenial little room, sleep was light and fleeting and broken by twinges of headache and nausea. The zero temperatures with which Mr Tse Xiu threatened us didn't materialize and when I should have been sleeping I was engaged in an energy-consuming nocturnal striptease, peeling off the various layers of clothing I'd gone to bed in and dropping them out of my sleeping bag one by one.

Open the curtains to find a yak calf helping itself to a bowl of water which has been put outside my room.

Wash in what's left of it and join the others for breakfast. On the way there I notice a big satellite dish in one corner of the courtyard. There's no evidence of a television anywhere about the place.

This is my first chance to have some time with Migmar, who has so far been preoccupied with getting us into China. He's 27, the son of Tibetan nomads who were enlightened enough to send him to school, from where he won a place at Lhasa University. He read Chinese (the Dalai Lama would have approved) and English, which, despite the fact he's never left Tibet, he speaks pretty well.

I'm impressed by the richness of the decoration on almost every inch of the timber columns, beams and ceiling boards, and Migmar explains that in the 9th century a Tibetan warlord tried to eradicate Buddhism and the only way that the culture survived was through a pictorial code. The Buddhist heroes were depicted as animals: dragons, tigers, even sheep. What began as a cipher developed into a rich tradition of imaginative painting, a particular target during the Cultural Revolution, when a renewed and virulent attempt was made to destroy Tibet's Buddhist past.

Instead of continuing along the Friendship Highway to Lhasa, we turn south on a dirt road, towards the heart of the Himalaya. Apart from the occasional four-wheel drives like our own, traffic consists of horses and carts trotting between isolated settlements, usually of low, whitewashed houses with prayer flags fluttering from poles at each corner of the roof. The harshness of life up here in this dry and windy rain shadow of the Himalaya is etched on the faces of the farmers and their families. Skin is weathered and faces prematurely aged. The children, noses running and cheeks red and rough from the sun, cluster round as soon as we stop, asking us to give them something.

At one stop the villagers are celebrating with music and dancing. Music seems to lighten the load, and getting out the three-string guitars is a popular move. Soon a circle is formed and the dancers are moving slowly round with a step that doesn't seem to vary, though, judging by reactions, the words they sing have been brought up to date. The women wear big, coral earrings, flower pattern shirts and the traditional Tibetan *chuba*, a long, sleeveless dress tied with a sash at the waist. Some of the men wear their version of the *chuba*, big, wide-sleeved coats, and one or two are in sheepskin jackets, leggings and heavy boots of the kind I haven't really seen since the pop festivals of the late sixties.

Migmar says that at times like New Year dances like this can be spun out for several days.

We move on, through desert scenery, with minimal vegetation but every kind of eye-catching rock formation: deep gullies, bluffs with soaring, scree-covered slopes, exposed synclines and anticlines, red and angry, as if freshly split from the cliffs around them. A brisk wind creates the only movement in this dead landscape, sending dust devils spiralling across the track in front of us.

A military checkpoint, beside a big, modern PLA (People's Liberation Army) barracks with a red-tiled roof, stands at the entrance to the Qomolangma National Park, and a metalled road, recently upgraded, leads us smoothly up to the next big pass, Pang La. This is the high point of our day's journey, in every respect. At the summit, a smooth, wide hill at 17,000 feet (5180 m), one of the finest views in the world is suddenly, almost abruptly, revealed. The full, majestic spread of the central Himalaya is laid out before us, like white-topped waves in a frozen ocean. It's an horizon full of giants: Cho Oyu, a huge massif that peaks at 26,928 feet (8210 m), Makalu 1 at 27,594 feet (8410 m), Lhotse 1 at 27,883 feet (8500 m) and the monumental pyramid of Everest, rising serenely above them all at 29,021 feet (8850 m).

The highest point of the earth's surface, which I am seeing today for the first time with my own eyes, is known to the Tibetans as Qomolangma (pronounced 'Chomolungma'), Goddess Mother of the Earth, to the Sherpas as Sagamartha and when the Imperial Survey of India first determined the mountain's precise height it was known on British maps as Peak XV. It was given the name Everest in 1865, in recognition of Sir George Everest, the man who pioneered the mapping of India. (To add to the confusion, what we call Everest should really be called Eev-rest, which was the way Sir George's name was pronounced.)

None of these things goes through my head as I stand at the top of the pass, unable to take my eyes off this stupendous panorama.

Like K2, the world's second highest mountain, which straddles China and Pakistan, Everest is divided between two countries, China and Nepal. In the 1920s and 1930s Nepal was a closed country and the pioneering expeditions of George Mallory all came in from Tibet and concentrated on the North Face.

When expeditions resumed after the Second World War, it was Tibet's turn to be closed off, after the Chinese Communist invasion of 1949, whilst Nepal opened up at around the same time.

The main bulk of Everest ascents, now running at around 100 a year, are made via the South East Ridge from which Hillary and Sherpa Tenzing had conquered the mountain in 1953. The North Face remains the more mysterious; aloof, daunting and much more dangerous. It was first climbed by a Chinese expedition in 1960. They laid a dirt road to transport their equipment up here, which is why we are able to drive up to Base Camp. The track bounces over impacted, corrugated earth strewn with small boulders, but the four-wheel drives don't find it too difficult, and by late afternoon, after winding our way through valleys fed by glacial melt from the slopes of Everest, we turn past the Rongbuk *gompa*, the highest monastery in the world, and in to the walled courtyard of the guesthouse, administered by the monastery.

It looks, for a moment, like the most wonderful place in the world. The same long, low, Tibetan-style layout as the Snow Leopard in Tingri, but with a hugely more spectacular location. This turns out to be its only redeeming feature. From the filthy, littered courtyard to the soulless concrete rooms with broken windows and the foul, doorless lavatories, Rongbuk Guest House is pretty much a hell hole.

The redeeming feature, however, is not to be underestimated. There is only one mountain to be seen from here and that is Everest. It stands, massive, grand and solitary, only a few miles away across the end of the valley. It is the horizon.

Day Sixty One : Rongbuk

Last night was desperately uncomfortable. A fierce wind blew, occasionally gusting with such ferocity that I feared it might tear the windows out. I lay awake, mouth dry despite regular swigs of water, listening to the village dogs fighting and detritus in the yard being flung about by the wind. As soon as I drifted off to sleep my breathing slowed and within moments I was wide awake, gasping for breath. I need the sleep so much, but I find myself fighting it, forcing myself to stay awake and breathe slow and deep.

The latrine is almost subhuman. It's hard enough to aim through a hole reduced to a slit by the calcified accretions of many previous visitors, without at the same time having to flash a torch to warn other guests and extract thin sheets of Boots travel tissue in a freezing, force 8 gale. Many years ago, encountering similarly appalling conditions in a boat on Lake Tanganyika, I took Imodium to prevent me having to go to the toilet ever again. As I squat in this howling tempest three miles up in the sky, I think cyanide might be the better option.

One advantage of this fierce wind is that when daylight comes it is clear and pristine. The summit of Everest trails a plume of spindrift, blown off the mountain by winds which, at that height, must be in excess of 100 miles an hour. The rest of the mountain, including the long, flanking shoulders below the arrow-head peak, is crystal clear.

The remainder of the guests who were here last night – Spaniards, Norwegians and a group of Australians – all leave today. They can't believe we're here for three nights, and whoop with joy as they're driven away.

Our cooks are making yak butter tea, which the Tibetans call Bo Cha, in the traditional, long, thin, cylindrical churn. It's a mixture of yak butter and tea leaves, with salt and milk added, and is a taste I've yet to acquire, and I'm sure I shall have plenty of opportunity to do so.

We had hoped to move up to Base Camp today, but with the wind still strengthening the decision is taken to stay down here and acclimatize. With atmospheric pressure about half that at sea level, everyone is suffering to some degree and Mr Yang, our minder, and John Pritchard, our sound recordist, are particularly uncomfortable.

Apart from the guesthouse and a new, red-brick hotel nearby, ready but tantalizingly un-opened, Rongbuk consists of a line of low cottages and the monastery, which looks old but was built less than 20 years ago to replace the one destroyed, along with thousands of others in Tibet, by fanatical Red Guards in the 1960s. Outside it stands a sizeable *chorten* topped with a small, black pyramid and hung with prayer flags like ribbons on a maypole. I walk into a courtyard of two-storey buildings with a painted balcony running round for access, and I follow the sound of chanting up a flight of steps on the far side of the square and into the temple. There are 30 monks and 30 nuns here at the world's highest monastery. With their shaven heads and loose robes, it's difficult to tell them apart.

After prayers they gather outside and I present them with a *thangka* (from Kathmandu). It's accepted by the abbot, a big, amiable man with a very dirty, cherry-red duvet jacket over his robes. The monks gather round and study it with great interest.

By evening the wind has dropped as forecast. I sit in the room I share with Basil and make my notes as Everest, now completely clear of the cloud, turns pink in the dying sunlight. Apart from the very top, Everest is not one single, symmetrical shape like a Kilimanjaro or a Machhapuchhre, its outline being composed of a series of huge blocks.

Suddenly my view is obscured by two women banging on the window, staring in at me and holding their hands out. They're some of the saddest people I've seen and for a moment I feel a sense of frustration that the monastery can do so little for them.

Getting in and out of my sleeping bag are the most uncomfortable moments of the day. The cold snaps at my heels and yet dressing and undressing cannot be hurried at this altitude.

Day Sixty Two: Rongbuk to Everest Base Camp

Last night I slept. Indeed, I slept so long and so deeply that Basil thought I might be dead.

What a difference it makes to everything. The sky looks bluer, the food tastes better, the yak butter tea is like nectar and the prospect of a trek beyond Everest Base Camp and up towards the Rongbuk Glacier is the only thing I want to do with the rest of my life.

It takes us 20 minutes to drive the eight miles from Rongbuk to Base Camp, passing on the way the remains of the old monastery.

Some of the walls still stand, but it's little more than a skeleton, barely distinguishable from the rubble-covered slopes on which it stands. Above these desiccated ruins a flock of blue sheep are nosing some nourishment out of the rocks.

Everest Base Camp is nowhere near as romantic as it sounds. Part of it is protected by a 100-foot-high moraine, a wall of stone and shale, carried down and dumped by the glacier that has gouged out the valley. A stream trickles through but any standing water is frozen solid. In high season, between June and August, this area and the rock-strewn valley floor beyond are packed with mountaineers and trekkers. This year there were 32 separate expeditions.

Now, in early November, the camp is all but deserted though the legacy of the summer lies around: discarded brandy bottles, playing cards, batteries and bits of sodden, scrumpled clothing.

A couple of motorbikes are parked beside a caretaker's tent, outside which a young man sits in the sun, having his hair cut by two ladies. Nearby, the yak herders with whom we shall be walking up to the glacier have set up two or three small tents of their own, while the yaks graze nearby, nibbling at the scatterings of wheat and dry grass laid out for them. One has made a small hole in the ice and is drinking from it. Their hair is mostly black, though some have white faces. All have the soft eyes of cows and the same sad, long-suffering look, as if resigned to whatever's going to happen. Despite looking eminently embraceable, they don't seem at all interested in my friendly advances, and I'm warned that they can turn very truculent.

I learn, too, that though yak is their generic name, it refers only to the male; a female is called a *dri* and a yak crossed with a cow is a *dzo* (this is a useful word to know when playing Scrabble, as my ever helpful Bradt guide points out). They are the preferred carriers at this height, stoical and persistent, sure-footed on the rocks. They thrive at altitude, protected from the cold by a thick saddle of insulating fat across their backs, and the big expeditions rely on them to transport heavy equipment up as high as 21,500 feet (6550 m). It's on the lower slopes that the yaks suffer. Anything below 8000 feet (2440 m) can be very uncomfortable for them, as they tend to overheat.

Though the herders seem not the slightest bit sentimental about their furry charges, theirs is one of the most one-sidedly symbiotic relationships between man and beast. In return for some grass the yaks give their owners milk, cheese, butter, meat, fuel, building materials, clothes and transport.

I join the herders around a fire of brush wood and bamboo kindling, which they keep alive by tossing on the odd yak nugget and pumping hard with an ancient sheep's bladder bellows. Sitting in a circle, eating cake made from *tsampa*, the barley flour and tea mix, they're jolly company, naturally given to smiling and cracking jokes, most of which are at my expense.

Their clothes are made from skins and fur and look as if they have been part of their bodies since they were born. Their complexions, skin textures, their whole physiognomy is a reflection of the life they lead. Coloured by the wind and rain, stunted by the bitter cold, their features sculpted in a craggy resemblance to the weird and wonderful landscape around them, they're elemental figures, created by and in the likeness of the mountains.

Maybe all this accounts for the ease of their manner. They know what to do here. They know what to expect and how to deal with it. They have slope cred.

This morning means having fun with foreigners, and being paid for it. First of all, it's tea, invigoratingly salty, with a knob of yak butter thrown in, then it's time to get out the *chang*, a fermented barley beer, for me to try. It's poured out of a stained, dusty container, the sort of thing you might find at the back of the shed ten years after you put it there. Before drinking, Migmar shows me the important procedure of giving thanks. I must dip my third finger into the brew, and, flicking it each time, give thanks first to the mountain, second to the Buddha and third to the assembled company. It's a pleasing taste, *chang*, like chilled ginger beer, with a hint of apples.

This is the start of one of those magical meals that may not win any gastronomic medals but are unique and unforgettable – a Sunday lunch 16,900 feet (5150 m) up in the heart of the Himalaya. The ingredients include perfect weather, cloudless blue sky, light breeze, generous sunshine, the comforting presence of the yaks and the cheeriness of their owners, the reassuring company of big black crows, and the presence, at our backs, of the highest mountain in the world.

The conquest of Everest in 1953 was one of the milestones of my childhood. I was ten at the time and, like every other Briton, bursting with national pride (we somehow dealt with fact that Everest had been conquered by a Tibetan and a New Zealander). What happened on the mountain behind me 50 years ago defined the heroic, and led to a fascination with exploration that I suppose has brought me here today, completing the circle.

Only later did I learn that Everest might have been conquered 29 years earlier, when George Mallory and Andrew Irvine disappeared into a cloud close to the summit and were never seen again.

As the years went by, this heroic failure came to fascinate me more than Hillary and Tenzing's success. The fact that Mallory and Irvine left from a base camp almost exactly where we are now and lost their lives on the face of the mountain I can see so clearly ahead of me makes this a very special place, somewhere that has been in my imagination for so long.

Lunch completed, the yaks are loaded up, the tents struck and we begin the walk up to the glacier.

The warmth of the sun and the gentle tinkle of yak bells makes up for the grimly lunar landscape of grey stones and boulders. The herders seem in no hurry, whistling every now and then to keep the yaks together and occasionally singing as we plod slowly upwards. As the afternoon wears on, and the snowdrifts become less avoidable, it becomes increasingly obvious that the requirements of filming are slowing us down and we shall not reach the glacier before the light goes. We've also lost Basil and John Pritchard, both of whom seemed fine at lunch but, unable to cope with the increased altitude, have had to turn back.

We carry on for as long as we can, past valley walls hung with rocks eroded into wonderful sculptural shapes: pinnacles of mud with enormous boulders poised on top of them and Stonehenge-like slabs teetering on the edge of mud cliffs. At just over 18,000 feet (5480 m), I get as close to Everest as I think I ever shall. A moment of regret as we turn back. The ribbed stone pyramid above looks daunting but beckoning at the same time. I can see why it makes people do crazy things. In the 1930s a man called Maurice Wilson planned to crash-land a plane on the side of Everest and climb on up to the summit. In 1980 Reinhold Messner made a successful ascent of the North Face, on his own, there and back, in four days, without oxygen.

As I take one last look, I put myself, as I have done so many times in the past, in Mallory and Irvine's stout walking boots and tweed jackets and feel what it must have been like for them to stand here 80 years ago, knowing that only two miles separated them from the top of the world.

Day Sixty Three : Rongbuk to Shigatse

Howling packs of dogs, yelping and snarling in the village last night, and, closer to home, some angry argument in the passageway outside my room, hoarse shouting and a man being restrained.

The words of Captain Scott on arrival at the South Pole come to mind: 'My God, this is an awful place.'

Today, though, I wash in the metal bowl for the last time, pay my last visit to the stained, encrusted lavatory, and take my last look at Everest framed in one of the squares of my cracked and much-repaired windows.

A Dutchman and his wife who stayed here last night are on their way from Lhasa to Kathmandu, on bicycles. It's taken them a month to get this far. I never thought anyone would make me feel pampered in a place like this, but as they wobble off on their bicycles and I climb into my four-wheel drive, that's exactly how I feel. A sturdy, smiling nun in a maroon robe, with a milk churn strapped to her back, stands to one side as our convoy pulls out. I'm torn between admiration for her indomitable cheerfulness and indignation at the grinding poverty that is the way of life for her and the villagers of Rongbuk. This is a beautiful, bleak place.

We run down into the valley, stacked high with glacial rubble, then climb up through a landscape of bare, brown, undulating hills, over a couple of spectacular passes and down through villages with snooker tables in the streets and horses tethered up outside front doors. We've almost 200 miles (320 km) to go before Shigatse, Tibet's second biggest city.

By the time we've passed through the town of Lhatse we've dropped down to 13,500 feet (4110 m) and are running past ploughed fields. There's not much traffic on the Friendship Highway: a few trucks lumbering along, a lot of horse and carts but hardly a private vehicle to be seen. As dusk falls we're in wide, desolate country, with dust blowing and the setting sun catching the tops of the smooth, brown hills and turning them a rich, mournful maroon. As we get closer to Shigatse we pass brand new electric pylons, at first lying in the fields awaiting construction, then, a little later, upright but unconnected and finally cabled up and striding over the last hilltops into the city.

It's a major culture shock after Rongbuk. I really feel as if we've come in from the outback. With its red lanterns and gold and stainless steel trim, the Shigatse Hotel, in the heart of the Chinese-built new town, gleams and glitters like a Las Vegas gambling joint. As we wait to check in, three girls in white coats emerge from a door off the lobby, marked, in English, 'Beauty and Massage', and ask us, quite ingenuously, which one we would like to choose.

This is all too much for us to get our heads round and we politely decline their services and, joy of joys, are taken up to rooms with carpets, lights, double beds, hot running water, no dogs and, luxury of luxuries, a bedside table.

This has to be better than sex. Sorry, Beauty and Massage.

Day Sixty Four : Shigatse to Lhasa

Shigatse, with a population of some 60,000, is the second city of Tibet, and boasts the second largest monastery in the country, the Tashilunpo, which is the seat of the second highest incarnation in Tibet, the Panchen Lama. In many ways, his recent history has been more interesting than that of his more illustrious superior, the Dalai Lama. In 1952, three years after the Chinese invaded Tibet, they brought the Panchen Lama to Shigatse and set him up, with his connivance, as their official choice of spiritual leader. After the Chinese had raided the Tashilunpo monastery in 1961, the Panchen Lama became increasingly critical. He sent a report to Chairman Mao calling for freedom of religion to be restored. Mao called the document a poisoned arrow and kept it secret. After a speech in Lhasa demanding Tibetan independence, the Chinese lost patience with their man and he was imprisoned for ten years in Beijing. His death, in Shigatse, at the early age of 50, created further confusion. The Dalai Lama and his advisers in Dharamsala found his reincarnation, a six-year-old boy from northern Tibet, and the Chinese promptly arrested him.

Tashilunpo once again became the centre of a power struggle, when, in 1995, Tibetan monks favourable to China came up with another candidate for Panchen Lama, and he was duly enthroned at the monastery.

No-one seems to know where the Dalai Lama's choice is at the moment. He's been kidnapped, and the Chinese-nominated Panchen Lama is rarely seen in Shigatse.

We drive to the monastery along modern, urban streets decked with ads for China Mobile. The temple, however, is resolutely Tibetan and mightily impressive. Its complex of buildings is laid out on a slope leading up to the row of tombs of the Panchen Lamas and a chapel that contains the tallest Buddha in the country.

A steady line of pilgrims, many in sheepskin coats and clutching prayer beads, are making their way up the stone-flagged pathways, flanked by juniper trees, that lead between the low, long buildings housing the various living quarters (there are 800 monks here) and the colleges where they can study Tantric philosophy, astrology, Tibetan medicine and history. Inside the colleges, small courtyards and whitewashed walls give the whole place the look of a mediaeval Spanish village.

Migmar tells me that boys are sent away to monasteries from the age of six, and they're only allowed back home once a year. He admits that when he was young all he wanted to do was become a monk, but his family sent him to school.

I ask him if it's right to say that education at a monastery would be more exclusively Tibetan, and school would offer a more international approach.

He agrees but says things are slowly changing.

'Today, in a monastery most of the monks try to study other languages, something like English or Chinese. In the past it was only Tibetan.'

We join the crowd, who seem to be heading for the Maitreya chapel to see the Buddha. Migmar says that the majority of the pilgrims are from the rural east of Tibet and some may have travelled over 1000 miles to get here. Not only that, but they would try and make the journey once a year.

Everyone who goes into the chapel, man, woman and child, has to squeeze up one of three steep and narrow stairways, about as precipitous as ladders, that can barely take two people abreast. The steps on either side are for going up and coming down and the ones in the middle are reserved only for the Dalai Lama and the Panchen

Lama. Everybody struggles up and down. Quite happily.

Once up the steps the familiar sour smell of hot yak butter suffuses the chapel. Many of the pilgrims have brought butter and knives with them to cut slices, which they then drop in the copper bowls that contain the lighted candles.

Migmar explains that in Tibetan Buddhism the spirit leaves the body when you die and the more you can help the burning of the butter lamps, the stronger will be the light that will guide your soul to its next body.

The chapel has a powerfully devotional atmosphere. The lower recesses are dark and smoky, but a shaft of sunlight catches the face of the Buddha, 80 feet (24 m) above us. The lines of the eyes, nose and lips are beautifully drawn and, with elegant simplicity, create an expression of profound compassion. Buddha statues are usually made of stone, but this one, commissioned by the 9th Panchen Lama in 1904, is made of copper, which enabled it to be such a great size. And the size works: the expression, the long fall of the robes and the lotus leaf base combine to convey a feeling of strength, serenity and immutability.

The new paved road from Shigatse south to Gyantse runs alongside streams and between pollarded willows. We pass through a village that has a big wheel made of wood with boxes fixed to it for local children to sit in and be hoisted aloft. In a field a road gang are having a picnic lunch, shovels all neatly stacked to one side.

Gyantse was once a rich wool town, on the lucrative trade route between Lhasa and India. A huge fort (*dzong*) dominates the high ground to the south of the town. Migmar and I stand on the battlements and look out over a flat plain that belies the fact that we are at 13,000 feet (3960 m) and still way up in the mountains.

Migmar points out the plastic-sheeted greenhouses and the modern housing blocks.

'This place has changed so much in last 20 years. Before, all houses were Tibetan.'

Whereas the Chinese seem to have invaded Tibet many times, the British largely left it alone, though in the mid 19th century they did train up Indian spies, known as pundits, to infiltrate this secretive land. In 1903, however, on a trumped-up pretext, an army, under Colonel Francis Younghusband, crossed over from India, fought a bloody battle not far from Gyantse, in which some 3000 Tibetans died, before storming the fort from which we're looking out and going on, unopposed, as far as Lhasa. The British left four years later, leaving behind in Gyantse a post office and a public school. All that remains now is the Anti-British Museum, housed in the *dzong*.

A smiling lady attendant gestures to me to go inside. She makes sure all the lights are switched on in the 'Memorial Hall of Anti-British', where murals depict the ghastly acts of Young-husband's army and the heroic resistance of the Tibetans. This is echoed on a TV screen on which runs a recently made Chinese epic called *Red River Valley*, which also deals with the British invasion. There is nothing here, of course, that deals with their own invasion of Tibet.

We have a cup of tea (black tea this time, not yak butter) in front of the ruins of a walled monastery that contains an enormous and very ancient *chorten*. According to Migmar, there were many such monasteries here. Now they have been cleared and in their place are wider roads, high-rise buildings of tinted blue glass, and, as we drive down from the fort, a concrete pleasure garden, half completed, with ragged grass, fountains that don't spout and twee, concrete bridges running over a stagnant pond.

The road from Gyantse to Lhasa runs through lonely and very wild landscape, first of all beside a rocky, steep-sided reservoir, then curling round the sinuous shoreline of Yamdrok Tso (Turquoise Lake), the biggest single stretch of water in land-locked Tibet.

Night falls and we're still hugging the lake. Eventually the road rises steeply and winds slowly over what seem interminable passes over interminable switchbacks. I must confess to being fast asleep as we roll across the Yarlung Tsangpo (the mighty Tibetan river that U-turns round the end of the Himalaya and enters India as the Brahmaputra) and when I wake we're on a fast dual carriageway that is the long, western approach into the world's highest capital. We've reached Lhasa, the Forbidden City where, judging from the rows of shining, gaudy, neon-encrusted buildings on either side of us, it doesn't look as if much is forbidden any longer.

I want Lhasa to be as dark and different as I'd long imagined it, a remote place of romance and possible menace, but the drive up the long approach road along West Dekyl Yam dispels illusions. The buildings we pass are more Las Vegas than Lhasa and to be wel-comed into the world's highest capital by flashing neon palm trees suggests the Chinese have well and truly won aesthetic control of this ancient city.

I'm aware that the bludgeoning tiredness I feel after crossing the mountains may well be souring my judgement and that once we're bedded in at what is purportedly one of Lhasa's swankier hotels all will be well again.

The shining, recently built Himalaya Hotel rises portentously from lower buildings in a quiet but characterless side street. It's clad in glass and as we pile wearily from our vehicles we're greeted by smiling doormen protected from the cold by fur-trimmed great-coats. Unfortunately, the staff at reception are also protected from the cold by fur-trimmed greatcoats, as are the waitresses who take our orders at the Yak Bar. The Himalaya Hotel may have glittering, gold-wrapped pillars, shiny mirrors and ceilings encrusted with every shape and size of light fitting, but it is the dazzling gloss of an ice castle.

I pile all the bedclothes onto one bed and, stripping down to a vest, sweater and thermal underwear, climb in. I feel desperately dis-appointed. This was to be our reward, a hotel in the heart of the capital, the Holy Grail after some pretty savage days on the road. As it is, the Himalaya Hotel seems to be everything its name might suggest.

Day Sixty Five : Lhasa

Though for a while suffocation seemed more likely than sleep, I actually pass a reasonable night beneath my sarcophagus of blankets and when I wake a pale morning light is leaking into the room. My bags, still packed, squat around the doorway where I dropped them last night, looking mournful and expectant, like neglected pets.

With an enormous effort of willpower I heave myself out of bed and across to the window. The curtain opens jerkily to reveal a mottled sky and an horizon of crumpled, grey mountains framing dusty, undistinguished, largely modern buildings.

A view that could only lower already jaded spirits, were it not for one thing. Away to the northeast, rising gracefully above the city, like a mountain in its own right, are the white walls, russet towers and gold-tipped roofs of one of the most dramatic and serenely powerful buildings in the world, the Potala Palace.

It's probably a couple of miles away, but even at this distance and this oblique angle it is mesmerizing, especially to one brought up with its black and white likeness in a volume of *The Children's Encyclopaedia*. To be honest, I was never quite convinced of the existence of the Potala Palace. Because its size and shape was so unlike anything I'd ever seen in the West, I always assumed that it was something mythical, an ambitious piece of artistic licence.

But now I see it with my own eyes I realize it is everything it appeared to be: a great Buddha of a building, looking gravely out over the city that was for so long the heart and soul of Tibetan Buddhism. The only thing I can see that is taller than the Potala Palace is the flagpole at its eastern end, from which flies the red flag of China.

Shave, dress, wrap a scarf around me and head for the dining room. A rubber mat in the lift reads 'Wednesday'.

Bas and Nigel are already at breakfast, dressed like Tenzing and Hillary. The staff are apologetic. The hotel is about to close for the winter and the heating has all been turned off. They do have portable radiators and will try to find some for us.

The bad news is that John Pritchard, ace sound recordist, has been examined by a doctor and found to have pulmonary oedema, an accumulation of fluid in the lung that normally occurs in small amounts at high altitude. He's also showing early indications of pneumonia and must be admitted to hospital at once.

Later in the day we go to visit him at the People's No. 1 Hospital, getting lost in a series of functional modern blocks separated by strips of lawn, which they've tried to cheer up with pagodas and play equipment.

Eventually find the Mountain Sickness Unit (largely financed by the Italians) and in a small, friendly ward John sits up in bed, a drip inserted into the vein in his right hand and an oxygen feed taped, rather ineffectively, to his left nostril. Even John, who suffers from almost terminal cheerfulness, cannot disguise the fact that he is in quite a bad way, though not as bad as the only other occupant of the six-bed ward, a young Korean with the much more serious cerebral oedema, or fluid in the brain. Both are casualties of the punishing pressure that the body progressively suffers as oxygen levels decrease. It can affect anyone who climbs above 8000 feet (around 2500 m), and no-one really knows why some suffer more than others.

We find a more congenial place to eat tonight. A small, Western-style, climber's bar and restaurant called the Summit Camp a few doors down from the hotel, cold as the grave, but at least built of brick and wood rather than the self-important chrome and glass of the Himalaya.

Over a Tibetan pizza we have to face the reality that John will not be able to continue with the journey. A temporary replacement is coming in from Beijing, and until that time Pete will carry the tape recorder and microphone, as well as everything else.

Day Sixty Six : Lhasa

'Thursday', the mat in the lift reminds me, as I descend from my seventh-floor eyrie, in which a mobile radiator with one broken wheel is engaged in a life or death struggle with the air of the Tibetan plateau.

We make for the Barkor area in the heart of the old city, where a rabbit warren of side streets leads off a main square. In fact, the rabbit warren once included the square, which was cleared less than 20 years ago, ostensibly to celebrate the 20th anniversary of the Tibetan Autonomous Region (as the Chinese renamed central Tibet), but also, some think, to allow the army easier access to the potential trouble spots of the Old Quarter.

A wide, granite-paved approach now leads up to the Jokhang Temple, the most ancient and holiest site of Tibetan Buddhism. Some of its remarkably modest stone walls date back to the mid 7th century, when Queen Bhrikuti, the Nepali wife of Songtsen Gampo, the unifier of Tibet, set up the temple on what was considered to be a powerful geomantic point representing the heart of a supine ogress. Much changed over the years and in the 1960s it was com-mandeered as a barracks for the PLA. Today, the Jokhang is once again a religious building.

A low, piercing sunlight bounces back off the flagstones and at first it's difficult to see 30 or 40 figures, hidden in the deep shadow, prostrating themselves before the walls of the temple. Most have bed-rolls, on which they flatten themselves, using pieces of cloth or cardboard beneath their hands to push themselves forward. Then they stand, hands pressed together above their heads, in front of their faces and then in front of their chests, before prostrating themselves and beginning the whole process again. Many of them, Migmar tells me, will have begun their prostrations outside Lhasa, with some coming from up to 600 miles (960 km) away, and taking two or three years to get here.

They fight for space with pilgrims from out of town, with matted black hair and deeply grooved faces, who pause on their devotional walk around the temple to pull juniper branches from plastic bags and feed them into the two small kilns whose smoke drifts across the square. They believe the pillar of smoke that rises from these fires creates a conduit between the earth and the sky down which the Buddha can travel. A very old lady with prayer beads in one hand and a stick in the other inches painfully slowly past the temple entrance.

The Jokhang Square seems to be the social, as well as the religious, heart of Lhasa. There are Tibetans from the east with complexions like old, weathered wood, pale Chinese immigrants, Muslim stallholders in white skull caps and farmers wrapped up in greasy sheepskin coats, wearing Stetsons with curled-up brims, looking almost identical to the people of the high Andes. Bored soldiers sit at strategic points, supposedly keeping an eye on things. One is having his shoes shined while trying to figure out the controls on a new radio, another sits, with great concentration, picking hairs out of his chin with a pair of tweezers.

Migmar and I join the clockwise perambulation, which they call the *kora*, passing rows of stalls set in front of old houses with Spanish-style, wrought-iron balconies. We stop for coffee at one of them, the Makye Ame restaurant, hung with red, tasselled lanterns, which manages to feel very Tibetan whilst serving Jim Beam whisky, playing The Grateful Dead on its sound system and offering 'Chicken à la King' as Dish of the Day.

It was here, on the first floor of a corner house overlooking the Jokhang, that Tsangyang Gyatso, the sixth and naughtiest of all the Dalai Lamas, used to drink and entertain a succession of lovers. In his book *Tibet, Tibet*, Patrick French quotes a contemporary Jesuit priest's verdict on the sixth Dalai Lama: 'No girl, or married woman or good-looking person of either sex was safe from his unbridled licentiousness.'

As if that wasn't enough, he also wrote poetry. Such apparently unrestrained love of life is not as incompatible with Buddhism as it is with Christianity, and later in the day we climb up to Sera, one of the great monasteries of Lhasa, to witness an activity that would probably be classed as highly eccentric in any religion other than Buddhism. Around 100 young monks gather beneath the trees of a shady, walled garden to take part in ritual arguing, a sort of verbal martial art. The idea is that one of a group has to stand and defend a proposition, which can be as provocative as possible (Migmar says he heard one monk arguing that there is no such thing as water) and the sitting monks must debate with him. Possibly because Sera has a long tradition of supplying fighting monks, the whole thing is very physical. The arguer, arms flailing, thrusts aggressively at his opponent and each error in the opposing argument is marked by a wide swing of the arm and a ricocheting slap of one hand against the other.

Old Lhasa can still be found – the Sera monastery was established in 1419 and the Jokhang Temple long before that – but new Lhasa is growing with an overwhelming momentum, and it has nothing to do with religion. This is a secular, consumerist boom, and from the lingerie ads to the health clubs to the main street boutiques with names like Ku-La-La, Eastern Camel and Gay Mice, it's clear where the new influences are coming from. America, via China.

Take some food to John, as the hospital doesn't provide anything. He now has the ward to himself, as the young Korean with cerebral oedema checked himself out in the middle of last night. John thinks he simply couldn't afford to stay.

Day Sixty Seven: Lhasa

Woken this morning by sound of soldiers being drilled in an army barracks somewhere below me.

Down to breakfast, all muffled up. The usual little awkwardnesses as we try to communicate the difference between toast and a heated slice of bread to a bemused Tibetan staff.

Why we persevere with these esoteric demands I don't know. Probably because Nigel has produced a pot of Cooper's Oxford Marmalade, and eating Cooper's Oxford from a limp patch of warm bread is like playing the Cup Final on tarmac.

We drive out to the west, passing the Golden Yak roundabout, where two of these great beasts are impressively mythologized, and a number of monumental government buildings. The six-lane highway is virtually empty, save for a rickshaw with a live pig sitting in the trailer behind it, and an official convoy of black limousines, which appears from nowhere and fades into the void ahead, sirens blaring and lights flashing as if it was trying to negotiate Fifth Avenue or the Champs Elysées.

Drepung Monastery, once the biggest in the world, with 10,000 monks living and studying here in the mid 17th century, stands slightly outside the city, overlooking Lhasa from high ground to the northwest.

We disembark and begin the long climb up to the heart of the complex (Buddhism is a very steep religion), until we reach the impressive portico of the Prayer Hall. Monks' shoes, most of them modern trainers, litter the ground outside. I remove my own shoes and, pushing aside a heavy, patchwork curtain, its edges dirty black and waxy from continuous use, find myself in a candle-lit interior, the size of a small cathedral, with long lines of red-robed monks sitting cross-legged on their cushions, chanting prayers from small strips of text on boards in front of them. A number of novices race through the hall dispensing butter tea. One of them trips over Basil as he's photographing and both he and his load fly into the air and land with a resounding crash on the stone-flagged floor. No-one bats an eyelid.

At the back of the hall, behind the line of candles, is a chamber that contains huge plaster characters from the rich cosmology of Tibetan Buddhism. Incarnations of the Buddha and various Bodhisattvas (beings who have reached enlightenment but rather than enter nirvana have chosen to return to earth and help others) as well as fierce, snarling, pop-eyed, horned figures who are their protectors.

The Communists came close to expunging Buddhism from Tibet. Six thousand monasteries, 95 per cent of all those in the country, were destroyed. But Buddhism is 2000 years old and

Chinese Communism was only 60 years old, so it was not a battle they could win. Now the Chinese, comfortably in control of the political and economic life of the country, have adopted a more pragmatic attitude to the old religion. Buddhism is seen as being good for tourism, and the revival of the monasteries has been accelerating, though possession of any image of the Dalai Lama remains a political crime in China.

At Nechung, half a mile down the hill, there is a thorough restoration going on. In a courtyard some 200 feet square a small team, mostly of women, is working away. Two of them are smoothing and shaping the plaster over an incense-burning oven, others are slowly and meticulously restoring the superb 14th-century murals on the walls of the arcades. Graphic, Hieronymus Bosch-like motifs of human torment are a recurring theme. Faces and skulls alternate, bodies hang upside down from serpents like clothes on a washing line, entrails are ripped out by wolves and naked bodies sundered by leering devils.

The work force goes about its task with quiet application. The only noise comes when they get together for an *arka*, a song and dance routine that they use to help them flatten the newly laid clay floors. Holding long bamboo sticks with stone pads on the end, they go into a sort of builder's line dance, rhythmically thumping the clay into place.

Someone hands me a stick and asks me to join in. Though I find myself regularly facing the other way to everyone else, I can now add Temple Restoration to my CV.

Back in the Barkor, we take lunch at a cheery upstairs café called Petoc. It's shamelessly aimed at foreign travellers and our Tibetan drivers are frankly embarrassed at having to eat behind a yak-hair curtain in a recreation of a nomad's tent. We, on the other hand, love it for its eggs and bacon, yak burgers and espresso coffee machine.

Halfway through this intercontinental fry-up our new sound recordist, a tall, thin Chinese, arrives from Beijing. Though he's got here impressively quickly, his expression is apologetic and his face a ghostly shade of green. We later learn that he's suffering from altitude sickness and won't be able to work for the rest of the day.

Recount this story to John when we take him food and supplies at the hospital tonight. It cheers him up no end. He's a lot better generally and now has only one aim – to get out of the People's No. 1 Hospital by any means possible.

Day Sixty Eight : Lhasa

Potala Palace and Potala Square should never be confused. One is the greatest building in Tibet, and the other is a large open space created by filling in a lake and flattening a neighbourhood of old Tibetan houses in order to celebrate 20 years of the creation of the Tibet Autonomous Region.

The only use of one for the other is that the best view of the palace is from the bleak square, where the wind blows the water of the ornamental fountains into your face and tourists pose in the middle of the emptiness to have themselves associated with the now equally empty palace on the hill.

The Tibetans call the peak on which the palace is built Mount Marpori and the soaring upward curve of the Potala's walls, rising 13 storeys and nearly 400 feet (120 m) high, stirs memories of the Himalayan rock faces we've seen to the south. Until the first skyscrapers were built, the Potala Palace was believed to be the tallest building in the world.

The mighty edifice that swallows up the mountain top today was built on the foundations of the 7th-century original. The White Palace was completed by 1653, and the central block of upper storeys, known as the Red Palace, was added some 50 years later. The entire complex has 1000 rooms. Despite that, it wasn't considered sufficient for the Dalai Lama of the time and within 50 years another palace, Norbulingka, was constructed on a 40-hectare site, a couple of miles to the west, in which His Holiness could spend the summer months.

A series of perilous staircases, as thin as firemen's ladders, lead remorselessly up from level to level, through dim and dusty apartments, until we're on the roof of the White Palace next to a room with deep red walls labelled 'Eastern Sunshine Apartment'. This was the Dalai Lama's bedroom and a more magnificent position could hardly be imagined. If you want to feel the monarch of all you survey, then this is the place to be, and I can imagine the young Tenzin Gyatso, the present Dalai Lama, making his early prayers as

Above: Women are prominent in Nepali rural life. In the Himalayan foothills, a woman carries home scrub for cattle feed. *Below:* Shopkeeper in crimson sari on the road to the Tibetan border.

Above: Road-sweeping gang takes a breather in Nyalam. *Left:* A circle dance takes shape in a village on the way to Everest Base Camp. These folk get-togethers are an important time for match-making.

OPPOSITE PAGE Man of the plateau. Sheepskin coat, earring and extended sleeves instead of gloves.

Above: Chomolungma, 'Goddess Mother of the Earth'. The best name westerners could come up with for the world's highest mountain was Everest. *Below:* Everest Base Camp, just before Sunday lunch.

Tashilempo Monastery, Shigatse: boys are sent away to monasteries from the age of six, emulating the traditional English boarding-school approach to education.

Above: The magnificent Potala Palace in Lhasa. *Below:* Walking with Migmar in the Barkor, one of the few areas of Lhasa where the traditional Tibetan houses are still preserved. In the foreground, a prostrating pilgrim.

Above: Am I right? Monk makes his point in ritual debating at the Sera monastery.
Below: Images of the gatekeepers, and other treasures, behind the altar in the Drepung Monastery, outside Lhasa.

Top: Makeshift lutes. *Above:* The essence of bleakness. The grey, windswept waters of holy Namtso Lake, 15,500 feet (4570 m) above sea level. Prayer flags show that pilgrims come from all over Tibet to make the 18-day walk around it, or shorter walks around these towering rocks at Tashidor.

Top: Yak herding on the summer pastures of Qinghai province. *Middle:* Yak husbandry continued. *Bottom:* Sonam the yak farmer prepares a calf for shearing.

OPPOSITE PAGE Tall in the saddle. Feet of horsemanship by the Kampas.

Left: Meeting monks at the Festival. Later they inveigled me into a game of football. *Below:* Well-restored *chortens* at Gyanak Mani. They are symbolic of steps to enlightenment.

Top: In Tiger Leaping Gorge. Behind me, Li Yuan, who we christened Mr Nice Man on account of his ineffable patience, leads the donkeys, keeps an eye on me *and* carries the sound boom. *Left:* Message in a bottle. Mr Feng's connection with the outside world. *Below:* The end of Tiger Leaping Gorge. The Yangtze below me has fallen 700 feet (213 m) in a series of 21 lethal rapids. I've walked 20 miles along the edge of a cliff and I'm going to bed.

Top: Luoshi, Sichuan. The jetty of Namu's hotel. *Middle:* Namu's aunt is more concerned with hospitality than the interview. *Right:* Namu, the nicest narcissist.

Above: Auto-rickshaw delivers me to Dr Ho's clinic. *Below:* (*left*) The Famous Dr Ho in trademark white coat. (*right*) Mrs Ho in the traditional costume of the Naxi, a minority people of Yunnan.

Right: Xuan Ke, Lijiang's local hero, takes his place in the front row of the Naxi Music Orchestra. *Below:* Sweet, beautifully played flute solo brings the concert to an end. Painted on the wall behind are black-necked cranes, a rare and sacred Himalayan bird.

Left: Trainee snake charmer? No, local man shopping for walking stick. *Below:* Dongba checks the instructions during purification ritual.

the first rays of the sun reached these gold-tipped rooftops, well before they reached anywhere else in Lhasa.

It must be 45 years since he last looked out from here over his capital and his country.

From the sublime to the ridiculous. We end our last night in Lhasa at JJ's nightclub, whose red neon strip lighting pierces the night air, down on the square in the shadow of the Potala Palace. Conspicuous consumption is evident. Cars, some substantial, are drawn up at the door, while inside beers are ordered in 12-pack slabs and delivered by pretty hostesses to tables filled with anyone from Tibetan girls on a hen-night and Chinese businessmen entertaining clients to shifty groups of underworld heavies. It's a big place, dominated at one end by a deep stage on which, to the accompaniment of a bellowing, distorted soundtrack, a show erupts. Strobe lights, pulsating disco music and John Travolta lookalikes alternate with Tibetan folklorique in a raucous mish-mash of old and new. I suppose it represents what's happening in Lhasa now. The power, the technology and the marketing is all Chinese, the past that is thrown into this mix is Tibetan.

Day Sixty Nine : North from Lhasa

We check out of the Himalaya Hotel this morning. Last images: porters wrapped in greatcoats and looking as if they were in their third month at Stalingrad, cleaners moving three-foot-wide brushes soundlessly across a spotless marble floor, a girl at reception smiling as if it were Christmas as the doors swing shut behind us. Fond farewells to John P, released from the People's Hospital and due to fly out to Kunming, Hong Kong and London later today.

The drivers are late. Most of them stayed on at JJ's until the small hours. Migmar stamps his feet against the cold.

'Tibetan people never tired,' he reassures us.

North of Lhasa, the trans-Tibetan Highway 109 runs alongside extensive railway construction. A billboard not far from the road depicts a speeding, white, high-speed train, the Potala Palace and a joyful group of ethnic minorities dancing and celebrating. Below runs the slogan, 'The Tibet-Qinghai railway benefits all the peoples of China'. It's a little disingenuous, as 91 per cent of the peoples of

China are from the same ethnic group, the Han. But the fact remains that the railway is likely to change Tibet as much as anything in its history.

By 2008, the year of the Beijing Olympics, a 700-mile (1120 km) high-speed line across the Tibetan plateau will connect Lhasa, for the first time ever, to the Chinese rail network. It's a fair bet that farmers and nomads, who make up 80 per cent of the indigenous people of the TAR, will find this less useful than the millions living in overcrowded conditions in the heart of China, for whom it will offer the chance of a new life, out west.

We pass two prostrating pilgrims, pulling themselves along the side of the road towards Lhasa, from which they must be several weeks away. The railway taking shape beside them will cross the entire plateau, one quarter of the land area of China, in 15 hours.

At Yangbajing a side road leads to a hot springs complex, where, in addition to storage tanks and a treatment plant that converts the geothermal power into energy for Lhasa, there is a lido with an open-air, Olympic-size pool. Immersed in the sulphurous water at 14,104 feet (4300 m) above sea level, surrounded by tundra and gaunt, grey hills, my body is, for the first time since arriving in Tibet, truly, unequivocally and luxuriantly warm.

Seventy miles further on, a town springs out of nowhere. A casual mess of a place called Damxung, where rubbish blows round and round in tight circles and hard men with pinched faces and red braids in their hair squat on the steps and watch us go by. Turning off here, we follow an unmade road up to Lhachen La, a 16,700-foot (5090 m) pass where the wind tears at the prayer flags and the sky looks ready for a storm.

This is the last pass before Namtso Chukmo, a sacred saltwater lake with great significance for pilgrims from all over Tibet.

First views of Namtso are dramatic. It lies, gun-metal grey and fringed with snow-dusted mountains. On a day like today it seems to discourage company. Yet down by the lakeside, near a cave hermitage called Tashidor, is a small town of tents and vehicles. The cliffs and rocks are festooned with flags and white scarves cling to a tall promontory like candle wax. A pile of mani stones (stones with mantras on) rises at one end of the shingle beach and despite the appalling conditions, people are out walking their *koras* or *mini-koras*, and a number of people are not even walking, but dragging themselves face first through the grit and gravel.

There are men in balaclavas and women with babies on their backs and scarves tied tight across their faces against the penetrating dust. There are figures whose big fur hats and robes of leopard-skin trim show them to have come from Amdo in the east. There are young men who weigh down their *katags* (white scarves) with stones from the shore, swing them round their heads and send them sailing up onto the cliff. The higher they go and the more firmly they stick the more merit for the thrower.

The hundreds, no, probably thousands of pilgrims who have defied the elements to come here and worship a lake, are largely poor, rural people. I don't know quite what to make of their tenacious dedication. My rational, enlightened, Western self recoils from the tackiness of it all, the parade of plodding, vacant faces. Another, more instinctual side of me is fascinated by and even a little envious of the deep belief that can bring them all this way and turn this remote and unforgiving lakeshore into a sanctuary.

Day Seventy One : Near Yushu, Qinghai Province

Keep going due north from Lhasa, across the Tibetan plateau that makes up a quarter of the land area of China, and you will come to Qinghai, the largest of China's 22 provinces.

It is not one of the world's great tourist destinations. *The Rough Guide* is, uncharacteristically, lost for words: 'Qinghai for the most part comprises a great emptiness.' *The Penguin Encyclopaedia of Places* (which has 12 lines on Grantham alone) doesn't mention it at all. Even when it does rate a few lines, as in Jan Wong's *China*, there's little to set the pulses racing. 'Qinghai,' she writes, 'was the heart of China's notorious gulag. Mention the place to ordinary Chinese and they shuddered.'

This morning in Qinghai it's raining, but, aside from that, this land of prison camps and nuclear weapons laboratories looks dour, but not depressing. We're running along a road not far from the town of Yushu, in a glacial valley 14,500 feet (4420 m) above sea level, hoping to meet up with a yak farmer called Sonam.

A sulky, grey sky sits low on the surrounding mountain tops as we pull off the road and bounce across rutted meadowland dotted with horses and cattle. In the centre of the herd is a black yak-skin tent with a motorbike outside.

Sonam greets us and Duker Tsering, the young Tibetan fixer who's brought us here. Sonam is slim, around 30 I should think, and not at all what I'd expect a yak farmer to look like. His face is oval, quite unlike the broad, squarer features of Duker, and with soft, sleepy eyes and delicate, almost feminine features, he looks like the model for a Renaissance Madonna. He's turned out in a smart brown suit, with a designer label sewn on the outside of the sleeve, and a natty pair of imitation crocodile-skin shoes. It crosses my mind that he might not be a yak farmer at all but an actor brought in to play the part.

Giving him the benefit of the doubt I follow him into the tent. It's surprisingly spacious, some 30 by 20 feet inside. Sacks of grain and flour fill one corner, a milk churn and a pile of dried yak dung fill another. There are three beds, all piled with brightly patterned rugs, blankets and bolsters. The only light, spilling down from a hole in the roof, falls around the handsome head of Sonam's wife. Tall, with a straw hat, woollen shawl, striped belt with red tassels and a big sand-coloured sweater, she's stirring a bubbling bowl of yak cheese at a stove built from turf and topped with dried mud. Two of their three small children run in and out. The eldest girl, Sonam tells me, has just started school.

We sit down on one of the three beds. Salty tea is poured for me from a big, blackened kettle, and in lieu of sugar, a rarity on the plateau, Sonam adds a small slab of butter, which liquefies into a greasy scum across the top. It tastes, well, not bad, just different. As someone wisely said, if they called it soup rather than tea we'd have no trouble drinking it at all.

Sonam doesn't speak much English and I don't speak Tibetan but we sit there quite happily without saying much, listening to the spitting gurgle of the cheese and the yaks feeding outside. Not that yaks make much noise either, beyond the occasional low, respiratory grunt, like old men dozing in a library.

I offer to help Sonam's various relatives herd the yaks and I walk beside an old lady who moves them along with sharp, chirruping cries and the occasional clod of earth thrown in the direction of any that step out of line. A grid of woven yak-hair ropes is laid out by the tent, to which the animals are tethered for milking. With Sonam's encouragement I have a go, leaning in, head up against the rear quarters, catching the toasty smell of the thick fur, hands groping about wondering where the udders are and what I should do with them when I find them.

By the time Sonam returns to check on my progress I have coaxed out about enough milk for a cup of cappuccino. He's far too nice a man to tell me off, but his laugh says it all. I must be much firmer with the udders, he says. I shall remember that next time I milk a yak. Sorry, a *dri*. (See yak sexing notes, Day Sixty Two.)

When the time comes to move on into Yushu for the Summer Horse Festival, the reason for our coming here, Sonam offers me a ride on the back of his motorbike. No helmets or anything like that, just hang on and go. Bounce across the meadow, accelerate up a steep embankment and onto the road, then down the hills, offering silent tributes to Chinese road-building skills as we race past shrines, beneath garlands of prayer flags, through a shallow river and into town.

Day Seventy Two : Yushu

The Yushu Hotel, its entrance garishly painted with the usual conflation of ill-tempered dragons, snowy mountains, lions, tigers and minor devils, was noisy with pre-festival singing and shouting last night.

My room has the usual idiosyncrasies. In this case, a basin pointing downwards at an angle of 30 degrees, which I don't use, not because of its peculiar tilt, but because no water comes out of either of the taps. This is unimaginable luxury compared to the other rooms on my floor, which share a communal bathroom and a pungently malodorous lavatory, from which I can hear the sound of throats being graphically cleared. Nevertheless, this is the best hotel in Yushu, or Jyekundo as it's known in Tibetan. This morning the narrow driveway is an ill-tempered place as dignitaries from as far away as the provincial capital Xining wait to be collected by their shiny four-wheel drives and taken the mile or so out of town to the festival ground. I meet an American in the lobby.

He's in water-management and is very excited.

'This is the water-tank of the world, Michael.'

For a moment I feel another plumbing story coming on, but then I see his gaze is directed out to the mountains.

'The Salween, Irrawaddy, Mekong, Yellow, Yangtze. They all start round here.'

He shakes his head reverentially.

'Water-tank of the world.'

We have taken a tent at the festival site. All around us people are getting ready for the parade. A man with bells around his short leather boots waves red and white scarves and tries out a few dance steps. The dancers' outfits look central Asian, even Cossack, with embroidered sashes across chests, baggy, peppermint-green silk trousers, dark hair squeezed into nets and covered up with fiery red headscarves.

The main stand is beginning to fill up. Men in suits are arriving, TV crews running backwards before them, to be greeted with white scarves and shown to their seats. The political officials are accompanied, more discreetly, by military top brass.

Around the other three sides of the parade ground is a vibrantly colourful crowd, dressed to the nines: women in long patterned dresses, hair carefully braided, ears, necks and hands adorned with coral and turquoise and men in calf-skin shoes, shades and imitation Armani suits, which I'm told can be picked up in town for about $7 each.

A sharp crackle of fireworks starts the parade, which is led by massed motorbikes, decorated with mountains of flowers and coloured sashes, followed by the massed blue trucks from local co-operatives, bearing politically sound placards lauding the policy of opening up and developing the wildernesses of the West.

Tub-thumping commentaries in Tibetan and Chinese evoke the spirit of the Soviet era, an impression re-enforced by the arrival of massed formation tractors, motors rumbling, exhausts belching. People have only good feelings towards tractors. They are the one symbol of progress that everyone approves of and they receive by far the biggest round of applause.

By now quite a head of traffic has built up at one end of the ground, with the massed tractors finding themselves banked up against the massed trucks, who are waiting for the massed motorbikes to clear. The result is an almighty fug-filled jam, a sort of pageant of pollution.

Once cleared, a po-faced detachment of the PLA enter the arena, take up position by the ceremonial flagpole and present arms to the dignitaries in the stand. No spontaneous round of applause here.

Then, by turns, the show-ring fills up with horsemen wearing cowboy hats and jingling bells, sword-brandishing dancers in red lamp-shade hats, monks sounding long curved trumpets, children in matching blue and white track-suits and Tibetan dancers in traditional double length sleeves, which they whirl around like windmills to a tempo as jaunty as an Irish jig.

Day Seventy Three : Yushu

Much jollier up at the parade ground today. The speeches are over, the big-wigs have gone and a holiday atmosphere prevails. Screeching disco music blares out from the PA system, boys race through on scooters with girls they've just met on the back, children are paddling in the river, horses are being washed, a lady wearing a post-SARS face mask sells fresh-made yogurt from a bamboo churn. Picnics are breaking out, an elderly monk is shouting into his mobile phone and horses are feeding from nosebags made from plastic footballs, cut in half.

We're quite an attraction. The children are particularly interested by my notebook and Nigel and Peter's arms, handwriting and bodily hair being endless sources of fascination.

Occasionally I look up and think what an English scene this is. Many of the women favour wide-brimmed straw hats, others carry parasols, making parts of the camp look like a sea of Eliza Doolittles or Frith's painting of Derby Day, yet when I look on the map we're in the middle of nowhere with nothing for 1000 miles around. I suppose that's why these festivals, especially one on this scale, are so important. They bring people in from their tough lives in inhospitable places to enjoy, fleetingly, the seduction and security of the crowd.

In the arena, meanwhile, dancers and feats of horsemanship alternate. The Khampa horsemen who perform with such panache are renowned for being the toughest and most warlike of the peoples of Tibet, and the only ones to offer any serious resistance to the Chinese 'liberation'. Spurring their mounts into a full gallop, they ride in with ancient rifles, which they twirl around their heads, bring down to a firing position and aim to blow a hole in a 9-inch square of white paper sticking out of the ground. Others do handstands, bareback and at full speed, or hanging head-first down from the saddle try to grab as many scarves off the ground as they can while racing past.

The junction opposite our hotel, where the Xining-Lhasa road meets the southeast turn-off to Sichuan, is a hive of activity. Shops and cafés line crowded pavements where it seems everything is traded. Women are selling butter and yak cheese, which is hardened, cut into small blocks and carried on a string round the neck. More conventional necklaces are also available. They're expensive too, made up of the highly sought-after amber and coral, as well as cowrie shells (exotic luxuries for people so far from the sea). More furtively traded, but fetching high prices, are withered black shoots called caterpillar fungus or *Cordyceps sinensis*.

Difficult to find, and detectable only by a thin shoot sticking above the ground, it is apparently a potent tonic highly prized by the Tibetans. A herbal cure, says Duker.

'What does it cure?'

'Everything.'

I buy five of the shrivelled pieces of grass for 50 yuan, nearly £4, and find them several weeks later down one of the seams of my bag.

Day Seventy Four : Yushu

Today we leave Yushu/Jyekundo, the northernmost point on our journey.

On our way out of town, Duker insists that we stop at Gyanak Mani, believed to be the largest collection of mani stones in Tibet. Mani stones are a prominent feature of any sacred Buddhist site, and this one is particularly blessed, as it's believed that Princess Wengcheng, the Chinese bride of King Songsten Gampo, spent time here, 1400 years ago. Mani stones usually have the mantra 'Om Mani Padme Hum' ('Hail to the Jewel in the Lotus') inscribed on them, but this stone field and accompanying walls are much richer, with some having carvings of gods and whole sections of the sutras (Buddha's sayings) carved on them.

Recently, and controversially, the Chinese authorities moved a lot of the stones to build lavatories, but I'm told there was such an outcry that the ground was reconsecrated after the work was done. This morning a regular stream of pilgrims walks, and in some cases crawls, around the temple, each circumambulation guaranteeing more merit points in the next life.

I buy a stone, make my prayer and place it in a wall.

Time to say farewell to Duker, a helpful and patient guide with a good sense of humour. He's a true Tibetan. His father is a nomadic farmer 60 miles from here. An aunt helped educate him at a monastery school and as soon as he learnt English he knew he would never return to the nomad's life. He fled to India for a while and learnt more about Tibetan tradition and culture in Dharamsala then he ever did in Tibet. Now he recognizes the importance of learning Chinese and his great hope for his son is that he will be truly international.

'At home in Lhasa or Oxford or Beijing.'

The road accompanies a meandering stream through a pleasant tree-lined valley. About 20 miles (32 km) from Yushu, the bubbling, fresh flow is swept into a faster, darker river, which will carry it 3500 miles (5600 km) from here to the shores of the East China Sea. It will also take us back into the Himalaya. Its name here is Tongtian He, the 'River to Heaven', but we know it as the Yangtze-Kiang, the longest river in Asia.

Yunnan, China

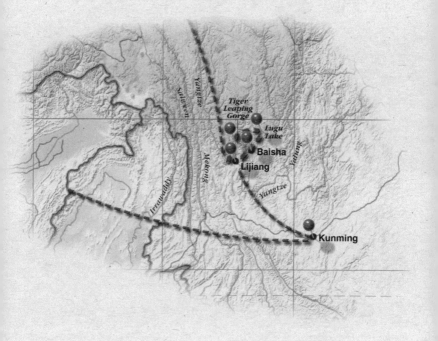

Day Seventy Six : Shigu to the Tiger Leaping Gorge

In eastern Tibet and western Yunnan something quite dramatic happens to the Himalaya. They change direction. Crushed up against two unyielding plateaux, the world's mightiest mountain range meets its match and is turned inexorably southwards. The meltwaters of the Tibetan plateau, gratefully unleashed, pour south through a series of plunging, often impenetrable gorges, to spill into the Bay of Bengal or the South China Sea.

All except one.

At a small town called Shigu, some 100 miles into Yunnan, the Yangtze, like the Himalaya, changes direction, a quirk of geography that Simon Winchester, in his book *The River at the Centre of the World*, regards as being responsible for the very existence of what we know as China.

Having carved its way off the plateau and running hard alongside the Mekong, the Salween and the Irrawaddy, the Yangtze-Kiang, now called the Jinsha Jiang, River of Golden Sand, meets an obstruction. A thousand miles of tumbling water heading for Vietnam and the Gulf of Tonkin is, within a few hundred yards, spun round to the north and, though it twists and turns and tries to find its way south again, it is now effectively a Chinese river, heading east to create the enormous bowl of fertility and prosperity that is the heart and soul of the Middle Kingdom.

Such is the fame of the Great Bend at Shigu that I expect to see a battleground of the elements, some evidence of a cataclysmic confrontation between rock and water; but the Yangtze goes meekly, and Cloud Mountain, which blocks its way, is little more than a large hill. Sandbanks rise from the river and Shigu itself is a warm, sleepy little backwater.

Maybe it's worn out by its history. Shigu means 'Stone Drum', which refers to a marble tablet commemorating the epic defeat of Tibetan invaders that took place here in 1548. It describes 'heads heaped like grave mounds', 'blood like rain' and 'dykes choked with armour'. Another memorial reminds us that Mao's famous Long Marchers, pursued by the Nationalist army, crossed the Yangtze at Shigu in 1936. It took four days and nights to get all 18,000 of them across.

Popular legend believes that the limestone buttress of Cloud Mountain that turned the Yangtze north was put there by the Emperor Da Yu, with precisely that intention, some 4000 years ago.

There's a huge tourist car park by the river with restaurant attached. Early on this Monday morning it's quiet and there's only one bus parked up, but I'm told that the rest of the time Shigu makes a very good living from Da Yu and China's most famous U-turn.

No sooner has Da Yu's carefully placed mountain done its work than the river is flung into the thrashing, frothing, unbelievably turbulent passage of a 13,000-foot (3960 m) ravine known as Tiger Leaping Gorge. Despite the fact that the escaping tiger that gave it its name would have had to leap a half-mile or more to cross it, legend is as important as fact in China and this is the name by which it is known, loved and increasingly visited.

At Quiaotou, a few miles downstream from Shigu, they're pushing an ambitious new road through the gorge. This will be the easy option: the Low Road, but we're going to walk the High Road, a trekker's trail that clings to the sheer side of the mountain. Our guide, Li Yuan, is a tall, stooped figure with close-cropped, greying hair and a livid scar running down one side of his face. He has six horses to carry our equipment. They're waiting patiently on the edge of town, tiny specks beside an army of bulldozers and earth movers. Adding a touch of surreality, women of the local Yi minority step daintily through the rubble on their way to market, dressed in sweepingly long, bright dresses, huge silver earrings and square, black hats, perched, like mortarboards, on the back of their heads.

We purchase tickets for the two-day walk from a small tourist centre beside which is a map of where we're going and a warning in English that 'Tiger Leaping Gorge is one of the most dangerous gorges in the world which is not convenient to sail', before concluding poetically, 'However there is a kind of beauty making of magnificence tugging of people's heartstrings'.

Before we can have our heartstrings tugged, we have to survive a mile-long walk along the road out of town, as coaches swish by, stirring up clouds of dust. As we cough our way along in their wake, we can at least feel morally superior to the bus-bound tourist and soon we can feel physically superior as well, as our track winds up the hillside and the road slips out of sight below. We climb steadily upwards through scrubby woodland with big views of the southern end of the gorge unrolling below. Following a stone-built irrigation channel, we arrive at a farmhouse, in whose courtyard we loosen our boots and sit down at a table set with bowls of walnuts, sunflower seeds and crisp, delicious pears as round as apples.

The farm also has rooms and is run by Li Yuan's wife. Like him she is quietly efficient, attentive and smiles a lot. She's also a fine cook, providing us with a sumptuous lunch of rice, fresh mushrooms, liver and green chillies, kidney, pork, tomato and egg and a bowl full of quivering grey tubes that no-one touches.

They're both from the Naxi (pronounced Na-hee) people, one of the rich mix of ethnic minorities in Yunnan.

Lunch is easily walked off on a thigh-stretchingly steep climb known as the 28 Bends. Trudging upwards in a tight zigzag, I count off each one carefully and still find another 20 left at the end. The reward is a long, level pathway following an old trade route along which horses from Tibet were exchanged for tea from Yunnan. It leads through warm slopes of camphor, bamboo and pine, across a stream, then downhill through a grove of walnut trees. By now the valley has become a gorge, and I have to concentrate carefully on the increasingly narrow and precipitous trail. It's narrow and the drop precipitous. Far below are the angry, white-whipped waters of the Yangtze, dropping 700 feet (213 m) in a dozen miles. A lethal series of 21 rapids took many lives before two Chinese made the first passage of the river in 1986, entirely encased in a sealed rubber capsule. Sometimes the water is so far away and so hemmed in by mountainside that we can only guess at its ferocity from the distant roar.

As the evening light slants across the gorge a terrific panorama unfolds. On the other side of the gorge the Jade Dragon Snow Mountains, easternmost bastions of the Himalaya, rise in a series of smooth columns, sinuous ravines and needle-sharp pinnacles, their dark grey sides streaked with waterfalls. What makes this place different from Annapurna, Everest, even the Karakoram, is that the tremendous height is so close. When I stop on a narrow ledge to look around me, I find myself having to plant my feet very securely, for it feels as if the soaring vertical walls across the gorge are exerting some magnetic force, determined to tear me from my flimsy ledge.

No-one speaks now, and as we plod onwards round the mountainside, silenced by the sheer scale of the place, there is only the reassuring sound of the horse bells, and the distant hiss of the river unthinkably far below.

It's dark by the time we reach Bendi Wan village and an overnight stop at a place called The Halfway House, run by the redoubtable Mr Feng De Fang. I've felt rather Hobbit-like for the past hour, as the scenery increasingly grew to resemble a *Lord of the Rings* backdrop, and the feeling that I might have morphed into Frodo Baggins is only increased as we pull the doorbell in the dim, lantern-lit entrance and are shown into a stone-flagged courtyard hung with gourds, pumpkins and stacks of drying corncobs.

Mr Feng is a slim to cadaverous young man, quietly busying round and making sure we have a warm fire to sit beside, and from his dark barn of a kitchen he and his wife produce an excellent meal of pork and fresh-picked wild mushrooms.

There's a small, very hot shower down below and the rooms are like those in an old alpine chalet – cosy, cool and with very thin walls.

Kept awake by a noisy game of Chinese chequers on the balcony below, I bundle myself up in the duvet and tot up the day's work. A 12-mile walk, a 2500-foot climb and, apart from the quivering grey things, two of the best meals since we started out all those months ago.

Day Seventy Seven : Tiger Leaping Gorge

On the steps leading down to the lavatory of The Halfway House a wooden board is nailed up with a Chinese inscription that translates as 'Number One Toilet in Heaven and Earth'. As a bit of a connoisseur, I put this ambitious claim to the test. I can report a plain and simple squat toilet, in a room half open to the elements and cantilevered out over the mountainside, with a narrow, angled channel running away into the garden below. Once in the crouch position, however, the real beauty of this little facility becomes apparent. The land seems to fall away, and all that can be seen are the walls and saw-tooth peaks of Ha Ba Snow Mountain on the other side of the gorge. In normal circumstances I'm out of these places as fast as I can, but here, feeling myself suspended above the earth, halfway to the realm of the gods, I am tempted to linger long after my work is done.

This morning an ethereal mist lingers over the mountains, making breakfast on the terrace a chilly affair. Mr Feng De Fang produces coffee or green tea, walnuts, pancakes with smooth local honey, scrambled egg and fresh apple pie in a crisp batter.

We sit and eat too much and look out over the terraced fields below, where beans, sweet corn and wheat defy the forces of gravity and an odd mixture of walnut and palm trees cluster around farm buildings whose stone walls are set solid and sturdy against earthquake impact.

It's a serenely calming view, timeless save for a mobile phone inside a doctored mineral water bottle which hangs out over the balcony on the end of a stick. I ask Mr Feng if they keep it out there for security reasons but he says no, it's the only place they can get reception.

Mr Feng speaks good English, which he says he learnt from British hikers on their way through. Maybe this accounts for the fact that, as we have a group photo taken, he encourages us all with shouts of 'Lovely jubbly!'

The track continues north, clinging to the side of the rock face, the Yangtze a boiling froth 4000 feet (1220 m) below. At one point a sizeable waterfall comes bouncing off the rocks above us and we have to pick our way beneath it, over 50 yards of wet stones. I'm most concerned about the horses but they're a lot more sure-footed than I am; perhaps there isn't such a thing as equine vertigo.

The stony, slippery path reaches its narrowest point. The other side of the gorge looms so close that perhaps a tiger might just have made it after all.

Then we're descending fast on steep and potentially lethal tracks of crumbling, chalky rock past bulky rhododendron bushes.

An almost unstoppable momentum delivers us eventually to the river as it emerges from the gorge. It's 100 yards wide here and the jade-green stream twists and turns and eddies and swirls between banks of bleached brown boulders. We've been told that a ferry crosses here but it seems highly unlikely. There are no moorings or jetties and the water looks decidedly tricky.

Then I make out some movement on the far bank and a small, steel-hulled boat emerges from beneath the shadow of a colossal overhang and, after taking the current in a wide arc, runs in towards us and docks by ramming its stern hard up between the rocks. Painted lettering on a metal arch at one end of the boat announces it to be the 'Tiger Leaping Gorge Ferry'. We clamber in and a man with a long bamboo pole and the looks and physique of a Spanish gymnast pushes us out onto the Yangtze with a flourish.

The boat seems very fragile all of a sudden. Its two outboard motors do their best but the current seems in control and swings us downstream beneath the overhang, where it's very hot and very quiet. For a moment I'm anxious. The power of the river and the power of the boat seem unfairly matched. The looming rock face above us offers no comfort.

The outboards surge, choke and surge again, but we hold our own against the current and soon we're grinding up onto a gritty beach.

An hour later we've climbed up to where the vehicles are waiting and I look back at the Yangtze, silvery in the twilight and calm and serene now after the trauma of the gorge, and I turn my back on it with a pang of regret.

Day Seventy Nine : Lugu Lake

There are 26 officially recognized nationalities within Yunnan, the most ethnically diverse province in China, and this morning, after a drive over the mountains and through gentle foothills spotted with Yi farms, we're entering the homeland of the Mosuo, who, like the Yi, are primarily Tibetan in origin. Their numbers are small, around 36,000, and are concentrated around a lake that straddles the border with Sichuan Province at a height of nearly 9000 feet (2740 m).

I'm going to meet Yang Erche Namu, known simply throughout China as Namu, a Mosuo woman who, after winning a national singing contest, ran away from home and found fame and fortune as a singer and later a model in China, Europe and America. Already I've had a glimpse of what to expect at Lugu Lake. The tourist authorities, as anxious to bring people to these ethnic areas as they once were to keep them away, have made much of the matrilineal tradition of the Mosuo. A billboard on the way here showed inviting girls in local costume above the slogan 'Lugu Lake Women's Kingdom. God Living There'. They meant 'Good Living' but for the men who troop out to the lake in search of liberated ladies it comes to the same thing. The irony is that there aren't enough Mosuo women willing to live up to this hype and they have had to import Han Chinese sex workers masquerading as Mosuo to satisfy the demand.

It seems to be working. With 60,000 tourists visiting Lugu last year, the lakeside village of Luoshi has become a boom town, with property prices rising as fast as the multistorey, log cabin-style hotels.

Today the waterfront has an out-of-season feel to it as I set out to find a boat to take me to the hotel Namu has just opened on the other side of the lake. A few tourists are out photographing each other, an elderly Mosuo woman walks beside the water, spinning her prayer wheel, and a line of little black piglets trots out from beneath the timber-framed buildings. In almost every shop, whether it's selling groceries, Mosuo jewellery or tourist tat, there is a stack of Namu's books and CDs. She's prominent on all the covers, her trademark dark hair centre-parted and framing her face mysteriously, like a half-open curtain. She displays a range of personas: Namu looking ruminative, Namu looking beguiling, Namu looking distant, Namu showing a shapely, fish-netted thigh. She certainly looks like someone who's outgrown Lugu Lake.

A canoe paddles me across to a wooden jetty on which Namu is waiting to welcome me. Grabbing at the steps and clambering a little clumsily upwards, I already feel she has the advantage over me, and a kiss on the cheek followed instantly by the buzz of her mobile confirms that.

Her hotel, built on the site of an apple orchard, only opened four months ago. It resembles a Wild West fort. A walled outer yard leads to a pine log facade with tall double doors that open onto a court-yard, enclosed on all sides by two floors of accommodation. Between phone calls Namu escorts me, effusively, into a dimly lit room with a flagging wood fire at one end, a huge television at the other and, somewhere in the middle, the sewn-up, cured carcass of a pig. She insists on butter tea for us all, 'made by my mother', fiddles with the TV remote until she finds a pop video for us all to watch, then, with a lingering flutter of her big dark eyes, disappears to deal with a group of her fans who are staying here tonight.

My timber-clad room is draughty and bitterly cold, and Namu's fans are in celebratory mood, drinking down in the courtyard and committing Karaoke, very loudly, until the wee small hours. Eventually, they stagger to bed and I hear doors slamming shut. Unfortunately, they're noisier asleep than they ever were awake and snoring that must be seven or eight on the Richter scale shakes my pine-clad peace. Around dawn I fall into a deep sleep, from which I'm woken by the sound of fierce and powerful expectoration.

Day Eighty : Lugu Lake

I'm becoming quite endeared to Namu's superstar pretensions, partly because she's so unashamedly open about them and partly because I'm pretty sure that deep down she knows it's all a game.

Joshua, a Beijing-based American journalist, is following her around. She introduces him with an airy wave of the hand.

'He's doing a story on the real Namu,' she says, without much enthusiasm.

We talk at breakfast about the strength of superstition in modern China. Joshua lives on the fourth floor of his building in Beijing, because the number four is considered unlucky and so the apartment is correspondingly cheap. Eight, on the other hand, is auspicious, and mobile phone numbers with eight in them are only available at a premium.

He sees I'm reading Namu's book about her childhood, *Leaving Mother Lake*, and we talk about the world it describes: a society that has no words for husband, wife, marriage or virginity; in which women make all the decisions about who they go with and who they stay with. A man may be an *azhu*, a close male friend, but that's as close as they get to any form of marital obligation. They practise *Zouhun*, 'walking marriage', in which a man and a woman may spend the night together, but he walks back to his own home in the morning. Couples share neither ties nor possessions. Women inherit all the property and bring up the children.

We're interrupted by Namu's piercing voice, rising from the courtyard.

'It is my uncle's house, we have to bring something!'

J-P, who wants to film Namu at the childhood home where her uncle and aunt now live, suggests we take some Yunnan ham.

'No!' barks Namu. 'Not good enough.'

A little later, bearing Yunnan ham, augmented with cigarettes, sugar, a bottle of brandy and a bottle of whisky, we're picking our way across a ploughed field, over a suspicious-looking stream, past a sow with a gaggle of piglets in tow and into a dark, old, smoky, timber farmhouse. In a small courtyard chickens peck away around feeding troughs made from hollowed-out tree trunks. The main room has no windows, only a hole in the roof, whose rafters are coated with thick black grime from the fire. Chitterlings and pigs' bladders hang from the beams. Smoke-veneered, wooden panels around the sides of the room are hung with celebrity calendars, posters of pop stars, and cut-outs of glamorous ladies. While Nigel lights this atmospheric but gloomy interior, Namu preoccupies herself with her looks, holding up a hand mirror and adding a touch of make-up before producing a pair of clippers from somewhere and trimming her eyelashes. Her aunt, a good-looking woman with a black, turban-like coil on her head, whose sole concern seems to be to provide us with refreshment, puts three large lumps of pork fat in a bowl on the fire and drops tiny pancakes filled with wheat flour into the bubbling mix.

When we start filming, a black cat nestles down beside me, looking very sweet but tormenting our sound recordist with loud meows at unscheduled times.

Our talk turns to Namu's relationship with her mother, which is clearly at the heart of everything that's happened to her.

Not only was she not the boy her mother wanted, she was also what she calls 'a crying baby', to such an extent that her mother was driven to give her away and she was sent to live with an aunt. At the age of eight she was sent away again, this time to stay with an uncle who had lost his loved one in an accident and lived alone with his yaks up in the mountains.

Namu speaks of this with a nice touch of understatement.

'That was a very interesting time, and very hard. My uncle never speaks and the yak never speaks, so...' she gives a short, piercing laugh, '…so I had a really interesting childhood in the mountains.'

At 13 she went through the Mosuo woman's rite of passage, the traditional skirt ceremony.

'The *lamas* help you choose the day,' she recalls. 'And then in the morning, very early, mamma prepared the skirt, beautiful, long, long skirt, and beautiful jacket and hair things and flowers and the key. The key that is the power for you to continue to take care of this matriarchal family.'

The key fits what they call the Flower Room or Flower Chamber, which was Namu's first room of her own. From that time onwards she was entitled to choose who she wanted to share her room with.

Mosuo boys, on the other hand, have to wait until 18 for their freedom, which is marked by a ritual burning of their bed.

She describes the process of courtship.

'When a man come to your house, normally he leave three things, one belt, one knife, one piece of clothing. If the woman doesn't want him back any more she lays them outside the door as a sign.'

'What if she decides she's made a mistake and wants to see him again after all?' I ask.

Here it becomes wonderfully Victorian.

'She will ask her grandmother to go to tea with the boy's grand-mother. They will bring like a bamboo box, some chicken meat, some Tibetan *momo*, some Tibetan wine, and when the lady receive all this she will tell the boy, why don't you go one more night there.'

The freedom of choice offered to the girls did not fool Namu. She recognized that it was another way of keeping her tied down, and all her instincts were to break out of the confines of the village and see the world.

'I want to go to Beijing, wear high-heeled shoes and pink lipstick, you know.'

So she ran off to Beijing and Shanghai and became a successful singer, until she damaged her hearing. Far from giving up, she turned to fashion and went to live and work in San Francisco, New York, Paris, Italy and Japan. She lived with a Norwegian diplomat but that now seems to be over and she's fallen for a Frenchman.

She tells me all this as the fire crackles and the smoke drifts lazily up into the rafters of what feels an essentially mediaeval cottage. Her aunt, thinking Namu is talking too much, tries to get at the fire to make us all a cup of salted butter tea.

The interesting thing about Namu is that she bothered to come back to Lugu Lake at all. Though she calls herself, wryly, 'a five-star gypsy', the claustrophobic world that drove her away still seems to have a hold on her.

I put it to her that she's still trying to win the approval of the mother who rejected her and she nods. But it hasn't been easy for either of them. What Namu did, and how she did it, was in every way extraordinary, but it nearly severed her links with her mother for ever.

She also seems genuinely fond of her people, describing herself as a 'Mosuo cultural ambassador'. This seems to excite her and she leaps up. There is something we must see.

We're whisked away to a nearby promontory, rising a few hundred feet above the lake. Here, looking like a half-built million-aire's home in California, is Namu's latest contribution to the Lugu Lake property boom, her own half-built museum.

She talks vaguely in terms of some sort of Mosuo cultural centre, but as we step carefully over pipes and piles of dust and rubble I get the distinct impression that this is a museum of Namu.

She waves towards a substantial three-sided space.

'I'm going to put the translations of all my books from all over the world here.'

'That's huge, Namu. That makes the British Library look like a newspaper shop.'

But she has already moved on.

'And this is my kitchen.'

She enthuses about work spaces and artists in residence, and 'rooms for my best friends'. On a terrace outside we look down on the concrete shell of a swimming pool.

'That's the most beautiful view on the lake,' she says, and it certainly is a glorious position, out there with the mountains beyond and small, wooded islets rising out of shimmering, silver-blue waters.

There are problems, however. The architect backed out halfway through, she's had to sack the last lot of builders and is down to her last 5000 yuan (about £350).

She looks around at the mess, apparently unperturbed.

'My mamma think I'm crazy.'

I walk down some steps to a long, curving room with floor-to-ceiling window spaces, and there is the woman who so affected her life. There is Mamma, almost silhouetted against the declining sun. She's short and wiry, wears a Mao-style fur hat and is smoking a cig-arette. A doughty little lady with shrewd, quick eyes. She sees me taking in the bare walls and empty sockets of the unfinished room and when I turn back to her I can see the ghost of a smile. A quiet smile of satisfaction. Or is it just the smile of experience, the smile of a mother who knows that she understands her daughter better than her daughter will ever understand herself.

On the way back to the hotel we pass by the local village, to which Namu donated a school for 60 children. We detour to look at it. It's run down and neglected. We can't get in but we circle it and try to peer inside. Namu mutters something. She looks puzzled and vaguely hurt by the state of it, but I have the feeling she's not sur-prised.

A little deflated, we return to the road. Namu dives into a car and heads back. Needing a bit of a breather, I walk back beside the lake, which is peaceful and unspoilt here.

Day Eighty One : Lugu Lake

The fans have gone and we have the 37-room hotel to ourselves. Well, ourselves and Namu. Namu, a little force-field of her own, is the centre of attention even when she's not around. She either retreats, with her mobile, to deal with her complicated international life, or sweeps out, usually in a different outfit, firing on all cylin-ders, organizing, cajoling and demanding.

Having talked about the importance of the Flower Chamber in her upbringing, she wants to recreate one for me. Orders are given and we all repair to the Karaoke room and watch pop videos until Namu, now in a long, black, satin dress with green silk lining, arrives, flicks off her mobile, then swings herself up on a raised plat-form before the fireplace and, with the relish of a natural actress, begins the half-interview, half-performance. I am expected to be both interviewer and supporting actor.

Though the Mosuo have this reputation for sexual generosity, the process she describes seems conventional enough. The first sign of attraction may well have taken place at one of the circle dances, a touch of pressure on the hand, a piece of skilful position-ing. But the Mosuo girls are always in control, she says. Before anyone got as far as the Flower Chamber she would have been playing the field, asking one to prove his love by throwing a stone further than anyone else, or singing more sweetly, or riding a horse faster.

Once allowed in, the lucky man would be offered butter tea and little delicacies such as a potato, an orange or sunflower seeds. If things were going well, some wine might be offered as well.

'All this at 13?'

Namu shakes her head. At 13 they don't usually go with men, but they begin to learn about sex from cousins, sisters and in her case from her mother, who, she says, gave her advice on 'how a woman should sit to show she had self-respect', and at the same time, 'how to walk to show herself off'.

Namu digs at the fire.

'The Chinese very secret, we're quite open about things,' she says, sliding a potato towards me.

'My mother told me sex is very good for the skin. You get good sex, you don't get pimples.'

I'm trying to find a polite way of asking how many men she slept with in her Flower Chamber, but she answers for me.

'In my Flower Room I was still virgin.'

I ask her if they used any form of birth control. She shakes her head. It's rather the opposite.

'Many Mosuo women want to get pregnant but can't,' she says. 'So they go to the Penis Cave on Gemu Goddess Mountain.'

'The Penis Cave?'

Namu's almond eyes widen.

'It's unbelievable. All stones look like a penis. They all different sizes.'

'Does it work?'

She nods.

'They go there to pray and normally after that they get pregnant.'

As a result of being allowed to choose their male partners and to have as many as they want without stigma, the Mosuo are seen in some way as less than civilized, but Namu sees it as quite the oppo-site. Theirs is a society that has no place for sexual jealousy and all the judgemental possessiveness that goes with it.

She says that her people are very like the native Americans she met in Albuquerque, New Mexico.

'I walk in there and feel that I'm like their sister.'

Tonight is our last night at Namu's and she has ordered a lamb to be grilled on the spit. First of all, though, there's entertainment around an open fire in the centre of the courtyard. Everyone's expected to sing. The crew are terrified and have been practising 'The Lumberjack Song' for days. The Mosuo women sing powerfully – hard, back-of-the-throat sounds that are often harsh and strident to our ears – but their range and control as they fly up and down the keys can be thrilling.

Then, with the men dressed like cowboys, they go into what they call Mosuo disco. Music thumps out from loudspeakers, but the movements owe more to line dancing than John Travolta. Namu talks often of East meeting West and Mosuo disco does seem to have brought Yunnan and Idaho a lot closer together.

Finally, a few rounds of circle dancing. Namu pulls me up and seems unfazed by my inability to get the footwork up to Fred Astaire or even Fred Flintstone standard.

'It's good exercise,' she says blithely, and suddenly I see the real Namu. She tries hard to be the vamp, but at heart she's the gym mistress. Must tell Joshua.

The drink flows and Namu's brother, who runs the hotel, is full of bonhomie. After bottles of Dynasty Red, gin and cognac have been passed round, he insists we have one last toast in the local corn wine.

'Tashi Delek!' we all shout, clinking our glasses and knocking back the smoothly fierce brew.

Namu is nowhere to be seen.

Day Eighty Two: Lugu Lake to Lijiang

There's a cockerel somewhere close by that wakes me every morning, long before it's light. Today I time its first call at 3.29. To make matters worse, it crows only on one note, a monotone cry like someone pretending to be a ghost.

It gives me plenty of time to get my head together and prepare for an early start. Breakfast is basic and heavy. Noodles, hot, spicy cabbage and coils of pudgy, white, steamed bread, washed down with butter tea, made, of course, by Namu's mother. Our drivers, like most other working people in China, carry plastic flasks of green tea at all times, wedging them perilously on the dashboard. Soon we're packed, have said our farewells and are making our way on a slow loop round the lake, passing the Coca Cola Hope School, proof that Namu is not the only philanthropist in Lugu Lake. The red soil has turned to mud with recent rain, and the 12,000-foot (3660 m) summit of the Gemu Goddess Peak is lost in the clouds. Compared to where we've been, Gemu seems no more than a foothill, but we are still above 8000 feet (2440 m) and, even here, the snow will soon come and shut the passes and Lugu Lake will be cut off for three months of the winter.

This has been the easternmost point of our journey. We are some 2000 miles (3200 km) from the Khyber Pass, as the crow flies, and now we must turn back towards the Himalaya and follow the mountains as they make their great southern arc towards India and Burma.

Within a few hours we are riding into the Yangtze gorges again, this time on the other side of the Jade Dragon Snow range from Tiger Leaping, but into canyons just as stomach-tighteningly spectacular.

Shanzidou, at 18,350 feet (5590 m) is the tallest of 13 limestone pinnacles that crown the summit of Jade Dragon Snow Mountain. With its brilliant white scarf of snow, this jagged diadem of ice and snow effortlessly dominates the northwestern horizon as we enter the village of Baisha.

Surrounded by a fertile plain, it's a quiet, attractive little place. Its main streets are more like lanes, with water rushing down open culverts, past houses of traditional mud-brick built on stone bases and topped with alpine-style, wide-eaved roofs. Some of the buildings, including a fine stone gate-tower, suggest grander times, and, indeed, Baisha was once the capital of the Naxi kingdom, before it was conquered by Kublai Khan 800 years ago.

In recent years it has rediscovered fame as the home of He Shixiu, known to the world as Dr Ho, one of the leading lights of Chinese traditional medicine. It's not hard to find his house, partly because the bus stops right outside and partly because of a battery of display boards leaning against the trees and covered with press headlines.

'The Famous Dr Ho', 'Dr Ho – He Has Many Friends', 'He Loves

Open-Door Policy' and 'Bruce Chatwin – 17 Years Ago He Stayed Here for Two Weeks'.

His son, Ho Shulong, emerges from the front door of a modest, two-storey house to welcome us. For a moment, it's hard to get a word in edgeways, as he reels off details of his father's worldwide fame. Some 500 articles about him in 40 languages, 300,000 people treated in 40 countries. National Geographic Channel are here today to talk about making a film about him, as is a British woman who already has made a film about him, called *The Most Admired Man*.

The walls of the front room are adorned with hundreds of visiting cards as well as pictures of Mao, the Queen, Princess Di and Deng Xiaoping. Several of Bruce Chatwin's books, in plastic wrapping, hang from the ceiling like holy relics. My own visit has caused enormous excitement, for apparently I have been here before, with John Cleese, my fellow Monty Python.

Before I can clear this one up, Dr Ho appears, sidling diffidently into the room. He must be in his mid-seventies, and sports a black, knitted scarf and hat and a white lab coat. His face is that of the classic wise old Chinaman, thin, with a wispy white beard and moustache. His eyes are bright and responsive.

He clutches my hand and says how nice it is to see me again.

I'm aware of other visitors hovering – a French girl, two Japanese and two Australian doctors, who tell me they are here to discuss Dr Ho's treatment of prostate cancer. Ho Shulong, hearing our conversation, thrusts a sheaf of documents in front of me. They're from a physician at the Mayo Clinic in America, acknowledging the part that Dr Ho's herbal treatment played in the recovery of a patient from prostate cancer.

I'm taken through to Dr Ho's consulting room. It's modest, like the house itself, and a bit of a mess. The floor is covered with red plastic buckets and there are various preparations open on the shelves.

'So, old friend, nice to see you again,' he repeats.

I can't lie, but I don't want to spoil whatever game he's playing.

'You're looking well,' I offer, neutrally.

'I'm 80 years old and getting stronger,' he grins.

He sits me down on a lab stool and I tell him of the hard travelling I've been doing and the fatigue and all that.

He asks me about my lower back, then asks me to put out my tongue.

He nods.

'Take care of the food,' he advises. 'Eat simple food.'

'The pork is very good in Yunnan,' I suggest.

'I think pork not so good.'

He checks my pulse and nods reassuringly.

'Good pulse, no high blood pressure. No high cholesterol, no liver fat, no kidney stone, no gall bladder stone.'

I feel like someone who's just won a scholarship. And Dr Ho isn't through yet.

'This morning many French people come. Some have high cholesterol.'

'Yes?'

'Fat liver.'

'Ah.'

'Diabetes.'

'Really?'

'High blood pressure.'

'It's all that French food.'

'But your chi is weak.'

'Oh.'

'You know "chi"? It is your energy levels.'

I nod. Here comes the bad news.

'And your stomach. And you have a Chinese cold, a little Chinese cold. I see it from your lips.'

'Oh dear.'

'But be happy, happiness is best medicine you know.'

Happiness alone is clearly not going to be enough for me, and he sets to work preparing some of his herbal remedies. He will make something up for me. I glance at the labels as he measures out the powder. Fennel, Plantain, Wrinkled Giant Hyssop, Indian Madder, Chinese Sage, Nepal Geranium.

The slopes of Jade Dragon Mountain are famous throughout China as the Home of Medicinal Plants, with over 600 species available. Dr Ho takes pride in the fact that all the ingredients he uses are either grown here or collected from the surrounding hills by himself or members of his family. No outsiders involved, and nothing bought from markets.

Clutching my various powders in brown paper cones, I return to the now even more crowded front room to be met by Dr Ho's son with an open visitors' book bearing incontrovertible proof that Michael Palin and John Cleese did indeed come here some five years ago. Unfortunately, our names and comments are the work of a man from Woking who clearly thought he was being very funny.

I try to explain the error but Mr Ho Junior is not really interested. He's now jettisoned the visitors' book and is showing us out through a small back garden, where seeds are drying in wide, shallow baskets, and onto a wooden verandah where food is being set out. Dr Ho's wife, a beautiful woman, and a calming presence too, is supervising what turns out to be a wonderful meal, served in dishes that spread over the table and beyond: hyacinth, water-lily, anchovy, baby pig, Yunnan ham, tofu, broccoli and more.

She wears traditional Naxi costume: a blue bonnet and deep blue top with a white apron and a quilted cape tightly secured by two cross-ribbons and on its back a slip of white fur, representing the day, and above it a dark blue cloth representing the night.

Dr Ho joins us and I learn a little more about him.

Though he was always fascinated by herbal medicine, he was reviled by the Red Guards, who smashed his place up, and he was unable to get back his licence to practise until the start of the 'Open-Door' policy in 1985. Even then, he could practise only at public hospitals. Nowadays he will see anyone and only asks people to pay what they can afford.

He was clearly inspired by the work of Dr Joseph Rock, an irascible, dedicated Austro-American botanist who lived and worked in southwest China for 27 years, until forced to leave after the Revolution in 1949. He admired the ethnic minorities and was apprehensive of their domination by the Han Chinese. He compiled an English-Naxi dictionary and sent back to the West a collection of 80,000 botanical specimens.

It was 'Rock's Kingdom', Bruce Chatwin's report for the *New York Times* in 1986, that brought Dr Ho to a world audience.

Which is why we're here today. And as far as everyone at Dr Ho's is concerned, I'm a regular visitor.

Day Eighty Three : Lijiang

From my hotel window two things compete for space in an otherwise clear blue sky. One is Jade Dragon Snow Mountain and the other is the great glass and steel tower of the China Construction Bank.

Lijiang is a tale of two cities: one a modern concoction of business district office blocks and shopping malls, the other an immaculately kept old town, with clay-tiled roofs, cobbled streets and a canal system that evokes Venice, Amsterdam or Bruges. Lijiang became rich and famous because of its key position on the Tea-Horse Route from Tibet into China, but its idyllic situation, set comfortably in a shallow bowl of hills, is deceptive. A fault line at the edge of the Tibetan plateau runs below and the ripple effect of the tectonic collision that created the Himalaya has been responsible for over 50 strong earthquakes here in the last 130 years. The most recent, which registered over seven on the Richter scale, hit Lijiang in 1996, killing 300 and injuring 16,000. Many buildings were damaged or destroyed. The majority of them were in the new city.

The wood and stone houses of old Lijiang were built by people who knew about earthquakes and how to withstand them. They remain, thanks to UNESCO money, as an example of how to create harmony, line and proportion on a human scale. The result is a labyrinth of cobbled streets and squares, car free, perfect for walking, but also a victim of their own success. Large-scale preservation of the past is so rare in China that Lijiang has become a big draw, pulling upwards of 3 million tourists a year into an old town of 25,000 people.

It's around nine o'clock when I set out for breakfast. Wooden shutters are being taken down from shops and cafés. The first tour groups of the day have been disgorged from their coaches and totter awkwardly on the cobblestones behind the upraised yellow flags of their guides. Many of them already wear the dogged, mule-like expressions of those condemned to another day of organized enlightenment.

The agglomeration of gift shops that always accompanies a tourist boom has hit Lijiang like anywhere else, but the shops are small and well kept and the streets clean and sparkling. Feeling slightly ashamed of myself, I choose a café offering 'England Breakfast'. It's served with wall to wall Sting.

Gorged on egg, bacon, fried bread, toast and many other delights denied to me for several weeks, I finish my fresh-ground Yunnan coffee and explore the area around the main Sifang Square. There are no big vistas here. The streets twist and turn on each other, often running alongside or over the streams of clear, cooling water that flow from Black Dragon Pool at the foot of Elephant Mountain. No wonder that one of the most powerful Naxi deities, and the one they pray to for prosperity, is Shu, the water god.

In this morning of rediscovered pleasures I find a second-hand copy of a classic book on the city, *Forgotten Kingdom* by Peter Goullart, a Russian-born Frenchman who lived and worked in Lijiang in the 1940s until forced to leave by the zealous xenophobes of the Communist revolution. 'A book about paradise by a man who lived there for nine years', says a *Times* review of 1957.

It contains tantalizing snippets of information that you never find in the guide books: that the Naxi were born gossips and the despair of missionaries; that their preferred poison was black aconite boiled in oil, which was characterized by a paralysis of the larynx. 'In convulsions the victim could only stare frantically at his helpless friends without being able to utter a word.'

Goullart was particularly impressed by the Naxi women, who 'silently and persistently, like the roots of growing trees…evolved themselves into a powerful race until they utterly enslaved their men. To marry a Naxi woman was to acquire a life insurance and the ability to be idle for the rest of one's days.'

Echoes of Namu and the Mosuo women here, and once again evidence that Yunnan's ethnic minorities have more in common with each other than with the rest of China.

Day Eighty Five : Lijiang

I meet the most famous man in Lijiang outside the traditionally decorated, red lacquered portals of the Naxi Music Centre. 'Naxi Ancient Music' is written in English above this doorway, at which people are already gathering, asking when the ticket office opens. A man in his seventies, quite trim, whose quick, lively, intelligent eyes dominate his

PREVIOUS PAGE Kunming, China. Girls in tribal costumes compare umbrella-opening techniques at the Yunnan Nationalities Villages.

Left: Elephant basketball at the Nationalities Villages. *Below:* Nagaland. An old warrior, with fern accoutrements.

Above: Belly up. Konyak Naga head-hunter outdoes me in stomach decoration. Nor are my Paul Smith belt and Craghopper trousers any match for his hornbill feather, wild boar's teeth and neck-chain showing he's taken five heads. *Below:* Shingwong translates the words of the chief of Longwa Village, on my right, as we talk to him in his hut. This picture has a distinctly period flavour. Hard to believe from the look of the place that most of them here are baptized Christians.

Above: With the morning shift at Tipong Mine, near Digboi, Assam. *Below:* Safety is the big issue at Tipong. I suppose they could start by giving them overalls.

Above: With Manoj Jalan (on leading elephant) in his Mancotta Estate. *Below:* Never saw anything like this on my bike rides in Sheffield. Mishing fisherwomen put their catch down their cleavage.

One of the great experiences of my travelling life. Washing an elephant at Kaziranga National Park. I'd never made an elephant rumble with pleasure before.

OPPOSITE PAGE *Top left:* The monastery (*satra*) on Majuli Island. With Jadab Burah (*right*) and his older roommate Lila Ram. Because of vows of purity they would have to wash themselves completely after touching anything in the room that I'd touched. *Middle and below:* Jumbo football at the 2nd Kaziranga Elephant Festival.

Above: Gantey village. With Dasho Benji, wearing traditional *kho*, on the lookout for elusive black-necked cranes. *Below:* Successful sighting. Rare black-necked cranes on the wing.

Above: Evidence of the cult of Drupka Kunley, the 'divine madman', on a house in Gantey village. Painted penises are believed to ward off evil spirits. *Below:* Workmen take a teabreak at the Gantey *gompa* (monastery), which is being refitted. Quite slowly.

Left: The extraordinary precipice on which Takstang is perched.
Below: Doje and I visit Choni Dorje, poet and yak farmer, who has lived up here for 82 years. He sings me his ode to the yak, which made him a national celebrity.

Top: The gravel banks of the Pijain River. *Above left:* The engaging Abdul Rahman, who became a poultry magnate in the Midlands before returning to Bangladesh to build homes for his family. *Above right:* Toilets that have travelled the world. Nothing is wasted at the ship-breaking yards near Chittagong.

Top: The bane and bounty of Bangladesh. Millions of tonnes of Himalayan water combine with the heaviest monsoons in the world to make the landscape both fertile and fragile. *Above:* A very few of the estimated 700,000 bicycle rickshaws in Dhaka, Bangladesh's capital.

Mission accomplished. With the help of the Ganges and the Brahmaputra I'm swept out into the Bay of Bengal, along with millions of tonnes of mud that was once Himalaya.

OPPOSITE PAGE In downtown Dhaka it's quicker to deliver by hand, or shoulder, or head.

Above: Saga Platoon (with apologies to young Peter Meakin) meets the Dalai Lama. (*left to right*) Roger Mills, Thingy, DL, Nigel Meakin, Peter Meakin, Vanessa Courtney, Basil Pao, John Pritchard. *Below:* With (*right to left*) John-Paul Davidson, Nawang Dorjee Sherpa and son, and Wongchu Sherpa, at the Yak and Yeti Hotel, Kathmandu.

face, is dealing with fans. He's darker, darker than most Chinese, dark enough to remind me, with his impish smile, of Desmond Tutu. His hair is black (blacker than might be expected in a man of his age) and brushed forward quite self-consciously. He's dressed in jeans, smart leather shoes, two sweaters and a jacket. His name is Xuan Ke and he is the conductor of the Naxi Music Orchestra.

Last night he and his orchestra were playing for the Prime Minister of Singapore. In the foyer of the theatre is a photograph of Chinese President Jiang Zemin, with flute, playing with the orchestra on a visit here.

This morning the great man has agreed to show me Lijiang, but as soon as we start talking I know that his own story will be much more interesting. He was born in 1930 and received an early musical training from American Pentecostal missionaries. In 1949, after the victory of Chairman Mao, which he refers to, wryly, as 'something called liberation', he became a conductor in Kunming. He wasn't a Communist, he says, but in a group allied to the Communists. Mao's Hundred Flowers campaign, eight years later, initially seemed good news for people like himself. 'Let a hundred flowers bloom,' Mao declared, 'and a hundred schools of thought contend.'

It turned out to be a trap. Having encouraged intellectuals and artists to come out and help the party, Mao, fearing their criticism, turned on them and ordered them to undergo 're-education'. Xuan Ke was sent, at the age of 28, to forced labour in a tin mine.

'Animal living,' he says, unemotionally. 'No human rights at all. Animal food, animal living and working a lot, from daybreak to the midnight.'

He was nearly 50 when he was released.

With Deng Xiaoping as leader of China, tradition was no longer seen as a threat, and, while working as an English teacher in a local school, Xuan Ke slowly began to pick up the pieces of his musical career. Many of his friends had died and the most precious of their antique instruments had been hidden, some embedded in walls to prevent them being found and destroyed by the Red Guards.

In 1986 Lijiang was opened to foreigners for the first time since the revolution and, as the years went by, traditional Naxi music became a big draw. Now the rump of the old orchestra, invigorated by younger singers and musicians, plays every night, and the top people come along to hear them.

As we walk through Lijiang, Xuan Ke is frequently recognized and breaks off from his story to shake hands, exchange greetings, pose for photographs and tell jokes.

He takes it all in his stride, a man seemingly completely at ease with it all.

'This must be the best time of your life,' I ask him.

He smiles and shakes his head.

'Not yet.'

He has a big garden to look after in his house outside Lijiang, and an autobiography to complete. Most of all, I suspect, he relishes his role as satirist, court jester, respected subversive. All the things he was sent to the tin mines for are now not only expected of him, but officially sanctioned.

He chuckles as he tells me that he had 22 American congressmen at the show the other night. After the orchestra had played a particularly quiet and soothing number, he asked the audience if they'd thought that was peaceful.

There was general agreement and appreciative applause, to which he responded, 'Then why not play it on the border with Israel and Palestine?'

'Very big applause,' he says, 'but not from the congressmen.'

Before going to see his show in the evening, Basil and I eat a bowl of delicious pork crackling washed down with Mekong River Beer beneath the bending, canal-side willows at our new favourite eatery, Old Stone Bridge Snacks (Basil admits it loses a bit in translation). Tour groups are still out, plodding submissively over the bridge, eyes glazed and heads lolling. After we've eaten, I buy a collection of old photographs of Lijiang from a stall opposite and notice four of Namu's books on a lower shelf.

From the heroine of the Mosuo, to the hero of the Naxi. Xuan Ke and the orchestra are performing at eight and the queues are already forming. The narrow entrance of the Concert Hall leads to a courtyard converted into a galleried auditorium. Cherry-red lacquer dominates and Chinese lanterns are hung about. Baskets of carnations, dahlias and roses are set out along the front of the stage, and on the back wall there is a colourful mural of black-necked cranes in flight. Above the stage, and in sharp contrast to the swirls of red and gold decoration, is a sombre display of black and white photographs of faces, some blurred, some blank and expressionless like prison photos or police IDs.

Which is probably what they are, for these are all members of the original Naxi orchestra, who have either died or disappeared.

The present orchestra take their places, with the most elderly members, venerable and white-bearded like a troupe of former emperors, being led on by young women in Naxi costume. Xuan Ke makes an inconspicuous entrance, slipping quietly on from the wings to stand at a microphone at stage right. He's wearing a long blue robe, like a priest's soutane, whose simplicity makes him stand out from the dazzling brocades and silks of the older musicians behind him.

He clearly enjoys being at the microphone and addresses the audience in a mixture of Mandarin, Naxi and English, milking the laughs skilfully, in all three languages. I can see the schoolteacher in him as the orchestra sit patiently through a leisurely monologue that touches on all sorts of pet peeves. He makes sure we know that the Naxi Orchestra still needs help. It receives no financial support from the government. And he sounds a warning. Here on the Chinese borderlands, where Han and Tibetan meet, 'the music and musicians are in big danger.'

Young people change their minds faster and faster, going for Karaoke, rock 'n' roll and what he calls 'nonsense lyrics'.

At this point his voice rises and the teacher becomes preacher.

'The music,' he declaims, with arm raised heavenwards, 'is disappearing in the shadow of the Himalaya!'

By now, I'm sure I'm not the only one in the audience thinking that the chief threat to Naxi music might be Xuan Ke's monologues. It's at least 15 minutes into the programme before bow is laid to string or stick to drum but, when it comes, the music, a piece written by the Tang Dynasty Emperor Li Hu over 1000 years ago, is fascinating and unusual, featuring early versions of familiar instruments, lutes, three-string violins and cymbals, accompanied by high soprano vocals.

The only wrong note is the jarring ring of a mobile behind me. Not only is it not turned off but the man proceeds to have a series of long conversations into it, quite oblivious to whatever's happening on stage.

The next song is 750 years old and was written, as Xuan Ke announces cheerfully, 'to express hatred of Kublai Khan'.

After this, he does a whacky impression of Pavarotti jerking manically about to reinforce a point about how even serious music in China has become infected with insidious pop star mannerisms.

The concert is brought to an end with a spare and soulful, if a little anti-climactic, bamboo flute solo, played by one of four young women who have also sung quite exquisitely.

At the end I try to get to Xuan Ke to congratulate him and thank him for our day together, but he's almost invisible between a wall of young female fans. And smiling happily.

Day Eighty Six : Lijiang

Our hotel is impressively located high up on the cusp of the new and old towns, a short, energetic walk from Lion Hill, which is considered the highest point in Lijiang. This is not strictly correct, as on the top of the hill stands a pagoda over 100 feet high, which claims to be the tallest wooden building in China. It's not old and has been put up to pull in the tourists, who, like us, feel duty-bound to walk up every one of the steps that climb steeply through five spacious floors. The view you expect to be rewarded with is quite disappointing, as someone's planted a girdle of conifers near the base of the pagoda that successfully masks much of the ink-black tiled rooftops of old Lijiang.

The designers have attempted to decorate the interior of the pagoda in local style, which includes several symbols in *dongba*, the old language of the Naxi.

Despite the best efforts to introduce a pan-Chinese orthodoxy during Mao's years, a rich and diverse cultural life has survived in the mountains of Yunnan. The Dongba, a Naxi word meaning not just 'the scriptures' but those who interpret them, are important guardians of the old traditions. They have their own cultural centre in Lijiang, where the 30 of them still alive work on translation of the old Naxi texts. Part shaman, part priest, the Dongbas also perform ceremonies and rituals based on the Bon religion, which pre-dated Buddhism in Tibet. In *Forgotten Kingdom* Peter Goullart describes his horrified fascination as he watched Dongbas dancing themselves into a semi-trance to reawaken the spirits of two young lovers who had killed themselves in a suicide pact.

'Just for an instant…we all felt that the lovers had returned… I thought at first the impression was entirely mine: but with a burst of weeping the two families prostrated themselves as one man before the little altar. The guests looked startled. Nothing was seen and the impression was gone in a flash. But they had been there and everyone knew it.'

Later in the day, we witness a Dongba at work a few miles outside Lijiang. When the last light of day has faded on the ice turrets of the Jade Dragon Snow Mountain behind him, he begins the ceremony. He's a sprightly old man, who I'm alarmed to find is only five years older than me, dressed in a long, mandarin-style, red robe and embroidered waistcoat with an amulet hanging from a cord around his neck. Wound round his head is a red cap with a headdress of five pointed leaves. He holds a drum in one hand and cymbals in the other, and, after striking the drum, he sets about purifying the area where the ceremony is to take place, which is unclean because of our presence here. With a handful of burning branches he moves around the courtyard and then the garden, chanting and passing the smoking branches over arches, walls and, finally, over all our equipment. Then, with ever-accelerating speed and more frenetic chanting, he races to the door of the building, runs out and with shouted imprecations hurls the branches away, casting out all the bad spirits he's collected from within the compound.

I must admit that there is an extra element of confusion, which is nothing to do with the Dongba, for at precisely the same time that devils are being cast out in Yunnan, England are contesting the Rugby Union World Cup Final in Sydney. While working flat out to set up equipment, change film, filters and lights when necessary, Peter has his mobile phone on and progress of the game is being texted through to him from a pub in England.

Meanwhile, we turn our attention to the Dongba's young assistants, who are preparing to sacrifice two chickens.

The birds have their legs trussed and, after being anointed with water, their necks are cut and the blood drained into a bowl.

'14-5, England,' hisses Pete.

The chickens are dangled over the fire and the air fills with the smell of scorched feathers. The two assistants, one boy and one girl, seem uncertain what to do next and they lay down the blackened chickens and wait for the Dongba to help them out. Their confusion is hardly surprising. Tradition dictates that ancient scriptures are only communicated to males, and then not until the Dongba who communicates them is over 75 years old. So the chicken's fate is currently in the hands of a girl who can't know what to do, and a boy who won't know what to do for another ten years.

The ceremony now shifts inside to a room with a fire and a candle-lit altar. As he makes various moves, the Dongba peers closely at an old book of pictographic texts, rather like someone following the instructions on a new video.

At one point he lays the book down and fumbles around. We watch in some suspense, as he reaches deep into his robes, only to produce a cigarette, which he lights up before carrying on reading.

For what seems like an interminable time he moves around the fire, passing chickens over the flame, before indicating to his assistants to fetch him a big black cooking bowl. The bowl is filled with water and the hapless, still-feathered chickens (which some of us think are not absolutely dead) are dropped in and imprecations muttered. At the edge of the firelight, behind the crouching Dongba, I can see Peter, face pale and eyes round as saucers.

As we come to the end of a roll of film he has time to get the news out.

'14-all! Extra time.'

What follows, as events in Lijiang and Sydney become inextricably entwined, are 20 of the more bizarre minutes of my life. Two rituals on continents thousands of miles from each other are approaching their climax, and as the Dongba becomes more agitated, Peter veers between ecstasy and anguish.

'17-14!'

It must be all over.

'17-17!'

It clearly isn't.

All I know is that the night air has turned very cold and the shaman, lit by a flickering firelight, is whirling around like a madman, eyes staring, sword in one hand and finger-cymbals in the other, as the news comes through.

'20-17! Whistle's gone!'

Our reactions have necessarily had to be whispered, like partisans in an occupied country, but now it's impossible not to let out a whoop of joy.

The Dongba, finishing his dance, leaps in the air with the athleticism of a much younger man and comes to a standstill, acknowledging our appreciation with a broad smile.

Intense as the ceremony has been (for many reasons), I don't think any of us felt the sensation of the supernatural presence that Peter Goullart had described so vividly. But a week or so after we got back, Basil called me with his usual report on the photos he'd taken. No problems, except for all those taken with a flash at the Dongba's ceremony. Despite his camera being fully charged up, all the prints came back over-exposed and burnt out. It has happened to him once before, when photographing the Ghost Festival in Penang. All his shots were fine except those taken when the shaman entered a trance.

What's more, he knows colleagues who've experienced the same thing. Everything seems to point to some powerful force or energy current being emitted on the same frequency as the strobe of the flashlight.

Back in Lijiang, Nina, our hardworking Chinese assistant, orders the meal tonight. Something a bit different she says. I'm not so sure. One of the dishes, a chicken stew, has a claw rising from the middle of it.

Day Eighty Seven : Lijiang to Kunming

Goodbye to the friendly Qian Xue Lou Hotel, though I never found out what its name means. In Lijiang New Town, by contrast, English signs are quite prevalent. So it's farewell to the Finance Hotel, the Education Hotel, the Greatness Drugstore, the Belief Supermarket and a menswear store called 'Clench'. All slip away behind us as we head to the new highway that will convey us smoothly to the new airport.

The casualties of this rush to modernize are the remnants of old Lijiang. Those traditional wood and mud-brick houses that have the misfortune to lie outside UNESCO's protection can be seen like fish left behind by the tide, circled by the diggers and graders, waiting to be swept away.

Kunming, with a population just short of 4 million, is the biggest city we've seen since leaving Lahore. Armies of bicycles, traffic lights with numerical count-downs and paradoxical reminders every-where that this burgeoning expanse of glass and concrete is a garden city, boasting one of the most generous climates in China.

For us, the City of Eternal Spring is another welcome step down from the high plateau. At a little over 6000 feet (1830 m), it's half as high as Lhasa and a third the height of Everest Base Camp. The air is positively balmy and a premature holiday mood grips us all as we put some distance between ourselves and the high mountains.

We lunch at a restaurant that serves Kunming's speciality, Across the Bridge Noodles. The story behind the name is both romantic and utilitarian. A scholar seeking peace and quiet retires to a cottage on an island. His wife brings him his food, but the bridge is so long it's cold by the time she gets across. She discovers one day that by pouring a layer of oil on top of the broth it would stay hot. So she poured on the oil, took the broth over the bridge, put in the various cuts of meat when she got there and a new dish was born. (I think the story says a lot about the importance of food to the Chinese. In England he'd have been lucky to get a sandwich.)

So we have set in front of us a bowl of very hot soup flavoured with chicken stock, duck and spare ribs and arrayed round it, with no regard for the size of the table, a multitude of side dishes includ-ing raw chicken and Yunnan ham, liver, fish, pork, spinach, onions and all sorts of other vegetables as well as chilli pepper to add to the fun.

It's a huge but quite delicate meal, with impeccably fresh ingredi-ents.

Kunming is not only a floral showplace, still basking in the glow of having hosted Expo '99 Flower and Plant Festival, but the capital of a province with more ethnic minorities than any other. Gardens and ethnic diversity meet in a landscaped, 90-hectare site on the shores of Lake Dian, south of the city. Called the Yunnan Nationali-ties Villages, in essence it's an ethnic minorities theme park.

I'm taken round on a white golf buggy by an obliging, if a little brisk guide called Ms Mi, who is herself in minority national costume.

Rather like feeding times at the zoo, there is a strict schedule of which minority is 'performing' when, and we're swiftly off to the Dai village, where, in front of a tall, white, instant pagoda, men and women dance, the women conspicuous by dainty scarlet straps over their red schoolgirl shoes. Along with light blue and orange tunics they look rather odd, like a tribe of air hostesses. Then we're off to the Tibetans, who dance in front of an impressive reproduction of the Jokhang in Lhasa, incongruously set against a backdrop of banana trees and bougainvillea. A small crowd, watching without any apparent engagement, becomes even smaller as the show goes on, leaving only ourselves and an old sick man in a wheelchair, who stares mutely ahead, his grandson perched on his lap.

If it's four o'clock it must be the performing elephants, and soon Ms Mi, who is Yi, and me are at the back of a somewhat larger crowd, watching a group of rather dry elephants being led into position in a concreted performance area.

'Are elephants a minority in China?' I ask Ms Mi.

She looks at me with vague irritation.

'I'm sorry?'

'I wondered if elephants were a minority in China.'

She looks deeply concerned, more, I think, for my sanity, than anything else. After appearing to consider the question for a polite amount of time, she frowns and shakes her head.

The attempt to make elephants look cute by pumping disco music from the loudspeakers and then tugging at their legs is a most depressing spectacle and the jokey compere seems thoroughly unpleasant. Maybe I'm just not getting the jokes, so I ask Basil, who confirms that he is indeed thoroughly unpleasant.

The weather's clouded over and the vast area of the park is almost empty, but the shows must go on and at five o'clock we're at the Mosuo stand. Their 'event' takes place in a smaller version of Namu's hotel, with log walls and lots of cowboy hats and line dancing. The audience walk in and walk out, talk and photograph each other as if the performers were invisible. There seems not the slightest respect, or, indeed, enthusiasm for the fact these are live performers.

This whole Yunnan Nationalities park has been like a weird, dreamlike playback of many of the places and the people we've met these past few weeks, and has the effect of making me feel enormously fortunate to have met our minorities in the wild, as it were.

Day Eighty Eight : Kunming

The first English-language newspapers since we left Kathmandu. It's not often I read the papers these days and feel cheered up, but *The China Daily*'s news of the first full ceasefire in Kashmir for 14 years is heartening. Kashmir was the most traumatized of all the areas we've been through on the Himalayan journey and its problems seemed insoluble. Now, President Musharraf has ordered a ceasefire along the Line of Control and there is a suggestion that he will allow talks to go ahead on the future of Kashmir without prior conditions. Previously, the Pakistan government has regarded a plebiscite in Kashmir as a *sine qua non* of any talks.

The Bank Hotel in Kunming is one of exceptional comfort but in the short time I've been here I've had to call someone to fix both the heating and the lights. Now I find that my bathroom scales don't function. This is not, I realize, a big deal, but we're paying for this little bit of luxury so we might as well get it right. I ring for assistance and have a not altogether satisfactory conversation with someone who seems unfamiliar with the word 'scales', but happier with 'bathroom'.

Within less than a minute the doorbell goes. Standing there is a hefty girl with a plastic cap on, flanked by two men in protective overalls, one holding a red rubber plunger and the other an enormous wrench. They stand there motionless for a moment, like figures on a coat of arms. I have the distinct feeling they would rather not be here.

It's quite a squeeze with all four of us in the bathroom, and, as we shuffle round, the man with the plunger gestures nervously towards the toilet bowl. When I shake my head and hand them the defective scales, their manner changes completely and, with lavatory-unclogging off the menu, we are one happy family, nodding and smiling and joking.

Taps are turned on and off as if to demonstrate something, but it's only after they've gone that I notice a small sign on the side of the shower apologizing for problems with the water supply.

'Please bare with us,' it reads.

Catch up with my notes, then walk into the central square of Kunming. The old city has been razed but the tall, arched West Gate has been rebuilt. This was once the Chinese end of one of the most famous highways in the world. Marco Polo knew it as the Southern Silk Road, an extension of the trade route that connected Asia with Europe, which we've touched on in several places on our journey. In the Second World War it was reopened as the Burma Road, a supply line that cost thousands of lives to build and extended through the appallingly difficult country of the eastern Himalaya to come out in Assam in north India.

Little is made now of its wartime connotations, but 100 yards away is the Hump Bar. The Hump in this case refers to the name given to the 500 miles of Himalaya between here and India by the AVG, American Volunteer Group, known as the Flying Tigers, who flew perilous supply flights across this towering mountain wilderness from 1941 until the end of the war. Six hundred and seven planes were lost crossing the Hump.

The walls of this comfortable, congenial old bar are covered in memorabilia of the period: maps and posters and black and white photos of the Flying Tigers standing beside planes with bared teeth painted on their sides.

The next port of call on our journey will be over the other side of the Himalaya, where the planes landed and the Burma Road broke out of the jungle.

Two last good memories of China, both meals. A lunch of fish in lemon grass, asparagus, chicken and delectable pork cooked beneath a vegetable crust, and a last evening thank you to our long-suffering Chinese fixers, minders and helpers in a chic restaurant, with photos of the old Kunming railway on the walls.

So I'm very happy tonight, and only wish John Pritchard were here to share our enormous sense of relief at having, in not much more than a month, crossed the hardest terrain we've ever travelled.

Nagaland
and Assam

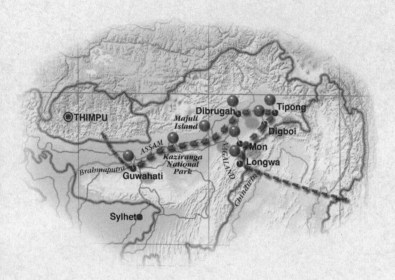

Day Ninety : Longwa

In the remote hill village of Longwa I can stand with one leg in India and the other in Myanmar, or Burma, as it used to be known. (I like the word Burma and take heart from the fact that Myanmar's national anthem remains 'Gba mjay Bma' – 'We Shall Love Burma for Ever'.) Longwa, a collection of palm-thatched huts, a tin-roofed church and a huge satellite dish, isn't marked on any maps I have. It's at the end of the line, on the very edge of Indian administration.

It's also the home of the largest building made entirely from vegetation that I think I've ever seen. The chief's hut, or in this case, mega-hut, is some 200 feet long and covered with a striking roof of palm leaves that sweeps down from an apex of 50 feet or more to within 3 feet of the ground.

The hut occupies the highest point of a 4700-foot (1430 m) ridge, on either side of which the land falls away in a series of crinkly valleys. Along the top runs the India-Myanmar border. In fact, it slices right down the middle of the chief's hut, so he can walk between the two countries without ever leaving home.

Throughout the Himalaya, in Kashmir, on the North-West Frontier, in Tibet and Nepal, we've encountered a tension between the hill people, determined to preserve their customs and traditions, and the plains people wanting to build nations and impose control and conformity. It's no different here. There are a dozen different Naga tribes in these hills, who until very recently fought each other and themselves, took heads as trophies and were generally left alone. From the middle of the 19th century, the British took an interest, but of an avuncular sort, never trying to subdue them but keeping them as a loose but friendly tribal area, which they called Nagaland. They were followed by American missionaries, who tried to persuade them to love God, grow crops and stop fighting.

When India was granted independence, the Nagas were not happy. Assimilation and domination by their Assamese lowland neighbours was seen as infinitely worse than staying with the British, and they made things difficult for India, boycotting general elections and fighting a fierce independence war against central government right up until the 1990s.

In January 2003, after 40 years of bloodshed, the NSCN, National Socialist Council of Nagaland, met in Delhi and announced that the war was over. Others are not so sure. They claim that the dream of an independent Nagaland will never go away.

The problem is that the Naga tribes remain essentially a trans-border people who don't fit neatly into any of the boxes that the politicians have created for them. This may vex central government but it also means I can stand astride this particular frontier without fear of being mined, electrocuted or shot.

The people of Longwa are Konyak Nagas, the most numerous of 16 sub-tribes. They used to be known as the Naked Nagas, the title of a book by an Austrian anthropologist who worked here in the 1930s, some of whose observations, such as 'Virginity wins no halo in the Naga heaven', suggest reasons for his fascination with them.

Today, things are very different. Such has been the success of the American Baptist Church that 99 per cent of the Naga have been converted to Christianity. Nakedness is a thing of the past, as is the once common custom of head-hunting. (Though a recent *National Geographic* article reported evidence of active head-hunters as recently as 1991.)

We have come here with Shingwong, whose official title is Extra Assistant to the Deputy District Commissioner. He's a soft-spoken Konyak, with square, grave features, more Tibetan than Indian. He wears a Western jacket and trousers. Tomorrow there will be a big spring festival here and the guest of honour will be the local MP.

The MP has asked to meet us and after our meal tonight Shingwong takes us to see him, in a small, dark barn, with a hard earth floor. By the looks of things the MP's had a few. His eyes are unfocussed and his mouth seems to have collapsed at one side, making him look not only unattractive, but dangerous.

Squatting on stools around him and lit only by flickering firelight is gathered a cross-section of mountain people, who seem to be from a completely different world. Most have red shawls thrown over bare shoulders and round their waists are aprons, held in place by belts made of bamboo cane. Some have bones in their hair and through their ears and small bronze skulls hanging from a necklace. These represent the heads that man has taken.

They grin vaguely at us as our purpose is explained.
'BBC. Journey round the Himalaya.'
But none of it's going in. They're all completely rat-arsed.

Day Ninety One : Longwa

The concrete walls of our rooms in the government guesthouse
seem to attract and trap the cold. I get up early. Outside, the mist lies
in the valleys, as thick as fresh snow. I walk around the chief's hut, in
and out of India, measuring its circumference as 250 yards. I'm full
of admiration that something on this scale is built entirely from
leaf, stalk, bark, branch and trunk. Shingwong tells me the whole
village helps in the construction of these longhouses.

A little further along the ridge, a cluster of tall stones rises from a
grassy mound. It looks like a graveyard but is more of a trophy
room. These stones represent the number of heads brought into the
village.

A crudely dug, stone-stepped pathway runs down from the top
of the ridge to a wide flat area with the white cross of a newly built
church (by far the biggest building in Longwa) looming over the
festival site. Stalls have been set out round the side of it, selling
antique gongs, rattan umbrellas, wooden figurines as well as essentials like clothes, cooking pots and local medicines such as cinnamon sticks for toothache. Food ranges from lemon grass and betel
leaves to porcupine, bred for eating. Its strong, tangy, venison-like
flavour is considered a delicacy round here, and the quills are cut up
and made into necklaces.

In fashion, the generational difference is marked. The young
favour saris, jeans and T-shirts but the grannies and grandfathers
still go barefoot, their thin, spindly legs often pocked with sores and
unhealed grazes.

One very senior citizen leans proudly on an old flintlock rifle.
Bamboo sticks have worn long, distended holes in his earlobes. He
has skull medallions round his neck and is clearly very proud of his
hunting past. He obligingly confirms that he has taken five heads.

His face, like those of many of the older generation, has what
looks like a black stain running across it. On closer examination I
see these are tattoos and not black but deep indigo, made of a

number of very fine pin-prick marks. He pulls aside his shawl to show me that the tattoos extend across his chest and stomach and round onto his back. The old man knows Shingwong. He used to help his father, a surveyor working for the British on the first maps of Nagaland. He says he was ten years old when he first saw an Englishman. At first he had been frightened to go near them, they were so white he assumed they had no blood.

I ask if this old man with the skulls round his neck and headdress of boar's teeth and hornbill feathers is now a Christian and he nods emphatically.

Shingwong thinks that conversion was made easier among the Nagas because their belief system was always based around one invisible god, one creator, which made the transition to Christianity seem less drastic.

Despite the grip of the Baptist church, the Konyak culture is still taught in schools and pre-Christian dances form the highlight of today's festival.

Women process down from the ridge, four abreast, holding hands and wearing coral bead necklaces, headdresses, blue or black tunics and skirts with striped hoops. They form wide circles and move round infinitely slowly, chanting almost sotto voce. The slow, dirge-like pace is dictated by purely practical considerations. The jewellery of each dancer weighs 10 to 25 lb (5 to 10 kilos) alone.

The men then perform a war dance, which recreates the story of a head-hunting party. They appear, ironically enough, from behind the Baptist church, armed with machetes in one hand and rifles or spears decorated with goats' fur in the other. On their heads are bear-skin caps and hornbill feathers, round their waists aprons and cane belts, squeezed tight to help puff out their chests, and on their feet incongruous black leather shoes of the sort you might wear to the office. On their backs are baskets in which to bring the heads home.

There follows a dramatic enactment of a raid on another village. Children cover their ears as the rifles are discharged, and the men end up with a celebratory python dance, in which their gyrations cause the sun to catch the glaze of their feathers and thus recreate the sinuous movement of the snake.

In the afternoon the arena is cleared and football posts are put up for a game between Longwa and Khemoi, a village in Myanmar. As there are no official games between the two countries, this is the closest there is to an India v Myanmar international. Despite a hard-fought first half, the Blues of India pip the Reds of Myanmar 8-2 and, to add insult to injury, the defeated team from Khemoi has a two and a half-hour walk home.

In the evening I have an opportunity to see inside the chief's house. He's agreed to be interviewed, and, armed with a bottle of rum as a present, I clamber through an entrance at one end. It is a cavernous space inside, like being in the upturned hull of some great ship. As there is hardly any natural light coming in, the soaring height of the roof is lost in gloom. I find myself in a long chamber, empty save for two huge, hollowed-out tree trunks, which Shing-wong says are war-canoes, and an aircraft seat, which they say came from a bomber shot down in the war. The Nagas are proud of the fact that they saved nine Allied airmen.

In the heart of the house, the chief sits at the centre of a semicir-cle of elders, an impressive number of brass heads hanging on their chests. A fire blazes. Above it hang various trophies, animal skulls and horns, and a number of ceremonial gongs.

The chief doesn't look like a man who needs another bottle of rum at the moment. As I hand it over, his wide, bloodshot eyes meet mine for a moment, and I feel like someone who's arrived very late at a party.

He has been the Ang, as they call the local headman here, for 25 years. It is an hereditary title, and will pass to his son, provided that son is by the daughter of a fellow Ang, and not by one of the chief's concubines. I ask how many concubines he has. Ten, comes the answer, after a longish pause for calculation.

He will probably be the last Ang for whom head-hunting was a condition of office. He has taken five heads, he claims. He is now a Christian and was baptized, by total immersion, in a nearby stream. When he was young, he says, the village was ruled by fear; now it's ruled by the fear of God.

I still can't get used to hearing such Sunday School sentiments from a group of people who, with their bleary eyes, boar-tusk head-dresses and monkey-fur decorations, look like every missionary's idea of the unapologetic heathen.

Tonight a huge thunderstorm breaks over Longwa. Torrential rain rakes the tin roof like machine-gun fire and a mighty rushing wind sets doors banging, dogs howling and curtains blowing. Good weather to lie in bed to.

Day Ninety Two: Longwa to Digboi

After the rains, the dirt road out of Longwa is heavy-going. We're in reconditioned Second World War jeeps. Comfort is sacrificed for nimbleness and they're alarming but agile on the slippery stuff. Our driver puts on a dusty cassette of Beatles hits. 'Help!' could have been written for this trip.

Shingwong's daughter, Pang Nou, shares the car with me. She's just completed a Master's degree in English Literature at Delhi. Her theses were on Plato's Concept of Love and the Book of Job. She tells me that, though in Delhi she felt her homeland seemed unbelievably far away, the Indian government is taking Nagaland very seriously. The roads are free, they pay no tax and the benign attitude to local culture is all part of the greater worry that Nagaland might fall into the clutches of the hated enemy on the other side of the border. Not Myanmar, but China.

After some 40 miles, the town of Mon appears like the new Jerusalem on a hill ahead of us, its Baptist church perhaps the largest and longest of the great white mini-cathedrals that rise above the palm and thatched terraces of the Naga Hills.

Our jeep, which has skated through the mud so athletically up to now, slithers to a halt at the last quagmire and we take a while to get started again. Our driver, chewing on the betel with grim determination, does his best to make up time, narrowly avoiding an 'After Whiskey Driving Risky' sign, but by the time we reach the church, the service we've come to film has long begun.

The Konyak Baptist Church is as big as an aircraft hangar, and every seat in the gallery and the body of the church is taken. Shingwong estimates there are 2500 worshippers here. The church was built in 1952 and the services are invariably packed.

The preacher is a Konyak who has been working as a Baptist missionary in Bhutan for the last nine years. In that time he's made fewer than 100 converts, which, I must say, makes me want to go to Bhutan right away. He speaks at great length on this and related matters, then everyone stands to sing 'Onward Christian Soldiers' in

Konyak, after which the congregation, largely passive up till now, is exhorted by the pastor to speak their minds and give thanks to the Lord.

A sedate, middle-aged lady next to me is transformed into a wailing ecstatic. As the prayers flow, her voice rises to a near scream. Stretching out her arm, she begins to rub her hand up and down my back.

'Hallelujah, Praise the Lord!' she screams.

The pressure from her hand increases and it moves up to my head, ruffling my hair one way and then the other.

'Halle-LU-JAH,' she crescendoes, leaping to her feet, arms flung wide above me, eyes tight shut.

'PRAISE...THE...LORD!'

Day Ninety Three : Digboi, Assam

Another night in a government guesthouse, this time on the plains of Northeastern Assam, a fertile salient pushing up into the tail of the Himalaya. The tropical lushness of these gently rolling hills is the work of the heavy monsoon rains that are channelled up the Brahmaputra valley. Overflowing flower beds almost reach up to the door and the guesthouse boasts the only 18-hole golf course in Assam.

The money in Digboi comes from oil, discovered here in 1889 and commemorated at the Digboi Centenary Museum of Oil, at which it is obligatory to remove your shoes before entering.

Also commemorated a few miles northeast of Digboi is the Indian end of the wartime Burma Road. Having so recently stood at the Chinese end, in Kunming, I'm interested to see what's left here.

There is very little. A strip of the old tarmac, which soon gets lost in the undergrowth, is all that remains of the road itself, and beside it is a patch of garden, complete with concrete furniture, that's called the Stilwell Information Park. The main feature of this display is a 20-foot-high hoarding with a painted map of a section of the route, named after the American General 'Vinegar Joe' Stilwell, who pushed this supply line through.

On top of the map, an unequivocally modern message is delivered. 'Rejuvenate our Life Line, Revitalize our Relationship, Reach out Beyond the Borders,' it reads. A reminder that if you look at the geography of Assam you will see that its border with the rest of India is only a few miles wide, but its borders with China, Tibet, Burma, Bangladesh and Thailand run for 3700 miles (5900 km), and Beijing is as close to Assam as Delhi. But nothing much seems to be happening out to the east today. For now, it looks pretty much as if everything stops here.

An hour's drive from the oil town of Digboi there is a coal mine. This isn't itself surprising, given this fossil-rich little corner of India, but Tipong Mine is a singular place indeed. A red-brick Nottinghamshire pit village in the middle of a jungle.

It's a still morning and shreds of mist have not yet dispersed. A smell of sulphur hangs in the air and the jungle gently steams. Miners are arriving on Hercules and Hero bicycles for the first shift of the day. I join a group of them on a narrow, cable bridge, which bounces like a trampoline as we cross. Below is a 40-foot drop into a sluggish river, transformed from a mountain stream into an industrial sump, stained with oil streaks and oxides.

The men have lamps and hard hats but the rest of their clothes and equipment are flimsy. Sandals, flip-flops, old gym shoes, vests and torn trousers are the order of the day. Before going underground they gather round a brazier made from pipes and old railway parts. There seems no sense of urgency.

A priest in dhoti and thick, knitted sweater moves among them, offering a plate of sweets and a prayer. He gives me a *tika* mark on my forehead. I want to tell him that the last one I had was put on by the King of Nepal, but he'd only think I was mad.

The protection of the gods is taken very seriously. Built above one of the mine entrances is a small, pink temple to the goddess Kali (alias Parvati, Sati, Uma and Durga), and as she is the consort of Siva the destroyer, she must be constantly propitiated. When the motley group of miners does eventually enter the mine shaft, I notice each one first touch the tunnel entrance, then his forehead and then his heart.

No sooner have they gone down than a greasy cable stiffens and begins to turn. Out of a second tunnel emerges a line of wagons filled with slack. As they reach the top of a low rise they're grabbed and pushed on by a work gang largely composed of elderly women in grimy saris. These ladies roll the narrow, coffin-like wagons down a short slope and assemble them into a train. When enough are

ready they are collected by a very old saddle-tank steam engine
called 'David', built in Lancashire in 1864. Its boiler is now so caked
and encrusted with deposits that it resembles a moving fossil.

Our host, Mr Das from Coal India Ltd, won't allow us to film any
of this until we have an armed police escort, and they haven't turned
up yet.

We suggest doing a discreet wide shot while we're waiting but Mr
Das shakes his head.

'This is a very disturbed place.'

He smiles tolerantly, like a teacher dealing with hyperactive
pupils.

'It is our headache to look after you.'

He seems a decent man, around 40, a Bengali, with intense dark
eyes, a thick moustache, brown bobble hat, a windcheater with
'Herod Active' written across it and an uncle who's an accountant in
Guildford.

He invites us to his office. It's a low, brick building, painted pistachio green, inside and out. There is a concrete floor and a board on
the wall with three columns marked 'Production Totals', 'Targets',
'Achievements'. A one-bar electric fire glows and two or three of his
colleagues are introduced and sit at the table with us. Our two
armed guards, thin men wrapped in headscarves, walk by outside
the window.

Sidestepping any further questions about security with a brisk
'there is some insurgency', Mr Das clambers onto the safer ground
of statistics. In quick succession, I learn that India is the fourth
largest producer of coal in the world (after the USA, Russia and Australia) but the biggest employer (600,000 people), that Tipong produces a particularly valuable high calorie coal, that they have had no
fatal injuries of any kind since 1994, when nine were killed after an
electrician tried to mend an electrical motor without turning the
current off, that, instead of shafts and lifts, the miners here walk to
work down inclined passageways that reach 1150 feet (350 m) below
the surface. The only shadow over Tipong is that they only have
technology to bring out 40 per cent of the coal deposits. The rest
they have to leave in the ground.

What really animates him is an obvious and glowing pride in his
labour relations. Tipong has a cosmopolitan work force, from
South India, Nepal, Orissa, Bihar, comprising Muslims, Christians

and Hindus, but everyone looks after everyone else and they provide schools and communal activities for everyone equally. Women who are widows of company employees are offered surface jobs.

David's wheezy whistle announces that the 140-year-old tank engine is coupled up and ready to leave for the depot two miles down the line. I'm privileged to ride the footplate as we bowl gamely down the hill past lineside exhortations like 'All Time is Safety Time' and 'There is no Substitute for Hard Work and Sincerity'.

We cross the river on a girder bridge with elegantly functional red-brick piers bearing a construction date of 1923. The line levels out. Bicycles overtake us easily. Goats and chickens stroll by. The fireman doesn't so much toss coal into the boiler but places it there by hand, positioning each piece carefully before ramming it home with a metal rod. Once away from the cleared area of the mine, the jungle closes in and David has his work cut out to push us past over-hanging branches and bushes. It's an enchanting run, a blend of *Thomas the Tank Engine* and *The Jungle Book*.

After lunch at the Tipong Mine Guest House, a once elegant, plantation-style building, now surrounded on all sides by coal heaps, Mr Das takes us up onto one of the hills overlooking the river to hear a selection of Safety Songs, specially written for Tipong. A five-man choir, accompanied by a harmonium and a tabla, a pain of small hand-drums is set up in the garden of a red-brick terraced house overlooking a hillside of mango, pineapple, jackfruit, guava, betel and banana trees. Across the river a slowly moving plume of white smoke rises above the trees, tracing the progress of David back up the valley again. Against this background of an industrial Arcadia, Hahmid Rachmar and his group, all sweatered up like a glee club, perform the safety song they've written themselves. It's a catchy song, beautifully performed, and in the abundant goodwill after-wards Mr Das shyly reveals that he's learning the violin at home.

'Does your wife mind?' I joke.

His brow furrows. 'No, she is very helpful.'

I leave Tipong with some doubts as to whether there really is a mine here at all and thoughts that this grubby Garden of Eden might simply be kept going by Mr Das and his friends so that they can learn music and write hit songs.

The last thing I do is ask him to write down the words of the catchy Safety Song.

I try them at the guesthouse, in the bath.

'Safety First, Safety First

In every step of work, be it the rule,

It is for us to remain awake all the time, There's danger in every move.

If we obey the rules

There will be no sorrow for us,

Safety First, Safety First.'

Perhaps we should adopt it as the crew's anthem. On second thoughts, it's too late now.

Day Ninety Four : Digboi to Dibrugah

A pack of pye-dogs circles the entrance to Digboi station, backing away with wary reluctance at the approach of my cycle-rickshaw. I buy a ticket for Dibrugah, 52 miles (80 km) down the line, for 18 rupees, about 25 pence. I notice that a ticket on the sleeper service to Delhi, over 1000 miles (1600 km) away, would set me back £8.

That the railway extends here at all has everything to do with oil, tea and coal and very little to do with passengers. The wooden bench seats are functional rather than comfortable and progress is slow and punctuated every few hundred yards by a blast of the engine's horn to clear the railway line of all those who use it as a highway, meeting place, or just for grazing.

Fortunately, I have some good companions. Sitting opposite me are two women, one tall and slim with classic English features, the other a short, stout, bespectacled Indian lady whose face wears an expression of such serene good nature that it's impossible not to want to talk to her. The reason why they're travelling together is a remarkable story that unfolds as the train shrieks its way westwards.

Anne, the older of the two, is the daughter of an illicit relationship between an English tea-planter and one of the women from 'the lines' (i.e. a tea picker). Such liaisons were strictly forbidden and Anne's father could never publicly acknowledge his child. He went off to the Second World War and died in Singapore in 1942. Anne's mother, poor, uneducated and illiterate, had no idea how to find information about him. She didn't even know how he spelt his name.

Anne, neither English nor Indian, never really fitted in with the tea-planters, who, embarrassed at such situations, were unapproachable and unhelpful. Enquiries about her father were stonewalled.

Anne was sent to a convent school and later met and fell in love with an Indian fighter pilot, who wrote to her every day, and even once dropped a letter to her from his plane. They had a daughter together, but he was a married man and, in a mirror image of her mother's situation, they kept their relationship secret. He eventually returned to his wife. Anne got a job as a secretary in a tea company, where she saw a copy of the London *Daily Telegraph* in her office. She noted down the name of their defence correspondent and, on a whim, wrote and asked him how she might find out about a tea-planter called Stuart who went missing in 1942.

Thanks to his help, she eventually learnt her father's name, one of many on the wall of a mass grave in Singapore. Armed with this lead, and with some help from one of the tea company's directors, she finally made contact with her father's family in England, 47 years after his death. His sister Mary was still alive and asked to meet Anne. Mary's granddaughter Sarah is the girl travelling with Anne today.

The two women derive so much pleasure from each other's company, that one can only wonder what things might have been like if they'd known of each other's existence years earlier.

It seems years have passed since leaving Digboi when the train finally pulls into Tinsoukia, less than 30 miles down the track. As we approach Tinsoukia station the view on both sides is of decommissioned steam locomotives, row upon row of them in overgrown sidings. Some lie on their sides, some are hung around with vines and creeper and, as there seems to have been no attempt to strip them down, they remain intact, as if a spell had been put on them.

We move out of Tinsoukia at a pace that would make a snail seem nippy. Seeing our impatience, a jolly, bespectacled lady in a gold-trimmed sari smiles broadly across at us.

'This is a train for people who have no work.'

We talk about local things. She's a professor at Dibrugah University and has strong views on the need for India to look east. She is a firm believer in an economic development initiative, ungracefully mnemonicized as BIMSTEC, to encourage co-operation between

Bangladesh, India, Myanmar, Singapore, Thailand and China. A recent meeting, however, was hobbled by the Indian government refusing visas to the Chinese delegation until the night before the conference. Understandably, they cancelled.

'The Indians don't really empathize with the Chinese then?' I ask.

'I don't think our mind-set is still yet fully open to Chinese co-operation,' she replies.

I take that as a no.

She agrees with Mr Das the coal-mine manager's point about the cosmopolitan make-up of Assam, but has a different explanation for it. In 1823 a Scotsman called Robert Bruce first noted the com-mercial potential of the wild tea plant and within 20 years it had become a major and highly labour-intensive crop. The Assamese, being partial to opium at the time, were not good at hard labour, so it became necessary to look further afield for the work force, hence the widening of the gene pool in Northeast India.

We stay tonight at a tea plantation house called a *changa*, which is in effect a bungalow on stilts. Beneath the extensive boughs and trailing tentacles of an old rain tree, we sit round a fire and watch a delicately energetic dance performed by girls who look more Thai or Burmese than Indian. Assamese specialities are brought round. Long, rolled rice-cakes called *bithas*, made with molasses and sesame seeds, a grilled root with tomato and aubergine dip, feather-light *pooris*, chicken and fish from the Brahmaputra.

As night falls the handsome house behind us looks like an ocean liner, with its deep well-polished decks and white balustrade. It belongs to a local tea-planter called Manoj Jalan and his wife Vinita. His plantations employ 8000 people, and tomorrow he's going to show me round. On an elephant.

Day Ninety Five : Dibrugah

The first thing I notice about my elephant is that it has no howdah. A howdah is a seat to make riding more comfortable, and I don't have one. So I find myself being unceremoniously thrust up onto the elephant's back and ordered to move forward until I'm tight up behind the mahout, the elephant driver. The elephant's back is nar-rower here and there's less chance of my doing the splits. Once I'm in position, the elephant is given an order and I feel myself rearing skywards as it straightens first the front and then the back legs. I'm now some ten feet off the ground and hanging on for dear life to a thin piece of rope that runs across its shoulder.

Manoj, a carefully turned-out, trim figure with boyish features, is next to me. He's riding his own elephant and doesn't look altogether happy.

My mahout shouts the order 'Agit!' ('Forward!'), one of 20 words of command the elephant has to learn, and this, accompanied, I notice, by a sharp blow to the back of the ear, sets the animal moving slowly ahead. There are three females and three young in our procession. The young elephants are not particularly interested in anything other than getting in the way and practising their trumpeting.

Feeling more secure, I look around. The mahout uses his feet tight up behind the elephant's ear to control direction and, far too often it seems to me, strikes the animal with the blunt end of a machete. Elephants' ears, seen from behind, look surprisingly delicate and vulnerable. Pale, curled at the edges and marked with long purple veins, they're like giant leaves in autumn. I'm surprised, too, how much hair there is on an elephant's hide, short little shoots on the full-grown females, much longer and thicker on the young. The prehensile trunk is always working away; on the lookout for a quick snack, a leaf or two, some shoots to strip and, if possible, an entire bush to uproot.

According to Manoj, the Assamese were the first to harness the natural skills of elephants to help with human activities, and their use became widespread in the logging industry when the railways were being pushed up into the plantations and oilfields. They showed the rest of India how to control and domesticate wild elephants but now, with logging drastically cut for environmental reasons, many of the mahouts and their elephants can no longer find work. A few, like these, are retained to clear bamboo cane or tidy up the tea plantations, but it's a dying art.

Having overcome my fear of falling, I'm enjoying this slow, powerful progress through the undergrowth. I'm hardly aware I'm on a living creature. It's more like being on board ship on a gentle swell.

All of a sudden there is the most enormous blast of sound, not unlike a foghorn at full volume. We've emerged onto a metalled road into the path of a group of men on bicycles. The cyclists are laughing and ringing their bells, the elephants are frightened and the mahouts and Manoj are shouting frantically.

'*Ghat! Pich-oo!*' ('Stop! Go Back!') My driver rains blows down on the back of his animal. It seems only to get her more distressed and she bellows again and starts off up the track at a canter, which for one stomach-tightening moment I think might turn into a full-blooded charge.

The mahout brings her under control, but I've had a glimpse of the power of the beast and I'm not unhappy when, after two hours straddling her back, my elephant kneels once more and I can clamber off.

For a while I think I might never be able to close my legs again.

Among the many pleasures of Mancotta Bungalow is its collection of old books. I pick up a copy of *The Survey of Assam 1825–1828*. This was the first time this part of the world had been mapped and the provenance of the areas covered has a nice personal touch to it. We learn that the details of one large area of Himalayan foothill is 'based on information of a Persian sent by Mr Scott into Bhotan (sic)', and the entire map between Assam and China is 'from information collected by Lieutenant Wilcox'.

A survey of Bengali exploration published in Calcutta in 1998 intrigues me in a different way. The index at the back of this book appears to record every word mentioned. A random glance at the 'R' column lists not only 'Ranpur' but 'reached', 'reasonable', 'rather', and indeed 'random', as well.

Day Ninety Seven : Dibrugah to Majuli Island

After a restorative break, it's time to move on from the world of fresh bed linen every night, a whisky every evening and a copy of the *Assam Tribune* every afternoon. I think they used to call it the colonial life and I can feel myself slipping into it.

The danger is that in faithfully and tastefully recreating the colonial lifestyle you recreate colonial attitudes as well. There is no shortage of labour in India, and this, along with residual effects of the caste system and poor education, results in there being a lot of people happy to wait around and be told what to do. I look forward to my Scotch at sunset but I know that if I pour it myself, jobs might be at stake.

So servility is perpetuated.

The gates are unlocked for us and we leave Mancotta's past behind and drive west. For several miles a vast plain of small, trim bushes, all neatly clipped and standing at a uniform height of about 36 inches stretches away on either side. Tall trees rise from among the bushes to shield them from the full glare of the sun. In this quiet period before the new shoots start to appear women in brightly coloured shawls and scarves move through the glades, grooming and trimming. It must have been a listless time for plantation managers. A time for chota pegs and perhaps a visit to the lines.

These great prairies of tea, still referred to as 'gardens', produce 340,000–390,000 tons (350–400 million kg) a year, half of India's total tea production.

The source of this bountiful fertility lies close to a snow-capped mountain in the arid desert of southwest Tibet. Mount Kailash is considered by Hindus, Buddhists and Jainists as one of the most sacred places on earth, the abode of their fiercest gods, the navel of the world from which life-giving rivers flow. The Indus and the Ganges both rise in its shadow, as does the Yarlung Tsangpo, which flows east through the length of Tibet, before entering the great bend of the Himalaya, plunging through a series of wild, barely accessible gorges and emerging in Assam, flowing due west and with a new name, Brahmaputra, 'Son of Brahma, the Creator'.

It is by now an immense river, with 1000 miles (1600 km) of water behind it, and it endows Assam with a rich alluvial flood plain, 445 miles (712 km) long and an average of 60 miles (96 km) wide.

It sustains not only the tea industry but a rice bowl too, as well as wheat, sugar cane, banana, tobacco, mustard, jute, silk and just about anything you care to put in the ground.

My first sight of the mighty Brahmaputra is from the ferry boat station at Neamati ghat, a few miles from the crowded town of Jorhat.

There is an air of lassitude to the place. A bus is drawn up, waiting to collect disembarking passengers. Dogs chase each other sporadically before curling up on one of several coal heaps. Tarpaulin-covered shacks offer tea and samosas.

The river seems very still and very silent. It's around 500 yards wide, I would guess, but it's difficult to tell, as it fills more than one channel. The land is endlessly flat. Out there all the lines are horizontals, subtle pastel shades fading into distant perspectives. The Brahmaputra is like an inland sea, as magnificent and implacable in its own way as the plateau where it was born.

Somewhere downstream is Majuli, the world's largest river island, and we're here to try and get ourselves aboard one of the embattled ferry boats that are the only means of reaching it.

The bank on which we're waiting will probably be submerged after the monsoon rains swell the river, which might account for the lack of any jetty. When the boat arrives, embarking passengers have to slither down the bank as best they can and cross two wooden beams that serve as a gangplank. The 100-foot-long flat-bottomed boats set no store by elegance. There is a basic cabin below, which is covered by a corrugated aluminium roof. Passengers pack in as best they can. From the anxious shouts and gesticulations you might think this was the first time a ferry had ever docked at Neamati but, as ever, remarkable order comes from the chaos, and by the time we cast off, every late-comer is aboard, as well as several bicycles, one or two motorbikes and a white Ambassador car. The women gather below and a mixture of men in Western and local dress sit, stand, squat and generally make themselves comfortable on the corrugated sheets above.

With a steady chug of diesel, we pull out into the wide brown stream, which, judging from the tree trunks, leaves and clumps of jungle scudding by, is not as lazy as it looked. We pick our way carefully among low sandbanks, some of which are cultivated. Ruddy shelducks sunbathe on the beaches. Cormorants perch on the fishing poles. Colours are soft and vaporous: muted greens, strips of golden sand and a huge haze-blue sky above.

My travelling companion is a well-informed young man called Maan Barua, whose father owns a resort hotel in nearby Kaziranga National Park. He's 20 years old and knows an awful lot more than I ever will. From him I learn the sex of the Brahmaputra, one of only two male rivers in India, and that ruddy shelducks mate for life. He's also promised to show me a river dolphin, if one passes.

After an hour and a half on the water the engine beat slows and the traditional man with a stick (in this case a bamboo pole) prods the shallow mud banks as we approach the island. As soon as the bank is within leaping distance, half the roof-class passengers fling themselves off and race up the hill to the bus. The bus driver, clearly enjoying his moment of power, sounds the horn again and again, prompting more and more people to death-defying leaps.

Majuli Island covers nearly 250 square miles (650 sq km), which, Maan tells me, is half as big as it was 50 years ago. It's been continuously settled for 3000 years, but since the arrival of a saint, Shankara Deva, at the start of the 16th century it has become best known for its religious institutions, a form of monastery called *satras*. These differ from mainstream Hinduism by preaching devotion to only one god, Vishnu, and rejecting the use of icons or images.

The Uttar (meaning 'North') Kamalabari *satra* is in a peaceful rural setting among rice and mustard fields criss-crossed with well-trodden mud paths and dotted with small bonfires. We are required to remove our shoes and socks when we reach its arched gatehouse entrance, with the date of foundation, 1673, inscribed on it. Purity is a very important part of the tradition of the *satras*. The *bhakat*, the community of monks, has taken a vow of purity and if they prepare food or touch someone who is impure they must immediately wash.

In the centre of the monastery complex is an east-facing prayer hall called the Kirtanghar, some 200 feet long and surrounded by vegetable gardens and tropical fruit trees. The living accommodation is set round the perimeter of this intimate site in four residential terraces called *haatis*, which are themselves broken down into two storeys of rooms called *bohas*, lending the *satra* the air of an Oxbridge college marooned in the jungle.

The thing that strikes one most of all is the handsomeness of the monks. All look very healthy and lissom, with pale brown skin and hair worn either close-cropped or in long, lustrous black tresses, tied at the back.

Accompanied by an older monk called Dulal, dressed in a white robe and dhoti, we're shown preparations for a play called *Rasa Lila*, which involves many of the most beautiful boys transforming themselves into beautiful girls. In this particular celibate sect, all the women's parts are danced by men.

The whole play lasts five to six hours and they only perform it once a year, so they are doing an excerpt for us in which Krishna, a dashing romantic incarnation of the god Vishnu, appears to a group of milkmaids, who all fall in love with him.

Inside and outside the *bohas* the young men are rapt in concentration, applying make-up to each other, rubbing white base over leg hair, or in the case of the monk who is to play Krishna, covering himself with a mixture of calamine and indigo, blue being the traditional colour in which Krishna appears.

Dulal, who has spent 35 of his 41 years in the monastery, tells me that some of the young men are sent here by their parents because they can't afford to keep them at home. Families who have experienced pain or disease might send one of their children to the *satra* in the hope of improving the family fortunes. A ten-year-old was being offered for sale in a market in Uttar Pradesh when one of the monks heard about it and brought him here.

By now, some of the young monks are pulling on skirts and blouses and another is, with great concentration, strapping on a pair of small artificial breasts, which he then covers with a bra. Krishna is having trouble coping with two wigs and a crown.

The dance is accompanied by a flute, harmonium, finger cymbals and three drummers, each with a *kohl*, a cylindrical drum only found in Assam, about 20 inches long, made from jackfruit tree stems with leather at either end and carried round the neck and across the chest.

The dance, which involves Krishna, 14 milkmaids and a demon who Krishna fights off with a tree, takes place in the Kirtanghar. It's exquisitely executed, requiring the most concentrated co-ordination, as every tiniest body movement, of arms and legs and hands and feet, is precisely choreographed, and every facial expression has to be exactly in accordance with tradition. Fingers must always be turned up at the ends to resemble the lotus, and when they make their delicate curlicue movements the eyes of the dancer must always follow them, creating the effect of the whole body as a stream in motion. A white butterfly flutters across the room as if to set them an example.

The performance attracts a small audience, and I notice that women spectators who wish to watch these men dressed as women are not allowed inside the prayer hall, but have to watch from behind bars outside.

Day Ninety Eight : Majuli Island

The air is warm and the light soft as I cycle along the high track between the fields. The bike I've been given is enormous, but then the sandy roads of Majuli are full of people riding bicycles much bigger than themselves. Maan is with me and we stop to see flying foxes hanging from the branches of a capacious banyan tree. A well-placed missile lobbed at the tree wakes a few and sends them soaring into the air on wings over three foot wide. The banyan is intertwined with an equally magnificent bo tree, with a geometrically elegant rattan palm somehow squeezed in there too. The rank luxuriance of the island is the result of regular flooding, which probably accounts for the impermanence and adaptability of human settlement. Bridges are light and mainly bamboo, houses are on stilts with grain and hay stores well off the ground. Nothing looks as though it expects to last long.

One of the minority people on the island are the Mishing. There are an estimated 45,000 of them, believed to be the original lowland people, animists, believing in the sun god, Donyi, and the moon god, Polo. They took refuge on the island, where they could practise their unorthodox Hinduism without interference.

It's the custom throughout Indian villages that the men plough and carry, but the women are responsible for the more specialized tasks of cultivation and harvest. In one of the many small ponds left behind by the floodwaters I witness the extraordinary sight of Mishing women catching fish.

About 20 of them, dressed in off-the-shoulder saris, walk through the shallow water, leaning on upturned conical baskets held out in front of them, rather like Zimmer frames. As they move forward, they stamp the baskets up and down to flush the fish out of the mud. Once they have a fish trapped in the bottom of the rattan frame, they pick them out, still wriggling, and drop them down their cleavages. Pausing only to tighten the waist band on their saris, they move on, the odd tail flapping defiantly between their breasts.

The whole process is carried out with much singing, chanting, laughter and general exuberance, which only adds to the strangely erotic quality of this particular harvest.

Day Ninety Nine : Majuli to Kaziranga

At 6.30 in my monastic cell in the *satra*'s guesthouse in Kamalabari town, I'm woken with a cup of 'bed tea'. The tea, milk and sugar have been boiled up together in the Indian fashion. There are no windows in my room but I can tell the sun's up by the pattern cast on my wall from a ventilation grille. A cow moos brusquely, crows screech in the trees nearby.

A bucket of hot water is delivered next and I take it into my dark, stained cubicle of a bathroom, looking round rather hopefully for the giant spider with whom I shared it last night. He seemed a friendly sort. Unable to find him, I wash carefully, nose pursed against the reek of the drains.

I'm at the *satra* by seven. From inside the Kirtanghar comes the sound of ragas being practised, and outside a class of a dozen young boys are being taught the 64 exercise positions needed to learn dancing. They're pretty good at back rolls and walking on their hands but less deft at the *ora* position, which requires them to balance on one leg, with the other straight out, almost doing the splits.

A young monk who has just finished milking the cow is washing himself clean under one of the old handle pumps. There's no running water here.

Dulal has agreed to give me a lesson on the *kohl*. First, he ties a dhoti around me. Dhotis, a variation on the sarong, must be worn when playing. I sit cross-legged facing him on the smooth, mud-floored passage outside his room. The first surprise is the weight of the cigar-shaped drum. When I draw attention to this, Dulal, a man of supreme calm, whose brother is a taxi driver, smiles. He teaches children of seven on that same drum.

Dulal shows me three basic movements. *Tao*, a slap with open palm on the smaller end, *dhei*, the same on the wider side and *khit*, resonating then damping the sound with the fingers.

He nods generously and compliments me on having grasped the basic moves. I wipe a few beads of sweat from the brow and allow myself a moment of smugness, which is swiftly despatched.

'You will need another five years to get it right.'

Hearing that we're leaving today, Jadab Burah, who played a

milkmaid yesterday, and Lila Ram, who played the devil, invite me to have a last tea in the room they share. Jadab is 18 and first came to the monastery when he was nine. His parents live less than a mile away and he still attends the local school and has friends, including girlfriends, outside the *satra*. He came here to learn dancing and is quite sure he'll stay for life. Lila Ram, who has been here for 16 years, is learning *gayan*, the art of cymbal playing.

They are delightful company, but when I leave they have to work out what I've touched in the room, as that object will now be impure and their vows require them to wash thoroughly should they come into contact with it.

All this is done with great ease and much laughter. In most institutions, however benevolent, you feel like an outsider looking in, but the special quality of Uttar Kamalabari is that everyone, from the young boys to the grey-haired older monks, has gone out of their way to include us in the life of the *satra*.

It seems a place of rare and genuine happiness, where the hardest disciplines are artistic rather than religious and the goals are more concerned with fulfilment than denial. I catch myself thinking it's too good to be true, but maybe that just sums up the difference between our world and theirs.

Back on the river, the wide, open reaches of the Brahmaputra are as calming as the monastery. Most of the vast, impermanent mud flats are devoid of humans or livestock. A few other boats pass, including a travelling theatre group in a green barge, noisy and low in the water. Mobile theatre is highly popular in Assam.

Time drifts by. A flock of lapwings from the other side of the Himalaya wheels above us. A solitary vulture turns slowly over the southern bank. Maan takes my binoculars and has a closer look. He is searching for more vultures and their absence confirms his worries over their dramatic decline in numbers, thought to be largely the result of chemical pesticides.

Where we shall be tonight is considered a shining example of how environmental protection can work. Kaziranga, which boasts the disconcerting slogan 'Come. Get Lost', is a 293-square-mile (760 sq km) reserve on the banks of the Brahmaputra. It was the first wildlife sanctuary in India, set up 100 years ago, by the Viceroy, Lord Curzon, after his wife had gone to see the famed horned rhinos of the area and returned without encountering a single one. Since the

Rhino Protection Act of 1913 the horned rhino has returned from the brink of extinction, and Maan tells me there are now 1500 to 1600 of them in the park, 70 per cent of the world's population, protected by 400 staff and 120 anti-poaching camps.

Not everyone sees this as a fairy tale. Serious concerns have been raised that animals matter more than people and that the local population has paid a high price for Kaziranga's 'success'.

We shall see.

Day One Hundred : Kaziranga

We're at the gates to Kaziranga National Park, awaiting the opening ceremonies of the much-publicized 2nd Elephant Festival. There could hardly be a greater contrast with the serenity of Majuli Island. Crowds are gathering on both sides of the road and, occasionally, a policeman will stride into the middle of them, waving his hands and blowing a whistle as if his life depended on it.

A constant blast of truck horns reminds us that the road we're standing beside is the NH 37, Assam's equivalent of the M1. Large signs call this stretch of it the Elephant Corridor, but it takes more than a sign or two to turn truck drivers into conservationists, and the presence of the crowd only seems to encourage them to drive faster.

The rich are here, men in suits and women in gorgeous saris, and the poor, in extended family groups, stand and watch them. A procession of elephants is gathered further up the main road, but nothing can begin until the local big-wigs are here.

Maan and I pass the time talking about Indian politics. He gets vociferously angry about the general level of corruption, but even more worried about the BJP, the right-wing Hindu nationalists currently in power. They're communalist, anti-Muslim and suspicious of ethnic minorities of any kind. A travesty, he thinks, of the principles of tolerance and diversity on which India was founded. He's about to tell me more when hysterical police whistle-blowing announces the arrival of a ministerial convoy accompanied by a jeep with a machine gun mounted on the back. This, it transpires, is only the Minister for Environment and Forests and it's a further hour before incandescent whistle-blowing and ferocious arm-waving narrowly avoid members of the public being mown down by the vehicles bearing Chief Minister of Assam and his party.

Priorities having been duly established, the long-suffering elephants begin to process down the road towards us. I count 41 of them, all colourfully attired in the national colours of red and green and carrying advertising for the Numaligarh Oil Refinery, whose tankers have been scattering us to the sides of the road all morning, and who are, astutely, chief sponsors of the Elephant Festival.

The elephants walk slowly, silently, with expressions of infinite patience. Their mahouts, in freshly pressed brown overalls and matching safari hats, look solemnly ahead. The crowd streams after them along the avenue of rosewood trees that leads through the fields to the arena. Many of them are representing local groups and organizations. They carry their pro-conservation banners aloft, shouting, singing and sidestepping the increasingly generous piles of elephant dung.

Once in the arena, a short speech explains that the motivation behind the elephant festival is to encourage local people to see the elephant as their friend and not something that tramples through their villages, damages their crops and destroys their livelihood. Unfortunately, this is but the first of many speeches on the theme of elephants as our friends, which the elephants and ourselves have to stand and listen to for over an hour in the hot sunshine.

Once the long paeans to biological diversity and ecological integrity are over, the elephants can get on with what they're there for. Playing football. It didn't seem a very bright idea when I first saw it in Kunming and it doesn't seem so here. Elephants are not natural footballers. You might as well get the Arsenal squad to pick up tree trunks with their noses. It's just not their field of expertise. They do their best, of course, but their ball skills are painfully slow and their ponderous movements and the commentator's attempts to present this as the last few seconds of a World Cup Final hint at desperation.

The elephant tug of war, on the other hand, is much more promising. The point here is quite simple – to show how much bigger and stronger elephants are than humans. Not an oft-disputed fact, you might think, but the proof of it is wonderful to watch. No matter how many men rush out of the crowd to grab the rope, and I reckon there were at least 60 clinging on to it at one point, the elephant merely has to walk a couple of steps to have them tumbling after him like the tail of a kite.

Later in the day, when the elephants have been taken away from the arena to be fed and watered, I encounter them in a different and quite unforgettable light. We are allowed close to three elephants and a calf as they trundle down to a muddy creek for their evening ablutions. At first, like all of us, I'm a spectator, impressed by the rapport between the mahouts and their charges, marvelling at the ease with which they persuade these colossal creatures to lie on their sides in the water. This is a rare thing to see, and can only happen if there is absolute trust between elephant and man and an environment with no outside threat.

Then they ask me in among them. At first I'm apprehensive. I have once in my life, in Africa, seen the terrifying power that can be unleashed when an elephant takes a dislike to you, and I approach very warily, stepping gingerly into the ankle-deep mud. As I do so, one of the elephants, a 55-year-old bull called Joiraj, decides to stand up. Like a small island coming to life, he rears up above me, stretching up to his full 14 feet and proceeding to fling water from his trunk over his back.

He's a magnificent animal with a proud set of long, curved tusks and not someone I'd mess with. The keeper, however, has no such qualms.

'*Boit!* (Sit!) *Tere!* (Lie On Side!)' he shouts and within a matter of seconds he has several tons of bull elephant crumpling down into the water and rolling over like a dog waiting to be scratched.

The mahout beckons me forward and indicates where Joiraj most likes to be washed.

So it is that at the age of 60 I find myself rubbing an elephant of 55, behind his ears and particularly at the point where the tusk disappears into the folds of his cheek. His eyes roll towards me, registering languid approval. I'm told that he likes nothing better than to be slapped quite hard on the bridge of his nose. Tentatively at first, then, at the mahout's urging, rather more powerfully, I strike the top of his trunk. But it's only when I give him a really good whack that he appears to enter elephant heaven, rolling his eyes, stretching out his legs and emitting an infinitely appreciative rumble. The sound of a contented elephant is a wonderful thing, and I'm amazed that this battleship-grey hide, and these hard, immemorially ancient flanks can be as sensitive as a cat's chin.

In the evening we're driven into the heart of the park for a barbecue organized by the Minister for Forests at one of the anti-poaching camps.

One of the guests is a fellow Englishman, Mark Shand, who knows about conservation and knows his Himalaya well too. We swap a few stories. He is very keen that we should film a man he's just met who claims he can call rhino.

'Looks a bit like Benny Hill, round glasses, big grin. And he's best after lunch, when he's had a bit to drink.'

Day One Hundred and One : Kaziranga to Guwahati

In the park at first light, a layer of mist draped like gauze across the cotton trees. Maan and I are climbing aboard for an elephant safari, getting on the easy way, up an access tower and then straight onto one of the wood-frame howdahs that can accommodate six people.

By happy coincidence we're aboard my new friend Joiraj, and as we step ponderously out into the park, I ask Maan about the future of the elephant in Kaziranga. He thinks that it's all part of a wider picture. Unlike in Africa, there has been a long tradition in India of domesticating and training elephant, primarily for the logging industry. Now the pendulum is swinging away from cutting down and more towards the preservation of forest, so a different role must be found if the elephant is not to return to its natural state, with all the damage that can cause to local inhabitants.

As far as Kaziranga is concerned, there is work for them, not only on tourist rides like these, but in patrolling the park itself. Wet, often swampy ground and stretches of thick grassland standing 15 feet high make large swathes of the park inaccessible by motor vehicle. For surveillance and accessibility elephant is still best. But they are expensive to run, in feed, maintenance and, believe it or not, elephant pensions, paid on retirement to the animal rather than his keeper, so some form of culling may have to be considered. Of course, as far as Joiraj is concerned, this is unthinkable and I might have to ship him back to London.

This morning, though, he earns his keep and from our perch we have a wide view over the tall *ikora* grass and the shorter grass in front, where beads of dew catch the morning sun and storks and pond heron strut about. We see swamp deer and hog deer, wild buffalo and a few energetically chomping wild boar, with their thin, bristly black hair parted across their backs like cheap toupees. A long-legged, duck-like bird flies by and Maan becomes very excited. It's a Bengal florican and there are only 400 to 500 left in the world. Which makes the rhinos of Kaziranga seem positively commonplace.

And at last we come across one, a greater one-horned rhino, with its wide lip and protruding upper jaw for better grazing, encased in almost colourless armour platelets, and standing still as a statue, like a great silver-grey rock. It measures about ten feet long and four high and Maan estimates it must weigh nearly a ton and a half, some 1500 kilograms.

Unruffled by our presence, the rhino lowers its head and carries on with breakfast.

By evening, we've left this expanse of unpolluted nature behind and are ensconced at the Dynasty Hotel in the Muslim quarter of Assam's capital, Guwahati. From my window I look out over an urban panorama, a mosque, a row of shop units, endless lines of mottled, blackened apartment buildings, offices and warehouses.

And not an animal in sight.

Bhutan

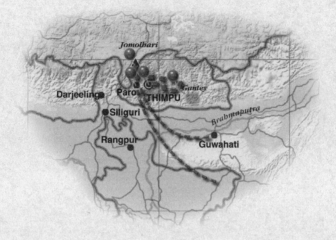

Day One Hundred and Three : Gantey

Having been lulled into lowland warmth and balminess in the Brahmaputra valley, I find myself tonight dressed in several layers of winter clothes, in a candle-lit room, hugging close to a wood-burning stove and gratefully accepting the offer of a hot-water bottle to relieve the icy chill of my bed. I'm a mere 140 miles (225 km) from steamy Guwahati but have forsaken the lazy horizontals of the Brahmaputra for a return to the rugged verticals of the Himalaya, and the bustle of the streets and markets for the silence of one of the most tranquil countries in the world.

Bhutan is the only independent Buddhist kingdom and one of only two remaining Himalayan kingdoms (Sikkim having gone to India and Tibet to China). It's a little larger than Switzerland, with a population less than the city of Birmingham, so there is room to swing cats. Add to this a deliberate government-imposed surcharge of $65 a day and you can begin to understand why we flew in to an airport that looked like a mediaeval palace on one of the only two planes that comprise the national fleet.

Bhutan (the name means the end of 'Bhot', the old name for Tibet) is a country of very strong character. The cultural confusion of East and West, of temples and shopping malls, robes and baseball hats, which marks so much of Southeast Asia, doesn't seem to have done much damage to a country where the official language is Dzongkha, the official currency is the *ngultrum* and the official policy is Gross National Happiness before Gross National Product.

Of course, there are telephones and cars and satellite dishes and laptop computers, but they are inside traditional buildings and used by people wearing traditional dress. Bhutan sees no contradiction between its past and its present. Its history is not to be found on display in tourist-friendly heritage parks, but on the street and in the countryside, as a part of everyday life. National costume is worn throughout the country, quite unselfconsciously, and very elegant it is too. The men wear the *kho*, pronounced 'go', an ankle-length robe with prominent white cuffs, pulled up to knee height and tucked into a belt. Women wear the *kira*, a length of silk or cotton wound around the body, and a short jacket called a *togo*. The fabrics are locally made and distinctive, varying from plain, utilitarian designs to complex weaves and intricate patterns.

Concrete has not yet rolled over Bhutan. Thanks to careful husbandry, over two-thirds of the country remains forested and the majority of the houses I've seen from the single-track main road that runs east from the airport at Paro are combinations of colourfully decorated wood frames and rammed earth walls, reminding me of alpine chalets and Tudor manor houses.

The village of Gantey, at which we arrived late in the day, is set in restful landscape in the central part of the country, on a hill overlooking the broad glacial valley of Phobjika. Surrounding and enclosing this peaceful place are the Black Mountains, which rise above 16,000 feet (5000 m).

As if to confirm this bewilderingly thorough and barely believable change in our circumstances, light snow is falling outside as I take one last look at the ghostly outlines of wide roofs around us and begin the delicate process of inserting myself, and hot-water bottle, which all of us have been thoughtfully provided with by the management, into the narrow neck of my sleeping bag.

Day One Hundred and Four : Gantey

Breakfast conversation is dominated by wet bed stories. As the only one whose hot-water bottle didn't leak, I feel rather left out.

My Bhutanese host and guide has been up for some time doing crossword puzzles, to which he's addicted. Dasho Benji ('call me Benji') is what one might call a larger than life figure. A colourful character. He's the King's cousin, and, over a period of 30 years, has held positions of power in Bhutan from Home Affairs to Chief Justice to Minister of the Environment. No longer a member of the government, he uses his considerable influence to pursue the environmental causes that are his first love. He also likes to go to Calcutta for golf and horse racing and is generous with his drink. He makes no apologies for enjoying the fast life, but now, at the age of 60, he's having to move into the middle lane as his body registers the toll of many happily misspent years. His broad, ruddy face is dominated by a pair of deep-set, ever so slightly bloodshot eyes, which seem naturally attuned to merriment and give little indication of the hard times he has known. His father, who was Prime Minister of Bhutan, was assassinated while in office.

Today, though, he is in impatient mood. He wants to show me something of which he's intensely proud. A colony of black-necked cranes, one of the world's rarest birds, winters in this valley.

The black-necked crane was first identified in 1876, by one of the great explorers of the Tibetan plateau, Count Nikolai Przhewalski of the Imperial Russian Army. Of the 16 species of crane, it was the last to be found.

Before 1990 the general estimate was that there were only 800 black-necked cranes in the world. Since China opened up and began to share information that estimate has risen to between 3000 and 5000. They fly down from Tibet and Ladakh every winter and gather here, attracted by the marshy wetland of the valley floor. But there is a complication. The Gantey valley recently discovered a potentially lucrative source of income from the raising of seed potatoes. The soil and air here are free of all the most common diseases from which potatoes suffer, so the seeds are much in demand, especially in India. Plans were afoot to drain the valley and build more farms. Benji fought to prevent the destruction of a unique habitat.

'The government said that, you know, we cannot stop the development of the country for 20 birds. But we found 80 of them.'

He gives a smile of satisfaction.

'And today there are 270.'

He is certain that his close relationship with the King helped. King Jigme Singye Wangchuck, educated in Britain, succeeded to the throne after the death of his father in 1972. He was 27. Before that, I get the impression that he and Benji had some pretty good times together, a sort of Falstaff-Prince Hal relationship. As Benji puts it to me.

'I was his court jester. I used to make him laugh.'

'So saving the cranes was a payback for the times you've cheered him up?'

Benji nods. 'I believe that. I believe that very strongly.'

We aren't far from the village when we have our first sight of them. In the brilliant morning sun, some 30 or 40 birds are pecking around for grain and insects in a recently ploughed field. They stand about three feet tall (1m) and look to me like a cross between a goose and a heron, with slender, pale grey bodies, black tails and, of course, black necks. The only splash of colour is a tiny red cap. They aren't arrestingly beautiful by any means, and I suppose I'm a little disappointed that rare doesn't necessarily mean resplendent. Indeed, Benji, in his red and green check *kho* with black, knee-length stockings and pristine white trainers, is a lot more exotic than the birds we've come so far to see. But their rarity has won them respect and the black-necked crane is thought to have great religious significance, proven by the fact that when they first arrive in the valley they always circle the monastery on the hill three times.

Benji takes me up a lane past timbered houses, fenced green paddocks and piles of fresh-cut wood, which looks like Switzerland in old photographs. He points out darting finches and snow pigeons with fawn backs and black and white tails, which, he says, are usually to be found much higher up.

At the end of the lane, beside a tumbling stream, is a modern, well-equipped, decagonal building, which houses the Black-Necked Crane Information Centre. Here I learn a little more about these celebrated creatures. Like the shelducks of the Brahmaputra, they mate for life (which adds to religious status, I'm told). They can live for 30 or 40 years.

Two or three mounted telescopes are trained on the swampy valley floor below us. A river dawdles through it, full of brown trout that are never fished, it being against the Buddhist religion to take life. A number of black-necked cranes are already gathered, and more fly in, until there must be 150 birds down there. J-P and Nigel become very excited and discreetly move the camera into a closer position. It's very hard to catch the birds in flight and it's not until Peter walks right round the far side of them (ruining a pair of trousers in the process) that they take, languidly, elegantly and prematurely, to the air.

'I didn't see you do that,' says Benji in his capacity as founder of the Black-Necked Crane Preservation Programme.

In the afternoon we ride a pair of small and very truculent horses up the hill to get a wider view of the valley. Last night's snow lies crisp and even up here, and we unpack our lunch and make a fire.

Benji, once again, didn't see us do this. So strict are the environmental laws in Bhutan's national parks that timber and branches must be left where they fall, and cannot be moved by anyone without special permission. As 28 per cent of Bhutan is designated national park, there's a lot of firewood going begging.

Benji points above us, to the hanging lichens that cover the trees like dust sheets in a shuttered-up house.

'This is an indicator of good-quality air, you know. Shows the air is very good up here.'

We return the horses to the park-keeper and walk back through the village. The houses are good-looking, rectangular in plan and usually of two storeys, the lower one for livestock, the upper for the family, with an open loggia below the roof, not for cocktails or deck chairs at sunset, but for drying crops and storing wood and cattle fodder.

As in Tibet, decoration of the houses is of great importance. In Bhutan an added refinement are the finely drawn paintings on the white, half-timbered walls, some of which are not for the prudish.

I counted about half a dozen painted penises in Gantey village, erect and beribboned, and often emitting a thin trail of cosmic sperm. They seem to be as unremarkable here as a box hedge in Dorking. Françoise Pommaret's *Odyssey Guide to Bhutan* explains that they were inspired by the teachings of one of the country's most popular religious figures, Drupka Kunley, who lived around the turn of the 16th century and was known as the 'divine madman'. He was from a distinguished family and, though he refused to take holy orders, he wandered the country with his own brand of Buddhism, which put the sexual act at the centre of religious experience, and from what we know, he practised what he preached. The fact that his phallocentric ideas are still celebrated says a lot for Bhutan's relaxed attitudes to sex. If you painted a penis on your house in Dorking, you'd probably be arrested.

Benji's enthusiasm for the rural way of life – and over 80 per cent of Bhutanese still work on the land – seems to be greater than his powers of mobility, but he insists in clambering up steps cut out of a tree trunk to show me the interior of one of the village houses.

A bright girl called Dawa Zangma, which means 'moon', lives here and helps the family income by weaving. She can make a *kira*, with all its complicated colours and patterns, in eight days.

Dawa Zangma is 13, apple cheeked with straight, thick, dark hair. She's about to leave the home and the loom to go to boarding school.

She lays aside her work and helps her mother prepare butter tea, which we drink sitting cross-legged on a small carpet, which is rolled out specially for us. There are, as far as I can see, no chairs in the house, which she shares with her mother, father and two sisters. Benji confirms that in a traditional Bhutanese house where there is little money around life is lived on the floor (which is why they move with much more agility than myself). There is no cutlery and no glass in the windows, which are covered at night by sliding bamboo shutters. Everyone eats or sleeps in the one big room, dominated by the stove at its centre.

The attractive appearance of the houses belies the condition of the villagers. We are still in the Bhutanese winter and those inhabitants who can afford it will have packed up everything and moved to lower slopes with their livestock. Those who stay on may be employed in the reconstruction work at the monastery, but that's about it. A woman, well wrapped up, sits behind the counter of the single local store. On display is a pretty meagre selection of chillies (the *sine qua non* of Bhutanese cuisine), cabbage, cauliflower, beans, potatoes and dried fish from Bangladesh. Though they seem to enjoy eating meat and fish, the Buddhist prohibition on taking life means that it all has to be killed by designated butchers within the country or brought in from outside.

As night falls and the warm sun is replaced by steadily falling snow, we sit around the stove, eating red rice and yak stew and a fierce plateful of what must be one of the oddest national dishes in the world, *hemadatsi*, chillies in a cheese sauce.

Bhutan, which has only had a king since 1907, must now rank as one of the most successful monarchies in the world. The current ruler is a widely respected, modest man who prefers to live, not in his palace, but in a log cabin in the grounds.

He tours the country regularly, consulting local people and hosting big meals at which he himself serves the food.

'He's not a king who goes on European holidays,' says Benji.

He is, nevertheless, an absolute ruler. Though he himself is working on a constitution that will limit his power, King Jigme is, to all intents and purposes, free to do as he likes. Benji sees no problem with this.

'It's very important to have an absolute monarch, a guy who cares for the country, who knows where he's taking us. Left to ourselves…we'd be squabbling.'

His policies are all geared to the preservation of Bhutan's cultural identity, and this has led to allegations that outsiders, particularly Nepalese immigrants in the south of the country, are not allowed the same rights as the Bhutanese. Benji sees this as justifiable.

'Small countries like Bhutan, surrounded by larger countries with fast-growing populations looking for land…have to be on the lookout. We don't want the Sikkim syndrome, where Sikkim was just overpopulated by Nepalese. The original people of Sikkim became a minority in their country…they got voted out of power, and then they all voted to become a state of India.'

Bhutan's survival after the war was a triumph of diplomacy and timing. Independence from India was agreed in 1950, just before the Chinese invasion of Tibet. If it had been after the invasion, Benji thinks India might well have wanted to keep control of Bhutan. As it is, the two countries have maintained good relations. Bhutan's biggest export is hydroelectric power, all of which goes to India, and recently the Bhutanese army flushed out insurgents who were using the country as a base for operations into north India.

Benji positively glows with pride.

'Led by our King…we took these terrorists on and in one swift fall knocked them all out in two days. It's amazing how we did it.'

The question is how much longer Bhutan will be able to walk this tightrope between the feudal system (officially abolished in 1953) and a forward-looking future. The King knows what he wants. In May 2004, he announced, 'Bhutan and its people are ready to have a democratic political system.'

Day One Hundred and Five: Gantey to Thimpu

The Gantey valley has turned grey overnight. A fresh coating of snow has picked out the field boundaries and transformed the gently sloping, treeless slopes from straw brown to light silver, making this beautiful corner of Bhutan look like the Yorkshire Dales.

From my window I can see a woman from the house behind, in a blouse and long pink skirt, stepping gingerly across the ice to the public water pipe. She brushes a white cap of snow off the top of the tap and starts to wash. The flying droplets of water, back-lit by the morning sun, splash round her face like particles of gold.

Before we leave, we pay a visit to the monastery, or *gompa*, at the far end of the ridge above the valley.

Benji explains that Bhutan may be a Buddhist kingdom, but the sects here are different from those in Tibet. The Galupka school, the Yellow Hats, dominate in Tibet and the Drukpa Kagyu school, the Red Hats, in Bhutan. The Je Khenpo, head of the Drukpa school, is the religious authority here. The Dalai Lama has no jurisdiction in Bhutan and has never visited the country.

The monastery has been undergoing renovation for two years and outside the main door a temporary roof has been erected to shelter a timber yard and workshop. Four craftsmen are at work carving a complex decorative motif on a 50-foot-long, blue-pine beam. One man is using a dagger to carve out a *dorje*, a diamond thunderbolt motif that is a recurrent theme in Bhutan. It's all done by hand, and each has a line of wood-handled tools and a portable radio laid out beside him.

An ancient gateway leads to a big courtyard, in the middle of which, in the Bhutanese style, is the impressive main temple, with the monks' accommodation surrounding it, in single-storey cells with painted lintels, door frames and eaves. It's a building site and looks as though it will be for some time to come.

Over the barking of a pack of dogs I can hear prayers are being chanted from somewhere. The restoration work is largely being done by *gomchens*, lay monks who don't have to be celibate or live in the monastery. The monks who remain here support themselves by offering their services out for family occasions, providing blessings for births, marriages, deaths, new houses and performing any cere-monies these innately religious people require.

On our way out a dishevelled, tousle-headed young man who can barely walk, approaches us and shows us a deep and nasty gash low on his right leg. Pete, who is a saint in these matters, washes the wound and advises him to go to hospital before it turns gangrenous, but the man says it's been like that for four years. He then starts to sing a love song to me. Benji shakes his head disapprovingly. He says the man's obviously mad. I try not to take this personally.

We head back towards Thimpu, but conditions on the road are much worse than when we came in. Stopping to take a shot of a herd of yaks against the snow, we find ourselves victims of an admirable piece of retail opportunism. A small, doughty lady races out of her tent and sprints a couple of hundred yards through the deep snow up towards us. For a moment, we imagine she's come to shoo us away, or demand a BBC contract, but nothing of the kind. Scrambling up onto the road, she produces a range of yak-hair tote bags and sells all three of them more or less instantly.

Once over the 11,000-foot (3350 m) pass out of the valley, we expect things to get better. Quite the opposite. The snow is deeper and the road icier and much more treacherous. Lichen-clad conifers plunge steeply down on one side of us, disappearing into a cold shroud of mist, so it's hard to tell just how far we might fall if, as seems all too likely, the minibus slides off the road. From marvelling at the delicate beauty of the snowbound forest, thoughts turn swiftly to problems of survival. The normally nerveless Nigel, who, not long ago, was in a serious accident on the ice in Alaska, has the window open on the other side of the bus, ready for a quick exit. We negotiate a score of steep hairpin bends at a snail's pace. The snow is falling more thickly now, and every now and then the wheels slide and we prepare for the worst. After almost an hour of hearts in mouths the snow turns to sleet and the conifers turn to rhododendrons and the dirt track to paved road and we can at last breathe normally again.

The Central Road, which is the only road connecting east and west Bhutan, is less than 20 years old, an indication of the government's ambivalent attitude to the opening up of the country. It twists and turns dizzily around the spurs and shoulders of the mountains. They say the longest stretch of straight road in Bhutan is the runway at Paro airport.

Nevertheless, journeys that took two days now take two hours, and we are in Thimpu by afternoon, and the near white-out on the pass already seems a distant memory.

So too is the gentle timelessness of the Gantey valley.

Thimpu, the capital of Bhutan, is no rip-roaring metropolis, but it has roads and roundabouts (where policemen direct traffic with wonderfully flowing arm movements, as if they're doing t'ai chi) and car parks and cosmopolitan restaurants and banks and hotels and, according to Benji, its very own property boom.

When Thimpu was chosen to be the capital in 1952, it was little more than a few houses clustered around the majestic Tashioed-zong, and it grew slowly until 1974, when Bhutan was opened to foreigners for the first time. Since then it has mushroomed and has a current population of 50,000. To accommodate everyone, the rules on traditional house-building seem more liberally applied here and the streets of boringly respectable four- or five-storey blocks look more Mitteleuropean than Bhutanese.

At the Arts Café I meet Tsewang, a young actor and film maker, recently returned from showing his new film *Travellers and Magicians* at the Deauville Film Festival. It's set in the Bhutanese countryside and in it he plays a man trying to get away from the restrictive world of the village.

He himself was the son of farmers and recognizes that, by many international standards, Bhutan remains backward. Literacy is a little over 50 per cent and television only came here five years ago. But though life is hard, he doesn't think this is a bad thing. Unemployment is quite high here and this worries him more than lack of money.

'The Buddhist version of poverty is a situation where you have nothing to contribute.'

He feels that in Bhutan there is still a strong sense of, as he puts it, 'unison with the earth'.

'In San Francisco I felt lost. Everywhere you go you have billboards telling you that you need to buy this or that, or the latest Cherokee four-wheel drive, but here we have different kind of billboards.'

A coach pulls up and a line of docile tourists file past us into the café.

'We have the prayer flags, we have the temples. These are our markers, you know, reminding you, in the Buddhist way, that you are not here for ever.'

Bearing this in mind, I end the day sampling one of the nightspots of Thimpu, a decorous, well-behaved snooker bar called Rumours. Pretty girls smash balls around the table like old pros and a television set is tuned to live coverage of England's cricket match with the West Indies in Barbados.

Benji, who doesn't like to miss a get-together, is sitting at the bar with me and his attractive and urbane cousin Khendum. The talk meanders round to reincarnation. Khendum admits she has 'a little problem with reincarnation'.

She doesn't believe in it.

'I can't reconcile my practising of Buddhism with that aspect of it,' she says with an admirable directness.

Benji has definite preferences.

'I'd like to be reborn as a black 7 foot 6 basketball player who earns a lot of money.'

Khendum gives me a wry smile.

'He'll be a cockroach.'

'Thank you. Thank you very much,' says Benji courteously.

She and Benji are both part of Bhutan's privileged, wealthy, cosmopolitan elite. Like Tsewang, they're outward-looking and internationalist, and though they are fiercely proud of their country's cultural protectionism, all of them accept that change is accelerating and inevitable. As Khendum says, 'We're not romantic or idealistic enough to think that things will always be the way they are now, but we'd like to slow the development process up to a degree that we can handle change when it comes.'

Realistic, sensible and a trifle wistful at the same time.

Day One Hundred and Six : Thimpu to Takstang

The slopes of the Himalaya are rich in plants that have medicinal properties. Used for thousands of years by rural, mountain people, they are now increasingly attractive to an international market seeking an alternative to chemical drugs. The canny Bhutanese government, together with the World Health Organization, recognized this demand and in 1979 set up an Institute of Traditional Medicine, which researches, catalogues and produces herbal remedies. Recent newspaper reports suggest that they might have hit pay dirt, with a product already being tipped as the first 'herbal Viagra'.

The word 'Institute' fills me with ominous images of two-headed dogs and white-coated men with small spectacles, so, as we approach the heart of Bhutan's traditional medicine establishment on a hill above Thimpu, I'm much relieved to find that it's a colourfully decorated, half-timbered building that looks like a well-preserved Elizabethan manor house.

We're welcomed by three serious men, two of whom are called

Dorje. They show us around an immaculately laid out display of traditional medicines in a long, library-like room with beamed ceiling and glass cabinets. The debt to Tibetan medicine is acknowledged in the old anatomical charts showing the five wheels or *chakras*, the centres of spiritual power that control all our bodily systems. Traditional Bhutanese medicine also borrowed from the Indian idea that the balance of the Three Humours, bile, wind and phlegm, dictates the state of our physical and spiritual health.

Of their prize discovery they are as bashful and cautious as you would expect government scientists to be. They admit that they are working hard to produce products that will have a commercial application, as it brings in the money to keep the Institute going, and that they have recently concocted a mix of five herbs that 'could possess spermogenetic powers'.

'Increase virility,' adds one of the Dorjes, helpfully.

Their mixture is currently on a two-year test, after which conclusions will be examined. When I enquire about its constituents, glances are exchanged and there are mutterings about bio-piracy and international property rights, but it seems the key ingredient is none other than our old friend *Cordyceps sinensis*, or caterpillar fungus, five pieces of which I bought off the street in Yushu for £4, and which are currently stuck in dust and fluff at the bottom of my bag. They confirm that the tiny little shoots are very difficult to find and though it grows up in the Bhutanese mountains, there is often a fight with Tibetans from across the border to get to it first.

Our hosts line up to bid us goodbye. The idea that these grave and courteous men in matching *khos* might be onto a world-beating sex aid seems as unlikely as it would be desirable.

Early lunch with Khendum at a trendy new restaurant called the Bhutan Kitchen, opened two days ago and alarmingly empty. I meet two of her international friends. Linda, a buxom American, is married to a Bhutanese *thangka* painter and has lived here for seven years.

'I love Bhutan. Bhutan is so relaxed and peaceful.'

'Everyone says that.'

She nods and shrugs.

'But there's nothing else to say about Bhutan.'

Françoise, a lively, funny French lady, who I feel I know already, as she's written the guide book that's become my Bhutanese bible, is a touch more analytical.

'I won't call it Shangri-la but there is a certain magic here, which isn't about wealth,' she says. 'Once you're trapped in, you can't get out. It's a magic trap.'

Khendum has lined up some local gastronomic specialities. As a sharpener, I take rice wine with an egg in it and, noticing the ubiquitous betel nut on the table, I decide that the moment has come for me to sample the Himalayan lorry-driver's staple diet. Khendum prepares it carefully, wrapping the hard nut in its own leaf with a smear of lime paste. The sharp bitterness of the leaf is an ugly taste, but it wears off and after a few minutes of chewing my head begins to heat up as if from deep inside. I feel my eyes water and my cheeks redden as the betel rushes my body onto full alert and soon, like everyone else who chews it, my teeth are stained red and I'm looking for somewhere to spit it out.

The main dishes are challenging. A long, stringy vegetable of some kind seems determined to strangle me from within, smashed chicken and red rice is dotted with small bone fragments and the cow-hide is, well, an acquired taste. One which, I fear, would take armed men with rifles at my head to acquire.

Our time among the flesh-pots of Thimpu is distressingly brief. Tomorrow we head north to Jomolhari mountain to begin a valedictory trek, a farewell to the high Himalaya.

By way of preparation, I plan a short training climb with my guide who, almost unbelievably, is not called Dorje. He's called Doje.

In the foothills near Paro is a complex of holy buildings that draws pilgrims from all over the Himalaya. Takstang, meaning 'Tiger's Lair', is built on precipitous rock ledges and, though it remains almost impossibly difficult to get to, there is now a well-trodden tourist trail up to the crags opposite.

We pass a farmhouse, whose walls are painted with motifs of tigers, devils and the curious symbol of a weasel disgorging pearls. Doje explains. The Guardian King of the North Direction traditionally holds a weasel, so anything emanating from a weasel's mouth denotes good fortune. Obvious really.

The clouds pile up as our trail climbs through oak and pine forest. Souvenirs are laid out for sale at every other corner. After an hour and a half's walking, the track levels out at a *chorten* with prayer wheels inside, from which a wide path leads to a log-cabin tea house with wood-burning stove and good local food. Outside is a terrace with fine views of the temple. It is believed to have been founded by the saint Padmasambhava, also known as Guru Rinpoche, who rode here on a tigress in the 8th century and took on terrifying form to chase away the evil spirits and convert the valley to Buddhism.

In 1998 a fire gutted the main sanctuary. Its restoration proved a formidable technological challenge, but it's almost completely rebuilt. Newly carved sections were hauled up from workshops 1000 feet below by a system of ropes and pulleys.

From across the valley, the white walls with the maroon band gleam from the top of the sheer tongue of rock that marks Takstang out as one of the most spectacular holy places anywhere in the world.

Day One Hundred and Eight : Jangothang

Just short of 24,000 feet (7315 m), Jomolhari is one of the highest mountains in Bhutan. Seen from our tiny, fragile campsite, it fills the northwestern horizon, an immense hemispherical slab, hung with mighty crusts of snow and ice save where the rock flanks of the mountain, too steep to hold anything, stand out raw and sheer.

Unlike Everest, which kept a majestic distance, Jomolhari looms very close, a presence so powerful and all-pervasive that at times it seems to be growing before our eyes. Unsurprisingly, this is a sacred mountain and no-one has ever stood on its summit.

The far side of Jomolhari is in Tibet and around it wind narrow passes that have long been used for trans-Himalayan trade. Proof of this lies in the half-collapsed dry-stone walls of a castle, built to control this meeting of two valleys. A track continues up beyond our camp and we follow it towards Ngile La, a pass at 15,700 feet (4785 m). Another mighty mountain rises close to us. Jichu Drake, at 22,300 feet (6795 m), is a classic Paramount peak, more shapely than Jomolhari, from which a beautiful glacier trails, covering the rocks in gleaming, blue-tinted ice sheets. A milky-green stream leaks from beneath it. We're above the tree line here, but there are yaks and the odd farm, on one of which lives a national character whom Doje is keen for me to meet.

The farmhouse is of the traditional manorial style, surrounded by a compound protected by a five-foot-high wall made from stone and topped with birch twigs and dried yak dung.

Inside the compound is a solar panel unit and a number of archery targets. Archery is the national sport of Bhutan.

We climb an outside staircase, at the top of which waits the bony figure of Choni Dorje. He's 82, and has lived here all his life. He's that happy combination, a yak herder and poet, and a few years back wrote a song extolling the virtues of his favourite yak, called something like 'Jewel of the Mountains'. Describing the beast from horn to tail in loving terms, it struck a national chord and he was asked to Thimpu to sing his song to the King. He doesn't look strong. He has a cataract in one eye, turning it milky blue, white hair tight around a prominent skull, sunken cheeks and a wispy Fu-Manchu beard.

But he seems cheered to see us and happy to give us a tear-jerking rendition of his big hit. Just to bring the tone down, I reply with a verse of the Lumberjack Song, which, sadly, I can never fully remember.

Choni Dorje's granddaughter invites us inside to the big, open, timber-floored room, where four generations live together. Bed-rolls are neatly stowed at one side of the room, along with the woven rugs and blankets to keep out what must be bitter cold. A little marmalade cat peers at us from a dark corner. As befits the house of a man who wrote a love song to the animal, there are bits of yak all over the place; haunches of dried yak meat and coiled entrails hang from roof beams and a pile of yak dung is stacked by the cast-iron stove. A small shrine with a Buddha lies behind a curtain off to one side.

As we drink our butter tea, I have to remind myself that Choni Dorje, his family, his yaks and his marmalade cat have lived their entire lives higher than the summit of the Eiger.

Day One Hundred and Nine : Jangothang to Takengthanka

One by one we stumble out onto the frosty grass after a bitterly cold night. The tents are comfortable enough when you're inside, but squeezing through that tight-zippered door is like coming out of the womb. Doje tells me that Jangothang means 'land of ruins' and looking at the state of us, it seems appropriate. I think we've been in the mountains too long. Last night was a sharp reminder of the high-altitude conditions that we thought we'd left behind.

Of course, the payback for the pain is tremendous scenery, unpolluted air, brilliant light and utter silence. And once I'm up and dressed and have splashed some water on my face, I know I shall miss all these things. By tonight the majestic peaks of the Himalaya will be behind us for the last time, so, while the tents are being struck and our ponies loaded up for the journey, I pick my way up past the monolithic boulders rolled down by the glaciers and through the birch scrub and the tough little juniper trees towards Jomolhari. It's a final act of homage to the high mountains and, as Jomolhari fills the sky, I feel a bit like one of the characters in *Close Encounters of the Third Kind* when the spaceship has landed.

The Himalayan peaks are seen by the people who live among them as awful places, abodes of jealous gods and places where the dead are gathered, and I have the feeling they've got it right. What do we know, we who romanticize them? We who fly in and use them to prove something to ourselves, to plant our flags, talk of 'conquest' and then go home. I can almost feel the shoulders of Jomolhari heaving with laughter.

I find a mossy rock and just sit for a while. I look down at our camp, with flocks of alpine choughs swooping noisily in to look for morsels of food, and feel my own personal pangs of regret at leaving all this behind. There are few places outside the Himalaya where the relation of man to nature can be experienced on such a gigantic scale, and something like that may not change your life, but it does stretch it a bit.

Jomolhari is draped in cloud as we set off across the stream and down along the broad, treeless meadow of grass and stones that leads down the valley. Within minutes the mountain is out of sight.

A yak caravan sways up towards us. Doje says he prefers to use horses and donkeys for carrying. He says they're much brighter than yaks and look where they're going.

Jomolhari is 11 miles (18 km) behind us by the time we reach our next campsite. It's in a tight neck of the mountains, where the valley becomes a gorge. Thickly wooded slopes of cedar, blue pine, maple and larch rise behind us and the stream we've followed since it left the glacier is now a river, some 30 feet wide and running fast and clear. A fire has been lit and internal warmth is taken care of by a slug or two of Special Courier Bhutanese Whisky. The description on the bottle, 'brewed at Gelephu Distillery (a unit of Army Welfare Project)', suggests that we are not only warming ourselves but helping the Bhutanese military at the same time. Very odd. Food is served early and I'm one of the last to bed. It's a quarter to nine and snowing.

Day One Hundred and Ten: Takengthanka to Sharna Zampa

My tent flap is heavier when I push it aside this morning. A layer of rime has built up overnight and, as I squeeze out into the world, it brushes across my back, propelling me forwards with a shock.

The sun will take some time to penetrate this steeply enclosed ravine, so breakfast is eaten with gloves, hats and scarves on. Our horse drivers are tucking into mounds of red rice and chillies.

'They can't move without rice and chilli,' says Doje. 'Each man eats a kilo of rice a day.'

I ask him what they eat on special occasions.

'Rice,' he says, predictably. 'Rice with green chilli. Pork slices, dried spinach.'

The horses, meanwhile, nuzzle dried corn from what I've come to call Himalayan nose-bags: plastic footballs sliced in half.

The business of reducing our travelling village to whatever fits on a horse's back is elaborate and time-consuming. Homes are demolished, restaurants closed and packed into boxes, kitchens disappear into bamboo baskets. This morning the horses haul their loads up and over a series of switchbacks, some steep and slippery, before the path begins to flatten out. Very occasionally, we meet people coming the other way. Locals carrying supplies up to the nomads in the higher valleys and, at one point, out of the woods ahead, a party of immaculately dressed Japanese. We descend from the conifer forests and into richer temperate woodlands with flowering laurel and luxuriant rhododendron swelling on either side, and strips of meadow thick with edelweiss and gentian.

But it is a long way and by the time we reach the patch of grassy riverbank near the bridge of Sharma Zampa we've covered another 12 miles (19 km). Nigel is limping from a blistered toe and Basil is appalled at what he's just done.

'No Pao has *ever* walked as far as this.' He shakes his head in disbelief. 'Never in the entire *history* of Paos has anyone walked 23 miles!' And there's more to go.

But we're down below 10,000 feet (3050 m). The valley is wider and more inviting, the river has broadened to 100 yards wide, and there are some substantial farmhouses on the far bank, where the forest has been cleared and the land terraced for cultivation. Though there is a bridge a mile upstream, most of the traffic from the other bank comes through the river. We watch a packhorse, fully loaded, followed by two women and half a dozen children, pick its way through the shallow but fast-flowing waters, and later two cows and a calf, almost submerged as it struggles desperately to get a grip on the wet rocks, make their way across.

Day One Hundred and Eleven: Sharma Zampa to Paro

I must really have been walked out yesterday, the result being a long, deep, wonderfully restorative night's sleep. Trekking beats any sleeping pill. Doje is tall, good-looking and, until he's had a drop of Special Courier in the evening, quite a serious young man. His mother was the Queen Mother's equerry and maybe that's where his rather dignified correctness comes from. So it's all the more gratifying to hear him getting quite worked up at the breakfast table. Admittedly, it's only about Bhutanese history, but there's a yelp of unalloyed chauvinism as he talks of the Tibetan invaders who used to come down trails like this.

'16th century, 17th century. I think there were nine invasions. And we trashed them!'

Doje shakes his head with relish, as if it had all happened yesterday.

'We sent them back. We sent them back!'

A herd of cows is crossing the river towards us. I think this verdant bank where we camped must be their grazing ground, for, once here, they tuck into whatever doesn't have a tent on top of it, including my jacket. The women who keep an eye on them are a feisty pair. While one looks through Nigel's camera in wonderment, another attacks one of our horsemen after he's made a joke about her, grabbing at his crutch, shrieking with laughter and revealing a perfect set of totally black teeth.

Doje keeps well out of it. He says the ladies up here are tough and can out-wrestle any of the men.

We move on. A magnificent landscape of interlocking, conifer-clad spurs stretches way above us to a mountain with a little tongue of snow and ice still clinging to its north-facing summit. On either side of us are meadows and the widening waters of the River Paro.

Civilization is gradually stretching its fingers up the valley. We pass a large army camp, more and more farms, emerald-green paddy fields, orchards ripe with plum blossom. Pigs scuttling about. After five hours of walking, we cross the river on a steel-slung suspension bridge (financed by the Swiss, I notice) and at last onto a paved road. An hour and a half later, we reach the famous Drukyel *dzong*. This fortress, raised around the time that England was fighting its only Civil War, commemorated one of Bhutan's rousing victories over the Tibetans. Reduced now to little more than a circular keep after a fire started by a butter-lamp in 1951, Drukyel *dzong* must once have seemed impregnable, standing as it does on a strategically commanding crag overlooking the valley, with Paro on one side and Jomolhari and the Tibetan border, 35 miles (56 km) away, on the other. Now it's a little forlorn.

At its foot is a small, picturesque, alpine village, with two huge cypresses looming above it. The very first house we come to has a fine selection of wall paintings, including a chubby pink penis with wings attached. But best of all, the village contains a bus that will take us the rest of the way into Paro, and the bus contains cold beers.

I pull off my boots and peel down the socks with wondrous relief. One of my toes is bloody but otherwise no ill-effects of the longest, if not quite the most arduous, of our treks so far.

Day One Hundred and Twelve : Paro

The great religious festivals of Bhutan are known as *tsechus* and commemorate the deeds of Padmasambhava, aka Guru Rinpoche, the saint whose rocky perch in Takstang I climbed up to a few days ago. *Tsechu* means 'tenth', which was the day of the month when, by tradition, these deeds took place. Today is the start of the annual five-day *tsechu* in Paro. Primarily a religious event, it's also a big social occasion, with people taking time off from work to dress up in their best outfits and watch dancing, have picnics, attend archery contests, and generally let their hair down. Opening and closing days are the most important and the crowds will be the biggest, so we're up at 5.30 to make sure of a good position. This is also a big draw for tourists and, though only a few thousand come in every year, the hotel accommodation is easily overrun and we're staying in a rented bungalow a half-hour out of town.

We drive in past the airport, so neat, tidy and largely uncontaminated by aircraft that it looks like a toy lay-out. Northeast of the airport and commanding the valley are the imposing white walls of the Paro *dzong*. Like the fortress at Drukyel, where we ended our trek from Jomolhari, it was built in the 1640s, in the flush of national victory over the Tibetans. By coincidence, it also suffered a serious fire, being virtually razed to the ground in 1915. Unlike the Drukyel *dzong*, it was restored to its former glory after a special tax was levied throughout the country. Its two longest walls extend for some 500 feet (150 m) and taper gracefully upwards in the Tibetan style. The uppermost of its five storeys have long windows, the main ones projecting out from the wall, and all surrounded by finely carved frames and lintels. A band of ochre paint connects them all up and marks it out as a religious as well as administrative building.

At the main gate stalls are already set up and at one of them a bearded old lay monk, or *gomchen*, stands beside a small table, on which is a brass and silver miniature temple, with drawers that open to reveal various gilt figures of the gods. As people go by, they tuck the odd *ngultrum* note into his temple. He makes no acknowledgement of the contribution, but stares ahead, keeping up a low, monotonous, gurgling chant. He's not the slightest bit fazed when a sudden yowling and barking breaks out beside him, as two packs of

Bhutan's ubiquitous stray dogs (which, of course, no-one is allowed to cull) fight for territory at the bottom of the entrance steps. After some vicious teeth baring, they're seen off and we climb up to the grand, carved doorway. The *dzong* is as impressive inside as out. There are two main stone-flagged courtyards on either side of a massive central tower. Timber-frame galleries run above the squares, connecting up the accommodation.

The opening ceremony takes place in the smaller, lower court-yard, which is hung with swathes of yellow silk, billowing out from a beamed loggia.

Out of 6000 monks supported by the government of Bhutan (there are 3000 others who live off private patronage), 200 live and work in this *dzong*, and before the crowds gather, I take a peek inside their rooms. The atmosphere seems very much like that of a Victorian public school. There are wood-panelled partitions, pegs on walls, dormitories with bare wood floors and rows of shoes at one end. I almost expect to see Dr Arnold striding round the corner of one of the dim and dusty corridors, heels clicking on the stone floor.

The courtyard is filling up. In the buildings on the far side boys' faces peep out and figures in maroon robes flit across the windows, their shaved heads catching the sunbeams.

There are a few tourists, but they're heavily outnumbered by local people, and heavily out-dressed as well. Not for the Bhutanese the polyester or the Gore-Tex. For them it's fine cotton and silk brocade, or hand-woven wool, individually patterned. Colours and designs are bold but never brash. I've rarely seen showing-off done with such subtlety.

There are no rows of seats, no tickets, no security staff bristling with head-sets. Spectators are left to sort themselves out, though there is a jolly, smiling actor brandishing what looks like a cat o'nine tails, who occasionally intervenes to help little children and per-formers get to the front.

First in the arena are the *atsaras*, clowns with bright red costumes and face masks dominated by exaggerated, beaky noses. They look like Mr Punch. Some carry painted wooden phalluses, which they use for crowd control. In their half-frightening, half-funny masks they are extremely effective at everything, from keeping the crowd back to chasing off stray dogs who want to take part. They also keep the crowd's spirits up with slapstick routines. Doje tells me that the *atsaras*, like court jesters, have licence to mock anyone involved in the *tsechu*, including the monks. This is quite necessary, as the long dances can become a bit tedious and are notably short on laughs.

They are, however, astonishingly rich in costume. From the very first number, described in the programme as Dance of the Lord of Death and His Consort, the profusion of colour and design, the sheer quantity of brocaded silk on display, the exuberance of the ankle-length robes with their wide, swirling sleeves, is marvellous to behold.

Big, expressive, brilliantly coloured masks complement the sumptuous costumes. If the deities are to be portrayed then they must be portrayed in all their terrible, magnificent glory. The music that accompanies the dance is played on eye-catching instruments ranging from the seven-foot-long Tibetan trumpets they call *dungchen* to painted and tasselled double-sided drums that look like cushions. Oboes, bells, cymbals, conch shells and a small horn made from a shin bone contribute to the clashing, tinkling, plangent sound.

As the morning goes on, the crowd swells, more and more people squeezing into the limited space around the perimeter until it's barely possible to avoid being pushed forward. It gets hotter, the high bright sun slicing the courtyard in two, reminding me of the *sol y sombra* of a Spanish bullring.

The Dance of the Lord of the Cremation Grounds is followed by the Dance of the Black Hats. I don't know the significance of these dances and the English translations are not always enlightening: 'on the external edges of a symbolic mandala where the assembly of the secret tantric deities are residing.' What is impressive is the poise of the dancers, often carrying enormously heavy costumes and headdresses, as they trip, turn, whirl and pirouette on the hard stone flags. In the last dance I see, the Dance of the Drum From Dramitse, the Black Demons are vanquished by the splendour of the White Gods, who swirl round in golden silk skirts hung with precious jewels. It is outlandish, frequently inexplicable and very wonderful.

Day One Hundred and Fourteen : Paro

After two days at the *tsechu* I take back all I said about Bhutan being an empty country. It feels as if, apart from two or three people left up in the mountains to look after the yaks, the entire nation is here in Paro. At certain times of the day, it's queuing only on the elegant covered footbridge leading across the river and up to the *dzong*. I've heard rumours of over-booked hotels with tourists having to camp out in the grounds.

Dust rises from the crowds wandering through the temporary market, which has spread between the *dzong* itself and the out-buildings nearby, where much of the dancing now takes place. There are makeshift cinemas and fairground games like hoop-la and even bingo. I pass a packed tent where a Bhutanese man calls the numbers in a remarkably plummy English accent.

'How do you do? Three and Two.'

Nearer the dancing, every inch of grass is taken up by picnicking families, many of whom look as if they have come down from the mountains. They unroll portions of seasoned pork and chilli, mushrooms and eggs and drink butter tea from thermoses. For them, *tsechu* is both pilgrimage and party.

Having devoted most of this morning to the Dance of the Judgement of the Dead, I feel in urgent need of some light relief and take up Khendum's invitation to join her for an archery match.

For her, this means watching only. In one of the rare examples of sex discrimination in Bhutan, women are not allowed to take part in traditional archery competitions. Two other reasons why I'm relieved to be, like her, a spectator, are that it looks pretty difficult and most of the participants are roaring drunk.

The hospitality tent, set on a pretty, willow-strewn meadow, is full of bonhomie. Long, rambling stories are told, one man sings 'Waltzing Matilda' at full volume, another lurches by with a whisky and loud yell, another becomes droolingly amorous. Khendum introduces me to them.

One is the Secretary of Employment, another the Managing Director of the National Bank. Others are chairmen of this and that. I realize this is no ordinary hospitality tent. These are the movers and shakers of Bhutan, letting their hair down. And why not?

Well, I suppose one reason why not is that they will shortly be loosing off arrows at enormous speed in a field that contains not just the target but also women, dogs and small children.

The national game, they keep trying to tell me, is taken extremely seriously and any young Bhutanese boy, in a village or a palace, learns the skills early on. However, it's clearly not a solemn sport. Though women are not allowed to play, they have an important role as vocal supporters.

Khendum tells me, with much amusement, that the night before a match the men sleep together in a dormitory with the door locked, as sex before a big game is considered bad luck.

She shakes her head in some disbelief.

'So the women are integral to the game, but the night before they don't want anything to do with them.'

Taunting is also an integral part of the game. Before a man shoots, it is the duty of his opponents to put him off by any means short of physical contact. Personal comments demeaning his appearance, physical irregularities, masculinity and the disloyalty of his wife are not only permitted but encouraged.

When the time comes, the team stagger out of the tent, exchange their drinks for huge, deadly, metal alloy bows, do a little dance, then line up to fire at a target 30 inches high, and 150 yards away. The extraordinary thing is that most of them either hit it or come damn close. I suppose that's the ultimate macho achievement. To be able to drink yourself silly and deliver a bull's eye while being told by your opponents that they've been shagging your wife for the last three weeks.

End up the day on a very different note. In the Queen Mother's Temple, a ceremony has been laid on to wish us good fortune for the rest of the journey. In a room, covered in beautifully detailed paintings of the various stages of the Buddha's life and incarnations, a group of eight monks has assembled for music and prayers. The chantmaster, or *udze*, sits on a dais and leads a chant in Cholkay, a variation of the Sanskrit in which Buddha himself wrote. The other monks chant with him or play oboes, drums, cymbals and the *dungchen*, the long trumpet that rests on the floor and makes a deeply mournful sound.

It's a serene and rather moving ceremony, quite unexpectedly interrupted by the sound of a mobile phone. An elderly monk, next to the chantmaster, fishes around inside his habit and switches it off.

Day One Hundred and Fifteen : Paro

The highlight of the last day of *tsechu*, and, indeed, the highlight of the festival itself, is the unfurling of the greatest treasure of the Paro *dzong*. It's a *thangka* measuring almost 100 feet (30 m) by 150 feet (45 m), and is known as a *thongdrol*. The survival of this huge tapestry when the *dzong* burnt down in 1915 only added to its reputation and merely to look on it conveys the very highest merit. *Thongdrol* means 'liberation by sight'.

To avoid such a precious object being damaged by the direct sunlight, it is unrolled at dawn, so our last full day in the Kingdom of the Thunder Dragon begins at 3 am.

When our bus pulls out onto the main Thimpu to Paro road, the valley seems to be already awake, if indeed it ever slept. Lights are on in the houses, buses and taxis are picking up people along the roadside. To add to the sense of great events, a full moon stares down from a cloudless sky.

Pilgrims are pouring over the covered bridge, fingers telling prayer beads and lips moving as they join a candle-lit procession winding its way up the hill. It's a quiet crowd. Buddhism is celebrated in song and chanting, but prayers are never shouted or hymns bellowed, and this morning the great throng, which must number several thousand, is almost silent.

In front of the five-storey building that will be completely covered when the *thongdrol* is unfurled, a line of butter lamps is lit. The men wear *khos*, of course, but today they also have white scarves across their shoulders and some wear them over their heads, lending an incongruous touch of the mosque.

To the sound of drum and bell, monks in procession emerge onto the forecourt and, dividing into two lines at right angles to the building, sit on the ground while the abbot, in a gold silk robe, takes his place on a raised dais between them.

Once this glittering scene is settled, the *thangka* is rolled out, up from the ground to the roof. At its centre is the figure of Padmasambhava, 20 feet high, flanked by his two consorts. In a circle around him are depictions of his eight manifestations.

The pilgrims press forward and, one after the other, pass along the base of the *thangka*, touching it, saying a prayer, and, in some cases, covering their heads with it.

Dancers come out now and some particularly intrusive, flash-popping tourists meet their match. As they push forward for their trophy close-ups, a couple of them are sent flying by a whirling dancer.

The dawn light slowly fills the sky, and as the time draws near for the *thongdrol* to be put away for another year, the line of pilgrims wanting to touch it surges forward. Not for the first time at *tsechu* I fear for the children and the frail older people who get caught up in this religious fervour. I count only six police at the front to deal with any emergency. But somehow, it never gets nasty or aggressive. The joy on the faces of those close to the *thongdrol* speaks of fulfilment not frustration.

The chill of the night softens and the sun begins to climb, revealing the full glory of this immense tapestry and the size of the crowd, banked right up the hill on both sides, that has been drawn here to see it. I turn away and look out over the shining walls and towers of the fortress to the mountains rolling away towards the looming Himalaya. This is a ceremony to match the landscape. A collective act of belief, bringing together the mountains and the faith that people need to survive them.

Bangladesh

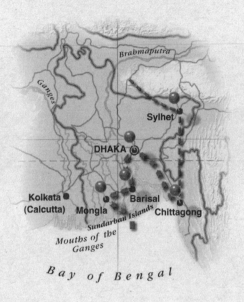

Day One Hundred and Seventeen: Near Sylhet, Bangladesh

At their closest point Bhutan and Bangladesh are some 25 miles (40 km) apart, yet they could scarcely be more different. One is entirely composed of mountains, the other flat as a pancake. One is among the least crowded countries in the world, the other the most densely packed. One is an absolute monarchy with a stable government, the other a people's republic that has just topped the list of the world's most corrupt countries. But there is something that unites them: the Himalaya.

Bhutan's seclusion and stability is due largely to the physical inaccessibility of the Himalayan mountains. Bangladesh's survival is due to the water that pours off them.

Bangladesh, three times as big as Bhutan, with 75 times the number of people, has a population of around 135 million, and the only reason it can support so many is because two of the greatest mountain rivers, the Ganges and the Brahmaputra, funnel down through the country on their way to the sea, depositing billions of tonnes of rich, recycled Himalaya.

Combined with the heavy monsoons that are the blessing and the bane of Bangladesh, this gives the country some of the most productive land in Asia. The price they pay is frequent and frighteningly destructive. The most recent serious flood, in 1998, inundated two-thirds of the country and left 22 million people homeless.

The River Pijain, in the northeast of the country, falls, not strictly from the Himalaya, but from that older rock on which Nagaland and much of western Myanmar rests. As soon as it enters Bangladesh it is harvested. Not so much for fish or crop cultivation but for stones. The country is strong on mud but very short on stone and the river bed at Jaflang, just across the border from India, is like an open-cast quarry, combed by several hundred freelance quarriers. Men, women and children, in narrow flat-bottomed skiffs, put out onto the lazy, meandering waters and dredge for stones and gravel, which they take ashore to be carried by trucks to the crushing plants that line the road for many miles.

In the West all this would be done by machines and conveyor belts: in Bangladesh, human labour is abundant and cheap. For a day's work collecting stones, unskilled workers earn the equivalent of 70 pence.

To survive in such unregulated conditions you need an eye for the main chance and while the boatmen are arguing over who gets the BBC's custom, a bright-eyed, obliging young man seizes his opportunity and offers me a ride out onto the river. It's only after the smoke-belching little outboard has kicked in and we're heading towards a very low, makeshift bridge with ten-tonne trucks rolling across it that I first take a good look at my crew. The captain is probably no more than 14 and his first officer 8 at the most.

None of the boats on the river look like the sort you'd find at Henley Regatta, but ours is easily the scruffiest tub on the Pijain. The metal hull is leaking quite spectacularly. A series of small fountains erupt from the bottom of the boat as if it had been raked by tracer fire. The eight-year-old picks up a plastic bottle and bails out enthusiastically, stopping every now and then to flash me a big, reassuring smile.

By the time we reach the furthest of a succession of gravel bars I've developed considerable respect for my under-age crew.

All around us there are people sieving, sorting and sifting alluvia. Pencil-thin wooden punts are packed with boulders and gravel until they are so low in the water that it seems one extra pebble might be enough to sink them. This low-tech quarrying looks to be a family activity largely undertaken by the very poor. Out in mid-stream young boys dive for stones. From the bank a line of elderly men toss roped buckets into the water and slowly draw them in. Wives and sisters are sizing the stones and putting them in piles.

Wandering in the middle of all this are relatively affluent day-trippers, who obviously see this stretch of the Pijain as something of a beauty spot. They sit in chairs, buy soft drinks off the heads of itinerant salesmen and have their photos taken. A group of boys and girls walk arm in arm, suddenly breaking apart to splash water at each other. Bearing in mind that Bangladesh is 90 per cent Muslim, it's interesting to see girls, unveiled, hand in hand with boys in public. It's a reminder that, unlike Pakistan, Bangladesh is not an Islamic republic, it's a secular democracy.

As I scramble off the cheerfully leaky boat back onto the shore, thinking what an odd and unfamiliar world this is, where holiday-makers mingle with crushers, trucks and small hills of gravel, I hear my name called in a Bangladeshi-Cockney accent.

'Michael!'

A man detaches himself from a family group and bounds up to me.

'I'm from Milton Keynes.'

He's a chef in a restaurant there, coming back to visit his home country, a rich man by Bangladeshi standards. He says there are many like him from this part of the country.

On our way to Sylhet, we see the other side of the coin. The roadside is lined with piles of stones, carefully sifted and laid out to be crushed, either in machines or by roadside gangs, very often female. Many of these stoneworkers have come across the border from Myanmar and are not welcome. The Burmese immigrants in Bangladesh are as much of a sore point here as the Bangladeshi immigrants are in India.

Near Sylhet, the stone industry is replaced by undulating tea gardens, and we spend the night at a plantation home turned into a guesthouse called The White House and run by a slow-moving, chain-smoking, very bright, very laid-back man called Kais Chowdhury.

This was his family house. It was burnt down in the vicious war of 1971, when this country was called East Pakistan and the Pakistan army came in very hard to quash any hopes of secession. They lost and, helped by the Indian army, Bangladesh came into being at the end of that year. But it left behind scars and a lot of people who claim to have been 'freedom fighters' at that time. This substantial, spacious and attractive house, with its deep verandahs, is, sadly, in slow decline. Water squeezes arthritically from the taps and disappears even more slowly down the plugholes; the wiring is eccentric and some switches require considerable effort just to find them. The White House has some grace and charm but it also has a fatal inertia, as if it's being slowly strangled by the rich profusion of tropical flowers and shrubs that spill over onto it, mounting the walls and climbing over the balustrades.

All evening and long into the night, trucks from the stoneworks thunder along the road close by. Kais says that the opposition party has called a *hartal*, a protest strike against the government, for tomorrow, and the truck-drivers are hurrying to get their work done before the morning.

It's apparently the second *hartal* this week. After the steely discipline of Bhutan, my first day in Bangladesh has been, well, different.

Day One Hundred and Eighteen: Sylhet

'The Londonis' is the local name for those Bangladeshis who have made a lot of money from running restaurants and allied businesses in places like Brick Lane in East London and brought the money back to build opulent houses in their home country. Sylhetis, more Assamese than Bengali, have a reputation for being clannish, for sticking together and helping each other, and have done particularly well in England. The evidence is all over the town, in row after row of fresh-built mansions in the International Rich Style. The paint is hardly dry on some of these urban palaces, stacked with a riot of cornices, columns, pediments, balconies and burglar-proof fences. They should, one feels, all be set in ten-acre compounds, but there's no room here, so they jostle together in streets that have not yet been paved.

Abdul Rahman was one of the first successful Sylheti emigrants to Britain. He meets me outside a multistorey block of apartments he's just had built. He's dressed simply in a lungi (a long white cloth worn round the waist and legs) and a hand-embroidered white shirt. He is carrying a hookah and puffing at it nervously. His wife died five days ago and he's not sure whether he should be talking to us at all. But in the courtyard back at his house, with various members of his family watching from the doorways, he proves to be engaging company. Mr Rahman has had three nationalities thrust upon him in his lifetime. Born an Indian in 1929, he became briefly Pakistani, when Muslim East Bengal was hived off at Independence in 1947, and finally Bangladeshi in 1971.

Despite being in his late seventies, he's an energetic, impulsive and tactile storyteller, all eyes and teeth.

'When I went to England first,' he turns towards me, wide-eyed, as if about to divulge an enormous secret. 'There was not any motorway *at all*. Wasn't *any* motorway in England.'

The conversation veers from the Pinteresque, 'Do you know Bewdley?' to the Pythonic, 'The only word I knew was "garlic"'.

This didn't help when he got his first job, in a steelworks. When a workmate asked him how old he was, he had to guess at what he meant.

'I gave him my tongs.'

The man asked him again how old he was.

'Then I give him my overalls.'

Eventually, Abdul Rahman learnt English well enough to attempt his first, and perhaps most important, deal. He sold a chicken he'd bought for two shillings and sixpence to someone for ten shillings. By the end of the next year he was a poultry magnate, selling 12,000 birds a week, and, in the process, becoming the first official halal butcher in England.

With colourful hand gestures he illustrates why he considers halal killing to be superior.

He mimes a man holding a chicken.

'English way, squeeze and pull. We think this is a cruel way.' He pauses again, mouth open wide.

'Muslim way, you cut like this. Very sharp knife, quick throat, let the blood out, and she very nicely sleep. This is halal way.'

He maintains that the houses he's put up in Sylhet are for his extended family and not for profit.

'That is our tradition here.'

In any case, it cost him a lot of money. Land is expensive here, he says, more expensive than London or New York.

'Because the people who run my country, they always want money for this and that.' Bribes, he alleges darkly, are an essential part of any transaction. His hand is on my arm again and his eyes bore into mine.

'I speak true. I always speak true.'

There is a pause, and then a last big, toothy laugh.

Day One Hundred and Nineteen: Chittagong

Have a lie-in this morning. Unfortunately, it's at the Harbour View Hotel in Chittagong. I have a distinct feeling that they are demolishing the room above me. Roars, thumps and metallic crashes above my head mingle with a tumult of car horns in the street below and ear-splitting bursts of pneumatic drilling from a building site opposite.

I pull back the curtains for a view of the harbour, but can't see it anywhere, and I'm on the tenth floor. Instead, there is a wall of concrete right opposite me, smeared grey-black as if it had been in a fire. Dozens of slight, spindly figures are at work on top of it, either demolishing it or building it. It's hard to tell.

I fear this unpromising start to the day is not entirely fair on Chittagong. We've come here, after all, in search of industrial destruction and dereliction, at the legendary ship-breaking yards further down the coast, and have no time to investigate the old bazaar or the wooded hills that rise out of the heart of Bangladesh's busy second city.

We drive out to the south, past the port that stretches along the banks of the River Karnaphuli, with its armada of mixed traffic, from break-bulk freighters to sailboats that look like sampans, waiting out in the roads. We follow the coast road through straggling suburbs and villages. Our driver hurtles along, firing off blasts of the horn at anyone and anything that moves. Basil notices that the driver's thumb is in such continuous use that it's worn a hole through the plastic on the steering column.

With some relief, we pull off the main road and up a narrow dirt lane to the ship-breaking yard, one of several along this coast that have taken advantage of a plentiful cheap labour force to grab a lion's share of what was once a lucrative market. We're welcomed by the manager of the yard, a bearded, thoughtful man with dark glasses and a wide, embroidered shirt, not the sort you'd expect to be running such a rough and ready business. He leads us up a concrete stairwell and out across a patio, past serried ranks of toilets and washbasins that have been stripped off the ships. He shows us into a room where refreshments have been prepared and we take coffee and biscuits looking out over a panorama of sanitary fittings and hear about the state of the industry. It's not good. A quarter of a century since ship-breaking businesses first sprang up on this stretch of coast only two or three remain. The privately owned Bangladeshi yards are finding it very hard to compete with their state-financed Chinese rivals.

We walk outside and up onto the level above for a view of the yard. It is an extraordinary sight. Dismembered sections of once-mighty ships are scattered across a blackened, oily beach, like the remains of some disastrous invasion. Two ships stand off-shore, awaiting their fate. Furthest away is the *Ocean Breeze*, a sizeable cruise liner. With her trim white superstructure and matching navy-blue hull and funnel, she looks more like she's on a maiden voyage than in her death throes. Nearby is a supertanker, the *Luccott*. Every now and then, a shower of sparks spills down her hull as the oxy-acetylene torches begin eating her away from inside.

I hardly notice the Bay of Bengal. It's grey and neutral here, like a workshop floor, and it comes as something of a jolt to realize that this is my first sight of the sea in six months of travelling.

Above the shoreline, slices of ships sit marooned in the sand like giant sculptures. The further they are from the sea, the less recognizable they become, until great leviathans are finally reduced to their component parts, piles of pipes, cylinders, air vents, staircases, propellers, lamps, doors and portholes, stacked neatly next to each other.

The manager, who says it takes six to seven months to break down a big ship, tells me that the money is not made from spare parts but from the bulk steel. There is enough in each supertanker to build two skyscraper blocks.

I walk down onto the beach. The stranded sections, an entire boiler room, a beehive of exposed cabins, pipe systems like prehistoric animals, have a mournful beauty, but otherwise it's like Dante's inferno. The once golden sand is in a chronic state, pock-marked with grease, oil, human and animal excreta, sinister patches of blue asbestos and scarred by trenches gouged by steel cables dragging heavy metal up the shore. The work force, supplied by private contractors and brought in from other parts of the country, swarm like ants over corpses. Surrounded by jutting, often jagged, edges of solid steel, flying sparks, falling metal and billows of evil-smelling black smoke, they seem desperately short of protective clothing. Headscarves, oil-stained trousers and T-shirts, baseball caps and sandals seem to be the order of the day for labourers, but even skilled men like welders can be seen operating without goggles or workboots. Tools are basic. Apart from the oxy-acetylene torches, most of the demolition work is done with hammer and crowbars. I see a cylinder block being carried away by two boys of school age.

It's not only ships that are on the scrap heap here.

On the main road outside, almost every shop is selling some kind of marine salvage, from taps and towel rails to crockery and capstans. One salesman stands proudly in front of a pond full of orange lifeboats.

Later, as our Biman flight from Chittagong descends into Dhaka, the Bangladeshi capital, I can see for the first time the full extent of the watery plain created by the great rivers. From up here I can easily believe the astonishing statistic that Bangladesh has 5000 miles (8000 km) of navigable waterways. Sometimes it's hard to see where earth and water separate, as the coiling river courses twist and turn and tangle with each other. Villages, marked out by clumps of trees, cling to raised mud banks like vessels adrift in a flat green sea.

Nearer Dhaka the riverbank is lined with brick kilns, all built on the same pattern, symmetrically laid out around a single towering chimney, looking like ancient temples.

Apparently, there are 2000 of them around the capital, and though they look rose-red and eye-catching in the evening sun, every one belches out clouds of unfiltered smoke particles that drift across what they say is already the most polluted big city on earth. Well, whatever it is, we're in it.

Day One Hundred and Twenty One : Dhaka

You need help to enjoy Dhaka. You certainly need help to understand Dhaka. Otherwise, you might easily be scared off. In 1971 the population was one million. Even conservative estimates believe that number to have grown to 15 million, and with 80 per cent of the country's jobs located here, there's little sign of this headlong growth rate slowing down. I've been warned that getting around can be slow and uncomfortable, but I have great faith in my companion Ishraq Ahmed, a short, canny man with a trim beard and an immense list of contacts.

This morning's *Bangladesh Observer* carries front-page reports of the second *hartal* this week. Both leading parties use these one-day strikes as political weapons and there are reports of marches, arrests, accusations, counter-accusations and several deaths in violent clashes with the police. The paper's mailbag seems united in condemning yesterday's action. Today, Dhaka is back to normal. This means unmoving lines of cars, trucks, buses, and over-revving, smoke-belching tuk-tuks, interwoven with any number of the estimated 700,000 bicycle rickshaws that offer a sporting alternative to the traffic jam.

There seem to be very few rules of the road. Road sense, in Dhaka, is knowing how to get to your destination by any means possible.

'It's the only country in the world where every one has right of way,' says Ishraq, with, I detect, a certain quiet pride.

There's a bracing, nerve-shredding excitement to Dhaka's street life, especially as we near the river, at the heart of the old city, where the traffic is infiltrated by hundreds of people weaving in and out of the crush, dodging from warehouses to shops to dealers with heads and shoulders full of anything from fish to electric fans and company ledgers to car parts.

There are women in black burkhas and women in riotously coloured saris, men in white skull caps and long robes, men in dark glasses with two-piece suits. Ishraq is emphatic that Bangladesh is ideologically tolerant and politically diverse. This may be part of its problem but it also explains the relative absence of the religious fundamentalism we saw in Pakistan.

We emerge from the press of markets and wharves and out onto the wide open spaces of Friendship Bridge Number 2, a graceful, grey curve slung across the River Buriganga by gift of the Chinese government. Adverts for 'Green Love' condoms have been slapped onto its concrete columns and beneath it is surely one of the most tumultuous stretches of river on earth. It reminds me of those paintings of the lagoon in Venice or the Pool of London in their heyday, before there was any other way of shifting goods and people en masse. The parallel is relevant. Only a few miles upstream from downtown Dhaka, the Ganges (known here as the Padma) meets the Brahmaputra (re-christened the Jamuna) and a combined total of 3357 miles (5730 km) of water sweeps on down to the sea. The only form of transport that can adequately deal with the delta is waterborne. Hence the ranks of multistoreyed ferries, drawn up offshore like floating new towns, the broad-bottomed junks fat with sacks of rice, the smeared and shabby freighters carrying steel rods twisted like barley sugar, the barges almost invisible beneath cones of sand and, everywhere, the slim, low-slung, cigar-shaped water taxis waiting to launch out into the middle of this mayhem.

I walk down to the shore below the bridge. A line of men, teeth clenched and bow-legged with the weight, scuttle up the riverbank with blocks of ice on their heads. Others emerge, like a line of ants, from within the dark hold of a barge, balancing wide baskets full of sand ballast as they negotiate a wobbling gangplank. A pye-dog, all sores and clouded eyes, collapses in the shade of a van. When I get out my notebook, a curious crowd presses against me. The *Lonely Planet Guide* devotes a whole column to 'Staring': 'The Western concept of privacy is not a part of the culture in Bangladesh,' it warns, and I can see what they mean. I find it as much comical as threatening, as 20 or more people all peer over my shoulder to try and see what I'm writing in a very small book. When I stop writing, all eyes turn to my face, watching expectantly. When I resume, they go back to the book, following every line and curve with the utmost concentration.

Just when I think they may be with me till the end of the series, they're distracted by shouts of indignation from the film crew, who, it appears, have been peed on from the bridge above. Whether intentionally or not, no-one seems to know. I try to console Nigel by telling him there's a first time for everything, but he's not in a humorous mood.

Despite the oil, the grime, the smell and the procession of unspeakable things flowing along it, the River Buriganga is lined with impromptu laundries. The crew of a timber barge wash their clothes by treading them inside old oil drums, before taking them out and beating them hard on wooden planks and tossing them onto a pile, from which they're picked up and laid out to dry on the sand. The odd thing is that they do look sparkling clean.

I am intrigued, and impressed, by the number of women in high positions in Bangladesh. The two main parties, the Bangladesh National Party and the Awami League (the ones responsible for the current wave of *hartals*) are both led by women. One of the most successful groups of garment factories, employing 7000 people and exporting 68 per cent of their output to the USA alone, is run by the highly charming Rubana Huq and her husband, but she is the one who travels the world and brings in the orders.

In early afternoon Ishraq takes me to meet Naila Chowdhury, a director of Grameen Phone, one of the great success stories to come out of Bangladesh. Naila, impressively built, with a strong hand-some face, is, like Rubana, charming, accommodating and, I suspect, pretty ruthless when necessary.

'Grameen' means village and the villages of Bangladesh are poor. To try and help break the spiral of poverty, a man by the name of Muhammad Yunus came up with the idea of micro-loans aimed at the rural poor, who maybe need a few extra *taka* to buy a cow or a plot of land or a sewing machine. He set up the Grameen Bank 25 years ago and now it has over three and a half million borrowers, 95 per cent of whom are women. (Grameen prefer to lend to women, as they're less likely to run off with the money.) The Grameen Phone project is an extension of the idea. A woman in the village takes out a loan to buy a mobile telephone and a solar panel with which to recharge it. She earns money to pay back the loan by charging local people for calls, both within the country and internationally. A lot of Bangladeshis are migrant workers in places like Saudi Arabia and the Gulf.

The women have three years to pay back the loan, and to prevent the whole scheme suffering the fate of well-intentioned causes in a cruelly commercial world, the interest is a hefty 20 per cent.

The results, as Naila explains to me, as we drive out to the countryside some 25 miles (40 km) from Dhaka, have been impressive. Grameen Phone has led to the empowerment of women and the empowerment of local village communities.

Not only are villagers able to talk with family members abroad, but villages themselves are able to talk to each other. They can compare prices of basic goods like seed and fertilizer and avoid being ripped off by unscrupulous suppliers.

'They can't be hoodwinked,' as Naila puts it.

Watched by a small caravan of Grameen advisers and feeling rather like a royal visitor, I'm led by Naila, wearing a smart orange and yellow *shalwar*, black, medium-heeled, leather shoes and rolled umbrella, along a narrow mud path between the fields. Pumps chug away, irrigating the rice paddies, and families of ducks are scudding about among the young shoots. Naila finishes a call and snaps her mobile shut.

'I love my work,' she says, steadying herself to cross an unsympathetic patch of wet, sticky mud, 'I love it so much.'

She apologizes for her executive outfit, but she has a big business meeting later. I ask her if the endemic corruption everyone talks about here hinders her work. She shakes her head. Bribes are a commonly accepted part of the system, if you want things to get done fast.

'They call it speed money,' she says. 'It's not always such a bad thing.'

Passing by a field of lentils, with fragrant blue flowers and clumps of bamboo with bee-eaters darting in and out of them, we reach Athalia village. In a month's time, when the monsoon starts, we could not have walked here, for the surrounding fields become a lake and stay that way for half the year.

A reception committee is waiting to meet us as we scramble up the bank, and we're led into the village, composed of around 30 huts of palm thatch and corrugated iron. The huts are built on hard, smoothed mud, freshly treated with liquefied cow dung, which seals the clay and keeps it waterproof. There is no electricity here. The village phone has been held for the last four years by Mrs Abida Sultan, a short, middle-aged woman with prominent, gold-rimmed glasses and matching gold watch. She is shy and rather quiet today, continually readjusting her pale pink sari modestly over her head, in a way that makes me think she wouldn't wear it like this if we weren't here. Her phone is in a plastic cover with a purple trim, and she grips it tight as she answers Naila's questions.

Being the only phone-lady for miles around means Mrs Abida Sultan is in demand. She must be available 24 hours a day, 7 days a week. She is making between 7000 and 10,000 *taka* profit every month, about £70 to £100. A rural family needs about 5000 *taka* a month to survive, so, unlike most of those who live in Athalia, Mrs Abida Sultan can comfortably break out of the life of subsistence. Grameen Phone has enabled her to send her 19-year-old daughter to university, something she could previously never have dreamt of.

Naila says that, despite Grameen's success, the potential has barely been tapped. Only one million of the 140 million in Bangladesh have been connected through the mobile system, and Grameen Phone, half owned by the Norwegians, is now the biggest single investor in the country. The concept has been exported to poorer rural communities in places like Malaysia, Thailand and Ukraine.

The pace at which Naila and her PR team work is very different

from the leisurely diurnal rhythms of this soft, warm, inviting countryside and once away from the village her mobile starts up again
and doesn't stop until we're back in Dhaka.

For those able to survive the sound and fury of the capital there is
a reward. Ishraq puts it simply.

'The best international cooking in Southeast Asia.'

And he's determined to prove it. Last night we ate some fine
Chinese, surpassed tonight by a wonderfully authentic Lebanese
dinner. And tomorrow, yet another strike day has been called, so we
can stay in bed and sleep it off.

Day One Hundred and Twenty Three: Dhaka to the Delta

Life down in the delta rarely makes the news. Goings on in Dhaka,
Chittagong and Sylhet hog the headlines. But today is different. In
between all the *hartal* horror stories, the *New Nation* has a mention
of the Sundarban Islands, my final destination. Apparently, the
decomposed remains of six villagers, killed by man-eating Royal
Bengal tigers, have been discovered deep in the mangrove forest. I
sort of wish I hadn't read that.

On the way to the boat terminal, through lanes crowded with
commerce and alleyways of go-downs where old men, still calculating by abacus, sit cross-legged beside sacks of rice or swat flies away
from fruit stalls with feather dusters, we pass an incongruous set of
cast-iron railings. Behind them rises the Ahsan Manzil, a wedding-
cake pink building that was the palace of the Nawab Abdul Ghani, a
Muslim and the largest landowner in East Bengal at the time of the
Raj. By all accounts, this influential man was also a man of learning
and culture, and his son Salimullah founded the Dhaka Medical
School. The Pink Palace, as it's known, has been restored to its
former glories and is a reminder of the beauty that lurks beneath
the surface of this scuffed and overworked city, and makes me wish
I'd had more time to explore.

The Sadarghat boat terminal is Dhaka at its most exasperating
and exhilarating. Everyone fights for everything: parking and
unloading space, space at the ticket counter, space on the long pon-

toons, space on the boats that moor up against them. No-one is actively hostile, they're just there. There where you want to be, and in huge numbers.

After many wrong directions, I eventually find our boat and can't understand why I hadn't seen it earlier. With an ochre-painted superstructure and massive paddle wheels, the PS *Ostrich* is an old-fashioned, pleasing shape, like a great nautical sausage. It is part of the Rocket Service, pride of the succinctly named Bangladesh Inland Waterway Transport Corporation. The identification plaque records that its Year of Built (sic) was 1929 and that it was 'Reno-vated and Dieselized' in Narayagonj (just outside Dhaka) in 1996. It accommodates a total of 700 people on two decks and has 24 places in First Class.

I step onto the gangplank. Below me, the water is thundercloud grey. An evil-smelling, viscous grease-slick covers the surface of the Buriganga like lacquer. Then I'm shown to a flight of steps with a banister rail in polished wood, which leads up to the first-class accommodation. Here, the world is transformed. The cabins, their numbers in polished brass, lead off a long and gracefully propor-tioned state room, down the centre of which runs an elegant mahogany table. The wood panelling on the walls is painted a subtle combination of light and dark grey, and interspersed at intervals with fluted bas-relief columns picked out in gold leaf. Outside, a covered deck set with tables and chairs offers the enticing prospect of cocktails at sunset. Sadly, this being a Muslim country, there is no bar on board, but Ishraq, ever ingenious, has access to supplies of his own.

Five minutes before our scheduled departure time the *Ostrich* emits two sonorous blasts from its horn, warning late-arriving passengers and waterborne tradesmen selling hard to the open decks below us that departure is imminent. We cast off and pull away from the seething Sadarghat dead on time, narrowly avoiding collision with one of the many ferries fighting for our place at the pontoon.

Ishraq has invited a friend of his along, a delightful lady called Mahjabeen Khan, but known to all as Moni. She is probably not far from my own age, but is blessed with a good head of glossy dark hair and intensely dark eyes. She was born in Guwahati, Assam, but at Partition in 1947, her family, being Muslim, moved from there to

Sylhet in what had become East Pakistan. Looking back now, she can see that trying to turn East Bengal into a part of Pakistan was a terrible mistake.

'They wanted us to behave differently, look differently, eat differently, dress differently. We were always a secular country.'

She and her seven siblings, six sisters and one brother, were sent to high school in Dhaka and encouraged to study a musical instrument. Moni discovered a talent for singing as well as playing and turned professional, until she married an ambassador and spent 15 years in Washington and Bangkok. Her husband, Abu Zafir Obaidullah Khan, was not just a diplomat and scholar but one of Bangladesh's leading poets. Her story seems to paint a portrait of a charmed life and it's quite a shock when Moni reveals that before she met Abu Zafir she had spent 12 largely unhappy years in an arranged marriage.

But before all that, when she was 13 or 14, she and her family took the Rocket Service when they went on holidays down south. She remembers its formality: the crisp linen tablecloth and gloved waiters in white uniforms with braided epaulettes, brass buttons and matching white turbans.

Tonight, there's less ceremony. People eat at different times. A tasty, fleshy local fish called *bekti* is served, but not with white gloves.

A thin, bespectacled man introduces himself after supper. He spent several years at the Botany Department at Sheffield University and, in one of those serendipitous moments that give travel a good name, I find myself on both the Ganges and the Brahmaputra swapping stories with a Bangladeshi botanist about the church I used to go to when I was nine.

The waterways of Bangladesh seem to operate on the same philosophy as the roads of Dhaka, an improbable synergy that, by the most dangerous means possible, successfully accommodates every kind of river user. None of them seem to have lights or horns. And as we don't have radar, Captain Mohammed Rahman has to rely on instinctive judgement.

I'm in bed in my cabin reading Patrick O'Brian when we make our first stop at Chandpur. There is a lot of noise and light and the sound of shouts and the slap of sandals, and the loading and unloading is still going on when I put down my book about

Napoleonic sea battles, feeling that, perhaps, past and present aren't so far apart.

Day One Hundred and Twenty Four : Chandpur to Mongla

Up at six. It's a soft, drowsy morning. The banks are shrouded in mist, from which fields and trees occasionally emerge, tinged with diffused morning sunlight. The mist and the water mingle, giving the impression that everything, on water and land, is floating.

From a map on the wall of the state room and a few enquiries of the waiters, I work out that we are west of the main river channel and south of Barisal, heading slowly through a maze of curling rivers in the rough direction of the Sundarbans National Park. Breakfast is a disappointingly routine affair, enlivened only by discovering that my bottle of 'Mum' mineral water is proudly labelled 'Official Drink For the 10th Asian Conference on Diarrhoeal Diseases'.

At half-past seven we reach a place called Jahlokati. An archetypal scene of passengers waiting beneath a spreading neem tree, a few thatched buildings and a tin-roofed warehouse, its walls stuck with political posters and daubed with slogans. The signs are only in Bangla, reminding us that we are well away from the cosmopolitan world of Dhaka. Well away from the hustle and bustle too. Though a lot of people are getting on and off here, the noise is as muted as the morning light.

As the gangplank goes down, the line of disembarking passengers begins to move, most of them balancing their possessions in bundles or cardboard boxes on their heads. Then the porters come aboard and take off the big stuff: massive, tight-strapped, white bundles that are manoeuvred slowly up the gangplank to the accompaniment of a chant.

The river is low and the root systems of the mangrove trees run along the banks like exposed wiring. A slew of fresh-cut logs is floating up against the shore and a man, balancing on one of them, dips his hand in the water and cleans his teeth with his finger.

The timeless rural peace is shattered by the warning sound of the ship's horn, which reverberates around this quiet little place like the roar of a bull elephant. After ten minutes or so, the gangplanks are raised, provoking the usual last-minute rush, as people leap out of the bushes and race aboard.

Our kitchen staff have secured a sackful of green coconuts, which they split open for us, and we drink the sweet but cool milk as we pull out onto the stream again.

A few minutes later, a modern concrete bridge materializes, silently, shockingly, out of the mist, then slips away behind us and we're back into the past again. Spreading rain trees, rubber trees and date palms cluster tight along the bank. A white-robed figure strides dramatically among them. Deep-hulled, tall-prowed boats, like Chinese sampans, bob up and down in our wake. I watch an immensely distinguished-looking man with a bushy, grey beard carefully prepare his fishing net. He tosses it into the water and slowly pulls it in and examines it. There is nothing there but mud. With infinite patience, he gathers the line, tosses it out and draws it in again. Nothing.

There is something about the dignity both of the man and his slow work that leaves an impression. And the fact that he never once looks up as a yellow 1920s paddle steamer with 700 people on board goes by.

The morning wears on. The sun grows stronger, but I find it hard to tear myself away from the deck rail. The dancing silver patterns of light reflected on the water, the gradual release of the countryside from the mist, the sound of a flute drifting across, all create a feeling of the world slowed down, a seductive and fragile sense of peace.

Moni and I are talking about this, about how the world's most crowded country can offer such a sense of calm, and she asks if I've read any of Tagore's work. I'm ashamed to say I haven't. Rabandranath Tagore was the Shakespeare of Bengal. A crude metaphor, perhaps, but it reflects his status here. He was a poet and playwright and, though he was a Hindu, he wrote of the universal preoccupations of Bengalis and particularly of the countryside, which, Moni thinks, has changed not at all since he died over 60 years ago. He had an international reputation, winning the Nobel Prize for Literature in 1913, and being awarded a knighthood by the British, which he returned in protest at the massacre in Amritsar in 1919. (Evidence of which I saw on Day 30.)

A lot of Moni's favourite songs are Tagore's poems set to music and she sings some to me as the countryside he celebrated slips past. As Moni points out, he was sympathetic but never sentimental about the rural life. We are in what they call 'cyclone alley', and in Tagore's time, just like now, this golden panorama of huge skies and wide water, of rice paddies and thatched houses, bordered by the long, dark outline of the mangrove forest, could be transformed overnight into a killing field by the storms that brew up over the Bay of Bengal.

One of the songs Moni sings tells of the bruised Bengali people standing in a line, crying, and asking their god to 'speak into our ears and into our hearts and tell us there is good news'.

We stop more frequently now and in the middle of the afternoon pull up at the jetty of a small settlement rejoicing in the name of Moralgunj. Big crows eye us from the bare branches of a dying mangrove tree.

I've worked out that the relative importance of our ports of call can be determined by the number of gangplanks the ship puts out. Chandpur was a four-plank stop, but Moralgunj is only a two-plank stop. Mongla, where we arrive after 13 hours, is Bangladesh's second port after Chittagong. It's also where we bid goodbye to the *Ostrich*, and disembark down five planks, with a security rail on either side.

Day One Hundred and Twenty Five : Mongla to the Bay of Bengal

There is one task we have to complete today and that is to cover the remaining 90 miles (144 km) between here and the Bay of Bengal, and rendezvous with a forestry department launch, which will take me out onto the ocean and off into the sunset for the final shot of the series.

I'm up before five. Shower, pack my things together, grab a basic breakfast at the Hotel Pashur, then walk out past the bus station and down to the jetty, where two of the three boats on which our day depends are bobbing up and down on the water. They don't inspire confidence. Named *Feni 1* and *Feni 3*, after a frontier town north of Chittagong, they're ex-lifeboats with a Do-It-Yourself viewing platform built on top and furnished with plastic chairs. The boat is steered from the top deck by a Heath Robinson rudder extension made from various pieces of scrap metal, into which is fitted a handle made from a tree branch. Well, not made from it exactly. It *is* a tree branch.

This whole unsteady collation is topped with a few lengths of domestic, wrought-iron railing and a sun canopy suspended from four sticks.

The crew is lively and enthusiastic. Unlike the engine.

We cast off at dawn and, as the light slowly improves, we can see our surroundings are as magical as yesterday. We chug through a clinging mist, past the temporarily exposed mudflats they call *chars*, islands that appear briefly after the flood waters recede and are instantly planted so that at least one crop can be harvested before the next monsoon washes the island away.

About an hour south of Mongla, the cultivated land comes to an abrupt end and we are hemmed in by the dark, impenetrable walls of the largest coastal mangrove belt in the world. There are few settlements down here, and the short, steep, slimy banks offer no landing opportunities. If one needed any further reason for staying away, the forest is also the habitat of the much feared Royal Bengal tiger, whom the people of the forest refer to as 'uncle'. It's considered bad luck to utter its real name.

Occasionally, we come across some fishing boats, at which, oblivious to our deadline, the cooks insist on stopping so they can investigate luncheon ingredients. They eventually settle on crab, sweet-water lobster and some of the largest prawns I've ever seen. Ishraq says these are of such quality that these small fishermen sell them on to bigger trawlers, which take them up to freezer plants at Mongla, from where they will be sent to the dining tables of the USA and Europe. It's a business worth $100 million a year.

I watch kingfishers skimming along the shoreline and a fish-eagle with bold, rufous wings hunting in our wake, snapping up tiny fish and eating them on the wing. After a while, I drift into a deep sleep in which I dream someone shouts.

'Michael! Crocodile!'

I wake up to hear someone shouting.

'Michael! Crocodile! Look!'

And I do, just in time to catch sight of a grey metallic shape the size of a small submarine turn its panto-villain face towards me and slide into the river, sending out waves of repulsion and muddy brown water. I feel sorry for crocodiles. Just because God gave them teeth too big for their mouths and yellow eyes that open and shut like Porsche headlights you can't imagine them ever having a single decent thought. But for all I know, they might be quite lovable, salt-of-the-earth reptiles who, given half a chance, might well help an old lady across the road and surprise us all by not eating her.

Worn out by all this mental exercise, I go back to sleep until lunch. And what a lunch. The cooks have achieved a minor miracle. In a tiny space beside the toilet they have cooked up the crab, prawn and lobster with turmeric, quince, chilli, coriander, onions and ginger into a perfectly balanced and gorgeously fresh-tasting stew, which must rate as one of the best meals on the entire journey.

After this celebration, sober reality intrudes. Time is no longer on our side. One of the boats is not even making nine knots and, in a last hope of reaching our rendezvous, we lash the two *Fenis* together and use the power of the better performing engine.

From here on, it's all anxiety. Looking at watches and trying not to look at them at the same time. Watching the sky, cursing the slightest headwind, fearing the worst at every change in engine tone.

With less than an hour to go until sunset, the waterway opens out into a wider bay and suddenly we are at the sea. Not far ahead, with huge relief, we catch sight of the jetty at Katka, where we have arranged to meet up with our forestry launch. The only thing missing is the forestry launch.

By the time we reach the tall, mud-encrusted pier and the launch still isn't there, we have resigned ourselves to the fact that it's never going to be there in time. We look around helplessly.

The place is silent and empty apart from the curved ribcages of boats long since abandoned to the mud.

Then into the bay comes another boat, a plain but picturesque small trawler with pointed prow, central cabin and some heavy structure at the stern. It's moving steadily towards the jetty. Ishraq issues orders. As soon as the fishing boat reaches the shore, the bemused crew find themselves, literally, roped into the final sequence of a BBC television series.

Feni 3, acting as camera boat, is roped up to the trawler and a complicated procedure worked out, in which, having delivered my last piece to camera from the fishing boat, the ropes will be loosened and I and the plucky little trawler will drift off into the sunset.

It is a crazy, impossibly risky idea, depending on split-second timing, but, with total credit to everyone concerned, we complete a successful take minutes before the sun and the Bay of Bengal merge.

In the last words of this last shot, I say that, despite all the wonders I have seen, the majestic scenery of a half-dozen countries, the power and majesty of the highest mountain range on earth, it is the people I've met that will stick in my mind.

The enjoyment of the world is immeasurably enhanced not just by meeting people who think, look, talk and dress differently from yourself, but by having to depend on them. The trio of Bangladeshi fishermen who learnt the arcane art of television filming in a little less than half an hour are only the last of a long list of those who had every reason to think that we were completely mad, but who decided, against all the odds, to be our friends instead.

In the heady rush of our emergency ending, I almost forgot why we were here. Only after the camera's turned off for the last time and we're heading for the muddy shores of the Sundarban Islands do I have time to feel that umbilical connection between the water I'm on now and the remote mountains where it all began for us, many months and several thousand miles ago.

Acknowledgements

At four o'clock on the morning of 25 September 2003, in a cheerless hotel foyer in Delhi, Roger, cameraman Nigel Meakin and I celebrated, as best we could, an anniversary of sorts. It was 15 years ago to the day that, at the Reform Club in London, Roger had called 'Action!' and set *Around the World in Eighty Days* in motion. One thing we all agreed on that morning in Delhi is that not for one minute had any of us imagined we'd still be travelling together five series and a decade and a half later.

I owe Roger a great debt of thanks for being patient and tolerant, careful, critical and above all wonderful company. As series producer, he took the lion's share of responsibility for *Himalaya* and, as co-director, led Saga Platoon through Pakistan, India and Bangladesh.

John-Paul Davidson, who directed us in Nepal, Tibet and Yunnan in China, Nagaland, Assam and Bhutan, is a veteran of the Himalaya and his unflagging mix of energy, enthusiasm and invention was only matched by his empathy with the people, his love of the countries and his ability to produce fresh-brewed ground coffee at any altitude. Nigel Meakin made a mockery of the passing years by producing superb work in often awful and uncomfortable circumstances. Peter Meakin, his son and heir, is not only a credit to the family filming business, but also a dab hand with the sound recorder who got us out of a hole or two when altitude sickness struck. For a few weeks we were sadly deprived of John Pritchard's affable company, as it was he who the altitude struck. His replacement, Chris Joyce, came out from England at very short notice, and ably picked up the baton (or whatever it is that sound recordists hold).

Vanessa Courtney, iron fist in velvet glove, negotiated us brilliantly through the choppy waters of security-ridden Pakistan and

India, and the manic delights of Bangladesh. Claire Houdret soothed frayed nerves in Nepal, Nina Huang Fan was a tower of strength in China and Havana Marking and Natalia Fernandez kept morale up in the rarely trodden pathways of Nagaland and Assam. No-one could have looked after us better in the high Himalaya than Wongchu Sherpa, Mingmar Dorji Sherpa (who reached the top of Everest on 17 May 2004) and Nawang Dorjee Sherpa. Mingmar was both on-screen and off-screen star in Tibet.

Life on the road would not be complete without Basil Pao, gastronomic adviser, menu translator, peerless photographer and, I suspect, closet trekker.

In the front office, the experienced hands and cool heads of Anne James and Mirabel Brook once again set our journey up with speed and great efficiency. Anne watched us through to the end, whilst Sue Grant stepped into Mirabel's shoes with aplomb. Natalia Fernandez worked tirelessly throughout the series, counting us out and counting us back. Lyn Dougherty and Steve Abbott took on the care of finances, and kept us both above the law and in the black. Paul Bird has done just about everything for us, short of coming on the journey, and Alison Davies has been wonderfully encouraging, as ever, as well as uncomplainingly taking on perhaps the worst job in the world – deciphering my sound tapes.

Special thanks to the sage of Harlesden, Alex Richardson, who should by now have been made the first saint of the editing world. Thanks too to Saska Simpson for taking on Alex's role on one of the shows. And to Lorraine Heggessey, Nicola Moody and Tom Archer at the BBC for their continuous and constructive support.

Apart from those mentioned in my text I would like to thank others without whom Himalaya would have remained just another mountain range: Jonny Bealby, Abdul Kadur Jaffer, General Rashid Quereshi, Anuraag Jacob, Onkar Singh, Holly Williams, Mr Yang Le, Sun Shuyun, Mr Ding Duzhang, Yatish Bahuguna, Fazal Kamal, Doug Scott. We would have got nowhere without Maqsood Ul-Mulk and Hindukush Trails in Pakistan, Royal Expeditions in New Delhi, Peak Promotions in Nepal, Chhundu Travel in Bhutan and Purvi Discovery in Assam. Special thanks to all at Whitehouse Cox who made me two shoulder bags that went with me everywhere, and to Mike Griffin for all those farewells and welcomes.

Enormous thanks, too, to all those at Weidenfeld & Nicolson

who have worked wonders to produce a complex book in such a short time, Michael Dover, my editor, whose unflappable and generous support was never more necessary, David Rowley, my art director and designer, who has done a fine job at a furious pace, ably assisted by Austin Taylor and Justin Hunt.

To Claire Marsden for making sure I spelt her name right, as well as about 4000 others. Thank you also to Tara Redmond and Angela Martin for making sure the world knows we exist and, finally, special thanks to Richard Hussey, who rejected a life of ease to stay on and see this book through production.

Reading Matter

Footprint, Lonely Planet and *Rough Guides* were never far from my side, but Isobel Shaw's *Pakistan Handbook*, Michael Buckley's *Bradt Guide to Tibet* and Françoise Pommaret's *Odyssey Guide to Bhutan* were outstanding. The beautifully illustrated *Insight Guides* add a touch of local colour. I eagerly devoured Patrick French's three books on the history of the region: *Younghusband, Tibet Tibet* and *Liberty or Death*, whilst among other favourites were Kathleen Jamie's *Among Muslims*, Peter Matthiessen's *The Snow Leopard*, Geoffrey Moorhouse's *To The Frontier*, Peter Hopkirk's *Trespassers on the Roof of the World*, Sun Shuyun's *Ten Thousand Miles Without a Cloud*, Namu's enchanting *Leaving Mother Lake* and Romesh Bhattacharji's travels in Assam, *Lands of Early Dawn*.

MICHAEL PALIN established his reputation with *Monty Python's Flying Circus* and *Ripping Yarns*. His work also includes several films with Monty Python, as well as *The Missionary*, *A Private Function*, an award-winning performance as the hapless Ken in *A Fish Called Wanda*, *American Friends* and *Fierce Creatures*. His television credits include two films for the BBC's *Great Railway Journeys*, the plays *East of Ipswich* and *Number 27*, and Alan Bleasdale's *GBH*. He has written seven bestselling travel books to accompany his series *Around the World in 80 Days*, *Pole to Pole*, *Full Circle*, *Hemingway Adventure*, *Sahara*, *Himalaya* and *New Europe*. He is also the author of a number of children's stories, the play *The Weekend* and the novel *Hemingway's Chair*. In 2006 the first volume of his diaries, *1969–1979: The Python Years*, spent many weeks on the bestseller lists. In 2008 an updated special edition of *Around the World in 80 Days* was published to coincide with his BBC documentary *Around the World in 20 Years*. Visit his website at www.palinstravels.co.uk.

BASIL PAO began his photographic career in 1980 on his return to Hong Kong after ten years in the United States, where he was an art director for Atlantic, Polygram and Warner Bros. He first worked with Michael Palin on the design for book accompanying Monty Python's *Life of Brian*. They have since collaborated on the books based on his seven travel series. In 2007 he wrote and photographed *China Revealed: A Portrait of the Rising Dragon*.

FULL CIRCLE

MICHAEL PALIN

Photographs by Basil Pao

PHOENIX

A PHOENIX PAPERBACK

First published in Great Britain in 1997
by BBC Books
This paperback edition published in 2009
by Phoenix,
an imprint of Orion Books Ltd,
Orion House, 5 Upper St Martin's Lane,
London WC2H 9EA

An Hachette UK company

3 5 7 9 10 8 6 4

This edition copyright © Michael Palin, 1999
Photographs copyright © Basil Pao
Maps by David Atkinson

The right of Michael Palin to be identified as the author
of this work has been asserted by him in accordance with
the Copyright, Designs and Patents Act 1988.

A CIP catalogue record for this book
is available from the British Library.

ISBN 978-0-7538-2325-5

Printed and bound in Great Britain by Clays Ltd, St Ives plc

The Orion Publishing Group's policy is to use papers that
are natural, renewable and recyclable products and
made from wood grown in sustainable forests. The logging
and manufacturing processes are expected to conform to
the environmental regulations of the country of origin.

www.orionbooks.co.uk

CONTENTS

INTRODUCTION

The Pacific Ocean covers one-third of the world's surface and around it lives one-third of the world's population. Its 70 million square miles of water spill onto the shores of a richly contrasting assortment of countries. Some are global giants – Russia, China, Japan and the United States. Others, such as Malaysia, Indonesia, Australia, New Zealand, South Korea, Chile and Canada, are becoming increasingly important and influential. The coastline that unites them is now more than just a physical entity. It is a political and economic state of mind, called, for want of something more poetic, the Pacific Rim.

Experts predict that the Pacific Rim will be the power-house of the twenty-first century. Commentators point to the final decline of the Mediterranean-Atlantic axis which has dominated the world these past two thousand years. The future, we are told, belongs to the other side of the earth. The Pacific century is about to begin.

Many times, over the last couple of years, I have found myself nodding in agreement with these sage judgements without being at all sure what I was nodding about. Where exactly is the Pacific Rim everyone talks about with such authority? Which countries does it include? What are the people like in these countries? Do they share a sense of the destiny so many think lies ahead of them? I felt it was time to stop nodding and to learn something.

After *Around The World In 80 Days* and *Pole to Pole*, the question I was most often asked was 'Is there anywhere you haven't been?'. As soon as I started getting out my Pacific maps, it became clear that there were lots of places, and that a journey round the Pacific Rim would cover a great many of them, as well as shedding some light on a huge part of the world I knew so embarrassingly little about. Having made the decision to set out again, with much the same team, we began to join up a few dots on the map. The more closely we looked, the more the journey grew in size and scale. A circle may sound a neat controllable entity, like a hub-cap or the face of Big Ben, but when its diameter is 11,000 miles it takes on epic proportions. And *Full Circle* indeed proved to be an epic.

The eventual distance we covered was around 50,000 miles, more than all the mileage on *80 Days* and *Pole to Pole* put together. We set ourselves the deadline of one calendar year and were on the road for more than two hundred and seventy days of that year, returning home briefly to do some laundry and save our marriages.

There were times when resources ran low and the whole effort seemed overwhelming. But, as with the best journeys, this was often because there was no let-up in the sheer richness of what we saw and experienced. It was a journey of dazzling surprises and jarring extremes. Beauty and ugliness, sophistication and squalor, unceasing urban noise and monastic tranquillity were often to be found within a few miles of each other. It was not always easy to keep an account of all this and yet I managed to write something in my little black notebooks each day. These diaries, spotted with sand, curled by sea-water, besmirched with everything from Japanese rice-wine to chicha beer from the Andes, form the basis of *Full Circle*, augmented by my tape recordings, postcards and letters home.

If *Full Circle* succeeds in painting a portrait of life around the Pacific Rim, it is through the eyes of a traveller looking for enlightenment, not an expert dispensing it. Often I learned the hard way. But I learned, and now the countries on the other side of the earth are less of a mystery and more of a revelation. This is a record of a year of wonder.

Michael Palin
London 1997

ACKNOWLEDGEMENTS

First and foremost, my undying gratitude to my fellow travellers. Most of them have trudged round the world with me before and they know that I can never convey in words my esteem for their work, their ability, and the fact that none of them makes a lot of noise at breakfast.

Clem Vallance, once again, set about the onerous task of pulling all the strands of the production together, as well as directing half the series. Roger Mills marched at the head of the troops for five of the ten episodes. Nigel Meakin, on camera, and Fraser Barber, on sound, maintained their legendary high standards in often impossible conditions. Nigel's assistant, Stephen Robinson, was calm in every crisis and Jude Tyrell and Vanessa Courtney quite brilliantly smoothed our way around the Pacific despite recalcitrant hotels, waiters, immigration officials and others less convinced of our purpose than ourselves. Basil Pao, our photographer and gastronomic adviser was, as usual, indispensable.

It is quite something to spend two hundred and seventy days of the year with six other people. To enjoy it as well is a credit to our simple rule of travel – that everyone depends on everyone else.

Along the way there were many others we depended on to help us through, over and between tight spots. We greatly miss Igor Nosov, who conquered Siberia for us, and who sadly died a year and a half later. Enormous thanks to him and to all who helped us round the Rim – especially Yukiko Shimahara, Shin-Na, John Lee and Susan Xu Xu, Mai Thu Ha, Marissa Floirendo, Philip Yung, Eko Binarso, Stephanie Hutchinson, Patricio Lanfranco Leverton, Barry Walker, Marcela Gaviria Quigley, Chloë Sayer and Bill Boatman of the US Coast Guard.

Mirabel Brook and Jane Sayers held things together at the London base and Emily Lodge arranged the currency deals.

At Prominent Television Anne James was both a beady eye and a great inspiration, and Eddie Mirzoeff at the BBC was always a guiding hand. My thanks too, to the patient editing team who put the series together – David Thomas, Alex Richardson, Victoria Trow and Kathy Rodwell.

The short sharp shock of putting this book together has been made immeasurably easier for me by the tireless patience of my assistants Kath James and Kirsten Whiting and my hard-working and long-suffering editorial and production team at BBC Books, especially Sheila Ableman, Anna Ottewill and our designer Bobby Birchall.

And last but not least, my thanks to Suzanna Zsohar for letting the world know it's been written.

Travel Note: Thanks to the *Lonely Planet Guides* for information on almost everywhere. *The Rough Guides* and the *Insight Guides* were invaluable too.

Little Diomede
Magadan
RUSSIA
BERING SEA
SEA OF OKHOSK
Petropavlovsk
Vladivostok
Qingdao
Seoul
KOREA
JAPAN
Sado Island
Tokyo
Hiroshima
Nagasaki
Chongquing
Wushan
Shanghai
Guiyung
Nanning
CHINA
YELLOW SEA
Hanoi
Baguio
VIETNAM
Manila
PACIFIC
PHILIPPINES
Saigon
Zamboanga
Sandakan
Kuching
MALAYSIA
INDONESIA
Jakarta
Surabaya
TIMOR SEA
Darwin
CORAL SEA
AUSTRALIA
Alice Springs
INDIAN OCEAN
Adelaide
Sydney
Auckland
NEW ZEALAN
Dunedin

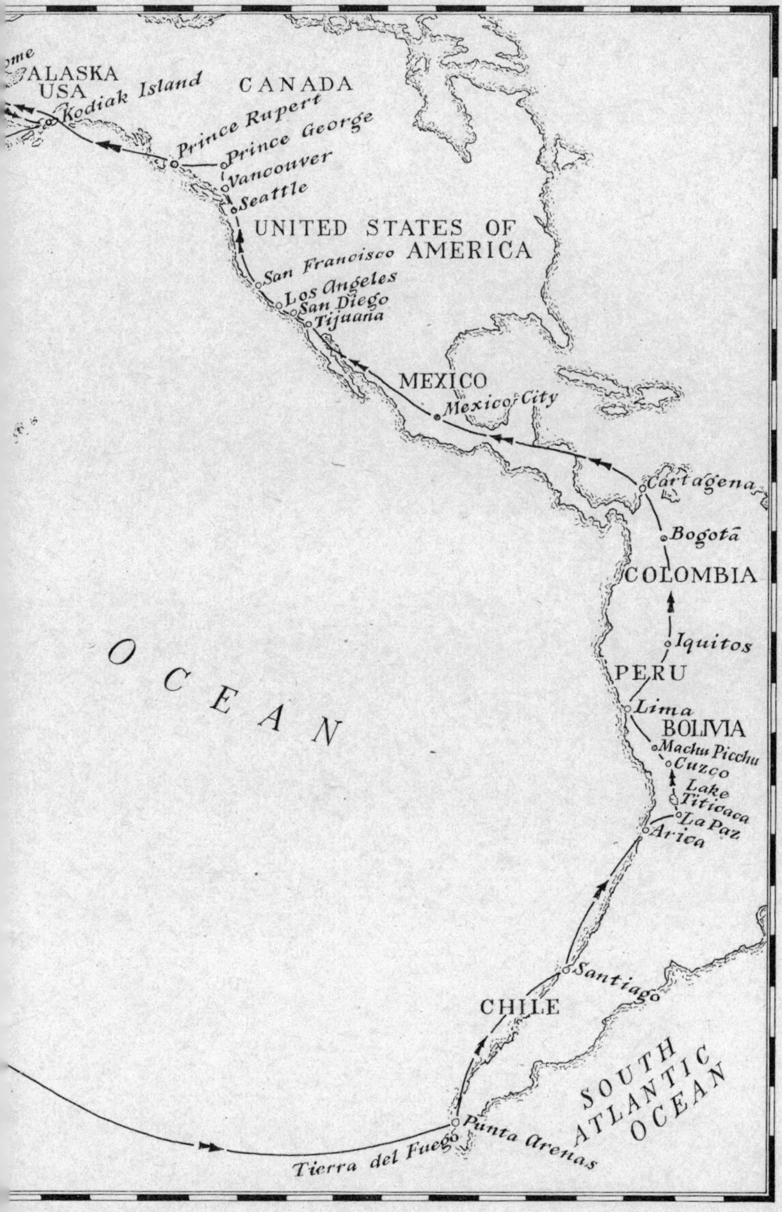
ome
ALASKA
USA
Kodiak Island
CANADA
Prince Rupert
Prince George
Vancouver
Seattle
UNITED STATES OF AMERICA
San Francisco
Los Angeles
San Diego
Tijuana
MEXICO
Mexico City
Cartagena
Bogotá
COLOMBIA
Iquitos
PERU
Lima
BOLIVIA
Machu Picchu
Cuzco
Lake Titicaca
La Paz
Arica
O C E A N
Santiago
CHILE
SOUTH ATLANTIC OCEAN
Punta Arenas
Tierra del Fuego

ALASKA, USA

DAY 1: *Little Diomede Island, Bering Strait*

It's mid-morning in late August and I'm sitting on a rock in the middle of the Bering Strait.

I'm not the only one here. As well as the six other members of my film crew there are a hundred and eighty-two Inaluk Eskimos for whom this mile-long granite outcrop is home. Down below me they go about their business. Fishermen dismember walruses, cutting the precious meat into fat, stinky chunks which they conceal beneath shrouds of plastic sheeting like objects in a murder investigation. Their wives spread the skin of the walrus out to dry on wooden frames, alongside braided lengths of seal intestine, strips of herring and morsels of beluga whale. Others repair boats, tarring and painting and tinkering with outboard motors. Most of the sixty children who live on the rock spill noisily onto the school playground for a lunchtime break. A handful of men in hard hats disappears into the treatment plant beside the huge water storage tank that dominates the small, steep waterfront settlement.

From my precarious perch I look down at the messy jumble of huts with something approaching despair. Everyone else on this rock seems to know what they're doing and why they are here.

I try to concentrate – Nigel is pointing his camera expectantly and Fraser's wind-baffled sound boom is aimed at me like a cattle prod. A documentary series waits to begin. Yet, as I sit here, I feel less like a television presenter, more like Alice in Wonderland.

Only five days ago I was filming in a cupboard in Buckinghamshire with John Cleese and a tarantula spider and now here I am, just short of the Arctic Circle on a Monday morning, looking across at a Russian rock where it is Tuesday morning – the explanation for this twenty-four hour time difference being the invisible presence of the International Date Line which slices through the Bering Strait not much more than a stone's throw away. The Russian soldiers staring out at me from across the water have already had the day I'm having.

Now the wind is strengthening, carrying the sickly, pungent smell of seal blubber up the hill towards us. It also carries the smell of changing weather and I'm aware that we cannot stay up here for much longer. I must focus my mind and try to make sense of all this.

The rock I am sitting on is called Little Diomede Island and it is the most extreme north-westerly possession of the United States of America. It lies just south of the Arctic Circle at a latitude of 65.40° and is separated from the Russian territory of Big Diomede Island by a narrow, racing, two-and-a-quarter-mile channel. A few thousand years ago, before the end of the Ice Age, Diomede was part of a huge land bridge, across which, many scientists now believe, came the first human inhabitants of the Americas. The Russian mainland is only 30 miles away and the American mainland even less. Asia and America come as close to each other here as London is to Oxford, and in winter, when the sea freezes, it's possible to walk from one continent to the other.

The Bering Strait is the northern gateway to the Pacific. From here the great ocean swells southwards until it extends 11,000 miles from eastern shore to western shore and covers one-third of the surface of the planet. Many people have explored its islands, or sailed down the Asian or American coasts, but I have never come across anyone who has been full circle, who has followed the countries of the Pacific all the way round. I hope to be back on Little Diomede one year from now. Or however long it takes to circumnavigate the Pacific Rim.

Once I've confided my intentions to the camera I feel better, clearer in my mind. But as the rising wind licks around this bleak and treeless cliff so there rises in me a dawning apprehension of what is to come, of how much there is to do, and how little I will see of my family in the year ahead. I look around the crew and wonder if they are thinking the same thing but they are already packing up the gear, hoisting bags onto shoulders and starting to pick their way through the grassy rocks down towards the village and the sea. We're off.

The village into which we are descending is called Ignaluk. It is the chief, indeed the only settlement on Little Diomede and within it are evident all the contradictions and complications of Eskimo life. The weather is fierce and pitiless. There is no shelter from the elements apart from the huts they build themselves and the few modern public buildings provided by the government. Living is still largely subsistence, and hunting methods ancient and traditional. Puffin-like sea birds called auklets are caught in nets at the end of 12-foot long poles. 'We basically scoop them out of the air,' one man told me. They hunt whales, though nowadays they shoot rather than harpoon them. When the first ice of winter, the 'slush ice' as they call it, comes down from the north, they lie in wait for the polar bears that come down with it. It's a hard life, but none of those I've met would dream of abandoning the island.

Eskimo culture is emphasized in school and in the local council. Alcohol is banned here, as in many communities in western Alaska; the Eskimos have a low tolerance of it. Half the population worship at the local Catholic church. Their Eskimo names have American counterparts – I've met Eskimos called Andy, Marlene, Orville and Anne-Marie. They may not have fridge-freezers (they bury food in the permafrost instead) but they do have satellite television and it's not long before word gets around that one of the actors from *Monty Python and the Holy Grail* is on the island. The last thing I have to do before leaving one of the most remote corners of the world is to sign autographs.

DAY 3: *Nome*

'You will find a magic city,
On the shore of Bering Strait;
Which shall be for you a station,
To unload your Arctic freight.
Where the gold of Humboldt's vision,
Has for the countless ages lain;
Waiting for the hand of labour,
And the Saxon's tireless brain.'
                    The Goldsmith of Nome
                    Sam Dunham

Breakfast at Fat Freddie's restaurant in Nome, a very whacky town, taking pride in bizarre statistics such as the fact that it is 75 miles away from the nearest tree. It lies on the south-west coast of the 200-mile-long Seward Peninsula, named after George Seward, the American Secretary of State who bought Alaska from the Russians in 1867 for 7.2 million dollars. (Even though this worked out at roughly two cents an acre it was not a popular purchase and the territory was referred to at the time as 'Walrussia' and 'Seward's Ice Box'.) We are quartered at a sea front hotel called the Nugget Inn which lies on Front Street next to the Lucky Swede Gift Shop.

There were in fact three Swedes who, in 1898, struck lucky in nearby Anvil Creek and started a classic gold-rush which in two years turned a stretch of Arctic desert into a city of 20,000. There are different versions of why it was called Nome, all of them suitably eccentric. One Harry de Windt who passed through in 1902 and described the gold-mad town as 'a kind of squalid Monte Carlo', claims that it derives from the Indian word 'No-me' meaning 'I don't know', which was the answer given to early white traders when they asked the natives where they were. The most popular explanation is that Nome came about as a misreading of a naval chart on which a surveyor had noted a nearby cape with the query 'Name?'.

Despite these inauspicious beginnings Nome has survived ninety-seven years of fire, flood and disease and though its population has settled down around the five thousand mark, it doesn't seem to have lost any of its spiky individuality. From the outside, the clap-boarded Nome Nugget Inn looks like a fair-ground attraction, with carved figures of doughty moustachioed gold-panners and the obligatory multi-branched milepost: 'London 4376, Siberia 164'. Inside, it's a cross between a bordello and a natural history museum. The burgundy walls around the narrow reception area are hung with picks, shovels, harpoons, an Eskimo drum made from dried walrus stomach, a fishing float, even an entire kayak. A stuffed ptarmigan scratches itself above an old-style Western bank grille and the skins of grizzlies, wolverines and Alaskan lynxes lie flattened on the back wall like the bodies of cartoon characters who have just run into it.

I take a walk up Front Street, clutching my place-mat from Fat Freddie's which is full of useful information. 'Nome has thirteen churches, three gas stations, nine saloons and eight points of interest.' All I can see at the moment is a large number of unsteady people weaving their way up the sidewalk, occasionally shouting some blurred greeting.

'You Korean?' is the one that throws me most.

Over the counter in a gift shop across the street I get talking to Richard Benneville. 'Sure there's a booze problem,' Richard nods across the street at a cluster of watering holes – with names like the Board of Trade, the Polaris, the Breakers Bar, the Bering Sea Saloon and the Anchor Tavern. 'Those bars on Front Street take ten and a half million dollars a year.' But he doesn't believe Diomede-style prohibition is the answer. 'The modern Eskimo is changing. They have their own corporations now. They can make up their own minds. There used to be two Alcoholics Anonymous groups here, now there's twenty-two.'

Later, Jim Stimpfle, a local businessman, enlarges on the changes, though with the discretion of a real estate salesman he refers to the Eskimos by their politically correct name: 'This is not a native American town. It's a gold-rush town. A town of outsiders, laid out on the traditional US grid plan. That's why Nome is special and that's why property developers like it.'

Two hundred thousand dollars for a property on this bare windswept coast still sounds a lot until one remembers that Alaska now has more than gold. Huge oil resources lie beneath the rock-hard permafrost. Already the share of the Permanent Oil Fund, which is what Alaska gets back in royalties, stands at thirteen billion dollars. Not only are there no state taxes but every Alaskan man, woman and child gets one thousand dollars a year back from the state government.

Perhaps not surprisingly, the locals express great affection for this wild place. They emphasize the lack of crime; the fact that, despite appearances, you can safely leave your door unlocked at night.

And, as Nancy Maguire, editor of the impressive local weekly, *The Nome Nugget*, reminds me, 'Our drunks are the friendliest in the world'.

17

DAY 5

I drive a little way out of town along the beaches to search for what remains of the Golden Sands of Nome which once attracted a stinking tented city of thirty thousand prospectors. Today, under cold grey skies, the description seems only ironic. The foreshore is grubby, more grey than gold, and there is a tidemark of bleached wood spars which I imagine must have been swept over from Russia, as there are no trees here.

But these unpromising surroundings do not deter eternal optimists like whippet-thin Andy and his thirteen-year-old son Rob. They sleep in a little shelter on the beach and pan laboriously by hand. Rob is sensible and articulate and after a brief conversation convinces me that there is absolutely nothing more normal than to spend an entire summer with your father, scraping grains of gold off a windswept Alaskan beach. He regards the financial rewards as quite sufficient enough to compensate for the lack of school chums. He reckons he can clear six and a half thousand dollars in a good summer.

Further down the beach, an Englishman by the name of Stan Cook uses sea water out of a high-pressure hose to dig out the sand. He's scoured a snaking six-foot channel down the beach but scoffs at suggestions of environmental damage.

'One storm'll put all this lot back.'

When I ask him how much gold he's found he laughs coyly, 'If I told you I'd be lying.'

Stan and the other half-dozen prospectors working this stretch may appear to be oddball recluses but he assures me that most of them meet up in the pub at the end of a day. And lie to each other.

On the way back, in a desolate landscape, broken by rickety cabins jacked up on oil-drums and discarded dredge buckets from previous gold mining activities, we stop for a beer at the Safety Bay Inn run by a lady with two-tone vanilla and chocolate-coloured hair. Dollar bills are stuck on the ceiling and the lavatories are marked 'Women' and 'Animals'.

DAY 6

Overnight a powerful storm rolls in from the north. I hear the rain and wind beat against my windows and when I peer out I can see the Bering Sea is agitated and alarmingly close; long, rolling white-tops rush at the sea wall like lemmings.

Wake with a dry cough, incipient sore throat and constipation. Roger prescribes me various preparations from the homeopathic remedy kit he carries with him in a smart little case. There seems to be a pill for every ailment, physical or spiritual, including one for homesickness. It's a bit early for that yet.

Down to breakfast. Fat Freddie's is a warm, fuggy diner on the edge of the continent which produces fry-ups all day long. These seem to be largely consumed by big men with beards and baseball hats wearing fleece-lined Gore-tex jackets and given to staring out to sea and not saying much. The waitress takes our order, adding chirpily that fresh fruit is off today. I flick through a copy of the *Tunnel Times*, published in Anchorage, which describes itself as the official organ of a group lobbying for nothing less than 'the most ambitious construction project in the history of the planet'. This turns out to be the digging of a railway tunnel beneath the Bering Strait which would connect North America and Asia. It raises the prospect of some tantalizing rail excursions. Waterloo to Grand Central. Windsor to Washington. Bangkok to Bogotá.

I admire their audacity. Make a mental note to include them in my will.

Spread out some maps. At this moment an intercontinental railway could solve a few of our problems. We have to try to work out the quickest way to get on to our preferred route round the Pacific – anticlockwise down the Asian side and back up through the Americas. Because much of Siberia is inaccessible wilderness, the most northerly landfall we can safely make in Russia is on the Kamchatka Peninsula. The United States Coast Guard has offered to airlift us through the Aleutians – a necklace of islands stretching 2000 miles out across the Northern Pacific – if we can get ourselves to their base on Kodiak Island, a few hundred miles south of Anchorage.

DAY 7: *Kodiak Island*

I confess I've never heard of Kodiak and was chastened to learn that it's the second largest island in the USA (after the Big Island of Hawaii) and the country's second largest fishing port. It has a jagged squiggle of a coastline, slashed by sharp, steep cliffs and headlands which are green, thickly-wooded and dramatically beautiful in an Alpine sort of way. That we are now well and truly on the volatile Pacific Rim is grimly clear from the natural disasters that mark Kodiak's history. Nearby Mount Katmai blew in 1912 with a force greater than that of Krakatoa. Five cubic miles of material were blasted into the air and the ash that fell on Kodiak choked salmon in the streams and plunged the island into total darkness for three days. On Good Friday 1964, the most powerful earthquake ever recorded in America created a tidal wave, which swept into Kodiak harbour at a height of 35 feet destroying the fishing fleet and flattening the downtown area.

This Sunday morning the town looks serene and neat and well-scrubbed and oddly un-American. I put this down to the dominating presence of the sky-blue domes and white clap-board walls of the Holy Resurrection Russian Orthodox Church. Kodiak was originally settled by Russians who, with the British, Spanish and French, were setting up trading posts on the Alaskan Pacific coast before the United States was even created. There is still a full congregation for this morning's Divine Liturgy, a service which lasts several hours. Most of it is sung, and very beautifully too. The cherubic anthem is hypnotic, gentle and compelling. Although the ritual, the priest's vestments and the architecture are thoroughly European, the Stars and Stripes hang against the iconostasis alongside likenesses of the saints, and in our prayers we are asked to remember not only 'all those suffering from the disease of alcoholism' but also 'our armed forces everywhere'.

This reminds me of our appointment with the US Coast Guard. All being well, we shall leave for Attu, at the end of the Aleutian chain, on Tuesday morning. That leaves us a day and a half to try and cover some of the attractions of Kodiak. Down at the harbour an outfit called Uyak Air offers a sporting menu that includes 'Scuba Diving', 'Horseback Riding', 'Fly In Fishing' (whatever that is), 'Kayaking' and 'Bear Viewing'. As my guidebook describes the Kodiak Brown bear as not just big, but the 'largest terrestrial carnivore in the world', there's really only one option.

I climb aboard the steeply-angled fuselage of an Uyak Air De Havilland Beaver float-plane. The pilot is Butch. That's his name, Butch. Early thirties, laconic, except when extolling the virtues of his aeroplane, he could be straight out of a *Biggles* adventure, as could his machine. Like so many aircraft that ply the world's remote places, the Beaver is no longer new – this one was built thirty-three years ago. Butch describes it, without irony, as 'a really good rough weather aeroplane'. Fortunately, we're spared the rough weather this time and, skimming the mountains at 3000 feet, we're treated to the sort of view you rarely get from commercial airliners. Ridges and peaks rise up to meet us then plunge down and away in a folded carpet of green that spreads itself around turquoise bays and quick, tumbling rivers.

Sixty miles south-west of Kodiak city we touch down on Karluk Lake and turn towards a small wooded refuge called Camp Island. We're met by Scott, the local ranger, and shown the tents and plain cedar cabins we shall be sleeping in tonight. Butch is soon away, racing up the lake and turning steeply off to the north-east. Peace reigns. There is barely a sound besides our own voices.

Scott reckons that, with the weather holding, we should stand a good chance of sighting bears. He and Kent the carpenter (who seem to be the only two running the place) load us, and the only two other guests – a very jolly German couple called Siggi and Rosie – into two aluminium dinghies which take us half a mile away to the point where a small river enters the lake. Scott, rifle slung over his shoulder, though he vehemently disproves of bear hunting for sport, leads us through shoulder-high banks of fireweed and extols the richness of the lakeside life. Apart from the Sockeye salmon and the Red-breasted Merganser ducks that feed on their eggs, we should see beaver,

21

otter, weasel, deer and eagles. All I can see at the moment are black flies, which gather in such persistent clouds around our faces that we all end up wearing the anti-insect equivalent of beekeepers' bonnets. The first time I see any bears – a broad-shouldered fat-backed mother trundling down the stream with two cubs in tow – I am so impressed that, without thinking, I whip the net off my face for a better view. Within seconds, squadrons of flies home in on my eyes, lips and nostrils.

The bears are less than a hundred yards away and we are advised to keep quiet and not attempt to move any closer. (As usual, the experts are divided when discussing wild animal behaviour, between those who insist they wouldn't hurt a fly and those who saw them rip someone to pieces only last week.) There are not many Kodiak Brown bears left, maybe two and a half thousand on the whole island and, though they can roam up to 50 miles, Scott knows the regulars in this river. Olga, the female we first saw, is now sitting back, staring down intently at the brisk stream spilling around her great haunches. Food is abundant at this time of year as the river is bulging with red salmon returning from three years at sea to spawn in the same river in which they were born. Fully-grown bears like Olga will eat about thirty of them a day.

Another two females come sloshing up the river with yearling cubs in tow, distinguished from the adults by their collars of white fur. Maggie, the leading female, makes a grab at a passing salmon which darts away. Instead of waiting for another, she doubles back and galumphs off after it. Eventually she finds something to her satisfaction and collapses on top of it, front paws out like a cat when it traps a mouse. Then, with delicate precision, she lifts the salmon, tugs the skin off with her teeth and carries the fish back to her cubs.

It's our cameraman Nigel's birthday today (on *Pole to Pole* it was celebrated while watching a belly dancer in southern Egypt) and we've smuggled a couple of bottles of champagne onto the island to celebrate. Timed perfectly to coincide with this moment of rejoicing, my incipient cold, which I have been trying to hold at bay with an alphabet of vitamins, finally hits with a vengeance. I take to my bed and end the day sneezing and snuffling in my tent beside the lake as the sounds of 'Happy Birthday' drift out over the water.

DAY 8: *Camp Island*

This morning I feel awful. I long for a hot bath, clean clothes and solitude. As I unzip the tent and emerge snuffling like Badger from *The Wind in the Willows*, I'm aware of a scuttling in the long grass, from which, after a short pause, the heads of two foxes peer out, one a dark ash-grey, the other russet, and regard me curiously. Their ears prick backwards and forwards, alert and wary. Scott is cooking omelettes as I reach the main cabin. He says there are three foxes on the island, Emily and two cubs. They're pretty tame but we should on no account feed them.

I see Emily again as we are leaving for another visit to the bears. She's down on the foreshore, rather daintily turning over pebbles with her stick-thin forelegs. Fraser says that last night he caught one of the foxes trying to prise open a bottle of champagne which he'd left among the rocks to cool.

Three o'clock. The float-plane to take us back to Kodiak was expected two hours ago. We're all packed up and ready to go. The weather has certainly deteriorated since yesterday but the cloud cover is still above the mountains.

Six o'clock and we're still here. There is no radio or telephone with which we can contact the outside world. The splendid isolation of Camp Island is beginning to lose some of its charm. Siggi and Rosie remain stoically calm, but they aren't on their way around the Pacific Rim via the Aleutian Islands. Scott cooks a fine meal of Sockeye and halibut with rice and chopped vegetables. Kent can be heard in the distance sawing and banging until well after dark. Basil thinks he's chopping up previous visitors.

When it becomes clear that no one is coming to collect us today, we unpack and settle down to another night beside this beautiful lake, so delightfully far from the insidious temptations of plumbing, drainage and laundry.

DAY 9

Tuesday morning. My head still feels as if it doesn't belong to me. Breakfast has a doomy air to it. No omelettes from Scott today, just a realistic assessment of our predicament. Visitors have been stranded here on seven separate occasions this summer. The only radio with which we can contact the outside world is in the nearby Parks and Wildlife Department hut but it is behind locked doors and Scott has no key. He is prepared to kick the door down only in the case of a 'life-threatening' emergency. Roger, our director, is not a happy man. He looks bleakly down at his filming schedule. 'Would a job-threatening emergency count?'

Later: Roger is writing a stiff letter of complaint to whoever it was that led us to believe we could be in and out of here in twenty-four hours. Otherwise a certain listlessness has set in. Vanessa (Roger's assistant) sits beside the pebbly beach, draped, like a dowager, in an anti-mosquito veil, reading Homer for her Open University course. Basil has his blow-up doll out. (She's an inflatable version of the tortured figure in Munch's *The Scream* and he plans to photograph her in every place we visit.) Nigel is trudging round the island, Rosie is making a home video, and I am in the woods, looking out from the picturesque, triangular, red-cedar lavatory hut at a bald eagle wheeling and turning above the lake.

Later: There *is* a radio which Scott can listen in to, although he cannot transmit from it. He has managed to pick up word that Kodiak city is fogbound. The only good news is that if no planes can leave Kodiak, our coastguard flight will not have left either.

The bad news is that the wine has run out.

DAY 10

We have now been marooned here for almost two days. The weather is worsening. Cloud and rain are descending and we can barely make out the low mountain horizon which we have all been scanning instinctively for so long.

Desperate situations breed desperate solutions. There is a plan that we should try to walk out from here to the town of Larsen Bay, 12 miles away. Scott reckons we would be risking injury and further delay if we tried it. He says that most of the grassland is bog. Kent flatly contradicts this. He claims he has made the journey before and 'it's like a walk in the park'. It sounds sheer unadulterated lunacy to me but there is an understandable fear that if we do nothing we shall not only lose our coastguard flight but also jeopardize our plans for filming in Siberia, which will then affect plans for Japan and so on.

The argument is temporarily decided by the increasingly poor weather conditions, as bad for walking as they would be for flying. Then, as the afternoon fades and we are resigning ourselves to a fourth night on the island, there comes the sound of a distant engine and, when we least expect it, the Beaver approaches low from the north.

Apparently there has been a brief lifting of the fog in Kodiak, fog that came down so low that, as Butch put it, 'if you'd dug a hole in the beach you'd have found fog in it'. Now the immediate problem is getting us back. There are strong winds and a forecast of heavy rain, so no time for fond farewells. My relief is tinged with a little sadness as I catch a last glimpse of the foxes on the shore gazing as curiously at my departure as they had at my arrival.

The journey back to Kodiak, at times, is perilous. We tumble about in the buffeting air currents and are flung around in the thick of ugly, unavoidable black clouds but relief replaces fear as we break through the last low barriers of mist and catch a glimpse of the flat-grey waters of the harbour below us. Butch becomes a national hero and the thirty-three-year-old Beaver the best plane in the world. Back at the hotel, the little box-like room with its smelly floor tiles is Paradise.

There is a message waiting for us. It's from the US Coast Guard. Their plane left this morning.

RUSSIA

DAY 13: *Kodiak Island to Petropavlovsk*

Aboard Flight 203 from Anchorage to Petropavlovsk – from America's last frontier to Russia's last frontier. Our airliner bears the striking, folksy livery of Alaska Airlines – on the tailplane the huge head of an Eskimo, weather-beaten features smiling out from beneath a fur-trimmed hood, and along the fuselage cartoon bubbles curl out from the windows which read: 'Swell', 'Good Choice' and 'Thank you'. We've been very lucky to get aboard. It is their last flight of the season.

Our route across the North Pacific traces, in reverse, that taken by the Danish explorer Vitus Bering in 1741 when he was employed by the Tsars to try to find out if Asia and America were joined by land. In 1740 he reached the Kamchatka Peninsula and founded Petropavlovsk, which he named after his two ships, the *St Peter* and the *St Paul*. A year later, he sailed some of the stormiest waters in the world to reach what is now Kayak Island, a mile or two off the Alaskan coast, before being forced to turn back by bad weather. To prove he had crossed continents, he brought back an American blue jay and a species of raspberry not found in Asia.

In the twentieth century the spirit of exploration and expansion was replaced by suspicion and secrecy. After World War II the Russians developed Kamchatka as a military region and it was closed to foreigners until 1990. Now the historical cycle is turning again, and with bewildering speed. On my seat I find a copy of an English-language publication called *Russian Far East Update*. It's aimed at foreign businessmen and paints a stark picture of an economy desperate for outside help.

The Pacific Rim is responding. Australians are coming in to save a steel-mill with debts of 56 million dollars, Canadians are building houses in Yakutsk, South Koreans are financing a business centre in Vladivostok, and the immaculately dressed American sitting next to me is hoping to open a string of luxury salmon-fishing lodges.

26

'It's unbelievable,' he enthuses, 'some of these rivers haven't been touched for years.'

I'm a little depressed by all this. I have long fostered romantic notions of the vast, uncompromising grimness of Siberia. Now it's beginning to sound like an industrial estate.

Two hours out of Anchorage we cross the date line and, quite effortlessly, teatime on Saturday becomes teatime on Sunday.

A short time later we are over Siberia. A bright, unclouded sun reflects off the burnished surface of the Anodyr River. Every variety of natural feature seems laid out below us. Flat, table-top plateaux, perfectly rounded craters, neat volcanic cones, deep ravines, glacial corries and the silvery ribbons of river courses meandering through wide, purple valleys. As we begin the long descent into Petropavlovsk, the volcanoes grow taller, wider and more perfectly proportioned. I feel as though I have happened upon a great secret. Our stock images of mountain grandeur – Switzerland or the Rockies, the Himalayas or Mount Fuji – are well-worn and familiar, but all this beauty, being Russian, hasn't yet been tapped for the calendars or place-mats of the world.

We swing wide over Avacha Bay, protected by high cliffs and massive crow-black headlands, and make a final approach over a delta carpeted in many shades of green. Now I can see the outskirts of Petropavlovsk below me. We have passed into a different day and a different world. This is not the world of highways and shopping malls, but of drooping power lines, sparsely-filled two-lane black-tops, and shabby, broken buildings. Where steel can rust it's rusting and where paint can peel it's peeling. The aircraft that line the rutted rim of the tarmac are of strange and unfamiliar design. Most of them are mothballed, their engines hooded and in some cases removed. Ground transport consists of two chunky military vehicles which trundle out to the plane bringing with them the portly, faintly theatrical figure of our Russian host and minder, Igor Nosov.

I have been warned about Igor's extrovert technique, so I am not entirely surprised when, from the front of the aircraft, rings out a command guaranteed to endear us to all our fellow passengers: 'Please! BBC to leave plane first!' Nor am I

27

entirely surprised to find Igor hustling me towards a reception committee. This consists of a man with a video camera, a half-dozen bored-looking women in national dress, one of whom is carrying a cake and another a big bouquet of flowers. Like a general escorting the Queen, Igor directs me along a line of broad-shouldered, slightly bewildered dignitaries. We shake hands and exchange mutually incomprehensible pleasantries. I am about to move onto the cake when Igor steers me firmly away towards our waiting vehicle.

'Wasn't that a bit rude?' I ask him. Igor shakes his head firmly. The welcoming committee wasn't for me anyway. They were waiting for a trade delegation from Alaska.

Igor bustles us onto an ancient bus which reeks of diesel oil. Hanging on the glass behind the driver is an English-language calendar, with a photograph of three spaniels peeping coyly over the top of a basket. The calendar is dated 1987.

We drive to Olga's Hunting Lodge which sounds romantic but is in fact situated next to a disused factory at the end of a cinder track in Yelizovo, a suburb of Petropavlovsk. Igor, who seems intent on giving himself a heart attack on our behalf, wheedles, cajoles and berates various members of Olga's family until he has set before us a magnificent repast. He is desperately keen that we enjoy ourselves and, as we tuck in to red caviar, smoked and poached salmon, borscht and cream, cucumber and tomato salad, Moldavian wine, Moskovskaya vodka and freshly-picked raspberries, alternate expressions of joy and deep anxiety pass across his face like clouds on a windy day.

There is a burly, middle-aged American staying at the lodge, on what seems a virtually permanent basis, with a striking long-legged lady friend who, we're told, is his translator. (Sniggers from the crew.) He is anxious to be of help to us. There is a firework display in town tonight to celebrate the two hundred and fifty-fifth anniversary of the founding of Petropavlovsk. Pressed for details as to when and where, he shrugs.

'We'll find it.'

For some reason, no one believes him. And it's raining.

DAY 15: *Petropavlovsk*

Wake to the sound of lowing cattle. Slept well but was chilly. One thing that hasn't changed since I was last in Russia is the width of the bed sheets, a little wider than the human body but a little narrower than the bed, so you tend to wake up like a badly-wrapped mummy with the sheets coiled around you. Similarly, the curtains, if there are any, are always a half-metre narrower than the window they have to cover. Which means, I suppose, you waste less time drawing them back. Looking outside this morning I see the rain has passed over, the day looks settled and pale sunlight is catching the damp, thick grass on which Friesian cows are munching unhurriedly. Wooden fences heighten the unexpected similarity to an English pastoral scene. But then, Petropavlovsk is on practically the same latitude as Stoke Poges.

To breakfast. No sooner have I poked my head round the door of the dining room than I'm met by Igor who thrusts a spoonful of fresh raspberries into my mouth.

'Tradition!' he shouts. 'Start the day with a raspberry!'

He enjoys it that we laugh, though I don't think he understands why we laugh so much.

He is also highly satisfied with the weather for today we are to visit the Kronotsky Nature Reserve. It covers one and a half million hectares around Petropavlovsk, and the only way in is by helicopter.

I drive to the nearby airstrip with Sergei Alekseev, the director of the reserve. He is a slim, good-looking man in his late thirties, dressed in jeans, thick rubber-soled boots and a bright green fleece. He pulls on a pair of sun-glasses as we climb into his four-wheel drive Subaru. He swings it expertly around pot-holes and stray dogs screeching to a halt only once to buy cigarettes. His car, he tells me, is second-hand from Japan. Does anyone buy them new? I ask him. Sergei flicks out a lighted match, pulls on his cigarette and smiles at me as if I'd asked if he knew anyone who owned a Picasso.

There is quite a crowd waiting by the lumbering ME-8, a twin-engined helicopter operated in the new Russia by a

29

private company. Apart from the pilot, there is a co-pilot, an engineer, the pilot's six-year-old son, a lady called Svetlana who is going to prepare a picnic for us, Konstantin our interpreter, and Igor's assistant, Sasha. It feels more like a family outing than a commercial enterprise.

Once aboard, we are issued with industrial-style ear mufflers which cut down the engine noise to just below deafness level. Take-off is a long, laborious elephantine process, but once in the air all is magical. We leave behind the low hills on which the trees are showing the first traces of autumn and run north alongside the Pacific, climbing slowly across bare rock and scree to the snow line that rings a spectacular volcano. There is steam drifting from the summit. Over the din of the engines Sergei reminds me that there are twenty-five volcanoes within the reserve alone, twelve of which are active.

Quite suddenly we are up to and over the rim of the caldera. Inside, ringed by sheer walls of brown and black rock, twisted and scored by the force of eruption, is a turquoise-blue lake. Its beauty lies not just in its appearance but in its lonely serenity, completely hidden from the world below.

We touch down on the much wider caldera of the Uzon volcano. This has been dormant long enough for a heath-like flora of pine and gorse to establish itself. But thermal energy still hisses and bubbles to the surface in sulphurous plumes of steam and the undergrowth is broken by stretches of deep-grey mud in which blow-holes belch and gurgle softly.

For the moment we have this odd, suppurating landscape entirely to ourselves, though there are clear signs that bears are not far away. Sergei points to a fresh pile of droppings.

'Here,' he calls us over, 'you see this here. It is . . . what you say?'

'Shit.' Nigel suggests helpfully.

'Yes . . . ' Sergei seems to be searching for something more scientific, 'Yes, it's . . . er . . . shit . . . yes.'

He leads us on past a sub-lunar landscape of bleached white, scalding sands. Much of it is quicksand and we are given a lecture on the perils of straying from the track. But life survives even in the hottest part of this great oozing stew. Sergei shows me a translucent, almost jellyfish-like plant, trailing fine white tentacles, which grows around holes from which water flows at a constant temperature of 90° centigrade. It is unique to Kamchatka.

A more spectacular thermal display is on offer in the nearby Valley of the Geysers, described as the world's largest concentration of hot springs outside of Yellowstone National Park. Whereas Yellowstone is one of America's busiest tourist attractions, Kamchatka's geysers are inaccessible by road and visitor facilities are confined to a single rickety wooden lodge and a network of duck-boarded pathways. Sergei is not unhappy about this. He is anxious that plants and wildlife be given preference over tourists.

The valley consists of a series of narrow fissures opened up by a fault line, through which steaming hot water from nearby volcanic systems emerges in various ways, ranging from the impressive to the frankly theatrical. You can almost set your watch by the great spout they call Velican (the Giant). This shoots a plume of boiling water almost 100 feet high, once every three hours. Sergei, checking his watch, leads me right up to the blow-hole. I peer down 35 feet into the earth's crust. An ominous bronchial wheezing rises from the darkness, as if the earth itself is not at all well.

A path leads along by the river to a gorge, one whole side of which is punctured by dozens of horizontal geysers. Some spurt neatly out over the river, others wildly loose off in all directions. The entire 200-foot cliff wall emits a great wheezing chorus of steam which reminds me of King's Cross station in the 1950s. On our way back we pass other delights such as the Gates Of Hell – two dark chambers whose cavernous entrances can be glimpsed only briefly through the clouds of foul-smelling sulphurous mist that guard them. Nothing is safe and sound and settled here; the earth seems to be in perpetual motion. This is nature at its most extravagant, melodramatic and bizarre.

Our day in the Kronotsky Reserve ends at a woodman's hut – a pitched-roof, log-walled affair where we eat Svetlana's rich salmon stew and the mosquitoes eat us. A pretty stream, fed by a hot spring, struggles past through thick beds of wild celery and cow parsley. If we can find the stream Roger thinks it would be very nice for me to be seen bathing in it. Eventually we locate a pool idyllically set with the log cabin in the background. I strip off only to find that the pool is little more than a sluggish reservoir of mud, stones and other nameless slimy objects, above which all the insects in Kamchatka have decided to hold their annual convention. The fact that the water is blood-warm only makes things worse. Despite the verdant beauty all around I shall remember this particular dip as the Jacuzzi from Hell.

DAY 16

So inadequate are my bedclothes that I have augmented them with various items of my own and I wake dressed like an SAS paratrooper in thick socks, tracksuit bottoms, a sweatshirt and a woolly hat. Igor is shrieking at someone down the telephone and, through the thin partition wall behind my bed, I can hear a lot of giggling as the American construction engineer discusses the day ahead with his 'translator'. In the bathroom, a thin trickle of water totters out of the shower-head but dries up before it gets to me.

Outside there's water everywhere. An elderly woman with a shopping-bag picks her way along the cinder track through flooded potholes. Sergei had hoped to take us up into the mountains to try and track down the Evenks, a nomadic tribe who live almost entirely from their reindeer herds but no helicopter will go up in conditions like this.

It is a frustrating day of delay. Igor spends much of the morning teaching me a suitably sad Russian song called 'Poliushko Pole' which he says is very expressive of the Russian soul. We drive into Petropavlovsk and I walk along the shore in the dripping rain, watching freighters moving slowly across the bay. I'm not the only one looking out to sea. Behind me is a 30-foot high, 65-ton bronze statue of Lenin, clutching his cap and gazing purposefully at the Pacific, his cape billowing out behind him.

It's a fine statue and I was glad to hear that, despite *Perestroika*, the citizens of Petropavlovsk had voted against a move to have it sent to South Korea to be melted down.

Like many Russian cities, Petropavlovsk still has a public water-heating system. It runs across the city delivering water from massive central boilers to homes and apartments. On our way back to Olga's we pass one of the distribution pipes, hanging, severed, from a metal frame above us. Steaming hot water pours uselessly, but abundantly, onto the road beneath. We all regretted not having brought soap and towels with us.

DAY 17

Woken by Igor's scream: 'Breakfast!'

No raspberries today. Instead a sense of barely controlled panic as we have a flight to Magadan on the Sea of Okhotsk this evening, and we still haven't seen the Evenks or their reindeer. The helicopter has agreed to fly today, but the bus to take us to the helicopter has not arrived. Igor paces about in the road looking like Napoleon on the retreat from Moscow.

An hour or two later, the helicopter, another chunky old ME-8 with petrol tanks outside *and* inside, heaves us up over woodland of willow and silver birch and onto slopes of purple tundra where the mist swirls dangerously low. I have doubts that we shall ever see a reindeer or an Evenk. My record of reindeer hunting is not good. On *Pole to Pole* we wasted the best part of a wet day in Lapland looking for them. Sergei sits hunched at the window, brow furrowed. He makes regular visits to the cockpit after each of which the helicopter veers abruptly off in a different direction.

All at once Sergei is on his feet gesticulating. He's found the Evenks. Well, *an* Evenk, anyway. A lone figure of indeterminate age and sex, swaddled against the elements, looks curiously up from a hilltop as the ME-8 lowers itself down through rain which is now turning to snow. As soon as it is on the ground Sergei leaps out. Camel cigarettes are exchanged and lit with difficulty in the wind. Then we're off again, this

33

time taking our Evenk along with us. There is, apparently, a very large herd of reindeer close by.

As we bank and swoop our way down yet another valley, the weather worsens by the minute. Icy rain streaks and streams down the windows and the mist is thickening on the slopes above us.

Now we can see reindeer tracks and the remains of a small camp, but no sign of either reindeer or their owners. 'Herd Not Seen' runs through my mind as a possible episode title. Then, miracle of miracles, I catch a glimpse of two antlered beasts, racing across a clearing and disappearing almost instantly into the trees, obviously terrified by the sound of the helicopter.

Sergei won't give up easily and orders the helicopter to attempt one more perilous landing beside an encampment in which lives a man they call the Brigadier, in charge of a herd of a thousand animals. Around him families gather outside tents, constructed from black plastic sheets and birchwood frames. A diminutive lady, swaddled in layers of clothing, with a face more Mongol than Russian, invites me inside. There are six or seven dogs and one or two senior nomads gathered around a stove made of vehicle parts. Smoke rises from a silencer and drifts around the tent. She makes room for me on a reindeer skin and pours me tea from one of a set of little enamel mugs. It's a welcome break from the hysteria of the chase, sitting in a pool of warmth with the rain hitting the sides of the tent like a hail of arrows.

I never saw another live reindeer the whole day, but at least I can say I sat on the skin of a very recently deceased one.

DAY 18: *Magadan*

A bright, clear morning in Magadan. Seagull cries scrape away at the borders of my consciousness. Peer out of the window. Bright sunlight picks out the cracks in the walls, the threadbare curtains, the mottled paintwork, the shabby unfinished drabness of the concrete blocks opposite. A half-mile beyond, this same crisp, unsparing brightness sparkles on the waters of

Nagaev Bay, where the Pacific is known as the Sea of Okhotsk. Below me people are making their way to work across rubble-strewn courtyards. They favour imitation leather jackets and carry plastic bags and saggy holdalls. Despite the sunshine it looks bitterly cold out there.

The Ocean Hotel, Magadan, at which we arrived late last night, is the newest hotel in a city built by forced labour in the 1930s. It was created as a port for the gold, silver and other precious metals dug from the inhospitable mountains of the nearby Kolyma region. From Magadan the most infamous of all the Gulags – the Soviet labour camps – were administered. Between 1933 and 1953 millions of 'enemies of the people' (writers, artists, lawyers – anyone on whom Stalin's suspicions fell) were shipped into Magadan during the ice-free months. It is conservatively estimated that three million of them died here.

Although it was always officially denied that the Kolyma camps ever existed, the numbers of those murdered by the state is now being acknowledged. It has just been made possible to visit the remains of the camps, which is why we are taking another helicopter today, this time in the company of a citizen of Magadan, Ivan Ilych Yakovlev. He is one of that small, exclusive and ever-dwindling band – the survivors of the Siberian Gulag.

The mountains of the Kolyma region are dreadful and forbidding. They rise in wave after wave of bare and broken rock, little more than petrified clumps of ash and dust stretching to the horizon. A vista of endless, hostile anonymity. It is ironic that these grim spoil heaps are full of all those things we find so desirable – gold, silver, diamonds – and particularly that most sinister and sought-after metal of the twentieth century – uranium.

The uranium mines were the worst of all. The work was hard, the food appalling. The winter temperatures dropped to −50° centigrade and there was the added risk of radiation poisoning.

Ivan Ilych points down at the raw scree-covered slopes below us.

'I know there is uranium there,' he says, 'because nothing else grows.'

Ivan sits close up to the window, staring out, preoccupied. We're heading for the camp at Butugychag. He has not been back to the Gulag since he was set free in 1946. Watching him reach down into a pocket, pull out a neatly-folded blue handkerchief and dab at his brimming eyes it's hard to imagine him as the 'young and dangerous boy' the secret police arrested in Moldova at the age of twenty. He's still a handsome man with a broad, strong face, bright eyes, quick to smile, and a thatch of silver hair peeping out from beneath a thick woolly hat. He lost his left arm in a prison accident and he walks slowly and stiffly. Yesterday was his eighty-first birthday.

One hundred and fifty miles north of Magadan we land on a silent hillside strewn with cracked and broken fragments of rock. On the surrounding mountain slopes the tracks and low walls of the abandoned mine workings are still visible.

The remains of the prison cemetery can still be seen. Wooden stakes, bleached by wind, rain and sun, stand in broken rows marking makeshift graves, some overgrown with tenacious pine bushes and trailing clusters of cranberry and blueberry, others open to the sky. Bones are exposed in many of them – even a skull – but the only record of their occupants are marker discs, made from the tops of tin cans, stamped with a number and attached to the top of each post. Nearly all are multiple graves.

I begin to count the posts. I give up after three hundred.

Ivan stands for a moment, perfectly still. His eyes could be full of tears or they could be smarting in the cool gusty breeze. He dabs at them again with his blue handkerchief, still neatly folded, then beckons me over.

We walk down to see what's left of the camp. In one corner there is a pile of old boots, made from rubber tyres, which has survived the forty-five summers and winters since the camp was abandoned. Some sections of the stone walls, including the roofless commandant's house, escaped destruction.

'He had hot water and a balcony built so he could enjoy the view,' says Ivan.

Ironically, it is the punishment cells, the prison within a

prison, that have lasted the best. Today, brambles wind decoratively around the bars and coarse grass is clumped around the heavy studded doors.

'No one ever escaped,' Ivan tells me.

I try to imagine what it would have been like to have been here, hauling barrowfuls of rock 1000 feet down the mountainside for thirteen hours a day, rations dependent on how much uranium you delivered, knowing that whatever trivial offence had brought you here – it could be something you wrote, the birthplace of your parents, or even a look in your eye – the outside world would never know. To come to a place like this would have been to vanish off the face of the earth, to cease to exist.

Ivan Ilych survived because he could play the piano and make things out of wood. So he was given privileges – a few ounces more salted fish, a coat for the winter. At the end of the day, when we are safely back at his cluttered flat in Magadan, lined with editions of Dickens, Balzac and Shakespeare, he has only two things he wants to show me. One is his release form from the Gulag and the other is a certificate thanking him for all his hard work in The Great Patriotic War. That's the final surprise, I suppose. That despite all that he went through at the hands of his own people, Ivan Ilych still loves his country.

There is a general feeling amongst those I have met here that post-Gorbachev Russia is as rotten as the Communist state it replaced. There is already a keen nostalgia developing for the days of queues and scarcity, which are associated with an equality, a sense of common purpose. Everything has a price now – education, housing, fuel – and it is a price most Russians can't afford. So the black market flourishes and the sharp and aggressive and unscrupulous are the new top dogs. At the Ocean Hotel tonight we have a glimpse of them.

Halfway through dinner, Fawlty-esque sounds emanate from the kitchen. Breaking of crockery, raised voices. Then a waitress backs out of the serving-door followed by a big, lurching heavyweight in light-blue denim jacket and trousers. He makes a grab for her and a vodka bottle. He misses both and sends a stack of other bottles crashing to the floor. Leaving the waitress to clear the mess, he turns his aggression towards the band, a sad little combo who play carefully and tentatively as though at any moment they might suffer an electric shock from their equipment. The thug leans against the stage, staring up at them, menacingly. There is a flurry of bum notes. Then, with sudden and surprising agility, he leaps onto the stage, head butts one of the amplifiers and, flinging aside the drum kit, he pursues the band backstage. Assorted cries and thuds are heard, culminating in a distant crash of breaking glass. No one from the staff has lifted a finger to restrain him.

Next morning I come down to see a part of the reception boarded up and fresh glass being put in the front door.

It transpires that the man who did the damage was well-known. They say he often comes here, collecting protection money for the local Mafia.

DAY 19: *Magadan to Vladivostok*

It's another bright sunny day and I'm out looking for a *probka dlia vanni* – a bath plug. Do they exist in Russia? I'm assured by our interpreter, Anastasia, that they do, but she doesn't hold out much hope of finding one in Magadan.

Magadan feels, and is, remote. Despite the fact that 30 per cent of Russia's gold and a considerable amount of her oil is located here, the cost of developing communications in these bitter, inhospitable conditions is enormous. There is no rail link with the rest of the continent, air travel is more expensive than it ever was in the Soviet days, and the nearest big town on the road north is Yakutsk, over 700 miles away.

But walking the streets, even in an unlovely place like Magadan, I can see that some things in Russia have changed for the better. There are fewer men in uniform, much less blatant surveillance, more stalls and street traders, more food in the shops. Christmas was restored by Yeltsin two years ago and the KGB has been renamed the Federal Department of Security.

But I still can't find a bath plug. Not even in the biggest store in town – The Everything For Home And Life Store, where car body parts are sold next to bone china, and tampons are found in the stationery department.

Later, at the airport, when I say goodbye to Anastasia with her jet black eyes and her turned-up nose I experience momentarily that tug of the emotions that characterizes every Russian farewell. Politely she puts me right about bath plugs. The Russians regard sitting in your own dirty water as something quite distasteful. I want to ask her why they bother having a word for 'bath plug', but it's too late. The plane's leaving to take us, as Roger is fond of saying, 'decisively south'.

Over the mouth of the Amur River, where the stream is a mile wide, snow flashes by the window and, as we descend into Nikolayevsk-na-Amure for refuelling, over the mighty marshy slough of the delta, visibility is so bad I fear we shall never get up again.

The small airstrip is lined with mothballed aircraft. In the swirling snow I count ten Antonov bi-planes and a further twenty small jets and helicopters in Aeroflot livery – some of which are for sale at less than 10,000 dollars each. Most Russian planes are out of date now, our pilot tells us. The one we're flying in today, a Yak 40, uses a lot of fuel and has no on-board computers.

'This is our computer,' he says and holds up a slide rule.

Five hours' flying time from Magadan and we are over Vladivostok, at the southernmost tip of western Russia. It's a perfect sunset. The mountains are less sinister than those of Kolyma and less spectacular than the peaks of Kamchatka. We are 3000 miles south of Little Diomede and only 35 miles from the Chinese border.

DAY 20: *Vladivostok*

The Vlad Inn is a long, low prefabricated building on the outskirts of the city with nothing Russian about it whatsoever. It's a joint-venture project between the government and the Canadians. In the bar last night the predominant language was English, as American Peace Corps workers mingled with

London accountants. I was pounced on by one of the accountants who couldn't contain his enthusiasm for life in Vladivostok.

'It's set to boom,' he kept saying, 'set to boom. And the women are the best in the world. If it's girls you want, this is the place . . . '

I asked him where he met them. He looked as if he hadn't considered this for a while.

'Oh, in the street,' he said, vaguely.

There are taxis outside in the hotel car park, even a limousine. I find myself becoming positively nostalgic for the rigours of Magadan.

Then I discover the secret garden. Not entirely by accident. I could hear the sound of trains close by and was told that the last few miles of the Trans-Siberian railway pass close to the hotel. The path that leads down to the line passes through the tranquil precincts of an old military sanatorium. The main building is a big, elaborate, neo-classical edifice, from which two curved staircases descend between thickly-plastered balustrades. On top of the building are perched three male statues depicting various post-athletic activities. One lies back, resting languidly on his right arm, trailing a plaster tennis racket over the parapet. Another reclines, leg draped, clutching a football (not an easy task) and between them rises an heroic figure in bathing trunks, immortalized in the act of towelling himself dry. Trees form an arch over the path which runs down the steps and out through a pair of big metal gates to a railway track and a beach.

A train rumbles by, headed by two of the old Soviet-style locos, hammer and sickles still intact on their sides, the dull green coaches interspersed with net-curtained windows. To add to the sense of unreality, it's a train from Moscow, 6500 miles and seven days away.

I walk up the line to a small station enclosed by birch and willow trees. It's called *Sanitornaya* (Sanatorium). I sit myself down on one of the mustard-yellow wooden benches, with a breeze wafting gently off the Pacific, and wait for the 10.30 into Vladivostok.

The local service, the *electrichka*, follows the line of the bay into the city. Although Vladivostok has its fair share of lineside decay, empty workshops and grey apartment blocks, it has a lot else besides. The ebullient main station is a fusion of the Alps and the Kremlin with stucco-work on the arched windows, cone-shaped bell towers, columns and curlicued balconies, decorated drainpipe heads and painted panels; the whole lot recently restored by an Italian film company. Beside it there is a statue of Lenin. It has him in urgent, proactive pose. His right arm, extended as though putting down a heckler, provides some ten feet of pigeon-perching space from shoulder to forefinger. (I'm indebted to Erik and Allegra Azulay's book on the Russian Far East for informing me that Lenin never visited the city and only ever mentioned it once. 'Vladivostok is far away but it's ours,' were his immortal words.)

There are solid, turn of the century red-brick buildings which could be in Leicester or Derby, as well as a Gothic church with a steeple which survived the atheistic Soviet years as a military museum. There are attractive streets of wooden-balconied houses, and on the crests of the sylvan hills around which the city is built are grand apartment blocks with curving roofs, domes and ornate pediments.

This all goes to show that there was plenty of money here in Tsarist times when Vladivostok – the Princess Of The East – was founded. I have the feeling there could be again. Japan is 750 miles away, China much less than that. There is a railway connection with Europe and a superb natural harbour. If Russia is to start looking towards the Pacific then Vladivostok could become its Hong Kong. There are certainly plenty of signs that the Pacific is looking towards Russia. Vladivostok's football team is sponsored by Australia's Castlemaine XXXX beer.

DAY 21

A day off in Vladivostok. I had hoped to spend it mastering the Russian song 'Poliushko Pole' which Igor has taught me and which I am to sing tomorrow with the Pacific Fleet Choir.

However, Anatoly, the conductor of the choir, with the dark moustache and debonair smile of a 1930s band-leader, has suggested an outing. He's laid on a helicopter to take us to Russkiy Island, out in the bay, and brought along some of his colleagues from the choir. The island is dominated by a massive gun battery built in 1913 by Tsar Nicholas II to protect his Pacific fleet. Each cannon weighs 50 tons and is dug down 50 feet into the ground. The whole emplacement is meticulously preserved, and we clamber down into the cool underground chambers where the 1100-pound shells were stacked. Then, after the serious work, the party begins. Accordions and vodka and a video camera are produced and an impromptu song recital from Anatoly and his colleagues leads to dancing and general festivity in the shadow of the Tsar's gun barrels.

The spontaneity, the music and the infectious need to share feelings is very Russian. It's what makes them great huggers, great embracers, great celebrants of either joy or gloom. Mood-swings are part of the national character and I know of few countries where they are so unconcealed.

Perhaps this accounts for the schizophrenic attitude to the Russian Pacific Fleet. This was one of the great, if not the greatest, naval forces in the world. Vladivostok, its home base, was so jealously guarded that the city was off-limits to foreigners until 1992. Now, only three years later, we are allowed to fly over, and even photograph, coves and inlets choked with beached and rusting warships. The helicopter pilot makes no attempt to prevent us catching sight of the half-submerged deck of a frigate, its revolving gun turrets peeking up above the water; or a submarine belly up on a sandy beach, with others keeled over in the turquoise water beyond.

The idyllic patchwork of waterways around the islands is one huge naval graveyard.

DAY 22

A day with what remains of the Pacific Fleet. The Deputy Commander, Vice-Admiral Chirkov, invites me aboard the

Admiral's launch *Typhoon*. It's small and travel-worn with a modest stateroom where bright orange chair-covers fight for survival with yellow curtains.

Once out in the bay the Vice-Admiral points out one of their newest warships, a 7300-ton anti-submarine vessel, bristling with radar scanners, communication masts and clusters of rocket launchers. It was built on the Baltic in 1985 and, such is the remoteness of the Pacific from European Russia, delivered to Vladivostok via the Cape of Good Hope.

Vice-Admiral Chirkov is at pains to point out that a lot has changed in the Pacific. Collective security has replaced cold war. Only recently they took part in joint exercises with the American and Chinese navies. With images of rotting and abandoned warships still in my mind from yesterday, I ask why there seem to be so few ships in this, the fleet's home port. I receive a diplomatic answer.

'The fleet is much smaller, that is true. But it is much better equipped.'

He is a likeable man who entered the Naval Academy here and became one of the youngest Soviet submarine commanders. He took nuclear submarines into the North Sea. I feel a pang of homesickness. I ask him if he has been to England.

He smiles, almost apologetically.

'No, but I have seen Scotland – through a periscope.'

My hour of shame, or glory, with the Pacific Fleet Choir can be postponed no longer.

After lunch I make my way to an intimidatingly large theatre on whose ample stage is a set comprising various naval accessories – rope ladders, flags, nets – against a painted backcloth of drifting clouds.

The band is warming up and most of the choir is already in traditional sailor outfits. I'm half-undressed when a small, muscular man with curly fair hair darts towards me and starts to apply make-up from what looks like a child's paintbox. He makes me purse my lips and applies a slash of scarlet lipstick, swiftly powders my cheeks and is gone. Meanwhile, I can hear the not-so distant sound of the slow, rising rhythms of the introduction to 'Poliushko Pole'. A broad white-brimmed sailor hat is thrust into my hand and I'm on – fortunately in the back row.

What I hadn't bargained for in all my rehearsals was that they don't just sing, they also sway. And, although I may be powdered up pink as a baby, I must remember to sway proudly. I look along the line of my fellow sailors and there they are, every rouged chin at a Churchillian angle, every crimson lip set defiantly. I hear my cue and start to sing, as lustily as I dare. This is a mistake. There are another three verses of humming still to go. The Pacific Fleet Choir is big on humming. Together with the swaying it builds up into something almost hypnotic. A mood, a very Russian mood, of uncontainable soulfulness is conveyed before a word has been uttered.

When the time does come for the words I am, of course, still humming. To sing in Russian requires considerable concentration, but once I am through the first verse, the sheer passion of the piece takes over and, as surge follows surge and the volume rises gently and remorselessly, I can feel myself, just for a moment, at one with the Pacific Fleet, at one with Russia and all its powerful longing. 'Poliushko Pole' is not an aggressive anthem, it is not even a marching song. No enemy is identified and reviled. It is a song about solidarity and pride and comradeship. The words, written in 1934, may lose something in translation:

'Girls! Wipe your tears . . . and let the song grow louder . . . the heroes of the Red Army are passing through the field' – sort of thing – but, when Anatoly thrusts his baton skywards one final time and the sound of the mighty last chorus hangs in the air, I feel ready to start the Revolution all over again.

JAPAN

DAY 23: *Vladivostok to Toyama*

Grinding out to Vladivostok airport in a bruised and ancient Lada. Every gear change is followed by a second or two of torsional limbo. Forward momentum cannot be taken for granted.

Most passengers arrive at the airport by bus, but there are plenty of new Russians – gum-chewing, bangle-dangling George Michael lookalikes, with hostile smiles, hitting the car park at speed, music pounding from their Japanese four-wheel drives, long-legged women at the ready.

It's a far cry from the cakes and flowers of our arrival at Petropavlovsk. Even Igor has become subdued as we have moved south. Maybe he feels his hustling bonhomie is out of place in the comparative sophistication of Vladivostok. Whatever it is, I liked the old raspberry-toting Igor better.

We take off past another sign of rapidly-changing Russia – the profusion of new aircraft liveries bearing the names of private companies that have sprung from the wreckage of Aeroflot's monopoly – Domodedobo, Orient and the unfortunately-named Kras Air.

An hour and thirty-five minutes later our Tupolev 134 is making its final descent into Toyama airport on the north coast of Japan's largest island – Honshu. The landscape is a patchwork of efficiency. Every single square inch below me seems to be accounted for, either by neatly tilled fields, carefully placed houses or state of the art factories set amid precisely marked roads. Basil leans across to me: 'Welcome to Toyland.'

The customs area is immaculate and empty, like an operating theatre awaiting its first patient. Toyama is a provincial airport and they are not used to dealing with British film crews, especially ones coming from Siberia. My bags are politely and thoroughly searched. I have to mime the function of every pill in my toilet-bag. After a particularly graphic portrayal of the reasons for taking Immodium, I am politely, but firmly, waved through.

So we pass from Russia to Japan, from the land where everything is difficult to the land where everything is easy; where there is a machine on every corner dispensing drinks hot and cold, and snacks, hot and cold, twenty-four hours a day, three hundred and sixty-five days a year; where restaurant windows sport not just menus but spotless acrylic models of every dish on that menu; where packaging is an obsession yet litter virtually non-existent. A free, open, affluent, sophisticated society in which, according to a recent poll, eighty-seven per cent of the population wants to look like everyone else.

At the hotel I make the mistake of ordering a particularly revolting cocktail called 'Around The World In Eighty Days' and take to my bed with a severe case of culture shock.

DAY 26: *Niigata to Sado Island*

Much recovered. Am now in Niigata, an unremarkable city a shortish train journey up the coast from Toyama, waiting to board the ferry to Sado Island, home of the world-renowned Kodo Drummers, with whom I hope to make contact.

The eccentric customization of the English language in the cause of Japanese fashion has been acknowledged before but the sight of a T-shirt bearing the legend 'D.O.N.U.T.S. – Driver Oriented New Ultimate Tyre Science', gives me pleasure as I board the ferry.

After two hours at sea we are approaching Sado, a small butterfly-shaped island fluttering off the north-west coast, once used by the Japanese emperor as a place of exile as Siberia was by the Russian Tsars. This information, together with 'The Song Of Sado', a mournful refrain swelling from the ferry's PA system, creates a very melancholy effect. The weather is dull, warm and hazy. Typhoon Ryan is heading for Japan. Not that anyone seems worried; it's the fourteenth typhoon of the season.

We drive across the island, dotted with rice fields, themselves dotted with stooping ladies in straw bonnets secured with headscarves, to a pension near to the Kodo Drummers apprentice school. I feel big and clumsy in Japan, especially here in the sticks, where the accommodation is not at all geared to foreign tourists. Here in the Pension Nagakura I have to bend my head to enter my bedroom and when I stand in front of the bathroom mirror I have a clear view of my neck.

The proprietors are charming and cannot do enough for us. Having served a meal they leave us in the tiny dining room to watch one of their laser discs. We end our first day on Sado Island watching highlights from Queen concerts.

There is one nasty shock in store. Having heard that the Kodo apprentices do a daily run as part of their training I have asked if I can join them for some much-needed exercise. They've just rung the hotel to say they're delighted to have me. The run leaves at 5 a.m. On the dot.

DAY 27: *Sado Island*

Woken by alarm at 4.15 a.m. Strike head on door to bathroom. The only vaguely encouraging thought as I climb into my shorts and trainers is that this will probably be the earliest I've ever run in my life. We tip-toe out of the Pension Nagakura to find Japan is still very dark.

Up at the school the eleven young apprentices, eight men and three women, look blearier than I do, and they've been getting up before five every day, except Sunday, for the last five months.

It's not easy to join Kodo, which translated into English means both 'heartbeat' – as in the rhythm of a child's heartbeat in the womb – and 'children of the drum'. Once accepted, pupils are required to spend a year living communally in a spartan, highly disciplined regime – no tobacco, alcohol, TV or radio – practising five or six hours drumming a day. As I am being told this by Sayo, a twenty-four-year-old Tokyo woman who once taught English, I can't help noticing a dusty TV set in the corner.

'Yes we do have a television,' Sayo corrects herself.

'But we don't have an aerial. So we can watch only videos.'

'What sort of videos?'

'Oh, videos of drumming.'

There is a strong element of tradition and ritual in all this. Though Kodo itself was founded less than twenty-five years ago, it harks back to a pre-industrial, rural Japan when the size of a village was defined by how far the sound of the taiko drum would travel.

The run is quite bearable. As we pad along by the side of the road, a flat, warm, humid dawn comes up, heralded by a light, unrefreshing drizzle. The pace is steady but polite. No one seems to want to offend their guest by leaving him behind – not for the first few miles anyway.

The serving of breakfast is preceded by the cracking together of two drumsticks. We file in and are seated on the ground around one long table. I find the lotus position quite painful, and breakfast is more athletically demanding for me than the run.

I'm introduced to the delights of fermented bean curd. Apparently Japan is divided into those who love and those who loathe it. I come down rather heavily on the loathing side. After fermented bean curd, the raw egg that follows it is like ambrosia. The hardest part is actually eating the egg, with a pair of chopsticks.

At nine the first period of instruction begins. In a plain and basic plaster-boarded room, in essence nothing more than a big garden shed, the apprentices sit, straight-backed on the floor and begin to hit the drums to a rhythm dictated by the sound of a flute and the striking of a small gong. One of the senior Kodo drummers walks amongst them, loosening wrists and correcting shoulder positions. The apprentices move from drum to drum and vary the pace of the beat they play and the position from which they play it, but essentially they keep going continuously and powerfully for forty-five minutes. When they stop the effect is extraordinary. If there is such a thing as a deafening silence, this is it. Total calm descends. Nothing and no one moves for a minute or more. After a short break they play for another forty-five minutes. At the end of it Sayo is dripping sweat. She looks shattered, but laughs at my concern.

'On a good day,' she says, 'I don't notice it. The energy comes from right here,' she indicates her stomach. 'It goes through my breast, shoulder, arm and then finally goes into my drumming. The drums become the sound of my heartbreak.' I think she meant heartbeat but it was a nice Freudian slip.

After a year's apprenticeship only one or two students will be deemed good enough to join the elite at the Kodo Village a few miles away. Here conditions are more comfortable and the atmosphere more relaxed. Among the trappings of success are tour trucks marked 'Kodo, European Tour 95', and the presence of foreign musicians in the village, come to learn from the masters. One is an Englishman, Chris Slade, drummer of the band AC/DC. He shows me a blistered and bloodied pair of hands. He grins. 'It's worth it, I tell you.'

I have to ask why. 'Well, it's not just the drumming. It's the whole way of life. The whole Japanese thing. Unity of mind and body to produce the perfect sound.'

Obligingly they fetch out for me the giant drum, *O-daiko*, which weighs 1000 pounds and can be moved only on a heavy black, wood scaffold. Only two men in the world know how to play it properly. One of them, Eichi Saito, shows me the Kodo stance and hands me the sticks. The sound is tremendous. Saito can play this huge drum without a break for fifteen minutes. I, lacking the required unity of mind and body, release the sticks after fifteen seconds. I already have two soft pink blisters to show for it.

It's been a long hard day by the time I arrive at the Red Pear House in Ogi village on the southern tip of the island, and I am quite ready for the legendary hospitality of this traditional Japanese inn, or *ryokan*. But Japanese hospitality, like Kodo drumming, does not come easy.

I'm greeted at the doorway by Mama-san, a tough-looking little lady standing five-foot two with her clogs on, and four-foot eight without. We exchange bows and I am shown onto a slate floor where I take off my shoes. Water is sluiced across the slate to eradicate my footprints. I then step up onto a low, stripped wooden floor on which a pair of slippers awaits me. I put them on and they reach about halfway up my foot. As I'm shown upstairs I admire the reticent Japanese aesthetics. The well-crafted wood used throughout (it's *hinoki*, a juniper of sorts), the vase of fresh cosmos (picked out by an artfully placed spotlight), beautiful pieces of porcelain, and somewhat surprisingly, a Chagall reproduction. Mama-san, who claims to speak no English, accepts my compliments with a series of chuckles and further bows. At the threshold of my room I have to take off the slippers I've just put on. A sliding rice-paper door gives onto a low simple room with tatami mats on the floor. Apart from a black-lacquered table, raised about a thigh's width from the ground, and a chair with no legs, there is no other furniture.

Bathing is done in communal premises downstairs and if I want to use them I must first don a *yukata* – a cotton robe. Feeling like some foul-smelling giant who's just come down a beanstalk, I gratefully slip off the hot sticky remnants of a long day, don the *yukata* and make my way downstairs. I forget my slippers and as I go back for them encounter Mama-san on the stairs. She shakes her head in despair and starts tugging at the belt around my robe. The *obi*, as it's called, must be tied, samurai-style, across the hip. To tie it *on* the hip, as I have, is considered deeply effeminate. Having tidied me up, Mama-san leads me downstairs and for one awkward moment I think she's going to accompany me to the bathroom. But she confines herself to a little cluck of disapproval as I go in without exchanging my *downstairs* slippers for my *bathroom* slippers, and pulls the rice-paper partition closed behind me. To my surprise I'm confronted on one side with a mediaeval Japanese bath and on the other by a positively twenty-first century toilet.

Mission control at Houston seems anti-diluvian when compared with Mama-san's state of the art appliance. The seat warms automatically on contact. The pressure-pad control panel offers a variety of delights. Eight separate 'Shower Positions' direct varying strengths of spray over the general posterior area, eight separate 'Bidet Settings' propel water jets at more specific targets, and finally four 'Dry' settings round off the whole experience with anything from a light, warm breeze to a mistral. Over the next few hours there is a constant background noise of soft, unmistakable cries of surprise and pleasure as various members of the crew discover its delights for themselves.

Pausing only to change my lavatory slippers for my bathroom slippers I make my way into the washing area. I soap myself first then squat down on a three legged wooden stool, and rinse myself using a small bowl and a bucket of water. Only when every sud is banished from my body can I remove the stout wooden planks from the tub itself and settle myself in the very hot, very clear water of the *o-furo*.

There remains only the ceremony of the evening meal, taken robed and cross-legged. This consists merely of seafood with garlic, bream, tuna and squid sashimi, seaweed, cooked vegetables with bean curd, abalone steak in soy sauce, fried seabream with limes (served whole with head and tail curved artistically upwards) teriyaki of tuna stomach and rice pickles and bean paste.

Mama-san serves this in impeccable style and with almost religious ritual. So pleased am I to see the jug of hot sake arrive, that I make the dreadful faux pas of reaching for it myself. The sake goes flying and I am covered in confusion and rice wine. One of the last lessons I learn on this crash-course in Japanese etiquette is that a guest must never, ever, pour his own sake.

I can barely shuffle upstairs at the end of all this, but I reach my room with relief, pull aside the balcony door and refresh myself with great gulps of muggy night air. Soundlessly, Mama-san's daughter slips in behind me to lay out my futon and bean bag pillow for the night – and to remind me that I really shouldn't be wearing my *upstairs* slippers inside my bedroom.

DAY 28: *Sado Island to Maki*

After a chromatically immaculate breakfast of green tea, yellow radish, red pear, straw-brown yam slices and cream tofu we leave Mama-san's *ryokan*, marvelling that such exquisite

51

elegance could be found in a flimsy-looking house on an unexceptional street in a featureless seaside town in one of the poorest parts of Japan. But then, one of the pleasures of travel is having to readjust perspective and re-examine assumptions. Ironically, it's the very Britishness of Japan's character, its insular off-shore reserve, that makes it much less easy to penetrate than the up-front brashness of Alaska or the manic honesty of the Russians.

Typhoon Ryan has hit Tokyo, but only lightly slapped Sado Island, and we are ferried safely back to Honshu in time to drive along a depressingly Americanized urban sprawl of malls and fast-food outlets to the town of Maki. Here, in the Cultural Hall, we catch the Kodo Roadshow, the ultimate result of all the rigorous, demanding training we saw yesterday.

It is quite an experience. The display of controlled power, the extraordinary dexterity, the scale of athleticism and agility, is thrilling. Great feats of group strength and stamina are interspersed with quiet, almost wistful solos, and the whole performance, lasting nearly two hours without a break, is staged with a sparse, austere beauty. Yoshi Kazu is their star, and his solo is the supreme demonstration of the Kodo technique. He begins on the massive *O-daiko*, deceptively gently, almost tapping, teasing out a beat, then gradually turning up the intensity. A single white light picks out every straining sinew as his body piles on the pressure. He pushes the tempo forward, beyond what you think is humanly possible, raining blows down on the skin of the drum with a fierce, irresistible, compulsive rhythm. Then he leaps from the scaffold to the drums on the floor and continues pummelling away at a speed the eye can barely follow, before slowly and deliberately bringing back the beat and the volume to the barely perceptible level at which he started. It is a stunning display of strength and energy. And he'll be forty-eight next week.

DAY 30: *Sanjo to Kurohime*

Overnight in Sanjo, another forgettable town on the rice plains of Niigata. All these towns seem to be alike, and considering how important a part aesthetics play in Japanese culture, remarkably unattractive. There is a constant feeling of being cramped. The houses are small and narrow, the streets have no pavements, the architecture of a shanty town in Ethiopia is more inventive.

Then, suddenly, this dismal place is wholly redeemed. In a copy of the English-language *Japan Times* I read: 'Sheffield United's improvement continued with a 2–1 win at Huddersfield.' My day is transformed at a stroke. Everywhere that was poky is quaint and every cramped street is picturesque and unspoilt. The train ride, taking us slowly but surely off the plain and up into the mountains, becomes an incomparable pleasure. Rice meadows are replaced by rice terraces whose crop, less advanced than it was lower down, is a deep golden green. Gradients get steeper, gorges deeper and dark green conifer forest crowds in on the train. At last there is fresh air and space. And more besides. The lodge we're staying in at the resort town of Kurohime is the most spacious domestic building I've yet seen in Japan, with tall public rooms open to the rafters, wide windows and long mountain views. The menu is a clever combination of western and Japanese, proving that sukiyaki and mashed potato can co-exist harmoniously. And to cap a day on which we have touched the depths and reached the heights, the owner, Eiji Nakahara, produces twenty-year-old Macallan whisky as a nightcap.

DAY 31: *Kurohime*

One of the most well-known people in Japan lives in Kurohime. He is tousled, weather-beaten, ruddy-faced, fifty-five and Welsh. C.W. Nicol – C.W. as he's affectionately known – has a CV which seems to encompass several lifetimes. He has worked for the Canadian Environmental Protection service, been the first game-warden at the Simian National Park in Ethiopia, and is currently Vice-Principal of the Nature Conservation College in Tokyo and an honorary member of the Ainu tribe, the most ancient of the peoples of Japan. He is a black belt in judo and a 7th dan in karate. He has had seventy books published here, including bestselling novels, children's books and conservation treatises. He has his own television programme, has recorded a CD of his songs and is an authority on everything from whisky to *shiitake* mushrooms. He's shot polar bears and is proficient at the ancient Japanese art of stick fighting.

He first came here thirty-three years ago to study martial arts. I asked him what it was about the country that made him stay.

'It was a country I'd never dreamt existed, a country of virgin forests, a country that has, even close to a large town, wild bears, wild boar, wild deer, such a rich nature and such a very vibrant culture.'

This is so unlike what I've seen so far that I ask him to show me what I've missed. The first thing I notice about the 'virgin forests' are unpromising great scars where trees have been felled to make way for concrete viaducts. C.W. explains that this is the infrastructure needed to bring the 1998 Winter Olympics to nearby Nagano. He mutters darkly about the level of corruption which secured the games in return for Japanese help with contracts elsewhere in the world.

Surprisingly, sixty-seven per cent of Japan remains either forest or woodland, and an hour away from the bulldozers and graders he shows me four-hundred-year-old beech, oak and horse chestnut.

These forested mountains which climb to 7500 feet are among the oldest inhabited areas of Japan, settled for over ten thousand years. They've served as a refuge for many clandestine organizations, including the Ninjas, master assassins who were always devising new and ingenious methods of knocking people off. One of these was a common or garden brush with a spike, tipped with deadly poison from the monks-hood plant and secreted amongst the bristles. The Ninja, disguised as a humble servant, would work away at the leaves until his victim passed by, then smartly bring up the brush and deal him a lethal sweep up the backside.

C.W. loves stories like this and all the rich legends of the local gods, and regrets the spread of urban life and the disappearance of much of the Japanese folk history. I ask him whether the Japanese are religious.

'I would say they're happily agnostic. There are some cults, as we all know, but mostly they're very, very tolerant . . . they'll have a Christian or a Shinto wedding and a Buddhist funeral.'

DAY 32: *Togakshi*

C.W. and I lunch in the village of Togakshi, where there are huge, enveloping thatched roofs steep-pitched against four or five months of winter snow, and an eight-hundred-year-old cedar tree rising 350 feet above the copper-ridged rooftops. This was once the Mecca of the mountain religion. Now it is squeezed tight with members of the tourist religion, its inaccessible beauty tarnished in the process. We sit down to eat at a fine, traditional restaurant which specializes in its own, home-produced buckwheat noodles. C.W. instructs me in the proper way of eating them.

'Don't nibble . . . ' he says reprovingly, ' . . . slurp! Forget you got bashed for doing it as a kid, now you can do it *and* be polite.'

Of course, it's like everything else, when you have to slurp, you can't.

To wash it down C.W. orders *doboruku* which looks to me like rice milk. He chuckles greatly at this. *Doboruku* is in fact white sake, traditionally only made at home. It's a lethal concoction, he warns me, as the yeast continues to ferment inside the stomach for an hour or so after you've drunk it. He knocks a glass back in one and swiftly orders another.

In his book *Traveller's History of Japan*, Richard Tames notes that what makes Japan exceptional among developed countries is its homogeneity. Ninety-nine per cent of all the Japanese in the world were born and still live in Japan. No minority, either racial or religious, comprises more than one per cent of the community (whereas sixteen per cent of Americans are non-white and four per cent of British are Muslim). Japanese is only spoken in Japan. Many Japanese are, deep-down, still uncomfortable with what they perceive as the loss of their uniqueness which followed the arrival of a US naval vessel in Tokyo Bay in 1853, ending two hundred years of self-imposed isolation. All of which makes C.W. one of that very rare sort indeed, an outsider assimilated into Japanese life.

He admits that it is not easy. The Japanese are self-absorbed and wary of the *gaijin* – the foreigner. But C.W. has persevered and been rewarded now with full citizenship.

It seems very apt that one of the last memories of my visit to the mountains should be a line of verse from Issa, a local Haiku poet, reproduced, with English translation, at Kurohime railway station: 'The ant's path, does it not reach to yonder cloudy peak?' The translation, I notice, is by C.W. Nicol.

DAY 34: *Tokyo*

Hachiko Square, Tokyo. Hachiko was the pet dog of a professor at Tokyo university who used to meet his master off the train as he returned from work each day. After his master died while at work, Hachiko still turned up at the same spot, every day, for the next seven years. In admiration of this display of loyalty the people of Tokyo had a statue built at the place where he waited.

Today I doubt if a dog would spot anyone in the great seething crowd that pours out of Shibuya station. Above the heads of the crowd, a reminder of where I've just been, is a clock already counting down the days to the start of the Nagano Winter Olympics. 860 days to go.

I'm on my way to meet Mayumi Nobetsu, a girl from Tokyo whom I've exchanged letters with for more than twenty years without ever meeting. She first wrote to me in 1974 when, to everyone's surprise, *Monty Python* briefly reared its head on Japanese television. The handwriting and spelling of her first letter were immaculate, the grammar ambitious. 'I am fourteen years old Japanese girl,' it had begun. She kept writing to me, sending protestations of love and valuable information on the erratic affair between *Monty Python* and the Japanese public. Now in her thirties, she is managing a hotel.

Our rendezvous is at an open-air café in amongst the walls of skyscrapers that have mushroomed all over the centre of Tokyo. As it turns out, there is only one table with an unattached occupant, a striking woman, all dressed in black with hair cut carefully in a bang, like some exotic star of the silent screen. This is the 'fourteen years old Japanese girl' twenty years on. I have had a lurking worry that she may have got the wrong Python, but she opens the locket around her neck and there is a picture of me as a thirty-one-year-old Sir Galahad in *The Holy Grail*. We have a drink and make plans for her to show me some of her city. As we set off Mayumi smiles gravely at me.

'I still cannot believe that you are here, talking like a human being.'

DAY 35

A six-lane elevated expressway runs down the centre of the road outside my hotel. A few hundred yards away it broadens to accommodate an intersection 30 feet above the ground. The concrete walls that support this massive structure are decorated with huge colour photographs of the countryside.

It doesn't fool anybody. Tokyo is a massive, unapologetically pragmatic modern conurbation. It is a hectic, hurtling city where everything is on the move except the traffic. Into each tall, implausibly narrow building are squeezed a dozen businesses: hairdressers, massage parlours, jacuzzis, restaurants, night clubs, health clubs, strip clubs and book stores. It's something of a relief to find that the place Mayumi takes me to first is an exception to the rule – a single storey building on a corner. It's a restaurant called The Dojo Nabe which has been doing business on the same spot for one hundred and eighty years.

The Dojo Nabe is run by the egregious and voluble Mr Watanabe, eighth in a line of Watanabes who have run the place through earthquakes, bombing and fires. He bustles out to greet us in traditional *yukata* robe, only to slightly spoil the effect by revealing that he once trained at Berni Inns in London. In good English, he likens his restaurant to a pub. It is a place for rich and poor alike. Certainly it is unpretentious inside. I have become used to eating at restaurants without chairs, but this is the first that has no tables either. Mayumi and I sit cross-legged on bamboo mats with a wooden board on the floor in front of us.

Mr Watanabe is punctilious in observing tradition. A man bent double by the door as if praying is in fact one of the staff laying three piles of salt out on the street. This particular little trick dates back to the time when people travelled into town with their cows. When they found salt the cows would always stop to lick it up, giving their owners time to size up the restaurant.

Mr Watanabe also likes a joke. He's particularly pleased with his slogan 'People who eat here never die'.

'Because if you're dead you wouldn't be able to eat here, you see?' He laughs gleefully.

What has brought hungry Japanese to this restaurant for nearly two hundred years is a thin freshwater fish about eight inches long called a loach. It has two attributes which the Japanese value highly – it aids digestion and virility. These may well be achieved at the expense of the fish's comfort for the loach are tipped live into wooden tubs full of *sake*. As the loach suck the oxygen out of the water, so they absorb the alcohol into their intestines. Or, as Mr Watanabe puts it, 'Many fish are marinated from outside. Only in Dojo are they marinated from inside.'

Later we take a walk through an unglamorous working-class part of Tokyo called Asakusa. The streets are full of betting parlours and punters studying the Japanese equivalent of the *Sporting Chronicle*. Mayumi doesn't care for the place. She points out the *yakuze*, the Japanese Mafia, moustachioed, close-cropped hair, eyes darting about, lolling against walls, keeping an eye on the action. But there's a horse race coming up and on impulse I suggest laying a bet. We approach an elderly couple sat behind a trestle table. Mayumi translates the names of the runners. One is called Super Licence which sounds suitable for a BBC enterprise. We put 1000 yen (about seven pounds) on the 3.40 at Osaka. The old couple are not allowed to take our money and direct us into a nearby building where, in a room as long as a station, bets are taken and money paid out. A vast crowd of Japanese Andy Capps stands, wreathed in cigarette smoke, their heads raised to a bank of television screens. When we get to the front it turns out that the old couple have by mistake marked our card as a *10,000* yen bet. There's no getting out of it either. We have to pay.

Then back into the street to listen to the race on the portable radio. Hard to follow, but much excitement and a late challenge by Number 7 is successful. Much consulting of papers then Mayumi leaps in the air. Number 7 is Super Licence. Rush back into the smoke-filled concourse and tension builds as we move closer to the cashier. Odds were 12 to 1. We've won one hundred and twenty-six thousand yen, or eight hundred and forty-five pounds and sixty-three pence.

Exit Mayumi skipping up the street.

Given the virility of the yen, eight hundred and forty-five pounds is just enough for a meal for us all at a decent Tokyo restaurant. The restaurant is located in an area called Ebisu. Ebisu, Mayumi tells me, is the name of the Japanese god of prosperity.

DAY 36

Every Sunday they close Yoyogi park to traffic and allow anyone with a guitar and drums, or even just a tape of someone else playing guitar and drums, to come and set up on the roadway beside the 1964 Olympic stadium. The result is a one-and-a-half-mile noise. Sixty or seventy bands all play at once, creating a mighty discordant cacophony totally at odds with the deferential orderliness of Japanese public behaviour.

The key to this uncharacteristic display is disguise. Most of the hundreds of performers in Yoyogi Park are pretending to be someone else. Many of them, far too young to remember that this park had once been a barracks for the American troops who occupied their country until the early fifties, are dressed as American heroes of their parents' era – Marlon Brando, Bill Haley, Buddy Holly and, of course, Elvis. D.A. haircuts and shades abound and black biker jackets sport names like the Tokyo Rockabilly Club. There are boys in winklepicker shoes and girls in bobbysocks and wide skirts jiving to grotesquely over-amplified tapes of Del Shannon and Billy Fury. There are reincarnations of the Sex Pistols and the Beatles. A Japanese Bob Dylan struggles with 'Subterranean Homesick Blues', while next door a Japanese Rob Roy, hair dyed scarlet, is leaping around to a thunderous heavy metal accompaniment. It looks wild but is in fact oddly decorous. The anarchy in Yoyogi Park is as carefully controlled as every other aspect of Japanese life. It's an acceptable way of showing off in a country where showing off is not encouraged.

Trying to find somewhere to recover from the bombardment, Basil and I end up in an unobtrusive little restaurant close to Shibuya station. It turns out to be the only whale restaurant in Tokyo and, although the meat is strictly from the quota they're allowed by law to catch, I'm not entirely comfortable with some of the delicacies. 'Whale's Tongue In Soy Sauce', 'Special Bits Of The Whale Put Together' and 'Upper Jawbone Distilled In Sake' are not for the faint-hearted. Decide on a green salad, but ask for a Greenpeace salad by mistake.

End an eclectic day at the Hot 6 Rocket Club in Roppongi listening to reggae. If Japan has a popular music culture of its own, I haven't found it so far.

DAY 37: *Tokyo to Fukuyama*

Leave Tokyo on the Hikari super express, heading south-west at a furious but almost imperceptible pace on a specially constructed high-speed track. Pass the austere, perfectly formed icon of Mount Fuji, reduced to an indistinct blur by clouds of pollution. The Japanese may wear face masks to avoid spreading germs when they have a cold, but still seem happy to allow industrial chimneys to belch away.

Disembark at Fukuyama, a small city on the shores of the Inland Sea, and make our way out into the countryside, dotted with buildings more attractive and distinctive than any we've glimpsed on the 400-mile journey from Tokyo. The most attractive of all are those of the Zen temple of Buttsuji where we are to spend the night.

Set in meticulously ordered grounds with each piece of gravel in its right place (not an exaggeration, for in Zen Buddhist belief a piece of gravel is as important as a mountain), the temple is approached from a humpback wooden footbridge over a rocky stream. Inside the compound are a number of solid wooden buildings topped with decorated wide-eaved roofs, tiled with heavy, high-glazed, gun metal grey tiles. Inside are chilly, sparsely furnished passageways. It's austere and timeless, though I did catch a tell-tale glimpse of computer screens behind a half-open rice-paper door.

Zen is about living, being and becoming. It seeks true awareness by bringing man back to the centre of his original experience. This I'm told by Almon, a novice from Holland in his first year here, who has been charged with looking after me at the evening meditation. I am required to wear a black robe and bare feet as I enter the *Zendo* – the meditation hall, which is dark and old and woody, like a mediaeval barn. Even for an overnight guest like myself there is plenty of ritual to deal with. I must make a fist of my right hand and cover it with the left. I must count from one to ten on every out breath and I must know the right places to bow – *gasho* – at the entrance to the hall. I must know when and where to dispense with my slippers and how to mount the prayer platform which extends around the perimeter of the hall at a height of some two feet. Once on the platform I can either assume the lotus position or kneel back on my legs (I choose the latter), but I must keep my back absolutely straight. Each period of meditation lasts 45 minutes (the length of time it takes an incense candle to burn down).

I surprise myself not only by finding a comfortable position, but also by feeling the immediate benefits of the dim light, the deep, regular breathing and the silence. The sounds of insects and birds and a stream running somewhere nearby become clear and loud but never noisy, and a soothing mind-cleansing tranquillity descends upon me. Just as I am slipping towards a blissfully raised state of awareness I hear a strange sound, a sharp crack as though something is being struck. I raise one eyelid cautiously and see that something is indeed being struck. It is the man next to me.

Perhaps it's just as well that no one had bothered to tell me about the *keisaku* – the warning stick. It is applied, with the full approval of the participant, to stop you slipping off to sleep during meditation. And I am to be treated just like anyone else.

With infinite care the *shika* – the head monk – arranges my body; arms crossed, hands on shoulders, head bent forward. Incredibly gently he feels for a spot on my upper back then brings the stick down straight and sharp. Before I can feel anything he gives me another light tap, followed by three enormous whacks, leaving a sting and a burn like the aftermath of a school caning. By now I've forgotten all about counting up to ten on the out breath, and am about to utter some good old Anglo-Saxon expletive when I become aware of my inflicter standing before me, presenting the stick and bowing low before me. I bow back with as much gratefulness as I can muster.

He must like me because twenty minutes later he comes back and does it all over again.

DAY 38: *Fukuyama to Hiroshima*

3.45 a.m. A monk with a wake-up bell comes softly along the passage outside the communal room in which we've slept. At half-past four I accompany him and his colleagues back into the meditation hall. After half an hour's contemplation, they get up, without warning, and flit very silently and swiftly out of the room. By the time I've got my sandals on, they've all gone. Fortunately I'm out in time to catch a flash of habit disappearing round a corner, and I hitch up my skirts and make after them. It has rained in the night and some of the stones are so slippery that I very nearly lose balance. Skidding round the temple buildings after them, grabbing at maple branches like a Keystone Monk, and trying to do all this soundlessly gives rise to a most un-Zen-like fit of hysterics.

Breakfast, like the accommodation, is frugal. The warm, wet tasteless rice is fortified with a bracing combination of pickled plum and radish and green tea. Not a bad start if you want to avoid using the squat lavatories. Afterwards, I want to ask Almon lots of mundane questions about his life here. He is patient up to a point, telling me that the monks shave their heads once every five days and that once a year the great temple bell is struck a hundred and eight times, a hundred and eight being what Buddhists believe is the number of man's delusions.

I think Almon would like to talk more but feels constrained. Zen tradition, he reminds me softly, insists that wisdom comes only when men are reduced to silence.

These words come to mind an hour or so later when I am interviewing the abbot and my question about the importance of peace and seclusion is drowned out by an aeroplane passing overhead. The abbot is an impressive man; wise, composed and gently mischievous. He looks young, but as Fraser, our sound man, says rather gloomily, he could be sixty-eight and a wonderful advert for clean living.

'If I am only here for one night,' I ask him, 'what can I learn?'

He smiles. 'That,' he says with obvious amusement, 'is a question you should ask yourself.' I have to conclude that Zen Buddhism and television interviewing are just not compatible.

The monks line up to wave us goodbye. Though the older ones smile serenely, Almon looks earnest. He's thin and his shaven skull stands out almost blue against his white skin. Find myself feeling sorry to be leaving him here, but as our bus honks, revs up and pulls out into the wide world I wonder, in a Zen sort of way, who the prisoner is, him or me?

An hour later we are approaching Hiroshima on the bullet train. Though it is a totally rebuilt, bland, modern city which

63

looks forward to the future rather than back to the war, the symbolism of the place is disturbing and impossible to ignore.

We visit the famous sites, like the domed skeleton of the Industrial Promotion Hall whose walls survived the blast of 6 August 1945. At the Peace Memorial Museum today's children pull mock horror faces at the waxwork tableaux of yesterday's children, with hair burning and melted skin hanging from their arms. The younger generation doesn't seem to want to remember any more. They're interested in an abstract way but what does it mean to them now? Defeat and destruction? Hardly. Today's *Japan Times* carries a report that nine of the top ten world banks are now Japanese. Anger and resentment at America for dropping the bomb? Hardly. There is a baseball stadium just across from the Peace Dome. American movie-stars stare down from the billboards – Arnold Schwarzenegger advertising cup noodles, Madonna, air conditioners, Jodie Foster, Mitsubishi Cars, Michael J. Fox, canned tea. Japan was rebuilt by the Americans in the seven years after the war and it is the reconstruction, rather than the destruction, that is remembered.

DAY 39: *Hiroshima*

As far as I'm concerned there is nothing I shall remember about this city *but* the bomb. The fact that I'm lying in a hotel bed in the centre of Hiroshima sets my imagination to work vividly and uncomfortably. If I had been in this exact spot fifty years and two months ago, and not toddling round a garden in Sheffield, I would have been wrenched instantly from sleep by the sound and light of the greatest explosion ever made by man. One second after detonation a fireball, 1400 feet wide, would have filled the sky 1000 feet above my head. Only a fraction of a second after that I would have been one of seventy thousand people torn apart by a blast travelling at the speed of sound and incinerated by heat that, at the hypocentre of the explosion, reached 4000° centigrade. If I had been here fifty years ago, I would have been reduced to a pile of dust.

At midday we leave Hiroshima but not the shadow of the past. Japan Airlines flight 5035 connects Hiroshima with Nagasaki, less than 200 miles away. 'Fat Man', a bomb with a force equivalent to 22,000 tons of TNT was dropped on Nagasaki three days after 'Little Boy' (15,000 tons) had destroyed Hiroshima. These two bombs killed and maimed half a million people. But the first sight of Nagasaki clears away some of the complex negativity, the uneasy mixture of compassion and complicity that I can't seem to throw off. At last, a Japanese city that doesn't look like all the others. Nagasaki is a green city, set amongst rocky peninsulas and deep bays, hemmed in by waves of thickly-wooded mountain ranges. And as we fly lower I have the first sight of palm trees on the Pacific Rim.

DAY 41: *Nagasaki*

Nagasaki is smaller than it looks. Less than half a million people live amongst the folded hills that dovetail into the long narrow fiord of Nagasaki Harbour. This protected anchorage attracted the first European traders to Japan in 1571. They were Portuguese, allowed to open a base for commerce and missionary work. The missionaries were too successful for their own good and a reaction set in. Early Japanese Christians were crucified and the *shoguns* (warlords) withdrew into the two-hundred-year period of international isolation. Only Nagasaki kept the door to foreign trade ajar, allowing a small Dutch trading post on an island in the harbour, and it was Nagasaki that opened up to the West in 1859, encouraging entrepreneurs from Europe, anxious to spread the benefits of the Industrial Revolution, to use the city as their base. A Scotsman called Thomas Glover, whose European-style bungalow is now a major tourist attraction, brought Japan into the industrial age virtually single-handed. He introduced railways, laid the first telephone cable, opened the first coalmine, started the Kirin Brewery and, in 1868, set up the first modern ship-building yard. He sold it nine years later to a fledgling company he helped found. Its name was Mitsubishi. Today Mitsubishi's shipyards dominate the north side of the harbour and nearly twenty per cent of Nagasaki's workforce is employed by Mitsubishi Heavy Engineering.

All this makes for a city of character, and one proud of its history, much of which is re-enacted at the yearly Okunchi Festival, derived from the strong Chinese influence in the city. Today is the first of three festival days and I have been accorded the high and, as far as I can tell, unprecedented honour of being a foreign participant.

At the crack of dawn I find myself sipping green tea in a shop in the city centre which has been commandeered as a dressing room. I am to be a flag-carrier on the Treasure House ship, and Mrs Takashi is arranging me into a rather attractive off-white silk kimono with maroon and black trim. On my head I wear a red and white bow and on my feet yellow-beribboned white cloth shoes with two toe-holes. Not what I would choose to wear in my local but quite restrained compared to some of the outfits I've seen here. Mr Takashi, who will be with me to tell me what to do, puts out his cigarette and we go off in search of the Treasure House. It turns out to be one of several decorated floats, called *mikoshi*, each one representing a different neighbourhood. Twenty young men have been deputed to heave it through the streets – not as easy as it sounds as it has twenty schoolchildren aboard.

I fall in behind the elders, who wear complex outfits of black kimonos and black bowler hats. If you can imagine Ian Paisley dressed as a geisha girl, you'll begin to get the picture.

When we reach the Suwa-jinja Shrine our Treasure ship is hauled into the arena, amid much cheering. There are some foreign tourists in the crowd. I think they must be British, because one of them catches sight of me in my kimono and red and white bow and performs the wildest double take I think I've ever seen. After the ritual presentation of our float to the Shinto priests, the children sing and play and enact a short drama. Then we all stand back and let the frenetic display begin. This consists of hauling the fully-laden float backwards and forwards across the arena as fast as possible. It's flung one way, then the other, raced to the brink of a steep stone stairway, wrenched to a halt then turned laboriously back again. Teeth are clenched, eyes rolled and bracelets of sweat are sent spinning through the air. The boat keeps moving as long as the audience keeps cheering, and the more passes it makes the more successful they're deemed to be. An added hazard is the presence of half a dozen television crews, not including our own. I get clouted on the side of the head by a video camera and at one point Mr Takashi has to race into the arena to retrieve his flag which has become coiled round a TV cable and is scything its way through the crowd.

The rest of the day is a considerable anti-climax. Thank God.

DAY 43: *Huis Ten Bosch*

An hour north of Nagasaki on the way to the Korean ferry port at Hakata, we detour to an extraordinary place called Huis Ten Bosch. It is the apotheosis of the Japanese talent for imitation and re-creation. But here it's not just a car or a portable radio that's been reprocessed, it's an entire seventeenth century Dutch seaport, complete with Royal Palace, customs house, town hall, churches, squares, shops and canals.

It is the brainchild of Mr Yoshikuni Kamichika, who chose to celebrate the long historical connection between the Dutch traders and Nagasaki by founding The Nagasaki Holland Village Co. Ltd., pledged to combine Dutch city planning and Japanese technology. Two and a half billion dollars have been sunk into the project already. Four hundred thousand trees and three hundred thousand flowering plants have been introduced as well as a desalination plant and a self-cleaning canal system. There are no cars, no dirt and after seven o'clock, hardly any people.

I walk around, one of the four million annual visitors, and marvel for a while at the thoroughness of it all. Architectural detail is precise and well-crafted. There are occasional glimpses of actual Dutch people mainly engaged in ethnic activities, such as the cheese carriers or the bicycle band. The bicycle band is worth the price of admission alone. There is something almost transcendentally surreal about seeing a woman dressed in a large white bonnet, dirndl, black stockings and clogs riding a bicycle and at the same time playing 'Bohemian Rhapsody' on a trombone.

The trouble is that this is normal behaviour in Huis Ten Bosch. Everyone who lives here is doing a turn. It's an elaborate, beautifully constructed, ever so environmentally-friendly theme park. The windmills don't need wind, the bricks don't actually hold up the buildings, the street singers don't actually sing (they mime), the be-wigged and buckled footmen who patrol the streets carry walkie-talkies. The intricately reproduced tracery on the bell-tower of Utrecht cathedral conceals a massive loudspeaker from which the sound of real church bells issues from time to time. It's cultural karaoke, a fantasy land where everyone wears a smile until closing time. I'm told that Michael Jackson has been here twice, and I can well believe it.

DAY 45: *Hakata*

On our last morning in Japan a clutch of newspaper reports emphasize the fragility of life on the edge of the Pacific. In two of the countries we are to visit, there have been earthquakes measuring seven and above on the Richter scale. One in Mexico has killed fifty-nine people and over one hundred have died in Indonesia. Nearer home it's a story of human fragility – the Japanese Minister for Justice has resigned after accepting money from a religious group. I'm told the favour system is a characteristic of Japanese business, the giving of gifts here is generous, and always reciprocal. But the line between a gift and a bribe has always been blurred.

The Hakata ferry terminal, with its polished marble counters, granite slab floors and gleaming chrome-sheathed escalators, is as spotless, efficient and bland as the Toyama airport terminal at which we arrived.

The ferry passengers are mainly Korean. As we wait to embark they bring small, encouraging signs of eccentricity into this shining wasteland. One of a group of monks wears a straw boater, another an embroidered Russian fur hat. A long-haired vamp of a woman in high stiletto heels is travelling with them. They are arguing, good-naturedly, but publicly – very un-Japanese behaviour. The woman next to me sits smoking a cigarette, hugging one of her nylon-stockinged legs up on the bench beside her; an inelegance which is quite shocking to behold after these last three weeks. And the language sounds very different, the accent heavier and more guttural. Korean is a central Asian tongue, which has more in common with Hungarian and Finnish than anything oriental.

KOREA

DAY 46: *Hakata to Pusan*

Pitch darkness. Rudely awoken by a thunderous rumbling roar which sounds as though the ship is being disembowelled beneath me. It's the anchor going down which means that we must already have covered the 140 miles of the Korea Strait to Pusan.

Dawn: Our ferry, the *Camellia*, stands off the rocky undulating coast of South Korea, one of a queue of vessels waiting to pierce the hazy brown veil of pollution that all but obscures the country's second largest city. Several passengers are up on deck exercising. I'm going through my travel documents in an anxious pre-Customs and Immigration way, ticking boxes to aver that I am not carrying 'guns, knives, gunpowder, drugs, psychotropic substances or any items harmful to the national constitution, public security or morals'. (I always wonder what sort of person answers 'yes' to a question like that.)

With a mournful blast of the horn, our ship moves slowly towards the dockside. It's only 7.30 a.m. but South Korea is already at work, making itself bigger. Cranes are swinging and concrete is pouring into a vast land-reclamation project. Shoreline highways are choked with morning traffic and a powerful array of multi-storey blocks bear familiar names –

Daewoo, Samsung, Hyundai, Goldstar and Ssongyang – the *chaebols* (family-owned super-conglomerates) that have pushed Korea's growth rate ahead of that of its arch-rival, Japan.

I'm discovering that Japan and Korea are completely different, not just linguistically, but socially and spiritually. From 1910 to 1945 Korea was occupied by the Japanese, who did their best to suppress the Korean language and culture. The bitter resentment left behind is now channelled into an intense commercial competitiveness (Japanese cars, films and music are banned in Korea) and an almost manic drive to modernize in the international way. (As from last week it became official government policy to convert all Korea's toilets from squat to Western style.)

At the bus station in Pusan a man is selling ginseng roots from a red plastic basket, and several others are watching over my shoulder as I note this fact in my diary. Curiosity is bold and open here. The Japanese concept of deferential conformity doesn't apply. Women chew bubble gum and stare back at you. A big beef-cake of a man noticing the camera, walks up, flexes a bicep and proclaims, much to the delight of the onlookers, 'In Korea they call me Terminator.'

A squat man in flares and a tight, buttoned jacket pushes him out of the way. 'If he Terminator, I King-Kong!' He beats what there is of his chest, acknowledges the laughter and disappears into the crowd.

What Japan and Korea *do* share, which is why they're both so successful, is a sense of national destiny which transcends individual aspirations. Things like privacy, holidays and time off, which we value so much in the West, are considered luxuries, always ready to be sacrificed to the national effort.

The bus deposits us at the town of Kyongju, 55 miles north of Pusan. At my hotel personal cleanliness is tackled with a vengeance. An enormous communal bathing area offers just about everything you might want to do with water. There are showers enough for a small army; a hot tub and semi-hot tub, a cold tub with high-pressure waterfall simulator, several jacuzzis, a ginseng-flavoured steam room and two capacious saunas. This palace of hydrophilia is filled with the soft, soothing sound of sloshing and scrubbing, spraying and gurgling, swilling, slapping and lathering.

Full of well-being and cleaner than I've been since the day I was born, I tuck into a substantial supper. The main dish of deep-fried fish is accompanied by acorn with sesame seed, garlic, lychees, broccoli, tofu stew with onions, zucchini, red and green peppers and, of course the Korean speciality, *kimchi*. This delicacy brings together a palate-punishing combination of cabbage, garlic, red pepper, ginger, radish, onions and chilli powder and then pickles the lot in brine to produce what some deem the most unpleasant national dish in the world. I can't see *kimchi* bars threatening McDonald's, but it's too powerful to dismiss after only one tasting. I shall leave mouth, and options, open.

We talk, after the inevitable comparisons with Japan, about the state of things between North and South Korea. Shin-Na, a bright and funny Korean journalist who is guiding us around, tells a joke which sums up the national stereotypes.

The scene is a restaurant.

'Excuse me,' says the waiter, 'there is no more beef.'

The North Korean replies, 'What's "beef"?'

The Japanese, 'What's "no more"?'

And the South Korean 'What's "excuse me"?'

DAY 47: *Kyongju*

Cultural day in Kyongju, which has such a rich concentration of visible history that UNESCO has named it one of their ten largest world heritage sites. First stop is a modest equivalent of the Egyptian pyramids called Tumuli Park, consisting of twenty low, gracefully-rounded burial mounds rising from the earth like giant bubbles. They have been found to contain a haul of artefacts from the Shilla kingdom, which dominated southern Korea for a thousand years.

The treasures from the tombs are on display at the nearby National Museum, which also contains a twenty-ton bell cast in 770 AD, said to have within it the body of a young girl sacrificed during the casting. The museum complex is awash with school groups. The boys race about, pulling lemons off the trees, taking swipes at each other and evading the wrath of the attendants. The girls, most of whom seem to be wearing identical oval gold-rimmed glasses and Korean Doc Martens, are quite direct in their curiosity. Foreign tourists are obviously something of a rarity here and any glance you give them is met with a mixture of eye-rolling flirtatiousness or hoots of laughter.

The centrepiece of this great cultural complex is Pulguksa temple – Historic Site and Scenic Beauty No.1. It was begun in 528 AD and its scale and superb decoration is another example of the sophistication of Shilla craftsmanship, aided, of course, by a readily-available slave-labour force. It survived intact for a thousand years before being destroyed by Japanese invaders, and its intricate restoration is very recent, highly expensive and evidence of the growing pride in all things Korean.

We drive up higher into the hills to take some shots of the distinctive saggy-tiled roofs from above. By now I'm beginning to suffer temple fatigue, a sort of cultural cramp which causes my brain to lock against any further intake of information, however enlightening. There are low tables by the roadside where snacks can be procured from old Korean men with ochre complexions and deeply-lined faces. It is here that I clock up another gastronomic first – crispy grasshopper, sautéed with soy sauce and sugar, and by no means as unpleasant as it might sound. Basil sticks to dried cuttlefish.

DAY 48: *Seoul*

My third day in the Hermit Kingdom (as Korea was known in the nineteenth century, when, like Japan, she tried to hide away from increasingly attentive foreign merchants). Eight thousand miles away in London my wife will just be waking up on her fifty-third birthday. I should like to telephone her but I'm currently caught up in a demonstration in Seoul. There are a lot of angry people around me raising fists and chanting. Photographers retreat ahead of us, many of them dragging little aluminium step-ladders which they erect every now and then to grab top shots of the crowd. Television crews weave in and out of the lines of protesters. As they do so, I see a young man just behind me hide his face behind a placard. Fliers bearing ghastly pictures of mutilated faces and bodies are handed out to the crowd. The shouting and chanting is insistent. Drivers, afraid of being trapped by the march, are attempting perilous U-turns over the central intersection. Up one of the side roads I catch sight of coaches with green and white mesh window grilles. Inside are the riot police, parked and waiting.

The anger of the demonstrators is vented at proposals to drop proceedings against two leading generals whom they think were responsible for a particularly bloody repression of the political opposition in the town of Kwangju in 1981, in which an estimated two hundred students were killed. Shin-Na is marching with me and eyeing warily the behaviour of the police. Squads of reinforcements are arriving, quite dapper in royal-blue shirts, navy trousers and ties and white peaked hats. These, Shin tells me, are traffic police. Only if the demonstrators lose control will the riot police, with tear gas and possibly rubber bullets, be released from their waiting coaches.

Despite being swept along unwittingly from observer to participant, I feel quite secure among the marchers. It's as though I am taking part in some time-honoured ritual in which both sides know each other's moves.

As my initial apprehensions fade away I begin to enjoy myself. This is probably the best way to see the city. Along streets obligingly cleared of traffic by the police, with three thousand people making sure you don't get lost.

DAY 50: *Seoul to the North Korean Border*

Here in Seoul we are about 50 miles south of our first serious obstacle to progress around the Pacific Rim. It's called North Korea, and no matter how nicely you ask, North Korea is not really interested in seeing you, especially if you're from the West and carrying a film camera. Global glasnost has barely dented the protective shell of one of the last remaining communist dictatorships and the closest we can get to it is the Demilitarized Zone, the DMZ, which has separated the two countries since the end of the Korean War in 1953. And the only way we can get to the DMZ is with one of the strictly-supervised day-tours which leave Seoul every weekday morning.

Our coach is filled with a mixture of Japanese, Americans and Europeans. As the coach moves off some of the Japanese are already asleep (I've never come across a nation which falls asleep so easily) and the babble of excited European voices is soon quelled by our tour guides, who keep up a two-hour informational duologue until we reach the border. First, the rules. We are entering an area around which is assembled the largest concentration of fighting troops in the world; so no hot pants, stretch pants, shorts or flip-flops, no children under ten years old and no alcoholic beverage.

Then Joy, our English-speaking guide, gives us a few facts about her country. I learn that the Korean Peninsula resembles a rabbit and that in five thousand years it has been invaded nine hundred and seventy times. The current troubles began in 1945 when the most recent invaders, the Americans and the Russians, drove out the previous invaders, the Japanese, and forced Korea into partition – communist north, capitalist south. There are still thirty-seven thousand American troops stationed in South Korea, while the north has a standing army of over a million. Joy rounds off her history lesson with a poignant reminder of the human cost of partition. It was imposed so swiftly in 1953 that millions of friends and families were separated with little prospect of seeing each other again from that day onwards.

'Our greatest wish,' says Joy, with a depth of feeling not commonly heard amongst tour guides, 'is the unification. We will reach for the unification in our dreams with our whole heart and our whole efforts. It is the unification which shapes our people. Oh, unification, come through, come through.' While this is being translated into Japanese a bulky middle-aged American leans across to me.

'Have you been up here before?'

I shake my head.

'You'll love it. You'll *love* it.'

On Unification Road the republic of South Korea stutters to a halt in an assortment of symbols. The railway line that used to run from Pusan to Peking now stops in a field with a chicken farm built over it. The last building of any size is The Anti-Communist Exhibition Hall, a big white circular construction which resembles a recently landed spaceship.

Freedom Bridge (named for the thirteen thousand North Korean prisoners who chose to stay in South Korea at the end of the war in 1953) is the end of the road for South Koreans, unless they are members of the United Nations Command Force. The rest of us pass on between mesh fences and barbed wire. Our passports are checked by lanky, crop-headed GIs from the First Battalion of the 506th Infantry – motto 'In Front Of Them All'. We are now in one of the most intensely fortified areas in the world; a two-and-a-half-mile wide, 151-mile-long strip of mines, tank traps and barricades, enclosed by a double chain link fence which slices through the Korean peninsula from coast to coast.

The South Koreans make much of the fact that there is a farming community right here, close to the border. They call it Great Success Village. The inhabitants are guarded day and night and after dark everyone must be back inside their homes with their doors locked. In return for taking part in this propaganda exercise they pay no taxes. The village may be a bit of a sham but the North Korean counterpart, called Paradise Village, is believed by observers to be a total sham with the buildings themselves only one-dimensional cut-outs.

Another manifestation of the propaganda war is the battle of the flag-poles. As soon as one side erects a new flag-pole, the other side puts up a bigger one. North Korea has the edge at the moment. Their current pole is 524 feet high and carries a flag which weighs 600 lbs and is the height of a three-storey building.

The heavily-armoured countryside we are now passing through is gentle and quite pretty with extensive alder, beech and birch woods largely untouched by human activity. There is a thick carpet of flowers on either side of the road. Bird life thrives here, I'm told, with several rare species reaping the benefits of living in an official no man's land.

Before we can actually see the frontier itself our coach pulls up at Camp Bonifas, where we are subjected to yet more information, this time from the Americans, about the DMZ, its history and the threat posed to the security of the free world by the existence of North Korea. I wander down a short green slope behind the souvenir shop. Ahead of me is a barbed wire fence and a watchtower, but right where I'm standing is what looks like a single golf-hole ringed with artificial turf. This patch of greenery has, I'm told, been featured in *Sport's Illustrated* as the World's Most Dangerous Golf Course. I sit for a while beneath a spreading oak tree and watch a flight of ducks squawking noisily towards North Korea. Then I pick up another sound. It's coming from deep in the woods ahead of me and a turn of the wind gusts it more clearly towards me. It's the sound of martial music being pumped across the frontier. A North Korean Vera Lynn is bawling out some patriotic anthem, interspersed with rousing, distorted exhortations to the capitalist lackeys and imperialist stooges of the South to throw off their chains and join the revolution. It is about the only sound that breaks the peace.

At last our bus moves off towards the border. A young black GI with the rank of Specialist has replaced Joy and her companion as our guide. His delivery and indeed the text of what he's saying are strictly military, with no place for emotion or embellishment. The effect is that of a policeman reading evidence in court – a curiously gripping blend of the inessential and the startling, both delivered with exactly the same emphasis.

'The drop gate we just passed is drop gate 28,' does not prepare you for 'The large grassy area on this side of Checkpoint 4 was the focal point of the 1976 Axe Murder Incident' (in which American troops conducting routine tree-lopping operations became involved in a contretemps which led to one of the North Koreans taking an axe and killing two soldiers).

At Checkpoint Three we get our first and last decent view

of the only country on the Pacific Rim we are not allowed to cross. Misty mountains frame the background and on the mighty flag-pole flies the red star of North Korea. We are allowed only a minute at this checkpoint. Our guide indicates the presence of a North Korean guard-post on the opposite hill and adds, matter of factly, 'in all probability you are under close observation. Please refrain from making arm gestures or sudden hand movements at this time.'

The mood of tension, artfully managed by both sides, is sustained by a squad of crack South Korean troops who, as we walk into the Conference Room, snap into a *Tae-Kwon-Do* martial arts pose as if about to headbutt the building.

Inside the long low hut is green baize table, half of which is in South Korea and half in the North. Around it the longest-running peace talks in the world have been taking place for over forty years. We're allowed to walk round the communist end of the table so we can, I suppose, all say we have stood in North Korea.

At the end of the day, as we are driven back to Seoul past yet more tank traps and yet another Freedom Highway, it's clear that our South Korean and American hosts have taken every possible precaution to look after us and prevent us leaving with an open mind.

DAY 51: *Seoul*

Under a headline 'Armed Agent Shot Dead', the late city-edition of the *Korea Herald* reports the shooting of one of a group of North Korean infiltrators a mile south of Freedom Bridge. On his body, found at 7.15 this morning, were hand-grenades, an M-16 assault rifle, pistols, ammunition, flippers and binoculars. It is the first such incident for four years but puts the paper in a lather of indignation. It links this with a description of life in the North culled from a North Army colonel who defected a week ago. 'The North Koreans have established their own Gulag, the worst of its kind in all repressive totalitarian societies.'

From the top of Insam Hill, where the cable car stops, I take a last look at 'free' Korea. Below me the new high rises of Seoul sweep across the landscape, like a steadily advancing army. Having taken the smaller hills in their stride, they gather in serried ranks at the foot of the steeper, less accessible cliffs, until, invigorated by property demand and new technology, they can storm the next mountain. And so on, and so on. Seoul, it seems, will never end.

In the face of this voracious display of power and industry, North Korea, I can't help thinking, doesn't stand a chance.

CHINA

DAY 52: *Inch'on to Qingdao*

It's a wet, overcast, monochrome day at the dockside in Inch'on. The assembly compound for the ferry service to the Chinese port of Qingdao is squeezed tight with cars, pick-ups and mini-vans around which bags and sacks are being unpacked and re-packed with serious urgency. Anxious, fraught faces. Calculators are out and last-minute deals are being made before the vehicles are stuffed to their roofs with everything from knitwear to pharmaceuticals to bottles of Chivas Regal.

Later, from the deck of our departing ferry boat, the MV *New Golden Bridge*, I count fifty or sixty ships at a dockside carpeted with thousands of new cars. Beyond them cranes are bending and turning continuously as they apply themselves to the Sisyphean task of clearing mountains of grain, coal and concrete. This is commerce on a grand scale, something unknown to British docksiders since Victorian times.

Its sheer energy and scale produces a disbelieving numbness. Who produces all this, who buys in such quantities, what creates this relentless demand? Then I remind myself that I am on my way to China, a land area of six million square miles, bordering fourteen countries, with a market of 1.2 billion people, and an economy which has grown at an average of ten per cent every year over the last fifteen years. On this murky, unpromising day we clear two great locks at the mouth of Inch'on harbour and head across the Yellow Sea to a country shaping up to be the superpower of the Asian Pacific. The most feared and least understood country in the world.

DAY 53: *Qingdao*

At first sight China looks like Germany. Red-roofed turn of the century housing blocks ride up the steep hills. Looming above them are two unmistakably Nordic churches, one with tall, slim spires and the other with a copper-domed clock tower. I blink again and it's France, with avenues of neatly cropped plane trees and solid bourgeois seaside villas running down to white sand, rock pools and a harbour wall. Look along the shore and it's Manhattan, with a cluster of crested skyscrapers thrusting up from an undergrowth of cranes.

The eclectic skyline emerging from the early morning haze is the city of Qingdao, 'Green Island'. It was once a small Chinese fishing village which attracted the attention of German missionaries at the end of the last century. Traders and troops followed the missionaries and Qingdao quickly became part of a German concession. The local Chinese could only stand and watch as a naval depot, coaling wharfs, houses, hotels, churches, a brewery and a railway created Bavaria on the Yellow Sea. The Japanese took it over in 1914, lost it again after the First World War and regained it in 1938, but it remained little more than a seaside resort until the 1980s when South Korean and Taiwanese money transformed the local economy for a second time. Today 'Green Island' is a conurbation of 6.8 million people.

But not everything has changed. We are viewed suspiciously by the authorities. Soldiers in drab green greatcoats with fur collars and yellow-trimmed high-peaked caps hold us on board ship until long after everyone else has gone, and when we are allowed off it is only as far as another bureaucratic bottleneck where we are required to fill in exhaustive questionnaires demanding to know if we are bringing in 'biologicals, blood products or second-hand clothes', and if any of us is currently suffering from 'cough, sore throat, vomiting, bleeding or lymph gland swelling'. Concealing a patch of incipient athlete's foot, I eventually step out onto the streets of China. The obliging porters who load our baggage and equipment into waiting vans turn out to be the manager of the hotel we're staying in and his gardener. When we arrive the chefs are called out to help unload.

The Welcome Guest House looks about as Chinese as Windsor Castle. It was built in 1903 as the Governor's residence and it is a great big daft dumpy pile of a place built in rampant German Romantic style, part schloss, part Roman villa, part gingerbread house. Crenellated towers top half-timbered flanks, massive thick-thighed columns support red-roofed balconies and flanks of rough hewn stone blocks shore up plastered walls.

We are treated to an official banquet tonight. The banquet here, as in Korea and to a certain extent Japan, is a vital part of any business relationship. Unless you can drink a lot in the company of other men who drink a lot you are not really to be trusted.

Our host is the vice-head of the local Foreign Relations Department, which keeps an eye on overseas guests to make sure they have everything they want, except what you don't want them to have. He is a soft-spoken, civilized man who spent five years reading geophysics at Imperial College in London. He is saddened by anti-Chinese bias in the English media. Objections seem to revolve around a recent Channel 4 documentary about Chinese orphans called *The Dying House*. It's hard to understand how one programme can cause such damage. I point out that in Britain we are constantly criticizing our own institutions but this doesn't cut much ice. There is so much good in China, he asks, why search out the bad?

Then the toasts begin and all differences are set aside in a brain-softening combination of *maotai* – a 55 proof spirit made from sorghum and wheat – Chinese Chardonnay and Tsing Tao beer. So copious and fraternal are the toasts that I hardly notice the sea-slugs and crispy-fried silkworm grubs that I pop into my mouth between them.

DAY 54

From a rough-hewn granite balcony I look out over the garden. A group of young women wearing an ensemble of black jackets, trousers and high-heels, are sweeping the lawn with besom brushes. There is something passive and docile in their attitude to this largely pointless task and it doesn't much surprise me that, according to my *Insight Guide*, China ranks 132nd in the world in women's working conditions.

I haven't slept very well. It wasn't the *maotai* as much as the awareness that some of the most ruthless men of this century have slept beneath this roof and, for all I know, on my very bed. The Welcome Guest House was one of the great holiday homes for dictators. Mao Tse-Tung spent a month here in the room below mine, a year before instituting the first of his brutal experiments with the Chinese population – the Great Leap Forward. He lived on pills for insomnia and constipation. I swear I heard him pacing up and down last night. A plaque outside the room next door records the visits of Lin Biao, author of *The Little Red Book* and, with Mao, instigator of the savageries of the Cultural Revolution; while Ho-Chi-Minh of Vietnam, Prince Sihanouk of Cambodia, Mao's foreign minister Zhou Enlai and two general secretaries of the Albanian Communist Party all stared up at my ceiling. Though not at the same time.

The Chinese Chardonnay made such an impression last night that we are to make a trip to the Hua Dung vineyard from which it comes. This involves an hour's journey into the limestone foothills of the Laoshan mountains, to the slopes around a long, low white building, more convent than chateau, where Michael Parry, an Englishman based in Hong Kong, first began wine making in 1985. Production has increased by an average of thirty per cent every year since then and, though Parry himself went bust and died at the age of forty-three, the

Hiram Walker company took it over as part of a joint venture with the Chinese and this year it will produce 440,000 gallons. Wu Lizhu, the present wine maker, is thirty-one, short, amiable and intelligent. His two biggest competitors for the growing Chinese wine-drinking market are Dynasty white and Great Wall red, but he feels he is in a different league. In a quick tasting he drew my attention to the peachy flavour in the Chardonnay and the hint of pineapple in the delicate straw-coloured Riesling. Our attempts to recreate this elegant tasting for the camera, on the lawn below the vinery, are sabotaged by the sudden appearance of a gale force wind that blows the glasses off the table and into the flower-beds.

At the end of the afternoon we climb up to Parry's grave on the hillside. Below us smoke rises from brick kilns and children's kites strain in the gusty wind. There are some, like the present manager of the vineyard, who regard Parry as a saint, and others who see him as an ambitious opportunist who conned a million out of an insurance company; but the distant line of men with hoes and axes levelling more terraces for more vines shows how, in the new China, ambitious opportunism can reap healthy rewards.

DAY 55

The prettiest part of the Qingdao sea front is called Number 6 Bathing Beach. Despite a cold, crisp autumn morning a few intrepid souls are prepared to take on the Pacific. They enter the water with a certain panache, arms extended, muscles flexed like hopeful entrants for a Mr Universe competition. Most other people confine their adventures to scrambling across the slimy rocks in big overcoats. There are beach photographers trying to lure people into their peacock chairs and trinket sellers with pieces of coral and necklaces, stamping their feet against the cold. It's comforting to know that the Chinese can have as miserable a time by the seaside as the British.

On the pavement of a road behind the sea front is a line of

men in white coats holding red crosses and standing beside what look like portable operating tables. I look around to see if there has been some dreadful accident but am assured the men are masseurs waiting for business. Passers-by lie down on the beds without ceremony and without even taking their coats off. I join them and quickly realize why you don't *need* to take anything off. All the masseurs are blind with fingers so powerful they could probably reach you through a suit of armour. They have a technique of rotating clenched fists so fast that the heat almost burns. Walk away with a feeling of quite bearable lightness. I'm sure it helps me to cope with another banquet, this time in honour of a diplomat from the Japanese embassy, who drinks with uninfectious enthusiasm.

DAY 56: *Qingdao to Tai'an*

Today we leave Qingdao and head south. Rather than follow the coast with its familiar and predictable run of boom towns, we have decided to make an inland journey using Yangtze river boats to take us into the heartland of China, where Mao's revolution had its roots; and from there south-west to the Vietnamese border. Every journey in China is an adventure and fraught with complications. We have our own fixers (one from the film facilities company in Beijing and another a freelance photographer also from Beijing) but we must also have at least one local official with us. Here in Qingdao it has been Mr Li. He arrives to see us off, looking red and puffy in the face. He shakes his head unhappily. Hospitality is getting him down. Yesterday alone he had to eat four banquets.

Chefs, gardeners and chambermaids help us load up. Everyone looks with envy at a powder blue Mercedes-320 parked outside the front door of our hotel. It has Tibetan licence plates.

The attractive old city which first caught my eye from the Inch'on ferry gives way to a monotonous and apparently endless urban industrial sprawl. Most of the development is new, Pacific miracle stuff. Plastics and clothing factories,

'Monkey King Frozen Foods'. After an hour or more we get out into the countryside, only to find that most of it is wrapped in polythene sheeting. Seas of hot-house plastic stretch away on either side of the Jinan expressway, a long straight, almost empty, elevated toll-road which looks as if it has been imported lock, stock and barrel from Europe. Why else would restaurants be marked with a crossed knife and fork in a country where everyone uses chopsticks?

We turn off at an unpromising service area, only to find that a 'light lunch' consists of eighteen different dishes (and chopsticks). The Chinese may tolerate bad surroundings but they won't tolerate bad food. We snack on liver, pork knuckle, carp, raw crayfish, spring onions and mushrooms, jellied rabbit, shrimp, eggs, fish in lotus leaf sauce and rice pudding. Predictably I nod off after the journey resumes and when I wake up I notice Susan, one of our Chinese fixers, reading the copy of Jung Chang's *Wild Swans* which has slipped from my lap. She says that such a book would not be published in China.

In Jinan we take a sharp left on the broad banks of the Yellow River and head up into low and lifeless mountains. Stripped of trees during Mao's time, they are now being stripped of the rock itself. Quarrying activity erupts on all sides like an artillery bombardment. The bright sun of the coast has been reduced to an unhealthy orange smudge which barely permeates a waxy haze of pollution. The driving has begun to turn dangerous. There are very few private cars and the belching, overloaded trucks regard the road as little more than a conveyor belt on which to swing about as they wish. We scream to a standstill just in time to avoid colliding with a train of high, blackened wagons crossing the road where neither lights nor barrier work.

At six we arrive in Tai'an, birthplace of Mao's wife, Jiang Qing, ex-actress and leader of the notorious Gang Of Four who, after Mao's death, took the excesses of the cultural revolution to a new degree of viciousness. For the Chinese, Mao is a cherub compared to his wife and most of his ruthless deeds have conveniently been ascribed to her influence.

Another set of minders awaits us here. Both are called Mr Wang. They entertain us most royally in a private room of the hotel whose table is dominated by a sculpture of flamingos, carved entirely from radishes. The staff, in national dress, explain the elaborate theatrical name of each dish. Fish and dumplings, for instance, becomes 'Dragon Eating Pearls'. One of the Mr Wangs proposes a toast to us all. He is delighted to have us here in his ancient city. The station has been specially cleaned for us and of course he hopes that we will find time to climb the sacred mountain of Taishan. It has steps all the way up, he assures me. Only the next day do I learn there are six thousand, two hundred and ninety three of them.

DAY 57: *Tai'an*

Tai'an is at the centre of much Chinese history, and several strands of religion and philosophy come together here. Taishan Mountain, the most important of China's five sacred mountains, is an hour's drive away, and Confucius, whose philosophy, with its emphasis on discipline and respect for authority is still influential, was born 80 miles down the road at Qufu, over two thousand five hundred years ago.

All this may account for why they are playing 'The Ride of the Valkyries' over the dining room loudspeakers at half past six this morning. Wherever there is likely even to be a smattering of foreign tourists, western music, rather than Chinese, will accompany them. I would rather it didn't. It's not easy to eat a hard boiled egg to 'Ride of the Valkyries'.

Although we arrive at the base of the Exalted Mountain by eight o'clock, there is already a steady trickle of pilgrims on their way up. It is said that if you can climb to the top of the mountain you will live to be a hundred. An unlikely assortment of would-be centenarians push past me. Schoolchildren in parties, lithe and bony old ladies, women in high heels, newly-weds, and couples practically frog-marching elderly relatives onwards and upwards. The object of their efforts is the Southern Gate of Heaven, a massive two-tiered red arch. It stands way above on a sharp rocky ridge and can be glimpsed occasionally through drifting clouds.

Halfway up, at the Middle Gate of Heaven, are lines of souvenir shops, most of which sell hats and walking sticks for about a pound. There is also a cable-car station here for those who aren't so worried about living to a hundred.

After five thousand steps, we are surrounded by unmelted snow. The only people not stopping for frequent rests are the wiry, bandy-legged porters who ascend steadily with enormous loads of bricks, cement, roofing tiles, or food supplies slung from yokes across their shoulders. They make two trips a day and are paid thirty *yuan* (two pounds) a time, enough for three beers.

The view from the Nantiamen Gate, the South Gate of Heaven, is obtained after more than two hours climbing and comes with the satisfaction of seeing an ant-like stream of figures still toiling up the pale white ribbon of stairs below. The centre of Paradise is a hundred and fifty steps away up the Scaling Ladder to the Gate of Heaven through Immortalization Archway and into the Temple of the Princess of the Azure Cloud. No azure clouds today, but a murky, clinging white mist which binds the cold air tight around me. The monks wear army greatcoats and rub their hands, and the pilgrims, having made the long journey, kneel at the blood-red doors of the temple, throw a money offering into what looks like a horizontal British pillar-box, bow three times before the Princess, raise their incense sticks, and move out pretty smartish.

As we retrace our steps away from this, one of the most revered sites in China, a sound drifts in the air above the chatter of the tourists. It's the sound of 'Moon River', played by Richard Clayderman.

We leave Tai'an in the evening on the overnight train to Shanghai. The station is spotless, as Mr Wang and Mr Wang had promised. Almost alone on the platform are a party of German tourists, a handful of Chinese businessmen, ourselves, and our fifty pieces of baggage. When the train is announced a rectangle of light spills out onto the platform as the waiting room door opens and a long silent line of shadowy figures is escorted by rail staff to their appointed position on the platform. These are the Hard Class passengers.

The difference between them and us in Soft Class is that we can enjoy the benefits of individual lighting, two layers of curtains and advertising in the corridors. There is even an ad on the door of the toilet. It is for a product called 'Love', which Susan tells me is an anti-haemorrhoid cream.

DAY 58: *Tai'an to Shanghai*

Wake up to first glimpse of the River Yangtze. The Chang Jiang, as the Chinese call it. Third longest river in the world, after the Nile and the Amazon, although there's only a couple of hundred miles between the three of them. It is suitably immense here and the bridge we are rumbling across, just north of Nanjing, is one of the great engineering feats of communist China. The rail span is over four miles long. Before it was opened in 1968, there was no direct rail link between Beijing and Shanghai, the two most important cities of China.

There has been a *waterway* system connecting them since the thirteenth century when the rulers of the Yuan Dynasty finally connected up a system of smaller canals and rivers dating back to the fifth century BC. It's known as the Emperor (or Grand) Canal and, if I lift the net curtain, I can see it, briefly, from my seat in the dining car before it merges into the green, vaporous wetland of the Yangtze Delta. This occasionally beautiful, limpid landscape, with elegant pagodas and flotillas of white ducks on flooded fields, is soon submerged by progress. Powerlines, factories, apartment blocks and assembly plants suck us into Shanghai.

I was last here seven years ago in the steps of Phileas Fogg. Then it was a city of awesome scale, bursting at the seams. Since then old seams have burst and new ones are already under threat. The pace of construction is relentless. Once the foundations of a tower block are laid, a new floor can be added every three days. But the difference I notice is not so much that there's more of it, but what there's more of. On streets which saw the violent birth of Chinese communism you can now buy a suit at Harvey Nichols, a coat at Ralph Lauren, a shirt at Gieves and Hawkes and a pair of shoes at Charles Jourdan. The streets on which Mao's plans for a Cultural Revolution were first made public are now as mercilessly franchised as any American shopping mall. Haagen-Daz ice-cream and Kentucky Fried Chicken fight over property with Mickey Mouse corner shops and Hollywood Wonder arcades. Girls here are no longer shy of fashion. They cycle by in black mini-skirts and Italian designer sweaters with an air of self-confident, almost Parisian hauteur.

Later, at our hotel, we are rudely reminded that the wind of change blows only in certain directions. Economic liberalism should not be mistaken for political relaxation. Over the weekend we have lined up three interviews with Chinese who have benefited in different ways from the Shanghai boom. Despite the fact that we have a fixer from Beijing accompanying us, and dealing with all the relevant permissions, our two *Shanghai* fixers are not at all happy. They are content for us to go out into the streets and shoot views of their city, but not to talk to those who live here. Clearly their interpretation of 'views of the city' is different from ours. But they will not be moved. We are faced with little choice. These Foreign Relations departments have tentacles all across China. If we try to talk to people in Shanghai whom they don't want us to talk to we may well find life becomes very difficult on the way down to Vietnam. On the other hand to retreat in high dudgeon and re-route through Taiwan and Hong Kong would waste our chance of a rare glimpse of the Chinese interior.

So we capitulate and agree to cancel the interviews. Despite the fact that tomorrow will be an unscheduled day off, it's a low point of the journey, only slightly relieved by the almost comic reaction of the Shanghai apparatchiks to the idea of a day off. What does 'day off' mean? Where will we be going? At what time?

Basil is of the opinion that the interference is not politically motivated. It's most likely that the Shanghai people want some of the money we're paying the Beijing people. And he's Chinese, so he should know. One good thing about this little crisis is that the flow of banquet invitations has dried up.

DAY 59: *Shanghai*

Rain, which fell in torrents overnight, has cleared, skies are bright and a man in the lobby eyes me suspiciously as I step out of the hotel. Next door is the neo-Stalinist bulk of the Shanghai Exhibition Centre. Already crowds are flooding in to the International Audio and Visual Exhibition, the International Textile Machinery Exhibition and the International Modern Fabrics, Apparels, Accessories and Materials Exhibition. None of these interests me as much as the 'Exhibition of Yangtze River Area in Rapid Development', which is advertised on a large board with an arrow pointing to a small side door. I try the door, but it's locked. Will come back later. Potter around the lively, walkable streets of the old French Concession, where nineteen-twenties red-tiled roofs, wooden balconies, turrets, chimney pots, back extensions and gardens survive incongruously amongst encroaching walls of skyscrapers. A helpful estate agent who speaks good English tells me that a two-bedroomed apartment in this part of Shanghai would rent for around three thousand US dollars a month.

Walk down to the Bund, the great riverfront thoroughfare. The soberly solid stone relics of colonial rule still dominate, but the brick terraces and warehouses on the other side of the Huangpu River have been swept away to create the New Economic Zone of Pudong. Proudly it is said to be the biggest commercial centre of its kind in the world. A huge, rude, pink television tower that looks like some giant internal probe dominates a sprawling building site from which sprout World Finance Towers, the new Shanghai Securities Exchange and many more capitalist sanctuaries.

Twice on my walk I am approached by Chinese wanting to practice their English. A very eager man, who says he works in a bookshop, accompanies me for almost half an hour repeating the middle names of my children slowly and reverentially until he is satisfied. To relax after the bustle of the streets I go for a massage back at the hotel. But there's no respite here either. It isn't easy, believe me, to give a sensible answer to questions like 'Manchester important textile centre. Yes . . . No?' when you're squashed head down on a massage table.

DAY 60

Walking through the grounds of the Exhibition Centre, I see that the door to the Exhibition of Yangtze River Area in Rapid Development is open. As I enter a couple of uniformed officials step forward threateningly. I mime, a little testily, looking, learning, walking around, etcetera. They shake their heads uncomprehendingly. This makes me more testy and even more determined to see anything to do with the Yangtze Area in Rapid Development.

Glances are exchanged and eventually my persistence is rewarded. I am directed to a ticket booth. Proffer a 50 *yuan* note and am given a ticket and 45 *yuan* change. I walk on into the darkened interior, muttering bitterly about Chinese bureaucracy. After a walk down a long, unpromising passage-way I emerge onto a dance floor. Hundreds of pairs of eyes turn towards me from a sea of densely-packed, smoky tables. A small band is waiting to strike up. The conductor turns and looks in my direction.

Back at the hotel, Basil examines the Chinese writing on my admission ticket. It reads 'Friendship Dance Hall. Tea Dance.'

DAY 61

At seven o'clock this morning they are ballroom-dancing on the Nanjing Road. Thirty or forty couples are waltzing on the sidewalk to the sound of an old Vera Lynn tape. It's all quite unselfconscious and matter-of-fact, as though this is what people all over the world do on their way to work. In terms of musical taste, China is the Middle of the Road Kingdom.

The old and middle aged, who were probably Red Guards twenty years ago, now love to hear Vera and Jim Reeves and anything by the George Melachrino Strings. They also assume, mistakenly in my case, that every Englishman dances like Fred Astaire, and I am soon at work on the pavement, joining this slow, rhythmic moving mass as the bicycles and cars stream past us down the road.

My partner is an attractive Chinese lady with a sleepy smile. At the end of the number I am congratulated on my deeply inept display. A very old, sprightly man in white gloves winks at me and says in English:

'You are Chinese Romeo.' He indicates my partner. 'And she is your Julie.'

DAY 63: *The Yangtze River – Yichang to Wushan*

Seven-thirty in the morning. From my window in the Ping-Hu Hotel in Yichang I enjoy a view of urban desolation – a featureless cityscape of dull, dirty blocks, unalleviated by any living colour, sprig of greenery, or man-made element one might consider graceful or uplifting.

'Welcome To The Three Gorges' reads a dusty red and yellow concrete sign on the other side of the road.

It's difficult to believe that this is the focal point for one of the greatest construction projects in history. Work began on the Three Gorges Dam in 1993 and will not be finished until 2009. The reservoir it creates will be the largest in the world, stretching back 400 miles. It was Chairman Mao's greatest unfulfilled ambition and now, twenty years after his death, it seems to be coming true. The mighty Yangtze will become the Ping-Hu – the Placid Lake.

All Ping-Hu means to us at the moment is a filthy hotel with delightful staff. Breakfast conversation takes a depilatory turn. I had found long black hairs on my pillow. Steve, our assistant cameraman, had found pubic hairs in his washbasin.

Yesterday we travelled over 600 miles from Shanghai by plane and bus, through rain and nondescript countryside,

so today we are all looking forward to slower progress and
finer scenery as we board the *Oriental Star Number 1*, a broad-
bottomed Yangtze ferryboat shaped like a great green marrow.
It has four levels of accommodation ranging from double
cabins to open decks. The last docking cable is cast off two
minutes after our scheduled departure time and with a
sonorous blast on the horn the *Oriental Star* pulls out into the
stream. Hooting our way past greasy tugboats, sampans,
colliers, junks and small two-deck local ferries we make our
way towards a cavernous lock beside the present Yangtze dam
at Gezhou. The doors holding back the river are 100 foot high.
I feel vaguely uncomfortable trapped at the bottom of these
black slimy walls. Cyclists and pedestrians pour across the top
of the lock gates way above us. When the Three Gorges Project
is finished there will be five locks this size.

Once released from the lock we find ourselves in open water,
narrowed by the steep sides of the Xiling Gorge into a funnel for
a cold, hard head-wind. A tourist boat, the *Yangtze Paradise*,
passes us on its way to Yichang. It's virtually empty.

After three hours on the river we reach the village of
Sandouping, site of the Three Gorges Dam. Despite considerable debate about whether or not there is money to build it
(costs are currently estimated at twenty billion dollars), a
graceful suspension bridge, about two-thirds of a mile long, has
been built across the river to connect the two construction sites,
cliffs have been stripped and blasted, spurs of rock blown away
and the rubble used to create the foundations for what will
be a 600-foot-high dam wall, one and a quarter miles long.
Bridges have been thrown across subsidiary inlets and new
roads have been dug into the mountainside to cope with the
lorry traffic. Cement silos tower into the air, conveyor belts run
down to barges, whole townships have been built on the banks
to house the eighteen thousand workers. The current stage of
this operation, which involves a temporary diversion of the
course of the Yangtze, is gigantic enough.

Up river from the construction site we enter the most unspoilt
pastoral landscape I've yet seen in China. A panorama of
traditional cultivation patterns – terraced valleys winding back

into the mountains, contours picked out by stone walls and winding paths. Hamlets of whitewashed stone cottages with wide-hipped roofs are tucked away amongst the trees, or dotted along sandy bays. Quite soon all this will have vanished beneath the waters of the reservoir. The occupants of those whitewashed farmhouses will be among the one and a half million who will be sent elsewhere, their homes and livelihoods sacrificed to the industrialization of the Yangtze Basin.

Meanwhile the river narrows. Whirlpools, eddies and races force the *Oriental Star* into long, time-consuming zig-zags as it labours against the current. One of the arguments in favour of the Three Gorges Dam is that it will calm the flow of the water and make navigation easier. It will also, its supporters claim, help prevent the recurrent and murderous Yangtze floods and provide thousands of megawatts of cheap electricity. At 4.15 we make our first stop at Badong, on the southern bank. It is built on steep slopes with a commanding view of the river, and an impressive edifice that resembles the Potala palace in Lhasa dominates one end of town. The reality is less glamorous. The Potala Palace turns out to be a power station and the banks below it are coal tips. Any coal not used at the power station is sent slithering down the mountain in long open chutes, and flung out into waiting barges in a series of sooty ejaculations. Badong does not look healthy. Dust from uncovered coal tips has blown across the town and the apartment blocks that stride so confidently up the mountain are stained and grubby. Much higher up however are brand new apartments. Fresh, clean and gleaming. They, of course, will be above the flood.

Through the Wu-Xia, the Witches Gorge, 25 miles long and flanked by twelve towering peaks. Kites cruise the cliff-sides. The river has lost all tones of green and is now a fiercely flowing mud-brown. The captain watches it carefully. He is the personification of riverine experience – an elderly man with close-cropped grey hair, shrewd eyes and compact, formidably serious features that transform like a clown's mask whenever he smiles.

As the light begins to fade, the walls of the gorge grow taller and more dizzily vertical – looming stacks of rock, black at their base, peaks tinged orange by the setting sun.

The Witches Gorge is the gateway to Sichuan, the largest and most populous of China's twenty-one provinces. With a hundred million inhabitants and an area slightly greater than that of France it consists of a prosperous eastern plain encircled by mountains. For centuries the Yangtze gorges have been its only communication with the outiside world. The easternmost city in Sichuan is Wushan, which we reach at eight in the evening.

Porters on the landing stage fight over the heaviest pieces of baggage, and enormous loads are tied to individual shoulder poles and carried off up a steep flight of stone steps separating the river from the road. We are then transported through narrow, winding, darkened streets in the hotel coach, horn blaring and everything in our way – cars, cycles, motor tricycles, men, women and children – cast to one side.

Wushan is small town China. Foreign tourists doing the gorges spend the night on their cruise ships, and the hotel, off a scruffy courtyard on the main street, is not sophisticated. We decide the rooms might be more beautiful after a beer or two and the man who is hiring us boats for tomorrow offers to find us somewhere. He will not hear of us exploring on our own.

'I will come with you. Wushan is a dangerous town.'

The tree-lined main street looks about as dangerous as Disney World but he walks ahead of us like a Chinese Robert Mitchum, jacket hung loose across his shoulders, chewing on a matchstick. It's clear, after passing one or two attractive street-side establishments, that his idea of 'having a beer' means more than merely having a beer. We leave the main street and walk a little way up a side road where he conducts some business with a middle-aged woman who casts repeated and unimpressed looks in our direction before finally indicating a doorway. We climb three floors past dimly-lit rooms. We are shown into a glum reception area with leather sofas and are given a plate of biscuits. But it is not until the ladies actually appear that we finally catch on. Hasty exits all round. Honestly.

RIGHT: *Little Diomede in the Bering Strait.*

BELOW: *The Nugget Inn, museum with beds.*

LEFT: *The largest terrestrial carnivores in the world.*

BELOW: *One of the twenty-five volcanoes in the Kronotsky Nature Reserve near Petropavlovsk.*

RIGHT: *Ivan on his way back to the Gulag site.*

BELOW RIGHT: *Day off. Dancing on Russkiy Island.*

FAR LEFT: *On the Sado Island Ferry.*

LEFT: *Outside the Dojo Nabe in Tokyo with Mayumi.*

BELOW: *The Kodo apprentices in class.*

LEFT: *Lone British participant. Okunchi Festival, Nagasaki.*

BELOW: *Learning their culture: South Korean schoolchildren at Pulguska Temple.*

RIGHT: *Climbing Tai-Shan mountain, Tai'an – only another two thousand steps to go.*

INSET: *Hair wash and scalp massage: value for money at Wushan, China.*

OVERLEAF: *On the Danning River with Victor.*

Unlike most small provincial towns, Wushan actually grows noisier as the night goes on. At midnight I set my Martin Amis to one side and pull the duvet over my head. The dissonant chorus of karaoke, bus engines, firecrackers, drunken arguments, riverboat sirens and the sharp, ugly 'eek!' of tricycle-taxi horns make rather a mockery of the 'Do Not Disturb' sign I've hung on the door. (Only in the morning do I find that it actually reads 'Do Not Disturd'.)

DAY 64: *Wushan*

Mr Huo, who insists I call him Victor, is to be our guide to the Three Little Gorges of the Danning River, a tributary of the Yangtze. He is slim and dapper with lightly tinted glasses in very big frames. Mindful of what we have heard about rapids and low temperatures in dark gorges, we all look dressed for an Arctic expedition. Victor wears a thin, oatmeal-coloured sweater and carries a handbag.

We drive down to the waterfront past the coal-loading area. Below a faded mural with the English legend 'You are welcome my dear friends. May the beautiful scenes in Mount Wu make a deep impression on you', coal is being loaded from wind-blown heaps by a constant shuttle of blackened, bandy-legged labourers with hods and shoulder poles. This is the old China, where machines are few and expensive and human effort plentiful and cheap.

But once on the unspoilt jade-green waters of the Danning River with spectacularly sheer walls enclosing a huge stillness, the beauty of the natural landscape is breathtaking and, with the prospect of the water level being raised 570 feet once the dam is built, there will not be long to see it.

We are travelling in a fragile sampan which adds to the drama of the scenery, and Victor is pointing out the graves in the cliff walls and the holes from which there once projected, during the Han dynasty, about the time of Christ, the supports for a walkway running 60 miles up the gorge. He also answers my questions about the Chinese predilection for giving animal characteristics to natural features. At one point he congratulates me on spotting a small outcrop looking vaguely like a dog.

'Good,' he says. 'Good imagination.'

His English is quite fluent but spoken with a rolling American accent which can create misunderstandings. Dragon, for instance, sounds like 'jerking', and it's a while before I realize what 'Jerking' Gate Gorge really is. At another time he talks of 'hawk' regularly descending over the gorge. I look up but can't see anything. Birds are pretty rare in China – outside soup and cages. Fraser, our sound man, seeing my bafflement, asks:

'Do you mean fog?'

Victor nods vigorously.

'Yes, Yes! Hawk . . . *thick* hawk.'

DAY 65

Main street, Wushan, less riotous by day than by night, is still quite remarkable. Every other business is a hairdresser, and every hairdresser's shop has its obligatory western glamour posters on the walls. The models, usually hunky American men with rippling muscles and women with breasts billowing from loosely-tied shirts, loom above the tiny people of Wushan like creatures from another planet as they toil slowly by, like survivors of a war, pulling cartloads of coal brickettes, or bamboo baskets full of potatoes or firewood.

The gutters are being carefully swept by a man with a brush made of bamboo stalks, who pauses every now and then to deliver a fresh gob of spit onto his handiwork. The restaurants serve pretty gruesome local specialities like pork belly and bull's penis.

It's hard to believe that in seven years' time the waters of the Yangtze will begin to lap over the coal yards and rise up the steps and along the alleyways and spill into the streets and, slowly but surely, drown every hairdresser's shop, every restaurant, every brothel, until the ferries we are now leaving to catch will eventually chug by 100 yards above our heads, and the twenty-four hour noise will be reduced to eerie silence.

Perhaps it is the acceptance of this fate that accounts for the manic liveliness of Wushan, one of the least comfortable places I have been to, but one I'm most sad to leave.

DAY 66: *On the Yangtze*

'Build Wanxian Into A Big City With 5,000,000 Population In 2000.' This huge hoarding, which looms up on our starboard side at breakfast time, is recklessly optimistic. Two-thirds of Wanxian, including nine hundred of its factories, will be inundated by the Three Gorges' floodwaters. Whatever big city it is built into by the year 2000 will not be the one we look out on this morning.

Which may not be a bad thing. From the river it looks hellish. Countless smokestacks and factory chimneys feed every shade of smoke from deep black to rust brown into a sky already turgid with low, pus-yellow cloud. A rubbish-tip smoulders on the shore and murky water streams from the town walls through great cavernous sluices. Trails of white scum, residue from an up-river paper factory, swirl past the boat, too thick to be broken up and not heavy enough to sink. My clothes retain the stink of sulphur long after my walk on deck.

These are the dark satanic mills of the Yangtze and, pausing only to set down and take on passengers, we proceed onwards, adding our own dose of diesel smoke to the thick, sticky gloom. I'm feeling quite seriously deprived of the sight of a sunrise or a sunset, a star at night or just a puffy cloud or two – anything to break the dispiriting colourlessness that has hung over the country since we left Shanghai.

The gorges are behind us now and the river turns quite sharply southwards. We are almost exactly twenty-four hours from our destination, Chongqing. All this and other information is relayed to us by the ship's announcer, a pretty twenty-three-year-old, with dark hair combed in a fringe, small mouth and full lips, who won the job in a competition. She would rather have been an actress but she's settled for announcing. Her own neat little cabin on the upper deck has the top half of the doorway curtained off as in a photo booth. When she's not at the microphone, she sits behind the drawn curtain, knitting demurely.

The scenery is pastoral again. An atmospheric mist shrouds tranquil terraces and villages. At Shibaozhai we pass a fine pagoda, eleven storeys high, built into the black-stained limestone rock of the west bank. Its blood-red walls and blue and white trimmed roofs inject a rare burst of colour into the landscape.

The day passes slowly. Chinese passengers hang over the deck rail clutching flasks of green tea which look like dumb-bells. At Zhong Xian more coal-black concrete factories pile up the river bank. In the fields around crops struggle to push their way through a layer of soot. But bad air and bad buildings don't necessarily mean bad food. Zhong Xian is the gourmet centre of Szechuan bean curd. As our ferry pulls alongside, choice delicacies are being freshly-cooked on the jetty. Frantic buying and selling goes on. As we leave, last purchases of bean curd are hurled across the water to the departing boat.

DAY 67: *Chongqing*

A rude awakening. First, low-grade awareness of the ship's ubiquitous music. A Chinese Olivia Newton-John seeping out of the wall. This followed almost immediately by a fierce throat-clearing retch from the cabin next door. But what has me diving for the floor is a series of thunderous explosions. The film *Yangtze Incident* leaps to mind. Has war broken out without us knowing? More explosions. Smoke rises from the bank, less than 100 yards away. This is followed by the sound of slithering rock, and relief that it is nothing worse than the Chinese blowing their mountains apart again. I can only think the quarrymen must have waited till we were passing to detonate the explosion. Probably cheered them up no end.

A metropolitan feel to the river traffic as we approach Chongqing, the largest city in China, with a population of at least fifteen million. A succession of hovercraft, hydrofoils and river cruisers with names like *Fantasy Fairyland* and *China Dream* pass on their way north.

We edge slowly closer to the great grey walls of the city, sombre but undeniably impressive as they culminate in a mini-Manhattan on the crest of a curving promontory carved out by the confluence of the Yangtze and the Jialing Jiang rivers. Though we leave the Yangtze here, it meanders on in a series of great loops for another 2500 miles, through the mountains of the south-west and into Tibet. At 10.15 we are alongside floating pontoons. Our equipment is carried ashore by a procession of twelve agile porters over narrow gangplanks and across mud-flats littered with river detritus – cast-off shoes, polystyrene boxes, bits of rope, cable and the odd bicycle wheel. On either side of us is an almost biblical scene as passengers from other ferries stream across the black mud and up the steep steps leading to the city gates. Until the 1930s, when Chongqing had a piped supply, all the water used in the city had to be carried up these steps in buckets. An army of twenty thousand coolies was constantly on the move.

Alongside the modern city there are still streets and alleyways where old two-storey ochre-washed houses survive, patched and peeling, the holes in the daub and wattle plaster exposing their wooden frames as though they're slowly dying of hunger. They have survived worse times. The Japanese bombed the city with ruthless persistence between 1939 and 1941, when Chiang Kai-shek and his anti-communist Kuomintang Nationalist Army set up their headquarters here.

Although there is much evidence of poverty – barefoot street sellers with shoulder poles, a mess of shanty houses clinging to the lower slopes of the cliffs – there is also a certain metropolitan confidence. We are back among mobile phones and traffic jams for the first time since Shanghai. I lunch with Miss Liu, a twenty-three-year-old local girl who last year graduated in English from Chongqing University. We eat in a street where we know the meat is fresh because it's hanging up all around us. A score of butchers' stalls form a gently receding pink and white perspective up the hillside. The food is spicy – the steamed pork is mixed with chillies and the vegetables glow with garlic and ginger. This is typical of Szechuan cooking, says Miss Liu, though she thinks that young Chinese are opting for less spicy food. There is now a Kentucky Fried Chicken house in Chongqing, she admits darkly. But this is about as far as her criticism of China goes. She professes serious enthusiasm for the 'opening up' policies of the government, its spectacular economic growth rate and growing awareness of environmental problems. Though she claims to listen to the BBC, her view of England is still of a land of rain and fog, Dickens and Shakespeare, and gentlemen with good manners. But in one way she gets it exactly right.

'I have some impression of the British people,' she says solemnly. 'That they are very preserved.'

The people of Chongqing, on the other hand, are much less preserved than their compatriots in Shanghai and Beijing. There is more eye contact here, a much more direct and friendly response to my curiosity. I have a long, intimate, mutually incomprehensible conversation with a boy who cleans my shoes for three *yuan* (twenty pence) and my passing interest in a stall serving take-away pig's head is cordially reciprocated with an invitation from the stallholder to try her stomach, heart and liver.

I'm beginning to be less wary of the Chinese and perhaps less mystified by them. I hope the feeling's mutual.

DAY 69: *Chongqing to Guiyang*

A Jack and the Beanstalk of a tower block is going up beside the hotel. There are lights on, cranes swinging and tiny figures working on its concrete summit throughout the night. I can't bear ear-plugs and don't take sleeping pills so I have to learn to live with the noise. The one sound that always lulls me to sleep is the sound of the sea and I'm beginning to miss the Pacific. I reckon it's now about 1,500 miles away. I have seen more of China than ever before but now I want to move on to where I can hear the waves breaking.

This is easier said than done. Our way out of China is by

train into Vietnam, but we have heard conflicting reports as to whether or not a railway link between the two countries actually exists. To reach the frontier means finding our way through the two rarely visited provinces of Guizhou and Guangxi. When, and if, we reach the frontier, my guidebook warns of a ten-minute walk into Vietnam and 'some of the most unwelcoming border guards you are likely to have encountered'.

These glum dark-hour thoughts are banished by the arrival of dawn and the repetitive practicalities of packing, loading and moving on. Our driver this morning wears white gloves and is used to driving Vice-Premiers and other luminaries. Instead of a siren he has a loudspeaker on the front of the vehicle through which he can hurl abuse at anyone who gets in his way. It's thoroughly effective and we arrive half an hour early at Chongqing station (which boasts the largest Marlboro ad outside of Times Square) for the train to Guiyang. At the next door platform an overnight train from Kunming disgorges one and a half thousand bleary travellers. Staggering beneath huge burdens of crates, sacks, planks and coils of rope they look like sappers of an invading army.

An hour out of Chongqing we have our last view of the Yangtze, trailed by heavy industry along both its banks. I have to say it looks pretty despondent at this point. Broad, limpid and lazy, a dull inscrutable silver-grey glimpsed behind steel and concrete installations from which God knows what noxiousness flows.

We, on the other hand, climb slowly up into a rich, vertiginous, sub-tropical landscape of rice terraces secured with elegant mud-red walls, interspersed with bamboo groves and banana plantations. Every now and then, of course, a bauxite mine or an aluminium smelter rears up, a sharp reminder that after Mao Tse-Tung's disastrous agrarian revolution, Deng Xiaoping gave industry priority over every living thing.

Another motive for government investment in these previously neglected hills and valleys is that good old chestnut, national security. Here on the southern borders of China the homogeneity of the Han Chinese, who make up ninety-three

101

per cent of the population, breaks down into a number of ethnic groups whose allegiance to central government cannot be taken for granted. The Tibetans may have been shown the stick, but the minorities here have had a few carrots. The electrified railway was built in the 1960s, and there is heavy investment in the local coal industry. In 1982 foreigners were allowed in for the first time.

After a slow climb, culminating in a stretch of tunnels, we emerge onto a wide limestone upland, carpeted with wheat and rapeseed fields, often substitutes for the opium which used to be grown here. Tall rocky outcrops pierce the flat plain. The human landscape looks traditional – haystacks with laundry laid out to dry, stone boundary walls and the occasional half-timbered farmhouse. But the greatest joy and pleasure of this long, slow journey is that, after two and a half weeks in China, we are blessed with a sunset. Not the wan, pale grey substitutes we've seen so far but a red and gold full uniform affair. And, as we step off the train at Guiyang, the stars are visible again.

DAY 70: *Guiyang*

A few years ago we would not have been allowed to travel in this area at all, much less visit minority villages, as we are to do today.

Since the 'opening up' began things have started to change. Our hotel, a thirty-one-storey joint-venture project between China and Singapore, is one of the results. It's lavish in concept but dreadful in detail. The exterior wall is covered in thin bands of tiny white tiles, all hand applied, like the interior of a public lavatory. The rooms look as though they have had teams of kick-boxers staying in them. The walls are scuffed and smeared and the wallpaper is already peeling. 'Guest is God' says the brochure, which sounds reassuring until you realize that China is officially atheist.

A happier consequence of the 'opening up' is the presence of Priscilla Wan as our guide. Her Chinese name is Sheng Wan.

She holds a degree in English from the University of Beijing. Favourite book, *Wuthering Heights*. Priscilla comes with a half-dozen other minders – advisers from the Minorities Ministry and apparently indispensable members of the Foreign Relations Department. It is a stuffy, crowded little bus that sets out for the villages in the mountains east of Guiyang where the Miao people live. There are five million of them in the country. A sizeable minority anywhere else, but in China only 0.2 per cent of the total population.

After an hour or two the narrow, metalled road becomes a track which twists and turns in a series of hairpins, around which every fragment of land is tilled. The combination of drifting wet mist, green grass and stone walls reminds me more of Wales or the west of Ireland. When the weather is as wet and cold as it is today the peasants' labour loses its picturesque appeal and the reality of wading, bare-legged and knee-deep in cold mud to plant rice stalks, as rain runs off hats and down backs, is there to see in hard-set, deeply-lined faces. We end up at 5000 feet.

At the first Miao village we come to we are treated to a traditional Miao welcome which, judging from the faces of the participants, is something that the Minorities Ministry and the Foreign Relations Department are more keen on than the Miao. (No wonder they're confused. Mao Tse-Tung spent years trying to get rid of all traditional culture; now the government can't get enough of it.) Lined up to meet us are a dozen young girls in coiled head-dresses with scarves of pink, green, yellow and white tucked into them. They have tasselled silver earrings and silver discs attached to colourful woven scapulas which are tied at the waist and then round at the back where an elaborately embroidered device, a sort of breast-plate in reverse, is worn. Blue track-suit pants and trainers peep out from beneath this finery. The young men who accompany them are having some trouble tying indigo cloth turbans. Two elders of the village wear black cotton robes with scarves and sashes around head and waists. Both have thin, pointed faces and goatee beards and one of them grimaces as he inhales from a cigarette, revealing a single large tooth in the centre of his top jaw.

Songs are sung to the accompaniment of the *lusheng*, an L-shaped bamboo instrument which requires great skill to play as you are supposed to dance at the same time. Then the girls step forward and offer Priscilla and me a buffalo horn full of local rice wine.

As my hands go up to take it, Priscilla cries out:

'Don't touch it. Don't touch the horn!'

It's too late.

'I've touched it, what does that mean?'

Priscilla looks disapproving.

'That means you want to drink. Now you have to drink it all.'

I knock it back. It's musty and quite strong. The girls look on with mild boredom. I have the feeling that the locals are used to this little pantomime.

'They've done this before, haven't they?'

Priscilla chides me a little.

'It is to show the hospitality of the Miao people,' she explains. 'It is to show respect to extinguished guests.'

A benign warmth has begun to spread up from my throat.

'Extinguished is the word, I think.'

After the wine there is dancing which I am invited to join. As I've had a hornful it's not as embarrassing as these moments usually are, when clod-hopping foreigners with no sense of natural rhythm feel bound to join in intricate national dances.

Their village is like something out of *The Seventh Seal*, with timber-framed, bamboo-walled barns and smoke rising from the curved tiled roofs of the huts. There is a modern red-brick school building in clumpy socialist style, from which children wearing 'Shanping Village National Minorities School' tracksuits spill out and make their way home across the paddy-fields. Four miles away is a market to which any surplus maize, tobacco or vegetables are taken. As we drive there I'm told of the Miao marital customs. Apparently couples can have trial marriages for a week, after which they can continue to live together or not. But as soon as the woman becomes pregnant the man she is with must marry her. As the child may well have been conceived during an earlier round of this marital musical chairs it is, in Miao culture, the second child that inherits, not the first.

The market takes place in the lee of a grey rock bluff on top of which stand the remains of a Miao castle built six hundred years ago. Children are carried, always by the women, in bright embroidered cloth baskets slung on their backs. Many of them seem to have an affliction which causes one eye to appear almost sealed. Alongside one of the buildings are lined up thirty or forty bamboo cages with songbirds inside. In front of them moves a line of men, who every now and then drop to a squat, listening intently to the quality of their song. There are stalls full of rope, spectacles, hats, pills, clothes, steamed dumplings and other refreshments. One section of the market is devoted entirely to raw meat, great hunks of which are laid out on trestle tables, where they are picked up and turned over by prospective buyers as if they were examining antiquarian books. Home-made pipes are smoked and, judging by some of the flat, blank faces and sudden, explosive arguments, much wine and beer has been drunk. As we leave, a woman with a pig on the back of her bicycle passes a man with an unwrapped leg of raw meat sticking out of his trouser pocket.

These are very poor people but, as ever, those making a life out of adversity are much more interesting than those making a life out of comfort.

In my hotel room at 10.30 when the phone rings. After I have said hello a couple of times a soft, breathy voice speaks.

'You like missy?'

'No . . . ' Feel foolish for not catching on earlier. 'No thank you.'

The phone goes down and almost instantly I hear it ring in the room next to mine.

DAY 71

Shimeng is another Miao village on the edge of plateau surrounded by a patchwork of green and gold rice terraces. It can only be reached from a dirt road by walking for half an hour along an intricate system of narrow mud causeways. On either side the wet earth is being turned with a wooden plough consisting of a single curved shaft with a steering handle at one end and a blade at the other, yoked to the shoulders of a water buffalo. It's a slow process, only as fast as the beast itself, which plods on, great eyes gazing forward, occasionally glancing wearily to the side. I watch a very old man communicate with his animal by a series of short, sharp hisses interspersed with loud grunts. It seems to work.

The villagers rush out to see us, many of them holding half-empty lunch bowls, jaws slack with disbelief. The women laugh, the men frown. One family allow us in to their house. They are sitting around a table on a mud-baked floor. Beside them is a brick hearth in which charcoal smoulders. Bowls of pork, chillies and sunflower seeds are on the table. In the room off to the right is bedding and a strip light; in the room off to the left there is a water buffalo.

We are the first people from the West they have ever seen. I ask Priscilla what strikes them most about us. She laughs with embarrassment as she translates.

'How do you say . . . big noses?'

As we look around the village I notice that some progress has reached Shimeng. There has been electricity here for the last nine years. There are a few lights, a radio. Not much else, but it must only be a matter of time before television comes and then a road and cars and motor bikes and the wider world.

It is selfish, I know, but with dragonflies on the ponds and swallows and swifts dipping and diving over the terraces and no sound louder than the human voice I'd rather Shimeng didn't change at all. This feeling is only reinforced by what I see on the journey back into Guiyang – the pervading dirt, the indiscriminate smear of pollution from new, unfettered industries, the apparent disregard for basic living standards. Everything that can be seen in photographs and engravings of Victorian Manchester or Sheffield or Glasgow or Birmingham or the East End of London.

The people of Guiyang don't seem to mind. They carry on –

busy, purposeful, preoccupied, their sense of optimism and determination as palpable as the foul air they breathe. Despite the mess they live in their faces show little doubt or sorrow. Some are hurt and some are desperate, but for the rest there is a sense of self-belief, a feeling that the tide of history is turning their way. They are probably right. China is on the verge of success it has not tasted for a thousand years. There is precious little that can prevent it from becoming, in the lifetime of the Priscillas and the Miss Lius, if not the most powerful nation on earth then at least a first among equals. The difference between now and Mao's time is that the Chinese are looking out at the world and wanting to join in. The lead story on the ten o'clock news is the visit of the Finnish Prime Minister and Giscard d'Estaing, ex-President of France. China no longer ignores the foreigner.

As if on cue my telephone rings.

'Excuse, please, Sir. Are you in need of a Miss?'

DAY 72: *Guiyang to Nanning*

Very tired but slept badly. Sure sign of mental fatigue and we are not yet a third of the way round the Pacific. Lie awake, listen to the rain and think of the days ahead. A twenty-hour train journey south to Nanning and then a border crossing into Vietnam. Borders are the stress points on a journey like this. No country in the world welcomes a film crew with open arms, but this one looks particularly sticky. Communist country to communist country. Not a time for the weak or wounded.

It's 8.15 in the morning.

Turn over and try to grab another half-hour's sleep.

The telephone rings.

'You like Miss?'

Later. On the way to the station we pass a 30-foot statue of Chairman Mao. It is the first one I've seen in China. He is, I'm told, admired, but definitely no longer revered.

South of Guiyang our train runs through Mediterranean-like

107

alpine scenery. Pine trees and sandy heathland. Dusk doesn't linger here and it's quite dark by the time I visit the dining car with John Lee, our Shanghainese fixer who has been a tower of strength on this leg of the journey.

John pours me a local Wanshi beer. 'In China the food is very important. Especially for peasants, you know. If they can eat well it means they have a really good life. I think that's their thinking.'

John, who's particularly partial to a bit of stomach, admits that the Chinese will eat most things if they're cooked properly.

'Rat?'

He nods emphatically.

'Oh yes, mountain rat. A delicacy.'

When I ask how mountain rat is cooked he has to consult fellow diners. The consensus seems to be that braised rat is best.

I talk to John of what I've seen in China and the sense I feel of tremendous national resurgence. He cautions against thinking that society has changed much. Overseas travel is still the privilege of a tiny minority and the old communist 'unit' is very much alive and well as the basis of social organization. Everyone in China is expected to belong to a social unit, and to report to that unit regularly.

As we turn in for bed we are flung round steep curves at a heart-stopping pace, only to jerk suddenly to a screeching halt. Not a peaceful night as we are hauled over the mountains from Guizhou into Guangxi Province.

DAY 73: *Nanning*

7.30 a.m. We are stopped outside the functional green-and-yellow concrete canopy of the station at Liuzhou, chief industrial city of Guangxi. Not a remarkable place. Basil tells me that the best coffin-wood in China comes from here.

After Liuzhou we are into the rough limestone scenery known as *karst*. Peaks of every shape and size are distinguished only by the degree of abruptness with which they spring from the landscape. We pass oleander bushes and cactus walls and bedding airing in the sunshine. Red-walled mud brick houses have replaced the grey stone. We're finally out of the mountains we've been amongst since we left Yichang eleven days ago. Mercifully we are also out of the coal measures. The difference is distinct and encouraging. The air is clearer, lighter and warmer. The pace of life looks slower. Bicycles lean against tall, wilting eucalyptus trees and their owners sleep beside them.

At Nanning station there is a fully operational 2–10–0 steam engine complete with smoke deflectors. It looks as though it has been made out of scrap metal. The drivers think I'm mad the way I stare at it. Clearly they don't have trainspotters in China. They tell me, with considerable satisfaction, that steam locomotives like this will all be in museums by 1998. Then, with a fierce opening of the valves and a jetting of white steam, the great beast heaves its way clear of the station, and snorts and snuffles off into the distance. I ask where it's going and am told that it's a local, running down to the coast. The coast! To my utter disbelief, the Pacific, masquerading as the Gulf of Tongking, is now less than 100 miles away.

The Vietnamese border is not much further, but the rail link to Hanoi is closed. The local trains to the border town of Pingxiang only run twice a week and the next one is in three days' time. Into Nanning to try to arrange alternative transport.

Nanning is a pleasant, airy green city with parks and avenues of trees. I go out for a stroll and the hotel receptionist, going off duty, asks if she can walk with me and practice her English. She's nineteen and very serious.

'The bicycle,' she asks me, brows knitted in concentration. 'What do you think . . . is it safe?'

She says the job is badly paid but she stays because of the opportunities to speak English. Did I know that many American adoption societies come to Nanning looking for Chinese children?

We walk round the White Dragon Park behind the hotel. It is spotlessly clean and well-kept, with a lake and pavilion in the middle. On the way back she stops at a florist's and spends a long time choosing a single red rose.

'For my boyfriend,' she says and, with a quick, unexpectedly glowing smile, mounts her bicycle and is gone.

VIETNAM

DAY 74: *Nanning to Hanoi*

In order to reach the border by bus and to have time for all the formalities we are advised to leave early. Wake at five and pack my bags. It is Sod's law that we spend the least time in the most attractive places. Nanning, warm, airy and cheerful, slips away and we roll steadily and unspectacularly south-west along soft-wooded valleys and through scrub-covered hills. The road is straight and empty. As recently as 1979 troops and tanks rolled along here when the Chinese, angered by the Vietnamese invasion of their ally, Cambodia, fought a seventeen-day war before withdrawing. Until 1992, when the Cambodian situation was settled, this border remained firmly closed.

Last images of China. A late breakfast in a candlelit restaurant, outside which a turtle shell is being skinned for soup. Despite a power cut we are served omelettes, pumpkin leaf, tarot and sweet potato. A huge 'One-Child' poster at the border town of Pinxiang, a reminder of the birth control policy.

The frontier is eight kilometres beyond Pinxiang at a place called Friendship Pass. The road bursts out from thickly-wooded hills and high cliffs onto a run-down square. In one corner is a handsome, disused cream-and-white French colonial residence, with elegant ironwork balconies, pilastered façade, and louvred windows, a relic from the days when this was a northern outpost of French Indo-China. Opposite stands a three-tiered stone pile as clumsy as the other is elegant. It bestrides a triumphal archway called Friendship Gate. Through the arch is a parking area with cypress trees planted around it, where two or three heavy trucks are drawn up. Beyond that is Vietnam.

The last rites of Chinese bureaucracy are given from what

looks like a requisitioned cow-shed. Behind desks, in stalls separated by concrete partitions, sits a trio of black-uniformed and epauletted officials from customs, immigration and quarantine. There is no sign of ring fences, barbed wire or the usual trappings of military surveillance. This sleepy, tree-shrouded backwater is a most unconvincing exit.

The barrier is raised and we make our way down the muddy track to Vietnam. Only then do we notice a big new circular concrete and glass building under construction amongst the trees. This is what will replace the cowshed. To the very last, evidence of China being reborn.

A cold wind blows through Friendship Pass, and there is not much one can do to avoid it. The facilities at the Vietnamese border post at Dong Dang are basic. The steps and wall outside are monopolized by a large and rebellious German tour group which has obviously been here for some considerable time. There is a toilet, situated in a blockhouse behind some nearby bushes, but this reached saturation point years ago and no one goes inside it any more, preferring to use the bushes themselves. Small, sad-faced Miss Ha, our fixer in Vietnam, waits with inscrutable calm as the enigmatic processes of customs and immigration slowly evolve.

The road to Hanoi is equally slow, picking its way between sharp, irregular limestone peaks that give the landscape the look of a workshop, where new mountain designs are tried out. According to my guidebook this frontier area is still heavily mined. Considering that the Chinese were fighting their way through here only sixteen years ago and eight years before that the Americans were bombing the place flat, the countryside looks remarkably unscarred. The red and white kilometre markers the French left behind are still intact, and the rocky fields are carefully tended by men in olive-green pith helmets and tiny old ladies in the conical coolie hats I had expected to see everywhere in China, but never did.

After an hour on a rough, meandering road through the mountains we emerge onto the rough, straight road that leads across the rich plain of the Red River delta. The countryside is filled with people. A great throng moves in both directions, like a scene of refugee exodus. Few have cars, most are either walking or on pedal and motor cycles. Every few miles, usually on a low rise beside the road, are monuments to the Vietcong army that defeated the French and the Americans. Nothing grandiose or militaristic; often nothing more than a white-washed obelisk. The box-girder bridges across the Red River still show patches and repairs from the American bombings of the seventies.

We are in the centre of Hanoi by six o'clock – twelve hours after leaving Nanning. Two hours later I'm sat in a *cyclo*, something like a bath chair attached to a bicycle frame. My driver, who pedals from behind, moves me at a stately pace up the dimly-lit streets towards the highly recommended 'N6' roof-top restaurant. Roof-top means exactly what it says – eating on a roof, beside pipes and chimneys.

Walk back to the hotel marvelling at the night-time activity, the small-scale bustle on the streets. Shops and workshops lit by single strip-lights. There's no neon, no bright-lit billboards, no seething lines of stationary cars. This seems to be a city on a human scale – busy but not oppressive. I catch myself wondering how it could be so different from China, and making the mistake of merging these countries of the Asian Pacific into one homogenous 'oriental' mass. Vietnam is as distinct from China as South Korea was from Japan. It has its own ancient culture, language and alphabet and its own, instantly appealing, style.

Tired, but unable to drag ourselves away from these dim, congenial streets, Basil and I take a last beer in a small Thai restaurant by the hotel. The proprietor is friendly.

'You like Thai food?' he asks.

'Oh, yes.'

He looks out into the night and sighs.

'Yes, one day,' he says, '*I* will go to Thailand.'

DAY 76: *Hanoi*

The characteristic sound of Hanoi traffic is the tinkle of the bicycle bell and the squawk of the scooter horn. It's a discordant sound, but discordant in quite an acceptable way, like that of a farmyard. It's the sound of traffic at an early stage of evolution, lacking the hi-tech swish and roar of Western cities.

But Vietnam, like China and Russia, is opening up. Here they call the process *Doi-Moi* – 'renovation' or 'new thinking' – and it has informed government policy for almost ten years. A managed market economy has replaced the communist command economy. Foreign participation in business is encouraged. It is obligatory for Vietnamese civil servants to learn a foreign language. Walking into town I pass the fruits of this policy. A four-star hotel called The Standard is being developed in partnership with Singaporeans and Malaysians and a South Korean company is building on the site of the old French prison, the Maison Centrale. In the Vietnam war this was the main holding and interrogation centre for captured American servicemen, known, mockingly, as the Hanoi Hilton. Many were tortured here. Now cranes and reinforced concrete piling rise from behind the prison walls and it could indeed become the Hanoi Hilton once again. Only, this time Americans will come to be pampered.

While the big developers try to spring their monumental schemes on Hanoi, the city remains defiantly small and low slung. Ninety-five years of colonial rule have left behind a passable imitation of a warm French provincial town based around shady avenues of two and three-storey buildings with stuccoed fronts, wrought iron balconies, pantiled roofs and tall green louvred shutters. Baguettes are sold by the roadside, bicycles are stacked along the broad pavements, *cyclos* re-route round old ladies with shoulder poles and baskets. I pass a long wall, hung with jackets, in front of which is a heap of clothes languidly supervised by a hollow-cheeked old man and a young boy. A passer-by stops, rummages around, pulls a jacket out from beneath the pile and puts it on. It's hopelessly crumpled, and far too small for him, but the old man and the boy, like men's outfitters anywhere, nod approvingly.

In Hanoi you don't need to hail a taxi, they hail you. Constantly.

'Hey you!'

I always fall for it, wheeling round as if I'm about to be karate-chopped. So when I do choose a *cyclo* I go for someone who doesn't seem to be the slightest bit interested in me. His name, it transpires, is Than, an elderly man with a Ho Chi Minh beard, broken teeth and one wandering eye. He wears a workman's blue cotton jacket and a grey-brown pith helmet. Before he mounts the saddle he takes a long gurgling puff from a bamboo pipe, which he then tucks down behind the seat, and mounts the saddle, exhaling slowly and skilfully.

With Than I visit the bleak, triumphal square where the remains of Uncle Ho, the father of modern Vietnam and the architect of the victory over the Americans, lie in a forbidding, columned mausoleum of black granite and marble. It's a depressing place for many reasons. For a start he shouldn't be here. Ho Chi Minh expressly requested that he be cremated and his ashes scattered over the countryside.

'Ho Chi Minh Will Live For Ever In Our Life', proclaims a red and gold banner beside the tomb.

There is not much life around this portentous monument today apart from two boys on bikes practising wheelie turns and a middle-aged woman learning how to ride a motor-scooter.

Beside a lake in the middle of town is a theatre where the internationally-known Thang Long Water Puppet Troupe performs. The show is based on the traditional agriculture of Vietnam and particularly the vital importance of the flooding of the paddy-fields to ensure a successful rice harvest. The 'stage' is a 20×12-foot water tank and the puppets, which range from peasant figures to birds, animals, ceremonial barges and legendary dragons, are all operated on the end of long submerged metal rods by puppeteers you never see.

The Water Puppet Theatre reminds me once again of the heady pace of political change in Asia. Twenty-three years ago the Americans were raining bombs down on this city. Now a show which celebrates the resilience of the peasants who defeated them is sponsored by AT&T, one of the largest companies in the USA.

DAY 77

There *is* cricket in Hanoi. A league of expatriates plays on a pitch belonging to the Vietnamese Air Force. Unfortunately it's a football pitch. When we arrive there is a game in progress between a Russian team and a Vietnamese military side. The Vietnamese are, head for head, an average of eight inches shorter than every one of their opponents, and they're a goal ahead.

After the football has finished, the cricket will begin. England will take on a combined India–Sri Lanka team, most of whom are already here, tossing the ball about and practising slip catches. The English team is in some disarray; the captain hasn't arrived.

'And he's bringing the pitch,' says an anxious colleague.

Eventually Martin, the captain, appears and produces a case of beer and a roll of straw matting twenty-two yards long from the back of his car. The matting is nailed into position across the centre circle and the crease marked out with white aerosol spray. Their previous pitch was underneath a bridge and every time the river flooded it had to be temporarily evacuated. Someone remembers this with fond nostalgia.

'There were turds *every*where.'

I talk to some of the team. Peter, a twenty-nine-year-old architect, has his own practice here in Hanoi. In the last year he has seen remarkable changes. There used to be very few shops, what little there was for sale coming from baskets by the side of the road. There were buffalo-carts in the main streets. Now the main talking point is the installation of Hanoi's first set of traffic-lights.

A Canadian who sells telecommunications equipment is amazed by the demand.

'They want everything we've got. It's like kids at the candy store.'

It is the infrastructure and the bureaucracy which everyone complains about. The local head of the BBC, who is having a frustrating time trying to learn Vietnamese – 'There are five different ways of saying each word' – notices that, despite *Doi-Moi*, very little dissent is permitted. The Vietnamese government, like the Chinese, believes it can expand economically while keeping the lid on politically.

As if on cue, a military observer appears, eyeing us suspiciously. He has a broad peasant face and his uniform hangs loosely from him. The Indian team, in matching caps and full whites, take to the pitch to be followed by the two English openers, one in shorts, the other in navy tracksuit bottoms.

After the first over the observer insists that we stop filming the game immediately as this is a sensitive military area. The players wax indignant and mobile phones are produced as they try to contact anyone with influence who might be able to help us. At one point a phone rings on the pitch. The fielder at short square leg fishes it out of his pocket, listens, then tosses it to our director.

'It's for you.'

Filming stops, but the game is still going on when troops appear on the track beside the pitch. Half of them are women with black pigtails trailing from beneath peaked hats. In the back row two soldiers march by holding hands.

None of this, or any of the surprise British victory over the Indian sub-continent, are we allowed to record.

DAY 78

It is Teacher's Day in Hanoi. To show their gratitude and respect, children bring gifts, or cook something for their teachers. Parties are held and shows put on. I call on an English teacher called Mr Hung at the English for Special Purposes Department of Hanoi Foreign Institute. Like many Vietnamese it is impossible to tell Mr Hung's age from his face. His skin is smooth and un-lined and yet I know that he fought in the

Vietnam war. He speaks quietly but with authority and clarity. He harbours few grudges against today's Americans.

'Let bygones be bygones,' he says. 'We have no quarrel with the American people, only their leaders at the time.'

When you consider the casualty figures – four hundred and forty-four thousand North Vietnamese killed, fifty-eight thousand Americans – this spirit of reconciliation is remarkable. (There is a street in Hanoi called Dwong Thien Thang B52 – Avenue of the Victories over the B-52s – but this is the exception rather than the rule.)

Most of all, Mr Hung feels let down by Russia and China.

'From 1975 to 1986 we looked to them as our models.'

But when he came to London and Paris to study in 1979 he came across books like George Orwell's *Animal Farm* which, he says, made him reconsider the behaviour of heroes like Stalin and Mao Tse-tung.

His fellow teacher, Mr Fang, young and intense, proudly shows me their English library – Georgette Heyer and Jane Austen, copies of the *New Yorker* and *Scientific American* and a range of language tapes with titles like 'English For Secretary', 'English For International Banking', 'Scottish English' and even 'French English'.

In the evening we leave Hanoi on the Reunification Express bound for Saigon, following the 1500-mile Pacific coast of Vietnam that curls like a sea horse from the Red River delta to the mouth of the Mekong. It's a two-day journey at an average speed of 25 miles an hour.

Even 25 miles an hour seems optimistic as we struggle to extricate ourselves from Hanoi. The railway line may have been a great symbol of peace and unity when it was opened at the end of the war in 1976, but it doesn't look as if a penny (or, more correctly, a *dong*) has been spent on it since. At times the narrow-gauge track is nothing more than another Hanoi backstreet. The locomotive threads its way through the heart of densely-packed neighbourhoods, its cyclopean headlamp illuminating a tide of humanity on the line ahead – old ladies, mothers and babies, bikes, scooters, men with filing cabinets on their heads, children balancing on the rail

117

like acrobats. The horn blasts. The crowd parts instinctively, skilfully, and at the very last minute. As soon as the Reunification Express has passed, it re-forms and the railway line becomes a street again.

Around midnight we reach the coast at Hoang Xa and out there in the darkness I can just make out the first glimmer of Pacific since we left Qingdao over three weeks ago. As I'm turning in, the train guard cautions me against sleeping with my head by the window. Miss Ha translates.

'He says you must be careful when the train stops at night. People may try to get in.'

'Can I lock the window?'

'The window *is* locked,' Miss Ha explains, reassuring me for a brief moment. 'But they may break it.'

DAY 79: *Dong Hoi to Hue*

Dong Hoi station in a downpour. Little children, wet through, beg at the windows, smiling ever so sweetly, raising their palms out at arm's length until little pools of water form in them. They are chased away by the guard. Catering ladies, middle-aged and motherly, with grey suits and incongruous white frilly aprons, come by with breakfast. This consists of a dry, vermicular collection of noodles sloshed into a bowl, accompanied by a cream wafer. When I ask if there's anything else they look at me pitifully and move on.

Feel a bit dejected. It could be all sorts of things – the weather, the breakfast, lack of sleep after a night being rocked and rolled about on my couchette, or the side-effects of the strong anti-malaria pills which I shall be taking from now until we leave the tropics.

I'm struggling to stuff the cold sticky noodles into my mouth when, with loud protestations, the ladies in grey reappear, seize back my bowl and pour a helping of hot pork broth on top, giggling gently, as one might at someone who had tried to eat Weetabix without milk.

From my window I look out on a grey-green, washed-out

world of paddy-fields and palm trees. White specks of light fleck the grey as a flock of egrets rises and curls away. A cemetery offers a brief splash of colour, bright blue and green paint peeling off the gravestones. There is an animated game of cards going on in the compartment next to mine. I count nine people squeezed around an up-turned suitcase. Next to that a man with a full-length keyboard across his knee is giving music lessons to a vivacious lady in a pink and black jumpsuit.

Forty miles south of Dong Hoi the rain has passed out to sea and a hot sun is breaking through as we roll slowly across the Ben Hai River, better known by its line of latitude as the Seventeenth Parallel. Between the years of 1954 and 1976, it marked the division between North and South Vietnam.

Thirty years ago President Johnson's huge 'Rolling Thunder' bombing offensive swept across this soft, sylvan countryside. Some of the craters can still be seen, though most have been filled in to prevent them becoming stagnant breeding grounds for malarial mosquitoes. Defoliants, like Agent Orange, have left their mark too, but the trees they burned and poisoned have been replaced, mostly by fast-growing eucalypts. Mines, planted by both sides, are still being discovered.

For someone of my age the Vietnam War remains a source of appalled fascination. For ten years or more images of the utmost cruelty came out of this green and pleasant land. Today nature has covered up most of the scars and, seeing it with my own eyes for the first time, the landscape looks as innocent as a baby.

We arrive at Ga Hue at midday. (*Ga*, meaning station, is a phonetic Vietnamization of the French '*gare*'.) Nothing much advertises the fact that we are in what was once the imperial capital of Vietnam. An ugly concrete girdle has been grafted onto the crumbling pink wash of the old French station building. Across a dusty square white metal tables are set out beneath a pair of thin acacia trees.

We leave the train here and take a boat up the Song Huong – the Perfume River – as far as the famous Thien Mu Pagoda. Its popularity as a tourist attraction is evident from the amount of transport available, ranging from catamarans, their prows decorated with gaudily-painted tin dragons, to the bobbing sampans with semi-circular rattan cabin covers, fan shaped bows and long-stem outboards, nimbly steered by foot or groin even. As we chug up river I see a woman bending over the side of a boat washing her hair. She rinses it with scoops of water from an American army helmet.

At the jetty below the elegant seven-storey brick pagoda, children gather round, hands outstretched.

'Pen? . . . Chewing gum? . . . Money?'

There is a small monastery up on the hill behind the pagoda. It was from here that a monk called Thich Quang Duc left for Saigon in June 1963, and became the subject of one of the most famous photographs of the century by setting himself alight on a public street as a protest against President Diem's treatment of Buddhists. His car, a four door light-blue Austin sedan, registration DBA 599, which appears in the background of the photo, is now on display in a corner of the monastery. In colour, make, model and quite possibly year of manufacture, it is identical to the one in which my father used to drive to work every day.

Back in Hue, *cyclo* drivers outside the hotel offer us 'Dancing', 'Boom-boom' and 'Eighteen-year-old girls'. But in the end we settle for Princess Diana. Her *Panorama* interview, filling a huge screen, plays to an almost empty hotel bar.

DAY 80: *Hue*

Eighty days around the Pacific Rim and we are only a third of the way there. Circumnavigating the world was a doddle compared to this. What's slowing us down is the quality and quantity of things to see. There hasn't been a day so far when we haven't encountered something remarkable.

Today it's the Forbidden Purple City at Hue, a massive palace and administrative complex built for Gia Long, first Emperor of Vietnam nearly two hundred years ago and protected by a six-and-a-half-mile wall. It was built near a river – a 'stream of light' which keeps away bad influences. Its three main

120

enclosures all face south; south being the best direction for a king to rule his people from. Two miles away is a small mountain, essential 'to protect from evil spirits'. The alignment of buildings to bring good luck, what the Chinese call *feng shui*, is still important in the east. A geomancer, one who calculates such things, will be consulted on everything from family houses to state-of-the-art office blocks.

My guide, Miss Huong, who wears *ao-dai*, the graceful national dress, a tunic with long panels over slim-fitting trousers, reminds me that the Nguyen dynasty, for whom this was built, ruled Vietnam from 1802 until 1954. There is still a Vietnamese emperor – alive and living in Paris.

We walk around, which takes a long time, ending up at the sacred Third Enclosure. This, says Miss Huong, was bombed by the Americans which is why it is now almost empty. I asked her whether it was true that the Vietcong hid in here deliberately, assuming the Americans would not bomb it, but she didn't know. I asked her about the reports of atrocities committed by the Vietcong against the priests and intellectuals of Hue. No, she knew nothing of that either.

At a bar called DMZ across the road from the hotel, I fall into conversation with an American who fought in the war and was captured and tortured by the Vietcong. On two occasions they lined him up before a firing squad, which then deliberately missed. He had been in a special army reconnaissance group and I asked him whether he'd have got off more lightly if he'd been an ordinary GI. He shakes his head vigorously. 'If I'd been an ordinary GI I'd have been dead.'

After the war, his marriage broke up because he couldn't speak about what had happened. He's now married again and coming back to Vietnam is part of coming to terms with horrors that still haunt him. Tomorrow he's going to surf China Beach with a bunch of other vets.

There are two dishes which catch my eye on the menu tonight: 'King Prawns Steamed In Gutter' and 'Tom Rang Me', which for a moment I thought was a message from my son.

DAY 82

Breakfast overlooking the Perfume River. Rain falls from a low, flat sky, as it has done for the last thirty-six hours. A shiny green kingfisher stares intently into the limpid water. A village of sampans lies strung out on the stream and the slim boats look like driftwood in a monochrome morning light.

At Hue station, *cyclo* passengers arrive encased like babies in multi-coloured rainproof sheeting. Children are sheltering under one of the arcades, taking it in turns to see who can slide their sandal furthest along the tiled floor.

As we progress slowly down the coast towards Da Nang on the southbound Reunification Express I can see why water puppetry is such an art form in Vietnam. The entire countryside looks as though it is about to float away. Short, fat, lazy rivers merge with waterlogged fields. Canals join up with impromptu creeks and ponds, which are in turn swelled by streams spilling merrily over mud walls. My bowels seem to take inspiration from all this and I am forced to face the Chinese toilet-paper torture, Hong-He Sanitary Tissues, the only lavatory paper that could also be used for sanding down.

Outside Da Nang the prospect changes dramatically. Our single line track winds up through tunnels and across steep, bridged gorges until we reach Hai Van Pass, nearly 4000 feet above the ocean. Waterfalls and tumbling streams have replaced the listless rivers of the plain. Far below, the flat, dull-silver surface of the South China Sea is transformed into tossing, turbulent breakers.

DAY 83: *Da Nang*

Bach Dang Hotel, Da Nang. I pay dearly for asking for a river view. There is a night-club next door which doesn't really get going until just after you've got off to sleep. It isn't the music that keeps me awake so much as the revving of scooters and the high-pitched voices of people trying to make themselves heard over the revving of the scooters. When the din dies down just before dawn, the noisiest fishing boats in the world start chugging up the Han river and out to sea – leaving the quayside clear for thunderous trucks to come and unload.

Miss Ha is wearing her Cliff Richard T-shirt this morning. Despite considerable official apathy, Roger, our director, has a full programme for us here in central Vietnam and we are heading through the suburbs of Da Nang at first light. Familiar urban landscape of sheds, shacks, uncollected rubbish, corrugated iron roofs, the mottled concrete of half-finished buildings. Cities out here in the East tend to grow according to need. There is no concept of civic architecture or town planning.

The Vietnamese, however, have a very strong concept of order in the natural world. A few miles south of Da Nang are the Marble Mountains, which rise short, sharp and sheer from the flat, flooded fields around them. Each one, they believe, represents a different element – Wood, Fire, Metal, Earth and Water.

'You are now on Water,' says Miss Tanh, a bright sixteen-year-old guide who climbs one of the peaks with me. 'The Gateway to Heaven is up there.' She points out a scruffy scrub-covered hill nearby, but doesn't volunteer to accompany me. I can't really go back without at least trying to get to Heaven, so Nigel, Fraser and I start off up a steep rubble-strewn path. Halfway up, the path peters out and we have to scramble the last 100 feet through cactus-filled gullies, grabbing what holds we can on rock that is fissured and fluted as if giant fingernails had been drawn down the face of it.

The view from the Gateway to Heaven is almost worth the effort. Away to the north the waves are breaking on the golden sands of China Beach where American troops used to come for R & R (rest and relaxation) during the war. Nearer to us is the deserted, blackening bulk of their huge arsenal at Da Nang, hangers still intact, the long lines of revetments in which hundreds of helicopters were hidden now overgrown and empty.

If the massive American base can be said to epitomize the Western way of making war, the nearby Van Thong cave is a perfect example of the guerrilla alternative. The way in is through a well-hidden cleft in the rock and along a pitch-dark tunnel. Tourists cling to their guides as the path descends wet and slippery steps in pitch-darkness. It gives onto a great subterranean chamber, 100 feet high, into which a single shaft of daylight falls from a hole in the roof which Miss Tanh maintains was gouged out by an American bomb. A pair of kneeling griffin-like beasts stand guard at the base of the steps. On the far side of the cave, a golden Buddha, with an uncanny resemblance to Grace Kelly, sits in a tenebrous candlelit alcove. The temple was used as a Vietcong army hospital and a plaque on the wall commemorates the downing of nineteen American aircraft by the Lady Machine-Gunners Brigade.

Later we travel down the coast to the town of Hoi An. Until the Han River became silted up it was one of the chief ports of Vietnam and, like a mediaeval English wool town, it reflects old time mercantile prosperity.

Walk along the waterfront and back down the main street, taking in the delights of a place that has eight hundred and fourty-four official 'structures of historical significance'. Past weathered wooden walls, galleries with fine carved balustrades, dark beamed and lamplit interiors, with the smell of joss drifting gently out into the evening air. Cross a handsome covered bridge of pink-washed stone built by the Japanese trading community over four hundred years ago to link up with the Chinese quarter on the other side of the stream. Clustered out on the river are the steep curved hulls of wooden fishing boats with boldly painted black and white eyes almost meeting at the top of each prow. This is a little treasure of a town, a reminder that its long mid-Pacific coastline gives Vietnam a perfect trading position.

DAY 84: *Saigon*

Morning flight to Saigon. At the end of the American war in 1975, the city was renamed Ho Chi Minh City but most of the locals still call it Saigon. For the sake of brevity, and because

I love the sound of the name, so shall I. Lunch on the roof of the Rex Hotel, another icon of the war. It was here that the journalists gathered for daily briefings from the US military. So little information was gleaned from these sessions that they became known as the 'Five O'clock Follies'. The rooftop, with a fine fifth-floor view of the seething intersections at the centre of the city, is a wonderland. It combines a garden, dining-room, bar, swimming pool, zoo and aviary, all decorated with compulsive, eclectic abandon, like an over-stocked junk shop or a family attic. Heraldic flags hang out from the parapet on either side of an illuminated revolving crown. Everything, from plates, cups and saucers to the carrot in my salad has the hotel name stamped on it. Most eccentric of all are the topiary deer, but I am reliably informed that topiary is very popular in Vietnam, as are the mountain deer.

I'm here to meet John Brinsden, a banker who has lived in Asia for thirty-four years. Beside our table is a large, hunched, crow-like songbird which makes sudden piercing shrieks as though trying to attract the waiter, and another which looks as though its perch is electrically charged, so persistently does it leap for the roof of the cage.

John, who is drinking Tiger beer in a hair of the dog attempt to mitigate the effects of last night's St Andrew's Ball, is confident that Vietnam will join the second-wave of Asian boom economies, after Singapore, Taiwan and Korea. 'They're remarkably open-minded people,' he says. 'In other parts of Asia you find a certain innate suspicion of foreigners and foreign ideas. In Vietnam that doesn't seem to exist.'

When John arrived in 1988 there were only five banks, all French, operating in Vietnam; now there are seventy. Certainly Saigon, with its mobile phones and Italian cafés, is fast and lively and much more cosmopolitan than Hanoi. There are more scooters than bicycles down here and there is nothing in the staid northern capital to rival the *chay rong rong* – the 'big ride round' which takes place on the Nguyen Hue Boulevard in the evening. Thousands of young men make circuits of the central streets on motor-cycles. For an hour the centre of the city becomes a deafening mile-long swirl of bescootered youth.

That's not all scooters are used for in Saigon. On returning from a meal on Dong Khoi Street (a.k.a. the Rue Catenat where the hero of Graham Greene's *The Quiet American* lived) we are propositioned by motorized prostitutes who cruise along beside us on 50cc mopeds offering 'massage' or 'boom-boom'. They won't accept 'no sex please – we're British' as an answer and, getting no satisfaction, one of them heaves her bike up onto the kerb and pursues us along the pavement.

DAY 85: *Saigon to Tay Ninh*

We are on our way north from Saigon, heading for the town of Tay Ninh, near the Cambodian border, in search of an international religion found only in Vietnam. It's called Caodaism and its secrets were revealed to a minor official in the French administration called Ngo Van Chieu at a seance in 1921. Through Ngo Van Chieu God made known his 'third alliance with mankind', which turned out to be a fusion of existing religions – Roman Catholicism, Buddhism, Confucianism and Taoism. This eclectic ecumenical grouping was based on direct psychic communication with great figures of world history and at times Descartes, Pasteur, Joan of Arc, Lenin and even Shakespeare have been contacted (though Shakespeare has not been heard of since 1935). The most regular respondent has been Victor Hugo, who was honoured for his availability by being made spiritual chief of Foreign Missions (which have so far extended only as far as Cambodia, 40 miles away).

At Tay Ninh this youngest of world religions is alive and well and the red-and-white trimmed, ornately-towered ochre walls of the Caodaist cathedral, rise from a wide and empty compound the size of Red Square.

The general shape of the cathedral is open-plan Western-style, but there the similarity ends. The floor is on nine different levels – representing the nine steps to heaven – and from it rise columns wound round with lumpy, luridly-painted green and orange dragons. The tracery is wildly and fantastically floral with what looks like great cabbage stalks growing up around the windows. The dome at the far end is painted to represent the star-spangled heavens and beneath it is a huge globe on which is painted the single eye in a triangle, the symbol of Caodaism.

The service is very laid back. The mood is gentle and contemplative, the music precise and delicate, and quite haunting. Women enter from one door and men from the other and all sit cross-legged on the brightly-tiled floor wearing ethereal expressions and chanting gently. Above them birds swoop in and out of the building.

Irrepressible roving bands of ten-year-old salesmen lurk outside.

'What your name?'

'Michael.'

'Oh. Your name beautiful.' An ice-cold can of 7-Up is thrust against my arm. 'You very handsome.'

'Not now thank you.'

'Maybe later. Yes?'

On the way back to Saigon we stop at the Cu-Chi tunnels, a system of passageways and chambers dug from the hard red earth during the guerrilla wars against the French, and later the American and South Vietnamese forces. Despite being close to enemy bases, their cover stripped by dioxin defoliants and carpet-bombed by B-52s, they were never destroyed in thirty-five years of warfare. I crawl down the tunnels to see preserved hospitals, war-rooms, and the kitchens with their special system of underground ducts which funnelled cooking smoke two miles away before letting it out above the surface. The tunnels are hot and tight, and I found my back scratching and scraping painfully against the mud wall.

The Cu-Chi underground system could accommodate five thousand people for up to two weeks. My guide, Le Di Phuoc, has shown high-ranking American generals round the tunnels. I ask him what their reaction is. 'Well,' he says, with a trace of a smile, 'they understand why they lost.'

DAY 87: *Saigon to My Tho*

One of those mornings. Sit on my glasses and break the frames. Then, getting grumpily into the bus, rip my trousers on the arm of my seat. These things always come in threes so I'm in a state of irritable anticipation as we drive south into the Mekong Delta.

I have never seen as many people in the countryside as we see on our way south. It is quite easy to believe that this slim country is the twelfth most populous in the world. The rice fields are raked by long lines of women bending and picking. A small town like Cao Be has as many people living on the water as on the land. I join the shoppers at a floating market. Housewives paddle their dugouts from boat to boat in search of the best bargains. On one boat we're offered a pair of snakes. Two boa constrictors at one hundred dollars each. I have to tell them it's too late, I'm already packed.

This is the hottest day of the journey so far. An unavoidable lethargic humidity which seems to steam and ooze off the river as the sun climbs. It doesn't surprise me to hear that Noël Coward composed 'Mad Dogs and Englishmen' while travelling in Vietnam.

At the town of My Tho we take an early lunch while we wait for the Mekong ferry. The tourist board restaurant has a menu which promises such delights as Eel, Frog, Snake (pounded), Tortoise, Swid and 'Teared Chicken Into Small Pieces'.

Cross-river ferries are a great focus of life. It's as though you are standing on a street corner that suddenly sails away. I find myself crossing the Mekong with four trucks, a Mercedes hearse with a handsome yellow casket inside it, motor bikers wearing reversed 'Lakers' and 'Raiders' baseball caps, a bus with a Buddhist shrine on the dashboard and a boy in a Guinness T-shirt asleep on the luggage rack, a group of chattering women wearing black pantaloons and straw hats, and an old lady carrying a bag of green apples on one side of her shoulder pole and a live cockerel on the other.

The river is broad, brown and sluggish. Like the Yangtze, it rises 2500 miles away in Tibet. At the height of its annual flood, it shifts over a million cubic feet of soil every second, expanding Vietnam with grains of Tibet, chunks of China and Burma, swathes of Laos and great lumps of Cambodia.

PHILIPPINES

DAY 88: *Saigon to Manila*

I'm drinking in a bar with the crew when I see Sir Winston Churchill come in. He's a little bit the worse for wear. He approaches Lady Churchill and her friends and it's quite clear from their half-hearted 'Hello, Winston's' that they aren't interested. I don't like to see a great man treated that way, even if he has had a few, so I ask him to dinner. He accepts. I am about to ask him a terribly important question when our food arrives in a baby buggy.

Why I should have to go to Vietnam to dream about Churchill I don't know, but this is just one of a series of odd and vivid nocturnal imaginings which seem to be increasing as the journey goes on. I lie awake in my hotel room feeling rather ill and think of the scene with Martin Sheen going crackers in Saigon at the start of *Apocalypse Now*.

Maybe it's just a side-effect of where we are in the journey. A long way from the beginning, and a very long way from the end. At Little Diomede, the Pacific was 50 miles wide. From Saigon it is over 10,000 miles to the opposite shore. At the rate we're moving it could take us another six months to get back to the Bering Strait.

Summoning up the bulldog spirit, I forego breakfast, pop another malaria tablet, pack my suitcases for the thirty-second time and slip a guide to the Philippines and a tab of Immodium into my shoulder bag.

Manila is two hours and ten minutes flying time north-east of Saigon. Like many of the islands off the coast of Asia, from Alaska southwards, the Philippines were, until quite recently, linked to the mainland by a land bridge. It sank beneath what are now the waters of the South China Sea only five thousand years ago.

I expect some similarities with Vietnam but find total differences. The famous observation on Philippine history: 'Three hundred years in the convent, fifty years in Hollywood' explains most of them. The Spanish took a firm hold of the islands in 1565. The Americans bought them from the Spanish in 1898. The Filipinos had to wait until 1946 to run their own affairs. Culture, traditions and social attitudes reflect Europe and America. Not the East.

The great, sweeping, sometimes intimidating free-flow of bicycle and scooter traffic in Vietnam has evolved here in Manila into the fully-fledged immobility of the late twentieth-century traffic jam. Traffic management is a constant topic of conversation. Tomorrow an 'Odd/Even' scheme comes into effect (cars with odd numbers only will be allowed into the city on Mondays, Wednesdays and Fridays, evens on the other days). This replaces a colour-coded system dropped last year after only three days in operation. Meanwhile, we wait in a mile-long jam on Roxas Boulevard, the strawberry-flavoured air-conditioning of our minibus shielding us from the sticky 86° humidity, as we do our bit to further pollute a city of ten million, forty-four per cent of whom are officially homeless.

Despite, or perhaps because of, such grim statistics there is considerable liveliness to the place. It's December and getting on for Christmas time. American carols play on our minibus radio. Artificial gold and silver-foil Christmas trees are on sale by the side of the road and all around us in the traffic are the gleaming chrome hulls of a very particularly Philippine form of public transport – the jeepney. At the end of the Second World War, when the Americans took back the Philippines from the Japanese and turned it into a huge military depot, opportunist locals took surplus US jeeps and customized them into small buses studded with every sort of lethal attachment and covered in stickers, transfers, multicoloured stripes and names ranging from the simple ('Jackie' or 'Fatima') to the sentimentally religious ('Mother of Perpetual Help' and 'Gift of God'). Fifty years on and, despite the advent of air-conditioned buses, taxis and even an overhead light rail system, the jeepneys are thriving.

You don't have to be long in the country to appreciate that the jeepney expresses the Filipino spirit: emotional, exuberant and celebratory, endearing and unwary. We are following a truck marked 'Careful Movers', which lurches forward, its back door swinging wildly open.

On a stretch of reclaimed land along the curving sea front of Manila Bay are a series of portentous concrete pavilions built by Ferdinand and Imelda Marcos in the 1970s to glorify the presidential family that headed a pitifully poor nation. The buildings were regarded as so extravagant by a visiting Pope that he refused to stay in one. Beneath the foundations of another are workmen, buried when their scaffolding collapsed. Rumour has it that work was carried on and concrete was poured in over the bodies.

Later I brave the traffic canyon of Roxas Boulevard and walk down to the Metropolitan Museum of Art which I think must be the only art gallery in the world with the sign: 'Please Deposit Your Firearms Here' at the entrance desk.

I spend the rest of the day sleeping, eating (*Lechon*, roast suckling pig, seems to be the lone speciality of Philippine cooking) and trying to digest a fat dollop of culture shock.

DAY 89: *Manila to Banaue*

On the BBC World Service this morning Alastair Cooke is talking about the design of the dollar bill, and the specific Christian symbols on it, including the all-seeing eye of God appearing in a blaze of light at the top of a Pyramid. I get out a dollar bill. Sure enough there is the Great Seal and the eye enclosed in the apex of a pyramid. I knew I'd seen it before. It's the eye framed in a triangle that figured so prominently at the Caodaist cathedral in Vietnam.

The extent of American influence in the Philippines is unashamedly obvious. The fruit-growing industry is run by them, they have only recently vacated two major military concentrations at Clark Air Base and Subic Bay and any Filipino musician worth his salt must be able to play a passable rendition of 'West Virginia'. The rugged crests of the Bataan Peninsula and Corregidor Island at the mouth of Manila Bay are reminders of what it cost the Americans to keep a presence in these islands. In the Second World War both places were the scenes of some of the fiercest battles America ever had to fight.

This morning we can see them clearly from the helicopter which is taking us far into the mountainous north to see the fifteen-hundred-year-old rice terraces at Banaue, which have been called nothing less than the Eighth Wonder of the World.

We bank out over the bay and inland to where the city suddenly ends and the wide green fields and golden-brown agricultural plains of central Luzon begin. Smoke drifts from burning rice stalks and rivers meander lazily through villages squeezed around with thick green trees. Our flight is reflected in the mirror-like surface of flooded paddy-fields. The pilot, Luis, an archetypally dapper, moustachioed Spanish-American, follows the broad course of the Magat River for an hour or more. The mountains begin to close in around us. The weather deteriorates and Luis wheels and turns and banks and tries to find a break in the cloud base. I begin to suspect that he's not absolutely sure where the Eighth Wonder of the World is. After some consultation Luis explains the situation. We are at 2700 feet. The cloud base is a further 500 feet above us. The Eighth Wonder of the World is 1000 feet above that. He cannot fly into the cloud, but will fly us down the valley to a town called Lagawe where we might find alternative transport. Luis now becomes Action Man. Briskly he lands the helicopter in the only place where he has room. This happens to be the school playing field where a game is in progress. Oblivious to the scattering footballers, Luis sets us down, hailing a passing jeepney as he does so.

The driver, Rodolfo, stocky, with Burmese-Indian looks, cannot believe this sudden bounty from the sky. He packs us all in the back of his pillar-box red vehicle, with bald tyres and a 'Thank God' window sticker, and screams off up the hill, round the hairpins and into the clouds. The road gets worse. There has been heavy rain here and it has loosened great chunks of the hillside and swept them across the road. Rodolfo scorches onwards and upwards, dodging goats, little black long-haired pigs and landslides. When the road surface turns to a sea of treacherous, slippery mud there are various attempts to restrain him, but he doesn't stop until he can deposit us proudly at the point from which the very best views of the Banaue rice terraces can be obtained. There is only one snag. We cannot see a thing. The cloud is so thick that the most ancient rice terraces in the world might as well be Leyton Orient Football Ground.

A group of Ifugao tribespeople, descendants of those responsible for the feat of agricultural engineering that we can't actually see, clearly think we're mad to be up here on a day like this, but drift towards us anyway and begin what is obviously their tourist routine. A thin, stick-legged old man in an embroidered red tunic, holding a spear and smoking a pipe, and a lady in a feather head-dress, wait to be photographed in front of the cloud. Somewhere a flute starts playing. A shopkeeper pulls the covers off rows of carved wooden bowls, statues of the Virgin Mary, animals and rosaries. Then, for a brief and tantalizing moment, the mist breaks to reveal a breathtaking amphitheatre of tiered embankments. Fields cultivated since the time of the Romans rise 1000 feet up the mountainside supported by a system of walls and terraces which channel rainwater through a series of thirty or forty controlled falls before allowing it to join the churning caramel-coloured flow of the river far below. Nigel barely has time to press the camera button before the great white wave obscures the Eighth, and Most Elusive, Wonder of the World once again.

DAY 90: *Baguio*

The Reneca Hotel in Baguio, self-styled 'Summer Capital of the Philippines', has very noisy neighbours. Dogs bark on and off for most of the night, but at around six in the morning, when I'm at last sinking into sleep, a talking bird wakes up. After a lot of muttering in Spanish it begins a series of piercing wolf-whistles.

Baguio is a Philippine hill-station, a cool, piney retreat from the heat and humidity of the plain. Up here at 5000 feet the edge seems to have been rubbed off the hard brashness of Manila and replaced by American small-town orderliness. Fire trees and native three-needle pines fringe well-kept parks and picnic areas aglow with poinsettias. The grass is green and healthy and the city signs are sponsored by McDonalds. The city was designed and laid out by an American called Daniel Burnham, apparently for nothing, and a huge park is named after him. (A much smaller park is named after Rizal, the Filipino writer and patriot executed by the Spanish in 1896.)

Not everything in Baguio is ordinary however, and on this fresh, sunny morning I find myself turning up past the wonderfully named Macadangdang's Grocery Store to Number 114, Lourdes Grotto Road to witness internal surgery performed without scalpels, drugs or anaesthetics. Psychic surgery.

The surgeon who welcomes us to his modest apartment is called, a little disconcertingly, the Reverend José Segundo. He is a short man, a member of the local Inguin tribe, more Asiatic than Spanish in his features. He wears grey flannel trousers and sports a neat black waistcoat over a dark striped shirt. He extends a soft warm hand. His own, I'm relieved to see.

He was born into a poor family up here in the mountain region where a strong tradition of faith-healing was already established. At the age of fourteen, he tells me quite matter-of-factly, a cloud appeared and a voice from within told him he had the power to heal. Since then he has become an international celebrity, very popular in rationalist strongholds like Switzerland and Germany.

I ask him if performing surgery in your own back room next door to the toilet might not carry a risk of infection. He shakes his head firmly and points to the success of a Brazilian healer called the Rusty Knife.

'Because he used a rusty knife?'

'Yes . . . a kitchen knife.'

'And people were not infected?'

'No . . . people see his power,' insists the Reverend. 'So with me, I do not wash my hands. The wound will not be infected because of the power that is in them.'

I ask him if he has any medical training. He shakes his head confidently.

'No.'

'Have you ever read any medical books?'

'No.'

We enter a small room which smells of damp. Its grubby white walls are empty save for a crucifix, rosary and a consulting couch with a plastic mattress and two towels laid out on it. Segundo rolls his sleeves up and beckons over his assistant, Rudy, who sports pink trousers and a pink and blue check shirt. The pair of them look as though they're here for a late night poker game.

In fact they are to administer surgery to a young white boy called Gustav, who, after seeing a film about the Filipino healers, has come all the way from Hungary to seek a cure for his persistent rheumatoid arthritis. Now he has realized his dream and lies face down in his underpants in a dingy room in Baguio.

'Will this operation be a bloody one?' our director asks, hopefully.

'I don't know,' says the Reverend. 'It is not in my power.'

Segundo closes his eyes and recites a prayer. Then he dips his fingers in the water from the green plastic bowl that Rudy holds out to him and begins to rub hard on the affected part of Gustav's leg. After a few moments all of us hear a snap, almost as though the flesh has parted under the pressure, and watery blood oozes out over the back of Gustav's thigh. He repeats this on the other leg, and quite quickly the operation is over and Rudy is gathering up the blood-stained cotton-wool. I later see him shuffle across the hallway with it and disappear behind a door marked 'Comfort Room'.

Gustav dresses himself as nonchalantly as he would had he just had a button sewn on. He says he feels fine but will not know if the 'operation' has worked for two or three weeks.

Segundo has by now washed his hands and is ready to deal with further questioning in his usual breezy, matter-of-fact style.

'I have only one question,' I say. 'Do you use blood capsules?'

Segundo brushes away such a suggestion.

'You cannot see what I am doing without the third eye,' he says. 'What you see with two eyes is nothing.'

To my two logical, rationally-conditioned Western eyes none of what I saw at 114 Lourdes Grotto Road adds up to a row of beans. The snap sounded suspiciously like a pop, the blood looked phoney and there was no evidence of a cure. But superstition and magic have been so eradicated from our culture that we no longer know how to deal with them. In a way Reverend Segundo is right. To begin to understand the history, traditions and powers of the ethnic, pre-Hispanic mountain people from which he is descended, and many similar societies, we need at least to have an open mind – or a third eye. In the meantime, I have his business card.

Ambrosio Pelingen who works nearby at 28 Mystical Rose Street, is a very different character from José Segundo. Quieter, less flamboyant and, speaking English with ease and confidence, he reminds me of a rather liberal head-teacher. He's giving his psychic surgery free of charge today for the poorest of his patients and is quite happy for me, and our camera and microphone, to follow him as closely as we like. From six inches away I see his fingers manipulate the flesh until, with no perceptible sound of any kind, dark 'blood' (of a much more convincing shade and consistency than seen at Reverend Segundo's) begins to seep through the skin, and he appears to extract from the wound a small dark patch of tissue which he calls 'toxins'. But there is no wound and no cut in the flesh. Though Pelingen has better props, and a sort of academic authority, both men seem more like magicians than surgeons. Their patients seem entirely happy with this.

We leave the town in the early afternoon, our bus winding its way round long steep hairpins into a narrow gorge. All roads lead to Manila, but agonizingly slowly. The reason for much of our delay today is the same as the reason why Great Britain had a bad summer in 1992 – Mount Pinatubo. When this volcano erupted in June 1991 it was one of the biggest explosions of the century. It hurled ash and mud 25 miles into the air, high enough and thick enough for it to reach the band of cloud that circles the earth and to affect the weather all over the globe.

As night closes in, our bus passes eight or nine miles east of Pinatubo. Ash, like heavy winter snow, has submerged the fields on either side. We cross over a broad river whose course, like that of the road we're following, has been nearly throttled by hard, grey sludge which is still seeping down from the volcano burying homes and villages. The water struggles through but the banks are stacked 15 to 20 feet high with ash and mud, ghostly grey in the rising moonlight. A limping dog barks at us as the cars pass slowly south.

DAY 94: *Samal Island*

We are resting up at Pearl Farm Resort on the island of Mindanao, having escaped by plane and boat from the noise and pollution of Manila, now 600 miles away to the north-west. The stresses and strains of South-East Asia have been soothed away, to the sounds of 'Winter Wonderland' and other Christmas favourites, on the palm-fringed shores of Samal Island, one of over 7000 that make up the Philippine archipelago. It's an hour's ride away in an outrigger canoe from Davao, the bustling, Chinese-influenced second city of the Philippines. Davao claims, in terms of urban area, to be the largest city in the world, but from the wooden balcony of my cabin on stilts it is a mere smudge on an horizon dominated by the sprawling rain-forested slopes of Mount Apo, a 9600-foot active volcano.

Today has been something of a milestone for the crew. Nigel has had a tooth pulled out in Davao and I have learnt the combined joys of scuba diving and underwater photography. I had only a day to learn scuba diving. (I didn't like to let on that in 1970 I had spent a morning underwater filming with no instruction at all. It was in Ealing Swimming Baths and

I was playing a man in a *Monty Python* sketch whose house was suffering from rising damp.) Today, thanks to the patient guidance of my instructor, Louie Barrios, I learn the ins and outs of negative and neutral buoyancy, nitrogen narcosis, embolism, ear-squeeze and eustachean tubes before lunch. I entered the clear jade waters of the Pacific knowing all sorts of useful things about the underwater world: that objects look twenty-five per cent closer and twenty-five per cent larger, that sound travels faster and in all directions, that blood is green rather than red, that toothpaste rubbed on the face mask stops it steaming up, and that a wobbly hand sign means you're in trouble. The latter saved my bacon when, feeling confident, I had strayed down to 40 feet or so only to find myself suddenly unable to breathe except in increasingly short bursts. A wobble of the hand brought Louie alongside. Seeing my air level had run dangerously low, he deftly reattached my tubes to his own air supply and brought me to the surface. It was mid-way through the afternoon before I suddenly got the hang of it, lost my clumsiness and began to move the way fish do.

As I lie in bed, my mind swooning under a celebratory combination of Margaritas and Australian white wine, a tropical storm breaks overhead, hurling stair-rods of rain against the thatch roof. Signalling, perhaps, that the holiday's over and it's time to move on.

DAY 96: *Samal Island to General Santos*

A superb morning. The night's downpour has freshened the air and scattered the clouds. As we skim across towards Davao, the shallow sea is a mix of pale green and deep blue. Nothing of course is ever as innocent as it looks and one of the problems in this idyllic bay is the use of explosives for fishing. Not only does it kill the fish but it shatters irreplaceable coral as well.

On the dockside we transfer our bags to a jeepney that will take us due south over the mountains to General Santos from where we hope to catch a ferry to Zamboanga, from where we hope to catch a ferry to Borneo.

Drop in at the Insular Hotel for an international paper. Pass a very fat man across whose T-shirt is written 'I Look Much Better Naked'.

The lead story in the *Herald Tribune* is the news that the President of South Korea has bowed to pressure to reopen the case against the two generals who were held responsible for the Kwangju Massacre. A victory for all those marchers whose protest I was caught up in a month and a half ago in Seoul.

Jerry is our driver. He has a radio all wired in on the driving seat which means he can't sit straight on to the steering-wheel. This doesn't seem to worry him any more than the fact that none of the gauges on the dashboard work. Maybe he has some ancient 'third eye' intuition as to when we are short of fuel, for he pulls confidently into a filling station off the Carlos P. Garcia Highway and pours several gallons into a tank alarmingly situated directly below his feet.

At Sirawan the Carlos P. Garcia Highway becomes the Carlos P. Garcia Dirt Road which tilts and sways us through a lush tropical sprawl of coconut and banana plantations. This is fishing and copra country and the poorest part of the Philippines. Another jeepney rattles by, going north. There must be forty people aboard, including three on the bonnet.

Stop for lunch at a small waterfront restaurant called Dolly's Seafoods. It's a bizarre place. Sounds of Roger Whittaker singing 'Danny Boy' fill the dining room and young girls are employed to walk round the tables keeping flies at bay with fluffy white nylon switches. Specialities include fresh squid, shrimp and tuna and the indulgent attentions of the owner, Dolly Hale, a jolly Filipino (not that I've met a Filipino who *isn't* jolly) married to an Oklahoman.

On through the maize fields of the T'boli people – an egg box landscape of little hills and valleys, to the outskirts of General Santos where we pass 'The Immaculate Conception Funeral Parlour'.

Evening. The dockside at General Santos is hot, fierce and manic. As departure time nears, the last containers are rushed aboard our ferry by a fleet of fork-lift trucks, their harsh horns blaring. The stink of hot fuel and human sweat mingles with the reek of cow dung from cattle crates bound, I'm told, for Japan and Korea from Darwin, Australia.

We pull out past a freighter from Manila – the *Lorcon Luzon*. The crew are playing basketball on deck beside a wall of containers from which rise the high-pitched squeals of pigs, bound for the *lechon* restaurants of the capital. They add another infernal element to this desperate place.

DAY 97: *General Santos to Zamboanga*

Aboard the MV *Princess of the Pacific*. Uneventful voyage on a flat calm sea. Dawn heralded by not one but possibly a hundred cockerels travelling with us, each one in his own cardboard box. Once one starts to crow, another picks it up and then another, like a crazed close-harmony chorus, until the noise is deafening.

As we turn in towards Zamboanga we pass on our port side the volcanic cone of Basilan Island about which my *Lonely Planet* guide is uncharacteristically guarded. 'For your own safety you would be advised to think twice about visiting Basilan.'

At the deck rail I fall in with a Filipino insurance salesman who is scarcely more encouraging. He nods towards the smudgy blur of Zamboanga. 'This used to be the worst of all the ports in the Philippines,' he observes with the relish of one who is not stopping there.

How is it that Zamboanga, referred to in the *Nagel Guide* as the city of the Five 'Fs' – 'Flowers, Fruit, Friends, Femmes and Faith' – can be surrounded by so much controversy? My friend says the answer lies in the word Faith. Of the sixty-eight million people in the Philippines, three million (four and a half per cent) are Muslim. In Zamboanga twenty-seven per cent are Muslim. Here in the far south-west of the country they have consistently fought for some degree of autonomy and religious liberty. The last twenty-five years have seen an intensification of this struggle and a cost of over fifty thousand lives. Meanwhile the area stagnated. The fishing industry was so underdeveloped

140

that it was said that in Zamboanga 'the fish die of old age'. A highway was said to have been completed seven times but in fact this was the number of times funds were allocated, only to end up in the pockets of corrupt officials. Now central government, anxious not to be left out of the Pacific Rim economic boom, wants a settlement. Potentially prosperous trading links with Indonesia and Malaysia could be threatened if the violence continues. Compromise is in the air. President Ramos has even suggested incorporating the Muslim crescent moon into the Philippine flag.

The fly in the ointment is a radical and violent fundamentalist group whose leader Abu Baker Janjalani has a price of one and a half million pesos on his head. His base is in Basilan Island, and his group is dangerous.

We steam into Zamboanga on a tide of warnings but no overt signs of trouble. A fleet of stick-like fishing boats follows the ferry in to harbour. In them are local islanders – 'water gypsies' my friend calls them. Their children call out for coins to be thrown into the water and they dive in and grab them before they hit the bottom, stuffing as many as they can into their mouths before returning to the surface. They are incredibly fast and agile but by the age of ten many of them have become deaf from the effects of water pressure.

Ashore by mid-morning. Crowds, noise and almost intolerable heat. Well, it *is* nearly Christmas.

DAY 98: *Zamboanga*

Intrigued by the whereabouts of all the cockerels on the boat I make my first visit to a cock farm. High up in the mountains north of Zamboanga, Boy Primalion raises some of the most sought after fighting birds in the Philippines which gives him considerable status in a country where cock-fighting is rated the Number One pastime, after basketball.

Primalion's farm is set at the end of a long, bumpy ascent. A muddy, red-earth track emerges from light jungle onto green and pleasant slopes whose summits are the first to catch the drifting clouds. These hills are alive with the sound of two and a half thousand crowing roosters and covered with orderly ranks of wooden, A-frame hutches. In each of these is a tethered cockerel, separated from his neighbour by a regulation distance of six to eight feet, which is the closest they can get without actually attacking each other. Outside their huts they cluck, pick, nod, strut, primp, preen, shake and ruffle themselves – a great army of first-time home-owners. The only drawback to this life of luxury is that they will soon have to exchange it for the cockpit and the strong possibility of being pecked to death.

Against the sound of mass crowing I talk to Boy Primalion's son, who is a courteous man with soft, fleshy features. His father set up the farm twenty-two years ago and now, with two thousand five hundred birds in residence it is, he says proudly, 'one of the biggest farm in the whole world'.

I ask him what's required to produce a champion fighting cock. 'It's simple. We give them fresh mountain air, carbohydrates and the protein to develop their muscles.'

It sounds like much the same system for raising any kind of prize fighter. And the breeder's trophies in the family guesthouse are as grand and monumental as any Lonsdale belt.

DAY 99

Sunday in Zamboanga. A hot, sticky, airless day which feels as though it's sickening for something. Throughout the night my air-conditioning unit rattles, wheezes and shudders like a dying man.

Boy Primalion has invited us to see his cocks in action today at the Galleria de Zamboanga. Two middle-aged ladies sit demurely behind a wrought iron Spanish-style grille selling tickets for what is billed as a Five-Cock Derby (which means each owner can enter five cocks). Total prize money of 450 million pesos (over 10 million pounds) is on offer.

The gallery is of wooden construction and built on three levels around a sand-covered arena, the same size as a boxing

LEFT: *Friendship Gate, the way out of China and into Vietnam.*

BELOW: *A bathroom by the Perfume River in Hue, Vietnam (the basin is an American army helmet).*

LEFT: *Saigon style.*

BELOW LEFT: *Full colour religion: a service in progress at the Caodaist cathedral, Tay Ninh, Vietnam.*

RIGHT: *Mekong Delta. As elsewhere in Asia, rice planting is done by the women.*

BELOW: *My bag's bigger than yours controversy.*

ABOVE: *Mesmerising glimpse of the two-thousand-year-old Banaue rice terraces, Philippines.*

LEFT: *Grid-lock in Manila.*

RIGHT: *Boy Primalion's cock farm outside Zamboanga.*

ABOVE: *Enjoying a head-hunting joke with the longhouse chief, Sarawak.*

LEFT: *Sepilok Orang-utan Rehabilitation Centre, Sandakan, Borneo.*

FAR LEFT: *Rio Hondo, the Muslim village in Zamboanga.*

OVERLEAF: *Iban children near Nanga Sumpa longhouse.*

ring (why *are* boxing rings called rings when they're always square?). This is lit from above by a rig of fluorescent strip lights. There is a tremendous noise inside which at first I assume to be a fight in progress. In fact it's the much more animated business of pre-fight betting. The fighting cocks are presented and then thrust at each other so that aficionados can judge their chances from the way they spar up. Then a prolonged process of laying money goes on led by bookies called *Kristos*, because of the way they spread their arms wide as they invite bets. Sign language is used to denote the amount of the bet and nothing is ever written down.

The fight itself is almost an anti-climax. Every bird has a three-inch curved blade secured to its left leg and these are what do the damage as the cocks fly at each other. A white cockerel, generally believed to be the strongest and most aggressive is pitted in the first fight against a brown. Feathers fly as they make contact and when the white comes out the other side of the fray his feathers are blood-flecked. But the blood is from the brown cock which wobbles unsteadily as the white goes in again pecking at its opponent's neck. The brown cock keels over. The seconds pick up the birds and they are held beak to beak. If both still make to peck, the fight continues. If only one, then the fight is over. The contest has lasted no more than twenty seconds. There is brief hollering and cheering from the crowd, then they get down to business. The winning bets are paid out – crumpled wads of money are tossed about the audience – and the cockerels are taken backstage where a blood-stained vet is on hand to stitch up cuts or pronounce the creature ready for the next stew.

Suddenly there comes a hissing, rattling sound which can be heard even over the screams of the next round of betting, and spectators in the top rows, where the stadium is open to the sides, rush to move forward as a massive tropical storm bursts overhead.

I have not experienced rain quite like this before. These are not drops or even stair-rods. It is as if a dam has burst a hundred feet above us. I walk out of the arena and round to the outer area. Niagaras of rainwater tumble off the corrugated iron roof, but life goes on as if nothing had happened. Food and drink is served (no drinking or smoking allowed at the ringside) and men wait patiently with their cockerels under their arms as lightning and thunder and the shouts of the punters and the crowing of two hundred eager competitors mingle into a great cacophonous uproar. Boy Primalion told me cocks on his farm are played tapes of fights in order to get them used to the noise of the cockpit. I laughed at the time but now I can understand why.

It could only happen in the Philippines, but I find myself, a few hours after the cock-fight, judging a beauty contest by the sea at Vista del Mar, in an atmosphere made markedly fresher and cooler by the afternoon storm.

The contestants for the crown of Miss La Bella Pacifica must be of 'at least' High School age, 'of good moral character, physical beauty, talent and intelligence'. And presumably women. I settle myself down for a delightful and relaxing evening, only to find that I am required to work as hard as I have in any three-hour period since taking my final exams at Oxford. Not only are we judging Miss La Bella P but also Best in a Swimsuit, Best in a Gown, Best Ethnic (traditional outfits), Miss La Bella Tourism and Miss Photogenic.

What with all the scores to add up it becomes a serious exercise in mental arithmetic. But I did get to kiss the winner. Once.

DAY 100

A hundred days on the road. Should be celebrating. But what? An awful long way still to go? Ironically this milestone (if such it is) coincides with one of those occasional vortexes in our journey when all we seem to be doing is flying round in ever-decreasing circles. The reason for our continued dalliance in Zamboanga is that, until quite recently, the Sulu Sea between here and Borneo was out of bounds to regular foreign travellers. Gavin Young, in *Slow Boats To China* talks of the 'treacherous water' between Zambo and Sandakan on the 'pirate-haunted Sulu Sea'.

Spent most of the day at the Rio Hondo, a Muslim village built on spindly stilts above the water. Rio Hondo is tough, wiry and welcoming. A network of unfenced bridges and walkways leads like a spider's web through the labyrinth of improvised wooden houses in which ten thousand people live. They have no sanitation other than the flow of the Pacific tide but they have billiard-halls, tailors, halal butchers, schools and a makeshift mosque with green tin walls and a silver tin dome, which is one of the most curious buildings I've seen on the journey so far. The rickety houses may have ten or fifteen people living in them, the walkways may be perilous and the wood planks holed and split, yet there is a sense of civic pride here. Pride in making the most of very little.

DAY 101

Basil is puzzled by his horoscope in the *Zamboanga Times*. 'Be grandiloquent', it says. Basil says he would if he knew what it meant. Better news on the shipping pages where there is confirmation of a ferry service across to Borneo run by an outfit called Aleson Lines.

On our way to the shipping office to check on the existence of the Borneo ferry we pass rich street life – psychic dentists on the street corners offering to remove teeth for fifty *pesos* a time, and businesses whose names you couldn't invent, such as The Golden Buddha Investigating Agency and The Transient Electrical Corporation.

Aleson Shipping Line is located out on Veteran's Avenue in the grounds of a rusting old rice-mill. To get to the head office you must cross a courtyard and step over a slumbering dog.

Feliciano N. Tan, who's known to all as Nonoy, is an engaging, self-deprecating middle-aged man with smooth olive skin and a head of flourishing curly hair. His mother, aunt, sons and daughters all live and work here.

The problem is that Nonoy has had an engine fire on the ferry that usually does the journey and it will not be repaired for another two weeks. He has another ship, the *Danica Joy*, named after his daughter, which is smaller and slower but which will be leaving tomorrow or the next day, or certainly the day after that.

One thing we need not worry about are pirates.

'No pirates,' he assures me categorically, 'ever boarded a ferry on the Sulu Sea.'

I'm quite happy with this until he adds: 'They couldn't have done. We have security.'

'Armed men?' I ask.

'Well,' he chuckles, 'not exactly armed but they have sticks.'

There is no option. We buy the tickets. For sometime . . . soon.

DAY 104

The *Danica Joy* is to leave Zamboanga this morning. Nonoy is at the dockside, smoking heavily, more preoccupied and a lot less avuncular than when we last saw him. Looking at the boat on which we are to cross the 'treacherous' seas between here and Borneo, I understand his anxiety. The *Danica Joy* is a squat 400-foot roll-on, roll-off tub, still moored to the dockside and already pitching about like a drunk. Nonoy knows, and he knows that we know, that she is a substitute for the bigger ship that should normally be on this run and is not built for ocean work. Like the rest of us he is hoping and praying she'll make it. Certainly there is a sense of occasion. Crowds, noise, shouts, blaring of car horns create an atmosphere of amiable frenzy, as if this were the first ship ever to leave Zamboanga.

Eventually all those who have to be on board are on board, the folding green gangplank has been winched up and we heave away hard to starboard and out past the gorgeously named MV *Magnolia Grandiflora*, a ferry even more battered and desperate than the one we're on.

Select a bunk on the open-plan upper deck. Some people are already curling up to sleep, others lie and watch the incredibly violent guns and Kung-Fu video on closed-circuit television. A man called Bert is feeding his prize cockerels on a concentrate of yucca oil from a plastic bottle. Cockerel sperm, he confides, is where the big money is made.

I wander up to the bridge. The captain is 'resting'. The helmsman is beating his hands up and down on the ship's wheel in time to a Queen tape, and the first officer, a genial, portly man, secures a chart and shows me our route, south and west, parallel with the Sulu archipelago.

They ask me what I do. Playing it as low key as possible I say I'm a writer. They all seem vaguely impressed. One of them points at the book I'm holding, Robert Payne's *The White Rajahs of Sarawak*.

'You write this?'

I shake my head.

'What you write?'

'Er . . . well . . . '

It's too late. I've lost his attention.

'You give me your book. Yes? You give me your book. You sign it.'

Whatever I say will make no difference. I don't have any of my books with me. I have Rob Newman's *Dependence Day*, so I sign that and give it to him and he seems very happy.

Meanwhile the first officer is explaining why the *Danica Joy* is not an adequate ship to be on. It was built to ferry people across the Inland Sea in Japan and has a flat bottom and a draught of less than 10 feet.

'These are not meant for high seas.'

I think I've heard that once too often and would rather talk to Bert about cockerel sperm.

Night falls and the ship is beginning to roll about laboriously. The lavatories are not for the squeamish. Even if you could stay sitting on them, there is no paper. Unsecurable doors swing crazily on their hinges and the flush is no more use than a bead of sweat. Some people opt for a short cut and pee in the showers.

I don't know when it is I wake, or if I've slept, but I am conscious of extreme, unpredictable movement. First I am pitched one way, then, after what seems like a very long pause, I'm pitched to the other. The blood rushes to my head just in time for my body to be corkscrewed around. Then I'm on the way up again and hard down as the hull belly-flops, spinning and reverberating like a boxer bouncing off the ropes. To start with it's physically quite exciting, like being on a never-ending fairground ride, but the more I wake up and the more I remember of the first-mate's warnings and the look of the ship and the owner's shifty anxiety as we loaded at Zamboanga, the more I become convinced that this is it. The luck's run out, and I have only myself to blame. The storm roars and, as the *Danica Joy* ricochets off another wave, I raise myself desperately from my bed to see how many other people are praying. But all I see, in the bottom bunk, across the gangway from me, is a woman in an immaculate deep blue *sari*, gold chain on her wrist, sleeping with such total and complete serenity that I suddenly feel rather foolish. And strangely safer.

MALAYSIA

DAY 105: *Sandakan, Sabah*

Morning after the night before. The weather has spent its anger and retreated into a low, grey sulk. We are 300 miles north of the Equator, making 10.7 knots and I am up early to catch my first glimpse of the coastline of Borneo, the third largest island in the world.

Though visibility is poor I know we are close to shore because the sea is muddy cream and its surface is littered with terrestrial debris – leaves, branches, sometimes whole tree trunks, swept down storm-swollen rivers and out into the ocean.

On the bridge a slim, young Malaysian pilot has taken the wheel. The captain, an elderly, unsmiling man, stands, stomach spilling from his vest, looking out at a rainswept island ahead like some grumpy general waiting to be dressed. On closer inspection, what he's looking at with such jaundiced eye is not an island at all but a huge, slow-moving timber barge, stacked

30 or 40 tree-trunks high, being hauled across our path by two tugboats.

Then, all at once, looming tall and sheer on our starboard side, water pouring down their flanks, are the orange and violet limestone cliffs of Sabah – formerly the British Crown Colony of North Borneo, formerly the property of the British North Borneo Chartered Company, formerly the property of the people who lived there.

The first buildings slide into view. The silver-grey minaret and dome of a thoroughly modern mosque dominates the northern headland, a Chinese temple straddles the ridge behind the city and along the shore is a long line of houseboats. Then the unlovely concrete blocks of Sandakan begin to emerge from the wet low cloud. High-rise blocks, grander than anything in Zamboanga.

The docks are at the far end of town. They are scrupulously clean. The stevedores wear matching green anoraks with black hoods. A police vehicle with a dog in the back waits on the quayside. There are two or three other people buttoned up against the rain. After Zamboanga it's like a morgue.

We are met by Philip Yong, a studious Chinese in his early forties, born and brought up in Sarawak, who will be our guide through Malaysian Borneo. He it is who tells me that this continuous rain is quite common. The State of Sabah may be just south of the typhoon belt, but it's not quite far north enough to avoid the monsoon. Borneo in a monsoon sounds exotic but the streets of Sandakan could be in Surrey. Raised kerbstones, neat road-markings, clipped verges, lawns, herbaceous borders and civic clocks abound.

Compared to the rigours of the *Danica Joy*, the Renaissance Hotel is a palace. After a hot bath and a good scrub, I stand at the window marvelling at the soaring beauty of the rain forest outside. Tall, elegant trees with bare chalky barks rising from thick, impenetrable cover. An emerald forest indeed.

Fall asleep to the steady, persistent sound of rain plopping onto my balcony.

DAY 106

Wake to the steady, persistent sound of rain plopping onto my balcony. In the smartly tiled coffee shop the waiters serve breakfast while deftly adjusting towels to catch drops from a leaking ceiling.

For some reason Philip and I are talking about the most revolting things we've ever eaten. He suggests that every culture has its 'test' taste (some defining food, prized by locals and generally repellent to outsiders). In his part of the world, South-East Asia, it is the *durian*, a fruit much sought after for its sweet creamy texture and powerfully foul smell.

'And in Britain?' I ask him.

Philip, has no hesitation.

'Cheese!'

Underlying all discussion of affairs in Borneo since half of it became part of the Malaysian Federation (now simply Malaysia) in 1963, is the highly charged subject of logging. The products of the lush tropical rain forest are in great demand, and over the last thirty years generous logging concessions were granted to foreign companies to help provide materials for the expanding Pacific Rim economies, especially that of Japan. Environmentalists say far too much has been cut down, the government protests that the clearing is sustainable and controlled, businessmen wait to grab what they can at the best price. Sandakan once boasted the greatest concentration of millionaires in the world; almost all of them Chinese timber-traders.

This morning, we pass by their huge, gaudy villas on our way to see a rare environmentalist's victory. Fifteen miles outside the town are 10,000 acres of lowland rain forest and 2500 of mangrove forest which became a jungle reserve in 1984. It contains two hundred and twenty bird species, four hundred and fifty separate tree species, ninety different mammals, and an extraordinary enterprise called the Sepilok Orang-utan Rehabilitation Centre.

One of the by-products of deforestation was the removal of baby orangs for domestic pets. The Sepilok sanctuary was set up in 1964 to try and reverse the process and save the orangs from extinction.

The heavy rain has flooded most of the paths into the forest, and we have been issued with rubber boots and advised to wear shorts. This has not been a sensible strategy. The flood-level is now well over the duckboards and warm muddy water rises quickly to the rim of my boots and starts to trickle down the inside. By this time Sylvia, our guide, is warning us that snakes and scorpions *do* sometimes come to the surface at this time of year. My boots are full of water and my knees feel wretchedly vulnerable. To make matters worse an immaculately overalled, bone-dry party of Japanese is following close behind.

We emerge, dripping and squelching, onto a wooden platform at the base of a lofty, smooth-barked *belian* or ironwood. These are graceful, slow-growing trees, providing one of the most durable timbers in the world, the only one known to be resistant to termites.

There is a theatrical pause as we gather on our platforms to await the arrival of the orang-utans for 9.30 feeding time. We have been advised not to wear anything red or display any jewellery, both of which they're attracted to, and, because the orang is highly susceptible to human diseases, those of us with colds at the running and sneezing stage have already been weeded out and left behind at the visitor centre.

It's nearer ten o'clock when the great spreading leaves below us begin to move and the first orang appears. 'Obviously, they don't like the rain,' says Sylvia, checking her watch.

A small, five-year-old orang-utan makes her painstaking way toward the bowls of milk and piles of bananas on the feeding platform at the base of the tree. She looks like a ninety-five-year-old baby, hair patchy, her body shockingly thin. She's followed by others, their skins the colour and texture of coconut husks. Most ignore the thirty-strong crowd of spectators, apart from one called Alice, who, Sylvia tells me, likes handbags.

When I suggest to Sylvia that they seem tired and a bit sad, like hospital patients, she says this is exactly what they are. It is a long, slow business returning them to the wild, and they only know they have been successful when the orang-utans

151

they've looked after for so long disappear into the trees and never return.

DAY 108: *Kuching, Sarawak*

A brilliant morning. The first let-up in the rain since we arrived in Borneo. Which is ironic considering we're in Kuching, the capital of the Malaysian state of Sarawak, which has more rainfall in a month than London has in a year. And *this* is the month.

Kuching is a small, attractive, prosperous city much of which was laid out under the largely benevolent despotism of the Brooke family – the White Rajahs – who came from Bath to rule a quarter of Borneo.

In the museum there is a chart headed A Chronology Of Sarawak. It lists one thousand important events that happened in Sarawak between 1292 and 1981. Only twenty-two of these take place before 24 September 1841 when 'Rajah Muda Hassim hands over the government of Sarawak to James Brooke'.

The initials J.B. are curiously apt, for Brooke was a sort of Victorian James Bond: attractive, independently wealthy, and very English. He was also single-minded and effective and, having restored law and order to the pirate-ridden shores and the inhospitable interior of Sarawak, he passed on a stable, efficient and reasonably tolerant state to his nephew Charles, who ran it for fifty years from the end of the Crimean War to the end of the First World War, neither of which interrupted the administration of his fiefdom one bit.

Though Sarawak is now firmly part of Malaysia, our arrival has coincided with a three-day regatta, which, with the sun shining on white tents and striped awnings, does lend the riverside a distinctly 'Brooke-ish' air. It's not a rowing regatta, but a paddling regatta, more Dayak pirate than Henley-on-Thames, with up to thirty oarsmen and women in each longboat. It's crowded and noisy with crews in vivid colours and supporters yelling on their boats. Walk on into the town, which has some good looking colonial buildings and a modest bust of Charles Brooke, the second Rajah – long hair, high collar, confident moustache – a paradigm of Victorian respectability.

The Jalal India, traditional street of the Indian merchants is, for me, the liveliest place in Kuching. A blind band playing Jim Reeves' hits weaves its way through the throng of shoppers, traders and other street performers. The biggest crowd is around a wild-eyed, lithe man with matted hair and bloody weals across his chest, naked apart from a pair of torn jeans. He is selling his patent medicine pills and, in order to show how effective they can be, he crushes up anti-mosquito coils in a half-pint mug and drinks the contents.

While the gasps are still being uttered, he reaches down and pulls open the lid of a small suitcase to reveal a coiled python lurking within. He reaches for the snake and, to the horror and delight of the audience, pulls open the waistband of his jeans and stuffs it inside, headfirst. Then, choosing his moment with well-practised skill, he gyrates his stomach lasciviously, allowing the python to emerge slowly from the top of his trousers. Heads shake, women turn away, and his audience doubles.

Philip takes us out in the evening to the River Café, a restored wrought iron pavilion set in a small garden a short way back from the esplanade. We eat *laksa* – a local speciality of curried prawn stew with noodles. The rain holds off long enough for a tremendous firework display lasting almost an hour. This celebration coincides with my daughter's twenty-first birthday and the news that Malaysia's first satellite has been successfully launched into space by the Americans. *And* Steve's wife is expecting a baby any moment. Starbursts fill the warm night sky, each one wider than the last. If life were a movie then this is when his baby would be born.

DAY 109: *Kuching to Nanga Sumpa*

Alarm wakes me at six. Lie for a while and listen to the rain that I have heard coming and going, rising and falling in intensity throughout the night. It's settled now into a sheer, ceaseless downpour.

The rain was certainly my friend last night, putting a premature end to a poolside karaoke party just below my window. Repeated, unsuccessful attempts to hit the high note of 'The Great Pretender' were plunging me into terminal despair. This morning I'm not so sure about it. In two hours' time we shall be out in the downpour, making our way out of Kuching, up river and into the interior. Head-hunter country.

2.30 p.m. On the Batang Ai Reservoir, 175 miles south-east of Kuching, close to the border between Sarawak and Kalimantan (the Indonesian half of Borneo). The rain-clouds hang in a long, windswept grey veil across the coast. Where we are the skies are clear blue, and slopes covered with palm oil and pepper plantations stretch in bright green patterns across the low hills.

We are on the edge of the great inhospitable interior of Borneo. To the south lie hundreds of square miles of swamp, to the north and east, range after range of precipitous, densely-forested mountains. It is one of the secret places of the world. Unless you know the jungle tracks and the difficult, un-predictable rivers there is no way in by land – no roads or railways, only the loggers' trails, where no one but the loggers are welcome.

From here on in we are in the hands of the local tribespeople; in our case the Iban (formerly the Dayaks), who comprise one-third of Sarawak's population, and who still live largely in communal longhouses. We are picked up at a jetty beside the dam by Denis (whose Iban name is Luart), a compact older man with a shining smile, dark glasses and an air-force blue pork-pie hat, which he seems to wear at all times. With him is a quick, intelligent young man called Emong Tinsang. They will take us up the river network, into the jungle and almost to the Kalimantan border.

I clamber into a *prau* – a low, narrow, 20-foot-long wooden canoe, its hull painted bright green with a sky-blue strip – and, gunning the outboard, Andat, my driver, races us across the shining glass surface of the reservoir. Once into the river system the going gets harder. The water turns a deep metallic green, reflecting the denseness of rain forest. Lianas brush the water, wild-boar tracks scuff the muddy banks and entrail-like root systems, in weird and wonderful shapes, spread out from the jungle. Giant cicadas can be heard like small sirens going off and, although this isn't the best time of year for birds, as most of the trees will not bear fruit for two or three months, we can hear the high-pitched cry of the stork-billed kingfisher and the rising and falling cadence of a bulbul.

Twenty-five miles into the interior we reach the settlement of Nanga Sumpa. The river is so shallow up here that our boatmen have to get out and push. In this ungainly way we approach a small creek from whose mud banks knots of small children watch us curiously.

This is so far from anywhere that, as I scramble out onto the bank, I jokingly question Emong as to when the last film crew was here.

'November the fourteenth,' he says, without hesitation. 'But they were only interested in the life of the pigs.'

He leads us towards the longhouse beneath which black, wispy-haired pigs lie lazily about in muddy holes, doubtless recovering from the pressures of making a television documentary.

The 300-foot longhouse is raised a dozen feet off the ground on a wooden scaffold and finished with bamboo, palm thatch and the odd sheet of corrugated iron. Beneath it is a dark, dripping forest of wooden piling amongst which chicken, ducks and dogs scratch and pick their way and against which the more energetic black pigs rub their coarse hairy flanks. It's not intended to last for ever. The Iban are nomads and this building has been standing for twelve years, which, in their terms, makes it something of an ancient monument.

We climb a precarious notched tree trunk which acts as a staircase leading to the front door of the longhouse. We take our shoes off before walking along the covered communal verandah, which opens out onto a shared terrace. On the opposite side of the verandah are the doors and plank-wall partitions of each family's private quarters. This is a twenty-eight-door longhouse, meaning that there are twenty-eight families here, about a hundred and ninety-six people. The place is lit by candlelight, although there are two, highly prestigious, neon strip lights at the centre of the public area, beneath which longhouse meetings take place. On the walls are calendars, cuttings from newspapers, faded pop-star pin-ups, fishing nets, baskets, a fact-sheet about malaria, a pheasant-feather head-dress, woven mats and blankets, and a sun-bleached colour photograph of Dr Mahatir, the Prime Minister of Malaysia. Although it gives the impression of a completely communal lifestyle, I'm told that money and food are not shared, though gifts are.

Denis calls the local men together and we all squat down on the floor in a circle. *Tuak*, the local rice wine, is dispensed from big old kettles which lend the occasion the air of a slightly surreal school tea. We introduce ourselves. I am asked to explain why we are here, which, considering we're cross-legged in a longhouse in the depths of Borneo, seems a suitably existential question.

DAY 110: *Nanga Sumpa, Sarawak*

As the morning fires are lit, smoke pours from inside and outside the longhouse. I can hear what sounds like a radio news broadcast, reminding me that, though we may be at the end of the settled world, we are not outside it.

Today Denis has promised to take us about as far upstream as it is possible to go. We are quite an expedition as the river is so shallow and the rapids so steep that the *praus* must be as lightly loaded as possible. This is wild orchid country and in March, the flowering season, collectors from all over the world will come out here. It's also leech country and we're advised to cover up when we walk into the forest. I'm told there are two kinds of leech. The black leech goes for the ankle and the brown leech for the privates. You will likely not feel the black one attach itself but if a brown one takes a fancy to you, you will know about it instantly, and so, I should imagine, will anyone within screaming distance.

The long low canoes are negotiated over the bed of this narrow, shallow stream by a mixture of machine and muscle. Up front the pole-man continually tests the depth, indicating to the man in the stern when it is safe to use the outboard. A full throttle charge may get us halfway up a rapid, but then the outboard has to be raised to avoid jarring the propeller, and the pole-man must use his own strength alone to push against the boulders and lever us up to the next patch of deep water. Occasionally both of them have to leap out and push, leaving me sitting there feeling about as useful as the Queen of Sheba.

Between these testing rapids are limpid pools of great beauty, where the sun occasionally pierces the tree-cover turning the dark, bottle-green water into a milky jade. Here we find fishermen, or more accurately fisher boys, wading in, slinging out a weighted net then diving in after it, sometimes pulling out fish in their bare hands. The damming of these rivers has not been good for the local fishermen. Variety has declined as tilapia fish, introduced artificially to boost production, have driven off many indigenous species. Others cannot survive in waters rendered increasingly murky by the slower flow and the erosion of deforested slopes.

However, our boatmen are pleased today to have caught a rare *semas* – the Sarawak state fish – and at lunchtime we pull the boats up onto a stony beach and a fire is made and the fish eaten with rice and a fresh-made *sambal*, a spicy condiment consisting of onion, garlic, peppers, limes, dried shrimp, chillies, soya sauce and other delicacies pounded together in a chunky granite mortar. Big, brightly-coloured butterflies – coffee brown, primrose yellow, malachite green – flutter about in the patches of sunlight.

A lot of the older men have tattoos. Denis tells me that because of the old tradition that tattoos be done away from the longhouse, they have become the mark of a gentleman who has travelled, someone who has seen the world. 'Good sign to women, too,' he assures me, grinning.

After lunch we press on, past the last house on the river and into a no man's land. We reach a waterfall that plunges out of the jungle and stop, strip off and bathe. The day has turned humid and it's wonderfully refreshing to be so thoroughly doused. Completely forget about leeches, and fortunately they forget about me.

Seven o'clock. We're back at the longhouse. The Iban are sitting around cooking and chatting gregariously. The world travellers are silent and exhausted. Steve is at his diary, Fraser is at his laptop, I'm writing my notebook. The irony of a long filmed journey such as this is that the effort and energy, which all of us have to put into recording what we see, means we never see enough. I want to make the most of my limited time in this rich and remote place and yet my body knows I have two-thirds of the Pacific Rim still to go and it is rationing out stamina quite severely. Emong is dying to take me on a walk up the hill behind the longhouse – I'm aware of him pacing the balcony and sighing meaningfully – and, although I'm sure it will be an instructive, possibly unforgettable, almost certainly enjoyable experience, I simply do not have an ounce of energy left.

One hour later. Have just returned from an instructive, enjoyable, possibly unforgettable walk up the hill with Emong. He showed me the profusion of plants and trees in the forest and how almost every human need can be supplied if you know what to look for. There is a seven-candlestick flower whose leaf, called *petai*, cures ringworm and which, when ground up and taken, cleanses the kidney; the *ilbepi* tree which produces a valuable emulsifying agent currently of interest to a German cosmetic company; and another tree, the *pendok*, a thin strip of whose bark is strong enough to carry a weight of 110 pounds. At the top of the hill we came across a small burial area. A few Heineken bottles, a can of Coke and some dusty jam jars lay around cracked and crumbling graves. When I asked Emong why such a sacred place is so badly looked after, he told me that the mess is deliberate. The Iban believe that a well-tended graveyard means you are happy that the people in it are dead.

After an evening meal of roast duck, beef curry, tapioca leaves, jungle fern and bamboo shoots, some highly disturbing news. Apparently James Masing, Sarawak's Minister of Tourism and the guest of honour at tomorrow's feast, is coming here straight from a conference in Nepal, of all places, and may not make it. If this happens I will be guest of honour instead. Which all sounds very nice except that it is Iban custom that the feast cannot take place until the guest of honour has slaughtered a pig.

Fall into light unhealthy sleep, dreaming for some reason, of Sainsbury's.

DAY 111

A loud thwack shakes the roof of the guesthouse where we sleep. Then another, closer to, followed by a third directly above my head. It's like an aerial bombardment in which none of the shells explodes. Extricate myself from the mosquito net and peer out gingerly. A low mist hangs over the forest, somehow amplifying every sound. Denis is already up and quite unfazed by another resounding report.

'War?'

Denis looks at me pityingly, shakes his head and nods towards the shiny green foliage above the guesthouse.

'Mango fruit.' He grins.

I am just about calmed down again when the sound of an over-throttled outboard engine rises up from the river bank.

'Mr Masing has arrived?' I ask eagerly.

Denis lifts his pork-pie hat, rubs his forehead and shakes his head.

'Fishermen,' he says. 'Big day.' No sooner has that noise died away than an unearthly snarling roar emanates from the depths of the jungle, culminating in a shrill, angry whine, a crash and silence. 'Chainsaw,' says Denis. 'Sago palms. For the feast. Big day.'

From across the bridge, beside the longhouse, comes a chorus of terrified, trumpeting squeals.

'Pigs?' I ask, getting the hang of this. 'For the feast?'

Denis nods cheerfully.

159

'That's right.'
'Big day!' we say in chorus.

By the time I'm up and out, two or three pigs have already been killed and chopped up into pieces which are being carefully laid on a log fire by a half-dozen Iban in shorts and T-shirts, who are already enjoying the benefits of a bottle of palm wine. Once the pieces are lightly scorched, they are carried down to the water, scrubbed clean of any remaining hair and taken back to the fire. At the same time glutinous rice is being cooked inside lengths of bamboo. Dogs prowl hopefully.

Inside the longhouse, plaited palm leaves are being wound round the central columns and bunting hung from the roof beams. Along, the headman, is well enough to talk to us. He is a tiny, stick-like figure, skin hanging slack from his arms which, like his back, neck and throat, are copiously tattooed. His face is strong and alert and he has a head of thick grey hair. Emong interprets for me as the old man describes the stomach operation he's just undergone, proudly hoists his shirt, peels off the dressing and shows me the wound.

I am introduced to his friend Badan, who is, at eighty-six, one year older than the headman. He says their tattoos were done many years ago and very painfully, using the traditional method of soap, a pin and soot from the fire.

Both Badan and Along are old enough to remember the time when head-hunting was part of the Iban way of life. They witnessed it as recently as the Second World War and the emergency with Indonesia. The heads would be smoked and there would be a festival to celebrate the event. But the chief dismisses the practice now. 'It was useless. Not good. It was only to show you were stronger than the next man.'

He hasn't much time for the past. He thinks that most things are better today. 'Today generation is good. We not only meet Iban but also meet white people. Meet white people and we eat together, play together, we talk together. There's no more fighting. That's good.'

Before we can play together (and I've heard that the Iban love to party), we have to observe the ritual start of the feast and just as I'm deciding which pair of trousers would show the blood least the arrival of James Masing is announced.

Everyone is delighted to see him, none more so than myself. He is the first Iban ever to become a government minister in a country run politically by Muslims and economically by the Chinese. He looks much more like a real guest of honour, anyway, having with him local politicians and a police escort. Also with him are his daughter Karen and wife Marcia, who wears an 'I Love Kathmandu' T-shirt. Masing is a smallish, powerfully built man with the hunch of a boxer and dark, wary, almost Latin-American looks. He wears a baseball hat and greets everyone with apparently genuine personal interest.

After climbing steps dug into the butterscotch-coloured clay of the river bank he is met by female dancers in silver-bell head-dresses, silver-beaded skirts and glittering tasselled shoulder pieces beneath which can be glimpsed heavy-duty brassieres. Drums and ceremonial gongs are played as the sacrificial pig is brought out, legs trussed, hanging upside down from a pole. As it's laid on the ground, it rolls its eyes as though it now knows what's going to happen and just wants to get it over with.

After ritual sharing and passing around of a cup of *tuak*, a spear is handed to Masing. Some politicians have to kiss babies, but if you want to get re-elected in Borneo, a passing knowledge of butchery is useful. With admirable cool, he places one foot on the pig's head and swiftly punctures its throat.

The ladies in the silver head-dresses and sturdy brassieres then precede him up the plank to the door of the longhouse, where a white cockerel is passed backwards and forwards over his head to ward off evil spirits – though I should imagine jet lag is his main problem at the moment.

Despite having arrived back in Sarawak only the night before, Masing seems to have time for everybody. I talk to him in the guesthouse before the evening celebrations. He defends the building of the Batang Ai dam, saying that before the water level was raised, a place like this would have been virtually inaccessible. (Naturally he regards this as a bad thing.) He's more cautious about Prime Minister Mahatir's much vaunted

161

aim of a developed (i.e. fully industrialized) Malaysia by the year 2020. He doesn't think the Iban will be ready to play much of a part in such a society.

They are an egalitarian people, he says. An Iban headman only holds his power by consent. They dislike being told what to do and will not accept hierarchies, which is why he thinks they have not produced many politicians. Nor are they willing to give up their animist beliefs despite great efforts to bring them into the Muslim or Christian fold. 'They are pragmatic,' says Masing. 'They will see what a god has to offer and take what they want.'

The evening party is a bit of an anti-climax. Most of the men of the longhouse have been drinking throughout the day and the presence of so many politicians and administrative officials seems to have dampened whatever spontaneity they have left.

The highlight of the evening is a group drumming round. Long, thin drums made from bark with tight-stretched deerskin tops are struck hard, fast and ever more furiously with the flat of the hand until one member of the group breaks the rhythm. He then has to down a tumbler of *tuak*, which makes his chances of surviving the next round even more unlikely.

The last thing I remember, as the *tuak* takes effect, is someone describing Iban hospitality as a contest. The host must provide far more food and drink than is strictly necessary and the guests must consume as much as possible without falling over. From what I can see around me as I find my shoes, slither down the plank and head across the bridge to the guesthouse, it appears that the host has won this one hands down.

And the rain is back. Drumming on the roof in a soft, soothing, all-embracing rumble.

DAY 112: *Kuching*

Early in the morning, in a small flotilla of canoes, we take to the river and head south and west, back towards Kuching, leaving a line of chickens at the waterside to peck away at the remains of the feast, and Nanga Sumpa to recover from its hangover.

The surface of the reservoir shines like patent leather in the clear morning light and suddenly we are back amongst schools and fish farms and rubber plantations and the bus is waiting by the dam to take us ever onwards.

Waiting at the hotel in Kuching are two faxed messages from our office in London. One for me and one for Steve. Steve can hardly wait to get upstairs. His new baby is due any time. I'm not expecting any babies – that happened a long time ago – but whenever I'm away I still worry subconsciously about my three children, even though they're better able to look after themselves than I am.

So I ring with some trepidation, and talk to my wife and this is how I learn that she has a meningioma, a benign brain tumour. We must have spent weeks, if not months on the telephone together since we met thirty odd years ago but I never remember a call quite like this. Helen is magnificent, giving me a clear, unsensational explanation of what has happened and bringing me down from near panic-stricken to merely shaken by the end of a fifty minute call.

The facts are that she has had a series of severe headaches, the last of which were accompanied by loss of feeling in her arm. Encouraged by friends and family she had a brain scan two days ago which revealed a large, benign growth, outside the brain, but inside the skull. The neurosurgeon says removal is safe and routine and proposes to operate in four days' time.

My first reaction is to abandon the journey and fly home, but the more we talk, the more Helen persuades me that the time she really wanted me there was over the last few nights when I was incommunicado at the longhouse and she was suffering the worst headaches she has ever had. Now that time is over she feels much better. She is on medication to reduce the chance of any further headaches and she has complete trust in the surgeon. The children are all at home and so many friends and family are helping out that she would rather I stayed working than came home to answer phone calls and pace up and down with worry.

163

She cannot, of course, see me pacing up and down with worry in a hotel room in Kuching.

We both agree that I must talk to the surgeon as soon as possible. This is arranged and he gives me a long, detailed and thorough assessment which concludes that Helen's case is straightforward, will not involve surgery inside the brain and that he doesn't think it necessary for me to return until after the operation.

This is the decision which Helen and I come to.

By the time I finish this, and many other emergency calls, it's dark and I've no idea of the time. My bags lie where I dropped them, unopened, full of muddy boots, wet plastic capes and four days' dirty laundry. The curtains remain undrawn. I walk to the window and stare out at the Sarawak river. It's high tide and the palms that line the opposite bank are half-submerged. Must eat, though I don't want to, so bathe and clean off the mud of the jungle and join the rest of the crew. By appalling coincidence Steve has heard that during the last three days his youngest daughter has had a fall from a window and injured her head. A few hours later his wife went into labour and he now has a third daughter.

We sit in the River Café on Kuching waterfront. A glum, tired, downbeat group tonight, the bad news outweighing the good.

DAY 113

The noonday heat burns like a blow-lamp in the grounds of the Istana, the palace from which Rajah Brooke ruled Sarawak.

I'm talking to Stephen Yong, a lawyer, prominent member of the Chinese community in Kuching and father of Philip, our fixer, about the rule of the White Rajahs. Because of their tolerance of all the different customs and ways of life of their subjects, he thinks they left a valuable legacy of racial harmony in Sarawak. Their major fault, if local tradition is believed, is that they didn't pay enough attention to local superstition. It was foretold that if the tower of the Istana Palace was ever repainted, bad luck would follow. In 1941, the last Rajah,

Vyner Brooke, decided that the whole place should be re-decorated to celebrate a hundred years of Brooke rule. The paint had barely dried when the Japanese army swept up the Sarawak River in armour-plated barges. The country was plundered and Vyner Brooke fled to Australia.

Stephen Yong thinks that their influence survives and certainly, looking across at the immaculate river front, Kuching glows with the civic pride of an overgrown English market town. But rising in the distance and for some reason strangely segregated from the rest of the city, are grandiose corporate towers with more echoes of Seoul and Shanghai than Cirencester. This is where the future lies, and it won't be quaint.

INDONESIA

DAY 114: *Kuching to Jakarta*

The realization of how far away and how helpless I feel is so acute this morning that I make plans to return home and see Helen after the operation and about the time she leaves hospital. It will mean breaking, but not necessarily abandoning, the journey. Both of us are in absolute agreement on this. H continues to sound up-beat. She's been out shopping today for something to wear in hospital. She says she can hardly wait to get in there. Steve's news is also better. His daughter's fall has caused no lasting damage, but she must still undergo tests on one of her eyes.

Time to leave Borneo. Apart from the tantalizing glimpse of life in the rain forest it has not been the wild place I expected. Sabah and Sarawak impress as orderly, efficiently-run states with freshly-painted kerb-stones and corporate comforts. They radiate a glow of soundly-based prosperity, quite unlike the rough and ready Philippines. On the drive to Kuching airport I read in my *New Straits Times* that the Malaysian government is to make whipping mandatory for anyone forging immigration documents. Booming economy, stern society.

Across the South China Sea, across the Equator and into the Southern Hemisphere. From the massive, inaccessible bulk of Borneo, to Java, a long, slim island one fifth Borneo's size with ten times its population. There is nothing inaccessible about Java. A hundred and fifteen million people live on a strip of rich volcanic soil no bigger than England. From what I can see from the plane the only thing it has in common with Kuching is torrential rain. Our plane circles paddy-fields so thick with surface water that it's difficult to tell where the sea ends and the land begins.

Many of the roads are flooded and long lines of traffic crawl towards the centre of the Indonesian capital, Jakarta, beneath the skeleton of an unfinished overhead road system. As we reach the downtown area a forest of corporate high-rises springs up along Jalan Thamrin, towering above the spray and swirl of the twelve-lane highway.

This is the big city, probably the biggest in the southern hemisphere. Its energy is palpable, its size impersonal and, after the soft, warm space of Sarawak, it cannot help but sink the spirits.

DAY 115: *Jakarta*

'Ramadan – Month of Self-Restraint', headlines the *Jakarta Post*, poked under my door at six o'clock. Ninety per cent of the Indonesian population is Muslim so the life of the country will be seriously affected by the festival, which requires true believers to refrain from eating, drinking and sex between dawn and dusk for twenty-nine consecutive days. More seriously it is announced that *Baywatch* has been temporarily removed from the television schedules.

'Muslims see Ramadan as a month of blessing that provides them with the opportunity to purify themselves', the paper explains. Only the sick and aged, pregnant women, nursing mothers and those who are travelling long distances are exempt. But what about those travelling only short distances? Will they be weaving about the road, concentration sapped by tiredness and hunger? How dangerous is the journey we are about to embark on?

All of these questions I put to my Indonesian travelling companion, Eko Binarso as we pull out onto the wet, steamy streets of Jakarta shortly after eight o'clock on a 650-mile drive between here and the north-eastern port of Surabaya from which we shall try to find a boat through the islands and on to Australia.

Eko, short, thick-haired, mid-thirties, founder of a successful trekking business, reckons that on the whole people drive more calmly during Ramadan as their stomachs are less full, and because true Muslims are not supposed to lose their temper with anyone during daylight hours. It's not really worth my while challenging these theories because Eko delivers them all with a twinkling, inscrutable smile which makes it very hard to know whether anything he says is true or not.

On the other hand, it may be that he is inhibited from saying what he really thinks owing to the presence of Mr Suherto. As in Vietnam and China, we have to take with us a government minder – someone who makes things more difficult by helping us. In Indonesia it is the short, amiably anxious, terminally confused Mr Suherto. He refers to our work as our 'activity' – as in 'What is your activity today?' or 'Where is your next activity?'.

We drive for a while on a stretch of well-kept motorway, flanked with huge billboards advertising golf ranges and polo-playing holidays. It lasts only 37 miles before petering out into a clogged two-lane hard-top.

For a fasting country there is an awful lot of food about. The roadside is stacked with bananas, yams, melon, rambutan, avocado and, of course, the famously smelly delicacy *durian*, which, as they say here, 'smells like him, tastes like her'.

About 55 miles out of Jakarta, we stop off at Gunung Mas, a sprawling tea plantation where the short, carefully cropped bushes spread in a great green crust, close and tight over the hillsides. In amongst them move the redoubtable lines of pickers, all women, in their uniform of wide-brimmed rattan hats, headscarves, blue and white track-suit tops, skirts over trousers and stout rubber boots. They move across the hills like human locusts, metre-deep baskets slung on their backs, snipping remorselessly.

The man in the tea-tasting room pulls in his cheeks, gurgles, spits and talks of 'a good plucking'. Although soil and climate are vitally important for quality (we are at 3000 feet here) the skill of the pickers is what can make the difference. The welly-booted women of Gunung Mas are not just formation hedge-clippers they are, in their way, experts, looking for the precision of one bud and two leaves from the most succulent young growths – what they call the PG (Premier Growth) tips.

Our destination for the night is the city of Bandung. A couple of traffic lights' distance from our hotel we are ambushed by a well-drilled squad of young men selling city maps, carvings, bits of batik and large colour pictures of the stars of *Baywatch*.

DAY 116: *Bandung to Yogyakarta*

Mox Salvus Redeas – 'May you soon return safe' – is a fine motto for any traveller, especially for those, like ourselves, plodding round the Pacific Rim with many thousands of miles still to go, but it is not one I would expect to find in a hotel in Java. But here they are, curling round the top of an arch as we leave the Savoy Homan Hotel in Bandung. It is a colonial hotel and, as the Dutch were the colonizers of much of Indonesia, it is not surprising that its extraordinary art-deco design is the work of a Dutchman, Aalbers. Completed in the 1930s, the Savoy Homan's elegant lines and stylish decoration would not look out of place in the swankiest parts of Manhattan. In fact its current state of health is largely the work of an unflaggingly enthusiastic American, Frances B. Affandy. She describes its design as 'Streamlined Deco' on the outside and 'Tropical Deco' inside. She has restored rich, detailed decorative work, including a fine 15-foot bas-relief mural, which superimposes the brave new world of European technology onto a giant map of agricultural Java.

Colonial affinities still influence the patterns of tourism. As we leave, a group of Dutch arrive. They stand in the lobby marvelling at the optimism of their forefathers. But it was only six years after Aalbers completed his work that the Japanese invaded. Here, as in the rest of South-East Asia, the Japanese lost the war but dragged European colonial rule down with them. The Dutch tried to hang onto the East Indies after 1945, but four years later, defeated in a War of Independence, they pulled out of Java for good.

Not far along our way this morning is evidence of the seismic instability that makes this island a farmer's and a vulcano-logist's paradise. Piles of rich black soil stacked by the roadside are the remains of deposits from nearby Mount Galunggung, one of Java's thirty active volcanoes. Galunggung had its fifteen minutes of fame in 1982, when its plume of freshly-discharged volcanic ash enshrouded an over-flying 747, shutting down all four of its engines. The plane plunged, but by some miracle the pilot was able to restore enough power to enable him to land safely in Jakarta.

The violent, unpredictable energy of the volcanoes has created a Garden of Eden as well as a killing field. These plains may have seen devastation and destruction but for now the rich, intensively cultivated countryside on the road between Bandung and Ciamis is unequivocally friendly. Amphitheatres of terracing rise on both sides of a narrow valley. I count forty-eight levels on one side alone, all still worked by traditional methods. Men with long-handled rakes push the mud back and forth to make it ready for sowing and women, wading in up to their knees, insert the carefully husbanded rice shoots. The colour and quality of the soil on these slopes is unlike anything I've seen. It's deep maroon, a rich plum-coloured satin.

One of the pleasures of Java is that so much of the island is as yet unspoiled by agribusiness. The main road remains a single carriageway and we are as likely to be held up behind a pony and trap as an over-laden banana lorry. The houses, standing amongst green fields and flower-strewn verges, are solidly built. Unplastered red brick walls are softened by shady wooden porches, louvered shutters and pantiled roofs more

169

reminiscent of Provence than the East Indies. Nearly every one of them, however humble, sports a satellite dish.

Once into Central Java, the countryside becomes less intimate and regimented lines of spindly white rubber trees stretch away on either side of us, bowing and bending in the wind like mourners at a funeral.

At Yogyakarta, where we spend the night, I put a call through to the National Hospital in London. Helen's operation was completed thirty minutes ago. I'm assured that it has been 'textbook' and asked if I would like to send her a message. So I send my love and, best of all, she is already conscious enough to send hers back.

DAY 117: *Yogyakarta*

Marhaban Ya Ramadan – 'Welcome to Ramadan' – reads the white lettering on green banners strung across the Dutch colonial streets of Yogyakarta, the ancient cultural capital of Java. Ramadan means many things, including waking up very early, whether you're a Muslim or not.

If you are a Muslim then your first meal must be prepared and consumed before sunrise. Calls to prayer rend the small hours and at 4.10 I am woken by what sounds like the start of a revolution but turns out to be a salvo of firecrackers.

Our hotel is on the Jalan Malioboro, which is named, not after a cigarette, but after the Duke of Marlborough, a name it must have received during the brief period at the start of the nineteenth century when the British ruled Java. Malioboro leads down towards the Kraton, the eighteenth-century palace of the Sultans of Yogyakarta. It is set within four square walls, each one about two-thirds of a mile in length, in which there are nine gates, symbolizing, we are told, the nine entrances to the human body. (In the bus afterwards none of us could come up with more than seven. Or eight at most. Not including bullet holes.) None of these gates opens directly onto a courtyard – usually there is a wall facing it. This was intended to confuse evil spirits who might rush headlong in. Nowadays there are more mundane admission controls. A sign beside the brass-studded teak doors depicts two cartoon torsos, one of which is squeezed into a lurid patterned pair of Y-fronts, while the other bulges out of a clinging pair of white shorts. Alongside both is the word 'NO'.

Having changed out of our Y-fronts, we pass through into an eclectic mix of buildings ranging from Hindu-Javanese temples, Islamic mosques, classical-columned pavilions to a wrought iron and stained glass, belle-époque, French bandstand. Elderly retainers in long batik sarongs brush the gravel in the courtyards and sweep the dusty tourist footprints off the tiles. There is a slightly seedy air to the huge place typified by the condition of the Golden Pavilion. This glorious concoction of gold leaf, marble floor and teak pillars supporting a magnificent tiered roof is said to represent Mount Meru, the centre of the universe. Yet at the very centre of the pavilion and, by extension, the very centre of the universe, is a growing pile of droppings from the birds' nests in the roof.

Another disappointment is that the recitals of gamelan – the best known and most admired of Java's traditional music – have been temporarily suspended. A large blackboard explains, crisply: 'During Ramadan, there'll be no dance, no music'.

Later: With the help of Joan, a Hawaiian married to a gamelan instructor, we have a chance to hear a gamelan orchestra at work at an impromptu session organized in the garden of a house in a quiet neighbourhood not far from the centre of Yogya.

Gamelan, deriving from the Javanese *gamel*, meaning a hammer, is percussive music played on gongs (gong is a Javanese word too), hand drums and bronze xylophones, though flutes and a two-stringed instrument called a *rebab* often supplement the percussion. The sound of gamelan music has been likened to that of flowing water.

Tonight we'll have chance to hear for ourselves as a fourteen-piece orchestra assembles and the gongs are laid out, some flat in a frame, others hanging. The musicians are all men, a number of them well beyond middle-age, with thick pebble glasses. One is an albino.

While they are warming up under the mango and jackfruit trees that offer some cover from the occasional drifting shower, I make a phone call to the surgeon who has performed Helen's operation and who has been so patient and reassuring with all my questions over the past few days. He confirms that all went well, that the meningioma was benign and has been completely and successfully removed. Then he breaks off and asks me what the noise is in the background.

'It's something called a gamelan orchestra,' I begin, about to embark on a long explanation.

'I thought so!' He exclaims. 'The man who's teaching me to play the saxophone leads a gamelan orchestra.'

'In London?'

'Yes.'

This unlikely piece of synchronicity is oddly comforting. Ridiculous, I know, but when I go back into the garden the music of Java reminds me of home.

The music is only half of the evening's entertainment. Joan has also found a *dalang*, a puppeteer, to present the traditional shadow play which they call *wayang kulit*. A good *dalang* is a bit like a pop star out here. They have their own 'roadies' who set up the cotton screen, arrange the lighting and bring them cups of tea during the performance. The best of them can command three million *rupiah* for the night (around three thousand pounds). For that they have to create an entire epic; working, providing the voices and doing the sound effects for forty or fifty separate puppets.

When tonight's performance is about to start, the children sit, legs drawn up, on the floor in front of the screen. Most of the adults are more interested in watching the musicians behind it. Clouds of flies buzz around them in the sticky warmth of the evening as the *dalang* settles himself cross-legged behind a long white cotton sheet, slips on a chunky old-fashioned neck microphone and selects the first two stick puppets from a long line of them stuck into a length of soft banana palm bark. The lights dim leaving only a large white bulb illuminating the front of the screen and a single green one behind it. A spindly, demonic figure appears on the screen with hands and arms swinging. A high, shrill voice comes from the *dalang*. The bronze gongs start to sound, softly at first, like leaves blown in the wind.

Wayang kulit is not for the faint-hearted. The stories are based on the great Hindu epics like the *Mahabharata* and the *Ramayana* and each performance lasts eight hours, though the dalang can interpret them, edit them and embellish them as he or she wishes. *Wayang kulit* has been used to disseminate political propaganda and, during the struggle for independence, was widely used to spread anti-Dutch sentiment. After an hour and a half of sustained performance the *dalang*'s assistant slips him his first cup of tea. My head's already dropping. The battle scenes temporarily rouse my flagging spirits. The puppets twist and turn and hurtle about in a frenzy of splits and scissors and somersaults. The musicians join in with grunts and shouts.

As the night wears on Joan assures me that we've done very well. The longest show they usually do for tourists lasts one hour.

DAY 119: *Yogyakarta to Borobudur*

The monsoon rains are back as we leave Yogyakarta. It's the morning rush hour. A swirl of people on gurgling mopeds, hoods down and plastic capes flapping, head into the city like a flock of strange birds.

Out in the countryside, swelled by twelve hours of continuous downpour, rivers the colour of strong tea are running wide and fast. In the rice fields work goes on under a forest of plastic umbrellas.

Not far from Yogya there rises one of the great monuments of the world, the huge Buddhist temple of Borobudur, a massive construction of black larval stone that has stood on a low hill surrounded by rice fields and coconut groves for twelve hundred years. Rather like the Nileside temples in the sands of the Sahara, Borobudur was neglected, overgrown and

173

half-submerged when, at the beginning of the nineteenth century, it attracted the attention of European colonists. Stamford Raffles, founder of Singapore, who once administered Java, wrote a book about the 'rediscovery' of Borobudur that captured the Western imagination and from that time on it was progressively repaired and restored. Work still goes on, supervised by UNESCO who have spent over twenty million dollars here.

The huge complex is designed as a series of five terraces which represent a *mandala*, a symbol of the harmony of the universe. The terraces form a path to enlightenment that runs around the temple for almost two miles. It is flanked by walls intricately and profusely decorated with stone relief carvings depicting the Buddha's own search for enlightenment.

The great black basalt mass looks dour and unpromising as Eko and I mount the first steep steps. But rich rewards for perseverance are to be found along the way. In the soft, friable rock, beautiful panels have been carved. Although there are other abstract designs, it is the scenes of everyday life which are most affecting. Human figures and facial expressions are caught with an intimacy and immediacy that is almost shockingly modern. At various points on our way intriguing notices read 'No Scratching!'. A jovial, hard-hatted UNESCO official who is checking moss deposits sees me puzzling over them. 'It does not mean no scratching of the *body* sir! . . . No scratching of the *stones*.' Six hundred builders and stonemasons, he says, were required to replace two million stones during the recent nine year restoration period so they're understandably touchy about them.

On the top of Borobudur, a single solid *stupa* – the pointed bell-like dome common to Buddhist temples – is surrounded by concentric rings of smaller domes. Eko surveys the view.

'We are in heaven now,' he says.

'The centre of the universe?'

'Of the *galaxy*.'

As he explains, the location of a monument like this would not be arbitrary. Enormous importance would have been attached to its exact positioning. Looking around me, I can, for

PREVIOUS PAGE: *Welcoming the Minister outfit.*

ABOVE: *With tea pickers at Gunung Mas.*

LEFT: *Gamelan musician and gongs which help to produce music like 'moonlight and flowing water'.*

TOP RIGHT: *'The centre of the Galaxy': stupas and surrounding volcanoes at the top of Borobudur temple, Java.*

RIGHT: *Raine, Bluey and the crocodile midwife.*

LEFT: *The Mount Cook massif – highest point in Australasia.*

ABOVE: Monty Python's *definition of a king – the only one who's not got shit all over him.*

RIGHT: *The shrine of a thousand plastic bottles on the road to Puerto Natales, Chile.*

the first time, appreciate why this great man-mountain is where it is. It is equidistant from five volcanoes, three of them over 10,000 feet high, not only putting it at the symbolic centre of a universe but acknowledging the symbiotic relationship between man and the volcanoes from which this land was created. Eko says that now only one thing remains to be done. 'You are ready for climbing now, Michael?' Tomorrow, he promises, we shall look into the mouth of a volcano.

DAY 120: *Mount Bromo to Surabaya*

My alarm clock sounds at 3.10 in the morning. It doesn't take much to wake me as I've been kept on the edge of consciousness by bone-numbing coldness. The surroundings are unfamiliar. A timber cabin. And the smell. Not since we left the northern Philippines have I smelt pine.

Gradually I assemble the pieces. After yesterday's drive across into East Java, during which we avoided certain death about once an hour on a treacherous road packed with cars, fuel tankers, goats, men with grass strapped to their bicycles and coaches hurtling down the middle of the road, accelerators and horns hard down, we ended up in the foothills of the Tengger Highlands. Steep gradients and hairpins brought us up slowly but surely into cool refreshing mountain air, 7000 feet above sea level.

Cool and refreshing it may have been last night, this morning it is just bitterly cold as I delve into the bottom of my suitcase for every sweater I can find, all the while cursing sunrises, volcanoes, television documentaries and everything that has brought me to this god-forsaken place at this god-forsaken time.

A cup of coffee and a bar of chocolate later, it's 3.45 and I'm sat astride a small pony heading off into the darkness. The sky is clear, there is no wind and the stars are out. A group of local guides watch their ponies anxiously as they bear us off down a stony track. We are a motley posse. Some Japanese, an Australian or two. The only thing we have in common is an inability to ride.

After half an hour the stony track levels out and I feel a little more confident astride my podgy little mount, comforted by the warmth he emits as I put my hand to his neck. We strike out across a solid, dusty plain. The first pale shades of blue and white creep into the pitch-black sky and it's like having a blindfold lifted.

At first sight we are in a stark, silent, vaguely menacing landscape, unlike anything I have ever seen. And the more the light fills the sky the stranger it becomes. We are crossing a deeply fissured surface between looming ridges of volcanic ash stretching, like giant splayed fingers, up to the top of the nearest peak. A lone cloud hovers above the peak and I catch an unmistakable smell of sulphur. We are near to our destination, Mount Bromo, active volcano. Height: 7639 feet above the sea. Latest substantial eruption: last October.

We leave our horses and climb two hundred steps to the rim of the cone. The scene behind us is biblical. A column lit by lamps and torches is crossing the dusty plain and heading towards us, occasionally vanishing from sight behind the dunes of freshly-spewed lava.

I pick my way cautiously along the narrow lip of the volcano and, when I have found a secure footing, peer down inside for the first time. Five hundred feet below me at the bottom of a great blasted bowl of earth is a black hole from which rises, slowly and steadily, a hissing plume of white steam, soft as a sigh at the moment but brooding and threatening, like a fuse attached to explosive.

This is for me as great a manifestation of the earth's natural power as was looking over into the Victoria Falls. There everything was falling in. Here on the edge of Mount Bromo, I'm looking at what has been blasted out. Brand new landscape, oven-fresh and still steaming. Rock so new that you could write your name in it.

I stay as long as I can, until the crowds of gabbling visitors have gone and a hazy pale-lemon sun has risen. Apart from myself there's only Fraser left on the rim of the volcano, microphone boom pointed downwards, recording the sinister wheezing of the earth.

We leave Bromo and the Tengger highlands mid-morning. In my case, reluctantly. It is not only the spectacular land-scape I shall miss. The weather I was so rude about early this morning is now almost perfect. The sun shines from a sky skimmed with high cirrus cloud, the air is dry and fresh, the temperature 70° Fahrenheit with a gentle breeze that comes and goes.

The people in the villages we pass on the way down are mostly Hindus, pushed to the farthest end of the island during the Muslim conquest of Java in the seventeenth century. They make a precarious living in every sense of the word, growing onions, leeks, cabbages and other crops on sheer slopes that seem to defy gravity.

Surabaya, a city of four million and the capital of East Java, lacks the beauty of its name. It's a city of red roofs rapidly being superseded by the bland, modern, high-rises typical of so many Pacific Rim boom towns. Like many of them, it had very little option but to modernize. Having survived the Second World War, Surabaya was almost destroyed by the peace. After the Japanese surrender in 1945 young members of an Indonesian republican party were suspected of assassinating the British General Mallaby, sent to oversee Allied occupation of the city. A battle ensued which raged for three weeks, during which the city was flattened by Allied bombing and thousands of its occupants killed by Dutch troops. It was one of the key moments on the road to Indonesia's independence four years later and earned Surabaya the title of Heroes' City.

As we drive into the centre we pass a roundabout dominated by the Hero Monument. It portrays a massive crocodile wrestling with a shark.

DAY 121: *Surabaya*

In the oldest part of the harbour in Surabaya the *pinisi* boats are moored. The *pinisi* are the old, tall-masted, high-prowed sailing boats that carry most of the goods between the islands of the Indonesian archipelago. Made out of wood, they are constructed entirely without plans or written designs. In this they resemble the state of our journey at the moment.

We had hoped to find a route across the Timor Sea through the islands to Australia, now a little more than 1000 miles away. Normally this would have been well within the range of the *pinisi* but it is late January and the winds and currents are all in the wrong direction. No one will take us east. This is doubly frustrating as I like what I see of these traditional trading ships. They remind me of the dhows of the Persian Gulf and the people who sail them. There is the same sense of local, native skills, operating outside the international mercantile system, the same feeling of family and friends doing business in the same way they have for centuries. It's not a world which welcomes outsiders.

We may have reached an impasse, but it could not have come at a better time. I ring the hospital. Helen has made such good progress that she has been cleared to go home. Thanks to the vagaries of the Timor Sea, I am going home as well.

AUSTRALIA

DAY 126: *Darwin*

Darwin, Australia, is 1200 miles from Surabaya. I don't recommend going via London unless you really have to as it adds 16,000 miles to the journey. For Steve and myself the long loop around the world, and the short, sharp shock of exposure to a northern winter, have been worth all the effort. Steve's daughters, old and new, are fine and Helen is well enough to request me not to go interviewing head-hunters for a while.

Jet travel can so compress one's sensations of time and space that last night, as we crossed the Australian coast, descending into Darwin to rejoin the crew, the grey estuary of the Thames and the blood-red effluent of the Daly River below seemed only a few miles apart. Though we have been away four days it's almost as though we had never left the tropics.

This morning, however, as we roll south on the long straight road out of Darwin there is a great sense of change. We are out of the crowded Asian Pacific seaboard and into the great empty spaces of Australasia. In Java there were eight hundred and fifty people for every square kilometre of land, in Australia, just two.

A nineteenth-century Welsh naturalist called Alfred Wallace, who made a detailed study of animal life on both sides of the Timor Sea, argued that there was a clear evolutionary distinction between the Oriental and the Australasian land masses. Recently his conclusions were borne out by geologists who now seem sure that a hundred and fifty million years ago a vast continent called Gondwanaland, which comprised what we now know as Australia, Antarctica, India, Arabia, Africa and South America, began to split and drift apart on the moving rollers of the earth's crust called tectonic plates. Australia moved the least of all these great land masses and has remained stable and largely unchanged for millions of years, except for the long, slow processes of erosion. While its near neighbour Java is one of the newest, least stable and most fertile lands in the world, Australia is one of the oldest, driest, and most inhospitable.

The Australians themselves are not at all inhospitable. And they're certainly not dry. My *Rough Guide* describes alcohol consumption in Darwin as 'legendary', estimating that they knock back about 50 gallons a year for every man, woman *and* child. After Ramadan this all comes as a bit of a shock.

Up here in the green and scrubby north which Australians call the Top End, we are as close to Singapore as Sydney, and a sturdy independence prevails. The locals do not take kindly to rules, reckoning that if you're mad enough to come and live here the last thing you want is someone telling you what to do. This is the general impression I get from talking with Scotty (soon or later everyone's name is rounded off with a 'y' here) who is driving me, and 170 feet of trailer, down the Stuart Highway towards the town of Katherine. Scotty is short, stocky with a solid black moustache and dark, curly hair squashed beneath a baseball cap. He drives the longest, heaviest commercial truck combinations in the world, the road trains. They move food and goods enormous distances right across Australia.

It's like being aboard some great mediaeval war machine. I'm in a cab perched seven feet above the road surrounded by a shining assortment of air cleaners and exhaust stacks. Below me are about 2000 litres of fuel slung in six gleaming heat-reflecting chrome tanks. Eighteen gears operate a Cummins 500 horsepower diesel engine which rolls three Fridge-Trans trailers down the long straight highway at a maximum permitted 56 miles an hour. Visors protect lights and windscreens against stones and bugs, leaving the four-foot high bull bars to deal with anything bigger.

Scotty last hit a kangaroo a week back. He was quite un-happy about it, as it struck the side and damaged his wheel.

'Best place to hit them is straight on. If you see them bounce off you know you're all right.'

In front of us is a mini flight deck of dials and gadgets, computers and radio equipment and, behind, a capacious sleeping compartment upholstered in padded and buttoned leather like a corner of a gentleman's club.

By lunchtime we're out of the green swampy coastland and beginning to hit hot, reddish-brown rock and scrubland sparsely covered with spear grass and the peeling black and white barks of fire-damaged gum trees. Scotty pulls us off the highway at a place called Emerald Springs, which appears to consist only of a pub, the Riverside Inn. Signs are hung by the door. 'G'day Mate', 'Welcome' and 'All Pets To Be Tied Up Please'.

Honey-eaters perch in the rafters, swooping with a loud *whee-k*! to clear crumbs off the tables or strut cheekily along the bar, which is made of sleepers from a single-track railway which, until 1977, ran from Emerald Springs to Katherine. There is talk of building a railway right the way from Alice to Darwin, but Scotty doesn't think this will happen in his lifetime. Transport up here means trucks. As far as I can see the only reading matter in the pub is a copy of *Big Rigs – The National Newspaper For Truckers*. The cover features a full-frontal of the Ford Aeromax-120. After lunch we prepare to head south again.

'A good feed,' Scotty reckons as we climb aboard. The Cummins starts with the kick and roar of a startled horse.

'It's an air start,' Scotty advises, 'not an electric start.'

Now I know.

In the blazing heat of the afternoon I see my first emu. It's little more than a heap of feathers lying by the roadside, and if Scotty hadn't obligingly pointed it out I wouldn't have known it was an emu at all.

We roll across the Eugene Betty bridge over the Katherine River at five in the afternoon to be confronted by the most celebrated traffic lights in Australia. Recently installed in the centre of town, they are the only set of lights for 1000 miles.

DAY 127: *Katherine*

Very early this morning, while the temperatures are only in the upper twenties, we make our way out to a small airstrip a mile or two from Katherine to join the Flying Vet, Peter Trembath, who has agreed to let us accompany him for a couple of days to see the land and its animals.

The airstrip is deserted when we arrive, apart from two single-engined Cessnas. Air Control, who's called Dave, and his dog Jabba, come out to greet us. Just before 7.00 a.m. Trembath arrives. He's as lean and trim as Dave is big and pudgy. He wears a green golf shirt and matching baseball hat bearing the words 'Katherine Vet Care', and carries a cat called Arthur in a cage. He has just had a hip operation – Arthur that is – and is mewing disconsolately. Jabba plods over and sniffs curiously at the freshly-stitched scar.

Dave is not happy. 'Landing problems. Fitzroy's out, 38 millimetres last night. Coolibah's too wet.'

This is the monsoon season. 'The Wet' as they call it here. It accounts for why much of the area around Katherine is good cattle country, and why the flies are already out, worrying away at my face and settling around my eyes and ears.

Peter Trembath seems unfazed. He smiles a wholesome toothy grin and decides to get up into the air 'and see what we can find'. After the rains, flying conditions are more stable, the air currents less volatile. He flies his own aircraft. Such are the distances he has to travel on his rounds, there's no other way of getting to his customers. We bump and bounce off the red sand and sparse grass of the airstrip and head north. The Northern Territory is bigger than France, Great Britain and Germany put together but has only 160,000 inhabitants, a quarter of whom are descendants of the Aboriginals who came to Australia across the islands of Indonesia, forty thousand years ago. The first white man to reach this remote land was the explorer John McDouall Stuart a hundred and thirty-four years ago.

We're crossing a tableland of intricately incised escarpments, red crusts of rock pushing clear of a thin green carpet of trees. The canyons grow deeper and more spectacular as the Katherine River cuts into the high plateau of Arnhem Land and Peter banks and turns to give me the best view. Below us the river turns this way and that, being harried into dramatic ninety degree swings as it picks its way through pale-red gorges.

Having shown me the sights, it's time for business. Peter swings the Cessna to the south-west, heading for 'Bluey' Pugh's farm, or 'station' as they call them out here. After a couple of hours Peter checks his course then leans forward over the joystick.

'That's his place down there, I think.'

'You don't seem very sure?'

'No, never am.'

He settles for another cluster of buildings further on, where mudbanks squeeze the lazy red waters of the Victoria River into a narrow stream.

'That's the one!'

Bluey and Janelle Pugh have been farming crocodiles for five years. This being Australia, 'Bluey' has red hair and a red moustache. Together with their young daughter, Raine, they live in a characterful outback house with a corrugated iron roof, brick-floored verandah and cluttered, companionable concrete-floored living rooms. A flock of white cockatoos flies up as we land in the field outside, and kites and the small but distinctive wedge-tailed eagles circle above, constantly in attendance, waiting for what the crocs don't eat.

Bluey is a big man, given to running his hand lazily across his close-cropped hair. When he talks his delivery is slow, soft and unhurried. The crocodile market is mainly French, he says. His best skins go to Gucci, Cardin and Hermés, and currently fetch around twelve dollars fifty per centimetre, about five times as much as those of alligators. Alligators, on the other hand, are cheaper to feed, requiring only prepared food in the form of a biscuit.

'And crocodiles?'

Bluey strokes his head.

'Wild horses. Feral animals. Horses are good – high in phosphorus, low in fat, lots of good protein.'

'You feed horses to crocodiles?'

He nods amiably.

'Mince 'em up. Add a few vitamins.'

My eye is drawn unwillingly to a large wall-chart above the sofa, 'Land Snakes of the Northern Territory'.

'Do you get many round here?'

'We get a lot of Western Browns . . . '

His nine-year-old daughter Raine comes in, trailing long red hair like Alice in Wonderland.

'There was one in my towel last week.'

'Then there's pythons,' Bluey drawls on, 'they're not a problem, they eat all the rats and the frogs. No, it's the King Browns you godda look out for. They chase after you. We had one come through that door once, didn't we?'

Janelle shouts back from the kitchen.

'I hit it with a shovel and the shovel bounced right off its back!'

They all laugh nostalgically. Janelle appears and lays a plate of fresh-baked chocolate cake on the table.

Out on the farm you can tell which are the crocodile sheds long before you get to them. A rank, rotten smell of ammonia and dead meat hangs in the noonday heat. Bluey shows me inside. The temperature is kept at a constant 32° centigrade (which today is a good three degrees cooler than it is outside). As soon as Bluey lifts one of the polystyrene covers there is a sudden thrashing, clacking scuffle as dozens of metre-long crocs slither over each other, jaws snapping angrily. The underside of the cover is crawling with cockroaches. 'Our secret food source,' says Bluey. He reaches in, picks up a croc by its tail and, without ceremony, whacks its head on the side of the pen.

'Green dream,' he says and grins.

The ex-croc is taken to a shed next door where Peter sets to work opening it up in order to try to trace a mystery infection which has affected a growing number of the two and a half thousand animals on the farm. He traces it to a lung and takes a section away to be analysed. In the back of the shed, industrial fridges hum away protecting Bluey's newest investment – hundreds of crocodile eggs which he and his men risked life and limb (particularly limb) to collect from nearby swamps. Janelle must have noticed my look of disapproval.

'Only one per cent of those eggs survives in the wild,' she points out. '*Seventy* per cent survive in controlled conditions here.'

As if to convince me of this haven of crocodile happiness, Bluey appears with a tray of eggs, about four inches long, one of which he hands to me.

'What do I do?'

'Just break the top.'

(The use of the word 'just' by an Australian means that whatever it is you have to do, it will not be easy, as in 'Just pull that sword out of the stone' or 'Just split that atom'.) Sure enough my hands begin to tremble as I pick away at the shell, feeling as I do so the corresponding thrust of a sharp pointed object trying to help me from inside. Then all at once we are united. A slimy, wriggling, miniature dinosaur strains to get out of my fingers as it strained to get out of the egg. Only then does it occur to me that I've just delivered a crocodile.

After lunch (crocodile curry, cooked by Bluey) we toil out into almost intolerable heat, now over 100° Fahrenheit, to watch Peter's most difficult consultation. A fully grown, 14-foot-long croc has to be hauled out, sedated and examined. Bluey and Patrick, one of his men, get a line over the croc's snout, and he is dragged from the grass and mud of his enclosure, lashing, turning and twisting out of a gate in the fencing. His jaw and back legs are unceremoniously gaffer taped, a piece of sacking is thrown over his head, and he's given a Valium jab. While Peter goes to work on a nasty raw nasal abscess I ask Bluey, who has been at the thick of the battle to get him out, if, after all we've seen today, he's still afraid of crocodiles. 'Oh, yeah,' he smiles and tugs on the ring in his ear. 'That's what keeps me going. Fear.'

I remember these words an hour or two later. We are half-way through our 200-mile flight back to Katherine when the darkening sky ahead of us is rent with tremendous flashes of lightning. Two great black slabs of rain-cloud are rolling at extraordinary speed towards us, like a massive pair of gates closing. I'm the only other occupant of Peter's Cessna, which suddenly seems very frail and fragile. Worst of all, Peter, normally full of wisecracks, has gone very quiet. He keeps looking down at the instruments and speaking rapidly into his headset. The storm is terrific to look at but I'd rather be seeing it from below. The black shrouds of rain are by now blotting out all but a tiny crack of the horizon ahead of us. Peter has the plane at full throttle but it looks for a moment as though this will not be enough. We are within an ace of being engulfed when we slip through and put down at an Australian Air Force base.

At seven o'clock, safely landed, the rain is sheeting down and we stand tired, but happy, waiting for Peter's wife to come and pick us up. With us, in two long tubes with wooden, punctured ends, are four live crocodiles.

DAY 128: *Eva Valley*

Peter has a real treat in store for me today. He wants me to help him castrate dogs at an Aboriginal settlement in the Eva Valley. 'Beautiful bit of country down there,' he adds, in case I'm not already champing at the bit.

185

By ten o'clock we're coming down low over scrubby wattle and gum trees, interspersed with termite mounds and the occasional drifting herd of wild donkeys. Since the Land Rights Act of 1976 about half of the Northern Territory has been returned to the Aboriginals, many of whom, like the Eskimos of Alaska, live away from the cities, have their own native councils and reject the whole idea of assimilation into a predominantly white culture. The community we are heading for is called Manyallaluk, and supports one hundred and fifty Aboriginals in aluminium frame houses set amongst newly planted trees and trim green grass. It operates a tour company and there is a shop selling Aboriginal arts and crafts. There is a strict no alcohol rule here. Peter reckons it's one of the best Aboriginal settlements. I have the feeling from the way he says it that he does not rate the competition very highly.

As we bounce down on another red earth airstrip a tall man with a big saggy belly, broad shoulders and a wide smile steps out to greet us. This is Peter the headman and he's followed by half a dozen curious little boys. They show particular interest in a Wet Wipe with which I'm cleaning ink from my fingers. I hand them one each and they set to cleaning their entire bodies with great enthusiasm.

Peter and his English assistant, Trish, who visit here three times a year, are looking for somewhere to hold the surgery. They settle for a spot beneath the shade of a low-hanging flamboyant tree. A collapsible table is produced. 'This is luxury,' says Trish as she lays out the containers, the serums and the hypodermics. I'm despatched to fill a bucket of water. (The tap is right next to a particularly evil-looking dog who eyes me with brooding malevolence, probably mistaking me for whoever clipped his balls off last time.) The two Peters calculate how many candidates there are for castration (15 dollars) and spaying (30 dollars). Many of them will also have to be 'needled' – given a jab against worms, mange and scabies.

Then the rounding up begins. It is complete mayhem. The dogs race off in all directions, barking frantically. Their owners race after them. Most agile of these is a very elderly lady with wild grey hair and a Mickey Mouse T-shirt who sprints round the flower-beds and eventually grabs her dog in a full-length tackle and drags it kicking and screaming towards the table. Peter, nimbly avoiding its snarling jaws, prepares a quick jab of Metamil, a heroin-based sedative, which will have it ready to be operated on in fifteen minutes. As Peter moves in with the syringe, the dog's eyes roll upwards and it howls to the heavens as if possessed by demons. Gradually the terrifying noise subsides and, as the Metamil begins to take effect, the ground beneath the flamboyant tree is littered with canine casualties in various stages of consciousness.

Peter and Trish get to work and I stand by with the bucket to collect any odd testicles and bits of ovary that might come my way. The process evokes nostalgic reminiscences from the crew. Basil had once photographed a horse being castrated in Kalgoorlie; Fraser had been the sound recordist when the broadcaster Tom Vernon, having watched a castration in Argentina, was offered the testicles fried for supper that evening. When I ask if anyone amongst us has ever eaten them Steve nods modestly.

DAY 130: *Katherine to King's Creek*

Katherine (population 11,000) was named after the daughter of one of the patrons of the explorer John MacDouall Stuart, who, in 1860, first successfully crossed the Red Centre of Australia and finally laid to rest the myth that a huge lake existed there. The 730 miles from Katherine to Alice is a lonely ride. South of Alice Springs the Stuart Highway shares the desert with a railway line begun in 1877 and finished in 1929. It was called the Ghan, because it was largely constructed by Afghan cameleers whose beasts were best suited to the harsh, dry, desert conditions. When construction finished the camels were turned loose. They bred so successfully in the outback that nowadays the wild camels of Australia are not only in demand from zoos and game parks but much prized in countries like Oman and Saudi Arabia for breeding and racing.

Today, heading south and west of Alice in search of camels,

we stop for lunch at a remote roadhouse called Jim's Place. It's a comfortable, friendly, no-frills establishment whose visitors book typifies the outback Australian. It's full of entries from those who'd fought fires and been hauled from rivers and helped build roads across the desert, including one man who gratefully records that he got 'drop-dead drunk' and had his first 'naughty' at Jim's ranch. Jim is the son of Jack Cotterill, an English emigrant who became a legend round here. (There seem to be only two fates out in this hard, hot place – to become a legend or to be forgotten.) On his father's death in 1976 Jim inherited a thriving tourist business and built up a successful ranch. A few years later his young daughter died and his ranch was found to be on Aboriginal land and ordered to be handed back to them. Jim was so devastated that he took a bulldozer and flattened every building, saying at the time that if the Aboriginals wanted the land they could have it the way it was when his father found it.

The new Aboriginal owners were given a grant and some portable cabins but they never made a go of the ranch. Now, a little further down the desert road, amongst the spinifex and the saltbush, all that's left of Jim's dream is a water-tower frame, some fencing, a couple of smashed cabins and a small flat gravestone. On it is the name 'Katherine Charlaine Cotterill', and the three months that she lived.

Later: Evening by the fire at King's Creek camp-site with cans of VB (Victoria Bitter) and plates of corned beef, potatoes and veg. Around us, in a circle of flickering light, are the men, and women, who catch wild camels. Their leader is Ian Conway. Through his maternal grandmother he's part Aboriginal, which is why he has been able to keep the property. He's about my age, with a lazy eye. On the rare occasions he takes off his bush hat, he reveals a high forehead topped with fair hair turning silver and worn in a fringe, giving him the look of a decadent Roman emperor. With him is his team: daughter Megan, a big dark-haired girl, who laughs a lot, Dave Wurst ('Wursty'), lean, serious, a biologist working for government, whippet-thin 'Westy', black-bearded Nicko and Gunnar, a Dane with thick prospector's beard and a dense and disordered thatch of straw-yellow hair through which a pair of bloodshot eyes can just be seen.

Ian and the boys are indulging in that favourite Aussie pastime – winding up the poms ('pom', abbreviated from pommy, meaning anyone British, may have come from the letters POME – Prisoner Of Mother England – stamped on the clothing of the early convicts). Each is trying to surpass the other in describing the perils of camel-mustering – the 180° spins, the high-speed chases, the near-certainty of being flung from the vehicle at some point, the legendary exploits of Big Steve, who leapt onto a camel at full speed and grabbed the one next to it as well.

'And he was over eighteen stone,' adds Ian admiringly.

It'll be an early start and a long day so we turn in around 10.00 p.m. There is a cabin nearby which is a toilet and bathroom for the whole camp. As I push open the door I'm confronted by a stark naked man from Leicester. (He tells me this later. It wasn't apparent from his body.) His mouth falls open and he gasps: 'Michael Palin!', before grabbing his towel and wash-bag, and rushing off into the night.

It's ten past ten in the centre of Australia. I'm lying in my swag, looking up at a glorious sky, clear and sharp as only desert skies can be. Far away, shooting stars blaze briefly; closer to, bats sweep and curl across the sky. A cooling south-easterly breeze wails through the wispy, mournful branches of the desert oaks. There's a clean, clear, elemental purity to the world out here which is so pleasing that I fight to stay awake. Across the other side of the encampment Basil has no such problem. He's been bitten, quite painfully, by two bull ants.

DAY 131: *King's Creek*

Wake to the sound of galah birds (pink-throated, white-winged members of the parrot family) calling to each other like doors on squeaky hinges.

Over a swagman's breakfast – eggs, bacon and sausage cooked on a wood fire – Ian, dressed for the day in blue and white check shirt, jeans and trusty bush hat, promises me that what I am about to take part in is one of the great adrenaline rushes I shall ever experience. Westy doesn't help by adding that bungy-jumping is tame compared to what we're going to do. It's the 'we' that alarms me. I can feel my sausages resurfacing as they speak.

At 7.30 a.m. our armada of vehicles leaves camp and drives off down bumpy red earth tracks into the bush. This is *Mad Max* time. Wursty, wearing a turquoise cut-off and a scarf tied, bandanna-style, beneath his baseball hat, drives a high chassis all-terrain Land Cruiser. Westy rolls up and down the column on a Yamaha 350, a black tube leading from his helmet to a water bag slung on his back. A helicopter is somewhere ahead of us, in the high wide skies, searching out the camels. Thin cassia trees provide the only escape from a hard unblinking sun. This is the sort of place where flying saucers land and things fall out of the sky. Land that is old and tired and has seen everything.

It's also *Monty Python* time. Even in my state of heightened anxiety I cannot hold back a smile as Ian strides to the top of a scrubby ridge, spreads his hand Moses-like out over the wilderness and declares: 'Great camel spotting country!'

There is a flurry of radio exchanges with the helicopter. Craig, the pilot, has spotted camel and they're heading in our direction. Ian beckons me towards his vehicle – a dusty, hard-worked, short-wheel base Toyota pick-up, known in this land of abbreviations as a 'shortie'. Attached to the screen is a fiercely explicit window sticker: 'Get In, Sit Down, Shut Up and Hang On'.

Immediately behind the cab are two parallel sets of metal bars and he orders me to stand between these alongside Gunnar. I'm handed a wooden stick about 4 feet long with a rope loop on the end which (and now there is no question of a choice in the matter) I must drop over the camel's head when Ian gets the vehicle close enough. In theory it sounds no more hazardous than tea-picking, but Ian's last words before he starts up give me a flavour of what's to come. 'When it's over his head for Christ's sake get down. If you get your body entangled with the rope it could take your leg off.'

Then we're off. Off the track, for a start. Ian blasts the shortie through the bush, cannoning up and down slopes, twisting and turning in pursuit of a bull camel which runs, rather than races, away from us with its nose in the air. Ian tries to match it movement for movement and, after a few desperate attempts, over which Ian screams advice, I make one last lunge which the camel disdainfully avoids. Westy and Wursty succeed where I have failed.

But Ian, I know, is not going to let me rest until I have lassooed my very own camel. We drive a little way further on before the next sighting. I cannot capture the sensation of what happened next better than in the lines I scribbled in my notebook immediately afterwards.

Ian will simply not let me give up. Trying to keep my balance and re-hang my stick lasso after the last attempt, I'm thrown one way and the other, banging the small of my back on the rear bar and the bottom of my ribcage on the front bar. Grabbing for a hand-hold only to be sent spinning by one of Ian's swerving high-speed ninety degree turns. Winded by the blow. Gasping for air as Ian yells at me to get ready. Pull myself upright, catch my balance, seize the forward bar just in time as he swings the wheel and accelerates so fast over a low rise that both my feet leave the floor. For one moment I want nothing more than to continue the ascent and rest quietly in the arms of St Peter.

Down to earth. Just in time to duck as we race under a low tree. Ian is almost up with three sprinting camels. He veers with them, I'm thrown forward, my rope loop hangs down over the cab, Ian shrieks at me to get it out of the way, before it catches in the steering wheel. Turns for another attempt. The camel's far too canny by now. Every pass is an effort. But no let up. After each failed pass he turns and takes me in again. I'm full of so much anger and frustration. Nowhere for it to go. Again Ian yells over the roar of the engine and the whine of the helicopter. 'Ready!'

The camels veer off as I throw. The vehicle spins and whines, flinging up the dust. I've hit my lower ribs going forward. The stick feels as heavy and unwieldy as a small tree. I want just to

191

stop. Please let me stop. Ian re-adjusts his course and we fire onwards again. I'm pitched forward. He screams at me 'Get that bloody rope out of the cab. I can't drive with it like that!' And that's when I explode. That's when all the pain and the anger and the emotion and frustration all comes out. I hurl abuse at Ian. I shriek Fs and Bs at him. I call him every foul name under the sun. But he probably can't hear for the screech of the tires, the thumping of the helicopter, the whine of Westy's motor bike and the hysterical revving of the Land Cruiser. It's all pain and noise and desperation but now he has me alongside again, beautifully positioned. One last lunge, one last call on resources I don't believe I have and the loop is over! And then I know what he meant about adrenaline rushes. I know that everything is as he said it would be. I get down and clasp his shoulder and apologise for all I said, but he just beams and rubs the back of the lassooed camel and hands me a ball of fur. 'There y'are. Last of the winter coat.'

On our way to Alice Springs it's sunset and the rocks we pass glow like live coals. Though I know I shall be black and blue tomorrow I'm still buzzing with the exhilaration of what has been the most physically demanding day's filming in my entire life. What happened today was a rare experience, well outside the world we are all increasingly used to living in, a world of rules and regulations and sensible precautions. Today I was protected only by my own instinct and my trust in a group of people I barely knew.

I understand a little better now why people come out to earn a living in the burning heat of this hard unfriendly land, why Ian and Westy and Wursty and the others still pit themselves physically against the camels instead of using, say, tranquillizing darts. There are easier ways to do it. But that's not the point.

DAY 132: *Alice Springs*

I'm not a pleasant sight at the poolside this morning. My body looks like a crossword puzzle. The white bits are interspersed with an impressive array of black bits – all around the ribcage, on the hip, small of the back and on the thigh. Decide to stay and rest, though conditions not ideal. The wind has dropped, the thermometer is showing 42° centigrade and the most intrusive flies in the world are about, seeking out every facial orifice with single-minded persistence.

Retreat to my room and, towards the end of the day, watch the light changing on the brittle, cauterized rock walls of the Macdonnell Ranges, which turn from bronze to copper to ochre and, at night, when the moon is up and there is total silence, to a ghostly, silvery grey.

DAY 134

The short history of white Australia can be traced in the names on any map. The Alice of Alice Springs was the wife of Charles Todd, Superintendent of Telegraphs, who in 1872 set up a repeater station beside a waterhole, used by the aboriginals for ten thousand years. Here he connected up the overland telegraph line which, at a stroke, according to the *Illustrated London News*, 'brought all the Australian colonies into electric communication with Europe, Asia and America'. The Todd River, which flows through the town on anything from two days to two weeks a year was named after the superintendent. It is the venue for the Henley-on-Todd Regatta, the only regatta in the world that needs no water. The boats are all bottomless, and the crew simply stick their legs through and sprint along the dried-up river-bed. There is also the Todd Tavern, with its low orange-coloured tin roof and hot, heaving saloon called, without apparent irony, the Animal Bar. It stands on the corner of Wills and Leichardt Terraces – both named after nineteenth-century explorers.

The rivers, waterholes and mountain ranges had Aboriginal names long before the explorers came. Modern developments have often ignored their significance. Barrett Drive, a new tarmac road that runs past our hotel, is known by the Aboriginals as Broken Promise Drive, as it was bulldozed through a sacred site after planners reneged on a commitment to find alternatives. We drive along it for the last time today, on our way to the station to take the Ghan train south, across the Simpson Desert and down to Adelaide, to complete a 1900-mile crossing of the continent.

The original railway was a disaster. Laid on the sand without a properly surveyed permanent way, it was susceptible to flash floods and the stress of dizzyingly high temperatures. Trains were constantly subject to delay, the longest recorded being three months. The new line, opened in 1980, is safer, more efficient and considerably more predictable. It was built primarily for freight, but the old Ghan name is still attached to the eighteen silver-ribbed coaches which convey travellers in varying degrees of luxury from Alice to Adelaide in twenty-two hours.

At the functional, unromantic modern station, metal steps are set out at each doorway like a long line of Zimmer frames. Our three-thousand horsepower diesel engine is called City of Port Augusta and will, we are told by our informative Train Manager, reach a top speed of about 70 miles an hour.

Colony wattles, desert cassias and witchetty bushes provide sparse cover as we roll over old, tired landscape, ribbed with low red ridges like some primaeval seabed. The Finke River, which we cross two hours out of Alice, is said to be the oldest river-bed in the world. It's a damp patch in the sand today.

Sunset is a violent crimson slash in the western sky. By the time it's over we have slipped past Kulgera and into South Australia.

DAY 135: *On the Ghan to Adelaide*

Seven o'clock in the morning at Port Augusta Station. The train has stopped and the car attendants are collecting their Sunday copies of the *Advertiser*. An Aboriginal family is disembarking from the train, clutching mighty mounds of bedding, like so many Mrs Tiggy-Winkles. The air smells of scorched grass. As we pull out, the train winds round a tight curve and the coaches look for a moment like burnished gold as they catch the full power of the freshly-risen sun. It's going to be a wonderful summer's day.

The seared desert is at last yielding to more familiar, less exhausted scenery as we run south along the shore of the Spencer Gulf. After a week of barren dryness the sudden profligate presence of wide blue water is scarcely believable, like a mirage. Then everything begins to change quite quickly. Industry looms into sight. Port Augusta, Whyalla and Port Pirie – Australia's Iron Triangle – mean smelters and smokestacks and the biggest lead refinery in the world. Then hedgerows and wheat farms, freshly-harvested fields and herds of sheep, then barbies and bungalows and Holden cars and cricket pitches. After a flurry of station names familiar to any Londoner – Kilburn, Islington and Mile End – the trim red roofs of the 1930s suburban city give way to the 1990s corporate skyline, the mammon mushroom, a confident and uncompromising reminder that this is how things are going to be. We are in Adelaide.

South Australia, unlike New South Wales, was never a convict colony. It has a tolerant tradition and according to my *Rough Guide* was 'the first state to legalize gay love'. Adelaide, its capital, is a city trying to wriggle free from a solid, serious provincial past and have a bit of fun. The lavish Italianate town hall is open for weddings and concerts, the stern mercantile buildings of King William Street are likely to have a live band playing at a bar in the basement. There is a casino in the old railway station and behind the reverently inscribed sandstone façade of the Adelaide Fruit and Produce Exchange – 'The Earth is the Lord's and the Fulness Thereof' – lies a whole new neighbourhood of expensive apartment housing. Beneath the sober classical portico of the Parliament Building is a banner reading 'Stop media persecution of the rave community!' A young blonde woman is assuring a large vociferous crowd of ravers: 'My party is the only one that will offer you unequivocal support.'

Rundle Street is a gauntlet of pleasure spots, everything from pubs and wine bars to cafés, coffee shops and restaurants. The

195

pavements are laid two or three deep with tables at which sit a lot of young, modern Australians in chinos and collarless cotton shirts or flimsy summer dresses eating olive bread and drinking the latest Chardonnay. After ten days in the Outback I feel as if I've landed on another planet.

DAY 136: *Adelaide*

At breakfast Roger, who listens more assiduously to the BBC World service than I do, says he has heard reports that the seventeen-month-old IRA ceasefire has been broken with a serious explosion in Canary Wharf. This chills me. For the last few months one of my sons has been working for a newspaper group on the nineteenth floor of the Canary Wharf Tower. I ask Roger what time the bomb went off. It was around seven in the evening. I know that Will works mostly at night, so he could have just been arriving. It's late in England, but I ring home. There is no answer. My mind races ahead inventing scenarios of Helen, barely recovered, having to deal with police and hospitals. With no other facts or details to go on beyond the ominously unhelpful phrases – 'substantial damage' and 'serious injuries' – the imagination runs down all sorts of dark alleys.

The gently rolling countryside of the Southern Vales south of Adelaide may be comforting to look at but it is maddeningly irrelevant to what preoccupies me at the moment. But worse, or better, is to come at the little village of Mount Compass which boasts 'Australia's Only Cow Race'. This is such a bizarre event that for the next few hours it takes my mind off everything except milking demonstrations, venison stalls, clay brick making (paint your own cow on the side) and the almost unbelievable Les. Les is a massive man, an heroic figure, a Falstaff of the farmyard, who for twenty-two years has been master of ceremonies at the Compass Cup Country Show. He keeps up a non-stop stream of politically incorrect banter for almost three hours. In a sack race in which contestants have to pick up an extra participant halfway through, he's in his element. 'Well he's got the girl in the sack – I wish I could do it as easy as that.'

Even an apology for an error provides Les with an opportunity too good to miss. 'Sorry about that,' he booms. 'It just slipped out. The word I mean.'

An auction is in progress. As a result of an inadvertent sneeze I win the opportunity of riding a cow called Udderley Yours in the second race of the Compass Cup. The first heat is a shambles. The starter releases the cows from the paddock by firing a double-barrelled shotgun quite close to their heads. They emerge rearing up, eyes bulging, legs flailing. Young men and women try desperately to attach themselves to these bovine berserks, but by the end of the race the arena looks as if the Light Brigade has charged through it. One rider is eased onto a stretcher by a St John's Ambulance team, another looks proudly at the place where the pad of skin between thumb and forefinger used to be and a girl jockey – a 'jockette' according to Les – has a suspected broken wrist.

Fortunately Udderley Yours proves to be so docile that Les refers to it over the loudspeaker as the Valium Cow. With the help of my three 'urgers', I was not only able to mount it, but to stay on it for the entire 200-yard course. As a result of this prudence I come second in my race, twelve and a half minutes behind the only other finisher.

Back at the hotel I ring home, wake Helen up and hear to my relief that Will had not been at work when the bomb went off yesterday.

DAY 138: *Adelaide to Sydney*

Having crossed Australia from north to south we must now head east again, back to the Pacific coast and on to New Zealand, the most southerly landfall on this side of the Rim. There is a train, suitably called the 'Indian Pacific' which winds its way in leisurely fashion across flat plains, past Broken Hill, where an Aboriginal by the name of Charlie Rasp came across one of the richest seams of silver, lead and zinc found anywhere in the world, through the Blue Mountains and into Sydney twenty-four and a half hours later.

DAY 141: *Sydney to Auckland, New Zealand*

I take a walk out onto one of the most momentous water-fronts in the world. The Sydney Harbour Bridge, epitome of the no-nonsense age of heavy engineering, looms like a great protective patriarch over the delicate, playful outlines of the Opera House. One a practical solution to a practical problem, the other a work of art in itself. I am surprised what a successful pair they make.

Until yesterday they were joined by a long, gleaming-white temporary structure whose size and elegance seemed to complement them both. The liner, *Oriana*, six weeks out of England, left the dockside with a big resounding farewell blast, at midnight last night. Our time in Australia has run out and today we must leave too.

Later: Flying across the 1000-mile stretch of Pacific that separates Australia from New Zealand. It is called the Tasman Sea, after the Dutch explorer Abel Tasman, the first white man to record a sighting of New Zealand, three hundred and fifty-three years ago. Tasman, one of the great explorers of the southern fringes of the Pacific, was trying to find a route from Java to the gold-rich coast of South America (which, for slightly different reasons, we are as well).

From the windows of a modern jet the first sight of the rolling, misty green hills and the long precipitous North Island coastline looks dramatic and also familiar, like Ireland or Cornwall. To Tasman they were daunting proof that he was at the western edge of a huge southern land mass stretching right across to America. Had he been able to understand the language of the Maoris, with whom he had one bruising encounter before packing up and going home, they would have put him right, for they had sailed from Polynesia to northern New Zealand eight hundred years earlier. They called the place Aotearoa – 'Land of the Long White Cloud' (which has been adapted by some Maori activists to 'Land of the Wrong White Crowd'). And they knew it was an island.

As we make our way through customs and immigration at this, our eleventh frontier on the Rim, there is a palpably British look and feel to the place. Though both Australian and New Zealand flags incorporate the Union Jack, you feel it means a lot more to the New Zealanders. Much of this is down to perhaps the greatest Pacific explorer of them all, Captain James Cook. When he wasn't naming fiords in Alaska or islands in Polynesia, Cook and the crew of the *Endeavour* sailed the entire coast of New Zealand, mapping it for the first time. He had a Tahitian tribal chief on board who understood the Maori language and, though this enabled Cook to strike up friendly relations with the inhabitants of Aotearoa, it didn't stop him annexing the country. In 1769, while keeping the existing Dutch name of New Zealand, Aotearoa became the property of King George III of England.

Once the Maoris had the benefits of Western technology they were able to kill each other in larger numbers than before and be killed by a variety of interesting new diseases. As the early European settlers flourished on the rich, well-watered grasslands, Maori numbers fell – by the end of the nineteenth century, from over a hundred thousand to less than forty thousand. Since then they have grown to half a million, and the Europeans to around three million. The only inhabitants whose numbers have fallen in the last few years are sheep, down to a mere fifty-three million.

NEW ZEALAND

DAY 142: *Auckland*

Auckland is a city surrounded by water (apparently there are more pleasure boats per capita here than in any other coastal city in the world), and today it's coming down from above as well. After 20,000 miles hard travelling one of my trusty bags has sprung several leaks so I have to go into the city for running repairs. My taxi driver is an Indian from Fiji.

'Polynesian?'

'No! I am *not* Polynesian. I am from Fiji.'

'Ah!'

'If it was not for you British, I would still be in Fiji.'

As we head down Queen Street, tyres hissing, rain streaming, he gives me a short run down on the recent revolution there and the subsequent injustices suffered by the Indian merchants.

'And Britain did not lift one finger to help!'

'I'm sorry.'

'I am sorry too.'

There is a moment's silence. The exchange seems to have cheered him up.

'So, how do you find New Zealand?'

On the way back my cab driver is a big, bull-like man from Tasmania. His father is Irish, and wants to go back there.

'He wants to take his wife,' he says, incredulously, 'to the North too, would you believe?'

'The North of Ireland is very beautiful,' I say, anxious to stir it just a little bit. He ignores this.

'Of course she won't let him. She says they're all bloody mad.'

For some reason these exchanges make me see New Zealand as a refuge. The kiwi is perhaps an apt national symbol. A flightless bird that survived here because it was never threatened. There were no predators. Until, of course, the foreigners started arriving.

DAY 144: *Wellington*

'Another day in Paradise!' chortles the D-J from station More FM after a forecast that temperatures may rise as high as the twenties. Considering it's mid-summer and we are on the same latitude as Barcelona, this sounds like a joke. But in Wellington, New Zealand, days like this don't come very often. Storm systems seem fatally attracted to the nearby Cook

Strait and the high winds that funnel up the harbour are part of Wellington folklore. Aucklanders laugh at Wellington's windy weather, but as they say down here: 'Wellington blows, Auckland sucks'. Unfortunately this sudden tranquillity has rather wickedly coincided with a Festival of Wind taking place this weekend. Paragliding and kite flying displays may not get off the ground.

Wellington, with a population of 330,000, may be smaller than Auckland (where almost one in three New Zealanders live) but it *is* the capital and from what I can see from a walk around the streets it seems determined not to be stuck with an inferiority complex.

It looks different, for a start. Auckland sprawls horizontally, lazy with space around its bays and off-shore islands. Wellington is compact and vertical, compressed into a horseshoe of land at the head of a ten-mile bay and below a range of low, sharply sloped hills. Some of them are so steep that on Mount Victoria wealthier citizens have their own cable cars.

This verticality leads to fanciful comparisons with San Francisco. Wellington certainly seems to be making strenuous attempts to promote an image that is more in keeping with the affluent, liberal, middle-class sophistication of the American Pacific than the old, grey, British Empire.

There is the almost inevitable arts festival in progress, and the gastronomic badges of the new Pacific Rim are proudly worn – espresso coffee bars, imaginative cooking (I have goat's cheese with honeycomb for lunch), superb wines from across the Cook Strait. Gay and new age bookshops jostle Salvation Army hostels. Walls, painted in bold colours – slabs of azure blue, crimson and canary yellow – stand out hard and bright in the keen sunlight.

Climb up the hill to the suburb of Kelburn, which has a fine view and attractive tree-lined streets of clapboard houses, with gabled balconies, cantilevered terraces, dormer windows, secluded gardens and shady verandahs. Stroll back through the Botanical Gardens to find an open-air jazz concert in progress. Couples with picnics laid out in front of them, sit beneath

Phoenix palms listening to numbers like 'You can't play the blues in an air-conditioned room'.

Perhaps the D-J was right this morning. It has felt pretty close to a day in Paradise. But something is missing and the New Zealanders know it. They want more than all this. In the bedrooms of the comfortable villas of Kelburn, teenagers are making plans to get out – to Africa, America and Europe. To see the roots of the culture they're fed every day.

This morning's *New Zealand Herald* carried a story of two men who broke into a sex-shop and escaped with an inflatable sheep, a blow-up doll and a store dummy. The report notes that police have reassured the public that 'the dummy was dressed'.

DAY 146: *Wellington to Kaikoura, South Island*

New Zealand was the staple diet of my O' Levels and whereas North Island had the odd volcano and a hot spring or two it was, in my sub-teenage mind, tame compared to the glaciers, mountain ranges and storm-lashed black cliffs of the wild southern coast, beyond which there is no landfall before the shores of Antarctica.

The morning looks unpromisingly free of wildness. The Festival of Wind being over, a stiff breeze has picked up. Though it is enough to flick up the anorak hoods on the ferry, the Cook Strait remains uncommonly tranquil as we move across the 25-mile stretch of water that has a reputation of being one of the roughest in the world.

By the time we enter the first of the jagged network of sounds and channels that mark the submerged valleys of the South Island coast, the sea has turned an astonishing jade-green in the sunlight and the day is as dazzling as the fresh-painted white hull of our Danish-built ferry, *Arahura* – 'Pathway to Dawn'. The crew is relaxed. There's not much to do but take in the warmth and wait for landfall at Picton. They're employed by New Zealand Rail, which has recently felt the full force of the sledgehammer deregulation of the old state industries.

Its workforce has been cut from twenty-five thousand to five thousand in four years. Most of those I talk to grudgingly accept that the nation's economy is now leaner and fitter as a result of the changes – 'Australia'll have to do the same thing soon,' they say. 'You watch.' One of the crewmen is thinking of trying emu farming. He maintains they're low in cholesterol, low in fat. The pelt's good for body leather and the feathers are in big demand in China. 'I reckon I can fit two hundred in eleven acres.'

At Picton we disembark and board a train grandly named the Coastal Pacific. There is nothing remotely grand about it. It's little more than a tourist shuttle, four coaches running once a day on an old single track. We move on, past distant vineyards, apple orchards, and dry, brown fields aching for rain.

Kaikoura Station is not much more than a wavebreak away from the Pacific Ocean. It calls itself, rather cookily, a Whaleway station, on account of the main attraction of the town. Two hundred thousand people a year come to Kaikoura to watch whales and the whales come to Kaikoura because the ocean here is special.

'It's globally unique,' says Wally Stone, a small dark-haired Maori who looks like a university professor, and who started Whalewatch. 'Three deep trenches meet out there. They're like huge rivers that run under water. You've got a cold current coming up from Antarctica, meeting a warm one coming down from the Pacific, meeting a third from the west coast of America.'

They meet in a trough one mile off shore which is so deep that, as Wally puts it:

'You can take the biggest mountain around here, drop it in the water and you still wouldn't see it.' He points to the western horizon dominated by the snow-capped summit of Mount Tapuaenuku, not far short of 10,000 feet.

The depth and the mix of currents make for fertile waters and sperm whales come to feed within a few miles of the shore. The sperm whale is a 'toothed' whale and feeds on squid and other fish. According to Wally, they once found one with a 15-foot shark intact in its stomach.

The weather is deteriorating, but may be much worse tomorrow, so he recommends we go out tonight. Our boatman is a lean young man with curly pre-Raphaelite locks. He's called Snow. 'Everybody sweet?' he asks as our aluminium-hulled dinghy is tractored into the sea off the shallow beach.

Then we're off like a rocket, slapping the waves at 50 miles an hour. Apparently oblivious to the thudding and whacking he's giving us, Snow points out rare and wonderful things en route – like the Western Black Petrel, a shoal of Dusky dolphins or anything else we might have missed while being hit with a faceful of sea water.

We have a merciful breather while Snow makes radio contact with a boat which has a device on board to enable it to pick up an 'eco-location' signal – a high frequency sound wave given off by a whale preparing to surface. As soon as one is located we race off again, twin outboards throttled up, just in time to see a tail, or fluke, to give it the correct name, disappear beneath the waves.

'Bummer!' says Snow, as we rise and fall on the heaving swell. 'That'll be another fifty minutes.'

Evidently whales keep regular appearance times. And they have names. Snow thinks that it was Henry's tail we saw disappear, but he assures us that Hook, Scar and Knuckles won't be far away. Another message on the radio and he flings us into a 180° turn. 'Time is the game!' shouts Snow, scudding over the waves, but I don't think anyone hears him.

We are lucky. A 14-foot male lies like a long rock, two-thirds of his body submerged, blowing a spout of water languidly into the air. 'Cleaning out his system,' says Snow. He takes us as close as he's permitted – about forty yards – and points out scars on the whale's back, just below the dorsal, probably from underwater battles. From the spout he can tell when the whale will dive.

That is the most impressive moment of all. The tail fin flicks up, seems to poise motionless above the water before disappearing with extraordinary smoothness and economy of movement, leaving behind a circle of absolutely clear water, an imprint no bigger than a drain cover.

'Sweet!' says Snow, admiringly.

DAY 147: *Kaikoura*

Kaikoura is an important Maori centre. The Whalewatch operation is owned and run by them. Before I leave I am to be received by the local Maoris in a traditional ceremony at the marae or meeting place. As I am a *pakeha* – a fair-skinned foreigner – I shall have to be guided through the complex procedure and will be required to give a short speech, and, horror of horrors, sing a song!

Introducing me is Rik, a very senior local Maori, currently pursuing a compensation claim for several million dollars arising from the government's failure to observe the Treaty of Waitangi, signed in 1840. He has a mobile telephone tucked into his trousers. Two Maori women accompany us. As we walk up to the *marae* I ask Rik how important the tribe is these days. 'To a Maori,' he says gravely, 'it is tribe first, Maori second, New Zealander third.'

Feeling rather as I did on the day I got married, I am led into the garden before the meeting hall and told where to stand and what to do. Two young men, dressed in warpaint and carrying spears and shields, come out to issue the *willigi*, the Maori challenge. It is an exercise in controlled intimidation. They thrust their bodies towards me, waving their spears up and down, grunting, chanting, stamping the ground and pulling frightful faces. Apart from some of the London reviews of my play, I have never encountered quite such a display of naked hostility. (Or, in this case, semi-naked hostility.) Eyes are rolled, tongues extended, mouths stretched in sneers of disgust and loathing that would make a gargoyle look like Julia Roberts. At the end of this display one of the men comes forward and lays a small green branch on the grass in front of me. If I pick it up it means I have been suitably frightened and agree to come in peace. I pick it up. The two rude warriors smile like babies.

We progress a little further toward the tall, intricately-carved gable end of the Council House. One of the women on the home side issues a call to us – a long wail with high rising and falling cadences, which is responded to by a woman on my side.

After this exchange we move a little further still, onto a green sward where benches are laid out for us 50 yards from the welcoming group. Then the *mihi* – speeches of welcome, interspersed with song – begin. A Maori with Irish and English blood called Taare Bradshaw tells me of the history of the place. I give a short speech, preceded by a couple of sentences in Maori I've been up all night learning, and then it's time for the song. Had toyed with 'Every Sperm Is Sacred' from Monty Python's *Meaning Of Life* but on grounds of taste settle for my old school song, in Latin. As I start I realize I've never sung it with less than five hundred people accompanying me. The strains of '*Rex Edwarde, te canamus, Pium Fundatorem . . .* ' drift thinly across the *marae*.

The Maories are genuinely, pleasantly, and completely confused. Rik gives yet another speech on my behalf and we are then allowed to cross to the home side for *hongi* – shaking hands and rubbing noses. Rubbing is a bit of misnomer, it's actually much closer to a pressing movement. It's an awfully good use for noses, I think. We are led indoors at that point to the final part of the ceremony, known as the Breathing. 'We breathe the air through the food we eat,' Rik explains, grabbing a sausage roll.

I must admit, I'm finding Rik increasingly difficult to understand and suspect him of having broken the no alcohol rule. But the green-lipped mussels are gorgeously, lusciously tasty, as is the local speciality, taken from the Pacific this morning, probably from the very jaws of a sperm whale. It is crayfish, or as they call it in Maori – Kaikoura.

DAY 148: *Kaikoura to Christchurch*

Last night I was lulled to sleep at the Norfolk Pines Motor Hotel by the sound of waves breaking and the comforting assurance of having the Pacific Ocean on the other side of the road. This morning the Pacific seems to have gone. A thick chilly mist shrouds my little cabin. I could be anywhere. Then I hear a light tap on the sliding door and the voice of my terminally happy host, John, announcing breakfast. He assures me it's only sea fog and will lift before long, which is as well as I have an ambitious plan to cycle to Christchurch today. John can't resist a chuckle and, as he brings in my breakfast tray, he has to tell me the latest mirthful event in his life. In this case it's an old friend's funeral he went to yesterday. Evidently the coffin wouldn't fit in the hole – 'They tried it every which way'. In the end the gravedigger had to hack one of the handles off with his shovel. The cups and glasses rattle with his laughter as he sets them down.

There is a call from London to say that the *Daily Express* has run a story about Helen's operation. Other newspapers are very interested and at least two are thinking of despatching reporters to find me in New Zealand.

Time for me to get on my bike. As John predicted, the sun quickly burns off the mist and I'm curling along the coast road in perfect conditions with a Mediterranean mixture of pine, palm, gorse and scrub on one side and, on the other, rocks thick with flabby fur seals, lying on their backs, enjoying the freshly-unwrapped morning sun.

There is a big vintage car rally in Christchurch this weekend and fifteen hundred cars have been given a week to drive there on a choice of twenty-eight different routes. There are so few cars generally on the roads of South Island that it is all too easy to slip into a time warp as 1930 Chevrolets with running boards and leather cases strapped to the back overtake me and Ford Prefects and chunky Austin Twelves appear out of side roads. By lunchtime the signs show over 60 miles still to go, so I cut my losses, pack the bike in the bus and enjoy my first sight of the wide rolling grassland of the Canterbury Plains in comfort.

Ostrich farms, racecourses (there are more of them in this country of three and a half million than in the whole of England), fat healthy cows and a wonderful collection of town and village names – Parnassus, Belfast, Styx – lead us into Christchurch, third city of New Zealand.

It looks as English as its name suggests, but the reality is more complex. The English-sounding public schools like St Bede's and Christ's College are certainly there, but their intake is increasingly Asian. Our hotel may be called the Park Royal, but most of its rooms are taken by Japanese, Korean and Taiwanese tour groups. There are as many *sushi* bars in Christchurch as there are tea rooms.

I've been asleep an hour when the phone rings. It's the *Sun* newspaper. A very apologetic lady wants to talk to me about my wife. I don't want to talk to her about my wife. As I put the phone down I wonder if I should check the cupboards for photographers.

DAY 149: *Mount Cook*

While I am complaining about being kept awake by the *Sun* newspaper, Basil claims he's still being kept awake by the bull-ant bites he sustained in Alice Springs. I think all of us could do with more sleeping and less staying awake, but we still have a few hundred miles to go before we reach the end of this side of the Pacific and can take a breather before turning east and north.

After three hours' driving the great tented ridge of Mount Cook blocks our way. The road leads as far as the front door of the magnificently situated Hermitage Hotel, and no further.

No sooner have we arrived than we are told that, because of bad weather approaching from the west, we must leave immediately if we want to fly up onto the nearby Tasman glacier. Cold-weather gear is provided for us by the manager of the hotel and, as we have no rooms yet, we scramble into it right there in the car park.

Within half an hour we have been helicoptered up 8000 feet onto the silent white world of the Tasman glacier. The views are enormous. Buttresses of rock rise sheer above us, a great ice dome capping one of them. Mount Cook looms close by, a majestic pyramid of ash-grey rock, its perfect Paramount Films peak reduced by a massive landslip four years ago. At one point two tiny figures on skis appear round the ice dome, moving tentatively towards us. Much speculation that these might be *Sun* reporters.

Back at the hotel. For a magic moment, as the sun sets, the broken tip of Mount Cook looks like molten metal. Later, at dinner, a forceful New Zealander is regaling us with his views on the Maori problem. As far as he's concerned there isn't one. It's all the invention of what he calls 'hairy-armpitted feminists'. The Maoris are only interested in integration. The old land-rights issue, which we had heard about in Kaikoura, was down to a very small minority. The strength of his views reminds me of the way many white Australians talk of the Aboriginals. He tells us that New Zealand's Prime Minister sees his country's future firmly in the Asian-Pacific bloc. After Australia, Japan is their second biggest trading partner. Korea is the fourth biggest, overtaking Britain. The majority of the new immigrants to New Zealand are now Korean or Taiwanese.

How changed everything is since I took my 'O' Levels. One last time before I get into bed, I look out of the window at Mount Cook, bathed in moonlight. Even that is 34 feet shorter.

DAY 150: *Mount Cook to Dunedin*

I'm hauled out of breakfast this morning to see a kea that is nosing around the garbage at the back of the kitchens. The kea is a mountain parrot with a large, sharp, lethally-curved beak with which it and its comrades have been known to strip a car down in thirty minutes. It is completely unafraid of human beings, which I find rather alarming. The fat, fearless little bird struts around like a newly-appointed alderman, occasionally fixing me with a beady, supercilious eye.

Decide I'm suffering from parrotnoia, an irrational fear that all the world's parrots know about the sketch I once played with John Cleese, and are waiting to take their revenge.

Mid-afternoon: The two-coach 'Southerner' diesel-hauled railway service pulls into Dunedin. Dunedin station was built for great things. It is a magnificent, florid Flemish Renaissance building that anywhere else in the world would be proud to

have as a town hall let alone a station. The walls are solid
and baronial, built from rough stone blocks. The booking-hall
is galleried with Italian cherubs looking down on windows with
stained glass panels which depict a locomotive, complete with
cowcatcher and orange glass headlamps, trailing a plume of
grey steam. On the tiled floor various features of the railway
are picked out in mosaic panels – a telegraph pole, a semaphore
signal, a goods wagon. Outside, a sturdy colonnade supported
by pillars of polished Aberdeen granite was built to protect
arriving passengers from the rigours of Dunedin's weather as
they awaited their carriages. Only two trains a day unload
passengers here now.

DAY 151: *Dunedin*

The name Dunedin (literally 'Edin on the hill') sounds like a
hybrid of Dundee and Edinburgh, which is actually not a bad
description of the place. Robbie Burns' statue dominates the
main square. This is Scotland in the South Pacific.

At first glance it is a dour, damp, chilly place, its buildings
heavy with ponderous Presbyterian civic pride. The travel writer,
Paul Theroux, called it 'cold and frugal' and looking out over
the steep hills, shiny with last night's rain, I can see why. But
beneath a grey and sober façade there lurks a wild heart. Or so
I'm assured by a number of New Zealand friends who attended
the city's highly prestigious University of Otago. To find out a
little more about this alternative Dunedin I have agreed to join
the students of Selwyn College on the ancient and traditional
Leith Run. 'Dared to join' is actually more accurate than
'agreed', as the run is part of an initiation ceremony which, I'm
warned, is extremely uncomfortable.

When I arrive in the august red-brick quadrangle of the
one-hundred-and-two-year-old college, freshmen are already
dragging each other through a thick, specially prepared bed
of mud, on the end of tug-of-war ropes. When they are all
satisfactorily filthy they, and I, spill out of the college gates and
run up a long wide road of small clapboard villas, which, I

assume from the piles of beer cans and wrecked chairs in the garden, are no longer occupied by old ladies. This, nevertheless, is our last glimpse of civilization before we descend into the black, rubble-strewn waters of the River Leith. What has been, up till now, good exercise, becomes a fight for survival. The new students have to run, scramble, slip, swim or somehow make their way down a mile or so of rocky river while being pelted with eggs, flour, mud and anything else those on the bank think might improve their chances of enjoying life at Selwyn College.

The rocks are sharp and treacherous and, after overnight rain, the water level varies from a stony trickle to a brusque six foot plunge. As I'm probably thirty years older than most of these others I seem to give them some hope. Here, after all, is someone who's actually *volunteered* for the Leith Run.

I discover that it's best to hang out with the girls. The boys plough on in their macho individualistic way, as if this might be the sort of event you should win, whereas the girls just decide to enjoy it, linking arms and wading through the devastation like a chorus line caught up in the First World War. Every now and then one of them will miss their footing and disappear beneath the waters of Leith, taking one or two others down as well. To give the girls credit this reduces them to hysterics, which is clearly the only suitable frame of mind for such an event. The wrought iron bridge beneath which the race ends is a last bottleneck where we are sitting, dripping and shivering targets for any dairy products the tormentors on the bank still have left.

But, as we are finally deposited from this hell onto the neatly clipped lawns before the great Gothic portals of the main building, I look on the bright side. It's been a chance for me to meet New Zealand's philosophers, brain surgeons, judges and prime ministers of the future. I only hope they remember me.

Sobering news on the six o'clock bulletin. A boat taking tourists to see the whales of Kaikoura has overturned. No one knows why, but someone on board has been drowned. Wally Stone is interviewed. For a man so dedicated to the enjoyment, appreciation and preservation of wildlife it seems a cruel blow.

DAY 153: *Dunedin to Milton*

Twenty-five miles south of Dunedin, at the small, inconspicuous town of Milton, we reach the southernmost point of our progress down this side of the Pacific Rim. At no point on our journey will we be further away from Britain. Yet nowhere has looked more like Britain. A Gothic spire rises from a red brick parish church. There is a Salvation Army hostel, a Cosy Dell Rest Home and an advert for 'Frosty Boy' lollipops – 'Often Licked, Never Beaten'. The gardens, and the fields beyond, could be straight from my Yorkshire birthplace. At around the time of my birth.

The South Pacific Ocean rolls in a couple of miles from Milton, the same ocean that I stood beside at Diomede, 22,000 miles and twenty-two weeks' travelling time ago. We're halfway there.

CHILE

DAY 156: *Cape Horn to Tierra del Fuego*

I'm surprised to find a chapel on Cape Horn. It's small, not much more than 15 feet long. The walls are made from planks of wood sheathed in rough, pine tree bark. A tin-roofed porch protects the entrance and rubber matting covers the floor. The altar is a wooden slab resting on two tree trunks. A plaster statue of the Virgin surveys the empty chairs. What light there is falls from two small windows, one on each side, both of them murky with sea salt.

Out of one window is the Pacific Ocean and out of the other the Atlantic. Nowhere else do the coastlines of the world's two greatest oceans come so close that by a simple turn of the head you can see them both. And that's not all. Behind me, through the doorway, I can see the point where America ends, where 15,000 miles of coastline peter out in a cluster of grassy rocks.

I walk down towards them, close my eyes and try to concentrate so I can remember what it feels like to stand on the tip of a continent, for it's not something you do very often. After a while I'm no longer aware of land. The sound of the sea drowns every other sound, the consciousness of sea, covering almost everything for thousands of miles around, overwhelms all other sensations.

The first westerners to land on this spot were William Shouten and Isaac Le Maire, who arrived in 1616 and named it after Hoorn, the town they came from in Holland.

Bobby the black collie, part of a three men and a dog team who make up the entire population of Cape Horn, bounds down towards me, tail waving and head turning insistently back up the hill to the single-storey wooden hut which serves as naval communications station, living quarters and post office. The Chilean navy vessel that brought me here, the General Patrol Boat *Isaza*, stands off-shore, grey and discreet, riding the swell, a compact 600 ton, hundred-and-fifty-footer, the unmistakable outline of its 45 mm forward cannons showing it to be more than just a supply vessel.

The weather is kind. On the way down Commander Merino, our escort, was at pains to point out that the odds on making a safe landing at Cape Horn at this time of year (early summer in England, early winter in Chile) were against us. But for now the clouds have rolled back and a pale sun warms a big, but well-behaved sea. It must have been a day like this when Magellan first came up with the name for the ocean he had never seen before. Pacific. Now Commander Merino is anxious to get us back on board for we have forty-eight hours sailing between here and the safety of Punta Arenas, the nearest mainland town. The weather can change with startling speed.

Bobby follows us down the wooden steps to the landing stage. He clearly doesn't see many other dogs on Cape Horn, and has taken quite a shine to Nigel's left leg. An eagle wheels slowly in the skies above the cape as our Zodiac landing craft carries us out to sea, back to the *Isaza*.

This is the start of a long journey up the American side of the Pacific coast, from Cape Horn, the southernmost point, to

Little Diomede, the furthest point north, to complete the circle. By the time we reach Puerto Williams, a Chilean naval base, and the most southerly permanent settlement in the world, outside Antarctica, we have made almost 100 miles. Only 14,900 still lie ahead. It's dark and a smell of wood-smoke hangs over the town as we come alongside.

DAY 157: *The Beagle Channel*

The *Isaza* is a working naval vessel, not equipped with any luxuries. Accommodation is cramped, even without the seven of us and our forty-eight pieces of gear. My bunk, one of six on either side of a small cabin, has no more than 12 inches of clearance from the one above. With some difficulty I have developed a technique for getting in and out of it while remaining flat. I feel I must look rather grotesque, like a great tongue emerging from between clenched teeth. Charles Darwin would, I'm sure, have been fascinated by this example of adaptation to conditions. He might even have had the same problem himself when he came through here in the 1830s.

His journey is not forgotten. The waterway we are following today is called the Beagle Channel after the ship on which he sailed. The hydrographic information provided by her captain, Fitzroy, in 1831, is still used on the bridge of the *Isaza* today.

The Beagle Channel provides a valuable, sheltered alternative to the hazardous passage round Cape Horn. So valuable that in 1979 Chile and Argentina almost went to war over it. Tierra del Fuego is split between the two countries and the mountainous shore of the Argentinian side is a mile to starboard as we run west out of Puerto Williams. A jet airliner appears from nowhere and glides down into the town of Ushuaia; once a place of exile, an Argentinian equivalent of Siberia's Magadan, now a tourist boom town with three flights a day bringing skiers from Buenos Aires.

Slowly we leave its smudge of pollution behind and enter a world of natural wonders devoid of any human settlement. The southern coast of Tierra del Fuego is marked by a series of great turquoise glaciers, clinging to mountainsides turned away from the warming northern sun. Gravity-defying shelves of ice hang perilously suspended between jagged peaks before sagging and spilling into the valleys and beginning their slow, remorseless progress towards the sea. Cracks and crevasses show the effort of their progress – glacial stretch marks frozen into their muddy blue surface. As the glaciers near the sea, streams of rubble and meltwater leak from beneath them and tumble off the mountain in a series of dizzying waterfalls.

It is majestic, endlessly creative scenery – 'Nature's workshop', Darwin called it – and I stand on deck, unable to take my eyes off it, until finally driven below by the intense cold. As the sun sets so the weather begins to change. On the charts our captain shows me a short stretch of water called the Brecknock Channel where, for an hour or so, we shall be out of the cover of the islands and facing the full brunt of a Pacific storm. He recommends we lash down the gear before we go to bed.

I insert myself into my bunk and wait. Around one o'clock we begin to feel the weather. For the next thirty or forty minutes the Pacific gives us a good thumping and I'm positively glad I have so little room in which to move.

DAY 158: *The Straits of Magellan to Punta Arenas*

During the night we enter the Straits of Magellan. The weather appears to have changed, certainly the storm has abated, but I am not at all prepared for what I see as I push open the bulkhead door this May morning.

We are in a small curved bay, half-surrounded by low coastline. The wind has dropped and the land is completely covered with snow. The sky is silver, matching the surface of the sea and the military grey paint of the *Isaza*. Sea birds – black cormorants and white gulls – are motionless on the water. Flakes of snow drift down vaguely. Looking out on this eerily silent, monochrome landscape, I feel like the Ancient Mariner, wondering for a moment if last night's storm was even worse than it appeared and we are now in frozen limbo.

The charts assure me that this place is not a figment of a storm-stressed imagination. It's called St John's Bay and the first captain of HMS *Beagle* is buried here. Fifty yards from the shore is a low hill into which is dug a small cemetery. In it is a gravestone with a cross and on it the words 'In memory of Captain Pringle Stokes RN, HMS *Beagle*, who died from the effects of the anxieties and hardships incurred while surveying the western shores of Tierra del Fuego. 12.8.1828.' The truth is he committed suicide here, in this lonely place, in the middle of winter.

The Straits of Magellan widen out until it is almost twenty miles from the Chilean mainland to the western shore of Tierra del Fuego, now no longer a place of glaciers and mountain peaks but a low, bare plateau, piebald under the snow. It is a land of ghosts, for the Indians Darwin found here were systematically wiped out in the century ahead by the European farmers who came out here and took their land for sheep farms.

By mid-afternoon I catch a glimpse of the multicoloured roofs of Punta Arenas, the gateway to Antarctica, which I flew from and returned to on my *Pole to Pole* journey four and a half years ago. I was pleased to see it then and I'm pleased to see it now. It's a proper town, with hotels, an airport and eighty thousand inhabitants, isolated at the bottom of South America, with no settlement of comparable size for thousands of miles around. It began life as a penal colony as did the Falkland Islands, one hour's flying time away.

The *Isaza* squeezes into a crowded dockside at which the battered Polish factory fishing-boat *Pollux* is landing a huge catch of krill. After three days under the protection of the Armada de Chile we walk down the gangplank for the last time. To the Cabo de Hornos Hotel for a bath and a drink. From the window of my room I can see increasingly fierce squalls sweeping across the Straits of Magellan and console myself that we have got out just in time.

216

DAY 159: *Punta Arenas to Puerto Natales*

Chile is a long, narrow country, divided into thirteen administrative regions each with a name and, apart from the capital, Santiago, with a Roman numeral as well.

We are on Highway 9, in Region XII, Magallanes y Antartica Chilena. It is cold and very wet and I find it hard to believe that when, and if, we reach Region I, we shall be in the heat of a desert, parts of which have never seen rain.

Telegraph poles and sheep the size of large huskies are all that stand out against the low skyline of exposed, soggy brown grassland north of Punta Arenas. If there are trees at all their barks and branches are a spectral green colour. They look dead but it's just a coating of moss formed in the sodden air.

Chileans were not much interested in this desolate southland and the names on the few farms we come to – 'Estancia Otway', 'Estancia San Geronimo, Prop. P. Schmitt' – are reminders that it was Europeans, particularly British, German and Yugoslavs, who first settled here and pioneered the sheep farms. The Chilean attitude to their remote southland is best summed up by the name on a sign we have just passed which announces this to be: Provincia del Ultimo Esperanza. Last Hope Province.

By the side of the road on a windswept hill is a shrine consisting of enormous numbers of empty plastic bottles gathered around a small glass container in which candles are burning. This is, I'm told, in memory of a woman who died on a road crossing the pampas. Despite the fact that she perished from dehydration, her child survived by feeding on milk from her breast. It was considered to be a miracle. There is a picture of the woman lying flat out on the road, a ray of heavenly light striking her nipple, and it is believed that if you leave a bottle of water here at the shrine someone who is sick will be healed.

Puerto Natales is a wide low-slung town at the narrowest part of Chile, only three miles from the Argentinian border. It is spread along the shore of Last Hope Sound where flocks of cormorants, tufted ducks and the characteristic black-headed swans gather in large numbers, undeterred by low cloud

217

and cold, driving rain. Before supper I walk along the front, wrapped up like an Arctic explorer, my feet crunching over mussel shells dropped by the seagulls.

DAY 161: *Puerto Natales to the Torres del Paine*

Breakfasts in Chile are definitely disappointing. Quite apart from the obligatory slice of pale yellow cheese, about as tempting as a skin graft, there is the vexed question of coffee. Sachets of instant coffee and jugs of hot water are usually all that's provided. This morning I have high hopes. The coffee order arrives on a tray covered in white linen. Two silver pots are laid on the table. No sign of any sachets. Nostrils twitching in expectation, I raise the lid of the first jug. It's full of hot water. Move quickly to the second, it's half full of cold milk. I look desperately round for the waiter, but he has anticipated my every need and with a triumphant flourish produces another silver tray on which is a tin of Maxwell House, exquisitely opened for me.

A gorgeous pink sunrise offers cautious optimism as we continue northwards into the Torres del Paine National Park on a holed and pitted dirt road. This used to be sheep country but demand for wool has fallen in the last few years, and the *ovejeros*, the 'sheep boys', have had to become cowboys. We pass them, astride their horses, wearing ponchos, muddy leather jackets and wide hats, herding beasts from field to field, with the help of earnestly scampering sheepdogs who seem to have happily become cowdogs overnight.

The Torres del Paine erupt from the wide rolling grassland like a geological Manhattan. The Torres themselves are stupendous – two soaring, pale yellow pinnacles, slender, graceful and shining in the sunlight. But they are only part of a rearing, twisting, galvanic upheaval of rock which has also created the Cuernos (the Horns) del Paine, two twirling, twisting peaks, and the king of the range, the Cerro Grande, over 10,000 feet high.

As we drive deeper into the park, the patterns of light and

shade change constantly so that from every new angle the peaks seem to alter their shape and size, one stepping grandly forward for a moment, another shrinking modestly into the background. Dazzling clear blue lakes offer the chance to see this stunning landscape twice.

It's four o'clock and the light is beginning to fade as we reach the small hosteria on the shore of Lago Grey where we shall spend the night. From the shore in front of our windows the lake stretches north to the base of a glacier from which slabs of blue ice have calved and drifted down the lake towards us. Eroded by the wind and rain they lie beached on banks of gravel, like abandoned carnival floats.

Few souls have ventured far into the park at this time of year and we have the hosteria almost to ourselves. Sit by the wood-burning stove, playing dominoes and drinking seven-year-old Scotch with seven-thousand-year-old glacier ice. Sometimes work is almost bearable.

DAY 162: *Torres del Paine National Park*

Distinct feelings of remoteness and vulnerability. The wind rises in the night and blows so hard that at one moment my window is wrenched open with such a crash and a howl that I am convinced some mountain banshee has entered my room.

By dawn the wind has whipped itself into an even greater fury, tearing at the threadbare trees, sending them straining and stooping for the ground. The good news is that it has cleared the sky of clouds and as we eat breakfast we can drool over the view of the great saw-toothed array of peaks, gilded by sharp morning sunlight.

I struggle down to the shore of Lago Grey. The black, crystalline sand is littered with gnarled branches and tree-trunks stripped white by the elements. Every now and then there are gusts so strong that I feel the unpleasant sensation of having my eyelids peeled back by the force of the wind.

Just before lunch we make a brave and probably foolhardy attempt to reach Grey glacier. The wind has lessened but rain has started to fall. Once out of the lee of a small inshore island our dinghy is caught by high-peaked waves which crash in over the bows, filling us with water. The boatman takes the brunt of it, standing with one hand on the outboard and the other on a steadying rope.

We are soon soaked and the camera and sound equipment is facing permanent damage, but it is the sight of our boatman closing his eyes as each wave breaks and the wind lashes spray across his face like machine-gun fire that persuades us to turn back. The peppermint blue cliffs of the glacier remain tantalizingly inaccessible, a reminder that real beauty rarely comes without a price.

A continuous road north through Chile does not begin until 230 miles north of here. It is separated from us by a permanent ice tableland and some of the highest mountains in the Andes. If we want to make further progress we must take to the sea.

DAY 163: *The Chilean Fiords*

Have slept, badly, aboard the MV *Puerto Eden*, a solid, red-hulled cargo ship that wends its way up through the Chilean fiords. A handful of passenger berths are available and it is from one of these that I tumble, after a bitterly cold night in which I dream constantly of farmyards.

What I see turns my dreams into reality. Overnight the *Puerto Eden* has become a Noah's Ark with trucks full of sheep and cattle, parked nose to nose on two decks. The sheep, some of them squeezed so tight they stand one on top of the other, shift from leg to leg, sniff expectantly at the sea air and blink through the bars that enclose them at the rosy glow of sunrise. The cattle are being taken north to be fattened. They will have to endure four days and nights like this.

There are few passengers on board and nothing much to do. An Israeli student and his girlfriend are playing cards with Linda, a voluminous chain-smoking American, and her young male companion. A Japanese father and son give the lie to the idea that Japanese never travel anywhere except in groups. There is an Italian boy on his own and a Chilean businessman who takes the ship because he loves the landscape. He's tall, bearded, baggy-eyed and looks infinitely sad. He has a teenage son with him and spends a lot of time on deck gazing at the snow-capped mountains while his son buries himself in his headset, or watches game-shows on television.

There is some excitement later in the day as we reach the Kirke Pass. There is no other way through the lace-work pattern of islands than this narrowest of channels, squeezed by rocky headlands and shallow banks. As we inch our way through with less than 7 feet to spare beneath our keel, an impressive crowd of wildlife comes out to watch. Seals offer synchronized swimming displays while sea lions bask in the sun, blubber against blubber, a wonderful parody of a Mediterranean beach in high season. They gaze blinkingly back at us, as if they've been waiting years for a ship to run aground here.

But most of the time there is only the sea, its surface black and shiny as fresh-drilled oil, the majestic cliffs, precipices, icy ridges and stark, rocky pyramids of the Andes to keep me company. That and those wholly incongruous smells of the farmyard and the sad lowing of cattle as the night comes on.

DAY 166: *Castro, Chiloé*

The town of Castro on the island of Chiloé. Rain drumming hard on the roof of my turreted room overlooking the bay. Fishermen in wet suits unloading catches of mussels, conger eel and octopus from boats with vivid yellow hulls.

Inside the hotel the gloom is total. There has been an early morning power failure and the staff are knocking at the door with candles.

'*Mal vente,*' says our driver at breakfast. The wind has indeed changed. The dry, cold, settled mountain weather has been replaced by the prevailing maritime depressions that make this island one of the wettest places on the Chilean coastline.

Into the bus and out through the streets of Castro past a

metal-sheathed, lilac and orange cathedral, and plain but pretty wooden houses with shingle tiles covering the walls. Nearly pushed into the ditch by two coaches hurtling out of town on their way to Santiago, 750 miles north on the *Carretera Austral Longitudinal* – the highway that is southern Chile's lifeline.

Turn onto an unmade road. Each pothole is a small pond after last night's rain, and on either side stripped-down cars lie about in untended gardens. Amongst a motley collection of domestic outbuildings is the home of Felipe and Sonia who are hosting a *curanto* – a sort of Chilean clambake – cooked outdoors in the traditional Chilote manner.

Felipe is in his forties, with a shock of dark curly hair, anorak and jeans. He looks like a favourite professor at a progressive university. Sonia looks older. She has short dark hair and a round, strong face, like that of a boxer. Dogs, cats and a cockerel follow her everywhere. The rain has slackened to a raw drizzle, but it is still the sort of weather you wouldn't wish on your worst friend's barbecue.

I help Sonia peel potatoes (Chilotes, as they call those who live on Chiloé, maintain the potato, which the Spanish brought to Europe, was discovered here on the island). I ask how many people are expected. She says thirty-eight.

'*Un grande curanto?*' I ask.

'No, *pequeño*,' she replies, small.

Before now she has prepared *curantos* which used a thousand kilos of potatoes. Meanwhile friends are digging out a four foot square hole for the fire and others are collecting the turf sods that form part of the cooking process. A number of wooden stones are being laid on a platform of solid slow-burning *manio* wood beneath which the fire is lit. Sonia shows me how to make two sorts of potato cakes called *milcao* and *capelele* (I remember the names by thinking of them as a firm of Spanish solicitors) while we wait for the stones to reach the right temperature. This is a crucial moment. When it is reached everything must be done fast so that they lose none of their heat. As the wood is pulled apart and the stones revealed, Sonia, looking like some revolutionary heroine as the smoke

ABOVE: *Paulino Esteban, reed boat-maker.*

LEFT: *Test sailing a reed boat on Lake Titicaca.*

ABOVE: *Corpus Christi Festival. Saints are paraded in front of the cathedral.*

TOP RIGHT: *On the streets of Cuzco.*

RIGHT: *The lost city of Machu Picchu, with the peak of Huayna Picchu in the background.*

LEFT: *Wembley in Peru. Listening to penalties in the Pongo.*

BELOW: *Cosquez, Colombia:* guaceros *scour the mudslide for emeralds.*

RIGHT: *The* murallas, *Cartagena's eighteenth-century city walls. Beyond, the Caribbean and the gold route to Europe.*

TOP LEFT: *Mexico City – largest in the world, covering 1200 square miles.*

FAR LEFT: *Los Angeles: epicentre of the American Dream.*

ABOVE: *Flagging down the Royal Hudson, outside Vancouver.*

LEFT: *Man on edge. Scottish Loggers Sports.*

OVERLEAF: *Back in the Bering Strait: not as welcoming this time.*

billows around her, summons the ingredients forward. Clams and mussels are laid on top of potatoes, salmon wrapped in *pangue* leaf is laid on top of the shellfish, strings of sausages and a couple of hams are laid on top of the salmon, my very own *milcao* and *capelele* are dropped among the sausages and they in turn are battened down with more clams. The whole gastronomic pyre is sealed with squares of turf, through which smoke, though dampened, still escapes gently, like the aftermath of some sinister nuclear catastrophe.

After that there is nothing much to do but drink *chicha* – the local cider – and not mention the word microwave.

The food, when extracted from the fire two or three hours later, looks visibly shaken and rather muddy, like something dragged out of a collapsed building, but, with the exception of my *milcao* and *capelele*, it is very good. Especially if you like smoke. The rain, which has obligingly held off until we have taken the food indoors, now comes down hard. Singing and dancing begins.

I usually run a mile when I hear the words 'folk dancing', but this is special. The dances are strong and simple and solemnly performed by everyone from the youngest child to the oldest man. A tall girl with lustrous black hair manages to be both graceful and funny while dancing with a half-full wine bottle on her head. The oldest couple in the room become hen and rooster to perform the strutting courting dance they call the *cueca*, waving white handkerchiefs above their heads and circling in a tight shuffle around each other as the audience urges them on. The music is provided by a unique Chilote combination of accordion, acoustic guitars and horse's jawbone. The correct way to play a jawbone is to run a stick up and down the teeth, though you *must* make sure the horse is dead first. It's a token of the liberating effects of *chicha* and *curanto* that I end this bizarre celebration with my first ever, and almost certainly last ever, jawbone solo.

DAY 169: *Valparaíso*

After nearly two weeks poking about the islands, much of the time in rain and bitter cold, it's good to see warm sunshine and the open Pacific. Darwin must have felt the same when he reached Valparaíso almost to the day, one hundred and sixty-two years ago. 'After Tierra del Fuego,' he wrote in his diary, 'the climate felt delicious . . . all nature seemed sparkling with life.'

Valparaíso *is* an attractive city. Big enough to have a presence but not weighed down with the heavy responsibilities of a capital. It spreads comfortably along wide hillsides around a capacious bay. There is an atmosphere of lively, run-down gentility to the place that reminds me of some of my favourite Pacific ports – Vladivostok, Qingdao, Wellington and Nagasaki. The houses have colour and style with nice flourishes like turrets and wrought iron balconies and orange trees in the gardens. It's also a navy town, and with a 2,500-mile coastline to defend, Chile takes its navy seriously. British-built Leander-class frigates and minesweepers stand out in the bay, the florid portals of the Armada de Chile's headquarters dominate one side of the Plaza Sotomayor and the equally exuberant monument to Chile's great naval hero, Arturo Prat, dominates the other. Chile's most commemorated naval action was the battle of Iquique in 1879. Prat's wooden hulled *Esmerelda* was rammed and sunk by the Peruvian ironclad *Huascar*, but he and his men boarded the Peruvian ship and fought to the death. They were defeated but you certainly wouldn't think so from this triumphant monument.

I spend much of the afternoon riding the *ascensores*, a series of short funicular railways which have survived the regular earthquakes and are still going up and down after one hundred years. Each one has two cars, looking like garden sheds on wheels, which are hauled up along rails, thick with oil and grease, balanced on a wood and brick ramp. The Ascensore Artilleria, which runs from the waterfront to an old iron bandstand on the hill, was built in 1893 and is approached through a turnstile that bears the imprint 'Stevens and Sons Ltd., London. Silent Reversible Patent 1887'.

British engineers may have serviced the world in the 1890s, but the huge assembly plants and factories we pass on our way from Valparaíso to Santiago belong to the new lords of the Rim – Hyundai and Gold Star of Korea, Nissan of Japan. The only link with a past I remember is my street map of the city of Santiago – sponsored by Shell.

DAY 170: *Santiago*

Chile is not a densely populated country, it's just that everyone wants to live in the middle. Santiago and its surrounding heartland are home to seventy per cent of a population of thirteen and a half million. The capital itself has five million people and, as soon as we arrive here, the familiar big city disadvantages like traffic and pollution seem worse than usual. Partly because we've come from the empty, unsullied south and partly because they *are* worse. Santiago, set in a bowl between the Andes and the Cordillera de la Costa is windless today and cold air traps the chemicals and the exhaust fumes. Like Manila they have alternate day controls on traffic, and like Manila it doesn't seem to make any difference.

But, as is the case with pollution, you don't notice it when you're in the middle of it, and though the sun is wan and pasty it seems suitable for late autumn, and in the General Cemetery golden leaves are dropping to the ground unassisted.

If you want to know about the life of a city, the municipal cemetery isn't a bad place to start. The hopes, aspirations, ambitions, even life styles of inhabitants past, are laid out here for all to see. The General Cemetery in Santiago is enormous, like a city in itself. Two million people of every sort and condition are remembered here, from those who lie beneath grass mounds to those laid to rest in expensive marbled bunkers, Moorish palaces, Aztec temples or Greek basilicas, as if money could somehow temper mortality.

There is one place in this vast and wonderful museum of Chilean life and death which seems to achieve the most that a memorial can hope to achieve. It is a rectangle of marble panels 180 feet long and 20 feet high, resting on a bed of massive boulders. It's called the Memorial to the Disappeared. Two sets of names cover the panels. At one end the *Detenidos Desaparecidos* (those who disappeared in detention), lists names, ages and the dates of those who were taken. At the other are the *Ejecutados Politicos* (those executed for political beliefs). The ages here range from three-years-old upwards. They commemorate not some old and bitter colonial war but events that happened less than twenty-five years ago – following the military overthrow of Allende's government in 1973 when Augusto Pinochet seized power. For the next seventeen years the country suffered severe restrictions of civil and human rights under a punishing dictatorship. Two thousand victims are listed altogether. When completed there will be four thousand names on the memorial.

It seems almost inconceivable that this urbane and civilized country should have allowed such fear, cruelty and hatred to run loose. Chileans of both the Left and Right now accept that the poison that entered the system in the 1970s was the fault of both sides.

'Everyone made mistakes,' says Patricio, whom I first met while passing through Santiago on *Pole to Pole*. This simple, powerful memorial is not just a list of names but a tangible act of expiation, a deliberate admission of national failure.

DAY 174: *Santiago to San Pedro de Atacama*

6.15 in the morning. We are on our way through the streets of Santiago. Running along by the flood walls of the Mapucho River, past the striking glass vaulted roof of the Museo de Belles Artes. A full moon is still up. Huddled groups of men, windcheatered and bobble-hatted against the cold, wait to be picked up for work. The city looks an edgy sort of a place at this time of day, full of shadowy figures, standing at roundabouts and intersections hoping to be hired and taken somewhere.

We are being taken some 900 miles due north, across the Tropic of Capricorn to the mining town of Calama on the edge of the Atacama Desert, in that part of Chile they call the Norte Grande, in some parts of which it has not rained in human history. Our flight, from the restrained autumn mists of Santiago to the brash heat of brick red, bone-dry hills in just a few hours is a short, sharp, shock to the system.

The desert road out of Calama starts unpromisingly. Rubbish lies piled on either side of the tarmacked highway. Nothing corrodes or deteriorates in the dry air. It just lies there in heaps where it's dumped. We pass a dead dog which has been pulled off the road and left on the dusty verge, legs sticking straight out as if petrified in the act of rolling over. There is a temptation to assume that we are in the middle of nowhere but in fact this road, Highway 23, is to be widened and extended in the next few years to give Argentina and Paraguay road access to the Pacific for the first time. Soon we pull away from all evidence of human habitation. We cross over a pass and in front of us is a measureless expanse of dried up salt lake. The terrain is not white as you'd expect, but dusted with red sand, the colour of raw meat. It is completely without cover and the sun shines day in, day out, three hundred and sixty-five days of the year.

Though this hard-baked, ridged and fissured saltscape feels as though it must be at the bottom of the sea, we are in fact at nearly 8000 feet. In the clear, unpolluted air, the views are tremendous. I can see the detail on a snow-capped mountain that the map tells me is a 150 miles away. We dip down again and enter the Valley of the Moon. When we stop to film, I'm aware of the utter silence. There is not a breath of wind and even if there were, there is not a tree leaf or a blade of grass in sight. This is desolation. The salt cliffs and ridges are crumbly and friable, worn into shapes unlike any I've seen in a landscape before and, as the sun sinks, the colours change. From white to cream to pink, terracotta and chocolate.

The last valley before San Pedro is the Valley of Death. The light has almost run out and yet the rock is still changing colour. This time into its most intense shade of all, a rich deep violet.

San Pedro de Atacama is a small oasis town of single-storey

houses with white adobe walls and cobbled streets. It was one of the stops on the drovers' trail in the golden days of nitrate mining.

My monastic cell at the Hosteria San Pedro feels just right for a place like this, but no sooner have I switched the light off and tried to remember the silence of the Valley of the Moon than the lights of a coach swing across my window. A moment later a party of fifty schoolgirls is disgorged into the car park. The generator has gone off so I have no light. Lie awake and listen to a sound that no stranger to the Atacama Desert could have expected to hear on his first night – fifty schoolgirls trying to find their rooms in the darkness.

DAY 175: *San Pedro de Atacama*

A knock on the door wakens me at four. Assume it's a schoolgirl still looking for her room, but realize with pre-dawning horror that it's time to get up.

It's also dreadfully cold. As cold as I've been on the journey so far, Alaska included. Our plan today is to continue north-wards into the Andes to try to reach El Tatio, the highest geyser field in the world. Locals tell us it has to be seen at dawn, before the air heats up and the steam disperses. It is more than sixty miles away on a dirt road, which is why we find ourselves driving through the silent, cobbled streets of San Pedro at the unearthly hour of half-past four. In the silver-grey glow of the moonlight the old town looks surreal, like something that should still be in my dreams.

I take a slug of grappa from my Sheffield United hip-flask as we pursue the twin cones of light cast by the headlamps of our four-wheel drive. Our driver, trying to avoid the worst of the potholes, rolls the wheel back and forth so we enjoy a bracing combination of horizontal and vertical disorientation.

I have brought a new toy with me on this leg of the trip, a digital altimeter, and, straining to read it by torchlight, I can see that we have climbed over 13,000 feet. I become aware of my breathing, of having to think about a process I don't normally think about. (I noticed that lacing up my boots this morning had been an unusual effort.) There is just enough light in the sky now to pick out fantastical silhouettes of piled, coiled, congealed lava formations, all around us.

At 14,000 feet ice forms on the inside of the windscreen. At 14,700 feet I am at the highest point I've ever reached on the planet. I ask Nigel, who has been everywhere, if he's ever been seriously affected by altitude sickness. 'Oh yes,' he replies breezily, 'after two or three days above fourteen thousand feet your face and hands swell up.'

All in all, I'm glad to get to the geysers in one piece. They are worth getting up for. From a distance the columns of steam rise from a bowl in the mountains like smoke from hundreds of camp fires. We can get close, but not too close. The surface of this thermal lake is a fragile crust and recently two tourists have fallen through into the boiling water beneath. One, they say, was never found.

At 7.45 the sun breaks over the rim of the mountains, backlighting the spray from the bubbling earth. It is still well below zero and the steam immediately condenses and freezes into tiny particles which glitter and sparkle as they catch the light. It is a wonderful show.

For breakfast we have eggs *a la fumarole* – eggs boiled in a blow-hole. Afterwards I walk a little way up the mountain where clumps of spiky *corion* grass, and not much else, grow. A great gusher of steam issues from an opening in the mountainside and I stand above it, enveloped in the cleansing, comforting billows of natural energy, marvelling at the richness of colour and texture that the sunlight has revealed in a land that half an hour ago was dead.

At the end of a long day's drive of great beauty we find ourselves at our hotel, comparing notes, not on the glories of the day, but on how much sleep we all lost last night as the schoolgirls swept in from the desert.

We have spoken too soon. The ominous hiss of air-brakes cuts the night air and the familiar sound of high-pitched female laughter is not far behind.

DAY 176: *Calama*

Back at Calama. Half the crew was billeted on the same wing as the schoolgirls, so half the crew haven't slept. Roger has had strong words with the teachers who shrug and apologize, but what can they do? It's a school journey. The children have come all the way from Santiago. They're over-excited. As we leave the hotel the girls are clustered, six deep, around the single public telephone.

There is only one reason why there is a hotel at Calama, and an airport, and a good, hard-top road, indeed a town at all, and that is copper. The Atacama Desert may look like a wasteland, but beneath it lies enormous mineral wealth – gold, silver, manganese, zinc, molybdenum, but particularly copper.

The Chuquicamata mine, five miles from Calama, has been producing almost continuously since reserves were discovered by prospectors in 1911. It is of such size that a hiccup in output causes indigestion in markets all over the world.

Copper production is a hugely wasteful process. Five hundred and fifty thousand tons of rock are extracted every *day*, of which only 160,000 tons are processed, and only one per cent will contain copper. There are now cliffs and plateaux and mountains of spoil around the mine so vast that they are almost indistinguishable from nature itself.

The search for copper has gouged a hole in the earth two and a half miles long, one and a half miles wide and 2500 feet deep. The mine has its own town for the twelve thousand workers and their twenty thousand dependants. It has its own river system – six pipelines bring water 75 miles from the mountains, for this mine in the middle of the desert needs four hundred and fifty million litres every day. And it has its own cloud formations, coils of black and grey smoke from the smelting plant that drift lazily upwards, the only stains on a piercingly clear blue sky.

Chuquicamata is a world of giants. Excavators with shovels that can lift 60 tons at a time fill dump trucks as high as houses.

Owned and run by the American Anaconda Mining Company for most of its life, the mine was nationalized by President

Allende in 1971 and is now run by the Chileans. They have kindly, many would say foolishly, allowed me to count down their weekly controlled explosion. In the operations cabin high above the amphitheatre of terraces I sit surrounded by football posters and pin-ups, aware that any flinching in my Spanish could jeopardize days of preparatory work. And I have to count backwards. I lean into the microphone. '*Cinco . . . Cuatro . . . Tres . . . Dos . . . Uno . . . Fuego!*'

Before any sound reaches me, I see black plumes squirt out of the ground, almost a mile away, and several acres of hard grey rock buck and rear up in slow motion before crashing back onto the ground in fragments. These then tumble down the hill until obscured by a swelling cloud of dust that columns into the sky and obscures the fading sunlight. I'm glad they didn't tell me before the countdown that the total cost of preparing an explosion of this size is about 600,000 dollars.

Despite the running costs of this enormously wasteful operation, world demand for copper is so high that the Chuquicamata mine made a billion dollars profit on last year's production. By order of the Chilean government ten per cent of this goes straight to the military.

It may be a blot on the strikingly beautiful landscape of the Atacama Desert, but in two years' time it will not be the only one. A new mine is due to open nearby, jointly financed by companies from Britain, Australia and Japan.

It will be even bigger than Chuquicamata.

DAY 178: *Arica*

At the port of Arica, only 12 miles from the Peruvian border, it is Army Day. Which is quite suitable really as it was through military action that Chile acquired Arica in the first place. In the War of the Pacific, between 1879 and 1883, Chile seized Arica and Tarapaca province from Peru as well as a large chunk of Bolivia, including all her coastline.

The sound of a twenty-one gun salute early this morning

and the presence of General Pinochet in town, reinforces my impression that the traditional hierarchy of Chile – rich landowners and old families in alliance with conservative and highly trained armed forces – is still firmly in place.

Stir myself for an early morning run by the Pacific. The sea must be rich here for there are seabirds everywhere. Great gangling pelicans, storm-petrels, boobys, skuas and shearwaters skim the waves while red-beaked oystercatchers scuttle up and down the foreshore and forbidding red-headed turkey vultures glare balefully from the rocks. The clouds are low, thick and depressing. The cold, offshore current which bears the name of its nineteenth-century discoverer, Humboldt, condenses the warm desert air into a low and formless mist which blots out the sun and envelops the Pacific coast as far north as Panama for eight months of the year. It looks like rain-cloud, but it never rains here. Odd to think that the world's most abundant source of water and its driest desert can exist side by side.

DAY 179

Roger has made the sensational discovery that General Pinochet was beneath our roof last night, being fêted at an Army Day banquet. Just to prove it, he got out his rarely-seen camera and took his first photographs on the entire Pacific Rim journey – twenty-four views of General Pinochet leaving the El Paso Hotel, Arica. 'They are for history,' he says, modestly.

Instead of following the fog-bound Pacific coast, we have decided to travel by rail and river from Bolivia into the Peruvian interior, across the *altiplano* (the high plains of the Andes) and down into the river system that leads eventually to the Amazon and the remote southern reaches of Colombia. It is potentially by far the most difficult and dangerous stretch of our journey. 'No gain without pain' will be the motto of the next few weeks. When, and if, we emerge from the Colombian jungle, the reward will be the prospect of North America and a relatively 'civilized' race to the finish.

Arica's tiny station is only a few hundred yards from the ocean, where hefty breakers smash onto the rocks with lazy, effortless strength. We needn't have hurried. There is no sign of the eight o'clock departure for La Paz. A half dozen mangy cats lope off behind the bushes as we unload our bags. On the tiny platform there is a memorial to one 'John Roberts Jones, *Ingeniero*, who oversaw construction of the line into Arica and died of malaria on the 18th of February 1911'. My mind goes back to Pringle Stokes of the *Beagle*, whose memorial lies two and a half thousand miles away, beside a snow-covered beach at the other end of Chile, and I wonder what it was that induced both men to come so far from home and risk their lives in such pitiless climates.

They didn't even have the BBC as an excuse.

A single ticket to La Paz costs 52 dollars, 'in clean US bills only', my guidebook adds. Once paid, there is nothing to do but wait. When the train that is to take us over the Andes finally arrives there is a palpable sense of anti-climax amongst the sprinkling of mainly foreign travellers who have been checking their watches with increasing anxiety for the past hour. All that stands between us and Bolivia is a single dusty, silver-grey railbus, designed and built in Germany thirty years ago to potter round the suburbs of Munich. Like Pringle Stokes and John Roberts Jones it seems destined to end its life far from home. And, from the look of it, quite soon.

Every item of heavy baggage, and we have forty-eight, is hoisted onto the roof by the stationmaster assisted by his wife, an endlessly cheerful lady in a beige cardigan. Vitaliano, the driver, helps from time to time. He has been driving the Ferrobus since 1992, he says, and adds proudly: 'I have been filmed four times.' (Not exactly what we want to hear.)

We leave precisely on the hour, though not the hour we were meant to leave precisely on. We have a driver, an assistant driver, a steward and twenty-five passengers on board, including Linda, the big American we last saw on the MV *Puerto Eden* and her boyfriend who today sports a 'Name Your Poison' T-shirt with a death's head on it. No one dares ask when we might reach La Paz. The word 'nightfall' is vaguely mentioned.

This could be optimistic, at the rate we're going. The first stop is not for a station, but to change the points, a cumbersome business which requires the assistant driver to climb out, walk up the line, unlock a padlocked lever, change the points and repeat the whole process in reverse after the train has passed.

About 20 miles out of Arica we ride a long left hand bend over the river and are suddenly and dramatically into the desert. The orchards, pastures and maize fields of the Lluta Valley recede below us like a thin, green glacier. The last remnants of the coastal fog are burnt away. The sun glares down. Our little coach, reduced to a speck in a mighty landscape, climbs slowly, with frightening gear changes. We seem to hang on the mountainside in a perilous limbo, as the cogs struggle to sort themselves out. And it is steep. Within a distance of 25 miles we climb 7500 feet.

A thin plastic water-pipe runs beside the line. Without it we probably wouldn't get across the Andes. Wherever there is a spigot the driver stops the train, fills a red plastic bucket and refreshes the engine cooling system, which is working harder as the air gets thinner.

I'm beginning to feel light-headed myself. We've all been warned of the effects of altitude sickness, but all I feel at the moment is a curious elation, a kind of couldn't-care-less contentment. Now I know why they call it being high.

Six and a half hours after leaving Arica we have reached the Chilean frontier. A faded sign shows the official altitude to be 13,305 feet. There is not much here. A few derelict sheds, some stone buildings from a more prosperous time which now provide little more than walls to pee behind and shade for those getting off the train for a smoke (not allowed on board). All around us stretches the *altiplano*, a wide, treeless plateau of boggy grassland in shades from rich emerald to lemon green, bordered by implacable white peaks – Putre, 19,102 feet, Larrancagua, 17,712 feet and the mighty volcano Sajama, its cone rising 21,500 feet. The air is clean and pure and the sunshine quite blinding. I stride off up the line to get the best view. Feel giddy after a few steps and have to slow down. I notice too that the ink flows more thinly from my pen as I try to make a note of what happened.

A mile further on, across a no man's land, populated only by grazing llamas, is the Bolivian border town of Charana. It's pretty clear from the look of the people and the condition of the buildings that we have crossed more than just a line on the map. Chile has a per capita GNP of 2730 dollars. Bolivia is the poorest country in South America, with a per capita GNP of 680 dollars. Most Chileans are *mestizos*, of mixed Spanish and Indian blood, sixty per cent of Bolivians are pure Indian. No one in Chile wears a bowler hat. In Charana all the women seem to have them. The military in Chile are always immaculate. The soldiers on the Bolivian frontier wear shapeless baggy trousers, tight, creased jackets and cotton forage hats.

The only sign of any investment in Charana is a gleaming new set of *Banos Publicos*, certainly the finest public conveniences I've seen since Santiago. I find them firmly locked. I suppose it makes sense; the public would only make a mess of them.

Linda, the American, is taking the altitude badly. She says she had been told there was oxygen on the train and there wasn't and she had mimed to the steward that she badly needed to sniff something and he had said rather huffily, 'No, that is Colombia, we do not have that here.' In the end they sorted it out and he gave her a large mug of coca leaf tea, which he was not allowed to serve in Chile. Coca leaves contain cocaine and are chewed by the people of the Andes as commonly as we smoke tobacco.

We are now over the watershed and rattling downhill. The driver bounces up and down on his seat like a man on a pogo stick, and the coca tea is flying everywhere. This does wonders for comradeship and soon the two New Zealand girls who are travelling with their mother, 'to all try and get to know each other', are talking to the German with the Peruvian wife and nineteen-month-old baby, Linda and the Dutch backpackers are comparing altitude sickness and the two Norwegians who were robbed in Ecuador are chatting up two heavily tanned girls from Brisbane. Outside it grows dark and very cold. The cold stops everyone talking and after we've eaten our chicken and chips we try to sleep as the little railcar bumps and grinds precariously towards La Paz.

It seems wholly predictable when, shortly after our twelfth hour on the train and within an ace of La Paz, there is a jarring whine, a lurch and silence. We are derailed. The driver reaches for a torch and climbs down. Voices are raised, a small crowd of people emerge from the darkness. The front wheels are off, and the baggage mountain on top of the train is tilted at a dangerously jaunty angle. Opinions are passed round. The driver disappears into the darkness with a shovel. He comes back with a pile of earth and stones which he tips into the space between the line and the unclosed point. Others dig around for stones and throw them on as well.

There are two small children among the crowd of locals which has gathered. I ask them if they have ever seen anyone try to put a train back on the line like this before. They nod cheerfully. This is how they always do it. I shouldn't worry, they say, it only takes half an hour. Sure enough, half an hour later, after some frenzied throttling, the whirring wheels catch the rubble and climb back on the line.

Cold and tired we may be but our adventures are not over yet. The approach to La Paz is dramatic. The city is built in an enormous canyon into which we descend in a series of corkscrew spirals. The glittering lights of the city below promise excitement and glamour but the closer view is depressing. The line is unfenced and neglected. At times the track disappears from sight beneath sand, dirt and stones. Packs of bony dogs prowl ahead of us, picking at the scattered piles of rubbish. Two drunks are caught in the headlamps walking along the line, balancing shakily on the rail and laughing. Perhaps the final indignity, as we wind our way down into the city, is finding two tall iron gates closed against us. The drivers, whose patience has been saintly, grab torches and climb down yet again. Eventually a lady in red shawl and a billowing pink dress emerges from a shed, takes out a key and carefully unlocks the gates. The drivers remount only to find that, while they were out, a passing drunk has climbed into the train. He's mistaken us for his bus home and is quite confused. The driver ejects him and we edge forward through the gates, which the lady in the pink dress locks after us, only to find ourselves in the middle of a city street. The driver hoots back at cars, themselves indignant at finding the train from Chile in the middle of their traffic jam. It is a wondrous, surreal finale to a journey which comes to an end a few minutes later at a deserted, unexpectedly handsome station, fourteen hours after leaving Arica.

We've covered the distance at an average speed of 16.4 miles an hour. But no one's complaining. There were many times during this momentous day when I thought we'd be lucky to get here at all.

BOLIVIA

DAY 180: *La Paz*

Soroche. That's what I'm suffering from. It's a Spanish word, and has a glamorous ring to it that the English counterpart, 'altitude sickness', sadly lacks.

All of us are, in varying degrees, 'soroched', and we shall spend two days here retuning our systems for a further week of high-altitude travel that lies ahead.

La Paz, or La Ciudad de Nuestra Senora De La Paz as it was named by Alonzo de Mendoza, its Spanish founder, in 1548, is a strange place. The highest capital in the world at 12,000 feet, but at the bottom of a hole. The rich live at the foot of the hill and the poor at the top. Mud-walled houses are piled up the walls of the canyon, while a modern high-rise city occupies the centre. Between the two is a labyrinth of steep streets that tempt the eye but test the unacclimatized walker.

Street traders seem to have taken over the centre of La Paz. The pavements groan beneath sackfuls of socks, piles of shoes, mountains of embroidered brassieres and hectares of Stayprest trousers. Beside them sit Indian men and women, known as *cholos* or *cholas*, in from the country. The women are particularly distinctive, wearing felt bowlers perched on top of dark, centrally parted, often plaited hair and carrying their worldly goods in fat cloth bundles. Their dresses are made from various combinations of bright, shiny material and worn wide and full over multiple petticoats. Apparently the whole outfit was foisted on the Indians by Spanish law over two hundred years ago.

Despite, or maybe because of this, the Indians resolutely refused to take Spanish as their first language and even today most speak only the Indian languages of Aymara or Quechua. And they don't like being photographed. Basil has had water flicked at him by several ladies and aspersions cast on his legitimacy. In Aymara *and* Quechua.

Higher up the hills behind the fine stone façade of the Basilica of San Francisco I find very odd things for sale, including dried llama foetuses. Apparently they bring good luck. I'm told that no self-respecting new building goes up in La Paz without a llama foetus in the foundations. (Other bits of llama are put to good use as well. La Paz was the first capital in South America to have its own electricity supply. It was powered in those early days by llama dung.)

Minibuses squeeze past me through the streets with children at their open doorways shouting a list of destinations in a lilting monotone, like a priest absolving sins. Shoe blacks who can't be more than eight or nine years old, shout '*Blanco!*' and point accusingly at my travel-worn trainers. It's a disorderly, entertaining city and I return to the sober, more expensive anonymity of the commercial district tired but happy in time to watch the sun slip behind the surrounding hills and the canyon walls turn into a carpet of sparkling lights.

DAY 182: *La Paz to Copacabana, Lake Titicaca*

Back on the *altiplano* heading for Lake Titicaca and the Peruvian border. It's the dry, winter season, cold and brilliantly clear. Scrubby grass, adobe farm-houses with walled enclosures attached for the animals – mainly healthy-looking llamas and less healthy-looking cattle. The eastern horizon dominated, as always, by a string of snow-capped volcanic summits.

So still is the air on this tableland that when Lake Titicaca comes in view it is hard to know if it's an illusion or not. On the map it looks like a bullet hole through the Andes, yet in reality it has a strangely insubstantial appearance. Its waters are a striking, almost absurdly deep blue, the sort of sheer over-emphasized blue that you get in badly-printed holiday brochures. At its shoreline water and land seem to float into one another, and the islands on the lake look as though they're suspended a few feet above the water.

Once I've rubbed my eyes and found it still there, the lake becomes more beautiful and beguiling all the time. Over 5500 square miles in surface area and 1500 feet deep, it is an enormous stretch of water to find three miles above the sea. The Incas believed it to be the fount of creation, the birthplace of the Sun God. It is still known as *El Lago Sagrada*, the Sacred Lake.

The reason for its ill-defined shoreline are the wide fuzzy beds of *totora*, rich yellow-green reeds that fringe the lake and from which fishing boats are still made. In the early 1970s the traditional skills of the local Aymara boatbuilders attracted the Norwegian explorer Thor Heyerdahl, who had them build two reed boats, *Ra I* and *Ra II*, in which he successfully sailed across the Atlantic. Paulino Esteban, one of the Indians who sailed with him, is working with Heyerdahl on a new project to build a boat strong enough to sail the Pacific from Peru to Tahiti. Esteban still lives by the lake and, though there is now a shop and small museum here, he and his family still turn out fishing boats for the locals. It's difficult to tell his age. He's a small, energetic, obliging man. His face is leathery and weather-beaten but his eyes are quick and alert, and his hands still fast and dextrous.

Everything is made from the *totora* reeds themselves. The cut stalks are kept stacked in the water to keep them flexible. The twine that binds them is stripped from the outside of the reed. The skill in building the boat is to know the thickness required to make the bundles of reeds waterproof and when and where to tie the twine that gives them their shape. All this is done by hand and eye. And even foot. Once Paulino has assembled a thick enough sheaf of reeds he makes an extra-strong cord by plaiting the twine, using his big toe to secure it. This is surely the only working shipyard in the world where the big toe is an intrinsic part of the construction process. He can turn out a finished boat in six days. Like the adobe houses, they are made from a renewable local resource and make sense for self-sufficient communities. But the modern world hovers seductively. A big tourist hotel has gone up near Esteban's shipyard and the whine of newly-acquired outboards shows that, with the money from tourism, fishermen who can afford it are quickly abandoning the traditional boats that the tourists have come all this way to see.

Titicaca is in fact two lakes connected by a half-mile wide channel crossed in a ferry from the village of San Pablo Tiquina. There is a strange, stunted little statue by the waterfront of one Don Edouardo Avaroa, a hero of the War of the Pacific, who sits awkwardly on the plinth, like an abandoned puppet. Below him is a tableau which shows a Bolivian soldier in sandals sticking a bayonet through the neck of a Chilean in jack-boots. '*Lo Que Un Dia Fue Nuestro, Nuestro Otra Vez Sera*' reads the motto. 'What was once ours, will be ours again.' Remembering the size and scale of the Chilean monuments I somehow doubt it. But it makes me warm to the place.

Across on the other side of the lake, an unmade, stony road runs along a gorgeous stretch of unspoilt coastline that reminds me of the Greek islands. It takes us, and our bus, to the town of Copacabana, 100 miles north of La Paz, where we are to spend the night. It's a solidly attractive town with cobbled streets and old stone buildings and a huge white cathedral in the Moorish style, which the Spaniards began building in 1605.

My room is a small, simple white-washed square with a hot shower provided by bare wires leading to a heating filament in the shower head. It looks like an early design for an electric chair, so it's a cold shower or nothing. Settle for nothing except a quick splash of the offending parts and into bed. Feel very excited to be where I am. Not many people I know have slept beside Lake Titicaca.

PERU

DAY 183: *Copacabana to Puno*

Last night's enthusiasm was premature. I didn't get to sleep beside Lake Titicaca. I did get to lie awake beside Lake Titicaca, and every now and then scramble out of bed and scour my bags for fresh clothing, beside Lake Titicaca. When morning came, I was dressed like an Arctic explorer and still shivering. I have not been as cold in a bedroom since I was at boarding school and woke one particularly hard winter to find an inch of snow on the end of my bed. To make matters worse, at the dead of night, a child screamed somewhere in the hotel, its cries echoing round the courtyard for what seemed like hours. Early this morning explosions rent the air. Someone told me at breakfast that it is St Anthony's Day, as though that explained everything.

I'm at a low ebb. I haven't slept well since we left Chile. The altitude has not given me headaches or nosebleeds or any of the colourful symptoms I can boast of when I get home. Just a steady, energy-sapping deterioration in quality of sleep. At far too regular intervals I wake short of breath, heart pounding and mouth dry. And today, in preparation for the Amazon jungle, I start on the high-strength anti-malarial drugs again.

At 10.30 we are at the border town of Kasani. 'Town' is a flattering description of a small settlement of ugly, half-finished modern buildings grouped around a square of patchy grass, which is being slowly nibbled bare by a pair of white llamas. Beside the pistachio-coloured customs house, the red, gold and green bands of the Bolivian flag droop in the rising windless heat. There was frost on the ground early this morning; now I'm down to shirtsleeves.

There is no one else here so we are kept waiting for some

time. Then, once our papers have laboriously and leisurely been checked, a border guard unhooks a chain slung between two dry-stone walls and lets us out of Bolivia. We climb over a rise, through an arch, off Bolivian cobbles and onto Peruvian tarmac. Outside the Peruvian *Migraciones*, bowler-hatted ladies home in on us slowly, holding out every kind of alpaca accessory – gloves, sweaters, bags, ponchos, pullovers, socks and knitted hats with ear flaps. Inside, the large-spectacled Japanese features of Alberto Fujimori *Presidente de la Republica del Peru* gaze down from a frame on the wall. He looks keen, healthy and ready for business, as though he might be a model for the glasses he's wearing.

Run along by the pale-brown totora-fringed shores of Lake Titicaca, two-thirds of which extends into Peru, until we reach the town of Puno, lively with St Anthony's Day crowds and street music.

Puno is the chief port of Lake Titicaca and it was here that, one hundred and thirty-five years ago, an English built steamship, the *Yavari*, arrived like us across the mountains from Arica. Unfortunately it arrived in two thousand pieces, each of which had to be small enough to be carried on a mule's back. Delivery took six years. The *Yavari* was laboriously put together and launched on Christmas Day 1870. It is still to be found at the dockside at Puno, moored today in a rich green sludge of algae, her hull and funnel looking businesslike under a coat of fresh black paint. Her survival, rather like her arrival, is the result of dogged determination in the face of overwhelming odds and quite probably, sensible advice. An Englishwoman, Meriel Larken, with the help of her Peruvian captain Carlos Saavedra, has made it her ambition not just to save the hundred and twenty-five year old steamer but to have her sailing the lake she was made for once again, carrying tourists who want to take in the beauty of Titicaca in comfort.

There are *some* changes. A 1913 four-cylinder Bolinder diesel engine (which is itself an antique) has replaced the original steam engine which, like La Paz's electricity supply, ran on llama dung.

'They had to collect fresh droppings at every port they put

into,' Meriel tells me. 'Of course it filled up most of the cargo hold.'

Meriel hopes to put paying guests where the dung was once stored.

'Ten twin cabins with baths. Great luxury,' she assures me.

DAY 184: *Puno to Cuzco*

Wake at 5.45. Immense view over the reeds and mud-flats from my window. Our hotel stands on a promontory near the town. It's long, low and modern, like some sinister medical research centre. They have provided a thoughtful English translation of the Spanish telephone instructions, but I gave up after reading it twelve times.

We have to be at the station early to catch the Cuzco train. First news at breakfast is that there is a railway strike. Rumour races around fed by a wealth of information, all completely contradictory. But when we get there the train is in the station and a man is selling fluffy llamas on the platform, so all's well.

There are three classes on the train: *Primera* or First, which is quite rough, *Segunda*, which is very rough and *Inka*, which is for tourists. *Inka* class is air-conditioned and protected from the rest of the train by locked doors. These become a source of great frustration as we try to film. Tempers flare. As we've not even left the station this is not auspicious. But we leave Puno on time, despite the strike rumours, and, after much haggling, I am allowed to travel in the non-air-conditioned splendour of *Primera* class. It's axiomatic that wherever there is least space you will find people with the largest and most bulky luggage. Huge shapeless bundles are spread across the gangway. They are negotiated skilfully by a steady stream of vendors offering water, cigarettes, oranges, *empanadas*, chocolate, coca tea, even guitar solos. All human life is here, as the *News of the World* used to say, except of course for those who have come to see the country in style. They're locked in *Inka* class, looking at each other.

At Juliaca, a few hours down the line, we are to be joined to another train coming up from Arequipa and the coast. This is a far from simple operation. Instructions are shouted, arms waved and circled and crossed. Sections of the train keep disappearing off up the line, with a man clinging to the back, waving his arms, only to reappear, a half-hour later, on exactly the same line but without the clinging man. So Byzantine do these manoeuvres become that we can only assume that there *is* a strike and management must be running the railway.

Meanwhile passengers waiting to board at Juliaca are kept off the platform in a fenced enclosure until the train is ready. One old lady has a dog in her shopping bag. Every time it tries to stick its head out she whacks it quite severely. Suddenly there is a dreadful crash, followed by a judder, a brief jerk forward, another hammer-ramming crash and stillness. The trains from Puno and Arequipa are united, and we are ready to continue our journey.

Two big diesels pull us up a slow and steady ascent to the La Raya Pass, just over 14,000 feet high. At La Raya station the mud walls are scrawled with political slogans. Children run alongside the tourist coach, rubbing their palms. It is a dilapidated place in a most enthralling location. This is one of the great watersheds of South America. From here northwards all the water runs eventually into the Amazon. The springs that rise in the wild soggy grassland on the way out of La Raya will grow into the longest river in the world, and our way home.

Along this route Inca civilization was born. Long before there was *Inka* class, Manco Capac, son of the Sun God, and Mama Occlo, daughter of the Moon, rose from the waters of Lake Titicaca and travelled this way looking for somewhere to settle. Eventually they reached a place where Manco Capac plunged his golden staff into the ground only to see it sink and disappear. They called the place Cuzco – 'the navel of the earth' – and it became the capital of the Inca Empire.

DAY 185: *Cuzco*

Cuzco is the Oxford, Cambridge and Bath of the Andes, a cultural city not to be missed. I know this because someone is reading it out over their orange juice and croissant in a distinctly international dining room. And in case I should forget, it says so on luggage labels and city maps available in the tourist boutique in the foyer. The Inca Empire may have been seen off by the Spanish four and a half centuries ago but it is big business now. Which is perhaps curious as its heyday lasted little more than a hundred years, from about 1430 to 1572, and two previous and much more successful civilizations – the Chavin and the Tiahuanaco – are almost forgotten. But they left little behind them, whereas many huge Inca constructions are still standing five or six hundred years after they were built.

These form some of the unmissable sights of Cuzco and I sally forth from my handsome but lifeless Spanish colonial hotel to scout them out. As I get close to the Plaza de Armas, the very centre of 'the navel of the earth', I can hear a growing din of music and a jumble of voices and, turning out of a stone-flagged arcade, find myself in the middle of a great procession. A fifteen-foot effigy of a saint – Sebastian, I assume from the pin-cushion of arrows and the leafy tree he's tied to – is being carried out of the doors of the baroque cathedral and down the steps to the cobbled square below. The palanquin on which he is set is covered with four tiers of gold above which the saint nods and wobbles glassily. It is clearly very heavy indeed and is borne, with much grunting and grimacing, by at least fifty men, many barefoot. A very amateur band leads the procession, playing with more noise than tune. Behind them come the most interesting figures in the procession. Twenty dancers wearing sombreros and masks of grinning faces, with long noses, red cheeks, beards and moustaches. They brandish beer bottles and execute a drunken knees-up routine. I ask someone what they're meant to represent.

'They are the Spaniards. The parading of the statues was an Inca tradition which the Spaniards took over. So this was a way for the natives to make a subtle answer to the domination.'

Does this Inca spirit of protest have any relevance today?

My companion has no doubt.

'Oh yes. It is very strong. It is the spirit of Peru.'

As I am writing up these notes, six months later, news is coming in of three hundred people held hostage in Lima by a group calling themselves the Tupac Amaru Revolutionary Movement, after the name of the last Inca king, who was beheaded by the Spanish and his head stuck on a pole.

'The Incas were the Romans of pre-Columbian America,' writes Peter Frost in his indispensable guide to the city, 'and Cuzco was their Rome.'

The Spaniards dealt with this not with total destruction but by the infinitely more acute insult of building their own churches over Inca sites. In order to impress the natives, they made these churches as rich and elaborate as possible, so today the city is studded with domes and fine towers and richly-carved stone façades. Though the Inca foundations look austere by comparison, the masonry on the grey limestone walls is deceptively complex and subtle. One of the polygonal stones has twelve corners and still fits tightly into the side of an old palace. It is true that Inca stonemasons never discovered the arch, but their straight-topped trapezoid openings were built for extra strength and, in the great earthquakes that shook the city in 1650, 1950 and as recently as 1986, Inca buildings remained undamaged.

Then why was the Inca Empire so easily taken apart by the handful of Spaniards who arrived with Pissaro in 1535? Among reasons propounded are their lack of weapons to match the flintlock musket and the horse, their initial confusion of the Spaniards with god-like warriors of Inca legend and the invader's ability to exploit differences between rival royal factions. Add to that the sheer appetite for war and conquest shown by the Spaniards who had just defeated the Moors and, through their sponsorship of Christopher Columbus, opened up America for the Europeans. But the fact remains that a sophisticated, supremely well-organized empire was defeated by less than two hundred Europeans.

DAY 188

Though my body has had over a week now to create the extra red corpuscles it needs to adapt itself to the reduced oxygen at this altitude, I still find touching my toes or tying my shoelaces leaves me gasping. I'm not the only one. The hotel lobby is full of inelegant Westerners with sturdy white legs and droopy knapsacks explaining to their guides that 'My wife is not well. She cannot come with us today.'

The good news is that tomorrow we start to move on up the valley that leads to Machu Picchu and eventually down through the mountains and into the jungle, where doubtless far worse things than altitude sickness lurk. We shall be in open boats for more than a week, and even if it doesn't rain there are potentially dangerous rapids to negotiate, so much of today is spent packing all I shall need into a waterproof bag and wrapping everything else in black plastic.

Celebrate our last night in Cuzco at an excellent restaurant run by a Japanese family. It's Clem, our director's, birthday so a cake is prepared. Unfortunately he has put his back out – not a good present.

Back to the hotel for an early night before an early start. In the lobby a Japanese man sits on one of the plush red sofas with a mask over his face and a five-foot high oxygen cylinder beside him. His travel bag reads 'Ultimate Andes'.

DAY 189: *Cuzco to Machu Picchu*

Huddled next door to the domed colonial church of San Pedro is the station for Machu Picchu. Everyone is kept off the platform until the train rolls in. First class passengers behind smoked-glass, and second class behind iron-barred gates. In this way, though the waiting rooms may be filthy, they can keep the platform immaculately clean. It has a fresh coat of orange paint and hanging baskets. The Canadian-built diesel engine, which is to pull the train to Quillabamba, 100 miles away is, beneath its coat of oil stains and smears, also painted orange.

As we leave the station vendors appear from nowhere. The compartment is suddenly full of people selling tea, chocolates, cold drinks, tamales, and trinkets. One man has a fistful of watches and an array of torches and Swiss Army knives inside his jacket. It's all a bit premature, as the engine expires on the first gradient and we slide slowly back into the station. After one further attempt, the locomotive is changed and we tackle the steep hill and the salesmen once again. The haul out of Cuzco is so steep that the train has to zig-zag up it. Along a slope, wait, change points, roll back along the mountain and up the slope the other side, brake, change points, forward up the next slope, slide back and so on all the way up until we are at 12,000 feet and taking a last look down from the slums on the mountainside to the elegant squares and fine stone buildings of the city below.

As we set off across the high plains once again, life on board becomes more hectic by the minute. The corridor in hard class is now so congested that in order to move from coach to coach the vendors have to climb out of the door and swing along the outside of the train clutching their trays of food, drink, watches or whatever. Opposite me one woman feeds a baby at her breast, another has a baby fast asleep in her arms, which is pretty remarkable as, right beside her, two boys are fiercely strumming *charangos*, small ukelele-like guitars, while a third bangs two stones together with equal intensity. At the first station no one gets off and a lot of people with bags of onions get on. A huge woman with the classic Indian high cheek-bones, wide nostrils and swept-back, middle-parted black hair is somehow passing through the crowd with plates of freshly-prepared salads. She bulldozes by with rock-like serenity and never drops so much as an olive.

After three hours we come to the town of Ollantaytambo which marks one end of the Sacred Valley, a rich and fertile strip in which the Incas grew corn and maize. Being the efficient administrators they were, they kept the grain stockpiled in stone walled granaries which can still be seen on the precipitous sides of the surrounding mountains. The massive 200-foot stone terraces of Ollantaytambo from which Manco Inca won a rare victory against the Spanish conquistadors in 1536, still exist and can be climbed.

Sweetcorn is the local speciality and sacks of it join the onions, leeks, carrots and sheaves of coriander and basil which make this quite the most fragrant train on which I've ridden. The lady with the face of an Indian chief is now bringing round jelly and ice-cream, and something nameless is moving about in one of the bags on the seat in front of me.

The mountains on either side of the train grow steeper and wilder now as the train moves with care along a twisting track and the Urubamba River begins to toss and tumble and accelerate alongside us. The station, Aguas Calientes, where we disembark, comes as a surprise. Emerging from a dark and winding gorge, the train is suddenly surrounded by bright lights and bustle. On both sides of the railway line are souvenir and craft shops, cafés, restaurants and backpacker hotels. The reason for this sudden explosion of life is Machu Picchu. A bus service runs from here up to the Lost City of the Incas, climbing through a series of hairpins around steep, wooded cliffs, their overhanging walls dotted with bromeliads, plants that can only grow on the bare rock because they take their nourishment from the air, not the soil. The winding dirt track is known as the Hiram Bingham Highway, after the American who 'discovered' Machu Picchu in 1911. It ends at a small, low-slung hotel in front of which the coaches that bring the day-tourists stop and unload. It is the only accommodation at the site itself, with no more than thirty rooms. We are staying overnight, and arrive as the last of the coaches is leaving. It's a short walk to the ruins.

Machu Picchu is a world of dizzying verticals. Stone-built agricultural terraces and the skeletal walls of temples and houses cling to a narrow promontory around which the Urubamba River makes a tight loop, 1000 feet below. The sheer ridge of Cerro St Miguel looms to the east and the tree clad crag of Huayna Picchu – 'Young Peak' – is a towering sentinel at the north-west corner of the site. Many miles beyond, a great multitude of snow-clad summits circles the horizon.

The only intimation of a world outside is the presence, over distant peaks to the north-east, of trailing white cloud rising from the Amazon rain forest. I'm told that they call this land of green gorges, halfway between high dry altiplano and tropical rain forest, 'the eyebrow of the jungle'.

There is not much light left and by the time I am back in my room at the hotel the huge view has shrunk to silhouette. Swallows dart in and out of the eaves. The temperature plummets as the sun disappears. Open the window and peer out. If ever there were a place for peace and contemplation this, surely, is it.

Then the strains of music rise from the bar below. Night falls over Machu Picchu to the sound of Abba's 'Dancing Queen'.

DAY 190: *Machu Picchu to Quillabamba*

Despite its lofty situation, Machu Picchu is 3000 feet *lower* than Cuzco, which is itself 1000 feet lower than La Paz, which may account for the first unequivocally deep sleep I have enjoyed since we climbed up into the mountains. It's sod's law that I have to interrupt it at 5.30 so that we can be ready to film the sun striking the sacred rock. Unfortunately it is the first sunless morning since we left Chile, twelve days ago, so it looks as though we shall have to film cloud striking the sacred rock instead. Not that I am complaining. Apart from a half-dozen others who have spent the night up here, and an assortment of llamas who ramble proprietorially through the ruins, nibbling the grass and occasionally stopping to wrestle or mate, we have the Lost City to ourselves.

The sacred rock is called Intihuatana, meaning roughly 'the hitching-post of the sun'. It's a carved stone block called a gnomon, a sun-dial whose four corners are aligned not only with the four cardinal points but also in direct line to four sacred peaks in the surrounding mountains (the same synchronicity we saw at Borobudur in Java). The Incas were animists and believed the mountains were gods, and that the sun was the greatest god of all, so this stone, which indicated when crops should be planted, must have been the most

250

important site in the city of Machu Picchu. Sacred stones like this are now extremely rare, as the Catholic Spanish made it a priority to wipe out the most revered artefacts of what they saw as pagan sun-worship. This raises the as yet unanswered mystery. Why, when the Spanish so systematically destroyed Inca culture, did they leave Machu Picchu alone? It is now considered almost certain that the Spanish never knew the city existed. Yet, the Inca rulers of nearby Cuzco who first welcomed Pissaro would almost certainly have told him of the existence of such a significant strategic city. So perhaps the Incas of that time didn't know it existed either. Perhaps it had been built but already abandoned, possibly because of plague or war. The mystery is intriguing. It cannot have been quick or easy to build a city of such sophistication on these precipitous slopes, and it seems inconceivable that no word of such a supreme architectural feat should have leaked out of these gorges for four hundred years.

I walk as far as I can down the terraces to what I think is the end of the site, only to find that the stone walls disappear beneath a canopy of grass and trees and bushes which is still being cleared. This is another twist to the riddle of Machu Picchu. How much more is there of it? Latest excavations and clearances have revealed further extensive temples, burial grounds and terracing. Much more than would be required for the one thousand souls thought to have lived in the city. The Lost City, it seems, is still being found.

The present day intrudes. A diesel horn moans down by the river and a line of buses moves into position at the station far below as the ten o'clock tourist train from Cuzco rounds the bend.

Only a handful of foreigners ever takes the train on to the *other* end of the line. Quillabamba is not a place of great consequence, but twenty-five thousand people live there and it is the last town of any size on the Urubamba River, which a few hundred miles north becomes the Ucayali and then the Amazon.

By the time we reach it the transition from the mountains to the rain forest is almost complete. Warm, sweet smells replace the crisp air of the *altiplano*. Bugs are out to greet us and banana groves flank the river banks.

We appear to have caught the hotel by surprise. The menu features only Chicken Supreme and Chicken Milanese. I ask the waiter what the difference is. 'They are both the same thing,' he shrugs, 'flattened chicken.' As another diner enters, the door frame falls on top of him, catching him a glancing blow on the back of the leg.

Lie in bed, my eyes smarting from anti-mosquito spray, finishing Patrick Leigh-Fermor's *Letters From The High Andes*. He is drinking whisky to stay warm. Already his world seems a long way behind us.

DAY 191: *Quillabamba to Kiteni*

Wake with the daylight at 5.45. Cockerel and chickens already up and making a lot of noise, though I can't see them anywhere. Eventually find them strutting about the deep end of an empty swimming pool. A small deer wanders about the garden, so tame it will take a piece of fried banana from my hand.

The organization of our river trip, now tantalizingly close, is in the hands of Barry Walker, a Mancunian ornithologist who, with his Peruvian wife, runs a fine pub called the Cross Keys in Cuzco. Barry towers over the local Indians. With his greying hair and shapely beer belly he looks a cross between a seventies rock drummer and the model for the 'Skegness Is So Bracing' poster. He has almost limitless enthusiasm and is particularly excited about what lies ahead because, as he says, 'I've never seen this part of the river.'

Which is great for an ornithologist but not so good for a tour-guide.

We load our equipment into what he calls Barry's Big Bus and set out for Kiteni, which is where we shall transfer to the river boats. A long, slow drive during which I have time to get re-acclimatized to the tropics for the first time since we left Darwin, Australia. A dusty track through thick forest verges from which huge, slashed banana palm leaves rise like the tattered sails of a ship. We pass houses, often only detectable through the all-entwining greenery by a plume of woodsmoke. Trucks, packed with villagers, perched precariously on top of coffee bean sacks, sway by on their way to market at Quillabamba.

The day gets hotter. There are fewer people on the road. The Andes level off into foothills and, never far from us, the Urubamba grows swifter and stronger.

Travel in this part of Peru is not encouraged. A Maoist revolutionary group known as *Sendero Luminoso* – the Shining Path – pursued a guerrilla war against the Peruvian government for most of the 1980s and early 1990s which resulted in more than thirty thousand deaths. Since Alberto Fujimori, Japanese son of immigrants from across the Pacific Rim, was elected President of Peru in 1990, he has taken a tough line against the terrorists, culminating in the arrest and trial of the leader of Shining Path, Abimael Guzman. Officially they are no longer a threat, but the existence of armed police at road blocks, and checks on our travel documents, show that all is not completely resolved.

If Quillabamba was the end of the railway then Kiteni, which we reach in late afternoon, is the end of the road. There is a short trail beyond, but to all intents and purposes there is no way north from here except by river.

We rumble down the main street, which can only claim to be a street because it has buildings on both sides. In every other respect it is a patch of waste ground. A Peruvian flag hangs limply from a building with barbed wire-topped walls around it. There is a big satellite dish, a shop called 'Video Dick' and a whiff of sewage in the evening air.

We ask where we can camp for the night and are directed through the village to a hard grass football pitch. Local children are in the middle of a game supervised by a very white man who turns out to be a theology teacher from Armagh in Northern Ireland. As Barry and his team set up camp on the centre circle, the children watch our every move as if we are men from Mars. We eat around a table in an open-sided mosquito-netted mess tent. Feel like a circus exhibit. Still, I'll do anything for soup, chicken and rice and a carton or three of Chilean wine.

Pre-bed activity is adventurous to say the least. The lavatory is a sackcloth-covered frame of sticks over a hole in the ground (so foul that my fastidious bowels fail to function) and the bathroom is a boulder-strewn stream a short walk away. Slither about among the rocks trying to find a pool deep enough to immerse myself. A chorus of bullfrogs accompanies me. Wash, gather all my things together and make my way back across the stepping stones back to the bank. Only when I've reached my tent do I notice I have left behind the metal soapdish I've carried with me from Alaska. Think of going back but know I won't find it in the dark. For some reason, this loss affects me. It isn't anything very precious, but the fact that I've kept it safe for many months and thousands of miles seems important. At this stage, losing anything feels like a bad omen. A sign I'm falling apart.

As I lie in bed I can hear sounds of little feet approaching, withdrawing, whispering and approaching again. Somewhere disco music is playing.

DAY 192: *On the Urubamba River*

Up, a little before 6.00, as dawn breaks. Waiting for me on the table at breakfast is my soap dish, retrieved by one of the children this morning. I'd never expected to see it again, and am quite excessively moved by its return.

Over coffee and French toast Barry shows us a satellite photograph of our river route. It shows clearly the line of a last rocky ridge, a final buttress of the Andes, through which the river cuts before settling into a sinuous, meandering course through the rain forest. To get through this cut we shall have to descend the fiercest of all the Urubamba rapids, the Pongo de Manaique. The Pongo (the word means a ravine, gap or gorge) is seriously respected, and none of these boatmen would take us down it during the rainy season when the river runs fast and full.

Leaving our camp-site to scabby nose-to-the-ground dogs and obsessively questing groups of hens and their young, we make our way to the river to see our boats for the first time. They are simple wooden canoes about twenty-five feet long, their hulls painted in a selection of bright colours, all now faded. Barry introduces me to Gustavo who is to be my *motorista* – my boatman. He stands a little shyly to one side, arms folded, hands thrust tight into his armpits. He has a square, scarred face, handsome in a way, like a middle-period Marlon Brando. While he looks after the outboard, his friend Adolfo, short and chunky, with calves like table legs, will be up front with the stick and paddle, testing depth.

As the boats are being loaded the crews' families sit on the bank on a long driftwood bough offering advice and encouragement and frequently dissolving into raucous and inexplicable laughter. Perhaps Barry senses my apprehension. He indicates the crew. 'They're the best, absolutely the best,' he says, as if reassuring both of us.

Before we leave we are given life-jackets which we are asked to wear at all times. Laden to the gunwales (one boat looks as though it could sink under the weight of our drinking water alone) we cast off onto the waters of the Urubamba, which are a couple of hundred yards wide at this point and running fast enough over the rocks to throw up a lot of white water. We swing into a sharp bend and the waving relatives disappear quickly from sight.

We haven't gone far before Gustavo heads us in to a sandspit and moors up. Much shouting and gesticulating. A bit early for a mutiny, surely? It turns out he has done a very good deal on a week's supply of mandarin oranges from a local man, who happens to be his cousin. These are duly loaded and the boat sinks a little further.

Barry, who reckons we have three hours to go before reaching what he calls 'serious water', is beginning to take on the look of a little boy let loose in a sweet shop. His binoculars rarely leave his face as he scans the forest.

'Military Macaws,' he announces, pointing high overhead. 'Good sighting.'

'Rare?'

'It's not that they're rare, it's that they're an "indicator species". They indicate the healthiness of the forest, so if we've got macaws it means the forest is in good condition.'

In the space of an hour he's introduced me to the wonderful world of russet-backed orependulas, bare-necked fruit crows and drab water-tyrants. 'There are more species per square mile here than anywhere else on this planet,' Barry rattles on from behind his binoculars . . . 'Seventeen *hundred* species. And it's not just the birds. Peru has the highest bio-diversity on earth. Butterflies, rats – look! on the bank there, fasciated tiger heron.'

By the time we moor up for lunch even *I* can recognize a fasciated tiger heron. They have a slightly lugubrious quality, tall and thin like cypress trees in a cemetery.

By midday we are into land owned by the Machiguenga Indians. Their children splash about in the water and we can see them on the rocks washing their clothes or crossing the stream in perilously fragile balsa rafts. A young boy swings a fish-tail on a length of twine round his head and flings it out into the water. With their fringed haircuts and simple brown robes the Machiguenga look as though they are from a time long past. I wave, but they don't wave back.

As we draw closer to the Pongo de Manaique the cloud thickens and a light drizzle begins to fall. Not good rapid-shooting weather. We decide to make camp and hope for an improvement tomorrow. Pitch our tents on grey volcanic sand. Adolfo and friends take one of the boats out and come back with a three-foot catfish for supper.

Take my towel and sponge-bag and walk along the bank to find a suitable place to wash.

'Don't pee in the water,' Barry shouts after me. 'There's a small barbed fish which will latch onto a stream of urine and swim right up the penis.'

Bio-diversity is a wonderful thing.

DAY 193: *Pongo de Manaique, Urubamba River*

Slept a blissfully peaceful (and rare) eight hours, having at last found a corner of the Pacific Rim free from cockerels, dogs, traffic, discos, karaoke, bicycle bells, babies and Chinese firecrackers. Only the deeply comforting rush of the Urubamba River accompanied my dreams. This morning, as I clean my teeth in it, I fall to wondering how much of what I spit out will find its way into the Atlantic.

The weather has improved enough for us to have little excuse not to shoot the Pongo rapids as soon as camp is struck. Everyone seems remarkably calm at the prospect. Fraser sits decoratively on a rock reading an ancient edition of *Hello* magazine. Barry has Nigel's short-wave radio clamped to his ear in a hopeless attempt to locate some commentary on the England v. Spain Euro 96 game.

Under grey, dirty skies the river looks dirty too, as our three canoes set out, watched on our way by a yellow-headed vulture which has had an eye on us since breakfast. Everything has been extra carefully lashed down, including Basil, who can't swim, and Clem, who can barely move his back today.

Adolfo stands in the prow, feeling out depth with a stick, as Gustavo bounces the boat over a succession of increasingly high waves that back into us. As the river accelerates the forest on either side of us falls eerily quiet. Ahead of us the foothills of the Andes come to an end in a dark, mist-covered wall which there seems no way through.

Suddenly a remarkable thing happens. As we bob and bounce and slither towards the Pongo, Nigel's radio bursts into life and into the middle of the turbulent Urubamba comes a voice from Wembley. Barry screams at me over the sloshing and slopping of the water.

'Extra time! They're playing extra time!'

'Pongo! Pongo!' shouts Gustavo, pointing ahead.

A wall of rock sixty or seventy feet high materializes from the misty greyness.

'Eight minutes left!' yells Barry, as Gustavo searches the fast water for a route that will take us away from the rock without grounding on the gravel beds and flipping us over. There is something quite ridiculously coincidental that two of my great loves, travel and football, should thus converge; that, at the very moment we enter one of the most potentially dangerous passages of this nine-month journey, England should be playing for its life. El Tel and me, both in a dug-out.

Water slaps over and into the boat, forcing Barry to stow the radio as we sheer away from the foot of the cliff. We swing, twist, bounce against a couple of sturdy backwashes, then all at once are out of the frothing rapid and into the smooth limpid stillness of the gorge.

Nothing I have read or fantasized about has prepared me for this place. It looks as though high explosive, rather than a river, has split through this last mile of the Andes. The walls are sharply fractured, with rocky overhangs, sheared off like the stumps of shattered bridges. Lianas hang down to the water, some tipped with orange-red flowers like up-turned candelabra. Water, pouring constantly down smooth black mossy flanks, has worn the rock into weird and wonderful shapes – symmetrical fluted surfaces, perfectly smoothed bowls, caves and chambers.

It is an enchanted world. The air is quite still, parakeet cries echo from above, white-collared swifts dart along the water. A blue morpho, the largest butterfly I've ever seen, moves lazily among the rocks. The animist Machiguenga believe the morphos are forest gods patrolling their territory.

We put in to an inlet in the lee of one of the two last cliffs that face each other across the river like great grey walls, and on a radio, with the signal fading and surging, listen to eighty thousand people half a world away, cheering a goalkeeper's save and England's progress to the semi-finals.

After we sail past the walls and out of the Andes, everything is an anti-climax. The transition to lowland is swift and total. Volcanic rock and hard black beaches are replaced by soft red mudbanks with a tendency to collapse into the water. The scenery, released from the exciting confinement of the Pongo, spreads itself out, wide, low and flat. The river, though still prone to the odd stretch of difficult fast water becomes wider and more even-tempered. A cayman, one of the crocodile family, pale and chalk-white, perks its head at our approach, then slides off its sandbar and into the water.

We make camp for the night on a sandy beach where the river forks round a low island. A pair of bat falcons with black heads and yellow eye-holes are perched motionless on top of a dead tree. Tall stands of *cana brava* – wild sugar cane – rise behind us to a height of fifteen feet or more before folding over and bending gracefully toward the ground.

Later: Basil, who has been out by the river for a smoke, reappears in some distress. Apparently he had heard a snake slither by him, heading for the tents. The men have cornered it. Barry calms him down. Any snake here, he says, would be pretty harmless. Eventually he is persuaded to take a look at it. He jumps a mile. 'My God! That's a fer-de-lance!' Apparently it's the second most dangerous snake in the Amazon, after the bushmaster. Basil gives up smoking for the rest of the evening, and the snake, a thin hapless creature, is put to death by the boatmen.

DAY 194: *Urubamba River*

Diarrhoea throughout the night. Four times I reach for the torch and toilet paper, unzip my tent without making any noise (impossible) and tramp across the sand to the lavatory tent. Unzip this without making any noise (impossible) and then juggle torch and toilet paper while trying not to look in the hole, or worse still drop the torch in it. I'm not the only one struck down. On my way back Basil trudges past me muttering, 'If God had meant me to live like this he'd have given me four legs and fur.'

A cool, overcast day. Chilly headwind. At the mouth of the Camisea River, a tributary of the Urubamba, we come across a tall red and white marker pole which is the first evidence of the *petroleros* – the oil men who have signed a contract in the last month to open up the vast reserves beneath the jungle floor.

Walking a little way up the shore from our new camp-site we come across a young Indian, in green cotton shirt and jeans, fishing with a bow and arrow. He stands at the water's edge gazing intently and silently into the river. When he has selected a victim he coils into an absolutely motionless cat-like crouch. After holding this for what seems like several minutes, he suddenly unleashes the arrow. He steps forward and reaches into the water. It has gone straight through the head of a small white fish. In return for a cigarette he shows us the arrow, made from a length of *cana brava* with a barbed nail as its head and the bow, made from *chonta*, part of a palm tree. The fishing's good now, he says, the water level is down and they're easier to spot. He invites us up to his village for the Feast of St John celebrations tomorrow.

Later that night: On my way back from a 2 a.m. visit to the loo tent I see lights approaching along the water and in amongst the trees. All sorts of panicky thoughts go through my mind, from the scene at the end of *Apocalypse Now*, to our supper conversation about uncontacted tribes further up the Camisea River, to a fear that the villagers will have presumed we are *petroleros* and come to wipe us out. Into my tent. Zip it up against the world and sit there bolt upright with my heart thudding, until they're close enough for me to make out that the lights are from fishing boats and the men are not looking at me but staring silently and intently at the water.

DAY 195

In the Machiguenga village of Shivankoreni the Fiesta de San Juan begins with a series of mournful blasts on a conch shell summoning the villagers to ancient ceremonies. At least, this is what it sounds like as we scramble up the slippery clay path that leads from the river to a collection of wood-framed, tin-roofed houses raised a few feet above hardened mud and receding grass. In fact, any conch shell exists only in my imagination. The sound is produced by blowing through a length of plastic tubing and the ancient ceremonies turn out to be a football match. Even my illusion about the timelessness of this riverside village is quickly disabused when I ask the head-man how far back in the mists of time lie the origins of his village. He thinks for a moment before replying. 'Thirty-seven years.'

Shivankoreni is a settlement in transition. The wood-frame huts are traditional but the new tin roofs are a sign of prosperity. The football match, organized by the younger men with all the earnestness of a club game in England – a team list, distribution of shirts of roughly the same colour – is totally ignored by the village elders who lie about in their plain, sandy-coloured robes, on the stoops of their houses, propped up on one elbow like long-redundant emperors.

The football game, too, is a mixture of ancient and modern. The bow and arrow fisherman we met yesterday has neat skills, a sense of tactics and a pair of football boots, while others play in patched shorts and bare feet. The referee has no watch. A time-keeper keeps the first half to a strict forty-five minutes, but then mysteriously disappears, resulting in an epic second half of almost sixty-three minutes.

A women's game follows. This is shorter and much more exciting. There is no semblance of a team strip, most of them play in dresses and skirts. Nor is there any inequality of footwear. All are barefoot. It's a cracking game though. Skirts are hitched up and shots hammered in from 20 yards. The memory of a beefy grandmother weaving through the defence in a long cotton frock and finding where the net would be, if they had one, from 20 yards out, will stay with me for a long time.

After the football, a car battery is produced, laid on the table and leads are attached to what at first looks like some small generator but turns out to be a sound system. Spanish disco music fills the air but no one responds to it. There is much drinking of *masato*, fermented yucca juice, which is made by the women of the village. Only after I've tasted a wooden bowlful am I told that the older women still use saliva as a substitute for sugar in its preparation. It tasted quite harmless, like slightly sour raspberry yoghurt. Wait with some apprehension to see the effect of Machiguenga spittle on my troubled gastric system.

The feast itself is peremptory. The women emerge from their huts with various dishes and a circle is formed in the shade of a grove of trees, where rush mats have been laid out and banana leaves cut on which to place the food. The elders are roused from their porches and, when standing, look even more magnificently lazy and imperial, with striped habits and headbands. The more illustrious of them have deep red parallel lines painted on their faces with *achiote*, made from the ground-up beans of a hairy red fruit found abundantly on bushes here (and now much sought after by Western cosmetic manufacturers).

When everyone is assembled a grace is spoken – which must indicate a missionary influence – and *juanitos* (named after John, the saint whose day is being celebrated) are passed around. These consist of fish and rice, or tapir meat and rice, wrapped neatly in a *bijao* leaf. There is desultory talk but not much else.

It might be our presence that inhibits them, but I think it is more than that. As we leave, the headman confirms that the Shell oil company provided them with tin roofs in return for their co-operation and that he expects the *petroleros* to return soon, in numbers, to activate the wells they have explored, and in some cases, already dug. He is happy that they are coming back, but it might account for the listlessness of the village. Everyone in Shivankoreni knows that very soon things will never be the same again.

An hour or so back on the Urubamba when the high whine of a speedboat can be heard from a tributary river and there emerges a fast aluminium-hulled dinghy beneath whose sun canopy sit a dozen oil men. They are arranged in orderly rows, Lego-like, with matching yellow hard hats and orange life preservers. It's impossible to see their faces and they barely glance our way as they sweep past and disappear down river leaving us to rock about in their wash and their indefinable aura of hostility.

DAY 196: *On the Urubamba to Sepahua*

Fifth night under canvas. Food is running short. No more bacon and egg breakfasts. Bread rolls hard as pebbles. Worse still, only one box of Chilean Red for the next two nights.

'Banana Quit,' says Barry suddenly, looking up from his coffee. For a moment I think he must have cracked, but he's pointing across at a tree branch on the edge of the jungle. 'Can you hear it?'

The Urubamba is growing wider and more middle-aged as we move north, out of Machiguenga and into Piro tribal territory.

By late afternoon we have reached the mouth of a narrow creek in which the town of Sepahua is situated. There is a table on the beach where we want to make camp and behind it sit two young soldiers, the T-shirts of whose uniforms announce them as members of the *Batalia Contrasubversivo*. They are obliged to search all river craft coming in to Sepahua for smuggling in general and drugs in particular. The sun beats down as we wait for Barry to talk them round, show the right papers, etc. Evidently this is not enough and they demand an inspection of the bags before they will allow us onto their bit of sand.

Sepahua might well have been the town Colonel Percy Fawcett, the explorer who died in the Amazon in the fifties, was referring to when he talked about 'the sort of place that looks a dump on the way in and a metropolis on the way back'.

After six days on the river the mere fact that it contains a bar with chairs, tables and cold beer is enough to give it an air of Parisian sophistication.

Clem's back is giving him increasing discomfort and he is now seriously immobilized. Though we have to return to the sandbanks for another night in tents we cannot stay on the river much longer.

Tonight fork and sheet lightning split the western sky. Thunder rumbles, coming closer. The air is more humid here and the insects are giving us their full attention.

DAY 197: *Sepahua*

At seven o'clock the young soldiers from Lima, who have been given the unenviable task of guarding the beach at Sepahua, appear from the town carrying two chairs, a table and three Kalashnikov rifles. Their arrival coincides with the start of a slow, deliberate downpour and pretty soon they pack up and traipse off the way they've come. Their departure does not produce a tidal wave of *narcos* and *contrabandidos*. In fact the first boat to make a landing is a dug-out full of schoolchildren in neat grey pinafores and white cotton shirts, standing in a solemn line as they cross the wide Urubamba from the misty western shore. I expect them at any moment to break into 'The Hills are Alive!'. Clem is feeling worse today and cannot rise from his bed unaided. A marvellous improvised chair is made for him out of boxes and benches in which he can sit upright and supported. From a distance he looks like some mediaeval monarch.

I spend half an hour in a futile attempt to rid my tent of sand. Have no clean clothes left. It's just a question of wearing what is least disgusting. In the middle of the morning the last of the rain clears leaving behind a blanket of suffocating heat. The only possible defence against this energy-sapping airlessness is not to move at all, but enquiries need to be made about flights out, and Barry and I walk along the beach and into town.

Meet two American missionaries who are hoping to fly to Lima tonight. They have heard there are more thunderstorms to come and there is a danger of the river flash-flooding. An image of Clem as King Canute, helpless as the water rises around his chair, comes to mind.

There is absolutely nothing we can do today but sit out the delay, have a beer and hope that we can pick up the England versus Germany semi-final later in the afternoon. Sepahua is a place of convivial and infectious idleness. It's a frontier town where no judgements are made, no questions asked and no particular behaviour is expected. It is not twinned with anywhere or kept clean by any worthy group. It has no heritage trail or historic centre. It is just a place in the middle of the jungle and if you don't like it you don't have to stay.

Barry is unable to pick up the World Service, but manages to find a weak but detectable commentary from Wembley, in French. As Gareth Southgate steps up for '*le penaltie sixieme*' we are standing under a pomegranate tree in the shabby main square. Gustavo, the boatman, seriously the worse for drink, weaves his way towards us and slips his arm around our shoulders. Southgate's shot is saved. Gustavo loves us all, he really wants to tell us that, now the hard work is over, we should all have some fun, a few laughs, a drink or two to celebrate. Muller scores. '*Les Allemands ont prevalu*!' Germany has won. Gustavo grins affectionately and squeezes my shoulder tightly.

DAY 198: *Sepahua to Pucallpa*

After our seventh night by the Urubamba we carry all our gear up the river bank for what we hope and pray is the last time. Almost the first people we run into are the American missionaries.

'I thought you were going to Lima last night?' I ask them.

'So did we, but the flight never arrived.'

'Any reason given?'

They shake their heads.

'It's the way things happen here.'

The prospect of spending another night on a sandbank is so unthinkable that I find myself scanning Sepahua's fly-blown waterfront for some alternative accommodation. Nothing, apart from the bar and the snooker hall, looks a serious possibility.

There is a small airline office attached to the general store, and the lady who looks after it, having completed the sale of some powdered milk, comes through to give us news of our flight to Pucallpa. Fierce thunderstorms are forecast. She recommends we catch whatever flight comes in today. Wherever it's going.

Six o'clock in the evening: Beer at the Hotel Sol del Oriente in Pucallpa, 207 miles further up river.

This sprawling jungle town of a hundred thousand souls is a rude shock after the river banks. It swirls with noise. My room has a view of a wall topped with broken glass and beyond it an adult movie-house showing *Pretty Anal*. A visiting football team staying at the hotel is up most of the night replaying the game in the corridors of the hotel, and the restaurant can't even raise a chicken sandwich. Come back sand and toilet tents, all is forgiven.

DAY 200: *Pucallpa*

There could be worse places than Pucallpa in which to celebrate two hundred days on the road, but no one can think of one. The hotel is built to provide a cool refuge from the tropical heat. On a day like today when a severe cold snap has brought grey, chilly weather to the town, it is certainly cool, but offers nothing in the way of a refuge. Fall asleep wrapped in a sweater and wake with eight days' dirty laundry staring at me.

Breakfast at Don José's restaurant. It's a long, narrow, convivial, old-fashioned working café with check tablecloths and shrewd middle-aged waitresses who look as if they've seen it all. Shipibo Indian women drift in and out with sets of bows and arrows for sale, but the pace is slow and the coffee almost bearable. Don José's considerably improves my perceptions of Pucallpa, and I can almost understand why people might want to stay in the town for more than a couple of hours.

A neat, soft-spoken Frenchman called Didier Lacasse, has lived here for ten years. Originally he came out to research the traditional medicines of the Peruvian Amazon, and in particular the use of the *ayahuaska* vine. Local shamans prepare it in such a way that hallucinogenic trances can be induced in healer and patient to cure physical and psychological conditions. Now Didier has his own herbal surgery five miles out of town, to which he drives me on an immaculately kept motor bike. His treatment is based on restoring our closer links with nature and though it may sound a little vague and dreamy the increasing interest in the Peruvian rain forest by the international pharmaceutical industry confirms his enthusiastic assessment of the potential of jungle medicines. One vine, the *una de gato* (cat's claw) has been proved to stimulate the immune system and reduce inflammation and is now being seriously tested for use in the treatment of cancer and Aids.

Along with interest in, and demand for, the fruits of the rain forest, Pucallpa will continue to grow, to become madder and even more raucous. It has a direct road link to Lima, which may well be extended across the river, giving Brazil, only 65 miles away to the east, its first ever road access to the Pacific. Our next destination, the old jungle capital of Iquitos, can only be reached by plane or boat. Bearing in mind how long we took to make our way down the Urubamba we decide that a plane is the safest way through the next 450 miles of jungle.

DAY 203: *Iquitos*

Iquitos has the past that Pucallpa lacked. Whether or not it has a future is debatable. Its success was built on rubber and the river. The rubber trade is long gone, the trees being found to be susceptible to a virus not present in the rubber plantations of Malaysia and the Far East. Its pre-eminence as an Amazon trade route has been superseded by the Panama Canal, air cargo and construction of the trans-Andine highway which has missed out Iquitos altogether.

But there is still an honorary British Consul here. To find out more about the place, I seek him out at an address on Arica Street. It's a low, embattled frontage of two grey wooden doors squeezed tight by the smart new Telefonica Peru offices next door. A noisy tide of *moto-carros* – three-wheel taxis – ebbs and flows busily past. Press the bell beside a brass plaque which reads 'Consulado Britanico'. A small, neat, elderly man in blue sleeveless shirt with greying hair brushed carefully back from a pale, almost pasty face, answers the door. He introduces himself as Lewis Power, born seventy odd years ago to a French mother and Irish father. The consular office is in what was once the thriving warehouse of his father's import-export business and is now a dark and dusty shed more like the set of *Steptoe and Son*. There is a clutter of old wooden filing cabinets, weights, lifting chains, cables, engine cylinders, ledgers and trade directories nibbled by rats and mice – the rotting remains of half a century of commerce.

In his office a German game show is playing on television. 'Satellite,' explains the consul, nodding at the screen. 'I speak five languages, you know.'

Lewis can just remember the rubber boom, when eight ocean-going cargo ships left Iquitos for Liverpool every month. 'It was closer than Lima then. A ship could sail from here across the Atlantic to Liverpool in six weeks. It would take them over two months going round the Cape to Lima.'

Everything around him, apart from a framed photograph of his father – 'I cleaned it this morning' – is covered in varying thicknesses of dust. He blows some off a copy of the *Peruvian Times* for 1955 showing a confident, expanding Iquitos with modern buildings and new hotels, society weddings and un-apologetic ads for exporters of alligator, crocodile and peccary skins. Iquitos, he says, is still a city of consequence. Capital of the huge department of Loreto and full of people (350,000 at the last count), though I get the impression that the Consul considers them the wrong sort of people.

'Chinese . . . Chinese all over the place. Every corner. And of course the *Sierranos*.'

'*Sierranos*?'

'People from the west, from the Andes. They've taken over. They don't come alone either. They come with their families. Eight people come along with them.'

Lewis Power and his sister Edith, with whom he lives, are selling their flat and planning to move out.

'Why?'

'Why? Because I'm sick and tired of the Amazon.'

The Malecon is a new esplanade built overlooking the river. It is all curved balustrading and painted plasterwork and I approach it with ill-concealed excitement. One of my most tenacious childhood ambitions was to see the Amazon. (I was only partly put off by the disappearance of my hero Colonel Fawcett, missing, believed eaten, somewhere on the Bolivian border.) I had many dreams of the awesome size and power of the world's greatest river. Now, at last, they can become reality.

The reality is that this is the dry season and the promenades of Iquitos do not overlook a mile-wide swirling torrent, but low sandspits and grassy meadows across which arms of water stretch and peter out. I've not reached the Amazon yet. But there are compensations. A number of friendly bars and restaurants are strung out along the Malecon and there is plenty of human activity to watch, especially as the sun goes down. From behind a bottle of beer at Jaime's excellent restaurant (maps and books of the area line the walls inside), I watch a man with no legs and only one arm spin and twist himself around to music like a dervish, while a group of huge Americans, each one like Gulliver in Lilliput, pass through the crowd trailing a grubby retinue of street children in their wake – shoe blacks, candy sellers and sharp-witted opportunists on the cadge for a *sol* or two. A snake-skin seller comes by and stops at our table offering us the pick of his wares for fifty *sols*. We defer, but he returns as we're eating, carrying a black plastic bag from which he extricates a white skull. 'Jaguar,' he says, in the hushed tones of a car salesman. Seeing our immediate lack of interest, he proceeds to move the jaw up and down like a puppet. 'Fifty *sols*.'

DAY 205

At the southern end of Iquitos is the barrio of Belen. Seen from the Malecon, the outline of tight-clustered roofs and the houses on stilts make it look like a print of the Thames in seventeenth-century London. Closer to, it's a seething wreck of a place, manically bustling, worn from overuse rather than neglect. On a low hill leading to the river little children are selling sacks of charcoal, a man is rolling a barrel of *aguardiente* – the local sugar-cane spirit – while another spreads wild boar skins out to dry on the sidewalk. I expect Moll Flanders to come round the corner any minute.

The streets level off as they get closer to the river and wind along between forests of piling. This will become a lake in the wet season. For now it's full of people, stalls, and decomposing rubbish. On balconies, set above heaps of uncovered garbage, people grow the medicinal herbs they take for dysentery. Infant mortality in Belen is between 18 and 20 per cent, yet more and more people are coming to live here.

Alcohol and cigarettes are used to dull the pain of life in Belen. A big, attractive girl called Julia rolls cigarettes from rich dark tobacco called *mapacho*. In one swift, flowing movement, she uses a pencil to keep the paper straight, pulls the tobacco out of a plastic bag, fills, rolls, then trims the ends with a pair of scissors, all so swiftly that she can produce three thousand cigarettes a day. She gives me one free. The taste is powerful and very satisfying, like double strength Gauloise. It's the best I've had since giving up smoking. And that was twenty-seven years ago.

Once it reaches the riverside the town continues into the water, which is one big floating market. This is where the *canoeiras* work. The *canoeiras* are floating prostitutes, and you can't miss them. Their canoes are pink. A pimp in a water-taxi will take you out to them for half a *sol*, turn his back discreetly and bring you back for half a *sol*. The *canoeira* charges five *sols*, so the entire transaction, plus a trip on the Amazon, comes in at just over two dollars.

DAY 208

We are becalmed in Iquitos waiting for a river boat to take us to Leticia on the Colombian border. It is not a popular destination, it seems. Everyone has a rumour to cap a rumour about Colombia. Dark tales of narcos and guerrillas.

A group of very big Americans currently in Iquitos are said to be part of a US DEA (Drug Enforcement Agency) offensive against cocaine factories in the Colombian jungle. They claim to be tourists whose plane has been delayed.

Today, with luck, we shall be on our way. A ship is leaving this afternoon, travelling down the Amazon bound for Santa Rosa. Not a moment too soon. It's mid-summer. The temperatures have been back to the seasonal average over the last few days, in the high nineties, and, with little to do but think about families back home going on holidays without them, the crew is restless.

I've quite enjoyed Iquitos and its lazy, undemanding comforts. Its colonial streets have style and a run-down, understated elegance, and though it is surrounded on all sides by thousands of miles of jungle it feels open, expansive and civilized.

The *El Arca* is a three-deck Amazon river boat built in 1882 and restored by Paul Wright, an American who made a journey from Alaska to Tierra del Fuego by motor-bike and so liked Iquitos that he came back to live here. It's moored up near the old market and is approached via a narrow and precarious wooden stairway that rocks and sways with every movement. A man comes by me carrying seventy-two full Coca-Cola bottles secured by a woven harness across his forehead. An ant-like stream of travellers, porters and passengers runs to and from the *collectivos* – the wood-hulled, flat bottomed, thatched-roofed commuter ferries which fight each other for space at the pontoons. Children appear from nowhere taking one last chance to flog me anything from chewing gum to calculators, bracelets to boxer shorts.

By late afternoon we have pulled out onto the river. At last I'm on the Amazon. It's enormous, shapeless, difficult to feel romantic about. Take a final, fond look at Iquitos. The pilot of the *El Arca* tells me that because of the sediment brought down by the Amazon it will be totally cut off from the river in ten years' time.

At its full speed of six knots, the *El Arca* could have made the 300 miles between Iquitos and the Colombian border in under forty-eight hours, but the price we have paid for hitching a ride is that we have become part of a tour. It is a small and exclusive tour – an Indian family now living in San Francisco, two Australians in late middle age, an English couple, two single American women – but it is a tour all the same, and it will not be hurried.

This evening we have an introductory address from our resident naturalist, Daniel. He is small, dour, passionate about his country, the river, the rain forest and, you guessed it, bio-diversity. After almost half an hour of dazzling us with extraordinary facts about the Amazon he asks for questions.

One of the American ladies put up her hand straight away. 'There's a good two inches of water in my shower that I can't get to drain.'

DAY 209: *On the Amazon*

Today we are up at the crack of dawn to disembark into small boats and explore creeks overhung with mangrove trees and a jungle lagoon where utter peace and tranquillity is only disturbed by the braying cry of a bird whose name I particularly like – the Horned Screamer. On the way, we learn from Daniel that a greater volume of water is discharged from the mouth of the Amazon than the combined total of the world's next eight longest rivers put together, and that annual rainfall in the Amazon Basin has dropped from 350 inches per year in the 1920s to 150 inches a year now, mainly as a result of deforestation.

Reeling from so many facts so early in the morning, we return gratefully to the *El Arca* for breakfast. It is only a brief respite. The boat steams down river to a native village where we disembark once again and watch traditional dancing performed fairly badly by bored natives. By lunchtime the temperature has reached ninety-nine degrees. This whole long, hot day is made worthwhile for me by seeing, on the bank, an ocelot kitten, cradled in the arms of a young Indian girl. It is one of the most beautiful creatures I have seen. A long body with perfect spotted markings. A compact, graceful feline head with big black and white ears and an expression that was proud, wise and anxious at the same time. The little girl said she would sell it to me for 200 dollars. I declined of course. I'm going to Alaska – it wouldn't be happy there. That evening I ask Daniel what would become of it. He said it would be killed for its skin – quite soon.

DAY 210

The tour activities, which begin this morning at 5.45, are written up in chalk on a blackboard outside the dining cabin. Highlight of today is an evening expedition to a lake near the town of Caballococha to see and hear Amazon river night life. Bats, not baccarat. Once in the middle of this great black lake Daniel orders the engine to be cut and is in the middle of a deeply felt dissertation on the unity and interdependence of all natural life when a cloud of mosquitoes gathers around him, attacking him so fiercely that he is forced to sit down and order the boat to get moving, and fast.

When we are back on the *El Arca*, Daniel is at pains to correct any negative impression he might have given about mosquitoes. 'Like any insect, they have many uses. One. They pollinate a certain kind of orchid. Two. They are important as food for bats.' There is a pause and an expectant silence.

'So, tomorrow at six o'clock. OK?'

Later the ship's generator breaks down, so no air-con, no pump for water, no light in the cabin. We are moored up for the night and the air is stagnant, muggy and lifeless. I have doused myself in so many layers of insect repellent that my skin feels like fly-paper. Open the cabin window as far as it will go and wait for the bat food to start buzzing round me. And this was supposed to be the comfortable part of the journey.

COLOMBIA

DAY 211: *From the Amazon to Bogotá*

Generator still out, so wash myself with what remains of my Kwik-Wipes.

By 8.30 we are at *Las Tres Fronteras*, the only point from which Brazil, Peru and Colombia – the first, third and fourth largest countries of South America – can all be seen at once.

Key locations on the map are rarely up to much when you actually get to them and this is no exception. Under low skies and thick, oppressive humidity, this epic crossroads looks what it is – low, cleared banks alongside a wide, sluggish, muddy river. Just another corner of the huge Amazon basin.

Black-shirted Peruvian customs and immigration officers board us, then we bid farewell to our fellow-travellers, off-load our equipment into two fast dinghies and head across the mile-wide stream leaving behind the *El Arca*, and Peru, which we have taken a month to cross.

Leticia (Latin for happiness) is the Colombian frontier town. There are problems right away. The coca-fields we had hoped to film here have been destroyed by a recent US-encouraged offensive (surprise, surprise) and what hotels there are in Leticia are full of congressmen down from Bogotá for a bio-diversity conference. We rest and wash at the Hotel Anaconda while our redoubtable fixer, Marcey, kicks whatever ass she can to get us on a plane north.

She is successful with the last flight of the day. Around midnight our British Aerospace 146 carries us over the Equator and out of the jungle. From sea level to 8000 feet. From thirty-eight degrees to ten degrees. From the southern to the northern hemisphere. To our twelfth capital of the journey so far, Bogotá, Colombia.

The hotel, which we reach at 2 a.m., is classy and comfortable. Linen sheets and classical music playing on the radio. Only a chain of angry red bites around the ankles reminds me where I've come from.

DAY 213: *Bogotá*

It's hard to understand Bogotá. In one way I feel very much at home here. Oma Libros, a bookshop and café I discovered yesterday, is like an Aladdin's cave, combining under one roof all the things I've missed since leaving Santiago – books, tapes, good fresh coffee and English language newspapers. The Italian restaurant next door is as good as any of my favourites in London. Yet, this morning, when I step out into these same streets it's a Sunday and the steel shutters are down and private security men, all in black and looking like something out of an Oswald Mosley rally, are patrolling properties, pulling aggressively on the chains of large Alsatian dogs.

The centre of town, around the Plaza Bolivar, is full of gorgeous interiors reflecting the panache of a city whose full name – Santa Fe de Bogotá del Nuevo Reino de Granada de las Indias del Mar Oceano – shows the seriousness with which the Spanish regarded this part of their Empire. But as my companion, a Colombian lawyer, points out, less than ten years ago, on this historic square, the army blasted a guerrilla group out of the Palace of Justice with the loss of one hundred lives, 'decimating the legal profession', as she puts it, and reducing the standards of law, if not order, at a stroke.

There is a strong middle class in Colombia. The economy is in better shape than in much of the rest of South America and yet the newspapers carry the news this morning that Samper, the Colombian President, has been refused a visa to visit the US because of his alleged associations with drug barons. Central Bogotá has fine museums and galleries and old houses restored with a striking sense of style, while a few blocks away everyone turns a blind eye as '*los limpiadores*' – vigilante death squads – go about their business 'cleansing' the capital of undesirables at the rate of a dozen a week. There are the most up to date gyms and health clubs and yet only in Bogotá would you hear of a jogger being mugged, and his blood taken. I don't understand it, and I need someone to help me.

DAY 214

Tim Ross, an English journalist, with long greying Sixties hairstyle and a preference for shades and jeans, has an insatiable appetite for the lowest street life in the most dangerous city of one of the most dangerous countries in the world. He lives in a comfortable apartment on the twenty-sixth floor of a downtown tower block with a long-suffering wife and a very fat rabbit

'Oh, I've had the usual death threats,' he says, adding, with a hint of regret, 'not for a while though.'

Tim is clearly addicted, not to drugs, but to drug-users. His life revolves around the danger they live with, and from which he draws much of his own energy and passion. He offers to take us to the most dangerous part of Bogotá around the *Calle Cartouche* – Bullet Street.

He cannot take us all, as we must be in one car and on no account open a window or get out. So Nigel, Fraser and I find ourselves squeezed in the back of a twenty-year-old, black and yellow Dodge cab with Tim and his driver Herman. I ask Tim why he thinks there are so many drug addicts in Colombia. The reason, he tells me, is partly because it is a major producer, and where there is production there is use, and partly because the institutions of the country are largely controlled by a few rich families so that political life is inert. There is no national will to tackle the problems of the desperately poor.

Only six blocks from the Presidential Palace we are into streets which are as grim as any I've seen on this or any other journey. Figures lie about in the litter and rubbish; others stand, swaying and unfocused; others, on the look out for anything to pay for their next hit, eye us malevolently.

As we turn into the *Calle Cartouche*, shouts follow the car and later something cracks into the side of us.

'They're throwing rocks,' says Tim, turning his head quickly from side to side. 'They assume we're death squads or police or something.'

Nigel wants to go round again but Tim is reluctant.

'Next time it could be more than stones, it could be iron bars and machetes.'

In a street of once quite handsome houses, now burned out, trashed and lined with rubbish, the police have set up a roadblock and are stopping people. Tim has a word with them and returns to tell us that we can get out, but must stay close to the car. As Nigel films I notice a small group of men immediately react to the sight of a camera. Their looks of curiosity harden into hostility and I'm aware of words spoken and movement made in our direction. These are not the dazed druggies, these are harder, meaner people altogether. For the first time since the demonstration in Seoul, I feel that violence is not far away.

We extricate ourselves and head back to Tim's place. I invite him to come and relax with us over lunch at the Margarita del Ocho, a restaurant I've heard about where horses gallop up and down between the tables. He makes a face and shakes his head. The restaurant is owned by the Ochoa family. The father, Don Fabio, actually runs the place and, though he has never been in trouble himself, his two sons have just been released from prison after a five and a half-year sentence for large-scale drug trafficking.

Lunch at the barn-like Margarita del Ocho is off-putting, not only because of what Tim has told me but because I find it difficult to chew up the large chunks of red meat as horses strut and prance past my plate, pursued, at a discreet distance, by staff with dustpans and long brushes.

To the surprise of all concerned, Don Fabio has agreed to be interviewed by me. In Spanish. I have two worries. One, I don't speak Spanish. Two, what do you ask a father whose sons have been found guilty of drug trafficking? Is the weather always like this? What's your favourite novel?

There is precious little time to plan this interview. Don Fabio looms out of his office. Either he has modelled himself on Marlon Brando or Marlon Brando modelled himself on Don Fabio. Whatever, it is the Godfather I see before me.

I feel I should quake and yet looking at him I see only an old man. He wears a stetson and a black and white striped poncho. His eyes, strong and piercing, stare out defiantly from a pale and bloodless complexion, speckled with liver spots.

I confine my questions to those interests closest to him – horses, horses and horses. Marcey whispers each question to me in Spanish from behind my back and it goes so well that Don Fabio beams in a slightly dazed way and agrees to get on a horse and ride for us.

His lackeys are thrown into some confusion as a mount is summoned and he is hoisted into the saddle. For a moment it looks as though they will drop the Don or pitch him clean over the horse and down the other side. Throughout the whole undignified procedure the old man stares forward, eyes locked in an expression of mute suffering. But, once in the saddle, he is transformed. He is confident and, despite his bulk, a graceful, skilful rider. He trots off into the restaurant to demonstrate the strutting little *Paso Fino*, which he has taught his horses to perform. There is delighted applause from the families round their tables. I think he has already forgotten about us.

DAY 217: *Cosquez*

On our way out of Bogotá, in the Boyaca Valley west of the city where, in 1819, Simon Bolivar fought the crucial battle that won Colombia independence from the Spanish Empire, is Cosquez, the largest, richest emerald mine in the world. It opened over ten years ago but produced nothing for the first five years as the mountain in which the mines are located was fought over by rival bandit groups. Three thousand five hundred people were killed in the struggle for control.

Today, six thousand live on the mountain, but only twelve hundred of them are directly employed by the private company that has the mining concession from the government. They in turn employ a private army to help run it.

Weapons are carried openly. I see a man casually bouncing a pump action shotgun up and down on his foot. Rifles and double-barrelled hand guns are carried like shoulder bags. The women look as hard as the men. They wear tight jeans with revolvers tucked into the belt. It is a *McCabe and Mrs Miller* world of tired, hard, red-eyed faces, of black mud tracks along which four-wheel drives slide and slither to avoid horses and donkeys carrying supplies.

To keep the locals sweet, public access is allowed to a stream which runs out of the mine at the bottom of the mountain. Anything they find here they can keep. A crowd of two or three hundred people is drawn down into the heat of the valley in the hope of finding crumbs from the rich man's table. They are called *guaceros* – scavengers. They scrabble around in the trickle of inky-black effluent, some shovelling gravel onto sieves and examining it, others, less methodically, throwing the shale onto the side of the stream, while some dig desperately into the slurry as if trying to rescue a loved one. Occasionally, sodden figures covered in black slime emerge from the ooze like primaeval life.

Further down, away from the mouth of the stream, where the pickings are less good but conditions less frantic, I see a woman and her son working through the silt. She moves heavy stones out of the stream and squats to peer at what might be beneath them. Her son, who can't be more than five or six years old stares around. Behind them a dog laps at the black water.

From the bank above, where the *guaceros* have built makeshift shops and cafés, the scene around the gushing water-hole has an unnerving resemblance to images of disaster – a plane crash or a landslide. The unreality is compounded when I look a little further up the hill, where the steep slope that the mine-workings have not yet touched is covered with green grass, trees and flowers.

DAY 217: *Cartagena*

Cartagena is a city comparatively free of guerrilla activity, and therefore much sought after by Colombians who can afford it. (Though I did hear that Pablo Escobar, most notorious of all the drug barons, threatened to blow it to pieces when the government vacillated on the subject of his extradition.)

We're nearly back on course. Whilst not a Pacific city (the ocean is 250 miles to the west) Cartagena was the clearing house for the treasures of Spain's Pacific empire. The almost inconceivable wealth of the Andes, extracted by the conquistadors from what is now Ecuador, Bolivia and Peru, was carried across the Isthmus of Panama and assembled behind the walls of Cartagena, before being taken onwards to Europe.

The conquistadors, recognizing a good thing when they saw one, decided to become settlers. A land-rush followed the gold-rush. The colonists found that anything would grow here. The only trouble was that, as so many Indians had died either in fighting or from diseases like smallpox introduced from Europe, they did not have enough labour. So thousands of slaves duly arrived on the Spanish Main, carried from Africa in boats owned largely by Englishmen. With the settlers and the slaves came the missionaries, and there is still a Palace of the Inquisition in the main square of the old town. After the missionaries came the pirates and the privateers like Francis Drake, but Cartagena resisted them all (including, in 1741, the British Admiral, Sir Edward Vernon, who was fought off by Blas De Lezo, a commander with one eye, one arm and one leg). Its wild, unorthodox and entirely unpredictable history continued until 1811 when it became the first city in the New World to declare independence from Spain.

A brutal revenge was extracted for this audacity but when Simon Bolivar finally liberated Cartagena in 1821 he called it *La Heroica* – the Heroic City.

DAY 220

Today is our last day in South America. Nine weeks and a day after setting foot on Cape Horn and nearly eight months after leaving Little Diomede we are into the home straight. It's July, the hottest time of year on the Caribbean coast, the time of fevers and mals de mer. The pleasures of the city, with its living, breathing, civilized old town, not yet camp or chic or over-restored, have been tempered by 100 per cent humidity, which rings sweat from parts of the body I'd have never thought possible.

Colombia should be the perfect tourist destination – it's accessible, modern and, except for internal transport, quite efficient. Yet it remains in the shadow of the *drogistas* and the great and entrenched corruption which allows them such power and influence. I would urge people to visit, but at their own risk. This should frighten away the lazy tourists leaving the adventurous to reap the rewards of this huge, rich, beautiful but blighted country.

MEXICO

DAY 221: *Cartagena to Mexico City*

A sticky, stale dawn. Through the walls of old Cartagena for the last time, passing an elegant iron-work bullring, a fitting last image of a city that takes its pleasures in style. Out along the coast road to the airport. The Caribbean Sea looks tired, as if it's had a bad night. Colourless waves sidle towards the shore and collapse exhausted onto the sand. The air smells of yesterday's heat and the humidity is already suffocating.

At the airport, as they sit out a two hour delay caused by a military fly-past to celebrate Independence Day, smart Colombians are reading the latest offering from their world famous author and national hero Gabriel García Márquez who now lives in Mexico City. A Frenchman, living in Colombia, tells me a good story about the eccentric country we have just come through. After a recent air crash in the Andes, the black-box flight recorder went missing for some considerable time. It was eventually found at the house of an old lady living high in the mountains. She had covered it with a cloth and was using it as an altar.

My image of our next destination is forever tainted by a phrase I remember reading in Charles Nicholl's fine novel, *The Fruit Palace*: 'Fifteen million people live in Mexico City and it smells as if they all farted at once.' Not exactly a tourist-board slogan and I'm prepared for the worst as we land in the Mexican capital four hours after leaving Cartagena. It's raining and I'm told that's good. During the rainy season daily downpours wash the pollution out of the air and clean the atmosphere.

The bad news is that our previous destination casts a long shadow. All baggage coming in from Colombia has to be opened and searched by the anti-drug squad as a matter of course. Our film equipment is viewed with particular suspicion and it is not until three o'clock the next morning that it is finally cleared.

Mexico City, which the locals refer to simply, if confusingly, as Mexico, is a mixture of grim and grand. Modern highways sweep past a colossal spread of characterless concrete box houses, surrounded by scattered debris and brown choked rivers, in which live most of the sixteen million population of the largest city in the world. Eventually these huge *barrios* (slums) resolve into the grid plan layout of all the other Spanish colonial cities, but here in Mexico the distances are greater and the boulevards longer.

Distinctive green and grey Volkswagen-beetle taxis swarm up and down the monumental main thoroughfare, the Paseo de la Reforma, scuttling past statues of the great Aztec leaders, seen off so summarily by stout Cortez and his conquistadors four hundred and seventy years ago. Outside our hotel, looking like a giant stone traffic cop, a statue of Christopher Columbus stands on a roundabout directing us by an outstretched arm and pointed knee along the last few miles of the Reforma to the Plaza de la Constitucion, known as 'the Zocalo', the heart of Mexico and, as far as the conquering Spaniards were concerned, the centre of their New World.

DAY 222: *Mexico City*

Coffee on the seventh floor terrace of the Majestic Hotel overlooking the Zocalo, the city's enormous main square. Mexico's colonial history is spread out below. The stone paving was first laid by Cortés in 1520, rubbing Aztec noses in their defeat by using stone from their own temples. On the far side, in a scalloped niche above the main entrance of the Palacio Nacional, hangs the Dolores bell, originally rung in the town of Dolores Hidalgo to signal the start of the War of Independence against Spanish rule in 1810.

In the centre of the square a group of people, surrounding a portly figure dressed à la Superman, are painting a wooden construction fence with a bold, colourful mural entwined with political graffiti – *Libertad, Trabajo, Dignidad, Respeto, No a la Contaminacion, No al Credito bancario*. The masked man with several spare tyres bulging from beneath a red tunic and gold pants calls himself Super Barrio and he is announcing his candidacy for the forthcoming American election. I go down to listen to his election address.

Thinly disguised as stand-up comedy it is, in fact, a good old-fashioned attack on US imperialism. Even the word America, he says, has been misappropriated by the USA. '*I* am American!' he cries indignantly and the crowd of largely working-class Mexicans applauds. The gist of his message is that the Mexican government, having recently signed a trade agreement with the USA in return for twenty billion dollars-worth of credit, have effectively pawned the nation's pride.

Everything about Super Barrio is deliberate. His outfit is based on those of the masked wrestlers – the *Lucha Libre* (free fighters) – who are heroes in the *barrios* of Mexico City. By wearing masks, the downtrodden and oppressed can be transformed. In the wrestling ring an ordinary man can become a god. The impetus for Super Barrio's grass-roots movement is directly related to Mexico's geographical position. In September 1985 a massive earthquake, measuring 8.1 on the Richter Scale, killed nearly ten thousand people, most of them in the poorly housed areas around Mexico City. Indignation at the government's lack of efficient and effective relief spawned a number of local self-help groups all determined to raise awareness of the appalling conditions in which so many urban Mexicans live.

Leaving Super Barrio to work a growing crowd, I walk across to the Palacio Nacional. Government offices lead off an arcaded classical courtyard. Its walls are decorated with a monumental series of murals by Mexico's most famous artist, Diego Rivera. I could see in these powerful paintings the same sources of inspiration as those of Super Barrio's street politics. Rivera was Marxist and patriot at the same time, idealizing the Aztec past (playing up the weaving and dancing, and playing down the human sacrifices), demonizing the Spanish conquerors and talking boldly and directly to the people.

By the time I leave the Palace, Super Barrio has gone. Around the wooden hoardings stand officials solemnly noting down all the graffiti. A squad of workmen follows after them, painting over every inch of the mural. I stand and watch *Justicia* disappear letter by letter.

Later in the afternoon I go to the Coliseo Theatre to see *Lucha Libre* for myself. A wrestler called El Satanico is fighting Lizmark from Acapulco. The middle-aged lady next to me tells me he used to be a gravedigger. She's obviously a fan. She wears bright red lipstick and her hair is in tight black waxed curls. A large silver crucifix stands out against her red jumper, only to be flung to one side as she leaps up with lusty shouts of 'Kill him!', and 'Smash his teeth out!'.

Looking around I notice many women, some much older than my companion, watching with clinically appraising eyes as legs are grasped, groins clutched, arms wrenched, bodies slammed across bended knees and leapt on from a great height.

Relaxing after dinner at a pulqueria in the Plaza Garibaldi (*pulque* is the milky juice from the agave plant, a sort of tequila), I am serenaded by one of the many mariachi bands that roam the square, dressed in high-cut black jackets and tight black leggings with silver buttons down the side. As soon as the mariachi band moves on flower-sellers and lottery ticket salesmen appear. You're never alone in Mexico. Never.

I can't leave the Plaza without trying the electric machismo test. On a battered tray of cigars is a small box from which two wires extend, each with a metal cylinder on the end. When I have one of these in each hand the cigar salesman turns a knob which sends an electric current through me – or rather, it's meant to. It doesn't work at first and the man impatiently hits the box. Forty volts tingle instantly across my damp palm. He raises this to seventy or eighty before I decide that's quite macho enough. He looks down at the writing on the dial which, loosely translated from the Spanish, reads 'Very kissable'.

DAY 223

'Poor Mexico,' wrote Pofirio Diaz, a President in the early 1900s, 'so far from God, and so close to the United States.' Though we are not *that* close to the United States – there's still 1500 miles between us and the Pacific border at Tijuana – there are times when I feel as though I am already there. There are far more English language newspapers, magazines, TV shows and American fast-food chains here than there ever were in South America. The only way to avoid this cultural blur is to get out on the back streets of Mexico City. I'm rewarded by finding a restaurant whose cuisine is not just firmly Mexican, but pre-conquest Mexican. Sandwiched between a butcher and a dry cleaner on a modest square called Plaza Aguila, Fonda Tino specializes in *Comida Exótica y PreColombina* which turns out to be mainly insects. Tino, a huge Hardyesque figure (*Oliver* Hardy that is), lays a tapas of tiny creatures before me. Maggots, beetles, ants' eggs, mosquito larvae and baby grasshoppers are set out for my delectation and delight. They are seasoned, cooked in oil and served crispy. Tino looms over me as I eat. He watches my face with such anxious concern that I fear that anything less than a 'Magnificent!' after the maggots would bring him close to tears. And indeed, once you forget that they are creepy-crawlies and treat them simply as snacks, maggots make rather good grub.

   Apart from invertebrates, the Aztec menu is limited. Of course they ate fish, but cows, sheep and goats were introduced by the Europeans. For meat they relied on dogs, turkey and armadillo. All are on Tino's menu. Drawing the line at dog, I plump for armadillo and beans, which is delicious. Encouraged by my enthusiasm, Tino won't let me go without sampling his speciality, tuna in a mango and chrysanthemum sauce. To be able to eat the flowers as well as the food was just one of many firsts at my lunch in the Plaza Aguila.

Later that afternoon, I return to my hotel with the taste of ants' eggs fresh on my lips, to find that a script for the re-shoot of *Fierce Creatures* has just arrived. When I finish this journey they want me back in character again – as Bugsy, keeper of the Insect House.

DAY 224: *Mexico City to Queretaro*

Buses del Norte is one of four massive coach stations set at the cardinal points of Mexico City. I'm told that express coaches are preferred by most Mexicans to the slower more expensive railway system. We take a comfortable, air-conditioned coach, curtained like a hearse, north on a modern well-kept toll road – Highway 57. The landscape is unexceptional. Grassland, studded with olive groves and spindly stands of eucalyptus and fields of cactus and maguey, interspersed quite arbitrarily with factories, assembly plants and power stations. Much of this recent industrial infrastructure dates from the investment boom in the mid 1970s when the US, terrified by the instability of the Middle East, sought to switch its oil custom to Mexico.

Two and a half hours north of Mexico City is the handsome city of Querétaro. With soft stone facades, neatly kept squares and splendidly decorated churches it appears to be the well-behaved personification of Spanish colonial stability. In fact throughout its history Querétaro has been a thorn in authority's flesh. In 1810 the wife of the administrator of the city passed on vital information which saved the fledgling conspiracy that led to independence from Spain. Nearly sixty years later the Hapsburg emperor Maximilian was executed here after trying to reassert his imperial authority and, in 1917, revolutionaries drew up the country's present constitution here.

Rich from silver mines and local agriculture, Querétaro wears its wealth comfortably, but beggars and street children with outstretched hands still attend the tables in the smart restaurants of the Plaza de la Independencia.

My room, in the richly-appointed town house, the Casa de la Marquesa, is one of the finest I've enjoyed on the journey. It's decorated in the style of the Alhambra in Granada, with rich mosaic tiling, stained glass and a domed roof. A terrific thunderstorm breaks as I get into bed.

I lie propped up against the pillows with rain streaming down the dome. Every now and then a brilliant flash of lightning sends shadows of the downpour swirling across the walls. I'm reading a history of Mexico. It is now thought that the first Mexicans, like the ancestors of the Incas of Peru, were nomads who crossed from Siberia into America on a land bridge which later became submerged beneath the waters of the Bering Strait. Pampered as I am tonight I cannot wait to see those waters again.

DAY 225: *Tlacote*

Not far outside Querétaro we stop off at an unremarkable village called Tlacote. It achieved overnight fame when a dog, supposedly on its last legs, drank water from a local spring and made a miraculous recovery. For almost two years the village was inundated by the halt and the lame, but most of them left in exactly the same state, and eventually the fuss died down and the village went back, gratefully, to being unremarkable.

Don Antonio is a smallholder who grows maize, beans and squash. He has the dark, leathery face of someone who has worked hard, out of doors, for most of his life. He wears a wide-brimmed straw hat and his T-shirt is torn and stained with sweat. He owns his property but expectations are low. By the time he has fed his own wife and three children, and a further nine children he looks after, there is little left for him to sell to raise money to improve his lot. There is irrigated water nearby but he can't afford to pay the charge for pumping it so he relies, as he says with a smile and a finger pointed heavenwards, on *agua de dios*, God's water. Downpours, like the one that hit last night, cheer him considerably. He's cautiously optimistic that he might be able to afford two pigs by the end of the year. Cactus leaves squeeze out from between the dry stones which wall his property. His wife, Guadeloupe, greets us with a broad grin. She's dressed in a white T-shirt over a patterned floral skirt and white sneakers. She shows me how tortillas – the pancakes that are the staple of the Mexican diet – are traditionally made. A maize paste is rolled out on a granite slab and then slapped from one hand to the other, gradually increasing in size until it is ready to be laid onto a tray resting on a wood fire. Her skill in producing one perfect specimen after the other is one that will probably die out over the next few years as hand-presses become more common. She tries to teach me the rudiments, but by the time she's made twelve tortillas my first one remains, for some reason, firmly stuck to my left hand.

Don Antonio and Guadeloupe are fine company, amused by, and infinitely tolerant of, the strange demands of filming. Nor will they let us leave without bags of hand-made tortillas and hand-picked maize cobs for the journey. I wish they'd come with us as well.

DAY 226: *Tijuana, Baja California*

Over a thousand miles north-west of Tlacote, at the northern end of the narrow desiccated peninsula of Baja California, is the border town of Tijuana. Separating it from the USA is a 27-mile, 10-foot-high steel barrier known as the Tortilla Curtain. It was put up by the US authorities in the 1970s to curb illegal immigration. Such is the economic inequality between the two countries that ninety per cent of the illegal immigrants who entered the States in 1994 were from Mexico. In 1995 1.2 million were apprehended trying to cross the border illegally. Even today, as we stand and watch at a point where the Tortilla Curtain runs only yards from the main entrance to Tijuana Airport, there are a dozen people preparing to cross, without papers or passports, in broad daylight.

Huddled beneath a low bridge, in the gully of a dried-up river bed, shaken periodically by great dusty trucks thundering in and out of Tijuana and the desert that lies beyond, is a largely silent group of Mexicans, or, quite possibly, Guatemalans, Venezuelans, even Peruvians, waiting to slip under the fence and into the Promised Land. The hard brown earth around them is dotted with the remains of small fires and strewn with cigarette packets, plastic cups, discarded Coke bottles, cardboard sheets and even an old sprung bedstead. There are young men, girls, old women. If they are related you wouldn't know it. The mood is muted and watchful. A mile or so ahead of us, across the border, a helicopter turns lazily, high in the sky over the United States.

We've been brought here by Arturo, a middle-aged Mexican; stocky, bearded, with the looks of an overweight matinée idol. He has himself been across twice, once swimming the Rio Grande River on the Texas border and once on foot. The second time he stayed almost six months. He's the only person I've ever met who hates the smell of new-mown grass. 'It remind me of when I work in New York, cutting grass.' He shakes his head with feeling. 'It is a terrible smell. It reminds me of how terrible the world can be.'

Arturo is bitter about what he sees as American hypocrisy. They pass laws vilifying illegal immigrants whilst continuing to reap the benefits of their cheap labour.

'Michael, California produce one-third of all American agricultural product. The labour force they use is ninety per cent Mexican, sixty-six per cent of them undocumented.'

He looks around at the motley, shabby group, some crouched down, peering through a hole in the fence, like children with noses pressed against a window. He shrugs. 'That's why they still go.'

The migrants are known as *pollos* (chickens) and those who help them across are called *polleros* or *coyotes*. A simple crossing can cost a hundred dollars or more; if faked documents are required it can rise to a thousand. It's a risky business. Many *pollos* speak only Spanish and have no idea where they are. They are often cheated or preyed on by *cholos*, gangs of young Mexicans who take whatever money they have.

As we talk, a young man ducks under the fence and saunters

into California. He wears a white shirt, black trousers and carries his belongings in a plastic bag slung over his shoulder. He seems to make no attempt to conceal himself. Arturo is not especially surprised. Sometimes, he says, it is safer to cross in broad daylight than at night with the laser beams, infra-red lights and sensors.

Everyone on the Mexican side stops and watches the young man's progress. There is no excitement, just curiosity. Most of us seem to hear the sound of vehicles approaching before he does. Even when the two Border Patrol Ford Broncos converge on him he makes no attempt to run or even turn back. He waits for them to pick him up. He has gone no more than 300 yards. But by then everyone has turned away.

I ask Arturo what will happen to him. He says he will be questioned, finger-printed, possibly held in jail for a while, then bussed back across into Mexico. If he has a record of previous illegal crossings he could stay in jail a lot longer.

An hour later, with the sun at its highest in a cloudless sky, a girl, not more than seventeen or eighteen, better dressed than the rest, secures white strips of cotton over her trousers as kneepads and, gesticulating to the rest of the group to wait, squeezes beneath the fence and is gone. Unlike the man before her she moves like a soldier, at a fast cat-like crouch, weaving and ducking and using the river bed for cover.

Arturo nods and turns to me. 'She's the *pollero*.'

Nothing moves for several minutes. Then she's up and running on. At this point another seven people, their possessions in half-empty shoulder bags, dodge through and race up the river bed. They freeze, then move, freeze and move, following the girl as she switches across from the main river bed to a steep ditch alongside a fence. Arturo watches, this time with almost painful concentration. 'They only have to make another two hundred yards to the road then there will be cars to take them on.'

The group have now reached the girl and are momentarily out of our sight. For a moment all is absolutely still. Everyone here is silently cheering them on. Then someone points. I lend Arturo my binoculars and he squints into the distance. With slow, remorseless, almost choreographed predictability the Broncos appear and begin homing in on the *pollos*. For good measure, a helicopter chatters over and circles the group. One of the *pollos* next to me hurls a plastic bottle at the fence, but there's nothing anyone can do, and no one wants to watch any more.

The Tortilla Curtain runs right out into the Pacific. Down at the beach sunbathers lie beside its rusting graffitied sections. 'Welcome to the New Berlin Wall', '*Morta a los Migras*' (Death to Immigration Officers). There is quite a contrast on the two sides of the fence. The last few yards of Mexico are tatty, lively and busy. The first few yards of the USA are tidy, clean, laid with public picnic tables, and empty.

There is an obelisk on the hill overlooking the Pacific which was here long before the fence. It marks the fact that this border was drawn in 1848 when, after a war in which 50,000 Mexicans died, General Santa Ana sold California, Texas, Arizona and New Mexico to the United States.

From a whitewashed church a bell tolls for six o'clock mass as we head back from the beach to our hotel. Tijuana has always been the victim. The town of easy virtue, the cheap and cheerful haven where Americans could come and spend their money with no questions asked. But it is nowhere near as awful as I had been led to believe and there are odd, mischievous, very Mexican touches, which still defy the international blandness which seeps down from north of the border.

One of these is a house in the shape of a 30-foot woman. She stands, white-plastered, naked and voluptuous on an otherwise drab and litter-strewn hillside. Her left arm across her chest, right arm raised in a parody of the Statue of Liberty. She was built by an artist in the likeness of his much-adored wife. Now they've split up and the artist is living there with his new partner. Apparently, she's not at all happy living in the body of his first wife.

As we finish filming this unique accommodation, a hand appears from between the breasts and waves us goodbye.

USA

DAY 227: *Tijuana to San Diego, California*

It's around 10.00 in the morning and I'm walking the last few yards of Mexican territory, to the busiest land-border crossing in the world. Over thirty million people a year cross between Tijuana and the town of San Ysidro. On one side of me solid columns of cars, buses and trucks are lining up at every one of the twenty-four crossing gates. On the other an unbroken line of souvenir stalls sells mementoes for every religion, creed and culture on earth. There are Buddhas, batmen, bulldogs, gorillas and cowboys. Rows of Bart Simpsons stand next to figures of Christ on the cross. The last billboard in Mexico reads 'Herpes. Ring 800 336 for a cure'.

The United States is air-conditioned right from the start. I shiver for the first time in weeks as I wait in line for one of the immigration positions where officials sit before humming computer terminals. On the wall is a sign warning of the penalties of drug trafficking and a photograph of the President who never inhaled.

After Tijuana, Mexico, San Ysidro, USA is immaculate. Almost the first American I see is dressed as a hot dog, walking up and down outside the railway station (which is sponsored by McDonald's), a plastic lettuce protruding from his (or her) midriff like a lime-green tutu. The railway service is called the San Diego Trolley and it carries me along Imperial Beach past stops like Iris Avenue and Pacific Fleet and into San Diego in clean, efficient comfort.

The city of San Diego, only 25 miles from the chaos of the Mexican border, could hardly offer a more emphatic statement of US prosperity, power and confidence. Huge hotels rise like pinnacles along a bay through which glide the largest ships of the greatest navy in the world. Everything seems big, tidy, sober and corporate. On the San Diego waterfront, bad behaviour has, it seems, been themed out of the system.

Unpack, relax, eat smoked marlin and 'leaves', and look out over San Diego Bay into which Juan Rodriguez Cabrillo sailed in 1542, christening this new land California. Sir Francis Drake brought his ships here five years later, but five years too late. Although it was Spaniards like Cabrillo who shaped and moulded the early European settlement of the West Coast, it slowly sinks in, as I listen to the chatter of fellow diners, that, for the first time in ten weeks, I'm in a country where English is the first language.

By early evening I find myself back at the border, this time seeing it from the American side in the company of Ron Henley, Public Information Officer of the INS – the Immigration and Naturalization Service. Ron is a tolerant, good-humoured man in his late forties who never wanted to be a Public Information Officer and can't wait to get out in the field again. He's a military man who served in the Vietnam War. 'We mined Haiphong Harbour,' he says proudly.

His is a growth industry. The number of Border Patrol Agents has risen by forty-five per cent since Clinton was first elected in 1993. In an initiative called 'Operation Gatekeeper', set up two years ago, the law was toughened to include five- to twenty-year jail sentences for illegal re-entry, the fencing strengthened and Enforce, a new computerized processing system for IAs (illegal aliens) was set up. As Ron drives us to the frontier fence in the same white Bronco four-wheel drives we saw picking up the *pollos* yesterday, he admits that all this will never stop people trying to cross. 'Hell, if you can pick up four dollars an hour over here and four dollars a day over there . . . ' His voice trails off.

Ron is against what some see as pressure to 'militarize' the border. He sees the role of the INS as control and deterrence not armed prevention. He accepts that as long as the work is there, the migrants will find ways of getting to it. 'We're just a Band-Aid. We can't stop the problem.'

Recently he apprehended a portable lavatory being carried up the highway on the back of a truck and found seventeen people inside. 'To us it was very serious,' says Ron. 'Those people had paid five hundred dollars apiece to be in that toilet.'

The technology available to the Border Patrol is becoming even more sophisticated. At midnight I stand on a hill beside the Pacific on which is parked a vehicle with a camera raised on an 18-foot arm sending infra-red pictures of any movement within two miles. Working alongside these night-vision scopes are helicopters armed with powerful searchlights and sensors that detect body heat. They're thudding around above us relaying pictures to the monitors we're watching.

In all I have seen around the Pacific Rim, I have rarely felt the difference between the First and Third Worlds as strongly as I do now, watching the potency and sophistication of modern technology reducing human beings to helpless maggot-like figures on a screen. The Aztecs and the Incas were destroyed by gunpowder, armour and war-horses, and the Red Indians by rifles and whisky. Progress trundled over them and, here on the borders of the USA and Mexico, I can feel the same steamroller at work.

The American paranoia that is responsible for all this will not be assuaged by events filtering through to us over the car radios. A bomb has exploded at the Atlanta Olympics. Deaths are reported. Ron shakes his head. The helicopter's searchlight rakes the fence one last time and is gone.

DAY 228: *San Diego to Los Angeles*

The hotel flags are at half mast as we load ourselves onto another bus and head north towards Los Angeles. The San Diego Freeway is a belt of apparently unrelieved prosperity – evidence of the extraordinary rise and rise of the state of California, a far-flung outpost of the Spanish Empire when the Declaration of Independence was signed, now, with thirty-two million inhabitants, the most populous state of the Union. The long, low gleaming assembly plants of the high-tech industries and the big tinted-glass blocks of insurance and banking corporations flash by, catching the sun. The Californians have embraced 'environmentalism' with enthusiasm. Signs extol ridesharing, car pooling, and cleanliness ('Litter Removal for the Next Two Miles Sponsored by Mitsubishi', 'Wall Adopted by Huntingdon Beach Pentecostal Church').

After three hours we are well into Los Angeles and surrounded by the happy, dappy burble of unfettered commercial enterprise. This is user-friendly California, the land of Drain Surgeons, Topless Driving Lessons and Freefone numbers for Psychics.

DAY 229: *Los Angeles*

The feeling of being back on home ground grows as I spend a day off amongst the Hockneys at the County Museum of Art and up in the Hollywood Hills with Eric Idle and family and friends in the afternoon. Returning home from Eric's, things take a less familiar turn. My taxi-driver says he is an Armenian physicist who in the bad old days of the Soviet Union was imprisoned in Siberia for two years for being a member of Andrei Sakharov's reform party. I tell him we have been in the Kolyma region and seen the camps.

He glances in the mirror as if to check I'm serious.

'You see politic prisoners?' he asks.

I shake my head. 'Not any more.'

We turn onto the freeway and run down past the Hollywood Bowl. A fine, un-smogged vista of LA lies below us. My Armenian driver is looking at me looking at it.

'City of pleasure,' he says.

'Are you happy driving a cab?' I ask.

'No, of course not.'

DAY 230

Los Angeles defies definition. Is it a city at all or, as they say, 'forty-nine suburbs in search of a city'? The road system encourages a constant movement of people in, out and across a great sprawl of neighbourhoods. The long Pacific coastline offers a vista of limitless space. The only way to shrink the vast distances of Greater Los Angeles is to take to the air, which is why I find myself on this sharp, clear and cloudless morning at an office attached to a hangar in a corner of Santa Monica airport.

It is the home of a remarkable family business. Bob Tur, his wife Marika and mother Judy, along with Craig, a pilot, run a helicopter-borne news-gathering operation which is legendary even in this city of legends. The walls of their trim but modest office are covered with framed awards and citations. They have won two Emmys, and Tur's footage of the beating of truck driver, Reginald Denny, after white police officers were acquitted in the Rodney King case is compulsive, frightening and unique. He has rescued people from deserts and out of earthquakes and he was the first newsman to locate O. J. Simpson's Bronco in the famous freeway chase.

Bob Tur knows his Los Angeles and he's told us that if we're prepared to take pot luck he'll take us along with him on the day's business.

He bustles in late, a slim almost studious figure in chinos and a check shirt. Reddish-brown hair flops across his forehead. He's dabbing at a blob of blood on his neck where he nicked himself shaving.

'It's a violent city,' he explains, reaching for another tissue.

He gives off an air of constant, barely-controlled energy, managing to be both laconic and garrulous, at the same time. He was independent when he started with his first helicopter twelve years ago; now he's on regular contract to CBS News. He works ten to seven with regular spots to fill on lunchtime and early evening bulletins. It's not what he wants to do.

'I want to make low-budget monster movies.'

His wife, who has been monitoring the emergency service radio transmissions, picks up word of some action. It sounds unlikely to me.

'We have a shooting on Sesame Street.'

Bob raises his eyes briefly at this then moves into action like a man who wouldn't swap his job with anyone. Grabbing radio sets, headphones, cellphones, bleepers and any other attachments he can find, he bundles us into a car and drives fast to where two million dollars worth of helicopter and camera are waiting.

We're strapping ourselves in when word comes across the radio from Marika.

'Suspect in custody.'

Bob curses and we all bale out. This happens twice in the space of an hour.

'Something'll come up,' he reassures me. 'It always does.'

'Always?'

He nods vehemently.

'Look, there are ten million people here and five million are fucking crazy.'

Not crazy enough this morning it seems.

Around midday he decides to go up anyway and see what he can find.

'Okay . . . let's cruise for news.'

We've cruised for less than a minute when word comes in of a light plane in trouble approaching Van Nuys Airport in the San Fernando Valley. It's run out of fuel and might have to attempt a landing on the freeway. Bob instructs his pilot, talks to his office, his TV company and us whilst at the same time listening over headphones to his office, police radio and Van Nuys control tower. He presses a button and a new voice comes over the headset. It's the pilot of the light plane. He confirms he's eight miles out and has no fuel left. He doesn't think he'll make the airport. We race to where he estimates he'll land. It becomes as exciting as any Hollywood movie chase as we head for the airport from one side and the light plane, slowly sinking, comes in from another. Bob talks swiftly as information comes in. We bank and turn and there below us is the freeway. The light plane has just skimmed down and landed safely on the inside lane. The police have not managed to stop the traffic and the pilot just took his moment to settle between two trucks. It's an extraordinarily lucky escape. Bob gets close-up pictures using his pride and joy, a camera with a 72 to 1 zoom lens. Then, as news-gathering helicopters from two or three other channels arrive, he turns to Craig.

'Let's leave it to the vultures.' And we pull up and away.

Bob likens LA to a theatre. Killings and shootings are plentiful.

'A shooting in Los Angeles is not a big story,' he explains. 'On average, twenty-two people are killed here every weekend.' He pauses, then adds sourly, 'How many *decent* people are killed in a weekend, that I can't tell you.'

During the rest of the day, between a series of aborted police pursuits, Bob is first to cover a fatal accident on the freeway and a forest fire out in the hills. He seems almost disappointed as he turns low over the Pacific and into Santa Monica one last time.

'An ordinary day,' says Bob. 'Just an ordinary day.'

All of us are exhausted.

DAY 231: *Los Angeles to Carmel*

We move out of LA, quickly, before we can be seduced by the sun and swimming pools. Not that I'm complaining. I've rented a red Morgan Eight, an English-built open-top sports car, to drive the 400 odd miles up to San Francisco. We leave LA on Highway 101. Sunshine and clear skies. As we head along the coast to Santa Barbara, a bank of cold, grey sea-mist lurks beside us all the way, rolled back a quarter of a mile off shore, like a stage curtain. At Santa Barbara the highway is tastefully landscaped with thick flowering oleander bushes waving gently in the slipstreams. Past Buellton – the Split Pea Capital of the World – over the wide, dry course of the Santa Rosa River, and on to San Luis Obispo where we branch off onto Highway 1, a narrow road that hugs the tortuous coast-line from Morro Bay to Monterey.

In all my visits to California, over a period of twenty-four years, I have never been up to San Simeon, the estate built in the 1920s and 1930s, above the ocean by newspaper magnate William Randolph Hearst.

The Hearst family turned it over to the government in 1957 and it is run, with an iron grip, by the Department of Parks and Recreation. Rules and regulations abound. Cars must be left at the bottom of the hill and 'guests' must wear identity clips 'at all times'. I'm given special permission to take the Morgan up the two-mile-long driveway that winds up through parkland to what Hearst liked to call Enchanted Hill, a collection of guest cottages, landscaped gardens, terraces and pools, dominated by the massive, elaborate towers of the Casa Grande. Three hundred full-time staff are required to maintain what Hearst himself called the Ranch. Although the pervading theme is Spanish, it is full of art treasures, furniture and decoration from every period of European history. The Great Hall is a Gothic baronial fantasy, complete with wooden panels from French churches, Aubusson tapestries, silver candelabra and the like. Elsewhere marble is used like lino, and hardly a ceiling remains that is not coffered, inlaid or painted. Money was never an object. Hearst, one feels, would have had the Pyramids shipped out one by one if he'd lived long enough. As George Bernard Shaw put it, San Simeon is 'the way God would have done it, if he'd had the money.'

At least Hearst enjoyed sharing the place. He not only invited guests up most weekends, he also arranged to have them brought here either by plane to his private airstrip, up the coast on his yacht or on a private train specially hired from the Southern Pacific Railway. The guests, mostly from the world of films and entertainment, were driven up the last few miles to the Ranch by a taxi company whose entire fleet of Packards and Cadillacs was permanently at Hearst's disposal. Banquets were laid on and previews of films shown at his own private movie theatre, often in the presence of their stars and directors.

Much of Hearst's fabulous world has been carefully and lovingly preserved. But what cannot be preserved is Hearst's joy in devising such a place. It is a shell, a glorious, mind-bogglingly rich shell, but its spirit has long gone. You can look, if you have an identity clip on, but if you try to touch, alarm sensors will sound, and sharp voices will ring out if you stand on an unauthorized piece of marble.

At the main entrance to the Casa Grande, modelled on the finely detailed stonework of Seville cathedral, a party is waiting to be shown inside. Their guide addresses them solemnly.

'Would anyone using chewing gum please deposit it now.'

A man steps forward with a plastic bucket. Nearly everyone makes use of it.

Further up the coast, patches of sea mist have begun to drift inshore, catching me and my open car in sudden pockets of icy-cold air and fifty-yard visibility. Between the fog patches I can see the road rising steeply above the Pacific. Thick, dark tree-cover closes in. This is the area around Big Sur. A secretive place, squeezed between mist, mountains and forest. I try not to take my eye off the road but it's hard not to be distracted by the drama of the surroundings. Razor sharp cliffs rise sheer from rocky bays against which the Pacific breakers roll and shatter.

Reach Carmel by evening. It's affluent and arboreal; tidy and temperate. Clint Eastwood was once mayor here, and Carmel people have enough money to install low-flow faucets to conserve water.

DAY 232: *Carmel to San Francisco*

A beautiful morning, the sort of morning that should be deep-frozen and used again. I walk two blocks down to the ocean past discreetly rambling clapboard houses set in flower-filled gardens behind fences half submerged in purple bougainvillaea. Palms, pines and eucalyptus provide a generous greeny cover and the shore is lined with white sand. All the colours are fresh, and a general air of discreet good taste prevails.

Bill Fink, the Morgan dealer from San Francisco (who rowed for Oxford University in my last year there – 1965), tells me that this is no accident. There is a Carmel 'book', a book of rules for preserving the character of the neighbourhood. Trees must be pruned to the correct height, houses can only be painted certain colours, even house names have to be approved.

I fantasize a visit from Clint Eastwood, tipping back his hat and telling it to me straight. 'Michael, folks round here don't like 'Dunromin'. You gonna have to take that sign down or be on the next train out of town.'

Just over an hour north of Carmel, the countryside flattens out and in the wide fields outside Salinas a hundred Mexicans are picking strawberries. They work their way swiftly along the rows, picking directly into green plastic punnets which are then pushed on miniature wheelbarrows and loaded onto waiting trailers. As each box is delivered, the foreman punches a hole in the picker's card. They are paid one dollar forty a box. Picking has to be done bent double and most of the pickers have tracksuit hoods or scarves pulled over their heads as protection against the sun. Not a word of English is spoken.

Late in the afternoon my Morgan passes beneath the soaring orange arches of one of the icons of the modern world, then stops. Still, a traffic jam on the Golden Gate Bridge is a cut above most ordinary traffic jams.

DAY 234: *San Francisco*

A day off here has been enough to re-tune my system from the exotic to the familiar. It is a cliché and a half that San Francisco is the most European of American cities, but there are some truths in all that. The moderate maritime climate, the love of bookstore and café life, the fuss over art and culture (ninety million dollars was raised within the community for the new Museum of Modern Art), the impression of a class system based on old rather than new money, the proportion of houses as opposed to apartment blocks, the tram cars and the hills – all contribute to the sense of having shifted a continent. Or could it be because I fell asleep last night to the sound of a church clock striking?

There are aspects of the city that remain resolutely American and one of them is Alcatraz, perched on its island in the bay like a grounded battleship. Because Alcatraz was a high security prison for the most notorious long-term criminals, not many men passed through it, perhaps sixteen hundred altogether. Nor was it a prison for very long. It opened in 1934 and closed, after steadily mounting running costs, in 1963. But it is the most famous prison in the world and, now, very much on the tourist circuit, it is run by the Department of Parks and Recreation. They take their task very seriously. The large sign on the quayside, 'Alcatraz Easy Access Program', shows no trace of irony.

Two ex-inmates, Prisoners 586 Jim Quillan and 1103 Glenn Williams, now in their seventies, accompany me round what was always known as the Rock. They make one or two things very clear. The proximity of Alcatraz to the tantalizing freedoms of a busy city was one of its least tolerable aspects. Both Quillan and Williams were desperate to avoid a cell with a view. Escape was virtually impossible. Although it is only one and a quarter miles from the shore, the water is freezing and the fierce undertow of its currents deadly. There were only fourteen escape attempts in the history of the prison. None was successful.

Seagulls scream constantly. Summer is nesting time for the Western gull, and many other birds for whom the Rock is a sanctuary. I ask Jim and Glenn if they knew the Birdman of Alcatraz.

Jim nods. 'Sure. I thought he was a jerk myself. He was a guy that liked chaos and turmoil and upheaval.'

'And all the time he would create it,' Glenn added.

'Always at somebody else's expense,' Jim looks bitterly about him as we turn and walk slowly down the long gallery of narrow cells. 'He cost me seven and a half years of my good time.'

'What did you think of the movie?'

'The movie?' Jim looks at me scornfully.

'It was a comedy,' says Glenn.

Jim nods. 'Right. It was an excellent comedy.'

The two men reminisce like old school chums back at their alma mater.

'See now, Jim, this is the basement where the clothing was issued . . . '

'I didn't know that.'

'Yeah, that's where Rodrigues killed Bowers.'

'D'you remember there was a barber shop here? I came here just after Jimmy Gross took a pair of scissors to someone and killed him.'

Both Jim and Glenn are, in a way, American success stories. Hardened criminals who did their time here and are now forgiven and, in varying degrees, famous. Both have written books about their experiences and, down in the Alcatraz Gift Shop, among the mugs and the T-shirts and the videos, Jim Quillan, the ex-bank robber, signs his book *Memoirs of Life Inside*.

'One of the primary reasons I wrote the book was to tell the reality of prison to kids. We have this image through the media that it's something glamorous and macho, but you know what prison really is, it's tears and sorrow and heartache and loneliness, bitterness, insanity, murder, suicide and death. That's what prison's all about.'

San Francisco does not wear novelty quite as flashily as Los Angeles, but few cities have pioneered as many social experiments. The tradition of the Beat Poets, Haight-Ashbury and the Summer of Love and a wide tolerance of homosexuality has led to the establishment of the world's largest, most prosperous and most stable gay community in the Castro area of the city. I learn more about it in the company of a handsome woman with sparkling, steely blue eyes, born Evelyn Fondren in Mississippi some fifty years ago. Since her lesbian conversion she's swapped Evelyn for Trevor and Fondren for Hailey.

'This is the gayest four corners on earth,' Trevor enthuses, as we stand on the corner of 18th and Castro. Looking around it all seems about as gay as Guildford on a Sunday afternoon. The streets are full of smart, well-kept shops, there is a fine twenties art-deco cinema and pretty little bourgeois houses stretch neatly up the hill. There is nothing remotely sleazy about the Castro. The 260,000-strong gay and lesbian community has smartened it up no end and the rainbow flag now flies over one of the safest, most sought-after areas in the city.

'Can anyone move in here?' I ask Trevor.

'Sure,' she says brightly. Trevor has no prejudice. She calls heterosexuals 'those who enjoy an alternative lifestyle'. But there is still an air of zealotry to the place. The battle is not yet won.

'Remember,' says Trevor, 'in twenty-two states it's still basically illegal to be gay.'

Trevor reckons it's all in the geology. The liberal values of San Francisco can be traced back to the gold rush.

'All sorts of characters came over here and all sorts of

behaviour had to be tolerated.' I think of dear old Nome and have to agree.

'Michael, the average age of those goldminers was eighteen. They were playful.'

Trevor certainly has a new slant on local history.

'When the Panama Canal was opened San Francisco became a port city, and ports always tend to be more cosmopolitan and liberal. Then came America's entry into the Second World War and San Francisco became the major disembarkation point for thousands of young men and women heading out to war.'

And they were, presumably, playful.

As far as she is concerned, the achievement of the gays in the Castro has been to show that they can run a neighbourhood in a much sought-after part of a much sought-after city, and run it well.

'The Castro is to gays what Israel is to the Jews,' she explains.

They own their homes and run businesses, churches and local politics just like anyone else. Although, of course, the last thing Trevor Hailey wants to be, or thankfully ever will be, is just like anyone else.

DAY 235: *San Francisco to Seattle*

A death is announced in the paper today. 'American Liberalism, born 1933, died 1996.' It refers to President Clinton's signing yesterday of a Republican Bill committing him to the biggest cuts in welfare since the time of the New Deal.

The other big story is the bombing at the Atlanta Olympics. It is now rumoured to be the work of 'separatist militias'. Meanwhile the Californian flag flutters alongside the Stars and Stripes outside our hotel. America seems tight, uncomfortable, on edge. Of all the countries of the Pacific Rim, this is the one in which I have seen fear and mistrust most clearly. Of course people have been welcoming. The glad hand has been extended, but only after a split second check on who it is being extended towards. Could it be that the legendary warmth and spontaneity of the American people has been compromised?

Has increasingly sophisticated technology delivered the prospect of an electronic wall of security and surveillance, behind which those who have can at last hide from those who have not? Could it be that this generous nation has finally lost patience with those who won't fit in?

This morning the city is cloaked by a funnel of cold sea fog drawn across San Francisco by the heat of the Central Valley. The bells of Grace Cathedral and the clanging tramcars on Powell sound muffled and mournful. Time to move north, to close the circle.

DAY 236: *Seattle to Vancouver*

Seattle, the third largest of America's great Pacific coast ports, is 680 miles north of San Francisco, and within 130 miles of the Canadian border. Despite all the buses and trains and helicopters and motorboats and sailing boats and canoes and red Morgan sports cars, we have only been able to take strides like this thanks to good old boring jet aircraft. Without them we would probably still be foundering in the jungles of Borneo and our wives and families would have forgotten what we look like. So it seems only right that in our headlong race to the finish we should pause for a moment to give thanks at one of the temples of air travel.

The final assembly plant at the Boeing factory in Everett could probably accommodate most of the temples we've visited on this journey and still have room for a football pitch. It covers 90 acres and is the largest building, by volume, in the world. (The Pentagon in Washington has the largest 'footprint', i.e. actual floor space, but less height.) It is home to some of the great statistics of the world, all carefully detailed in a Fact Sheet for visitors. My favourite concerns the computer-controlled automated riveting machines. 'Each of the ten machines can drill, ream, countersink, insert, squeeze and shave smooth one rivet every ten seconds.' Pure poetry.

What strikes me most about this great assembly area, where (I feel a statistic coming on) eight 747s can be finished, side by side at the same time, is that from the moment I pass through the hangar doors – each of which is the size of an American football pitch – the place is as quiet as a library. Some of the most enormous machines made by man (make up your own statistics here) are produced in near silence. There *are* noises – the hiss of hydraulics, the hum of fans, the brief whoop of a high-speed drill – but they die swiftly, almost apologetically. Parts are carried around on noiseless buggies, employees cycle round the plant on bikes or tricycles. There is no dirt or dust and virtually no smell. This is not really a factory, it's an environment.

Everett is full of environments. The cafeterias which serve (here we go again) seventeen thousand meals a day, are immaculate and their Computer Weight and Calorie Analysis machines and non-fat espressos help overweight employees in their desperate struggle to achieve the trimness so natural to those on the other side of the Pacific. There is a garden environment, where smokers, banished from the rest of the complex, are forced to go about their sordid business, and a reception environment, orderly and uncluttered, which contains one book. Somewhat surprisingly, it's called *The Art of Indonesia*.

To someone who has spent many weeks of his life suspended above the earth in Boeing products, all this is immensely reassuring. Everything about Everett (or everything they let outsiders see) is clean and safe and controlled. It's almost a shock to see the airliners in the assembly process, the fuselage interior a naked aluminium and fibreglass shell, engines haemorrhaging coils and tubes. It all looks a bit indecent. But they are not long like this. Once the sections are delivered to Everett (mostly from the States but some from South Korea and Canada), a single 747 can be assembled in fifty working days. And a paint crew can cover the outside in just forty-five minutes.

Before I leave Statisticville the enormously obliging people from Boeing give me a chance to crash one of their 737s. I'm given a choice of locations at which to do this. We choose Seattle. From where I sit on the darkened flight deck of my simulator, I can see the approach to the airport projected on the screen in front of me. The engine noise is switched on and an uncomfortably realistic impression of the network of bays and islands around Puget Sound appears 6000 feet below me.

I think I do pretty well. I follow instructions, hold course and speed and, with eyes glued to the instrument panel, bring us gently down to earth. When I look round for some acknowledgement of my prowess all I can see is a white-faced and gibbering camera crew. Apparently I had missed the runway, clipped the corner of the control tower and landed in a crowded car park.

It's early evening by the time we reach the forty-ninth parallel and our eighteenth national frontier. A portrait of The Queen hangs on the wall of the immigration shed and ahead of us lies British Columbia, Canada's most westerly province. Vancouver, its largest city, has a population of a million and a half, swollen by a recent influx of Hong Kong Chinese who have chosen Canadian rather than Chinese rule after June 1997. A cosmopolitan, multi-racial crowd is making its way down Robson Street towards the waterfront for the last night of an international fireworks competition. There is a palpable mood of national rejoicing. Canada has beaten the USA in the Olympic 4 x 400 metres relay. I think we got out of America just in time.

CANADA

DAY 237: *Vancouver*

Sunday morning/*Dimanche matin* in/*dans* Canada/*Canade*, where/*ou* everything/*tous* is/*est* in/*dans* two/*deux* languages/ *langues*. The festive mood of the night before somewhat dampened by low straggly rain clouds.

I've been told that out here in the west there are so few people that railway trains can be flagged down like buses. Put this to the test on the bracing pine-smelling shores of Howe Sound, a few miles north of Vancouver, and am rewarded by a plume of steam and a piercing whistle as the Royal Hudson Express makes a spectacular appearance from among the densely-packed trees that fill the narrow space between rock and sea. The locomotive is an elegant and shapely 4–6–4 built in 1940 and it is run by two engineers in immaculate blue and white seersucker overalls which make them look like Andy Pandy. And it stops for me.

I judge from its pristine cleanliness and smiling staff that this is a tourist train and I am right. The original Royal Hudson Express ran right across Canada to commemorate the visit of George VI and Queen Elizabeth in 1939. Now, thanks to a consortium of local businessmen, it runs only the 40 miles up to Squamish. It comprises sixteen 1950s coaches and a palatial 1940 Parlour Car in which a fine lunch is served as an accompaniment to fine scenery. Or so I'm told. The weather, unfortunately, is not co-operating. People are constantly reassuring me that, if only I could see it, some of the most beautiful landscape in Canada is right outside the window. All I can see through the drizzle are saw-mills and huge log jams in the water below. There is a hint of desperation in the announcement that we are about to pass the second largest piece of granite in the world. (For Trivial Pursuit players, the biggest is the Rock of Gibraltar.)

At Squamish there is something very Canadian going on. A loggers sports, or, to give it its full title, the Squamish Days Loggers Sports. Now in its thirty-ninth year, this is a sort of Highland Games or Cow Cup of the logging community, a hearty celebration of local skills which has grown from a single day's competition to a long weekend of barbecues and bingo, hoe-downs, parades, decorated bicycle competitions and the crowning of the somewhat lumberingly titled Miss Squamish Youth Ambassador. Nowhere do I hear the word lumberjack. The talk now is all of integrated logging management, which means more costly operations for the companies for greater environmental benefit. Locals take great pride that round here eighteen per cent of the forest is protected from any logging at all.

But the sports themselves come as something of a reassurance that men are men and indeed women are men when it comes to logging prowess. Competitors have come here from Britain, New Zealand, Denmark and the Pacific North-West of America for axe-throwing and sawing and chopping, as well as the rather dainty sport of birling. This involves two men running on a 15-inch floating log to keep it turning, each one trying, by changes of pace and speed, to dislodge the other. The experts make it look like a Fred Astaire and Gene Kelly routine. The high point, in every sense of the word, is a race up to the top of a tree and down again. Dennis Butler from Washington state in the USA is the winner, negotiating a 100-foot tree-trunk, ringing a bell at the top and getting down again, in less than thirty seconds.

I am persuaded to take part in a chokermans race. Each contestant must run across waterborne logs carrying a choker (not a close-fitting necklace as worn by Jane Austen heroines, but a 25-foot collar weighing 75 pounds), which they must attach to a pole. Even without the choker I only managed to get halfway across the log before making the fatal mistake of looking down.

Later, wearing a dry shirt and trousers supplied by the master of ceremonies, I watch the grand finale: Powersaw Tree Felling. The mountains are alive with the sound of twenty-one power-saws grinding into twenty-one tree trunks, as each lumberjack (sorry, logger) fights to drop his or her tree onto a target. Funnily enough, no one asked me to enter this one.

DAY 239: *Vancouver to Prince George*

Restored and revived by a day off in Vancouver, I set off for the final push, by train through British Columbia, then by ship through the islands into Alaska. Looking at my map as our five-car train pulls out of Vancouver at 7 a.m., I estimate that now only 2200 miles separate us from the Bering Strait and a re-union on Diomede. Summer has come round again and the weather should hold, at least as far as Alaska.

Our train is called the Cariboo Prospector after the gold-rush of the 1860s that opened up the interior of British Columbia. Captain Cook had explored and charted the coast eighty years before that, trading with the local Indians, but, as we have seen in nearly every part of the American Pacific Rim, it was the lure of precious metals that drew the Europeans here in numbers.

We have become blasé over the last eleven months, but even by our own severely jaded standards this is a fine morning to be setting out. The waters of the Howe Sound are serene, still, and luminous. Two huge Hyundai car transporters move slowly down the bay towards Vancouver. After a few miles the railway line turns sharply north, clinging precariously to the base of towering cliffs, occasionally squeezing into the gloom of cuttings and tunnels blasted out of the hard black rock. Our route follows the Fraser River 460 miles north to Prince George. On the way there are eight scheduled stops and fifty-five 'flag stops', where anyone, provided they're holding the requisite metal rectangle, can flag the train to a halt.

At a place called Gates we're stopped by a ninety-one-year-old lady in a blue two-piece and a white hat. Her name is Mrs Ward and she's making her twice-monthly trip to buy groceries at Lillooet. She's a doughty woman, born in Belfast, and has lived out here in British Columbia for sixty years. She hasn't much time for television interviews. 'I've just told you that,' she keeps saying, rather testily.

The scenery has become majestic by now, but I find I can only take majestic for so long before my eyes start drifting back to my novel about New Jersey. But I'm glad I'm looking up when we pass a sign which reads 'Marne: Elevation 867, Pop.: 2.' Both of them have come out to collect the mail. An elderly couple with a black dog. They put the letters in the dog's mouth.

After Lillooet we are on the leeward side of the Rockies and the countryside is unexpectedly bone dry. The dramatically steep walls of the Fraser River canyon are the colour of cinders. At one point we are running on a narrow ledge 2000 feet above the valley floor.

The forests that have covered the mountains for the first 200 miles out of Vancouver are unsustainable here and the rock is covered with sagebrush and stumpy Ponderosa Pines. Salmon are fished in the waters far below (I see ladders to help them climb upstream) and giant swathes of protective black netting cover fields of ginseng.

Eventually we pull up and out of the canyon onto a flowery upland – the high Cariboo Plateau. Here there is water, in shallow, reedy ponds surrounded by fields carpeted with purple and yellow wild flowers, and swathes of a red flower they call Indian paintbrush. The sunlight flickers through stands of trembling aspen and white spruce. There are occasional houses, often dilapidated, their grounds littered with scrap metal and car wrecks.

Almost at the 330 mile mark we cross Deep Creek Bridge, one of the most spectacular of all the distinctive wooden-built trestle constructions. It looks like a matchstick bridge, thin and spindly above the trees. Vertigo sufferers should probably avoid the view at this point as the line runs across the bridge, narrow and unfenced, for a quarter of a mile, over 300 feet above the ground. It's one of the highest railway bridges in the world.

The setting sun brings one last surge of colour to this fuzzy grassland as we run the last hundred miles to Prince George.

We roll in at 9.30, an hour late over a fourteen and a half hour journey. My hotel room smells of drains, but when I mention this at reception they tell me not to worry. The whole town smells like this. And it's not drains, its wood pulp being processed, and everyone gets used to it. Sleep with my window closed.

DAY 240: *Prince George to Prince Rupert*

Another early departure. Unlike yesterday's train, this one has an observation car. There is not a lot to observe for the first few hours except the tops of trees. After a while the similarity of the trees becomes strangely mesmeric and I drink cups of coffee and go very slightly mad. Awakened from my reverie somewhere near Smithers on the Bulkley River. Lunch is roast beef or turkey. I choose turkey and the hostess nods approvingly.

'You look like a turkey sort of guy.'

Two hundred and forty days into the journey and I'm still learning new things about myself.

We're a small train – two aluminium shell Budd cars and one observation car – proceeding at a sedate but consistent fifty miles an hour. The 475-mile journey ends in a great climax of mountains, curving glacial valleys and steep cliffs through which the Skeena River flows towards the ocean. The weather that has held so obligingly for us through these spectacular railway journeys now begins to turn and the first flecks of rain begin to pepper the perspex dome above my head as we reach the end of the line, the Pacific Coast and the town of Prince Rupert.

DAY 242: *Prince Rupert to Nome*

Prince Rupert is known, ominously, as the City of Rainbows. It has the third deepest harbour in the world, after Buenos Aires and Sydney. (One of the dubious pleasures of travel in North America is the amount of information available. You can cross China, Vietnam and the Philippines and search in vain for a single fact about what you're seeing, but in the Pacific North-West no tourist enterprise, however mean and humble, is worth its salt without a brochure or three.) There is a small, extremely well laid-out and informative museum in Prince Rupert which made me feel rather ashamed. Ashamed to have assumed that there was nobody round here until the nineteenth-century European settlers came along. There have in fact been native tribes here for five thousand years and their totem poles, erected and carved to commemorate important events, carry a record of history before the Hudson's Bay Company introduced guns, medicine and religion. One quite trivial fact sticks in my mind. Tax K'walaam is a Tsimshian Indian name meaning Place of the Wild Roses. When the white man arrived he promptly renamed the same place Fort Simpson.

Yesterday it rained solidly and there were many rainbows. Today, although the downpour has eased, a watery mist clings to the islands as we embark on the MV *Malaspina* (named after Alaska's biggest glacier), which will take us up to the city of Juneau. It is an American ferry, commissioned in 1962, and this is its two thousand and eighty second voyage up the inter-island channel they call the Alaska Marine Highway. There is not a lot to see from on deck, but there is a selection of mind-improving talks given in the forward lounge by representatives of the US Forest Service. The first one is mainly about how wet Alaska is. Learn More About Bald Eagles is promised later. The History of Alaska lecture pumps out facts relentlessly: Alaska is one fifth the size of the USA, of the twenty highest peaks in the US, seventeen are in Alaska, the Alaskan flag was designed by thirteen-year-old Benny Bensen from Chignik and adopted in 1927.

Retreat to my cabin, away from all facts and figures, for at least three hours. After lunch I make a tentative sally out. In the forward lounge a young woman who looks like a square dance caller is talking about lichens. Up on deck, visibility is, if anything, worse. There is no one out there except a middle-aged Australian, leaning on the rail and gazing out at the enveloping veil of cloud.

'I've been looking forward to this for years,' he says, without turning.

DAY 243: *Nome*

The *Malaspina* drops us off at Juneau with one parting statistic to chew on. Juneau is the only US state capital not accessible by road. We have no option but to fly out, across to Anchorage and finally to the familiar streets of Nome where we shall prepare for the very last stage of the long haul back to Diomede. The sight of the Lucky Swede Gift Shop and the Bering Sea Saloon bring on dangerously premature feelings of elation, and the joy of seeing my old room could hardly have been greater had the Nugget Inn changed its name to the Journey's End.

But Little Diomede is still 130 miles away, and over a meal at a local restaurant where 'authentic' Chinese food is cheerfully served by a family of Koreans, we hear news that is both good and bad. The United States Coast Guard has a patrol boat coming to the end of a routine mission off the Alaskan Coast. If we can make our way to Cape Prince of Wales, the most westerly point on the American continent, they will try to pick us up and take us across to Little Diomede. The bad news is that they have run into thick fog on the Bering Sea and their progress has slowed to a crawl. Maybe mindful of their unsuccessful attempt to fly us down the Aleutian Islands in the first few days of our journey, the Coast Guard are anxious to help us and promise to do everything humanly possible.

DAY 244: *Nome to Wales*

On the wildlife bulletin board outside Fat Freddie's restaurant someone has written up the latest sightings. 'Bluethroats, Arctic Loon and Grizzly Bears (3).' There is no information on *where* the Grizzly Bears were seen. When I ask someone if any of them were in the vicinity of Cape Prince of Wales, they just shake their heads and smile broadly. (The broad smile, I've noticed, is very much an Alaskan phenomenon, valid in all emergencies from the mildly humorous to the life threatening.)

Wales, a settlement of one hundred and fifty Eskimos, lies at one end of a curving spit of land, between beach and low, spiky-grassed sand dunes, just to the north of Cape Prince of Wales. The cape, a 2000-foot granite outcrop, was once part of the Bering Land Bridge. This corridor between Alaska and Russia was estimated to have stretched 900 miles from north to south. Across it, scientists believe, came the first human inhabitants of Alaska, and indeed all of America, eight to ten thousand years ago. Since the end of the last Ice Age it has lain submerged beneath a sea which at this moment looks increasingly surly.

I have with me a book I started out with, this time last year. It's Harry de Windt's *From Paris to New York By Land*. He came across the Bering Strait from Russia in 1901. His description of where we are standing is not encouraging. 'There is probably no place in the world where the weather is so persistently vile as on this cheerless portion of the earth's surface.'

The Eskimos live in long low, modern huts. There is a landing strip, a schoolroom, a store, a washeteria, a post-office and not much else. I see Polar Bear skins hanging out to dry, but nothing grizzly.

We are as far west on the American continent as it's possible to be. Siberia is a mere 53 miles away, Little Diomede a tantalizing 25. Now all we can do is wait.

It's so close to the end of the journey that none of us can really concentrate on anything but getting there and spirits slowly sag as a night on the schoolroom floor becomes increasingly likely. Then, preceded by a sudden flurry of radio messages, the US Coast Guard cutter *Munro*, distinguished by a red stripe running diagonally across her bows charges out of the fog like the hand of God or the US cavalry.

From now on things happen fast. We receive word that the weather in the Strait is deteriorating. To speed matters along the *Munro* cannot dock here. We must pack our overnight bags and be ready to be picked up by ship's dinghy as soon as possible.

We can all see the ship's dinghy lowered and we all see it set out. A squat, robust orange-coloured boat, bobbing and bouncing against the waves. We all see it making heavy weather of the approach to the shore, disappearing altogether behind the bigger waves. And we all see the dinghy return to the *Munro*, unable to find a way through the low sandbars across which the waves are breaking with increasing force. The captain has one remaining option, which is to use his on-board helicopter to take us off. It will take a while to be made operational, but if the weather holds he will send it out within half an hour.

We film by a graveyard in amongst the sand-dunes. By the time we have finished the wind is howling round the cape and whipping sharp stinging grains of sand across our faces.

The helicopter makes the half-mile crossing, but there is a complication. Because of military regulations he cannot take all of us at once, so several time-consuming trips have to be made as the weather gets progressively worse.

The rest of the crew, with camera, film and unfortunately, as it transpires, with the radio as well, is taken back safely to the *Munro*. The helicopter does not reappear. Fraser and I, the only ones left on the mainland, can only huddle beside an aircraft hangar, out of the wind, and wait. We can now no longer see the *Munro*. Even Cape Prince of Wales, barren and treeless, is now an increasingly indistinct presence. I have rarely seen weather turn so angry, so fast. This, I suppose, is what western Alaska is really like. The dead calm, sun-drenched days when we were last here have lulled us into a false sense of security. I should have listened to Harry de Windt. What an absurd way to end a series, crouching behind a shed on the furthest westerly point of the American continent. An hour passes. We check our options. Fraser has nineteen dollars in his pocket. We're about to trudge back to the nearest hut when we catch the sound of an aircraft engine over the screeching of the wind. Though we are safely plucked from the tempest on Wales beach, the most perilous part of the whole operation is still to come. The helicopter must be landed precisely in the right spot on the stern of a ship pitching and tossing in a strengthening gale. In these conditions the slightest misjudgement could be fatal. The skill of the pilot and the co-ordination of the manoeuvre by Captain Gable on the bridge made me feel doubly embarrassed to be involving such people in our harebrained schemes.

DAY 245: *Bering Strait*

Safe aboard the *Munro*. Have been given the cabin of an absent Ops Officer called Kelley. It's very small, there is a computer beside me and books on code, environmental fishing regulations and celestial calculations on a shelf at the end of the bunk. My clothes are spread out to dry over every available surface. I don't sleep much. Whatever happens, this will be the last day of a nine-and-a-half-month journey. The day we close the circle.

It's August again, only this time round Alaskan August is not at all like anyone else's. The seas are high and the wind and rain rake the decks making it impossible to stay outside for long. I can see Little Diomede, but only as a black dot on a radar screen.

Throughout the morning we lie off the island waiting for a break in the weather to put us ashore. Last night's adventure was a clear warning of what we are up against so no one protests when, with the swell rising to 12 feet, winds blowing out of the south-west at 40 miles an hour and visibility down to a murky half-mile, Captain Gable abandons the attempt to land us on Little Diomede.

Besides ourselves he has one hundred and seventy crew on the ship, many of them itching to get back to California for their first leave in four or five months. As we criss-cross the international date line, tacking between the hemispheres one last time, I know how they feel and make no protest. I feel sad but not at all tearful. What the hell, after 50,000 miles of travel we are one mile out. As the Buddhists would say, only God is perfect.

MICHAEL PALIN established his reputation with *Monty Python's Flying Circus* and *Ripping Yarns*. His work also includes several films with Monty Python, as well as *The Missionary*, *A Private Function*, an award-winning performance as the hapless Ken in *A Fish Called Wanda*, *American Friends* and *Fierce Creatures*. His television credits include two films for the BBC's *Great Railway Journeys*, the plays *East of Ipswich* and *Number 27*, and Alan Bleasdale's *GBH*. He has written seven bestselling travel books to accompany his series *Around the World in 80 Days*, *Pole to Pole*, *Full Circle*, *Hemingway Adventure*, *Sahara*, *Himalaya* and *New Europe*. He is also the author of a number of children's stories, the play *The Weekend* and the novel *Hemingway's Chair*. In 2006 the first volume of his diaries, *1969–1979: The Python Years*, spent many weeks on the bestseller lists. In 2008 an updated special edition of *Around the World in 80 Days* was published to coincide with his BBC documentary *Around the World in 20 Years*. Visit his website at www.palinstravels.co.uk.

BASIL PAO began his photographic career in 1980 on his return to Hong Kong after ten years in the United States, where he was an art director for Atlantic, Polygram and Warner Bros. He first worked with Michael Palin on the design for book accompanying Monty Python's *Life of Brian*. They have since collaborated on the books based on his seven travel series. In 2007 he wrote and photographed *China Revealed: A Portrait of the Rising Dragon*.

POLE TO POLE

MICHAEL PALIN

Photographs by Basil Pao

PHOENIX

A PHOENIX PAPERBACK

First published in Great Britain in 1992
by BBC Books
This paperback edition published in 2009
by Phoenix,
an imprint of Orion Books Ltd,
Orion House, 5 Upper St Martin's Lane,
London WC2H 9EA

An Hachette UK company

3 5 7 9 10 8 6 4

This edition copyright © Michael Palin, 1999
Photographs copyright © Basil Pao
Maps by David Atkinson

The right of Michael Palin to be identified as the author
of this work has been asserted by him in accordance with
the Copyright, Designs and Patents Act 1988.

Thanks are due to A.P. Watt Ltd for their permission on behalf of Paul O'Prey
to reproduce the extract from his introduction to *Heart of Darkness* by Joseph Conrad
(1983 edition) on page 215, and on behalf of Ronald Huntford to reproduce
the extract from *The Last Place on Earth* on page 287.

A CIP catalogue record for this book
is available from the British Library.

ISBN 978-0-7538-2326-2

Printed and bound in Great Britain by Clays Ltd, St Ives plc

The Orion Publishing Group's policy is to use papers that
are natural, renewable and recyclable products and
made from wood grown in sustainable forests. The logging
and manufacturing processes are expected to conform to
the environmental regulations of the country of origin.

www.orionbooks.co.uk

CONTENTS

INTRODUCTION

For almost a year after my return from travelling around the world in eighty days, well-intentioned ideas for sequels were generously offered. I had only to show up with a suitcase for the 10.15 to Bristol for someone to ask, 'Off round the world again, Michael?' A chance sighting of me far from home would prompt a cry of recognition: 'What's this, Michael . . . round Penrith in eighty days?'. Taxi-drivers would hold me personally responsible for new traffic schemes: 'You should try going round *this* lot in eighty days!'. A moment's hesitation at a road junction would not go unnoticed: 'You can get round the world in eighty days but you can't find your way across Oxford Street!'.

It was beginning to drive me up the pole and Clem Vallance, ever the opportunist, suggested that if I was going up one pole I might as well do the other. His idea was simplicity itself – on an atlas, anyway. A journey from North to South Poles along the 30 degree East line of longitude, chosen because it crossed the greatest amount of land.

I wanted to call it *Pole to Pole by Public Transport*, but owing to the absence of a bus route through the African bush or an Awayday across Antarctica, this had to be dismissed as wishful thinking. In the event, though we relied on aircraft to get us to the Poles themselves, we completed the rest of the journey overland, on a mixture of ships, trains, trucks, rafts, Ski-Doos, buses, barges, bicycles, balloons, 4-litre Landcruisers and horse-drawn carts.

The bulk of the journey was made between July and Christmas 1991. With one ten-day break at Aswan we travelled and filmed for five months, passing through seventeen countries and making over seventy overnight stops.

We were unable to film at the North Pole in July as no plane would take the risk of landing on the summer ice, so the section from the North Pole to Tromsø in Norway was filmed separately, in May.

1991 was an exceptional year. A quarter of the countries we visited had undergone, or were undergoing, momentous changes. Communism disappeared in the USSR and apartheid in South Africa. We arrived in Ethiopia four months after the conclusion of a civil war that had occupied parts of the country for thirty years and in Zambia on the day Kenneth Kaunda's 28-year reign ended.

Pole to Pole is, like *Around the World in 80 Days*, based upon diaries and tape-recordings kept at the time. They describe the pain and the pleasure of the journey as it happened. I have deliberately not used the benefit of hindsight to change any of those entries. What you get is what we saw and experienced in those extraordinary months between the Poles – warts, bedbugs and all.

London, 1992
MICHAEL PALIN

ACKNOWLEDGEMENTS

Pole to Pole was in every sense a team effort. First and foremost on the team was Clem Vallance, whom I must thank for the original idea, the meticulous preparation to bring it to fruition and for his guidance and good company on the road.

Nigel Meakin, Patti Musicaro, Fraser Barber and Basil Pao travelled with me almost everywhere and I owe them enormous and almost inexpressible thanks for not only being the best technicians in the business but for being the very best travelling companions. Mirabel Brook shared the brunt of the preparation work and much of the travelling with patience and humour. Roger Mills, who had been my co-director on *80 Days*, made sure the work was fun, and after work was even more fun. Angela Elbourne, another *80 Days* veteran, was, if it were possible, less flappable than ever. Mimi O'Grady in the London office was our dependable and ever-present lifeline to the outside world. At Prominent Television I must especially thank Anne James for working so hard to get the show on the road, Alison Davies for painstakingly and encouragingly putting my ravings and ramblings in order, Una Hoban for signing the cheques and Kath James for keeping the world at bay while I was away.

There are many more people without whose help, energy and enthusiasm *Pole to Pole* would not have happened. Besides those already mentioned in the book, I would like very much to thank Paul Marsh, who patiently and valiantly tried to teach me Russian, Roger Saunders, Chris Taylor, Sue Pugh Tasios, Gabra Gilada, David Thomas, Alex Richardson, Jonathan Rowdon, Anne Dummett and last but not least Suzanne Webber, Suzanna Zsohar, Linda Blakemore and Julian Flanders at BBC Books.

For travel information I relied heavily on the excellent *Rough Guides* and the *Lonely Planet* series, and the *Insight Guides* and Martin Walker's *Independent Traveller's Guide to the Soviet Union* were invaluable.

NOTE ON THE TEXT

Not every single day is described. Rest days when nothing happened except laundry have been omitted out of consideration for the reader.

The word 'fixer' is often mentioned. Fixers are professional organizers whose job it was to ease our passage through their countries.

THE NORTH POLE TO TALLINN

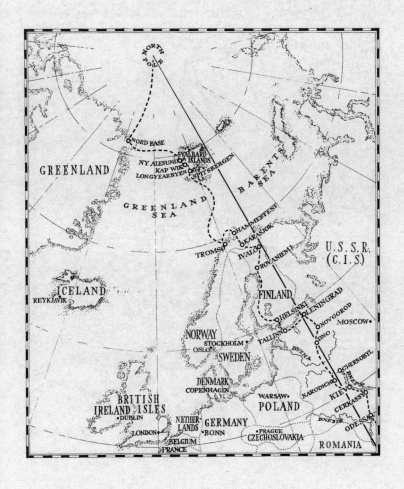

TALLINN TO PORT SAID

PORT SAID TO NAIROBI

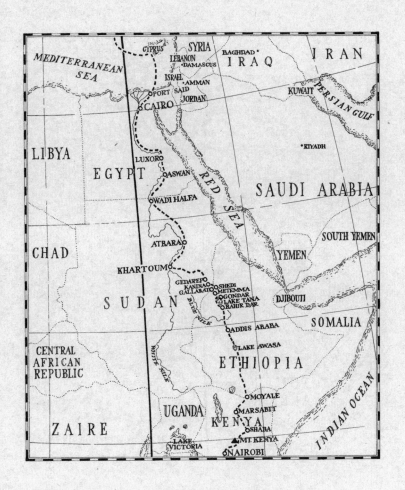

NAIROBI TO CAPE TOWN

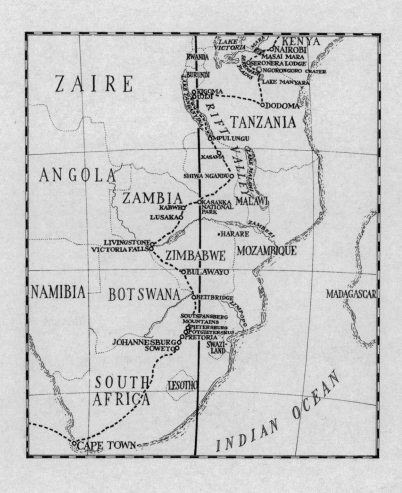

CAPE TOWN TO THE SOUTH POLE

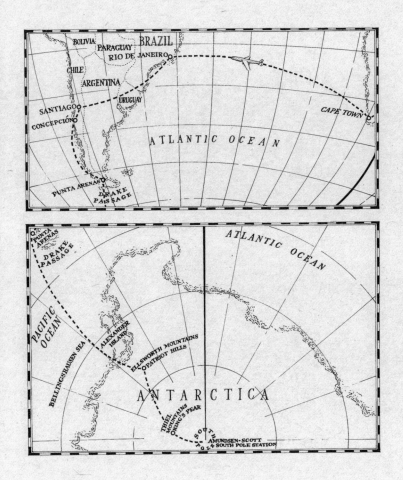

DAY 1: *The North Pole*

It's 3.45 on a Saturday afternoon and I'm seventeen miles from the North Pole. Somewhere, a long way away, people are doing sensible things like watching cricket or digging gardens or pushing prams or visiting their mothers-in-law.

I'm squeezed tight into a small, noisy aeroplane descending through stale grey cloud towards an enormous expanse of cracked and drifting ice. With me are Nigel Meakin and his camera, Fraser Barber and his tape-recorder and Roger Mills and his pipe. With our two pilots, Russ Bomberry and Dan Parnham, we are the only human beings within 500 miles. Outside my window one of our two propeller-driven engines slowly eats away at a fuel supply which must last us another six hours at least. In little more than ten minutes our pilot will have to fashion a landing strip out of nothing more than a piece of ice – strong enough to withstand an impact of 12,500 lbs at eighty miles an hour. Below the ice the sea is 14,000 feet deep.

I'm sure I'm not the only one of us looking down on this desolate wilderness who hasn't wished, for an impure moment, that the North Pole, rather than being in the middle of an ocean, was solid, well marked and even supplied with a hut and a coffee machine. But the cracked and fissured ice-pack offers no comfortable reassurance – no glimmer of any reward to the traveller who has made his way to the top of the world. The Arctic Ocean, known to the Victorians as the Sea of Ancient Ice, stares balefully back as we descend towards it, reflecting nothing but the question: Why?

It's too late to ask the producer now, too late to begin to speculate why I so eagerly agreed to come here, and completely out of order even to mention that if we survive this ice landing we have only another 12,500 miles to go.

At two minutes past four our De Havilland Twin Otter, designed in the fifties and much loved and trusted by Arctic flyers, is finally over the North Pole. One almost looks for a point, a peak, a curve offering tantalizing glimpses of those huge land masses – Alaska, Siberia, Scandinavia and Canada – which back on to the Arctic. But all there is to see is ice and the nearer we get to it the more evident it is that the ice is not in good shape. Russ, a self-contained, taciturn man about whom I know nothing other than that my life is in his hands, leans forward from the controls, scanning the conditions below and frowning.

Technology cannot help him now. The decision as to how, when and ultimately whether to drop the plane onto the ice is for his judgement alone.

He clearly doesn't like what he sees and, by my watch, we have circled the roof of the world for nearly thirty minutes before a change in engine note indicates that he is at last throttling back in preparation for a landing. We drop low, running in over a tongue of open water, Russ staring hard at the ice as ridge walls taller than I'd expected rush up to meet us. Brace myself for impact, but it never comes. At the last minute Russ thrusts the overhead throttle control forward and pulls us up banking steeply away. He checks the fuel gauge and asks Dan, the young co-pilot, to connect up one of the drums for in-flight refuelling. Dan squeezes his way from the cockpit to the back of the plane, where he begins to fiddle around with spanners and tubes until the aircraft is rich with the smell of kerosene. The Pole remains 100 feet below us, tantalizingly elusive, probably in the middle of a black pool of melted water. Russ takes advantage of some marginally increased sunlight to attempt a second landing. Once again hearts rise towards mouths as the engines slow and a blur of ice and snow and pitch-black sea rises towards us, but once again Russ snatches the plane from the ice at the last moment and we soar away, relieved and cheated.

I make a mental note never to complain about a landing ever again. Russ circles and banks the plane for another fifteen minutes, patiently examining the floating ice for yet another attempt.

This time there is no pull-out. Six hours after leaving Eureka Base on Ellesmere Island, Canada, the wheels and skis of the Twin Otter find the ground, bounce, hit, bounce, hit, swerve, slide and finally grip the slithery hummocked surface. We are down and safe. I check the time on my watch, and realize that at this point it could be whatever time I wanted it to be. Japanese time, Indian time, New York time or London time – they're all the same at the Pole. It is ten o'clock at night in London.

Home seems impossibly far away as we step out onto a rough base of ice and snow. It looks secure but water channels only a few yards away and the fact that Russ will not risk switching off the aircraft engines in case the ice should split reminds us that this is a lethal landscape. Finding the highest point in the vicinity – a pile of fractured ice-blocks, soaring to three and a half feet, I plant our 'North Pole' (kindly loaned to us by the Canadians) and we take our photos. The air is still, and a watery sun filters through grey-edged cloud giving the place a forlorn and lonely aspect. The temperature is minus twenty-five Centigrade. This is considered warm.

After an hour's filming, we defer to Russ's polite impatience and return to the aircraft. Concerned about fuel, he takes off quickly and unceremoniously, as if the North Pole were just another bus stop.

We have planned to follow the thirty degree East meridian all the way to the South Pole, but straight away there are problems. There is only enough fuel left to reach the nearest airstrip, a Danish base in Greenland. Even this is 480 miles away, and beyond radio range at the moment. We have no option but to fly in hope.

For some reason the only liquid we have been provided with for our journey is a litre can of tomato juice which doesn't last long between six people, and it is a thirsty, underfed, cramped and exhausted little group that puts down at Nord Base, Greenland, with only twenty-five minutes of fuel left. We have been away from the rest of the world for ten minutes short of twelve hours.

There is not a soul to be seen.

Russ, armed with registration documents and proof of identity, trudges off into the distance to try and raise someone.

We wait by the aircraft, in a curious state of mental and physical limbo. The only one who seems really happy is Roger, who is at last able to light up his pipe.

After what feels like an eternity, Russ returns with a young Danish soldier who is in a state of considerable shock. No one had told him we were coming, and it being three o'clock in the morning on the north coast of Greenland, 700 miles from the nearest settlement, a knock on the door must have been like the start of a horror movie.

He bravely tries to laugh it off, 'We thought it could only be Father Christmas', before offering us what we are dying for – food and drink and a bed for the night. So day one ends in country one, which turns out, quite unexpectedly, to be Denmark.

DAY 2: *Greenland to Ny Alesund*

The midnight sun is shining brightly when I climb into a bunk at 3.30 a.m., and equally brightly when I wake at half-past nine. From 15 October the sun will disappear below the horizon and not rise again until the end of February, but for now, in mid-May, day merges seamlessly into day.

Greenland is a part of the kingdom of Denmark – a massive, almost uninhabited ice-cap over fifty times the size of its mother country. The base at Nord is manned for the Danish government by five soldiers, but one of them is away, so Henny, Jack, Kent and Kenneth are running the place at the moment.

Two big supply planes come in each year bringing all they need – fresh videos, books, food and drink, and equipment. The only thing they don't like is that it means letters . . . 'Not receiving them, *writing* them,' they explain.

They're so friendly, open and hospitable that there is a great temptation to abandon the journey and stay here, drinking fresh coffee with rich Danish bread, half-listening to a rock-and-roll track by a Miss B. Haven entitled 'Making Love in the Snow', and gazing out to a view of icy fiords bathed in crisp bright sunshine. I ask Jack if the snow ever disappears.

'Oh yes,' he assures me, 'it melts in July. And starts snowing again in August.'

Russ is unable to make contact with our next port of call – Ny Alesund in Spitsbergen – and the Danes say they will try and raise a weather forecast from the American base at Thule. This takes some time, but at midday the news comes through that the weather is good, and after refuelling and repacking we squeeze back into the Twin Otter.

There are 325 miles between Greenland and the Svalbard Islands, of which Spitsbergen ('steep mountains' as it was named by the Dutch who discovered it 400 years ago) is the largest. Part of Norway since 1925, it is for us an important stepping-stone between the North Pole and Europe, and the first place where we hope to do without aircraft and continue our journey by land and sea.

Below us, a mixture of black clear-water channels, pale-blue icebergs and various shades of frozen and refrozen ice give the Greenland Sea a mottled effect, but as we cross the Greenwich meridian and enter the eastern hemisphere the effect of a warm current pushing up from the Atlantic changes the scene dramatically. The ice melts away and thick cloud hides the water for a while. When we see it again, it is only 1500 feet below the plane and a fierce easterly wind is flicking spray from the top of angry waves.

The Twin Otter is suddenly battling against a headwind and horizontally driving snow. Russ takes us down another 1000 feet but the visibility is no better, and before we hit slap-bang into the side of Spitsbergen he pulls us sharply up through the impenetrable but mercifully low storm cloud to calmer conditions at 2000 feet.

Judging from his expression Spitsbergen is not on Russ's regular beat and he seems as surprised as any of us to see the sweeping sides of a mountain range emerge above the clouds to the east. From the map these look to be the peaks of Albert I Land, and turning the little aircraft south we follow the coastline and descend through the angry, drifting remains of the storm clouds into King's Fiord, where glaciers roll down to the sea and fragments of ice speckle the dark water. Dwarfed by the massive landscape two golf ball early-warning domes, a couple of tall concrete structures and a cluster of brightly painted houses mark the settlement of Ny Alesund (New Alesund). We have crossed two time zones in our two-and-a-half-hour flight and passed south of latitude 80 degrees.

At Ny Alesund we rendezvous with David Rootes, our adviser on Arctic survival from the Scott Polar Research Institute, Engineer Geir Paulsen, the organizer of our land transport, and Patti, Nigel's camera assistant. Basil Pao, stills photographer and last member of our team, is to meet us in Tromsø. It's soon clear from the swirling snowstorms that sweep across the fiord and from the experiences David and Patti recount from their journey up to meet us that Greenland and the North Pole have been a picnic compared with what lies ahead.

But first the pleasure of a shower and clean clothes and a drink in the only bar in Ny Alesund. Everyone seems subdued, but this is apparently the result of multiple hangovers from a party held here last night to toast the news of our arrival at the Pole.

DAY 3: *Ny Alesund*

We're quartered in simple comfort in a long wooden hut comprising individual bedrooms, shared shower and lavatory, sports hall and a room for conferences and classes. It's owned, as is most of Ny Alesund, by the King's Bay Kull Company. Kull, or coal, is the main reason for a human presence on Spitsbergen but following a series of disasters in the early 1960s the Ny Alesund mines were closed down and the accommodation is now used for scientific research, intrepid vacations and the inevitable weather station. There is even a fledgling British presence here in the shape of Nick Cox and his wife Katie who are employed in setting up an Arctic research station.

Life is still run along the lines of a company town. Breakfast at 7.30, lunch at noon and supper at five are all served in a communal canteen, a five-minute walk along a snow-covered track. The preferred mode of transport is the snowmobile, often known by one of its trade names as the Ski-Doo. Built like a fat motorbike, it is driven by a caterpillar track with short skis on the front for steering. With flashy trims and names like *Exciter*, *Enticer* and *Phazer II* they make a lot of noise and give a great impression of speed although rarely hitting more than 45 m.p.h. They are to be our transport on the 155-mile journey across the mountains to the capital town of Longyearbyen.

Though we are crying for a day off after the polar adventure, Geir Paulsen, a round, pony-tailed adventurer with a considerable sense of humour, is of the opinion that we should try to leave before bad weather sets in. (One thing I've noticed in countries full of weather stations is that no one can give you an accurate weather forecast. They can tell you that palm trees will be growing in Iceland in seventy-five years, but nothing at all about the afternoon ahead.)

We load up and set off about 3 p.m. It is appropriate that our column of snowmobiles and trailers should pass, on the way out of town, a three-foot high bronze head of the explorer Roald Amundsen. It commemorates the first transpolar flight in his airship *Norge*, which left Ny Alesund on 11 May 1926 and landed in North America on 14 May, after a journey of over 3000 miles. Three years later Amundsen died in the Arctic attempting to rescue his friend Nobile, whose airship, like Amundsen's, left from the thirty-foot pylon which still stands on the edge of town, receding into the distance as we head for the mountains.

Determined to do all my own stunts, I send myself and my passenger David Rootes flying as I lose control of *Mach-One* (the name of the black Ski-Doo I've been allotted) round a tight bend. One handlebar is the accelerator, the other the brake, and at this stage I'm not entirely sure which is which. Fortunately the accident causes more injury to pride than to limb. The going is not easy. The sun is now lost in cloud and it's difficult to see the track. Heinrich, a young Norwegian with disconcertingly blue eyes, who can probably drive a snowmobile standing on his head, leads the procession as we climb towards the saddle of the mountain. Quite suddenly thick cloud envelops us and everything around is white. All sense of direction is lost, and when we do eventually have to pull up, David Rootes informs me drily that 300 yards to my left is a precipice, dropping sheer to a glacier. Defeated by the worsening conditions we turn back. Fresh snow is falling and a small drift has formed already on the side of Amundsen's huge and beaky nose as we re-enter Ny Alesund. Neither he nor anyone else seems surprised to see us back.

DAY 4: *Ny Alesund*

Wake to the sound of bird-song. As I haven't yet seen a single living creature in the Arctic, I wonder for a moment if this might be one of the crew, driven mad with homesickness, playing a Percy Edwards tape. But Peter Webb, a young Englishman and one of our Ski-Doo circus, tells me at breakfast that it's a snow bunting. We're also likely to see seals, reindeer and possibly Arctic fox on our way across the island. I'm desperate to see a polar bear (having been brought up on Brumas) but might have to shoot it if I do. I glean this from a warning poster, in Norwegian and English, displayed at the door of the canteen. 'Polar bears may be very dangerous,' it begins:

'The following precautions should be taken: (1) Always carry a weapon. (2) Do not attract bears by putting out food. Place your garbage at least 100 metres away from the camp, directly in view of your tent opening or cabin door. This may enable you to see a visiting bear in time. Report to the authorities if you have had to kill a bear, find out what sex it is, and take care of the skull and skin.'

Roger slept badly and suspects he has a sprained wrist following yesterday's excursion. This is his excuse for wearing a sinister black glove on one hand. Fraser dreamt that he gave every member of his family a Ski-Doo for Christmas. I can see why he thought of Christmas, for the snow is falling here as copiously as in any Disney cartoon, making it hard to remember that it's nearly June.

Geir is ever hopeful. The barometer is evidently rising and we should be packed and ready to leave at six this evening, after supper.

At 6 p.m. the snow is falling in great big fat lazy flakes, and we are about to settle, not unhappily, for an evening of table tennis and a good night's sleep when Geir and his colleagues suggest that the most settled conditions are often in the middle of the night and they would seriously ask us to consider a 2 a.m. departure. This is seriously considered, but not for very long. Another postponement, until tomorrow morning, is agreed upon. Back to the table tennis.

DAY 5: *Ny Alesund to Kap Wik*

2 a.m. The skies duly clear and dazzling sunlight picks out mountains and glaciers obscured for forty-eight hours.

8 a.m. I raise my blind in expectation. The sun has gone as if it were a dream, and the pile of snow at my window is half an inch higher. Walk through a blizzard to the canteen. I have said goodbye to the breakfast chef at least twice and he is now thoroughly confused and a little suspicious of my intentions. Am I really on my way to the South Pole or just trying out Great Mueslis of the World?

Heinrich is phlegmatic.

'Waiting . . .' he observes, 'everything about the Arctic is waiting.' After lunch the snow begins to ease off and in the square the Norwegian flag turns abruptly to the south. This is a sign of the arrival of the settled northerly airstream for which we have been waiting.

The journey to Longyearbyen is likely to take twelve hours at least, and it is suggested that we should break it with a stop at Kap Wik, about five hours away, where there is a trapper's hut with accommodation. This sounds suitably photogenic and fairytale-like and once the vehicles have been cleared of their carapace of snow, the sledge trailers lashed down and hooked up, and an anti-polar-bear rifle stashed aboard, we are once more ready for departure. Nick and Katie Cox honour us with an official British presence at the great moment, and Nick entrusts me with a bottle of whisky for Harald, the trapper. I am so embarrassed that we might have to slink back yet again that I avoid the chef's eye and Amundsen's severe stare as we finally pull away just after seven in the evening.

The mountains climb quite steeply to 2000 feet and we have to stop a lot in the first hour, partly to free snowmobiles bogged down by their heavy loads, but mainly to photograph the spectacular views out across King's Fiord, fed by three glaciers and rimmed with sweeping mountain peaks. As soon as the motors are turned off and the natural silence restored, the size and scale and majesty of the landscape is indescribable. There are no trees on Spitsbergen, and therefore few birds except around the coast, and with unbroken snow shrouding the valley below us there is an atmosphere of magnificent peacefulness.

Soon we are across the pass and putting the snowmobiles down a snow-slope so steep that we are warned not to use the brake. This is to prevent the trailers from swinging round and pulling the vehicles over – and presumably sending the driver hurtling downhill in a mass of wreckage, though they don't tell you the last bit. We twist and turn through some perilous gullies which Roger refers to with a certain relish as Walls of Death, as in 'Michael, we'd like to do another Wall of Death sequence'. The whole adventure seems to have gone to his head since he chose the codeword 'Raving Queen' for his end of the two-way radio. Fraser, at the other end, is 'Intrepid One', and I suppose it does take away some of the terror to hear, floating across a glacier, the immortal words:

'Raving Queen to Intrepid One, Michael's on the Wall of Death . . . Now!'

On the other side of the pass another epic wintry panorama is revealed on the shores of Engelsbukta – 'English Bay' – where an English whaling fleet under Henry Hudson took refuge in 1607 while in search of the north-east passage. Much of the bay is still frozen, and we see our first seals – nothing more than tiny black blobs – waiting beside their holes in the ice. A ptarmigan, in its white winter coat, peers curiously down at us from a pinnacle of rock, and a pair of eider ducks turn low over the bay.

We head towards a wide, level glacier passing ice cliffs of palest blue which are millions of years old and still moving. I ask Geir why they should be such a colour. Apparently it is caused by the presence of air inside the ice.

After the roller-coaster conditions on the pass, progress across the glacier is fast and reasonably comfortable. I am riding pillion behind David, and apart from nursing an occasional numbing cold in my thumb and fingers, I have plenty of time to sit back and take in the glories of this wide, unvisited landscape. A pair of Svalbard reindeer, not much bigger than large dogs, wander across a hillside. God knows what they find to eat.

After five hours we grind to a halt, our vehicles stuck in deep fresh-fallen snow at the top of a pass, still barely halfway to the trapper's hut. Bars of chocolate, nips of Scotch and stupendous views keep spirits up as Geir, Heinrich and the team make repeated journeys down the valley to bring up machines that couldn't make it to the top. Once all of them are up on the ridge they have to be refuelled, a slow laborious job, as is anything which involves unloading the trailers.

We are rewarded with a long exhilarating run on wide downhill slopes to our first ice-crossing – on the frozen head-waters of the Ehmanfiord. The surface is scratched and rutted, and it's only on the last stretch that the ice is smooth enough to open out, and we ride like invading Mongol hordes toward the tiny, isolated cabin on Kap Wik where, somewhat improbably, we are to spend what remains of the night.

DAY 6: *Kap Wik to Longyearbyen*

It's 2.45 in the morning when we arrive at Harald Solheim's hut. A tall wooden frame hung with seal carcasses stands on a slight rise, more prominent than the cabin itself, which is set lower down, out of the wind. The first surprise is Harald himself. Instead of some grizzly bearded old-timer, a tall, pale, studious figure comes out to welcome us. He does have a beard, but attached as it is to long, aquiline features the effect is more rabbi than trapper. The second surprise is how benignly and agreeably he copes with the appearance of ten tired and hungry travellers in the middle of the night. First we fill up his minuscule hallway with our boots and bags, then we burst his sitting-room to the seams while he heats up some stew on a wood-burning stove. His wood supply, neatly stacked in a workshop, is driftwood, probably from the Russian coast. His electricity supply is wind-generated.

He fetches out a leg of smoked reindeer, which is quite delicious, and over this and a mixture of stew, smoked salmon, Aquavit (the local spirit) and Glenmorangie whisky we thaw out and swap stories. Harald offers advice, comment and information, liberally laced with dry humour. It's like some wonderfully chaotic tutorial.

Around about 4.30 a.m. some of us start looking a little anxiously for the dormitory. Harald explains the arrangements. In a next-door room he has four bunk-beds and floor space for two. There is more space on the floor of his workshop. Everyone else will have to sleep in the sitting-room with him. There is one sit-down loo, but as this is a bag that has to be emptied men are requested to use the Great Outdoors whenever possible, but to refrain from peeing on the side of the house from which he draws his water supply. For cleaning teeth and washing he recommends the snow.

When I wake, it's half-past eleven. The sitting-room resembles some Viking Valhalla with recumbent Norwegians scattered about and Harald sprawled on the sofa like a warrior slain in battle. Then the telephone rings. Last night my tired brain was so busy romanticizing Harald's existence that I hadn't noticed the phone, or the remote control for the matt-black hi-fi, or the visitors' book, or the collection of Rachmaninov piano concertos on CD, signed 'To Harald from Vladimir Ashkenazy'.

Is it all a dream? Have we been hi-jacked in the night to some apartment in Oslo? I stumble outside clutching my toothbrush and there is the reassuring reality of empty mountains and frozen seas stretching as far as the eye can see.

I scrub snow all over my face and neck. A refreshing shock which dispels any lurking hangover. When I get back indoors Harald is off the phone and preparing coffee. This autumn, he tells me, he will be celebrating fifteen years at Kap Wik. He has family in Norway, but they don't visit much. His closest neighbours are the Russians at the mining town of Pyramiden, eighteen miles away. He reads a lot, 'almost everything except religious literature', and hunts seal, reindeer, Arctic fox (a pelt will fetch around £80) and snowgeese. '"Goose Kap Wik" was served to the King and Queen of Norway,' he informs me, with quiet satisfaction.

'So it's a busy life in the middle of nowhere?'

Harald shrugs. 'Some years I don't see a living soul from autumn to July.'

I ask him if he has ever felt the need for companionship. A woman around the house, perhaps.

'It's . . . er . . .' he smiles at his sudden inarticulacy, '. . . it's not easy to explain in Norwegian . . . but any woman mad enough to come here . . .'

He never finishes the sentence. The sound of a distant helicopter brings him to his feet.

'It's my mail,' he explains, almost apologetically, as a Sea King helicopter clatters into sight across the fiord.

After a late lunch and more stories our caravan is re-packed and re-launched. Harald, smiling, waves us away. I don't really understand why a man of such curiosity, fluency and culture should want to chase animals round Spitsbergen, but I feel he rather enjoys being an enigma, and though he is no hermit he is one of a rare breed of truly independent men.

The rest of the journey is less eventful. The slopes are not as fierce, and the snow is turning to slush in some of the valleys. It's becoming almost routine to turn off one glacier onto another, to roar up snowbound mountain passes and see the seals plop back into their ice-holes as we cross the fiords.

We stop at the spot where Patti had an adventure on the way up to Ny Alesund. She lost her way in a 'white-out' and was not found for almost an hour. I hope this isn't an omen for the long journey ahead.

Although we make fast progress towards Longyearbyen, the weather has not finished with us. Turning into the broad valley that leads to the town we are hit full in the face by a blizzard of stinging wet snow and as Heinrich accelerates for home it makes for a hard and uncomfortable end to the ride.

After five and a half hours' travelling we see through the murk the first lights of Longyearbyen, and the snowmobiles screech clumsily along the wet highway.

It's half-past ten and we have reached our first town, 812 miles from the North Pole.

DAY 7: *Longyearbyen*

Everyone in Ny Alesund was rather rude about Longyearbyen, and certainly as capitals go it is no beauty. It is another coal town, largely the property of the Store-Norsk Company, but unlike Ny Alesund, coal is still mined here and there is fine black dust in the air, trucks on the road and housing blocks set out in severe grid patterns down the sides of the valley. It is ironic that the chief product of this treeless island should be fossil fuel. There is a theory that at one time Spitsbergen lay near the Equator and was covered by tropical forest.

In my spartan room at Hotel Number 5, the information sheet on Longyearbyen reads more like a company report than a tourist brochure. The settlement was founded in 1906 by an American, John Munroe Longyear. For ten years it was run by men only but in 1916 the Norwegians bought Longyear out and the first women were allowed to accompany their mining husbands here. The population today consists of 250 women, 250 children and 550 men. 'However,' it adds, a little ominously, 'there are still important differences between Longyearbyen and other small towns in mainland Norway. Here there are neither pensioners, handicapped people, nor persons terminally ill.' I half expect my door to be flung open, and my birth certificate and pulse given a snap check.

There is no getting away from Ski-Doos. I dreamt about them all night and this morning I find that there is a Ski-Doo convention in town, and our hotel is at the centre of it. From ten o'clock onwards international buyers from the world's cold countries can be heard, if not seen, attempting to scale the near-vertical slopes behind the hotel. There is something about these vehicles that brings out the Jekyll and Hyde in a driver. Once in the saddle, he will sooner or later succumb to an uncontrollable urge to do something dangerous. They are vehicles for a world without roads or policemen.

Longyearbyen has a supermarket. It doesn't actually say on the self-opening doors 'World's Most Northerly Supermarket', but, at 78.15 degrees I can't imagine it has many competitors. Apart from an eye-catching range of canned vegetables called 'Sodd' there is not much to detain us except a well-stocked drinks section. As we have a long sea-journey ahead of us I fill my trolley, only to have to replace all the bottles as I don't have a valid air ticket into or out of Longyearbyen. Alcoholic refreshment is, it appears, severely rationed. The only way we can buy even a can of beer is with a special dispensation from the Sysselmann – the Governor. We traipse round to Government House to get our chitty, feeling like naughty schoolchildren.

DAY 8: *Longyearbyen to Tromsø*

We are to continue our journey south on the supply ship *Norsel*, which leaves today for Tromsø in Norway, refuelling, or 'bunkering' as they call it, a number of fishing boats on the way. They have limited accommodation on board and it will be a slow trip (estimates vary from five to seven days for the 600-mile journey), but beggars can't be choosers and there are no other ships operating out of Longyearbyen this early in the summer.

We bid farewell to all those who guided us across Spitsbergen, and I promise Geir that I will let the world know that most of our snowmobiles were made by Yamaha for whom he is the dealer, and not Ski-Doo. He in turn reveals that he's going to Tromsø anyway, but flying there in a couple of hours as any normal person would. I try to point out the delights of not being normal.

The *Norsel* is the only vessel at the dockside. Adventfiorden, on which Longyearbyen is situated, only became free of ice a week ago, and the coal ships will not start arriving for another month. She looks sturdy, if a little bruised, a slash of pillar-box red against the grey buildings of the port, and the flowing white cloaks of the mountains across the fiord. She is not a big ship, only 550 tons, and our cabins are the size of cupboards, but there is an appealingly warm and secure atmosphere below decks. Earlier in the day I had talked to a journalist from the Svalbard newspaper who raised her eyebrows when she heard I was crossing to Tromsø by ship.

'They call that sea the Devil's Dancefloor.'

I put this to the captain, Stein Biølgerud, who smiles quietly to himself in a not very encouraging way. He explains to me that the *Norsel* has an exceptional draught of 8 metres (26 feet) which means that when fully loaded most of the hull is beneath the water and much more susceptible to rolling and pitching.

'And are we fully loaded at the moment?'

His smile widens. 'Oh, yes.'

The good news is that the hull is composed of 28-millimetre-thick steel plates.

'The highest ice class,' he continues encouragingly. 'We can move through sixty centimetres of solid ice.'

'So we'll be safe in the ice?'

'Oh yes. Unless of course we have too much ice on the super-structure. Then the ship can topple over.'

Credit for the redoubtably solid hull of the *Norsel* must go to Hitler's shipyards, for it was constructed in Germany in 1943, but left unfinished until the Norwegians took it over in 1947. Since then it has seen service as a seal catcher, scallop trawler and expedition vessel.

There is a crew of seven. The captain, first mate, chief engineer, cook and three deckhands. At the moment they are supervising the unloading of what seems like a year's supply of toilet rolls. This uncharismatic little ship is a lifeline up here. The captain recalls arriving late one year with a supply of beer on board.

'They only had seventeen cans left on the island. There were guys waiting on the jetty.'

Shortly after seven o'clock on an evening of piercing sunshine we pull away from Spitsbergen, round the headland, past the coal tips and out into the broad waters that lead to the Greenland Sea.

Soon a wall of grey cloud looms ahead of us and the captain says a gale is forecast. His bridge bristles with all sorts of electronic equipment, but he prefers to slide down one of the window panels, stick his head out and see what the birds are doing. He's sceptical of weather forecasts. In these waters things change so quickly.

'Once thing you can be sure of, you can't be sure of anything,' he observes. Another piece of Arctic wisdom.

He has to set a course almost due west to avoid the pack-ice along the coast, but it is from the west that the gale is coming. Thinking it may be the last meal we can cope with for a while we eat well – a rich stew cooked by Anthony, a small pale man dressed all in white, like an anxious dentist. We don't think he's Norwegian and Roger hazards that he is Russian.

'Are you Russian?' he asks him over another helping of stew. Anthony gives a quick, brittle smile and shakes his head. 'Polish.'

It turns out that the three deckhands are Polish as well.

Later, on the bridge, the captain (Norwegian) is worried that the wind is veering west earlier than expected.

'Not good for us,' he mutters. At the other end of the bridge the moustachioed chief engineer (also Norwegian) sits reading a comic book and not laughing.

DAY 9: *The Greenland Sea*

A night of varying degrees of instability. Occasionally some steep pitching and tossing which has clocks, books and glasses sliding onto the floor. The engine noise is a loud, persistent, constant factor we shall have to get used to. Noise insulators, like stabilizers, were never part of the *Norsel*'s specifications.

Egg and bacon breakfast. Fraser is worried that we have been given no lifeboat drill. Roger had awoken in the night to find a large sailor in his cabin. He was a messenger from the captain who had seen some ice near by and thought that we might like to photograph it.

Wintry conditions. Snow flurries on deck and a heavy sea. Seabirds like tern, fulmar and kittiwake, rest on the ice-covered bow before resuming their graceful gliding search of the waters.

I show Fraser the findings of an American survey, published in the shipping magazine *Trade Winds*, which asked people for whom they would give up a seat in a lifeboat. Of men, 67 per cent would give up a seat to their wives, 52 per cent to Mother Teresa, but only 8 per cent to Madonna. Of women, 41 per cent would give up a seat to their husbands, and only 3 per cent to 'men not their husbands'. I don't think Fraser's even found the lifeboat yet, so the question is academic.

I ask the captain what our maximum speed is.

'Well,' he pulls heavily on a yellowing hand-rolled cigarette, 'with a light load, good weather and the current behind us . . . ten knots.'

I reckon it will take us thirty hours just to clear the coast of Spitsbergen and another two days before we reach the fishing fleets on the Barents Sea.

Such is the pitching and tossing of the ship tonight that as I lie in my narrow bunk I experience the not unpleasant sensation of being stretched. First of all my body tries to slide out through my feet, then a moment later everything tries to escape through the top of my head. Go to sleep wondering how one could design a machine to reproduce this effect.

DAY 10: *The Barents Sea*

At 10 a.m. I check our position on the satellite indicator – 75.47 North and 16.25 East. We're entering the Barents Sea, named after the Dutchman who first discovered it in 1596, and the waters are shallower but cooler, fed by an Arctic rather than Atlantic current. This means that as we head east to the fishing grounds we have to push through a thickening ice-field. Up to now the ice fragments have floated by rather forlornly, looking like upturned tables and chairs, or floats heading home at the end of a parade. But now, as the air gets colder, the ice-blocks are growing in size as the open water between them decreases.

Stein (pronounced Stain), as we now call the captain, picks his way carefully. Some of these ten-foot ice-blocks have wide, solid platforms below the water which could cause damage if met head on. The ideal way to deal with them, he explains, is to keep the bow riding high over the ice, which then passes along the keel and is split by the weight of the ship.

When we are in the thick of the ice, Stein cuts engines and our intrepid cameraman is winched off the deck onto a convenient floe. I personally think it's too early in the journey to get rid of him, but I'm overruled. The sight of Nigel's solitary figure drifting slowly away from us is quite disturbing and I'm sure we all take far more pictures of him than he ever does of us.

The eerie sound of ice scraping along the hull continues for much of the day, before we are through into clear but rugged seas again. Roger, puffing on his pipe and looking increasingly like Captain Pugwash, surveys the spray flung high by waves breaking on the bow, and smiles with satisfaction.

'The devil's coming on the dancefloor, Mike.'

DAY 11: *The Barents Sea*

Snowstorms and high seas. I don't feel nauseous exactly, but the sight of the breakfast table replete with fried eggs, gammon, sausages, yoghurt, mayonnaise, fish paste in tubes, cheese, bacon, prawn spread and two kinds of salad in plastic tubs moves me fairly smartly up on deck. It's furiously cold and bleak but I stare at the horizon, as recommended, and take a few gulps of Arctic air until the moment of queasiness passes.

This morning everyone is slipping and sliding about, and in one 60-degree lurch all the drawers fly out of the captain's desk.

The first sign that we have reached the fishing fleets is a parade of Russian stern-trawlers, tossing about in the waves. I ask Stein if he refuels Russians. He shakes his head. 'They don't have the money.'

A week and a half from the Pole and the good news is that we are almost exactly on our target of thirty degrees East. The bad news is that we shall be around here for at least forty-eight hours as all the ships we are bunkering are in a twenty-five-mile radius.

The sea is too rough for ships to be fuelled alongside, and Stein has to opt for the more tricky and time-consuming bow-to-stern operation. Once a ship is about twenty feet astern lines are thrown and when secured a black rubber pipe is hoisted across and the fuel is pumped through. Our first customer, the Norwegian fishing boat *Stig Magne*, has to stay connected for an hour. Great skill and seamanship is required on the part of both captains to keep their vessels the right distance apart, whilst both are soaring and plunging wildly on thirty-foot waves.

In the middle of it all a sleek, battleship-grey 'Kystvakt' (coastguard) vessel prowls by, supported minutes later by a four-engined Lockheed Orion which swoops low over us before flying off to the south. Stein tells us that the coastguard plane will be looking for illegal discharges of fuel and the surface vessel checking on things like net size. The catches are constantly inspected and anyone found taking too many young fish or the wrong kind of fish is liable to be escorted out of the fishing grounds.

Around midnight, drinking a Scotch too many and being soundly whacked at Scrabble, I'm looking forward to nothing more than the womb-like, cradle-rocking security of my bunk when Stein's tall pale frame looms above us. He looks rather pleased with himself.

'There is an improvement in the weather, and I have a factory fishing ship which is happy to take you aboard and keep you there whilst they trawl.'

'What time tomorrow will that be?' asks Roger.

Stein glances at his watch. 'In about two hours.'

DAY 12: *The Barents Sea*

My alarm sounds at 1.30 a.m. It has to work hard to be heard above the cacophony of an engine grinding, revving, reversing and thrusting frantically. Up on the bridge Stein apologizes. The last ship he refuelled 'didn't know what he was doing'. Feeling all the better for forty minutes' sleep I scan the grey waters for whoever it is that has invited us aboard. At around two o'clock the *Jan Mayen* materializes on our port side. She is two or three times the height of the *Norsel* and her stern-gate is bathed dramatically in a sodium orange glow. The ship-to-ship transfer will be by crane, and as I am to be hoisted out over the only recently unfrozen waters of the Barents Sea, I'm put into a survival suit. This is a big, clumsy, rubberized affair, which looks as if it would instantly convert to a body bag once I hit the water.

'Do not be afraid,' grins one of our Polish crew with relish as he slips a rope under my arms. He signals to some faceless figure high above me and I'm suddenly ascending, swinging like a box of toilet paper, a case of beer or any other piece of goods, over the side and across the water, then up and up into a different world. The sailors on the *Jan Mayen* are not scruffy and informal like our friends on the *Norsel*. They are smartly clad in yellow PVC with tall black boots, like policemen round a road accident. Unlike the *Norsel*, wildly bobbing below, the *Jan Mayen* is almost motionless. We are led indoors and shown an air-conditioned bridge with quietly clicking consoles and men sitting around as if they were in *Star Trek*.

The stern resembles a bowling alley along which the long green nets are wound out with a cacophonous crashing and clanging to fall 1500 feet to the sea-bed. It is an impressive and exciting display, and one wonders what mighty creatures of the deep demand such terrible power. The answer is, shrimp. The *Jan Mayen*, with her million-pound state-of-the-art bridge, her forty-strong crew, her trawling Datasyncro display and her 4080 horse-power Danish-built turbine engine, is nothing but a glorified shrimping net.

They *have* been shrimping round the clock for over a month and they do have 400 tons of the little red things aboard, and they do have a factory deck with processing facilities which can transfer the catch from sea-bed to freeze-pack in twenty-four hours, but somehow it all seems like overkill. Who eats that many shrimps? The answer, as in so many things, is the Japanese.

At eight in the morning, in the company of two coastguard inspectors, we watch the nets drawn in. Another magnificent display of technological expertise and human organization. Another three tons of shrimp.

At nine o'clock the *Norsel* totters alongside and we prepare once again to be swung out over the sea. Clutching our complimentary boxes, we are dangled down onto the deck like children returning from a school outing.

DAY 14: *The Barents Sea to Tromsø*

Wake to calm seas and clear skies. This morning we can see the mainland of Europe for the first time. The craggy snow-capped mountains of the island of Fugløy on one side and Arnøy on the other are suitably impressive portals through which to pass into our first continent.

The cold grip of the Arctic has finally loosened. The ice on the anchor winch has melted, the sea laps lazily and placidly around the hull and the first traces of vegetation are bobbing by on the water. On the bridge all the anxiety of the last few difficult days has gone. With twelve ships successfully refuelled Stein is positively expansive, the crew are scrubbed and shaved like choirboys and the chief engineer is wreathed in smiles, phoning home.

For us, it's far from the end of the journey, but as we slip south of seventy degrees I can understand why everyone on the *Norsel* looks so happy. We have all survived a foray into a world where conditions are extreme and the margins of error pulled dangerously tight.

At two o'clock in the afternoon the first mate spots a plane taking off from Tromsø airport. Within an hour we are moving down the Grotsundet, which I suppose is in a sense the Gateway to the Arctic, and there are all the trappings of civilization laid out – a Legoland of painted walls and roofs.

Five days and twenty-one hours after leaving Longyearbyen we arrive at the Tromsø dockside. Two small, attractive ladies from the Norwegian Customs come aboard and after a brief inspection we are free to step ashore.

Tromsø is the first city on my journey, and though it contains only 50,000 souls, it boasts three cathedrals, a university, a brewery and twenty-three night-clubs. It likes to call itself 'The Paris of the North' and, as I feel I should celebrate reaching Europe, I seek out the nearest boulevard café. I find myself sitting outside the Cormorant Bar dubiously eyeing a glass of beer whose brand name is apparently Muck.

Summer seems to have reached Tromsø early. Crowds of students enjoying the three gloom-free months of the year, when the combination of warm Gulf Stream and twenty-four-hour sunlight give the little town an air of nervous hedonism, are today joined by football supporters from Trondheim, nearly

500 miles to the south. The Muck is flowing, though I've found out, a little to my disappointment, that Muck is the local pronunciation of Mack, a brewery famous for the purity of its product and for the motto on its bottles: 'First on the North Pole'.

A short walk away from the Cormorant stands a bronze statue of Roald Amundsen – first on the *South* Pole. Amundsen stands purposefully atop his granite plinth, dressed in the loose Eskimo-style outfit he favoured, gazing down the fiord. A seagull stands on top of Amundsen. I stand in silence trying to draw some comfort from those gaunt, ascetic features. After all, there can't be that many of us who have left Norway for the South Pole.

In the evening we eat at a restaurant which offers an intriguing dish by the name of 'Seal Lasagne'. Ever mindful of the fury which greeted my consumption of snake in Canton, I check with the waiter.

'This isn't . . . *baby* seal, I hope?'

'Oh no, sir,' he assures me, 'it's very old seal.'

Later, I walk back to my hotel across the main square, the Storttogret. There are queues outside the night-clubs and a group of drunken boys are kicking over tables and upturning sunshades. Not violently, but with a lunging, lurching, bleary desperation. They probably think they're having a good time. Nearer the hotel two quieter lads are gazing out towards the snow-capped mountains that surround the city. It's only after a while that I realize they are actually peeing into the harbour. It's midnight and in the west, over the cold hills of the island of Kvaløy, the sun is already starting to climb again.

DAY 15: *Tromsø*

Is this the same city I was in last night? This morning it seems butter wouldn't melt in its mouth. People are vertical rather than horizontal, and the chaos of the night before has been replaced by a pristine calm.

We drive across the long slim bridge that connects Tromsø Island with mainland Norway. It's a bright, beautiful Sunday morning and bells ring out from the Arctic Cathedral, a striking modern building comprising eleven interlocking triangular sections – representing every apostle apart from Judas Iscariot. Inside is as modest, well-behaved and self-effacing a congregation as you'll find anywhere. The first few rows are completely empty and the hymns are sung softly, almost apologetically.

Who are the modern Vikings – the lusty, lurching lads overthrowing the tables in the square or these sober-suited pillars of the community?

Towards evening the sun becomes obscured by cloud and a north-west wind ruffles the waters of the bay. Locals shake their heads. The weather change reminds me how near we still are to the polar ice-cap. Basil has joined us in Tromsø as official photographer, and already he has managed to find a Mongolian restaurant with a Japanese chef. Sushi and sashimi 200 miles above the Arctic Circle. Very odd. Not that Odd is unusual in Tromsø, in fact it's one of the most common surnames. Should you ever wish to stay unnoticed in a Tromsø hotel, check in as Mr and Mrs Odd.

DAY 16: *Tromsø to Hammerfest*

The weather has changed. The clouds are low and grey, and Tromsø has shed its Mediterranean glow and taken on the aspect of northern Scotland. To cheer ourselves up we visit the Arctic Museum. This is a mistake. All it does is remind us how lucky we are to have lived this long. Polar life offers few comforts, and the faces staring back at us from seal hunts and shipwrecks are prematurely aged. Objects, on the other hand, survive well in the intense cold, and Amundsen's pipe, mug, comb, typewriter and sewing kit are all beautifully preserved, as is this menu for a special dinner to mark the safe return of Amundsen and his crew from the South Pole in 1912:

Polar Soup
Whale with fat oil
Saelhundsblod (Seal Dog Blood)
Pork from Haakon VII Plateau
Pigviner (Penguins)
Polaris mit Hvalrostuender (Polar Ice
with Sea-Elephant's Teeth)

And no vegetarian alternative.

We've strayed some way off our thirty degree meridian and should be striking directly across Norway, but the desolate mountain ranges of Finnmark provide such an impassable natural barrier that all land-routes east must first go north.

At four in the afternoon we board the MV *Nordnorge*, a stout, workmanlike vessel of 2600 tons which forms part of the Hurtigrute (literally 'rapid route') service from Bergen to Kirkenes on the Russian border. The ships take eleven days to work their way there and back through the channels and islands of this convoluted coastline. Also boarding at Tromsø are sacks of potatoes and onions, sides of meat, televisions, wash-basins and mail. The Hurtigrute is a delivery service, a bus service, a postal service, and for tourists a way of experiencing the life as well as the physical spectacle of the fiords.

This is not a good day for spectacle. A line of low grey cloud has settled a few hundred feet above the water, reducing fiord-spotting to an act of imagination. There is a restaurant, with a lady organist playing 'Beatles songs like you've never heard them before'. She's as good as her word.

When I repair to my windowless cabin in the bowels of the ship, we are making a steady fifteen knots and the organist is playing 'The Happy Wanderer'.

DAY 17: *Hammerfest to Karasjok*

My bunk is comfortable enough, but every time anyone in the vicinity turns on a tap the result is a series of sledgehammer thuds, and a short night's sleep. Up on the bridge at a quarter to seven to film our arrival at Hammerfest, only to be told we're running an hour late and we could have stayed in bed and listened to the taps. There isn't much compensation in the landscape. An unrelieved horizontal band of cloud hangs, like a pelmet, over the treeless headlands. When Hammerfest does appear, a smudge nestling in a bowl of tundra-covered hills, it lacks the sparkle of Tromsø. Bleak and beleaguered, one can well believe that when the town was first settled in 1789, early occupants had to be encouraged with the promise of a twenty-year tax exemption.

The *Nordnorge*, which has taken fifteen hours to bring us from Tromsø, unloads and turns toward the North Cape, leaving us on a cold, damp dockside. Norwegians grin and shake their heads wearily when I use the word 'cold'. Maybe they just take it for granted, as we might the word 'air'.

'There's no such thing as bad weather, Michael, only bad clothes.'

The town's Director of Tourism is almost lyrical about the weather. Did I know that only three days ago the temperature in Hammerfest had reached twenty-eight degrees Centigrade?

'Well, of course that's *too* hot,' he grimaced, rather spoiling the effect.

Did I also know that only yesterday the QE2 had been in port?

'Two thousand five hundred people . . . all shopping at once.'

I look round at the food stalls in the market-place selling reindeer sausages and cods' tongues and bright hats and sealskin boots and try, without success, to visualize the scene.

Was I familiar with the Royal and Ancient Polar Bear Society? Taking my look of incomprehension for one of curiosity, the Director of Tourism ushers me, without further ado, into the presence of the Mayor of the World's Most Northerly Town who, in fluent and persuasive English, enlightens me as to the role of the polar bear in the history of Hammerfest. It has clearly been a submissive role, requiring the polar bear to do little more than lie still and not get up, but the town is proud of its part in the hunting and fishing of Arctic waters.

With brisk Scandinavian efficiency I am enrolled as member 116,747 of the Royal and Ancient Polar Bear Society and issued with card, stickers, hat, badge, certificate and a carrier bag to hold them all in. Which all goes to show that if you run a town 300 miles north of the Arctic Circle with no sight of the sun for three months of the year, you have to make the best of what you've got.

One escape from the melancholy of the long dark winter months is through alcohol, and its use and abuse has forced the authorities into Draconian measures. I learn of some of them from Troels Muller, our Norwegian fixer, as I drive my hire car south towards Lapland. In Norway police in unmarked cars can stop motorists at random and breathalyse them. If they are found to have more than 0.5 millilitres of alcohol in their blood – that is the equivalent of one light beer – they can be sentenced to three weeks in prison. There is no appeal. This has led to some unusual problems.

'People are waiting one or two years to get in prison. And then when you go off to prison you don't want your friends to know obviously, so you tell them that you're going to travel.'

Troels pauses as I pull out to avoid a couple of dejected reindeer, wandering along the side of the road with all the panache of footballers sent off in a Cup Final.

'There is a prison near Oslo they call Costa del Ilseng, because everyone . . . you know, goes to Spain . . . and, well, they're not in Spain at all . . . '

Some way further on we come to a stretch of treeless hillside from which rises a pointed tent made from tall branches covered up to three-quarters of its height with canvas and skins. It's a laavu, the traditional dwelling of the Same (pronounced Sar-mi) people who are the original inhabitants of northern

Scandinavia and parts of Russia. Many of them still live by reindeer herding including the two we are going to visit, Johan Anders and his wife Anne Marie. Unfortunately their reindeer herd has disappeared. We return in the direction of Hammerfest, but even the stragglers I'd seen earlier on the roadside have vanished. The reindeer quest turns into pure farce when we find ourselves bouncing up a rocky track to what appears to be a rubbish tip. Amid stacks of rotting cardboard, waste paper, rusting machinery and frozen-food packets stands the unhappy figure of Mr Anders, arms spread in a rather unlikely 'they were here a minute ago' pose.

Somewhere between Hammerfest and the Same 'capital' of Karasjok, 130 miles to the south-west, I must have fallen asleep. When I wake the scenery has changed completely. The treeless plateau has given way to an endless vista of lake and forest. A comforting sign that we are once again heading in the right direction.

Elk for dinner. Almost impenetrable.

DAY 18: *Karasjok*

The SAS Turisthotell in Karasjok. Outside my window a flock of sparrows is breakfasting off a bed of newly-sown grass. I rang home last night, then remembered that the family are all on holiday in France. Rang France. It had rained since they got there. Here, above the Arctic Circle, the sun shines and I'd be in shirt-sleeves if it weren't for the mosquitoes. From what I can gather Lapland is where mosquitoes who can afford it go for the summer. Heavy-duty repellent is required, and I'm ready for them with 'Jungle Formula Repel – with added Deet'. Deet, like so many other deadly substances, was apparently developed for the US forces in Vietnam. I'm busy squirting it on any available patch of flesh, when Patti kindly offers the information that it's strong enough to strip paint off cars, and Fraser maintains that it once melted a wristwatch of his.

It's a day of *Boy's Own* adventures, starting with a ride up the

Karasjoka (the Karas River) on a low, swift, wooden canoe in search of gold. My guides are two Same yuppies – Nils Christian who's visited Beverly Hills, and Leppa who carries a radio telephone in his national dress. The river is big business. Though frozen for several months of the year, it is still, according to Nils Christian, the best salmon river in Europe, yielding 133,000 kilos last year.

The tributaries of the Karasjoka are also rich, and in a bubbling stream beside a cool, damp, mosquito-infested stretch of woodland I am initiated into the recondite art of gold panning.

Required: one pair of thigh-length rubber boots, a plastic pan, a shovel and a natural sense of rhythm. The plastic pan has replaced the metal pan (as used in the movies) because the gold shows up better against the blue of the plastic. The shovel is required to ladle mud and the natural sense of rhythm helps with the sifting. Gold, being the heaviest of metals, will always sink to the bottom, and the skill lies in the delicacy required to filter out the gravel and mud without losing the grains of gold as well. Being the sort of person not noted for either rhythm or delicacy I experience a childlike sense of glee when, after a few minutes of sifting and spilling, I catch a glimpse of gold amongst the pitch-dark graphite sand. Not enough to open a Swiss bank account and probably not as much as you might find on one of Elizabeth Taylor's eyelashes, but the mere fact of having retrieved it, by my own efforts, from the mud of this remote river gives satisfaction way beyond the value. My self-sifted fortune is estimated to be somewhere in the region of £9.50 sterling. Decide to buy the crew a beer and invest the rest.

Sven Engholm is the Martina Navratilova of dog-sled racing. He's won the *Finnmarkslopet*, Europe's longest race, nine times. Like everyone else in this inhospitable northernmost corner of the continent he has a mobile telephone and a shrewd eye for a tourist opportunity. In the laavu in his garden, a few miles from Karasjok, he and his wife Ellen serve us a traditional Same lunch. Smoked salmon, with egg and fresh-baked brown bread, is followed by reindeer bouillon and reindeer stew served from a smoke-encrusted black pot over an open fire. We sit on reindeer skins and eat off wooden platters. Just when you think the meal is getting conventional, Sven produces a large hunting knife, reaches for a charred brown lump hanging above the fire and offers each of us a slice of dried reindeer heart with our coffee.

The dogs which Sven breeds so successfully are outside in a compound. Thirty-seven adults and ten yearlings. They seem wildly hyperactive, straining at their leads, barking and lunging at Sven as he passes. I suppose the secret of being a good musher (as they call the dog-sled drivers) is to be able to translate this manic energy into forward momentum. That Sven and his team can race 1000 kilometres across the frozen Finnmark plateau in less than five days is an indication of his success. During our interview, as Sven is earnestly explaining the need for the dogs to relate socially, not just to each other, but to people as well, I notice the camera crew convulse with laughter. Seconds later I feel a warm, damp glow on my trousers. I look down just in time to see that one of Sven's dogs has just finished relating socially to my right leg.

DAY 19: *Karasjok*

There isn't much to see in Karasjok. It's a transit town, straddling the E6 Arctic Highway on the tourist route to the North Cape. But if you look a little closer, if you stop for more than the statutory half-hour the coach tours allow at the gift shop, there is evidence here of a thriving culture which is not Norwegian or Swedish or Finnish. It is Same, and it is alive and well, with its own museum, radio station and since 1989, a gleaming new Same Centre, incorporating their own parliament. I meet Gunhild Sara, who has travelled all over the world and lived and worked in Canada and Tanzania.

I ask her if this is not just Lapland by another name.

'Lapland doesn't exist. We are in Sameland.'

So she isn't Norwegian then? She shakes her head dismissively.

'I am Same. I shall always be a Same. Whatever passport I hold I shall die a Same.'

I ask what took her to Tanzania, and she smiles, which is rather a relief.

'Very common thing, you meet a handsome fellow and then you just go!'

She preferred the Tanzanians to the Kenyans, 'They have more self-confidence, more self-pride. The Kenyans just want to be British,' but she didn't have much time for Julius Nyerere's social reforms.

'He made long moral speeches on the radio . . . tried to get the local Masai to wear underpants when they got on the buses.'

Later in the day I witness a truly surreal piece of Same culture – a joiking ceremony. A joik (pronounced yoik) is an improvised chant, delivered in a semi-yodelling waver. It has no beginning, middle or end. It is musical but not actually a song. It contains the essence of a feeling or a character or an emotion that is wholly personal and cannot be transferred except possibly within a family. Our presence makes the joikers self-conscious to start with. They puff heavily on cigarettes (smoking is widespread up here) until some beers arrive and then the curious wobbly chanting begins. It all feels very Irish, or perhaps Indian, and later I find out that joiking is very much part of an international folk tradition. Indeed one of them had just come back from joiking in Reading.

Angela is of the opinion that we may well have been had, but I prefer to give them the benefit of the doubt. It's late when we drive back to the hotel. The light of the midnight sun combines with a gentle drifting vapour off the river to create a magical stillness and beauty around the half-harvested fields.

PREVIOUS PAGE: *The* Pole
to Pole *team (left to
right): Fraser Barber,
Patti Musicaro, Nigel
Meakin, Angela
Elbourne, Roger Mills,
Clem Vallance, Mirabel
Brook, A Hanger-on.*

OPPOSITE: *With our pole
at the North Pole.*

ABOVE: *Crossing the
glacier on snowmobiles
en route to
Longyearbyen,
Spitsbergen.*

RIGHT: *Television
presenters: Britain's
newest export.*

OPPOSITE: *Panning for gold.*

RIGHT: *Tea in a laavu in Karasjok, Norway.*

BELOW: *On Santa's knee in Santa Claus village, Finland.*

LEFT: *No-one knows who you are when you're naked.*

BELOW: *On the train in Leningrad, now St. Petersburg.*

OPPOSITE: *Lenin, Lenin and me at the Finland Station.*

OVERLEAF: *Newlyweds outside the Hermitage, Leningrad.*

DAY 20: *Karasjok to Ivalo*

South towards Finland on the Postilinjat, the post bus that is the only form of public transport available. I was beginning to feel becalmed in northern Norway and am glad to be on the road again. A shower has passed over, Nigel is napping and Basil is worried that he's spelt reindeer 'raindear' on a card to his daughter. The bus is a fifty-seater, but few of the seats are taken. A Japanese couple sit efficiently in front, a bearded Frenchman hunches over a backpack and a young Norwegian boy is off to spend the summer with his Finnish grandparents.

We cross the Norway–Finland border at a sleepy hamlet called Karigasniemi. The Japanese couple, who have been clutching documents for the last half-hour, cannot believe that no one wants to see their passports. I look, in vain, for signs of Finnishness. There's a Shell garage and a café, with a Mercedes outside, serving pizza. The only locals are clustered around a Space Invaders game.

There are quite a few more Mercedes on the ninety-mile run down to Ivalo. Many of them are towing hefty caravans on their way north, to the lakes and forests for summer with the mosquitoes. Finland strikes me as more obviously affluent than Norway. They even seem to have more reindeer, and the bus, when it's not stopping to deliver mail into makeshift roadside boxes, is pulling up to avoid them. I'm told that the reindeer, now that they are shedding their winter coats, are tormented by the clouds of flies and mosquitoes and find relief in the cooling wind that blows down the highway.

The switchback single carriageway is well kept and the time passes lazily as the colour on the lakes turns in the evening light from black to deep green to silver. At Inari, a lakeside town bristling with outboard motors, the intrepid Japanese get off to be replaced by a few locals, including a teenage girl who is on her way to a disco in Ivalo. She says she will have to be back home by ten o'clock this evening. Her English is good, the result, she tells us, of a summer spent in Hastings. Feel embarrassed, as always, at the efforts foreigners make to learn English, compared with the other way round. But by any standards Finnish is a tough language, unlike any other in Europe except Hungarian. Verbs have *sixteen* cases.

Travel, at its best, is a process of continually conquering disbelief, and to be in a Finnish hotel on the Arctic Highway, with a sign outside my window reading 'Murmansk 313 kilometres' and the sound of a plaintive violin accompanying daylight that refuses to disappear, is, I feel, after a beer or two, the sort of thing that makes life worth living.

DAY 21: *Ivalo to Rovaniemi*

I wasn't the only one at breakfast to have noticed that, apart from plaintive violins, our hotel in Ivalo also sported a full-blooded disco which set to work around midnight and was conveniently located beneath the bedrooms. At 7.30 we're on the way south again. A white reindeer crosses the road. These are rare, and hopefully as propitious as a black cat.

Troels left us at the border and we are now in the hands of Kari Vaatovaara, a young man from Helsinki, who, among other things, plays the lute. I ask him about reports I've read of the effects of nuclear fall-out from Chernobyl in this part of the world. His reaction is swift and dismissive.

'Everything was tested!'

The need for such tests must have been especially urgent here as the area was directly beneath the crescent cloud of contamination during a period of heavy rain. The staple grazing food of the reindeer is a rootless lichen which absorbs all its moisture from the atmosphere. Most of the forest foods – berries, fungi and the like – also absorb atmospheric pollution, and those who live off them and the reindeer that eat them must be at greater than average risk. So goes the theory (expanded on in the excellent *Rough Guide to Scandinavia*), but Kari would have none of it. Everything in Sameland is fine.

An unusual encounter on the bus. The crew have gone ahead to film and I am left in the company of an inebriated Finn.

He smiles blearily. I smile back. He starts to talk. I can't understand a word. He looks pained. I feel I must help. I speak slowly and deliberately, 'I am an Englishman'.

Amazingly, a look of recognition crosses his face.

'Ah . . . Eenglishman!' he cries, and before I have time to compose a smile of complacent acknowledgement, he blows a long and disgusting raspberry.

We pass summer homes in the forest and occasional clearances where grass has been cut and hung to dry on long rails or else swathed around single sharp sticks like gravestones. We pass through Sodankyla, which announces itself as the home of the Arctic Film Festival, and eighty miles further on, at 66 degrees 32 North, we pass the most southerly point at which the sun stays above or below the horizon for more than twenty-four hours, commonly known as the Arctic Circle.

There is a bus stop on the Arctic Circle and a sign halfway down a ditch marking it in several languages, but these are completely overshadowed by the bizarre presence of Santa Claus Village. This roadside complex, which resembles a small airport, contains, among other things, a shopping mall, a café, and Santa's Post Office. With brisk opportunism the Finns have managed to ensure that half a million letters a year, many of them vaguely addressed to Santa somewhere in the north, are directed to this particular spot. Presiding over the enterprise is a crew-cut ex-DJ and journalist who is so big that when he says he's Father Christmas you don't argue.

He doesn't seem particularly at ease with us, torn between being avuncular and jolly and protecting this considerable investment from smart-arsed snoopers and cynics. He talks evangelically about combining the 'commercial' and 'ideological' aspects of Christmas, but it's hard to keep a straight face when you can see behind him a line of oddly shaped women in red capes and tasselled hats emerging from a Portakabin. He catches my eye and turns.

'Ah, those are the elves coming on for the afternoon shift.'

The elves sit at desks, with red and white computers, dealing with the world's largest concentration of begging letters.

'Everyone receives a personal reply from Santa,' the Big Man tells me with fierce pride.

After Finland, most of Santa's mail comes from Japan – a hundred thousand letters last year. The Big Man spent six weeks last summer touring Japan dressed up as Santa.

As if to underline the Japanese connection, we later see our couple from the Ivalo bus emerging purposefully from Santa's Grotto clutching a certificate.

A steady stream of state-of-the-art tourist buses from Germany are pulling in off the Arctic Highway, and though it's high summer they too expect to see Santa. This has thrown the Big Man into a bit of a state, as he has agreed to give me a personal audience while one of his colleague looks after the tourists.

'It will not be good for them to see two Santas,' he mutters.

But eventually all is well, and for the first time in forty-one years I get to sit on Santa's knee.

A short distance beyond the village is the town of Rovaniemi (Finnish pronunciation accents the first syllable only: '*Ro*-vaniemi'). Flattened during the war, it was rebuilt by the famous Finnish architect Aalvar Aalto, who laid the roads out in the shape of a pair of reindeer horns.

'There are only 35,000 people here and they still get lost,' Kari remarks unpatriotically.

More importantly for us, Rovaniemi marks the northern limit of the Finnish railway system, and at 7.20 in the evening, with the sun about to set for the first time since we left the North Pole, we pull out of the station on the overnight train to Helsinki, finally turning our backs on the Arctic.

DAY 22: *Rovaniemi to Helsinki*

The railway line to Rovaniemi was built when Finland was a part of Tsarist Russia and the Soviet Union is still seen as a baleful presence, a lurking threat to the spectacular prosperity the Finns have experienced since their independence in 1917.

There are only five million people in Finland, and they enjoy the second highest standard of living in Europe. They also share a long border with a country that is cracking up, and one of their great fears is that Gorbachev's reforms will one day lead to a flood of Russian immigrants. I ask the daughter of a Finnish family I met in the train's restaurant car what she knows of Russia.

She grimaces. 'I have heard there is very robbery there. One of my friends is robbery in money and clothes and a clock.'

Kari joins in enthusiastically. A friend of his had been robbed by a taxi-driver in Estonia.

'Left him with no money, no luggage, no passport.'

I can't wait.

Our train pulls into Helsinki an hour early. It's a warm Sunday morning and after I've been filmed arriving we have the rest of the day off. Helsinki, with a population of half a million, is by no means a brash or daunting city, but it requires a conscious mental adjustment to be back where humans control the environment, rather than the other way round.

The station is a remarkable building, an example of what is known as the National Romantic Style, developed by Saarinen and others at the turn of the century to express, in architecture, a Finnish culture and tradition that was not dominated by either Sweden or Russia. It makes much of indigenous materials such as pink granite, brass, wood and copper, decorated with reliefs of trees and plants. Dark and mystical, redolent of mead halls and medieval castles, it contrasts strongly with early nineteenth-century Helsinki, down by the sea. This is light and graceful and neo-classical, a reflection of Leningrad, only 180 miles to the east.

I've found that the best places to aim for in a new city are stations, for the buzz and the newspapers; markets, for food and colour; botanical gardens, for peace and contemplation; and, whenever possible, harbours, for space and spectacle. The joy of Helsinki is that you can visit all of them in a couple of hours.

In the early evening I take my first run of the journey, around the Toolonlahti, a shallow lake close to the centre of the city. The temperature is in the low seventies and it's hard work. At 11.15, as I turn in, the lights are on along the Mannerheimintie – the main road in to the city from the north, where the sun will still be shining.

At a quarter to midnight the telephone rings. It's a particularly insistent Finn who wants to talk to me for his university newspaper. In vain I point out the time, the fact that I was asleep, and the work I have to do tomorrow.

'I am down here in the lobby,' he persists.

'Well, it's not really a good time.'

'I am doing an article, please, on John Cleese and I think you know him . . . '

That does it.

'I am *in* bed. I have four months' travelling ahead of me, and I have *no* time to talk about John Cleese!'

Somewhat surprisingly, this seems to amuse my caller greatly, and only then do I recognize in the cackle of non-Finnish laughter the unmistakable tones of a tall fellow Python.

'I just rang to see how you were getting on,' wheezes John cheerfully . . . and I remember how much he enjoyed doing Scandinavian accents.

DAY 23: *Helsinki*

Today I am to be initiated into the pleasures of the sauna, pronounced 'sow-na' in these parts. It is not a Finnish invention, for the Red Indians used hot stones to keep their tepees warm, and it spread to the West out of Asia. But the Finns have endorsed it with an almost religious zeal, and like any religion it has its orthodoxies and its heresies. One of the most kosher of Finnish saunas is in the grounds of a lakeside house called Hvittrask, a half-hour's drive from Helsinki. The house itself is remarkable. Built ninety years ago by Saarinen, Gesellius and Lundgren – the architects responsible for Helsinki's idiosyncratic railway station – it embodied many of the most advanced ideas in decoration and design, such as *en suite* bathrooms, central heating and the first use of textiles as wallpaper. All these things that the middle classes eventually adopted were at the time deliberately unconventional and anti-bourgeois.

The sauna is traditional, with a wood fire rather than electricity and the emphasis on dark beams, tiles, and log and granite walls. It's built, like a boathouse, where tall trees meet the lake, to which it is connected by a long wooden jetty.

My companions are a Finnish writer and ex-MP called Lasse, and Neil, an Englishman, who has produced comedy shows on Finnish television and hosted a controversial chat show here. But as Lasse says, as we squeeze our fleshy white bodies onto the slatted wooden shelves of the sauna, 'no one knows who you are when you're naked'.

Well, they certainly know none of us is Madonna. Lasse waxes lyrical as Nigel tries to frame shots which will be acceptable to BBC Television.

'It's meditative, contemplative, reflective . . . not a place for angst or anxiety or argument . . . that's why you have settled so many disputes in the sauna in Finland – political ones, economic ones . . . whatever. Because who wants to argue when they are naked, you know . . . '

'What are those twigs for?' I ask, meditatively.

'They're birch twigs. They must be picked about midsummer when the leaves are soft . . . '

Lasse picks up the bundle and proceeds to whack himself about the face and upper body, before offering it to me.

I begin to apply them gently. Neil looks unimpressed.

'No, you've got to get the circulation going . . . '

He grabs the twigs and lays into me. Lasse looks on with approval.

'Try it on the face, very nice on the face . . . you get a nice sort of scent from it . . . '

The flagellation does produce a pleasantly aromatic tingling sensation and I feel it's only polite to offer to scourge someone else. Lasse accepts and I go to work.

'Say when . . . '

This all seems very energetic and I'm still waiting for the contemplative and reflective bit when Neil suggests we go and jump in the lake.

The dip is very refreshing today, and apart from possibly frightening a group of schoolchildren swimming near by, fairly harmless. In the winter they break a hole in the ice.

'You can only be there for half a minute . . . then you roll in the snow.'

Back in the intimacy of the sauna, we discuss Finland and Finnish attitudes. They're anxious to dispel the myth that Scandinavians talk about sex all the time, but Neil says that in the north of Finland the girls are very direct. At a dance or disco they will always make the first move. 'Even the old and ugly ones,' adds Lasse.

'You should have got off with someone by eleven o'clock.'

For some reason my mind went back to the elves toiling over Santa's correspondence and dreaming of the evening . . .

The Finns, it seems, are egalitarian, eschewing formality and anything that smacks of class. They have a sense of humour, but not much sense of irony. Humour is introspective and personal; there's no tradition of getting together in a theatre to laugh communally.

An example of all of this is perhaps their national AIDS campaign. The fact that they have such an extensive campaign when there is a comparatively low incidence of AIDS in the country is very Finnish. Fastidious about their health and efficient and far-sighted enough to attack the problem before it becomes a problem. But it's all done very seriously. Neil tells me that public figures have gone on television to advocate the advantages of masturbation, under the slogan 'Give it a hand!'

'These are country people,' says Lasse, 'this is not an urban society, not yet.'

DAY 24: *Helsinki to Tallinn*

There is a swimming-pool at the Hesperia Hotel in Helsinki and though it means getting up a little earlier I feel I must take advantage of such luxuries, for today we enter the Soviet Union where things will be very different.

An hour and a half later I'm down at the dockside. The early sea mist has cleared and it looks set for another hot day. The harbour is busy with boats coming in from the surrounding islands – the Suomalinen. Some are bringing produce for the market: potatoes, carrots, onions, strawberries, cherries and plums; some are fishing boats bringing in crayfish, sea salmon and Baltic herring, and some are ferries bringing in commuters. The ship that will be taking us to Estonia is the *Georg Ots*, a slim, trim, Russian-registered vessel owned by the Baltic Shipping Company.

As we wait for clearance on our thirty pieces of film equipment, I get talking to one of the Customs men. He repeats what I've heard elsewhere in Helsinki about the existence of a Russian mafia which runs a drug and prostitution racket between penurious Estonia and prosperous Finland. It's hard to overestimate the contempt which Finns seem to have for all things Russian.

With a sonorous blast of the horn the *Georg Ots*, named after an Estonian opera singer, pulls away from Finnish soil punctually at 10.30. The copper domes and wide sloping green gables of the harbourmaster's house recede into the distance as the ship picks her way along narrow channels between the jigsaw of little islands and sandbanks that lead to the Gulf of Finland, and, fifty miles away to the south, Estonia. Not a wide gulf geographically, but in many other ways, enormous.

Thinking myself somewhere exotic, I scan my fellow passengers for clues to their nationality. The first one is reading the *Daily Mail*, the next *Newsweek*. Leaning artfully against one of the bulkheads, face turned towards the sun, is a striking girl in dark glasses and a black-and-white cloche hat. She could be Audrey Hepburn in *Breakfast at Tiffanys*, if it wasn't for the Lycra cycling shorts. I'm not surprised to learn that she is in the fashion business. She's German, and on her way to a festival in Riga, the capital of Latvia. It is, she explains, the one fashion festival held in the Soviet Union at which Russian designers are permitted to mix with their Western counterparts.

The man with the *Daily Mail* is English. His father, an Estonian from the town of Tartu, left at the end of the war to escape Stalin's ruthless purges of Estonian nationalists. In one night in 1944, he tells me, sixty thousand people from the Baltic states were rounded up and taken away.

'It may be that my grandfather was amongst the sixty thousand, or my relatives were amongst the sixty thousand . . . I'm not raising my expectations, but I do feel . . . it's an adventure out there . . . '

He looks out over the flat calm sea, and in a sense I know what he means. Three weeks in the empty untroubled wilderness of the Arctic and cosseted by the comfortable materialism of Scandinavia has done nothing to prepare me for what lies ahead in a land that has been on the receiving end of so much violence.

The *Georg Ots* has a shiny chrome and mirrored bar serving beers, vodka and coffee. American-made MTV pop videos run remorselessly on a screen. Everyone at the bar looks like a mechanic. Peter is a young Estonian who's done his two years' compulsory service in the Soviet army, who has a currency shop and a very smart briefcase which he bought in Singapore. He teaches me to say 'hello' in Estonian, and proffers other advice.

'Russian girls very good . . . '

'Do you have a Russian girlfriend?'

'Yes . . . ' he glances around to where the crew are sitting, 'but not in front of camera, I have wife too.'

He won't elaborate on what is so good about Russian girls but tells me where to find them.

'The night bar of the Palace Hotel.'

Later I ask Clem where we're staying in Tallinn. It's the Palace Hotel.

I'm unapologetically excited by my first sight of Tallinn, which appears to starboard from a low green coastline about one o'clock in the afternoon. I have never quite believed in the existence of Estonia. It always sounded more like a name out of fable than fact, this tiny country at the tip of a spur jutting out into the Baltic. Quite suddenly, since *glasnost*, the existence or non-existence of Estonia has become a crucial political issue, and as we approach I feel I am not only on the verge of satisfying a lifetime's curiosity, but of seeing some history in the making.

Rising around soft brown city walls are the spires, turrets and towers of a medieval city, but the docks present a dejected picture. In marked contrast to the bustling cosmopolitan harbour we left three hours ago, our only companions on the Tallinn waterfront are rusty-hulled colliers and cargo ships in need of a coat of paint. All bear the hammer and sickle on their funnels. The immigration forms are faint Xeroxes, and as there are long queues to process them I go back to take a last picture of the *Georg Ots*. A car pulls up almost instantly and a soldier gets out and eyes me with contempt.

I have tried to learn some Russian but this is not how I wanted my first stab at the language to be.

'I am from London, making a television programme,' I blurt out.

I don't think he understands a word, for his expression doesn't change. He climbs back in his car and drives scornfully away.

The feeling of being watched persists later as I take my first stroll away from the hotel. Both soldiers and police are much in evidence. The soldiers are thin, scrawny conscripts, some with the dark, smooth-skinned features of far-off Asian republics. They look lost compared to the police, who, while being no less thin or scrawny, patrol the streets more purposefully in groups of five or six, holding nightsticks. I feel myself being sized up on all sides. Some lads approach and offer to change my dollars into roubles at an absurdly generous rate. This is because the rouble is almost useless. When I tried to acquire some at the hotel earlier the cashier thought I was mad. She asked me how long I was staying in the Soviet Union.

'About three weeks,' I replied.

She pointed to an English five-pound note. 'That will be enough.'

Next door to the hotel is a small cosy-looking bar, but as we push open the door a trio of bouncers appear, and for the second time today I feel I'm expected to explain myself.

'We just want a beer . . . '

Heads are shaken unhelpfully.

'Only vodka or champagne.' Meaning, of course, only hard currency.

In the evening I visit a cabaret at one of the tourist hotels. The tourists are mainly Russian, some of them in family groups despite the fact that the floor-show features a full frontal strip-tease and a sinuous and erotic dance sequence spoilt only by the man dropping the woman at one point.

We end up in the Skybar Disco of the Palace Hotel. MTV videos pump out images of America, the lights circle and flash, but at least you can have a beer. And probably a Russian girl if you'd wanted.

DAY 25: *Tallinn to Leningrad*

I eat a breakfast of good fresh bread, honey and coffee to the strains of Marianne Faithfull's 'This Little Bird', then walk out into the city. The newspapers are full of the news that in Moscow yesterday President Bush demanded a measure of independence for the Baltic states as the price of 'most favoured nation' trading status for the USSR.

On the way up to the Toompea Castle huge blocks of rock and concrete lie across the road, moved there by the civic authority in response to the recent military repression in Lithuania. The present feels tense here and yet the past, in the shape of an extensive and beautifully preserved Old Town, seems serene and comforting. Not a modern or unharmonious building intrudes on long cobbled streets lined with merchants' houses and guild halls. At the centre is Raekoja Square, a wide and handsome area bounded on one side by the imposing and elegant fourteenth-century Town Hall. A weather vane called Vana Toomas (Old Tom) has topped the building since 1530.

The unpretentious beauty of the old town bears out Colin Thubron's observation that there's nowhere like a modern socialist state for preserving the past it replaced so vociferously.

On a side road a passer-by offers Patti something in a bag for fifteen dollars. It turns out to be a gun. Patti shakes her head categorically, at which, unfazed, he drops the price to ten dollars.

Pick up a copy of the *Tallinn City Paper*. It's in English; well produced, anti-Russian and easily available. It pronounces on politics – hoping that talks with Moscow may reduce the 180,000 Soviet troops stationed in the country but holding out little expectation; seafood – 'In this seaside city, the best fish . . . goes to Leningrad, Moscow . . . and not to Estonia'; and national differences – 'Estonians complain that the Russians here are hot-tempered, uneducated and haven't bothered to learn about the culture to which they've migrated. Russians . . . complain that Estonians are cold-tempered, arrogant and dull'.

Back in Raekoja Square a group called the Johanson Brothers are entertaining a small crowd. Jakov Johanson maintains that 'singing has been for the Estonians . . . the most effective way to use the language . . . to sing out loudly . . . that we are Estonians'.

He sees similarities with the Irish, whose songs they perform as well, and draws a parallel between the Russian occupation of Estonia and the British occupation of Northern Ireland.

For our last meal in Tallinn we take the advice of the *City Paper* and eat in a restaurant irresistibly described as 'about the best you will find anywhere in the Soviet Empire'. It's called The Maharajah, and to be eating fine and delicate Indian curry in a fourteenth-century Estonian town-house seals an intense, if confused, memory of this extraordinary city.

I would very gladly have lingered here a day or two more but we have another Pole to get to and having run due south from Arctic Norway to the southern shores of the Gulf of Finland it's time to turn eastward once again to pick up the thirty degree meridian, which will be our guideline down through Russia and Africa. To this end we assemble beneath a dominating bas-relief of Lenin on the wall of Tallinn station to make the eight-hour journey to the city to which he gave his name.

Every coach of the train bears the emblem of a wreath intertwined with a banner on which is written, in the languages of the fifteen republics, 'Proletariats of all Countries Unite!', and beneath this a crossed hammer and wrench. Bold design which makes British Rail's spectral swallow look pathetic. Prices, too, are competitive. My fare for the equivalent of a journey from London to Newcastle is eight roubles and forty kopecks – about thirty-five pence. The train is very hot and slow. Everyone seems helpful and friendly, none more so than the beleaguered proprietor of the buffet. He has two problems. One is having nothing to sell and the other is having to explain this to an Englishman who wants to try out his Russian conversation.

'Have you tea?'

'No . . . '

'Have you coffee?'

'No . . . '

'What do you have?'

His reply, being more elaborate than in previous exchanges, is quite incomprehensible, and I end up with a cherryade and a piece of cake.

We cross the Estonian–Russian border at Narva – from the smallest of the Soviet republics (27,000 square miles) to the largest (11 million square miles). Within two hours we have reached Leningrad. A hot and sticky night as we hit our thirty degree meridian for the first time since the fishing-grounds of the Barents Sea.

60

DAY 26: *Leningrad*

The Okhintskya Hotel has only been open for two months. It's a tall, anonymous, modern block about twenty minutes from the centre of the city and my room has, apart from a fine view of the river Neva, a fitted carpet, bidet, hot water and a massive throbbing Cheshinka 304 refrigerator, which I have to unplug in the night after dreaming of a tank coming through the wall. There is a huge party of Italian tourists here which explodes into the lobby every now and then, but apart from them and us the place seems empty.

Our Russian hosts give us an introductory tour of the city. The roads are in terrible condition, holed and pitted, and the ubiquitous tramlines have often completely parted company with the road surface, sticking out of their sockets like ribs on a corpse.

We're taken in the evening to a gypsy restaurant. Our regular drivers have the day off and Volodya, one of our Russian fixers, is at the wheel. He always looks harassed, but tonight as the vehicle jerks erratically forward he seems more than usually unhappy. Reaching for the indicator as he swerves to avoid a pothole, he succeeds only in activating the windscreen wiper. Unfortunately there is no wiper in the fitting and there is a horrid screech as the metal claw scrapes blindly at the windscreen, which is already broken anyway. Almost everything to do with the vehicles is a headache for Volodya and his team. The chronic shortage of petrol means that to be sure of supplies our regular drivers have to fill up at three in the morning, and the chronic shortage of glass is why every other windscreen in the city is cracked. At the restaurant we have zakuski – an hors d'oeuvre comprising slices of tomato, cucumber, pickle, tinned ham, beef and pork on a bed of lettuce, hard-boiled eggs in mayonnaise, fish paste and caviar. Vodka and wine are liberally supplied, and because the wine is so rough and beer seems impossible to come by most of us attend to the vodka. This leg of the journey is going to be quite a test of survival.

DAY 27: *Leningrad*

Alexander 'Sasha' Godkov is my guide to Leningrad today. He is a professional Lenin impersonator and the very fact that he can walk the streets masquerading as the father of the Revolution without being removed to the nearest branch of the KGB shows how lukewarm traditional communism is becoming. He takes me to the Finland Station at which his factual predecessor turned up twice in 1917, once courtesy of the Germans, who encouraged the growth of communism to help win the war, and the next time disguised as a railway fireman. The locomotive he fired is preserved in a Perspex case, which, considering it contains one of the icons of the Revolution, is remarkably grubby and uncared for. Outside the station a single withered rose lies at the base of the full-length bronze likeness of the great man.

From the melancholy of a past no one seems to want any more to the liveliness of a tram-ride down the Nevsky Prospekt. Our driver is a stout blonde lady in a flowery print dress. Tickets are bought in carnets and then stamped in a knob and spring device mounted on the side of the tram into which you insert your ticket and give the knob a sharp bang. Some burly men on the seat opposite are watching me cope with this and smiling broadly. Sasha gets into conversation with them. They are from Armenia and having heard me speak English wish to shake my hand and tell me that English and Armenians worked closely together after the earthquake (of 1988) and how much that had been appreciated. More big smiles and handshakes and at the next stop they disappear. We reach Winter Palace Square, a massive and belittling open space surrounded by classical and Baroque façades that places Leningrad firmly as a European city. The Alexander Column in the centre of the square was designed by a Frenchman, Montferrant, even though it was to commemorate the victory over the French in 1812. The Tsar's specifications insisted it should be taller than the obelisk in the Place Vendôme and taller than Trajan's Column in Rome. It weighs 610 tons and is carved from one single piece of granite.

A few minutes' walk away is the equestrian statue of Peter the Great. Set on a huge granite rock, garlanded Peter, his bronze horse rearing into the air, looks as if he is about to leap the Neva river. It is a powerful and stirring embodiment of controlled strength and so much loved by the people of Leningrad that there is nearly always a line of newlyweds waiting to be photographed beside it. This set me to thinking of Lenin's statue at the Finland Station and its solitary faded rose. It's clear that Peter, old despot that he was, retains a much stronger place in the affections of the inhabitants. The city was built by him and may well go back to him. In a recent poll fifty-two per cent voted to change the city's name to St Petersburg.

We eat at a Georgian restaurant tonight. Set in an anonymous block in a side street it has a striking avant-garde interior, which I think is meant to recreate the centre of an Egyptian pyramid. It looks to be full of fashion models. Very tasty Georgian meatballs and a fresh bread called lavash. Fraser has ordered real French champagne for us to toast the third birthday of his son Jack. The only problem is that Volodya has to drive the van again. As we swerve and shudder our way home I ask Volodya where he spent his two-year national service.

'In tanks,' he shouts, and we end the day on a laugh.

DAY 28: *Leningrad*

A rough night's sleep. Had to dig out the paracetamol for the first time on the journey so far. At breakfast, found that two others in the crew had suffered as well. We reluctantly agree that the champagne must have been too good for us.

I take a launch from the front of the hotel and am swept upstream to the Monastery of Alexander Nevsky. Nevsky is a great Russian hero who defeated the Swedes by the river Neva in 1240. The monastery, the third biggest in Russia, was built as a tribute to him by Peter the Great in 1710. Today it's a very busy place, an indication that religion is alive and well despite seventy-five years of official atheism. Disabled people are lined up inside the grounds. They are brought here to beg because families receive only a pittance from the State to look after them.

Inside the main church, beneath domes and columns decorated with epic, brightly coloured biblical scenes, priests who seem to have been chosen for their likeness to the prophets are moving around, conducting services, swinging censers, and in one case receiving a line of penitents who approach, kiss the icons, wait for a few words of comfort, receive a blessing and move on. I cannot take my eyes off one encounter. A woman, young and headscarved, is talking urgently to the priest, but softly too, so he has to bend and listen intently. He asks her something, she pauses and looks ahead for a while, then nods slowly. It's an incongruous moment of intimacy in the middle of this crowded, bustling place. She wipes away tears and bows her head. The priest lays a cloth over her head and makes the sign of the cross. She kisses the icons, crosses herself and moves away. She has an expression of inconsolable sadness as she passes by me.

In the crypt they are preparing for the first public baptism of the day. Christenings were not approved of in the hard-line days and had to be conducted secretly, but now things have changed. There are two ceremonies a day and four on each Saturday and Sunday. I take my place among the families of the thirty or forty babies who have been brought along. Everyone but me seems to be in their best clothes. The priest is an imposing, charismatic figure, though not above sneaking a small comb from beneath his robes and attending to his thick black hair every now and then.

Impervious to a constant barracking of coughs, gurgles and whines, he gives a long opening address before making his way round the gathering to anoint those present on the fore-head, base of the neck and ears in the sign of a cross. As he approaches I notice men are rolling up their trouser legs. Nigel, tracking back at a crouch, whispers urgently,

'Better roll up your trousers. They're all doing it.'

I don't imagine the priest will notice me anyway, curled as I am into the curve of the vault. But I'm wrong. Not only does he notice me but brings the entire service to a halt as he looks at my knees with considerable suspicion.

'What is your belief?'

'Church of England' sounds rather insipid in the middle of all this, so I opt for the more general 'I believe in God'.

His anointing brush remains poised in mid-air. He turns to his assistant. They confer. He looks back at me. The Russian congregation look on, quite baffled.

'I have been baptized!' I add, helpfully.

More consultation. The priest regards me sternly, but with faint alarm.

'Do you want to change your religion?' he asks.

Life is complicated enough at the moment without becoming a member of the Russian Orthodox Church, so I politely decline.

'Now is the time . . . '

I'm desperately trying to become one with the wall.

'No . . . er . . . it's all right . . . thank you.'

The camera edges closer, and the priest breaks into a smile.

'I can act, if you like . . . '

He's already acting me off the screen so we don't pursue this offer. He moves on to the font. By this time the first baby is ready. Her clothes have been removed, and the chubby naked figure is lifted in the priest's massive hands, so high that for a moment the scene resembles one of those paintings of the Massacre of the Innocents. Then Tatiana (he has announced her name) is plunged down and through the water, not once but three times. The force of this triple immersion reduces Tatiana to stunned silence, and before she knows what's hit her she is passed on to the assistant priest who dabs oil on her eyes, nose, ears and chin and places a cross round her neck.

Soon the whole crypt is filled with the sound of wailing babies and cooing parents. Later there is chanting, singing and a candlelight procession which is still going on when I leave.

In the grounds of the monastery is the Tikhvin Cemetery,

which has a section reserved for the remains of 'Masters of Art'. The quality is impressive. In a ten-minute stroll I visit Dostoevsky, Rimsky-Korsakov, Mussorgsky, Borodin and Tchaikovsky. Tchaikovsky's memorial is particularly sad. The great man's bust, marooned in a bed of begonias and flanked by a gross pair of overacting angels, is like something on the top shelf of a junk shop.

Later in the afternoon, a visit to two contrasting food sources. One is the private market, to which people can bring their home-grown produce to sell. It looks much like any big covered market, though the standard of hygiene is low, especially on the butchery counters where stallholders are constantly swatting flies away from pigs' heads. But there is an air of bustle and good humour – one man is a brilliant mimic of bird noises, and whenever Fraser raises his microphone to do a wild track of market atmosphere, the place is suddenly full of exotic birdsong. According to Irena, our interpreter, the average Russian would not be able to afford to shop here. Even her parents, who are quite well off, could only come maybe two or three times a month, for a treat. A bag of seven pears costs me fifteen roubles. The average wage in Leningrad is seventy roubles a week.

The alternative, the State food shop, is across the road. It is clean, well lit, hygienic and almost entirely devoid of food. Assistants in starched white hats and overalls stand behind large mounds of margarine and unsold tins of pilchards. With desperate irony it's called Gastronomia. I try to buy a bottle of genuine Russian vodka here. The bottles look unusual and I check I'm asking for the right thing. Yes, it is vodka, but there is such a shortage of glass in the Soviet Union that they're having to put vodka in bottles that once contained children's orange juice. As it turns out, I can't buy vodka anyway, as it's all strictly rationed and I don't have coupons. I ask for wine instead but there is no wine on the shelves as Gorbachev's anti-drinking reforms have resulted in enormous cuts in production. Apparently sixty per cent of the Georgian wine crop was deliberately destroyed.

DAY 29: *Leningrad*

A rare honour has been accorded me today, and I wish it hadn't. I am to be permitted to fire the noonday gun from the roof of the barracks of the Peter-Paul Fortress. This is a tradition stretching back 250 years to the days when the sound of the gun was the only way of giving the city a daily time check. It's still taken very seriously and today everything depends on my ability to fire a 152-millimetre howitzer cannon, built in 1941 and with a range of eight miles, at precisely twelve o'clock. For obvious reasons practice is out of the question, so an elderly gunnery officer prepares me by describing everything that could go wrong, ending up by offering me earplugs. As the moment grows closer crowds of Russian tourists begin to assemble. I have never felt more like a condemned man. The crew adjust their earplugs, the officer orders everyone, except me, to stand well away, and I'm left looking out, beyond the barrel of my howitzer, towards the glinting towers and domes of this imposing city. My last thought is that there are over five million people out there and it'll have to be a hell of a loud bang, when down goes the officer's hand and before I know it, I've pulled the rope and ignited the cannon. There is a city-shattering boom and I am turned instantly from a jelly to an artilleryman, and can't wait to do it again.

The afternoon is almost as bizarre. I spend it in the company of Edward Bersudsky, who works in a small studio making what he calls his 'kinematic sculptures'. These are intricate machines, assembled in Heath Robinson style, which turn, whirr and animate in an hour-long performance.

One is called 'The Great Idea' and features a wooden Karl Marx in a loincloth, turning an old-fashioned handle to set in motion a manic scrapheap of cogs and pulleys, springs, levers and flywheels. Another construction, called somewhat forbiddingly 'An Autumn Walk during the Epoch of Perestroika', brings to life a suitcase from which appears a skeletal hand, a pair of automatically walking army boots on a red bentwood chair, an accordion which plays itself, a German helmet complete with lavatory chain, and a rocket which springs erect and with a loud pop discharges a tiny ball, very slowly. Edward sees his machines as a symbol of order rather than disorder. He wants to show that we are all at the mercy of the circle of life and death and paradise and hell. Everything moves but remains in place. The Hindus call it *Sansara*. He calls it 'Soviet Absurd'.

We end up drinking tea in a friendly, cluttered kitchen behind the studio. The tablecloth is a Soviet map of the world, but Edward has never been out of the country. He's Jewish, one of the 'nationalities' for whom travel is difficult. He is about to go abroad for the first time, to show his work at the Glasgow Festival, but his passport will still make specific mention of the fact that he is Jewish. As a soft sunlight warms the room I feel for a moment as if I'm back at home on one of those Sunday afternoons when time slows down and people drop in and the talk goes round like one of Edward's machines. I find Edward and his helpers very sympathetic. Kindred souls, I suppose. He laughs a lot. He says the Russians all do. They couldn't survive without laughter.

'And politics?' I ask.

He makes a face. 'We're sick of politics! . . . We've had politics for the last seventy years!'

DAY 30: *Leningrad to Novgorod*

Wake up to my thirteenth-floor view of Leningrad for the last time. I shall miss the comforting presence of the broad river, with its embankment pathway along which I ran in the early evening, past boys fishing and men walking dogs and lovers arguing. One evening I discovered a dream house along there, number forty, Sverdlovskaya. It must have dated from the eighteenth century – the golden age of Tsarist Leningrad – for it had an elegant three-storey classical façade from which extended curving crescents, each one culminating in a perfectly proportioned pavilion. The front of the house was guarded by a heavy chain running through the mouths of fifteen stone lions. It was deserted, a relic of another time, of Leningrad's aristocratic past, now almost lost among the factories, warehouses and apartment blocks of the proletarian present.

At the bus station in Leningrad is one of the small-ads boards which offer details of neighbourhood services, things for sale, and lost and found. The preoccupations of Leningraders look pretty similar to our own – 'Back massage, manual therapy', 'Rottweilers Club' – though there was one which surprised me: 'Seal . . . intelligent, lovable, tender'. Required for lasagne?

The bus is comfortable. There is even air-conditioning, though when I adjust it the ventilator falls apart in my hand, so I have to content myself with opening the window, which is what everyone else has done anyway. Pass a sign reading 'M20. Kiev 1120 kilometres'. Kiev is another city on the thirty degree meridian but on the way is Novgorod, 117 miles from Leningrad down the main road to Moscow. One of Novgorod's eternal claims to fame is that it is twinned with Watford and I have been charged with helping to cement the relationship by taking Novgorod a gift from Watford. (How do these twinnings work? Is there an agency? Maybe they advertised: 'Handsome walled town, icons, gilded onion domes, seeks English town/city with railway connections, pref. handy for Gatwick/Heathrow'.) Most of the traffic on the single carriageway south consists of noisy, smoke-belching trucks, and the scenery consists of flat fields, interspersed with birch and poplar trees and occasional small settlements, some of which boast brightly painted wooden houses, surrounded by allotments and beds of sunflowers. We've been travelling south for over a month, and I'm tempted to think we must soon be in Mediterranean climes, but in fact we are still at the same latitude as the Shetland Islands.

The weather feels continental, hot and humid, still and muggy. Combined with the unevenness of the road and the miasma of truck exhaust fumes, it doesn't make for a good introduction to Novgorod. I'm just jotting in my notebook that everything, as far as the eye can see, is filthy, when a mirage appears in the distance. Rising between a screen of blackened roofs and smokestacks, are four shining domes, one gold, the others silver. It's my first sight of the historic heart of Novgorod, squeezed and surrounded by unrestricted industrial expansion, a jewel on a rubbish tip.

We are staying at the Party Committee Hotel, which looks like a seventies police station on an Essex housing estate. I have been allotted a suite, very grand and shining with freshly varnished wood. It comprises a hallway, reception-room complete with glass cabinet full of crockery, a small sitting-room with a television and a sideboard, a bedroom and a bathroom with two lavatories, but no soap and only twelve sheets of toilet paper, which I think might not be toilet paper at all, but a notepad. In the lobby of the hotel are bound copies of *Pravda* and *Isvestia*, the two party newspapers. Both are very thin – eight closely printed pages each. I'm told that *Pravda*'s readership has fallen from ten million to three million in the five years of *perestroika*.

A local photographer drives me and Basil out a little way from the city onto the flood plain of the river Volkhov. The flat countryside is dotted about with churches, and once again I'm struck by the paradox of an atheist state going to such lengths to keep them standing. I think perhaps the key lies in the other monuments amongst these low watery fields – war memorials. The impact of the war on this part of Russia was so savage that the restoration of the churches, like the memorials of tanks and aeroplanes, is an act of defiance and pride – to show that the soul and spirit of Mother Russia can never be defeated.

DAY 31: *Novgorod*

Woken by the sound of mowing-machines. Not one or two, but a squadron of them, unleashed on the grass surrounding the hotel in a rare and impressive display of formation lawnmowing.

In the morning I make the acquaintance of a film-maker and

vodka-maker by the name of Edward Ranenko. I find him at the Correspondent Film Centre, situated in a long, low, whitewashed building on a leafy avenue. He is tall and thin and stands as straight as a Guards officer. Long silver-grey hair is swept back from a high, domed forehead, and he sports a moustache. A charismatic figure for whom people will clearly do anything. How else can I explain the fact that we all solemnly follow him to a muddy pond surrounded by housing blocks, a main road and a building site, to shoot a film about crayfish?

Edward is about to offer me a part in the proceedings, possibly as second crayfish, when word comes that I must return at once to the Party Committee Hotel and vacate my room. A VIP is arriving from Moscow. This must explain the onslaught of the lawnmowers. It's no use protesting. The receptionist is firm but apologetic. The Deputy Prime Minister of the Soviet Union needs my room.

'The Deputy Prime Minister of *Russia*?' I ask.

'No.' She spreads her arms wide. 'Of the whole Soviet Union.'

As I go through the hotel every shiny floor is being made even more treacherous by an army of cleaners, and there is an elderly, bald and very sweaty plumber in my bathroom trying to fix the heated towel-rail. He finishes his work and shuffles off. I complete my packing and take a last look at my bed, soon to be occupied by the second most powerful man in the Soviet Union. Toy with the idea of leaving him a note – 'Keep up the good work . . . we know everyone in Russia hates Gorbachev but we think he's doing a good job', that sort of thing – but, as I've discovered, the notepad is actually toilet paper. I'm about to close the door when I become aware of a widening pool of liquid creeping out from the bathroom. A jet of water is gushing merrily from the end of the heated towel-rail.

Edward Ranenko has offered me traditional Russian hospitality at the Correspondents Club tonight. He wants to treat me to crayfish and samogon – home-made vodka that he brews up in his garage.

He assures me: 'Mine is only the best. With samogon you have no headache in the morning'.

Dinner is laid out on the most remarkable table I've ever seen. It's ten feet long, carved in an irregular outline, varnished and stained the colour of raw meat. The surface is engraved and from the centre of the table rears a horse's head with a brass harness of bells attached. It is, Edward tells me, the work of Vladimir Grebenikov, a father of five and a great and un-appreciated genius. His fantastical designs are evident in the rest of the decoration – intricately worked chairs and elaborate lampshades the size of Roman breastplates. The whole effect is as if someone had gone berserk with a Black and Decker.

So begins the Night of a Thousand Toasts. Edward has assembled a party of family and good friends, none of whom speaks much English. There is Valery, quiet and uncomfortable, but a great crane operator; Igor the cook, jolly and companion-able, with a son in the army; Edward's son Michael, whose names, in the Russian way of using a patronym, come out the same as mine – Michael Edvardovitch; and Sasha, a journalist from Moscow radio. Edward's illegal vodka is served with slivers of garlic in it from a litre Coca-Cola bottle. To get the best effect he adds another refinement – two fresh-picked cherries to be placed in the mouth before each glass.

The toasts start early and follow rapidly. Almost anything will do . . . 'To the guests!', 'To Michael!', 'To the crayfish' . . .

After each toast the glass must be drained. Pretty soon I can hardly stand up and am laughing insanely at everything, including a toast to the Romanov dynasty, rightful rulers of Russia, which is not a joke at all but taken very seriously by Edward. By the end of the meal I have put away at least a bottle of vodka, and sung 'The Lumberjack Song' from Monty Python to a rapturous reception. Mindful of the fact that I have to do my stuff as an ambassador for Watford in the morning, and that my hosts are beginning to sing long, maudlin Russian songs, I make my farewells. Never was there such a kissing and a hugging and an embracing. It was as if the world had ceased to exist outside the Correspondents Club. All the warmth and the sadness and the madness of the Russians poured out in a waterfall of emotion as we clung to each other.

I just about remember ending the evening sitting on a seat outside the Party Committee Hotel, impervious to the clouds of mosquitoes, enjoying the hot, humid night, and waiting for the Deputy Prime Minister of the Soviet Union to arrive. The hotel staff were still in a high state of excitement and at one point the receptionist rushed out into the night holding a cardboard box at arm's length.

'What is this?' she cried. 'I think it is a bomb!'

Everyone recoiled except those of us who knew exactly what it was – Basil's box of exotic sauces for improving local cuisine. To be known from now on as 'The Bomb'.

DAY 32: *Novgorod to Dno*

Edward Ranenko was right about one thing: considering the prodigious amount of samogon I consumed I have a remarkably clear head. But my stomach is not happy and I've been bitten to pieces by vodka-loving mosquitoes. Reduced to a room the size of a samovar I suffer further indignity when the basin I lean heavily on in the bathroom proves not to be attached to any other part of the bathroom. It turns a half-somersault into my arms which gives me such a shock that I quite forget what I wanted it for. After yesterday's jollity and exuberance, this morning is a let-down. Even the Deputy Prime Minister has come and gone by the time I get up.

With its history, its handsome buildings and two hundred small churches one might expect Novgorod to be rather proud of itself. But there seems to be not even a postcard in sight. I'm directed to the souvenir shop which bears a hopeful sign, 'Open, 9 till 6'. The door is locked and barred though it's 10.15 in the morning. I give up and prepare myself for the twinning ceremony. This involves taking a couple of Arret capsules to make sure my bowels behave, and giving a little thought to the virtues of civic togetherness.

It appears that Novgorod has not been altogether faithful to Watford, for when I go to inspect the silver birch tree planted on 9 September 1983 to symbolize the accord between the two great cities, I find the place positively littered with tokens of friendship. There are trees from Nanterre and Bielefeld, Uusikau Punki in Finland and Rochester in New York.

The ceremony is to be held outdoors, in the most prominent part of old Novgorod, with the domes of Saint Sofia rising behind. A folk group has turned out and a bulky but impressive sound system has been erected and tested. I am wearing a jacket and tie, for the first time on the journey, and clutching the Watford glass decanter inscribed 'Presented to the People of Novgorod, August 1991'. The only element missing is the Mayor of Novgorod. A couple of lads with hands in their pockets observe our discomfiture with polite interest. It turns out that one of these lads *is* the Mayor of Novgorod.

He delivers a shirt-sleeved speech in fluent English, extols the benefits of free enterprise in Novgorod and hands over a beautiful but delicate ceramic dish, which will be lucky to reach Kiev in one piece, let alone Watford. He then goes back to running his city, leaving me with the athletic folk group, who are anxious to involve me in a Russian Kissing Dance. This is a particularly frenetic activity for which a jacket and tie and a set of loose bowels are not helpful.

If only I had been able to spend more time with the Mayor, and less in the dances, I could have asked him why, in a city of 250,000 people, there are only five restaurants. And why the one we end up in is described as a restaurant at all. It's part of the Palace of Culture, a huge, desolate, shabby, modern building in the suburbs of Novgorod, which must once have been the face of a golden proletarian future, and is now, literally, rotting. In the middle of its drab and dusty halls is a canteen serving the worst pizzas I've ever eaten. This is only a minor cloud over a grim day. Earlier this afternoon one of our drivers collapsed in great pain and is now in hospital with a perforated ulcer.

It's a subdued team that sets off from the Palace of Culture to drive sixty miles south-west to pick up the Leningrad–Kiev express at the town of Dno. Dno, in Russian, means literally the bottom, the pits. Three hours later we are completely lost. Total darkness and the lack of anything resembling a road sign have completely floored our drivers, who are all Muscovites, and know nothing of these marshy flatlands.

Eventually, negotiating country roads by a process of elimination, we bump into and over what miraculously turns out to be a railway track.

DAY 33: *Dno to Kiev*

It's one o'clock in the morning at Dno station. The main lines from Tallinn to Moscow and Leningrad to Kiev cross here, and it has enjoyed its moment of history, too. On this station, in April 1917, Nicholas II was persuaded by his generals to abdicate, ending 450 years of Tsarist rule.

I know it's not fair to judge somewhere after a one-hour wait for a train in the middle of the night, but it does seem a place of desperation. A group of teenagers emerge from beneath a goods train, run across the line and jump up onto the platform. They are wild-eyed and grubby and very drunk. One boy looks heavily beaten around the face and there is mud and blood in equal parts on his clothes. They push close to the little circle of light where we are set up to film the train, demanding we give them beer. We're used to people wanting to join in the filming but this time there is an ugly air of aggression and potential violence. There is no help from the railway staff and the other travellers are completely uninterested. We're all relieved when the mournful boom of a diesel horn heralds the approach of the Kiev express. All its compartments are dark except for a silver light in the buffet car where a few staff are watching a soft porn video. Console myself with the thought that though Dno may be the pits, it is the start of a 620-mile run, due south, in less than twenty-four hours. Compared with our recent progress, this constitutes a sprint.

To bed at two, wake at six and stumble to the uncongenial toilet and washroom which serves the entire coach. There is a wooden frame for a washbasin in my compartment but the basin has gone, as have most of the light fittings.

At breakfast time we are passing Orsa, 100 kilometres west of Smolensk. We are now in Belorussia, our third Soviet republic, after Estonia and Russia. From here on down to Odessa and the Black Sea we shall be following the Dnieper, Europe's third-longest river, and a significant part of one of the great trade routes of history, linking Russia and Scandinavia with Asia and the Mediterranean. There is a real sense of putting the north behind us and heading towards the centre of things.

I walk along the train. Windows are lowered as the temperature rises. The open mixed-sleeper coaches are crowded, but oddly peaceful and intimate. Everyone makes the most of their own space, people sprawl asleep, unembarrassed by public exposure. I squeeze past bare feet, stockinged feet, recumbent grandmothers, chess-playing old men, children clustered at the window. The click of wheel on rail is the loudest sound, and even that is lulling and hypnotic.

At the town of Zlobin, some 200 miles from Kiev, we cross to the left bank of the Dnieper and into the Ukraine. I'm sitting with a Ukrainian writer and film-maker, Vadim Castelli, and we drink a toast to his country in pomegranate juice. He is vehemently proud of his homeland.

'Ukraine is potentially such a rich land . . . we produce about one-third of all industrial output of the USSR, we produce more than one-third of all agriculture of the USSR. About eighty to eighty-five per cent of all these riches just go . . . to this bottomless pit which is the Soviet economy . . . '

I ask Vadim if he thinks there will ever he an independent Ukraine.

'It's not going to be very fast. We are still conservative . . . we've seen what's happening in the Baltics, we've seen what's happening in Lithuania – we wouldn't want this . . . but the process of secession is inevitable . . . I hear people on the streets of Kiev speaking Ukrainian . . . the culture which many people thought is gone for ever. If one feels Ukrainian, if one feels it's one's roots, this is a very exciting period to live through.'

It's moving to hear feelings like this expressed with such eloquence, the more so when I hear Vadim's personal experience at the hands of Soviet institutions. His father, a writer and film director, was arrested by the KGB in 1977, after works of his, critical of the regime, were published in the West. A healthy forty-nine-year-old, he was sent to a KGB prison in Kiev, from which he emerged six months later, paralysed and confused. He was taken to hospital but died six months afterwards. Two months later, his father's prison diaries appeared in the West. The KGB were furious and yet could find no way in which these writings had leaked out of his high-security confinement. For twelve years Vadim was subject to harassment, until the extraordinary effects of *glasnost* enabled him to publish both his father's original work and the diaries in the Ukraine. But all is not over for him. The authorities still have his father's papers, and as Vadim warns again, 'The KGB is still very strong, the military are very strong . . . we have to be very cautious . . .'.

Somewhere between Gomel and Cernikov our steady southward progress comes to a halt. We go to see the train 'chief'. In his cabin there are two pictures, one a scantily clad dancer with high-sided boots and tasselled nipples, the other a Madonna and Child. He says there is a broken rail ahead and we will be held up for two and a half hours.

The passengers accept this news quite philosophically and most of them leave the train, some crossing the rails to a house where ducks, goats and scrawny chickens run round a well in the garden. From this well, and for no apparent payment, the locals are drawing buckets of water to fill a collection of jugs, tins and plastic bottles produced by the passengers. Other passengers have slipped on bathing costumes and made off through the woods to a large flooded gravel pit. This turns into an impromptu holiday beach. Some men build a diving-board from tree trunks, others hoist each other onto their shoulders. There's terrific crashing and splashing and laughter. Others, less extrovert, watch from the edge of the forest, or walk through the bushes picking blueberries and redcurrants. The wind half-heartedly rustles a tall willow, but can do little more than waft around the heavy heat of the afternoon.

After a swim I return to the train, to find our coach supervisor and two colleagues tucking into a smoked fish and vegetable stew which she has cooked up on a small Primus. She smiles as I look in, and offers me some. The effects of Ranenko's vodka and crayfish orgy are still upon me and I mime a stomach ache. Much laughter.

At half-past five the engine's whistle reverberates through the trees, and the bathers and sunbathers and lovers and loners and berry pickers and water gatherers make their way slowly back to the train, and I feel quite a pang of regret as we jerk into motion. I search the map and locate this spot in case I should not believe all this ever happened. As I do so, I notice, less than 100 miles to the south-west, the name of the small, almost insignificant town of Chernobyl.

At 9.45 in the evening we are at Nezin, two hours late already and still no sign of Kiev. Even with the windows and doors open there is no relief from the clammy heat. The train chief has pulled off his shirt altogether and his huge white gut hangs out of the window. As happens on train journeys that have gone on long beyond their appointed time, no one seems to care any more. The layered dirt and dust gradually attaches itself to the passengers who only a few hours ago looked scrubbed and glowing. Try to read. Vadim and Roger are deep in discussion as to whether or not Lenin died of syphilis.

At a quarter to midnight we pull into Kiev, capital of the Ukraine, third-largest city of the Soviet Union. The station is packed solid. I've seen nothing like it since India. Our admirable fixers find trolleys and somehow we're out of this madhouse within an hour and driven to a tall new hotel overlooking Dynamo Kiev's football ground. No porters to be seen but the room is fine. Until I draw the curtains, when first one then the other slides slowly up to the end of the rail and off onto the floor.

DAY 34: *Kiev*

I celebrate the end of my twenty-four-hour, post-crayfish fast with a slap-up breakfast at the Warsaw Hotel. This consists of a thin sliver of cheese, some equally thin slivers of bread, a jam smear and a cup of coffee.

Soviet restaurants exist for one purpose, and that is to keep the customer out, and if by any chance he or she should get in to make life so uncomfortable that they wish they hadn't. Even to get as far as the sliver of cheese involves a considerable amount of bureaucratic negotiation. A card, which can only be issued at reception, must be produced and exchanged for a voucher, which is thoroughly scrutinized by the restaurant gauleiter, who will then turn you over to the waitresses who will ignore you.

It's all very depressing and is, I suppose, just the Soviet system in microcosm – unwieldy, paranoid and impersonal.

This morning I witness evidence of an encouraging change when I accompany Vadim to see the Deputy Procurator of the Ukraine, who has been examining the case for returning Vadim's father's papers, held by the KGB. For whatever reason, this senior Soviet law officer is welcoming and affable, even happy for the meeting to be filmed. Short, square-shouldered, with a wide, strong face and a well-cut suit, he personifies Gorbachev Man, assiduous in attention to the smallest public relations details.

He reassures Vadim that the rehabilitation committee set up by Gorbachev last year to investigate the cases of political prisoners in the USSR has cleared 1200 people in less than five months, and that he himself will personally try to expedite matters in the case of Vadim's father. Then he offers us all green tea from Uzbekhistan complete with a special herb which, he tells us proudly, he has grown himself. It is altogether a smooth performance, but Vadim, who has grown very cynical about Soviet justice, feels that there is substance there as well.

We take a quick tour of Kiev, which looks a green and handsome city with broad boulevards and trees everywhere. It's hard to imagine that, in my lifetime, these green and pleasant hills were the scene of unspeakable suffering. During the time the Nazis occupied Kiev – from October 1941 to October 1943 – 400,000 people were killed, either in the city or in extermination camps, 300,000 were deported to forced labour camps in Germany, and eighty per cent of all residential houses were destroyed. The reconstruction of the city, especially the fine old buildings like the Monastery of the Caves, must be one of the more tangible achievements of the Soviet regime. There has been a price to pay, such as the erection of an enormous stainless steel statue of a female warrior, 320 feet high, dominating the heights above the Dnieper. Huge, gross and unavoidable, it dates from the seventies and is known locally as 'Brezhnev's Mother'.

Kiev has been very close to modern tragedy as well. If the prevailing wind had not been blowing from the south on 26 April 1986 – the day the reactor blew up at Chernobyl – Kiev, only fifty-five miles away, would have been a dead city. No one knows how serious the effects might still be. The wind started blowing towards Kiev five days after the explosion, but the reactor wasn't sealed for a month. Looking down from the old city walls I can see people splashing about in the Dnieper. I ask Vadim if it's safe. He tells me a friend of his, a nuclear physicist, told him that it was fine to swim as long as he didn't touch the bottom, for radioactive material always sinks. But, he shrugs, on a day as hot as today there will always be people who will take risks.

Back at the hotel, Volodya has defused a potentially embarrassing situation. Two months ago a local girl was made pregnant by an Englishman staying in this hotel, whose name was Michael. Since then her mother has scoured the guest lists for an Englishman called Michael, and this morning she turned up trumps. With her wronged and freshly impregnated daughter in tow she spent all day camped in the lobby, waiting for Michael Palin to return. I'm just relieved not to have been first through that door.

DAY 35: *Kiev to Narodichi to Kiev*

Today we are going close to Chernobyl to visit towns and villages that have been, or are about to be, evacuated as a result of the disaster. We shall not be entering the thirty-mile exclusion zone but will be in contaminated areas and Volodya, Irena and the rest of our Russian team will not be coming with us. Mirabel too has decided not to risk it. Roger has been in contact with the National Radiological Protection Board at Harwell, whose advice offered mixed comfort. They said radiation levels would be the same, if not less, than at the Poles, with their concentration of magnetic forces. However, the knowledge that there is still confusion and debate over the effects of the disaster, and the advice from scientists that we wear shoes and clothing we could throw away afterwards, add a frisson of danger to the journey and there is some nervous joking over the slivers of cheese at breakfast.

We head north and west from Kiev, making for the town of Narodichi. It's forty-two miles due west of Chernobyl, two of whose reactors, Vadim reminds us, are still operational. The Ukrainian Parliament has voted unanimously to close them down. The Soviet government has refused. The Ukrainians claim that 8000 died as a result of the accident. The official Soviet figure is thirty-two.

We are passing through woodlands of pine and oak scrub interspersed with harvested fields and cherry and almond orchards. An army convoy of forty trucks passes, heading south. After a while the woodland gives way to a wide and fertile agricultural plain. The first indication that this abundance is tainted comes as quite a shock. It's a sign, set in brambles and long grass, which reads, 'Warning: It is forbidden for cattle to graze, and to gather mushrooms, strawberries and medicinal herbs'.

We stop here and put on our yellow TLD badges, which register radiation levels, and which will be sent back to Harwell for analysis after our three-hour visit. Armed with these and a radiation detector, we enter Narodichi where people have lived with radiation for over five years. It's a neat, proud little town with a chestnut-lined main street and a silver-painted Lenin in front of the party headquarters. In a year's time there will be no one here.

In the municipal gardens the grass is uncut but a fountain still plays. There are several memorials. One is a scorched tree with a cross on it – local people think that the forest protected them from the worst of the blast. Beside the tree are three large boulders, one of which commemorates four villages and 548 people evacuated in 1986, another fifteen villages and 3264 people evacuated in 1990. Twenty-two more villages and a further 11,000 people will be going in 1991. An inscription reads: 'In memory of the villages and human destinies of the Narodichi region burnt down by radiation'.

One of the most polluted areas is the children's playground, with thirteen to seventeen times normal gamma radiation levels. The red metal chairs hang down from the roundabout and blue steel boats swing gently in the breeze, but no one is allowed to play here any more.

Michael, the local schoolmaster, is short and podgy and his face is an unhealthy grey. There were 10,000 children in the region, he tells me; now there are 3000. Two of his pupils pass by on bicycles and he grabs them and introduces us. The boys, just back from a Pioneer camp in Poland, look bored, and reply in monosyllables, which Michael translates thus: 'The children send fraternal greetings to children throughout the United Kingdom'. He smiles proudly and a little desperately. I ask if the children's work has been affected by their proximity to Chernobyl. He sighs and nods.

'There is not a single healthy child here.'

As we drive out of Narodichi, Michael talks with pride of the history of his town, interspersing this with casually chilling present-day observations.

'This is the bridge over the Oush river. It is area of highest pollution.'

We come to the village of Nozdrishche, which was evacuated last year. There are no ruins, there is no devastation or destruction. Wooden cottages with painted window-frames stand in their orderly rows. Flowers are in bloom and grasshoppers dart around in lush overgrown gardens. It is a hot, soft, gentle summer's day. Yet scientists who have visited the area say it could be 700 years before this place comes back to life. It is hard to know what to believe, for whatever curse lies over these villages is the more frightening for being invisible. It is how one has heard the countryside would be after a nuclear war – benign, smiling, deadly.

A year's exposure to the weather has not yet dissipated a faint smell of disinfectant in a small, deserted maternity hospital. A poster on the wall depicts the American space shuttle spinning round the earth, with the single word 'Nyet!' beneath. There is a book on breastfeeding, its leaves nibbled by mice, an examination chair, medical records still in files, and a portrait of Lenin which has fallen out of its frame and lies in a corner beneath a scattering of glass slides and syringes. Conscious of the limited time we have been advised to spend here, we move on through the village. I catch sight of two figures down a lane to one side of the main street. One is a very old lady whose name is Heema, and the other her nephew. Heema is ninety years old and has refused to be moved from the village. She says she has been moved five times since the disaster and now she is too old and ill. Her one wish is to die in the house in which she was born, but that is now cordoned off with barbed wire, so she will remain here with her daughter. They are the only inhabitants of Nozdrishche.

Further along the road, at the village of Novoye Sharno, the radiation detector bleeps for the first time.

'Pay attention, please,' says Michael, 'the radiation is very high here.'

This is one of the villages evacuated in 1986, immediately after the explosion and fire, and the village shop is now almost submerged in the undergrowth. Inside it is a mess of broken shelves, abandoned goods, smashed bottles.

'There was a panic here,' Vadim explains, unnecessarily.

We drive back through Narodichi, where, as in Novoye

Sharno, Nozdrishche and over forty villages in this region alone, the grass will soon grow around doors that will never be opened again, and anyone who comes here will be informed of the dangers and the risks which those who lived here were not told about until it was too late.

Back in Kiev, two and a half hours later, I'm struck once again by the spruceness of the city compared with Leningrad or Novgorod. A Russian, writing in the *Insight Guide*, relates even this to Chernobyl. 'The terrible effects of the tragedy made many people, in Kiev and other towns, take another look at themselves. Kiev is cleaner, and not merely because the streets are watered twice a day now; once the people were shown the frailty of human existence, they changed.'

We end the day in a brick-vaulted cellar in the Andreevsky Spusk, a Montmartre-like street full of cafés and shops and predominantly student meeting-places. The food is the best we've had in the Soviet Union – Armenian-Georgian cooking – kebabs, rabbit stew, aubergine and onion salad. An excellent jazz trio of bass, fiddle and piano plays local music and well-served-up classics like 'Take the A-Train'. Vodka flows freely. It is one of the best evenings, and in a sense, the only way of dealing with what we have seen today.

DAY 36: *Kiev to Cerkassy*

Alarm wakes me at six. It's a Sunday, but no day of rest as we continue southwards. We are travelling by river as far as Cerkassy on the *Katun*, a 215-foot barge with a canary-coloured hull, carrying a mixed cargo of bottles, fabrics, sports equipment, clothes, children's push-chairs and electrical appliances down the Dnieper to the port of Cherson on the Black Sea.

The *Katun* is a barge of character. She's forty years old next year, and her interior features wood rather than plastic or the ubiquitous Formica. Two small cabins below the bridge have been set aside for our use. One has a writing-desk and chair, an old oak wardrobe and an enamel washbasin, with an alcove containing what looks like the world's most comfortable bed. Sitting at the desk, looking through a porthole, I imagine I could be Joseph Conrad, though the football team photo above my head, featuring the chunky lads of Metalworkers Zaporozje, doesn't quite fit the romantic illusion.

On the bridge there is a big and handsome ship's wheel and a book of river charts painted in watercolours. So much of the image of the Soviet Union is of vast institutional spaces and faceless buildings that it comes as a constant surprise to find warm, intimate, friendly corners of life like the *Katun*. We progress at an unhurried ten knots beneath the bridges of Kiev, leaving behind the remarkable prospect of Baroque church towers, whitewashed walls, malachite-green roofs, and spires crowned always with gold. Roger is leaning over the side, examining the water.

'Have you ever been to a sewage treatment plant?' he asks me after close study of the Dnieper. 'Well, this is what it looks like before it goes in.'

It's a pleasantly lazy day, which I think is what we all need. Basil sleeps, Irena sits at the desk with a copy of Longman's *Dictionary of Common Errors*. Her English is fluent but she's desperately keen to polish up her Cockney rhyming slang.

We pass through a network of small islands and beaches busy with holidaymakers. Hydrofoils, scuttling along the surface like great white cockroaches, drone past at frequent intervals. Barges pass, mostly carrying coal. The captain says that the Dnieper is navigable as far north as Mogilov, about 300 miles from Moscow. Since the Chernobyl catastrophe (as he describes it) he doesn't go north of Kiev. There's nothing to bring down any more.

He's a slim, weatherbeaten, good-looking man who roundly refuses to be interviewed. 'I'm not an actor,' he says. Even filming on the bridge causes some consternation. There is a flurry of activity as the first mate hides something the captain doesn't want us to see. It turns out to be his brown jacket which he says is 'very old'. Later I notice that they only have one pair of sunglasses between them.

The Dnieper has been dammed at a place called Kanev where a lake two miles wide is squeezed into one lock, with a fourteen-metre drop. The smell inside the dank and slimy walls of the lock is appalling, and as it takes a good fifteen minutes to fill up, there's very little escape from the odour of decay and dead fish.

All this is made up for by a Sunday lunch of stew and mashed potato, a lazy afternoon reading and a drop of Scotch as we sit on the top of the hold taking in a glorious sunset that dazzles and fades over a landscape of low, wooded sandbanks. I realize that what I missed in the Arctic was not so much darkness as the sunrises and sunsets that go with it.

At eleven at night we reach Cerkassy, threading our way towards a container-stacked dockside with the help of a sharp, stabbing searchlight.

Our drivers have followed us down from Novgorod, and the ill-luck which has already put one of them in hospital has persisted. One of the vehicles, a Volga limo, has been written off in an accident, and the other, the 'Latvia' minibus, has survived two blow-outs, one at full speed.

DAY 37: *Cerkassy to Odessa*

Breakfast at the Hotel Dnieper in Cerkassy offers some odd fare. There's very sweet yoghurt, served in a glass, cottage cheese with sugar, and a choice of either dry hard white bread or dry hard brown bread with slices of sausage. There is no coffee, but tea from the samovar.

As I'm upstairs packing for what I estimate to be the seventeenth time on the journey so far, I look down at my bed and experience a most unusual feeling of foreboding. I'm not normally given to precognition but something warns me against proceeding to Odessa by road. Two out of three vehicles are damaged, one beyond repair, and I've experienced enough of the haphazard inefficiency of Soviet life to make me fear for the safety of the third.

Our problems in the end aren't mechanical as much as navigational. Somewhere between Cerkassy and Uman we get horribly lost on unmarked maps and unsigned roads, finding ourselves stranded in sprawling landscapes of weed-ridden wheatfields. Eventually we find ourselves on the Kiev–Odessa main road, which is narrow and fortunately not busy. We cross the fast-flowing river Bug, and twelve miles north of Odessa we pass the first vineyards I've seen in the Soviet Union. The people down here are darker, almost Turkish in looks, and the blonde hair of the north gives way to the lustrous jet black of the south.

By six, after a drive of 300 miles, we reach Odessa safely. From the top of the Potemkin Steps, a few hundred yards from the hotel, I give thanks beside the Black Sea.

DAY 38: *Odessa*

In the middle of the night I'm woken by the sound of voices from the street below my window. A man and a woman are talking. The woman's voice is deep, rich and smooth. The talk turns into an argument. I lie for a while contemplating rather enviously the exotic, Mediterranean feel of Odessan street life when the argument turns into a violent shouting match. Suddenly the woman screams repeatedly and with such primal intensity that I'm up and rushing to the window. There is a sound of car doors slamming, an engine revving, tyres squealing, but by the time I've pushed the curtains back nothing is there but the disturbing echo of her cries.

We're staying at the Londonskya Hotel, situated on a tree-lined esplanade overlooking the port. It has a heavy neo-classical façade and was built in 1910; it had its name changed to the Odessa Hotel in 1948 as part of a policy called 'anti-cosmopolitanization'. Thanks to *glasnost*, it has, from last week, returned to being The Londoner. The lobby is a reasonably accurate representation of a London club, dark and rather grand, with columns, stained-glass windows and a wide and self-important marble staircase.

Equally decorative but much more seedy is the Kuyalnik Sanatorium, one of the most famous institutions in Odessa, to which people from all over the Soviet Union repair for mud treatment. The mud is drawn from a nearby lagoon which was once open sea, and which retains mineral deposits believed to be good for arthritic and respiratory complaints, as well as for the nervous system, slipped discs, thromboses and kidney trouble. Built in 1892 as a series of rococo pavilions, it has never quite recovered from being submerged in 1941, when a nearby dam was blown to try and halt the advance of the German armies. It stayed underwater until 1948.

After the rigours of our journey from the north I'm ready to try anything with soothing properties and so find myself following the holidaymakers up the steps of the sanatorium. Ahead of me are three women, dressed for the sun and chewing corn on the cob. Once inside the building I am led along corridors past waiting patients and through small atria whose damp and grubby walls are decorated with peeling stucco. A sulphurous, bad-egg smell becomes more intense the closer I get to the treatment room, and I am beginning to regret the whole thing.

The beds, or treatment tables, are laid out in two rows on either side of a tiled sluiced floor. There is no privacy at all and gentlemen in various intimate stages of treatment are on full view. One man is heaving his blackened and naked body off the bed like someone escaping from a swamp. Another is being administered a mud enema with the aid of a white plastic plunger. The whole grotesque scene resembles a cross between a hospital and an abattoir.

My time has come, and I'm led by the supervisor, a benign, motherly sort with pink earrings the size of ships' lifebelts, to a changing cubicle, from which I emerge, uncovered, to find a lady with a white coat, red hair, pink spectacles and a rubber pipe squeezing a layer of evil black slime onto a stained brown undersheet. She beckons to me to get into the middle of all this. My first surprise is how warm the mud is, the second how soothing it is to have it rubbed all over me, and the third how deeply tranquillizing it is to lie wrapped in the stuff like a piece of *boeuf en croûte*. Everything, the dreadful smell, the cattle-shed conditions, the slurping of distant enemas, is forgotten in the sheer tactile pleasure of lying in warm mud.

Glowing with health and smelling very gently of marine deposits I take a walk on the beach from which the therapeutic mud is gathered. Because the mud is best applied only to those parts which need it, and because most of the applicants are very white, the shoreline offers the bizarre sight of what appear to be human crossword puzzles. A local lady doctor strides into the sea with her daubed legs looking like thigh-length black boots. 'I bathe and then I don't wash it off for five days,' she enthuses.

At lunch I meet a local historian. Discussing the recent past it's clear that sunny, seaside Odessa has not escaped the tragedies that have befallen most of the western USSR. Romanians occupied Odessa in the war – Hitler had promised their leader Antonescu large stretches of the Black Sea coastline. They burnt 20,000 locals in an arsenal and hanged 5000 from trees around the city to frighten the populace. Today the major problem is severe industrial pollution. The Sea of Azov, a huge area east of the Crimea, is so badly affected that its beaches have been totally evacuated.

Later I go down to the Arkady Beach, one of Odessa's most famous, and find that there is not a space to be found, and – as in the waters of the Dnieper at Kiev – there are still plenty of people for whom cooling off on a sunny day is more important than any health risk.

We have dinner at the Krasnaya Hotel. Huge bare-breasted ladies support the balustraded balcony above the door, and the whole pale green and white façade is like a richly adorned cake. Inside there is a mirrored and chandeliered barn of a dining-room, the inevitable zakuski, and a very incompetent band fronted by a fat lady in a gold dress. She probably gives mud enemas in the daytime but at night she murders Beatles songs.

We have a party on the balcony of my room to celebrate

having made it this far. It's late when I get to bed, and when I get up there is a faintly detectable trace of black sediment on the bottom sheet.

DAY 40: *Odessa to Istanbul*

It's 12.48 by the digital clock in the main passenger terminal of the port of Odessa. As far as I can remember it's the only public clock I've seen in the Soviet Union that is still going. After a day of rest, the crew and myself are in transit again, bound for Istanbul. At the moment we are in the limbo land of Customs and Immigration, waiting for something to happen. They have tried to brighten up the arid bureaucratic wasteland in which we are confined by sticking travel posters to the walls – rugged mountains, ski slopes, folk dances and children gambolling on beaches. The pleasures of these places may be beyond the range of most of the Soviet people and yet they do represent one of the more acceptable aspects of this country, an ability to relish, whenever the opportunity arises, an escape from the surrounding gloom. We have seen the petrol queues and the empty shops, the shabbiness of the surroundings and the hard face of privilege, but we've also seen spontaneous delight in the countryside (as on the train to Kiev), happily packed beaches, and just this morning, holidaymakers on the Potemkin Steps asking me if I would mind taking a family snap for them. All you can say is the Soviet Union is never quite what it seems. We have eaten old, tasteless bread in hotels, but found, here in Odessa, a shop around the corner baking fresh baguettes. We have seen one bag of fruit costing over twenty per cent of a weekly wage and country gardens groaning with produce. We have looked into stony faces but never been hugged as hard.

Once cleared by Customs we are free to have a last lunch in the USSR. The good news is that the terminal has an outdoor restaurant, something we've been looking for for the last two weeks, the bad news is that it is on a crumbling concrete terrace which looks as if it has been reprieved halfway through demolition. The catering is standard to bad – our twenty-fourth zakuski, a gristly hamburger topped with fried egg, and coffee from chipped cups with broken handles. It's the sort of experience that makes you want to get to Istanbul as fast as possible, but we have a thirty-six-hour journey ahead of us, and to all intents and purposes it will be another day and a half in the Soviet Union. Our vessel is Odessa-registered and built in Bulgaria. She is a thirty-year-old, 280-foot-long, 1000-ton training ship. Her name, *Junost*, means 'Youth'. She has only recently been converted to take passengers and runs a ferry service to Turkey every five days. There is no alternative.

In the late afternoon the time comes to say our goodbyes to the team of Russian drivers, interpreters and fixers who have become our friends. They have guided us through the labyrinth of official obstruction with great skill and the fact that we have been able to film all we wanted and travel as and when we wanted is down to them. Volodya looks exhausted, and though there must be relief in their farewell waves, I think there is also regret, not just that we are going but that we can go so easily. For all the fatigue I feel after crossing the Soviet Union, the sight of their faces as the *Junost* pulls slowly away makes me aware of how fortunate I am.

Our bow swings round, pointing for a moment straight up the 192 stone steps, called the Potemkin Steps after a dramatic sequence shot on them in Eisenstein's film *Battleship Potemkin*, which rise grandly from the port to the tree-lined esplanade. A staircase into the USSR. Then we are turning away from this warm, unassuming city and slowly out of the immense dock area, past the hydrofoils they call Comets and Meteors which race about the harbour, the grey battlecruisers and a vast Soviet freighter improbably called *Mister Michael*. As we run slowly south-westwards along the low shadowy hills of the Black Sea coast, I enjoy one of the great pleasures of travel: exploring a new ship. The *Junost* is a rag-bag. The cabin space, which is shared, is cramped and basic. The lavatories are indescribably filthy, and I pray I don't have to use them for anything but the most cursory visits, but the main deck is a very congenial space, with a strip wood floor and a number of spacious and superior deckchairs, complete with footrests. Slung over the stern of the ship is what looks like a hastily erected shed, fashioned from corrugated plastic and painted brown. Inside is a small bar and a job lot of swivel chairs upholstered in red nylon. As well as serving nothing useful like beer and wine but only the dreaded hard-currency tariff of champagne, vodka and brandy, it embodies every fire risk known to man.

Roger has decided that the toilet facilities are so bad that we should film them. The purser, a trim, hairless man called Felix, walks past as we are emerging with all our lights and equipment and gives us a very odd look. Unfortunately we have to re-shoot. Once again we bump into Felix on the way out. This time he looks positively alarmed, but by the time we go down to dinner the lavatories have been thoroughly cleaned.

Felix is quite a character. Crisply dressed in white shirt and trousers, he not only announces dinner, but physically assists potential diners towards the restaurant. The longer you dally the more urgent are his attentions. The last arrivals are practically frog-marched to their table. I notice on the wall of the dining-room the only photo of Gorbachev I have seen publicly displayed. Is it just that he's unpopular or did he specifically discourage any personality cult? We all notice that his birthmark has been masked out.

End the day on deck with a Scotch and water and a sky full of stars, unobscured by city lights.

DAY 41: *Odessa to Istanbul*

Up on deck at 7.45. To my horror, Felix is there and appears to be having a fit. He's standing half naked with eyes rolling and hands flapping wildly out in front of him. Only after a while do I realize he's doing his exercises. He smiles in my direction, a grotesque rictus of a smile which virtually slices his head in two. Fortunately this turns out to be another exercise.

I'm beginning to wonder if this is a Soviet ship at all. There is Peter Gabriel on the PA and porridge on the breakfast menu. Among the passengers is an eighteen-year-old girl from Ilkley, travelling with her brother who has been studying in Moscow for a year. They have just returned from a trip to Lake Baikal in Siberia, the deepest lake in the world, so far miraculously unpolluted. Their descriptions of its beauty, purity and tranquillity I found very tantalizing.

There are fifty-four crew on the *Junost*, ten more than there are passengers. The first officer who told us this is engagingly frank. If he had his way he wouldn't stay in the Soviet Union. He worked once with Norwegians and they asked him how much he was paid in the USSR. '"A hundred and thirty dollars," I said. "Per day?" they asked. "No! Per month."' He smiles wryly at this.

I suggest that 130 dollars buys you a lot more in the Soviet Union than in Norway. He doesn't fall for that old one.

'I would rather live in expensive Norway.'

I'm growing fond of the *Junost*. Life on board has an innocent, anarchic quality. It's rather like being in a Monsieur Hulot film. A man in swimming trunks claiming to be the chief electrical officer bumps into me on the main staircase. He's dripping wet from a shower but anxious to know if we're happy with everything. I ask him why we are only going at nine knots. He drips a little and considers the question.

'Well, who wants to go any faster?'

Up on deck, the girl from Ilkley has a fierce nose bleed, and all sorts of previously unseen crew members appear to help her. Felix, clutching an ice-bag, orders them all around, having her blood pressure checked and her brow wiped. But the strangest encounter is with the lovely Lyuba, proprietress of the bar. I had discovered that, up in the bows, the *Junost* sported a swimming-pool. All of six feet long and five feet wide, it is in fact nothing more than a large packing case with a tarpaulin draped inside to hold the water. Deep end and shallow end change places with each roll of the ship. It's hardly large enough for one fully-formed adult, so when I see Lyuba's neat but ample figure clambering down towards me I adopt an air of nonchalant British lounging, as if there's nothing more normal in the world than sharing a waterlogged packing case with a Russian barmaid. But Lyuba is in the box for some fun, and having told me that her name means 'Amore . . . love' she splashes me with water and asks if I have a woman.

'A wife . . . yes,' I reply, as if the two things are quite incompatible.

'Is she engineer . . . technician?'

An image of Helen with the Black and Decker comes to mind, and as we splash around in our boxed fragment of the Black Sea, Lyuba and I fall into intimate conversation about schools, children and how we miss our families.

DAY 42: *Odessa to Istanbul*

Sleep almost ten hours, and wake with a sense that our engines have slowed, if that's possible. Push aside the curtain to see that we are only a few hundred yards from land. We have left the Black Sea and are halfway down the Bosporus, the winding eighteen-mile channel that leads to the Sea of Marmara, the Aegean and eventually the Mediterranean. On deck Roger is contemplating a couple of weeks' recovery time before rejoining us in Egypt. He's in professorial mood. Did I know that Bosporus and Oxford mean the same thing? In Greek legend, a priestess called Io was seeing Zeus, after work as it were, and Zeus, in order to prevent Hera, his wife, from finding out, turned Io into a cow. Hera, not fooled, sent a gadfly after her, causing the tormented Io to seek relief by jumping into the nearest stretch of water. This happened to be just about where we are now and became known as the Bous (ox) poros (ford).

Everything is so different from what we have just left. Minarets and cypress trees stand out from the green hillsides, houses are being built, and many are crowned with satellite dishes. Lines of private cars are weaving their way along

ABOVE: *The Russian kissing dance.*

LEFT: *Two-hour train delay – Russian style.*

OPPOSITE: *Odessa: the Potemkin Steps.*

ABOVE: *Istanbul from Süleyman's mosque.*

RIGHT: *Massage à la Turk.*

ABOVE: *The great theatre of Ephesus.*

OPPOSITE (TOP): *A 'blackbird' from the wedding at Limassol, Cyprus.*

OPPOSITE (BOTTOM): *Over-zealous celebrations at the Polycarpu wedding.*

OPPOSITE: *The Hypostyle Hall, Karnak, Egypt.*

ABOVE: *Felucca ride on the Aswan.*

Above and below decks on the Sinai.

crowded coast roads flanked by balconied apartment blocks on one side and white-hulled yachts on the other.

The *Junost* looks what it is, a poorly maintained, over-manned country cousin of a ship, a bit of an embarrassment in the midst of this burgeoning capitalist neophilia. The *Junost* is like the Soviet Union itself, inefficient and ill-equipped but full of character. Its shortcomings create an atmosphere of closeness and warmth in the face of shared adversity. I can't wait to get off and enjoy a few creature comforts but I know I shall miss Lyuba and Felix and the dripping chief electrical officer.

As we move slowly past the 540-year-old Ottoman fortress of Rumeli Hasari, entirely built in four months, all of us on the deck-rail are excited and uncertain. The girl from Ilkley will be hearing her A-level results today. Two Afghans who have come through Russia to set up business in the West will face commercial reality for the first time. The first officer will look longingly at the glitter of capitalism, before turning his ship back to a country that's falling apart. Only Felix seems un-affected, flicking his head round in a series of neck-wrenching turns, as if desperate to achieve a full 360-degree rotation.

The sweeping, graceful span of the first bridge ever to link two continents soars above us as the incomparable skyline of Istanbul comes into view. Set on headlands and curving around the inlet known as the Golden Horn, it is one of the great cityscapes of the world. Modern buildings are there, but the overall impression of grace and harmony is set by the mosques, with their clusters of domes and their attendant minarets pointing heavenwards like defending rockets, and the sprawling beauty of the Topkapi Palace, leading the eye downhill to the ramparts of the old city walls and the harbour, teeming with overloaded ferries.

The stealthy, tentative, introverted public face of the USSR is replaced here by shouts, waves, imprecations, noise, bustle and urgency.

We dock at ten past nine at a quayside that seems to be run by a very proprietorial black-and-white cat which, surrounded by a mangy harem, watches us tie up and sniffs each passenger as they disembark.

The formalities of Customs and Immigration are all conducted in a congenial and good-humoured way. Our new fixer Sevim, a formidable and energetic middle-aged lady, is organizing everyone. When there is trouble with the porters who object to being filmed because they are not in their best overalls she dismisses it briskly: 'These complexes . . . it is a problem in a Third World country . . . '.

As we leave the Customs hall the two Afghans are the only two passengers left. The contents of their suitcases, mainly cheap gift accessories, samples of local cloth and rugs, are strewn out on the inspection table. Maybe Turkey will not be their promised land after all.

For me, things taken for granted like waterfront cafés and fresh orange juice, even a traffic jam, are new and wonderful. The young man from Ilkley, returning from a year in Russia, shakes his head in disbelief.

DAY 43: *Istanbul*

Woken by the distorted sound of a pre-recorded muezzin calling the faithful to prayer. It's 5.30. Breakfast of orange juice, cereal and honeycomb – things I have not seen since Helsinki, three weeks ago. Fraser has had a nightmare in which he had to wire every minaret in Istanbul for sound.

Istanbul is a very noisy city, much of the noise from a huge construction programme. A companion to the famously crowded Galata Bridge across the Golden Horn is almost complete. A last massive section of its six-lane highway, waiting to be lowered into position, rears up at a right angle, a huge phallic symbol of regeneration. Sevim says the reconstruction is going on at such a pace that her husband, given a month's notice of redevelopment, went in to work one Monday morning to find his shop had gone. There are those with reservations about the pace of change. One is Altemur Kilic, a Turkish writer, diplomat and friend of Turgut Ozal, the President. He remembers Istanbul only thirty years ago as a city of 750,000 people, home to a flourishing number of foreign communities – Greek, Jewish, Armenian and what was known as the Levantine, comprising Italians, English and French who had lived in Turkey all their lives. He himself went to the English-run Istanbul High School for Boys whose headmaster, Mr Peach, he knew affectionately as Baba (Father). The teachers caned him regularly. He smiles happily at the memory. 'My father authorized them to do so. It helped my character.' In between canings Altemur played cricket, read the *Boy's Own Paper* and grew up in an Istanbul which was small enough to give him 'a sense of rather being somebody in a big city'. Now the city population has swelled to eight million and the real Istanbuliots, as he calls them, are very few.

As I step out of his elegant, unostentatious house on a small sloping street in Emirgan, I could be in the South of France, with the blue waters of the Bosporus catching the sunlight, people taking a drink or a coffee beneath the shade of ash and mimosa trees, and the almost unbroken line of passing traffic.

Down by the Galata Bridge, close by the old spice markets, the pace of Istanbul life is at its most frenetic. Ferries are constantly loading and unloading, providing a regular and copious passing trade for the street food-sellers. Fishermen dart in, light up charcoal braziers and, rocking crazily in the wash of the ferries, sell their grilled catch then and there. You could have a street dinner every night of the week here and never eat the same menu twice. Apart from the fish, served in luscious sandwiches of hot fresh bread, tomato and onion, there are kebabs, pretzels, walnuts, pancakes and stuffed mussels, corn on the cob, succulent slices of melon and as much sweet tea as you can drink.

Back in England, it's the first day of the football season and in my hotel the new BBC World Service Television is showing Episode five of *Around the World in 80 Days*.

DAY 44: *Istanbul*

The crew are up early to shoot the sunrise from the top of the 600-year-old Galata Tower, where in May 1453 the Genoese Christians handed over control of the city to the Ottoman Muslims, a key moment in European history. It is at breakfast at the Pera Palas Hotel that I hear the first news of modern history in the making. Those with short-wave radios have heard word from the Soviet Union that Gorbachev has been overthrown in a right-wing coup. Nothing more is known at the moment. I think of all the friends we made – Irena and Volodya and Edward and Sasha the Lenin impersonator – and I know that if the news is true things can only be worse for them. Selfishly, we can only be thankful for our extraordinarily lucky escape. If this had happened three days earlier, the *Junost* might never have left Odessa and we would have been stranded. If it had happened three *weeks* earlier we would never have been allowed into the Soviet Union.

The shadow of this great event hangs over the day, giving everything else we do a certain air of unreality. Some of the unreality is there already, especially in Room 411 of the Pera Palas Hotel. This is the room in which Agatha Christie wrote *Murder on the Orient Express*. It's small and rather cramped and you wouldn't get much writing done nowadays as they've just built an eight-lane highway below the window. After Agatha Christie died in 1976, Warner Brothers wanted to make a film about the mystery of eleven lost days of her life. An American medium, one Tamara Rand, said that in a trance she had seen an hotel in Istanbul and in Room 411 of this hotel she had seen Agatha Christie hiding the key to her diary under the floorboards. On 7 March 1979 the room was searched and a rusty key was found. The president of the hotel company, sensing Warner Brothers' interest but miscalculating their generosity, put the key in a safe and demanded two million dollars, plus fifteen per cent of the films profits. Here the key remains. Its age has been authenticated and as Agatha Christie was highly secretive about travel arrangements it's considered unlikely that the medium can have known about the Pera Palas before she saw it in her trance.

It all makes Room 411 rather a creepy place and I'm glad to get out and into the bustle of Pera Street – the mile-long main thoroughfare of Istanbul. The best way to see it is from one of the venerable red-and-cream trams that run its length, though I must confess I do catch breath when I notice the number of the tram we're on – 411.

I buy a Panama hat for under £6 from an elderly French-speaking Turk at a shop by the tram stop. I'm not keen on hats, but with the weather getting hotter by the day I can see the advantages.

As a result of climate, history and geographical position, Istanbul is the quintessential trading city. Russia and the Mediterranean and Europe and Asia meet here, and though a walk through the endless arcades of the old covered market gives an overwhelming sense of richness and variety, there is no better place to see trade in its rawest, purest form than the square outside the gates of the Beyazit II mosque and the impressive Islamic-arched entrance of Istanbul University. Here an extraordinary dance of commerce goes on. Groups are constantly gathering, splitting and reforming. Eyes are always on the move. These are furtive people on the very edge of the law, buying and selling in the spirit, if not the currency, of this great commercial city. There are Azerbaijanis, Iranians, Poles, Romanians, Ukrainians and Afghans. Most of them sell out of black plastic bags. I see Marlboro cigarettes traded for dollars, and plastic train sets, cheap East European trainers, an anorak, some metal ornaments – all attracting the crowds.

By the end of this hot, hard day the ministrations of a proper Turkish bath, a hammam, are irresistible.

The Cagaloglu Hammam, a splendid emporium of cleanliness, is this year celebrating 300 years in business, during which time it has cleaned, amongst others, King Edward VII, Kaiser Wilhelm, Florence Nightingale and Tony Curtis. I can choose from a 'self-service bath' (the cheapest option), a 'scrubbed assisted bath', a 'massage à la Turk – you'll feel years younger after this vigorous revitalizing treatment' or the 'Sultan service', which promises, modestly, that 'you will feel reborn'. At 120,000 Turkish lira, about £17, rebirth seems a snip, and after signing up I'm given a red-and-white check towel and shown to a small changing cubicle. Through the glass I can see a group of masseurs with long droopy moustaches, hairy chests, bulbous stomachs and an occasional tattoo. At that moment a Turkish father and son emerge from a cubicle and the little boy, who looks to be only eight or nine, is ushered towards the steam-room by one of these desperadoes with a reassuring gentleness and good humour.

The steam-room, the hararet, is set to one side of an enormous central chamber with walls and floor of silver-grey marble, and a dome supported by elegant columns and arches. While I work up a good dripping sweat from the underfloor heating I get talking to a fellow bather, an Italian. He has driven to Istanbul from Bologna, and had come quite unscathed through Yugoslavia, where there is a state of civil war, but had found newly-liberated Romania a dark and dangerous place. Gasoline was almost unobtainable. He bought a can which he found later to be water. I asked him if there was any more news from the USSR. He said he had heard that Leningrad had been sealed off and tanks had moved into the Kremlin.

Then it's my turn on the broad inlaid marble massage slab called the Gobek Tasi. I'm rubbed, stretched and at one point mounted and pulled up by my arms before being taken off and soaped all over by a masseur who keeps saying 'Good?' in a tone which brooks no disagreement. He dons a sinister black glove the size of a baseball mitt. (The brochure describes it as 'a handknitted Oriental washing cloth', but it feels like a Brillo pad.) Never have I been so thoroughly scoured. The dirt and skin roll off me like the deposits from a school rubber. How can I have been so filthy and not know about it?

There is a small bar giving on to an open courtyard at the back of the hammam. Sitting here with a glass of raki and a bowl of grapes luxuriating in the afterglow of the bath at the end of a long day, I feel as content as I ever could.

The last news of the day is that the port of Tallinn, which we entered three weeks ago, has been closed by a blockade.

DAY 45: *Istanbul to Selcuk*

Up at 6 a.m. to get down to Sirkeci station to buy a rail ticket for Izmir. Fraser is becoming more Cassandra-like each day. This morning he's heard news that a British businessman has been killed in Istanbul and British travellers are advised to be on their guard. Unfortunately no one's told us what to be on our guard against.

On the concourse of this station at the very end of Europe, where the Orient Express used to terminate, there is a large bas-relief of the head of Kemal Ataturk, founder of modern Turkey. His presence is as ubiquitous as Lenin's was in the Soviet Union, but unlike Lenin he is still widely revered and respected fifty years after his death. Even the cheerfully cynical Sevim, while telling us that he died of cirrhosis of the liver and had a prodigious sexual appetite, declares: 'This was a *great* man'.

We leave Istanbul at nine o'clock on the ferry MV *Bandirma* which takes four and a half hours to cross to the town of Bandirma on the north coast of what my school atlas used to refer to as Asia Minor. She is carrying nearly a thousand passengers – a mixture of Turkish students, businessmen clutching laptops, veiled Muslim women and foreign backpackers. The bars and cafés are already open and salesmen with drinks and sandwiches are working their way through the crowds.

Sevim looks scornfully round at some of the passengers. Turks are nomads, she feels the need to remind us, they've never settled anywhere, they use things, destroy them and throw them away. Fall into conversation with a Turkish actor, heading south to play a series of one-night productions. He misses the sixties, when there was a wealth of good writers. I ask him if there is a National Theatre in Turkey. 'Oh yes, they do the classics,' he smiles wryly, 'in a very classical way.' I wish him well and he gives me his newspaper which is full of the news of Gorbachev's fall. He is evidently under arrest in the Crimea, but information, like everything else in the Soviet Union, is in short supply.

At half-past one we land on the continent of Asia, and fighting past the sunglass salesmen, the pretzel-pushers and the shoe-shiners – 'White shoes very bad, sir,' they cry, pointing at my trainers – we find the station and board the four-coach, diesel-hauled Marmora Express for Izmir and the south.

The train passes through brown, dry fields and open treeless country. At a military air base jets are taking off at regular intervals – an ominous sight, remembering the news this morning and Turkey's border with the USSR.

In one of the fields a group of white-veiled women are tossing turnips, or possibly watermelons, into a tall trailer. Behind them rises the first substantial patch of high ground since we left Hammerfest twenty-eight days ago. As we near Balikesir the flat plain disappears altogether and we are winding our way through tall, wooded limestone hills that give way eventually to rocky gorges.

By nightfall we are in the land of legend and ancient history. Troy is nearby, Smyrna (now Izmir) sprawls by the sea and it's quite late by the time we pull into Selcuk, a couple of miles from the ancient city of Ephesus, where legend has it that the Virgin Mary died at the age of sixty-four.

At the guest-house I have a small whitewashed room with a plain pine table and a kilim that provides the only touch of colour. Outside my window at midnight the sound of street talk merges with the incessant swish and slap of sandals on the roadway.

DAY 46: *Selcuk to Ephesus and Marmaris*

At the entrance to the ruins of Ephesus by nine o'clock, to avoid the crowds. There is a gauntlet of stalls to be run before reaching the gates. Alongside the usual stacks of guide-books, fezzes, sun hats, pipes and dresses is a small army of little figures with enormous phalluses. They are reproductions of images which date from the earliest, pre-Christian history of Ephesus when it was the centre of the fertility cult of the goddess Cybele. They're now available as car key-rings. Basil buys a few as Christmas gifts.

I'm not a great one for ruins. Generally it requires an enormous outlay of imagination and patience for relatively scant reward, but the site at Ephesus is so rich that I can walk on 2000-year-old flagstones with recognizable buildings on either side – fountains, libraries and temples donated by the rich of Ephesus to extend their influence and generally impress people. The decorated columns and friezes are often still standing, whilst others lie broken and scattered on the ground. I stumble over history, down the hill, past the remains of a pre-Christian brothel and public latrine to the graceful façade of the Library of Celsus, built around AD 135 to house 12,000 scrolls – all destroyed when the Goths sacked the city in 262.

The latest invasion of Ephesus is well underway by mid-morning as the crowds flock to the largest classical ruin in existence after Pompeii, reducing it to yet another sight, robbing it of magic and atmosphere. The sun, reflected off the stones, burns from above and below and I'm glad when our filming's over and we can move on down to Marmaris and the sea.

This is the first unequivocally hot day of our journey. The bus passes through dry and buzzing hillsides covered with scattered bushes, low pine trees, and the occasional cypress-ringed graveyard. A heat haze rises from roadsides where peppers are laid out to dry in the blistering sun.

My thermometer registers 94 degrees at Cine, where we eat an excellent lunch at an otherwise empty roadhouse. Above our heads a dim TV picture shows army vehicles and flashing lights in Moscow. The waiter looks up and shakes his head. It's serious. People have been crushed to death by tanks. But this heat wraps everything in a blanket beneath which time and the outside world cease to exist.

103

Then, sixty miles further on, an extraordinary moment. We have stopped in the pine forest above Marmaris to film my bus descending into town. A car with a couple of drowsy picnickers is parked, doors wide open, in the shade of a tree. A Turkish voice chunters on from its radio. Sevim stops suddenly and listens, with a frown of concentration which gradually relaxes into a look of disbelief. She talks to us as she listens:

'The news from Moscow is that the coup is over . . . some generals are dead . . . ' She listens again. 'Gorbachev is coming back to Moscow.'

On this languid, lazy afternoon in southern Turkey, it seems unbelievable. History shouldn't happen as fast as this.

A few minutes later we have reached the shores of the Aegean, though the town of Marmaris is almost separated from the open sea by two tall headlands curving like crab claws to enclose a handsome blue-green bay. They call this the Turquoise Coast. The view from the harbour is wonderful, but the harbour itself is fringed by restaurants with tourist menus and expensive yachts, the fattest of which sports the red ensign and is rumoured to have Princess Margaret aboard.

DAY 47: *Marmaris to Rhodes*

When we leave our hotel some guests are already staking out sunbeds, and frankly, I wish I could join them. Our journey across the Mediterranean now looks a lot of effort. There is no direct maritime connection between Turkey and Egypt, but if we can reach Limassol in Cyprus there is a connection from there to Port Said. However, the Greek Cypriots, still bitter about the Turkish invasion of Cyprus in 1974, will not allow Turkish-registered vessels into their ports. Our only chance is to travel to Greece first and hope to pick up a boat to Limassol from there. This will add to our schedule and our workload which, with the whole of Africa still to go, is the last thing we need.

We join the queue for tickets on the ferry to Rhodes, the nearest of the Greek islands, fifty miles to the south. The fact that we are carrying equipment and luggage for a world trip does not make things easier. These small boats are hard pushed to squeeze 200 people aboard. But persuasive and persistent work by Clem and Angela secure us the places, and we join the backpackers and the Italian bikers. My last memory of Marmaris is a quayside shop sign advertising the services of 'Doctor Satan, Gynaecologist'.

The crossing to Rhodes starts idyllically as we push through the narrow gap of the bay and run out alongside the Bozburun peninsula in what is unarguably a turquoise sea. But a stiff westerly wind lurks round the end of the peninsula and whacks us hard on the starboard side. The Italians rush to the stern to lash down their BMWs, and it only takes one substantial wave across the upper deck to cause an exodus of distressed sunbathers clutching soggy paperbacks.

Around lunchtime we land below the well-preserved medieval fortifications of Rhodes town. The Knights of St John built them when they took over the island in 1309. The Turks then ruled for nearly 400 years until they were evicted by the Italians in 1912. Rhodes has only been a part of Greece since 1945. We book into a tiny, characterful guest-house called the Cava d'Oro built into the city walls and bearing the date 1281. Accommodation is simple and cramped and seems to attract backpackers with huge loads who get wedged in the doorway.

A fellow Yorkshireman – the astrologer Patric Walker – has invited us for tea at his house in Lindos, some fifteen miles away. Lindos is a compact little town with the neat, clean, sharp lines of its whitewashed buildings gleaming in the sunlight, which, this afternoon, is hot and hard and destructive. The thistles by the roadside are bleached yellow, and the wild flowers which apparently enjoy only two and a half weeks' glory have long since shrivelled. In the pebble-floored courtyard of an attractive corner house beside orange and lemon and tangerine trees, Patric Walker serves us a grand English tea (he's even had a cake decorated with a map of our journey) and warns us about Mercury being in retrograde. 'It's when the planet Mercury appears to be travelling backwards in the heavens – it isn't, but it appears to be . . . and it's a time when all forms of communication and travel plans tend to be disrupted.' Apparently it happens about three times a year, and it doesn't surprise me that it's in retrograde at the moment, and will be for the next week. As the last days of any period 'tend to be the trickiest', we should expect mounting problems between here and Egypt. He consults his book of planetary movements and offers us the cheerful news that it will happen again at the end of November – when we hope to be setting off from South Africa for the South Pole.

I don't think Patric likes to be the harbinger of bad news and seeing our glum faces he seeks to reassure us. Astrology, as he says, is an art, not a science. 'Everybody expects the astrologer to be infallible – you're not, you know. I can be as wrong as anybody else, particularly about . . . you know, my own life.'

His own life looks very nice to me. Especially over the top of the glass of champagne he offers us, looking out to sea beyond the rooftops of houses built by the Crusaders, as the sun begins to set. For the second time today I feel the insidious pull of the sedentary life.

DAY 48: *Rhodes*

Wake at 2 a.m. from a recurring dream of tanks in Moscow to a far worse cacophony from the road outside. Motorbikes skidding round corners, music and loud arguments. I should have realized, the day is for TV crews and the night is for the locals. Shut my balcony doors and wake an hour later pouring sweat. Open the doors and lie there rigid with sleeplessness as dogs take over the streets. Try to prop the doors half-open and nearly break the window but at least fall asleep from the effort. Not for long. An agonizingly slow street-cleaning truck finally lumbers by at half-past six. Half an hour later Clem and the crew are ready to go.

'Why so early?'

'Best time. Before the streets get busy.'

Vangelis Pavlides, a political cartoonist and local historian, has agreed to be my host in Rhodes. He appears on his vintage BMW motorbike and we grab some fresh bread from a local bakery before taking a walk round the Old Town. Vangelis is a good companion. He loves the city, though not uncritically. In his opinion it had a better sewage system 400 years before Christ than it does now. It also had a population of 300,000, now shrunk to 80,000.

One of the most handsome thoroughfares in Rhodes is the Street of the Knights. It's said to be the oldest street in Greece, following a line originally laid out in the fifth century BC. A collection of fine medieval stone façades rises up the hill, testimony to the great wealth accrued by the mysterious order of the Knights of St John, despite being sworn to poverty and chastity. The story, which Vangelis relishes, is that they infiltrated the island disguised as sheep. Though there were never more than 400 knights (if they wanted soldiers they employed mercenaries) they held the island until 1522. The Order, which took refuge in Malta, remains in existence to this day. It has close links with the Vatican and still owns properties on the oldest street in Greece.

Back in his apartment which is paved with slate slabs from Northern Greece, Vangelis kicks off his shoes and shows me some of the drawings for his history of medieval Rhodes. There is a lot of humour in the work – one knight encased in heavy armour is relieving himself through a large household tap. The apartment has many other delights, including a very old box camera which Vangelis inherited from his uncle's father, who used to say the Lord's Prayer to determine the length of the exposure. For lunch we eat pizza on his balcony which looks out towards a beach solid with holidaymakers. A thousand pink bodies propel a thousand red pedaloes slowly across the bay. Vangelis says many of his old neighbourhood friends have been driven away by the remorselessly increasing crowds of visitors, and he himself is away to Crete tomorrow for two weeks' peace on a sailing boat.

We are off even sooner. I just have time to ring my daughter and hear her GCSE results (I think this may be the real reason I didn't sleep last night). They're good and I'd like to celebrate, but we only have time to get down to the dockside and check ourselves on board the *Silver Paloma* – a cruise liner bound for Limassol. Her final destination is Haifa, and the majority of the passengers are Israeli families returning from holidays on the Greek mainland. The security implications are explained to us at some length, and we are told to take all precautions and report any unauthorized objects. Most of our gear has been stowed securely below, which produces a gem from Basil at dinner. When asked by Clem if he has one of his sauces to enliven a dull carrot soup he says loudly and with some exasperation, 'Oh no! The Bomb's in the hold.' (Readers who've just come in, see Novgorod.)

DAY 49: *Rhodes to Limassol*

Everything about the *Silver Paloma* is depressing. Breakfast is the first meal I've turned down on the whole journey. The smell of stale cigarette smoke hangs around the passageways and clings to the walls. The decks are empty but the slot machines are busy. Families bicker and argue. There seems little joy in it all.

Arrival at Limassol is protracted. We sit in one of the ship's reception areas, which is fitted out in a barren blend of vinyl, chrome and plastic, and wait over an hour for the disembarking queue to clear. This is followed by another half-hour's wait on the quayside in airless, muggy heat until we are allowed to begin unloading our equipment.

Times such as these are the low points of the journey. None of us is much refreshed after a night on the boat, and after thirty-two days of filming in the last five weeks and four national frontiers crossed in the last seven days alone we are all expending energy much faster than we can replace it.

We drive west from Limassol beside plantations where

oranges, lemons, avocados and kiwi fruit are grown in long orderly lines protected by avenues of eucalyptus and fir, then out onto higher ground where there is no shelter and the grapes on the vines are burnt brown by the sun. A fine Corinthian arch standing forlornly among thorn bushes, an amphitheatre which is still used for plays, and the remains of the Roman city of Curium lie next door to the ninety-nine square miles of the British Sovereign Area with its bobbies and post-boxes. (They were allowed only ninety-nine square miles because one hundred would have constituted an occupation.) For five miles, the road from Limassol to the west is effectively part of Britain and I suppose we could call this the eighth country we've passed through.

We are heading for a village near Paphos where Ariadne Kyriacu is today marrying Polycarpus Polycarpu. We have been invited to join the guests, which is not quite the honour it sounds, as there are likely to be over 3000 of them. A Cypriot wedding involves not only relatives but also the local community. It is not uncommon for a couple to advertise for guests in the newspaper. It's all seen as good for business.

A wedding is quite an affair, especially if it is, like the one today, traditional. About three o'clock the show gets on the road with a public shaving of the groom. Polycarpus is a modern Cypriot, a student in Germany, who looks very different from his beaming, ruddy-cheeked father who is the current head man of the village. He sits in the half-finished shell of the house that is being built for him and his wife, and with a brave smile submits to the attentions of an elderly barber who has a disconcerting habit of swatting flies away with his cut-throat razor.

After what is certainly the longest shave I've ever witnessed we all walk through the village to the church. I fall into conversation with the best man's wife, who turns out to be from Kent. She married her Cypriot husband after a holiday romance. They had a thousand guests, 'but then I didn't want a big wedding,' she explains.

At the church Polycarpus's bride arrives, dramatically attired in white with her pitch-black hair swept up through a band of flowers and spilling out in a mass of carefully disordered curls. She looks wondrous, like some Edwardian actress, tall, very slim, with a strong face and a long, straight nose. Then three priests, in no particular hurry begin a long recitation of the liturgy. A professional video recording is being made and the director, a man in a yellow jacket which clashes with everything, rushes about amongst the priests moving sacred objects and generally getting in everyone's way. The church is far too small for all the guests and people come and go as they please. Only the old widows – the 'blackbirds' as they call them – follow the service intently, their lips moving in time with the priests' words. Polycarpus and Ariadne remain standing heroically throughout this curious mixture of the spiritual and the secular until the moment comes for them to be linked with white ribbon, take communion and then process in a circle around a Bible.

But their work has hardly begun. At the wedding feast, held in the huge courtyard of what was once a monastery, they sit for three hours receiving guests. I am told that it is the custom on being received to slip the happy couple a small financial gift, and by the time I get there Polycarpus's pockets are stuffed with notes, of which he is occasionally relieved by one of the family.

We sit at long tables and tuck into lamb kleftiko, moussaka and To Rezi, a thick but tasty oatmeal mix which takes two days to cook and almost as long to eat. There is music and dancing, including one dance in which the marital bed is blessed, and four men in suits have to perform a particularly tricky soft-shoe shuffle while holding a mattress on their shoulders. There is still no respite for Polycarpus and Ariadne. They are dragged up on stage to cut the cake, and all goes well until the best man opens the champagne over-zealously and a stream of foam deluges the bridal pair. As champagne drips down his forehead I see Polycarpus's smile wither for a split second before he's back to being man of the moment and leading the hastily mopped-up Ariadne into a slow, rather inelegant dance which could be called the Lumbago. The reason it is so slow is that during the dance relatives and friends come up and pin money to the couple. Polycarpus is no Fred Astaire at the best of times and having to trip the light fantastic festooned with currency doesn't help. By midnight they must both be carrying close on a thousand pounds each, and I now understand those who say that these weddings, besides being good for public relations, can be run at a considerable profit. Not that that can be much consolation for Polycarpus, who is now quite seriously wilting, and the night still young. But his wife is beautiful and 3000 guests are having a great time and there's a near full moon in the cloudless sky.

DAY 50: *Limassol and Akrotiri*

Seeing families around the swimming-pool of our hotel reminds me of the summer holidays our family have enjoyed and the one I'm missing at the moment. Basil, detecting a sniff of homesickness, cheers me up with an account of a local festival he dropped in to see last night at which he witnessed the crowning of Miss Grape 1992. Her prize was £15 worth of chicken and a large fish.

There is a copy of the *Sunday Times* in the hotel – the first up-to-date English newspaper I've seen for two months. Gorbachev is to disband the Communist Party. The Ukraine and Estonia have declared independence. I have to read it again to believe it. Only ten days ago we were in the Ukraine, which even optimists thought would not see independence for thirty or forty years, and in a Soviet Union whose existence was inseparable from communism. Only five days ago the country was led by a group of hard-line generals. The USSR has blown up in spectacular fashion.

We are to spend this afternoon with the British forces at the RAF base in Akrotiri. Here very little has changed, or that's how it seems. There is a water shortage, which means that pitches have to be watered with 'treated effluent', i.e. sewage, but there is still polo and cricket and cream teas and brass bands.

111

In reality things have changed quite a bit. The garrison at Akrotiri has been reduced to 1500 from a peak of 5000. There is concern that the Turks and the Greek Cypriots may patch up their quarrel and the three bases the British still have on the island could be the first casualties of rapprochement.

Our papers checked, we are escorted onto the base past a weather bulletin board on which is scribbled the chalk message 'Cyprus will have a public holiday on the first day of rain'. A cricket match is in progress between a Youth XI and a Veterans XI, though how they can play in this heat, and on grass watered with recycled sewage, is beyond me. There is no alleviating breeze here, just air so thick with humidity it practically bubbles. But being British means not letting that sort of thing worry you, and during the interval the teams are tucking into cream buns and cups of hot tea as though it were a spring day in Hove. I ask one of the Veterans if he felt he'd lost much weight out there.

'Oh, about seven bottles of Carlsberg.'

The talk is mostly of sport rather than fighting, though the base had been on full alert during the Gulf War five months previously, when an extra 400 medical staff were drafted in to deal with expected casualties. The men I speak to regard Cyprus as a good 'tour' but some of the women are less keen. Because many of the civilian jobs on the base are open to local Cypriots, the forces wives find it very hard to get work, and life, after the initial euphoria over the sun, sea and sand, can become very routine. As one of them said with feeling, 'All you can do here is have babies'.

The band of the third battalion the Queen's Regiment brings 'Sussex by the Sea' to a stirring climax, the teams come out onto the pitch again, and I'm hoisted aloft in a Wessex helicopter to have a snifter with the commander of the British forces in Cyprus, Air Vice-Marshal Sandy Hunter and his wife Wilma. They live in a long, comfortable house on top of a fortified ridge, complete with their own helicopter pad. Our drinks are served by a Sudanese butler called Ahmed, a man of great presence and gravity who has worked for the

British for thirty-five years. He has family north of Khartoum, 'near railway station Number Six'. Hearing that it is on our route he urges me to visit their riverside village.

'We got island sir and we got home sir. Island very nice, we give you one very good day sir.'

We drive away from Sandy and Wilma's house along a ridge from which we have a fine view of the most beautiful sunset. On one side a long, wide, pale crimson sky stretches across hazy hills, while on the other a full moon is rising.

At midnight I walk along the beach by the hotel. A mile or two further on is Aphrodite's Rock. Legend has it that if you swim three times round it on the night of a full moon you'll live for ever. Well, to paraphrase the chief electrical officer on the *Junost*, 'Who wants to live for ever anyway?'.

I turn and head back to the hotel.

DAY 51: *Limassol to Port Said*

Today we embark on the last stage of our zig-zag progress across the Mediterranean, aboard the *Princesa Marissa*, a Cyprus-registered, 9500-ton vessel built in Finland in 1966, which now operates a two-day 'fun-filled' cruise from the 'Island of Aphrodite' to the 'Land of the Pharaohs'. As the fun-filled cruise costs a mere £100 all-in it's well subscribed, mainly by the British, who make up around 600 of the 750 passengers on board.

The party begins on embarkation as we are given a brochure with a programme of events: 'Enjoy the sailaway music of the Duo Zorba on Deck 7' . . . 'Relax to the sounds of Rainbow in the Ledra Lounge'.

The constant pounding of disco music above and below decks is broken only by loudspeaker announcements which all seem to feature the phrase 'Deck Sexy'. It turns out to be the Greek for Deck 6. A voluble Filipino steward shows me to my spacious cabin, complete with bath. 'Anything you want, you ask for Johnny,' he keeps repeating. I never see him again.

The journey due south to Port Said is a distance of 203 nautical miles, and will take fifteen and a half hours. Somewhere at sea we shall cross the thirty degree meridian, curling round to come in at Port Said at 31.17 East. Kill some of this time at the Gala Show, which features the impressively hard-working Melody Dancers, a group of showgirls who, backed by a Polish band, climax their act with a cancan of extraordinary athleticism and energy.

DAY 52: *Port Said*

My alarm sounds at 4.30. By five o'clock I'm packed, shaved, showered and off to the bridge for a first sight of Africa. My watchstrap breaks and I pray it isn't going to be that sort of day. The moon is still the only light in the sky, but way ahead on our starboard side is a tall flashing beacon and a long row of orange and white lights which must be Port Said. Below us a line of red and green flashing marker buoys indicates the mouth of the Suez Canal. As we pass another cruise ship – the *Romantica*, also from Limassol – one of her tugs breaks away and comes to manoeuvre us into position a little way out from the palm-fringed waterfront.

The first light of day breaks in the sky behind us. It's as if a veil has been lifted from the city and the dark, unfamiliar outlines resolve into handsome old colonial houses, with tall louvred doorways opening onto wrought-iron balconies, an elegant, arcaded Canal House, with its mosaic-covered dome and a fine lighthouse of yellow brick.

Port Said is not a major port of entry for passenger ships, most of which use Alexandria. This may partly explain why Louis Lines, who operate the *Princesa Marissa*, can keep their costs down, and why there appears to be no means of getting from the boat to the shore.

Then, slowly, a brown and rusty pontoon is uncoiled from the waterfront by men in boats all shouting at each other. When at last this steel snake reaches the ship, a crowd of salesmen rush along it and stand at the doors, making it almost impossible for anyone to disembark without tripping over a brass tray, a bubble pipe, a copper gong or a pile of cut-price Lacoste T-shirts.

Once the Cairo-bound day-trippers have left, we go with some relief for breakfast, but there isn't any. Even worse is to come. As the porters unload our gear the camera tripod rolls unnoticed into the Mediterranean. Could this be Mercury in retrograde? Should we have made other plans? I think it's just Egypt, where confusion seems an essential part of everyday life. There is no feeling here that life is a series of problems to be solved, rather that there is a human state, which is chaos, and that peace, calm and order is a heavenly state to which, Inshallah, we wretched mortals may one day aspire. Meanwhile six men are staring into the murky depths of the Mediterranean as if some Egyptian Lady of the Lake might suddenly hoist the tripod aloft, whilst six others are improvising something with a fish-hook on the end of a piece of string.

Romany Helmy, our good friend who looked after us on *Around the World in 80 Days*, suggests that we should go to Customs and get the formalities over with while he supervises the raising of the tripod.

The tripod is retrieved half an hour later by a diver whom Romany got out of bed, but it is another seven hours before Nigel, Fraser, Patti and Basil are cleared to leave Customs. Every single item on their lists is checked and double-checked, and in some cases triple-checked, during which time they are not allowed beyond the gates of the port. There are several problems. The Customs officials have never had to deal with a foreign film crew before. Port Said is a duty-free zone, and they cannot believe that we are not here to take advantage of this. But what seems to throw them completely, what they simply cannot comprehend, is that we are leaving the country, by land, through the Sudan. It appears to be quite beyond belief that anyone would want to do such a thing.

Those of us not directly responsible for the equipment can only wait, guiltily, at the Helnan Port Said Hotel, which is run, ironically, by a Scandinavian company.

In its grounds and along the Mediterranean shoreline Egyptian holidaymakers are engaged in frantic physical activity – running, judo, soccer, tennis and what appear to be aerobic classes. The screams of children playing in the pool mingle oddly with the wailing chant of the call to prayer.

The day's filming is wrecked by the long wait in Customs and for the crew the last straw is that all the restaurants in Port Said are dry, the work of a zealously Islamic mayor.

There are also mixed opinions over what it is safe to eat. Should we eat the salad, which looks appetizing but which my medical bible – Richard Dawood's *How to Stay Healthy Abroad* – does not recommend in Africa? Or the crayfish from the Med? In the end I eat both, because I'm terribly hungry.

DAY 53: *Port Said to Cairo*

Refreshed after eight and a half hours' sleep, and tempted by the cool of early morning, I go for a run with Patti along the beach. Fishermen are examining their catch which they have hauled up in long nets. A man with a child calls out to me as I pass. My Western reflex says beware, but it turns out that he only wants to ask where I am from and to wish me welcome.

Port Said doesn't figure on Western tour itineraries and happily the seafront remains typically Egyptian, complete with a ladies' beach where Arab women bathe fully clothed. Bathe is perhaps too strong a description for what consists essentially of wading into the waves and standing there.

The Customs nightmare of yesterday may well be repeated for we have to go through another check today when we leave the free port and enter the rest of Egypt, so we decide not to delay our departure for Cairo. We drive down Palestine Street, where we came ashore yesterday, and through squares with duty-free shops at ground level and rows of washing and occasional mattresses hung out to dry above. At cafés men – never women, I notice – play backgammon, and every now and then there is a reminder of the proximity of the Suez Canal, with a dramatic glimpse of a 50,000-ton tanker gliding across the end of a side street.

At the outskirts of the city there is a cheerful sign above the road: 'Have Nice Trip'. It is here that our troubles begin.

We are turned back at the Customs barrier and sent along a dusty carriageway to an address in the suburbs of Port Said. This turns out to be another Customs area, for buses only. As soon as our minibus pulls up outside salesmen cluster round brandishing chocolate, sunglasses, coffee cups, razor blades, make-up, watches and even plastic rattles. We sit and wait. The temperature is climbing up towards 100 Fahrenheit. Eventually we are let through into a courtyard and after some deliberation asked to unload all our equipment for examination. Romany is doing his best to prevail upon the officer in charge, telling him we have been through all this for seven hours yesterday and he has the paperwork to prove it. After an hour we are allowed to repack our bus and leave. As the imperious senior officer barks orders at the soldiers lounging by the gate, I notice his right hand is playing with a string of beads. We pull out into the road. A man supporting himself on a crutch toils by. He has a child on his back.

Egypt offers no gradual assimilation into Africa, no comfortable cultural transition. The strangeness of everything begins at the coast and doesn't let up.

For a while we avoid the busy Ismailia highway, and take a side road that runs alongside the Canal. It's quiet and restful down here. There is a station through which no train seems to pass, and a narrow side canal called the Sweetwater where kingfishers swoop, butterflies flicker in the reeds and there is not much noise until the wind sets the bulrushes hissing and whispering. Even when the northbound convoy comes up the Canal these massive vessels, hundreds of thousands of tons in combined weight, pass by almost soundlessly.

As the day fades we drive south, passing through canalside villages, past small children guiding donkeys at tearaway speeds, makeshift ferries caked in Nile mud plying the

117

waterways, orange-sellers at the side of the road. At Ismailia we turn west to run for seventy-five miles across the Eastern Desert to Cairo. Having extricated ourselves from Port Said morale is improved, and there is a further bonus in the shape of a breathtaking desert sunset. After the sun sets a rich peach afterglow remains, which as it dies seems to intensify to a raw golden red, like the embers of a dying fire.

Cairo seems more enormous and manic than I ever remember it. It's 9.30 in the evening but every road and side street teems with traffic, often blocked solid. The Egyptian theory of driving is simple – everyone else on the road is in your way. There is nothing else to do but call on whichever God you feel closest to and hold on tight.

DAY 55: *Cairo to Luxor*

Cairo, hard up against thirty-one degrees East, is the only point at which our Pole to Pole course coincides with my *80 Days* route. This time we stay only long enough for a day and a half of rest and recuperation. Not that anywhere beyond the confines of my hotel room can be described as restful, but if you can endure the demanding pace Cairo is a city of all sorts of hidden delights. Before we leave for the station I take a walk out onto the Nile Bridge and a long look at the river with which our destinies are to be linked for days and weeks ahead.

Late afternoon, stuck in traffic on the way to Rameses Station. At busy intersections everyone drives through red lights until they have to stop, which is usually when the light turns green. Nobody can then move until it becomes red again.

At the station, all the destination boards are in Arabic, and I have to ask a porter the platform for Luxor.

'Nine,' he assures me with confidence.

'No, no!' another man shakes his head with equal confidence, 'eight.'

I appeal to a sensible-looking man with glasses, 'Is it eight or nine for Luxor?'

'Luxor? . . . Eleven.'

By now it's beginning to sound like a bingo session, as passers-by helpfully shout numbers in my general direction. Fortunately a passageway is marked '8, 9, 10, 11', so I take that and am met at the other end by an extremely helpful and courteous railway official: 'Yes . . . it is Number Eight, sir'.

The train for Luxor leaves at half-past seven, from Platform Ten.

The sleeping-cars on the train are run by the Wagons-Lits company and are modern and well equipped, with air-conditioning, carpets, towels, coathangers, and venetian blinds. I'm served an airline meal on a tray and while Joseph, the coach steward, makes up my bed, I wander down to the bar. I had heard how badly the Gulf War had affected tourism in Egypt, and the sight of the barman quite alone seems to suggest things have not recovered. Andy and Bridget, an English couple on honeymoon, are the only others who come in. They couldn't take any more of Cairo. Apart from finding 'a cockroach as big as a cat' on her bed, Bridget professed herself disillusioned with the way friendship never seemed innocent, 'it always led to a shop'.

After a drink together I wish them *bon voyage* and they ask me if I'm going anywhere beyond Luxor.

I nod and try to reply as nonchalantly as possible, 'The South Pole'.

Not for the first time do I notice what a conversation killer this is.

DAY 56: *Luxor*

My sleeping-car berth is comfortable but the ride is ferocious. For the last two hours to Luxor the train seems possessed by devils, and Joseph has no need to knock so hard at my door, I'm awake and hanging on for dear life.

'It's 4.45,' he announces, and he lays a tray of unidentifiable clingwrapped things beside me, ' . . . nice breakfast, sir.'

119

At 5.35 in the morning the train pulls into Luxor, known by the Greeks as Thebes, 420 miles south of Cairo, in Upper Egypt. I cannot conceal my excitement at being here for the first time in my life. Basil, never even in Africa before, is finding the whole journey beyond description: 'This is a great picnic,' he raves, 'this is the Mother of Picnics'.

Luxor station is tastefully monumental in decoration, with tall columns, gilded details on the doors, eagle heads and a hieroglyphic design somehow incorporating power-stations, railways and ancient history.

Opposite this grand façade there is a bicycle leaning against a wall, and lying in the dust between the bike and the wall is its owner, who hasn't had to get up as early as we have. Figures materialize from the pre-dawn gloom to offer us taxi rides. You will never stand on your own for long in Egypt.

We shall be joining a Nile cruise for the next leg of our journey, and as we drive along the river to find our boat – the *Isis* – I can see serried ranks of chunky four-storeyed vessels, maybe a hundred in all, lined up along the river bank, awaiting the day the tourists come back.

My guide to Luxor is a tall, straight, matchstick-thin aristocrat of the business whose name is Tadorus but who asks me to call him Peter . . . 'It's easier'. I would rather call him Tadorus, but he doesn't look the sort you argue with. He wears a white djellabah and cap and carries with him a Chaplinesque walking-stick, which he often rests across his shoulders. An enormous pair of Esprit sunglasses almost obscures his striking but emaciated face, and when he removes them they reveal a pair of moist, sad eyes. He is eighty-three years old, and as a boy of fourteen was present when the archaeologist Howard Carter first pushed open the door of Tutankhamun's tomb.

Peter takes me across on the Nile ferry to a cluster of mud buildings on the West Bank opposite the city. We are driven past fields of sugar cane and alongside an irrigation canal financed by the Russians in 1960. The greenery ends abruptly as we climb a winding road up into barren, rubble-strewn desert. We pass an ostentatious modern cafeteria. 'The Temple of Coca-Cola,' Peter announces, permitting himself a shade of a smile. Then we are into the Valley of the Kings, which resembles a gigantic quarry, littered with rock debris, bleached white by the sun. We leave the bus and walk up towards the tombs in dry and scorching heat. Peter estimates the temperature at forty Celsius, 104 Fahrenheit. I ask him if it's usually like this.

'No . . . no,' he shakes his head dismissively, 'last month was hot!'

This vast necropolis contains the remains of sixty-two Pharaohs of the New Kingdom, established in Thebes 3000 to 3500 years ago. It was discovered – 'rediscovered', as Peter corrects me – in 1892. Only forty of the tombs have been found, and all, bar one, had been emptied by robbers. That's why Howard Carter's discovery of Tutankhahmun's burial chamber was of such significance. Because it had been built beneath another tomb (that of Rameses VI) the rubble left by the robbers had helped to hide the entrance, and what Peter saw with Carter that day in 1922, was Tutankhamun's treasure exactly as it had been sealed in the tomb 3300 years earlier. I asked him what he could remember of the moment of discovery.

'We find all the beds and the chairs and the statues . . . stacked one on top of the other up to the ceiling.'

'What was Howard Carter's reaction?'

'He became crazy . . . when he have a look to the state coffin, which it is made of solid gold, that thick gold, not like our gold, twenty-four carat gold, he became crazy, you know . . . hitting like that.' Here Peter slapped at the sides of his face with his long bony hands in a passable imitation of a pools winner, 'Unbelievable, unbelievable'.

I asked him about the curse that was supposed to have been visited on anyone who opened the tomb.

'No curse . . . no curse at all.'

'It was said that a mosquito flew from the tomb as it was opened.'

'No mosquito. They say there is a mosquito came out of the

tomb and bite him and he died . . . he discovered the tomb in 1922, he's still inside the tomb up to 1927 . . . he died in 1939, he died a very very old man.' And not from a mosquito bite apparently.

We walk down into the tomb of Rameses III. The walls are covered in rich paintings and complex inscriptions illustrating the progress of the Pharaoh on his journey through the underworld which is filled with wicked serpents, crocodiles and other creatures waiting to devour him. Because of the dry desert air, they are well preserved, an extraordinary historical document.

The sun is setting behind the Valley of the Kings when we return on the ferry. At this indescribably beautiful time of day, when the rich golden brown of the lower sky spills on to the surface of the Nile, turning it an intense amber, and the palm trees along the bank glow for a few precious minutes in the reflection, it is not difficult to imagine the power and spectacle of a funeral procession bearing the God-King's body across this same river three and a half thousand years ago, at the beginning of his last and most important journey.

DAY 57: *Luxor*

An early start to catch the sunrise over the ruins of the Temple of Karnak. The name is taken from the town of Carnac in Brittany and is a reminder that it was the French who, in 1798, rediscovered this temple under thirty feet of sand. We have a local Egyptologist with us who has obtained permission for us to climb up onto one of the pylons – the massive 150-foot high towers that flank the entrance to the temple. This involves a scramble up a narrow passageway enclosed between the tomb of Seti II and the pylon wall. We must have disturbed a colony of bats, for the dark tunnel is suddenly filled with flapping creatures trying to find a way out. My hat is knocked off as they brush my face. At the top, the view is splendid but the sunrise isn't and the crew return to our boat for breakfast.

I decide to stay in the temple and enjoy some pre-tourist solitude.

The buildings and the monuments here are as impressive as any man-made thing I have seen in the world. They were created to extol the power and strength of the Pharaohs and the gods whose likenesses they were, and it is impossible to walk amongst the columns and beside the obelisks and not feel the presence of this power. In the Hypostyle Hall, where 134 columns rise in a symbolic forest, sixty feet high, from bases whose circumference could just be contained within a ring of twelve people with outstretched arms, I feel a sense of awe and wonder unlike any I've experienced before, compounded by the awareness that similar feelings must have been experienced here over thousands of years.

I'm brought back down to earth as the first wave of tourists appears, adjusting cameras, complaining about meals the night before and arguing over who has the air tickets. Then I catch sight of Tadorus, whom I must remember to call Peter, like a white wraith among the massive pillars, stick resting across his shoulders. If you need a lost sense of wonder restored, then Peter is the man. Despite his eighty-odd years spent in and around these buildings with scholars and archaeologists, he still finds some things unexplainable. A statue of Rameses II, ninety-seven feet high and made from a single piece of granite, weighs 1000 tons. Cranes nowadays can only lift 200 tons, yet this massive statue was brought to Luxor from Aswan overland, 3000 years ago. Peter strikes a theatrical pose, 'How, Tadorus, they say?' He pauses and his big, round, sad eyes blink slowly. 'My answer, magic.'

The temple of Abu Simbel, further south, was, he tells me, aligned by the ancient Egyptians so that the sun shone onto the face of Rameses twice a year – once on his birthday and once on his coronation day. When Abu Simbel was re-sited in a forty-million-dollar operation to save it from the rising waters of Lake Nasser, all the calculations of the world's experts could not enable the sun to shine on Rameses' face more than once a year.

Peter shakes his head sorrowfully, 'Nothing better,' he sighs, 'nothing better.'

Here is surely a man born 3000 years too late. I'm sad to say goodbye to him.

It is September now and there are little things a traveller tends to forget, such as haircuts. I repair to a barber's shop in the back streets of Luxor. My barber is called Allah Gmal Idil, and he is very proud of his establishment, and of his two sons who stand and watch the whole procedure. I fear the worst and get the best from Allah: a good haircut, a cut-throat shave, a rub with pomagne scent, a trim of the eyebrows and even an assault on the nostril hairs.

In the evening, back on the *Isis*, I'm on deck looking out over another Nile sunset and dreaming off into the past when the present rudely reasserts itself.

'You don't know how Sheffield Wednesday went on last night?'

Pat and Gerald Flinders, two of our fellow passengers on the cruise down to Aswan, are from the town of my birth. Gerald has been studying Egyptology at night school.

'He can write National Westminster Bank in hieroglyphics,' says Pat proudly.

'Why would he want to do that?' Roger asks.

Pat seems surprised at the question. 'Because he works there.'

They join about twenty others whom we meet this evening, including a family from Watford, one of whom by extraordinary coincidence works in the council department responsible for twinning arrangements with Novgorod. There are three middle-aged Danish ladies on a girls-only holiday, a French couple, two handsome Italians, two Montreal Canadians, and assorted English and Americans. There is a resident archaeologist called Abdul – a big man with a shaved head. We shall set sail in the early hours of tomorrow morning for Aswan, which is a little over 120 miles upstream. It will take us a leisurely three days.

DAY 58: *Luxor to Aswan*

I'm up on deck at 7 a.m. The light is soft and gentle, and the air dry and warm. *Isis* glides along the lightly rippled surface of the Nile with solid ease. On either bank smoke rises from huts of mud and straw. A line of people who have just landed from a felucca – the traditional single-masted sailing boat of the Nile – winds up the short, steep, hard-baked mud bank in the shade of locust and palm trees. Two boys in a rowing boat, painted the green of Islam, moor up by a fishing net. One of the boys smacks at the water with a long pole while the other bangs a drum to attract the fish. A buffalo grazes, donkeys wait in the fields. There are no roads or cars or railways, there is no concrete or neon. It is a timeless scene, containing almost unchanged all the elements of nature that cover the walls of tombs and temples.

By nine o'clock the surroundings have changed considerably. We have reached the lock at Esna, thirty miles from Luxor, a bottleneck of quite serious proportions which they don't mention in the brochures. The lock was built by the British in 1908, and it has room for only one ship at a time. It takes thirty-five minutes to get each one through and, as they alternate between those going north and south, it can mean a seventy-minute wait; if you're lucky. But the lock also incorporates a swing road-bridge so it is closed every alternate hour. There are four ships ahead of us, and Wahid, our cruise director, estimates that we will not be through until late afternoon. 'And this is not the busy time,' he adds gloomily, 'from late September it will start to be the busy time . . . during, let's say, New Year's Eve, sometimes it reaches up to twenty-four ships each side.'

He remembers once being held up for forty-eight hours.

So we drop anchor beside the noisy construction site of the new two-berth lock which will not be ready until 1993. It's easily the least beautiful stretch of the Nile, and we have seven hours to enjoy it.

As we watch one of the cruise ships negotiating the lock like a fat woman trying to get through a turnstile, our Egyptian pilot – Mohammed Ali Abu el Makeran by name – sits by the wheel, one leg hooked up under a striped djellabah. He has been with Hilton Cruises since they began in 1963, and has the quiet smile of one to whom patience is not a virtue but a way of life. He has fourteen children, he says, and they all live in his house. He tells me their names but apologizes for not being able to remember the last five.

To pass the time, Wahid and Abdul the archaeologist decide to mount an expedition to the temple at Edfu, and to this end the *Isis* draws up alongside the river wall, where we are immediately besieged by traders. They obviously know what Nile cruise tourists like to buy and it's revealing that most of their wares are for women and consist largely of flashy sequinned dresses – probably good for a night on the Nile but a bit of an embarrassment back in Widnes. If anyone on board shows the faintest glimmer of interest they throw the item up in a plastic bag, shouting 'One pound to look!. One pound to look!' One bag lands with a soft plop in the swimming-pool. No one pays the pound but persistence pays off. One of the Danish ladies has bought a slinky black number with 'Egypt' picked out in gold and Pat from Sheffield has just caught something in blue.

'We women can't resist shopping,' she says and leaning over the side, shouts down a price. She looks pleased at the aggrieved response.

'I love to haggle!'

The sound of Yorkshire and Arabic haggling drifts across the Nile. Pat's husband is more interested in our mutual connection with Sheffield than shopping. Did I know that the British Open Barber's Shop Quartet Champions hail from Sheffield?

I'm more worried about tonight's fancy-dress party at which everyone is required to 'do a turn', and I use the quiet time after the others have gone off to Edfu to learn the Percy Bysshe Shelley poem 'Ozymandias':

> I met a traveller from an antique land,
> Who said two vast and trunkless legs of stone
> Stand in the desert . . .

Two curly-headed local boys approach the lock wall making signs on their palms for baksheesh. Instead I give them 'Ozymandias', at full volume and with attendant mime. As I reach the end, they applaud as enthusiastically as only a couple of natural actors can.

After an Oriental buffet the evening's fancy-dress party gets under way, presided over with enthusiasm by Abdul. I have secured a makeshift Roman centurion outfit which is not quite long enough to cover an expanse of Marks and Spencer underpants, and Mirabel and Patti have sportingly agreed to be a pair of concubines and lead the audience participation by holding up the words of 'Ozymandias'. At the last minute I think it might be a bit sexist to call them concubines and suggest that Abdul announce them as handmaidens.

'Oh no,' he says briskly, 'concubines is *much* better.'

The glamorous Italians come along as Pinocchio, and Pat and Gerald as a pair of music-hall artistes. Roger bravely dons drag as Mrs Mills and sings 'The Mighty Dnieper', and the people from Watford as the Mayor of Edfu and his family, despite being mercilessly rude about the Egyptians, win first prize, largely as a result of some virtuoso belly dancing from their daughter. But for me the unquestioned highlight of the evening was seeing Nigel operating the camera dressed as a Pharaoh. This was surely the period of history his body was intended for.

DAY 59: *Luxor to Aswan*

Up on deck to watch the sunrise. It's Nigel's birthday, but he's already out and about trying to find somewhere to set up the camera, and muttering darkly about the vibration of the ship's engines. It's cold enough for a sweater as I settle down to watch the show. By six o'clock the first reflections of pre-dawn light can be glimpsed in the water. The concentration of light grows slowly, expands and then widens into an expanse of pale pink, extinguishing the stars. A half-hour later the crest of the sun edges into a whitening, cloudless sky and within a matter of seconds it is riding free of the mountains, growing in power and brilliance until it is a ball of molten gold. At this point, as if sunlight-activated, the onboard muzak tinkles into life . . . 'Raindrops keep falling on my 'ead'. I'm not sure they'd know what a raindrop is round here.

After breakfast we put in at Kom Ombo, twenty-five miles from Aswan, to visit the Temple of Sobek, the sacred crocodile. Pat is persuaded to come along despite claiming she has 'temple fatigue', and despite a brisk wind which is continually blowing her straw hat off.

'This hat's a mixed blessing,' I hear her muttering, as she chases it across the Hypostyle Hall.

Abdul, his hairless skull protected by a knitted white cap, is a proficient but intimidating guide. He reels off facts, figures, details and explanations with unassailable authority and then fixes us with a piercing gaze,

'Any questions?'

Having learnt in the last thirty seconds that the frog is a symbol of life, that this temple is dedicated to a sparrowhawk as well as a crocodile, that women in ancient Egypt delivered babies in a sitting position and that in the mummification process the brain was pulled out through the nostrils, no one really knows where to begin.

At 2.15 in the afternoon we reach Aswan, the capital of Upper Egypt, 550 miles from Cairo. The Nile begins to break up at Aswan, and will not, for several hundred miles, be the orderly river we've come to know and love. It is divided by the bulk of Elephantine Island, then broken by a series of cataracts and two dams.

My thermometer, laid out for five minutes in the sun, registers 121 Fahrenheit, 50 Celsius. The river seems busier here. Maybe it is because the town itself is bigger than Luxor, and contains modern high-rise blocks and a four-lane Corniche, or perhaps the narrowing of the river around the islands concentrates the traffic. Feluccas with weirdly misspelt English names, like *Hapey Tripe*, drift about, looking for tourist business.

Bid our farewells to Wahid and Abdul and Gerald and Pat and seek out the Old Cataract Hotel. Try out one of the fiacres lined up hopefully along the Corniche. My driver is called Shehan, and he's very proud of Abla, his black horse with white copper blinkers and the hand of Fatima on the saddle. Shehan says that the Gulf crisis has been very bad for business: 'For a year nobody come'.

I ask him what he did during that time.

'Sleep,' he replies matter-of-factly. 'My horse sleep at my home. I sleep in the car.'

It's belly-dancing night at the Cataract Hotel. The audience consists almost entirely of tour groups, but Romany assures me that the belly-dancer is the real thing. Every now and then she will lead some victim from one of the tables to dance with her. All this does is demonstrate that belly-dancing is not something anyone can do after a few beers. One grey-haired man is so confused by the encounter that he wanders the room in a daze, unable to find where it was he was sitting.

Romany, who has already given Nigel a djellabah for his birthday, goes down to the floor for a word with the dancer, and glances over in our direction. Nigel disappears like greased lightning, not to be seen again until his birthday's over.

DAY 60: *Aswan*

There is a wide wooden balcony outside my room at the Old Cataract Hotel, and from it one of the most extraordinarily rich views one could wish for. It's a mixture of the mundane and the dramatic. Directly below me are the terraces and gardens of the hotel, lined with chairs, tables and sunshades. Below them, at the waterside, are the feluccas, their tall masts and angled sail-booms rising above the clusters of palm trees. Elephantine Island rises up in mid-stream; the smooth granite rocks at its water's edge resemble elephants bathing, and above them is a collection of ruined buildings dating from as far back as the 3rd Dynasty – 4000 years ago – when Elephantine Island was the centre of the worship of the god Khnum, who, among other things, created mankind. Beyond the island is the desert. Low, bare, dusty hills, in the middle of which, solitary and exposed, stands the domed mausoleum of Aga Khan III, spiritual leader of the Ismaili Muslims, who died in 1957. The story goes that he suffered from severe rheumatism, and was told that a cure would be to rest his feet in desert sand. He came to Aswan, stuck his feet in the sand, was duly cured and gave orders that he be buried here.

I spend some of the day relaxing in a felucca, sailed at a leisurely pace by Captain Peckry, a twenty-one-year-old Nubian. Clasping a cigarette between his lips, he moves the heavy single-sailed boat with some skill, but seems quite bored by the whole thing, only coming to life as we are heading back to shore. Out of the blue he asks if I would like to go to a Nubian wedding tonight.

'Will there be anything to drink?' I inquire, knowing the Moslem views on these matters.

'Beer, whisky . . . hash,' replies Peckry, cheerfully. I feel rather pathetic for saying I might go and knowing full well I won't, though he has a felucca to recover in tomorrow, and we have a long, long way to go.

DAY 61: *Aswan*

We are on our way out of Egypt at last. From tomorrow we shall cease for a while to be tourists and become travellers. Soon we shall exchange the cosseted comforts of Cataract Hotels and Hilton Cruises for the uncertainties of a public ferry into a country which my guide-book describes as 'fraught with political turmoil, economic chaos, civil war, drought, famine, disease and refugee crisis . . . '

We travel in hope rather than certainty, having met people who have waited six weeks for the ferry into Sudan. We drive one last time along the Corniche, past acacia trees in bloom, and the Police Rowing Club, and the intriguing sign 'Pedaloos for hire', out of the town and along the first dam ever laid across the Nile, by the British, in 1902.

The British dam looks like a toy now, compared with the Soviet-built monster which replaced it three and a half miles upstream, creating Lake Nasser which stretches over 300 miles, into the Sudan. The approach to the High Dam is beneath a web of overhead power lines, past soaring concrete monuments to Soviet-Egyptian co-operation, and all the trappings of modern military security – radar, anti-aircraft guns, camouflaged helicopters, silos, dug-outs, bunkers and early warning systems. This could be described as overkill, but, as someone chillingly pointed out, the dam at Aswan is 650 feet higher than Cairo and Alexandria, and if it were to burst Egypt would be virtually wiped out.

This complex is the nerve centre of Egypt, from which half of the country's electrical power and ninety-nine per cent of its water flow. Its importance is colossal, but so is the investment needed to keep it going. Hamdy Eltahez, the Chairman of the High Dam Authority, who showed me round, was blunt about the need for outside help. A massive programme to replace all twelve Russian-built turbines with American models is currently under way. But there is now a new problem. The lake behind the dam is silting up rapidly. Since 1964, there has been an eighty-two-foot build-up of sediment at the Sudanese end of the lake. At this rate the water flow will be rapidly reduced and in some cases cut off altogether. Eltahez and Egypt are looking for a new international saviour, someone to invest in the vast costs of digging a by-pass canal around the silted-up area. To invest in nothing less than diverting the Nile.

Some people question the wisdom of building the dam at all, pointing out that the yearly flooding of the Nile provided vital fertility, which now has to be provided artificially; this is expensive and destructive. The Nubians question why they had to lose seventy-five villages and have thousands of their people resettled to make way for the lake. But Eltahez is adamant. The Aswan Dam saved Egypt in the nine years of drought between 1979 and 1988.

Whichever way you look at it, it is a truly extraordinary

undertaking, the only project in modern Egypt to rival the works of the Pharaohs.

DAY 62: *Aswan to Wadi Halfa*

At the gates of the Eastern Harbour, beneath an imposing sign announcing the jurisdiction of the 'Aswan Governate, High Dam Ports Authority', an official wearing a 'Port Police' armband attempts to hold the world at bay with a red loudhailer. Cars and trucks piled with crates and packing cases hoot their way past men and women piled with refrigerators, cabinets and bulging roped sacks. Porters in frayed blue cotton jackets stand, confused and vacant, waiting to be shouted into action. A boy with a dustpan and long-handled brush dabs ineffectually around the feet of the throng. There is not a white face to be seen, and even Western clothes are a rare exception in a sea of chadors – veils covering the heads and bodies of the women – and grubby djellabahs, the long wide-sleeved robes of the men.

Slowly, patiently, this mass of people and possessions moves through the Customs building and out towards a buff-hulled 160-foot ferry boat called the *Sinai*. It's a hard worked, stocky, unglamorous vessel with an apparently unlimited capacity to absorb everyone *and* their kitchen sinks. The authorities, for their part, have done what they can to make getting aboard as difficult as possible. Passengers must squeeze between unloading trucks on one side, and barbed wire, a link fence and sandbags on the other. Their progress is further impeded by an official of the Port Authority with wavy black hair and a wonderful repertoire of hand gestures who seems unable to communicate on any level less than uncontrolled fury. The slightest thing sets him off, igniting a Fawltyesque rage which quite cheers people up.

As this is the first ferry out of Aswan for two weeks it is full to capacity, which I'm told, with a vague shrug, is anywhere between 500 and 700 passengers, though I can see only two lifeboats, neither of which looks capable of taking 350 souls. We shall be on board for one night, covering the 186 miles to Wadi Halfa in roughly fifteen hours.

There are three decks on the *Sinai* and the good news is that we have cabins to ourselves. The bad news is that it's almost impossible to reach them as the central companion-way fills up with crates, sacks, boxes and their owners. No one is able to move anyone else out of the way as there is nowhere out of the way to go. I walk up onto the top deck to watch the loading, but there is little shade and the temperature is over 100 degrees. Return to my cabin to read Alan Moorehead's *The White Nile*, only to find my cabin has filled up with some of the thirty boxes of drinking water we are carrying with us. Once I've sorted these and my bags onto the top bunk I lie down, but the commotion in the gangway outside makes sleep impossible. There are no locks and every now and then an Arab face peers in before slamming the door again.

At 4.15 the barriers have gone up at the dockside and it appears everyone is aboard. The passengers, mainly Sudanis who have come to Aswan to buy things not available in their own country, sit cocooned by their possessions, waiting patiently. Despite the overcrowding there is no feeling of pressure. People talk and joke with each other, and children play up and down the ladders. On the top deck prayer mats are being laid out and small groups (always of men) are gathering around the mullahs, as pupils before their teacher.

With an ear-splitting blast of the horn the *Sinai* pulls away from the jetty at a quarter to five, past one of the old ferries, of which only the bows can be seen, rising out of the water at an angle of forty-five degrees.

We are on the waters of a lake that is younger than I am. Beneath the waves are the granite cliffs of the Nile Valley from which so many of the great monuments of Ancient Egypt were carved. Many of these monuments of the past, luckier than the Nubian villages of the present, were saved from the floodwater by a massive international aid programme to dismantle and re-site them. The Temple of Kalabsha, built around the time of

Christ, is now perched on a headland close to the Eastern Harbour, after being moved thirty-seven miles in 13,000 pieces. As we sail slowly away to the south the sight of its pylon and the columns of its Hypostyle Hall are a last reminder of the extraordinary and enigmatic power of Ancient Egypt.

At seven o'clock the captain, Mahmoud il Sudani from Alexandria, turns muezzin and broadcasts prayers from the bridge. Almost 200 people gather on the deck, bowing, in ranks six deep, towards the low ragged mountains in the east, beyond which lie empty desert, the Red Sea, and the holy shrine of Mecca, 500 miles away.

Our own polar Mecca is still many thousands of miles off, but as the sun sets we cross the line of the Tropic of Cancer, and feel we are making progress.

Basil, busy avoiding the attentions of a mullah who is trying to convert him, has discovered the dining-room and, with the proviso that we bring our own plates and cutlery, is recommending it for dinner. Carrying my camp cutlery set (made in China) I fight my way to the galley, only to find the door barred by a tall, turbaned figure with a gaze of dervish-like intensity. Like some *maître d'* gone berserk he occasionally emerges to deal very fiercely with the queue, thrusting them back and shooing them away. It turns out that the dining-room is also the immigration office and very few people are queuing for the food. Chicken noodle soup, followed by macaroni (which I am assured is a typically Egyptian dish) with a pungent meat and tomato sauce, chicken, chips and fresh baked faturia – crisp, bap-like bread rolls – are eaten to the accompaniment of constant tapping at the portholes by those wanting to have their passports (pale blue for Sudan and green for Egypt) examined and processed.

Whenever I have ventured into the washing and lavatory area it has been full of people cleaning their feet before prayer, and now the basins are blocked and water sloshes around the floor. The squat toilets are foul-smelling and permanently full.

To bed, climbing into my own sheet sleeping bag for the first time, and donning my head-torch to read about conditions during the siege of Khartoum in 1884, which don't sound a lot different from what we're undergoing now.

DAY 63: *Aswan to Wadi Halfa*

On the deck of the *Sinai*, directly in front of the bridge, is a three-piece suite, upholstered in claret velour, with worked wooden legs and decoratively curved arms. No one seems to know to whom this fragment of living-room belongs, but all sorts of people rest in it for a while. So it is that I find myself entering the Sudan on a sofa.

Sudan, the largest country in Africa, stretches from the Red Sea in the east to within a few hundred miles of Nigeria in the west, from the Tropic of Cancer almost to the Equator. Foreign visitors are not encouraged.

The first sight of its northernmost town, Wadi Halfa, is of an exposed rocky headland, on which stands a collection of open-sided tented structures, a handful of vehicles and a number of waiting figures moving across the rocks as we approach. Their djellabahs are caught by a light breeze, giving their movements a dreamlike quality.

There is no port, and there are no other vessels. The Sudanese Customs officers are slow and thorough, removing personal items and laboriously copying serial numbers. The cumbersome process of examination and paperwork seems to bear out the rule that the more forms you have to fill in the less efficient the country is likely to be.

In the end they confiscate two videos of *Around the World in 80 Days*, which are taken off for inspection, while we are allowed, after a three-hour wait, to step ashore and find transport into the town, which lies three miles away. Accompanying us are two minders from the Ministry of Information (and any country that has a Ministry of Information must have something to hide). I squeeze onto the back of a pick-up truck in which a dozen people are already standing, and we drive off across a sandy wasteland dotted with rocks and scrubby bushes. Then dwellings of the most primitive kind appear, some of them little more than cloth or skins stretched across four poles. They give way to small mud huts and eventually to a sprawl of long, low, painted buildings, one of which is the Nile Hotel.

The hotel comprises a series of concrete courtyards with communal washing facilities – there is cold running water between six and seven, morning and evening – and basic rooms with brightly painted walls. It's plain and unadorned but a haven from the bleak and burning desert.

There will be no cold beers for a while as Sudan is run according to strict Islamic law, which forbids the use of alcohol. Nor is there any lunch at the hotel. We have to dig into the stocks of cheese spread, tinned tuna and Marks and Spencer chicken breasts, which Angela has assembled in what must have been the Mother of all Shopping Expeditions. I place my thermometer in the sunshine on the window-sill of my room, where it registers 128 Fahrenheit, fifty-four Centigrade. I have been nowhere hotter in my life.

The proprietor of the hotel, Ibrahim Abbas, a tall, dignified, melancholy character, brings out two photographs, and I understand his sadness. One shows an elegant waterfront of distinctive wooden-balconied houses alongside a fine mosque with decorated minaret. The next shows nothing but water lapping around the pinnacle of the minaret.

'The waters come at night,' he remembers, ' . . . pushed down the houses. It was terrible.' It was in August 1964 that Lake Nasser finally engulfed the old Wadi Halfa.

4 p.m. I lie on a thin grubby mattress in my room. The air is unmoving. The thermometer shows ninety-eight Fahrenheit, but it's dry heat, just bearable. Flies settle on my mouth and nostrils until I grow tired of waving them away and fall into a light sleep. The room seems hotter when I wake. I blink out at an implacable sky. Beside my bed my Braun alarm clock sits on a pink metal table next to a chair with a plastic strip seat. The walls are bare, with a pale blue wash over chipped and scuffed plaster.

Around five o'clock I hear the wailing sound of a distant

locomotive, and within minutes the hotel is galvanized. This is the moment for which they have been waiting a month – the arrival of the Khartoum train. The hotel suddenly fills up – every bed, inside and outside, is mobilized.

At the cooler end of the day we pay a visit to the Governor of Wadi Halfa, an imposing, charismatic man with a greying beard who speaks good English in a soft deep voice. He has only recently been appointed. He is critical of the way things have been run.

'Since twenty-six years when old Wadi Halfa was flooded they have done nothing . . . only wait for the train and the ferry.' And, he might have added, the possibility of being flooded again if the water behind the dam should rise to 182 metres. It has once reached 178. But this governor is a quiet optimist and is pushing ahead with various projects to drag Wadi Halfa out of its lethargy, including an irrigation programme to help the town grow all its own wheat.

He offers us tea and sweets and talks of the diversity of these big African countries – there are 270 languages in the Sudan alone. The Governor reveals that he was once Member of Parliament for Darfur in the far west, but concludes, 'I have enough of politics, now I like to work with the people'. I can't help feeling, as I leave, that this capable man has been sent as far away from the present government as possible, and that for a politician Wadi Halfa is the Siberia of the Sudan.

The 'Nile Hilton', as the crew have christened our hotel, is packed tonight. There are bodies everywhere, and voices and shufflings and comings and goings, but the cold shower is spectacularly refreshing, and it's down to ninety-two degrees in my room. As I lie down to try and sleep I feel exhilarated but a little apprehensive. I have never experienced anything quite like this in my life, and I have the distinct feeling that there is worse to come.

DAY 64: *Wadi Halfa to Atbara*

Sleep is not easy at the Nile Hotel, what with the heat and the almost unbroken nocturnal soundtrack of rasping, hawking, spitting and snoring from just outside my window.

At one point in the night, despite stern instructions from my brain, my bowels are wide awake. I reach for torch and toilet paper, seek out one of the plastic jugs which are scattered around the hotel, fill it from one of the earthenware Ali Baba jars full of muddy Nile water, and, picking my way carefully between the sleeping bodies, head for the lavatories like a condemned man. There are fewer flies to contend with at night, but the smell is very bad, and it's best not to breathe through the nose if you can help it. This is not easy if you have to hold the torch in your mouth to keep both hands free.

Up at seven o'clock. Fraser has found a scorpion in his room and killed it with a shoe. Wash at a communal trough, into which oozes a thin trickle of water. Breakfast consists of dark red beans, cheese, jam and two eggs sprinkled with turmeric.

The train leaves at five o'clock this evening, so I have time to stock up on some provisions for a journey that is scheduled to take thirty-six hours.

The desert begins at the door of the hotel. Across an empty expanse are houses surrounded by long, low, mud walls, the same colour as the sand and the hills, so all seem to blend together in one wide, dim-brown desiccated vista. No rain has fallen here since 1998.

In the market most people seem to be either eating or washing their hands. Dogs hang around waiting for scraps, children play with sticks and hoops, and the stalls sell onions, beans, some cucumber, dates, bananas, garlic and rice. Flies cluster round the already decomposing fruit.

As we film we seem to attract friends and enemies in equal measure. Among our friends is the Customs man who returns my confiscated video of *80 Days*, grinning broadly, a little boy wearing an 'Egypt No Problem' T-shirt who attaches himself to us, and a group of Sudanese from our hotel who invite me to share some fresh grilled Nile perch with them. Our enemies are sour-faced men who appear from nowhere scowling and finger-wagging. They have taken great but unspecified objection to our presence, and quickly gather around them a small angry group, swelled into a threatening crowd by curious onlookers. Their wrath can be insistent and disturbing. One of them takes a stick to Basil, and they seem to regard the presence of Patti and Angela, unveiled and working, as particularly provocative to Islamic sensibilities. Their own women keep a very low profile. I see one move swiftly past swathed in a 'World Cup 1990' sari.

At four o'clock we cross the sand to the station. Crowds are already milling around the long train, which is made up of three open service wagons at the front, eighteen passenger coaches and eight freight cars at the back, a total of twenty-nine vehicles behind one American-built diesel.

The Governor arrives to see us off. He's exchanged his robes for the characterless but ideologically sound safari shirts favoured by Kenneth Kaunda and others. He presents me with a box of dates for the journey, and smiles and shakes hands with us all most warmly.

'When the train leave you will see a sight,' he chuckles, and indeed as the whistle wails across the desert at five o'clock sharp and this huge, unwieldy combination begins to move, the low embankment is filled with a mass of running figures, hurtling towards the train, leaping onto the coaches and eventually clambering up onto the roof.

Apart from the Roof Class travellers who, if they are prepared to risk extremes of heat and cold and blowing sand, are not officially discouraged, there are three classes on the train. Although we are in First it's quite basic – we are four to a compartment, few of the lights or fans work, and the basin in the lavatory has disappeared. The train superintendent, another big, friendly man, reckons there could be 4000 passengers altogether, though he doesn't know for sure.

A milepost in the sand indicates 899 kilometres (557 miles) to Khartoum.

The long, straight, single-track line was built on the orders of General Kitchener in 1897 to help in the relief of Khartoum, which the Mahdi had seized from General Gordon twelve years previously. Despite the punishing heat and lack of water, the British and Egyptian forces laid track at the rate of more than one kilometre a day, covering the 370 kilometres (230 miles) to Abu Hamed in ten months.

Once the pride of the Empire, the Nile Valley Express is now much reduced. Nearly all the coaches are in need of repair, and the wooden struts of their frames can often be seen through the rotten panelling. Delays are almost obligatory, sometimes extending to days.

But for all its inadequacies, riding this train is an exhilarating experience. As night falls on the Nubian Desert and a pale half-moon lends a ghostly glow to a landscape of silver sand and occasional low jagged peaks, I sit at the open door of our coach, with a little Van Morrison on my Walkman, and marvel at the sheer beauty of it all.

Twice we come to an unscheduled halt – once for a broken vacuum pipe, and once for 'engine failure'. As soon as the train stops, passengers on the roof jump down and curl up to sleep on the sand, usually in groups of three or four, with one person on watch in case the train should start. Some get out to pray, others to stretch their legs and cool off in the light desert breeze.

Then, miraculously, the train rumbles into motion and they all rush back as we continue into the night, shadows from lighted compartments forming an abstract pattern of cubes and squares on the floor of the desert and spent cigarettes flashing from windows like fireflies.

DAY 65: *Wadi Halfa to Atbara*

At some point in the night I wake feeling as if I have a rock lodged in my throat. Swallowing is piercingly painful, and only partly relieved by a swig from my water bottle. I'm relieved to find that I'm not the only one suffering. The cause is fine sand blowing off the desert and inhaled in sleep. There is dust over everything in the compartment, and only our precious bottled water to wash with.

At 6.30 a.m. Nigel, who must have been born on wall-bars, is already up on the roof filming the sunrise. Fraser is also up there and I know I shall have to join them. The train never moves at more than a steady forty-five m.p.h. but the scramble onto the top requires an act of faith in the shifting, creaking fittings between the coaches. There are about twenty people riding on our coach, and the atmosphere is friendly. Ali Hassan is young, maybe eighteen or nineteen, travelling to Khartoum to study civil engineering. He seems surprised that people in England cannot ride on the top of trains. I explain about bridges.

We talk about the state of the country. He is optimistic. There is no famine any more and the civil war in the south is less severe than it was. I ask him if it is a religious struggle between the Muslims of the north (comprising about seventy per cent of the country) and the Christians and non-Muslims of the south. He says it is political. Garang, the leader of the rebels, wants to be prime minister, and if he would only content himself with a position in the existing government the war could be over. The Sudanese need no friends, he adds, they will solve their own problems.

Our roof-top deliberations are interrupted by the arrival of a robed bundle of a man carrying a huge kettle swathed in cloth and a stack of glasses. Ali Hassan insists on buying me a cup of tea, and a cloth bung is removed from the spout and my glass filled with a sweet but refreshingly sharp substance. I'm lingering over the pleasure of this unusual feat of catering, when I notice a bony hand impatiently extended. The tea-man wants the glass back so he can continue along the top of the train. He sways off into the distance and Fraser shakes his head. We'll get botulism, he declares, that's for sure. Still, that was the least of my worries when I climbed onto the top of a moving express.

At eight o'clock we pass Station Number 6 (none of the stations across the desert have names). I remember a Sudanese butler in Cyprus insisting I visit his family here, but there seems no sign of life, family or otherwise, for miles around. I make my way through the shredded and rusting remains of a connecting corridor to the dining-car. There are six tables set beside dirty, shattered plastic windows and a number of empty wall-fittings where fans used to be. The breakfast of bread, chunks of beef, a boiled egg and lentils is not bad.

We reach Abu Hamed as the day is beginning to boil up. This is where the Nile, having completed a wide loop, turns south again.

The engine that has miraculously survived the night is taken off here, and while it is being refuelled I walk down to the river bank. A number of long, low boats with outboard motors are filling up with passengers to cross to the far shore. I notice that the women travel separately from the men, as they are required to do on the train.

By midday my thermometer reads 100 degrees in the compartment. Outside, the rock-strewn desert floor is bleached white. Inside, I'm eating a tin of 'Stewed Chicken with Bone', canned in China, bought in Wadi Halfa. The rest of the crew are opting for health, safety and Sainsbury's tuna. No one has much energy left, and when I squeeze a plastic tube of mustard so hard that the end flies off and covers Nigel in a pattern of yellow blobs, there is a sort of weary resignation that this is the kind of thing that happens on the Nile Valley Express.

About half-past one someone falls off the roof and the train backs up for half a mile to collect him. He was flat out at the time and the whole episode gives a new meaning to falling asleep.

Between Artoli and Atbara we run close to the Nile, which is thick and muddy here compared with Egypt. The villages are squashed along the bank, and there seems to be no systematic irrigation. The houses are square, of mud brick; simple shelters from the sun. There are goats, but no vehicles. It looks a hard life out there despite such a bounteous river.

In the dining-car, desperate for anything to relieve the relentless heat, some people are drinking Nile water, complete with mud. I stick to tea bought for me by three Khartoumers, two of whom are returning from a honeymoon in Cairo. One is an agricultural engineer, another a lawyer. They are anxious to tell me of the damage they think the present government is inflicting on their country. The fundamentalist hardliners are aggressive, they have killed many opponents and, says the lawyer with a frustrated shake of the head, 'They really do dislike educated people'.

As we step off the train in the cool of the evening at another Nileside stop, I watch a roof passenger unwind his turban and lower it down to a water-seller who ties it around the handle of a bucket, which is then hoisted up again. Locals sit beside their wares with hurricane lamps burning, and little girls walk up and down with kettles kept warm on a base of burning charcoal. The river has a rich, sweet smell here and the bleached and silent rock of the desert rises, bare and uncompromising, against the last of the sun. As I'm thinking how utterly and wonderfully strange it all is I notice that the coach in which we have been travelling across the Nubian Desert bears the maker's name: 'Gloucester Railway Carriage Company, 1959'.

We reach the busy town of Atbara, 193 miles from Khartoum, seventeen hours after leaving Wadi Halfa. From here we are to continue south by bus. I can remember only shadows, soft smells of cooking and a lot of carrying as we disembark. At a government rest-house we celebrate the successful conclusion of a potentially very difficult stretch of the journey with a jug or two of *karkaday*, a pleasant Ribena-like beverage made from the hibiscus flower. Well, it's all there is.

DAY 66: *Atbara to Khartoum*

The room which I share with Basil has, like its occupants, seen better days. The washbasin sports hot and cold taps, but only cold water, and that flows into a basin covered in a thin, waxy layer of coagulated dirt. The beds are narrow and the linen grey enough for me to bring out my own sheet sleeping-bag.

Surrounding the room is a wide balcony with a couple of cane chairs, and it is from here, soon after 6.30 in the morning, that I look down onto a green and pleasant garden, in which a pair of security guards are fast asleep. They are not just asleep at their posts, they are asleep in their beds, at their posts.

Having packed my bags for the thirty-fifth time since the North Pole, I make my way to what is proudly signposted as the Dinning Room, and after a remarkably good breakfast, including porridge, we catch the bus to Khartoum. The bus is built onto a Bedford chassis, *circa* 1956, and richly decorated in bright primary colours like some 1960s hippy caravan. It is 'air conditioned', which means open at the sides.

Our equipment is roped on top by a number of porter-helpers, who travel with us. One is jovial and speaks good English. When I ask him how long the journey will take he says, 'Eight hours,' and adds with a twinkle, 'eight *hard* hours . . . '

We are on our way at 7.15, to make the most of the cool of the day. This is a fairly hopeless objective as it is already ninety-two degrees. My excitement at being aboard such a colourful, ethnic form of transport is rapidly moderated by my acquaintance with the sticky plastic seats, leg room that would have tested Toulouse-Lautrec, and the hard metal of the seat frames, which means that if I nod off I run the risk of splitting my head open.

Atbara is a railway town, the junction of the lines to Khartoum from Wadi Halfa in the north and Port Sudan on the Red Sea coast, and we climb up over lines and past sidings full of derelict steam engines before rattling into the shantytown suburbs, where mud walls give way to semicircular constructions of the utmost simplicity, covered in rush matting, goatskin, cardboard or whatever is available. They sprawl across the sand like patchwork tortoises. Less than thirty minutes after starting off we leave the metalled road behind and, passing a huge open rubbish tip, we bounce into the desert. Bounce is an understatement. There are jolts of such severity that the whole bus leaves the ground, flinging us towards the metal roof. Away to the west a train passes, heading north, with a human crest stretching back along the coaches.

By nine o'clock the temperature has reached 100 degrees once more and huge stretches of silvery water and thick stands of palm trees fill the horizon – the most vivid mirages I've ever seen.

Our driver, Ibrahim, is laconic, and has one white eye which stares fixedly ahead. There is no visible road, but he concentrates on the rocky, sandy surface as if negotiating Piccadilly Circus at rush hour. Occasionally he reaches into a small plastic bag and extricates a wad of tobacco which he rubs, breaks and sniffs into each nostril. We pull up every now and then and Nigel, Patti, Fraser, Clem and Angela toil off into the distance to set up for a passing shot. The moment we stop an eager, bright-eyed young boy, who appears to live on the roof, leaps down, pulls open the bonnet and fills up the radiator with water before scampering back up among the cases.

Ibrahim cannot understand the need for all these stops, he just wants to get to Khartoum. It is Mohammed's birthday and there will be festivities tonight. My porter friend is much more chatty. He says he is a schoolmaster and asks me such imponderables as, 'Do you know Richard Burton?' I shake my head. There is a short pause. 'Do you know Roger Moore?'

We stop at a Nileside village. The river, swollen by the rains in Ethiopia, has risen eleven metres and will continue to rise until October. But the great, wide, generous Nile flows by on its way to make electricity for the Egyptians, leaving these Sudanese villages to try and extract what they can with, in this case, one steam pump and wooden sticks and boards to scrape out irrigation channels.

Its one of the puzzles of history that such hardship and poverty can exist in a land which over 2000 years ago was renowned for an iron industry and a rich agriculture. The area we are passing through still has some of the remains of the ancient kingdom of Meroe, including a group of broken and leaning pyramids, some topless, which stand in the desert like a row of bad teeth.

We reach the town of Shendi, 132 kilometres from Atbara, after six hours of hot and desperately uncomfortable travelling. With great relief we step down at the Taieba Tourist Hotel. This proves to be closed, the gardens overgrown and unwatered, the spacious public rooms empty and smelling of decay. We are allowed to use the toilets, from which a couple of mangy cats emerge and skulk away. This must once have been a fine riverside hotel. Now it gives pleasure to no one.

We find a café which serves cold Pepsi and a hot vegetable dip of okra, tomatoes, shallots and cucumber. Very tasty, though not all of us risk eating it.

At a quarter to seven, as lightning flashes on the eastern horizon, we are stopped beside a canal bridge at our third army checkpoint of the day. An hour later we are crossing the Nile at Khartoum. Someone is pointing out the confluence of the Blue and White Niles but I'm staring downstream, transfixed by what appears to be a thick cloud obscuring the rest of the sky and drifting rapidly over the river like a curtain being drawn across the city. Then suddenly we are surrounded by a rushing wind, breathtakingly cool, and a hissing, crackling shower of sand, which douses lights and whips into eyes and mouths. Those of us not already wearing them reach for the face-masks we were issued with at the start of the journey. We are in the middle of one of the violent local sandstorms called a *haboub*, sparked off by a storm out in the desert (the one we had seen earlier). It is an absurdly theatrical entry into the capital – on Mohammed's birthday, with the wind whistling and the sand swirling round the lights and tents specially erected for the celebrations.

How the camera and the rest of the equipment will survive is another matter, and it's with considerable relief that we roll up outside the Khartoum Hilton thirteen hours after leaving Atbara. The first white faces we've seen since leaving Aswan look apprehensively at us as we approach the reception desk, shabby, unshaven and caked with desert sand.

Never has a hot shower been quite as exquisitely welcome, let alone a double bed and a mini-bar – empty, but still a mini-bar.

The *haboub* is still howling round the buildings as I fall asleep.

DAY 69: *Khartoum*

After a weekend of recovery from the journey into Sudan it's now time to investigate how we are going to get out. This necessitates a visit to the Ministry of Information. We drive out along what was the Corniche and is now El Nil Avenue, beneath majestic mahogany trees and alongside colonial remnants like the Grand Hotel and the People's Palace – a much restored version of the building where General Gordon lost his life in 1885. Khartoum seems to be a city without an identity. It grew up in the 1820s on a curved spit of land between the White and Blue Niles which resembled an elephant's trunk, *khartoum* in Arabic. It prospered as a centre of the slave trade, a gateway to the vast human resources of central Africa. In 1885 the local hero, the Mahdi, took the city from Gordon and the British, but was defeated by Kitchener in 1898, after which Khartoum was rebuilt in the Western style – even to the extent of laying out the streets in the form of a Union Jack. A pleasant, easygoing way of life was ensured despite the enervating climate, and the centre of the city still resembles Greece and Rome more than Africa or Arabia. Since the pedantic but house-proud colonialists left, no one seems to know quite what to do with Khartoum. There are not the seething millions here to energize the city by sheer weight of numbers, as there are in Cairo, and the present government, supporting Saddam Hussein and the Generals' coup in the USSR, is not much interested in international appeal. All this, combined with a comatose economy (inflation is currently running at 240 per cent), leaves the capital city lethargic, a junk shop of the past, lacking any internal dynamism.

The threat of violence is more real here than in any of the

other countries through which we have travelled. The American ambassador was assassinated recently. In 1988, a bomb was thrown into the restaurant of the Acropole Hotel, a popular rendezvous for Western aid workers and journalists. Five people were killed. Last year a bomb was tossed into the lobby of the hotel at which we are staying. A notice by the lifts reminds guests that there is a curfew in the city between 11 p.m. and 4 a.m.

Despite the presence of tanks and troops at various points in the city, especially around the bridges, access to the Ministry of Information seems very relaxed. People come and go in the forecourt including a trim, urbane gentleman with short silver-grey hair who turns out to be Sudan's leading film director, Jed Gudalla Gubara. He is a man of spirit and humour, fluent in English. He says he is shooting two films here at the moment. I ask him what they are. One, he says, is about National Savings, and the other about mining.

The news from inside the Ministry of Information is not good. They refuse to give us a permit to travel south. A state of civil war has existed there for years and they cannot guarantee our safety. Even if we were to fly into the southern capital of Juba, it is surrounded by Garang's SPLA (Sudan People's Liberation Army) fighters and it would be highly dangerous for us to try and get through to Uganda.

Our attempt to follow the thirty degree meridian, in which we have succeeded, give or take a degree or two, since reaching Leningrad forty-two days ago, seems to have ground to a halt.

Back at the hotel we consider our options. There is no shortage of advice. The expatriate community here has grown close as it has diminished, and the lobby of the Hilton is one of the places where it meets the outside world. We talk to an Englishman who has worked here for three years and who thinks that if the present government continues its policies most of the aid agencies will be forced out of Sudan in the next year. He looks up with weary resignation: 'They don't like us'. The aid scams are a joke, he says. 'Twenty million pounds' worth of stuff is unaccounted for.' He finishes yet another fruit juice.

'Welcome to the Sudan,' he keeps repeating with a shallow laugh.

Still feeling low on energy, I content myself with a game of table tennis, a lazy swim and a wander round the undernourished hotel bookshop, which must be the only one in the world which has Jilly Cooper next door to *The Cultural Atlas of Islam* and Jeffrey Archer side by side with *The Sudanese Bourgeoisie – Vanguard of Development?*.

I finish Alan Moorehead's *The White Nile* looking out across the river itself, swollen and grey, inundating fields and trees a few hundred yards from my window. If I could follow it, it would lead me due south across swamp and desert to the Equator and the Mountains of the Moon, the very centre of Africa, to which the great names of Victorian exploration, the Spekes and Burtons and Stanleys and Livingstones, had been drawn 130 years ago. Now it seems that my hope of seeing any more of the White Nile must be abandoned – a casualty of war.

DAY 70: *Khartoum*

There may be a way out of our predicament. Clem has made contact with a group of Eritreans who are experienced at cross-border transport. Where, when and whether they'll take us will depend on a meeting later today. Meanwhile we go to film in Omdurman, across the Nile.

The British never bothered to incorporate Omdurman into their new plan for Khartoum and it remains very much an African city, without high-rise buildings or great monuments.

In the souk – the market – there is every small item one might want. These are essentials, not luxury goods. Spices, oil (for cooking and lighting), piles of metal buckets, cooking utensils, cloth, cottons and food – bananas, limes, lemons, mangoes, dates, onions, huge bowls piled high with nuts.

On one side of an open area a line of men are sitting crosslegged on the ground. Each one has the tools of his trade arranged neatly in front of him. One has a short spade on a bridge of bricks, another a light bulb on top of a tool bag, another a bag of paint-brushes with a plasterer's trowel on top. They are waiting to be hired for work and seem to be quite placid and patient until we raise the camera, when all hell breaks loose. A man with a pickaxe gestures at my head so graphically that I automatically shield myself. He smiles broadly at this, thank God.

The absence of any form of tourism in the Sudan results in many small pleasures, one of which is to be able to watch the extraordinary skills of the felucca-builders beside the Nile without having to buy model boats or 'I Have Seen . . .' T-shirts. A thick trunk of mahogany is hoisted by as many as ten men onto a frame about six feet off the ground. Then two men, one on top and one underneath, saw down through the trunk until it falls neatly apart into four planks. Apart from the back-breaking work involved in sawing manually through mahogany in conditions of extreme heat, the two men are shaping and curving the wood as they cut through it, making precise calculations without benefit of any instruments except their own eyes. What comes out at the end of this remarkable toil are boards perfectly fashioned to the shape of the hull. They can build a felucca from mahogany stump to sailing vessel in forty-five days.

Our meeting with the Eritrean transport contacts is set for the afternoon, back across the Nile, in Khartoum itself.

A neat modern villa is the incongruous headquarters of the EPLF – the Eritrean People's Liberation Front – and also of Ayusha Travel, an organization set up to capitalize on the experience gained driving to and from northern Ethiopia during the thirty-year war which ended with the overthrow of Colonel Mengistu only four months previously. On the walls of the bungalow are murals depicting idealized freedom fighters – women armed to the teeth, about to hurl grenades, tribal warriors brandishing spears, and the skulls of enemy dead grinning grotesquely. Hassan Kika shows me into his office. He is a soft-spoken, quietly authoritative man. It's much easier to think of him as a transport manager than a freedom fighter, though he does have things like bomb fragments on his desk and talks of the '10,000 martyrs' who died fighting for Eritrea against Ethiopian dictatorship.

Now the victory they always believed in has come and in two years' time there will be a United Nations sponsored referendum in Eritrea to decide whether it will become a new independent state. Hassan Kika thinks the result is a foregone conclusion.

I put our more mundane problem to him and we look at the map together. There is a way he can take us into Ethiopia. It would involve a six- or seven-hour drive on a good road to Gedaref, and from there on what he calls 'rough roads' south to the border crossing at Gallabat. He cautions that the rainy season has been much later this year and parts of the road could be washed away, but with his Landcruisers he doesn't anticipate a problem. I ask him if there is still any fighting across the border.

'No . . . no, I don't think so, no. The TPLF (the Tigrayan Forces who defeated Mengistu) was controlling all this part of Ethiopia. But there are some, you know, who doesn't want to join with them, so they have made their own band.' Bandits? He smiles, but not very convincingly.

'The people in the village will chase them out, you know.'

Hassan Kika and the Eritreans appear to have saved our bacon. They say that they can let us have the vehicles we want by the weekend. They estimate it will take us about three days to drive from Khartoum to Gondar in Ethiopia.

Back to the hotel, much relieved, only to have my enthusiasm dampened by an English couple who have just spent five weeks in custody in Eritrea after their yacht strayed into a restricted area. They were not treated well. There had been some 'physical stuff' and no legal representation. 'And don't believe any estimate of time they give you.'

The couple, who are on their way back home, have with them a white parrot called Gnasher, who is a Category B protected species, so all sorts of export licences are required. They now have the paperwork but Air France will only take him in a special box, which they are having made at the moment. Meanwhile Gnasher is getting very twitchy and nibbling at anything he can find.

'I've already had to pay for two pairs of curtains he's eaten in Asmara,' says his lady owner resignedly.

Never a dull moment in the Khartoum Hilton. And it's British night tonight in the buffet.

DAY 71: *Khartoum*

The modern British presence in Khartoum has dwindled to a handful of aid workers and teachers. Since the Gulf War even the embassy has been reduced to fewer than ten people. There remains the Sudan Club, once open only to those of British and British Commonwealth nationality, now extended to include anyone from an EC country. It occupies a villa in the middle of the city. It has a swimming-pool, squash courts, a pale green lawn and a membership that has shrunk to 230 from a colonial high of over 1000. I meet Alan Woodruff for lunch here. He is Professor of Medicine at the University of Juba. He's seventy years old and plays tennis three times a week.

Talking with him offers a bracing corrective to any dewy-eyed nostalgia for a British Sudan. I ask him what it was like during the Gulf War, when Sudan took Saddam Hussein's side and most European governments advised their nationals to get out.

Professor Woodruff brightens visibly at the memory. 'Well . . . I had the whole place to myself . . . dined in state, on my own!' He says he felt quite safe and secure. The country's myriad political problems and the fact that he is, as he admits, living in a 'war situation' does not seem to worry him half as much as the salad.

'Maju,' he calls to the waiter, 'you know I never eat salad!'

He turns to me forbiddingly, 'Salad is one of the worst ways of contracting dysentery.' (I presume he means one of the best ways.) 'One of the first principles of keeping fit in the tropics is that you avoid salads.'

He claims he has not lost a day's work in ten years here, so I move my rather succulent plateful of tomato and onions as far away from me as is politely possible. I would think the rest of the menu, which contains items like Scotch egg and 'twisted fish' could be a problem, but not for the professor. Anything that is served hot, out of the Club's kitchen, is safe. Twisted fish?

'Very good; fillets of fish twisted round and fried.'

The 1500 students of Professor Woodruff's beloved University of Juba were recently airlifted from the south when the war made it impossible for life and work to continue. He has high praise for his students, and says the Sudanese make very good doctors. But there are not the resources to train enough of them. 'The World Health Organization recommend that there should be one doctor for every thousand of the population – in the Sudan I think it is still one doctor to ten or twelve thousand.'

Later, and much against my better judgement, I'm lured into a game of squash with Noshir, an Indian working here in Khartoum. He is clearly used to playing in the heat, and is very understanding when I am reduced to a state of total collapse after less than ten minutes.

'It must have been about 100 degrees in there,' he says consolingly. May and June are the hottest months. His wife, he recalls, once left some eggs in the car by mistake and they were boiled when she came back.

He is happy in Khartoum. He sends his children to the local schools and thinks it is a good thing that they have to learn Arabic.

'It's nice out here, you don't have a drug problem, you don't have mindless violence, and the family gets together.'

On my way out of the Sudan Club I stop at the notice-board. There's a Disco Buffet on 4 October, an International Swimming Fun Day, a European Quiz Evening, even a Hallowe'en Fancy-Dress Ball. To the outside world Khartoum is the sluggish centre of a war-torn, famine-ridden country on the brink of economic collapse, but to those living here, the Noshirs and the Professor

Woodruffs, it is, for better or worse, the centre of their world. For them, and even for me after half a week here, Khartoum ceases to feel remote or difficult, or dangerous. It is where we are. It is home.

DAY 73: *Khartoum*

Still no sign of the permits we need for the journey south. Pass the time with a visit to the camel market, out in the desert. Huge numbers of cattle and camels are gathered here from all over the country, accompanied by herdsmen who have walked with them for hundreds of miles. I ask how much it would cost to buy a camel – one owner, good condition – and am quoted 25,000 Sudanese pounds, which is £1000 sterling.

On the way back we run into trouble. We have stopped in one of the featureless desert settlements that border the city. Our several minders have gone to buy drinks. Through the car window Basil photographs a beautiful robed figure against a background of drifting smoke. His camera is spotted and two or three men approach the car pointing and demanding the film. Basil refuses to hand it over. A crowd gathers and soon the atmosphere is as hot as the day itself. Arms stretch into the car in which we are sitting, fingers jab at the camera. Someone shouts to us not to get out of the car – as if we could. We are surrounded and people are banging on the roof. All the fuss is because they thought that Basil was snapping not a fine figure of a Sudani but the rubbish tip in the background. With a smart piece of sleight of hand Basil passes over to them an unexposed film.

We end up filming the least provocative thing we call think of – the point where the waters of the Blue and White Niles meet.

A group of pelicans bobs obligingly along the line where the waters merge, and, yes, it is possible to distinguish the different colours. The White Nile is clearly grey and the Blue Nile undoubtedly brown.

To bed, with another sandstorm howling into town.

154

DAY 74: *Khartoum to Gedaref*

Woken at five o'clock. The permits have arrived at the eleventh hour and we must load the vehicles for departure as soon as possible. The Eritreans turn up with three spanking clean Toyota Landcruisers and a smaller Nissan Patrol to take our baggage. Water, food, fuel and some of the camera equipment are roped expertly onto roof-racks and we are on our way by 7.30.

After the bouncing desert ride from Atbara to Khartoum, our progress towards Gedaref, 260 miles south-east, seems almost serene. The powerful, well-sprung vehicles glide along the metalled highway that is Sudan's vital supply line, connecting the capital with Port Sudan, on the Red Sea.

The scenery is as flat as Lincolnshire and wide green stony fields on either side of the road continue to invite the comparison. Tall minarets dot the countryside like church spires. There is industry here, in the shape of cotton and flour mills and factories producing medical packaging, glucose and glass. A grey Mercedes 500 with the red stripe of the government races past, cutting in front of an advancing truck by a narrow margin. My immediate thought is that it must be another president fleeing, and that the Sudan, like the USSR, is collapsing beneath us.

10.20 a.m. Petrol sprays out across our windscreen and we pull to a stop. The carburettor has come loose and the engine is awash with precious fuel. After some time spent trying to mend it with rope, it's decided that a spare part is required. Fortunately we are on the outskirts of the town of El Hasaheisa, and our driver Mikele goes off to locate what is required while we wait beside a brown, burnt-earth roadside ditch topped with a row of usha bushes, whose fruit looks rich and seductive but is deadly poison. A group of children gather to stare. My unbounded confidence in the Eritreans has taken a bit of a knock.

12.30 p.m. We are on our way again.

Just outside Gedaref is a huge refugee or 'displaced persons' camp, housing 22,000 Ethiopians. It has been here for sixteen years. The Sudanese pursued a benevolent but not altogether altruistic policy of support for those fighting the government of Colonel Mengistu and these camps, filled largely with political refugees, were recruiting and training centres for the Tigrayan resistance. This one is as big as a small town, well laid out with long lines of circular huts capped with conical thatched roofs, and surrounded by high fences. A big crowd gathers around us. I have the feeling that visits such as ours are a spot of welcome entertainment in an otherwise confined and routine existence. The presence of the camera is also an opportunity to air grievances and appeal to the world. Refugees, some wearing 'Desert Storm' and 'Rambo' T-shirts, tell us that there is not enough food, that they have to do the most menial jobs for the Sudanese in order to make money to live, and that now the war is over they want international pressure to be used to get them back home again.

'What can you do for us? What can you do for us?' they keep repeating.

The worst part is leaving. Being able to leave.

In Gedaref we are quartered at another government rest-house. Our shared rooms are set off a verandah which is screened with netting to keep out mosquitoes. The floors are covered in badly-fitting vinyl, the walls are bare plaster. There is a fan that doesn't work and basins with no running water. It is a cheerless place. We sit, before supper, with glasses of lemonade, feeling like occupants of an old folks' home.

DAY 75: *Gedaref to Kanina*

Alarm sounds on the chair beside my bed at 5.15. Slept well despite a rich assortment of noises off – dogs barking, cockerels crowing from an indecently early hour, cats, crickets and muezzins. It was as if someone had broken into the BBC Sound Effects Library and put on all the African tapes simultaneously.

The dawn temperature is a refreshingly cool eighty degrees,

and an encouraging contrast to the stuffiness and claustro-phobia of the night before. There is no breakfast, so after a bracing argument over the bill we pack up the vehicles, in which our Eritrean drivers have spent the night, and head for the border. It'll have to be another Sainsbury's picnic on the way.

Surveying my Michelin map (*Africa North-East and Arabia*), I notice the road to Gallabat is clearly marked but lined with a series of blue notches. The key reveals that these indicate 'roads impassable in the rainy season'. The rainy season, though late, is past, but its aftermath is the only thing that seems to cause the Eritreans any concern.

We are only ninety-six miles from the frontier, and with luck could be in Gondar, Ethiopia, by this evening.

Fifteen minutes later comes the first, ominous, sign that things might not be so easy. We pull up at a crossroads in the centre of Gedaref. The town is already full of people, buying bread, selling hot corn on the cob or just hanging around. A shabby group gathers curiously by the vehicles, peering in. Normally we'd either get out or wind the window down but this morning we want to keep moving. Instead the drivers are consulting, pointing and arguing. It's clear that they're already lost. After a few minutes they climb back in and haul us round in a bad-tempered U-turn.

We follow an unmade track, the rain-softened soil already churned up by trucks from the border. This is where the drivers earn their money. They must be able to read the tricky surface ahead, riding in the grooves when there is clearance enough to do so and switching onto the ridges when the grooves run too deep. The driver must match decisiveness with delicacy – as if the walls of hardening mud were made of eggshell.

As happens in Africa, there are people walking in the middle of nowhere and Mikele stops twice to give rides – once to an old woman and her daughter, and further on to a farmer whose name is Ibrahim. He is going to visit his fields in the village of Doka. He has twenty cows and also grows *simsim*, which I'm told is sesame. He wears a crisp white djellabah and a neat lace

157

takia and argues loudly with Mikele about religion. Arab versus Christian.

We pass the carcass of a cow, picked clean by the birds of prey. Yellow butterflies flutter about the bones and alight on the skin, which has shrunk in the sun and now looks like an inadequate blanket put there by someone trying to conceal an accident. Nigel films it and Fraser dangles his microphone boom over it. Basil asks Fraser why he is recording the sound of a long-dead animal. Fraser seems genuinely hurt by the question. 'The flies are alive!'

Ibrahim chews tobacco and displays a surprising knowledge of idiomatic English.

'What is it you English say . . . ?'

'About what?'

He shifts a wad of tobacco across his mouth and back again.

' . . . you say about English ladies . . . '

I crane back to try and catch this over the revving of the engines.

'What do we say, Ibrahim?'

'All the same with the light off?'

He giggles helplessly. I'm quite shocked.

We have been travelling for nearly six hours when we reach Ibrahim's destination. His parting shot is to tell us that in his opinion we shall not reach Gallabat before dark. The drivers laugh this off, but it raises awkward questions for us. Transport from the Ethiopian side is to meet us at the border this evening and we have absolutely no means of getting a message to them if anything goes wrong.

We move on, encouraged by a faster, more solid surface out amongst the corrugated iron shacks of the village.

Then we take a wrong turning. There are no signposts and the Eritreans have not a map amongst them. Eventually we find what appears to be a dried-up river-bed. We drive along it until the Nissan gets stuck and has to be towed out by Mikele. Then Mikele gets stuck and has to be pulled out by the Nissan.

The landscape is changing from semi-desert to savannah. Acacia trees proliferate. At a village where we stop to fill the radiators the look of the people has changed too. There are fewer djellabahs and more colourful robes and cloths, as well as armlets and necklaces and other ornate jewellery.

The track is now so badly pitted and potholed that our drivers are forced to seek the drier, less well used ground on either side. It is less well used largely because it is planted with crops, and as we charge through, flattening maize and sesame, I try not to think of the grossness of our action.

As the sun declines the colours of the countryside become more beautiful. The blackness of the soil contrasts with the pale lemon of the grass and the glowing russet of the eucalyptus trees' bark.

When our drivers are not pulling each other out of the mud they are questioning anyone who goes by. Little children, old women bearing piles of wood, young girls, all are asked with increasing desperation, 'Gallabat . . . Gallabat?'.

Night falls and one of the Landcruisers is stuck at an angle of 45 degrees, another sprays an arc of mud from its back wheels as it tries to drag the beleaguered vehicle onto the level. A donkey trots quietly past bearing an elderly man who gives a hint of a sad smile as he overtakes us and disappears into the distance.

Seven o'clock. One Landcruiser is now seriously damaged, with a crack in the suspension. This necessitates much unloading and redistribution of baggage amongst other, already crowded vehicles. It is pitch dark. As we are doing this three figures appear from the undergrowth. One of them is a little boy holding a candle. Behind him the horizon is momentarily illuminated by a flash of lightning. We are tired, dusty and saddle-sore but there is something about this moment which is unforgettable.

By eight o'clock, after thirteen hours' driving, we find ourselves in a small settlement. There is no electric light, just a collection of dimly lit huts and dogs prowling about beside a smelly stream. We are told this is the village of Kanina. Being near the frontier, it has a police presence. Their advice is that it would be highly dangerous to travel further tonight and they agree to put us up in the compound of the police station. They gather beds together and by the light of oil lamps and torches we rustle up a meal of cheese spread and pressed chicken and other slithery things out of tins. The 'bathroom' consists of a large urn of water in one corner of the mud-floored compound. The lavatory is outside. Anywhere.

DAY 76: *Kanina to Shedi*

In Kanina the dawn chorus lasts all night. Never have I heard such a symphony of grunting, chattering, hooting, whooping, howling, barking and honking. And that was just the crew. The village by daylight looks quite pleasant and green, a mixture of straw-thatched conical huts and, settled in a hollow, more substantial structures roofed in corrugated iron.

Once again we decide to move on as early as possible and stop for breakfast after we have covered some ground. It's still frustratingly difficult to gather any accurate information but Gallabat is said to be no more than thirty kilometres (eighteen miles) away.

We leave at ten to six, just before sunrise. Dust and dirt of travel is ingrained in everything – our bodies, clothes, bags and bedding. The Landcruisers that were gleaming and pristine forty-eight hours ago are unrecognizably filthy.

The Eritrean drivers, who have worked much harder than we have, are a little chastened this morning. After yesterday's unproductive free-for-all they have developed a system which involves following rather than racing. The lead driver goes ahead and inspects the route, then comes back to give instructions. The problem, however, remains fundamental. There is no road to Gallabat. There is not even a continuous track to Gallabat. Whatever track there might be is likely to be obscured by an ever-thickening carpet of low trees and undergrowth. The dark shape of the Ethiopian highlands remains elusively distant.

We carry on where we left off yesterday, bulldozing through fields of maize and millet, and sliding and swerving onto the thick mass of trenches ground into the mud by vehicles much heavier than our own. Though Mikele and his team ride the ridges bravely, flicking into four-wheel drive and plunging ahead at full throttle, there is more sound and fury than actual progress. The pervading smell of burning rubber and freshly-gouged earth merely underlines the fact that we are in the wrong place with the wrong kind of transport. Not only does the earth seem stickier and heavier, but trees are flicking at us through the windows, and as I am helping push out the Landcruiser for the umpteenth time a thorn bush drags me back. I survive, but my trousers are ripped like paper.

By ten a.m. we have moved seven and a half miles in four hours. This is our fourteenth day in the Sudan and the country seems increasingly reluctant to let us go.

The police escort given to us by the authorities at Kanina has now broken down. As they struggle to fix a water-pipe an army unit draws up, insisting that we take armed guards with us to the border. They say there are men from Mengistu's recently defeated army roaming the hills, 'living off their wits'. Now we have in addition to our own damaged vehicle a disabled police escort, and two soldiers to fit into an already overloaded convoy.

An hour later, about midday, the scenery is becoming more picturesque and we stop to allow Nigel to climb a low hill and get some shots. The soldiers become very agitated and order him back. One of them, who is travelling with Angela and Patti, has told them both that these hills are full of armed men who will not hesitate to shoot on sight.

We pile back into the vehicles only to find, round the next corner, an upended truck with its load of salt sacks scattered on the road. This, it turns out, is the first sign of a northbound convoy which pins us down for an hour or more as forty or fifty trucks and tractors pulling trailers trundle past us. These swaying, overloaded old Austins and Bedfords, all of which have five or six armed men travelling on top of the cargo, make light work of the road conditions, but I feel sorry for Mikele as he looks balefully at the deepening ruts they leave behind, over which he and the others will have to return.

At 3 p.m., having moved fourteen miles in nine hours, we emerge from the trees into a collection of army huts at the top of a hill. Down below us is Gallabat.

Like Wadi Halfa the town itself is endowed with less than its oft-quoted name might suggest. But for us Gallabat and its Ethiopian counterpart of Metemma on the other side of a shallow valley is the Promised Land, the end of the worst stretch of the journey since leaving the Pole.

Our battered convoy rolls down the hill towards a collection of thatched huts and crowds of people milling around a small grubby building marked 'Democratic Republic Sudan Customs'. It all looks unfamiliar and potentially threatening, but to our enormous relief our Ethiopian contacts – Graham Hancock, who is a journalist, and Santha Faiia, a Malaysian photographer who has lived a long time in the country – are there to meet us. They bring the welcome news that we are cleared through Sudan Customs and there are no Customs on the Ethiopian side before Addis Ababa.

The Sudan-Ethiopian frontier is a stagnant creek, over which a concrete bridge has been recently erected. It doesn't surprise me when Graham warns that it is an area of high malaria risk.

I walk across, through a jostling mass of donkeys, trucks and curious faces, into Ethiopia, where, as they use the Julian calendar and not the Gregorian, the year is 1984, and the month, I think, January.

While the load is moved onto a new set of Landcruisers, I revel in the pleasure of the first beer since Aswan, just over two weeks ago. It is almost body temperature but quite wonderful.

Because it's now so late in the day we are advised not to attempt to reach Gondar as the roads pass through bandit territory, and we put up for the night at a village about twenty-five miles from the border. I don't think any of us cares much where we stay so long as there is a comfortable bed and some hot water. There are neither in Shedi. The accommodation, though looking quaint enough by candlelight, is rougher than anything we've experienced so far. My room is reached through a small dimly-lit bar which gives onto what smells and feels like a farmyard. In the middle of it are people sitting around a fire, and off to the sides are rooms that look like rough stables. Mine has an earth floor and wattle-and-daub partitions. There is a corrugated iron door and ceiling. The proprietress finds me a chair and a couple of stones to wedge one of the legs of the bed. Cockroaches and beetles scuttle away in the torchlight as I unpack. Electric light would be terrifying here.

This 'hotel', in which only Basil and I are quartered, is nevertheless more luxurious than the rest in that it sports a shower. This consists of a large plastic drum with a supply valve controlled by a piece of wire. The stream of cool water is heavenly. Not so the lavatory next door. I have become used to the squat technique, so I'm not unduly worried to find myself poised above a shallow hole filled with sawdust. It's when the sawdust starts to move that I feel just the slightest bit queasy. What I thought was sawdust is in fact a cauldron of maggots, over which the occasional cockroach stumbles.

Despite this revelation I partake heartily of Fray Bentos corned beef, Garibaldi biscuits and several Ethiopian beers before turning in.

DAY 77: *Shedi to Gondar*

I don't sleep for long. I don't think any of us does. Though I remain wrapped tight in a sheet sleeping-bag and covered up from head to toe, I cannot reconcile myself to the fetid smell from the sticky rough cloth of the mattress, the treasure trove of insects concealed within it and the presence of bodies only a breath away on the other side of the thin mud wall. Because of my protective cocoon I become very hot and push open the door to let some air in. I must have dozed, and wake to find a face peering down at me and a moment later hear the door slamming shut. When I do nod off I'm woken sharply by a peculiar, violent and inhuman sound. It sounds like a donkey having a nightmare.

I've never risen at 5.15 with less reluctance. Splash a little bottled water on my face and tiptoe to the door, only to find it has been locked on the outside. Fortunately Basil is within shouting distance. We assemble in the pre-dawn light and recount our various experiences in this most ethnic of stop-overs. Angela had an armed guard in her room, though not all night, I'm assured, and Nigel's nerves of steel were shredded when a cat jumped onto his bed in the small hours. For once Fraser seems to have found nothing in his shoe, ear or any other orifice.

We set off for Gondar before dawn. The roads are straighter and in better condition than in the Sudan, but the river-beds here are not dry and consequently must be crossed with greater care.

I travel with Graham, who fills me in with the history and politics of the country as we pass through scenery which resembles the Welsh borders. He says it's a good time to be in Ethiopia, in the euphoric aftermath of the fall of Mengistu's government and just after the rains have turned the countryside green.

Colonel Mengistu had ruled the country for sixteen years after deposing Emperor Haile Selassie, who had ruled for fifty-seven years. Under Mengistu, poverty and corruption went hand in hand with totalitarianism and an irrelevant pro-Soviet policy. The Eritreans opposed him because they wanted independence for themselves and the Tigrayans opposed him because they wanted political change in Ethiopia. In the end it was a people's army from Tigray in the north-east that formed the driving force behind the EPRDF (the Ethiopian People's Revolutionary Democratic Front) that swept through the country and forced Mengistu to flee to Zimbabwe just over four months ago. Meles Zenawi became head of the new government at the age of thirty-five. It is, as Graham says, a young revolution. 'People between sixteen and thirty have completely changed the face of this country in the last six months.'

The soldiers who are travelling with us as protection are part of this volunteer EPRDF army – paid only in cigarettes, food and accommodation. The emblems on their tunics are inked in by hand, they wear cut-off jeans and carry Kalashnikov AK-47 rifles. They are probably fifteen or sixteen years old.

The scenery outside is now almost alpine. Green meadows are filled with the short-lived but intense yellow flower called maskal, which is the national emblem. There are butterflies and gold and green weaver birds and brilliant red bishops. A Soviet-built tank stands abandoned in the long grass. It looks idyllic out there, but there have been frequent attacks on the road since the end of the war and our escort slips a bullet into the breech and pokes his rifle out, looking watchfully around at the mountains.

We stop at a village for refreshment. We buy some tea while our guards sit talking quietly with colleagues. I'm impressed that they don't swagger or behave loudly or aggressively. They sit there quite gravely, as if prematurely aged by their responsibility as liberators.

There are casualties of war. The children have had no schooling here for several years. A number of them are pitifully thin. Often their heads have been shaved, and their pointed faces and big eyes bring to mind pictures of concentration camp victims. All this in surroundings that resemble Switzerland.

Graham sees cause for optimism, 'The former government structure was one of total control of the whole country . . . they had their cadres in every village . . . neighbours were encouraged to spy on each other . . . these rebels fought to get rid of that. At every level people are more free than they were before.'

By mid-afternoon we have reached the village of Aykel, which is entered through a tall, ungraceful metal arch bearing slogans like 'People's Power' and 'Ethiopia Shall Be the Home of Heavy Industry'. Below them a cluster of wrechedly poor children gather around us.

'You! . . . you!', they shout, holding their hands out for anything. I give one of them a 'Wet One' – one of the cleaning tissues we carry with us – and mime what to do. He is still vigorously wiping his face with it when we leave twenty minutes later.

165

Beyond Aykel we follow a stony track over a wide upland plateau.

Thunder has been rumbling and clouds building; finally the heavens open and down come hailstones the size of marbles. It is hard to believe that ice is falling on us less than twenty-four hours after we were sweating our way out of the Sudan.

It is a wonderfully refreshing deluge and as the clouds pass on and the sun begins to come through we find ourselves on the outskirts of Gondar. Our three-day journey has turned into four hard-travelling fifteen-hour days and everyone is tired, crumpled and desperate for a creature comfort or two. As we drive into this sizeable town, 7000 feet above sea-level and for 200 years the capital of Ethiopia, we come up behind a large and forlorn crowd of men who look in a worse state than ourselves. They are walking disconsolately down the hill carrying cans or plastic containers. Apparently they are some of the 70,000 government troops garrisoned in Gondar who surrendered to the EPRDF without a fight. Deciding what to do with them is one of the problems facing the new administration – Mengistu had one of the biggest standing armies in Africa and there are an estimated 400,000 to 500,000 of his men still in custody, and two million of their dependents neglected.

The Gohar Hotel is spectacularly sited on a bluff overlooking the city and the wide panorama of mountains that encircle it. We have been nowhere like this. Built for a tourist industry that never happened, the hotel combines a museum, a repository of local arts and crafts, with interestingly designed public spaces and a decently stocked bar.

There is a sign on the back of my door which could be an offer or a dire warning: 'Room Service. Express snakes available at all times'.

Apart from the danger of express snakes the chief delights of the Gohar Hotel are electric light, hot water (for a whole hour in the evening) and a freshly made bed. It is chilly enough for me to huddle to sleep beneath two blankets.

DAY 78: *Gondar to Bahir Dar*

A cool morning. Mist clings to the mountain ranges, enveloping all but the tallest ridges and summits. The only other people staying at the hotel are a couple of Red Cross workers and ten EPRDF troops, who are quartered in one wing free of charge.

In the foyer there is evidence of the stillborn attempt to bring tourists here. 'Ethiopia, thirteen months of sunshine', reads one poster, playing on their calendar difference. Another extols the wonders of the nearby Simian Mountains: 'The splendid Roof of Africa – peak after rugged peak stretching away to the limitless horizon; pastoral scenes of shepherds and their flocks, carpets of Alpine flowers'.

Down to the centre of town. The place looks better from a distance. Below the picturesque patchwork of red and grey roofs are streets thronged with people, most of whom look downtrodden and threadbare. The djellabah, a simple, sensible, economical garment, is hardly worn here, partly because of the climate and partly because only fifteen million of the country's forty-five million people are Muslim. Here they seem to wear whatever they can get their hands on. One little girl appears to be dressed in a nightie, another in a torn crocheted sweater. Some have shoes, many don't. Food is stacked next to open drains, and it's easy to see how disease thrives. A lot of the children quickly gather round us, despite the efforts of some of the older men who try to clear them away by throwing stones. They look very unhealthy, with bulging stomachs and sores on their faces around which flies gather. They watch us quietly through big protruding eyes. One or two of the livelier ones try to interest us in packets of American army rations which found their way here after the Gulf War. I'm offered freeze-dried 'Cherry Nutcake', 'Tootsie Roll', 'Tomatoes au Gratin' and 'Beef and Rice Meatballs', all in identical grey sachets.

One boy, Mohamed Nuru, speaks English well. He is one of a family of seven. Large families are common in the poorer parts of Africa as they represent an economic asset – a family work-force. He has lost friends and family in the war. He is Muslim but many of his friends are Christian and the two religions get on well here.

English is taught in schools as a second language and Mohamed listens to the BBC World Service.

'I have a great chance to listen for football . . . particularly England football . . . club football. Every Saturday from four to six.'

His favourite team is Manchester United, but I try to put him right.

One thing there is no shortage of in Gondar is sewing-machines. A line of machinists stretches up the hill and all seem busy. I take one of them my trousers, severely ripped in the cause of leaving Sudan, and with ninety seconds of work on his foot-pedalled Mansukh machine he has restored them to full health.

To get away from the relentless pressure of the market, Graham and I go off to look at Gondar's fine stone-walled castles. The first one was built by the Emperor Fasilidas in 1635 when Gondar was made capital because of a superstition rife at the time that the capital should begin with a 'G'. The five emperors who followed him all built their own castles, in the grounds, as it were. The distinctiveness of these dark towers has much to do with Ethiopia's curious history. It is unique in Africa in having been ruled by a direct line through forty-five generations, and though these fortified palaces reveal a distinct European influence, Ethiopia was never colonized. The link with the Jews is fascinating. Graham has a well-researched theory that the Ark of the Covenant is held in a chapel not far from here, and he has just completed a book on his findings.

In one corner of the grounds there is a cage and in it the first lion I have seen in Africa. His name is Tafara and he once belonged to Haile Selassie, the last Emperor. Selassie died in 1975, a year after he was deposed by Mengistu, and with him died imperial Ethiopia. Tafara, the lion that was the symbol of his power, lingers on, an embarrassment, one feels, to almost everybody. His cage is small and he paces it restlessly, with only flies for company. There are raw wounds on his back and legs.

He had a partner who has long since died. Now he is twenty years old and one can only hope that he does not have to suffer this indignity much longer.

By the time we leave Gondar darkness is falling, and we are soon in the thick of a tremendous electrical storm, the longest and most spectacular I've ever witnessed. Torrential rain pounds the vehicles, and for over two hours fork and sheet lightning rip and burst across the sky. The flashes occasionally reveal dramatic pinnacles of rock and abandoned tanks by the side of the road, frozen into negative for an instant by the intensity of the lightning. At other times they reveal my suitcase, riding uncovered on the roof-rack of the vehicle in front. This is the sort of test they write commercials about.

We arrive at the town of Bahir Dar, 110 miles from Gondar, at ten o'clock at night, having dropped about 2000 feet in the process. The rain has stopped. The storm has passed on. There is a chain barrier across the road, and after some moments a bleary soldier wrapped in a pink blanket with a rifle over his shoulder emerges and looks at our 'safe passage' note. I can tell by his face that he doesn't understand a word of it. He stares hard at it, then back at us, yawns powerfully and waves us on.

My suitcase hasn't survived the onslaught. Red dust and rain have turned some of my shirts an interesting colour.

DAY 79: *Bahir Dar*

Our hotel gives onto the placid grey waters of Lake Tana, which is considered to be the source of the Blue Nile. It has taken us the best part of a month to follow the river down from Cairo. The gardens running down to the lake are rich with hibiscus and poinsettia and the approach to the hotel is dominated by a flowering euphorbia, a goblet-shaped tree that looks like a giant cactus.

We gather at nine a.m. to make an expedition to the Blue Nile Falls, or the Tissisat ('Smoking Water') Falls as they are known locally. Leaving Bahir Dar we pass a huge and graphic anti-Mengistu painting by the roadside. Leering horribly, he has one arm raised in a dictator's clenched fist salute, and the other securing a crutch beneath his armpit, as the lower part of his body decomposes onto a heap of skulls.

Outside the town a pair of storks rise lazily from the fields and away over a road busy with groups of people carrying bundles of wood into town. These resilient figures are of indeterminate age, with legs as thin as the sticks they carry.

At the village of Tissabay, eighteen miles from Bahir Dar, we have to disembark and walk the last mile to the falls. We are not to be alone. No sooner have our vehicles been glimpsed than we are pursued by a crowd of boys waving and shouting. They all want to be our guides. Their technique is to press long sticks into our hands and as soon as anyone should grasp one, to stand proprietorially beside them. After much heated and exhausting negotiation we choose a group of guides and bearers and set off across a difficult stony path through the fields. Tadesse, twenty-five years old, and Tafese, a couple of years younger, are my 'guides' and I am their 'foreigner'.

'He is *our* foreigner!' they shout at anyone who tries to muscle in, and to me, solicitously, 'How you are now? Fine . . . ?'.

What with our bearers carrying the film equipment, and me in my Turkish straw hat, we must look like every clichéd pictured of the Great White Explorer. We cross a picturesque four-arched stone bridge.

'Bridge built by Portuguese,' Tadesse tells me, a few seconds before Tafese tells me the same thing. 'Cement made of egg yolk and sand' . . . 'of egg yolk and sand,' echoes Tafese.

It's hot and increasingly clammy as, after a forty-five--minute walk, we climb a long green slope, mount the brow of a hill and look down on one of the greatest natural spectacles I have ever seen. It is the central fall of the three that catches the eye. An immense torrent of water is plunging over it, a cascade so massive that it appears solid, as if the land itself is crashing down. A continuous subterranean rumble seems to shake the ground. Locals say they have not seen the falls so full in their lifetime.

I'm aware of Tadesse looking expectantly towards me:

'How you find it? Attract . . . ?'

'Oh yes, attract all right . . . sublime, stupendous and stunning.'

'So . . . you like?'

A rainbow hangs over the gorge and the clifftops below us are covered in tropical jungle, a mini ecosystem created by the billowing clouds of spray. An explorer called James Bruce came here in the 1780s and described the sight as 'stupefying'. He claimed to have been the first white man to see the falls, but two priests challenged his claim. Queen Elizabeth came here in 1965, and they built a viewing platform specially for her. Today there is nothing between ourselves and a 100-foot drop, except slippery grass. Patti nearly goes over, taking most of her guides with her.

2.15 p.m. At lunch in the Fountain of Life Restaurant beside the lake there is a loud crack on the plate-glass window. We dive for cover, but nothing has broken. A huge hornbill has flown into the glass and now lies stunned and flapping feebly on the patio outside. It flies off but only as far as the water. Santha and one of the waiters rush out and help it onto the bank, where it all but attacks them.

The sky is darkening over the lake this afternoon, and it looks as though we shall have our third storm in three days in Ethiopia. But the wood collectors still cross the water in their distinctive narrow papyrus boats. These delicate, insubstantial craft also service the islands of the lake, about twenty of which contain monasteries. Some of these are closed off to the outside world; many more will only allow men to land.

The storm does not come today, but the low dark clouds make Lake Tana even more mysterious and secretive.

DAY 80: *Bahir Dar to Addis Ababa*

Six times in the last seven days we've been up before dawn, usually to catch the coolest time of day. This morning it is because we have a very long drive ahead if we are to reach Addis Ababa on schedule. The capital is 300 miles away and we are taking a gamble by using a subsidiary road for the first 160 miles to avoid the busy truck route. My Michelin map has the first part of our journey picked out in yellow and white stripes, indicating, elegantly but rather unhelpfully, 'road liable to be impractical in bad weather'. As there is also a rumour that a bridge is down this could be quite an adventure.

We leave at a quarter to seven, apprehension mixing with elation at the prospect of a great step forward. If we can reach Addis by tonight we shall be less than a thousand miles, on long straight roads, from the Equator.

At the first checkpoint, we ask a soldier with boots, but no laces, if he knows anything about the bridge being down. He shakes his head. A mile further on Sayem, our driver, pulls up and there is much argument between him and his colleagues about fuel. As in the USSR and Sudan, petrol is strictly rationed here and cannot be acquired without coupons and permits. Sayem is worried that the garages on our back road will not know anything about our permits. Bearing in mind the misfortunes that have attended our transport from Khartoum he's right to worry, but calculations are made and we all start off again. A few yards later we stop again, this time to interrogate a bus-driver as to the state of the suspect bridge. Smiles all round – the road is passable.

Once clear of settlements we are into a beautiful, Arcadian landscape of green terraced fields, with a silver river winding its way down through the valley towards ragged mountain peaks half hidden in haze.

It's a stick culture here. Everyone we pass seems to have a stick – for rest, for protection, and for herding the sheep, cattle and goats, which are constantly on the move by the roadside. The silhouetted walking figure, stick slung across shoulders, could be the trade mark of pastoral Africa.

In the villages the main street is always full. Men, women, children, donkeys and dogs mill about and our driver blasts his horn and ploughs into the middle of them. South of Mota, where Mussolini's six-year occupation of the country has left behind some chunky and incongruous European-style public buildings, we climb onto a broad and grassy plateau from which distant mountains rise to 12,000 feet. Chocolate-coloured streams drain away some of the billions of tons of rich Ethiopian soil which will eventually end up behind the Aswan dam, clogging the desert waters of Lake Nasser. Up here the wood-and-thatch dwellings are often surrounded by carefully cut and dressed drystone walls, but the villagers are very poor. Clothes are patched up and threadbare. Trousers are worn into strands, boots have holes in them. There is no sign of the pick-up trucks and tractors which could still be seen in the poorest parts of the Sudan. Graham thinks the explanation for this lies in foreign reluctance to invest in Mengistu. Under his communist regime Ethiopia received the lowest *per capita* amount of development aid of any country in the world. Long-term development aid, as opposed to short-term emergency aid, is what really matters to a country, though often it is strung around with so many conditions and debt repayments that it ceases to be of real help.

We reach the junction with the main Addis road after six hours of bumpy but uninterrupted progress, and are soon descending through a patchwork of green and yellow fields into the Blue Nile Gorge, where the south-flowing river has cut a mile down into the rocky massif before slowly turning west and north into the Sudan.

The heat rises, trapped by towering red sandstone walls. When we stop for lunch beside a lazy waterfall my thermometer shows 100 degrees and the cool, clear air of the highlands is a just a happy memory. As we dip once more into our dwindling supplies of peanut butter, Treacle Crinkles and Fruit Rustics, we are not alone. From somewhere on the cliff wall above us come high-pitched, almost human cries and an olive baboon lopes away along a rocky ledge. Graham says that there are few wild animals left in Ethiopia now. They have been hunted to extinction.

At the bottom of the gorge a single-span steel bridge crosses the Blue Nile, flowing fast and muddy below. This bridge, a vital link between the north and south of the country, has apparently never been filmed. Under Selassie and Mengistu it was strictly out of bounds. It is our good fortune to have come along so soon after the liberation, and instead of hostility and secrecy we are greeted with curiosity and co-operation. This EPRDF army seems to feel so secure in its achievements that there is no need for striking poses of aggression or intimidation. It must be unique in the world, an army that smiles.

Taking full advantage of their helpfulness, we end up driving across the bridge four times. The soldiers look increasingly bemused as we keep coming back through the checkpoints, grinning manically.

About three o'clock in the afternoon we drive up the steep hairpin bends to the south of the gorge, and take one last look at the Nile which has led us two and a half thousand miles into Africa. Once over the mountains and beyond Addis we shall pick up another natural route – the Great Rift Valley – to push a thousand miles further south, into the heart of the continent.

As we near Addis the road surface is increasingly cracked and broken, the result of the enormous movement of troops down from the north in the last months of the war. A lot of military hardware, mainly personnel carriers, armoured cars and tanks, has been left by the side of the road. With the sky darkening behind them, a hyena loping across the road in front and lightning once again splitting the western horizon, it is an apocalyptic sight.

Darkness falls, and it is after eight o'clock when we first see the lights of Addis. The drivers have been at it for thirteen hours, which is quite a feat of concentration on damaged, unlit roads.

The last plateau we crossed was at 10,000 feet and Addis Ababa, at 8000 feet, is one of the highest capitals in the world.

There is a smell of wood smoke in the air, and for the first time in Ethiopia I notice private cars. A burned-out tank, slewed halfway onto the pavement outside the Presidential

Palace, is a reminder of the resistance the EPRDF encountered when they took the city. Between two and three thousand were killed here when the presidential guard put up a last fight.

Culture shock as we arrive at the Addis Hilton, into a world of white faces, blond hair, thick legs, full bellies. Curfew from 1 a.m. to 6 a.m, but telephones and mini-bars. Gorgeous, sensational and wonderful shower. The dust runs off in muddy channels. My eyes are red-rimmed and sore, and I have picked up a cluster of flea bites from somewhere but I suppose that's a small price to pay for what we've just been through.

Can't help noticing that the only postcards available here carry fine colour photos of the Blue Nile Bridge – the bridge no one had ever filmed.

DAY 82: *Addis Ababa*

Addis Ababa was chosen by Emperor Menelik II to be his capital in 1887. The name means 'New Flower' in Amharic, the official language of Ethiopia, which is a Semitic language, closer to Arabic and Hebrew than anything African. It is a nondescript city set handsomely in a bowl of mountains but reflecting no great sense of civic pride. Under Mengistu it was adorned with roughly painted metal arches and towers celebrating communism in Ethiopia. This morning one of these towers is lying on its side on a road close to the hotel. Men in green overalls dismember it with hammers and oxy-acetylene torches. The thin panels offer little resistance. A severed red star is flung into the back of a truck.

We make our way down the hill, past the grand but overgrown gates of the old Palace of the Emperors, and the empty plinth where a thirty-foot-high statue of Lenin used to cast a beady eye in the direction of Revolution Square. Lenin has gone and Revolution Square is now Maskal Square. We approach it through an arch bearing the green, yellow and red colours of Ethiopia and surmounted with the faded legend 'Long Live Proletarian Internationalism'. It is a wide, long, rectangular space with a grassy bank, ramparts and a city museum on one side and dull modern constructions on the other.

Children wearing 'New Kids on the Block' T-shirts shout 'Money! . . . money!' at us. Above their heads hammer and sickles in lights still hang from the lamp-posts.

Rumour reaches us that a big crowd is heading for the square to demonstrate in favour of the United Democratic Nationals, a party opposed to the government's plans to allow self-determination to Eritrea and any other independently-minded provinces. A couple of police jeeps with machine-guns mounted in the back cruise anxiously. Any form of public protest has been unheard of for so long that the general mood in the approaching crowd seems celebratory. But as the first flag-waving rows of demonstrators reach the square, there is a sound of crackling gunfire. Some people throw themselves to the ground, and we make a brisk retreat towards our vehicles.

Gunfire breaks out again, and for a moment it looks as if there will be panic. Members of the crowd are running towards the centre of the square. Whoever, or whatever, tried to stop them has been silenced. Apart from a lady from Agence Presse we seem to be the only foreigners present. As our brief is to get to the South Pole in one piece rather than be Kate Adie we leave the field open to Agence Presse. There are no further incidents but over 10,000 people are later reported to have protested against the new government.

DAY 83: *Addis Ababa*

It's a damp morning with light rain and moderate temperatures as we make our way past the hillside of corrugated-iron roofed huts behind the hotel to the big hexagonal and corrugated-iron roofed church of St Michael. Crowds move slowly through the rain towards the church. Umbrellas are up, salesmen are out offering candles and tapers. Beggars line the path, and a number of people are standing up close to the church wall, their lips moving urgently in prayer. A stand of eucalyptus trees, tall and tired, surrounds the building, adding a little gloom.

There are twenty-five million Christians in Ethiopia out of a total population of forty-five million, and church attendance is taken very seriously. The services are long – this one began at 6 a.m. and will last three and a half to four hours, after which there will be a ceremonial breakfast followed by another service. Serious worshippers are expected to attend twice at the weekend and on ceremonial days, when services can last up to six hours. There is a mixed bag of ages and sexes in the congregation (many of whom never get into the church itself), including elderly men in army greatcoats, young girls in white robes and young men in headscarves who stand, eyes closed, chanting to themselves. Someone estimates that there are at least 1000 people here.

We have to remove our shoes before going inside the church, which is arranged in a series of concentric circles running outwards from the holy of holies at the core of the building. There seem to be separate sections for men and women. One arcade is full of the elders of the congregation – white-robed men holding sticks with a crosspiece that I notice is often of ornately worked silver. The colours proliferate as you go further in, in fact the centre resembles a fabric warehouse. Elaborate use is made of curtains and carpets and fringes and pelmets, and the priests themselves wear highly decorative robes and capes, often in shimmering brocade. The walls where they are not covered with cloths and rugs have painted scenes; some show Christ's miracles, others the Virgin Mary, and one has St George plunging his spear into the dragon's mouth. It's reminiscent of the services in Cyprus and Leningrad and again indicates Ethiopia's links with the North and East rather than the rest of Africa.

Ceremonial is very important, as are props. A Bible, said to be 300 years old, with pages of skin, not paper, is paraded around in a gold frame. Worshippers touch it with their forehead and then kiss it, and when it is read it is in the ancient language of Ge'ez, which is not commonly understood outside the priesthood.

177

The most extraordinary part of the service is the music, which is played on three big barrel-shaped drums (*kebros*), accompanied by *sistras*, which are small wooden-handled instruments on which a line of silver discs is shaken to produce a sound not unlike that of a castanet or tambourine. The three drummers and twenty other musicians slowly build up a rhythmic counterpoint to the increasingly fast and strident chanting of the priest, and as they do so they begin a swinging forward movement with steps to left and right. It is a hypnotic routine and presumably intended to play worshippers and participants into some heightened state. We leave after nearly three hours of the service. The charismatic and indefatigable chief priest is in full flood at an open balcony as the rain drips past him off the roof and onto the patient crowd below.

If all goes well I am to travel into southern Ethiopia with an Oxfam team, and this afternoon I go out to meet them at the home of Belai Berhe, who has worked with Oxfam since it began operating in Ethiopia seventeen years ago. He has a comfortable, sparsely furnished house on the outskirts of the city, and while I talk with him and Kiros, a water and wells specialist, Neggar, who designed the new village wells, and Nick Rosevear, the only Englishman of the group, Belai's wife performs the coffee ceremony. It's not a ceremony in the sense that it is done on rare and special occasions, in fact it happens several times a day in nearly every household in the country. The Ethiopians adore coffee and grow some of the best in the world.

It is about as far from instant coffee as you can go, and involves first roasting the beans over a charcoal burner. A bracing, pungent smell rises from the fire as the white beans turn brown. When the beans are roasted they are offered round for us to smell, then pounded in a wooden mortar with what looks like a spider wrench from a car kit. The grains are laid out on a straw dish before being squeezed into a tall, elegant coffee pot with a narrow head, into which is poured boiling water. The jug is then put back on the coals to keep warm.

The coffee, needless to say, is excellent, sharp and fresh and powerful.

The ceremony, Belai tells me, should take an hour – twenty minutes for the preparation and forty minutes for the drinking. We spend at least forty minutes drinking and talking over the recent 'take-over', as people here prefer to call it. Someone points out that the removal of Mengistu was not a revolution, that the revolution happened in 1974 when Haile Selassie was overthrown. What happened in May was just putting it back on course.

Neggar is optimistic that things will get better, particularly if farmers are allowed to farm their own land and sell their own produce, but at the end of it all Nick sums up the difference between now and then.

'Six months ago we couldn't have sat here and talked like this. Under Mengistu Ethiopia was to all intents and purposes a closed country.'

Belai's hospitable wife and family have prepared supper for us as well and it's my first experience of a staple of the Ethiopian diet – injera. Injera is made from a low-grade cereal called tef. It is not unlike a rubber mat in size and consistency, sour to the Western palate but very useful for mopping up the various side dishes – an all-purpose spicy stew known as a wat, spinach, and a feta-like cheese. A meady liquor called tej completes a collection of unfamiliar tastes.

DAY 84: *Addis Ababa to Lake Awasa*

Clusters of small, deep-red spots on my arm, stomach and around my ankles indicate, according to Dawood (*How to Stay Healthy Abroad*), the activities of *cimex*, which sounds like a Swiss drug company but is in fact the Latin name for bedbug. I found it in the chapter entitled 'Fleas, lice, bugs, scabies and other creatures', which I defy anyone to read without scratching. After a lot of misunderstanding I manage to persuade hotel housekeeping to come up and spray my bed.

'Make the bed?'

'No ... no ... the bed is made, but it has some bugs in it, which need to be removed.'

'You want your bags removed?'

The combination of bugs in the bed and a bug in my digestive system has meant little rest, but nothing much has gone right here. The management even chose our day off to empty the swimming-pool.

Now, a little after seven in the morning, we are leaving Addis, to no one's regret, and heading south again. I am in an Oxfam Land-cruiser, accompanied by Nick, with an Oxfam helper, Tadesse, at the wheel.

The road out of Addis is metalled and we make good progress. We pass factories and power-stations on the outskirts of town. Nick reckons that the industrial infrastructure is enough for Ethiopia's needs, but is run at only thirty per cent of its potential.

Most Ethiopians are farmers anyway – ninety-two per cent of the population, in fact. Of these, eighty-nine per cent are subsistence farmers, growing only what they need for themselves. Our journey from the Sudanese border has been through the provinces of Gondar, Shewa and now Arsi, the only three that produce a surplus. The other eleven provinces survive at a basic level or in the recent cases of Wollo, Tigray and Eritrea not even that.

This is the grim background to Oxfam's seventeen years of work out here, but Nick is hopeful that the Ethiopians will be able to solve their own problems.

'If one thinks about the fact that more than half the gross national product for the last seventeen years has been spent on the civil war, that is an awful lot to ask of anybody, let alone a country where there are such intractable problems.'

If the new government can give some encouragement to farmers to grow for profit, he believes that Oxfam, along with other non-government agencies, could help the country to a stage at which, as he puts it, 'Oxfam hopes to do itself out of a job.'

The landscape is changing again as we come down from the plateau and into the Rift Valley, part of a 4000-mile split in the earth's crust running from the Red Sea to Mozambique. Acacia trees have replaced fig and eucalyptus, their flat tops reflecting the flat, wide plain between distant mountain ranges. The dusty terrain is studded with termite mounds – white, chunky blobs like the droppings of some giant creature that has moved across the countryside.

Outside Meki we pass two priests standing beside the road beneath wildly colourful umbrellas. For a moment it looks as though they're hitch-hiking, but in fact they're collecting for church funds. As a vehicle goes by they upturn their brollies and people throw money in.

At Bulbula, cattle are being driven down to drink at a palm-fringed pool fed by a narrow river and here we encounter our first baobab tree. These ancient growths are sometimes referred to as 'upside-down trees' and with their wide, stumpy trunks and scrawny branches they do indeed look as if they have been thrust into the earth the wrong way up.

By lunchtime we've covered 150 miles with ease and have reached the noisy, vigorous road-junction town of Shashamene. Kites and eagles circle above a busy main street with video stores, garages, stationery shops and public table tennis by the side of the road. Little children chew sugar cane, while their older brothers and sisters sell corn on the cob off charcoal fires. A huge parked Mercedes truck offers shade to a sheep suckling its young, a sleeping dog and, under the back axle, a cow, possibly hiding away from the legendary Ethiopian butchers' shops in which you can order a slice of raw flesh off the carcass and eat it then and there. We look into one. A huddle of men in the back of the shop are chewing away surrounded by walls of meat. Roger is very keen for me to join them but they are, thank God, not the least bit interested in appearing on television. We encounter similar resistance from the voluble and entertaining spokesman of a Rastafarian community in the town. Maybe it's because he's from Peckham in South London, but Tony, who talks to us outside a neat and well-kept collection of plain wooden huts with washing spread out on the grass to dry, is paranoid about the media. He's also fascinated by the media. His heroes are John Arlott, the cricket commentator, and Max

Robertson. He is canny enough to know that people are curious about a Jamaican who supports Manchester United and claims to be a member of one of the lost tribes of Judah. He is also convinced that for some reason we will misrepresent him.

'You people! . . . What can you ever know or understand about what we do here!'

Understanding only comes from knowing, but Tony is adamant: 'Come back in three years when we have got it together'.

Janet, also from Peckham, smiles helpfully, says she can't change his mind, but she does recognize me from Monty Python. I feel our stay at Shashamene has been in the very best Python tradition.

Having failed with raw meat and Rastas we fetch up for the night at a lakeside hotel in Awasa. It's rather like checking into a zoo. A monkey sits at reception chewing the rubber off a pencil. In the grounds a pair of black-and-white casqued hornbills crash about in a cover of lush and exotic trees.

A tunnel of hibiscus bushes leads to a pair of old iron gates that give onto Lake Awasa itself. The water is fringed by a reed-bed in which Nick points out to me at least four varieties of kingfisher, an African jacana, or lilytrotter – an Audrey Hepburn of the avian world – and a tall, red-necked Goliath heron who appears to be monarch of all he surveys until with a rush of black and white and a brief cry of protest he is seen off by an African fish eagle.

The hotel bar fills up at dusk with locals and the ubiquitous aid workers or 'aidies' as they're known here. Unfortunately the beer runs out and not many people are left when at ten o'clock there is an English-language news programme on the television, preceded, inexplicably, by a short film on ankle injuries.

Our dinner conversation is becoming increasingly dominated by bowel talk. Since the crossing into Ethiopia all of us have been afflicted in some way. Is it the beer? Or the hotel salad? Nick can cap all our stories with his experience of *giardia lamblia*, which sounds like the ultimate in these sort of problems. I look it up in Dawood before I go to sleep and wish I hadn't.

DAY 85: *Lake Awasa*

Out today to see Oxfam's water resources programme at work. Like many people I have contributed to Oxfam for many years and it's rare to have a first-hand chance to see how the money is spent. We head for Boditi, a small town, two hours' drive away along dirt roads.

Oxfam's programme is designed to require the minimum amount of cost and technological expertise. There is little point in pouring money into sophisticated technology unless the local people can use it and repair it when it goes wrong. The village well that Kiros and Nick take me to see uses a simple pump with only two replaceable parts, which can be installed with nothing more than a spanner. It has been dug to a depth of ninety feet to tap an almost infinite source. A possibly tainted water supply from a river two hours' walk away has been replaced by a safe, regular supply of pure water in the centre of the village, at a cost of around £2000 provided, in this case, from Comic Relief funds. It's too early to tell how significant a difference it will make to the lives of these 600 villagers but aside from the obvious health advantages Nick thinks that one of the chief benefits will be to the lives of the women of the village whose job it traditionally is to walk to the river to collect and carry back the water. Suddenly they have three or four hours a day given back to them.

There is some bad news waiting for us at the hotel. Monty Ruben, a friend who had looked after us in Kenya when I was filming *The Missionary* there nine years ago, has been taken to hospital after a heart attack. He was to meet us at the border and guide us to Nairobi, hut now we must make alternative plans, and quickly too, for we should cross the border in two days' time.

DAY 86: *Lake Awasa to Moyale*

Scatter the monkeys from the vehicles at seven o'clock as we load up once again. It's our eleventh day in Ethiopia. By tonight

183

we hope to be in the border town of Moyale, 325 miles away. We pick our way through the Awasa rush-hour, in which we are about the only vehicles. Everyone else is walking: school-children, farmers, soldiers, workers on their way to the textile factory or the production lines of the National Tobacco and Matches Corporation.

There is not much public transport down here. People either walk, or pack into the back of precarious and overladen pick-up trucks which travel at lethal speeds. There is the occasional bus, so occasional that it is usually packed to the gunnels. The only other alternative is to hitch a ride on top of a truck. This sounds to me a novel way of seeing Africa, which is why I end up jostling with banana-sellers in the main road at Yirga Alem at nine o'clock on a Thursday morning. After a half-hour wait we persuade a small truck packed with sacks of kef to take us some of the way to Moyale.

The roadside buzzes with life on this stretch of green, fertile, lushly tropical valley, and besides the usual firewood and charcoal vendors are small children waving sugar canes four times their own size, and squatting figures laying out white peanuts to dry on the hot road surface.

Pedestrians – mostly women – toil by with enormous loads on backs or heads. A mountain of cut grass almost obscures the old lady beneath it, giving the impression that it is moving up the road of its own volition.

We pass a crowd of people on a bridge staring down into the gully below. A truck has plunged twenty feet and lies there on its back, wheels still spinning. An hour later on a deserted stretch among acacia scrub a pick-up truck which had earlier roared past us packed with standing figures lies flipped over on the road, its cab crushed, and two of the passengers dead.

By early afternoon the countryside has changed from the fertile valleys to a scrub-covered semi-desert. I've seen camels for the first time since the Sudan and the termite architecture is increasingly Gothic. One mound, at least fifteen feet high, is the most extraordinary feat of building I have seen since the Hypostyle Hall at Karnak.

The people are changing too. We are now in the land of the Borena, animists and gatherers. The women are very beautiful, exotically dressed in bright swirls of jade green, deep blue and lemon yellow. They smile broadly as we pass.

At 5.30 a rattling truck takes us through the last of the army checkpoints and into the town of Moyale. The barrier – a bar stretched across the road and weighted at one end with an old cylinder block – is raised and lowered by one of the boy soldiers holding a length of rope.

The town is divided into Ethiopian and Kenyan Moyale by a muddy stream and some sophisticated link fencing on the Kenyan side. Judging by the lights and the noise and the crowds in the street, Ethiopian Moyale is the hotter of the two spots. It has the rakish brashness and heightened energy of a frontier town. Arguments are louder here, drivers more impatient, demands more urgent. Music blares out from shops. Graceful pale-blue jacaranda trees add a little style to its streets, but really, the place is a mess.

At the Bekele Molla hotel we are greeted by the good news that Monty Ruben is not seriously ill and that Abercrombie and Kent, the safari people, have at the last minute organized alternative transport for us to Nairobi.

Our hotel is described by its manager as the best hotel in Moyale. I cannot imagine what the opposition must be like. The rooms are set off a yard in motel style. I *do* have a double bed with slightly damp but, I think, clean sheets and there *is* electric light, but the bathroom has no running water or flushing lavatory. A half-full plastic bucket of water must serve all my needs. The curtain is a fragment of torn sacking and there is a heady smell of stale urine.

I'm told that there is a serious water crisis in the town. Wells have been sunk but the water is brackish. Southern Ethiopia and northern Kenya are becoming part of the Sahel – the sub-Saharan area that is turning rapidly into desert. This information only serves to turn my particular gloom into a general gloom. So little of what I have seen so far in Africa can by any stretch of the imagination be described as progress, with the possible exception of the pump and well I saw yesterday near Boditi. Maybe 'progress' is a Western concept, irrelevant in African terms. Talk of 'solutions' and 'ways forward' may make us feel better but can mean nothing until the yawning gap between Western and African culture begins to narrow and that probably requires a lot more listening and a lot less talking.

I finish the day writing up my notes in my hotel room. I feel a light tingling on my left arm and look down to find that I have diverted a column of ants off the wall and across my body.

Later. After a last taste of injera and wat at a restaurant in the town, I have doused myself with Repel, lit one of the spiral anti-mosquito burners provided and taken a large swig of Scotch. I hope my dreams of Ethiopia will not be affected by this grim place, for so much of what I have seen of the country has been a rich and surprising revelation.

DAY 87: *Moyale to Marsabit*

Wind rose during the night. I rose several times as well. It seems that the restoration of digestive stability after Addis was only temporary. My alarm sounds at six. Reach for the light, but there is no electricity this morning. Wash in mineral water as my bucket supply has all gone.

After breakfast we climb into new vehicles marshalled by Wendy Corroyer, an impressively competent lady from Abercrombie and Kent. There are four altogether, Landcruisers again, but larger than we have had previously, bought as one-ton trucks and converted into sturdy, elongated jeeps for work on safaris. My driver is short, muscular and middle-aged. He smiles easily, but cannily. His name is Kalului. Our other drivers are Kabagire, a young, slim, shyly handsome man, George, and William whose T-shirt reads 'Born to be on Vacation'.

At half-past eight we roll down the hill out of Ethiopia. Out of 1984 and back into 1991.

As the Kenyan customs officer plants an entry stamp on a fresh page of my passport I remark on how odd it is that it should be seven years later here. He looks across the page at my Ethiopian visa and nods sagely: 'They will never catch up with us'.

Further up the hill, in the main square of Kenyan Moyale, we wait for the armed guard who will accompany us as far as Isiolo. This is the third country in a row to have bandit problems. Here the blame is laid on Somali guerrillas.

We are now in Swahili-speaking Africa and I can dust down my Jambos (Hellos) and my Akuna Matatas (No Problems). Less auspiciously for us, Pole Pole in Swahili means 'Slowly Slowly'.

This does not deter Kalului from setting off like a man possessed once all the border checks are completed. Unfortunately the British were never as keen on road-building as the Italians, and the smooth tarred Ethiopian road north of Moyale becomes dirt track to the south. A fine dust soon settles over everything and I now know why they laughed when I appeared at breakfast in a clean white shirt.

Every now and then we hit a run of shallow ruts and for fifteen seconds it's like being in a cocktail shaker. I cannot imagine how the vehicles survive this kind of treatment. The answer is they don't and at 11.20 we have our first puncture.

Wendy is philosophical about the delay. She has been in the safari business for years and as she says cheerfully, 'I haven't lost anyone yet'. Born in South Africa and now living in Kenya, she describes herself unapologetically as 'an old colonial'. She thinks that there have been many improvements in the country, but the fast-growing population has brought problems. Wild animals are now increasingly confined to expensively maintained reserves, with results that include a sharp growth in elephant numbers. From being almost an endangered species elephants are now in danger of damaging a fragile environment. Richard Leakey, the Director of Kenya's Wildlife Services, is, Wendy reckons, facing a tough decision.

'We made this stand on elephant poaching and we burned all that ivory, so now we have got world attention we've got to think of a solution other than culling.'

Apart from the security checkpoints – nail-studded wooden strips laid across the road – there are few breaks in this silent wilderness.

After an incongruous picnic of Brie cheese, frankfurters and fresh pineapple, we rattle and roll on towards our goal for the day – the town of Marsabit, 155 miles south of Moyale.

Scrub gives way to desert. We cross a desolate coverless landscape of black basalt rocks called the Dida Galgalu – the 'Plains of Darkness' – and then, as we begin to climb out of the plains and up on to the 6000-foot plateau of Marsabit, the 'Place of Cold', the scenery changes dramatically. We begin, at last, to see wild animals – such as dik-dik, the tiniest of the antelope family, gerenuk, which stand on their hind legs to nibble thorn bush branches and apparently never need to drink, and the ubiquitous Grant's gazelle, poised and graceful. Higher up, at the rim of a magnificent volcanic crater, we are watched closely by a greater kudu, a fine, tall antelope with lofty spiralling horns.

Our resting-place for the night is the Marsabit Lodge, set in rich green woodland beside a crater lake within the National Park.

No sooner have we arrived than a slow procession of elephants – three adults and three young – emerge from the trees and make their stately way round the lake towards us. They are the descendants of the magnificent Ahmed, the only elephant to be protected by presidential decree. He used to live in this park, constantly attended by his own personal rangers. To sit with a beer at sunset watching a young descendant of his being taught how to flick earth onto its back is well worth the price of the ticket. On the tree beside me hangs a sign, 'Animals are requested to be silent when people are drinking, and vice versa'.

By a stroke of luck there is a complete power failure in the hotel. We eat by candlelight and sit afterwards beside a log fire. Sprawled out in front of us is an unkempt and indolent hotel cat. Now and then we can hear from out of the darkness a tearing of undergrowth as the elephants plod slowly about, feeding voraciously. The combination of cats at the hearth and elephants in the garden outside is quite surreal, and oddly comforting.

DAY 88: *Marsabit to Shaba*

At first light we are on our way up the bumpy tortuous track and out of this mountain-top forest, passing by some extra-ordinary trees with sinewy roots twisting down the outside of the trunk. Wendy tells me these are strangler figs. They are seeded by birds and grow around an existing tree, becoming stronger and stronger until they kill off the host.

The road south – still no more than a dusty track – descends from Mount Marsabit to the hot and rocky plain. We pass a group of Rendille tribesmen, tall and very straight, wearing head-dresses, bare-chested apart from coloured beads around the neck, taking their cattle to water. One carries a gun, another a stick tipped with a plume of ostrich feathers, a sign that they come in peace – unless you're an elephant. One looms closely and the men fling stones at it to keep it away from their herd. A little while later a group of Rendille women pass. These nomadic people walking barefoot along the dusty rutted tracks of Africa look as effortlessly graceful and immaculate as anyone on a *Vogue* cover. From a band around their heads hang discs of what looks like gold or silver, their long necks are held erect by a stack of beads, and they wear loose flowing garments of red and white striped cotton. They lead donkeys hung about with every kind of plastic container. They're looking for water.

Weaver birds nest in the low, flat-topped acacias. Those with tidy nests are the sociable weavers and those with the scruffier nests, constantly having to rebuild, are known as the sparrow weavers. Two white-bellied turacos, known, because of their cry, as the 'go-away' birds, shriek at us from a high branch.

We are now entering the land of the Samburu, or 'Butterfly' tribe. They are a branch of the Ma people, of whom the best known are the Masai, who many years ago split from the Samburu and went south. The Samburu remain, like the Rendille and the Borena in southern Ethiopia, a colourful, un-Westernized tribe still practising male and female circumcision. They love dress and display, especially favouring ear ornaments – rings in top and bottom and lobes pierced then stretched into holes an inch wide.

I have fond memories of filming *The Missionary* in Samburu territory – at the village of Lerata. We built a mud-and-wattle chapel, complete with stained glass windows, in which I played 'From Greenland's Icy Mountain', which the local children specially learnt for the occasion. Our construction crew put a new roof on the schoolroom, and I wanted to return and see if it had survived and what, if anything, they remembered of us.

It is baking hot again – 112 degrees in the sun – as we reach the village. The schoolchildren, neatly turned out in gold and blue uniforms, have obviously been told to expect a celebrity, and as soon as we stop they crowd around Wendy, chanting, smiling and clapping. When eventually they are pointed in my direction they are confused and cannot whip up quite the same degree of enthusiasm. But Henry the teacher is still there and so is the schoolroom roof, and beneath it I tell the children about the journey I am doing with the aid of the inflatable globe that stood me in such good stead on *Around the World in 80 Days*. At the end I donate the globe to Lerata School, which they all seem to think is wonderful and proceed to play football with it.

A boy called Tom, who remembers singing in the film, has come all the way from Eldoret University in the west of the country where he is a sociology student. We look at photos taken during the filming, while the bonily photogenic elders of the village debate how much it will cost for them to be filmed.

This is a poor part of the country and the liveliness and eagerness of the children is moving. Henry, who is the sort of opportunist the place needs, tells me they are building a dormitory for children who have to come in from a long way. They have everything but the roof.

By the time I leave Lerata they have money for another roof.

As we drive away, a dust devil, a column of dust whipped up by the wind to a height of thirty or forty feet, snakes out of the bush and across our path. It seems an appropriate image for our visit to Lerata. A rush of hyperactive whites, a windfall and we're gone.

At four o'clock we are staring into the eyeless sockets of two massive water-buffalo skulls which mark the entrance to the Shaba National Reserve, 160 miles from Marsabit and not much more than fifty miles from the Equator.

The Shaba Lodge is a wonderful hotel, unashamedly modern but not ostentatiously luxurious, skilfully landscaped among tall trees along the Vaso Nyiro river. Last night at Marsabit we had water but no electricity, the night before that we had electricity and no water, tonight we have a swimming-pool, double beds, mosquito nets, a bedroom and a sitting-room. But the shock of comfort brings with it less pleasant shocks. One is the realization that, for the first time since leaving the Old Cataract Hotel, Aswan, we are back on the tourist trail – back in the world of aimlessly pointing video cameras, bandy white legs and loud, complaining voices.

'Where are those bats coming from?'

'I don't know where they're coming from.'

'They came right down and zoomed my head. It was horrible!'

I have to physically restrain myself from shouting, 'Then why come here? Why ever leave home at all?'

Maybe it's just that I've been away from home too long.

DAY 89: *Shaba to Nairobi*

A significant day ahead. By the time it's over we should be in the Southern Hemisphere, over halfway to our goal after three months' travelling.

Wendy thinks we should be up at 5 a.m. if we want to see the summit of Mount Kenya before the clouds form over it, but long-term fatigue wins the day over short-term shot-chasing and we gather for breakfast soon after six o'clock. Sparrows and starlings are already in attendance in the dining-room. The sparrows are familiar but the starlings here look a lot sharper than their British counterparts. They're known as superb starlings and are luridly turned out with metallic blue backs and chestnut bellies.

The Shaba Lodge has a bookshop and while we wait to leave I'm able to acquire the indispensable *Field Guide to the Birds of East Africa* (650 species described) and the equally illuminating *Mammals of Africa*.

Straightaway I'm able to identify a greenbacked heron (rare) and the more common marabou stork. Two of these are moving, with measured strut, along a sandy spit in the middle of the river. Seen from behind, with their heads down and their voluminous white wings clasped behind them they look like a couple of elderly dons debating some fine point of moral philosophy.

Isiolo is a place of mixed blessings. Roads from predominantly Moslem Somalia and predominantly Christian Ethiopia converge here, on the northern edge of the prosperous colonial heartland around Mount Kenya. A fine mosque, with delicate filigree work around the windows and a cluster of beautiful domed alcoves atop the minarets, shares the main street with a branch of Barclays Bank, video stores, one-room hotels and churches of the Seventh-Day Adventists and many others of the 140 religious sects alive and well in Kenya. The roadside salesmen are hard and aggressive, but at least the going is softer, with the road metalled again after 320 miles of dirt-track.

Lying between here and Nairobi, and forcing a long detour to east or west, is the soaring bulk of the Mount Kenya massif. The highest of its ragged peaks, Batian, rises to 17,000 feet. It is the second highest point in Africa, after Kilimanjaro, and was first climbed by a Westerner, Sir Halford Mackinder, in the last year of the nineteenth century. Even from the hot plain beyond Isiolo one can make out the glaciers and ice-fields at its summit, which ensure that there is always snow at the Equator.

As the road climbs, I can see that Wendy was right – a helmet of cloud is beginning to form around the top of the mountain and may well have concealed it altogether by the time we are close enough to film.

The scenery has once more undergone an amazing transformation. We could be in the American Rockies, with the towering crags of Mount Kenya on one side and rolling prairie on the other.

A secretary bird, quills bristling, struts self-importantly through a fresh-cut cornfield, an augur buzzard beadily scans the terrain from the top of a telegraph pole. Higher up, fat fluffy flocks of sheep graze in the shadow of the mountain.

'Great sweater country,' says Wendy. We grab a shot of the summit with seconds to spare, and the road coasts downhill to the town of Nanyuki, passing signs for 'Jack Wright Ltd Family Butcher', 'Modern Sanitary Stores', 'Kenya Insurance', 'Marshall's Peugeot' and finally, 'The Equator'.

Clem and Angela have driven out from Nairobi to surprise us – and a lot of onlooking souvenir salesmen – with a bottle or two of champagne. This reunion of the entire crew not only celebrates a certain achievement, it also averts potential anti-climax, for the Equator line, marked as it is by power cables, a main road and an electricity substation, could just as well be in Croydon as Kenya.

In the ruins of what was once the Silverbeck Hotel, which straddled the Equator and offered punters the prospect of buying a beer in the Northern Hemisphere and drinking it in the Southern, a young African called Peter demonstrates the Coriolis effect by which energy in the Northern Hemisphere appears to be directed to the right, and in the Southern to the left. Peter drains a bowl of water in the North, and, by means of a floating stick, we observe that the water drains away in a clockwise direction. Then we (myself and a group of American tourists) wander with Peter, his stick and his plastic bucket into the Southern Hemisphere, where we observe that in exactly the same operation the stick turns anti-clockwise. On the Equator line itself, the stick doesn't turn at all.

Peter politely acknowledges our expressions of wonder and then prepares for the next demonstration while we collect certificates to show that we have seen what we have seen.

For a proper celebration of Sunday at the Equator we adjourn to the unashamed luxury of the Mount Kenya Safari Club. Here, amidst immaculately coiffeured lawns patrolled by ibises, cranes, peacocks and marabou storks, is a sign telling us we are eating our Sunday joint on Latitude 00.00, Longitude 37.7 East at 7000 feet.

The run into Nairobi is full of reminders of a way of life very different from what we have seen in our last six weeks in Africa. Tribal costumes give way to T-shirts and jeans. There are traffic jams of private cars, road signs, newspapers, irrigation sprinklers, villagers on bicycles (why were there so few bicycles in Ethiopia and Sudan?) and polite notices at the end of towns and villages saying 'Kwaheri'. Goodbye.

For us it's goodbye to the Northern Hemisphere after three months on the road. I don't really think about what's to come. It's hard enough to accept that we have to do that distance all over again.

DAY 95: *Nairobi*

It seems to be an odd psychological and physiological fact that on a journey like this time off is trouble. The system, geared up to movement and rapid adjustment to changing conditions, is caught off-guard and may begin to wind down, thinking perhaps that it's all over. The adrenalin is switched off and all sorts of little ailments appear. I have the feeling that after five days' break in Nairobi all of us will be very glad to be on the move again. We all know that the only way back home is via the South Pole.

This morning I'm to be fitted for an outfit in advance of the next stage of our journey – an Abercrombie and Kent safari into the Masai Mara game reserve. I'm collected at the hotel by a London black cab. President Arap Moi was so impressed with them on a visit to Britain that he allowed them to be imported into Kenya free of duty, and there are now over 100 operating in Nairobi. I ask Michael Nqanga, my driver, if anything has ever gone wrong with his vehicle. 'Not exactly,' he replies, but doesn't elaborate.

Downtown Nairobi is compact and modern and not particularly beautiful. Bland concrete blocks are being superseded by bland aluminium and glass blocks. The reflecting walls of Lonrho's new headquarters dominate the skyline. If cranes and scaffolding are a sign of confidence then Nairobi appears to be doing well, though local people I have spoken to regard Moi's maintenance of a one-party state as a source of weakness and potential future chaos. Opposition is tightly muzzled, both by the imprisonment of its leaders and by restriction and censorship of the press.

But at Colpro, safari suppliers to the rich and famous, it's business as usual. Well, not quite as usual, for as Chetan Haria, the proprietor, tells me, the tourist market still hasn't recovered from the Gulf crisis. There was a time, he remembers fondly, when 270 Americans came in at once, 'all wanting to look the same'.

His family began the business as an army surplus store thirty years ago and it has grown to be the leading supplier of safari gear, much of which is based on military uniform. Now that the Hemingway days are over and hunting is strictly controlled the outfits are a mass of anachronisms, a matter of fashion rather than practicality. The jacket design seems entirely pocket led. Some models have as many as twelve in various places. What earthly use, I ask Chetan, is a pocket sewn into the lining in the middle of the back? He glances towards the door.

'There are thieves outside,' he confides darkly.

I settle for what is described as a 'photo-journalist's jacket' as I know it will be good for a laugh from the crew. It is.

A photograph of Prince Charles – a previous customer – is tacked onto the wall beside the changing booth from which I eventually emerge with my ensemble: a cotton shirt with a map of Kenya printed on it, my photo-journalist's jacket and a pair of trousers which can be unzipped at the kneecap should I prefer shorts.

Apart from being an extremely helpful place, Chetan's store displays none of the colonial snobbishness I had associated with safari-ism. He is just as happy to sell you a tape of local tribal music, or a 'Wild Thing' T-shirt, or a 'Horny Friends' bag.

Outside, many of the city's buildings are being draped in the national colours for Kenyatta Day, tomorrow's national holiday in honour of the man who led Kenya to independence from the British twenty-eight years ago.

Like Colpro the outfitters and the Republic of Kenya, Abercrombie and Kent have been in business for almost thirty years. Their safari stores are located in a solid stone-walled building in one of the burgeoning industrial estates around Nairobi. Here two Isuzu trucks are being loaded up with the eleven and a half tons of equipment we shall need over the next three days. Travel-hardened wooden and tin crates are filled with everything from toilet paper and fresh-cut flowers to hot-water bottles and cases of Blanc de Blancs. In the storeroom are rows of trestle tables, bed frames and barbecues, sackfuls of mallets, shelves of hurricane lamps and coathangers, piles of doormats and shovels and lavatory seats. There is even a wood-framed double bed. 'Usually reserved for honeymooners,' explains Martin, who is in charge of our preparations.

The drive to the Mara can be tricky, with dirt roads for most of the way. Martin is anxious to get the big trucks off as soon as possible. 'In the last four years the rains have gone crazy.' (They call rain 'rains' out here, but elephants they call 'elephant'.)

This year they are expected two weeks early, which could mean tomorrow, and an eight-hour journey to the camp can take as long as four days in bad weather.

DAY 96: *Nairobi to the Masai Mara*

Up at 5.15. On the move, away from the world of CNN and English newspapers and telephone access to life at home.

Pulling back the curtains, I can make out the dark clouds which have hung over the capital these past few days with still no sign of them emptying. Below me a border of white, purple, orange and blue bougainvillea almost obscures the chain-link fence which, like the corridor outside my room, is patrolled by guards with nightsticks.

I'm reunited with Wendy and Kalului and our caravan sets off at 6.30. The streets of Nairobi are quiet on this Kenyatta Day holiday, but as the sun rises and we head north along the Trans-African highway, the roads soon fill up with the tearaway minibuses they call Matatus, whose names indicate their driving style – 'Exocet', 'Sidewinder', and most ironic of all in view of their appalling accident record, 'Gateway to Heaven'.

Up and over a string of fertile valleys and cultivated hillsides, where roses, carnations and poinsettias are grown to be sold in Europe. Behind neatly trimmed hedges is a picture postcard tea plantation, with rows of green bushes radiating from a cluster of low red-roofed buildings. It looks like a country without a care in the world, yet so many here feel it is heading into serious political trouble.

We climb to the top of the eastern wall of the Rift Valley, about 8000 feet above sea-level. There is an almost dizzying view of a great expanse of sunlit plain dominated to the north by the grey, deeply fissured walls of the extinct volcano Longonot.

The valley floor is rich ranchland, and when in the film *Mogambo*, Clark Gable looks out over this same view and shouts 'Gorilla!', every true Kenyan cracks up. The nearest gorilla is at least 500 miles away.

Our reverie is broken by the roar of a Mack truck on its way from Rwanda in central Africa to the port of Mombasa. It barrels dangerously down the hill, sending up a shower of dust and stones around the words on its tailgate: 'Praise the Lord. He is Merciful'.

197

We stop to buy a late breakfast of fresh-grilled corn cobs from some children at the roadside. A troop of baboons is scattered across the road, extracting bits of corn and wheat grain that have, literally, fallen off the back of a lorry. Some have their young slung beneath them, where they remain until five weeks old, after which they're transferred onto mother's back for three months and only much later allowed to run and play on their own. Wendy says that most safari tours miss all this. They are air-lifted straight out to the Mara.

The entertainment goes on. Giraffe glide with effortless grace through the pale gold grass. Hartebeest and Thomson's gazelle graze beneath the predatory eye of vultures, kites and buzzards. A black-tailed mongoose scuttles across our path. As we climb the western wall of the Rift Valley we come upon a flock of fifty or sixty goats who have mounted the bank at the side of the road, nuzzling the earth and sticking their heads into a honeycomb of small holes from which they are trying to extract salt.

We are now running west, back a little way towards our thirty degree meridian. At Narok we leave the metalled road again and are soon bouncing our way over mercifully dry tracks, past tall, long-striding Masai, usually wearing red cloaks or blankets across one shoulder. Their villages, enclosed by a stockade fence, are known as manyattas. The men maintain the fence leaving the women to the less glamorous job of coating the stick-frame houses with dung.

By late afternoon we have covered about 145 miles from Nairobi and are crossing into the Masai Mara National Reserve. Unlike the Serengeti to the south, the Mara is not a National Park and the Masai farmers are allowed to graze their flocks here. This mixture of the wild and the domestic, cows and sheep grazing alongside giraffe and elephant, gives the Reserve a special Noah's Ark quality.

But man is now very much a part of the Mara, and as we near the river the afternoon session of tourists are being transported out of their lodges in a fleet of open-topped minibuses.

Wendy is a bit sniffy about them. 'If you've been to Africa

and stayed in a lodge, you've been on a holiday; if you've been to Africa and stayed in a tent, you've been on safari.'

When we reach our campsite by the banks of the Mara river, the tents have only just been pitched and lavatories not yet dug or beds erected. Patrick, the *maître de camp*, who has safaried with Hemingway, but still looks only twenty-five, welcomes us, quickly introduces the staff of thirteen, makes us cups of tea and leaves us to look at the local river life. This consists of a colony of around thirty hippos puffing and wheezing like a lot of old men in a club after lunch. They apparently spend most of the day there, emerging at night to feed and, I'm told, wander through the camp. 'It's perfectly all right so long as you stay in your tent,' Martin advises, cheerfully.

We are on what is known as the 'Out of Africa' safari – one up from the 'Hemingway', which is one up from the 'Kenya under Canvas'. This certainly isn't how I remember school camp. The tents are spacious. At the back, and under cover, there is a sort of dressing area, with a table and mirror, and a plastic toilet over a freshly dug hole. Beside the hole is a pile of earth, a small spade and a sign: 'Hippos cover it up, will you do too'. I have an old-fashioned bed, a solar-powered light and a rail for my clothes, and outside the roof of the tent extends over a wash-stand and a couple of canvas chairs, excellent for sitting out in before supper, and drinking a Scotch to the accompaniment of awfully rude noises from the river.

Dinner is served after a slight delay owing to the activity of baboons in the kitchen. Martin tells the story of one guest who felt a baboon against the side of his tent and whacked it with a heavy torch. It turned out to be a hippo, which charged off through the kitchen tent. The tent offered little resistance, and the hippo vanished into the bush with the kitchen wrapped around him.

10.20 p.m. The river is silent. A big moon casts a silvery light across the trees and the banks of the river. A group of Masai from the local manyatta guard the camp, sitting by a wood fire and talking quietly. One of them, an elderly man with close-cropped grey hair, walks up and down between our tents and the river, ear-ringed, blanketed and carrying a spear. I feel very strongly that I am in a dream I once had, a long time ago.

DAY 97: *The Masai Mara*

Roars, splashes and hippo hoots mark the end of the night and I'm already awake when I hear the first human cry.

'Jambo!' comes from outside a nearby tent, followed by the sound of a door-flap being unzipped and bleary greetings from the occupants. It's six o'clock. There are no lie-ins on safari.

I'm Jambo-ed a minute or two later. A flask of tea, a plate of biscuits, and milk in a china jug are set down by the bed and hot water poured into the washing bowl outside.

Dressed in my Colpro safari outfit, looking and feeling like a cut-price David Attenborough, I set out at 6.45, with the sun struggling to make an impression on a cloudy lifeless sky.

We make our way along the damp uneven track from the riverside towards the tall slope of the escarpment, passing zebra, impala and a grazing warthog. Warthogs – ugly, endearing creatures – live in the remains of anthills into which they insert themselves backwards. For some reason this makes me even more fond of them.

Six elephants, mighty ears flapping and trunks ripping at the croton bushes, move down the hill away from us. They only sleep about two hours a night, I'm told. Kalului, who has an extraordinary sixth sense about the presence of animals, spots a lion couple away in the distance. As we drive closer they turn out to be a somewhat battered male and a lethargic female. Neither seems to bat an eyelid at the circling presence of three vehicles and a clutch of cameras only yards away. The female after washing and yawning, unhurriedly raises herself and the male immediately follows. He is limping. Lions spend about a week together mating, sometimes coupling as often as eighty times in twenty-four hours, but this affair looks to be over, if it ever began.

Meanwhile, in another episode of the Masai Mara soap

opera, a male ostrich is doing his best to attract the ladies' attention. He cannot rely on subtlety as his legs turn pink during the mating season, so he goes for broke with an outrageous fan dance, a wonderful spectacle of feather control, which does seem to have several female beaks turning in his direction.

In the midst of life we are in death. We pass Nubian vultures tearing away at the corpse of a zebra. These birds are known as the butchers, the only ones with necks and beaks powerful enough to open up a carcass. The coarse grass of the plain is littered with skulls, bones and skins, and the constant presence of vultures, eagles, buzzards and land scavengers like jackals, with their sharp faces and big ears, is a reminder of the precariousness of life.

Our feeding is a little more decorous. We are treated to one of the set-pieces of an A and K safari – the 'Out of Africa' breakfast. While we have been ear-wigging lion couples, the staff from the camp have set up a long table, complete with fresh flowers and cut-glass butter-dishes, on the top of the Olololo escarpment. Eggs, bacon and sausage are sizzling on an open fire and the waiters are in dinner-jackets. The plain stretches away, flat and wide, between the escarpment walls of the Rift Valley, south towards Tanzania. A thousand feet below us the sunless Mara, which we know to be teeming with living things, looks grey and empty, except for a Second World War DC-3, which makes a wide, banking turn before settling down onto the airstrip only a few hundred yards from where we watched the lions.

Later in the day grey clouds have filled the sky and the rain comes in, straight and heavy, putting an end to safari for the day.

Our journey through Africa has been planned to tread a fine line between the rainy seasons, but nature has not played along. The late rains in Sudan and now early rains in Kenya will not make our progress any easier.

The temperature falls to 63 Fahrenheit – the coldest we've experienced since northern Norway. There isn't much to do but sit and watch the water drip off the tents and listen to the blowing, wheezing, gasping, gurgling pleasure of the hippos.

Later some of the local Masai come to the camp to perform a traditional dance which tells the story of a lion hunt. I ask one of them afterwards if this is all now a thing of the past. He shakes his head firmly. Although it is not officially permitted to kill a lion in the Reserve, he and his fellow villagers recently took the law into their own hands after a lion had persistently attacked their goats. They hunted the lion down and killed it, with spears and arrows, not guns. Would he do it again? He nods, equally firmly, but says that the leader of their manyatta has now been recruited by the conservation people. 'This makes life more difficult for us.'

DAY 98: *The Masai Mara*

Wake to a sky of cloud and drizzle, which is unfortunate as we are to begin the day with a balloon ride over the Mara.

It's chilly and still dark when we arrive at the launch area, at the place called Little Governor's Camp. Surrounded by trees and stone-built, thatched cottages with hanging baskets by the doors, it is not unlike an English village green on a wet morning in November. However, the rain is not strong enough to abort the trip, and as a glum sunlight struggles through, instructions are given to fill the envelopes – the gasbags – of the two balloons. The envelopes are made by Thunder and Colt of Oswestry from six and a half miles of polyester fabric, and are thought to be the largest in the world. By the time they are inflated, each with 330,000 cubic feet of air heated to 100 degrees Centigrade, they will stand ninety feet high. Dawn breaks to the roar of the burners with their piercing yellow tongues of flame, and the slow tumescence of the multicoloured giants.

Each balloon can carry a dozen people and an apprehensive mixture of English and Americans is gathered in the half-light. I feel a sharp sting at the back of my leg, and turning to scratch, I notice that everyone else is doing the same thing.

'Safari ants,' says an Englishman cheerfully. 'Touch them and they bite.'

As a large number of them are halfway up my trouser leg and the ground is full of reinforcements this isn't particularly helpful, and trying to extricate myself from them is like a coping with a series of very light electric shocks.

Eventually the towering balloons are ready and we climb into our baskets. Each one is traditional, made of wood and cane, and divided into partitions, so once inside we must look a little like milk-bottles in a crate. Most of my co-passengers are American but the pilot is very British.

'My name is John Coleman and I'm your pilot this morning. As you can see I have three stripes on my epaulette – one for each laundry.'

He keeps up a steady stream of such observations as we rise slowly into the sky above the murky treescape below.

'If you feel a little frightened, don't worry. I get scared whenever I fly. Chicken in the basket.'

The Americans are a bit bewildered by all this and also a little disappointed at the lack of wildlife talent this soggy morning.

Still, they point in hope.

'Hey, look at that bird!', 'Look down there, there's one of those things . . . '

As John Coleman steers us along the tops of the trees, we learn from him that the hippos who keep us awake at night are amongst 2500 in the reserve, that the lungfish survives in the ox-bow lakes of the Mara river by burying itself in the mud during the long dry season and re-emerging when the rains come, and that elephants can drop their blood temperature eleven degrees just by flapping their ears.

Coleman takes the balloon down until we are almost on the ground, slowly skimming the surface at animal height, but not having found much he climbs swiftly to 1500 feet. He makes it all look very easy, but as he says, this is good ballooning country, no power cables or barbed-wire fences to worry about and a climate good enough for 350-days-a-year operation. The only danger is of straying across into Tanzania and having to put down there. It's easily done and recently a balloon safari was arrested and held by the Tanzanians for illegal entry.

The landing is a bit of a drag and a bump, but not uncomfortable, and we find ourselves within cork's distance of another Masai Mara champagne breakfast. Our glasses of pink champagne match the legs of a randy male ostrich racing about in the distance, but otherwise our bacon, egg, sausage, mushroom and croissant 'kill' is observed only by a yellow-bearded kite, a predator kept from the long, low breakfast-table by a line of spears.

Coleman brings the proceedings to a close with a toast to wives and girlfriends – 'May they never meet' – after which we collect another certificate.

I feel as though I've done a day's work, but it's not yet ten o'clock as a pale sun at last begins to warm the grassland and the indefatigable Wendy leads us off on another grand nature ramble.

We return to the donga, which is the Swahili word for a small overgrown creek, where yesterday we saw the two lions conspicuously not mating. Today things have changed. Same lioness, different lion – probably the brother of the failed suitor. This time they are obviously interested in the same thing. They sit eyeing each other until, as yesterday, the female gets up and strolls off. As if on an invisible lead her partner follows and waits for such time as she squats down. This is the signal for him to settle on top. They couple for no more than twenty-five seconds, to an accompaniment of low growling and neck-biting. Then the male stands back and the female rolls over onto her back. After a decent interval of nine or ten minutes the whole thing starts again.

Then, from down in the undergrowth, another lioness appears, leading four very young cubs. (Wendy estimates them to be about six weeks old, and probably out in the open for the first time.) One stays close to his mother but looks bright and adventurous, two others follow a little further behind, but number four is clearly the runt of the litter, unable to keep up. Meanwhile, up on the low hill, uncle and aunt are at it again.

They all seem quite oblivious of each other and of the intrusion of a half-dozen telephoto lenses. More distressingly, it seems at one point that the mother is oblivious to her fourth cub who is floundering way behind in the long grass, but just as we thought she'd forgotten, she raises her head, turns, pads slowly back down the hill, picks the runt up in her mouth and carries it back to the family. It's mesmerizing activity and we remain absorbed for the best part of an hour. By which time, as I calculate it, the happy couple have mated six more times.

A short while afterwards we come across a stately column of giraffe moving across the landscape in what appears to be slow motion. At the back of the procession is a smaller lame giraffe, walking awkwardly and falling further behind. This time it doesn't look as if anyone is going back to help.

Wendy shakes her head. 'They just carry on, it's the survival of the fittest. That's why it's probably better if some predator comes along . . . they wouldn't be able to kill them standing up like that . . . they'll wait till they lie down.'

Birth, reproduction and death. We've been close to it all today.

Though it doesn't actually rain again, the grey clouds pile up to bring on a premature dusk. Sweaters come out and the camp staff light a fire beside the river for us. I wander round to the kitchen. A big pizza is being loaded into the oven. Patrick is busying around and I probably get in the way, but I can't leave here without talking to someone who's been on safari with Hemingway. Was Hemingway as good as he said he was? Patrick nods.

'He must have learnt to shoot with the American cowboys. Some shoot in the stomach or the leg, but not him. He was good.'

Others of Patrick's illustrious companions were not as naturally gifted. President Tito generally had to be assisted. 'We had some problems . . . he doesn't shoot on the best part.' Prince Charles, whom he accompanied on a camel safari up to Lake Turkana, wasn't interested in the hunting but was himself nearly hunted.

'He stepped on the back of a crocodile thinking that it's a stone, or a log lying by the sand. Then this crocodile started moving – he was frightened!'

I have the impression that Patrick preferred the old days, when risks were greater but groups were smaller, when you ate what you hunted and slept in the open.

Now that tourism has taken a firm hold here it seems that safaris have become a parody of themselves. We dress like white hunters. We are treated like white hunters, brought whiskies at sundown and bacon and eggs for breakfast, yet we hunt with Canon cameras from within solid vehicles. Maybe one day visitors will be able to see, enjoy and learn about animals in the wild without having to go through the pretence of being latter-day Hemingways.

But for now we remain pleasantly cosseted. After a farewell barbecue dinner of impala and hartebeest, the staff bring in a cake for us and dance around the table singing 'Jambo Bwana'. It may all seem a bit colonial, but they have made us very happy here and I don't think they've hated it any more than we have.

DAY 99: *The Masai Mara to Seronera*

Of course, the day we have to leave our camp is better than any since we arrived – clear skies and a fine sunrise to shave by. A generous traveller's breakfast, including fresh pineapple, melon, porridge and all sorts of cholesterol, and fond farewells to Patrick and his staff, and particularly to Wendy who has been such an excellent and informative companion and guide – giving us just about the right balance of carrot and stick. Addresses are exchanged and family safari holidays promised. Not that we shall be leaving Abercrombie and Kent behind altogether. Kalului and Kabagire have agreed to drive us down through the Serengeti to pick up the train at Dodoma, in Tanzania, over 450 miles to the south. Craig, a young, athletic Kenyan, will be taking over Wendy's role as troubleshooter and animal-spotter. Craig was born and raised in Kenya of white English parents.

PREVIOUS PAGE: *Nubian mother and child, Sudan.*

ABOVE: *The Nile Valley Express: riding Roof Class.*

LEFT: *The start of another felucca.*

OPPOSITE (TOP): *Omdurman: camel shopping.*

OPPOSITE (BOTTOM): *Ethiopian border country: tea with the troops.*

ABOVE: *At the Blue Nile Falls, Ethiopia.*

RIGHT: *Back to school in Lerata, Kenya, where I leave the world behind.*

OPPOSITE: *Woman from the Samburu, or 'Butterfly' tribe, Kenya.*

RIGHT: *Lions in the Masai Mara II.*

BELOW: *On safari.*

RIGHT: *On the Kigoma Express, Tanzania.*

BELOW RIGHT: *Baby born in the restaurant car of the Kigoma Express, Tanzania.*

ABOVE: *Boat to Ujiji.*

'Over here they call us Vanilla Gorillas,' he grinned.

We leave the Hippo Riviera at a quarter to eight, heading south and east towards the Tanzanian border.

Our thirty degree meridian remains elusive, as Lake Victoria, with irregular and unpredictable ferry crossings, blocks our way to the west. The good news is that this morning I exchange the dusty, threadbare map of *Africa North-East and Arabia* which has accompanied me for seven weeks – since Port Said – for a crisp and pristine *Africa Central and South*.

I have a feeling it will be worn in very quickly as we venture into rarely visited territory to complete the last thousand miles of our sweeping detour round southern Sudan.

Animal-spotting is every bit as obsessive as train-spotting and one of the gaps in my book is filled after little more than half an hour's driving when we catch our first sight of a cheetah. It's a solitary animal but its presence has a magnetic effect on the supporting cast. Thomson's gazelle grazing nearby freeze in mid-mastication. Impala heads turn and stare as if hypnotized. There is very little point in trying to run away from an animal whose 'maximum speed in emergency' can, according to my book, 'reach 110 k.p.h.'. The cheetah looks made for speed. Its head is small, body long and powerful, legs lean and slender. Cheetahs stalk their prey with infinite care and patience, moving to within a hundred yards before attacking. The suspense is so sustained, the build-up so painstakingly slow, that in the fifteen minutes we are there nothing moves except eyeballs.

Near the border we catch our first sight of migrating wildebeeste. They are returning south in long columns after feeding on the short rich grass of the Mara. We have to wait twenty minutes for one procession to pass across the track. They seem in good spirits, butting each other playfully, cavorting, facing the wrong way and generally displaying all the characteristics of a school outing on the way home. I can't imagine why these heavy-shouldered grey-pelted beasts should be quite so happy. Each year, a quarter of a million of them die on the migration. Some die natural deaths, but many more perish from drowning while crossing the river, snakebites (those carcasses are left untouched by other predators, who can tell there is poison on the body), and the activities of lion, leopard, cheetah, serval and others.

A little further on we come across two hyenas shuffling off with a piece of wildebeeste. They are shifty-looking creatures, round-shouldered and surly. I rather like them. They'll never get a decent part in a Walt Disney film, but they do keep the place tidy and I find it rather endearing that they giggle so much when they've made a kill that they give away their position and are often dispossessed by more lugubrious beasts.

Close by the Kenyan border-post a solidly built, light-blue truck is stuck in the mud. A small group of young whites stand looking dolefully at it. They are mostly Australians, New Zealanders and Brits on an overland adventure tour from Nairobi to Harare, Zimbabwe. Their leaders are a short, smiling young man with a *Just William* shock of hair and a girl called Dave.

'German . . . built for the Russian front,' says the young man, jabbing a spanner at the beached vehicle.

Despite its bulk Kabagire manages to pull it out of the mud with his Landcruiser. The overlanders remount and the truck slowly and unsteadily heaves itself up the last few yards to the border, leaving behind a pair of deep trenches and a baboon sorting through the remains of their campfire with the meticulous care of a forensic scientist.

After passing through Customs and Immigration without incident, we run a short way downhill to a bridge across the Sand river and up a rocky slope past a sign reading 'Welcome to Serengeti National Park'. Elephant herds, bigger than anything we saw in the Mara, crowd the brown-gold grassland studded with enough trees to give them cover and food. A family of warthogs sprints across the road in front of us, tails hoisted in unison. Nigel is particularly soppy about warthogs, and the sight of baby ones is almost too much for him. We'll probably find rolls of film full of them.

1.20 p.m. At the Bologonja border station. Set between solid stone posts topped with massively horned buffalo skulls is a gate with 'Tanzania' written on it. This is the first country I've seen with a gate and makes me rather warm to the place. It's 140,000 square miles bigger than Kenya, though a minnow compared with Egypt, Sudan or Ethiopia. Once part of German East Africa, it became the independent republic of Tanganyika in 1962 and merged with the People's Republic of Zanzibar to form the name on the gate in 1964.

We have a three-and-a-half-hour wait at the thatched bungalow that is the border-post, and we are still there, having all our permits laboriously described in longhand, when the overlanders catch us up. The truck has had no further mishaps, but they have to keep its engine running as the starter motor's gone.

Once through the gate, we appear to be in a Garden of Eden with trees, lush green grass and streams bubbling through, but this soon gives way to the Serengeti proper, a 57,000-square-mile expanse of scrubland. Unlike the Masai Mara, it is a park set aside for wild animals only. There are no cattle or herdsmen here. We pass more lion, this time about ten of them at a kill. A wildebeeste is the victim and by the time we arrive the male lions have already fed and are lying panting in the shade, while the females dismember what's left. A macabre chorus of thirty or forty quarrelling vultures and marabou storks stand some yards away waiting for the pickings.

Finally a very young lion approaches the stomach, which has been left intact. Though I will him not to, it's all that's left to him and he picks it up. Half-digested grass spills from the gut as he drags it along between his front legs, away to his own private place.

The altitude dial on Basil's watch reads 1750 metres (5500 feet) as we cross the Seronera river into a green cover of mahogany, fig and umbrella acacias, amongst which are set big smooth boulders of the sort that John Wayne chased Indians through. Our hotel is built around one of these outcrops, and offers the serious pleasure of being able to stroll across the rocks at dusk and watch the light fade over the Serengeti as a colony of hyrax – rabbit-sized furry creatures that look a little like draught excluders – scuttle about in the background. A full moon slowly rises as the immense plain merges with an immense sky.

DAY 100: *Seronera to Lake Manyara*

Pull back the curtains at 7 a.m. to find myself staring into the wide, curious eyes of a vervet monkey, nose pressed up against the window, watching me unblinkingly. I admonish him sternly.

'You monkey!'

Basil thinks this is very funny, but we have been on the road for three months . . .

It is a clear, fresh, glistening morning and I cannot quite believe that I am alive and in the Serengeti and only hours away from the Ngorongoro Crater, the second largest in the world. And me a schoolboy from Sheffield.

Just then I hear, from the passageway, the unmistakable sound of other ex-schoolboys from Sheffield.

'Hurry along, Clifford!' . . . An early morning chorus of Yorkshire accents recedes towards the restaurant. Later I see them being squeezed into a fleet of white mini-vans and driven off to the lions.

Twenty-five per cent of Tanzania is apparently turned over to conservation, a higher proportion than anywhere else in Africa. My driver Kalului worked here in 1960 and remembers when the Serengeti National Park was created and hunters were turned into poachers overnight. He was a ranger and responsible for apprehending those who didn't understand that their livelihood was now someone else's. Later he became a guide and has many tales of near disaster. I noticed that whenever we stopped in the Serengeti, Kalului very carefully examined the surroundings before letting us out of the vehicle. He has learnt by experience to be very careful.

Once, he recalls, he had checked the area around a tree before laying out a picnic only to find, halfway through the picnic, that a leopard was actually in the tree above them finishing off its kill. Someone noticed, screamed, and that brought the leopard tearing down.

I confess to him that my only disappointment of the safari has been an absence of rhino and leopard. Kalului attempts to redress this by an amazing park-full of impersonations, from leopard to rhino to tortoise to jackal, mating wildebeeste, and the animal he unhesitatingly names as the most dangerous of them all, the buffalo.

'Many times buffalo is chasing me . . . '

I ask him what he does in such a case.

'I running . . . up the tree!'

He grins broadly, almost as if remembering one of life's forgotten pleasures.

Kalului, small and wiry, with his energetic, humorous face that can easily turn truculent, has become too close a companion to submit tamely to an interview, and when we do get him in front of the camera he has fun turning some of my questions back on me. 'What tribe are *you* from?' he asks.

'British Middle Class,' I reply staunchly. It doesn't have quite the same ring as Akamba.

We drive on south-east passing the end of the Olduvai Gorge, in which Louis and Mary Leakey, and more recently Donald Johanson, found some of the earliest human remains on the planet, including, at nearby Laetoli, a 3.6-million-year-old footprint trail preserved in solidified volcanic ash.

We wind up from the plain to the rim of the Ngorongoro Crater, almost 6600 feet above sea-level. Spectacular views unfold, of the Serengeti on one side and the vast circle of extinct volcano on the other.

A group of Masai herdsmen approaches from along the ridge, preceded by the soft, delicate tinkling of cow bells – what Wendy used to call 'the sound of Africa'. They are young, mostly teenagers, dramatically turned out in ostrich-feather head-dresses, enormous wooden earrings and cloaks of intense purple and deep red. They are not unselfconscious. I notice one of them adjusting his outfit in the reflection from the car window. Nor is their initial friendliness and curiosity unprofessional. If we want to take a photo of them, or even of the crater below them, we must pay.

We continue on the road around the rim. All the way along are groups of children, decked out in beads, faces painted, holding spears and ready to go into a parody of the Masai dances for anyone with money.

Crater Lodge is a spartan, tidily laid out collection of huts which resembles an army camp, but is in fact a hotel with one of the finest views in the world. Spread out below us is the twelve-mile-wide crater with trees around a small soda lake at the bottom. A pelican, legs dangling lazily, glides in the thermals. The habitat inside the crater looks less dark, secret and Lost World-like than I had expected. In fact it looks suspiciously as though there is a car park down there. Certainly I can see more minibuses than I can see wild animals. But then it could be the effect of the deceptively strong beer I've been served. I look at the bottle for guidance but it has no label, only the words 'Beer Only' embossed on the side.

A Kenyan expatriate, working for the hotel, berates me for not going down into the crater.

'The Eighth Wonder of the World,' he announces, spreading his hand out to the view, before fixing me with a withering glance. 'You have seen it, but you have not *experienced* it.'

The truth is that I know what he means, but I am a traveller, not a tourist. I'm more concerned with the sailing date of the ships from South Africa than the departure of the next safari bus to the bottom of the crater. I'm trying to get to the South Pole, dammit, not Tanzania.

Not that I say this to him. He might ask why. And then I'd be floored.

Reluctantly leaving behind the second-largest crater in the world, we descend southwards through thick tropical rain forest and into a network of Mulu villages connected by red earth roads in poor condition.

At five o'clock we reach our destination for the night, another hotel with a stupendous view, this time from the top of the Rift Valley across Lake Manyara. A series of short, steep rivers with mantra-like names – the Yambi, Endabash, Ndala, Chemchem, Msasa, Mchanga and Mkindu – drain off the spectacular western wall of the escarpment through a forest of fig, mahogany and croton into the long slim lake 2000 feet below. The garden of the hotel is dominated by the vivid red and green umbrellas of three flame trees whose blossom looks even more striking tonight against the slate-grey skies of an impending storm. From my balcony I watch the storm approach, trailing curtains of rain across the lake. Then a fork of lightning slices the grey haze, dust from the shore is caught by the sudden fierce wind and swept in clouds up towards me. Wind rattles and batters at the glass, then the rain comes, and after the rain a double rainbow arches over the north-eastern shore.

Life indoors is a bit of a let-down after this. The hotel is full of Western tourists and the food is a bland chicken and leek soup and roast lamb.

To sleep over Hemingway's *Green Hills of Africa*, a well written but relentless account of his hunting prowess. I should think there was nothing more dangerous in the African bush than our Ernest on a day when he was out to prove himself.

DAY 101: *Lake Manyara to Dodoma*

We've 250 miles ahead of us today, so up at 6.15 for an early start. Peer out over the balcony to see baboons swarming all over the place taking apart the ornamental gardens.

Leave an hour later, taking the right turn at the end of the hotel drive. The safari traffic turns left and I feel a quite poignant sense of regret at leaving the animals behind.

A rough track, uncomfortably negotiated, brings us out onto the main road from Dodoma to Arusha. This is a fine, recently constructed highway. It even has white-line markings. We sizzle along it for fifteen miles, as far as a large phosphate factory at

Minjingu. I know it's called Minjingu because it's written several times on road-side hoardings: 'Have You Applied Minjingu Phosphate Fertilizer?', 'Have You Taken Your Sample?', and finally, 'Bon Voyage from Minjingu'. It's quite the opposite, as it turns out. Mal voyage from Minjingu to Dodoma, on a road surface once metalled but since left to break up into a cracked and pitted mess.

We're out of the dramatic scenery and bumping along between dry straw-coloured fields through which bare patches of an ash-grey rock can be glimpsed, with only the occasional 'sausage tree' to enliven the view with its long cylindrical fruit dangling from the branches.

The villages are plain and poor, growing staple foods like banana and papaya and tomato. At the junction town of Babati we buy samosa and bread for lunch. Even the children here seem to view us with caution, a sort of guarded suspicion which we have not met anywhere else but Sudan, where xenophobia seemed like government policy. What have the children been taught here? I know that Julius Nyerere preached self-sufficiency and non-alignment which may have delivered national pride but not much in the way of economic self-confidence.

For five or six hours we progress along a winding ridge, densely wooded with acacia resplendent in colours of deep green, pale brown and golden yellow, a splash of Vermont in the fall. Then we're running down onto the plain and the baobab trees are the star turn. Some of them are believed to be 2000 years old, massively built, twenty or thirty feet around the trunk, with flanks the colour and texture of gunmetal. Birds love them and owls, hornbills, bats and buffalo weavers nest amongst them.

Over ten hours after leaving Lake Manyara we finally reach the outskirts of Dodoma, a city of only 45,000 people, not even among the ten largest cities of Tanzania, but plumb in the middle of the country. It is announced by a faded sign beside a broken road, 'Welcome to Dodoma, Capital City'.

This is strong missionary country. On the way in we come across the incongruous sight of orderly rows of vines, tended by the Passionist Fathers and producing Dodoma Red, which I am warned against.

The Vocation Centre of the Precious Blood Missionaries and the Assembly of God Bible College beckon with their signs, as does the New Limpopo Bar. A stretch of dual carriageway around the refreshingly modest Parliament building passes the Roman Catholic bookshop, the Paradise Theatre – Elliott Gould and Kate Jackson in *Dirty Tricks* – and the headquarters of the ruling CCM party (attached directly to the Parliament) before we are deposited in front of the colonial façade of the Dodoma Hotel. Considering this is the best hotel in a capital city it's disappointing that there is no hot water on tap, but a bucketful can be brought to you on request. In the public rooms fat armchairs with their stuffing leaking out are set around an old John Broadwood piano with middle C missing. The food is dull but the beer is cool and welcome. My bed has a huge mosquito net, though I point out to the attendant that it has three very large holes in it. He smiles helplessly and produces a can of fly-spray the size of a bazooka which he uses so freely that I am unable to breathe inside the room for at least ten minutes.

There is a disco in the hotel tonight and it's a measure of how tired I am that the music blasts me to sleep.

DAY 102: *Dodoma to Kigoma*

I've noticed that everything in my room from the grey pillow that I didn't dare lay my head on to the mirror I don't shave in front of because there is no hot water is stencilled with a long serial number and the initials TRC – Tanzanian Railway Company. It's appropriate, I suppose, for our destiny is now in their hands from here to Mpulungu in Zambia – 800 miles through the heart of Africa.

When nine years old or thereabouts . . . while looking at a map of Africa, and putting my finger on the blank space then representing the unsolved mystery of the continent, I said to

215

myself with absolute assurance and an amazing audacity which are no longer in my character now: 'When I grow up I shall go there.' I read this last night as mosquitoes poured through the holes in my net, and although it is Joseph Conrad's recollection of his childhood in Poland it could as well have been an expression of my own boyhood fascination with somewhere as remote from my domestic surroundings as it seemed possible then to be. Lake Tanganyika, the second-deepest lake in the world (after Lake Baikal), set in the centre of the African continent, surrounded by mountains and jungle and God knows what, is what I was thinking of, I'm sure. It's now one railway journey away.

I like Dodoma. It's not beautiful but the people are pleasant. Tanzanians don't intrude, they aren't curious or reproving or obsessive starers. They quietly go about their business, which might include selling wooden whistles outside the Parliament building.

'How much?'

'Four hundred.'

'I only have two hundred.'

'I'll give it to you for three hundred.'

'I only have two hundred.'

'All right. Two hundred.'

Now that's the sort of haggling I like.

I meet an Englishman, a university professor checking out Tanzania prior to some investment from the World Bank. He is in despair over the paperwork needed to get anything done here. He shakes his head in disbelief: 'They have a saying in this country that bureaucracy is like God. It's everywhere'.

The servants of God are certainly here in force. Religion seems to be the growth industry. On one of the major intersections the Indian Christians' huge domed neo-classical château stands next to the sweeping modern red-brick lines of the Lutheran cathedral, which in turn faces across to the squat polygonal towers and domes of the Anglican church.

The English language *Daily News* has a sports headline with a familiar, almost nostalgic ring: 'Angry Fans on Rampage'.

Football is popular here, with a big match in prospect tonight as Black Fighters of Zanzibar take on Railways of Morogoro, whose players most likely have TRC stencilled somewhere on their bodies.

At ten minutes after midday a large metal cylinder hanging outside the office of the stationmaster at Dodoma is rung loudly, and the purveyors of nuts, eggs, bananas, dried fish, sweet potatoes, rubber sandals, fresh water, loaves of bread, toy aeroplanes and other travellers' fare edge closer to the railway track. Beginning as a distant shimmer, a diesel locomotive with a red cow-catcher and a distinctive yellow V on the front slowly materializes, bringing in the express from the port of Dar es Salaam, 280 miles to the east. It's an enormous relief to see it. This and the boat down Lake Tanganyika are two of the essential connections on the journey. Neither is easy. There is an element of uncertainty about our right to seats on the train as none of our bookings has been confirmed, and indeed all our compartments are occupied. Polite persuasion is not enough and we just have to move in and hope that the sight of thirty boxes of film equipment will put the skids under someone. An emotional farewell to Kalului and Kabagire, who have looked after us since the Ethiopian border. I leave Kalului my Michelin map – *Africa North-East and Arabia* – which I know he coveted.

The train is not in good shape. Most of the windows are broken, and that's only in First Class. There are, considerately, two types of lavatory, announced on their doors as 'High Type' (European) and 'Low Type' (non-European). Once we are underway, I approach the High Type, prepared for the worst, only to find that it is not there at all. The High Type has vanished, leaving behind only a hole in the floor.

It's seven in the evening. To the restaurant car for dinner. Hot and crowded, but there's something familiar about it. A metal manufacturer's disc by the door reads 'BREL, Derby 1980'. Of course; these battered coaches rolling across the East African bush are of exactly the same design as British Inter-City stock.

They may look as if they've had it but they're thirty years younger than those which many London commuters travel in.

Chicken or fish with rice and potatoes. Run DMC rap music sounds loudly from the next table, making it difficult to hear my dining companion who says he is a footballer with CDA Tabora. CDA stands for Capital Development Authority. Not an easy one to chant on the terraces.

We stop frequently, and I wish I hadn't eaten on the train. By the line-side is a feast of food – tables set up with chicken stews and rice and beans, all fresh from voluminous saucepans. Kebabs and live chickens and even a duck are bought and sold through the windows. At all these stops I've been aware of a persistent clicking sound. I thought it might be cicadas, but now I see it is made by children who carry their wares – cigarettes maybe, or bananas – in one hand and click loose coins in the other to attract business.

Craig and Nigel have ears pressed to a radio at the window, trying, in the midst of this line-side cacophony, to pick up the sound from Edinburgh where England are playing Scotland in the Rugby Union World Cup semi-final.

Nigel suddenly turns from the radio with a look of total disbelief. 'They've gone to the *news*! . . . They've gone to the news with two minutes left!'

As we pull away from Itigi, 105 miles beyond Dodoma, Mbego, our coach attendant, a wraith-like figure in white cap, blue tunic and trousers, appears dragging a shapeless green canvas bundle. From this he extricates my bedding, which he lays out with infinite care and precision. Later I see him sitting at the open door of the train gently and ruminatively stroking the head of a young man next to him.

Night falls and the electricity supply fails. To sleep reading *Heart of Darkness* by torchlight. Outside is Africa . . . 'its mystery, its greatness, the amazing reality of its concealed life'.

DAY 103: *Dodoma to Kigoma*

Dream of thousands of shuffling feet, a babble of strange voices, baby cries, chickens clucking, heavy objects being dragged close by me, clicks and curses and strange cries. My eyes are wide open, but I can see nothing. My window has been boarded up. The noises continue, growing in intensity.

Dawn. In the Low Type, which is filthy and caked with un-flushed waste, a sign reads: 'The co-operation of passengers is required to prevent waste of water and the misuse of this toilet compartment'. There's no water to waste.

Something is different about the train this morning. It's shorter for a start, and the restaurant car is different (the clock has stopped at 8.10 rather than 1.05). Over breakfast of fried egg, boiled potato, bread, marge and three cups of sweet tea, I hear the explanation of my dream last night. Soon after midnight the train stopped at Tabora in order to be split up and re-grouped into three separate trains. Patti and Craig had to spend three hours on the platform making sure our equipment was not sent north to Mwanza or south to Mpanda. Apparently Patti received one proposal of marriage. Craig none, sadly. Angela tried to help out with her torch until she found out that the entire shunting manoeuvres at Tabora were being co-ordinated by torch signals.

Later, to the restaurant car for elevenses. It is closed. All the windows have been covered up with some kind of material. Rueful smiles all round. No one seems particularly worried, except me. I try again in half an hour, only to find the rueful smiles turned to wholehearted joy at the continued closure of the restaurant. Then a soldier emerges from inside, positively wreathed in smiles.

'It is a girl,' he announces.

It must be almost as we touch the thirty degree meridian, for the first time since the Mediterranean, that a little girl is born in the restaurant car of the Dar es Salaam to Kigoma Express. It is certainly the best thing the restaurant car has provided so far and I take it as a very good omen for the rest of our journey.

Mercury being well out of retrograde at the moment, things do seem to be going, if not comfortably, at least smoothly and we are on the final curve into Kigoma by late afternoon, only three and a half hours behind schedule on a twenty-seven-hour journey. A lush, thick, heavy heat spills in from the open doorway. Children run out from groves of bananas, papaya and mango to wave at the train. Mbego sits on the step at the end of our coach, unselfconsciously tickling the ear of his friend. There is a marked absence of the heightened stress and strain that usually grips arriving passengers.

Kigoma station is a fine old colonial building, and looks as though it could be north Italian with its arches and loggia. Its grand clock, in the fine tradition of TRC, has stopped. Useless Facts Department: from a hanging sign above one of the doors I learn that the Swahili for Stationmaster is Steshinimasta.

We are driven to our lodgings by a soft-spoken, middle-aged man in a well-kept Toyota Corolla, with a transfer of the Pope on one window. He turns out to be a doctor as well as a taxi-driver and apologizes for not taking the direct road to the hotel.

'There are large holes in it, you understand.'

Our detour bounces us along a red earth track, scattering chickens and goats, which leads to the low, nondescript façade of the Railway Hotel.

We unload for the fifty-third time. Kigoma, elevation 2541 feet, population 50,044, is just about bang on course at 29.36 degrees East. We have completed our enforced long eastern swing from Khartoum in thirty days, and hopefully we've made it in time to make the infrequent but vital ferry connection to Mpulungu and Zambia.

Clem, who should be feeling very pleased with himself, appears from hotel reception looking quite the opposite. Apparently no one knows anything about our bookings, and they do not have enough rooms for us. Kigoma is by no means awash with alternative accommodation so this is a cruel blow. As Clem and Angela embark on the slow process of sorting out the reservations, I walk across a bare and uninviting lobby to be confronted with the sort of view that lifts the spirits however low they might have sunk. A descent of chipped concrete steps leads down to a grassy hank, studded with tables and parasols, beyond which the waves of a wide blue-green lake spill lethargically onto a beach of coarse red sand. Lake Tanganyika, confined here into a small bay between low grassy headlands, stretches away, across to the hazy cliffs of Zaire, once the Congo, Conrad's Heart of Darkness.

It is a breathtaking revelation of scale and space, as if I had opened a door onto the centre of Africa.

'*When I grow up I shall go there* . . . '

Well, I've had my cosmic moment and now the reality must be faced. The Railway Hotel, Kigoma, is not the heart of darkness. It is more like a cross between a pub in Earl's Court and a minor Hilton. Encamped on the unmown lawns are two dozen Australian and New Zealand overlanders drinking beer. A Japanese film crew are at work in the lake and another harassed European rushes past us clutching a sheaf of papers.

After hours of patient negotiation we are all found rooms. They are arranged in unglamorous functional blocks which do no justice at all to the splendour of the location. Mine has a small bed with a frame for a mosquito net, but no net. A concrete floor extends into a washing area with a shower and basin, but no hot water. My lavatory is of the High Type, but the cistern overflows gently and persistently. As if to further mock my dreams of solitariness and isolation, all I can hear as I unpack is a radio crackling out the last seconds of commentary from the Rugby Union World Cup followed by a roar from the darkness outside as Australia defeats New Zealand.

Later I settle down with Conrad on my narrow bed, and read myself to sleep to the sound of 'the howling sorrow of savages' and the gentle lapping of an overflowing lavatory cistern.

DAY 104: *Kigoma*

Day of rest and recuperation at the hotel. I have fixed the cistern by jamming a lavatory brush beneath the ballcock.

221

Examine myself in the mirror (Serial Number TRC HOT GM NM 024) to see whether three and a half months of travel have left any damage. I gaze into dull, weary eyes set in sun-reddened features. A bleached immobility of expression. I look like a survivor from some awful natural disaster. Laugh at the thought, and only then do I recognize something of myself.

At breakfast – omelette, chips and sliced white bread – the manager apologizes for the lack of facilities. 'We have hot-water boilers and supply all ready, but no one comes to fit them . . . ' He rubs a handkerchief across his face and shakes his head. 'They are simply standing in waste.'

A few African horror stories with our omelettes . . . Craig tells us that in his opinion electric shocks are the best cure for snake bites. He recounts the story of someone whose life was saved after a bite – from 'some sort of cobra' – when he was wired up to an outboard motor.

'Put the earth in one hand and the live wire on the bite. Five applications in fifteen seconds. Oh sure, his hair stood on end and he was lifted a foot or two off the ground, but the doctors said it saved his life.'

After breakfast, having ascertained that the risk of bilharzia is low as the water is not stagnant, that crocodiles would not come in this far and sea serpents are all I have to watch out for, I take a cautious bathe. The water is clear and cool, the surroundings quite beautiful. No sailing boats or water-sporters to disturb the peace. Only the barely perceptible wake of a passing dugout troubles the placid water. And I can tell my grandchildren that I swam in Lake Tanganyika.

I dry out in warm sun with a cold Safari beer. At the bar is a small, straight-backed European who turns out to have spent nineteen months in Antarctica. Had he enjoyed it?

He pulls fiercely on a cigarette, scouring it for every last ounce of nicotine, before answering, with eyes narrowed against an endless exhalation.

'Put it zis vay . . . it is an experience you should go through.'

He knows the MV *Agulhas*, the ship we hope to take to Antarctica, and asks me to remember him to the captain.

'Sure . . . your name?'

'Doktor Brandt,' he replies after an inexplicable hesitation.

I ask him what he's doing here in Kigoma.

'Teaching blacks to use the telephone,' he replies crisply.

Having nothing better to do, I begin to suspect him of being involved in some sort of racket; later I find that I could be right, when I overhear him asking the manager, *sotto voce*, 'Any news?'

This surely is the stuff of Conrad. At last a whiff of intrigue and corruption in the heart of darkness.

It turns out that he is inquiring as to the whereabouts of his lavatory seat.

The manager spreads his arms helplessly. 'We wait for them . . . '

But the Doktor is not in a mood to be trifled with.

'Vy cannot you take the lavatory seat from fourteen and put it in fifteen?'

I rush to make sure my door's locked against possible loo-seat predators.

Round off a bizarre day eating goat stew and drinking Primus beer from Burundi in a local restaurant in the middle of a power cut. Our host is the taxi-driver/doctor, William, who has become our self-appointed guide to Kigoma. The restaurant, or what I can see of it in the lamplight, is rough and ready, with an ancient, almost biblical feel to it. Above the doorway is a large hand-lettered wooden board, like a pub sign. I presume that to be the name of the restaurant and ask William for a translation.

'It says "Pay Before You Leave".'

Anyway, the goat is excellent, and best of all, it is not the property of Tanzanian Railways.

DAY 105: *Kigoma*

Another day to kill before the ferry leaves. Take a boat to Ujiji, a few miles down the coast. Once the centre of a thriving slave trade, it's also the place where Livingstone and Stanley met in 1871.

The location of this historic meeting is now a small museum in a well-tended garden on a hill above the busy waterfront. A forbidding, lumpish grey monument, 'erected by the Government of Tanganyika Territory' in 1927, stands beneath two mango trees said to be descendants of the one under which Livingstone and Stanley met. On it is carved a map of Africa with a cross incised into it. It's a brutal and arrogant image. The only visitor besides ourselves is an Englishman from Leicester, looking very red and unprotected in the sun. He is in his fifties and had decided, after reading a book about Cecil Rhodes's plan for a railway from the Cape to Cairo, to do the journey himself. Today he had only one thing on his mind.

'All I'm looking for, Michael, is a cold beer.' I suggest he makes for the Railway Hotel, Kigoma.

Things are more light-hearted inside the museum, despite its depressingly empty rooms and smell of disuse. Most of the work is by a local schoolteacher, A. Hamisi. There is a series of paintings of the great moments in the life of Livingstone – 'Dr Livingstone saving Chuma and Others from Slavery', 'Dr Livingstone Sitting Under the Mango Tree Thinking About Slavery in Ujiji'. Beside these are two life-size papier mâché models: Livingstone, looking like Buster Keaton in a dark-blue three-piece suit, raising his peaked cap to Stanley, looking like Harold Macmillan in a light-blue safari suit, and with a pink face. These are also the work of A. Hamisi of Kigoma Secondary School. There is nothing else in the museum.

We drive out of Ujiji, up Livingstone Street, then right at Lumumba Road and back via Mwanga – home of 'Vatican Enterprises Hardware Supplies' and 'Super Volcano Tailoring' – to the busy mango- and acacia-lined main street of Kigoma which is also named after Patrice Lumumba, one of the great heroes of African independence, who was assassinated in 1961.

At the Railway Hotel, half an hour before sunset. This is a magic time as the sun sinks towards the lake and the mountains of Zaire, always grey in the haze, sharpen to a deep black. At the lakeside tonight Australians and New Zealanders, Doktor Brandt, erect and smoking powerfully, two Dutch boys, the Japanese underwater cameraman, even my friend from Leicester, all gather to watch the sun go down; for a few minutes every sound, even the cries of the naked children plunging into water near by, seems to grow distant.

DAY 106: *Kigoma to Mpulungu*

Down to the waterfront at 9 a.m. to join the queue for tickets on the ferry which runs to Mpulungu once a week. Ahead of me in the line is Francis, a farmer from Karema, one of the stops on the way down the lake. I explain to him what we are doing, and, with more difficulty, why we are doing it. He listens carefully before asking politely, 'And will your film help to solve the problems it exposes?'

The MV *Liemba*, 800 tons, her lines as straight as the back of a Prussian cavalry officer, is said to be the oldest passenger ship in regular service anywhere in the world. Judging by her history she could have been better named the MV *Lazarus*. Built as a warship in Germany, she was carried in pieces overland and assembled on Lake Tanganyika in 1913. At the end of the Great War she was scuttled by the Germans, and lay on the bottom of the lake until raised and refitted by the British in 1922. She was in regular operation as a steamship before being converted to diesel in 1978. After eighty years she remains the only way out of Kigoma to the south or to the west. If we had missed today's sailing we would almost certainly have missed the sailing from Cape Town to Antarctica in a month's time

We pull away at 5 p.m. The Australian and New Zealand overlanders have taken over the stern deck, and the locals crowd into the bows or the lower covered decks, squashing in with their boxloads of plastic sandals, pineapples, and even Lion Brand Mosquito Coils – 'Keep Out of Damp' – and with apparent good grace accepting the presence of two white-owned Land Rovers, which further reduce the space. At least we can all feel ourselves better off than the several hundred tired and confused occupants of the *Kabambare*, a barge just arrived from Kalemie in Zaire. They are refugees from the inter-tribal violence which has recently flared up in their country. They do not know if the Tanzanian authorities will accept them.

A last look at Kigoma from the departing ferry. I had come here expecting dense jungle, snakes, monkeys and swamps. Instead the town at the centre of Africa resembles a small port on a discreet Scottish loch, with the railway line running picturesquely between the water and low grassy hills – reassuring, comfortable, rendered exotic only by the bright slash of purple from the jacaranda trees on the shore.

My cabin has the stamp of Tanzanian Railways all over it. It claims to be air-conditioned but the fan is missing. There is a basin but no water, hot or cold. All but one of the light bulbs is missing.

Three hours out from Kigoma I am unenthusiastically facing up to a plate of rice and scrawny chicken leg, when the engine note changes down an octave, the ship slows and within seconds the night air is filled with a growing clamour of voices. They grow louder and more insistent, and are mingled with the splash of paddles and the thudding of boats against the hull. Out on deck in some alarm to witness an extraordinary scene. Flooded by powerful shipboard lights, a dozen or more dugouts are clustering around the *Liemba* like maggots at a corpse, filled with vendors of every kind of food, families trying to get themselves and their belongings aboard and water taxis touting to take people off. Everyone is screaming to make themselves heard as a forest of hands extends from below decks, waving, beckoning, holding out money, helping some people aboard and others down into the bobbing mass of boats below.

Every boat is vying with its neighbour to get close to the *Liemba*. As soon as the tiniest gap is glimpsed paddles are applied furiously and very often one hull will ride up over another, until with cries of protest the offending canoe is thrust back. Babes in arms are passed to the hopeful safety of outstretched hands. Small boys frantically bale out their boats.

This is African business. The whites can only watch and photograph. There is an urgency about it all that is spellbinding and exhilarating and exhausting. And I'm told later that what looked like a fully-fledged native attack is just one of fifteen scheduled stops.

DAY 107: *Kigoma to Mpulungu*

Aboard the *Liemba*, Lake Tanganyika. The last day of October, 1991. Have taken a capsule of Imodium as a prevention against having to make use of the toilet facilities. I know it is unwise to meddle with my metabolism but the alternative is too frightful to contemplate.

It has rained before dawn and I step out of my cabin onto the head of a sleeping figure swathed in cotton robe and woollen shawls. I needn't have bothered with my profuse British apologies as he doesn't wake up. A row of passengers is sheltering beside him. Their heads turn towards me, defensive and unsmiling. My hot and airless little cabin may not be the last word in comfort but it is First Class, and I know that by the time I return from breakfast the officious policemen on board will have shooed these people back down below.

Later in the day the captain agrees to be interviewed. His name is Beatus T. Mghamba and he lives on the bridge deck, which is nearly always empty apart from the lifeboats (made by Meclans Ltd of Glasgow in 1922), a jolly group of ladies and a hard-drinking Englishman. At the appointed time for the interview – about five in the afternoon – I knock on Captain Mghamba's door. After some time it is answered by a handsome dreadlocked lady who is obviously surprised to see me. I ask for the captain. She disappears into the cabin. There is a long wait and some muttering before she returns.

'He is asleep.'

She bats not an eyelid, and as I utter the immortal words,

'When he wakes up, tell him the BBC are waiting', she closes the door on me.

The captain finally appears, dishevelled but surprisingly cheerful after his sleep. I ask him about the problems of running an eighty-year-old ship.

'The ship is big, but the engine is small . . . manoeuvring is a little bit difficult.' He shrugs. He has no chart of the lake.

'We are sailing this through experience. If you are one mile away from the shore you will be safe.'

The *Liemba*, he tells me, is registered to carry 500 passengers and thirty-four crew, 'but sometimes in summer seasons where we find that these people along Lake Tanganyika are harvesting their crops it can be more'.

'How many more?'

'Up to a thousand.'

At one of our fifteen stops a wedding party paddles out to welcome guests off the ship. Huge brightly-coloured flags and banners stream in the wind and there is great singing and chanting as they circle the ship. The progress of the *Liemba* reminds me of the Hurtigrute service which took us up through the Norwegian fiords three and a half months ago. In both cases the service is the only lifeline for communities unreachable by road or air. There the similarity ends. I cannot imagine the manic, uncontrolled exuberance of the *Liemba* surviving long in the cold Protestant waters of the North Atlantic.

As we progress south, some Zambians come aboard. Tomorrow they are voting for a new government, and I am quite shocked to hear that Kenneth Kaunda is so unpopular that he may well be unseated after twenty-eight years in power. I always had the impression that he was one of the most secure, successful and responsible of the post-colonial leaders, but Japhet Zulu from Chingola, who describes himself as 'a simple businessman', thinks Kaunda has ruined the economy and he will not be voting for him.

At dusk, unobserved except by me, one of the policemen who chases steerage passengers off the upper decks has removed his hat and boots and is praying towards Mecca. The sight of this man of authority so completely prostrating himself before a higher authority is oddly moving.

DAY 108: *Kigoma to Mpulungu*

Have taken another Imodium. This is quite definitely not wise, and may have contributed to a general feeling of malaise as we approach Zambia. The ship has emptied overnight. Apart from the crew there are now only ourselves, Japhet and his friend, and twenty-five overlanders left on the *Liemba* as we cross the border into our thirteenth country.

A new country and a new month, our fourth on the road. The small deficiencies of Tanzania have begun to grind me down, and the prospect of a hot bath and clean clothes and a bed away from heat and mosquitoes is a more alluring one than the network of forested bays and islets that is the coast of Zambia.

'It's the first day of spring,' I hear someone say as we crowd at the deck rail.

'Don't be stupid,' another retorts, 'It's November. Spring starts in September.'

Of course, they're Australians. Or New Zealanders. Looking around at them I do not see the faces of explorers but of pale, tired children. They look as if they might have got lost on a hike from Sydney to Brisbane or Auckland to Wellington rather than being in the centre of Africa. They wait patiently for a sight of their truck, which has been driven overland from Kigoma and should be waiting for them on the dockside. Their journey will cost them £1000 or thereabouts and they sign on for nine weeks. I admire them. It isn't the easiest way to see the world, but it may be the one they will remember most.

We bid them farewell as we disembark at the small dockside of Mpulungu. Looking back on it from a distance, with the chunky, upright *Liemba* and its attendant crane nestling among wooded cliffs, surrounded by a stack of oil drums and building materials, it looks like a set in a James Bond film. The sort that is about to be blown sky-high.

New Customs and Immigration to be gone through, a new production team – Roger and Mirabel take over from Clem and Angela – and new guides and fixers. For once I don't feel I have the energy to respond.

The thick woolly heat seems to be inescapable down here by the lake, and I miss the openness and space of Kigoma.

Lunchtime. Feeling much recovered. We are lodged at a small collection of rondavels set in a tree-filled garden and run in easy-going fashion by Denish, an Indian of unforced charm and dazzling smile who came to Mpulungu for a ten-day holiday and was so captivated that he stayed and built this place – for himself, and any guests who might drop by. The first people we saw as we drove in were the overlanders, already pitching their tents on the grass, washing out clothes, and forming a queue for the lavatory and the thin trickle of cold water that is the shower.

I'm sitting in the shade of an orange tree being fussed over by Jake da Motta, an engaging Hong Kong-born Englishman who, with others of his team, is in charge of our welfare over the next few days.

Up here, among the stone-walled huts and the hibiscus and the gentle breeze, Mpulungu has taken on an unexpectedly Provençal aspect. This is soon to be quite rudely shattered.

Roger, naturally anxious to get to work, has booked me an appointment with the local witch doctor.

After lunch we drive away from Denish's sanctuary and down a track which curves round the bay, away from Provence and back into Darkest Africa.

A crowd of people cluster around one of the more substantial bungalows in a lakeside village of thatched huts scattered messily about a patch of rising ground. Some of them are on tiptoe, straining to see through a window. Inside, I'm told, is an effiti, a man charged with being a black witch or warlock, who is thought to have secured the deaths of five or six people. The witch doctor, or inganga, has been to the man's house and found a leather bottle in which a mixture of blood and poison was found. This is thought to be the blood of the victims.

The room where the investigation is being carried out is not, at first glance, in any way sinister. At one end, where the pale light from an overcast sky spills through a wrought iron window grille, is a plastic-covered sofa and matching chair. The floor is bare concrete, the walls plastered and painted grey. Two half-deflated beach balls hang from the ceiling, and on one of the walls are pictures of footballers and a BP Zambia calendar. On a small table is a line of six doll-like figures, one of which I notice is of a white woman, with a short skirt wrapped around her.

Huddled in a corner, looking pathetic and helpless, with glazed eyes and glassy stare, is the accused. He wears a thin brown shirt and trousers, black moccasin shoes and a fat wristwatch. He bears an unnerving resemblance to Nelson Mandela.

The witch doctor, Dr Baela, is a young man from Zaire. He has pouting lips and big lazy eyes. He wears a head-dress of genet fur, a pink tunic with his name on the back and a pair of welding goggles. In one hand he holds a heart-shaped mirror with a border of shells and in the other a small pot with a mirror set into it. His helpers wear white cotton robes with red crosses on them.

It may be the effect of the presence of a camera, but they all look sheepish and rather awkward, like children at the start of a school play.

Baela's acolytes brusquely remove the victim's watch, then tear off his shirt and make a series of marks on his body. A curved horn with money tied to its base is placed on his head and a basket with a white cloth in it passed three times around him. Two young men – boys really – step forward, and with grubby razor blades make incisions on his neck and shoulders. Thin lines of blood ooze to the surface. He's questioned, but looks blankly back, and is then cut across the forehead. Some powder is rubbed into the wound which makes him start back. He is held still, his trousers are rolled up and cuts are made on the outside of his knees and toes. On the wall behind him is a text in a faded frame – 'True Love Never Ends'.

The bleeding victim is rubbed with polish and left in his

corner while Baela and his gang disappear outside to be interviewed by the BBC.

Dr Baela's eyes freed from the goggles are red and watery, he smokes a very wide cigarette and his voice is a high-pitched sing-song. I ask him if he can tell if I have any evil spirits and he, through an interpreter, concludes that I have what is translated as an 'evil shadow'. It is the shadow of a woman.

In his curiously hypnotic monotone, Baela asks if the woman he is seeing is my wife. I ask him to describe her.

His reply, 'Is not tall, fat a bit', lets Helen off the hook, but only adds to the confusion. Dr Baela goes on to say that my life could be in danger and things of mine will be stolen, but that he can give me medicine which will 'drive out' any evil influence.

It all seems slightly laughable when written down, but Baela, who describes himself as a healer, not a witch doctor, has had some success in the village, and being surrounded by a couple of hundred people who believe every word he says is unsettling enough for me to take my shadow and his medicine more seriously than I'd expected. His prescription is a piece of tree bark which he gives me from a suitcase, with instructions to cut, pound up and wash with it, in a private place, saving some to place in each nostril.

In the evening, back at Denish's, Jake and his colleague Paul Murphy, a lean, wiry English-born Zambian, cook us a splendid meal as a fierce thunderstorm breaks. I drink too much wine, but haven't come across any since Kenya, and feel the need to wind down after this extraordinary day.

As waves of rain lash through the trees I talk to Paul about the problems of the country, it being election day in Zambia. In his opinion what the place needs is discipline. Liberalism, in the Western sense, cannot work in Africa. He quotes Malawi as an example of the way things should be done.

I also meet Chris and Jean Bigereaux, who employ 300 people in Mpulungu's biggest industry, fishing. The talk turns to malaria.

'The first time you have it, you never want to have it again. You just want to die,' says Chris.

Denish agrees, adding that he now expects to have malaria attacks about four times a year.

My head is muzzy by the time I reach the hut I'm sharing with Basil. Pushing open the door with infinite care so as not to wake him, I drop my torch, trip over Dr Baela's medicine and nearly bring down my mosquito net.

DAY 109: *Mpulungu to Shiwa*

I can't help noticing that the lavatory on which I spend most of the night is called the Victory. A night of victory for myself and Mr Frederick Chiluba, the new President of Zambia. I only hope he feels better than I do. Acute stomach cramps and diarrhoea have kept me up since 2 a.m. I hear the sound of music from down in the town, the barking of Denish's dogs at the gates, persistent coughing from one of the overlanders' tents and, later, cocks crowing.

On the Victory at 5.30 a.m., my system seems on the verge of collapse. I'm not sure whether or not I've ever had cold sweats before, and maybe this is why the tingling in the hands, the shivering and the uncontrollable flood of perspiration is so alarming, even, to be honest, frightening. For five minutes I have no idea what is going to happen to me. My fingers are going numb, and I am shuddering and shaking and soaking in my own sweat. Isn't this what we were talking about last night? Isn't this how malaria begins? What happens to our journey if I've caught something bad? 'Pole to Mpulungu' doesn't have the same ring. It must be the evil shadow . . . I should never have had anything to do with Baela's world. We don't understand it and we should have left it alone.

This jumble of anxieties fills my mind until the attack passes. Basil fetches me a thick sweater and delves in his extensive pharmaceutical collection for some tablets. Breakfast is tea, Ryvita biscuit and honey, and a faintly sickly solution of water and rehydration pills.

I look around the garden of the lodge. This morning it all

looks different – the water drum at which I had waited patiently for much of the night to extract enough water to flush the Victory; the overlanders, blearily packing for another day of discomfort; the flies buzzing around the dogs.

Denish has done his best for us. His lodge, after all, was built for himself and a handful of occasional travellers, not for the thirty-five people who were sharing it last night. I'm sad to say goodbye to him but glad to leave Mpulungu behind.

On the road there is plenty of evidence of the euphoria following Chiluba's victory over Kaunda, which appears to have been a landslide. Men, women and children raise their hands in the finger-and-thumb salute of the MMD – the Movement for Multi-Party Democracy. I see a group of villagers clustered round a radio beneath a spreading mango tree, listening to Kaunda's resignation speech.

I remember Japhet on the boat telling me that whichever side won the election there would be 'no violence . . . Zambians are not like that'. Paul sees this as a negative quality. There are eight million Zambians, anything can grow here he maintains, but the economy is in ruins because the people are too easygoing and acquiescent.

We pull in to the Modern Kwacha Relax Hotel in Kasama where much beer is going down in Chiluba's honour. His photo has been hoisted above the bar. 'This is the man we have waited seven years for!' they cry.

My hot and cold sweats have mercifully not been repeated but my system is very delicate and I excuse myself from the celebrations. But as soon as they realize we are from the BBC they are queuing up to be interviewed, and from being a stretcher-case I'm suddenly a news reporter. Their message is the same – tell the British people that this is a new dawn for Zambia, a dawn of open and incorrupt government. No one seems quite sure how practical change will accompany political change. The World Bank is vaguely mentioned, but this is not the point. The point is to tell the world that democracy has triumphed. When we tell them that we will tell the world but not for about a year, their enthusiasm turns to incredulity. BBC News and their deadline is a year ahead? I just don't feel strong enough to explain, and we move on, leaving them to their beer and their joy.

The drive down south towards Mpika is a further 130 miles of flat Molumba woodland, much of it stripped and burnt for fuel and building materials. The road is metalled and quick, but darkness has fallen by the time we reach the extraordinary red-brick barns, Hardyesque cottages and gabled gatehouses of Shiwa – an English estate in the middle of Africa. John and Lorna Harvey and their son David receive us warmly, and David's dog Deeta takes my hat.

My system has survived the day without collapse, but after the bliss of a hot bath the stomach cramps return and I take to my bed, unable to eat.

DAY 110: *Shiwa*

Halfway through the night, as recurring twinges of cramp keep me padding off to the bathroom, I experience a quite irrational fear of being in the same room as a piece of tree bark handled by Dr Baela. I see it lying on the table with my notebooks and maps, and though I know I'm being ridiculous I cannot help blaming it for this sudden reversal of fortunes. After all, Mercury isn't in retrograde until the end of the month so I can't blame that.

By the morning I feel stronger and better able to look the bark in the eye. Breakfast of toast and home-made marmalade at a huge table of mukwa wood designed by Lorna Harvey's father – Sir Stewart Gore-Brown, the man who created Shiwa.

Sir Stewart came out to Africa early in the century as a member of the Boundary Commission, quite literally to draw the map of Africa, or at least that part of the continent bordering on the Belgian Congo and Rhodesia, and stayed on to construct Shiwa house, between 1928 and 1932, in an eclectic European style with towers and pitched roofs and a formal English garden. In an article about the house, written in 1964, *Horizon* magazine summed up his achievement. 'Shiwa gradually became the showpiece of Northern Rhodesia, where a courteous squire, possessed of a taste for diplomacy, ruled his estate with benevolence and a hand of iron.'

On Sir Stewart's grave, set on a hill a mile away from the house and looking out over the forest-fringed lake of Shiwa Ngandu, is engraved the name Chipembele. I ask Lorna its meaning.

'It means rhinoceros, which was his African name . . . a rhino charges and then actually stops, and he was just like that. He would get very angry with you and then five minutes later he would be asking for a loan . . . '

John Harvey saw this as a positive advantage.

'As a politician he was a tremendous chap. He was a sort of Churchill, and he just rode over everybody and got his own way.'

He ran the estate feudally, as Lorna put it, 'as you would in Europe; the gardeners and people came through the back door, not the front door', but he had no time for the apartheid that existed in Northern Rhodesia. 'We were brought up that you respected a person for their age, not their colour.'

John thinks Sir Stewart's influence helped avoid either a bush war of the kind that destroyed Southern Rhodesia or terrorism on the scale of the Mau-Mau in Kenya, though eventually he lost the political support of the Africans by championing a paternalist solution which fell short of the self-rule they wanted. He died in 1967 but Shiwa is full of his presence – not just in books and pictures and portraits and rhino motifs on beams and brickwork, but in spirit. The flag is still raised and lowered every day on the balcony outside the library, and the estate workers are still summoned by drum to a muster parade at seven o'clock every morning.

At dinner with the Harveys tonight, the talk ranges from the long-distance lorry drivers' part in the spread of AIDS in Africa to the scandal of agricultural chemicals, banned in Europe, still being sold to Africa, and on to superstition and witchcraft.

David Harvey, who farms in the south of the country and is as level-headed as you would expect from a graduate of agricultural college, respects witch doctors and has used them. He saw with his own eyes a witch doctor make his way down a line of farm workers, one of whom was thought to be guilty of stealing. He touched each man on the shoulder with his stick but as he applied it to one man the stick burned into his flesh and stuck fast. The man confessed.

Apparently many public figures believe in lucky charms and talismans. Even Kaunda, sober product of a mission school only a mile or two from here, was rarely seen without a certain white handkerchief. President Mobutu of Zaire never goes anywhere without his stick.

Back in my room I take the bark off the table and put it in my bag. At the bottom.

DAY 111: *Shiwa*

Still alive. Cramps lessen but still disrupt the night. Patti is evidently quite poorly and displaying the symptoms of malaria despite taking the pills – 'fever, malaise, chills with sweating and headache'. Looking at Dawood I think I may have been quite lucky until I read that though the incubation period following a mosquito bite is a minimum of five days, '*as long as a year* may elapse before symptoms appear, especially if antimalarial drugs have been used'.

Today we see more of the estate, from its own model post-office complete with red letterbox – the postmaster says he's bored stiff there and can't wait to be transferred – to the school where the children are taught to build and thatch using local materials, but lack, according to John their teacher, such basics as 'books, desks and pens'.

David Harvey, meanwhile, is putting 2000 cattle through a dip. This must be done once a week to kill off ticks that can cause death. Africa seems to be constantly in the process of eating itself – from strangler figs to cattle ticks to snakes and cheetahs and anopheles mosquitoes, everything is munching away at everything else. Even as we speak, white ants are chewing away at the wooden frames of the buildings, David reckons that any wood-based dwelling, unless protected against the devouring ant, will have to be rebuilt after two years.

Even Shiwa, with all the care that has been taken and money that has been spent, is fighting for its survival. The Great Man has passed on and John and Lorna are struggling to discharge all the responsibilities required in maintaining an estate of forty square miles in a country with 150 per cent inflation. They have tried timber, cattle-ranching, egg and poultry production, but none has survived for long. John is hopeful that the new government will improve matters; meanwhile he and Lorna have formed Shiwa Safaris to exploit the tourist potential of the wildlife on their land.

At the end of the day John takes me down to the lake. It's a tranquil place, unmarked by human ambition and the inconstancy of fate. I feel he's happy here, released momentarily from the effort of keeping someone else's dream alive. I look around for the wildlife on which he is staking his latest hopes. A heron gracefully skims the water, a wattled plover screams overhead and a line of hippo tracks leads through the mud and into waters that reflect the ochre-red of another sunset.

DAY 112: *Shiwa to Kasanka*

Wake after another uncomfortable night. My digestive system still unruly. I would like to have felt fully recovered before venturing Polewards again. Patti is in a far worse state. Huge doses of chloroquine seem to have knocked out the fever but left her head and stomach aching. She leaves before the rest of us for a blood test at the Chilonga hospital.

Bid our farewells to the Harveys, who have been generous with their time and hospitality. On our way out we pass another testament to the Gore-Brown brand of colonialism. This is the estate hospital, opened in 1938. Now it has been downgraded to a clinic, and many of the buildings lie abandoned, pitched roofs open to the skies, discarded bed-frames rusting against the wall. But it is still useful, and up-to-date. 'Sex Thrills, AIDS Kills. Stick to One Sexual Partner' reads a poster on the office wall, from which one of the nurses is removing Kenneth Kaunda's portrait.

Today is immunization day and 200 women and children have arrived to be inoculated against whooping cough, polio, TB, tetanus and measles. They are dressed immaculately, the children in the fussiest knitted caps and coats and some women in tweed skirts and high heels despite the 90 degree heat. But the decay of the place, the smell of dust and dirt and the sweet sweat of humanity, is unavoidable. Africa is rewarding but demanding.

Uneventful ride south through trees and scrub. At a service station in Mpika I make my first acquaintance with the gloriously named Eet-Sum-Mor brand of biscuits. Nigel manages to pick up commentary of the England–Australia Rugby World Cup Final as we bounce and weave through a forest. The more Australia score the weaker the signal becomes. This time no one complains when they break off for the news.

We fetch up for the night at another camp, this time in the small National Park of Kasanka, which is run under a ten-year management contract by a genial, enthusiastic and adventurous Englishman called David Lloyd, who once had an awful lot of money but lost most of it running up-market hunting holidays in Zaire. His lodge, situated beside a small, reedy lake, is clean, well-kept, and, thanks to the profusion of frogs, mosquito-free. I learn more about hippos here than in all my time beside the Mara river in Kenya. So thoroughly had this area been poached, says David, that when he took over the park in 1986 there were only three hippos.

'They didn't call at all for the first two years – dead scared.'

Now there are fifteen altogether, seven or eight of whom are offspring of the original three. I ask him about the extraordinary noises of the hippo wind ensemble in Kenya. David tells me that every grunt means something. Hippos are 'highly intelligent', with over 100 separate sounds in their vocabulary.

Before supper I decide the time has come to do what I have put off for too long. Just in case. Not that it means anything, you understand. I take out Dr Baela's strip of bark from my bag, cut a slice off it with my Swiss army knife, grate it into powder, and, taking care to choose a private place, rub the powder all over my body before showering, keeping just enough aside to fill each nostril. The results are immediate. I sneeze uncontrollably for twenty-five minutes. No one, not Jake or David or any of their helpers, seems to know which particular tree I have just inhaled, but for the first time since I left Mpulungu I feel well enough to really enjoy my dinner.

Turning in. Sounds of low voices round the remains of the fire and bullfrogs on the lake. Above, a clear, intense, starlit sky. No reflections from anywhere. Pure sky. Pure night sky.

DAY 113: *Kasanka to Lusaka*

Sometime in the night I wake to hear a big wind blowing. It heaves and sighs around the hut with inexpressible mournfulness. I lie awake and think of the day ahead. If all goes well we should be in Lusaka by tonight, then Victoria Falls, and from what I hear our troubles are over after that. Zimbabwe and South Africa are comfortable, efficient, Westernized. Akuna Matata. No Problem. Wild, uncomfortable, incomprehensible Africa will give way to tamed and tidied Africa – hot baths and iced beers, air-conditioning and daily newspapers, French wines and credit cards. Lying here, listening to the aching wind in a hut by a lake in a forest, I feel a pain of sadness at the prospect of leaving behind all I have been through these past months and returning to a world where experience is sanitized – rationed out second-hand by television and newspapers and magazines and marketing companies.

The next thing I hear is a knock on the door and a soft voice outside:

'Four and thirty minutes, sir.'

The dawn reveals a sky mottled grey from last night's storm, and a thin orange line cresting the trees across the lake. Another farewell, and along the stony track out of the Park and south towards Lusaka, capital of Zambia, over 300 miles away. We have moved and filmed for seventeen of the last eighteen days, and there's some good old-fashioned exhaustion about. Patti's blood test could not indicate conclusively if she had malaria as the drug level was so high after the doses she'd been taking, but the hospital thought the symptoms fitted. She is too weak to work at the moment, but still has to travel, and squashed in the back of a bumpy minibus is not the best way to recuperate.

Our first experience of Zambian Railways, on the train from Kabwe to Lusaka, is not auspicious. The train is late and, once arrived, so reluctant to move that a plaintive announcement has to he made over the PA: 'Would Express Two move from the platform to allow Express One to come in'.

This does the trick, but progress is still painfully slow. The interior of the Japanese-built coaches is in terrible shape. All the fans are broken and the upholstery torn and shabby. The track is badly maintained, so progress is not only uncomfortable but slow and uncomfortable. Not that any of the passengers seem worried. They sit reading newspapers and religious texts as the carriages lurch and swing. A kind gentleman, sensing my agitation, lends me his copy of the *Zambia Daily Mail*. It is full of sycophantic adverts taken out by public companies congratulating Mr Chiluba on his victory. 'The United Bus Company of Zambia says Bravo MMD. The Hour Is Now.' A leading article by one Leo J. Daka, headed 'Zambia, Which Way Now', is less amenable:

'Zambia,' writes Mr Daka, 'is a hospital with the citizens as patients. When we were under colonialists we had no worry of major concern, now, with independence promoted by fellow blacks, I wonder. The point is something has gone mentally wrong with our leaders.'

The fact that such a piece is printed at all is one of the better things about Zambia. It is ironic that one of the achievements of Kaunda – the establishment of a two-party state and a free press – should be the instrument of his downfall.

DAY 114: *Lusaka to Livingstone*

We are in and out of Lusaka without time to take much in. The hotel is bland and efficient. Patti is off her malaria-crunching course of drugs and perceptibly better. And the *Times of Zambia* carries barely believable evidence of the pace of the Soviet Union's Great Leap Backwards. The story, filed from St Petersburg (which was Leningrad to us, three months ago) reports that the Grand Duke Vladimir Romanov, heir to the throne of Russia, has arrived in the Soviet Union for the first time.

We leave early, departing Lusaka via Saddam Hussein Boulevard, and swinging away again from our thirty degree line to Livingstone, another 300 miles south-west on the Zambian side of the river Zambesi.

The main street of Livingstone is lined with low, run-down colonial-style buildings with verandahs. Money-changers dart out as soon as they see a bus-load of tourists, miming their occupation suicidally and jumping out of the way only at the very last minute.

Our hotel is called 'Musi-o-Tunya', which is the local name for the Victoria Falls, and means 'the smoke that thunders'. It is modern, but uncertainly run. A smell of drains wafts into my bathroom from a grille high on the wall. But I shouldn't complain; at least I have a bathroom. But I don't have either of my bags. The staff at the Lusaka hotel failed to collect them from my room, and inquiries are under way. Apart from my clothes, which are replaceable, my diaries and taped notes, laboriously assembled, are now unaccounted for, 300 miles away. But then, so is Dr Baela's bark.

DAY 115: *Livingstone*

A half-mile walk through the well-watered gardens of the hotel takes me out onto the Upstream Trail which leads to the placid waters of the Zambesi as they flow gently, this being the dry season, towards a 250-foot precipice. In March and April the river floods and, as the brochure describes it, 'the greatest known curtain of falling water', one mile wide, spills into this massive split in the basalt rock, formed by cooling volcanic lava.

I walk, unhampered by fences or warnings of any kind, across a river-bed, sculpted by the action of stone and water into a weird and wonderful honeycomb of bore-holes and clefts and pipes and basins, to the very edge of the falls, where what is left of the river makes its way innocently towards the void. Defying stomach-tightening vertigo, I stand as close as possible to the rim and peer over. Far, far below the falling streams accelerate into an inferno, smashing against the fissured black rock which streams with foam as the water is flung forwards, repulsed and hurled back again at the cliff. The spray that is the debris from this massive collision of rock and water is flung in all directions, blown by its own momentum skywards, way above the top of the gorge. In the flood season this cloud – 'the smoke that thunders' – can be seen twenty miles away, and it was this that drew Livingstone to the falls in 1855, apparently the first white man to set eyes on them. As I turn back, reluctantly, to pick my way home across the river-bed, I appreciate for once the laid-back, shambolic arbitrariness of Zambia, which has allowed me, with no fuss or bother, unhindered access to this gigantic, enthralling sight.

It even enables me to accept, without chewing the carpet, the news that my bags have been located and have reached Lusaka airport, but have not been put on a plane.

I can't wear my T-shirt in this state for a third day, so I soak it, wash it and go down to dinner dressed in clothes Basil has lent me. It is fish night in the restaurant and all the waiters are dressed in straw hats.

Jake asks where the fish is from.
'America!' is the happy reply.
'America? How does it get *here*?'
'By sea . . . '

DAY 116: *Livingstone*

The morning paper reports that President Chiluba has lifted Zambia's twenty-seven-year State of Emergency. The police have been ordered to remove all road-blocks (still common in countries like Sudan, Ethiopia and Kenya) and various powers of search and detention have been curtailed.

For myself and the crew another day of new experiences. If it's Saturday it must be white-water rafting, and we assemble by the swimming-pool to sign in, absolve the company taking us of any culpability and generally try to look cheerful. Basil is very silent. He has persuaded himself that the photo-opportunities outweigh the fact that he can't swim. But only just. Fraser has spent hours devising a waterproof method of recording my shouts, screams and cries. His solution is to encase tape-recorder, battery, microphone and all the wiring in a selection of condoms. 'I've never used so many in one day in my life,' he claims.

Nigel has a tiny waterproof camera on a huge harness, which sits on his shoulder like a parrot. Patti must be one of the very few who have been white-water rafting in the same week as having malaria.

The organizer of the expedition is a short, lean, bearded American called Conrad with an intense, some might say manic, look in his eyes, softened by a ready smile. We are issued with life-jackets and then briefed by Heidi, another American who manages to put over dreadful information with a disarming, gung-ho jollity. Most of what she tells us has to do with what happens when, rather than if, we are flung off the boats and into the water.

'Just let yourself go. Don't try to swim . . . When you come up to the surface be sure to take a deep breath before you go under again.'

My legs are like jelly at the end of this and Basil is white. We select our life-jackets and head for the river.

What neither Conrad nor Heidi has prepared us for is the descent into the gorge, which involves a rough thirty-minute scramble, in considerable heat, over smooth and slippery boulders. Bad enough at the best of times, but with camera gear as well it delivers us to the rafts in a state of terminal exhaustion.

We climb into the reassuringly solid, heavy-duty rubber rafts, made by Avon in England. Eight to a raft, with a driver mounted on a central cross-board. We pull out into the stream, dwarfed by sheer rock walls and pinnacles of basalt. The Zambesi, as it winds through the gorge, falls over a series of twenty-odd rapids, of which we shall be tackling the first ten.

My companions are local people, some of whom, thankfully, know what to do. Our driver, Alex, a rangy black Zambian, rehearses us in the technique known as high-siding, which seems to mean flinging ones body as far forward in the raft as possible to keep the nose down and stop us being turned over by the force of the water. Once rehearsed, we move across the deceptively tranquil, unruffled pool between falls and rapid number one and wait for the camera crew's raft to go over first. Heidi steadies them into position. Basil is tucked down at the back, almost on the floor of his raft, hanging on to everything it is possible to hang on to. Heidi guides them slowly to the lip of the rapid. Much depends on how she lines the raft up. Satisfied she's hit the right spot, she allows the raft to glide forward and into the rapid. For a split second it accelerates like a rocket, twists, turns, carves into a reverse wave and momentarily disappears in a spectacular eruption of spray before bobbing away into safe water.

Seeing it happen to someone else merely increases the thud-rate of an already overworked heart, and only when we ourselves fly down the rapid, fling ourselves forwards on Alex's command 'Go!' and experience the exhilaration of total immersion do I begin to relax and even to suspect that I might enjoy myself.

Rapid five is the most spectacular, with a steep drop of more than twenty-five feet. Exhilaration and excitement make up for fatigue as we progress into some longer but less steep runs. I suppose the maximum time we spend on a rapid is no more than forty-five seconds, but into that time is packed an enormous amount of action, and the outpouring of nervous energy can only be released by bawling one's lungs out.

The sheer relief at reaching the tenth and last rapid, with the day's filming done and soft evening light catching the walls of the canyon, leads me to do a Very Silly Thing.

The crew of my raft manage to persuade me that there is an even more wonderful experience than white-water rafting and that is to swim, or rather let your body be carried, down a rapid. I ask about the crocodiles we'd seen further up the gorge. No problem, they avoid moving water. I ask about the rocks. No problem, way below the surface. Such is their enthusiasm and my joy at having survived this far that I surrender to a dangerous streak of natural impulsiveness, and jump, with them, off the raft and into the waters of rapid number ten.

As soon as I leave the boat I know I should have stayed in it. The current is fast and there is no way of controlling my progress. Within half a minute I'm swept and spun along before being tugged helplessly beneath the water by a reverse wave. I strike what is incontrovertibly a rock, and what's more a particularly sharp and unyielding rock.

The full force of the impact is taken on my lower back, protected, thank God, by my life-jacket, and probably by Fraser's tape-recorder. My calf meanwhile cracks against another rock that wasn't supposed to be there either. Winded by the blow, I struggle up to the surface driven by a potent and uncontainable sense of indignation. This enables me to roar, 'You bastards!' and take in a mouthful of Zambesi before disappearing again.

My companions are already ashore and gazing around with expressions of beatific happiness when at last I fight my way clear of the current and clamber up the rocky bank. I don't want to spoil the party so I keep smiling and begin the slow ascent of the gorge, content in the knowledge that, whatever I might have done to myself, Fraser's condoms are still intact.

At the hotel another bruise to add to the two already growing – one of my missing bags has arrived, the other has been lost by Zambian Airways and no one seems to hold out any hope of finding it.

Whatever baleful influence has been at work in Zambia, it has persisted to the end.

DAY 117: *Livingstone to Victoria Falls*

Sleep for an hour with the help of two paracetamol tablets, then painfully and fitfully for two or three more hours fighting against sticky heat (the air-conditioning being completely ineffectual) and sharp pain from my ribcage whenever I try to turn over. At three o'clock I give up, manoeuvre myself awkwardly out of bed and begin to make some assessment of what was in my missing bag. Torches, my favourite boots, my favourite sweater, my personal diary (though not, thank God, my notebooks). What has vanished, to my great relief, is Dr Baela's bark. I feel a little better, almost immediately.

At nine o'clock in the morning we clear Zambian Customs and make our way across the Victoria Falls Bridge, which marks the border with Zimbabwe. Constructed nearly ninety years ago it is a road, rail and pedestrian bridge and, for today only, something more than that. A group of people are proposing to throw themselves off the bridge on lengths of elastic, in what the organizers, an outfit called Kiwi Extreme, believe to be the first ever bungi jump in Africa. Bungi, I'm told by Byron, the leader of the team, who has a world record jump of over 800 feet to his credit, is an Indonesian word for the particular rubbery twine they use in their descents. Having nearly given my life to the Zambesi I am not at all tempted to fling myself upside-down into a gorge, but I recognize someone who is. It's Conrad, our organizer from yesterday. Slim and insubstantial beside the chunky white men in beer-brand T-shirts who seem to make up the bulk of the jumpers, he grins nervously as a red towel is wrapped around his ankles and the rope lashed carefully over it. Tied only by his feet, he climbs onto the parapet of the bridge, moistens his lips, murmurs something – I think it's 'goodbye' – and hurls himself out and away from the bridge. As he goes he flings his arms out, plummeting in a Christlike free-fall nearly 300 feet to the river below. Then, when he looks set for certain death, he freezes for a split-second, and begins to return rapidly back towards us.

We leave Conrad bouncing up and down in the Zambesi Gorge, and make our way across into Zimbabwe.

Zimbabwe is younger than Zambia by sixteen years, and has just celebrated ten years of independence under the guiding hand of Robert Mugabe. On the wall of Immigration Shed A there is an old relief map of the country on which the word Rhodesia has been Tippexed out and 'Zimbabwe' scribbled in. The old capital, Salisbury, has been recycled more ingeniously – a piece of tape with 'Harar' on it has been stuck over 'Salisbur', so it reads 'Harary'. Perhaps they weren't expecting independence to last this long.

Check in to the Victoria Falls Hotel, an immaculately clean white-painted complex with red roofs and shining green lawns. The gift-shops on the Zambian side were pathetically empty, but here the shelves are full of all sorts of fluffy junk, though there is not a newspaper or book to be seen.

The room is comfortable and efficient. The carpets are soft and the curtains of flower-print pattern. The whole place feels like a very well appointed Old Folk's home.

The price for this soft-furnished cosseting is re-entry into the world of regulations. The 'I Presume' Bar has a sign warning that between 7.00 and 11.30, dress is 'Smart Casual. No Denims, No T-Shirts, No Takkies'.

A pleasant meal out in the open air, but surrounded by

package tour faces. Roger and others leave early to hit the casino, but when I eventually hobble off to my bed I find them all gathered in the 'I Presume' Bar looking very cheesed off. Apparently all of them were banned from the casino for being improperly dressed. The doorman picked them off one by one – Roger, sandals; Paul the driver, trainers; Basil, canvas shoes; and Nigel, denim jeans. It may hurt but at least I go to bed with a laugh.

DAY 118: *Victoria Falls*

I am taken to the local hospital for an X-ray. It's the sort of hospital you dream about when you nod off after a three-hour wait in a London casualty department. It has only been operational for a month, is spotlessly clean, well equipped and almost empty. The lady in X-ray has so little to do that before attending to me she has to set down the book she's reading – a slim paperback by one Dr James Dobson entitled *Dare to Discipline – Permissiveness Doesn't Work*. After four exposures she's satisfied and I take various studies of my ribcage along to the doctor who diagnoses a hairline crack and prescribes nothing more than paracodeine to help me sleep.

Nigel, who said all along that he thought it was a cracked rib, is sympathetic but realistic. 'There's nothing you call do. The pain wears off . . . in about six weeks.'

My biggest mistake was to do it off-camera. Now I shall creak all the way to the Pole and everyone will think it's old age.

DAY 119: *Victoria Falls to Bulawayo*

A bombshell of a telex has arrived from Cape Town. There are no berths available on the *Agulhas* – the South African supply ship which was our only means of transport to Antarctica. The full complement has been taken up by scientists and survey staff.

We must go on to the Pole somehow. It is inconceivable to have come this far and not to reach our goal. Phone calls to the office in London to double-check the *Agulhas* and investigate any possible alternative.

Meanwhile, life must go on, and that means packing and moving on, yet again.

On the way through the hotel gardens to reception a group of tourists stands frozen beneath a low covering of mango trees through which a troop of baboons is rampaging, bombarding the red-tunicked porters below with sticks, branches and half-eaten mangoes. It's amazing how little it takes to cheer one up.

We assemble at Victoria Falls station around 5 p.m. to take the overnight train to Bulawayo. Like everything else in the town, the station is in immaculate condition. It's a low, elegant, Greek-revival gem with freshly painted sky-blue doors and matching detail, and on the platform an ornamental pond, palm trees, frangipani and striking red flamboyant trees.

The train rolls in an hour late but is worth the wait. The coaches are in a dignified, rather unfashionable livery of brown and cream and the interlinked initials 'RR' – Rhodesian Railways – can be found engraved on the windows and mirrors of the older coaches, whose dark, mahogany-panelled compartments contain display photos of wildlife, the Victoria Falls and other Zimbabwean attractions. The past has been assiduously preserved here, in marked contrast to Zambia, where not even the present is well preserved.

The difference between the two countries is much on the mind of Elizabeth, a chatty Zimbabwean who quite unselfconsciously applies a squirt of underarm deodorant as she chats to myself and Angela and a very obliging Zambian.

'Zambians are . . .' she searches for the word, '. . . so humble. Maybe it is because of their poverty.'

The Zambian gentleman smiles benevolently, displaying patience rather than humility.

A few minutes after leaving, a guard comes by to check I have everything I need.

'Where are you from, sir?' he asks.

'London.'

He points to his tie.

'Do you have a badge? I will put it on my tie.'

I apologize for not having a badge, whereupon he smiles broadly, crosses himself and leaves. No sooner do I have my map out to check the route than the door slides open once again and an attendant appears with a litter bag. This country has a most un-African obsession with tidiness. On my way down the corridor to the restaurant there is an instruction from Railways of Zimbabwe urging us, with graphic underlining, not to 'Expectorate in Corridors'.

Darkness has fallen by the time we reach Hwange, or Wankie as it used to be called. There is a large coalfield here, and perhaps because of this a number of steam locomotives – Beyer-Garratt compounds, burning seven tons of coal a day – are still working, and the sight and sound of them under the night sky brings a lump to this old train-spotter's throat.

DAY 120: *Bulawayo*

From the moment our night train rolls at a leisurely pace through a cutting and past the line-side greeting 'Welcome to Friendly Bulawayo', the illusion of being in Surrey *circa* 1958 begins.

Steam engines are at work shunting goods-wagons and big yellow diesels bring in expresses from Plumtree and Mafikeng, made up of varnished wood coaches with clerestory roofs.

We drive out to our hotel along wide streets – when they were laid out by the early settlers they had to be wide enough for a team of oxen to turn without backing up.

There *have* been changes – Selborne Avenue has become Leopold Takawira Avenue, Rhodes Street has become George Silikunda Street, and Grey Street, Birchenough Road and Queen's Road have all been subsumed into Robert Mugabe Way – but this is still a city of boarding-schools and bowling clubs, and when whites talk about it being multiracial they mean it includes Scots, Irish, Germans and South Africans.

There are cricket pitches and even an Ascot Racecourse. The high street shops are British of the pre-Tesco era, with names like Haddon and Sly, Townsend and Butcher, Stirling House, Forbes and Edgars, while some, like Kaufmanns and A. Radowsky, established 1907, reveal a Jewish influence among the early settlers.

The roads are full of Morris Minors, Hillman Minxes, Ford Anglias and solid old bicycles with delivery frames on the front, and at Mikles Store the 'Early Xmas Sale' begins today.

Not everything is comfortable and assured – an ominous sign in the centre of the city reads 'Save Water. Only twenty-two weeks water left in our dams' – but after Sudan, Ethiopia, Tanzania and Zambia, I have to pinch myself to make sure that I am awake and that Bulawayo is not some figment of my paracodeine-drugged mind.

This evening there is a four-hour thunderstorm and a downpour which should add a day or two more to the water supplies. After the rains, which broke a hot and humid day, the air is full of winged insects, committing mass hara-kiri against the windows. Paul says they're flying ants, out to find a mate, dig a hole somewhere and breed. They're eaten all over Africa, apparently, usually fried.

DAY 121: *Bulawayo*

Water is not the only scarce commodity in Zimbabwe. A report in this morning's *Bulawayo Chronicle* is headed 'Shortage of Bibles'. 'The sudden eruption of religious organizations during the past five years is said to be straining the supply of Bibles written in local languages. Religious leaders in Bulawayo said the influx of Pentecostal churches, breakaway groups from the mainstream Roman Catholic church, have led to a high demand.'

Demand is falling, however, at the Bulawayo Bowls Club. Pearle Sheppard, the secretary, blames Independence. 'A lot of people have left the country . . . we used to have nearly 400 members . . . and now it's gone right down to about 120.'

When we arrive to film, Pearle is concerned that we don't get the wrong impression from a large sign which greets us at the clubhouse: 'BBC. Do Not Leave Things on the Verandah for the Thieves'.

'Oh dear no, BBC is for Bulawayo Bowls Club,' she explains apologetically.

Despite it being a dull, drizzly afternoon there are twenty bowlers out on the greens. The men are thin, erect and grey-haired. The women are generally, though by no means exclusively, buxom, and as you might expect, younger than the men.

'You get a very representative crowd, people from all walks of life and all ages and everything, they all come and play bowls.'

I ask Pearle if the club has black African members.

'Er . . . we don't have any, no. Actually the Africans are not particularly interested in bowls. The only black bowlers we've got in Bulawayo belong to the Blind Bowlers Association . . . It's really quite fantastic to see some of them play, because they might not be able to see anything yet they call out instructions to them and they sometimes play incredible bowls.'

A Scots lady is the current Zimbabwean National Champion and she is on the green today, broad and tanned, her hat at a rakish angle, with a cigarette permanently on the go. She encourages her opponents vigorously. 'Beautiful weight, Doris . . . Oh, magic adjustment Ethel, well bowled!'

When her turn comes she delivers the bowl with one hand and retains her cigarette in the other. As the bowl describes the gentlest of arcs she straightens up, pulling slowly and thoughtfully on her cigarette as she encourages it across the green, 'Come on, kiddo . . . come on, little one.'

About thirty-five miles outside Bulawayo, in the modestly spectacular and historically fascinating region of the Matopos Mountains, is buried the man whose foresight, determination and insatiable ambition created a country which bore his name for fifty-seven years before becoming Zimbabwe in 1980. In a short life he had a massive influence over the whole of southern

Africa – opening up farming land, developing the gold and copper mines, and setting up communications. When he died in Cape Town in 1902 his own personal train, designed by the Pullman Company of America, brought his body to Bulawayo. He was a year short of fifty, and had left precise instructions in his will. 'I admire the grandeur and loneliness of the Matopos in Rhodesia and therefore I desire to be buried . . . on the hill which I used to visit and which I called "The View of the World" in a square to be cut in the rock on the top of the hill, covered with a plain brass plate with these words thereon, "Here Lie the Remains of Cecil John Rhodes".'

Ninety years later, and despite threats by Mugabe to dig up the body and send it back to London, this is exactly how and where Rhodes lies. The area is now a National Park, a controversial move which involved the forced removal of local residents and accusations of desecration of holy places by the Ndebele people.

The grave lies on top of a great smooth pate of exposed granite, topped by a ring of massive boulders, some twenty feet high, frozen at a gravity-defying angle on the very tip of the slope.

This being Zimbabwe one cannot climb up to it without some official instruction. 'No one is allowed to take alcoholic stuff up to the grave. No radios. No noise. No domestic animals', reads the sign.

The view out across a rich and irregular landscape of rock-stacks, rounded hills and long smooth ridges shaded by woodland is very fine, and at sunset the dying light on the red and yellow lichen of the rocks creates a warm luminous glow.

In order to balance something against the pervasive influence of white culture I spend the evening in the Umtshitshimbo Beer Garden at the back of the Waverley Hotel where a band called Southern Freeway are playing live.

The Umtshitshimbo Beer Garden is not the sort of garden that Vita Sackville-West would recognize. The concrete tables and chairs are mounted on breeze blocks and the only greenery is on the wall in a series of ruggedly painted murals depicting

ABOVE: *The floating wedding party.*

LEFT: *Me and my prescription with Dr Baela in Mpulungu, Zambia.*

ABOVE: *English country life endures at Shiwa Ngandu.*

RIGHT: *White-water rafting on the Zambesi river.*

ABOVE: *Family outside their home in Soweto, South Africa.*

LEFT: *Reunion with the Gwangwas and a cow dung welcome.*

OPPOSITE (TOP): *Western Deep −2½ miles down.*

OPPOSITE (BOTTOM): *The closed virgin, Santiago.*

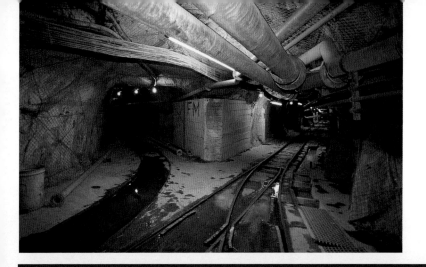

May the world stay in peace
May Antarctica be used for peaceful purposes only
May high-tech propel pollution-free motorization
with my gratitude to my family and friends for their support

January 1st. 1992
Shinji Kazama, at the south pole

scenes of African village life – cooking fires, drinking hooch, baboons scratching their bottoms. Around the front of the stage a crowd has already assembled. They sit right up close, beers lined up on the stage itself. Recorded music is blaring out and people are dancing.

Every now and then the music is interrupted for a long and explicit public service warning about the danger of AIDS, to which no one listens. The beer – Black Label, drunk from the bottle, or Castle – is often augmented with spirits. Quarts of gin seem to be the popular choice. By the time Steve Dyer and his band mount the stage, the crowd are restless and beginning to stagger a little. Looking around, I see no white faces apart from ourselves, one older man, a thin blond boy and Steve Dyer himself, who seems rather low-key and apologetic for the occasion. Once the band gets going there is an infectious and generous response, especially when an impressive diva by the name of Thandeka Ngoro takes the stage. She has a dramatic presence and a powerful voice which she may feel is more suited to La Scala in Milan than the Umtshitshimbo Beer Garden.

DAY 122: *Bulawayo to the Soutpansberg Mountains*

Up at six o'clock to pack and leave Bulawayo for our last African country. The next cities of any size on the line south will be Pretoria and Johannesburg in South Africa.

It all seems to be happening fast now. We can travel long distances on these straight tarmac roads and there are few diversions on the way. Today we are aiming to move another 400 miles closer to the Pole.

7.15. Bulawayo bus station. For a republic founded and led by an avowed Marxist, Robert Mugabe's Zimbabwe displays a healthy respect for private enterprise. Among the innumerable bus companies are Sun-Shine Coaches, Hit-Man Buses, the Hwange Special Express and the magnificently titled Dubies Megedleni Omnibus Service. The buses are circled by salesmen with travel-aids of every description from Afro-combs to balls of string with which to tie up baggage.

Lunchtime: After a long and uneventful morning's drive by bus and minibus across monotonous miles of dry bush, we have reached Beitbridge, a nondescript frontier town whose most recent claim to fame was an appearance in the film *Cry Freedom*, for it was the crossing-point where Donald Woods escaped South Africa dressed as a priest. (In Bible-booming southern Africa I can see that this was the perfect disguise to choose.)

After a mixed grill at the Beitbridge Inn on the Zimbabwean side, we drive across the Limpopo and into South Africa.

I wish I didn't have to dismiss the crossing of the Limpopo so lightly, for like the Ngorongoro Crater, Lake Tanganyika and the Zambesi, the Limpopo is one of the most mysterious and evocative of all African names. I wish I could say I bathed in it (as I did in Lake Tanganyika and the Zambesi) or at least paddled in it, or at least got a little closer to the hippos that wallow in its red and muddy water. But it has suffered the fate of all rivers that become national boundaries – it is a security risk. Nowhere more so than on this border between the white-run economic giant of the south and black Africa to the north. Although apartheid is being rapidly dismantled, the thousands of yards of coiled razor wire, the two ten-foot-high steel mesh fences, the guard-posts and the searchlight towers at twenty-yard intervals remain to guard the Republic of South Africa against the world, and the Limpopo from its fans.

The South African Immigration Office has a quarry-tiled floor, modern, efficient air-conditioning, computers and tinted glass. There are posters on the wall but they aren't displaying the beauties of the country. Instead, under the heading 'Look and Save a Life', they show you how to recognize an SBM limpet mine, a PMN (TMM) anti-personnel mine, a TM57 land mine and grenades M75, FI and RGD5.

Outside, the first white soldiers we've seen in Africa check the vehicles that go through. They seem an ill-disciplined, loutish lot, unhealthily red-faced and red-eyed. They deal mainly with commercial vehicles here, there are few private cars going through. Some African women are thumbing lifts on the big trucks belonging to Wheels of Africa or Truck Africa as they grind through the checkpoint bringing cobalt and copper from Zambia and Zaire.

Clem has rented for me not only a BMW but a white BMW. Hardly a discreet way to enter the country, but when you've been on the road for four months in fourteen countries you seize whatever bonuses come your way. I check the map, slip Bob Seger's *The Fire Inside* – noisiest and liveliest of my tapes – into the cassette player, and flicking on the engine ease southwards into the Transvaal. The economic transformation from the wild, unruly and unavailable to the comfortable, expendable and the infinitely possible, which began at Victoria Falls and continued in Zimbabwe, is complete.

DAY 123: *Soutpansberg Mountains to Johannesburg*

After a hot night at a motel in the Soutpansberg (Salt Pan Mountains), with my cracked rib giving me no relief unless I sleep sitting up, we are on the move, passing along a series of tunnels through the folded, faulted range that is part of the Drakensberg Mountains. If I'm not much mistaken the Verwoerd Tunnels (after Dr Hendrik Verwoerd, Prime Minister and staunch advocate of apartheid, assassinated in 1966) are the first tunnels we have been through in nearly 12,000 miles of travel. Forty miles further on I'm surprised to be reminded that part of South Africa is in the tropics, as we pass a tall, modern, chrome-tipped monument marking the Tropic of Capricorn.

How different my circumstances were when we crossed into the tropics nine weeks ago. From the Wadi Halfa ferry to a BMW.

We reach Pietersburg, to the passing eye clean, well-kept and affluent, and on through towns whose lumpy names, like Potgietersrus and Naboomspruit, declare their origin in the years following the Great Trek of 1837 when 10,000 Boer settlers, unable to coexist with the British, left the Cape and moved north. Now they are proud communities announcing themselves with weighty concrete signs. Hotels and shopping malls are going up behind false brick façades and the car parks are full of BMWs like mine. Sanctions don't appear to have caused much pain up here.

We run on towards Pretoria, across another immense and spectacular African plain. This is the High Veld. The four-lane highways are in good condition and not busy. Puffy altocumulus clouds are stacking up in a wide blue sky.

We arrive at Pretoria, over 200 miles from last night's stop-over, in good time for the afternoon's big football match. Christopher, the black driver of the minibus into which we have transferred, is becoming increasingly agitated the nearer we get to the Atteridgeville Super Stadium. Atteridge is a black area, he says, and will not be safe for us. Looking around at the township, set on a hill, with a church and a lot of brick houses with pitched corrugated iron roofs, I can't see quite what he's worried about. The streets are unswept and there has been no attempt to plant a public tree or two, but no one is shaking their fist at us. The traffic begins to build up as we near the stadium and Christopher falls apart completely. This is not a safe place, they are all black people here, and do we not know what they do to white people in a place like this? They kill them.

Then suddenly his fear subsides. He has spotted several white faces queuing up for tickets for the game. All of them are alive and well.

We follow an expensive red car into the ground. 'Soweto BMW' says the rear window sticker. Admission is five rand – about a pound, which is not bad value considering this is a cup semi-final between the local team, Sundowns, and the holders, Jomo Cosmos from Johannesburg.

The status of football being relatively humble here, Sundowns arrive squeezed into a minibus bearing their motto which, with an unfortunate letter missing, comes out as – 'Sundowns. The Sky is the Limi'.

The Jomo Cosmos team is as far as I can tell the personal property of Jomo Sono, a Pele and a Charlton of South African football. It has been managed for the past nine years by a Scot from Arbroath called Ray Matthews. I am privileged to hear his warm-up chat in the dressing-room. He exhorts his players in a broad Scots accent that gives no hint of twenty years spent in South Africa. 'Mothale, you feed Minkhalebe . . . Masinga overlap Singiapi . . . '

The players all nod as if they understand. I ask him how much difference he thinks his chat makes. He shrugs and shrinks even lower into his shoulders.

'It's like talking to children. You just don't know how they'll play on the big occasion.'

His team, nine blacks and two whites, run out onto a pitch respectably green considering the shortage of water. A concrete ramp surrounds the pitch. On it graffiti slogans like 'Viva Joe Slovo', 'ANC Lives', 'ANC Leads', 'Smash Capitalists', coexist with ads for Caltex, Shell and Philips. Under 'Socialism Never' someone has added 'Failed'.

The first half is a bit of a plod. Half-time comes as a relief, in more ways than one. The top row of the cantilevered terracing becomes an impromptu urinal from which a gentle curtain of golden rain descends forty feet to the ground.

There are few police in evidence and despite losing to a soft goal from Ray Matthews's team, the local crowd behaviour is good. Everyone, including the players, seems quite free of the surly posturing that was once so common in English football.

Thirty-five miles away down swift, modern highways is Johannesburg – capital city of the Transvaal with 1.6 million souls. Tall unblinking tower-blocks of glass and steel climb up into the sky. As we wait in the muzak-sodden lobby of the Johannesburg Sun Hotel, Nigel looks helplessly round at the chrome and the preserved plants and the water-effects and asks: 'What happened to Africa?'

DAY 125: *Johannesburg*

'Summer's here! Make it a good one with the Trimrite Trimmer. Only 179 rand! . . . This is High Veld Stereo on 94.95 *Eff*-Em . . . twenty-two to twenty-three degrees out there . . . real swimming-pool weather!'

A November Monday morning in Johannesburg. The silent skyscrapers are coming to life after the weekend and the traffic jams are growing on the freeways, like in any big city in the world. We are heading south-west, out of town, to visit somewhere quite unlike any other city in the world.

Soweto, twelve miles south-west of Johannesburg, comprises thirty-three townships with a population of 3.5 million people. The first buildings went up in 1933 and a competition was held to decide on a name. Verwoerdville was one of the unlikely contenders, but Soweto – South Western Township – was chosen. It's a cold and functional name for a cold and functional purpose: to house a cheap, disenfranchised workforce with which to exploit the mineral wealth of the area. That wealth, needless to say, went back into Johannesburg and not Soweto, which is why, nearly sixty years on, the contrast between the two is such a shock. The skyline of Soweto is unbroken by cover of any kind. Row upon row of basic single-storey houses sprawl across bare, unlandscaped hillsides. The streets are full of uncollected rubbish, some of which has just been set on fire where it lies. The rest blows and swirls in the wind. The stations from which hundreds of thousands of workers leave for the city each morning are currently patrolled by guards with Armalite rifles, following a spate of violent attacks on passengers. As many people as can afford it have taken to using the ubiquitous minibuses, privately owned, which cover the city. The stories of Inkatha violence are sickening. They have added to the fear in the city. As someone told me, 'When Mandela was released everyone was wearing ANC T-shirts, now you don't see any'.

This is the grim first impression of Soweto, but as soon as you look beyond the physical differences, beyond the outrageous disparity between the quality of surroundings in two cities so close to each other and so dependent on each other, there are plenty of signs of life and hope. I am here to visit a family from Soweto who were once our neighbours in London, and who have recently been allowed back into their own country. We are accompanied by a Sowetan called Jimmy, who has made a good living from guided tours of the area. Jimmy, full of wisecracks – he tells me in Soweto BMW means 'Break My Windows' – is by turns charming, congenial, garrulous, curt and businesslike. He is a professional and a survivor. He offers breakfast at his house, which is a long way from the traditional image of the tin-roof shack.

It is approached through wrought-iron gates and past newly-planted jacaranda trees. Inside is a fitted kitchen with all mod cons hung with pictures and paintings. He is particularly proud of a personally signed copy of a Robert Carrier cookbook.

While we eat breakfast he is constantly on the phone doing deals of some kind. He breaks off just long enough to give a public wigging to Roy, the gardener, who has arrived half-an-hour late this morning.

'Blue Monday,' nods Jimmy as Roy retires chastened, 'the people here they just drink all weekend long.'

I ask him if there are any whites in Soweto.

'Oh sure . . . twenty per cent of the taxi businesses here are white-owned . . . there's a lot of whites work at the power station . . . there's an area there called Power Park which has a lot of white residents . . .'

As we leave Jimmy's house, Roy is scooping dog-shit off the lawns.

In Jimmy's neighbourhood – the Diep Kloof extension, or Prestige Park as it is known – there are streets full of architect-designed, venetian-blinded villas with double garages, clipped lawns and herbaceous borders. Mercedes back lazily out of radio-controlled garages and one mansion boasts the ultimate in Soweto chic: a white security guard. These houses went up in the last five years and were bought by businessmen, doctors and lawyers. One was for a man who makes 150,000 rand a year profit from the butchery business; another cost the Reverend Chikane 800,000 rand (£150,000).

'Moneymakers in the name of the Lord,' muses Jimmy as we drive by.

At our insistence and with, I detect, a slight weariness, he shows us another side of Soweto, a shantytown known as Mandela Village. Looming in the distance, beyond the tin roofs and the undrained streets, are the long straight lines of the gold mine dumps.

A baby is born in Soweto every five minutes, says Jimmy. Fifty per cent of the population are under sixteen. Many thousands of them live in conditions like these, makeshift cabins which can be put up overnight, made of anything their occupants can lay their hands on. There are frequent fires and no sanitation other than a few plastic lavatories provided by the council. The shacks consist usually of one room, with maybe the added luxury of a scavenged gas-ring or an old car-seat. Very often the inside walls are papered with pages from sales catalogues or fashion magazines. Three-piece suites, televisions, showers, refrigerators and all the other things the occupants can't afford form a constant backdrop to their lives.

The 'Blue Monday' effect can be seen in a number of sad characters who lurch along the dirt track between the huts, but the children are wide-eyed and curious, quick to smile, easy to make laugh. It is fairly unbearable to dwell on their prospects in life – taken away from the simple, hard but traditional way of life in a mud hut in the bush to a life equally hard, but suddenly not as simple.

Having seen the unreal best and the depressing worst of Soweto I'm ready for a little normality – a dose of straightforward friendship uncluttered by projections and statistics. I repair to the Orlando district to see the Gwangwas. Outlawed from South Africa for belonging to the ANC, Jonas, a musician and co-composer of the music for *Cry Freedom*, his wife Violet and their two children took refuge in many cities including London. I never imagined I would ever see them in their own home, and the pleasure of the reunion is tremendous. Violet welcomes me with such a hug that I fear another rib will crack, and on the yard of their house is what I am assured is a traditional African greeting – 'Welcome Michael, To Gwangwa Family' – marked out in dried cow-dung.

Violet apologizes for Jonas's absence. 'He's at a meeting with Nelson Mandela.' Now there's an excuse.

We go to lunch at a shebeen, originally the name for an illicit liquor shop, but now applied to a rather decorous front room in a nearby street where, over a licit can of Castle lager, Violet talks about being back home.

After eight years away she finds the surroundings worse – 'seventy-five per cent of people can't afford the new houses they're building' – a growing middle class and a growing violence and uncertainty, but she recognizes the danger of the returned exile coming back to tell those who live here how to run their lives. Her travels round the world echo my own feelings. 'Most countries you go to, you find that people want to be hospitable, they're proud of their country, you know, whatever, whether they're rich or poor, they want to make you feel welcome and they want to sort of show you how they live, and I think that's the same here too.'

Later I meet Jonas – another short, sharp shock for the ribcage – back from his meeting. I ask how Mandela was.

Jonas smiles. 'He still has a powerful handshake.'

Jonas has been away for thirty years and is still dazed by the reaction, 'people I haven't seen since the sixties coming up and shaking my hand'.

When I ask him if he detects a difference in the people he nods very firmly.

'They're broad-shouldered now, you know . . . before they walk looking down, they were cowed so easily.'

On which optimistic note we leave Soweto.

The last thing I hear from High Veld Stereo, '94.95 *Eff*-Em', is that Terry Waite has been released.

DAY 126: *Johannesburg*

First good night's sleep – five unbroken hours – since my dip in the Zambesi. Probably just as well, for today promises no respite for the body. We are to go down one of the gold mines on which the wealth of Johannesburg and indeed the whole of South Africa is based. One third of the country's export earnings comes from gold, and the proceeds from coal, platinum, uranium and other minerals found in these rich seams raise this to almost two thirds. A new mine can cost twenty billion rand (£3.8 billion) to develop. It isn't surprising therefore that mining is a tight, white-run operation.

The Western Deep Mine, developed by Anglo-American, one of the six private companies that control ninety-five per cent of gold production, is kept almost pathologically clean and tidy. Despite the water shortage, sprinklers gently douse the lawns on the approach to the offices, and men with pointed sticks are at work removing kerbside litter.

We are briskly and efficiently processed, like patients at an expensive private hospital, into a reception-room where coffee and pastries are served under the clean-cut, clear-eyed gaze of the directors of Anglo-American whose framed photos are the only decoration. Then we are shown into a changing-room where every single item of our clothing has to be exchanged for a company outfit, and minutes later we re-emerge, in white boiler-suits, safety helmets and rubber boots, as Western Deep Visitors.

Martin de Beers, solidly-built, moustachioed in the style of a Southern Hemisphere cricketer, begins a long and doubtless ritualized public relations spiel as we are fitted out with headlamps and batteries.

Western Deep Mine is in *The Guinness Book of Records* for the deepest penetration of man into the earth's crust – 3773 metres, that's nearly two and a half miles. Within the next year that will be surpassed by a new shaft which will be sunk beyond the 4000-metre mark. It has been honoured on a thirty-cent postage stamp as one of the three best achievers in technology in South Africa since 1961, along with Christiaan Barnard's heart transplants and a machine for harnessing wave power. At any one time there are 7000 men working beneath the surface, and it takes four hours to get them all down. The workforce is seventy-two per cent migratory labour, the majority coming from the Siskei and Transkei (two 'homelands' set up in the spirit of apartheid to encourage Bantus to develop separately), but also from Mozambique – 'very placid, they are the only people who mix freely with all the other tribes'. Martin prefers to talk rather than be asked questions. I sense that there is anger in there, probably a lot nearer the surface than anything else at Western Deep.

I have seen no black faces yet, apart from the gardeners. I presume they're all underground. We pile into a lift to join them. It rattles and clangs towards the earth's core at seventy metres a second. Another form of transport to add to the list. Two kilometres down we are released into a world almost as spotless as the one we've just left. It smells of fresh cement – like a newly-constructed underground car park.

I ask Martin if this is a model mine, the showpiece of the company.

'This is Anglo-American standard, the model mine's the South Mine. They all drive around in Land Rovers down there.'

Temperatures at this depth are around 50 Centigrade, and so Anglo-American have had to air-condition the earth's crust to a maximum of 28.5 degrees . . . 'the limit set by the human sciences laboratory'.

So far the experience has been curiously undramatic, the surroundings clean and spacious. Then quite suddenly there comes a point where underground car-parking becomes potholing and all Anglo-American's environmental cosmetics cannot disguise the realities of mining.

The shaft narrows to a slippery rock passage, full of water. The only light is from my helmet, and footholds are not easy to find. A scramble up spilled rock-fall leads through to a narrower chamber. The noise of the drills makes it difficult to hear instructions and it is no longer possible to stand upright.

Away from the air-conditioning the heat quickly rises and the sweat begins to run. We edge carefully through into a man-made cave with little more than three-foot clearance where crouching miners are at work on the rock-face. There is great heat and terrific noise when the drills are in action.

Three-men gangs work at the face in temperatures approaching ninety Fahrenheit for six hours per shift. One operates the drill, another checks the equipment and a third directs water into the hole, keeping the dust down. A fourth man, and the only white in the team, is the mining engineer who has to check the face and mark in red paint the bands to be drilled. I am close enough now to the gold seam to reach out and touch it. It doesn't glitter. The gold here is in carbon form, in fact the gold-bearing strip only inches wide, studded with white quartzite pebbles against a dark background of limestone and lava, looks more like black pudding.

Before we leave Western Deep we're allowed limited access to the Holy of Holies – Number 2 Gold Plant – where at temperatures of 1600 Centigrade one of history's most ancient, magical and mysterious processes comes to its conclusion as black pudding is turned into gold. Security is tight; a steel-mesh doorway is locked behind us. Every camera angle is checked by armed security men, and Nigel is given strict instructions: 'You must shoot nothing west or your camera will be confiscated.'

Tension builds as the crucible is slowly upturned and the molten material begins to flow.

'Is that gold? . . . Is that gold?' we first-timers keep asking, but the experts peering through the green visors that enable them to look at the quality of the smelt shake their heads. For the first minute only slag appears. I should have remembered from the rivers of Lapland that gold is always at the bottom. Then a lighter, whiter stream comes through and everyone breathes a sigh of relief as each ingot tray is filled with gold worth £150,000.

I'm told that if I can lift an ingot I can have it. But they've only ever lost one like this.

On the way back from Western Deep through a landscape

scarred by flat grey spoil heaps fifty feet high and yellow and white plateaux of rubble hundreds of yards long I keep trying to find the answer as to why gold should still be so sought-after, so valued as to create monster technological feats like Western Deep Mine. No one seems to have a satisfactory answer.

Back at the hotel I ring my son whose twenty-first birthday it is today and realize after I put the phone down that I'm a very long way away from home, and still have a lot further to go.

Our future progress is still uncertain. The *Agulhas* remains adamant that there are no places, and the only alternative would be to approach Antarctica from a quite different direction, such as Australia, New Zealand or the tip of South America. But we are booked on the Blue Train to Cape Town, and as reservations on this exclusive express are almost as valuable as the ingots I tried to lift earlier, there seems no point in not completing our crossing of Africa, even if we don't know what on earth it's leading to.

DAY 127: *Johannesburg to Cape Town*

Discomfort in my back at night is still acute. Time will heal, people keep reassuring me, but I wouldn't mind a bit of help. A cheerful and obliging Johannesburg chemist recommends arnica, a homoeopathic remedy, and bonemeal tablets. They join the growing stash of pain-relieving drugs which have just about made up in weight for the bag lost in Lusaka.

Johannesburg station is deserted at 10.15 a.m. apart from a straggle of passengers and their porters booking in beside the sign 'Bloutrein Hoflikheids Diens'. The Blue Train porters must be the smartest in the world, in their blue blazers, grey trousers with knife-edge creases and leather shoes polished to a mirror-like sheen. Sadly, they wear rather sour expressions as if they all might have toothache, but as our man leads us into a lift he makes it pretty clear what he's surly about.

'Sorry about the smell,' he turns to pull the gate across, 'it's the coons. They piss all over the place.'

A group of fellow travellers is squashed onto a piece of carpet at a specially erected check-in area in the middle of an otherwise long and empty platform. They look a little nervous and exposed, as if the ability to take the Blue Train marks you out as one of the world's most muggable prospects. Some are scanning the information board which gives details of unashamed luxuries that await us.

'Dress is smart casual for lunch and elegant for dinner.'

Rack my brains to think of anything in my depleted wardrobe that could by any stretch of the imagination be described as elegant. Fail.

Two azure-blue diesel locomotives, bringing the seventeen coaches of colour-coordinated stock down from Pretoria, ease into the curve of the platform and quietly glide to a halt, whereupon stewards move smartly forward to lay out matching carpets, monogrammed with the letter 'B', before each door.

And so it goes on. My compartment has a wall of a window – big and double-glazed – air-conditioning, carpet, individual radio and temperature controls, half a bottle of champagne, a newspaper and an electronically operated venetian blind.

Just before 11.30 a husky female voice breathes over the intercom, 'The Blue Train is ready to depart,' and barely noticeably we begin to pull out of Johannesburg, due to cover the 900 miles to Cape Town in twenty-two hours. For the first time since Tromsø we are moving *west* of our thirty degree meridian and may not meet it again until, God willing, I reach the South Pole.

A travel-worn maroon and white local from Soweto passes us, heading into the city. We gather speed through grubby stations like Braamfontein and Mayfair, whose platforms are crowded with blacks in headscarves and sweaters, and accelerate into the smarter suburbs with names like Unified and Florida. It is the most comfortable train-ride I've ever experienced, and combined with the air-con and the thick glazing and the wall-to-wall carpets it is like being in a hermetically sealed capsule, enabling the passenger to observe the outside world while remaining completely detached from it – an unconscious paradigm, perhaps, of the apartheid system, officially abolished only five months ago.

There are ninety-two people in seventeen coaches – as opposed to 4000 in eighteen on the Nile Valley Express. No one is allowed to travel on the roof. On Zambian Railways the restaurant-car was out of food altogether; on the Blue Train I count thirteen pieces of cutlery in front of me at lunchtime. Terrine of kingclip (a local fish) and Cape salmon are served as we move across the wide, flat expanse of the High Veldt. Grain and gold country. Far in the distance the mountains are temporarily obscured by a thunderstorm.

The *Johannesburg Star* carries more evidence of the rapid emergence of the country from the years of isolation. South Africa is to be allowed to take part in the Olympics for the first time in thirty years. There is an advert for the resumption of South African Airways services to New York and a report that Richard Branson hopes to bring Virgin Airlines into Johannesburg by 1993. Meanwhile uniformed attendants move discreetly along the carpeted corridors collecting clothes to be pressed. Muzak lightly dusts the tranquil atmosphere, occasionally interrupted by train announcements.

'You can look out for some rhinos now on the compartment side.'

We search unsuccessfully for rhinos. All I can see are telegraph poles.

'Well, we don't seem to be in luck today.' Fade up Strauss waltzes.

But they don't give up easily. Fade down the Strauss waltzes.

'Ladies and gentlemen, you can now look out for flamingoes on the corridor side.'

Have a shower before dinner, and taking my all-purpose tie out to add that indefinable touch of elegance, saunter down to the bar. The windows are of such a size, with minimum partitions giving maximum view, that one has this strange sensation of floating, unsupported, over the countryside. Fraser says he saw a car coming towards him on a road running alongside and instinctively moved to one side. Poor old sod.

The barman Matt is put to work by Basil to make the perfect martini, but after three attempts Basil drinks it anyway. Matt comes up with the surprising information that the noisiest tourists he deals with are the Swiss.

'Swiss people are noisy?'

He relents a little. 'Well, not noisy, but they're happy drinkers.'

A glorious sunset over the town of Kimberley, which boasts of being the home of the World's Largest Man-Made Hole. At one time there were 30,000 frantic diamond prospectors digging in the hole at once. When it was closed in August 1914 it was three and a half thousand feet deep with a perimeter of a mile.

Meet one or two of my fellow travellers. A couple from Yorkshire whose daughter manages a vineyard on the Cape; a Swiss tourguide (Swiss and Germans are the most numerous tourists); a lady from the Irish Tourist Board who thinks that they have similar problems to South Africa's in attracting visitors – beautiful countries but political problems – and an exotic couple, she Colombian, he German, who are working in Gabon. We get back to the hoary old subject of malaria. Their view is that the pills are as bad for you as the disease, quite seriously affecting digestion and eyesight.

Fortunately my digestion is, for once, settled as I move through to the restaurant and the mountain of cut-glass that awaits me.

DAY 128: *Johannesburg to Cape Town*

5.30. Woken with piping-hot tea in a white china pot. For the first time since Victoria Falls I was able to sleep without a painkiller, and for the first time in Africa I was able to sleep well on a train. I now regret that I gave such enthusiastic instructions to be woken at sunrise.

We are travelling across the Karoo, a wide landscape of bare mountains and scrubby plain, deriving its name from the Hottentot word meaning 'thirstland'. Stimulated by this information I make my way down to the restaurant-car, past train staff already polishing the door handles.

We are close now to the end of Africa. Beyond a succession of tightly folded mountain ranges lies Cape Town, the richest corner of a rich province. God's Own Country. Sit and watch the sun warming the mountains and allow myself a nostalgic drift back to a sunrise in August as we drew in from the Mediterranean and saw the lights of Africa for the first time. It's now late November and high summer has turned to early spring. I don't exactly know what lies ahead but I have a sudden surge of optimism that everything is going to turn out right. We have been tried and tested by Africa in every possible way and, bruised and battered maybe, we have survived. My children call these moments of mine 'Dad's happy attacks', and as we glide out of an eleven-mile tunnel into a dramatic, sweeping bowl of land filled with vineyards I know that this one may last some time.

The magnificent landscapes of Africa build to a tremendous climax. Towering haze-blue mountain ranges – the Matroosberg, the Swarzbergen and the Hex – part like stage curtains to reveal the final epic image of Table Mountain and the wide Atlantic. It is a breathtaking display of natural beauty and one which raises all our tired spirits.

DAY 130: *Cape Town*

Yesterday I stood on the Cape of Good Hope, a low stack of rocks pounded by the ocean and strewn with giant seaweed, and this morning I sit on top of Table Mountain, a sheer cliff rising 3500 feet above the city of Cape Town. It's a warm spring morning and the rock hyraxes start mating wherever we point the camera and the magnificent view extends towards Cape Point where the warm waters of the Indian Ocean meet the cold waters of the Atlantic. Everything about this coastline is on the grand scale. The rolling breakers steaming in from thousands of miles of open sea, the long white beaches and the tall craggy walls of exposed rock that circle the city to the east – Signal Hill, the Lion's Head, the Twelve Apostles and Table Mountain itself. A brisk wind blows in off the sea, combining with the sun and the scenery to cleanse and reinvigorate an over-travelled system.

Looking down at the massive natural harbour it is ironic to think that this most prosperous corner of Africa was dealt a serious blow by one of the poorest when de Lesseps chose to build a canal through the Egyptian desert 130 years ago. All at once the trading ships from India and the East had a shorter, more convenient and more sheltered route to Europe, and Cape Town's 200-year monopoly as a supply and maintenance base for east–west shipping came to an end. There isn't much activity in port today, with the poignant exception of a sturdy red-hulled survey vessel making final preparations for an eight-day journey to the Antarctic. With a pair of strong binoculars I can just about make out the name on the hull – MV S. A. *Agulhas*.

Though there could be worse places to be marooned than Cape Town the good news is that after some feverish international telephonic activity we have secured an alternative passage to the Antarctic via the town of Punta Arenas in southern Chile. The bad news is that we must abandon any hope of clinging to the 30 degree meridian and any further surface travel. We have only two options left open to us; to fly into the Antarctic or to fail altogether.

DAY 133: *Santiago, Chile*

Santiago. Tuesday morning. It took us nearly three months to travel 6800 miles down the length of Africa, and only forty-eight hours to travel 6200 miles from South Africa to Chile.

Nor, after all this, are we any nearer our final destination.

Santiago and Cape Town are both, at 33 degrees South, some 4200 miles from the South Pole. There are other similarities. Both cities have a temperate climate and a distinctly European feel, reflecting the style and taste of the early settlers – Spanish in Chile and British in the Cape. Both produce good wine. Both have a recent political history of violence, oppression and varying degrees of international ostracism. The father and two brothers of Patricio, our guide and fixer in Santiago, were arrested and imprisoned in 1973 for supporting President Allende, General Pinochet's socialist predecessor, and Patricio himself was expelled from the university for his political views. He is not angry any more, nor does he regard himself as particularly unfortunate. Pinochet's police arrested 250,000 suspected Allende supporters and held them in national sports stadiums for up to three months – 2000 are still missing without trace. Though Chile now has a reformist, liberal president, Patricio Aylwyn, they are still missing and Pinochet is still Commander-in-Chief of the army.

This morning it's sunny at the foot of the Andes, with temperatures rising into the seventies, and the army band is parading outside the Moneda, the elaborate colonial-style presidential palace whose name means 'the Mint', which is what it was designed to be in 1805. It was here that President Allende committed suicide nineteen years ago after the building had been rocket-attacked by Hawker Hunter fighters ordered in by Pinochet and his rebellious armed forces.

A well-drilled changing of the guard takes place and then, with much preparation and flourish, the sixty-piece military band breaks into the unmistakable tones of 'Happy Birthday to You'. Not just one chorus, but a long symphonic variation which keeps a small crowd mystified for some five minutes. It's presumed that this is for the President, but no one seems at all sure.

We eat lunch in the glorious covered market, a classical façade outside and an elaborate and elegant cast-iron construction within. The produce looks plentiful and fresh – asparagus, strawberries, avocados, cherries and pineapples, and a rich and exotic selection of sea fare, especially conger eel and some things called picorocos, strange sightless rubbery creatures living in rocks. In order to eat them you have to buy the rock as well and drop it in boiling water for a couple of minutes. Piures, an even less attractive delicacy, resemble marine cowpats and contain some evil-looking orange parasites which Patricio recommends highly.

'Pure iodine . . . '

'Iodine?'

He nods enthusiastically. 'Very good for sex.'

Having restaurants in a food market seems such a sensible idea, and my meal with Patricio at the Marisqueria Donde Augusto is one of the best. Good food, good wine and an introduction to the Pisco Sour.

Pisco is an eau-de-vie served with a third of lemon juice, some white of egg and a lot of ice. It's fresh and quite fierce. While we're drinking some musicians come by, playing traditional instruments like the quena, a set of pipes, preferably bamboo, now plastic, and a charrango, a ten-stringed instrument, preferably of armadillo shell, now, for ecological reasons, made of wood. The sound is haunting and, according to Patricio, so old and traditional that Pinochet tried to ban the instruments for being too representative 'of the left'.

For a panoramic view of the city we take a funicular railway up beyond the zoo, onto a hill crowned by a forty-foot statue of the Immaculate Conception. Following a bent metal sign reading 'A La Virgen' we toil up paths and steps only to find that the Virgin is closed. Peering inside I can see a small chapel. The wall outside is extensively decorated with sentiments of a non-religious nature – 'Norma! Te Amo!', 'Mejay 2000', 'Depeche Mode' and, intriguingly 'Gladys y Dario 1/08/91'.

Above me the steel Virgin, cast in France in 1908 and brought here 'To celebrate the 50th anniversary of the dogma of the Immaculate Conception', stands arms outstretched, head slightly raised and eyes gazing into the middle distance, which is I presume how you are when that form of conception occurs.

DAY 134: *Santiago to Punta Arenas*

6.30 a.m. It's nine degrees Centigrade as I leave the hotel, wearing a thick shirt and sweater for the first time since northern Norway. We carry with us bulky bags of Antarctic clothes hastily flown out from London. Santiago airport is packed, and with forty-one pieces of baggage to check-in amongst the six of us we have few friends in the queue for LanChile's flight to Concepción and Punta Arenas.

Punta Arenas, at the tip of South America, only a mile or two across the water from Tierra del Fuego, is somewhere none of us in this well-travelled crew has ever been before. Because of the rapid change of plan at Cape Town even Clem, who reconnoitred as much of our route as possible, is a stranger to the next 4000 miles.

As we wait to board we can only talk in rumour and speculation about what lies ahead. There are so few facts to go on. A company called Adventure Network does exist – well, at least they answer telephones, take bookings and have headed notepaper – and they do claim to have direct flights from Punta Arenas to an Antarctic base at the Patriot Hills, and to be able to provide further air transport from there to the South Pole. The fact that none of us can find the Patriot Hills on any map of the Antarctic only adds to the confusion. Some gloommonger remembers our visit to Patric Walker in Lindos.

'When was Mercury going to be in retrograde again?'

'Late November . . . early December, wasn't it . . . ?'

The public address system bursts into life again. 'LanChile Flight 085 for Concepción and Punta Arenas is ready for boarding.'

I take a last look at the destination board. It's 27 November.

The first, moderately disconcerting, thing about the flight is that the plane is a Boeing 707, a perfectly fine aircraft, but not in service on any airline I've travelled with for a while.

As we take off, a Walt Disney cartoon plays on the cabin video.

It's a short hop to the city of Concepción, but already the

275

landscape is changing. The hills are steep and pitted, the narrow valleys running down to the sea are green and forested. The cabin announcement as we taxi to the terminal advises us to remain on board. 'Our staying at this airport will be approximately twenty minutes.'

Seven and a half hours later we are still at Concepción. We have played cards, read books, drunk beers and coffees and have even been bussed into a city-centre hotel for a gloomy set lunch. Patti and Fraser have managed some time for shopping, or retail therapy as they call it. I've met a scientist who is off to do coastal research in the Antarctic. He has stood on the South Pole. It had been 50 below . . . 'and your breath just gets swept away. It's so short anyway. You're at 10,000 feet'.

It had never occurred to me that besides being bleak and inhospitable and pitch dark half the year, the South Pole was as high as an Alpine peak.

The reason for our delay, Mercury apart, is all to do with the 707, which I have a feeling was a last-minute replacement. When the time came to re-start the engines there was no generator at Concepción airport powerful enough to provide the necessary charge. The engines are eventually re-started and we take off again in late afternoon. This time the air-conditioning has failed and as we begin to see icy peaks and glaciers below, the temperature on board verges on the Sudanese.

Somewhere below us the Trans-America Highway runs out and with it all road connection to Punta Arenas. The long Chilean coastline fragments into a breathtakingly spectacular array of mountainous islands, straits and fiords, of which the thickening cloud cover offers only tantalizing glimpses.

At half-past seven, ten hours into what should have been a two-and-a-half-hour flight, we turn and bank over the Straits of Magellan and down across sparsely-covered grassland into Carlos Ibanez Airport, Punta Arenas. We have reached latitude fifty-three degrees South. I should feel at home; I was brought up on fifty-three degrees – North, of course.

This realization does bring home to me the scale of the

276

travelling that still lies ahead of us. Punta Arenas may be the last stop before Antarctica, but it is still as far from the South Pole as Sheffield is from the North Pole.

DAY 136: *Punta Arenas*

Woken by the sound of a car alarm, which makes me think for a happy moment that I'm back in London. Consciousness slowly clarifies my surroundings into the narrow, unadorned walls of a room in the Hotel Cabo do Hornos, Punta Arenas, Chile. The Cape Horn Hotel is a romantic name for an unromantic eight-storey slab of a building, whose pale-yellow brick walls and low gabled roof stand on the brow of a hill dominating downtown Punta.

I sent off a postcard to my daughter yesterday and wanted desperately to lie to her and say that my room looked out over Tierra del Fuego. Basil's room looks out over Tierra del Fuego, but on my side of the corridor we look down on the main square, with its labelled trees, as neat and proudly kept as those of any French provincial town, protectively clustered around a flamboyant bronze statue of Ferdinand Magellan. The great man stands, one foot on a cannon, atop a plinth on which striving mermaids hold aloft the shields of Spain and Chile. Patagonia is marked on one side and Tierra del Fuego on the other, together with a bronze relief of Magellan's plucky little boat fighting its way between the two, as he became, in 1520, the first Westerner to sail from the Atlantic into the Pacific. Whoever designed the statue wouldn't let it lie and added two subjugated Indians beneath Magellan's feet. To kiss the toe of one of these Indians is supposed to ensure safe passage back from Antarctica. Since Dr Baela's bark I've been rattled by all superstitions, so I give the toe a quick peck.

Some last-minute shopping in Punta. Short on underpants, I make my way to a promising emporium only to find that this is not Africa and people do not speak English. I have to mime. It isn't very good and the assistant brings me a pair of trousers.

My next mime is shamelessly graphic. She colours a little and brings me a belt. By now I'm desperate and reach into the top of my trousers to show her the actual garment itself and find out that she can speak English after all, even if it is only to shriek, 'No! . . . not here!'.

On to the nearby Hotel Navigantes to meet our fellow polar travellers for a briefing ahead of tomorrow's planned departure.

Some are dauntingly well qualified. Graeme Joy, a keen, humorous New Zealander has skied to the North Pole. It had taken him fifty-six days and they had seen polar bear tracks regularly.

'That kept us together,' he grinned, 'no one wanted to be last.'

He leads a party of seven Australians and New Zealanders who are aiming to climb Mount Vinson – at 16,000 feet, the highest point on the continent of Antarctica. For some of them it will be the last in a series of expeditions to climb the highest peak of every continent. Graeme's co-leader is Peter Hillary, son of Sir Edmund, the first man known to have climbed Mount Everest.

A woman in the party, an Australian doctor, has flown a light plane from California to Sydney, across the USA and Europe. There is much talk of self-reliance, of testing themselves. An Australian lawyer and company director quotes Peter Hillary as his inspiration.

'It's the challenge of knowing what the limits are within which you can go, and pushing it right up to that limit.'

I'm quite relieved to meet Rudolph – 'Rudy, please' – W. Driscoll, a quiet, somewhat lugubrious American, who was already booked to fly to the Pole when we arrived. Rudy has not climbed mountains or flown light planes but since his divorce ten years ago he has been to the North Pole on a Russian ice-breaker (with eighty-nine others) and on the Trans-Siberian Railway.

'My son said, "Go on Dad, have a go". And I did.'

The rest of the party are Japanese – three neatly and

identically attired mountaineers and the rest aiding and abetting a genial, shaggy-haired character called Shinji Kazama. Kazama-San, as his team refer to him, is attempting to make the first motorbike journey to the Pole. He's already driven a bike 15,000 feet up Everest. He has an assistant, Antonio, and an immaculately dressed film crew of three.

In England many people thought I was mad to attempt to go from Pole to Pole overland. Here, in the lounge of the Hotel Navigantes in Punta Arenas, I reckon I'm about the sanest in the room. Excepting, that is, the local head of Adventure Network, who is not a wild man in a beard or a lean and weathered six-and-a-half-footer, but a slight, delicately attractive, soft-spoken Scot called Anne.

She conducts the briefing, telling us that Adventure Network, and an outfit splendidly named Antarctic Airways were founded in 1983 by two Canadian mountaineers and 'a seasoned Antarctic pilot, Giles Kershaw'. This last she said without flinching, which cannot have been easy as Kershaw, by all accounts a brave man and an extraordinary character, died in an accident out there a year ago. She had been married to him for eighteen months.

Two years later Adventure Network set up a permanent base camp at the Patriot Hills, 78 degrees South.

The main dangers in Antarctica, she warns us, are the cold and the wind and the snow. Exposed areas will get quickly frostbitten, and snow-blindness is painful and easily acquired. A snowstorm can come down at any time so 'always move in a party of people'. When we leave the hotel tomorrow morning we must be wearing and personally carrying everything we need; 'You must be a self-contained unit, and able to operate should the aircraft put down anywhere in Antarctica.'

We're assured there is a permanent doctor on the base. His name is Scott, and, as some wag shouts from the back of the room, 'his rates for open-heart surgery are very reasonable'.

'His success rate isn't quite as reasonable,' comes the reply.

I'm surprised, talking to Anne afterwards, to find how few people have ever been to the South Pole. Higher, colder, less accessible than the North, it remained unvisited for forty-four years after Scott left in January 1912. The US Navy landed there in 1956 and scientists have worked at the Pole ever since, but few outsiders have visited. Anne estimates that in six years of operation Adventure Network have taken no more than twenty-five or twenty-six people all the way to the Pole.

Which makes me feel even more special, and even more apprehensive when, later, I look out over the multicoloured roofs of this compact, characterful town, and go through my check-list for the last time.

DAY 137: *Punta Arenas*

At the airport, but the news is not good. Bruce Allcorn, our pilot, a white-haired, white-bearded, broad-shouldered Canadian with twenty-five years' flying experience in the Arctic and three years down here, is bent over the computer in the meteorological office. He beckons me over and points out four low-pressure systems between here and the Patriot Hills. A few days back there had been nine frontal systems in the area. He shakes his head.

'This doesn't happen anywhere else in the world. If you saw a weather map like that in Europe you'd all move.'

He's worried that there is a lot of wet weather around, and the combination of wet weather and height leads to icing. Also it's important to have 'good visual' on the mountains. What this actually means is that he won't believe they're there unless he can see them. There's no guided navigation down here. In fact below about sixty degrees South there is not even satellite coverage. All of which is why Bruce likes to see where he's going.

He introduces me to his co-pilot, Louie. 'He's a fully qualified stuntman, you know.'

A youngish, angular, handsome face. Eyes that look back impassively. These two, like everyone else on the edge of the Antarctic, are straight out of Central Casting.

'So . . . we're not going in today?' I ask Bruce.

280

'We're definitely not going today.'

'Tomorrow?'

Bruce shrugs. 'I'll come over here at about 7.15 tomorrow morning . . . we'll make a decision by 7.30.'

I must be looking at him like a dog waiting for its dinner. He doesn't want to disappoint me but he can't bear me looking at him like that.

'It's very common to have five- to ten-day delays, with the weather . . . not to put you off.'

Back to the Cabo do Hornos with its plaintive sign in the elevator: 'Please Push Only One Time the Button'. I'm in limboland. All dressed up and no Pole to go to. We visit a nearby penguin colony but a fierce storm hits us and Nigel is unable to film.

An early night after a bad paella. Lie awake worrying about footling things. What happens if we're stranded there until Christmas? Did I buy enough underpants? Is Mercury still in retrograde?

DAY 138: *Punta Arenas to Patriot Hills*

December already. Christmas cards. Present lists. Parties. A telephone rings. My bleary eye catches the clock as my hand reaches for the receiver. It's 7.15, and a voice is telling me that we leave for Antarctica at midday. Into my thermal vest and long-johns, Gap denim shirt, faithful moleskin trousers, thick knitted sweater, two pairs of socks, Asolo boots and down jacket made by RAB of Sheffield. Ring home to tell them I am leaving for the South Pole. There's no one in. Leave a message on the answering machine.

'Going to the South Pole. Byee!'

Hopefully for the last time I push 'only one time the button', and say farewells once more to the helpful staff at the Cabo do Hornos. They seem to be quite accustomed to being used as a jumping-off point for Antarctic explorers, and will keep our rooms free tonight, just in case.

Collecting various hung-over Australians on our way, we drive out of Punta Arenas past Unisex Pamela and Unisex Splendid Hair Salons and the Club Hipico – 'Horse Racing once a Week'. Someone mentions the oft-quoted statistic that Punta Arenas has more brothels per head of population than any town in South America, and a local Chilean is surprised that I haven't visited the Red Zone . . . 'the cathouses', as they call them. They were a notable omission from the list Adventure Network issued us with on arrival: '101 Things to Do while in Punta Arenas'.

The classic outline of a Douglas DC-6, blue and red streak along its white and silver fuselage, stands in a corner of the airstrip. Beside it, instead of Bogart and Bacall, are Bruce Allcorn and his wife Pat, supervising the loading and refuelling. Yesterday Anne Kershaw told me the plane was built in 1948. Bruce shakes his head as if to reassure me:

'No . . . no . . . no. 1953.'

I'm about to reply 'before my time', when I realize that this was the aeroplane of my childhood. This was what I drew when I drew an aeroplane.

We board by a perilously slim extending ladder, with a piece of rope for support. Inside there is none of the squash and squeeze of a conventional airliner. Basically it is an empty shell into which whatever is required for the flight has been fitted. There are twenty-eight of us going to the Patriot Hills, so there are some thirty seats set out in readiness. A bulkhead separates the passengers from the cargo hold, where Kazama-San's motorbike occupies pride of place. Pristine white, it stands on its frame like a knight on a tomb. Bruce, in his captain's overalls with four stripes on the epaulette, and Louie the qualified stuntman insert themselves into the cramped cockpit and make their final checks.

There is a general air of nervous excitement. Bruce's dry drawl comes over the speakers:

'It's going to be a little bit rough to start off . . . a bit of turbulence over the mountains . . . We'll be landing on a blue-ice runway . . . the ice is a little rough and the aeroplane

wiggles around a bit . . . Lots of engine noise . . . It's all normal
. . . You're welcome to come to the cockpit, but if you use
a flash camera, please warn me . . . Kinda startles the hell
out of me.'

Louie adds a reminder that the aircraft is not pressurized and
there is no air-conditioning, and asks us to observe the no-
smoking sign. This raises a cheer and a shout of approval from
the Australians. 'There are human beings on board!'

I see Basil, who would like nothing more than a relaxing puff
or two before heading into what the old maps used to write off
as Terra Australis Incognita, sink further into his seat.

At 12.10 the first engine is started, and as all four come on
stream and the frame of the aircraft rocks and shakes, everyone
is filming everyone else, and Anne is waving a relieved goodbye
as we taxi out for take-off.

At 12.30, after final weather clearance, the DC-6 rumbles
down the runway, rises confidently into the sky, then turns and
heads south down the Strait of Magellan away from the oil
refineries and the brightly coloured roofs of Punta Arenas and
the wide treeless plateau of Tierra del Fuego.

As we climb to our cruising height of 10,000 feet the first
wisps of cloud drift by the windows and we catch a last glimpse
of the majestic, snow-capped Andes mountains running 4500
miles north from here to the shores of the Caribbean.

Using a *National Geographic* map of Antarctica pinned to
the partition, Rob, a tall, slim young Canadian from Adventure
Network, runs down the eight-and-a-half-hour journey for us:
1700 nautical miles at 220-knot cruising speed, estimated time
of arrival 8.30 this evening. First four hours over the Drake
Passage. Nearer to the continent the first sight of icebergs
and the ice-shelf as we cross the Bellingshausen Sea. Landfall
over Alexander Island, at 70 degrees South, and in over the
Ellsworth mountain range.

Unlike the Arctic – a moving ocean covered with ice several
feet thick – Antarctica is a landmass, covered with an ice-sheet
12,000 feet thick in places. It is larger in area than the USA and
yet there are probably fewer than 4000 people on the entire

continent. (By my rough calculation, this means that if and when we land our film crew will make up one six hundred and sixtieth of the total population of Antarctica.)

About three hours' flying time from Punta Arenas, as we're all walking about finishing a serve-yourself picnic lunch, the plane appears to make a very quick jump, dipping and almost instantly regaining height. As we struggle to regain our balance Bruce's laconic tone can be heard over the intercom.

'We just went over the Antarctic Circle.'

The first ice-floes are sighted. Huge white floating platforms tinged a piercing jade green at the base, some of them as much as three-quarters of a mile across and 800 feet high (though only 200 feet may be above water). The pack-ice, which begins by looking like curdled milk on a cup of dark coffee, then fractured eggshell, coalesces into a continuous band of ice which makes it difficult to distinguish where the ice-shelf ends and the continent begins. Fierce winds are blowing, turning the sea white and whipping snow trails high off the cliffs. They call these katabatic winds, caused by a mass of intensely cold air sinking onto the polar plateau and flowing downhill, accelerating as it hits the coast, sometimes at speeds of 180 miles an hour. It may look beautiful and serene from an aircraft, crisp and cool as Hockney's Los Angeles, but the land below is the most inhospitable on earth.

Below us the flat white waste is broken by nunataks – peaks that are tall enough to break through the ice-sheet – and eventually by the longer ranges of crumbly black rock that make up the Ellsworth Mountains.

Much of Antarctica is still unmapped and a race to name new mountains, plateaux, bays and glaciers is under way. To prevent complete confusion there is an international committee that vets names and claims. From the latest map it would seem they've run sadly short of inspiration – one set of mountains is called the 'Executive Committee Range'. If they can get away with that, surely I can find a 'Palin Peak'.

One of the Canadians is enthusing about what Antarctica does for her.

'I go through a sort of cleansing process out here . . . I don't drink coffee, I don't smoke.'

I could certainly do with a bit of cleansing. Beneath my nose I feel a spot about to break through – my own personal nunatak – my throat is dry and sore and my rib aches. What sort of awful germs will I be unloading on this purest of continents?

We are getting close to landing. Bruce likens putting down on a blue-ice runway to landing on a cobbled street. The sun has melted pockets in the ice, called 'suncups', which makes it trickily uneven. The ice is so slippery that he cannot risk using brakes and must control the aircraft with engine throttle only. But a big-wheeled aircraft like this could never put down on snow.

At 7.45, turning one last time in the lee of a low rocky range, Bruce lowers the DC-6 onto the translucent, glassy, blue-green surface of the Antarctic ice-cap. There is much noise as the tone of the engines rears higher and we are bumped and swung. Snow swirls past the window as we create a temporary blizzard. After a moment or two of sound and fury, everything settles down and Bruce eases the aircraft round and taxis towards a cluster of oil drums and a converging group of Ski-Doo-hauled wooden sleds.

The dangers of Antarctic life begin as soon as you set foot on the ground. It is an extremely slippery continent, and all of us shuffle about trying not to fall over and generally getting in everyone's way. There is not much time for a welcome. It is probably the busiest day of the season at Patriot Hills. Twenty-eight people and their gear have to be unloaded and dragged across the ice to the camp, a half-mile away. The plane must be refuelled and on its way back again to Punta Arenas within two hours, otherwise the engines will freeze up.

I decide to walk to the camp.

Ahead of me, a crusty surface of wind-blown ice and snow ridges called sastrugis stretches to the horizon.

The sky is clear, and we are back in the Land of the Midnight Sun.

The wind is mercifully light and my thermometer reads twenty-two Fahrenheit. Minus six Centigrade. Nothing serious.

I think of where I am, now only 600 miles from the South Pole. On my globe at home I would be on that dark, unseen area at the base which never gets dusted. How ironic that the reality should be quite the opposite. Clean, clear, dazzling brightness. And silence except for the crunch and squeak of snow under my boot.

The Patriot Hills base is a collection of modern lightweight tents of varying sizes and colours – mostly red and white – made from Coldura, a reinforced nylon fabric. Patti has one to herself but five of us and Rudy will share. There is one tent which operates as kitchen, dining-room, drying-room, radio-room, office, library and general meeting-place. As far as I can see there is no such thing as a washing or bathing tent and the lavatory is a wooden frame over a plastic bag, with a low snow wall on three sides offering a degree of protection from the wind and the public gaze. It is easy to tell when it is occupied, and by whom, from the head above the wall.

I'm laying out my sleeping-bag when I hear the low roar of an aircraft, and get my head out of the tent just in time to see the DC-6 swoop less than thirty feet above the camp and away towards the mountains. Bruce is on his way back home and with him our only practical means of escape.

In the mess tent Scott, the doctor, and Sue from New Zealand have cooked up a hot, thick and nourishing meat and veg soup for everyone, after which the climbers – Japanese, Australian and New Zealanders – are ferried by single-engined Otter aircraft to the Mount Vinson Massif, one and a half hours away. Every bit of good, settled weather must be taken advantage of.

Peter Hillary is in the second wave of climbers to leave. He and his party will not be back for two weeks. I ask him if, as the son of Sir Edmund, he could ever have been anything other than a mountaineer.

'Well, I think if anything Dad really almost discouraged us

from going to the mountains . . . he really didn't particularly want any of his children to get into mountaineering.'

Whatever went wrong, Peter seems to have become the best sort of enthusiast – resourceful, adventurous and well aware of taking it all too seriously.

With Bruce and the Vinson party gone a certain tranquillity returns to the base. Kazama-San's team are putting up their own tents. His motorcycle stands, like a council sculpture, in the middle of the camp. Fraser is taking photographs of a shovel – 'through' a shovel, he insists. Nigel is sipping Scotch in the sunshine outside our tent. It's two hours after midnight but none of us can take our eyes off this shiny white landscape.

DAY 139: *Patriot Hills*

Away from the coast, there is no life, and therefore no bacteria; no disease, no pests, no beasts of prey, no human interference. It is a clinical environment . . . It can only be compared with life under the ocean or in space.

I read this description of Antarctica, from Roland Huntford's book *The Last Place on Earth*, over an early-morning cup of tea in the mess tent. Outside the air is barely moving. The silence is almost indescribable. It is as if everything you know that makes noise, that gives life, has been suddenly switched off. Bruce's wife had described it as a deafening silence, which is exactly what it is.

I slept fitfully, still troubled by a rumbling, discontented stomach, which has a knack of knowing when I'm furthest from a lavatory. It isn't just a question of getting out of bed and going next door. It is a question of getting out of bed without waking five other people, putting on trousers, a sweater, a jacket, two huge boots, a neckband, a headband, a Balaclava, sunglasses and a pair of gloves, walking a hundred yards across the ice, remembering you've forgotten your roll of toilet paper, coming back, treading on someone's head, and then finding a Japanese motorcyclist has got there before you.

Still, once enthroned in solitary splendour, one does experience an acute feeling of accomplishment at having got there at all. The view from the loo is immense and empty. There is no one out there, for thousands of miles.

No waste of any kind is allowed to be left in Antarctica. Any effluent, human or otherwise, will make an epic journey, not via some dark drain and sewer, but by Bruce's Douglas DC-6, 1700 miles back to South America to be finally disposed of. Later I notice one of the staff replacing the lavatory bag. It has 'Felices Fiestas' and pictures of Father Christmas all over it. Mike Sharp and his staff of five are, quite rightly, concerned to limit any pollution of this still pristine continent. Men are allowed to pee on the ice but only at a certain spot, marked by a red flag, which gives vital wind direction information as well. Anyone who thinks they can get away with a quick one outside the tent is in for a shock, as urine turns the snow bright orange.

There is a chance that we could go to the Pole tomorrow. Weather is being checked with the Amundsen-Scott base there. What little human activity there is in Antarctica is centred around a number of scientific research stations. (An international treaty bans, for the next fifty years, any exploration or exploitation of mineral rights, so the big-money boys are not here, yet.) These stations or bases rely on each other for information and they chat at various times of the day, like fellow members of an exclusive club, often without ever meeting.

Adventure Network is the only tourist operation on the continent. There would be more if Mike Sharp had his way.

'You get so many different people through here . . . sixty or so in a season . . . before, it was always closed up, and the governments had control over Antarctica. I mean, someone like the BBC, for instance, would have to follow the British government's line on Antarctica, whereas now they can just be free to look at the place . . . and it's made a difference. Government organizations are clearing up their fuel drums and getting their garbage out of here, whereas in the past they just dumped it.'

At the end of the season the camp is packed away in a snow cave, four feet underground, which is reopened the next year. Even aircraft can be buried and retrieved. A Cessna 185 was buried with its tailplane sticking out so they could find it again, but in the fierce winter gales the tailplane was broken by an overturned oil drum. Today it's being replaced by Bill Aleekuk, an Eskimo engineer in his first season with the company. There are no polar bears in the Antarctic and until Bill arrived last November, there were no Eskimos either.

Gradually the mess tent fills up. Tea and coffee is made from snow melted in a metal tank which is attached to a kerosene-powered heating unit. Beside the tank is a plastic container of freshcut blocks of snow – the Antarctic equivalent of a coal-scuttle or a basket of logs.

Kazama-San is preoccupied with the testing of his bike. It is a Yamaha, powered by a specially designed engine, low on noise and fuel pollution and with a thick tyre at the back, studded like a punk's belt for better grip in the snow. Kazama-San is a charismatic, infectiously jolly character. He has been by motorbike to Everest, the North Pole, and now, with luck, the South Pole. I ask him where next.

'Moon!' he shouts with a manic grin. I believe him.

2.45 p.m. Kaama-San and his team leave after due Japanese ceremony. He ties a yellow ribbon bearing good-luck messages around his waist and heads his white Yamaha out of the camp. It's so light and silent and insubstantial that he looks like a samurai on a poodle. He is followed by Rob, driving a Ski-Doo and pulling two sledges, one containing a solar-powered radio. It's all very environmentally conscious but the environment isn't appreciative. The sledge sticks on the very first rise and has to be pushed.

Later, in the distance, Kazama's bike leads the procession across the snowy wilderness like a pied piper. They hope to be at the Pole in twenty-eight days.

Less than two hours later Rob returns with the news that because of the unusually warm weather (only minus one Centigrade today) Kazama's environmentally friendly bike has become embedded in the snow. He plans to continue, travelling only at night.

In the evening I manage to make radio contact with my wife, via Anne Kershaw in Punta Arenas. To be speaking to my little house in London from the wastes of Antarctica is perhaps as much as I can hope for; the fact that owing to excessive distortion Helen's voice sounds like a strangled gannet is evidence that we are not in the mainstream of international communication. But apparently she can hear me and one of her gurglings is translated as wishing me luck and a warm hug.

Sue has cooked us pasta, which we polish off with Chilean red wine. Later Basil and Nigel disappear into the sun-drenched night with a Ski-Doo and an ice pick, reappearing triumphantly with a chunk of ice from beside the nearby hills which is as old as the rock itself.

Basil looks very pleased with himself as he drops a chunk into a glass.

'There we are. Ten-year-old whisky. Two-million-year-old ice!'

In this limbo-land of 24-hour daylight I lose track of time. All I know is that when I leave the mess tent, Billie Holiday's voice follows me from the cassette player and Basil is drinking in earnest with a stubbly-bearded, red-eyed old-timer from Canada called Dan who, weather willing, is flying us to the South Pole tomorrow.

DAY 140: *Patriot Hills to the Thiel Mountains*

Wake from utterly warm, comfortable, womb-like night, curled up half-dressed inside my RAB sleeping-bag, to the desolate sound of a polar wind, sighing, hissing, slapping at the sides of the tent like some irascible neighbour. As if pleased with itself for having at last woken me it seems to grow in intensity. Look around the tent. Fraser is invisible – somewhere in his sleeping-bag I presume; Clem snores reassuringly, as I feel he might do if the battle of Waterloo were being fought outside; Basil, his face masked against the daylight, looks like a cross between a bank robber and someone halfway through cosmetic surgery. Nigel lies awake, probably wondering, like me, if this change in the weather means a further delay. Rudy is already up and about.

Ablutions in the Antarctic are perfunctory, to say the least. We may be living on top of seventy per cent of the world's fresh water, but it is not easy to get at and unless some thoughtful soul has been up, cut some snow and slipped a block of it into the tank you might as well be in the middle of a desert.

The only washing point is in the kitchen, and shaving into the sink is discouraged. Even in the tent the temperature is only forty-two Fahrenheit, so taking clothes off is not comfortable. How on earth anyone has a proper wash in Antarctica I can't imagine, though Patti claims to have managed it.

When I catch sight of myself in the mirror I see disturbingly gaunt features. The cold has tightened my skin. My eyes have sunk and my nose seems to have grown an inch or two. A dark beard-line adds to the impression of a man at the end of his tether, if not at the end of the world.

Make a cup of tea and join Rudy who is deep into an account of Shackleton's expedition to the Antarctic. Shackleton made it to within ninety-seven miles of the Pole, three years before Amundsen.

We still have 600 miles to go. There is no sign of Dan the pilot or anyone else for that matter. The wind rises and falls. Through the window I can see trails of snow scurrying across the ice.

The door is pulled open with difficulty and a round, wrapped bundle is silhouetted against the bright sky before the door slams shut. This bundle stands for a moment, apparently frozen, arms stretched out in front like a penguin, before heaving a deep sigh and beginning to unwrap. Only after several layers of headgear have been shed can you be absolutely sure who has come in.

Scott cooks sourdough pancakes for breakfast. We eat them

with 'Lumberjack' syrup. Mike calls the South Pole for a weather check. Visibility is a little hazy, otherwise good. Temperature minus twenty-six Centigrade. Wind fourteen knots. There is no reason for us to stay here. The go-ahead is given to start loading the plane.

Dan, who looks like a plump Lee Marvin, learnt his flying in the USAF and later in Alaska. As we assemble our gear I catch him looking thoughtfully at the plane. I ask him if he knows the Pole well.

He scratches at a white-haired chin. 'Never been there.'

He must enjoy seeing my jaw move up and down, soundlessly, for his eyes have a twinkle as he adds: 'I'm from the north, I've come down south here for the winter . . . to enjoy the nice weather.'

I try to make the best of it, tapping the side of the plane.

'Still, I'll bet this aircraft must have seen plenty of polar action . . . '

'Nope. This'll be the first trip for a single-engine turbine Otter to the Pole.'

It transpires that neither pilot nor aircraft, nor even Scott, our Adventure Network escort, has ever been to the Pole. We're all first-timers.

Now I know what Mike Sharp was talking about when he told me yesterday that Adventure Network's success was 'based on enthusiasm, really . . . We're an ex-company of adventurers that . . . still want the adventure.'

At 3.45 p.m. we say our farewells, not just to Patriot Hills, but to Basil and Patti, who have to stay behind. Though they have known this all along, it doesn't make it any easier to leave them so close to our final destination.

We squeeze into tiny seats, made smaller by the bulkiness of our clothing. It is rather like sitting at nursery-school desks. We share the cabin with a drum of kerosene as well as camera, camping and catering equipment, pumps and ice shovels. The only empty space is the gangway, and that is soon filled with an aluminium ladder.

At 3.50 this tightly-packed collection of people and their props taxis out across the ribbed and rutted ice, turns, and begins the longest and most unconvincing take-off I've ever experienced. It's nothing to do with the pilot, who is completely unconcerned, it's just that the relentless bumping and buffeting of the aeroplane's skis over the sastrugis doesn't seem to be allowing us to gain momentum. The fragmented rock face of the Patriot Hills is approaching fast and my grip tightens on the seat in front. Then with two or three gazelle-like bounces we are airborne, and within seconds the waving group below become specks against the snow.

We are flying into what the locals call 'the interior' – a flat plateau with few distinguishing features, rising from 4000 feet at Patriot Hills to an official 9348 feet at the Pole, though local atmospheric conditions there give a pressure altitude of 10,600 feet.

On the way we have to put down at the Thiel Mountains for a refuelling stop, and to give Dan time to drop some fuel for Kazama-San's expedition, which will pass near by.

After two or three approaches as Dan and Scott search for the oil drums, we put down on the ice, at a spot called King's Peak. After two and a half hours sitting in the plane, unable to change position, it is a relief to clamber down onto the ice, even if it is into the teeth of a strong, bitingly cold wind.

Scott puts Rudy and myself to work, assembling a tent. It is, I'm sure, quite simple to those familiar with these matters, but I have never been a happy camper and the cluster of fibreglass rods spells nothing to me but confusion. Scott's patience is wholly commendable.

'They're all colour coded,' he points out, a little tersely. This is no help as my sunglasses distort most colours completely.

After much grunting and groaning and wrestling hopelessly to combine precision assembly with thick polar gloves, we have the tent up and crawl inside to drink tea and coffee and nibble chocolate while we wait for Dan to return from dropping Kazama's fuel, some fifty miles away.

Of course, in the dim recesses of one's mind the awareness

293

that we are in sub-zero temperatures 300 miles from the South Pole with no means of transport does cause a flickering of doubt. Not often can one's survival be said to depend on one man, but the prospect of Dan not coming back doesn't really bear thinking about.

The wind-driven snow licks around us. It must be infinitely worse out in the open, away from the protective barrier of King's Peak. All of us are more relieved than we care to show when the scarlet flash of the Otter comes around the mountain again.

Dan takes a last weather check with the Amundsen-Scott base. As with Russ at the North Pole, a great deal of responsibility rests on the pilot at times like this. Dan knows that there is no safe place, no fuel cache at which to land between here and the Pole. It's entirely up to him to evaluate the information and make the final decision. He decides we should go in.

11.30 p.m. We have seen the last of the rock-strewn slopes of the escarpment, now there is nothing but whiteness below in every direction. In front of me Clem settles to sleep. Dan has changed his sealskin hat for a baseball cap, held in place by his headset. Scott is concerned to know if any of us are feeling the effects of altitude – for we are at the equivalent of 20,000 feet above sea-level, in an unpressurized plane. I sense that I am taking shorter breaths, but apart from that I feel good, bumped by the excitement of my situation from the tired, almost melancholy heaviness I felt as we sat at King's Peak an hour ago.

DAY 141: *To the South Pole*

12.30 a.m. Over the noise of the engine Dan shouts back that we are forty-seven minutes from the Pole.

1.00 a.m. Radio communication from air traffic control at the South Pole base.

'There is no designated runway and the US government cannot authorize you to land. How do you copy?'

Dan: 'OK.'

'OK. Have a good landing.'

Scott gives Rudy a shot of oxygen. The effects of the height can now be clearly felt. Shortage of breath, every movement requiring twice the effort.

1.10 a.m. We can see the South Pole ahead. It is somewhere in the middle of a complex of buildings dominated by a 150-foot-wide geodesic dome. Vehicles and building materials are scattered about the site. It is the busiest place we've seen in Antarctica.

1.20 a.m. We land at the Amundsen-Scott South Pole Station, scudding to a halt on a wide, cleared snow runway.

Two well-wrapped figures from the base wait for us to emerge from the plane, and shake our hands in welcome, but the senior of them, an American called Gary, advises us that it is not the policy of the National Science Foundation, who run the base, to offer assistance of a material kind to NGAs – Non-Government Agencies – such as ourselves. Scott confirms that our expedition is self-sufficient and that Adventure Network has a cache of fuel and accommodation located near by.

Gary, having officially informed us that we are not welcome, brightens up considerably and invites us in for a coffee.

It's as we walk towards the dome, past Portakabins and stacks of wood, insulation equipment, all the flotsam and jetsam of a builder's yard, that I become aware of how much effort is required just to keep going. It's as if I'm in a dream. However hard I try, the dome doesn't seem to get any nearer.

After what seems like a lifetime we descend between walls carved from the ice to a wide underground entrance, above which a sign informs us that 'The United States of America welcomes you to the Amundsen-Scott South Pole Station'.

No pretence of neutrality here. After travelling 23,000 miles we have found the end of the earth, and it is America.

Pulling open a door as heavy as that on a butcher's deep-freeze we enter a warm, brightly lit canteen. Music plays. 'If You Leave Me Now', by Chicago. Fresh orange juice and coffee on tap. T-shirts read 'Ski South Pole – 2 miles of base, 12 inches of powder'. A man in Bermuda shorts is piling a tray with chilli dogs, turkey soup, potato chips and lemon poppyseed cake. One of the chefs even *recognizes* me:

'Hey . . . wow! Michael Palin . . . !' He rubs lemon poppyseed cake off on his overalls and proffers a hand.

'Welcome to the Pole!'

The South Pole is on New Zealand Time. Everyone is eating, not because it's two o'clock in the morning and they can't sleep, but because we have leapt forward sixteen hours, a time-shift of record breaking proportions. These people are coming in for their evening meal.

Gaze longingly at the hamburgers and French fries, wondering if consumption of either or both would contravene the rules of the National Science Foundation, but after a coffee we trudge back outside. Scott, Fraser, Nigel and Clem go off to dig up the tent which was left here last year, so that we can eat and sleep. Rudy goes back to the plane. I'm about to join them when I realize that in the midst of all these rules, regulations, coffees and poppyseed handshakes I have completely forgotten why we are here.

The temperature, with wind chill, is a cutting, almost paralysing minus fifty Centigrade, and it's 3.15 in the morning at 10,000 feet when I set out on the final lap of this extraordinary journey.

A few hundred yards from the dome, out on the snow, is a semi-circle of flags of all the nations working in Antarctica, in the middle of which is a reflecting globe on a plinth. This is the 'Ceremonial South Pole' at which visiting dignitaries are pictured.

Crunching slowly past it, numb-faced and short of breath, I come at last to a small bronze post sticking three feet above the ground. It looks like an unplumbed lavatory outlet but it exactly marks ninety degrees South. From this spot all directions point north. At this spot I can walk around the world in eight seconds. At this point with one bound I am back, on thirty degrees East . . . and thirty degrees West, and seventy-two degrees East and twenty-three degrees West. I am on the same longitude as Tokyo, Cairo, New York and Sheffield. I am standing at the South Pole.

In the distance I can see a group of anoraked figures pacing the snow, stopping occasionally, forming a circle, pointing then striking at the earth with a shovel. They seem to be repeating this strange ritual over a wide area. Eventually Clem and Nigel and Fraser and Rudy give up looking for the tent and we all stand together at the bottom of the world. Or the top. It depends which way you look at it.

AFTERWORD

The first newspaper headline I saw on my return home last December ran 'USSR Will End On New Year's Eve'. Months earlier such a thought would have been laughable. Now, so much has happened that some of our experiences on *Pole to Pole* seem, within less than a year, to belong to another era. Not only has the Soviet Union disappeared, other countries have sprouted in its place. The same journey done today would go through twenty countries instead of seventeen – Estonia, Belorussia and Ukraine adding to our tally and the atlas compiler's nightmare. Leningrad is now St Petersburg and the Hammer and Sickle nothing more than a good name for a pub. On a more serious note: Greenland has laid claim to Santa Claus – 'Greenland's PM Accuses Finland of Stealing Santa' was another recent headline; and the Novgorod plate, amazingly, reached London in one piece, only to be broken on the ten-mile journey from there to Watford.

The crew has proved there *is* life after *Pole to Pole*. Fraser was back at the Ngorongoro Crater within a few months of our return; Patti's malaria has, at the time of writing, made no reappearance; my rib healed in the predicted six weeks, and I have suffered no other side-effects apart from a recurrent fear of waking to find my body tattooed with a Tanzanian Railways serial number.

The saddest news was of the deaths of Lorna and John Harvey of Shiwa six months after we stayed with them. They, and many others, provided us with the patient, considerate, generous hospitality without which our journey from Pole to Pole would never have been possible.

MICHAEL PALIN established his reputation with *Monty Python's Flying Circus* and *Ripping Yarns*. His work also includes several films with Monty Python, as well as *The Missionary*, *A Private Function*, an award-winning performance as the hapless Ken in *A Fish Called Wanda*, *American Friends* and *Fierce Creatures*. His television credits include two films for the BBC's *Great Railway Journeys*, the plays *East of Ipswich* and *Number 27*, and Alan Bleasdale's *GBH*. He has written seven best-selling travel books to accompany his series *Around the World in 80 Days*, *Pole to Pole*, *Full Circle*, *Hemingway Adventure*, *Sahara*, *Himalaya* and *New Europe*. He is also the author of a number of children's stories, the play *The Weekend* and the novel *Hemingway's Chair*. In 2006 the first volume of his diaries, *1969–1979: The Python Years*, spent many weeks on the bestseller lists. In 2008 an updated special edition of *Around the World in 80 Days* was published to coincide with his BBC documentary *Around the World in 20 Years*. Visit his website at www.palinstravels.co.uk.

AROUND THE WORLD IN 80 DAYS

MICHAEL PALIN

PHOENIX

A PHOENIX PAPERBACK

First published in Great Britain in 1989
by BBC Books
Revised edition published in 2008 by Weidenfeld & Nicolson
This paperback edition published in 2009
by Phoenix,
an imprint of Orion Books Ltd,
Orion House, 5 Upper St Martin's Lane,
London WC2H 9EA

An Hachette UK company

5 7 9 10 8 6 4

ISBN 978-0-7538-2324-8

Printed in Great Britain by Clays Ltd, St Ives plc

The Orion Publishing Group's policy is to use papers that
are natural, renewable and recyclable products and
made from wood grown in sustainable forests. The logging
and manufacturing processes are expected to conform to
the environmental regulations of the country of origin.

www.orionbooks.co.uk

Contents

CONTENTS

CONTENTS

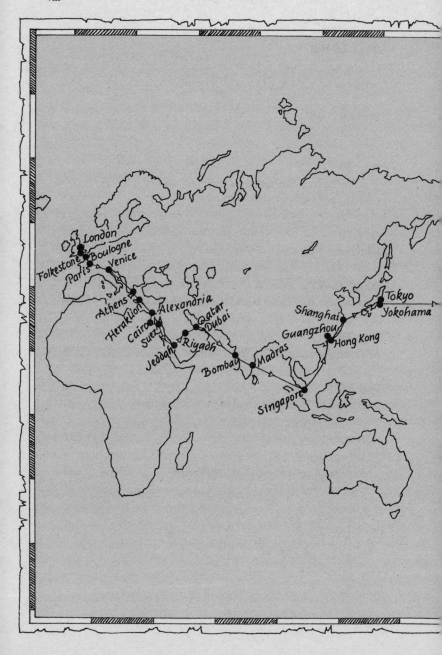

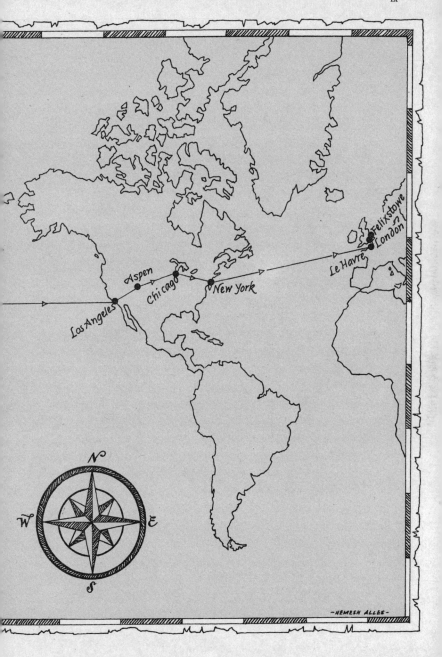

Preface to the new edition

Little did I imagine, as I was turned away from the doors of the Reform Club in London after completing my circumnavigation of the globe back in December 1988, that far from being an end to my travelling career, this was just the beginning. *Around The World In Eighty Days* was to become around the world in twenty years.

I had intended to stop once we reached the unyielding doors of the Reform Club and return to a normal life – slapping people with fish, running over Kevin Kline in a steamroller and singing the Lumberjack Song in German to selected audiences. The attempt to circle the world in less than three months without ever leaving its surface had, I felt, offered me enough adventure to last a lifetime.

But something had happened on all those long sea trips, on battered cargo boats and creaking container ships, on heaving Indian trains and racing dog sleds in the Rockies. Though I had travelled with a course of painful injections and bag full of pills and potions, nothing had protected me against the overpowering, aching desire to do the whole thing again. It was as if a door had been opened through which I could see a big beckoning world. I could see North Poles and South Poles and Equators and Tropics and rapids and volcanoes and it was all much more exciting than slapping people with fish. The success of *Around The World In Eighty Days*, and a very tolerant wife and family, made it possible for me to walk through this door and discover new people, new places, and experience sights and sounds beyond my wildest expectations.

Twenty years on, I and my crew, many of whom had accompanied me on that first journey, have been to every continent in the world, travelled hundreds and thousands of miles across every terrain from ice and snow to burning desert, and regurgitated it all in seven books and television series.

So I must thank my lucky stars, and Clem Vallance and the BBC in particular, for creating for me a role I never expected, that of a sort of tour guide to the world. I also have to thank those who so selflessly agreed to let our camera peer into their lives, for, as I've learnt in all my series, it's the people you meet who make the programmes work.

Bearing that in mind we decided that the best way to celebrate twenty years of travelling would be some sort of a reunion. The choice was easier than I'd expected. Looking back over the years no single experience has remained more powerfully in my memory than our dhow journey from Dubai to Bombay. It was the first time I realised quite how much the success or failure of our series depended on those with whom we were travelling, in this case a crew of eighteen Indian fishermen from a small village north of Bombay. Despite their assurances of getting us to Bombay in six days, we shared the boat with them for a week. We slept on deck, sacks of pistachio nuts beneath us, we learnt to use a toilet which was nothing more than a box suspended over the stern of the ship, we gratefully ate the curries they produced from nowhere and we tried not to think about the lack of life-jackets, or the fate of the captain's brother whose dhow and entire crew had perished in a storm the year before.

It was only when the time came to say goodbye in Bombay that I sensed just how close we'd all become. The combination of my gratitude and their affection made leave-taking difficult and surprisingly emotional. As I said in my commentary, 'It's almost impossible to accept that I shall never see them again.'

So, after twenty years, I took myself at my word and we went in search of the crew of the *Al Shama*. The result of this extraordinary trip is contained in a new chapter at the end of this book.

The way we made *Around The World in Eighty Days* can never be repeated. Now we have mobile phones and global positioning satellites and digital tapes instead of cans of celluloid. But how much the people and their lives have changed is less easy to tell.

There was only one way to find out, and the reissue of the book and our return to India and the Gulf is more than just a celebration of all twenty years on the road, it's an affirmation that, for this traveller at least, there is still no end in sight.

MICHAEL PALIN *London, September 2008*

Note on names

As this is a 20-year-old text, names are sometimes out of date. Bombay has become Mumbai and Madras, Chennai since then. To keep the flavour of the time, we've kept the old names.

Introduction

The compulsive urge to travel is a recognised physical condition. It has its own word, dromomania, and I'm glad to say I suffer from it. The ambition of every dromomaniac is a circumnavigation of the planet, but it's a less fashionable journey now than in Jules Verne's day. Part of the reason is that you can do it by air in 36 hours (a technological feat that Verne would have greatly appreciated). But air travel shrink-wraps the world leaving it small, odourless, tidy and usually out of sight.

There are container vessels which will take you round in 63 days, but you will see only water on 58 of those. The reason why Phileas Fogg's 80-day journey retains its appeal is that it is still the minimum time needed to go round the world and notice it. To see it, smell it and touch it at the same time.

Each time I look at the map and retrace my progress I become painfully aware of the countries I didn't visit, and I'm sure there would be a case for a zig-zag circumnavigation which would take in Australia and Thailand and Russia and Africa and South America and Canada. Nevertheless my route, following Fogg's as closely as possible, still took me through an extraordinary sequence of countries: from the European empires of Britain and Venice and Greece, to Egypt, one of the oldest civilisations on earth, through the heart of the Muslim world, across India into China and the awesomely energetic economies of the Pacific Rim countries – Singapore, Hong Kong and Japan – and finally to America, still the most influential nation in the world.

The pace of this kind of travel has not much changed since Fogg set out in 1872. Trains may be a little faster, but there are certainly no high-speed rail links yet across India, China or the USA. Passenger services have practically disappeared from the world's shipping lanes, whilst at the same time the armoury of bureaucratic obstacles – visas, permits, passports and carnets –

has proliferated. Recourse to air travel, even as a convenient means of escape, was not allowed.

But these were challenges and challenges help to make an adventure, and an adventure was what I was after when I signed up. This diary is a record of success and failure, of euphoria and deep gloom, of friends made and advice and help generously given on what must still be the ultimate terrestrial journey.

There was never time to dig very deep and those expecting profound international insights will be disappointed. I'm particularly aware of how traumatically China suffered only a few months after my visit. But my journey around the world gave me a sense of global scale, of the size and variety of this extraordinary planet, of the relation of one country and one culture to another which few people experience and many ought to.

For this I am eternally grateful to a lot of people. Not least to Clem Vallance of the BBC who dreamt up the whole crazy idea, and thought of me; to Will Wyatt who first asked me and made sure I didn't say no; to my wife Helen and the family who let me go; to my attentive, patient, incredibly hard-working, almost uncomplaining Passepartout* – Nigel Meakin, Ron Brown, Julian Charrington, Nigel Walters, Dave Jewitt and Simon Maggs, who between them shot and recorded film on 77 out of 80 days; to Angela Elbourne and Ann Holland without whose level-headed, panic-free presence I would probably still be at Cairo station; to Basil Pao, without whom none of us might have survived Hong Kong and China, and to Roger Mills who, along with Clem Vallance, directed, guided, encouraged, cajoled and tolerated me for many months.

MICHAEL PALIN *London, 1989*

*Note about my Passepartout

Clem Vallance and Roger Mills (with production assistants Angela Elbourne and Ann Holland) travelled all the way with me. Nigel Meakin, Ron Brown and Julian Charrington filmed me to Hong Kong, then Nigel Walters, Dave Jewitt and Simon Maggs brought me home.

Day 1 25 September

ILEAVE THE REFORM CLUB, Pall Mall, London one hundred and fifteen years, three hundred and fifty-six days, ten and three-quarter hours after Phileas Fogg. It's a wet, stuffy morning, I've had three and a half hours sleep and the only thing I envy Phileas is that he's fictional.

Few buildings could be more fitted to a Great Departure. With its 60-foot-high main hall, marble columns, galleried arcades and the grand scale of a Renaissance palace the Reform Club is a place of consequence, grand and grave enough to add weight to any venture.

This morning it smells of old fish, and glasses and bottles from the night before stand around. I can see no one sampling the sort of breakfast Fogg had taken the day he left: '... a side dish, a boiled fish with Reading sauce of first quality, a scarlet slice of roast beef garnished with mushrooms, a rhubarb and gooseberry tart, and a bit of Chester cheese, the whole washed down with a few cups of that excellent tea, specially gathered for the stores of the Reform Club.'

I have tried to follow Fogg's example and travel light. 'Only a carpetbag,' he had instructed his servant Passepartout, 'in it two woollen shirts and three pairs of stockings ... my mackintosh and travelling cloak, also stout shoes, although we shall walk but little or not at all.' I've managed to find a passable equivalent of a carpet bag and in it packed six shirts, six pairs of socks, six pairs of underpants, three T-shirts, a towel, a pair of swimming trunks, a short-sleeved sweater, three pairs of light trousers (long), two pairs ex-R.A.F. trousers (short), a pair of sports shorts, a sponge bag, various pharmaceuticals, a change of shoes, a jacket and tie, a Sony Walkman, six cassettes, a small short-wave radio, a Panama hat and one or two heavy and serious books with which to improve my mind on long sea journeys. In a shoulder bag I carry my diary, a small Dictaphone recorder for on-the-spot notes, a camera, the BBC's *Get By In Arabic*, a Kingsley Amis novel, some extra-strong mints, a packet of 'Family Wipes', an address book and an inflatable globe to enable me to check on our progress. Phileas Fogg would doubtless have regarded all this as clutter, but it's still less than I would take on a two-week holiday.

These bags I heave up onto my shoulders as the clock shows ten o'clock. I carry them down the stairs, out of the tall doorway and into Pall Mall. I've eighty days left to get back in again.

Fogg went from the Reform Club to Charing Cross station, I leave from Victoria.

Here I find Passepartout, who will travel everywhere with me. Unlike Fogg's Passepartout, mine is five people, has fifty pieces of baggage and works for the BBC. Roger Mills is the director of this first leg of the journey and is already bemoaning the fact that we've just missed some foul weather in the English Channel. 'If only this had been yesterday.' He draws on his pipe despondently. Ann Holland is his Production Assistant. She will keep full details of all the shots we take, and keep in touch with our base camp in London. Nigel Meakin and Julian Charrington are the camera team and Ron Brown is recording sound. The film equipment is in containers of many shapes and sizes and mostly very heavy. As I help them down the platform with a muscle-tearing case of film stock I think of Phileas – 'one of those mathematically exact people … never hurried … calm, phlegmatic, with a clear eye' – and how desperately unlike him I am.

However, I am leaving London in a manner of which he would doubtless have approved had it been available in 1872, aboard the Venice–Simplon Orient Express. Last farewells and a check on the exact time of departure by two friends acting as judges. Fogg's friends were bankers. Mine, Messrs Jones and Gilliam, are Pythons. Terry Jones eyes Passepartout, already about his business with the camera. 'You're going to have to look happy for eighty days.' 'No,' I reassure him. 'There'll be no cheating.' Then the whistle sounds, the last door slams and we're off.

I am installed in a sumptuous refurbished Pullman coach called 'Zena'. Behind me are 'Ibis', 'Lucille', 'Cygnus' and 'Ione'. Antimacassars, marble washbasins, upholstered armchairs and inlaid walnut panelling come as a bit of a shock to one used to the Gatwick Express, but I try hard to forget about guilt and silly things like that and sit back and sniff the fresh orchids and sip a little champagne. The leader of a crack force of waiters approaches, issuing brisk directives.

'We *do* advise you to be seated. We're coming through the train with hot soup.'

We are dealt a three-course meal and coffee in 55 minutes flat. It's delicious, but such is the precision with which it has to be served that you feel that any lingering over the menu might result in the aforementioned hot soup being lightly but firmly applied upon some tender area.

A huge scar slices into the landscape on the eastern side of the train. It's the site for the Channel Tunnel terminal, 16 acres of devastation. Jules Verne would surely have approved, being a man fascinated by transport technology. He'd probably have sent his hero to have a look at it. Or rather, he'd have sent Passepartout to do it for him, as Fogg hated sightseeing.

We're in Folkestone now, the last few hundred yards of England, and rumbling down a steep gradient past back gardens close up to the railway line; a world of sheds and extensions, corrugated iron and chicken wire, unself-conscious, domestic and reassuring. The sun breaks momentarily through the leaden cloud causing the mountain of cut-glass on my table to sparkle, but the word is that the Channel is 'rough' to 'very rough', and I'm glad I passed on the ginger profiteroles.

No longer do the ferries carry trains and at Folkestone Harbour I part company with 'Zena' and take up with the *Horsa*, a 6,000-tonne vessel which has been plying the 22-mile crossing to France for 16 years.

'It's that Monty Python bloke!' shouts one of the crew as I mount the first of many gangplanks of the world. He turns confidingly to me: 'If you want a farce, you've got one here.' The passageways of the *Horsa* smell of day-old school food, but we Oriental Expressers are ushered to our own private lounge.

It's a dispiriting place, decorated in International Cowboy Saloon Style. The walls are ringed with reverentially lit alcoves which look as if they might contain international art treasures or religious icons, but which, on closer inspection, are found to be full of duty-free goods.

Seeking refuge from the world of 'Antaeus, Pour Homme' and 'Superkings', I walk out on deck. It's mid-afternoon and the white cliffs of home are now little more than a blur. A huge black cloud seems to be sealing England off behind us. A sharp, squally wind that would test the stoutest toupee rips across from the West. With friends and familiar surroundings disappearing over the horizon, I catch my breath for a moment at the scale of what is just beginning.

The Channel crossing is bumpy, but to the director's chagrin nothing more. A Force 5. 'I've had her out in a Force 12,' says the captain, eyes skinned for stray fishing boats, tankers, ferries, yachts, channel-swimmer's support vessels and every floating thing that makes this one of the busiest waterways in the world.

4.30: On the bridge. From a mile out at sea Boulogne, France, looks to consist of one huge steelworks, but as we get nearer a hard skyline of soot-flecked concrete apartment blocks looms.

Down below, the Orient Express passengers are impatient to party. They so want to have a good time, and the expensive hours are ticking away and the luxury they were promised is not to be found on the *Horsa* or in the passageways of Boulogne's dockside. But spirits rise once they reach the platform of Boulogne station at which stand a dozen coaches sporting the navy-blue livery and solid brass letters of the Compagnie Internationale des Wagons-Lits et des Grands Express Européens. I am billeted in sleeping car 3544, built in 1929, decorated in 'Sapelli Pearl' inlay by René Prou and having been, in the course of a long and distinguished career, a brothel for German officers and part of the Dutch royal train. My cabin is small but perfectly formed, sheathed in veneered mahogany inlaid with Art-Deco panels. From this luxury cocoon I watch grey, seagull-ridden Boulogne slipping away and when its drab suburbs have gone, I turn once more to make-believe, and begin unpacking my dinner jacket.

I dine next to a couple from Southend who are celebrating their twenty-fifth wedding anniversary with an Orient Express trip to Paris. Nice people but, looking round, I'm rather disappointed at the lack of princesses, murderers and deposed heads of Europe. Most of the 188 passengers are either going to a pipeline conference in Venice or are Mid-Westerners on a tour. Instead of falling into risqué conversation with a Mata Hari of the 1980s, I end up in the piano bar with the pipeliners. They seem very interested to hear that, in 70 days from now, I hope to cross the Atlantic from Halifax, Nova Scotia. 'We've got a big pipe there, we could flush you through.'

My cabin has been prepared for the night by Jeff, a down-to-earth, well-informed Englishman who has responsibility for Coach 3544. The bed is soft but short. 'Yes, we do have a bit of trouble with our Americans,' he concedes. 'There's one tonight who's 6 foot 8.' He looks apprehensively down the corridor, listening no doubt for the giant's tread. Feeling for the first time in my life rather smug about being 5 foot 10 and a half, I turn in.

The train is heading for the Belfort Gap, my head is buzzing with an evening's champagne, and so far circumnavigation is a doddle.

Day 2 26 September

Slept as badly as I ever have in a really comfortable bed. Passepartout complains as well so it can't just be me. The ride of these old coaches is not as smooth as their interior design.

8.30: Jeff arrives carrying a tray of croissants, brioches, jams, hot, dark, intensely tasty coffee and the *International Herald Tribune*. More record-breaking from Ben Johnson in the Olympics. Pull back the curtain and there is Switzerland. The murky gloom of Northern Europe has been replaced by clear and cloudless skies, and the *banlieues* of Boulogne by neat meadows grazed by neat cows interspersed with neat factories. All this orderliness is contained within violently twisted cliffs of rock rising thousands of feet to left and right. As we slow through a small town people gaze at us, curiously but not censoriously. The conspicuous luxury of the Orient Express seems not so remarkable here in Switzerland. Perhaps it goes with numbered bank accounts and private nuclear shelters.

A little trouble shaving. There seems to be no hot water to fill my exquisite marble wash basin. Jeff is philosophical.

'Try the cold tap, sir.' Sure enough a steamy, near-boiling torrent pours out.

There's never a dull moment on the Orient Express and flakes of brioche are still fresh on my fingers when the first call comes for brunch. Before I embarked on this journey I sought advice from many experienced travellers, and it was John Hemming, the Director of the Royal Geographical Society, who advised me that a true explorer never turns down a meal. It might be the last he'll be offered for days. I decide to approach brunch in this spirit, tucking into Eggs Benedict but avoiding a 'light breakfast wine' at £24 a bottle.

We cross Liechtenstein between the second and third courses, and are entering our fifth country in less than twenty-four hours, when things begin to go wrong. We are diverted through the town of Buchs because of derailment (which I just can't imagine happening on such an immaculately run system) and worse than this, we are to terminate at Innsbruck as there is a rail strike in Italy. So the Venice–Simplon Orient Express will not, today, visit either Venice or Simplon.

A bus is to be provided at Innsbruck but they are unable to guarantee the arrival time. Nervous now because of our tight ship connection onward from Venice, there's nothing I can do but sit back and enjoy the view. We're winding up to the Ahlberg Pass, through sweeping panoramas of lush green slopes and mountainsides of acid-rain-crippled trees. The villages with their onion-dome steeples lie calm and drowsy in the valleys. From each one there fans out a network of grey pylons carrying the cars, cables and chair-lifts on which their livelihood depends, and in the winter here you'll hardly be able to move.

Twenty-four hours after leaving Victoria the Orient Express pulls into Innsbruck, Austria and from its seventeen coaches in orderly confusion come the pipeliners and the Mid-Westerners and the porters and the apologetic couriers and even the chefs bearing food on silver plates, all of which is carried across the station car park to a fleet of anonymous modern coaches. Everyone tries desperately to pretend that they're still having just as good a time, but the magic's gone.

At the Brenner Pass we are delayed interminably while Austrian customs search for the correct stamp for our film equipment clearance. As the sun sinks behind the mountains I make a quick calculation based on the time it's taking to leave Austria. At a rough estimate I could be spending eight of the next eighty days waiting at customs. Not a problem Fogg had to deal with. Nor was he ever faced with what the Austrians call, rather dramatically, a *streik*. His train would be rattling through the Alps by now.

At the Italian border, a bottle of Orient Express champagne is passed over and this seems to speed up the customs process. Soon, amid smiles, shrugs and assorted gesticulations we are off and running into the land where a *streik* is only a *sciopero*.

Crossing the lagoon which divides Venice from the mainland a dreadful smell assails us. It's sulphur from the massive chemical works at Mestre, sending up a malodorous halo around the Serenissima, and firmly deflating romantic anticipations.

Twenty minutes later: On the canals. Stuck firmly under a bridge. We are in a fully laden 40-foot barge trying to negotiate a 90-degree corner. Sandro, our boatman, skips elegantly but ineffectually about the vessel and blames the tides. A small crowd of Japanese tourists has gathered on the bridge above us. They seem to have eight cameras each. It's all rather embarrassing. When Sandro eventually pushes us, and a fair-sized chunk of sixteenth-century stonework, away from the bridge, we find ourselves backing into a funeral procession. Somebody popular by the looks of things, as fresh gondolafuls of mourners keep appearing round the corner.

Much later: Hot, tired and missing the Orient Express and the antimacassars and the ever-solicitous Jeff to guide me through life, I find myself at the Hotel Atlantide with my bag weighing heavy.

The Italians take being on film very seriously, but not quite as seriously as what they're wearing when they're being filmed, and this costs André, one of the hotel receptionists, the part of Man Who Shows The Presenter To His Room. He goes off to do his hair and put on a suit, leaving the way clear for his colleague Massimo, who is not so worried about his personal appearance, to turn in a splendidly moody performance. There's no lift. My room is at rooftop level with a small balcony which does not enjoy any of the classic views of Venice. As I clean my teeth the first cockroach of the trip scuttles across cracked bathroom tiles.

Day 3 27 September

A few hours to kill in Venice before leaving by boat for Greece, Crete and Egypt. The director thinks it would be nice for me to see the city from the back of a rubbish barge, and very soon, perhaps a little too soon, after breakfast I find myself hosing down the Riva degli Schiavoni and tossing plastic bagfuls of Venetian unmentionables into the garbage barge. Mario, 48 years old, with a 13-year-old son and a daughter of 20, is in charge of our squad. 'Even the rubbish in Venice isn't cheap any more,' he replies to my routine suggestion that this must be one of the most beautiful cities to grow up in. 'The young can't afford to live here now.' The other two members of our crew are Fabbio, who turns out to have weightlifted for his country, and is profoundly embarrassed by the whole filming, and Sandro, curly-headed, beautiful, pre-Raphaelite, and unreachable on most levels.

We move at a stately pace up the canals, hurrying for nobody. Refuse collecting gives one a smug sense of superiority. The veneered-wood and polished brass launches may huff and puff as they try to get past us with their expensive cargoes, but we know they know how much they need us. We've seen what they like to keep out of sight.

I enjoy my refuse-eye view of Venice and suggest to Roger that we make it the first of a Great Dustmen Of The World series, to be followed, if successful, by Great Sewers Of The World.

Ron Passepartout baulks at this. 'I've just spent five weeks in the sewers, thank you!' He is referring not to conditions at TV Centre, but to a programme he's just made about a man who had taken refuge in the war in the sewers of Lvov. Ron has been everywhere and met everyone. On the very first day of filming the phone rang on location and a P.A., covering the mouthpiece, shouted, 'Ron! Can you do the Pope, Friday?'

By boat to the Venice Post Office to send my dinner jacket back to London, the smartest part of the journey being already over. This is one of The Great Post Offices Of The World, located in the Fondaco dei Tedeschi, built between 1505 and 1508 as a base for German merchants in Venice. There's a wide brick-tiled courtyard with a stone fountain in the middle surrounded by three levels of pillared galleries. The walls were once decorated with the works of the great Venetians, like Titian – but of these only, as the guidebook has it, 'one much-impaired nude' by Giorgione remains. I notice a lot of young, beautiful women heaving mailbags out onto the quayside beneath the Rialto Bridge. They also work for the Post Office. The Grand Canal, at this point, is like Piccadilly Circus, and the driving is terrible, with motoscafi cutting up vaporettos and cement barges cutting up taxis and gondolas gliding serenely and suicidally between the lot of them.

I seek refuge at the Hostaria del Milion – good unpretentious food and wine in a tiny, intimate little courtyard. Two doors down there still stands the house where Marco Polo lived and from which he departed on his great journeys to the East. I stand and look up at the modest stone walls, as if there might be something I can learn from them. A photographer takes pictures of me doing this. He's an Italian. His real name's Renato but I've taken to calling him Posso which is the only word I've heard from him today.

'Posso?' Snap. I feel sorry for these still photographers. They're only doing their job, but they keep getting in the way of Passepartout and making him very cross.

Early evening: Our departure for the Levant is not, sadly, from some photogenic quayside flanked by the Lions of St Mark, but from the tourist-neglected backside of Venice, the docks of the

Stazione Marittima. The soft warmth of the day has given way to a chilly evening as our baggage barge chugs past the soaring hulls of a rough assortment of freighters – a Russian boat from Starnov, the *River Tyne* from Limassol (a poignant reminder of where the British shipping industry has gone) and finally the elegant wave-moulded bow and milk chocolate hull of my home for the next four days, the *Espresso Egitto, Venezia*. Maybe because we're all tired, or maybe because we can only count eleven portholes on her side, Passepartout and I are not as responsive as we might be to the promise of the *Egyptian Express*. A shout causes me to turn, lose my footing and almost disembowel myself on the camera tripod.

'Posso?' Snap.

Aboard ship after two hours in bureaucratic limbo on the quayside. 'People Who Need People' echoes from the PA system. 'People Who Need Portholes' would be more appropriate. Ron is in deep decline. His cabin not only lacks portholes but also lights. I keep trying to remember not to tell him what I can see out of my window.

What I *can* see is the delicate skyline of Venice at night, as we pass through the lagoon. A soft, almost insubstantial image, I feel that if I rub my eyes and look again it will be gone.

'The end of civilisation,' someone mutters darkly, as the stone quaysides and lamplit arcades recede into the distance. A bit of an exaggeration, especially if you're a Greek, but it is the end of temperate climates, seasons, and western ways for a month or two, and I allow myself a little homesickness.

Day 4 28 September

The *Espresso Egitto* is a vessel of 4,686 tonnes, built in Livorno 14 years ago. She's owned by the nationalised Adriatic Navigation Company and provides the only regular passenger service between Venice and Egypt. (Fogg travelled from Brindisi to Bombay, a service long since defunct.) The appeal of a two-hour air flight over four days at sea is illustrated by the fact that there are only eighty passengers aboard.

This morning, fortified by a good night's sleep and a lie-in, I set out to explore the boat. From a warren of identical passageways I eventually find my way to an open central area. Here there is a notice board on which, I'm told, will be displayed the day's entertainments. It's blank. Opposite, behind a curving glass panel sits the substantial form of Mr Lalli, the ship's purser. He's coughing.

'I should stop the smoking,' he growls gloomily, 'but I get nervous.' The thought of this massive primate-like figure being nervous is rather like hearing that Arnold Schwarzenegger cries when he can't get to sleep, and is not the only surprise about Mr Lalli. He's a Slovene who wants the Italians to give back Trieste and he sympathises with the separatists in the south of his country, who are currently embroiled in strife with their central Yugoslav government. 'That's why I can understand the Welsh, who also want their own country.'

He'd wanted to be an actor at one time, and remembers being dressed down for chewing a piece of gum during a Shakespearian death scene. Then he wanted to be a film director. He's seen *Battleship Potemkin* seven times. He reaches for a piece of paper and the microphone, and with a bleak smile of apology returns to the job he ended up with. Adjusting an incongruous pair of half-moon spectacles he sets to the laborious business of announcing, in five languages, that the clocks will go forward an hour tonight.

A handful of passengers are sitting in the main lounge watching Popeye dubbed in Italian. Ron is reading *Great Air Disasters* and a small elderly Scotsman is protesting at the bar: 'That's the smallest Coca Cola I've ever seen!' His wife nods in agreement. The barman shrugs and examines something his little finger has just fetched out of his ear.

Up on deck there is sunshine and an extended Egyptian family returning from a holiday in Nice. The womenfolk remain covered despite the heat, but the children chase one another round the empty sun-deck. Their father, Mahmout, grins throughout the voyage, like the cat that's eaten the cream. Maybe he's just done a pipeline deal with my friends from the Orient Express.

The out-of-season feel persists. The small swimming pool is dry and a safety net is slung across it. I ask a crew member if it will be filled. He looks at me in surprise and shakes his head: 'It is for crazies.' The whole of the lower sun-deck is full of Mercedes cars – an overflow from the hold, I suppose.

Passepartout has lost all the Sunday papers he bought at Victoria three days ago with the exception of *Sunday Sport*. As we cut through the deep blue waters of the Adriatic, on our way from one cradle of civilisation to another, I settle down beside the Mercedes and read of 'Lesley's Agony As Her Man Turns Into A Frog'.

Midnight: A last turn on deck. Cool enough to make me grateful for including a sweater in my minimal luggage. After the mad rush of the first 48 hours, the pace of the journey has completely changed. For the first time I'm beginning to sense the immensity of the distance ahead. We're making 18 knots, which is respectable for any ship, but it still means that I'm currently going round the world at less than 30 miles an hour. Trains now seem unimaginably fast, aircraft incomprehensible. We have been moving steadily now for 29 hours and have seen nothing but hazy pale-grey sea. Away to our right (I'm sorry, starboard) is Brindisi, from where my illustrious fictional predecessor set sail.

Back to my cabin, which I can now find with only one wrong turning. In the middle of the Adriatic I put my watch on an hour – the first of 24 time changes before I get back home.

Day 5 29 September

The haze has cleared and the sea is a terrific turquoise. Overnight we've changed course and are now heading due East (which is always welcome news for this circumnavigator) and I can see dry straw-coloured coastline on either side.

No one is lingering over breakfast today, for we are now only a few miles away from one of the most spectacular experiences of the journey – the passage of the Corinth Canal. Its construction began just nine years after Phileas Fogg set out and was completed in 1893. It saves 200 miles sailing and the *Espresso Egitto* is the largest boat it will take.

Our engines slow for the first time since we left Venice. Two small boats are now approaching us, one the tugboat that guides us through, the other the boat containing the pilots – not one, but three – who will assist the captain. They grab the rope ladder and scramble aboard. They're dressed in well-pressed chinos. The senior of them is elderly, bald with grey hair, then there's a younger man with a wild, Gaddafi hairstyle and another, rather distinguished, like a statesman. There's a considerable and quite exciting air of expectation about this operation which, as Roger says, is rather like threading something through the eye of a needle. Gradually everybody on the boat, even the most laid-back sun worshipper, even the catatonic lad on the till in the bar who hasn't taken his eyes off the television for 36 hours, gathers on the rails to watch our progress. The narrow cut ahead of us looks unreal, like a Cecil B. De Mille special effect.

A soldier with a machine gun patrols outside a tiny concrete guard hut as we pass. The trees on either side bend rather wearily: we're in the land of parched grass.

Suddenly we're inside the canal and in the middle of a picture from the *Boy's Book of Wonders*. Walls rise at 90 degrees with only 2 metres leeway on either side of us. The three pilots, one on each side of the bridge, and the chief pilot in the middle, now have their trickiest work to do. If the stern of the ship swings at all, it will strike the dry sandstone walls. The negotiation of the Corinth Canal must be one of the top maritime stunts, a display of navigational skills, not just by this boat but by the tug, which is guiding us and keeping us on course, our own steering being ineffective at this speed.

The pilot on the starboard corner cracks his fingers, occasionally calls out some warning in Greek, and the captain then goes to his gyroscope and checks our course. We're flying four flags at the moment, the red and white flag emblazoned with the lion of St Mark, which is the flag of Venice, the red, white and green flag of the Republic of Italy, the red and white flag to signify a pilot on board, and the blue and white flag of Greece. Also up the masthead is Nigel Passepartout with his camera, ever in search of the Great Shot. His presence provokes terrific shouts and consternation from the crew below.

Just over an hour after entering the Corinth Canal we're through, saving ourselves seven or eight hours on the journey round the Peloponnesian Peninsula. As we emerge into the Saronian Sea the land to our left is burnt and bare, and the pine trees that do exist are scorched. There's obviously been a considerable fire. A coach at the side of the road below us disgorges a party of Greek ladies with handbags. They rush towards the canal side to watch us go by. Our tug turns and heads back through the canal. A launch comes alongside to collect the three pilots. A round of applause should really be offered, but they do this sort of thing ten times a day.

Three o'clock in the afternoon: Vast numbers of boats of all kinds around the port of Athens at Piraeus remind you that the Greeks still regard themselves as a seafaring nation. But in a bay almost out of sight are dozens of supertankers, laid up and rusting, a reminder that the golden days of the 1960s and early 1970s are over and may never return.

Mr Lalli is having a harassing time on the public address system: 'Transit passengers wishing to visit in Athens are reminded that we set sail again at nine p.m. Passengers *must* be aboard by nine thirty ... I'm sorry ... eight, *eight* thirty ...'

The Greek word for 'strike' is *aperghia* and we've already run into one. There are no taxis into Athens and as far as I can see no sign of a public transport alternative. For a moment on the dockside I feel a keen sense of isolation in a foreign land. A compatriot approaches: 'Saw you on Wogan!' Turns out to be a native of Manchester on her way to work on a kibbutz, and complaining bitterly about a 40-hour ferry journey from here to Tel Aviv.

A minibus takes me into Athens. Earthquakes or the threat of them seem to have knocked the stuffing out of domestic architecture and we pass row upon row of bland, unremarkable concrete facades. Sad in a city which contains two or three of the greatest buildings in the world.

What I've really come to see in Athens are the Evzones. Not sore throat pastilles, but the bizarrely dressed Presidential guards who, among other things, patrol the war memorial, and raise and lower the national flag at the Acropolis every Sunday. Enormous, specially selected, highly trained, superbly fit fighting men whose uniform consists of tasselled hats, embroidered tunics, short flared skirts, white stockings and clogs adorned with black pom-poms. Any temptation to see all this as rather twee is dispelled by one look at the giants who wear them. The outfit reflects the fierce national pride of the Greeks, for it was originally worn by the guerrillas who fought to keep the nationalist cause alive during 400 years of Turkish occupation. Nowadays the Greeks and the Turks are theoretically allies, as both are members of Nato, but the Evzone lieutenant I spoke to was in no doubt as to who was still the traditional enemy.

The Evzone tradition is that the guards dress each other, and I watch, feeling like a pygmy, as these huge, solemn young men, arms entwined around each other's waists, arrange the skirts (which they call *foustanellas*) so that every one of the 400 folds (one for each year of the Ottoman domination) hangs in exactly the right place.

We are entertained at the barracks with great warmth and courtesy by the Evzone commandant, a Cretan who offers us considerable slugs of tsikudia, his local spirit, which tastes like slivovitz. Maybe it's because of the taxi strike but the restaurants that ring the Piraeus waterfront are very empty and their owners seem prepared to go to suicidal lengths to stop our minibus as we drive back to the ship. We eventually stop at the only establishment whose owner hasn't flung himself into the middle of the road ahead of us. It's called The Black Goat Restaurant and features a special called 'Fish in Slic'. The sea water which laps gently at our feet is so full of oil and rubbish it's a wonder it can lap at all. (Perhaps this is the 'slic' referred to.) It's quite a relief to get back to the *Espresso Egitto*, and Mr Lalli's plaintive cries: 'Said Achmed Sabra from Egypt ... please call at the Purser's office; Mr Neekolas Russell from England ... *please* call at the Purser's office.'

He was smoking a lot when I passed his window on my way to bed.

Day 6 30 September

'This is my worst day ... this is my *worst* day.' Mr Lalli is referring to the arrival of 100 extra passengers at Heraklion, on top of the 100 who boarded last night at Piraeus (including, rumour has it, 31 unaccompanied German girls). I collect my shore-pass from him and at 7.30 on a clear hot morning I'm running along the sea-front past the low, solid battlemented fortress that dominates Heraklion harbour. On its wall the lion of Venice in low relief marks its origins in the time when Crete was part of the Venetian Empire.

This dusty sea-front has seen a few empires come and go. The Minoan civilisation, 3000 years before Christ, had already given way to Greek, Roman, Byzantine and Saracen empires before the Venetians arrived in 1210, and the Turks were still to come. I assume they all looted each other. A massively protracted exercise in the redistribution of wealth.

I rather liked the friendly atmosphere and human scale of the city. Everything seems to be half-finished, but there's an intimate little square in the centre of town where I rest and, over thick coffee, fresh orange juice, bread and honey, catch up on Olympic news in a day-old copy of the *Independent*. Ben Johnson's disgrace has followed his success with a swiftness the occupants of Mount Olympus would have been proud of.

I run at a gentle pace back through streets with unexpected names like Evans Street (after the Englishman who excavated the nearby Minoan capital of Knossos) and Duke of Beaufort Avenue ('Leoforos Dhoukos Bofor'). Back on board ship, Said Achmed Sabra is still wanted at the Purser's office.

Today's passenger intake has changed the character of the *Espresso Egitto* considerably. The leisurely sprinkling of smiling Egyptians and dour Scots with whom we left Venice has now been swamped by dreadlocked German bikers and package holidaymakers on 36-hour excursions to Egypt. There are a lot of thin, badly dressed Egyptians with plastic carrier bags and resigned, unsmiling faces. The sound of hawking and spitting is almost as frequent now as Mr Lalli's increasingly desperate announcements. As we pass the long, medieval harbour wall and ease into the eastern Mediterranean, we're still 200 short of a full complement of passengers. What it must be like when full hardly bears thinking about.

The highlight of my last day aboard the *Espresso Egitto* is a celebration dinner. The people from Adriatic Navigation have been extremely helpful to us and want to lay something on. Ann Passepartout suggests that we put two tables together, only realising later that they are bolted to the floor. But before she can stop them, Bruno, the Adriatic rep., Eros, the lugubrious maître d', several of the waiters and an engineer have begun construction of a wooden bridge from table to table.

In the afternoon I'm shown the galley where Franco and a team of 11 are preparing dinner for 300. Franco, a Neapolitan who's been 27 years 'man and boy' with Adriatica, gives me a rapid lesson in bread-making. The essence seems to be controlled panic. Once the dough is prepared Franco sets to at a furious pace, kneading, twisting, tying, folding, muttering, cursing and turning out, in the space of a minute, about 25 little rolls which an uncharitable observer would compare to a series of exquisitely formed dog turds. Egomaniac to the last I produce, after two or three attempts, a passable letter 'P' which I shall eat later.

5.30: On deck to watch my last European sunset. As the sun swells and sinks, a flight of small birds appears darting and diving in front of me. They're swallows. The sun has so dazzled me that they appear crimson.

The Great Meal this evening is to be filmed and all the waiters suddenly have crisp white jackets. Eros, in full dress, resembles a fifties matinee idol gone to seed. Champagne, risotto di gamberi, loup de mer, cheese and profiteroles, red and white wine come on inexorably, severely testing not just the diners but the structural engineering beneath the table.

As the *vita* becomes *piu dolce* the ship begins to roll for the first time in the journey. Eros looms over us, becoming more and more like Frankie Howerd. 'Not for nothing,' he declares with a twirl of the fingers, 'do they call me Eros,' and with an outrageous wink he turns on his heel and walks straight into a minion bearing more profiteroles.

To my cabin. Through eyes blurred by fine wines, I can just make out my copy of the BBC's *Get By In Arabic*. I'm on page 2, and Egypt's only 180 miles away.

Day 7   1 October

Dark, unsettling dreams from which I wake to the sound of throat-clearing, scratching and thick irregular breathing. It's not mine either. It's on the other side of the cabin partition but feels disturbingly close, as if this nameless heaving, unhealthy mass is on the other side of my bed. This all happens at 2.30, and I never quite recover. Four hours later I'm up, packing, deflating the inflatable globe which is the only way to get an accurate picture of the real extent of the journey. We hardly seem to have started, though Roger, trying to be encouraging, tells me that Cairo is 2,000 miles from London and when we get there we'll be a twelfth of the way home.

Up on deck for my first glimpse of the North African coastline. There's a smell of fresh bread oddly contrasting with the largely silent mood of passengers who stand staring mutely forward, their feet hemmed in by unwieldy boxes containing microwave ovens and Kenwood mixers. They're conserving their energies for queues and customs.

I talk to a lone Englishman who is travelling to Sinai and then the Sudan, scuba diving. He's addicted to the sport and finances his journeys by letting out grazing land he owns in Brecon. He grins apologetically, 'Not a very responsible way to carry on.'

Well, I'm not one to talk.

I'm now on the threshold of an uncompromisingly unfamiliar world. Everything is different, from the minarets on the dusty skyline of Alexandria to the blatantly shady behaviour of a small unmarked boat which sidles up on our stern port side, collects a pack of 200 Marlboros thrown down by one of the crew, secretes it and stands off for a while before returning for a few more goodies, all of which are swiftly stowed under the steering column in the wheelhouse.

Trying to sense a little of what drew Alexander the Great, Caesar and Napoleon to this place I shuffle down the gangplank, barking my shins on a Magimix. I'm met by a very charming lady in white who checks my passport and for the first time I hear that soft, courteous Egyptian response to foreigners, 'Welcome'.

The German bikers are wheeling their monstrous machines from the ship's hold, a couple of middle-aged dock-workers pass by holding hands and a shabby shuffling figure in loose plimsolls dolefully works the crowd proffering a bucketful of Coca Colas on ice.

Once on Egyptian soil, I feel a curious surge of adrenaline, as if I've escaped from five days in cotton wool. There'll be no such thing as normal for quite a while now. As if to underline this I find myself in a fiacre, which is an open horse-drawn cab, being galloped out of the port and into the hurtling traffic. A gaggle of Egyptians, sipping tea, have presumably been told what the camera's there for.

'You are Michael Caine?' they shout.

'No. I am cheaper than Michael Caine.'

They all laugh, beyond the limits of politeness. 'We want to see this film very quickly.'

I just want to survive long enough to make it, but there's not time to tell them this as Achmed the driver applies his whip and we swing out into the streets of Alexandria. It's quite terrifying. The horse, which for some reason is called Larry, seems congenitally unable to move in a straight line and in a series of lurches and wild whip-assisted sprints, dodging within inches of passing cars, we eventually reach the famous Corniche – the long curving sea-front. It's like Cannes with acne. A wide and well-proportioned road and some handsome facades in the neo-classical style, but everything blotchy and half patched-up, giving it the odd air of a city that was abandoned long ago and is now full of people gingerly coming back to re-inhabit.

On the sea-wall, itinerant street-sellers are curled up asleep, their heads protected from the sun inside the baskets they'll later sell. Achmed and Larry deliver me physically, if not mentally, unscathed to the Cecil Hotel. Here hippies are having their shoes shined by ten-year-olds and within the space of a minute I'm offered sunglasses, black market currency and a trip to Alamein.

'Alamein … you know … Hitler! …'

Midday: To the impressive Misr Station to pick up a train to Cairo. The noise is incredible. This is a horn-blower society. Egyptian drivers make New York cabbies sound like librarians. They must specially modify their cars to connect the accelerator to the horn. They never use one without the other. And now the muezzin has started, his raucously distorted call to prayer adding to the cacophony, and causing prayer mats to be laid down in the middle of an already packed ticket office.

A blazing row has erupted as to whether we're allowed to film or not, and about four people are shouting at each other, clutching their heads. You'd think there'd been a death in the family the way they carry on. It all reminds me of a big, slightly out of control boys' public school, everyone issuing different orders, a few people trying to be serious, but everyone else finding it frightfully funny.

Watching the crowds come off the trains it's interesting to note how the traditional garb – jellabas and turbans and fezzes for men, and veils and long dresses for women – is now mixed with Western dress – Levi's, jeans, slacks, shirts, dresses and skirts. The contrast is extraordinary: some look like Old Testament prophets, others like James Dean. Sometimes there's a mixture with the women, of the old Islamic headdress and a modern slightly blowsy Orlon two-piece. It may be chaotic but life wouldn't be as rich as this at airports, where people are much more conditioned, directed and cowed into submission.

Four o'clock: At Cairo station, half an hour late after a 135-mile train journey from Alex across the fertile, feudally farmed Nile Delta. The temperature is 91 degrees.

It's Saturday afternoon and I've been promised seats for the big football match between local heroes National Sporting Club and some tough-tacklers from Middle Egypt – Al Minya. I arrive at Cairo Stadium, in a grandiose complex called Nasser City, halfway through the second half. The stadium is a wide, comfortable bowl with an electronic scoreboard and lush grass playing surface. The terraces are clean and well cared-for and put most British grounds to shame.

I'm rather confused by the colours and enthusiastically cheer an Al Minya attack by mistake. I'm then taken in hand by some local supporters who explain who's who and offer me sunflower seeds. They are exceptionally friendly and as Sporting Club score twice only moments after my arrival, clearly regard me as having Bill Shankly-like powers.

The 60,000 crowd is well patrolled. Ten minutes before the end riot police with transparent shields, visors, helmets and long white sticks take up position around the touchline, facing the crowd like nervous samurai.

Outside, the army, consisting of thin and petrified teenagers, waits in trucks. But there seems to be no trouble. Indeed, some supporters produce prayer mats and fall to their knees as soon as they leave the ground.

On the way back from the match, traffic is so solid along a half-finished eight-lane super-highway that we are passed by an old woman in black on a donkey, leading a herd of goats up the side of the motorway. A red, rather unhealthily flushed sun descends slowly behind a hazy city skyline. Last night it was the crimson swallows; tonight, more menacingly, sunset brings the kites, flapping lazily around the eucalyptus trees.

I check in to the Hotel Windsor, which, like everything else in Cairo, is remarkable. It's run by two brothers called Doss. The Doss Bros have resisted any pressure to convert this unprepossessing pile into a characterless modern hotel, much to Passepartout's dismay.

I rather like its surreal atmosphere. The stairs and the stickily hot hallway are decorated with old Swissair posters of the Alps, so as you climb, perspiring, upwards you pass red, chubby-cheeked German children smiling in St Moritz and Alpine walkers in Zermatt with thick legs protruding from bulky lederhosen. The hotel was once under Swiss ownership and there are reindeer antlers and hunting trophies on the walls of the bar.

But the food is Egyptian. For dinner we have lentil soup, then a plateful of spring onions, cracked wheat, rice and fried onions, falafel (deep-fried vegetable balls), a chilli and onion salad and a thick and treacherous local wine, which is about the only thing that doesn't have onions in it.

Later, whilst Passepartout sorts out the film he's shot of this day's madness, I take a walk for a late-night look at the Nile. A brutal network of flyovers bars my way and I end up lost. A courteous Egyptian helps me out. He asks me where I'm from and what I think of the weather.

'A little hot for me.'

He laughs. 'This is very nice. It's the first time it has been below 95 for weeks.'

Back in my room, the bath tap produces only dreadful bronchial shudders and a thin trickle of water before sinking into total unconsciousness. There's a washbasin, but no plug, and the lavatory's unflushable. However, I work out an Emett-like temporary solution involving twisting a coat-hanger around the ball cock. Later discover it's my only coat-hanger.

Day 8   2 October

Sunday morning in Cairo.

I wake with a greater than usual feeling of sensory dislocation. Where am I and what is the horrendous noise?

Most of it can be attributed to my air-conditioning unit which changed gear during the night with a splintering crack that sounded as if someone were trying to batter the door down.

I silence the air-conditioner and throw open the windows only to find there's even more noise outside. I now know why they had laughed at me in reception when I'd asked for a quiet room.

'In *Cairo*!'

I suppose it's sheer weight of numbers. There are over 10 million people living in Greater Cairo and a further million or more unrecorded refugees and squatters – many of them living in the eerily beautiful City of the Dead, a huge and ancient cemetery. I passed by it with fascination, but on enquiry found that cameras are not allowed inside, so, with a day to kill before my next boat connection from Suez, Passepartout and I take up the invitation of a man I met in the bar last night to visit an Egyptian movie set. Crossing the Nile by the Tahir bridge I have my first sight of the more prosperous side of the metropolis. Hilton, Sheraton and Meridien hotels, skyscraper office blocks. From here Cairo could be anywhere in the world and I'm glad to be at the eccentric Windsor, in the as yet unsmoothed heart of the city.

The film is a political thriller called *Inar Gahined* ('Hellfire') and it's being shot in a Safeway supermarket in the tidy, tree-shaded Zamalek area. Foreign diplomats live here, so it's well tended, well guarded, and dotted with twee boutiques with names like 'Mix 'n' Match' and 'Genuine'.

It transpires that my contact is Egypt's leading lighting cameraman and I'm treated royally, meeting the stars and, without any audition, being given the part of Third Shopper In China Department. My six steps to the left as the gang pass by are executed so successfully that I am upgraded to the more demanding Man In Lift. The terrorists have a gritty scene here in which their recriminations are cut short by the arrival of the elevator, whose doors slide open to reveal yours truly. I'm not quite sure what I'm doing but I stare hard at the gang leader as I walk past him and he seems very pleased.

I talk to him afterwards. His real name is Noor-el-Sherif and he is very big in Egypt – where they make over 60 films a year. He admits only about six of these are any good and blames much of the blandness on the censorship that is necessary to make pictures saleable in the rest of the Arab world. I ask him what sort of things they censor.

'Sex, politics, religion ...' he replies gloomily. 'That's all.'

Having arrived in Egypt 600 years too late to see one of the Seven Wonders of the World – the Pharos lighthouse – I felt I couldn't leave without seeing one that still exists – the Pyramids. I had always presumed they were in the middle of nowhere, marooned in the desert. In fact they are within five minutes' walk of apartment blocks in the suburb of Giza. My first view of them is from a traffic jam on Pyramids Road. The 4,600-year-old apex of the Great Pyramid pokes up from behind a block of flats. My first full-frontal view of the Pyramids provokes an heretical comparison with the slag-heaps which used to litter the South Yorkshire countryside where I grew up. They had the same solid bulk, shape and immovable presence. Once free of the straggling suburb we are straightaway in desert. There's no transition through savannah and scrubland, like in the geography books. The city ends, the desert begins, and it goes on until you reach Morocco. The dustiness of Cairo is explained. Every time a wind blows it dumps thousands of tonnes of desert on the city.

Closer now to the Pyramids and they are awesome. The blocks of sandstone at their base are twice as high as the small children playing around them. The structures rise serene and powerful above us, preserving an unmoving dignity, like great beasts surrounded by insects. Coaches ferry out an endless stream of human insects, deposit them at a tightly packed vantage point where they are assailed by camel-mongers, postcard salesmen, purveyors of trinkets and all the other free market forces which have ripped off tourists at this very spot for hundreds, if not thousands of years.

They have their patter well worked out, and very bizarre it sounds in the middle of the desert:

'You from Yorkshire? ... I am friend of Yorkshire!'

'You are English? Tally-ho!'

'What is your name?'

'Michael.'

'My camel's name is Michael!'

So it is that I find myself on a camel called Michael (or Ron or Julian or Nigel or Dwayne or Sheri-Anne) being flung skywards into the air as the creature raises itself on its forelegs. It looks and feels grossly unsafe, as it totters into the desert with me clinging on for dear life and feeling ridiculously conspicuous in an Arab headdress which the camel-owner, who I think is called Michael as well, has insisted I wear: 'Now you will be like Lawrence of Arabia!'

Behind me hot white people from all over the wealthy West are being given similar treatment. Every time they raise a camera to the Pyramids an Arab stands in front of it. The tourist adjusts his shot, the Arab follows. The air is full of the angry din of protest and dissension. This din is beginning to fade now as Michael, Michael and Michael wander further into the desert. In silence and sunset the Pyramids take on a potent, talismanic quality.

At supper at the Windsor, they appear to have unearthed a new and comprehensive wine list. Marked *Carte des Vins* and bound in thick, padded leather, it's presented to us proudly by Mahmoud, the small elderly head waiter. Inside it appears to consist of nothing but photos and press cuttings mostly featuring a squat, muscular man with very few clothes on surrounded by admiring groups of ladies. Mahmoud beams proudly. Of course, it's *him*. 'Yes!' he nods graciously and strikes a pose. He was once very famous for his body. We admire his pectorals, but would have preferred the wine. He retrieves the book, wipes its cover and presents it to an infinitely more appreciative group of Australian schoolgirls. They arrived at the Windsor last night, after a European tour which has left their teachers devastated. One of them tells me that Athens was the worst: 'All those sailors.' Then he shrugs and takes another gulp of Stella beer: 'So long as we get them home without any diseases.'

Seems a suitable epitaph for a long day, and I'm about to drink to it when Ann appears with a very long face. My onward connection from Suez – the SS *Algeria* – will not be leaving Suez tomorrow after all. Engine trouble. So it's back to the phone as soon as shipping offices open in the morning. Suddenly the schedule's looking shaky.

Day 9 3 October

Encouragement of a sort from my horoscope in the *Egyptian Gazette* (109th year of publication): 'Others may make demands on you today that you consider unreasonable, but you will come through with flying colours.' I wish I had their confidence.

My breakfast is served by a Nubian in a fez who was once a servant in the household of King Farouk. 'Nubians make very good waiters,' observes Mr Doss. What a dreadful reference for any nation. It's like hearing that Visigoths can iron well.

Better news from the shipping agent. Though I shall have to take a later boat out of Suez which will mean missing my planned connection from Jeddah to Muscat, a sister ship, leaving Jeddah later, has altered its itinerary to call at Muscat after all.

I leave the Hotel Windsor at 2. I was never able to have the bath I so much wanted and my coat-hanger remains a vital part of the lavatory system but there is an almost unreal individuality to the place which represents Cairo in a microcosm.

There is no train connection between Cairo and Suez, so I take a taxi. Within a few hundred yards I know that I should have gone by camel. This is going to be one of the most uncomfortable journeys of my life. The temperature is creeping up to the hundred degree mark. There is no air-conditioning, and the windows open onto a wall of noise and pollution.

The statue of Rameses II, discovered in Memphis in 1851 by French archaeologists, stands between two flyovers in front of the Rameses Station, moving no faster than we are. On my left is the railway line to Alex, which brought me in to the city what seems an impossibly long time ago, but is, in fact, less than two days. As if there isn't enough noise the driver flicks a cassette into his machine and loud Egyptian pop music fills the taxi. 'This was a very good song for Al Amkansoun,' he tells me. 'She was very famous lady from 15 years ago; she now very famous in Arab. More than 100 million population like to hear this song.'

We've been going now about 25 minutes, the heat, noise and smell of fumes still intense, but the roads have at last thinned out as we pass through Heliopolis. Lots of barracks around here, many soldiers. Howitzers and rockets are proudly displayed outside.

Suddenly we're on the edge of the desert, 96 per cent of Egypt's land surface, and mile upon mile of tips. All Cairo's rubbish; old furniture, rubble, twisted car wrecks, some of them burning. It seems to be an open dump. Pass a huge articulated truck which has swerved and overturned on the side of the road. The cab looks completely smashed in, and two men helplessly wander around the sacks of cement which lie scattered across the road.

Occasionally an advertising hoarding stands out in the middle of nowhere. We pass one which depicts a huge bidet and washbasin.

The meter ticks over. It shows about 40 Egyptian pounds – nearly £11 sterling. I pray that we keep moving. As soon as we slow down flies fill the car. Not a lot of traffic anyway. Trucks containing oil drums and pipes. At least there are some mountains now rising to the south, and a lower range to the north, something to look at.

Pass ten tanks and about thirty troop carriers by the roadside, with people playing on them. It's not really surprising the Egyptians were clobbered so often by the Israelis. They're not warriors. They're shy, rather jolly, humorous people. Can't imagine them taking military life and conquest very seriously.

It's 5.15 and approaching dusk when I catch my first sight of Suez, a flame high in the sky marking the first of many oil refineries. This does look a god-forsaken depressing place. What vegetation there is here on the edge of the desert, small scrubby bushes, blossom with a thousand plastic bags.

It's a quarter to six when I reach the gates of Suez port. We are not allowed to board tonight, and there seems some doubt as to whether we shall find a boat tomorrow. And we can do nothing until morning as the shipping office is closed. A battered sign in English at the entrance to the port gates reads 'Goodb'ye'. A harsh joke as we turn back and trudge into Suez to find a hotel.

In the centre of Suez two captured US-built Israeli tanks, taken in the 1973 war, are displayed. Alongside them can still be seen piles of rubble from the 1967 war when the town of Suez was almost destroyed.

Then all at once we are in an area of substantial houses with pillared porches and wrought-iron balconies, set along leafy avenues and around well-kept squares full of oleander bushes and Flame of the Forest trees. This is the Port Tawfik area and it was built as a cantonment for foreigners working for the Suez Canal Company.

Here we find the Red Sea Hotel with its plain, slightly depressing rooms devoid of any decoration. Worst of all it is

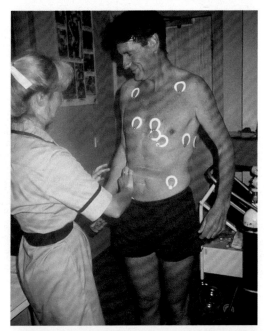

LEFT: *Pre-journey tests to ascertain my suitability for employment with the BBC.*

BELOW: *Passepartout and me. Left to right: Julian Charrington, Angela Elbourne, Ron Brown, Fogg, Dave Jewitt, Simon Maggs, Clem Vallance, Roger Mills, Nigel Meakin, Ann Holland and Nigel Walters.*

RIGHT: *Boarding the Venice-Simplon Orient Express at London Victoria.*

FAR RIGHT: *Great Dustmen of the World.*

BELOW: *Venice, after we've cleaned it.*

BELOW RIGHT: *With the Evzones of Athens.*

FAR LEFT: *The Corinth Canal: threading ourselves through the eye of a needle.*

LEFT: *Mr Lalli at his most relaxed.*

BELOW: *On a camel called Michael at the Pyramids.*

LEFT: *Captain Abbas of the Saudi Moon II (crossed out).*

BELOW LEFT: *Smoking hookah at a pavement café in Jeddah.*

RIGHT: *Warning: camels crossing.*

BELOW: *Living on the edge – the facilities of the* Al Sharma.

OVERLEAF: *Hoisting sail on the dhow.*

'dry' and more than anything in the world at this moment I want a cold beer. The receptionist, sympathetic to my plight, directs me to The Gulf Rose Restaurant and Bar where, creamed against mosquitoes, I sit for a while and take in the dark water ahead, the mouth of the Suez Canal and the busy flames of the refineries. A light breeze blows, and it has to be said that sitting in Suez is not at all unpleasant. Quite how *long* I shall have to sit in Suez is tomorrow's problem.

Day 10 4 October

Phileas Fogg arrived in Suez aboard the SS *Mongolia* six and a half days after leaving London. 'As to seeing the town, he did not even think of it, being of that race of Englishmen who have their servants visit the country they pass through.' One of the reasons for his superior rate of progress becomes clear this morning as I stand beside the Suez Canal just after dawn, watching the northbound convoy go through. There is not a single passenger ship among the fifteen or so which pass, one every seven minutes, rumbling away into the morning mist. The days when you could hop on a *Mongolia* or a regular P & O or Union Castle service are over. There are cruise ships and cargo ships and not a lot else in between. And that's why I'm already almost four days behind Fogg and every hour of this uncertainty in Suez puts me further behind.

There's no one else out here by the canal where the rusting sections of a pontoon bridge and the dug-outs, trenches and blockhouses are reminders of the bitter fighting that took place only fifteen years ago. The whole place is like one huge War Museum, through which ships pass at a stately pace, almost like mirages in the haze.

By mid-morning I'm back at the gates of Suez port. A steady line of brightly painted trucks and trailers is passing through, occasionally swerving to avoid a minibus packed to the gunwales which has in turn swerved to avoid a woman with her worldly goods on her head and a crying child on her arm.

Water-sellers clang brass rings together to attract attention, but vanish into thin air at the sight of a camera, which is a pity as their kit is extraordinary. It consists of what appears to be a long-spouted silver urn from which hang glasses and which is topped with a block of ice. A tin tray is worn on the waist to collect the money. Sometimes you can hardly see the boy inside all this, giving the odd impression of robot coffee bars whizzing around the dockside. On the roadside the beggars wait patiently, many with children sitting uncomprehendingly in their arms, flies buzzing at their nostrils.

At last it seems we are clear to go through. Reservations have been made for us on a boat carrying itinerant workers to Jeddah. At the immigration counters are long lines of people waiting patiently. Inaction is a fact of life, it seems. We are, I'm embarrassed to say, expressed through, but only as far as customs where we experience a lot of inaction.

There is nowhere to wait except in the minibus, and it's very hot. At the entrance to the dock they are preparing to resurface the road. The preparation consists of two men and a donkey drawing a small tank of liquid tar. One man holds a long leaky rod from which he sprays the tar on the road and his trousers whilst his accomplice shuffles alongside pumping a handle. The effect of the tar is wonderful to behold. Everybody treads in it. One man with green flip-flops discovers he's in it too late and each step he takes his flip-flops grow in size, so after a while he's walking like a huge duck. It affects everybody from the jellaba-ed peasant to the brisk, white-shirted self-important official. Soon all around us the dock is full of people scraping their shoes.

Can this be the same country that built the Pyramids, invented the column, the cornice and the capital?

After three hours of formalities we are aboard the M.V. *Qamar El Saudi II* ('The Saudi Moon II'). The II has, however, been roughly crossed out and I written in. Her sister ship, *The Saudi Moon I*, recently ran aground and sank on a reef outside Jeddah. The ship, of 5,342 tonnes, was built in Genoa in 1971 and began life as the *Dana Sirena* before being sold to a Danish outfit, DFDS Seaways, for North Sea ferry work. Now it's owned by an Egyptian company who bought it off the Saudis. The interior seems to have been left alone, and I find myself looking at a plan of the ship which still features the 'Hamlet Lounge', the 'Tivoli Club', 'The Mermaid Pub' and even the 'Dog's Toilet'.

Up on the bridge, beside an indicator with the ship's speed and direction in Danish – 'Frem', 'Bak', 'Halv' and 'Fuld' – the portly Egyptian captain is bent over charts of Suez harbour published in Taunton, whilst his first officer tends a radar scanner made in Bremen.

I've lost another half day on my schedule by the time we eventually pull away from the dockside, passing the stricken *Algeria* whose engine problems precipitated all these delays.

It's a 48-hour trip to Jeddah and our speed will not be much more than 15 knots, a much slower rate of progress than the *Egitto*. There are 650 passengers and 12 cars aboard (one of which is a gleaming Cadillac). Though Passepartout and I have comfortable cabins with plenty of portholes, we seem to be in splendid isolation, for most of the other passengers are squashed together in cabins below, and 200 of them are sleeping out on deck. The reason for this can be gleaned from a comparison of the per capita earnings of Egypt, 700 dollars a year, and Saudi Arabia, 8,000 dollars a year. Saudi Arabia is a magnet for labour in the Arab world, and many of these passengers have left wives and families to earn a year's good money in the still booming construction, oil and agricultural industries of their wealthy neighbour.

Sadly the Mermaid Pub is now much reduced. The bar and bar stools are still there, but only non-alcoholic drinks are available. Tea, coffee and things like Viva-Up and Santa – a dreadfully sweet fizzy apple confection. Stick to water.

Somehow drinking water in surroundings expressly designed for something more fun is a depressing experience.

Day 11 5 October

Ron tells me at breakfast that when his watch alarm went off on deck last night a lot of people woke up and started to pray. I had noticed yesterday that the deck passengers, who have very few belongings, do sport some impressive wristwatches. These are not only prestigious, but very practical for those who must remember to pray five times a day.

Apparently one is not advised to wear shorts. The sight of my knees would be frowned upon. I shall just have to get hot, secure in the knowledge that there is only cold water in the shower. And no towels.

There are four Arab women and a dozen men in the first-class lounge this morning. A video of expensive cars, prominently displaying 'Rothman's' signs, on some glamorous rally, plays in the corner. A group of children are chasing each other around the tables. The Arabs love children and when I show an interest in them there is a smile of contact from the parents. But that's about as far as it goes. Yesterday I had met some people on deck who were quite chatty. This morning with the camera about it is very different, and I sense a chill of hostility. A slim, intense young man with a beard and a brown third-world suit reads his Koran and very obviously avoids us. His attitude seems to affect a lot of the others.

The deck passengers all wear traditional clothes – tarbooshes or takaias (the white skullcaps), jellabas and sandals and have no interest in the small duty-free shop below with its VHS cassettes, lingerie, Lacoste shirts and bottles of 'Poison' eau de toilette.

I should assume no Arab, of whatever class, would have much interest in the information outside the main lounge that there was, once upon a time, a King of Denmark called Gorm the Old or that the present Queen, Margrethe II, is his direct descendant.

Lunch with Captain Abbas. He is a charming, enthusiastic and philosophical man. An Egyptian with fond memories of Liverpool, especially their football team. 'I follow the Reds!' he declares, beaming round at us, and scooping a little more beans and onion onto his plate. 'I am not a communist, but I love the Reds!'

He did not sleep at all last night, he tells us. He never does while going down the Gulf of Suez. It's a very busy waterway and now that they have discovered oil on both sides there are support craft flitting to and fro and fishing boats as well, for unlike much of the Red Sea the Gulf is only 50 metres deep. On the other side of Sinai, the Gulf of Aqaba is 2 kilometres deep, 'Which is why Moses decided to walk across the Gulf of Suez!'

Captain Abbas admires England: 'You have such a love for the sea.' Clearly he's not read the Greenpeace report on North Sea pollution. He regards himself and his fellow mariners as guardians of the oceans they serve, and is concerned at the way so many ships mistreat them, throwing unrecyclable rubbish overboard, flushing out oil tanks.

His ship may be tired, battered and grubby, but his love for his work and his affection for sea life and its special mixture of loneliness and comradeliness is very affecting. At the end of the meal he bids us all a most courteous farewell and excuses himself as he has to go to his cabin to listen to a football match on the radio. It turns out that his team is Sporting Cairo, whom I watched on Saturday. Today they have a midweek match against Ismailia ... 'Seaside boys, very young, very strong,' he winks and jabs both elbows out, dangerously.

By mid-afternoon the ship is beginning to roll quite noticeably in a six to seven foot swell. Jules Verne had noted that when the *Mongolia* rolled in the Red Sea, 'the ladies disappeared, the pianos were silent, the songs and dances ceased at once'. Not only was Fogg ahead of me, he was clearly having a much better time.

About six o'clock, as we are crossing the Tropic of Cancer, there is some bad news from Jeddah. One connecting ship which I had hoped might be delayed has left on time, and the next one will be missing out Muscat where I had fixed a dhow connection on to India, and going on to Dubai further up the Persian Gulf. Even if I were able to pick up a dhow in Dubai, the extra distance on both journeys would make me five days late in Bombay. The rest of the schedule would then fall apart like a pack of cards.

Meet Passepartout in the bar. Over water and Santas we discuss alternative possibilities. Unfortunately it's difficult enough to enter Saudi Arabia at all, let alone change plans whilst there, and all the shipping offices will be closed for the weekend. We are entering 'The Arabian Triangle', as Clem Vallance, director of this leg of the journey, puts it, where normal rules no longer apply.

We all need a drink: not a water, or a Santa, but a drink. At lunch Captain Abbas had eloquently defended the Muslim objections to alcohol. He reminded us of 'the phrase you drinkers often use – to get out of our minds'. Abbas wagged his finger and grinned sagely. 'This is not what we need. We need to get into our minds.'

Later I retire to my cabin and try to get into my mind. I can't concentrate, and head up on deck for a walk and listen to the World Service. Around me the 'deck class' are preparing for a second night under the stars. Some are already curled up, heads on crooked arms, others lying spreadeagled like dead men. In the stern the young man in brown, clasping his Koran, sits surrounded by a small group. He's making points on each finger, slowly, trying to bring in every one of his listeners. They watch engrossed.

I hold my short-wave radio out over the side, to receive the signal better. London comes through to the Red Sea loud and clear. They're talking about the Labour Party conference and Kinnock's fighting speech. Above me two shooting stars fall through a clear sky; below me a sleeping man's arms falls across my feet.

Day 12   6 October

Cheese, olives, omelette and hot rolls for breakfast. My system has been a little fluid recently. In fact everything I've eaten south of Cairo has turned to water. I dislike using drugs, but as I'm apprehensive about public lavatory availability in Jeddah, I've taken recourse to a couple of codeine phosphate. Ron swears by Imodium which, besides binding the bowels, apparently kept him as high as a kite in Cairo for 24 hours.

No sooner have we finished breakfast than the dining room is turned into a makeshift clinic. There is evidently a meningitis epidemic in Saudi and we must all be vaccinated. Soon the Elsinore room is full of children crying and adults screaming their heads off. It's all rather disorganised and I'm sure some people are vaccinated twice. I'm handed a certificate in Arabic which, they tell me, says I'm immune from meningitis until October 1990. As we approach Jeddah, we try to film the Saudi pilot coming aboard, but are asked not to. Later, on the bridge Captain Abbas has words of explanation for what he calls the prickliness of the Saudis. 'They are a desert people – and what do you get from deserts? Not roses ... cacti.'

Until five years ago, Jeddah, ringed by treacherous shoals, was one of the most dangerous ports to enter. Then, as part of his colossal investment in its improvement, King Faisal commissioned Gray Mackenzie, a British firm, to provide a decent chart. Now it's much easier and Captain Abbas has little time for the pilot, who looks about 16 and very nervous (as anyone with the expansive bulk and ironic eye of Abbas behind them would be). Pilots, he reckons, are very often a formality.

Any ship's master, with up-to-date charts, could make the approach himself.

As the sun burns off the morning mist, the skyline of Jeddah is clearer. If I shut my ears to the Arabic radio exchanges between the pilot and the shore I could imagine myself in America, Japan or Singapore. There's no minaret, dome or crescent moon in sight. Instead, the tall towers of a desalination plant dominate a waterfront of extensive jetties, state-of-the-art cranes and gantries, all set out spaciously and tidily, like an architect's model. Everything has been built in the last 15 years. It is the formidable face of a boom economy. I can't help thinking that this is what Victorian Britain must have felt like. Now it seems quite strange – the unfamiliar feeling of being in a country which can afford anything it wants.

In the last 48 hours I've grown very fond of Captain Abbas and we leave with regret. His boat I shan't shed many tears for, though. I feel travel-worn and grubby and haven't had a good bath since leaving the *Egitto*.

On the quayside at Jeddah we're met by Achmed, our man from the Ministry (of Information), and Nick, a young man from the British embassy in Riyadh. Everything is very formal here. Things have to be done the right way. The cheerful anarchy of Egypt is a thing of the past. For the grubby, flagged floor of the custom house in Alexandria substitute an air-conditioned plastic-finished international terminal. VDU screens shimmer behind colour-coordinated desks. The walls are covered with framed evidence of the Saudi boom – photos of dams, highways, power lines. For the Egyptian workers from off the *Saudi Moon* it's the Promised Land, but not *their* Promised Land. One of them has a last spit in a lined litter-bin before his passport is stamped.

Most of the menial work in Saudi Arabia is done by foreigners. As well as the Egyptians there are Yemenis and Filipinos and South-East Asians. The Saudis prefer to be behind desks, they don't really like to get their hands dirty. Difficult to know, quite inscrutable people, according to Nick from the embassy. As he says this I notice two men greeting each other with a rather delicate kiss on each cheek like a couple of French ladies in a café.

A Chinese boat, the *Cha-Hwa* of Keelung, is pulling into the harbour as we make our way through the white and grey marbled gatehouses and out of the port. The sign to the city centre is spelt in the American way – 'center'. Sony, Sharp and Panasonic signs abound. But perhaps the greatest shock is the Red Sea Palace Hotel. Not only is there hot and cold running water, there are valets in little hats and sachets of 'Foaming Bath Cream' and music seeping out of the ceiling. Nothing in the previous 12 days has prepared me for this, and I quite forget for a while that we have no idea how we're going to leave this place. Consult Dan Bannerman, a shipping agent and a Liverpudlian, born a football pitch's distance from Anfield. He confirms there is no alternative to the slow boat to Dubai, and indeed it's even slower than we thought, stopping to unload on the way.

The only way to make up time is for me to drive overland to the Gulf, a distance of about 1,120 miles. It will be very tricky to obtain permission for such a journey but Achmed agrees to try.

There is no such thing as a tourist in Saudi Arabia. Every visitor has to have a sponsor – a company or a government department – which guarantees his status and suitability. Saudi Arabia may look like America but it can behave like Russia. However, relations with Britain are good at the moment – we've just clinched a multi-million-pound defence deal – and Nick reckons we could be lucky. Achmed intervenes here to say that under no circumstances would a film crew be allowed to accompany me. Forward one step, back two.

Time to kill in the hotel bookshop. Look for something to follow *Stanley and His Women*. Find little more than a waterproof edition of *Red Sea Reef Fishes* and a stack of *Time* and *Newsweek* magazines on a shelf marked 'No reading please'.

I have to walk for a while before I find an echo of the conviviality of Egypt in the orderly Sony Panasonic world of Jeddah. It's a pavement café at No. 21 Tanaf Lane in the Al-Balad district, outside which sit two or three people smoking most elaborate hookahs. The old houses round here belonged to merchants who were very well off at a time when Jeddah was making money from two sources, one from the *haj*, the annual pilgrimage to Mecca, the other from the spice route to the Yemen. Most of these coastal areas would have been very rich, whereas Riyadh, now the capital, would just have been a collection of mud huts. In the middle of all this I chance upon the nostalgic sight of a manhole cover made by Brickhouse of Dudley, impressively inscribed 'The Pennine Drain Cover'. Pass a group of slim, bright-eyed smiling Sudanese guest workers touting for a bit of car cleaning. The Sudanese I've met on this trip I've liked very much indeed; they have a natural grace and wit and smile a lot, as though they like a good time.

To a courtyarded restaurant called El Alawey for supper. Delicious fresh fruit; and I eat couscous, with lamb, and then almond rolls and sesame seed rolls. The restaurant seems largely for foreigners – Saudis don't eat out much, and when they do they prefer Western-style restaurants. Very nice ambience here, with brass and silver pitchers. I sit with my shoes off and feet up, resting on my side, on a sort of carpeted pillow, like a Roman emperor.

A good chat with Nick from the embassy who used to be in Jordan. We talk about Middle Eastern affairs. Some foresee that Israel will cease to exist in 25 or 30 years because there are so many Arabs living within her borders and reproducing at a rate 50 per cent faster than the Israelis. In 25 years or so, half the population of Israel will be Arab. We walk back together and it's very hot and sticky. Still no word on whether I can move on tomorrow.

Day 13   7 October

I wake with sulphurous tastes emanating from my stomach and
decide to kill or cure by taking some exercise. I am a regular
four-times a week runner at home and yet, apart from hopping
over the Heraklion waterfront, I've taken no vigorous exercise
for almost two weeks. Out onto the Corniche, passing on the
way the remarkable Jeddah roundabouts, decorated with huge
and playful sculptures: at one a 25-foot-high bicycle, at another
a series of enormous Arab lamps, at another a concrete block
with the front and back ends of cars embedded in it. The
presence of these light-hearted civic ornaments is one of
the paradoxes of a country which takes itself and its role in the
world very seriously, which can in many ways seem severe and
intolerant, which won't allow theatres or cinemas but loves fun
fairs and garden centres. Sculpture is everywhere. No human
representation is allowed so the abstract and surreal flourish in
exuberant childlike designs – spiky cacti, boxes of treasure with
jewels inside, stranded ships.

Out on the Corniche beside the Red Sea, I can run in my
shorts, which it would be highly disrespectful to wear in the
centre of the city, and think myself to be in California,
especially when polystyrene Big Mac boxes from the nearby
fairground blow across my path.

And yet, though there are Big Macs and family playgrounds,
the women of Saudi Arabia cannot drive, nor, for instance, can
they find employment on their own airline, where the
stewardesses are English or Canadian. In the shops I can buy
every kind of sophisticated communications equipment and yet
the *Observer* newspaper I buy in the hotel is crudely censored.
A photo of Olympic athletes Mary Slaney and Yvonne Murray
has been scored out with black Pentel below the women's necks.
A half-page article on the drug Ecstasy has been partially cut
out and a feature on Lord Lichfield's Pirelli calendar entirely
black-pencilled. To a first-time Western visitor it is all most

confusing, this mixture between the primitive and the sophisticated, the plutocratic and the austere, the open and the tightly closed.

Another night in Jeddah. To pass the time Passepartout and I visit one of the fairgrounds. It's family night, which means women and children only. Inside there is neon and music and bright lights, but only a few children, supervised by women in black. On one carousel children ride farmyard animals to the music of 'Old Macdonald Had A Farm'. Another, more energetic ride carries with it the warning, 'for your safety this game is not allowed for those who suffer from ... hearts, diabetics, nerves, high pressure and the pregnants'. Beneath the sign a group of Arab women, black veils flying, are sitting together in a huge teacup as it whirls round a teapot. Sadly it's too dark to film.

Above the Atallah Happyland flies the Saudi flag, unique in the world for having an inscription on it. It reads, 'There is only one God and Mohammed is his prophet.' I must hope both are on my side tomorrow.

Day 14 8 October

My *Arab Gazette* tells me it's the start of Fifth National Cleaning Week. For me it's the end of Second Travelling Week and nothing is getting easier. The word is that Achmed has been up all night at the Ministry, and at 3.30 a.m. finally secured permission for myself, Clem and Nick from the embassy to drive across Saudi Arabia. It's now eight o'clock in the morning and there is no sign of Achmed or the permission. Nick is anxious to be leaving, for we have an 1,100-kilometre drive ahead of us. This will take us to Riyadh, and after that there are still more than 1,000 kilometres to the Gulf. It's like driving from London to the Black Sea in one weekend.

At last Achmed, with neat beard and fresh white thobe (as the Saudis call the jellaba) enters the lobby of the Red Sea Palace waving our travel permission like a latter-day Neville Chamberlain. Profuse thanks, then into Nick's Toyota Cressida and we head for the hills.

Not far from Jeddah the road divides on creedal grounds. A huge gantry saddles the motorway, indicating two lanes for 'Muslims Only' and a slip road for 'Non-Muslims'. Only Muslims may look upon the Holy City, so we must take the Christian exit.

Here also we must leave Ron, Nigel, Julian and Angela Passepartout. They will fly on to Dubai and try and fix up a dhow to take us to India. It's a sad moment, as we were enjoying seeing the world together, and regard going on aeroplanes as a cheat.

The main road to Taif is closed for repair and for 50 miles or more we toil slowly up onto the central plateau behind a line of water-carrying tankers, past scrubby pasture where goats and sheep graze and higher up where a few crops are growing in neatly terraced fields. The trucks are nearly all grey-green Mercedes with ornate fifties-style curved radiators. The Saudi market is intensely conservative and apparently Mercedes continue to make them in the old style specially for the Bedouins.

Just outside Taif we come to a police road block, and the first test of Achmed's rather flimsy note of authorisation. The policeman reads it with intense concentration, his lips moving over every word. Time seems to stand still. The unpromising frown on his face proves to be a natural expression rather than an ill omen, and after one last searching look we are waved through. Nick says there may be two or three more such roadblocks. Now the road is straight and almost empty. What's more, it's a beautifully surfaced brand-new six-lane highway. The only possible hazard might be hitting a camel. There are 'Beware Camel' signs at regular intervals and fences along the sides of the road, yet clearly the ships of the desert haven't grasped the full implications of the Saudi road improvement programme, and insist on strolling across as if nothing had changed. Occasionally in the stony wilderness I see a camel herd being rounded up by Bedouin shepherds in Nissan pick-up trucks.

At lunchtime we stop for fuel, still about 300 miles short of Riyadh. I lay my portable thermometer on a wall as we fill up. When I pick it up it reads 50 Centigrade, 112 Fahrenheit, but the air is very dry and the temperature as bearable as 90 Fahrenheit was on the humid coast. The road continues straight and empty.

Most of the cars we see are wrecks, dragged off to the side of the road, bleached and rusting in the desert heat. I suppose it's cheaper for the owners (presuming they survive) to go and buy another car than haul the wreck off to a panel beater.

In the hour before sunset, the desert springs briefly to life. The slanting refracted sunlight, reddened by the dust, turns the blank face of rock and sand into a land of many colours – orange, deep reds, rich ochres and golds. This is the pitted, craggy, sandstone escarpment which leads to the plateau on which stands Riyadh. All around us are weirdly shaped pinnacles of rock, jutting up – like rotting teeth one moment, like the Sphinx the next. On top of all this is the city of Riyadh, built almost entirely in the last 15 years and one of the hottest capitals on earth. It is here because this central part of Arabia, the Nejd, is the home of the ruling house of Saud. It is as big, brash and booming as it is because the Saudis regard themselves as the natural leaders of the Arab world. That they have greater oil reserves and therefore more money than any other Arab country is not to them a coincidence, but a gift from Allah to help the country guard and preserve the two holiest places in the Muslim world – the shrines of Mecca and Medina.

So in this desert miles away from anywhere is this Las Vegas-like symbol of the fusion of the spiritual and commercial. In the neon-glowing streets, all spotless testimonials to the start of Fifth National Cleaning Week and the success of the previous four, glittering modern buildings rise above the old mud dwellings. There seems no attempt here to preserve the old city, as in Jeddah. Perhaps there was no old city. All is new and confident. It's Riyadh, Texas.

To the Al-Khozama hotel. Rather an anti-climax to have made our way to the heart of the Arabian Peninsula only to find that businessmen of every western country have got there first. In reception deals are being done and an English couple are arguing: 'The trouble with Arthur is, that Arthur's been out here too long.'

My spirits are revived by a lovely meal at a simple Lebanese restaurant. A meze with fresh radishes, mint, onions, lettuce and tomatoes as sweet and succulent as those we ate in Egypt, tahini, houmus with aubergine, then a mixed grill of tender and flavoursome shashlik and shish kebab.

Day 15 9 October

The *Arab Gazette* has a list of 'Today's Prayer Times', as well as the more valuable news that Sheffield United beat Wolves 2–0 in yesterday's League game. Nick is waiting for us outside Budget Rent-a-Car. He has arranged a car and driver to take us the 360 miles to the border with Qatar. We are not allowed to take a hire car across national borders, but he reckons that we should either be able to hitch, or pick up a taxi for the 60 miles across Qatar to the border of the United Arab Emirates. He has arranged for another hire car with driver to meet us there.

We leave Riyadh at 9.15. The temperature is 100 Fahrenheit, but dry and bearable. As we head out on another immaculate freeway – the Dammam Expressway – past the King Faud Security College and the Hyatt and Marriott Hotels, it's America again (but of course not *entirely* America, for no corporations, however rich and famous, are allowed here if they have any Jewish or Israeli connections). We pass modern tracking stations and more wrecked cars. Apparently there is no such thing as a driving test here and you can get a licence at the age of 13. Off the expressway and onto a single-carriageway road which bounces on interminably. Presently pipelines appear, my first view of the substance on which Saudi wealth is based, criss-crossing the landscape on their way from the refineries on the eastern horizon. Long-haired black sheep nestle up against the pipelines. The desert is whiter than anything I've seen so far. Bleached white.

We come to the town of Hofuf where the taxis are incongruous yellow Chevvies, like the checker cabs in New York. There is a huge centre here for the study of land reclamation, irrigation and fertilisation. One of the more encouraging aspects in a world which seems to be making every environmental mistake in the book is the Saudis' success in greening the desert. Plants are so tenacious. They cling desperately to life, and the grasslands outside Hofuf show what a difference a little help makes. I fall asleep. When I wake up I can hardly believe it, I'm looking out at the sea. My first view of the Persian Gulf. The air is salty and sticky again.

In marked contrast to most other public places in Saudi Arabia, the border crossing at Abu Samra is shabby and down-at-heel. As I crouch down at a window, proffering my passport and our authorisation, I notice a sniffer dog being walked along a collection of carrier bags belonging to some Arabs of little wealth going the other way. The authorities are very confused as to what we're doing here, and we are eventually shown into the presence of the top man. He motions us to sit down on a couple of armchairs, in whose arms large holes have been gouged, revealing torn and fleshy sponge-rubber beneath. He is a handsome, softly spoken man. His subordinates are progressively fatter and uglier leading me to wonder if promotion can be based on looks. With an elegant economy of

movement he orders us to be looked after. A subordinate
thrusts a form at us. 'Fill this!' he shouts. Another crosses to a
rack of sports lockers on the wall, rummages around and
produces an official stamp.

At 2.35 we are shown out of Saudi Arabia and into Qatar,
country number ten in fifteen days.

The Qatari customs shed is not run down, just bare. I begin
to wilt in the heat as we are slowly moved from desk to desk.
One look around at this fly-blown place reveals a total absence
of the hoped-for taxi. When we make enquiries, we're made
aware of how much we need Nick, or someone with a little of
the language. There is no taxi rank for 50 miles. Clem goes to
try and phone up a car from Doha, the capital of Qatar, whilst
I try my luck at cadging us a lift. Three friendly Qatari
policemen let me share their hut. They assure me they'll find a
vehicle going our way, with the two words that mean you're
sunk in any language: 'No problem.'

They offer me their tea, and when I've drunk it, they order
an Indian to fetch some more. Their names are Saalem, Omarj
and Achmed. In between not getting me lifts, they ask about
England. Omarj is going to London in December. I nod grimly:
'So am I, I hope.' They find this very funny.

Omarj holds his crotch unselfconsciously and talks of
Princess Diana who came here a year ago. All testify to her
beauty.

By now there are hardly any cars coming through and none
want to take us. Clem is still in the guardhouse. We've been in
Qatar for two and a half hours and moved fifty yards.

A truck driver from England pulls into the dusty compound.
He's taken 11 days to drive his 40-tonner overland from
England. (The thought occurs to me that if I'd come with him
I'd be four days ahead.) He's not happy to be here at all. He had
to go into Doha, to have his cargo inspected by a three million
pound British Aerospace machine, for which he has nothing
but contempt: 'They stick this vacuum tube direct to the lift to

sniff for spirits. Well I've got half a hundredweight of paint-stripper aboard. It'll knock their bloody heads off!'

He waves a sheaf of customs papers in the direction of the guardhouse, now fading in the dusk: 'They're all new here. The old ones were alright. This lot don't know what they're doing.' It turns out that what irks him most of all is that he was asked to change into long trousers before they'd even look at his papers.

Neon lights flash on, off and finally on again at the top of the local minaret, bathing the place in a lurid blue glow. A pick-up truck goes through with two racing camels kneeling in the back. Amazing how neatly two camels fit in a Datsun.

At last our taxi arrives, and we are driven the 60 miles to Abu Nathil, the next Qatari border post. Here two bits of bad news are waiting. One is that though this may be the end of Qatar, it is not the beginning of the United Arab Emirates. There is another 60 miles of Saudi Arabia in between, and our driver is not allowed to cross this. Furthermore, the clocks are one hour ahead in the Emirates. The connection arranged for us by Nick will have given up and gone by the time we get there, and there's nothing we can do about it.

It's now 7.15 in the evening, and the Qatari customs here are even more obdurate. We wait our turn behind a Syrian truck driver, travelling with wife and children. More embarkation cards to fill in, more windows to be referred to. The sight of a cockroach at my feet making off with a crumb reminds me that I've only eaten a cheese sandwich since that far-off breakfast in Riyadh.

At last a piece of long overdue luck. A young Kuwaiti passes through with a brand-new red Mercedes 300, with the cellophane still on the seats. He speaks very little English, but his name is Hassan and he agrees to take us to the Emirates border. So we find ourselves racing across no-man's land, with the English channel of Emirates radio promising two hours of 'hard-driving rock' and Hassan tossing spent Pepsi cans into the desert.

Our next piece of luck is that our patient Indian hire-car
driver, Vijay, is still waiting for us at the Emirates border,
despite being treated shamefully rudely by a young, officious,
Arab policeman.

We stop for a coffee at a transport café in the middle of
nowhere. It's run by Indians, who sit outside, in the hot, dry
night air, watching a Charles Bronson movie on video, at full
volume. Sex and violence I can take, but sex, violence *and* noise
is the worst of all. At one point the tape, obviously bootleg,
mixes without an apparent break from the middle of a Bronson
love scene to a wrestling match between two very fat
Americans, before a crowd of many more very fat Americans.
The Indians watching – slim, gentle people – appear not to
notice the difference.

We drive off and I sleep again and in my dreams huge neon
signs appear like mirages – 'Desert Springs Village', 'The
Emirates Golf Club', 'The Dubai Metropolitan', 'Safeway
Emirates', 'Beverage Filling Industries', 'The Princess Crown
Beauty Centre, Specialists In Skin And Body Care'. But it's all
real, and it's Dubai.

Uncrumple myself from the back seat. 2.20 a.m. We've been
on the road over 17 hours, and travelled 660 miles. We're
outside the Intercontinental Hotel, and I shall soon fall into the
ninth bed since leaving London. And the most welcome.

Day 16 10 October

Woken from a five-hour sleep by the sound of a telephone at my
bedside. Good news and bad news. The good news is that we
have secured a dhow to take us to Bombay. The bad news is that
it leaves at dawn tomorrow. No time for recovery before a six-
day voyage on an open boat. On the other hand the sooner we
move on the better. I must not forget that Phileas Fogg, aboard
the *Mongolia* all the way, reached Bombay in eighteen days.

Walk out onto the quayside. My first sight of a dhow. Only nostalgic, crossword-loving Western romantics still call them dhows. To the locals they are 'launches' or 'coastal vessels'. They are wooden, built to a traditional design resembling in shape a slice of melon, with a high stern on which sits the wheelhouse, a draught of 15 or 20 feet, and a length of about 60 feet. There seems to be no shortage of them in Dubai. There are 20 or 30 lined up in this inlet of the river they call The Creek. One is loading crates of 'Tiger's Head' brand flashlights, made in China, 'Coast' full-cream milk powder, boxes of Tide washing powder, 'White Elephant' dry-battery cells, Sanyo radios and a twin-tub washing machine. Its destination is Berbera in Somalia.

Every one of the dhows is like a floating small business, and generally run by family and friends, though owned, as likely as not, by some shrewd import-exporter in a stretch Mercedes. They present quite a different dockside ambience from any I've experienced so far. Instead of cranes and gantries and hard-hats and bulk loads and lorries, operating behind guard posts and fences, the dhows are serviced, right in the centre of town, by small pick-up trucks, trolleys and men's backs. People bustle around, scrambling over the boats like ants, arranging, moving, heaving and hoisting the cargo. The reason for the great activity at the moment is that these are some of the first boats out after the monsoon season from May to August, during which the dhows are laid up because of storms.

In the afternoon we are taken by Kamis, an agent for the port and customs department, to see the boat that will be our home for the next week. The M.V. *Al Shama* (meaning 'Candlelight') is a trim, freshly painted ship, and her captain, Hassan Suleyman, bounds across the deckful of date sacks to welcome us. He smiles broadly and constantly, especially when giving us bad news, so it is a moment before it sinks in that he is telling us he will not be leaving tomorrow, but the next day, Wednesday, 12 October. Day 18.

All the time made up on the hectic scramble from Jeddah is suddenly lost again, but there is nothing we can do. Clem disappears to have words with the owners, Nigel and the other Passepartouts to the other end of the quay to film. I'm left with the taxi drivers. One nods towards the *Al Shama*. 'You go on that?' He clearly can't believe it. The other joins in. 'These boats no restaurant!' He shakes his head vigorously, mistaking my smile for disbelief. 'No clean, nowhere sleep!' Now they both shake their heads, like witches. 'It will be six, seven days, you know. Terrible ... Terrible! Three days on a dhow, fifteen in hospital!'

Day 17 11 October

A day's respite (which I am sure we will pay for later). Run along the side of the creek before breakfast, while the temperature is still down in the eighties. Much of Dubai is high-rise, prosperous and rich, but the area where the small ships unload must be much like it was before they first struck oil.

Kamis was telling me that the years of the Gulf War were boom years for these small boats. They could scuttle about the place, largely unnoticed, behind blockades, and away from heavily patrolled harbours. It was the dhows that kept Iran supplied throughout the war. I ask him who stands to gain from the peace, so recently broken out. The question perplexes him. 'For me ... they are all my people ... Iranians, Iraqis ... I see them all.' They're traders, not warriors, in Dubai.

Later in the day we visit the local supermarket for provisions. None of us is quite sure what we shall need, apart from my bag of rice, though drinking water seems a good idea. So in addition to 108 bottles of local spring water, we emerge with a motley assortment of Western delicacies, such as Spam, corned beef, tuna chunks, kitchen roll and digestive biscuits.

Buying bedding is more problematical. There seems to be no such thing as a camping shop and I end up buying a Czech Li-Lo from one shop, a soft cushion from somewhere else and at a third, a tastefully embroidered flowery pillow case, a stripy sheet and a blanket from China.

I make some phone calls home. Am I too garrulous? Do I betray in any way a nagging suspicion that I might never see anyone again? Steve at the office tells me that *A Fish Called Wanda* has now taken 53 million dollars in the USA. He must think my reaction ungratefully cool, but I'm wondering if I have enough codeine phosphate for the next week.

Day 18 12 October

Wake about 5.30. Recurring images of bags and baggage, loading and unloading, have filled my dreams. I'm tired but I can't go to sleep again. It's good old-fashioned nervous excitement. After all, I am about to experience something which nothing in my life has prepared me for. At breakfast an hour later even Ron Passepartout, who has been with the Pope to Paraguay and Madhur Jaffrey to Sulawesi, is strangely subdued.

According to the *Khaleej Times* the forecast for this part of the Gulf is a maximum of 99 degrees, waves 1 to 3 feet. Sea gentle and slight.

8.30: On board the *Al Shama* Captain Suleyman is beaming. Something must be wrong. It is. We won't be leaving quite as early as we thought, so plenty of time to settle in to our quarters. These appear to be on top of some boxes of sultanas where a flat space has been cleared and covered in a tarpaulin. The boat looks very spruce. The captain is proud of the fact that he has cleaned the paintwork, not just with ordinary water, but with drinking water.

Before we can leave, we must once again go through the tedious business of customs and immigration. Outside the immigration office several truckloads of gently bleating sheep stand in the sun. Inside a group of white-robed desert men cluster round our passports like surgeons at an operation. There follows the now familiar shaking of heads. Confusion followed by suspicion and aggression.

'What is *this*? Where is your Dubai visa?'

Kamis, dabbing at his face with a small white towel, argues wearily, brandishing papers. But like customs authorities the world over, these people always want the one extra piece of paper you never have.

On the wall above the unsmiling immigration officers are photos of the two sheiks of Dubai, who look worldly and cunning, with long, narrow noses and hard eyes. Clem says they live near Newmarket.

10.20: At last our dhow casts off. As we turn slowly out into the harbour I feel that regret at leaving which I've felt everywhere so far (with the exception of Riyadh and Qatar). Travellers depend so much on people, and have to place enormous trust in them. Strangers become friends quickly, but all too briefly, and I'm sorry to see Kamis with his ready smile and podgy, sweating face grow smaller on the dockside. Even our hard-bitten taxi drivers are waving.

We are flying the Indian red ensign, and a Muslim pennant with a crescent moon against a green background, and from the prow of the ship hangs a garland of flowers and paper decorations, an offering to the gods for a safe passage.

No sooner are we out of harbour than I am offered a glass of tea – of the kind Indians favour with evaporated milk and lots of sugar – by a burly man in a baseball hat who introduces himself as Osman. The rest of the crew, all Indians, Gujaratis from north of Bombay, cluster round me as I drink. None of them has more than a few words of English, but all insist on giving me their names, and they watch closely as I write them down, correcting my spelling punctiliously and sometimes gently removing my notebook and writing in it themselves.

There are eighteen of them, all from the same village, ranging in age from the two teenage cabin boys, Anwar and Hassan, to the venerable elders like Deyji Ramji, the navigator, who looks, in his brown corduroy cap, like some Oxford poetry don, and Kasim with the craggy face, beady eyes and stubbly grey beard of the Old Man Of The Sea. In fact there is a vaguely theatrical Arabian Nights air to the whole outfit. With their torn shirts and carefully patched trousers, shining teeth and wide smiles, they look like the chorus from a Christmas panto.

One of the quartermasters, Dahwood Adam, sets up two fishing lines trailing back on either side of the stern, making use of a hook, a length of nylon and a glittering piece of wrapping paper from a pack of biscuits. A huge container ship passes us. The bulky, top-heavy outlines of the stacked containers are so much uglier than the simple lines of the dhow. As she passes I notice her name – *Orient Express* – and feel perhaps there is a guiding and coordinating hand behind this crazy journey after all.

First lunch on the dhow: thick, juicy rice with lentils and curried vegetables; pears, grapes and apples (sliced) for us. The food is prepared in a galley the size of a large dog kennel by Ali Mamoun, whose hat says 'Buick'. We eat in a patch of shade provided by canvas sheeting slung across the boom and made fast to the temporary scaffolding rail which girdles the ship and is the only barrier between the date sacks and the deep blue sea. Beneath the tarpaulin it's 98 Fahrenheit. Eating a curry in such conditions is like taking a hot water bottle into a sauna.

Gingerly try out the lavatories which consist of two wooden barrels, open to the elements and suspended over the ocean on either side of the stern. The base of the barrel has two wooden footrests on either side of a T-shaped aperture. Both these appendages have been painted a tasteful pale blue. I clamber in and settle down, feeling slightly ridiculous, like a character in an Edward Lear drawing. Later I realise I was facing the wrong way. I should have been looking out to sea.

Talking later to Passepartout it transpires that what we all fear, even more than sharks, pirates or a resumption of the Gulf War, is to miss our footing whilst clambering onto the loo in the middle of the night. What a way to go.

In the middle of the afternoon Osman, with a shy, schoolboy smile which belies his bulk, brings us, not just tea, but a selection of Huntley and Palmers assorted biscuits which would not have disgraced a Knightsbridge soirée. We are nibbling at the corner of a Garibaldi when there is a shout and everyone rushes to the stern. Momentary anxiety that Ron may have fallen through the toilet is dispelled when it turns out they've caught a fish on one of the trailing lines. It's a *gedri*, which we think is probably tuna. The indefatigable Ali Mamoun has it cooked and served for us by sundown, with lentils and chapattis.

Afterwards, having ascertained that the captain will not be offended as the crew are Muslims and take no alcohol, we're enjoying a nightcap of gin and tonic or in my case a glass of Glenmorangie malt whisky when the engine cuts out. The captain and the engineer disappear down below. There are sounds of protest, indignation and recrimination from the engine room. Deyji Ramji lights two incense sticks and waves them before the flag, and Kasim and Sali Mamoun, a short powerfully built older man with a peaceful face, are praying in the bows. Suddenly, I feel a little vulnerable. It's getting dark, there's no wind to fill a sail, there's no radio or radar on board and we're drifting slowly towards the Straits of Hormuz.

Day 19 13 October

Sometime in the middle of the night the sound of the engine, now restored to life, mingles with shouts and the rustling of feet about the boat. Orders and counter-orders. Sounds like another crisis. Blearily look around me to find that there are enormous craggy rocks rearing up on either side of us. We are squeezing through a narrow channel, less than a mile wide, without the help of any navigational machinery, and in the dead of night. It's a considerable test of skill for the captain. What he seems most concerned about is the presence of other ships in these labyrinthine waters, hence his shouted orders to various watchers along the rails. None of this feels like the twentieth century at all. It's as if I'm back in some ancient legend, and I half expect the rocks to transmogrify into vast mythical creatures.

Wake again about six o'clock, with the first light of dawn. We are now through Hormuz and into the Gulf of Oman. There is nothing to see at all but flat, calm empty sea. Later, just to make sure that what I'd seen in the night was no dream, I checked the charts, and found that we had indeed made a complicated passage around the Mussandam Peninsula, past Perforated Rock and the Elphinstone Inlet, and other points in a ragged archipelago just off the northern tip of Oman.

All is pretty quiet aboard the *Al Shama* this morning, the crew lie curled up on various parts of the deck, sleeping off the night's activity. Ali Mamoun, of course, is awake, already making chapattis and brewing tea. A small rattan mat of many colours is produced for us, and our breakfast of omelette, chapatti, jam and fresh oranges laid out on it.

As we're eating the sea around us turns leaden and heavy. We're passing through the thick, viscous smear of an oil slick. It extends for several miles, and is so obscene it silences us all. Osman being flat on his back against a sack of pistachio nuts, Mahomet has taken his role as our guardian. Mahomet, wafer-thin and with a crop of curly black hair, is the father of Anwar, the cabin boy, and brother of the captain. He speaks more English than most because he worked for a while as an international seaman. He produces a carefully kept notebook which lists the details of all his journeys away from home. The time he left, the time he returned, all neatly rounded up to a grand total of nine years, seven months and three days away. He will receive 300 rupees for this journey, about £20, but he's much happier to be working for this company than for the P&O group. Here he's with friends and family and though no one gets rich, everyone is in it together. As they all wake up they're eager to see how we're getting on. First we practise the names. They try to catch me out, producing shy crew members whose names they think I'll have forgotten. 'Mi-kel ... who this?' The homework I did yesterday has stood me in good stead, and if in doubt I just say Mohammed.

They are fascinated by my map of Asia, and when I spread it out it gives the better-travelled crew members a chance to show off. Many of them have been down the East African coast, to Somalia and Kenya, and one has been as far as Madagascar. Only Mahomet and his brother, the captain, have seen the world.

The captain appears late, rubbing his hands through thinning hair and apologising for all the upheaval in the night. His ablutions are extraordinarily thorough, especially in the oral department. Using his forefinger and regular ingestions of water he massages the inside of his mouth with a zeal and ferocity which seems almost manic, as if devils are being expelled. I think he's quite concerned about health and hygiene for he comes and squats beside me later and says he is very keen to know if there is treatment in London for '(a) Cancer, (b) Diabetes, (c) Receding Hair'.

At about 10.30 Deyji Ramji produces his sextant and stands on the starboard side pressing the instrument to his eye and steadying it on his chin. Then he produces a small gold-backed pocketbook, makes a note, disappears into the wheelhouse, consults various charts and comes up with our position, which this morning, October 13th, is 57.30 E and 25.0 North ... about 100 miles south of the coast of Iran. The captain estimates our arrival in Bombay in six days. Ron groans. I don't think he's got into the spirit of the thing yet.

Kasim, The Old Man Of The Sea, is showing a marked interest in my Walkman. I'm listening to Springsteen. I offer him the machine and he seems delighted. Give him a quick rundown on the controls and leave him to it. A little while later I see him, face wreathed in a smile, head rocking from side to side, eyes wide with excitement. Only when I've taken the set back from him do I realise he's been playing 'Incident on 57th Street' at full volume.

Tonight there are flashes of lightning on the southern horizon. There could be storms tomorrow. To bed feeling a little apprehensive. Bad weather would hit a boat like this very hard.

Day 20 14 October

Somewhere a long way away it's my wife's birthday and *A Fish Called Wanda* is being shown to the British public for the first time. Here in the Gulf of Oman my chief preoccupation is avoiding seasickness. During the night I was aware of a freshening wind and a not unpleasant increase in the ship's movement. Now, at 6.30 I'm feeling rather ill. The waves are coming in at a height of five or six feet and the wind from the south is causing a sideways roll to add to the impressive pitching and rising of the bows ahead. We have some anti-sickness plasters which have to be stuck on behind the ear, from which a chemical called scopolamine is released into the system, preventing nausea. All of us stick them on, making ourselves look like initiates of some new religion, apart from Nigel Passepartout, who seems quite unaffected by the rise and fall of the *Al Shama*. He has his camera out already and is trying to set up a prize-winning shot of old Kasim asleep with the sun rising behind his nose. Unfortunately everyone keeps tripping over the recumbent old man and waking him. When he sees the camera he is delighted and turns and stares into the lens with a fixed grin. Nigel gives up.

The last few feet of the bow area are reserved for washing. A plank, laid vertically across the deck, serves to run the water away and allows a certain modesty cover, but basically, the bathroom, like the lavatory and the bedroom on the *Al Shama*, is al fresco. Once the morning ablutions are done (and the Gujaratis are compulsive washers) the bathroom becomes a kitchen extension and now (8 o'clock) Ali Mamoun is preparing the lunch, rolling red chillies on a stone, and then chopping aubergines and onions.

A fish bites and we all rush to the stern, where for a moment a *gedri* of Moby-Dickish proportions breaks the surface and skids and spatters along the water allowing us just enough of its time to create tremendous excitement before flicking off the line almost disdainfully and returning to the depths.

With breakfast before seven and very little to do for the next twelve hours, time passes slowly. I finish *Stanley and His Women* and wade into a thick Spanish novel called *Fortunata and Jacinta*. But mostly I sleep. The sun becomes so strong that most parts of the boat are too hot to stand on, and simply moving around is highly energy-consuming. There are regular false fish alarms. At these times the *Al Shama* resembles a Second World War aerodrome, with combatants suddenly scrambling into action, only to reach the stern, bearing cameras and tape recorders, to find that yet another has got away.

After yesterday's dose of Springsteen on the Walkman, today I offer the crew Oistrakh's Brahms Violin Concerto. Anwar listens for quite a while before pronouncing it, 'Great disco!' Anwar tries a little bit more English on me each day. He's learnt it at school. Hassan his colleague knows only two words, 'Mi-kel' and 'Jack-son'. Whenever he sees me he grins manically and shouts, 'Mi-kel! Mi-kel Jack-son!'

I, in turn, press on with my Gujarati. I'm pretty handy with 'Thank you' (*mehrbani*), 'Good morning' (*salaam aligam*) and today, after a very good lunch, I embarked on 'Congratulations'

(*Mubarakhi*) and the less problematical *Thik-Thak* ('Hey man! Everything's OK').

Weather conditions improve during the day and seasickness is avoided. The captain informs us that we have just left the Gulf of Oman and are now in what he calls the 'Big Sea', the Arabian Sea. There is no land south of us now until Antarctica. Only ocean, through which we are making our way, at eight knots an hour, a pace at which many marathon runners could overtake us. The natural world assumes a much greater significance out here. The sky and the sea are watched anxiously. Apart from the fish alarms, the sight of a school of porpoises loping by or flying fish skimming across our bows can be the highlight of a morning, and now, at five o'clock, I find myself waiting impatiently for the next entertainment – the sunset. It's quite a short show, only about half an hour, but on a clear day like today, the view is immaculate and of course quite unobstructed. I watch every detail down to the five-minute climax when the golden ball comes to rest magnificently on the horizon before being squashed, squeezed and distorted out of sight, returning for a final brief manifestation as a shimmering disc on the surface of the sea, signalling that it's time for the infidels to get amongst the gin and Glenmorangie.

There's no lights out, because the lights never go out. So we're in bed by 7.30, looking up at the stars. Ron tunes in to BBC World Service for the 8 o'clock news from London. Gorbachev's proposed reform of Soviet agricultural policy seems wonderfully irrelevant.

I drift off to yet more sleep with a last lingering image of Nigel's head, with a miner's lamp-style torch strapped around it, protruding from his sleeping bag reading about another dhow trip in Gavin Young's *Slow Boats to China*.

Day 21   15 October

Fourth day on the dhow and life increasingly resembling that of a nursing home – waking with the dawn, then visiting, first the barrel, then the bows, making sure we take a bottle of our 'Jeema' mineral water for cleaning the teeth. Like invalids, all our movements are a little unsteady, what with the roll of the boat, the unevenness of the sacks and the necessity of having to virtually climb overboard to reach the loo.

Our Gujarati nurses have meanwhile prepared us a morning cup of tea which we drink slowly, comparing our sleeping experiences. Having compared notes and confirmed to an increasingly despondent Ron that there is absolutely no chance of us being in a nice comfortable hotel for at least four days, we then tidy our beds away (to the self-contained Gujaratis, with their neat bedrolls, our elaborate deflating of Li-Los and folding of striped sheets must look ridiculous) and turn the bedroom into the day-room. Our mat is laid out and breakfast taken. The crew will let us do nothing to help with the running of the boat, further fostering the nurse–patient relationship.

It's mid-morning. A fish alarm goes unheeded by the camera team who are playing backgammon. It turns out to be a whale, about a hundred yards off the port side spouting water every twenty seconds or so.

What have my books taught me today in my odd waking moments? That *tertulias* were, in nineteenth-century Spain, semi-informal meetings for conversation. We have a *tertulia* over lunch, the upshot of which is that it's decided we should film the sail going up this afternoon. The captain checks wind direction and speed with a quick look at the flag and seems unenthusiastic. He's clearly more comfortable with his 280 h.p. British-made Kelvin diesel engine.

Good news – we have travelled 204 miles in the last 24 hours, as opposed to 197 the day before. But there are still 720 miles between us and Bombay. Like a model patient I'm in bed and tucked up at some ludicrously early hour. The soft lapping of the waves and the steady chug of the Kelvin set a soporific mood and the last detail I remember of the world is that Sheffield United have won 2–1 at Blackpool.

Day 22 16 October

The boat really comes to life at first light which, as we are moving east and have not yet adjusted our watches, comes a little earlier each day. I'm awake today at 5 a.m. The wind has dropped and the sea is flat and calm. Over the reassuring rumble of the engine I can hear the soft sound of singing. Pull myself up on an elbow and look towards the bows. There is Kasim, standing motionless and in perfect silhouette, looking out to sea and chanting. Beside him two or three others are gathering in the small foresail.

''ello Mi-kel!'

'Mi-kel, Mi-kel Jack-son!'

As soon as they see we're awake someone is taken off foresail lashing and sent to arrange some tea for us. One of the things this traveller has learnt is that those who have least are prepared to give most. This crew has given up a lot for us – sleeping space, living space and precious fresh water – without ever making us feel obligated or tolerated. Their life is communal, they depend on each other rather than machines, and maybe because of this their attitude to us materially overstocked and somewhat stand-offish Westerners has been unfailingly generous and helpful.

The captain takes a look at the sea and removes his cap, scratches his head and shakes it respectfully. 'We are lucky men,' he says. He's rarely seen it quite as calm, and he knows the power of the sea, for in a storm last year, his brother's ship was sunk and 18 drowned.

The captain and his navigator sleep in the back of the wheelhouse. A new music centre and a pair of speakers are the only luxury. The only printed books appear to be navigational charts and almanacs. The front of the wheelhouse contains, apart from the wheel, a compass, a clock that's stopped, a throttle control and a bell that's rung every time the fish-line is sprung. There is also a panel of dials indicating engine r.p.m., water temperature and oil pressure. None of these is working.

Under the wheelhouse is a fetid, windowless airless cabin which I hope we never have to make use of. The temperature in there hovers constantly at 100 degrees, and Julian and Ron, who have to go in to load film and change stock, emerge pounds lighter. The corresponding aft cabin is full of the crew's trunks. They are allowed one each in which they can import certain items free of duty. A perk of the job.

Captain Suleyman says the Indian customs are very strict. No gold or guns.

'Is there then much smuggling?' I ask him.

'Oh, plenty smuggling … in clothes, wristwatches … but,' he reassures me, '*we* are not smugglers,' and laughs uproariously.

Midday: 92 Fahrenheit under the awning. We're due south of Karachi. Looking at my map I observe that it has taken us a day to travel between the 'A' and the 'R' of 'Arabian Sea'.

Sunday afternoon on the *Al Shama*. The crew sit round watching us read or sleep or listen to our headsets. They're curious but never intrusive. My fat Spanish novel intrigues them. How could anyone hold a book of such size, let alone write it, and why does it make Mi-kel's eyes close so frequently?

Suddenly there is some sea-borne entertainment. Dahwood, at the wheel, has spotted dolphins approaching the boat. They gather ahead of us, lazily and luxuriously rolling around in the bow wave, weaving in and out, diving, backtracking, returning and always keeping just ahead of the boat. The crew encourage them with drumbeats and whistles. As soon as they know there's an audience the dolphins show off shamelessly. For a magical few minutes they stay and play. The sea is so blue and clear it is one of the most remarkable and beautiful sights of the journey so far, rivalled a little later by the raising of the huge sail.

All hands are needed for this task, for there are no mechanical pulleys, no cables or electric winches. It's all done by human effort. Rather as they encouraged the dolphins they now encourage each other, chanting and singing as they pull on the rope. Once it's up, Kishoor and Haroun shin deftly up to the top of the 20-foot mast and release the cords that bind the sail, which billows down, revealing a much patched and stained canvas. But against the sky at night with a big moon shining it looks impressive and very beautiful. Indeed this is the most pleasing evening so far. Lying in bed beneath the boom with the sail spread out above and beyond it the clearest of night skies is almost perfectly peaceful. There is a request from Nigel to make it totally peaceful by turning off the engine. This produces a sharp cry of horror from Ron's bed! But engine or no engine it is the sort of moment when you would be quite happy for time to freeze.

Day 23 17 October

Having overdosed on happiness and contentment I pay the price a few hours later when an ungrateful stomach has me out of bed and swaying dangerously toward the barrel soon after midnight. Fierce acidic discomfort persists and I have to make three visits to the stern during the night. Each time I feel worse and each time I'm greeted warmly by the crew. Any hopes of slipping quietly by and enjoying my misery in private are out of the question. They all seem to be awake, and as I totter across the sacks of dates, on the point of nausea and clutching my lavatory paper, a chorus rises from the darkness:

'Mi-kel! …'Ello Mi-kel …'

'Mi-kel, Mi-kel Jack-*son*!'

And even more poignantly, 'Mi-kel … 'ow are yoo?'

The first time I react very Britishly, with a complete fib: 'Fine … fine, thank you!'

But later when my resistance is lower it's not so easy to be British about it: 'Mi-*kel*, 'ow are yoo?'

'Not at all well!'

'Good, Mi-kel!'

It doesn't really seem to make a scrap of difference what I say. They're just pleased to see me, whether white as a sheet and carrying an ever-decreasing roll of loo-paper or not. On my third and most traumatic visit they actually ask me to come and eat something with them, which at that moment is a bit like offering a vegetarian a job in a butcher's shop. I clamber back into my pit feeling sorry for myself and a cockroach walks over my head. By the time dawn comes the idyll has gone. There's nothing like feeling ill to make you want to be at home, and the smell of the morning omelette and chapatti induces a sudden feeling of imprisonment.

But outside the boat things are happening this Monday morning. We are now in the much shallower waters of the continental shelf and the captain shouts as he sees the marker buoys of a large fishing net. Apparently there are always fish to be found on the periphery of these nets. He orders the quartermaster to turn the ship smartly about.

Soon both lines are twitching and a 25 to 30 lb *arbrous* practically falls into the ship. No one seems to know quite what to do with it especially as a *gedri* has been caught at the same time, and the wretched fish lies panting in the bows, its tail flicking ever more weakly until an expert can spare the time to kill it.

By 8.30 a.m, four sizeable fish have been caught and everyone's looking not only pleased but relieved. Up till now the sea has not been fruitful. Ali Mamoun sets to producing his much-vaunted fish biryani and suddenly all the talk is of food.

They must notice that I'm not joining in with my customary ebullience, and Kasim seems especially concerned. He stands over me like some craggy bird for a while then indicates my stomach and rubs. I nod and offer the appropriate grimace. Kasim then indicates that I should turn over on my stomach. The accumulated wisdom of many years at sea is not to be questioned, but I'm certainly not prepared for what happens next. Kasim starts slowly and agonisingly to walk up and down my body, starting at my ankles and working his way along my spine. He's surprisingly light, but when his prehensile feet come into contact with my tender muscles the pain is excruciating. Kasim, quite unmoved by my cries, continues his walk.

There's no doubt about it, Kasim's feet are precision instruments, even if they are applied rather ruthlessly, and inasmuch as I can no longer remember which parts of my body hurt before he began, he's been successful. As he was busy realigning my spine, and Passepartout, with a certain amount of sadistic relish, was recording my cries, the prospect of a new form of TV chat show occurred to me, in which the host would talk to famous people whilst walking on them.

We are 200 miles from Bombay. Ron gloomily observes that this is the distance from which planes begin their descent into Bombay airport. *Our* approach is going to take two days. I must say that I am now beginning to feel very Ronnish. A dhow is not a good place to feel unwell – there really is nowhere to go and lick the wounds. The thought of Bombay, bed and bath seems irresistibly attractive.

The captain is concerned about me. 'You are sick, sick man,' he says and orders me to be brought his patent remedy, a glass of 7-Up with drops of lemon, knocked back in one go. This causes me to belch thunderously, after which all is well for a while.

*

Evening: Have not eaten today and worst of all the Glenmorangie has lost its attraction, so I am ill-prepared for the news that I shall not be in my bed in Bombay tomorrow night after all. The reason is that we shall reach Bombay at 7 in the evening and the Indian customs (keeping British Raj hours) close at 5. The captain does not want to spend the night in a busy harbour and is proposing we cut speed and wait a few miles out, dragging out our final approach until the morning of Wednesday, 19 October. I'm now likely to be a week behind Fogg at Bombay. I've lost so much time since Suez that an extra day doesn't seem to matter any more. By the law of averages we must have some good luck too.

Day 24 18 October

An air of anticlimax hangs over the boat. The elation of the first few days has been replaced by impatience and now resignation. At one time on the dhow I wanted time to stand still; now that it is, I just feel frustrated.

Our speed has been cut to four knots, a pervasive odour of fish hangs over the boat, for most of yesterday's catch is being dried for the return voyage. *Fortunata and Jacinta* is a terrible translation and I'm going to have to abandon it after 150 pages, which I always feel is a bit of a defeat. As I'm not eating I feel my energy reserves dwindling. Nowhere on the boat is comfortable any more. The clear bright skies are gone and it's cloudier, humid and very still. Even the weather seems to be waiting for something to happen.

The captain is less relaxed the nearer we get to Bombay. An Indian navy vessel passes slowly and he eyes it unhappily. Apparently they occasionally come aboard and ask awkward questions about gold wristwatches, especially if they know you are from Dubai.

The navy boat disappears over the horizon. The captain has a new stomach-cure for me today, 7-Up and black pepper.

Kishoor, the slim, dark engineer with big sensuous eyes, erects a screen in the bows before having a shower. This occasions the only real guffaws of the day. Apparently he is going to shave his entire body. When I ask why, I'm told, with much giggling, that his wife prefers him that way. At dusk more oil platforms sprout on the horizon, flaming away like mini-sunsets. Kasim walks on me again, and perhaps because I'm prepared for it, I don't react quite so pathetically.

Our seventh and last night on the dhow should be celebrated but, as the *Al Shama* turns in aimless circles, wasting time, Passepartout and I are subdued and quite soon get our heads down, taking refuge in the world of personal stereo whilst the crew sit round in groups, talking, for most the of the night. There's an end of term feeling aboard, and I feel that our inertia must be something of a disappointment to them.

Day 25 19 October

Wake to the sound of crackling cooking oil. Ali Mamoun is making puris (deep-fried fluffy pancakes) as a farewell meal. My stomach has now recovered sufficiently to make me feel hungry for the first time in 48 hours, but there's precious little time to eat. The captain shouts and points into the teeth of a welcome easterly wind.

'Bombay!'

The engines, which have been idle most of the night, are restarted.

Anwar is very excited. 'Indies ... Indies!' he keeps shouting to me.

The grey mist is lifting and revealing a long, tall, unexpectedly modern skyline, which surprises me – I'd expected Bombay to be low-rise and cluttered. I can now make out my destination – the Gate of India, a triumphal arch erected for the visit of George V in 1910. But first we have to go on, southwards to the Hay Bunder, the dhow port, passing a lot of ill-kept and rusty-hulled freighters and the navy base containing the largest warship I've seen so far, the 16,000-ton ex-British aircraft carrier *Vikrant* (née *Hercules*).

At about ten o'clock we are opposite the port, but as the dhow cannot go alongside until customs and immigration have come aboard, the crew prepare to weigh anchor. This procedure, like raising the sail, involves all hands – old men and boys, side by side, releasing the anchor and lowering it into the murky water. Scavenging crows board the ship, followed by three well-built customs men in dark glasses.

So the time comes to say goodbye to the people in whose hands we have entrusted our lives for the last week. It's been a unique relationship, for I can't imagine any other circumstances in which we would have become so close so quickly to people like this, and of course it's hard to come to terms with the fact that it must end so peremptorily. But I clutch a batch of addresses and Kasim clutches me and I climb down the rope ladder to waves and smiles and 'Goodbye Mi-kels!' Then my launch speeds me to the quayside and I know I shall never see them again and I shall miss them.

Into Indian customs 'F' Division hut. Seeing men in unpatched shirts is quite a shock. Their uniforms are clean and crisply pressed, which is something of a contrast to the general condition of the hut, which looks like somewhere commandeered behind the lines in wartime – dusty with cracked walls and a sackcloth ceiling. There is no door, but a curtain. The officers are very charming. Then outside to meet the owners of the dhow. There are two of them, sharply dressed in the manner of international hairdressers – Cuban heels, expensive shoes, Afro haircuts. They stand holding hands on the quayside and seem to have little to say to us.

Then back into a small launch to take me to the Gate of India. Despite its name no one enters India through it any longer, apart from royalty I suppose, so it's a very curious feeling to scramble off here, with my bags, clothes crumpled from seven days in a dhow. There are snake charmers and drug pushers and men with monkeys and women with babies and outstretched hands. Indian life is no respecter of great monuments, especially one so prominently associated with alien domination, nor does Indian life have to be sought out in back streets and certain quarters of town. It begins, like the heady, warm smell of spice and manure, as soon as you set foot on the land.

A hundred yards further on I am confronted by a completely different world again – a world of turbaned doormen, Mercedes limousines, air-conditioning and American Express. The world of the Taj Mahal Hotel. I'd been dreaming about its soft beds and clean sheets for days but now I'm here, grubby and unshaven in the lobby, I find it sour and rather objectionable. For a week I've been in a world where rank, class and social distinction don't exist. Now I see it all around me. Of course I'm happy to be comfortable and to be looked after and to enjoy the style and splendour of the hotel but I hope I never forget the values of simplicity, honesty and unselfishness which I associate with the *Al Shama*.

A copy of the *Indian Express* is in my room. The government is thinking of lowering the voting age to 18. A stay of execution has been granted on two assassins of Mrs Gandhi and on the entertainments page I see there is a play in Bombay called *No Sex Please, We're Hindustani*. It's billed as 'The Ultimate Laugh Riot'.

Spend an afternoon unwinding, and checking my onward plans. I hear that all is not well for the next connection in Madras. The ship I was relying on has been delayed to mid-November and the only alternative, so far, has no room. All the timetables have been disrupted by a dock-workers' strike in Bombay.

In the evening I walk along the Apollo Bunder, which extends along the waterfront from the Taj, enjoying the street life, the old-fashioned and ubiquitous Ambassador cars, the smells, the crumbling hotels on the front called 'Evelyn' and 'Shelley's' – the ever-present parody of Britain. It's better than being a parody of America, which is what Saudi Arabia was. There's a big, bright noisy party being held out on a pier. Folk dance inside which looks like an Indian Morris dance. Much striking of sticks. Sends me to bed happy, on my first night in Asia.

Day 26 20 October

'It's out of the question for a sane man to spend his life jumping from one steamer onto a train and from a train onto a steamer, on the pretext of going round the world in eighty days! No, all these antics will come to an end in Bombay, you can be sure of that.'

I pondered on Passepartout's words as I lay in bed after waking at dawn from a night during which my room had very gently rocked from side to side. Passepartout's gloomy prediction is nearer to my experience than his own. He and Fogg arrived here in eighteen days, and left on a train across India within three and a half hours, during which time Fogg saw nothing of the city save for the inside of the station restaurant, where he was served with cat disguised as rabbit.

I'm eight days behind Fogg, and as yet I have no onward passage from Madras to Singapore. The dhow was a wonderful week out of life; now the realities must be faced and some clear thinking done. But somehow Bombay is not the best city, nor India the best subcontinent for clear thinking.

It's quiet now on the quayside below me, though I'm sure I heard marching bands and a confusion of drumbeats and explosions in the early hours. All I can see from my window are children and street sellers around the Gate of India and pigeons wheeling and flapping about the façade of the hotel. The fussy little balconies and turrets which project from every sea-view room are a pigeon's delight and, judging by the thick encrustations of bird lime, have been since the hotel was opened eighty years ago. Walk down to breakfast. The layout of rooms along open galleries leading off a central staircase gives the impression of a sumptuous prison. There are huge arrangements of flowers about the place and I make the mistake of asking the lady who's setting them out if they're real.

'Of course they're real,' she replies admonitorily, 'this is India, not Hong Kong.'

I glean from her the reason for the unnatural quiet on the Apollo Bunder, and the noises in the early hours which, like another traveller in the Indies, Waugh's Gilbert Pinfold, I'd begun to think were my imaginings. Today is a festival day called Durga Puja, the climax of a ten-day celebration of the triumph of good over evil. There are at least seven different New Years in India, depending on when the harvest is brought in. Effigies up to 50 feet tall will be carried through the streets and destroyed to commemorate the killing of the evil king Ravenah of Sri Lanka by Lord Rama. The celebration of myth and the belief in the supernatural is an important part of Indian life, and on this festival day it is customary to bless whatever brings you your livelihood. So the soldier garlands his rifle and the photographer his camera and the farmer his plough and so on. This is called *puja*, meaning worship, and would probably explain the garland on the prow of the *Al Shama* as she left Dubai.

I venture into the streets of Bombay in search of someone to remove eight days' growth of beard. If you look around with only reasonable diligence you can find someone on the street to do anything for you. I end up opposite the grand Gothic pile of Victoria Terminal – one of the most gushingly elaborate station exteriors in the world. Sandwiched in between a professional letter writer and a man who organises mongoose and snake fights, I find a barber who shaves me then and there on the grubby pavement with a cut-throat razor. Not something I shall tell my mother about, especially as I'm convinced from the way his fingers rather than his eyes seek out my face that he is blind. By the time he's finished shaving me, a crowd has gathered that would not disgrace a third division football club. The barber completes the shave by rubbing my face with a smooth piece of alum, a crystal-like stone which is used as an antiseptic.

Passepartout is more interested in the mongoose and snake attraction next door, but as soon as the presence of the camera is detected, the snakes are popped back in their baskets and a furious row ensues. It seems their owner knows all about world television rights and he negotiates with a single-mindedness that would assure him of a vice-president's job in any Hollywood studio. A man with a hooded cobra in one hand has to be listened to. The 'fight' itself is a pathetic and ugly affair. The mongoose, looking terrified throughout, is not only chained to a stone, but has its front legs tethered so that it couldn't kill the snake even if it wanted to. The snake man tries to introduce a note of danger by continually ordering back the fly-blown street children who are his chief audience. But the mongoose is clearly not interested in exterminating any snakes today and has to be forcibly yanked upwards to simulate aggression. Of the five snakes kept in baskets, only the cobra looks fit; the rest are dry and docile. This whole grubby spectacle takes place only a few hundred yards from the bewhiskered bust of Lord Elphinstone and his fellow Victorians whose idea of civilising India was to build massive public buildings in the architectural style of a continent five thousand miles away.

The oldest surviving English building in Bombay is a more modest affair than the Victoria Terminal. It's a church, with a simple perpendicular tower, completed in 1718 and full of sad memorials to those who, by and large, died young and far away from home. Of 'cholera, aged 32', of 'wounds received at Lucknow, in the mutiny, aged 23'. Now it is St Thomas's

Cathedral, the main Christian church of Bombay. I assume wrongly that it is frequented by the English community, but the priest in charge tells me that the congregation consists entirely of native Christians, and that Christianity, far from being a relic of the Raj, is the third most popular religion in India, after Hinduism and Islam.

The key to India's remarkable success as the world's largest democracy is, he says, tolerance. There are 16 different religions in India and all respect each other. There are, on one Indian banknote, 14 different languages, all of which are protected.

On my way back to the hotel I find the road blocked by chanting crowds who are milling around slow-moving trucks carrying effigies of the goddess Kali and making a lot of noise; banging cymbals, dancing and singing. They have crimson powder all over them and the Indian photographer who is with me says that their wild stares are probably the result of a certain amount of ganja. 'Join in!' he urges, and leaving me to be swept along towards the Gate of India he rushes off to get some shots. I don't know what's happening, except that I'm the only white man there and I'm being carried along in the crush toward the great arch and the sea. At about the spot where I landed yesterday they begin to submerge their goddesses, tossing in garlands, offerings in small clay pots and, very often, themselves. Some of the more intense disappear beneath the muddy waters for a minute or more, to reappear jubilantly soaked. There is an edge of hysteria which I'm glad to escape from unscathed.

Day 27 21 October

Extraordinary night of dreams. A series of benevolent nightmares on the theme of travelling but never arriving. Recurring images of friends and home veering wildly from the modern (new information systems being installed at Swiss Cottage Underground) to a Hardyesque world of country pubs and masques and morris dances. An Indian postal official dumps his sports bag in my car, I try desperately to ring my wife and tell her why I'm in Washington D.C. with George Harrison and the next moment I'm driving a Mini over a ploughed field. The reality is that I'm in India, which is more bizarre than any of my dreams. I read in my *Times of India* at breakfast that fourteen people were killed yesterday in a stampede at Jamshedpur during the immersion of their goddess in the local river.

Taxi to Victoria Terminal to collect my rail tickets for tomorrow. On the way we pass a shop called Dogy Items and another mellifluously named The Lovely Steel Centre. Traffic conditions in Bombay are anarchic. Pedestrians and cows have as much right to be in the road as cars and this makes for a constant disorderly fight for space. My cab has a sticker on the dashboard which reads 'Trust in God'.

Despite the noise and heat and smell at Victoria Terminal, the faces in the crowd show none of the tension, anxiety or pent-up anger which you can see any morning or evening at a London main-line station. I think it boils down to tolerance again. The Indians do not betray impatience. They accept everyone's right to be wherever they are. Thus poverty and appalling destitution, malnutrition and deformity are on public view, but nervous breakdowns are almost unknown. The ticket office presents the modern face of India, all smoked glass and VDU screens. They're very proud of it and I am asked if I will sign their Distinguished Visitors Book. The head man stands over me as I write and prompts me. 'Yes, just there please ... Staff all very cooperative, very good conditions ... nice and modern. Thank you.'

And I'm out again, clutching my seat reservation, into the street with its blind and limbless beggars alongside red pillar boxes and 1930s-style double-decker buses.

There are more aspects of British India left than just the buses and the pillar boxes. The world's largest democracy drives on the left and plays cricket. The English language unites north and south and east and west of a country that has no other common tongue. But India remains, like few other countries in the world, its own place, the archetypal non-aligned nation, putting self-sufficiency before luxury, a social and economic buffer-zone between the thrusting certainties of Western and Oriental capitalism.

I end the day at the Chowpatty beach. From here the tower blocks of Nariman Point make the Bombay skyline twinkle like Manhattan. Here on the beach at night is a public massage school, where students try out their technique on anyone willing to take the risk. I settle for a scalp massage. It's so powerful that I actually worry at one point that his fingers may enter my head, in a sort of digital acupuncture.

Day 28 22 October

In order to convince some of the sceptical friends who haunt my dreams at night that I am not mocking all this up in a BBC studio I have undertaken to try and bring back various items as proof of travel. One has asked for an Indian astrological chart for their first child, expected next April. It so happens that the Taj is the only hotel I know of in the world which has a resident astrologer. So this Saturday morning I repair to Mr Jagjit Uppal, a pleasant, soft-spoken man with a serene but disturbingly impenetrable smile. Astrology, he confirms, plays a big part in Indian life and he is regularly consulted by businessmen, politicians and film stars. He needs to know only dates, places and exact times of birth to give a fluent prediction. Having collected my friend's chart I ask him about my own prospects, especially for the next 52 days. Fixing me with big round eyes he assures that as bright stars, Jupiter and Venus, govern my future, all my problems are over. My journey from now on will be smooth and I am destined to arrive on time or even early. I see the director's face drop. It may be good astrology but it's bad television. Personally I'm rather relieved.

Having put the cost of predicting my future down on my hotel bill, I venture out for a last look at Bombay before I take the Madras train this afternoon. I find myself in one of the poorest parts of the city. For several hundred yards along a high wall are clusters of dwellings assembled from bits of old cardboard, corrugated iron, sacks and assorted pieces of wood and metal. It looks like a long rubbish tip but it is, in fact, the most basic form of terraced housing. Yet, as I walk along past these rickety tenuous little coverings, I see very little sourness and despondency. There is dignity in the faces of mothers washing in the water from the standpipe. Eyes are not averted in embarrassment or shame, the children are responsive, lively and curious. Once again I'm confused and surprised by the way India works. Poverty seems not to be judged as failure, as it is in the West. Here it is a fact of life. There are too many people and too few jobs. Those who have little or nothing are not cleared off the streets or shoved out of sight. To make something out of almost nothing, as in the case of these families huddled against the high wall, is an achievement, and that shows in their faces. But as soon as we start to film, and I cease to be a solitary wandering foreigner, the relationship changes and children who have hung on my arm and laughed when I've pulled silly faces become suddenly inquisitive. Some bigger children join the group. One feels in my pocket. By now the word has gone out that I have money, and money changes the group from hanging on to me in good humour to clinging menacingly, and with frightening speed inquisitiveness turns to anger.

Just before we leave the Taj Hotel I take a last walk by the sea. I'm approached by a man who says he'd seen me dancing at the Durga Puja festival yesterday. Had I enjoyed it? Having ascertained that I had, he falls into step alongside and proceeds to try and interest me in other aspects of Indian life.

'You want woman?'

We walk on for a bit.

'I can show you fifty thousand women.'

This is a bit of a leap. 'Fifty *thousand*?'

'More, more,' he adds hastily, misinterpreting my surprise. He is referring to the red light area of Bombay, known as The Cages, which someone had wanted to take me to on the first night off the dhow. I wasn't really interested then or now. He goes on to offer 'Good boys', 'temple carvings' and 'a joint' before giving up.

I feel like a paragon of virtue, but really I'm just trying to take in, on my own, some last impressions of the atmosphere of Bombay – like most of India, enticing, elusive, imprecise, uncertain and seductive. But a foreigner, strolling on his own in Bombay, will not be alone for long.

Now we're on our way to the station passing, outside the 'Ear, Nose, Throat, Deafness and Vertigo Clinic', a huge Bruce Springsteen hoarding, and a big rather ugly statue of Mahatma Gandhi, much less affecting than the modest one in Tavistock Square in London. This one appears to be made of shiny brown plastic and makes him look like a Martian.

We pull up at Dadar Station at two o'clock, our minibus driver sliding in beneath a sign reading 'Parking For Four Bullock Carts Only'.

Train travel in India is not restful, and the shredding of the nerves begins as soon as you enter the station. The Indians seem to revel in the arguments and mis-arrangements and hustle and heat and chaos. Though my name is clearly spelled out on the computer-printed list of passengers, posted on the platform: 'Michael Palin ... male ... 45 ... 194/64', it appears that there are two other people called Michael Palin in 194/64, and one of them is a woman.

Part of the problem is that Indian Railways is the largest civilian employer in the world, and for every single problem

Slowboat to India:

PREVIOUS PAGE: *Man with a BBC series on his mind.*

ABOVE: *Captain Suleyman and Deyji Ramji show me the way.*

RIGHT: *Anwar does his* Treasure Island *audition.*

FAR RIGHT: *The rising sun wakes Kasim.*

BELOW RIGHT: *With Clem and Ron in the library.*

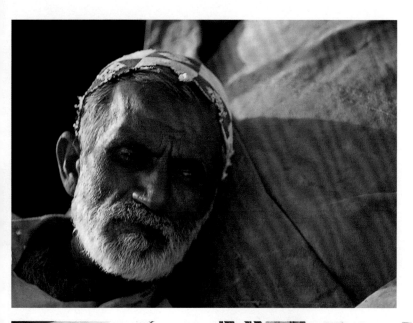

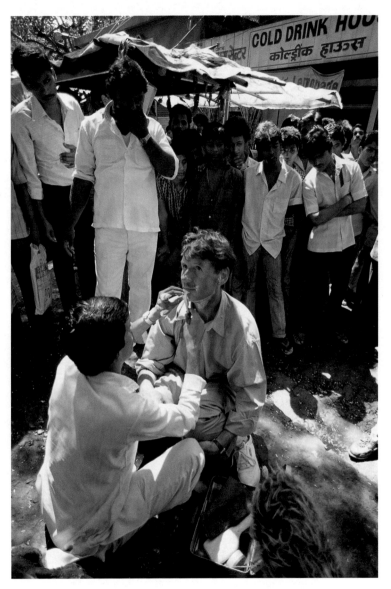

LEFT: *Preparing to leave the dhow at Bombay.*

ABOVE: *Shaved by a blind barber with a cut-throat razor.*

ABOVE: *Looking out over Bombay from the top of the hideous extension to the Taj Mahal Hotel.*

RIGHT: *A family in Tent City.*

ABOVE: *The hot and lively streets of Madras.*

RIGHT: *'Déjeuner sur la mer' or barbecue day on the Susak.*

you have there are about eight people all with different ideas of how to solve it. A hapless man called Mr Nitti has been detailed to accompany us and look after all our needs. He is nowhere to be seen.

We leave on time at 2.30. Our journey across 775 miles of India will take 27 hours and we shall make 30 stops. The implacable couple called Michael Palin sit resolutely surrounded by BBC equipment, quite unmoved by the entreaties of the recently located Mr Nitti. I sit in the corridor with the window open, glad to feel a breeze on my face and glad to be circumnavigating again. I could well do with a cool Kingfisher beer but the only bars on this train are across the windows.

The suburbs of Bombay slip by, presenting a Caribbean or West African aspect, with a cover of bamboo and palm trees amongst which are tethered cows and goats on small scrubby patches of land beside stained concrete shacks. These give way to battered shanty housing of great ugliness in the midst of which are people walking hand in hand, talking, smiling, sharing loads and generally behaving most cheerfully.

The train is progressing comfortably but unspectacularly, at 50 or 60 miles an hour. The lines are busy, with much more freight being moved than in Britain. Our meals are ordered ahead, so we have to decide on tonight's supper at 4.30 and tomorrow's breakfast about an hour later. Details are phoned through to the relevant stations, so if the train is late so is supper and breakfast.

My compartment is First-Class non-air conditioned. First-Class air-conditioned are apparently very cold and have windows tinted so thickly that you can hardly see out. There is a 'Western-Style Latrine' at one end of the carriage which has a sit-down lavatory and a push-button water dispenser that fires straight over the basin and into the trousers. As we begin an eye-catching climb out of the humid, tropical plain into the cool red hills of the Western Ghats, I'm allowed to ride in the cab. The locomotive, a diesel-electric, was made in Newton-le-

Willows 31 years ago. Though it would have been long retired in England, it heaves and shudders powerfully up the gradients and through the tunnels. Sweeping views of softly sunlit, wooded slopes below.

I notice that though every window on the train, even the small, thick side-windows of the engine, is barred, the track ahead is completely unfenced and clearly used as a public highway. Apparently oblivious to the oncoming presence of a 17-coach intercontinental express, a group of 20, mostly women, are picnicking between the rails at Karjat Station. Goats graze suicidally on the track until we're almost on top of them, cows amble across the line and even in the middle of a tunnel our headlight picks up a man in a white dhoti coming towards us carrying his shopping.

As the engine works harder and the air swirling into the cab becomes fresher and cooler I think of my father taking this train 60 years ago, for he visited the regatta at Poona when he worked in India as an engineer. A silver mug celebrating his part in a coxless fours victory and inscribed 'Royal Connaught Boat Club, Poona 1929' stood on our mantelpiece throughout my childhood, and now, as daylight fades, I find myself crossing the river where it was won. But Poona is now spelt Pune and it's an awful anticlimax, grey and industrial and no sign of flannelled fools.

At Daund our meal arrives on a tin tray, neatly portioned with yoghurt, dhal, chapattis and a small vegetable curry and rice. As we eat a station official peers in from the platform and advises us to shut our window, lower the bulky steel shutters and to sleep with our feet facing the window.

Part of the exhaustion of Indian travel is the profusion of things to see. At every station there is something going on. Some fierce argument, a pair of monkeys scouring the platform, a steam engine with *puja* garlands draped over its boiler, a line of military tanks on low loaders, their barrels hung with washing.

At Kurduvadi at ten past ten. We're now up on the wide central plateau, the Deccan, as I remember from 'O' level geography, and running about fifteen minutes late. I'm not much reassured by a board on the station which reads 'Trains Running Late May Make Up Time Or Loose Time'. No bedding has come aboard for us and Mr Nitti has disappeared again. I feel absolutely exhausted and fall asleep using my bag as a pillow. About 12.30 I'm woken from deep sleep by the arrival of our bedding at Solapur. Never really get back to sleep again.

Day 29   23 October

Another Sunday, and into my fifth week away. At this moment home seems very far off and the prospect of seeing family and friends again in 50 days utterly remote. But at least we are moving east, and there is daylight through the shutters. There's also an insistent pounding on the door. I open it and find a small, grubby, bearded man standing there looking disgruntled. He demands to know what I want for lunch:

'Chicken biryani very nice,' he proposes briskly, and when I don't show instant enthusiasm (it *is* seven o'clock in the morning) he looks irritated: 'Egg curry, Western style, very nice.'

An order for several biryanis, accompanied by payment, is all that will get rid of him, and I hear him go on to the next compartment. He knocks at this door persistently for at least 15 minutes, too afraid to open it, too dogged to give up.

Not wanting to wake the rest of the compartment, I visit the Western-style latrine, then consult the two railway officials sitting in the corridor as to our whereabouts. Guntakal Junction is the next stop. How long would that be?

'Fourteen minutes,' says one, very positively.

'Half an hour,' pronounces the other authoritatively.

We pull into Guntakal Junction 45 minutes later. When I next look, both men are gone.

Outside there are rain clouds in the skies. A boy waves at the train, further on an older man pulls his trousers up after depositing another load of what is poetically known as night soil.

The bird life is rich and I wish I knew what they all were. Egrets perch on bullocks and the rest pose on the telegraph lines as if in an ID parade – parrots, hooded crows, shrike, kite, humming birds. Some of the bullocks' horns have been painted bright blues and reds. Pride of ownership, I'm told. Like putting 'Les and Christine' across your car windscreen. There are no tractors in the fields, not even a bicycle.

Crowds of passengers disembark at Guntakal's 'Bathing Cubicals', which are lines of basins with a cold water supply running along them. They clean their teeth vigorously and wash themselves. I buy a newspaper. 'Punjab Ultras shoot dead 12 Harijans', '8 Killed in Lanka Violence'. Tolerance clearly has its limits. Inside there is a small piece on the arts page about the government's recent ban on Salman Rushdie's *The Satanic Verses*. The writer seems to think that the authorities have over-reacted and that the book is difficult and probably quite inaccessible to those it's being banned to protect. There's also a long letter of complaint about the number of soaps on Indian TV. *Ramayan* and *Mahabharat* (sponsored by Dunlop) come in for most criticism.

Mr Nitti is still with us and, as he couldn't find any room for himself elsewhere, is installed in our compartment. He's now been joined by his counterpart from Southern Railways, a Tamil. He has nowhere to sit either so we all move up. The irony is that they're here to make sure we're comfortable. They talk to each other in English as Mr Nitti has no Tamil and the Tamil no Hindi. The first thing they do is cancel my lunch order. Apparently I should not have given in to the small bearded man, however much he knocked on my door. He is not a good man and his lunch will not be good. They propose instead a Southern Railways Special, and are justifiably proud of what arrives. It's a thali, which is a sort of south Indian vegetarian meze, with all sorts of different fruits in pickles and curries and dhals and raitas, fresh and sharp.

After lunch we descend slowly from the plain to the hot coastal strip. We're now in the province of Tamil Nadu. The complexions are darker, the earth a deeper red, and the settlements less drab. Much smiling, from slim graceful faces, and a characteristic rolling wobble of the head as they speak. I talk to a much-travelled lady from Madras, a paediatrician in her mid-forties, brought up on English literature. She says that southern Indians feel infinitely superior to the northerners. It starts to rain. Gentle showers. More like sweat than real rain, and soon past. I buy a bag of nuts at one stop, to find that the paper cornet they're served in is made from a page of *Alice in Wonderland*.

Arrive in Madras 45 minutes late. I'm thrust aboard a rickshaw and pedalled off to the Connemara Hotel. A parting glimpse of Madras station. Imposing scale, big pink Gothic tower and a loggia on either side. The neo-Renaissance effect spoilt by an extensive corrugated-iron roof. Over a foul-smelling river we go, my straining Tamil and I, past lots of adverts mainly for films and cigarettes, past The Convent School of Commerce and over a succession of speed-breakers in the road – rather a cruel obstacle to throw at my driver, as he's only doing about three miles an hour anyway.

Down Marshall's Road and Monteith Road and into the gates of the Connemara Hotel – a low thirties-style building, which looks more Croydon than Madras. As soon as we pull up, we're waved out of the way by an officious doorman to accommodate a white Mercedes, from which descends a very well-dressed couple indeed. I have arrived in the middle of a wedding party. Rich Indians fill the foyer as I walk through. I catch sight of myself in the mirror. I look like a scarecrow.

Unshaven, unkempt, clothes crumpled after a night sleeping in them. A burgeoning cold sore. The manager pushes through the crowd towards me. I'm sure he's going to take me round the back and fumigate me. But no, someone has told him that this tramp is a VIP and I find myself garlanded, given the mark on my forehead by a beautiful woman, and led to my room by the assistant manager himself. I find myself gushing apologies for my appearance.

The bath and the cold beer that follow are two of the most wonderful experiences of the journey so far. I feel, perhaps prematurely, that I have survived India.

Day 30 24 October

Not out of the woods yet. The earliest boat to Singapore doesn't leave for 48 hours. It's a Yugoslav freighter chartered by a German company called Bengal Tiger Lines. The chief, and as far as I can see, insurmountable problem is that the ship has no space for passengers. There is a crew of 18 and only 18 places in the lifeboat, so it would be illegal and uninsurable to take any supernumeraries. There is no other sailing to Singapore until the end of the week. We have to try and put pressure on Bengal Tiger Lines for a compromise. Added to this uncertainty Roger Mills, director on this leg, who, like me, felt pretty lousy on the train, has come down with sweats and a temperature. So a day off is called, our first non-filming day since we left.

After a breakfast of paw-paw, fresh pineapple juice and brown toast I nose around the hotel. There is a pool and a small bookstore called Giggles, which doesn't sound promising but is a treasure trove inside. Though only the size of a couple of cupboards it seems to contain a comprehensive selection of all the latest novels, but the chatty, intelligent lady who runs it is still not satisfied. 'I'm after them every day for *Bonfire of the Vanities*, and every day they let me down.' She will stock *The*

Satanic Verses. 'After the elections the ban will be lifted. It's all so political.' I ask her why she called the place Giggles.

'Because I started it for a giggle,' she replies very seriously.

I buy Ellman's Oscar Wilde biography, a Ruth Prawer Jhabwala and a J. L. Carr novel, *A Season in Sinji.*

Meet two southern Indians who are staying at the hotel but working abroad, one as a bookie in South Africa, a country he thinks most highly of, and another in Singapore.

'What's so good about Singapore?' I ask him, a little peevishly.

'They work hard. Nobody cheats.' And he proceeds to warn me against the greed and duplicity of his fellow Indians.

The day passes most agreeably, reading, sleeping and generally behaving more like Fogg.

I attempt some sightseeing later on, but don't get very far. It's Mohammed's birthday and already hellish traffic conditions are augmented by processions and truckloads of flag-waving Muslims driving about, horns blaring. Retreat back to the hotel to find a crowd outside in the street, peering over the wall. A feature film is being shot in the hotel grounds by an outfit called Prasad Art Pictures. It doesn't look like an art picture. The leading actor is on the chunky side and dressed very early seventies in a black shirt with collar turned up and white pants stretched tight across his bottom, flaring to white leather boots with Cuban heels. He's obviously a big favourite with the crowd and a ripple of excitement goes through them when he occasionally glances over towards the wall and waves. When he's not looking a security man sprints across to the spectators and whacks them viciously with a stick. The star casts his eye cursorily over a script held up in front of him by a minion, whilst another pats periodically at his perspiring face. His female co-star wears almost as much make-up as he does. She too is on the stout side, but an undeniably good-looking lady. Their hands remain entwined after the take.

Whereas many hotels have taken to providing the freshly tooth-washed guest with a nice little chocky on the pillow, the Connemara provides instead a small but intriguing package with the words 'For Your Comfort'. Inside are two cotton buds and a nail file. The nail file is a bit chewy, but the cotton buds are delicious.

Day 31　25 October

Extraordinarily good English Sunday lunch at Roger's beautiful house on the Suffolk coast. Even as I scrape away at a meagre slice of paw-paw it's hard to believe it was another of my British Tourist Authority dreams. I've described the house to Roger and he's promised to get one like it as soon as possible. He's a pale shadow of himself this morning, having sweated through a day and night's fever, but at least he's up and about and we all go off together to film the news as it happens in two shipping offices.

It's nine o'clock when we leave the hotel and Madras is already, like its curry, hot and lively. The big film on the hoardings is *Grunt – The Wrestling Movie*. We pass the oldest Christian church east of Suez, St Mary's. It was built in 1680 and designed by a British gunner, who built the walls four feet thick and the roof a foot deep. Then we swoop down into a four-lane underpass which is being swept with a single straw brush by a lady in a green sari.

The office of the agents for the Bengal Tiger Shipping Company, Babuji Jetsea Freights, is located on the corner of Ebrahamji Street, where the countryside has come into the city. Wandering goats pick up what they can from broken sidewalks and sleeping dogs and naked children sit about. When we arrive Vikram, a young, personable Tamil who is in charge of our case, is talking to Lloyd's of London to try and effect some insurance deal for us on the Yugoslav freighter the *Susak*. He fails. Our only hope now is a plan of Clem's which involves substituting myself, the cameraman and sound man for members of their crew who would be flown to Singapore at the BBC's expense. Vikram promises to put this to the owners.

We go on to check out the next possibility at the New Indian Maritime Agency in Armenian Street. The street is a director's dream. Every image of India apart from the Taj Mahal is gathered here. There are street sellers and bullock carts and cars and stalls full of aromatic garlands of rose and jasmine and there is, across the street, St Mary's Cathedral in whose forecourt, beyond a sign reading 'Take Care Of Your Money Jewels And Things', an Indian priest in a white surplice is blessing a long line of supplicants. The beggars are everywhere. One man has a piece of string around his big toe and is tugging at it. Others display mutilated hands and limbs. The cathedral bell tolls.

Three floors above all this I'm shown into the office of a Mr Arul, who has another Yugoslav ship, the *Kamnik*, on his books. He is a most singular man, an ex-chief of police in Madras, living out his retirement as a shipping agent. He tells me that the bell is the sound of the angelus and on Tuesday anyone of any condition can come along to be blessed, hence the lepers and cripples. He describes all this quite matter-of-factly. He goes on to bemoan the water shortage in the city. Because the monsoon has failed here for the last three years water is desperately short and available on alternate days only. I ask about the hotel, feeling guilty about my luxurious baths.

'Oh, they will have private suppliers, of course.'

He assures me that the *Kamnik* will be our very best way of proceeding to Singapore. There is room for everybody and it leaves in three days. The catch is that whereas the *Susak* is a container ship, the *Kamnik* takes break-bulk, i.e. mixed, uncrated cargo, subject to much last-minute delay. I ask him what sort of thing they carry.

'Oh … granite, quartz, hair …'

'Hair?'

'Oh yes. Indian hair is highly prized in Japan. Many in India go to the temples to have their hair shaved off as a penance. The hair is sold for wigs in Japan. The temples pocket the money.' Here Mr Arul spreads his arms and raises his eyebrows as only an ex-policeman can.

Later in the afternoon: In a rickshaw, 94 Fahrenheit and humid. I've been looking at the grand imperial statues which have not been removed from sight in Madras as quickly as elsewhere. There is an equestrian statue of Munro, a governor in 1820, with stirrups missing. They say that the sculptor took his life as a result of this omission ... Edward VII (1903) stands in a well-tended garden whilst George V is slap in the middle of the flower-market and has bills stuck on him and families living around his plinth. Both the royal statues were given to the city of Madras not by the British but by local Indians. Back at the hotel, hot and tired again, we're revived by good news. The *Susak* will take two of us – Nigel Meakin, the cameraman, and myself. It looks as if I shall have to take a crash course in sound recording. Nigel says it's not difficult. Ron says it's very difficult.

So with the way ahead looking clearer my last meal in India is something of a celebration. I eat in the open air beneath a full moon and beside an enormous raintree, in the gardens of the hotel. The food is excellent. A buffet full of mixtures of yoghurt, carrot, coconut and aubergine, tomato, chillies, coriander, spinach, onion and peanut. No meat but plenty of fish. There is a fierce crab curry which is irresistible.

All this is accompanied by classical dancing of extraordinary precision, complexity and beauty. Folk dancing usually has me reaching for my room key, but this display is quite superb. The girl dancer speaks good English. She is fifteen, and has been learning classical dance full-time since the age of six. She reckons it will be another five years before she's any good.

Day 32 26 October

The Hindu reports yet another air crash. There has been one a day for the past week, two of them in India. Any tendency to smugness on the part of the non-air traveller is countered by a small headline at the bottom of the front page: 'Ferry Overturned By Typhoon In South China Sea. 500 Lost.' If all goes well I shall be crossing the South China Sea next week.

My more immediate problem is to get aboard the *Susak* by 10 a.m. The highly efficient Mr Vikram is out of town today and has deputed an assistant to help us. We wait for him outside his office for over half an hour, before deciding to try and enter the docks ourselves. We arrive at a level-crossing beyond which is a railway, a high wall with barbed wire and the gates to Madras Docks. Two trains roll by but the level-crossing gate remains lowered. One or two dockworkers amble across the line, but we have a vehicle so we're stuck.

Indians seem to have a knack for sniffing out agitation and discomfiture, and a small crowd has gathered staring patiently but implacably at our every move. This in turn adds to our agitation and discomfiture and the crowd, duly rewarded for its patience, grows. The level-crossing barrier is still down after 45 minutes and since no one can be found with the authority to raise it, we execute a rather grumpy three-point turn, and leaving a satisfied crowd behind us return to the goats, the naked children and the office of Babuji Jetsea Freights. We are half an hour late for the *Susak*.

Of course when Mr Vikram's assistant – a cool young sharply dressed Tamil called Jacky – eventually turns up, he is completely unflustered and assures us that ships never leave on time anyway.

4.15: Still in port. We are having a problem with immigration. Having been through the usual number of confused junior officials we are now in the senior immigration officer's presence. On the wall is a gaudy, gold-trimmed clock, hung up, but still in its wrapping paper. A metal cupboard is covered in violent stains, as if cans of paint had been hurled at it in some kinetic frenzy. In front of him is a desk diary for 1985. He sits examining our papers critically, like a headmaster with a bad report. His hair is thick and grey, but on closer inspection is growing out of one side of his head only and spread artfully across the rest, Bobby Charlton-style. He sniffs. Obsequious attendants lurk in the background. After he's finished a brief phone call one of them steps forward, uncoils the telephone wire and replaces the receiver for him. We are losing time, and I notice on a blackboard behind us that our only alternative out of Madras, the *Kamnik*, has been postponed five days. As if sensing our restlessness, the officer becomes even more leisurely. He asks me the purpose of my journey. 'Jolly,' he says, 'jolly first class.' He smiles across at me, pleased with his grasp of the colloquial idiom, then returns to my papers: 'But everything must be pukka you see.'

A separate letter, explaining yet again the intention to substitute two of us for two of the *Susak*'s crew has to be drawn up and brought to him. By this time it's five o'clock. Sailing time. The officer reads the letter very slowly. Beside him another acolyte stands, with a huge stamp in his hand, for at least ten minutes, after which, at a nod from the officer he brings the stamp smartly down onto the paper, and retires into the shadows, never to be seen again.

5.30: Finally cleared to leave India. We are shown aboard the *Susak* and meet the captain, a handsome man with greying hair and a face of infinite melancholy. He tells us they're still loading and will not be under way until ten o'clock. So, another twelve hours wasted. Nigel and I are shown to our quarters. A sign on the door reads 'Hospital and Medicine Locker'. Inside are two beds, high off the floor and equipped with various adjustment devices. There is a washbasin, complete with single, nonturnable hospital tap, a couple of lockers, two portholes and a bedside cupboard which contains the only evidence of medicine in the place – a litre bottle of Ballantyne's Scotch. Next door is a bath, lavatory and another washbasin. The room is air-conditioned, clean, and two towels are laid out on each bed. I ask the captain what will happen if someone has to go to hospital. He shakes his head wearily.

'No one will go. They are all young.' And here he smiles, a smile well worth waiting for, bleak and quite unexpected.

Midnight. Still loading. Nigel is down in the engine room with the effusive second engineer Ivan, who has limited English and unlimited supplies of slivovitz. I'm in the hospital, talking to Jacky. Indian shipping agents and their representatives are lolling about the officers' mess. Much Ballantyne's is changing hands, plus the odd video and gold timepiece. It's a seedy time of the night and Jacky is telling me about sailors and their needs. A man called P. C. Alexander, an ex-Indian High Commissioner in London, has cleaned up Madras. There's a very Puritan atmosphere here now, and the seamen are not happy.

'All ships crews very happy with Calcutta. Can bring many girls there. Bombay too – no problem.' Bombay is apparently the only city in India to license prostitutes. The girls are very often procured from local villages, where fathers or uncles are paid maybe 5,000 rupees by travelling pimps. This is a lot of money to a poor villager and the girls don't stand much chance. They are brought to the city and installed in a pimp's bungalow. He trains and looks after them for a year. Then they may have outlived their usefulness to him, and he turns them out. Indian girls are naturally very shy and nervous, says Jacky, and Western crews can be disappointed. Good prostitutes can be found, oh yes. The big companies, and here he names a prominent British-owned tobacco producer, will provide girls who will do anything for buyers.

It's a dispiriting conversation, and it seems likely to go on for a while, as through the porthole window I can see containers still being swung aboard. The operators in the huge gantries seem unable to get a trip on the containers first time. It all looks awfully amateur.

Jacky explains to me what is going on. Incentives are necessary for these workers. 'Speed money', it's known as: 25 rupees per container and the dock drivers will move at 40 miles an hour rather than 20.

I walk on deck. It's limbo time. No one is really comfortable. A solidly built, dark-haired Slav called Marenko, who is the Donkeyman on the ship, unburdens himself, in very limited and slightly slurred English, about the political situation in Yugoslavia. He's a Catholic and a Croatian and can't see why the people of Kosovo should not have their own republic, when the Montenegrins have theirs. He can't stand the Serbs.

'They are ... the secret police ... the controllers,' and he emphasises his distaste with a curious gesture – a flick of the back of the hand up the neck and out under the chin.

There are two communists on the boat, he tells me, the chief steward and the chief engineer. I ask if the captain is a communist. Marenko looks shocked 'No. He is a Catholic! Like me.'

It's when he begins to tell me of his prostate problems, 'but sex is still *goot*', that I know I've had enough. Apologising, I turn to go back to the hospital. Marenko presses upon me a little gift. It's a magnetic badge on which is a picture of the Virgin Mary and the words, in English, 'Christ Came Into The World To Save Sinners'. I stick it onto the door of my locker but it drops off in the night.

Day 33   27 October

The *Susak* seems more firmly attached to the Madras dockside than my badge to the door, for sunrise comes and we've still not moved. Nigel was up and out with the camera at a quarter to six, and an hour later, feeling rather guilty, I grab hold of the clockwork handbag, as Ron calls his tape recorder, and go out on deck to help him.

7.15 a.m: We finally set sail. Striking juxtaposition of thin, wiry, almost black Tamil stevedores, unlooping the ropes and huge, blond Schwarzeneggerian Slavs hauling them in.

So I sail away from the Coromandel Coast of India, in a Yugoslav ship, owned by a German company and registered in Cyprus. It's a Thursday morning, the delays in India have put me ten days behind Fogg's schedule, and unlike him I have no Indian princesses to show for it – only Nigel, who is not as far as I know of royal stock, and 30 pieces of BBC film equipment under my hospital bed.

The only ray of hope is that Fogg sailed from Calcutta, away to the north, so we should catch up a day or two by Singapore. Not that the *Susak* is a fast ship. Though only launched 18 months ago at the May 3rd Shipyard in Rijeka, she is making a mere 13 knots, slower than any ship I've been on so far, with the exception of the dhow. Doubtless there are sound commercial reasons for this fuel economy, but it's frustrating for the circumnavigator.

Breakfast is at 7.30. We are served it in the officers' mess (there is strict dining and accommodation segregation between officers and crew) beneath a photo of Marshal Tito, which emphasises his spectacles so strikingly that he looks like an optician's model. The various officers come in at various times and the food, cooked by Nino, is served by Szemy. The crew divide neatly into physical types. Either they're tall, blond and clean shaven or short, dark and bearded. The short, dark and bearded ones are the most jolly and whereas Nino has a twinkle in his eye, and has indicated that I can come into the galley for a snack at any time, Szemy (best pronounced like the Glaswegian 'Jimmee') seems not altogether pleased about our presence. Breakfast consists of two fried eggs on a bed of greasy luncheon meat (which I wolf down), thick slices of Nino's home-baked white bread with butter and jam, washed down with strong Turkish coffee.

It's hard to conceive of what sort of life it must be for Yugoslavs ferrying goods they hardly ever see between three Asian cities they know nothing about, and two of which – Calcutta and Madras – they clearly dislike. This 15-day round trip will be their lot until May next year. The young radio officer has already had enough and will be transferred back home in January.

The *Susak* is, at 4,000 tonnes, classed as a feeder ship, distributing containers, off-loaded from the big carriers, to secondary ports. It has a capacity of 330 containers and is carrying about 300 at present. Many of them seem to contain onions, and to prevent them rotting these have their doors kept open during the voyage, so a gentle shallotty aroma accompanies any walk on deck. The captain claims to have a computer print-out of all the contents of the containers, but is vague as to what their cargo might be.

'Cotton fabrics … leather … some dangerous cargo.' These are the ones with skull and crossbones markings and the word 'hazardous' stamped on the side.

We have 1,500 miles to go to Singapore. The sea is calm, the sky clear and sunny.

Lunch on board the *Susak* is at 11.30, and supper at 5.30, which takes a bit of getting used to, but it's all based around changing watches.

The cuisine is relentlessly carnivorous, and comes as a complete contrast to the delicate vegetarianism of southern India. The tea and fruit juices of India and Arabia have only limited appeal on the *Susak*, which amongst its cargo has 3,000 cans of Zlatorog Export, a high-quality Yugoslav lager which sports a cheery-looking mountain ram as its trademark and is available at most times of day, as of course is Ballantyne's Scotch, a bottle of which seems to be in every cabin, storage locker and maintenance room. With some of the meals, according to Jimmee's mood, there is Yugoslav wine, bearing the government name Vinoplod.

Much of the talk at the meal centres around shopping. Where did you get that watch? Did you know that you could get 17 track, triple re-wind, simultaneous play-back Dolby stereo music centres for 43 dollars in Singapore?

I find a place in the sun after lunch and lie on an unvisited deck high up beside the smokestack and listen to Billy Joel and Leonard Cohen on my Walkman and read the excellent *Travellers* by Ruth Prawer Jhabwala, which tells me a lot about India, a country which it's not easy to put out of mind.

At half-past five an intense golden sun sinks beneath the horizon drawing with it all the light from the sky, which changes from off-pink to lemon to light eggshell to murky grey. The long evening, which stretches from 6.15, or earlier if Jimmee is being brisk, is devoted to Zlatorog, Vinoplod and backgammon lessons from Nigel.

Day 34 28 October

The clocks have gone on by one and a half hours, so sleep later. Nigel and I try our most technically ambitious adventure this morning – an interview with the captain on the bridge. This necessitates me holding the tape recorder and mike (and remembering to keep both out of shot) whilst checking the level on the recorder and answering questions. The captain has chosen this moment to give long, discursive replies and my arm is practically breaking by the end.

Finish *Travellers*, a gentle, sensitive, sensuous tale, which has restored my faith in writing. Now embark on Anthony Burgess (*Little Wilson and Big God*) and a book on Islam, about which I know woefully little. On the *Susak* mental exercise is not as problematical as physical exercise. There is nowhere to run off the effects of the Zlatorog.

The sea and weather conditions become the main source of interest. There are no other ships to be seen, only a squall of rain and a sensationally prolonged sunset, during which the surface of the Bay of Bengal seems molten.

Spend an hour or so at the prow, screened by the containers from the noise of the engine, just gazing out over the glassy silent surface of the sea, and looking down at the wash from the bows which is filled with phosphorescent pin-pricks of light. I am taking a last walk around the ship when a door opens at the stern, letting out a long strip of light, into which a huge bull-shouldered deckhand steps, lifts his arm and sends a bottle of Ballantyne's arcing high into the ocean.

Day 35   29 October

Today is Jimmee's 32nd birthday and the celebrations start early. I've just finished my toast and jam at a quarter to eight when he produces two bottles of what appear to be a Yugoslav version of grappa, one of which is colourless and the other the dark brown of an amontillado sherry. I plump for the latter, which is called Pelinkovac and has a bracing taste like Fernet Branca. Two of these before 8 a.m. produce a warm interior glow to match the warm exterior glow from clear sunny skies and a deep-blue sea. We seem to have the Bay of Bengal to ourselves and the captain confirms that this is a little-used route, the main shipping lane being further south, on a line from the Red Sea to Singapore. I ask the captain who is doing the job of the two crew members we've been substituted for. The captain says he himself is covering for the 3rd officer by doing an extra watch. The other was a deckhand and in an excess of zeal, brought on I'm sure by the early application of Pelinkovac, I find myself offering to swab decks and help out with some painting. Ships are always being painted. It's a continuing battle against the sun and salt. I'm given a roller on the end of a very long pole and told to paint more or less anywhere. Nigel's efforts to capture this on film make him look like the one-man bands that used to entertain cinema queues. He balances precariously on a deck rail, a sheer drop into the sea behind him, with camera on one shoulder, tape recorder on the other, headphones over his ears, microphone between his knees and clapper-board in his teeth.

Mid-morning and we're 620 miles out of Madras, the sea calm.

We go below to film a sequence in the laundry. A crewman who doesn't speak any English is showing me how to work the washing machine. Unfortunately he keeps pouring the soap powder in before Nigel has the camera focused or the tape recorder on, and has to repeat the action. Eventually he times it right, but by then about six loads of powder have gone into my washing and we leave the scene rapidly before lather engulfs the entire below-decks area.

To the engine room, which is pristine compared to the last one I saw – on *The Saudi Moon II* (crossed out and *I* written in), which shuddered and rattled and leaked oil from the cylinder casings, where Filipinos worked at temperatures of over 100 Fahrenheit. The *Susak* engine room is like a library by comparison and the control room is cool and spacious. The chief engineer is anxious to show me how they can re-bore piston rings in their own workshop; Ivan, his assistant, is anxious to show us the comprehensive display of beverages in their fridge.

The engine room is unmanned from five in the evening until eight in the morning. The whole thing operates automatically, but has a system of alarms which ring through to the cabin of the engineer on duty. It's a far cry from the cinema image of the engine room, which always had Richard Attenborough or Michael Medwin about to be engulfed by seawater. Stuck to the walls are pin-up photos of great-chested ladies. One for each of the engine-room crew, according to Ivan, who seems to have picked the most statuesque for himself.

One would think it's a bachelor life at sea but the captain tells me at lunch that 80 per cent of the crew are married men. He has a wife and two children, whom he last saw in July and will not see again until next May. It's hard, but the pay isn't bad and his wife comes from a seafaring family and is used to the separations. Jobs are scarce back home, he says. Many young people, qualified as lawyers or doctors, are forced to make a living selling newspapers. I ask him if he would advise his own son to go to sea. He shakes his head.

'It's all changing,' and he smiles. Sadly, as ever.

In the middle of lunch, the young 2nd officer with the swallowtail of hair down the back of his neck suddenly bangs the table and points at me: 'You are Monthy Pyton!'

I have a dim recollection that the series was at one time sold to Yugoslavia. He looks awfully pleased with himself, but the captain rather spoils things by recognising Nigel as Bill Oddie.

'And you do all those bird programmes!'

This evening there is a certain amount of nodding and winking and leaving the table early. A blue movie is being run in the crew's dayroom. Everyone quite enjoys it to start with and there are the same shouts of encouragement, gasps of appreciation and groans of incredulity that you might hear at any Sheffield United game. Eventually the jollity wanes with the sheer relentlessness of it all, and a rather morose silence descends. Post porno omne triste est. The captain is one of the last to leave. He gives a hint of an ironic smile and a shrug of the shoulders.

Clocks on an hour again.

Day 36 30 October

Nigel says I moaned tragically in my sleep. He says it was like a horror film, each sound more heart-rending than the last. I try to tell him that that's the sort of thing he should expect, sleeping in the hospital. The real reason for my performance may have been a sea-swell, which appeared from nowhere and had us both rolling across our beds, perilously close to the edge.

After breakfast land is sighted on the port side. Radar and satellite navigation systems have made crows' nests and cries of 'Land ahead!' obsolete, but there's still a frisson of excitement when you've seen nothing but empty ocean for four days. The land in question is Great Nicobar Island – 27 miles long, the same size as Singapore, but almost uninhabited. Though we are now 950 miles from Madras the island is still Indian territory. On the bridge the captain has the Admiralty charts laid out. However exotic the location the names remain incorrigibly British. Wherever you look there's a Dreadnought Channel or a Ten Mile Channel or a Carruthers Deep. At the end of Great Nicobar is written 'Densely Wooded' and the highest point is marked as 211 metres.

Up onto the topmost deck for a better view. Great Nicobar does look like the stuff dreams are made of. Dark, wooded hillsides run down to the sea. No smoke to signal a settlement, no sign of a building, and what looks momentarily like a flash of light reflected on a window is the white foam of a wave breaking on an empty beach. (Later in my journey I was told of an outrageous but apparently successful attempt to bring tourists to Great Nicobar. During the monsoon torrential rain comes down spectacularly. A bright Indian entrepreneur advertised a tour for rich Arabs from the arid Gulf who could sit on their hotel balcony and watch rain for a week. It was a sell-out.)

Today's big event is a barbecue. The tireless Ivan has once again been the moving force, and the captain has agreed to pay for the drink.

Preparations start after lunch (i.e. about midday) when an oil drum, split in two and laid end to end, is filled with driftwood and set alight. Two 7 lb turkeys, skewered on a long metal rod and basted with salt and olive oil, are laid across the fire and turned continuously for about four hours. Everyone takes a turn, fortified with Zlatorog and mournful singing. Cans of Zlatorog tumble into the Andaman Sea and the singing becomes so awful that a huge cassette player is fetched out and a tape of Croatian songs blares out. More melodic than the deckhands' dirges but still no match for the sound of a 2,800 horsepower engine

The pathos in all this is that these are love songs, sung by a Yugoslav woman, and it will be seven months before any of the crew see Yugoslavia or a Yugoslav woman again.

3.15: First sight of the islands and coastline of Sumatra, and of a succession of vessels, 15 or 20 miles away, emerging from the Malacca Strait to head across the Indian Ocean to Socotra Island, Aden and the Red Sea. For a long time the land is a smudge on the horizon, barely distinguishable from the sky, but the moment when it becomes definably land, when features can be picked out, is for me one of the most exciting moments of sea travel, especially when it is a new land. Sumatra was just a name I'd pored over in stamp albums and inky school atlases and read about in explorers' tales and quite probably Biggles stories. Now as I sit with the smell of wood smoke, roasting turkey and diesel fumes wafting gently about me, it is slowly becoming a reality beneath a low band of dark rain clouds on the south-eastern horizon.

Along the deck two of the crew are fashioning a long table (for we all eat together at the barbecue, officers and crew alike). Jimmee produces acres of red cloth from somewhere and drapes it tastefully over everything, including one of the capstans on which the bottles of wine are arranged. The islands ahead loom slowly larger – silent, dark and peaked. The captain takes his place rather languidly at the head of the table.

He's in a T-shirt as usual. I ask him why I never see him in his uniform.

'Only in the port,' he grins. Can't imagine this happening on a British ship.

It is a wonderful meal. The turkey is succulent. Thick tender meat and a crackly skin. It's served at sunset, which is another beauty. 5.9 from all the judges. Smiling, singing, laughing and sharing incomprehensible confidences we enter the Malacca Strait. The music is an incongruous mixture of Yugoslav songs sung *a capella* and Kenny Rogers, Bob Dylan and the Beatles on the cassette. As the sky grows darker so does the conversation and after a while the sexual exploits of the small 3rd engineer, whose squashed face resembles that of a satanic baby, become a bore and I wander off to the bows, full of good food and too much drink and sober up with the football results from London. Wednesday lose at Charlton, United beat Bury and we are heading south to Singapore.

Back at the table a previously quite unobtrusive deckhand has seized a broom and is miming guitar to a Dylan song. He does it very well and after a final flamboyant riff hurls the broom overboard to a standing ovation from those who can still stand. This encourages him to delve into a maintenance locker and produce a shovel with which he does the same thing. It's only with difficulty that he's stopped from flinging my long paintbrush into the sea.

Day 37 31 October

Now we are in the Strait the swell has eased, the ship is once again on an even keel, and I can think of no explanation for a vivid dream of snakes beneath my feet. All I know is I wake kicking.

There is an air of melancholy about the *Susak* this morning. It's as if yesterday's conviviality was an aberration, and today life is back to being what it probably always is on board a cargo ship, slow, listless and repetitive.

On the bridge the captain indicates the print-out screen on the satellite navigation system. This is a relatively new but radical improvement. Eight satellites orbiting the earth send down signals against which the ship's position can be checked. The vagaries of the weather – clouds or fog – have been defeated, the days of the sextant superseded. This morning the screen indicates that our speed is down to 11 knots. A strong northerly head current is responsible. Time of arrival in Singapore has been put back to midnight tomorrow.

On deck the weather has changed completely, from the sunny to the surly, and from the Malaysia shore a low grey mass of cloud swings towards us from a pitch-black horizon. I realise how fortunate I have been so far. Since Day 2 the sun has shone from cloudless skies and the only complaints have been about the heat. I've forgotten about rain and lowering skies and thought we'd left them behind in Northern Europe. Now, as we draw near to the most southerly point of the journey, only 300 or 400 miles from the Equator, they're back.

The rain hits the *Susak* about two in the afternoon. Grey, flat and prolonged, dampening spirits and disrupting radio communication so that I'm unable to reach the rest of the crew in Singapore to tell them of our further delay. A succession of container ships and car-transporters pass us going north whilst others rapidly overhaul us going south. The effect of the weather on the visibility makes me uncomfortably aware of how potentially dangerous busy shipping lanes can be. Ferries and fishing boats from both sides of the Strait weave in and out of the transporters and supertankers, most of which cannot be brought to a standstill in less than half an hour. Even the little *Susak* would take two miles to stop.

Late afternoon: Playing Scrabble and looking out over grey seas and rain puddles on the containers. This should be one of the most exotic parts of the journey, slipping down between Malaya and Sumatra. Instead it's like a wet Sunday in Sheffield. Ironically the ship has run out of drinking water. On our last night on the Bay of Bengal, the rolling of the boat mixed residue from the bottom of the tank into the water supply, which is why Nigel's bottle of drinking water looks the colour of a prop from Dr Jekyll and Mr Hyde.

At dusk I take a walk on deck. A pair of dolphins has homed in on the ship, and, as usual, make for the bow wave. I hurry to the bows to watch them and whistle encouragement. They play for a while, but the sea is no longer blue and translucent, and they have to dodge polystyrene fragments, swirling tissue paper and bobbing cups – the trail of debris that heralds the approach of civilisation.

Even the meals fail to lift our spirits. Meat, meat and more meat, and the officers (apart from Ivan) seem dragged into a pit of Slovene moroseness in which nothing gives them pleasure. The news that we shall be later into Singapore compounds their gloom for it means even less time ashore in the only port they can bear.

If Nigel and I can be so desperately bored after six days, what can it be like for the crew after six months? I suppose they become numbed, their responses reduced to the minimum necessary. *They* don't rush to the rails every time they see a dolphin or climb to the highest point of the ship to strain for a view of a distant island. They just want it to be over. For them Singapore is not the gateway to new unvisited lands. Singapore means Calcutta and Calcutta means Madras and Madras means Singapore again, and this will be their life long after I've finished going round the world.

Day 38 1 November

At breakfast the captain announces that the *Susak* will pick up the Singapore pilot at 11 p.m. tonight, and will be in berth by midnight. 310 containers will be unloaded and 150 loaded. Departure from Singapore will be 3 p.m. tomorrow. Audible groans.

The crew disappear to their various jobs. To pass the time (breakfast having been cleared away by 8 a.m.) I look for a while at the framed map of the world, courtesy of Transjug, Rijeka. Looking at my route from London to the Equator I can see a symmetry. The Adriatic, the Red Sea, the Persian Gulf and now the Strait of Malacca, are all splits in a landmass, all aligned N.W. to S.E., giving the impression of progress, by a series of down escalators, from sea to sea – the Mediterranean, the Arabian, and, to come, the South China, where it's typhoon season.

A small seabird is trapped for a while in the kitchen. It flies, foolishly, into the oven. But before Nino can turn the gas on, Jimmee has chased it out with a brush (the only one that survived the Dylan impersonations). It flies down towards the engine room, then up again, fluttering along the passageway until one of the engine crew (who looks like Trotsky) happens to step in off the deck, whereupon the bird flies out past him, leaving him quite confused.

In the radio room, where tapes by Tiffany and Samantha Fox lie about the desk, I at last make radio contact with Singapore. Odd to hear guttural Yugoslav talking to tinkling Chinese using English alphabetic identification. I become 'Mike India Charlie Hotel Alpha Echo Lima, Papa Alpha Lima India November', and Roger, whom I'm calling at Raffles Hotel, becomes, much more exotically, Romeo Oscar. The news is that I shall not be spending a night in Singapore. A container ship, the *Neptune Diamond*, leaves for Hong Kong at 11.30. I tell Roger that we shall not berth until 11.30, and explain the problems of the head current. He says I shall just have to ask the captain to put his foot down.

Last lunch with the captain, Ivan and the radio op. The conversation ranges from the idiosyncrasies of the Albanians – at an Albanian port the crew of any merchant vessel is confined to the ship and soldiers with rifles patrol the dockside (the Yugoslavs seem to think it quite a good thing that Albania is cut off) – to a warmly appreciated recitation of the different brands of Scotch: 'Chivas Regal ... ah, yes ... Dewars ... yes ... Johnny Walker ... ah, yes ... Famous Grouse ... what is that?' I ask the captain if there are any restrictions on travel for Yugoslavs. 'Only money,' he smiles. 'If a Yugoslav have enough money he can go to Seychelles.' The captain himself is living with his mother-in-law but has bought a small apartment in Rijeka which he's doing up. Somehow I can't imagine him in the Seychelles.

We have a long and faintly surreal discussion in which the words 'cheap', 'ship' and 'chip' become hopelessly muddled. I ask the radio operator how he'd heard of Samantha Fox. He is surprised I should even ask the question. Every full-blooded male in Yugoslavia has heard of Samantha Fox. 'After Mrs Thatcher, she is the best-known woman!'

At this, the conversation lapses for a while. The captain sits, head on one side, toothpick in his hand: 'So, you will be home by Christmas.' I feel a pang of guilt as I nod.

We've talked about more at this last lunch than at any previously, and as always seems to happen you get to know people a little better just before you have to leave them. Both Nigel and I have grown to greatly like and respect Captain Sablic. He's a man of quiet authority and considerable understanding and I've never heard him raise his voice in anger. Significantly, that goes for the rest of the crew.

This afternoon the wind drops. A feeling of lassitude hangs over everything. A long, lumpen, heavy day, in a lazy, hazy sea. The sort of day when you fear you could stick fast here forever. The sort of day when the Ancient Mariner was 'sad as sad could be, and we did speak only to break the silence of the sea'.

Down in the engine room Ivan is getting very drunk. 'I believe in whisky,' he confides to me. 'But in my cabin you will see Jesus picture and the Virgin Mary.'

At a quarter to eleven after a last round of backgammon Nigel and I would normally be taking a last Zlatorog and heading for bed, but tonight an adventure is about to begin. The solitary days on the Bay of Bengal seem like another life as we make our way slowly closer to Singapore, just one in a long line of southbound ships, whilst another line, northbound, slips past us on the port side. There is very little noise but an enormous, almost frightening amount of movement. Our maritime progress is mirrored in the skies above as a constant succession of jets, their navigation lights flashing, descend to the airport. There is a feeling of heightened excitement – we are coming into the centre of things.

At eleven o'clock precisely a launch emerges from the darkness and puts the pilot aboard. Two hundred ships are processed every day through Singapore and things are done in a brisk, businesslike way.

Up on the bridge the pilot and the captain are lit by a spectral blue glow from the instrument panel. The pilot speaks softly but clearly into a walkie-talkie. We are to be taken straight into our berth at Keppel Harbour, which is good news for those of us hoping to catch the *Neptune Diamond* before she sails, but it'll be a close thing. I can see no sign of her at the dockside.

Down on the deck, I'm grabbed by Ivan who is soaking wet. There had been a leak in the engine's seawater cooling system, but he had plugged it. His face shines with achievement but his eyes are red and tired. He insists we have a last rum together in the engine room. When it's time to go, he says to me, 'You know for me the best sound in the world? Is the motor of aircraft,' and he looks up to the flashing lights in the sky, which one day will be for him.

After fond and emotional farewells all round I totter off the *Susak* and onto Singaporean soil at a quarter past midnight to be told the *Neptune Diamond* had already sailed.

I feel rather glad I've had that last rum. It helps to cushion the blow. But Roger, who has taken over the direction from Clem, is rushing me away from the dockside as if my life depends on it. What's going on?

They tell me as our minibus rushes Nigel, myself and our baggage to customs and immigration. It's to be another night at sea. Such is the power, might and influence of the BBC that the *Neptune Diamond* has agreed to wait for us, four miles out in the roads.

At 2.15 in the morning, after two hours in Singapore, all is cleared for our departure and we are at Clifford Pier, boarding a small but sturdy launch called *Carnival* which sweeps me in a curve past the prosperous, boomtown skyline – the Oriental Hotel and the Westin Raffles, which they tell me is the tallest hotel in the world. But at the pier itself I have seen some litter and a drunk or two – neither of which I thought were allowed on the streets of the city.

2.45 a.m.: Hurrying past all manner of ships in the harbour. First the section they call Smuggler's Corner, where the smaller, less conspicuous boats come and go with surreptitious cargoes, then out between the cruise ships, festooned with lights, past a surveillance ship with two bulbous deck structures, and in among a crowd of cargo vessels riding at anchor. Then voices are raised, the engine tone deepens and sputters and ahead of us is a sheer wall of steel, rising 40 feet above our heads. This is the *Neptune Diamond*. We've made it.

Climb aboard, up a 30-step ladder at ten past three. Met by a Singaporean officer who takes me upstairs to meet the captain who turns out to be a reassuring Geordie, Norman Tuddenham. His wife Pat, who's Scottish, is in her dressing gown. She fusses around us – showing us our cabins and offering us chicken salad and Tiger beer. My cabin is enormous after the *Susak*. The whole ship is enormous after the *Susak*. It carries 2,000 more containers than the *Susak* and travels twice as fast. There is a lift to carry us the six floors from the deck to our quarters. To transfer from a Yugoslav 'tramp service' (as Ivan once described his ship) to a Japanese-built, Singaporean-owned, British-captained 35,000 tonner between midnight and three in the morning in an unknown foreign port is overloading a sensory system already full of rum and Zlatorog, but as I fall asleep I can feel the throb of the engines and I know we're moving round the world again – and that's really all that matters.

Day 39 2 November

The ship as hospital analogy which first occurred to me on board the dhow is becoming remarkably literal. On the *Susak* Nigel and I shared the hospital, and on the *Neptune Diamond* I'm occupying the Doctor's Bedroom. The ship's doctor seems to be a largely fictional character these days. Norman and Pat Tuddenham seem capable of anything and I'm sure minor surgery wouldn't be beyond them.

Despite not getting to bed until the small hours I'm awake early. A new bed, a new ship, a new movement, a new engine note, a new set of circumstances, a new crowd of people to absorb and process into the film, together with my natural curiosity, all conspire to keep me from a lie-in. I have to realise that until I reach London in December everything that surrounds me is potential material. I'm on full filming alert for eighty days – or however long it takes.

A look at my copy of *Around the World in Eighty Days* is not encouraging. Fogg, aboard the *Rangoon*, was in and out of Singapore as fast as I was, but ten days ahead of me. He hoped to accomplish the 1,400 miles from Singapore to Hong Kong 'in six days at the most', but Captain Tuddenham is quite confident that we can accomplish it in 67 hours. Fogg was crossing the

South China Sea at the same time of year and hit seriously bad weather. Tuddenham checks his radar and his daily weather charts and says we have nothing to fear. Perhaps this is another chance to catch up.

Unlike the *Susak* which pottered along at 13 knots to conserve fuel, the *Neptune* ships earn their money by getting there fast and arriving on schedule. Gone are the days of pleasant lackadaisical dawdlings on the Bay of Bengal.

Norman and Pat Tuddenham try hard to inject some human interest into what is essentially a cool and unsentimental business operation. They show us the swimming pool, which has the brightly painted figure of Snoopy on the bottom. 'My wife says that's what I look like,' cracks Norman. They're both very game and go for a splash around for the cameras.

There was, as we know to our cost, no extra room for supernumeraries aboard the *Susak*, but on the *Neptune Diamond*, perhaps to compensate for the factory-like existence, wives are allowed, even encouraged, and Pat is one of three aboard.

We meet the others for a drink before supper up in the captain's cabin. The room, with patterned sofas and family photos on the table, is neat, tidy and domestic and could, one feels, be as easily at their home in Broughty Ferry as in the middle of the South China Sea. The chief engineer and his wife and the radio operator and his wife remain shyly silent throughout. It's a new crew. They mostly joined the ship at Singapore and are as familiar with the captain as we are. On deck earlier today I encountered a painter who asked me my nationality. 'British,' I told him, 'like your captain.' He looked surprised: 'Is captain British?' Norman and Pat propose a party for tomorrow night so that everyone can get to know each other.

'You've got to tell a story, sing a song or show your bottom,' he tells them. The Singaporeans look suitably terrified.

Dinner is a mish-mash of British specifications and Singaporean application. The captain's attitude is to resolutely avoid too much foreign stuff. 'I've ordered steak, because at least they can't muck that up,' he reassures us, inaccurately as it happens. It's interesting that someone who has spent most of his life abroad should be so inimical to foreign cooking. But I must stop making the mistake of confusing being at sea with being abroad. Being at sea is really being nowhere and I suppose you have to create a cultural cocoon in which to live. The Tuddenhams have chosen to survive by replicating familiar home conditions as thoroughly as possible.

On the charts earlier today I notice the words 'Many sightings of unlit sampans,' added in pencil. These presumably refer to the refugees from Vietnam, whose coast we are approaching fast. Captain Tuddenham's attitude to the boat people is as pragmatic as one would expect. He would set a course 20 miles longer to try and avoid them but 'of course I'd pick them up if I had to, poor buggers'.

Roger, who's recently completed some filming in Vietnam, scents a photo-opportunity, and tries to persuade the captain that it would be in everyone's interest for him to divert towards the coast and see if he could find any boat people to rescue. 'You'll bring glory to the company and a medal for yourself – you'll probably get the O.B.E.'

'The P.U.S.H. more likely,' replies Captain Tuddenham drily.

Day 40   3 November

My eighth consecutive day at sea. Exactly halfway through my ration of days, but far from halfway round the world. Ron wakes me with a cry of 'Mi-*kel*! 'Allo Mi-kel!' and a cup of coffee. We're 160 miles off the Vietnamese coast and a big sea is running, whipped up by a Force 7 wind from the north. The Beaufort Scale, on which these things are measured, is still internationally accepted as the wind speed criterion. On the bridge is a display board of photographs illustrating the various conditions. Force 7 is white caps and 10 foot waves. The hurricane that struck southern England a year ago was Force 11. The top of the range is 18, though it's hard to find anyone alive to talk about a Force 18.

I find a gym with table tennis, some weights and a rowing machine, and row for a quarter of an hour. At least I can say I've rowed across the South China Sea. I even manage a run on deck. I get soaked with spray every time I pass the bows, which is most refreshing.

The captain has to admit that the current is running against us and has forced a cut of one and a half knots per hour and our ETA in Hong Kong is now 2 a.m. on 5 November. But we are still in less of a crisis than Fogg, whose vessel had also hit strong North-Westerlies and Passepartout had begun to panic:

'Until then everything had moved on so well! Land and sea seemed to be devoted to his master. Steamers and railways obeyed him. Wind and steam combined to favour his journey. Had the hour of mistakes finally sounded?' On the *Diamond* the only precautions the captain advises is that not more than two of us should use the lift at the same time.

I ask the captain why he joined the Merchant Navy. Like most seamen he's been in the business all his life. (No one seems to drop chartered accountancy and run away to sea, however romantic it may sound.) His father was in the Merchant Navy too – which was true of the *Susak*'s captain and Abbas of the *Saudi Moon* as well. Merchant seamanship is an hereditary condition.

Captain Tuddenham remembers when he was a junior purser in Hong Kong in the 1940s, it was his job to supervise (i.e. lower the ladder and take it up again rapidly if the captain appeared) the embarkation of Chinese ladies, whose company you could then purchase in day-, week- or two-week lengths. 'Very civilised in those days,' he adds provocatively, and Pat is duly provoked:

'*Nor*-man!'

'Long before I had you, my love.'

Outside, the character of the sea has changed totally since we left. Now it's ceased to be a supportive friend or a calming influence – it's fierce and powerful and agitated. 'Only a moderate swell,' the captain insists, in between coping with telexes from the shipping agents in Hong Kong who want to know why he was hanging about in the Singapore roads until five in the morning.

The party starts, unhopefully, after supper, at seven. Shreds of streamer and strands of tinsel from the Christmas decorations remain stuck to inaccessible parts of the bar as Pat and Norman personally set out bowls of crisps, twiglets, prawn crackers and, for the Singaporeans, fragrantly roasted peanuts. 'They won't eat them unless they're like that.' One of the married couples arrives. The wife of the radio operator has been seasick and won't be here. Disco music blares out across an empty floor. Passepartout waits patiently to film whatever might happen, but without him probably nothing will. At last some of the 25-strong crew begin to filter in. The beer and the whisky begin to flow, and much to Tuddenham's relief there is talk, laughter and even dancing – albeit led by the captain himself. I talk to a Singaporean, aged 28. He joined the navy to see the world and is not disappointed. He loved distant places, different cultures, and asked me if I knew Felixstowe. It's only 20 miles down the coast from the little Suffolk town where my mother lives, but I can't imagine what it would offer a hot-blooded oriental. It turned out that when he was there he was doing Captain Tuddenham's old job and dropping the rope ladder down for the girls. Suffolk girls are evidently carrying on a time-honoured tradition. The rate of change is a common theme in conversations with the older officers. Smaller crews, more automated ships, tighter commercial pressures and the shift of the centre of trade to the Pacific Rim, all add a certain poignancy to the captain's reminiscences of the days when Britannia still ruled the waves and the depth of a continental shelf was determined by a weight dangled over the side until someone shouted 'Bottom!'

I ask him if he thinks the British Merchant Navy is in terminal decline.

'It's already dead. We only run ferries now.'

He starts on another reminiscence: 'A man came to my cabin one night holding his hand in his hand …'

Time for bed.

Day 41   4 November

A rough night. Wake at 5.30, with a sore head and the boat pitching and plunging. Unsteady progress to the bathroom, trying to time my movements to the roll of the ship. First Alka-Seltzer of the journey.

Later, on the bridge, last night's party is judged a success. The captain sounds surprised. 'They all came!'

Ascertain that 'they' comprise 18 Singaporeans, 1 Burmese, 1 Filipino and 5 Malaysians. I ask the captain what size of crew he thinks will be needed to run ships like this in the year 2000.

'One. An educated monkey.'

What is sad is that so much folklore will die with Captain Tuddenham and others like him. No one else could tell so richly the story of the woman who knocked on the door of the captain's cabin in the middle of a voyage, said she'd fallen asleep on the toilet after saying goodbye to her man, and could he drop her off at Cardiff.

'Well,' I said, 'I'm not goin' to Cardiff. We're in the middle of the Bay of Biscay and the next stop's Brazil.' She had been quite unfazed by this and in the end he'd had to put into port at Madeira and pay her fare home. 'She walked off that ship lookin' immaculate!' I ask him if he has any legal redress and he shakes his head. 'At sea, Michael, everything's legal after seven days.'

*

5.00: I try to run round the deck but the wind has shifted to the North-West and is hitting the ship at 50 knots (speed of wind plus speed of ship) and waves are crashing over the bows. There is a tropical storm heading north at Latitude 5 and the captain is hurrying for Hong Kong on full power. There's also news of a 'very severe' storm developing to the East of us. (This was the genesis of Typhoon Tess, which we missed by 48 hours and which was one of the fiercest in living memory.) Roger, thwarted of boat people, is gnashing his teeth that we seem once again to have just missed something truly dramatic. We all blame the astrologer. On my way to supper, I mention the smell of some unpleasant gas.

'Could be from one of the containers,' observes the captain. 'There were five seamen killed quite recently inhaling toxic fumes.'

(Twelve hours after we left the *Neptune Diamond* in Hong Kong, one of her containers exploded, starting a fire so severe it could not be controlled with the CO_2 on board, and Captain Tuddenham was forced to bring her back to Hong Kong.)

Day 42 5 November

At 5.30 Ron wakes me with a coffee. Counting six days pre-filming in London this is our 48th day together and our last. Nigel, Julian and Ron will hand over to another Passepartout today and by Monday will be back in England, having taken 14 hours to retrace the steps which have taken us 42 days. To have come this far and shared so much and still be brought morning coffee in bed is more than I could have hoped for. I lie and consider the days ahead. Confronted with the prospect of two weeks' intensive travelling through China and Japan with a rested director and a fresh and eager new Passepartout, the temptation to fly away to some beach or simply sleep for a week is momentarily strong. But having come this far, I mustn't weaken, especially as, for the first time since leaving London, I have gained some time on Phileas Fogg. His ship, the *Rangoon*, arrived in Hong Kong battered by storms, and 24 hours late, on Fogg's 36th day out of London. The gap between us is now reduced to six days. Fogg, however, left Hong Kong for Shanghai by sea, and I shall be taking a more tortuous railway route across China, which may be more adventurous, but offers little immediate chance of catching up time.

Physically I've held up well so far, with only the gripes on the dhow coming anywhere near immobilising me. A tan from five weeks' unbroken sunshine covers up some of the creases and helps to make me look better than I feel. Despite the lack of hard physical exertion since running in Dubai, I've managed to take some exercise every day, though much of this counteracted over the last few days by far too much to drink. Travelling light has paid off. There are only two casualties. Of my six trusty shirts one was aborted in Bombay, when the hotel laundry washed it in acid rather than soap, and another is terminally covered in oil from the rush through Singapore docks.

We disembark at 8 a.m. Verne observed as Fogg landed in Hong Kong that there is 'a track of English towns all around the world'. It's now reduced to one, and after 1997, none.

My bag breaks. The strap, unable to take the strain any longer, rips away as I set foot on British soil for the first time in six weeks. Unfortunately the camera has a fault as well and I am required to walk down the gangway twice more, pretending that the bag isn't broken. By this time I'm anxious to be away from the container port – so empty of people and full of the smell of diesel engines and the clang of metal resounding. Above my head huge gantry cranes are off-loading a 40-foot container every 80 seconds. I find that the Peninsula Hotel, where I am to stay for two nights, has sent a green Rolls-Royce, complete with chauffeur and champagne, to the dockside to collect me. The driver shows me, somewhat distastefully, into the snug, white leather seats, and soon we are in a traffic jam on a flyover. Somehow after ten days at sea a traffic jam seems singularly pointless even if you *are* in a Rolls-Royce. Ships may move at less than 30 miles an hour, but at least they're moving. You never find yourself pulling up behind another vessel. On either side the tall apartment blocks are huddled together, side by side and back to back, scrambling for space. The city feels unbearably claustrophobic, but my eyes are wide, taking everything in – the Chinese signs and the Union Jacks. Down into Kowloon, past sparkling and expensive hotels and office buildings. I'm back in the world of security men, outside prestige entrances with their two-way radios and swivelling suspicious eyes. Haven't really noticed this breed since they chased us and our camera from the front of the National Bank in Jeddah.

Outside the handsome period frontage of the Peninsula Hotel, Passepartout One take their last shot of me. As I come through the doors into the lobby Passepartout Two take up the story. The cameraman is still called Nigel (Walters, not Meakin). His assistant has become Simon (Maggs) and Ron has metamorphosed, and lost a stone or two in the process, into Dave (Jewitt). Far from looking fresh, Passepartout Two is grey-eyed and thick-headed, having struck a run of mini-flu since arriving a week ago.

There is hardly time to be introduced before I am led with an ever-increasing entourage into the lift and up to Room 417. The door is opened before me to reveal a small hallway with an antique table on which stands a bottle of every kind of sophisticated refreshment. A bottle of champagne nestles in ice and beside it is an invitation to a black-tie party tomorrow night to celebrate the halfway point of my journey. My broken bag is swiftly removed to be repaired, laundry is whisked away and, after some shell-shocked pictures of my reaction are taken for hotel publicity, I'm left alone for fifteen whole minutes!

Then to the Bird Market, a long narrow street devoted exclusively to the sale of birds and their accessories. The only other creatures well represented are grasshoppers – sold by the pound in plastic bags as bird food. Songbirds are very popular here, and punters looking to buy one bring with them birds they already have, for the birds won't sing unless there is another to sing to. Not all the birds are bred for choral purposes. Some are for fighting, and one stall has a large number of small angry birds, about the size and beauty of shabby starlings, which are specially bred for this purpose and imported from mainland China. There are also some very fine parrots and macaws if you want conversation, and while I am trying to teach one of them to say 'John Cleese is rubbish' I feel an affectionate tug at my trousers. A beautiful white cockatoo on a lower perch has taken a shine to my faithful cotton trousers and is shaking them at the knee.

I call the camera over to witness this charming rapport between man and beast only to find the hard-beaked little zygodactyl has bitten clean through the trousers and is now going for the kneecap. He is as tenacious as Norman Hunter and eventually has to be pulled off. Everyone seems to find this a lot funnier than I do.

This unprovoked assault on my costume reminds me that I have to acquire a black tie and suit to match before tomorrow evening – and it's the weekend. But Hong Kong is a 24 hours a day, 365 days a year city. The only reason for cramming onto these islands is to make money and do business, and if you want a new suit on a Sunday, Sam's tailors will make you one. Sam's shop is no Savile Row salon. It's a cramped narrow unit in a featureless arcade, but its fame is worldwide. It's full of westerners who've maybe heard about the place from Henry Kissinger or Cyrus Vance or Bob Hawke or Prince Charles or David Bowie or Derek Nimmo or George Michael or any of the illustrious names who appear in photos displayed around the mirror at which you have your fitting.

Within about seven minutes I'm measured for jacket, trousers and shirt, all of which will be custom-built for me in 24 hours.

Back to the hotel. As in any fast city, the traffic moves incredibly slowly, and there is no time for a breather before going into a press conference. I have been happily unrecognised for most of the journey, and it's disconcerting having to play the celebrity again. I agree with Paul Theroux and Norman Lewis that travel is best enjoyed by being as inconspicuous as possible. The newspapers want funny stories and lots of incident, but I haven't edited the journey down yet. It's still a big, rambling, extraordinary experience, not easy to sum up in headlines. Clem says there has been keen interest in the journey here and when he was talking to a radio station earlier in the week he was introduced, with an apt slip of the tongue, as the producer of *Around the World in Eighty Delays!* Thank God for the trouser-eating cockatoo. It's just what the press want to hear – and it even ends up in the London papers.

After a quick lunch I'm onto the Star Ferry from Kowloon to Hong Kong Island. I'm surprised that the enterprising Chinese haven't slung at least one bridge across the downtown area, but heartily glad they haven't. Today the water of the unstraddled bay ripples in bright sunshine. They call this millionaire's weather, and I'm off to millionaires' territory – the Happy Valley Racecourse. I reach it by tram, a well-worn vehicle of character that used to run in Glasgow in the 1940s.

Happy Valley is an extraordinary phenomenon. Billions of dollars change hands here on the two days of the week when there is racing, because it is the only legalised gambling in Hong Kong, and the people of the city love to gamble. (Living here at all is a gamble, I suppose.) The Hong Kong Jockey Club, a very exclusive and traditional band of gentlemen, have found themselves sitting on a goldmine, which they are permitted to continue sitting on if they redistribute a certain amount of profit in good works around Hong Kong. So everyone's happy and the place is aptly named.

Buildings all around the course form a natural amphitheatre. When it gets dark and the floodlights bathe the lush green turf and the shining outfits of the jockeys, it becomes curiously intimate. Thousands of spectators are easily absorbed in clean and comfortable surroundings, and there is, in the centre of the track, a huge video screen which gives up-to-date information and a simultaneous TV picture of every race. I'm given a tip by the racing correspondent of the *South China Post*, an amiable Australian. Though I don't much go for the name I do win 600 Hong Kong dollars (about £50) on a horse called Supergear. After a couple of hours, despite the cool clarity of the evening and the spectacular location, the crowds and the standing and the sheer weight of the day's activities get to me, and I return to the sybaritic clutches of the Peninsula.

My bag and my parrot-molested trousers are waiting for me, restored to life. I play the laser disc of David Byrne's movie *True Stories* and eat pigeon breasts and Dover sole. I ring my mother, secure in the knowledge that, at this moment, I can tell her how completely safe I am.

Day 43 6 November

Sunday morning. The only thing that irritates me about this marvellous room is that I can't pull the curtains open. Nose around behind chairs and up and down the walls searching for those pulley systems that hotels like to torment their guests with, and am about to give up in disgust when I notice the word 'curtains' on a space-age control panel beside the bed. One press and they soundlessly swing apart. The start of my seventh week away from home. Almost halfway round the world and yet so much about Hong Kong is familiar that I feel closer to home than at any time since I set out. There's an article about Jamie Lee Curtis and John Cleese in the arts section of the paper, talking about the film we all made last year. The *South China Post* leads with Maggie Thatcher and her triumphal visit to Poland. A long and sycophantic piece, and it comes as no surprise to learn that the *South China Post* is owned by Rupert

Murdoch. Breakfast of muesli, fresh orange juice, croissant, brioche and coffee.

Even the weather is passably English. The humidity and high temperatures that have dominated much of the journey have given way to dry, cooler, crisply fresh air as I walk to the ferry to Cheung Chow – an island known as the Hong Kong Riviera, where live my friend Basil Pao, wife Pat and baby Sonia – born almost to the minute as I left London.

Hong Kong harbour is, like the Happy Valley Racecourse, a great outdoor arena. In the centre of the stage are ships of every shape and size. Coasters, sampans, powerboats, tugs, hydrofoils, yachts, ferries, barges with two or three containers aboard, intercontinental carriers with two or three thousand, junks and rowing boats, floating restaurants, cruise liners and police launches, tankers and motor boats and frigates and rickety wood-built fishing vessels which look as if they have come out of the Middle Ages. (Clem says this is very deceptive and many of them are smugglers fitted with 200 horsepower motors which can move at 30 knots and outrun any police launch.)

I meet Basil at the Cheung Chow Ferry Terminal, an hour or so out from Hong Kong. The island has a Mediterranean feel. The low, white-painted jumble of houses and particularly the richness of produce in the market heighten this impression. Basil selects scallops, prawns and crab which we will take to a local restaurant and have cooked for lunch.

We wet Sonia's head with champagne overlooking a beach on which the Hong Kong Open Windsurfing championships are being held. They look to be dominated, as was the racing last night, by the Australians and New Zealanders. One feels the Chinese have more important things to do than windsurf.

Way beyond the windsurfers and tucked away almost out of sight on another island are the long ugly prison-like blocks that provide temporary accommodation for Vietnamese boat people. There are still thousands unhoused, and a repeated point of issue with the Mother country is her reluctance to take what Hong Kong sees as her fair share.

I have persuaded Basil to come with me to Shanghai. He speaks Mandarin, understands film, is a well-informed guide and brilliant photographer, and we have for many years intended to do a book together on Chinese railways. We celebrate with one of the best meals I've had in 43 days, at a very un-fancy restaurant, known locally as the Bomb Shelter. Basil tells me it's the only one on the island that doesn't use monosodium glutamate. Our scallops are cooked in garlic sauce, the prawns with black bean and chilli sauce, like the crab, and we also feast on calamares fried in spiced salt with black pepper, spicy bean curd and a large and delicious white fish (name unknown). All washed down with Tsingtao Beer, from the mainland.

Reluctantly back to Hong Kong Island after this pleasurable unwinding in a quieter place. The ferry is much busier than when we left this morning. Tourists, many of them German, fight for deck places in the sun. The local Chinese stay inside with the air-conditioning.

By the time we land there is no time for a wash and brush-up before the party. So straight to The 1997, a small, smartly furnished club which doubles as an art gallery and trebles as a jazz club. There to meet me is Sam with my suit. Before I can even try it on a photo has to be taken of the two of us together. The fact that I'm hot and a little irritable doesn't seem to matter, and I now understand why the smiles on so many of his celebrity photos look a little cracked. A fashionable young man sits at the bar and, taking him to be the manager, I ask where I might go to try on my new outfit. He indicates a door which turns out to lead to the gents. I am beginning to bitterly regret this whole enterprise when the door to the gents swings open as I'm in mid-change, catches me off balance and sends me spinning, and half de-trousered, into one of the cubicles.

Eventually all is well. I cool off with a beer and the reassuring attention of the club's real owner, a young man from Austria called Christian. He came to Hong Kong in the Foreign Service eight years ago, quit the job and has been running the club since 1982. He fully expects to be running it after 1997. The bubble of enterprise and energy and self-belief that sustains Hong Kong must not be pricked by premature speculation. I suspect that everyone is looking to the business community. If *they* can operate with the new regime then Hong Kong will probably stay much as it is. A young Italian at the party, confident and prosperous, says that the great attraction of Hong Kong is that almost every financial and commercial practice is legitimate. Stacks of money can be, and are expected to be made. There is a fierce battle for mainland Chinese business, with most governments standing firmly behind their companies in offering substantial discounts on loans. But the Japanese have so far pre-empted everybody, offering the Chinese money at zero interest.

Back at the hotel, the feeling of being back in London persists. There are two messages on the video screen in my room. One to say that Douglas Adams called and the other that Mr Alan Ricker (*sic*) was at the Mandarin. Alan, who was once approached by the BBC to do this journey and who gave me some advice before I left ('Faced with any trouble, I become *tremendously* British'), has rung to check if I'm still alive and Douglas is quite upstaging me with something like a two-year journey to various remote parts of the world for a BBC radio series.

None of the travellers meet tonight though, as I am off to a farewell dinner with Passepartout One at the Kowloon Hotel across the road.

Day 44 7 November

Up at six. Pay my bills and am asked, 'Taxi for airport, sir?' Glad to shake my head and notice momentary concern cross the faces at reception. Can one trust the credit card of a guest who doesn't travel by plane?

Eight o'clock at the Tai Kok Tsui ferry terminal, waiting in a queue beneath a sign 'To China'. Tour groups are pushed through ahead of us. Dishevelled and overladen and in need of sleep we may be, but at least we're not in a herd. Ron and Julian have sacrificed a lie-in to come and say goodbye. We shuffle through. Final farewells. I shall be in Guangzhou this evening. Julian will be in Fulham. As we board our twin-engined catamaran for the 110-mile journey up the Pearl River I talk to Nigel Walters, our new cameraman. He thinks we're doing it right. Travelling by ship, I mean. 'At least your mind gets there at the same time as your body this way.' A customs inspection. 'No spitting', 'No smoking', 'Keep clean please', read the signs. An American girl is worried whether she'll get on. I ask her why she's going to China. She looks nervously around: 'I'm going to Beijing to collect some stuff.'

At 8.20 a.m. the ferry *Long Jin* pulls out into the hyperactive waters of Hong Kong harbour. She was built in Norway two years ago and has a maximum speed of 30 knots. Soon we're passing the New Territories north of Hong Kong, leased from China in 1898 for a 99-year period. These are what will revert to China in 1997, and there is bad feeling here that Mrs Thatcher should have thought it necessary to include Hong Kong Island and Southern Kowloon in the deal.

Now, from the windows of the air-conditioned cabin I catch my first glimpse of Hong Kong's prospective owners. A huge country, but everything is on a smaller scale. Thatched huts stand in the water at the shores of the estuary, beside them long, low, elegant pencil-thin fishing boats. The river is as busy as the harbour in Hong Kong but less glamorous and cosmopolitan –

the boats here move more slowly, and produce is more likely to be shifted in slow-moving lines of multiple barges than in shiny new bulk containers. Most of these barges look as if they're also people's homes. One is black and grimy, straining under a pyramid of coal slack and coke waste, but beside the wheelhouse a man is doing his washing. Clothes hang on a line and pot plants decorate the grubby superstructure. Everywhere I look, on land or on the water, are lines of washing and potted plants. Launderettes and garden centres could be the businesses to get into in China.

Even before we reach Guangzhou (or Canton, as it used to be known) I sense a similarity between China and India, as strongly as the similarity between Hong Kong and Singapore. Though China has factories and modern docks, and even, I'm solemnly informed by the captain as we pass beneath them, the tallest pylons in the world, it's a land of small enterprises, highly labour-intensive, with most of the work being done by human rather than mechanical effort.

Down in the cabin the passengers are riveted to a beauty competition beamed out on Hong Kong television. Basil says the Chinese love beauty contests. He thinks maybe it's an identification with the rags to riches story, the refugee's dream of making it into the glamorous life; which is the motivation of Hong Kong.

As we draw closer to the centre of Guangzhou I notice that the tallest structures are not offices and apartment blocks but something I never saw in Hong Kong – factory chimneys. And they're all belching smoke, lending the skyline a Victorian aspect.

On TV Miss Chinese International 1988 has been chosen and her two dry-eyed rivals attend her simperingly while she, radiant and sparkling, allows a tear or two to trickle deftly onto her left cheek. Whatever is the Chinese equivalent of patriotic music surges and chord-changes its way up the emotions and rings in my ears as I step out onto the soil of the People's Republic for the first time in my life.

One thing a land of over a billion people does not have is staff problems, and this small, rather homely ferry terminal is manned by countless young people in Ruritanian uniforms – peaked caps, lots of braid and buttons and gold-trimmed epaulettes, bottle green for the police and navy blue for the Customs. Unfortunately none of these ornate uniforms fits very well, and no amount of twirly stripes and badges can disguise the cheap and shapeless material, nor can Dan Dare-style peaked caps disguise unflattering lumpy haircuts. But the set-up is extremely efficient and courteous and we are processed through in just 40 minutes, which must be a world record.

Taken to the White Swan Hotel. This is the real thing. A real replica of a Western luxury hotel complete with bellhops, receptionists dressed like lady barristers, a floor of polished granite, a marble-topped reception desk and a hanging gallery of trailing plants surrounding a waterfall, four storeys high, that spills into a little garden with bridges and paths that lead to the coffee shop. I sink gratefully down beside a gurgling pond, in which goldfish laze comfortingly. A lady barrister approaches and waves me away, 'No sit here!'

A constant stream of ruddy-faced, wide-eyed visitors perambulate around the lobby. Some of them are soldiers, some family groups up from the country who gaze about in awe. They all gravitate towards a peach tree made entirely of jade, and here they are photographed. There is a card beside this remarkable object with information in English. It is called, a little baldly: 'Big Sculptured Jade Article'. The blurb continues effusively, 'It has more than a thousand jade peaches and 15,000 jade leaves. It is beautifully shaped and it looks really lifelike. It is the biggest potted landscape in our country at present.'

Mingling incongruously with the Chinese proletariat are huge bronzed Western athletes, glowing with hairy good health and carrying sheaves of tennis rackets. They have come to take part in the first professional tennis tournament ever held in China. They look like men from outer space.

I have a room on the 16th of 28 floors with a stunning view down onto the Pearl River where it bends and is joined by a side canal. I could easily sit and watch the ebb and flow of craft along it all afternoon, but we have a film to make and after a bland international buffet lunch I'm out in the streets. The commonest, nay almost universal, form of transport is the bicycle. No racing bikes here, no sports bikes, mountain bikes or drop-handlebar affectations. These are solid traditional sit up and beg jobs, with wheelguards and racks on the back. Housemasters' bikes. There are occasional cars and the way they are driven suggests an apocalyptic future for China when the millions decide to forsake their bikes for Toyotas. As it is, rush-hour, apart from the occasional tinkle of a bell, is pollution free and wonderfully quiet.

As in India, there are enormous numbers of people about, but the Chinese behave very differently. They're more purposeful, they always seem to be on the move or intent on doing something. There isn't much of the drifting, gazing, eye-wandering of India. Nor are they particularly curious. Whereas Indians are always catching your eye eager to exchange a smile, the Chinese tend to avoid eye contact and it's difficult to get any response from the faces.

Just behind the White Swan is an area called the Shamian. This is where the foreigners who were allowed to trade with Canton in the eighteenth century were confined. I walk along its leafy avenues of cinnamon trees before supper. The great merchants' houses in elaborate Western styles – classical, rococo and baroque with wrought-iron balconies and pillared porticoes – still exist, but the people have taken them over. They have subdivided the huge rooms and hung their washing out on the balconies on bamboo poles and their plants have filled the window ledges and they've lit open fires in the porches.

Three little girls are running up and down an impressive staircase playing a game which involves energetic activities and much shouting at each other. I ask Basil what they're saying. '... and the next competitors are the Americans,' he translates. I remember that it's only a few weeks since the Olympics.

Basil points out several small shops offering earthenware bowls of what looks like stew, heated over a charcoal fire. I am quite tempted to indulge, until he tells me the attractive folksy bowls contain dog.

But greater gastronomic adventure lies in store in the evening. We drive down endless dimly-lit streets, some dark because of low voltage, others because of power cuts, all intriguing and full of atmosphere, to a restaurant at which snake is the speciality. There are one or two in the window, twined around a dusty branch in a cursory attempt to re-create a natural habitat. Inside there's a bustle of waiters and a family atmosphere at the tables. The Chinese, who take their food very seriously, like to select a snake of their choice before it's killed, and accordingly a number are brought to your table, or rather, thank God, to the floor beside your table. They are in circular baskets from which they are extracted and deftly displayed. Not wanting to see them twist and writhe in the air any longer than necessary, and having no clue as to what to look for in a snake, I leave Basil to choose. He selects a nice bit of cobra. The waiter makes a small incision in the chosen one, and deftly removes its gall bladder which is laid neatly upon a white saucer and which will later form the basis of a highly prized liqueur, available here but not in Hong Kong, from whence special tours are laid on to taste it. I'm told it's good for rheumatism and speeds up blood-cell regeneration. Once the gall bladder is removed, the head is cut off and, its forked tongue flicking desperately at thin air, laid beside the saucer on which the gall bladder nestles. The waiter then slits the snake's skin from top to bottom, and with rather too much pulling and tugging for my liking peels it away from the body. Spots of blood splatter onto the floor, but the whole operation is over in less than a minute and is watched, admiringly rather than sensationally, by the other diners. A moment or two to recover before the cooked snake appears (in many forms) at table. It tastes like rich chicken, and is served as part of a long, and I have to say, delicious meal of which I can do little more than relate the menu:

Snake bladder liqueur
Cat and snake soup
Shredded snake with broccoli
Snake balls (tender morsels of deep-fried snake)
Rice birds (these are the smallest birds I've ever eaten, and they come whole, but plucked. None of our party ate the head, which to the Chinese is the supreme delicacy)
Ginseng, chicken and mushroom soup (served from a silver steamer with coiled-snake handles)
Fresh fox (fruit-eating foxes, which live only on bananas and taste of venison)
Noodles
Melons

The proprietor assures us that all his snakes are free-range, from the warm and humid province of Guangxi, and that autumn is the best time of year to eat them, as they've fattened themselves for winter hibernation. And in case we still have any doubts, the Chinese Olympic team trained on snake and ginseng – and they were the most successful in Asia. There's a lesson there somewhere.

When I get back to the White Swan it's a little after eleven o'clock. I notice that people are still working on the building site next door.

Day 45 8 November

Up at 6.15. Misty half-light over the Pearl River. To Guangzhou station for the 8.30 train to Shanghai. Through the cycle rush-hour. Only older men still favour Mao jackets. Otherwise it's Western 1950s or, amongst the young, American casual. A Turnerish sunrise spreads over the city, silhouetting the forest of TV aerials turned, despite official discouragement, in the direction of Hong Kong.

The long, elevated motorway to the station is a Western commuter's dream; almost empty at peak travel time. At the station, an immense characterless building in a side square crowned with neon signs advertising Sanyo, Seiko and State Express 555s, there are few vehicles but a huge swell of people. Many are squatting in groups on the main concourse, their baggage consisting of two plastic or string bags, looped around a bamboo pole, and carried on their shoulders. They scan a state-of-the-art matrix indicator for news of their train.

Ours is already at the platform, which is clean and well-swept. The eighteen coaches are green- and cream-painted, of chunky old-fashioned design, ridged along the outside with air vents on top. A stocky girl with a pretty face and pigtails stands, in the uniform of the railways, at the entrance to our 'Soft Class' coach. Attendants in peaked caps abound (there are fifty to serve this train). One feels that part of China's achievement has been to put as many people as possible into uniform – of any kind.

The 'Hard Class' coaches are already full, their occupants leaning from open windows to buy sandwiches, orange juice and cola, or drinking their tea from big enamel mugs. The 'Intermediate Class' have bunks, but in an open-plan arrangement, and without the homely touches of 'Soft Class' compartments, which include four berths, complete with duvets and fluffy pink cushions, a small table with an embroidered red cloth on which is set a reproduction oil lamp with cut-glass shade, and, of course, a pot plant. Lace curtains are drawn back at the window. It's very cosy, an odd mixture between a bordello and my grandmother's.

We leave on time and are quickly out of the city and into a landscape of fields still worked by families with hoes and rakes. Our smiling, pigtailed lady appears with an enormous steaming kettle and fills up my thermos jug. Another attendant follows up with some cups and jasmine tea-bags.

Talk to a helpful railwayman who tells me, among other things, that we have 13 stops ahead of us on our 35-hour, 1,130-mile journey. He's called Mr Cha and has worked on the railways for more than 20 years. I ask him if there were foreigners riding on Chinese railways 20 years ago.

'Oh yes, indeed. But only from countries we were friendly with.'

'Such as?'

'Vietnam, North Korea …' He can't think of any more names. He gets off at the next stop and leaves me his cap badge as a memento.

At 10.30 plastic bags are brought round to collect our rubbish. Outside, the landscape is still, serene and peaceful. Every stage of rice production is in evidence: planting, growing, harvesting, winnowing and threshing, all non-mechanised, like a series of period tableaux. A couple of perky dogs march across a field, tails in the air.

'Lunch on a lead,' says Clem.

Lunch turns out to be dog-free and extremely good. There is one restaurant car, which appears to exist mainly to service the huge staff, who are to be found in there most times of day, with their caps off, laughing and gossiping. The kitchen is solid and heavy and full of people, with the cooking done by five chefs on cast iron ranges in woks the size of Jodrell Bank. The tablecloths are plastic and two bottles are at each table, one marked 'China Red Wine' the other 'Chinese Brandy'. I presume they're ornamental as I never see either drunk by anyone throughout the journey.

Those who don't want the restaurant, and haven't brought their own food, can buy carry-on lunches in white polystyrene boxes, which they then throw out of the windows.

At Ganzhou station a wall is being erected at enormous speed, by a workforce consisting of old men, young men, women and boys. Fourteen-year-olds are straining under bamboo yokes from which are suspended pails full of bricks. I counted 30 in one load.

We talk to some of the passengers in Intermediate, including an infectiously enthusiastic lady who has learnt English off the BBC World Service. When asked for an interview she agrees politely and just before we turn over cries, 'Wait a minute!' and rushes off to put on her lipstick.

Mid-afternoon and feeling drowsy as we pass into Hunan province – Mao's province. I talk to Mr Xie, one of our minders from China TV. He's very earnest and calls me 'Mr Mike'.

'Lot of people have deep feeling for Mao,' he says, 'but there have been economic changes that are visible, and the political changes must accompany economic changes.'

'Do you think there will be free elections in China, say, ten years from now?'

'Yes,' nods Mr Xie, frowning with concentration, 'is historical tendency.'

Now we are in amongst walls of rock rising sheer from the fields, eroded into fantastic shapes. Then we run along a narrow gorge beside a mud-brown river, down which stacks of bamboos are being punted. At Zhenzhou a couple of grimy steam engines stand tantalisingly close to our train. I hop out and ask if I might climb up into the cab. (For train buffs, the engines were 2–10–2s with smoke deflectors, built in 1981.) Whilst in the cab I notice that the engine is parked level with the roof of a long engine shed, roofed with small earthenware tiles, of the kind which Terry Gilliam, one of my timekeepers, requested I bring back. Very gently I prise one loose and return to the train, very pleased with myself.

At sunset *Swan Lake* is playing over the PA as we head out of Hangyang. The chef excels himself and provides the best train meal in 45 days. Pigeon in soy sauce, squid on a hot plate, with tomato, pork and sea-turtle casserole, fish cutlet, and in the Chinese manner, just as you think the meal is over, soup – in this case cucumber and egg-white. In Intermediate Class they're playing draughts. A lot of people are smoking. The land outside is very dark. The stations we pass through are dismally lit, though large crowds still wait patiently on the platforms.

At Zhuzhou station at 10.15, Dave Passepartout goes in search of digestive biscuits, a man goes along checking the axle temperature with his bare hands and Mr Xie wants to draw me into conversation about the book I'm reading: *The Horse's Mouth* by Joyce Carey.

'This look very serious book, Mr Mike.'

When I tell him that much of it is raucously funny, he seems very disappointed.

Later: I'm comfortable under the thick duvet but lie awake for quite a while, listening to the ever-changing sounds of the train. It seems wrong to waste any of China in sleep.

Day 46 9 November

Hot water arrives at twenty to seven. Hawaiian music is playing over the broadcasting system. Beyond the lace curtains the fields are already full. The countryside is like a Thomas Hardy novel come to life. One man is hoeing, another cutting the rice. A woman is washing, someone else is fishing, another feeding rice stalks into a thresher which two others pedal. An old man is setting the cut rice up in stooks, a woman tills the soil, two men pass carrying a threshing machine on a pole slung between their shoulders. A brick kiln is already smoking. The Chinese seem to have an insatiable appetite for building.

Into the loo for a wash. Only cold water and that is sporadic. The smells have increased overnight, and my Armani soap, a memento of what seems like days long ago at the Peninsula Hotel, adds an unlikely whiff of Beverly Hills to this stained and shabby place. As I return to the compartment, I find my way blocked by our attendant who is sloshing a filthy old mop across the floor of the corridor. It's a painful process to watch, as the floor is carpeted.

At Yin-Tang in Jianxi Province I alight from the train and take the morning air. I realise, with quite a start, that it is cool, even cold, and riffle through my bag for my short-sleeve sweater, which I haven't worn since the night we left Venice. There's an edge of autumn in the air which I suppose is to be expected as we've been travelling due north since leaving Singapore – from 150 miles off the Equator six days ago to over 2,000 miles north today.

More steam engines up here. One passes slowly in the dusty low sunshine, double-headed with a diesel. Interesting comparison. What makes steam engines so good to watch is that you can see them working.

The countryside continues to be fascinating. The Chinese manage their water carefully. Every village has its central pond (with ducks and geese in attendance), and a nearby river with channels and canals and waterwheels and stout stone bridges that Devon would be proud of. The water always seems to be still, reflecting the life that goes on around it, and setting off the constant movement of figures on the landscape. Tufted haystacks, tufted rice stooks, tufted children.

Our latest estimate of arrival is four hours late in Shanghai. Mr Xie can see I want to be left alone, so he slides up to me: 'What are you thinking, Mr Mike?'

Last night I gave him *Travellers* by Ruth Prawer Jhabwala and Graham Greene's *Ways of Escape*. He was absolutely delighted and has probably read them already. But I haven't enough stamina for a literary discussion and I mime exhaustion so effectively that he nods understandingly, like a hospital visitor, and settles down to watch me.

From the compartment next door comes the rasping prelude to a good spit. The Chinese are great expectorators and very often a hideous deep-throated rumble will belong to a petite lady.

I visit the train's DJ. She is a petite lady but would, I'm sure, never be heard to rasp. One of the qualifications of her job is 'impeccable Mandarin' and besides record requests and on-train information *and* pre-announcing every station, there's precious little time for a rasp even if she wanted to.

Her compartment is papered in dark-blue brushed suede. There is a tiny bed and a stack of cassette players, amplifiers and a mike. She has 30 cassettes, two of which are Western. One is classical, another contains an amalgam of such memorable tracks as 'Let's Go' by Magazine '60 and 'Scandal Eyes' by Fesh. Requests to play a track from my Springsteen and Billy Joel tapes have been vetoed by her superior, the Director of On-train Broadcasting, so I suggest a Mozart flute piece instead. She eyes my tape doubtfully. They don't know who Mozart is, so it's privately played first, approved and, much later, relayed to the rest of the train.

Talk to two journalists from Shanghai. She is 32, he's 33. In the last ten years they have seen their salaries increase and the freedom of the press widen. They are proud of the fact that their newspaper – *The People's Evening News* – is not a government mouthpiece and has a circulation of 1.8 million. The view of Shanghai people is that the process of opening up – Chinese *glasnost* – should continue. The irony is that it has not changed Shanghai, which always enjoyed a privileged and independent status, even under Mao. The recent improvements have allowed the rest of the country to catch up and Shanghai's privileged position is now threatened.

At Xiaoshan industry intrudes onto the Arcadian landscape, dust and smoking chimneys, coal heaps and piles of ballast everywhere.

I meet the nearest thing to a Chinese yuppy, a 24-year-old girl in smart Western-style outfit who has learnt English with an American accent. I ask her where she works and she replies, without a pause for breath: 'China National Light Industrial Products Import and Export Corporation Shanghai Branch.' She's returning from the Canton Trade Fair where she has been selling hurricane and kerosene lamps. I ask what she thinks of the Chinese one-child policy.

'Well, *I* don't want *any* children,' she says with great determination. 'We have too many people.'

But she concedes that most of her fellow Chinese wouldn't agree with her. She works a six-day week and for relaxation likes the cinema and going out with her old classmates. She likes Western films but *Waterloo Road* was the only title she could remember seeing recently.

One advantage of running four hours late is that we have time for another dinner. A lot of the standard ingredients have run out and the chefs are making the best of whatever they can find. So tripe and eels (in soy sauce and chilli) and duck's gizzards are presented.

It is a tired and travel-worn Passepartout who partakes of a whisky with me as we roll in darkness through the interminable hinterland of China's biggest city. We have been moved out of the corridor, and the much-mopped red carpet has been rolled up. We have been shifted around our compartment so they can collect the towels and sheets. It's the end of journey treatment which I have observed many times on British long-distance trains, that point at which you switch from being a customer to being an encumbrance. When there's nothing left for you to buy, you're in the way.

Nigel returns from the loo with a look of deep shock on his face. He's just seen all the plastic bags, into which they so punctiliously gathered our rubbish, being emptied out of the window.

9.30: At Shanghai. Cannot see any porters. Maybe people aren't allowed to be porters here. So long walk with bags down densely packed, featureless walkways, smelling of chlorine.

Then an hour's wait in a cold car park for all our film gear to be checked through. A female voice echoes across the emptiness from the station loudspeakers. I ask Basil what she is going on about. He says they are public service admonitions – advising people not to smoke within the station area as it pollutes the air for others and polluted air makes you dizzy and so on ... It doesn't seem to make much difference.

Midnight: In bed at the Peace Hotel, formerly the Cathay Hotel, built by the Sassoon family between 1926 and 1929. Noel Coward may have slept here. I *certainly* will. Slightly regret the gizzards.

Day 47 10 November

My room is spacious, but there isn't much to fill the space. The curtains don't quite meet in the middle and the carpet bears some prominent stains.

Down to breakfast, only to find it's being served on the eighth floor. As I climb back into the lift I'm horrified to see one of the uniformed attendants clear his throat vigorously and deposit a glob of spit, quite deliberately, in a rather attractive brass bowl which sits on a pedestal by the lift doors. Later I see someone else doing it and feel foolish that I didn't know such a beautiful object could be a spittoon.

The Peace Hotel is a curious mixture of dark and oppressive English thirties suburban mixed in with some fine examples of Art Deco, and a spectacular Chinese-style banqueting room with dragons in bas-relief curling round the walls and ceiling. Nobody knows much about Sassoon, the man who built it, except that he was a Jew, possibly from Baghdad, who came to China and made a lot of money out of the opium trade.

Drive out to see his family house, about half an hour from the centre of Shanghai. The well-trimmed lawns, the swinging garden seat and the mock-Tudor mansion with its beamed ceilings and latch doors, wrought-iron chandeliers and minstrel's gallery, are pure Sunningdale. But the grand piano is under covers and there's no one in plus-fours with a pipe standing by the fireplace nor any cucumber sandwiches to be enjoyed in the big antimacassared armchairs. It's an odd and melancholy experience to see this ghost of a past and to realise such quintessential Englishness survived the days of Mao Tse-tung intact.

Driving back into town, I sense a prosperous, confident city, with many of the manifestations of other boomtowns on the Pacific Rim. A huge amount of new construction, much of it hotels and trade centres, is under way in conjunction with foreign companies – Australians and Japanese and Americans. One sign beside a picture of towers of the future reads, 'Sister Cities Co-Operation, Shanghai – San Francisco'. It's very easy to forget that you are in a Communist country.

Lunch at the Shanghai Old Restaurant, in existence for 100 years, my first experience of traditional Shanghainese cuisine. The menu is nothing if not original: Preserved Duck Eggs, Crab Yolk and Sharks Fins, Smashed Chicken with Sea Slugs, Squirrel Yellow Fish, Minced Pork Ball and Potted Big Fish Head. Being conservative we stick to crabmeat and bean curd, and squid and eel with garlic and pepper – which is quite sensational.

An attractive and beguiling side of Shanghai exists only just off the main thoroughfares and the construction sites. There are narrow streets and squares of low buildings of some style, with louvred shutters and wrought-iron balconies, on an enjoyably human scale, lively and thriving. There are rice kitchens and small electrical shops, where, if you buy a calculator, your bill will be added on an abacus, and the elegant Tong Han Chun Tang Chinese Medicine Store (established 1783) whose speciality is the Zhang Guang Brand 101 Hair Regenerating Extract (formerly the Baldish Hair Regenerating Tincture). 'The outstanding invention of Dr Zhang has brought the masses of sufferers from alopecia happiness and good tidings.'

This is traditional medicine and the ingredients are organic and not chemical. I ask for a tonic, something to relieve travel fatigue and generally rejuvenate me. Various roots and mosses and ginseng extracts are gathered from their jars, mixed together and handed to me in brown envelopes. To achieve full potency, I must pour boiling water on these dry bits of debris twice a day for the next three days, and drink the brew.

The streets outside are meticulously swept, and appear to provide jobs for everyone. There is a car parking warden, with his white cap, and there is a bicycle warden with his red armbands. Old men and women, beyond retiring age, are employed as street attendants. They have red flags and megaphones and are deployed at busy junctions, bus queues and outside popular shops to regulate the pedestrian traffic.

As it is difficult for the average citizen to get permission to travel across China, let alone the world, the chance to speak to a foreigner is highly prized. A retired bus conductor spoke impeccable English, which he'd learnt to give him 'a better knowledge of socialism and its international application'. I keep forgetting that the theory of socialism is all of Western, not Eastern origin. For half an hour or so the bus conductor, and an engineer and a couple of younger Chinese, ask me about home, as a crowd gathers round.

This old part of the city around the sixteenth-century Ming dynasty Yu Garden, with well-preserved pavilions, gardens, ponds and rockeries, is much more amenable than the Nanjing Road, where I end up later trying to buy some protection against the sudden arrival of autumn.

It's getting dark and the crowds and the dimly lit shops remind me of Sheffield in the early 1950s. The fashions are certainly of that period, and I'm made aware of how much bigger most of us are than the exiguous Chinese. I tire very quickly of hearing 'No got' and return, empty-handed and exhausted, to the Peace Hotel.

Later, in the coffee shop, a jazz band composed entirely of elderly Chinese gentlemen is thumping out 'Alexander's Ragtime Band' and 'You Are My Sunshine'. This is a happier example of cultural miscegenation, as the Chinese seem to take to black American music with great style. They are retired players from the Shanghai Symphony Orchestra and have been resident here for years. Cities with a 'naughty past', like Shanghai and Havana, have always fascinated me, and as the band breaks into 'Tiger Rag' one can, even in the chaste surroundings of the Peace Hotel Coffee Shop, imagine a little more easily how lively things were in Shanghai in the days when Noel Coward might have slept here.

Day 48 11 November

Out early to film the Chinese at their mass, public, morning exercises. We're on the Bund at half past six, but the Tai Chi classes are already under way, and, horror of horrors, in the middle of 80 pairs of slowly circling arms is a television presenter, clutching his mike and delivering a long piece to camera. He is only one of three TV crews, not including ourselves, who are also recording this unusual and highly visual social phenomenon. I notice that they tend to concentrate their cameras on the group activities, whereas, for me, the fascination likes in the peripheral, individual behaviour. Respectable middle-aged gentlemen, looking like civil servants, can be found with legs up on a fence, foreheads bent low toward their knees, twirling swords about their heads, or literally spinning themselves around. A woman of advancing years bounces her back gently and repeatedly against a plane tree, a younger woman instructs a clumsy soldier in some balancing act, a silver-haired man who looks into his seventies is doing amazing things with an unfurled umbrella, sweeping the ground with lithe, balletic movements and ending in the splits.

All this is being done, not in any special area or with any special clothing, but on the way to work. There is none of the western paraphernalia of jogging suits and trainers and designer sweatshirts. Nor is the exercise punishing or demanding or violent. It's all controlled movement, bending, stretching; relaxing and coordinating rather than body-building. A young man comes up to me to practise his English. He's already done his Tai Chi – 30 minutes at six o'clock – and he's rather dismissive of the group everyone's filming. They are only doing 24 variations. Some people do 88.

How many does he do? '110,' he replies, without immodesty. He asks me about my business here. I start to tell him about *Around the World in Eighty Days*, and he interrupts knowledgeably: 'Ah yes, I know the book you are referring to. It is a work of science fiction.'

Despite a sore head from the beer and jazz last night, I attempt a run. The sheer weight of numbers prevents me. 12.5 million inhabitants on the move, and not an empty pavement anywhere.

Back in my room for a bath and some breakfast. It's eight o'clock and I feel I've already done a day's work. The *China Daily* bears news of the American Presidential election and a front cover photo of George Bush triumphant. Regulation grin, arms wide above his head, wife beside him, in one of those spontaneous gestures which ceased to be spontaneous years ago. The Americans seem to have voted for another four years of the same. Expected but depressing. I write postcards – dozens of them, driven perhaps by the knowledge that 60 years ago in Shanghai Noel Coward wrote *Private Lives* in four days.

Mental and physical energies recharged after a couple of hours to myself, I take a walk with Basil round the streets at the back of the Bund. My guidebook explains that 'visitors who have been to Shanghai before 1949 may find the names on the streets radically altered', and provides generous help to those who might be looking again for Bubbling Well Road (Janjing Road), Avenue Foch West (Yan'An Road), Avenue du Roi Albert (Shaanxi Road) or Robinson Road (Changshou Road).

There are a lot of comic books and magazines available on pavement stands. One has a lurid picture of a man carrying off a woman. Basil translates the title for me: *Silver Snake and the Beautiful Woman*. There are also a number of literary magazines – *Foreign Stories, Culture and Life*. Girls' faces are used to sell a lot of the mags, but I notice that the features of these alluring girls are never Chinese, always Western.

We eat dumplings and chives at a tiny table with two benches on the pavement. It's most satisfying to sit and watch the world go by. I realise, of course, that I can only do this with someone who speaks the language, and if I were in Shanghai with a tour group I wouldn't be sitting here.

Lots of food on sale at the street side. Confirms my impression that Chinese are the Small Businessmen of the World. Watercress, spring onions, fennel, red and green peppers, turnips, pickled cabbage, cauliflower and dried bean curd in chunks, like sealing wax. Live chickens and fish in small tanks, pigeons, bananas, noodles and, of course, snakes.

Along the Sichuan Zhong Lu, with its buildings in Venetian and Florentine Renaissance style, the door to an impressive office building bears the name 'Complete Sets of Equipment Corporation'.

The Opium Wars of the 1840s made drugs big business in China. Shanghai became the new centre, for only an hour up the river Huangpu was the Yangtze and a gateway to the heartland of China. This is what the reappearance of the Florentine Renaissance on the shores of the East China Sea is all about.

I'm soon to see the East China Sea for myself, for at five o'clock we're due to set sail for Yokohama. The ferry goes once a week and if there is any delay we are in trouble again. But with a deep blast of the horn it pulls out into the river, dead on time, executes a 360-degree turn opposite the Zhong Shou Road (formerly the Quai de France), which is rather like making a U-turn on the M1, and heads slowly up the crowded river to the confluence of the Yangtze.

A magnificent sunset to match this morning's spectacular sunrise. The domes and spires of the city are outlined in red and gold before sliding slowly into silhouette.

An hour or two later, after supper, I walk out on deck. I needed that coat I didn't buy. The night is clear, silent and chilly. We're free of the metropolitan sprawl of Shanghai, and the only lights I can see are coastal beacons, and small ships a long way off. We could be on the open sea, except that the water below me is muddy brown. We're on the Yangtze, and still two hours from the ocean.

Ten o'clock at night, Day 48. On the Yangtze River, heading due East, the Reform Club still over half the world away.

Day 49 12 November

Woken by the sound of inscrutable Chinese announcements on the tannoy. Knowing that, for once, we don't have an early start, I turn smugly onto my side, pull the sheets over my head and look forward to a long, late breakfast. An hour later, refreshed, bathed and relaxed I amble down to the canteen only to find that the inscrutable announcement was informing passengers that the clocks had gone forward an hour. It's now ten o'clock and breakfast has long since finished. I'm directed to the Coffee Room, where I find a bartender, a waitress and no one else. Order a coffee, orange juice and biscuits and sit by a low table spread with a Shanghai silk cloth. The room is full of fussy, abstract perspex fittings (which I come to recognise as a feature of Japanese interior design), swivel chairs and mournful piped music. The good-natured waitress brings me some carefully prepared Nescafé in a cup which bears the words 'Good Day,

LEFT: *Rough days on the South China Sea: Phileas looks out on a Force 7 gale.*

BELOW: *Owing to an error in the BBC computer, I'm met by a Rolls-Royce in Hong Kong.*

OPPOSITE: *Attacked by a cockatoo in the bird market, Hong Kong.*

RIGHT: *Joining in the gambling at the Happy Valley Race Course.*

BELOW: *On the ferry to Cheung Chow I note that they call this 'Millionaire's Weather'.*

RIGHT: *On my way into China.*

BELOW: *Life on the barges.*

FAR RIGHT: *At Zhen-zhou station – China is the last great refuge of steam.*

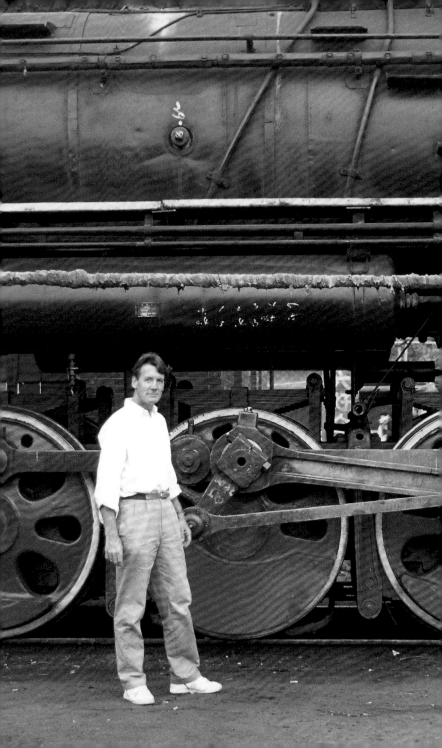

LEFT: *Boy looking out of the window on the Shanghai Express.*

BELOW LEFT: *On the train to Shanghai: Englishmen are a curiosity in Intermediate Class.*

RIGHT: *Mr Cha making a kind gift of his cap badge.*

BELOW: *Faces of Shanghai.*

OVERLEAF: *The great Chinese workout.*

nice friends'. She speaks a little English and tells me that the ship, called the *Jian Zehn*, is a Sino-Japanese ferry, operated by the Chinese, built in Japan. Her capacity is 560 passengers, but there are only 165 on board today. I ask her how long she's worked on the ship, and she says eight months.

'Do you like it?'

'Only a little.'

The cassette runs out and in selecting one to replace it, she picks up a tape called 'Songs of a Stormy Night'.

'Beautifurr music,' she sighs, and slips the tape in lovingly.

The first minute or so consists entirely of the sound of rumbling thunder and heavy rain, which seems to be tempting fate a little. Eventually some strangulated synchronised chords are added to the bad weather. I smile, she smiles back, distantly. The recorded thunder rumbles. Glance out of the porthole to reassure myself it *is* a tape making these noises, and find a calm sea and the sun high in a sky of cotton-wool clouds. She smiles, I smile, the bartender smiles. It seems the only thing to do.

Later I explore the boat. Past the sign 'Gentles toilet' and endless slot machines dispensing beer, soap, coffee, noodles and sticky soft drinks.

There turns out to be another film crew aboard. Some 25 strong, from NHK, the Japanese BBC, shooting a drama about a woman of mixed Sino-Japanese parentage, born in Shanghai when the Japanese occupied it during the Second World War, who is bringing her children to China to decide what nationality they will adopt. They are shooting a scene of a waiter walking up some steps to a cabin. As these are the steps up to my cabin, and as the waiter always seems to get something wrong, I decide to go out on deck for a while.

In a forlorn games room stand two or three well-worn ping-pong tables with legs missing. A group of Japanese students are playing cards at plastic tables in the stern, set below a circular striped plastic canvas stretched across slender plastic poles to create a little plastic gazebo. I can only see two Europeans, who

I think may possibly be a honeymoon couple so deeply are they involved in each other. Shirt off and sit for a while reading Anthony Burgess's reminiscences which often make me laugh out loud.

Later Passepartout, who has enjoyed a day off, is asked to be an extra in the Japanese film. The scene is to be shot in the bar and payment is as much to drink as they want. As Nigel, Simon, Dave and Angela walk onto the set there is a spontaneous round of applause from the Japanese. On deck at 10 before turning in for an early night, I can pick out the lights of small boats and some coastal settlement to the north. Consulting my map, I deduce that we are passing through the archipelago of the Rijuku Islands, off the southern tip of Honshu. This is my first sight of Japan, as we leave the East China Sea and sail into the Pacific, the tenth sea I've entered since crossing the English Channel. I brew up some hot water in my cabin and take another dose of my Chinese medicine. The taste sensation is roughly similar to lying face downwards, mouth open in a patch of damp woodland.

Day 50 13 November

Filming around the boat. Clem decides on a 'where is everybody?' angle, only to find that the warm sunshine and calm sea has fetched everybody out, and in order to get the feeling of emptiness we have to move people out of the way.

The 'newly-weds' turn out to be a society acupuncturist from Paris who has been walking round the world for two years and a Dutch student of Arabic studies who fell in with him on the way. Having walked from Paris to Pakistan (where he had talked with General Zia less than a week before his death), into Afghanistan where he had spent six weeks with the Mujahidin, it came as a rude shock to find that China, the country that had been his goal, proposed to charged him 45,000 dollars for permission to walk across it. He came in on The Great Silk Road. I expressed my envy. 'Forget it,' he flicked his hand dismissively. 'It doesn't exist any more … it's all just the same … temples, monasteries. You've seen one temple …'

He certainly had a bad case of disillusionment. I asked if the Chinese had been welcoming.

'The minorities, yes,' said his companion … 'in Tibet especially; but in mainland China, no.'

They had been viewed with deep suspicion, followed, asked for money and forced sometimes to spend a night in a local jail. They had a fund of horror stories about the country, a lot of them, to be honest, second-hand. One concerned a student who had her camera stolen on a train. At the next stop, the train doors had been locked and the police had come on board. They found a man with a camera and asked the girl if it was hers. She nodded. Then the policeman assured her that there were no thieves in China and shot the man dead on the spot.

We talk about medicine. I ask him what he thinks about the Chinese attitude to doctors – that you pay them when you're well and stop paying them when you're ill. He seems to agree with the traditional Chinese approach, and says he no longer believes in Western medicine. He taps his head. 'So long as you eat the right food, breathe the right air …'

At three o'clock in the afternoon the east coast of Japan can be clearly seen on the port side, rising in a series of rocky cliffs. The Pacific, meanwhile, is living up to its name, and time passes slowly.

In the shop down below I buy a book of short stories by a Chinese author, Lu Wenfu. He had joined up to fight the Kuomintang rule in 1949, but later found himself, as a writer of fiction, denounced during the Cultural Revolution. 'I was forced to confess my crimes and paraded through the street with a placard round my neck.' He was luckier than some. He escaped with banishment to the countryside. Others lost their lives, many were unable to write again. The fact that Lu Wenfu is being published again in China has to be balanced against the unhappy experiences of the Walking Acupuncturist.

I also buy a sweatshirt with a glamorous picture of the ferry on it and a wonderful example of Anglo-Oriental doggerel: 'Regular weekly service with gorgeous cargo-passenger boat. A Happy, Warmed Journey with Thrilling Sealine.'

Day 51 14 November

We're due in Yokohama at 8.05 this morning, but no ship I've been on yet has arrived on time. My now dog-eared copy of *Around the World in Eighty Days* reminds me that Passepartout came alongside the wharf at Yokohama aboard *The Carnatic* on 14 November 1872 – 116 years ago to the day – but without Fogg whom he'd lost in Hong Kong. Even with the run of misfortunes they were still only 44 days out of London. I could catch up on the Pacific which Fogg took 22 days to cross, if I'm able to find a vessel able to outrun his *General Grant*, '… a large side-wheel steamer of 2,500 tons, well equipped and of great speed'.

I pull back the thin orange curtains and there is Japan. The rays of the rising sun, appropriately, fill the little cabin, spilling out from behind a dark outline of ragged hills. Elaborate announcements in Chinese and Japanese.

We move slowly towards the indistinct brown-grey skyline of Yokohama. (The brown are the buildings, the grey is a corona of polluted air above them.) Pass two of the largest vessels I've ever seen, both car transporters with the name Nissan in 20-foot-high letters on the side. They are incredible hulks which make container ships look graceful, but their size is evidence of the commercial power of Japan. Behind them equally enormous super-tankers are queueing to unload their oil. As fast as the oil comes in, the cars go out.

In this harbour full of Leviathans it's good to see the occasional grimy freighter, like the *Asian Rose* of Panama, the

Chunji of Pusan, bringing scrap metal from Korea, and one whose name can only just be made out beneath the stains and scuffed paint – *Venus*, Manila.

The tug *Yokohama Maru* gives a prolonged blast on the horn to warn off about six other vessels which seem to be heading for our spot on the jetty and begins to heave us round and into position. The Chinese students who have come to study in Japan lean expectantly over the rails. The Walking Acupuncturist shoulders an enormous pack, the back of which is adorned with the names of his twin causes: 'Enfants Réfugiés du Monde' and 'Université Européenne de Médecine Chinoise'.

Dockers in uniform yellow windcheaters stand by to catch the ropes. Customs men in immaculate navy-blue uniforms ease on white gloves in preparation for boarding. A volley of poppers and streamers crackle out from a welcoming party for the students. Next to me are a Japanese family who had taken a bus across China for a holiday in Pakistan, only to be turned back at the Pakistan border because of a cholera scare. They seem to have taken it awfully well.

A Sousa march is blaring from the terminal loudspeakers, mingling in a musical Babel with the Viennese waltzes on the ship's indefatigable Muzak system. We are processed through customs and immigration politely and briskly, and driven the short distance to Yokohama Shin-Kensan station. *Shin-Kensan* means 'New Railway', better known in the west as the Bullet Train.

The Sousa march played as we landed is a fitting foretaste of the extraordinary Americanisation of Japan, the country America bombed into submission in the war, rebuilt in its own likeness and to which it has now ceded economic primacy.

So the forecourt of the station has a restaurant called The New York Lunch Box, an advert for the Home Town Express and Tom and Jerry selling something. The remarkable part of it is that few of the Japanese speak or write English. They know a few key words, culled phonetically from American records and movies and TV shows and thrown together to create a new and batty half-language which erupts on carrier bags – 'Trad Boy, Tradition succeeded to Men', or sweatshirts 'Soul Explosion', 'Funny Crazy', 'Hey Sexy'. There's a sock brand sold at one of the numerous little station shops, called 'Naughty Boy', and I was told that someone saw an immaculate, expensively dressed woman, wearing a huge leather belt on which the word 'Bullshit' was written at regular intervals.

The station is kept obsessively clean, not just swept with a brush but scrubbed with soap and water by an army of Lady Macbeths trying to get rid of any stains that might indicate poverty or economic back-sliding.

The Japanese are very well dressed. Their shape and style reminds me of the Italians. I'm afraid we stand out like a bunch of tramps. I feel like those Chinese peasants who came wide-eyed into the lobby of the White Swan to gaze in awe at what man could make of his world. Feel a little less impressed when a dapper businessman gets onto the train wearing a smog mask.

Inside and out the train resembles an aircraft. The pointed nose, with the cabin high up, looks like the front of a 747, cut off, then stuck on to a line of wingless aircraft fuselages. The seats inside are laid out like aircraft seats, and the driver wears a pilot's peaked and braided cap. Your ticket tells you exactly where to stand on the platform. The train arrives every 10 minutes exactly on time and the doors are open for 30 seconds only. They are meant for light-travelling businessmen, not round the world film crews, and feeling like participants in some game show we only just haul our baggage aboard in time.

A 15-minute ride into Tokyo through an unbroken swath of close-packed housing. Hardly a break in the jostle of low-rise, flimsy-looking boxes which I'm told cost half a million pounds minimum in the centre of Tokyo. So little room is there that the golf-crazy Japanese have to build their courses on the tops of buildings. Well-behaved, well-heeled fellow passengers read their papers which are headlined, as I'm told they have been since late August, with news of Emperor Hirohito's illness. Nothing is spared. The big news today is that he hasn't had a bowel movement for a week. Details of his pulse and blood pressure are as meticulously recorded as the Dow-Jones Index.

At Tokyo station the magazine racks are full of George Bushes with their arms spread out. A Japanese magazine bears the English title *Heart Washing*. I bend to look more closely and rest my bag which is heavy on my shoulders. I immediately have to pick it up again as a lady on a sweeping machine bears down on me.

Parties of schoolchildren, uniformed and well-behaved, are led through the crowds by teachers holding flags above their heads. The girls are in navy blue with pleated skirts, the boys in what looks like Prussian hussars' uniforms, with black tunics, buttoned high up to the neck. (I later learn these traditional boys' school uniforms are in fact based on Prussian army jackets.)

At the entrance to the park which surrounds Hirohito's Imperial Palace stand serried ranks of silver TV vans, topped with plastic-shrouded outside broadcast cameras, waiting, like hooded vultures.

I can see trees whose leaves are turning and I'm reminded that, though Tokyo is on the same latitude as Morocco, its climate is closer to that of Manchester and I am back again in a land of four seasons. I can't postpone augmenting my wardrobe any longer and in the spirit of Fogg's instruction to Passepartout – 'we shall purchase on the way' – I sally forth to the department stores. Japanese department stores are an institution, and they take their role in national life very seriously. Apart from offering an enormous range of everything they are also travel agents, concert halls, cinemas and art galleries. Picasso's *Acrobat and Young Harlequin* has just been bought for 38 million dollars, to be displayed not in the

Japanese National Gallery but in the Mitsukoshi department store. Rivals Seibu recently bought a Monet for 10.5 million.

At twenty to seven in the evening I'm drinking a coffee at the Concorde bar on the top floor of the Hankyu department store, Tokyo. I walked in here about 35 minutes ago, found a selection of clothes I liked, mostly from Italy and England, bought a jacket, a sweater and two pairs of trousers. Both the trousers needed taking up, and the assistant apologised that this might take half an hour! As I was paying my bill they noticed my finger had a small slightly bloody scratch and, within seconds, had produced a Band-Aid and dressed it for me. As I leave the store at seven, clutching my new outfit and dying to replace my embarrassingly creased stained and travelworn shirts and parrot-pecked trousers, the staff of each department, from Soft Toys to Dental Appliances, gather at the top of their respective escalators to bow. I may look like Worzel Gummidge, but for four floors I'm the Queen.

Both Shanghai and Tokyo have populations of around 12 million, but the difference in the look of the people is enormous. Japan seems to consist of one very affluent middle class, busy and assured of their place in a sophisticated urban technopolis. Shanghai's crowds seem out of another century. Central Tokyo at night is a blaze of light, an eruption of neon, trains rumbling overhead, roads full of cars. But there are no jaywalkers and no black plastic bags. Control is the name of the game here. I take a taxi back to the hotel with my new acquisitions. Not only does the back door swing open automatically, it also closes automatically, and like the bullet train you have to move fast or you'll lose something.

Cultural magpies, the Japanese have an ability to replicate with great skill whatever attracts them. So we end up eating Tokyo Irish, in Mother Maguire's beer and steak house.

Day 52 15 November

So highly automated is my bedside console that when I stretch to put the light on in the night I find the weather forecast for Southern California flashing on to my TV screen. The curtains swing open and the kettle starts to boil before I eventually locate a light switch, and several downlighters and uplighters later before I find one which sheds some light on the place where I actually need it. First thing in the morning I phone Mr Nakajima, the shipping agent. He's not there and someone else is put on to help me. The language barrier is too high to cope with the delicacies of circumnavigation, and I resign myself to having to wait before I know the fate of my Pacific crossing.

It's a sign of the times that when Fogg arrived anywhere there was an outward-bound passenger service leaving that same day. There are now no passenger services across the Pacific, apart from cruises. I have no option but to insinuate myself aboard some cargo boat, and this requires constant pestering of those whose business is goods, not people.

Look around the side streets near the hotel. The units are small. Cafés, businesses and shops cheek by jowl, with very few high-rise blocks. (This, I'm told, is because of the ever-present earthquake threat; there is an earthquake every day in Tokyo, they say, most of them too small to be felt on the street.) The group being more important than the individual in Japanese life, it is natural for shopkeepers and businesses to band together to look after their streets and to vet further development. The result is not architecturally impressive – there are no grand and sweeping facades – but there is a lively, varied, vigorous feeling of impermanence.

I go to check out what is still a Japanese phenomenon, but which is rumoured to be spreading west – the capsule hotel. These establishments offer a city centre bed for the night for 3,600 yen, about £17 or the price of a round of coffees in a downtown café. For this extraordinary value you have to put up with a certain degree of regimentation. The hotel I try is a cross between a high-tech school dorm and an executive morgue. Shoes must be removed before you even reach the front desk (this in itself must be quite a test for the late-night inebriates). Whereas in central London cheap hotels generally mean seedy hotels, the capsule hotel is kept, like everywhere else in Tokyo, pathologically clean. Interior surveillance pictures on a bank of video screens at reception roll over like ever-changing symbols on a fruit machine. You pay as you enter, and are given a locker key, a note on how to behave ('Persons whose bodies are tattooed are requested to keep out') and a towel. In the locker on the floor on which you are to be stored you exchange your clothes for a pair of pale blue shorts and a Hawaiian shirt. Businessmen are turned momentarily into butterflies. Finally you're issued with a razor and toothbrush. You are then shown to the allotted capsule. These are nothing more than plastic boxes, six feet long by about three feet wide, stacked one above the other in long rows. A thin but comfortable mattress is provided, the temperature is controlled from a panel by the right shoulder, as is light and a tiny colour TV. The less you value individuality the easier you will overcome the feelings of claustrophobia and loss of identity. For me, waking in the middle of the night in such a place would be profoundly depressing, if not terrifying.

I lunch with David Powers, a BBC radio man in Tokyo, at an automatic sushi bar. Thirty-seven varieties of sushi (raw fish with rice) move slowly round on a constantly replenished conveyor belt, in front of which the customer sits and takes off the saucer containing the sushi of his choice. The stack of saucers is checked at the end and your bill calculated. Tea and water are dispensed automatically. It's a triumph of what the Japanese are really good at – management, distribution and control.

My stack of saucers mounts as squid, cod roe, conger eel, boiled octopus, pickled radish, raw prawns, cucumber and seaweed, chopped tuna and onion and crabsticks slip down. There is one particularly vile looking delicacy which keeps coming past which David tells me is salted squid innards and almost unpalatable to Europeans. Being a bit of an innards man this sounds like a challenge that cannot be avoided and I pop one in. Mauve in colour, slimy in texture it is, to say the least, bracing. Rather as industrial adhesive might be bracing. It will definitely join fox, dog and snake and cat soup as party conversation for many years to come.

Waiting at a public phone box to contact Mr Nakajima again I'm caught unawares by the Japanese use of the sharply exhaled exclamation *Hai* in everyday conversation. It whistles out so emphatically that it sounds like someone's just thrown a knife at you, and you duck sharply only to see it's someone talking on the phone behind.

Mr Nakajima is in his office and I have had a great stroke of luck … *Hai!* … a container ship of Neptune Orient Lines is scheduled to leave Tokyo tomorrow evening for a ten-day journey to Long Beach, California.

This is good news indeed and demands a celebration. Clem is set on trying a *Karaoke* bar. *Karaoke* (which means 'empty orchestra') began 20 years ago as a way of allying Japanese technology to the Japanese urge to sing in public. It's refined a little since then but basically consists of a small bar at one end of which is a performing area. The one I visit with David Powers has on laser disc the backing track to 2,000 popular songs. For the negligible sum of 100 yen a tune can be played through the club's PA system whilst the punter stands on stage with mike in hand, words relayed on a screen in front of him, singing along as best he can. But this is not all, for on two screens behind, a video adds the final touch. Respectably dressed middle-aged men, and women, can croon mournful ballads whilst young lovers on video career through corn fields in soft focus and 4-wheel drive Subarus.

The atmosphere is very jolly and everyone is encouraged

and applauded, however dire their presentation. Whilst I gulp a beer for courage, David Powers sings, in Japanese, a couple of truly heart-rending ballads which bring the house down. A tableful of nattily dressed young Japanese launch into a chant of 'T'atch-er! T'atch-er!' Not trusting my voice to linger over anything sentimental I choose from the catalogue 'You Are My Sunshine', which I've been unable to banish from my mind since hearing the Shanghai jazz band playing it. The audience is supportive, the video shows streamlined images of Muscle Beach in Los Angeles, my next destination, a bouncy Japanese girl joins me in the choruses and at the end there are shouts of 'Bee-Bee-*Cee*! Bee-Bee-*Cee*!' which will, I'm sure, bring tears to the eyes of the taxpayer.

Back at the hotel Cleese tells me on the phone from London that Japan has been the only country in the world to show no interest in *A Fish Called Wanda*. Suggest *A Squid Called Wanda* might go better.

To bed in a blaze of glory with a glass of 'Super Nikka' Japanese Scotch, which is almost as bad as my singing.

Day 53 16 November

Before I leave Japan I have one last proof of travel to collect. Robert Hewison, one of my four trustees, has asked me to bring back a menu from a place called Caffe Bongo. Fortunately the Caffe Bongo is not easy to miss. It appears that an aeroplane has just crashed into it. A wing projects out of the window and into the street. Inside the wing is lodged about 8 or 9 feet off the ground. Bent girders on tilted metal columns snake upwards into, or downwards from, the aircraft, and classical columns, broken and tilting, seem to grow through it. Michelangelo's *David* is perched against a wall. The general effect is as if a Dakota had been forced to make an emergency landing in medieval Florence.

In the middle of all this exhilarating profusion of images, designed by a British architect, Nigel Coates, a few Japanese are solemnly sitting drinking coffee at £4 a cup as if they were in Betty's tea rooms in Ilkley. I ask for a menu, and then have to try and explain to the waitress that I want to keep it. She doesn't understand. Why should she? The more I explain my mission the more preposterous it sounds. I should have just pocketed the menu card, but it's rather large and unconcealable. I approach various other customers who try not to look at me, and on my third or fourth attempt, enlist the help of a businessman who tries his hand at explaining my quest to the staff.

Not a smile is cracked throughout the explanation. Instead frowns deepen, but eventually a solution is reached: the buck will be passed. Someone with more authority is to be summoned. How long will that be? The waitress doesn't understand. I point to my watch and try to indicate that I'm expected on the Pacific in a couple of hours. She goes away. Time passes. There's a distinct chance that I shall have to choose between getting a Caffe Bongo menu or getting around the world in eighty days. Order another £4 coffee. Am about to grab the menu and make a break for it when a smart lady appears and after I give another long and time-consuming explanation, I'm met with the same bewildered response.

'Look, a British architect designed this and so surely you realise the British occasionally do very silly things ...'

'You are architect!' Her eyes lit up.

'Well, not ... er as such, but I like architecture ...'

'Ah ... yes? ... architect ... good!'

From then on it's plain sailing and I emerge £8 lighter, but with a Caffe Bongo menu *and* a Caffe Bongo cup and saucer.

A digital sign above me reads: 12 degrees centigrade, 11.20, November 16. Buy a sweatshirt with highly prized example of Anglo-Japanese: 'Sporty Life. You ought to get do some a little exercise everyday'. Well, I'll have time to think about that on the Pacific, which is where I must now head for.

My home for the next week and a half is a big, fat, well-used ship which could do with some paint on the hull. At 800 feet and 42,872 tonnes, she's 10 feet longer and 6,000 tonnes heavier than the *Neptune Diamond* and her name is the *Neptune Garnet*. A container full of containers, built to circumnavigate the world every 63 days. She has come from Singapore, by way of Hong Kong and Taipei and Pusan in South Korea. She sails tonight at 10 for Long Beach, California, then on to Charleston, New York and Halifax, Nova Scotia, from where she sails non-stop to Singapore, via Suez, in 23 days.

After 30 days ambling across Asia, and with an American crossing still to come, I need the reassurance of a tight schedule like this, and we all need a break from loading, unloading, checking in and checking out, filming daily in heat and crowds and on the move.

At the top of the ship's long accommodation ladder I'm greeted by the master of the *Neptune Garnet*, an immediately likeable Indian – Captain Suresh Amirapu.

Although the *Garnet* is a bigger and more modern ship than the *Diamond*, most of the 'improvements' have been strictly commercial. Everything has been squeezed to make more room for the containers, so the crew's quarters are narrower, showers are preferred to baths and the swimming pool's disappeared altogether. The decoration is the same – Far Eastern Functional, all artificial materials, moulded plastic, bland colours, easy to use, easy to clean, difficult to remember. There are 24 in the crew: 3 Indians, 1 Pakistani, 14 Singaporeans, 2 Malaysians, 2 Burmese cadets, 1 Filipino cadet and a Ghanaian.

I'm in the doctor's quarters again, comprising a small bedroom and a day room, six levels up from the deck. The captain has given us all a computer-printed sheet covering things we need to know, and encourages us to visit the bridge whenever we like. The captain has leave every six months, when he's flown home. He has a six-week-old baby boy he hasn't even seen yet. We cast off at 11.25 at night, an hour and a half late.

The two 45-tonne cranes have been working up to the last minute and containers are now stacked five-high from the deck. Nigel and Dave, whose quarters are unfortunately on the fifth floor, saw their view disappear about ten minutes ago.

I watch from the bows as a tug heaves us round, leaving only a few feet clearance between ourselves and the *Neptune Crystal*, which is still loading. (This was the ship which was our second option out of Singapore, and which lost a couple of containers overboard during Typhoon Tess.)

A cool wind catches us as we head off south-west, to the mouth of Tokyo Bay. Sad to see the last of Asia, but glad to be moving east again.

Over a late night Tiger beer, Roger tells me of a plan he has to pass the long hours on the Pacific. I am to produce a play with the crew. Nine days' rehearsal, one performance. What sort of play do we do with Singaporean, Ghanaian, Burmese, Filipino, Indian and Pakistani merchant seamen? Roger admits that his choice was circumscribed by the availability of English plays in Tokyo, but he *has* secured ten copies of *Macbeth*.

Day 54   17 November

Thursday morning. Bacon and egg breakfast after strange dream in which Margaret Thatcher was very nice to me. Can it be that she is now intruding into the previously exclusive domain of royalty – the British dream? Resolve to lie awake all tomorrow night in case it happens again.

It's not easy to take in that we will not see land again until we reach Conception Point, 50 miles north of Los Angeles, a week this Saturday. That's eleven days – longer than our average family holiday. Talking of holidays, Dave Passepartout will not believe that we can cross the Pacific without hitting Hawaii. After all, he says, it is bang in the middle. But of course we don't go through the middle of the Pacific. We stay as far north as is safe, taking advantage of the curvature of the earth to shorten the distance. The 'summer route' is 4,606 miles from Tokyo to Long Beach, but Captain Amirapu is taking the winter route, 360 miles longer, because, as he shows us on the charts, 'it will avoid us being clobbered by these'. He indicates several clusters of tightly packed isobars hovering to the north and east of us.

'We just missed a big gale. If we'd left a day earlier …' More gnashing of teeth from director. More converts to astrology.

The clear skies, which last night gave such a fine parting panorama of Tokyo, have been replaced this morning by thickening grey clouds. A fresh north-east wind sighs round the plastic passageways.

After breakfast I have to go to bed again so they can film me getting up. After that I walk out on deck again so I can be filmed walking on deck and in this way a morning passes briskly, if derivatively. In the late afternoon I explore a running circuit around the ship. There is a narrow gangway between the deck rail with containers stacked above and to the side. A tight squeeze across the bows, but it's possible, weather permitting, to run the circumference of the deck which is a neat half-kilometre.

Evening: Almost all the crew apart from a couple on the bridge are watching *Stakeout* in the narrow room that serves as bar, games room, reading room and library, but which nearly always has the curtains drawn and a video on. It doesn't seem the time to get them out for a *Macbeth* rehearsal so the idea is indefinitely postponed. On the floor below there's a table-tennis table and Roger and I resume our rivalry.

We lose an hour tonight, one of eight time changes on this Pacific crossing. The 12 hours that we've progressively lost since leaving London, together with another 12 that we shall lose between the Pacific, America and London, will be refunded in full at the International Date Line in the shape of one extra 24-hour period. Though only ten days on my schedule, the crossing will be eleven in reality.

Day 55   18 November

The only waves troubling me this morning are waves of delayed fatigue. The supply of adrenaline which pushed me through Hong Kong and China and Japan has dried up and as I lie in bed this morning, having lost an hour's sleep to the clock, my body feels as immovable as the 6-foot-high anchor on the bow deck. Rain beats against the window. I look out on the first unequivocally wet day of the journey.

Eggs and bacon have run out already and breakfast is a Singapore dumpling that nestles, white, round and naked on my plate like a miniature early warning system. The intrepid eater is rewarded with a smudge of red bean curd at the centre. A mug of coffee, then a sorting out of clothes and a visit to the laundry room. There are two machines, above one of which is written 'Dirty Overalls Only'. This looks to be stating the obvious until I see one of the engine crew looking with satisfaction at a filthy, blackened, grease- and oil-stained boiler suit – which he has just taken *out* of the machine.

Up on the bridge at 11.45. 250 miles out of Tokyo and on a course East North East up to latitude 38 and longitude 165 at which point we shall head due East for the rest of the journey. Our speed is steady at 20 knots. I ask the captain why we are 3 knots slower than the more aged *Neptune Diamond*. He says it's all a matter of economics. At 20 knots his engine is using 10 tonnes of fuel a day. At 23 knots it would use 20 tonnes.

I manage a run later in the day, but only up and down the sheltered starboard side. The weather is worsening – rain pelting down and the wind's sighs becoming shrill screams. Roger looks cheerful. Apparently he's just encountered the captain who greeted him with:

'Bad news for me, good news for you.'

A fast developing frontal depression is advancing on us from the south west. Force 7 or 8, it should hit us this evening.

Up on the bridge the barograph has plunged and the captain is carefully marking the path of the storm from his own observations and from information he receives from Ocean Routes, a subscription weather information service run by the Americans, who supply a daily faxed weather chart and regular telex update of conditions.

The evening's video is *Live and Let Die*. The gathering storm makes for an interesting game of table tennis. Scrabble is brought out later in the Doctor's Day Room which Roger has christened 'Mike's Bar'.

Eleven o'clock: Mike's Bar has just closed and I'm in bed with Oscar Wilde – Richard Ellman's biography that is. The wind is moaning and the ship is shuddering as if reliving some awful childhood trauma. The containers creak and clang mournfully below my window. I haven't taken any anti-sickness precautions. I want to see if I need to.

Difficult to write now. In the bathroom poltergeists are at work. My shower curtain draws itself and undraws itself. First a toothbrush, then the toothpaste, then the tooth mug topple into the basin. Put them all to rights, but as I turn over to try and sleep, I hear the Scrabble slide the length of the table and spill onto the floor. It's an uncomfortable night. Impossible to lie in one position for more than a few seconds. As the ship rolls the body tenses waiting to counteract the roll. Instead the ship decides to quiver and pitch forward. It's like having your cradle rocked by a giant with a twitch.

Day 56 19 November

The worst of the gale is over, but on the faxed chart there is another approaching from the west. Our speed has dropped and America is still 4,000 miles away. We have just passed off my admirable Kummerly and Frey map of Asia on which I've been able to chart progress since we left Crete 50 days ago. Now

I have nothing but my inflatable globe to show me the vast distance I still have to travel.

Passepartout is scattered in various accommodations. Ann is in the pilot's room, Roger in the 2nd officer's, Nigel and Dave are cadets 'A' and 'B' and Simon is spare officer. At breakfast there is much one-upmanship over how badly we slept last night...

'An *hour*! You were lucky!'

'Nothing woke me up, nothing. I never went to sleep.'

After breakfast we assemble to discuss the day's work in the 'Meeting Room', seven floors above the deck, and just below the bridge. The wall is covered with certificates and mementos of the *Garnet*'s maiden voyage in January 1986: a silver and black model lifebuoy inscribed 'Bon Voyage' from the port of Osaka, a miniature ship's wheel from the stevedores of Terminal 18 at Port Seattle, and a pink, glass-eyed geisha doll presented by the Hyundai Shipyard, South Korea, on completion of the vessel.

Talk at lunch to the Pakistani chief engineer. He is anxious about the new Sulzer fuel-efficient engine, which is giving him 'many sleepless nights'. This sounds ominous.

Tonight, to celebrate the Indian festival of Deepavalli, a special buffet supper and party is to be held. We have managed to steer the Singaporean chef away from attempts at European food and he comes up with an Indo-Chinese spread which scores highly. Curried prawns, red snapper, chicken with mangoes and rice, followed by Tiger beers in the bar followed by introductions and speeches, emceed admirably by a Singaporean officer whose name I think is Hang On.

There is much laughter that I should be making such a meal of going round the world in eighty days when they do it in sixty-three. Six times a year.

Then the party begins. Such oriental specialities as Pass the Parcel and Charades are entered into with an enthusiasm that would delight the United Nations. The games are well organised and forfeits are very popular. The captain has to mime someone without money trying to grab an illegal ride on the Hong Kong subway, Simon has to sing 'Yesterday', Nigel has to give George Bush's first Presidential address and Roger to imitate his favourite animal. He gets down on all fours then lifts his leg on the captain's shoe, to great applause.

Charades are more problematical as none of our team knows any of the films the crew have given us. They're the video favourites and usually involve killing and retribution, and despite our energetic efforts with *The Evil that Men Do*, *Street Killer* and *He Knows You're Alone* the result is only bafflement.

We're more successful in the Tug of War. This takes place in the passageway outside, and as it's a hot sticky night, both deck doors are open, so there's always the danger that the team that loses its balance might disappear for ever into the North Pacific. But the contest is close and myself and Passepartout hold the young, fit, though well-Tigered, *Garnet* crew to a draw over three contests.

Pouring sweat, retire triumphantly to bed. Twelve thousand miles away in London my second son will be waking up on his eighteenth birthday. The fact that I'm missing this and an important university entrance exam he has to take in two days makes me momentarily regret being so far away and so helpless.

Day 57 20 November

Wake, very hot. Something is wrong. The air-conditioning seems to be sucking in moist, humid air, and the engine note has changed. Pull the flimsy curtain back from the porthole. The long causeway of containers – six high and thirteen across – stretches ahead, but there is no sign of the surging white wake from the bows. In fact, we've almost stopped. The chief engineer, raised at dawn from another sleepless night, is not a happy man. Captain Amirapu tries to keep cheerful. Precious time drifts away.

Mid-morning. The engines are up to power again. A feeder pipe had sheared off and we've lost three or four hours.

Run early today as the weather service has forecast another storm, marked this time on the fax with an S.W. (Storm Warning), a notch up on yesterday's G.W. (Gale Warning). Once again it's from the south-west, and once again it's expected about the time Mike's Bar opens for the evening session.

At five o'clock, I take a walk on deck and can see the edge of the approaching storm, spread diagonally across the southern sky like a huge grey wing, sheltering beneath it a mass of mist and rain which will soon overhaul us.

Even in this solid great ship it's easy to feel vulnerable, as the wind brings in the storm, and the pots and pans are battened down in the galley. At a somewhat shaky dinner I talk to the chief engineer about Benazir Bhutto's election – news of which I picked up on my shortwave radio earlier. He is not happy. She is an untried politician, voted in on a wave of sympathy for her father's death. Sounds as though people supported Zia in Pakistan for the same reason many support Thatcher in Britain. He may not have been personally popular but he was tough, forever standing up to people. Not those with money however. Zia was a good businessman and the chief engineer fears that Bhutto, elected by a popular rather than establishment vote, will squander a carefully built up international reputation.

Day 58 21 November

On the bridge early this morning. Remains of the storm still blowing, but it moved across us fast, says the captain, and the worst is long gone. Bulky low cloud and drizzle, a sluggish sea and not a strand of sunshine can be seen through the long, wide windows. In short, inauspicious conditions for an auspicious day – the return to the Western Hemisphere, the halfway point of my journey, the crossing of the International Date Line. Since nature has refused to play up and no international corporation has yet considered the advantages of sponsoring a line of Date Line marker buoys, we are reduced to marking this great occasion by watching the line appear on the satellite navigation screen, which is a bit like seeing the New Year in with Radio 3. There are no trumpets sounding, not even an extra electronic bleep to mark our passage into another hemisphere, just the split-second changes of little white numbers. 38.02 is our latitude (about the same as Benidorm), and at 8.20 precisely, longitude 180.00.E flashes for a second, then remorselessly moves on to 179.59.W.

As we have moved east with the sun we have gained a day over the rest of the world and must now mark time and let the others catch up. So we have an extra day. This was the coup for Jules Verne at the end of *Around the World in Eighty Days* when Fogg thought all was lost for he had seen eighty sunrises. His colleagues, stationary in London, had only seen seventy-nine. So the bet was won and Mrs Aouda became Mrs Fogg. But all this is jumping ahead. It's taken me 58 days to travel halfway round the globe, and I've 22 days to do the rest.

My fate depends ultimately on one propeller and the ability of the engine to turn it non-stop, 24 hours a day, in all weathers, for at least the next six days. The propeller weighs 55 tons, is cast in bronze and has four blades with a diameter of about 27 feet. The engine room area occupies five floors below decks, and the cylinders are three floors high. If noise were enough to drive the ship along I would have no worries. We are given ear-protectors, but I slip them off to feel the sound of so much power. It is just below the limit of aural pain. The chief engineer with his permanently worried look (either because of Benazir Bhutto or the problems with the Sulzer engine) is testing electrical circuits. With his white coat, neat black beard and moustache, obsessive enthusiasm and small frame dwarfed by pumping hissing machinery he reminds me of Willy Wonka in Roald Dahl's *Charlie and the Chocolate Factory*.

From the caves of heavy metal below decks I walk out before lunch to my favourite spot above decks. This is a gallery at the stern, open on three sides, low to the sea, on which are winches and capstans and stanchions of powerful appearance standing like sculptures at some futuristic art gallery. At the stern rail I am only a few feet above the churning propeller and I can happily stand for ages watching it send the water flicking up and flinging back to mark our progress across the Pacific with a green and white gash two or three hundred yards long, above which wheel half a dozen sea-birds, who have followed us for days. Along the sides run swelling waves, massive and unbroken after crossing thousands of miles of open sea, rising sometimes high above my head. With the noise of the engine and the wind, it's a sobering but exhilarating glimpse of power. So easy would it be just to slip through the rail. If I did what would be my chances? There's no one with me. The noise would drown any shouts. How long would it be before my absence was noted? Another half-hour at least. The ship would be 15 miles away by then and a full turn would take another half-hour. Decide to go to the quieter end of the ship. Today, because of a following wind the bows are almost eerily silent. Like cloisters.

The Table Tennis Competition is hotting up. Nigel Passepartout is now known as Hurricane because of his mercurial style. Sometimes unplayably deadly, other times unable to hit the table. The ball flicks and spins off radiator pipes, shelves, air-conditioning vents and opponents' heads. But win or lose, his approach is pure Welsh passion. Roger, on the other hand, is becoming a cool, calculating opponent, poker-faced and consistent, and now known as the Professor. The man to beat.

There is a bizarre announcement halfway through the evening meal: 'You are reminded that it will be Monday again tomorrow.'

Day 58   21 November

What one always wants. A chance to have the day again, and get it right this time. Long lie-in. The Professor has decreed that this shall be a no-filming day, and the signs are that it could become a non-day altogether. It's as if no one has any confidence in a day we've had already. I see nothing of Passepartout until late morning.

The sea is calm on the surface but a big swell is running at us from the south-east, and the captain is worried that this is somehow affecting our speed. We are over halfway across the Pacific now, the weather warm and humid and cloudy. A ship is sighted on the starboard side, heading west, the first we've seen for four days. The captain makes radio contact:

'Hello westbound ship … This is eastbound ship *Neptune Garnet*, do you read me?'

'Hello eastbound ship, we read you.'

'What is your name?'

'*Manila Prosperity*.'

'Where are you coming from?'

'Great Lakes and Montreal to Nagoya and Bangkok.'

'We are on liner service, Tokyo to Long Beach.'

'How is weather?'

'Two lows, quite developed, have passed up to the Aleutians. We hope we are in high pressure now.'

'You're lucky.'

'Not so lucky after all, we have swell on port side. Rolling and pitching badly. We've lost time.'

The Filipino ship doesn't sound convinced. She is a much smaller ship heading into a steady succession of depressions. Our captain signs off breezily: 'Have a safe voyage, avoid the lows.'

Investigate the library. It's that sort of day. Nearly all the books are in English, though there isn't an Englishman in the crew. A selection of sea classics – *Requiem for a Wren, A Night to*

Remember, Moby-Dick, The Iliad. Can't imagine container ships spawning any literature of their own – *In Which We Load, Voyage of the Canned*.

There are fat Micheners and Urises and Clavells. Long, thick and international. The container ships of literature. There are games – chess, draughts and Mah Jong – but videos are more popular. This afternoon they're watching *Silent Night*. Far from being a nice little tale of carol singers it's another load of screams and terror. These gentle people's capacity for watching other people's violence seems almost unlimited.

On the notice board outside there is information about stress and how to combat it, the danger of Aids and an invitation to participate in Vernons Football Pools.

Day 59 22 November

The swell shows no let-up and makes sleep uncomfortable. Wake to find my world rolling around on the floor. Sitting at a solitary late breakfast of coffee, toast and marmalade, I see only sky through the porthole, a moment later only sea.

It's the Professor's birthday, and I give him J.L. Carr's *A Season in Sinji*, as it's about cricket, which he is fond of, and is an excellent and absorbing tale. A clutch of letters from his family, all assembled unbeknownst to him at Tokyo, make his morning.

On deck the containers are groaning and wailing more spectacularly than ever. They sound like Stockhausen and the Professor thinks a symphony for containers should be commissioned. Simon, on the other hand, thinks they might be communicating something to the whales.

By mid-afternoon the flat, muggy, moist, overcast conditions which have prevailed since the weekend give way to sharper, clearer, cooler weather. Ideal, it is judged, for an initiation ceremony to mark the crossing of the Date Line.

Such is the nature of my relationship with Passepartout that when something potentially as unpleasant as this has to be faced, it is faced by me alone. The gulf between presenter and crew, normally the width of a fordable stream, becomes a Pacific Ocean. So it is I alone who represent the supernumeraries and gather down in the Radio Room at half past four to be prepared for this time-honoured and humiliating ritual. Fortunately there are members of the crew who have not been initiated – Francis, a 25-year-old Ghanaian, who served in his own country's merchant fleet until Jerry Rawlings reduced it to only four vessels, George, a tall, languid, 22-year-old Burmese cadet and a small slim Malaysian who we know as Saatchi – his full name being Sachithanathan and a bit of a mouthful.

The four of us are lined up and the crew members, dressed in an odd mixture of handmade ceremonial robes, with cardboard hats and in one case a Korean flag worn like a toga, start to make us ready. Parek, the mild-mannered chief officer, has become a monster for the occasion. He has the role of Neptune's High Priest, so he can shout louder and more abusively than anyone apart from the King. We are ordered to strip down to underpants, and are given only a thin strip of sacking to act as a loin cloth. Then our wrists are bound together with adhesive tape and a rope is looped round all our necks. Yoked thus, like the burghers of Calais, and preceded by a pounding gong, we are half-led, half-shoved onto the deck and up two flights of steps to the Captain's Bridge Deck.

Here is enthroned King Neptune, a cardboard crown and cotton wool beard barely disguising the dark Singaporean features of the chief electrician. He holds a trident and next to him sits the Queen – his wife Lily. Their little boy Rajiv, who is travelling with them, is not one of the participants but looks on in total amazement. We are ordered to kneel. Just time to notice there's a handsome sunset behind us before being shouted at to keep my head bowed. A scroll is then unwound and charges read to the effect that we transgressors have strayed over the Date Line without asking King Neptune's permission.

The King is then asked what punishments are required before he will be appeased. Already Passepartout, safe behind his camera and tape recorder, looks a little embarrassed at our predicament, but when the first punishment turns out to be that we must 'shit and urinate', I just have time to see four mouths drop open before being flung forward, and a small glass bowl (of the sort we have puddings in) placed beneath my groin. This is then rapidly filled with syrup from a tin of fruit salad, into which a frankfurter is then dropped. The next order, somewhat predictably perhaps, is that we should 'eat shit and urine!' This done we are dragged to our feet and daubed with tomato ketchup. 'Hands above your heads!' Despite the cold and the smell and general discomfort I keep my spirits high by thinking of Alan Whicker doing this. I think Clive James might have drawn the line at eating his own shit and urine. The tomato ketchup having been liberally applied, particularly to the armpits, we are then sprinkled all over with soy sauce, thrust to our knees again and flour rubbed into our hair, after which there is a momentary breather before an egg is broken over each of our heads. I feel the yolk, gratifyingly warm, as it slides down my back. Between all this there is much banter between the King and High Priest on the lines of 'Have they done enough, O King, to atone for their crime?' The King, of course, decides we haven't done enough and orders us to drink something very nasty. This turns out to be a half pint of some bilious brown concoction which contains coffee, Tabasco, curry powder, chocolate, raw eggs, soy sauce and mustard – to name but a few; we have to drink it in one go.

I think of Alec Guinness and tip the glass. George the Burmese gags halfway through and keels over, coughing violently. Saatchi, without an ounce of fat to protect him, is shivering visibly, and it's still not over. More shouting, and we're dragged up again to be stencilled on the forehead with a potato in which the red sign of a trident has been roughly carved. Something warm and red trickles down my face, but it's only the dye from the potato. This is worse than appearing in a Terry Gilliam film. And still it goes on. Hoses are prepared to sluice us with cold seawater. But a power behind the throne decides that it's gone far enough. We are ordered to shuffle up in front of the electrician (sorry, King Neptune), who after one last impassioned harangue, dubs each of us with his trident and hands us a scroll which confirms that, in my case:

'On the 20th November 1988, A.D. at 20.20 hours GMT I, Michael Palin, crossed the International Date Line on ye goode ship *Neptune Garnet*, and was humbled before the King Neptune, Great Ruler Of The Seven Seas, and thus accepted into The Brotherhood of Mariners.'

Except that I'm not accepted yet. Signatures have to be secured from both the King and the High Priest before the certificate is valid – these can be obtained at a separate ceremony this evening.

The evening ceremony turns out to be also a party for the Professor. Forfeits abound, and in order to get my signatures I have to impersonate a sexy model, a pregnant woman, a housewife *and* give a display of break dancing.

It's a very good party, attended by all except the two crew members on watch, and many games are played, a tug of war is pulled, which I'm sorry to say the BBC loses this time. The Professor reveals there is no end to his talents by singing a song in Russian to his own guitar accompaniment, and Saatchi having endured the afternoon with great dignity produces his guitar, and plays a long and rather mournful rendition of 'Hotel California'.

A day to remember, however much one might want to forget it.

Day 60 23 November

Eighth day on the Pacific. Woken at six by what I take at first to be a hangover. My cabin reeks of diesel fuel. Surely I hadn't drunk that as well. Somehow after the tomato ketchup and the Tabasco and mustard cocktail anything was possible. But it turns out to be another of the eccentricities of the *Garnet*, that when the wind is in a certain direction, it blows the engine fumes into the air conditioning.

Still suffering from ship lag. Last night was the 14th time I'd put my watch forward since crossing into France, 60 days ago.

Up to the bridge. 3,562 miles from Tokyo. Our speed is 20.9 knots with a Force 6 to 7 wind from the West pushing us along, but the rolling keeps our speed lower than it should be. The captain is still mystified as to why, and reiterates his preference for Japanese over Korean shipyards. The chief officer and ex-High Priest is more concerned about yesterday's ceremony. Was it too violent? I assured him that it was a great performance and will make television history. I didn't like to tell him that the language was so foul that the BBC will probably have to keep their bleep on throughout. He in turn assured me that it was usually much worse than that. He had had his testicles painted different colours and knows of someone on *Neptune Amber* who was given a Mohican haircut, and another who had his head shaved completely and was made to stand at the bottom of the accommodation ladder at Long Beach and escort customs and immigration aboard, dressed as Gandhi. Run eight laps of the ship this afternoon – four kilometres. There's hardly ever anyone on deck, except for a couple of people checking the container fixings, or the temperatures on the refrigerated containers, so I have the Pacific to myself.

Read further into Ellman's Oscar Wilde, watch a video of *Salvador*, iron some shirts and prepare for another evening at the table-tennis table and the Scrabble board. The rolling of the boat seems to be getting worse. Simon pours a Scotch twice and each time it falls off the table. Resign myself to another night on the move. Wedge everything that might roll and put pillows on either side of the bed to prevent me hitting the wall. It's close and muggy again and just when the air conditioning is needed it's impossible to have it on because of the diesel fumes. On all the ships I've been on there seems to be a psychological Sargasso Sea round about two-thirds of the way into the voyage. A period of lethargy and dissatisfaction between the excitement and novelty of setting out and the anticipation of arrival at the other end.

As I'm lying in bed, rolling gently, I reflect on the fact that India, more than any other country, has dominated this journey so far. Indians took me from Dubai to Bombay to Madras, now an Indian is taking me from Tokyo to Long Beach. A third of the journey altogether. Captain Amirapu couldn't be bettered. A polite and considerate host, a highly competent and inspiring captain and a nice, friendly and straightforward man. I was surprised to hear him today expressing interest in leaving the sea and taking a shore job. Sensible for a family man I suppose, but a great loss to the sea.

Day 61 24 November

Sleep in half-hour bursts. The ship feels like a tormented soul tonight, shuddering, quaking, tossing and turning, teeth chattering, as the rolls become steeper and longer. Up the hill one minute and down again the next. I nod off only to be woken moments later by a swingeing change to my centre of gravity, or the sticky heat of the airless cabin, or backache from the semi-foetal position into which I've concertinaed my body. When I do sleep I fall into a vivid dream of home. Clear details of collecting my mail from the Python office (which has added to its staff a lot of young men in red braces), hailing a taxi and at last turning into the street where I live. A hundred yards from my front door I wake in the middle of the Pacific. A warm glow of anticipation and happiness vanishes instantly to be replaced by frustration, then resignation, then backache.

There is a crash and the sound of breaking glass from the Dayroom. I totter through expecting to find a carpet awash with Johnny Walker Black Label, but fortunately it's only a couple of glasses that have broken free of their moorings. Later, on the bridge, the captain is apologetic about the boat's behaviour.

Saatchi shows me our position on the charts and I tell him we are going to have to re-shoot the initiation ceremony. He looks so utterly terrified that I have trouble persuading him it was a joke. We talk about football. Saatchi the Malay, like Captain Abbas the Egyptian, is a Liverpool supporter. He says people all over the world watch English football. For some reason it's more exportable than French or Italian or Dutch. Everyone he knew made sure they were near a television set to watch live coverage of the European Cup Final at the Heysel stadium. It's easy to forget the international repercussions of the disaster. The millions of Liverpool well-wishers let down, embarrassed and shamed by the events.

Still, he says, it's past and there has been a sympathetic backlash over the continued exclusion of English clubs from international football. 'You're not so bad,' he says, and, as if to cheer me up, 'Everyone knows Mrs Thatcher ...'

The captain has asked us to his cabin for a drink before supper. It's comfortable up there with soft sofas and plants and Mozart coming through elegantly on the hi-fi. The chief engineer (Mr Wonka) is there. They talk of cricket, the Japanese (admired but not liked), reduced manning levels on container ships (neither admired nor liked) and the experiences of Neptune Orient Lines in the Gulf war. Two company ships were hit. One was completely destroyed. The other, a tanker, was hit fifteen times, but only one crew member was killed.

After supper there's bingo in the games room. The captain joins in as usual, and takes it very seriously. He's hoping to win at least 50 dollars.

Day 62 25 November

Breakfast at 9.30. The Singaporean food on the *Garnet* has been good but I miss fresh-baked bread, freshly ground coffee and milk. I've been existing on instant coffee and Coffee-Mate, 'America's Favorite Non-Dairy Creamer', which I see is full of non-dairy goodies like: 'Corn Syrup solids, Partially Hydrogenated Vegetable Oil and any one of the following oils – Coconut, Cottonseed, Palm, Palm kernel, Safflower or Soybean. Sodium Caseinate, Mono and Di-Glycerides, Dipotassium Phosphate, Artificial Flavor and Annatto (a vegetable derived artificial color).' The outlook for fresh food doesn't look hopeful as I approach a new continent.

At ten o'clock our satellite fix is 36.35 North, 129.21 West, 4,380 miles from Tokyo and making 20.6 knots. Seven hours behind schedule.

Nothing much to do but wait. At lunchtime the sun comes out, and, for the first time since we left Japan, I feel its warmth on my face. Inspired to try and make 10 kilometres round the deck, and do so. Shower, read and bask in general feeling of achievement.

Rajiv, the three-year-old son of King Neptune, is going to be a world-class footballer. I confidently predict this after seeing him dribble my inflatable world up and down the passageway, and strike penalties with either foot through the cabin door. After saving the world from further punishment, I learn that his father was a footballer and his mother Lily (Mrs Neptune) trained as a parachutist until a particularly horrific accident in which her harness caught as she leapt from the aircraft and slammed her against the fuselage. She fell most of the way unconscious. They're a nice family, but I feel for Rajiv sustaining such a long journey with no friends of his own age.

Despite all the modern technology many traditional nautical terms remain and the deck crew is still organised by the bosun, who on this ship is Mr Ong. I find him taking measurements for an insurance claim for the 40-foot-long accommodation ladder which was torn off the ship by Typhoon Tess. He's sad to hear we're leaving at Long Beach.

'Why do you not come to Panama? Where else could you see a ship climb a mountain?'

I'm sorely tempted. After all I've seen the Corinth and the Suez canals, and the Panama where ships are raised up through a series of locks, must be the most spectacular of them all. I explain to him my targets and dates and deadlines, which he quite rightly doesn't regard as at all important compared with the splendours of Panama. 'Weather down there very nice … sunbathe,' he suggests hopefully. I think my sunbathing days are over on this journey.

Day 63 26 November

We are to land in America today. The long Pacific crossing is abruptly over. I wish I could hope, like Fogg, that 'the most difficult part was done … they had left the fantastic countries of China and Japan … they were returning to civilised countries'. But I have 17 days to cross America on an infrequent and neglected railway system, and then I have to find some way of crossing the Atlantic at the onset of winter, when as Captain Amirapu assured me, 'You can almost be certain of running into something nasty.' In short, I don't altogether share Fogg's confidence in 'civilised countries'.

But for now, at eight o'clock in the morning in the Santa Barbara Channel it's a day for optimists. A peerless morning, the best on the Pacific. The sun shines from a clear blue sky, the swell has dropped, and there's a crisp, fresh breeze high up on the bridge deck.

It was in these waters, 46 years ago, that a Japanese submarine surfaced and fired seventeen rounds in the direction of Ellwood oilfield – the only direct enemy attack on continental USA this century. There are now a lot more offshore oil rigs for them to aim at and a steady stream of tankers heading north for the Alaskan oil. The chart indicates that we are in a Traffic Separation Zone, one lane for north and one lane, further out, for south. Such zones are in operation in all the maritime traffic black spots – the English Channel, the Gulf of Suez, the Malacca Strait.

Plenty of signs now of approaching landfall. A profusion of pelicans, cormorants and terns. Fat seagulls perch proprietorially on the containers. A school of dolphins, small jets of water signalling their progress, arc lazily through the water to the east. I feel concerned about their safety as deep-sea fishing boats bob about in these waters, bristling with rods. The sea begins to smell salty, as it never does out on the ocean. The inevitable plastic and polystyrene detritus accumulates, there's a sudden profusion of radio stations and the sound of airliners again. There's also the sobering sight of a low cloud stained brown with pollution, extending about half a mile out into the clear air of the Pacific. It's frightening to see so clearly the mess we live in. It's like stepping from a rock pool into dirty bathwater.

By lunchtime we're down to 12.5 knots and passing Malibu beach. The stars and stripes flies from the masthead, alongside the flags of Singapore and Neptune Orient Lines. We may be an ugly duckling, stacked with boxes, scuffed and yellowing in the hull, but we're 40,000 tonnes and eleven storeys high. A sailboat flutters perilously close to us, like a moth drawn to a light. Our deep and sonorous horn blasts out and Captain Amirapu shakes his head, 'This is the land of the free, you see. Any rich American can take his boat out right into the lane, without knowing *anything*.'

Now experiencing, yet again, AES – Arrival Euphoria Syndrome. The adrenaline begins to flow, clicking my system into receptive mode, responsive to a whole new set of sensations. I feel as I did coming into Bombay after a week on the dhow – a quickening of the pulse, a need to be there. Sure signs of a landlubber.

At five past two the pilot comes aboard. Unlike any other I've encountered he is in a civilian suit, an elderly man surely near retiring age, with crinkly grey hair. The smooth efficient American accent goes into action. It's odd to hear the real thing after so many international imitations. It makes me aware that I'm a foreigner – along with Captain Amirapu and Chief Engineer Durrani and Lily and Rajiv and Bosun Ong and Saatchi, Hang On, and all of us aboard.

There are small boats all around us now, but the difference between here and anywhere else I've been is that they're not working boats. These boats are for play. All modern, well equipped, fibreglass-hulled. None of them looks more than six months old. One sweeps by close to us and its occupants wave. A classic American quartet of rugged men and huge honey-haired women. We're in the land of giants.

Escorted by our tug, the *Sea Robin* from San Francisco, we pick our way carefully to the container terminal, where the American stevedores wait beside their cars (no bikes here), shouting, joking, swaggering, flexing muscles – every one of them from Central Casting. Captain Amirapu gives his last instructions to the engine room: ''ard a port ... 'ard a starboard', an Indian bringing me to the New World. The temperature is in the upper 60s, a light wind blows from the desert.

The customs men come aboard. Passepartout and I are officially signed off the ship's register. 'OhhhhhhhKay,' pronounces the senior officer, a grey-haired black. 'You're clear for customs. Enjoy your time in the U.S. Don't drink the water or eat the food.'

Transfer to another ship, my tenth so far. It's also the biggest, the most comfortable and by far the fastest. But it's moored in concrete and hasn't moved an inch in 22 years. It's the R.M.S. *Queen Mary*, striving to maintain some dignity despite being stuck in a pond and clamped to the shore by a modern steel and glass umbilical cord of elevators and service towers, on one of which is attached an illuminated sign confirming her new status as 'Hotel Queen Mary'. An arrow, pointing inland, invites me to 'Cross the Parking Lot to London Towne'. I suppose I should feel at home, but it isn't easy.

The first words addressed to me on American soil come from a thin, epicene registration clerk, with a spiky peroxide blond haircut. He punches a keyboard and looks up only briefly, just to ascertain I'm not a gorilla or armed with an axe. 'Hi, I'm Randy.' With a flick of the fingers Randy summons someone of a different ethnic group to carry my bags to Stateroom 306 on 'B' deck. We pass groups of partying Americans. They are twice as big and twice as loud as anyone else in the world. It's not just the grunts and laughs and whoops but also the sheer volume of the voices which ring out as if they are trying to communicate over vast distances. I feel like a mouse amongst bull elephants. In no time AES (Arrival Euphoria Syndrome) gives way to PAP (Post-Arrival Pathos), which in turn gives way to TT (Transition Trauma).

Once on land everything accelerates. No sooner have I arrived in a place than I have to make plans for getting out. The only boat across the Atlantic leaves from New York. I have now to cross to the East Coast as soon as possible, which is easier said than done in the land where any alternative to flying is not really taken seriously. There is an express to Chicago, called the Desert Wind, but it doesn't blow until Monday afternoon.

Whether I like it or not I have a day and a half to cool off in Los Angeles.

Day 64 27 November

My face, with dreadful permed hair, stares out at me from the top of the television on a card advertising *A Fish Called Wanda* as one of the four in-house movie hits. As it's currently taken 55 million dollars in the States I resolve to shut up about the Americans and their taste. At least they saved the *Queen Mary* and enabled me now to relax in a heavy enamel bath the length of a sentry box with a choice of four fillings: 'Freshwater Hot', 'Freshwater Cold', 'Sea Water Hot' and 'Sea Water Cold', and a shower control which marks Tepid.

A short walk up on deck. The Art-Deco fittings of the interior, the inlaid wood and cut glass, the classical bas-relief figures in bronze and the murals of England in the thirties are superb. On deck, I find I've been pursued from Shanghai by Noel Coward, whose life-size photographic likeness graces the wide teak floor that he himself once graced, along with other swingers of the thirties and forties such as Fred Astaire, Spencer Tracy, Winston Churchill and Marlene Dietrich.

A display shows the *Queen Mary* up-ended, alongside the Eiffel Tower and the Empire State Building. She's taller than the first and only a touch shorter (at 1,018 feet) than the second. Fifty-one years ago she sailed between New York and Cornwall in 3 days and 20 hours at an average speed of 31.69 knots. If she still did I'd be home and dry. The very newest and most powerful container ships can make 26 or 27 knots.

To breakfast at the Sidewalk Café on Venice Beach. At the turn of the century a rich man decided, as rich men do in Los Angeles, to spend an awful lot of money to re-create something that already existed elsewhere, in this case Venice. Unfortunately Abbot Kinney's Venice wasn't as sturdy as the original and only lasted about twenty-four years. There isn't much left (a columned arcade scrawled on by street artists or just people leaving messages) but the name persists and suits the neighbourhood, which is light and sparkles in the reflected waters of the Pacific Ocean, a hundred yards away. Venice Beach is America at its least self-conscious. Loud, informal, brash, individualistic, ostentatious, tolerant and unapologetic. A perfect reintroduction to Western culture.

The Sidewalk Café is attached to a bookshop and you can buy a first edition Sinclair Lewis and read it over a generous plate of bacon, eggs, links (sausages) and hash brown potatoes with a slice of orange. I bought the *L.A. Times*, a bundle of newsprint that looks like a week's supply of any English newspaper, but when whittled down to what is actually readable is equivalent to Monday's *Independent*. Though Venice, Los Angeles, looks the only place to be on this heavenly, healthy Sunday morning, it's Florence, Los Angeles, that's in the headlines. 'Another weekend in L.A. Gang Violence and Death.' No country I've passed through is without its violence, and you get to hear about it pretty quickly. On another page under 'Saturday's Air Quality' is an analysis of air pollution in the city, monitoring daily ozone, carbon monoxide and nitrogen dioxide levels. Which newspaper will be brave enough to do the same for Britain? Sidney Sheldon's *The Seeds of Time* is top of the fiction chart and Stephen Hawking's *A Brief History of Time* top of the non-fiction. There's nothing about England except the football results.

Walk along Ocean Front Walk. Against a Hockneyed backdrop of palm trees sharp against blue sky, a man juggles with two balls and a rotating chainsaw. Whilst performing this extraordinary and terrifying feat he warns the crowd who've gathered to watch: 'The last time I did this the chain broke off and went into the audience.' At the end he passes around a hat, examining contributions with disgust: 'Ten dollars! Hey! This is what I do for a job, shithead!'

Another man does a robot act, so good that only when he breaks sweat are you actually sure it's not a machine.

At Muscle Beach the bodybuilders work out, pulling 225 lbs on a single cable without apparent effort. Like everything else here this is a spectator sport. There are tiered benches beside the weights enclosure that could accommodate a couple of hundred people. The crowds wander by, barely commenting on our filming. In India they stare straight in the lens, in America they ask: 'Is this a movie, commercial or local news?'

Though there's a crowd, there's never a rush. This is Sunday, in California. The sun's shining and no one's going anywhere.

Except of course the circumnavigators, who feel twitchy if they stay still for too long. So a couple of hours later I find myself in a quiet canyon off Sunset where Michael Shamberg, the American producer of *Wanda*, *The Big Chill* and other movies, gives a most un-Hollywood Thanksgiving lunch for me. No noise, no cameras (except ours), no one being paged to the phone, no live appearance of the Count Basie Band, not even a celebrity punch-up. A low-key get-together of sympathetic folk, who can't really comprehend what I'm doing and why I'm doing it. Jamie Lee Curtis comes by later and saves the afternoon for Passepartout, who had long since decided I knew nobody famous in this town.

By five o'clock I'm exhausted. Is it ship-lag or the hectic pace on land after the monastic days on the Pacific?

Buy the *New York Times* and *Bonfire of the Vanities* and retire to my 'stateroom' for an early night. The *Times* has a romantic piece in the travel section about Christmas in London. No mention of traffic jams and black plastic bags, but it does provoke a sharper than usual twinge of homesickness.

Day 65 28 November

Up at 7.30. Call my mother in Suffolk. There's been thick fog there for days. Today the fog's gone but the rain's begun. Outside in Los Angeles the sun shines once again on the walls of London Towne, and the TV weatherperson forecasts 75 degrees in downtown Los Angeles, but heavy snowfalls in the

Rockies, with 40 inches at Alta Lake. It's the latter part of the forecast that gives me pause, for our train will be crossing the Rockies this time tomorrow morning. Switch channels to a discussion of why families quarrel more at Thanksgiving than any other time of the year. Switch off. Farewell to the shackled *Queen Mary*. Leave with mixed feelings, as if having visited a good friend in prison.

Drive downtown to another great relic of the thirties. Completed three years after the *Queen Mary*, in 1939, Los Angeles Union Station had an even shorter life in the style for which she was intended. The last of the great American railway terminals, her moment of glory was cut short by the Second World War and pre-empted by the rise of air travel immediately afterwards. But at least she's not completely retired, and trains still run from beneath the slender and graceful tower of the Spanish-style building. A belittling sticker, 'Shoes and Shirts Required', is pasted on the grubby glass of the door, beyond which is a magnificent interior of marbled floors and colourfully tiled walls, soaring 52 feet, to a timbered roof, intricately beamed, from which hang massive wrought-iron chandeliers. The atmosphere of the interior is dark and comforting like the wood of which so much of it is composed. Shafts of sunlight pierce the gloom from windows high up. The seats in the waiting room area are big and comfortable with thick wooden arms. Outside there are two cloistered gardens full of bougainvillea and frangipani – the only self-contained gardens I've ever seen at a station.

Sadly, the nearer you get to the trains the tattier the station becomes. The platforms are so desolate and uncared-for that on first sight I thought the railway might have closed without anyone telling us. There is not a single sign bearing the name of the city. The platforms, along which run narrow, rusting metal canopies, are empty of all the usual railway paraphernalia, except for the occasional seat and a rank of pay-trolleys.

The Desert Wind is made up of Amtrak Superliners, two-

tiered coaches in silver, red and blue livery. Its interior, like the
bullet train in Japan, but unlike the trains in China and India,
owes much to aircraft design. A lightweight shell, moulded
seats in open coach formation, inadequate but neatly designed
individual lights, fold-down tables. There are also sleeping
cabins, utilising the space quite skilfully but failing to disguise
the fact that there isn't much of it. An attendant welcomes us
aboard.

'No hurry, we got problems with the engine.'

Most of the passengers look to be holidaymakers or train
buffs, so no one seems to care very much. I have the feeling that
I'm the only one chasing time. Two big diesels pull us out
almost an hour late.

'Thank you for travelling Amtrak train Number 36, The
Desert Wind.' The announcements come thick and fast, and we
are all issued with useful information on the country we're
passing through. All of it rather tame compared to the days
when Fogg crossed America and Passepartout had asked him 'if
it would not be prudent, before starting on the Pacific Railroad,
to buy a few dozen Enfield rifles or Colt revolvers'.

'We're now crossing the Los Angeles River, dry 350 days of
the year.'

Well-stocked railway sidings indicate that though passenger
traffic, run by federally financed Amtrak, is still struggling,
freight traffic, still in the hands of private companies, is healthy.
If I'd jumped a freight train I could have been in Chicago in 36
hours. The fastest passenger express takes 42.

Once out of industrial L.A. we pass a string of good-looking,
well-maintained stations in the Spanish Mission style like
Fullerton and San Bernadino, complete with domes, balconies,
wide-eaved tiled roofs, wrought-iron fences and twirly stucco,
built by the Southern Pacific railway, one of three working this
line, the other two being the Santa Fe and the Union Pacific.
'Here at San Bernadino the very first McDonald's hamburger
stand opened 50 years ago.'

The engine horn wails as we pull out of the station into countryside which seems to have turned suddenly lighter. The earth is now a rich golden brown. Is it an illusion? Is there really more light outside at four o'clock than there was at three? A knowledgeable couple in front of me, forest rangers from Colorado, assure me it wasn't an illusion, we're just out of the smog.

'On the left of the train, the birthplace of Richard Nixon.'

No one rushes to the windows. Perhaps they should, for it was under Nixon in 1971 that Amtrak was created. By unburdening private companies of the need to run passenger lines, his administration expected passenger travel to wither and die. But it has, against all the odds, survived, is popular and will not be cut again. Indeed Dukakis, until weeks ago a Presidential contender, had promised to double Amtrak's spending. Bush hadn't.

Dusk falls as we climb up into the Sierras. A red and dusty light catches the boulders strewn along dried up river beds. We pass a point where we can see the San Andreas Fault, a blue line of rock in the hills.

I scan through Amtrak's blurb: '... come to where the sun rules the earth ... where canyon walls give up the secrets of rivers long dead ... where desert winds carve steeples to the sky.'

The PA adds a more realistic note: 'We do advise all passengers not to place Kleenex tissues in the toilet bowls.'

As the last light of a good-looking day fades we move slowly up and over the Cajon Pass, and down into the Mojave Desert. After a couple more hours we're in Nevada. I know it's Nevada because the only signs of life are casinos, explosions of neon which dot the darkness like tribal fires.

At mealtime we move along to the restaurant car which is run with the same benign air as a prison canteen. Food here is strictly to be delivered and consumed. Enjoyment is not an issue. The menu is printed on an order form, which must be signed and the number of the car in which you're accommodated filled in. If all this is not done, frosty looks all round.

Midway through the meal, and six hours out of Los Angeles, Las Vegas appears, materialising from nothing, like a magician preceded by a flash of light. 'Stardust', 'Circus Circus', 'Caesar's Palace' … familiar names blaze out of the night sky. Las Vegas station is a cursory affair, like the rest of the city, not quite believable. Almost immediately we're in pitch darkness and emptiness again. Clocks on an hour between here and Salt Lake City. Not enough beds for Passepartout and myself so recline in the seat in coach class. A sociable atmosphere. Meet a man who uses the train for business. He's an accountant out of Chicago, with work spread out in front of him, even at midnight. 'It confuses some clients, impresses others.'

'This is the way I like to do it. If people don't understand that then I don't want them as clients.'

A lady called Beth, insubstantially slim and soft spoken, has set up a business of her own in upstate New York, making and selling her own dresses.

'Can you make a living out of that?'

'Not really,' she smiles almost apologetically. 'I deal in real estate as well.'

Onwards into the darkness of the land of opportunity.

Day 66 29 November

At seven o'clock I pull aside the curtains and look out on a silvery-grey morning. A light covering of snow lies between the tracks as we ease into Salt Lake City.

Fogg came here to 'the curious Mormon country' on the 6th December, his 65th day out of London. I'm only a day behind now, after the *Garnet* crossed the Pacific ten days faster than the *General Grant*. On my 66th day I find myself in Passepartout's footsteps, climbing down onto the platform 'to take the air'. The 6th December 1872 and 29th November 1988 sound much the same. 'The weather was cold, the sky grey, but it had stopped snowing. The disc of the sun, enlarged by the mist, looked like an enormous piece of gold, and Passepartout was busy calculating its value in pounds sterling ...'

Plenty of time at Salt Lake City this morning to calculate the value of the hazy sun as we are waiting for a connecting train from Seattle which is reported stuck in a snowdrift high in the mountains. The Seattle train, known as the Pioneer, combines here with the California Zephyr from San Francisco and the Desert Wind to form the California Zephyr service to Chicago. We are thirteen cars long when we eventually pull out of Salt Lake City, with three diesel locomotives to haul us up and over the Rockies.

One thing I do miss from Fogg's days are the bison. 'About three o'clock in the afternoon a herd of ten or twelve thousand blocked the railroad. The engine ... tried to plunge its spur into the flank of the immense column, but it had to stop before the impenetrable mass.'

The landscape we're travelling through has long been rid of bison and Sioux and Pawnees too, but it's a spectacular backdrop for a bacon and egg breakfast, with snow-sprinkled fields in deep shadow and sun-capped mountains in sharp contrast behind. The train snakes its way into the Rockies following half-frozen streams up curving valleys that are narrowing and steepening all the time. The rocks have been folded and faulted and weathered into tortured, crumbling shapes. Pinnacles and boulders rest on tiny stems, there are precarious overhangs and knobbly stacks.

Into the small town of Helper, Utah, about mid-morning. Helper is one of those functional names that abound in this literal, pioneering part of America. Towns with names like Parachute, Rifle, Gypsum, Carbondale and Basalt, Colorado. Helper was where additional locomotives required to help trains on the final assault of the Rockies were housed. The town, built for the railway crews, is now a coal-mining centre and has upgraded itself to Helper City.

Early lunch as we pull into Grand Junction, Colorado. Elevation 4,906 feet. Confluence of the Colorado and Gunnison Rivers. The chief steward, improbably called Abdul Mahmoud, exhorts his team of waiters in the fine art of service: 'Come on. Get 'em in here.'

Today's lunch menu features the forbidden delights of 'The Hot Open Face Sandwich. Your attendant will describe this to you.'

The sun spills into the train as we set off again alongside the Colorado River. It's about 25 yards wide here, and on its flat banks, protected from the winds, grow orchards of apple, pear and peach. Halfway down the train is an observation car. It's filling up fast on this clear and sunny afternoon.

There's a lady of late middle-age calling herself Mar-Mer, who became a clown two years ago. She sparkles with the delight of it all and bursts into song and jokes with the zeal of a new convert. How does her husband cope with her new profession, I ask. 'Oh … he's kind of an introvert,' she reveals, as if describing an incurable illness. There's a man travelling with his son simply because he prefers trains: 'Sure knocks heck outta driving.' His wife is a cellist with the gloriously named Mile High Orchestra in Denver. But I get the feeling these are not average Americans. They're people who care about their environment, who despise and fear what big business is doing to it and who are immensely knowledgeable about where they live and determined to protect it from unnecessary development.

Back to my seat and doze a little. The mother of the Colorado couple sings to her daughter, in a soft and lilting voice. 'Freight Train', 'When Johnny Comes Marching Home', and others. The combination of this gentle voice and the wide empty country by the winding river is enchanting.

The PA system has become a staff intercom as well as a passenger information service this afternoon. 'Get your cameras ready for some truly great photos' is followed abruptly by a breathless shout of 'Earl, come to the dining car. We need you bad!'

At a quarter to four we reach Glenwood Springs. Elevation 5,600 feet. I must take a decision. However short of time I am, I cannot go through the Rockies without a pause to look around. To travel and see nothing is my complaint about aeroplanes, and I can feel myself falling into the same trap. I alight here for a detour which I hope I can afford.

Whilst there's some light left I take a dip in the Glenwood Hot Springs – geothermal waters that soothed the Ute Indians a hundred years ago and beyond. Today they're part of a busy health spa peppered with notices – rules and signs and health warnings in thorough but bewildering American style. The waters, at 104 degrees Fahrenheit, are in the open air, which is currently 35 degrees Fahrenheit. My body quite enjoys this schizophrenic experience. Passepartout sets up on the side of the pool to witness my immersion, but the cloud of steam is so dense that the camera can't find me.

Then drive up to Aspen, about an hour away and two and a half thousand feet up into the Rockies. It's a sort of Christmassy Beverly Hills, but though it may be Californian in income it's East Coast in taste. To the Hotel Jerome whose placid 1889 brick exterior masks an exuberance of Victorian excess inside.

My room is wide and well-furnished in impeccable re-creation of the Naughty Nineties. I take a long, slow bath in a room floored in Carrara marble. Then in one of those cultural cross-connections that have characterised the journey I end up picking my way through the snow to a Mexican restaurant, walking through the neat streets of Aspen, treading carefully along icy sidewalks. The unfamiliar feel of ice-cold air on my face is very refreshing. Nothing brash or strident intrudes on the rows of carefully maintained houses. No sodium or neon lights allowed here. The town feels like a village, intimate and enclosed.

A last look out of the curtains at midnight. On the ski slopes behind the town, huge machines hurl white plumes of artificial snow onto the mountain.

Day 67 30 November

It's the last day of November and the outside temperature is minus 8. Checking through my notebook, I find that I passed the *first* day of November in a floating Yugoslav hospital on the Malacca Strait. The balmy heat of that wet tropical day could not be further from the bracing freshness of this morning, nor could my activity be more different.

I am to try a new form of earthbound transport, to add to trains and buses and ships and fiacres and taxis and camels and rickshaws and Rolls-Royces. Not to be outdone by Fogg who took a snow-yacht across Nebraska, I'm to cross a bit of America by dog-sled. At Krabloonik kennels in Snowmass village, Dan Maceachen and his colleagues have 250 huskies, some of whom are being trained for a 5,000-mile trans-Antarctic expedition next year, some of whom will pull sleds in the Iditarod – the annual race across Alaska, in which the dogs are expected to cover more than 100 miles a day for 17 days. The dogs spend the winter season pulling 'guests' as the visitors are called, on handcrafted sleds around beautiful mountain trails.

No one can sneak into Krabloonik kennels unannounced. As soon as the dogs hear a suspicion of a footfall they spring to their feet, tugging at their leads and barking and baying in an ever-swelling chorus that resounds through the woods. A young man with a mass of blond curls, padded out like a Polar explorer, is to be my musher – the human element in the dog-team. His name's Marion, and he's from Mississippi, where they give men names like that, and he left law school after a year to come up here. He's married to another Mississippian, who runs the library in Aspen, and they live in a log cabin up in the mountains, 'all by ourselves'.

He works hard for his idyllic life. Dog sledding, as Dan Maceachen says, is 10 per cent glamour and 90 per cent hard work. These are dedicated men. The composition of the 13-strong dog team is vitally important, and before anything else, Dan and Marion work out a team sheet, rather like the ones posted on the school notice board. There is a lead dog. His or her qualities are 'instinctively born', says Maceachen. 'It is not a trait I can breed or train.' This was the team chosen for me:

Dishaan (lead), Atangee, Tuliaan ('gentle one'), Liseen, Nunapik, Naken, Nutek, Twintoo, Akarta ('red fox'), Kuna ('great warrior'), Donawoo, Uquila and Takkuk ('moon spirit'). The names are Inuit, for these are Eskimo dogs.

The harnessing-up is a traumatic process for all concerned. So eager are the dogs for an outing, that they intensify their cries, fling themselves to the ends of their leash, straining and howling with all their might to catch the musher's attention. Dan and Marion have the assistance of one other musher, an ex-harbourmaster, steamboat captain and film school student whose card reads 'Pilot Lord Frieherr B'Wana Joe Edmonds, Adventurer For Sale'. He has the aspect of a true eccentric, unconventional even by mushing standards. An old sweater, straggly and very worn, sags off him. 'Put it this way, it's lasted longer than the girl who made it for me.'

The control over the dogs is based on cooperation rather than coercion. No whip or rein is used and the instructions are communicated verbally. At the moment there's a lot of 'Siddown!' and not much else as the dogs are forced, much against their instinct, to wait for Passepartout to find a camera position.

Marion asks me how I'm coping with the altitude. 'There's usually some nausea or headaches.'

LEFT: *Braving the stage for karaoke.*

BELOW: *Bedtime at the capsule hotel in Tokyo.*

LEFT: *Killing time on the 11-day Pacific crossing to Long Beach.*

ABOVE: *An international incident as we cross the Date Line. N.B. It's tomato ketchup,* not *blood.*

ABOVE: *On the phone to my agent aboard the* Queen Mary.

RIGHT: *Dog sled approaching, Aspen, Colorado.*

Inside the highest atrium in the world, at one of the world's seven-star hotels. The Burj Al Arab, Dubai.

Back at the Al Hamriya Port, Dubai, at the sport from which Al Shama *sailed twenty year earlier.*

Bhuj: The Jubilee Hospital, shattered by the earthquake of 2001.

Magic Moments. Reliving the journey of twenty years ago with (left to right): Captain Hussan Suleyman, Mahomet, Asimuth, the captain's grandson, Anif, Captain Suleyman's son-in-law and Anwar, the ex-cabin boy.

Funnily enough, until he said that I felt fine.

Then suddenly we're away. Any feelings of guilt at sitting like Queen Victoria in the back of the sled, covered in rugs and furs, whilst small dogs pull me along, are dispelled by the obvious delight the dogs take in being on the move. Marion leaps on and off the sled, running, sliding, leaning out over corners like a cycle speedway rider, and keeping up a running stream of imprecations and exhortations to the dogs.

The dogs, sadly, have to be constantly stopped, while Passepartout scuttles off to another position. Marion's hardest task is to keep them down. To this end he employs a length of rolled-up paper ('it's just an old dog food packet') with which he slaps them cautionarily. He is embarrassed about doing it. 'The whapping doesn't usually go on, I want you to know that.' He claims that it's the noise of the impact rather than any pain that calms them. And the embarrassment: 'They just don't want to be the one that gets told off like that.'

The less experienced dogs are showing increasing reluctance to sit and wait, and the moment one of the older ones rises, the others follow, and whilst Marion's back is turned they're off, hauling me helplessly over a mound of cleared snow. A branch flicks down taking out my hat instead of my eye, but only just. Marion screams them to a halt and quite a bit of paper is applied. Much surly whining. The phrase 'mutinous dogs' comes to mind.

On the occasions when they are allowed a run the sensation is wonderful. The sled moves silently over the snow, and the air smells good and clean (apart from the more than occasional pungent odours from the dogs themselves who have to learn to defecate on the move). As we toil back up the last hill, Marion becomes softer with the dogs. 'I'm going to barbecue you.' The dog gazes happily up at him. 'You're a real knucklehead today,' he tells another. I ask him if he knows every dog in the kennel by name.

'Yep! And I know their mother and their father and their grandfather and their grandmother.' Because of the exigencies of filming we've travelled maybe 4 or 5 miles, and it's frustrating when you think these dogs think nothing of 100 miles a day. A bit more snow and they could have taken me to Chicago.

Day 68 1 December

December arrives in Aspen, Colorado, which seems suitable. The air is very dry and I wake far too early with a thick, abrasive sore throat.

With another fine day dawning there seems little point in moving from this agreeable spot. But I have cut things very fine. I must not miss the California Zephyr this afternoon, nor its connection with the Lake Shore Limited in Chicago, for if I'm anything more than a few hours late in New York at the weekend I shall lose the last vital link in the chain.

But I've one adventure more before leaving the Rockies. It begins, prosaically enough, in the municipal car park at six o'clock in the morning. Two enormous vehicles are being assembled here. One is called The Rat, the other The Unicorn. There isn't much passenger space in either of them, they have no means of independent propulsion and once started they may end up anywhere. They are the one form of transport everyone connects with *Around the World in Eighty Days*, and yet Jules Verne never mentions them. I'm about to board a hot-air balloon.

Passepartout and myself and Jake the pilot – burly, moustachioed and, like everyone else in Aspen, aged between 22 and 35 – are squeezed into the 4-foot-square wicker and leather-padded basket of The Unicorn. Clem and the BBC New York film crew are in The Rat.

We have to ascend at this ungodly hour before the land warms up and starts giving off thermals which disturb the air current. Hot-air balloons do not, it appears, like hot air.

I feel rather silly standing in this little basket on the ground, like a piece of forgotten shopping, whilst each flame of propane swells the shroud above my head.

Then, quite suddenly, without a lot of fuss and bother, we're rising majestically above the car park, above the hotel, above the neat, clean-as-a-new-pin streets, above the substantial Victorian bulk of Wheeler Opera House, above the Aspen Fresh Fish Co. and The Great Divide Music Store and the eye-catching old bandstand in Paepcke Park. Over Highway 82 and Hyman Avenue and Pepi's Hideaway and suddenly the town is in miniature and there are shouts from the occupants of the other balloon for me to stand up and be photographed and I'm not sure if my knees will support me.

I can feel the blood draining from my face, God knows where to. If only Jake were wearing some sort of harness instead of just balancing casually on the edge of the basket as if he's going for a picnic up the Thames. There is nothing to stop me jumping out. I'm not attached to a damn thing. I stand up, feeling queasy as I've never felt since that night on the dhow. Think back to the astrologer's words of reassurance. Everything smooth … back in plenty of time … no problems. But I'd told him I was taking surface transport only. I've cheated, I've left the ground and now I'm paying the price.

'Where are we going?' I manage to ask in a voice as thin as the air.

'Aw … I dunno for sure.'

Oh, great.

Jake looks around. He looks around without getting off the edge of the basket! He just twists his unharnessed body on the thin leather rim 300 feet above Aspen!

'You see, it just depends on the way the air behaves.'

'You mean you don't know that?'

'Not until we get up here.' He consults one of the distressingly few instruments, which shows wind speed. Below me now Main Street has become Highway 82. A long line of

Dinky Toys thread their way slowly into the town. What's a traffic jam doing in a beautiful place like this? Remember to ask Jake this when my voice has broken.

'Y'see, the cold air flows down this valley like water in a river. It's not till you're in it you know where or how fast those currents are flowing.'

I know where. Aspen International Airport, that's where. A light plane is actually flying in beneath us.

'Er … Jake … Do …er … do … airport control … er … *know*. About us?'

'Oh, I guess so.'

So on a swell of currents and hope we drift slowly towards the mountains. And quite suddenly I've lost that fear of the unlikely and I'm leaning over the side with the rest of them. We can watch silently from up here without disturbing the wildlife, and I catch sight of a pair of elk in amongst the trees. The view is wide and majestic, from Aspen round to Snowmass as well as the snowcapped Mount Daly, a peak of classic Paramount Films proportions. I may be cheating, but by the time we drift down, making an endearingly clumsy descent into some prickly scrub, I calculate I've moved a mile nearer the Reform Club.

Back into Aspen for a late and hearty breakfast, such as the condemned man might enjoy after his reprieve. My *Rocky Mountain News* tells me that it's Woody Allen's 53rd birthday and that Michael Dukakis' waxwork has been removed from Madame Tussaud's after the shortest display on record.

Walk a last time around Aspen. Gaze enviously at the skiers, who, at this early stage of the season, have wide slopes to themselves. Feel glad that I kitted myself out with some new clothes in Tokyo. Everyone here looks as if they're straight out of the windows of the local boutiques, which proliferate under names like The Freudian Slip, The Hedgehog and Shirtique.

Christmas carols sound from somewhere, and I realise that I want to be back home. As if to acknowledge the wish, I find a bar serving Sam Smith's beer from my home county. A pint, a bowl of clam chowder, and a last lungful of the cold, dry, reviving air before heading back down to the real world.

Glenwood Springs station could be out of the Scottish Highlands. Rough-hewn stone, overhanging eaves and a feeling of having been nearly glamorous. The same could be said of The California Zephyr. 'A soft gentle breeze' as it's defined in the dictionary, and certainly it's no hurricane today. An hour passes and still no sign. A massive goods train goes by, quite possibly the longest train I've ever seen. Seven diesels of the Rio Grande and Southern Pacific Railroads hauling one and a quarter miles of trucks. The Zephyr arrives one and a half hours late and it's getting dark as we wind into the canyon, the tips of whose walls are caught by the last rays of a golden sunset and glow like the points of a crown.

All that's needed to enjoy it is sight and silence. But the train manager has other plans.

'I've collected all the Trivia sheets. Mrs Dorothy Connelly, you got all your questions wrong. I'd like to meet you. You're the person who got *all their questions wrong*!'

Pause.

'On our left Interstate Highway 70. In construction for fifteen years. The most expensive highway ever built in this country.'

And there it is, in the gathering gloom. Squashed in between sheer rock walls and the much-abused Colorado River – squeezed dry in its later stages to service the lawn sprinklers of L.A. and here in the canyon half-filled with the rubble and concrete of America's most expensive highway.

'Margaritas goin' for a dollar fifty cents in the lounge car. Why don't you come and join us?'

At five past eight we enter Moffat Tunnel, the third longest in the world. It runs beneath the watershed of the Rocky Mountains, the Continental Divide, reducing what was a five-hour journey for Phileas Fogg to ten minutes today.

Have a cabin to myself and Chuck, the attendant, warns me that tonight's ride could be a little rough, as we shall be moving onto The Burlington and Northern Railroad and we'll be switched to their secondary track to leave the fastest free for freight.

Dinner taken as we descend into Denver. Four thousand feet in thirty minutes. It looks as if we're coming in by plane.

Chuck has some bedtime stories for me. Mostly gruesome and to do with the dangers of modern travel for an elderly clientele. The more modern the appliances, the more neat and clever and labour-saving the designers try to be, the greater the scope for disasters. They can range from a simple dousing for those who mistake the shower button for the lavatory flush, to the Rabelaisian experience of a very fat lady whose fleshy bottom was sucked into the stainless steel toilet bowls by the electric flushing system. Chuck had the delicate task of trying to prise her free, but without success. The train had to be halted and the entire electrical system switched off before she could be removed. The stop was described over the PA as a 'routine electrical check'.

His most feared passengers are the Boy Scouts. Maybe the strain of hours tying knots and trying to light fires with two sticks provokes a vehement counter-reaction but their behaviour makes Attila the Hun sound like Beatrix Potter. They are in the habit of leaving sachets of tomato ketchup underneath the lavatory seat. At the first heavy pressure the sachets break squirting their sticky red contents down the next customer's leg.

Boy Scouts or no Boy Scouts, I lifted the seat carefully before turning in. Rocked to sleep on the Burlington and Northern somewhere between Denver and Omaha.

Day 69 2 December

7.45: Rosy-fingered dawn over the Midwest. The topmost points of leafless trees see the sun first and burn a light red. Fifteen minutes later at Omaha, Nebraska. Big railway centre. At one time supported nine railroads. The Union Stockyards, a huge cattle-shipping centre established in 1884. This is all culled from my excellent Amtrak Route Guide, something which British Rail could well introduce. It has a lot more practical value than any 'Inter-City' magazine.

I *like* small-town America. I'm not entirely sure why, because I've little practical experience of it beyond films and writers like Garrison Keillor and Nabokov and Updike. I fear it may be the curse of nostalgia. Nostalgia for a 1950s world culled from the pages of the *National Geographic*.

Today as we cross into Iowa, 'the land beyond', it's all there in the hard bright sun and it doesn't seem to have changed. Small, clean, white-painted clapboard settlements, bordered by woods and barns and ponds, focused around a steepled church. Modest and tidy, set in an easy rural landscape of low hills and tree-fringed streams. Only the ubiquitous presence of satellite dishes distinguishes them from the dreams that filled my schoolboy years in Sheffield.

'Are you meatless?' a waiter screams at me at breakfast. 'I've been called many things in my time', I'm about to reply when he jabs his pen toward the bacon and sausage section of my order which I've omitted to fill in.

Copies of *USA Today* are on every seat in the train. News from the present day. Benazir Bhutto is soon to be sworn in as the world's first Muslim woman leader. I think of the *Garnet*'s chief engineer. Not happy news for him. He's probably down near Panama. Mike's Bar empty now, I suppose.

Eddie Murphy has bought Cher's house in L.A. for 6.5 million dollars, and Spielberg's latest hit features 'a bunch of lovable dinosaurs'. Could well have been filmed aboard the California Zephyr.

There is a new man on the PA this morning and mercifully he is very good to listen to. This is because he gets everything slightly wrong. So, in a piece of historical information, Lucy Kilpatrick comes out as 'Lucky' Kilpatrick, and a film as *Who's Afraid of the Virgin Wolf?*

At 2.20 in the afternoon we're at the good-looking town of Burlington on the Illinois border. Spires pierce the skyline and bonfire smoke drifts across a graveyard in a wispy autumn breeze. We're about to cross the Mississippi and all seems well with the world, except that we are running ever later. Due in to Chicago at 4.30, with what seemed an easy 6.25 connection to New York, we're now looking at an arrival time nearer 6. Chuck isn't worried. He's going to call ahead and have redcaps and trolleys standing by for us.

Rumble over a three-quarter-mile-long Mississippi bridge. After crossing a world of largely empty rivers it's good to see such an unequivocal expanse of water. No rocks and sandbanks. Water stretching from side to side, a river of noble size.

'Our next stop is Princeton. The big capital of the world … I'm sorry, the *pig* capital.'

Four o'clock, and the sun is losing its intensity. Red and browns dilute the gold. It has been a magnificent day and it's a pity that it has now to be coloured, as have so many days on this journey, by a faint but nagging feeling of anxiety. Perhaps the Rocky Mountain detour had been an indulgence. I don't want to go home having seen nothing, and I've already sacrificed Muscat and Singapore to the pressures of the schedule, but having come so far and so close, it would be ignominious to end up on a deserted New York quayside.

4.45: America silhouetted against the dark blue horizon, the outlines of bare trees, trucks on the highway, sheds and factories rise and fall sharp and geometrical. Dear God, don't let the train stop, please. Into my mind comes a statistic from the *Queen Mary*. She never suffered a mechanical breakdown at sea, never had to use a single lifeboat, and never transmitted a distress signal on her own behalf. Reliability like this, plus a few extra miles an hour, is all I can hope for from Amtrak.

5.15: Christmas trees in the streets of Aurora, Illinois, in the Chicago suburbs. Six-lane tailbacks on the freeways, two-tier trains roll past, full to bursting with Friday night commuters.

At last the towering downtown skyscrapers come into view. The Hancock Tower and the Sears Tower, once the world's tallest building, now for sale at 2 billion dollars.

The only good thing about Union Station is that we are there with 35 minutes to spare. There are none of the promised redcaps to meet us, and we are at the far end of a bleak and grubby ice-covered track, without even a platform. We have much more than my bag to move and by the time we have a trolley, it's only 15 minutes before the Lake Shore leaves. By the time we've reached the departure platform, 10 minutes are left. Then Simon hears my name called on the station tannoy. 'Mr Palin, arriving from Los Angeles, please go to Station Information.'

This is a time for strong heads. Station Information is back the way we've already come. To go is to run the risk of missing the train, not to go is to run the risk of missing what could be a vital message. Go straight to Halifax? Ship leaving tonight from Montreal? About turn and race through the station. Find the information desk. A queue. Push my way through. Yes, there is a message. Lady disappears to collect it, scowls from others in line.

'Here we are, Mr Palin ....' With the exquisite timing of a B-thriller, she unwraps the note. 'A Mr Seth Mason says if you have any time in Chicago he'd love to see you. Please give him a call at home.'

6.35: Never been so happy to be on a train, and a comfortable one at that. The Lake Shore Limited left on time, seconds after we boarded, and it's racing out of Chicago most purposefully, like a train that has business to do, rather than the pleasantly peripatetic California Zephyr.

Through South Bend, Indiana, another good functional name. In England we so seldom have to make up new names. Apart from a few Skelmersdales and Telfords our cities, towns and villages have had their names for centuries. America has no such inheritance, and yet a much greater demand. No wonder they run out of inspiration and have to pinch other people's names. Most of the cities I've passed through in the last sixty-nine days have been replicated somewhere in the U.S. There's Bombay, New York; Madras, Oregon; Tokio, Texas; as well as four Venices, seven Cairos, and no fewer than seventeen Cantons.

Clocks go on an hour, my seventh lost since the Date Line, as we enter Eastern Standard Time. Hard to get to sleep for the sound of loud, grating voices from a very busy next-door compartment.

'We have been in court for custody, in ten years, a total of *seventy-four* days!' Rumbles of reaction from deeper voices over which a harridan cry rises once more: 'Seventy-*four* times, in and out of court in ten years!'

Do these people know there's anyone else in the world?

If all goes well this could be my final night on land before we reach Britain. And lying here looking out into the dark as we pull up at some unnamed Ohio station on the shores of Lake Erie, I'm having a last concentrated dose of America.

Forty-five-foot trailers are being humped noisily into a siding, the bare anonymous station is lit by a pair of cold overhead lights like an Edward Hopper painting and the soap opera continues next door ... 'I'm thirty years old and my life is goin' nowhere ...'

I take recourse to my headphones. Blank out the noise with Leonard Cohen.

Day 70   3 December

Sometime in the night we must have passed through Cleveland and Buffalo and Rochester on the southern shore of Lake Ontario. We're in New York State, heading due east along the gap in the Appalachian Mountains formed by the Mohawk River. The map is studded with classical names – Ithaca, Utica, Seneca Falls, Rome and Syracuse, the city we're drawing into as

Nigel and I, the non-meatless, dig into eggs and bacon and that strange burnt and watery substance that passes in America for coffee. Sitting across from us is a distinguished elderly man. He turns out to be 90 years old, an ex-air force commander called Skeel, who has traced back his Danish ancestors to the year A.D. 800 when they left Denmark and settled in East Anglia. He told us that this part of New York State, from Lake Ontario down to the Pennsylvania border, was given in gratitude to soldiers who had fought in the War of Independence. Most of the soldiers, wanting only to return to where they'd lived before, sold their share of the land, but a high-minded group of officers formed a co-operative to run the area, on the republican ideals of ancient Rome and Greece. According to Mr Skeel, naming the cities after the homes of these ideals 'was just about the only thing they ever did'.

Despite it being a Sunday this courteous gentleman was on his way to Albany for a board meeting of some industrial company of which he had remained a director. Albany, at the confluence of the Mohawk and Hudson rivers, presents a proud city skyline, as confident and serious as befits the capital of one of the most prosperous states of America. Here the 'Lake Shore Limited' splits, half continuing east to Massachusetts and Boston and half turning due south to New York along the Hudson Valley.

As a valedictory dose of American landscape the ride down the Hudson could hardly be bettered. Though the intense autumn colours have faded from the woods that climb the cliffs on either side, the wide valley and its steep rocky banks offer a long and impressive stretch of grand and unspoilt river scenery, brilliant today in the unflinching sunlight.

Enjoying it too are a group of jolly ladies in their forties from Albany, who are leaving their husbands for a girls' night out in New York. A little shy to start with, but once it's established they're not going to spend the evening at the opera but at a male strip club, and that all of us think they're quite right, they loosen up and more Molson's beer is called for. It's a little early in the day to start, but as the Professor puts it we're all feeling a little demob happy. High on the opposite bank is a long sprawling pile that looks like a Russian jail. On enquiring I'm told it's West Point Military Academy.

There's an air of heightened excitement as we approach New York, so different from the easy-going almost sleepy atmosphere on the train as we pulled out of L.A.

Across the Harlem River and into Manhattan rolling slowly above the derelict urban landscape described so enthusiastically by Tom Wolfe in the book I have by my side at the moment, Bonfire of the Vanities. Around 132nd Street the city looks more like Cairo. Rubbish is strewn everywhere, smashed cars and discarded beds are scattered over plots of land empty save for sheets of corrugated iron and people living beneath them. As if this might have been just a momentary waking nightmare, an aberration not to be confused with the real thing, we are swept away into the darkness of Park Avenue Tunnel.

Passengers begin to move to the doors. The garrulous openness of the Hudson River ride has been replaced by an edgy silence, as if everyone is mentally preparing themselves for the demands of this ruthless and impatient city. As in Chicago and Los Angeles, the railway approach to New York is not one to lift the spirits. We disembark in subterranean gloom and trudge along the platform sustained only by an act of faith that New York really is up there above us, and that we haven't all died.

The shabby tunnels lead to what could quite easily be Heaven and Hell combined – the great concourse of Grand Central Terminal. The massive celestial ceiling, pinpricked with gold-leaved constellations, shelters two sorts of people – those who are going somewhere and those who are not. In the latter, more interesting category, are flute players, those fighting off imaginary aerial assailants, those conducting urgent conversations with themselves, and those sitting with vacant eyes, staring down at the ground, unable to take life in New York any other way.

I'm neck and neck with Fogg now, for the first time since I left. He arrived on the seventieth day at 'thirty-five minutes after nine at night' at Jersey City 'near the very pier of the Cunard line of steamers, otherwise called the British and North American Royal Mail Steam Packet Company. The *China*, bound for Liverpool, had left thirty-five minutes before!'

Fogg of course had not panicked, and taken himself off to the St Nicholas Hotel on Broadway to sleep on the problem.

At least he had the choice of a dozen other transatlantic passenger carriers, none of them in business nowadays. My eggs are all in one basket – a 53,000-ton container ship, hopefully loading now at Newark Docks en route for Felixstowe. I must get over there fast, but cannot, at the vital moment, find Passepartout. They'd been filming on the concourse, but were no longer to be seen.

Search for them unsuccessfully. New York, for all its virtues, is not a safe place to hang around. The man who stands still in New York is either buying or selling. For what other reason would you want to stand still? Eyes turn toward me, eyeing me, sizing me up suspiciously.

At last Passepartout appears from a side entrance looking ruffled and in the company of one of New York's finest. Demands to know what we're doing, who gave us permission and so on. Clem strides over to deal with it, but the whole episode loses an unsettling amount of time.

Fight gracelessly for a taxi which is driven by a Haitian.

'I shouldn't think you get many passengers asking for the container terminal?' I venture.

He says nothing.

I have chosen the only New York cabbie with nothing to say.

4.30: at the Port of Newark. The penultimate connection has been made. We have berths on the *Leda Maersk*, a Danish container ship, leaving tonight and reaching Britain in eight days, given fair weather. Though this is by no means guaranteed on the Atlantic in winter (as Captains Tuddenham and Amirapu warned us), my chances of success have never looked so good.

The first surprise on climbing aboard was not how spick and span the ship was – after all, you expect that from the Danes – but that the first officer who greeted me was a slim blonde girl. She shrugs off our disconcertment. Apparently it's quite common to have women officers now, especially in the American merchant fleet, which has women captains. Still, she is the first lady merchant seaperson I've encountered.

10.45: Grubby, after two and a half days on the train, and looking forward to a shower before turning in. I've just walked the 880-foot deck and am looking towards the New York City skyline, crowned by the winking lights of the World Trade Center. Between me and Manhattan is Jersey City, and nearer still, a huge transportation complex. The docks themselves lie beside ten-lane turnpikes on the other side of which is Newark airport. The night is full of lights and activity. But by the time I sink into the twenty-eighth bed since leaving London, the ship has still not sailed.

Day 71 4 December

Wake up to feel us moving, but only just. Certainly not out on the high seas where we should be. It's now seven o'clock and we are moving gingerly out along a maze of wharves and into Newark Bay. Dress quickly and go straight up onto the bridge to catch a last look at New York on this brilliant morning. It's cold but clear and there is a magnificent panoramic view from New Jersey to Manhattan and Long Island beyond. The captain says that when he arrived from Charleston yesterday he could see the New York skyline from 50 miles away. The Statue of Liberty slides by, looking greener and sexier since her restoration, and so spellbinding is the view that no one goes down for breakfast until we have passed beneath the Verrazano Narrows Bridge, the East Coast's Golden Gate, and the pilot has been dropped at the Ambrose lighthouse. From here there are three traffic separation zones funnelling ships out of the crowded New York area. On the chart they point off like the arms of a country signpost. We turn north and east for Nantucket. The journey repeats itself neatly when I hear the captain's instructions.

'Frem ... Fuld.'

The sound of the words on the controls of *The Saudi Moon II* (crossed out and *I* written in). Captain Rodebaek looks like the archetypal sea-captain. He's round, ruddy-faced and smiles readily. He even has a slightly wandering 'Long John Silver' eye. He's not worried about the late start. The Maersk line is renowned for its timekeeping. He'll easily make up any backlog, and we should be alongside in Le Havre next Sunday at 4.30 a.m. It's a bit earlier than he'd like but he doesn't trust the French stevedores after Sunday lunch.

The only jarring note in all of this is the mention of Le Havre. Both Passepartout and myself were under the impression that next Sunday the *Leda Maersk* would be at Felixstowe. Ah, no ... that's the next day.

Over a breakfast of yogurt, coffee, eggs, bacon, and thick rich white bread baked on board by a German chef, we discuss the implications of the Le Havre delay, and various alternatives are proposed, ranging from catching the Le Havre–Southampton ferry, to a more tele-worthy ship-to-ship transfer at the mouth of the Thames and a launch up to Westminster Pier. No one feels we should waste time on the French coast.

There is an almost palpable sense of company pride about the *Leda Maersk* which did not exist on any of the other ships. A. P. Moller, the founder of the owning company, is a controversial figure in Denmark. The richest man in the country and an unapologetic advocate of private enterprise, his views rarely coincide with those of a liberal, progressive government. But his business, 'run with a rod of iron' I'm told, is the biggest employer in the country, including shipyards, oil exploration equipment, trucks and aeroplanes. This ship was built in Denmark in 1982 and registered there, despite worldwide trends to register in the cheaper free ports like Monrovia, Singapore, Panama and Limassol. The captain has been with the ship for its whole life, unlike the Neptune Orient captains who may do only six months before being transferred. The crew, with the exception of the chef and an Indian radio officer, is Danish, and the whole atmosphere seems to reflect confidence and top-dogginess rather than the retrenchment of Neptune's Singapore-based operation. Mind you, this impression could be the result of having a company man on board. This is Jesper, thin and sardonic, and with him two other 'civilians', Erik and Thorval, both office workers gaining travel experience. Erik is an accountant and Thorval isn't.

Pass the day in mundane activities with the rather traumatic exception of a haircut. The Professor has discovered that Lillian, one of the stewardesses, cuts all the crew's hair, and she and the gloating Passepartout assemble in my cabin after lunch for the ritual depilation. Lillian, armed only with a cigarette and a pair of scissors, has a strong lived-in face and a wearily enigmatic manner. Does she not feel that it's a lonely life at sea?

She pulls in a mouthful of smoke and exhales unhurriedly before answering: 'It suits me. I prefer to be alone … I would like to be an able-seaman. Then I could be always at sea.'

She seems to be spending a long time at the back of my head and hair is falling in divots. Is she not perhaps taking off a little too much?

'You are an actor. They will see only the front of your head,' she grins malevolently.

A marvellous Sunday dinner. Roast beef (though no Danish equivalent of Yorkshire pudding) and good red wine, a rarity on the journey, as Queen Margrethe and her French consort look down from the wall.

Day 72 5 December

A cold, presaged by a sore throat and a thick head since leaving Aspen, has finally come out of the closet and I wake feeling dull and drained of energy. The switchback course of the weather hasn't helped, and after our chilly, dry and dazzling days across the States, we are now in the warm fug of the Gulf Stream. So warm is the current that the sea this morning steams like a Turkish bath. Wraith-like wisps of vapour drift around the boat, blotting out the horizon. Instead of being on the wide ocean we are suddenly enclosed in caves of white cloud, through which a ghostly sunlight filters, and from which you half-expect to see a ship of lost souls emerge.

9.30: I'm halfway through a late breakfast when the alarm sounds for lifeboat drill. This is obligatory on all ships, but has been observed with varying degrees of thoroughness throughout my journey. It's typical of Maersk lines that they are the most conscientious of the lot, and there's clearly little chance of my resuming my breakfast. We are all given a lifeboat rendezvous position, which is not difficult to find once you've reached the boat deck. The real problem is finding the boat deck.

There are six floors of accommodation and all around us bells are ringing and doors swinging shut automatically. I find myself up in the crew's laundry with the second stewardess. Bente, the blonde first officer, clutching a two-way radio, eventually rallies us all, and we have to don chunky orange lifejackets and wait for the lifeboat engine to be started. The engine won't start today, so we're stood, out on deck, looking like Flowerpot Men, for some considerable time. Fall into conversation with the chef (or chief steward as he is officially known) whose blue and white check trousers poke out incongruously from beneath his life preserver. He's from Schleswig-Holstein, and has a sad face but humorous eyes. Like Lillian he smokes assiduously, and enjoys a drink too.

'Last night,' he confides, 'I was quite intoxicated, you know. I go to the door three times before I can go out of it.'

At this point Dave Passepartout appears, looking a little grey and rather hurt that no one had woken him up. 'I could have died,' he mutters, before being told he's at the wrong lifeboat.

Given the occasional unresponsive gurgle from the lifeboat's engine I imagine all of us on this deck might have died as well, if this were a real emergency. Eventually it spurts into action and is promptly turned off. Divesting ourselves of the lifejackets we are about to head back to breakfast when the alarm bells start jangling again, lights flash, and the doors start to shut themselves. Over the din voices are raised:

'Fire! … Fire! … Assemble on main deck … Fire!!'

Momentary panic that this *could* be real. Especially as I've gone one way and everyone else has gone another. Again, I'm rescued by Bente, and led down five flights to a demonstration of fire-fighting equipment.

Chris, the young solid chief officer, gets to let off an entire foam extinguisher over the side, which awakens schoolboyish envy in all of us. Chris has a rather pedantic delivery and a way of leavening all he says with figures, which soon completely befuddle the listener. A case of confusing with too much precision. So when he tells us of the tensile strength of the container connecting rods or the awesome foam emission pressure of the extinguishers, one knows one is in the presence of greatness, but is not particularly reassured.

However, he's a mine of information on the *Leda Maersk*. In 1986 she was extended by 80 feet. A Japanese shipyard sliced the bows off, inserted a new section, welded, made good and had the ship ready for work again in forty days. A year later the superstructure was heightened one tier to accommodate more containers. There is hardly a ship in the Maersk fleet which hasn't been enlarged. The next class to be built will narrow the accommodation, widen the hull and provide spaces for 700 more containers, making a carrying total of more than 4,000.

At present the fastest service they offer is Hamburg to Singapore in 17 days, which means among other things that a whole new range of tropical foods will be available in Europe in bulk, rather than for the lucky few who can afford the costs of air freighting. Refrigerated containers are the coming thing. They require constant supervision and a separate and self-contained power supply for each one, but pay good money. The *Leda Maersk* has 300 containing anything from prunes to helium. Chris can remember once carrying a load of 20 million grapefruit. Punch-drunk with figures I retire to lunch, which is the main meal of the working day and this morning is oxtail in a thick and juicy gravy.

After lunch Passepartout and I assemble in the Captain's Day Room, which has been generously loaned to us for the crossing, for the first read-through of *Under Milk Wood*, which has been organised by Nigel as a way of passing the time. Seven of my ten roles are women, I notice.

Day 73 6 December

Lie low for most of the day as my cold flourishes. At dinner the conversation turns to boat people again. Captain Rodebaek picked up 55 in one trip and 63 in another, 'many of whom are now working for the company'. In a side-discussion on world ports, Singapore comes out fastest, with five cranes per vessel capable of 125 moves an hour. Felixstowe, free-enterprise jewel of British container ports, can offer a maximum of 40 moves an hour. Still no decision on what to do at Le Havre. At the moment we opt for safety and an extra day on the *Leda Maersk*, especially as the weather has been kind and we are on time.

Day 74 7 December

Feeling no better. Headache persists. No appetite for breakfast but climb up to bridge in the hope that Atlantic breezes will clear my head. More than breezes. A Force 8 wind blowing East North East is covering the sea with spray, and the prunes and helium are rearing and plunging over the waves. We're lying 1,453 nautical miles from New York, a little more than halfway to Europe, Newfoundland is 580 miles North West and the Azores archipelago 600 miles South East. It's a warm 61 degrees but very wet. Looking out at the Atlantic from the rain-lashed windows of the bridge, ten storeys above the hard-running waves I can hardly conceive of the courage, or foolhardiness that would make anyone want to cross all that alone.

At lunch today there is a big discussion about the elegant damask tablecloth on the captain's table. Jesper, the A. P. Moller company representative, says that in future, because of a ruthless cost-cutting exercise, the new tablecloths will not have the white Maersk line star woven in to them. We all take the captain's side on this one and urge the company to reconsider!

It'll be the tureens next.

Talk to Christian, the second officer, up on the bridge this afternoon, alone amongst computers and VDU screens. It occurs to me that apart from the dhow, in all this journey I have hardly ever seen a ship steered by a human being, except when going into port.

Christian shrugs and looks gloomy. Even on a successful and expanding line like this one, the future is not good for seamen. He is from the Faroe Islands, of which I know nothing apart from their frequent starring roles in weather forecasts. I certainly didn't know that they have their own Parliament, flag and language, and have never been members of NATO or the EEC. They're remote but not cold, lying in the path of the Gulf Stream. Shotguns are allowed on the island, pistols and rifles are not.

Tonight, Danish cold table with beer and Aquavit. Try two or three of the latter for my cold. No obvious relief but recurring dream of my grown-up boys as five-year-olds riding Shetland ponies. Faroes ... Shetland?

Day 75 8 December

Wake feeling much better. Head clearer and though there is a coffee cup-sliding swell out there, the ship copes with it much better than did the *Neptune Garnet.*

Christian, the Faroean, is alone on the bridge. He is one of the most lugubrious people I've ever met, but seems quite happy about it. He calculates our position for me.

For the first time in 75 days the chart shows Britain, and on a nautical map our favoured position is very clear. The fish-rich Continental shelf extends right around the British Isles and in places a hundred miles beyond, whereas it is only a thin strip along the coasts of France, Spain and Portugal. And the North Sea is covered in a black rash of oil rigs. We're making a respectable 22.1 knots and are 1,929 miles from New York.

There is, on the aft deck, lashed into a space which would have accommodated 50 containers, a very interesting piece of cargo. It's the shell of a slim, elegant sailing boat. It has no name, no superstructure, and the planks of its all-wood hull are wet and rotting, but someone must value it enough to pay the substantial amount to transport it at the cost of so much container space. Today Jesper solves a little of the mystery for me. The yacht dates from 1932, her destination is Felixstowe and she's being transported by the Sea Containers Group, whose chairman, James Sherwood, was responsible for the re-creation of the Orient Express.

Abandon my afternoon exercise as a wind strong enough to prevent walking, let alone running on deck, has appeared from nowhere. The Professor is concerned that there might be supernatural forces at work on the ship. He had lost his faithful tobacco tin, his navy sweater and now it seems that his whisky bottle is suffering from the Widow's Curse syndrome. No matter how much he drinks it seems to maintain the same level. It has been a long journey and I suppose one of us was bound to crack up.

Day 76 9 December

The sea is calming. Quite the opposite of what's supposed to happen on the Atlantic at this time of year. I lie in bed this morning and seriously consider what it will be like to be back home. Up till now I've not allowed my thoughts to take such a morale-threatening direction for very long, but now it seems increasingly likely that the Bombay astrologer's prognostications will be accurate. I realise for the first time that I shall miss this journey, which many times I couldn't wait to end. At sea the pace of life slows to a very agreeable level, and the thought of a return to city life is not, this morning, as tempting as I expected it to be. In fact I could easily go round again.

The Danes seem private people, not given to drawing attention to themselves, and despite having been six days on the *Leda Maersk* we keep meeting members of the crew we've never seen before – today a thickly bearded Captain Haddock of a man appears in the engine-room lift. He, like one or two others of the crew, seemed determinedly uncommunicative. Not so the captain who is becoming quite mischievous at the expense of the company, whose representative, Jesper, supervises every aspect of our filming.

We're talking at lunch about lucky and unlucky ships. It took three attempts before the champagne bottle broke at *Leda Maersk*'s launch, which the captain says is not a good omen. I asked him if there were any likelihood of a ghost on board.

'Not on an A. P. Moller ship,' was his brisk reply. 'He doesn't allow them!'

Much laughter from the crew, less from Jesper.

The company will have the last laugh though. The captain admits that in future a ship of this size will only need five officers to man it, and Noel, the Indian radio operator, knows he will be one of the first to go. Plans are to do away with radio operators entirely within the next two or three years. Supervision of a largely automated radio-room will be added to the duties of one of the other officers. Noel is dubious about how they will cope without an independent operator, especially at times of emergency when the others may all be occupied elsewhere.

Even as we're talking to Noel, as if to underline the volatility and unpredictability which can upset the most rational man-made system, the news comes through of a massive earthquake in Armenia, with rumours of 100,000 killed.

Running on deck today for the last time, squeezing along the heavy-metal tunnels, with wind buffeting me gently and tugging at the tops of the waves, I realise I shall be very sad to leave the sea. I stop in the bows and look around me. Through 360 degrees nothing is to be seen. As far as the horizon, 15 to 20 miles away, there is only sea and sky. No noise except for the throb of the engines, the soft swish of the bow-wave and the flapping of the wind.

At supper Roger announces that he thinks his whisky bottle may be being replenished by a less than supernatural force.

Day 77 10 December

Today we should have our first sight of England. Make a big effort to fight ship-lag and get up for breakfast. At 7.30 it's pitch dark outside, and the temperature indicator on the refrigerated container outside my windows glows red '−0006F'. By 9 o'clock it's still dark, with a faint yellowing of the Eastern sky over a flat featureless sea. The terrors of December on the Atlantic have not materialised yet. Roger says he's now absolutely convinced someone is augmenting his whisky.

The captain doesn't come down for lunch today as he's promised his wife he'll lose a pound or two. Equally concerned crew members, including Lillian, gather in the engine room for a weekly weight-watcher's meeting, whilst outside we can see porpoises unconcerned with weight problems rise gracefully out of the sea, marking, along with wheeling sea-birds, our arrival in shallower waters. We're now on the Celtic Sea, in the evocatively named Western Approaches, familiar territory for all brought up on Nicholas Monsarrat's *The Cruel Sea*. On the bridge Bente takes out Admiralty Chart 2649 on which is the tip of Cornwall.

The richest detail on the chart is reserved not for land but for the sea, whose bed is annotated and named as thoroughly and richly as any corner of the countryside. We are sliding in over King Arthur Canyon, whose sides drop 3,430 fathoms and rise to 840. There's Haddock bank and Melville Knoll and Porcupine Sea Bight and Nymphe Bank and Shamrock Knoll. Inviting places one hopes never to see.

The charts have to be continually updated. A correction manual is issued each week. It's not that Newfoundland may have moved two inches to the right, but that things like oil rigs, traffic separation lanes, militarily restricted areas are changing all the time. Bente says that the big tankers will carry up to 3,000 charts on board at one time, because they rarely have fixed routes, being sent off to wherever the oil is available and most needed.

Also open on the bridge's wide map table is the next Admiralty chart – Lizard Point to Berry Head, a smaller-scale map of the English Channel, Central Part, a book of port operations and pilot services – open at Le Havre – and a Mariner's Routeing Guide Chart, incorporating passage planning charts. There is a book with full details of local currents. 'In the English Channel the streams separate on a line running Hastings–Dieppe.' As an old sentimentalist, I'm rather glad to see all this written material laid out beside the radar scanners and the computer screens.

After lunch we record for posterity our rendition of *Under Milk Wood* with Nigel bringing a fine Burtonian gravitas to the part of Eli Jenkins, the Professor giving the definitive Captain Cat and Dave scuttling between Willy Nilly, Third Drowned and the tape recorder. Angela, Ann and Simon all deserve Oscar nominations.

Considering only Nigel lays claim to Welsh blood it comes out well, and the final lines are still resounding as the pin-point of Bishop Rock lighthouse mounts the northern horizon. The Scilly Isles, then Lizard Point and the lights of the Cornish coast follow. Home base is tantalisingly close. If they could loan me a lifeboat I could be ashore in half an hour, and home three days early. As it is the English coast recedes as we turn away to the south for Le Havre and the estuary of the Seine, and soon the only lights I can see are those of other ships, and above me, of a magnificent night sky.

Day 78 11 December

Forty-eight hours to go before the deadline. Fogg at this same stage was literally burning his boat in an attempt to get the *Henrietta* to Liverpool. He's already got rid of the cabins, the bunks and the poop-deck. 'The next day ... they burned the masts, the rafts and the spars ... Passepartout, hewing, cutting, sawing, did the work of ten men. It was a perfect fury of demolition.' At least he was on the move. I have the uneasy feeling of being marooned.

In grey, characterless weather much like that when, eleven weeks ago today, I first caught sight of the French coast at

Boulogne, we are coming alongside the almost deserted container port of Le Havre. It's all rather anticlimactic. I remember the captain's concern to get his ship unloaded before the dockers had their Sunday lunch. Well, it's turned 10 o'clock and we're not even tied up yet. The Southampton ferry has sailed and all Passepartout and I can do is sit and wait. Remembering the dockers and their Sunday lunch gives us an idea, and as the trucks begin to roll past the gantry cranes and the unloading begins at a decent, if not manic pace, Passpartout and I leave the *Leda Maersk* and set off in search of a French Sunday Lunch.

We pass the smartest ship in Le Havre docks, a white-hulled multi-decked cruise liner, not from Monte Carlo or Bermuda, but from Russia. She's the only thing that is smart in what is essentially an industrial complex, and the French, cultivators of the comfortable lifestyle, builders of handsome cities and attractive villages, are quite unsentimental when it comes to industry, so there's not much attempt to conceal the grime as we walk up beside a railway track with silos and warehouses on one side and the sad and derelict remains of the transatlantic passenger terminal on the other. That the glamour of the place where the great liners docked should be thus reduced is quite a shock and reminds me how long ago it was that I fell in love with Jane Russell in *The French Line*.

An hour's walk brings us at last into the town itself. The centre, destroyed by bombs in the Second World War, has been rebuilt without flair. Long low terraces are dull in scale and finish and present a dour background to the waterfront area. Quick look in the cathedral, from which people in their Sunday best are emerging after mass. A slightly mad-looking man is trying to get the priest's attention. The priest eventually throws him out.

In these unpromising surroundings we come across a restaurant which serves us a superb five-course lunch and which is by extraordinary and suitable coincidence designed like a railway train. It is family-run and cramped in the French style, and we wonder if it's to save space that the patron employs his tiny son as a waiter. Nigel asks the boy his age. He looks about eleven but turns out to be even younger.

'He's seven,' translates Nigel after a brief conversation.

'No ... no!' the boy protests vigorously. 'Seven*teen*!'

We don't stint the wine, and drinking the likes of Sancerre and Gigondas after all we've been through is like finding a waterfall in the desert. The walk back to the *Leda Maersk* seems much shorter and more convivial, and though none of us is admitting it, this unscheduled lunch in Le Havre had a definite celebratory air.

We leave France at seven in the evening. The weather is settled. The Channel is millpond calm. There's a chill in the air as we move slowly out toward the harbour wall of the fishing port which Francis I christened Le Havre de Grace in 1516. Past the euphoniously named Bassin Théophile Du Crocq and a last illuminated Christmas tree and onto the high seas again.

As soon as we're clear of the sodium glare of the city lights another wonderful night sky is revealed. It reminds me of nights on the Bay of Bengal, but as Captain Rodebaek points out, it's better. There's more to see in the northern sky.

The day ends with a party, of which I dimly remember a tug of war in which a BBC team, sapped by over-confidence and French Sunday lunch, were pulled to defeat, and a 16-person doubles table tennis tournament in which the Professor and myself triumphed by a whisker over Jesper and Erik the accountant.

At one point we listened to our recording of *Under Milk Wood*. Noel, the radio operator, was so taken with it he asked for a copy to take back to his wife. Listening to it with him was particularly appropriate, for Noel has maintained the Indian presence that has been such a feature of my journey. If I were superstitious I'd say that this presence has brought us luck, and as I stand with a buzzing head at the deck rail at two in the morning, watching us turn North through the Straits of Dover on seas of almost freakish tranquillity, I think back to the twenty-eighth day when Jagjit Uppal told my fortune and wonder whether this whole journey wasn't made in Bombay. A last few deep breaths of sea air and back to my cabin to pack my bag and deflate my world for the last time.

Day 79 12 December

Four hours' sleep and up to catch the dawn over the Suffolk coast. A golden sun is rising slowly into a clear sky as we approach the low-lying, neat green shoreline, with Harwich's old church and surrounding houses sitting on their low headland and Felixstowe opposite. I didn't expect such a caricature of England. Felixstowe seems tiny compared to the ports I've visited round the world – a container terminal John Betjeman might have approved of. Not hugely out of scale with the undemonstrative coastline and giving way quite quickly to green fields beyond. There is hardly a ripple enough on the surface of the North Sea to ring the mournful bell on the big green buoy that stands at the entrance to the port. We are home on a morning of glassy calm.

The pilot is already on the bridge, supervising our approach. On this journey pilots have been like heralds, embodying the first sight and sounds of new places.

So I know exactly where I am as I hear, 'We're going to swing her in, we'll need two tugs,' spoken in the dry matter-of-fact English professional monotone. I'm back in police stations and Crown courts and customs sheds and airline cockpits and doctors' waiting rooms. 'Dead Slow,' he orders, and jokes to Captain Rodebaek about a friend who's just come back from a holiday in Spain: 'He got a whole year's rain in three days!'

The captain smiles but only out of habit. Maybe there is always this feeling of strain between captains and pilots.

With the tug *Brightwell* at our stern and *Victoria* of Liverpool at the bow, we wend our way between the marker buoys into the mouth of the Orwell. A seaman (and I realise that, unlike the *Garnet*, I know hardly any of the names of this crew) selects a Union Jack from the wooden pigeonholes full of national flags and goes outside to run it up the mast. The pilot talks to one of the tugs:

'Give her a helping hand, *Victoria*, starboard bow.'

We are aiming for a mooring beside *Canadian Explorer* of Hong Kong, and a Russian ship. Bente stands in the bow with her walkie-talkie, Danish flag fluttering above her, and blonde hair streaming from beneath her 'Maersk Line' baseball cap. A strange wild Nordic figure in her light blue deck overalls.

For me this is the end of an epic and unusual journey. I'm almost home. For Captain Rodebaek and his crew it's the first of a gruelling series of North Sea stop-overs. From Felixstowe they must cross to Antwerp, from Antwerp to Bremerhaven and Bremerhaven to Hamburg, before turning and heading down the Channel again to Singapore. This is where the crews earn their money, and while TV presenters drool at sunrises, they have only a week of sleepless nights to look forward to.

I unfold a small piece of paper given to me by the jolly German chef as I said goodbye to him this morning. He said it summed up the sailor's lot: 'We the Willing, led by the Unknowing, are doing the impossible for the ungrateful. We have done so much for so long with so little, we are now qualified to do anything with nothing.' As we disembark, Passepartout admits to having supplemented the Professor's whisky bottle each night of the journey – four before he even noticed.

Have to keep reminding myself that it's not over yet, and will not be until I'm inside the Reform Club again. A *Leda Maersk* truck gives me a lift through the tidy, well-kept streets of Felixstowe to the railway station. There is no train for an hour, so we repair to the Moat House Hotel across the road. Ironically the hotel bar has a colonial feel. The only other customers apart from ourselves are elderly ladies ordering scotch and sodas. I fantasise that they are widows of men who travelled, maintaining the tradition of the quick snifter before tiffin. A young barmaid with strident lipstick plays listlessly with a beer mat. Though I've been hurtling round the world, against the clock, my progress has been marked by moments like these, still pools at the side of the stream, where for a while, nothing at all moves.

At half-past twelve, well into my last twenty-four hours, I pick up the local two-car diesel and we rumble off towards Ipswich. England looks greener than anywhere else in the world. And much neater than I remember. On the Inter-City train from Ipswich to London I decide to treat myself to a Great British Lunch and receive instead a Great British Apology.

'I'm very sorry, sir, there's no chef and no food, but I can offer you afternoon tea.' So I have afternoon tea at five past one, and very good it is too.

Liverpool Street station is a building site and has been for two years, but we're in on time.

There then occurs something which could have put Passepartout, me and the astrologer out of business in a big way. Our Central Line train from Liverpool Street to Oxford Circus pulls into Tottenham Court Road station. No sooner have the doors slid open than a disembodied warning voice rings round the platform, which I notice with a shock is completely empty.

'Stay on the train! Stay on the train! There is a suspect package at the station. Stay on the train! Do *not* alight here.'

It's the first time that I've seen the Professor, a veteran traveller and hard man to scare, lose his colour. It drains from his face as I imagine it must be draining from mine. For a frozen moment we are stuck beside an empty platform far below the ground with a 'suspect package'.

We look at each other, the same thought crossing all our minds. After all we've been through. There is a moment's complete silence. Breaths are held. Then, not a moment too soon, the doors swish closed.

After that London never recovers. It is like being back in the very pit of hell. At Oxford Circus the Christmas lights stretch away into the distance, and the Christmas spirit is similarly stretched. We attempt to film me buying a newspaper, to confirm my date of arrival, and are subjected to a volley of abuse from the vendor such as we've experienced nowhere else on the journey. When we do buy a paper, the front page is full of grim pictures of the Clapham rail disaster, which had happened as we were docking at Felixstowe. (All of us were sobered by the thought that if we had taken the Le Havre–Southampton ferry we could quite possibly have been on one of those trains.)

We hurry through the crowds down Regent Street, and at five minutes to five, shabby, tired, rushed and ruffled I stand before the steps of the Reform Club, seventy-nine days and seven hours since I had walked down them to go round the world. Would love to have bought Passepartout a drink, but we weren't allowed inside.

Afterword

Reflecting on the journey from a safe distance of five and a half months back home I cannot imagine quite how I did it. After all, I was exhausted at the end of Day 1. My body must have produced a Niagara of adrenaline to keep me on the road for the next 79. There was only time to keep going.

Of course I would do it again, but I know it would never be quite the same. Despite the best laid plans of the BBC we ended up bustling, hurrying, rushing, improvising to get ourselves home only by the skin of our teeth. And that's what made it worth doing. The smoother the journey, the duller it would have been.

The generosity with which people we met along the way gave us their time and their help increased my optimism for the future. Travel of this kind, travel when the hands get dirty, when contact is made, brought home to me how much we all see of the world on television and in the newspapers, and how little we know of it. Journeys like this can only be good for us. Perhaps it's time for 80-Day Circumnavigating to become a recognised pastime, then a sport and who knows, eventually an Olympic event.

Another Afterword

A bit of sad news. Nigel, Ron and Julian Passepartout have faced prison for their pains. Together with Angela and Clem they were arrested for a train-spotting offence while filming extra shots for the series in Egypt. They were released after a few hours after giving the police some story about going round the world in 80 days.

Around the World in 80 Days

Revisited

Dubai 8 October 2008

TWENTY YEARS AGO, following in the steps of Phileas Fogg, the journey from London to Dubai had taken Passepartout and me fifteen days. Today an Emirates Airbus brought us here in seven hours. Twenty years ago, Dubai was a desert town with a population of 350,000. Today it numbers one and a half million and more are arriving as fast as they can build homes for them. And that doesn't include the six million visitors who stop off here every year.

In October 1988 we put up at one of a tiny handful of hotels. Now there are over five hundred to choose from, including the Burj Al Arab which calls ifself a seven-star hotel and serves a cocktail costing £3,800 a shot. The minarets and mosques which defined the skyline have been overshadowed by secular constructions, including the Burj Dubai ('burj' meaning a tower), currently the world's tallest building, in which you can live and work 2,500 feet above the ground. There are plans to top even this, with a tower that will be more than a kilometre high. The *International Herald Tribune* describes the city as 'Las Vegas on steroids'.

At the Dubai Off-Shore Sailing Club, I meet up with Bill Nelson. As Head of Ports and Customs Bill had been our first point of contact twenty years ago. Now eighty-six, in poor health and having to leave Dubai as his house is to be bulldozed to make way for the new airport, he was in remarkably good humour. He gives me the number of his one-time deputy, Khamis Ghamil, who actually found us the *Al Shama*, and who is now himself Head of Ports and Customs.

Captain Khamis agrees to meet us the next day, which gives me a chance to sample some of the delights of the new Dubai. As we head out to the Jumeirah quarter, one new tower after another rises on either side of us and progress on the twelve-lane Sheikh Zayed Highway is sluggish. Alongside runs an almost-completed monorail system which is due to open next year, though few believe that it will make much difference to the traffic. This is a shopping culture, and with the aid of modern technology the crowded souks and bazaars of the old Arab world have evolved into the colossal shopping malls of today. The New Emirates Mall, in which we find ourselves this morning, boasts one of the world's largest indoor ski slopes. The fact that the outside temperature is 37° C and that it hasn't snowed here for centuries is exactly the sort of reason why the developers created it. It seems that the only requirement for building schemes in Dubai is that they start with the impossible.

The brazen confidence of the city is personified in the face of Sheikh Mohammed, one of the Al Maktoum family which has run Dubai for 175 years. His likeness is everywhere, reminding the foreigners who comprise over 70 per cent of the population that the Arabs are still masters here. This morning I feel his craggy features and gimlet eyes on my back as I walk past a billboard on my way to take an *abra*, a water-taxi, to the Customs House. *Abras* are a rare example in this city of cheap and cheerful public transport. Little more than floating benches with a thin roof providing cover from the fiercest of the heat, they provide a continuous ferry service across the Creek at its most attractive point, close to the old Bastakia quarter whose narrow alleyways and shining domes remind me more of Venice than Vegas.

Captain Khamis greets me with a broad smile. His face has filled out and though he's now Head of Customs, and a husband and father, he wears his responsibilities with the same unhurried ease which I found both comforting and a little worrying twenty years earlier. He takes me to Al Hamriya, the same small cargo dock from which I sailed with *Al Shama*. Khamis tells me *Al Shama* would have been tiny by today's standards, with new dhows of two thousand tonnes being built, and horror of horrors, some of them made of fibreglass. But as I stand watching a chain of Indian labourers unloading apples, and the gentle rise and fall of wooden hulls two or three deep at the dockside, I can easily recapture that combination of fear and fascination with which I stepped aboard the boat that was to carry us across to Bombay all those years ago.

Khamis can't give us much help, as he hasn't seen *Al Shama* since the day we left, but he does offer to find me a similar-sized dhow leaving Dubai, so at least I can relive the past for an hour or two. He wangles me aboard a boat heading for Bandar-e Bushehr in Iran. As on *Al Shama* the conditions are still basic. The crew live, literally, on top of their cargo, and the only real change I notice is that they have an on-board, rather than outboard, lavatory. At the dockside the crew seems nervous and suspicious, but once away from the authorities they relax, asking me all sorts of questions in severely fractured English. I show them the DVD of the original dhow journey, which they watch with amazement. Though we don't have much time away from Dubai, it's long enough for me to feel strangely at home, whilst at the same time asking myself, as I try to get comfortable on covers of greasy tarpaulin, how I ever survived a week on a boat like this.

Mumbai 14 October 2008

Superficially it seems that Dubai reeks of opulence and Mumbai reeks of poverty. In fact both are illusions. There are armies of Asian construction workers living in Dubai on less than two hundred dollars a month, and, as well as the street beggars and the huge slums of Mumbai there are more millionaires here than in any other Indian city. Dubai is an indoor, air-conditioned world. In Mumbai life is out on the streets: noisy, demanding, relentless and inescapable. We've not been long in a traffic jam from the airport when I hear a persistent tap-tapping on the side of our minibus and a moment later the stumps of two arms appear at the window and a face, teeth bared and eyes wide, peers up beseechingly. Then the traffic moves on. Near the hotel women with babes in arms hold out cupped hands. Nothing seems to be very different from when I walked in through the Gate of India twenty years ago, except of course for the name of the place. Since 1995, at the instigation of the Shiv Sena political party, strong Maharashtrian nationalists, Bombay has become Mumbai and Victoria Station, from which I left for Madras, the Chhatrapati Shivaji Terminus. Not everyone approves of these changes, just as not everyone approves of the hard-line policies of Shiv Sena, whose leaders have whipped up sectarian hatred against anyone they see as outsiders, including fellow Indians, if they happen to be Muslim or born outside Maharashtra state.

The Taj Hotel is still here and thriving, and their welcome is friendly and congenial. Garlanded with marigolds, I'm for a moment tempted into thinking I'm to be given the Rajput Suite, the most luxurious accommodation in an already luxurious hotel, but it turns out they're just showing me where John Lennon, Yoko Ono and, later, George Harrison stayed. I'm in Room 276.

From the BBC files, we know the name of the ship brokers who chartered *Al Shama*, Dewkaran Moorjee and Sons. At first we draw a blank. The phone numbers have all had extra digits added to cope with Mumbai's growing population, which has increased from around 10 to around 18 million since we were last here. The new number puts us through to a company called Damodar Dharamshi and Co, which inherited Dewkaran Moorjee's business. Its run by a man called Digant Joshi, who sounds busy but agrees to look in his files for us.

I spend next day reacquainting myself with Mumbai in the company of a knowledgeable lady called Jyoti Namaste. We meet up at Churchgate Station. With only four platforms, two in and two out, this unprepossessing terminus performs minor miracles, managing to process six or seven million passengers every day. At rush-hour the trains come in and out every one minute, thirty-eight seconds. Two of them are reserved for ladies only. Jyoti says it only works because punctuality is near-perfect and the rolling stock, ancient and battle-scarred, completely dependable. Mind you, they don't have any doors on the coaches, which must help speed things up.

We alight from the train at Mahalaxmi station, beside which is the largest of the city's open-air, soap and stone laundries. Built in British times, it is worked by five hundred dhobis – laundrymen – all from the same 'fourth caste', the working class. They collect laundry, wash it in pens of water, then beat the dirt out on a stumpy granite stone.

I road-test their service with a pair of chinos, terminally oil-stained from my brief sojourn on the Iranian dhow. I was on the point of giving up on them, but after a good thrashing my dhobi hands them back to me without a stain to be seen. I'm raving about this new, natural, chemical-free approach to laundry when Roger brings me down to earth. 'So you'll be buying Helen a stone for Christmas, then?'

The offices of Damodar Dharamshi and Co, formerly Dewkaran Moorjee and Sons, are in an infernally busy street in the Dockyard area of Mumbai. A constant stream of men and goods passes by; handcarts piled high with plastic piping, enormous cardboard boxes balanced on tiny heads. Digant Joshi is a shortish, well-built man, mid-forties I'd guess, with thick black hair and neatly trimmed moustache. From him I learn the sad news that *Al Shama* is no more. She sank to the bottom of the Arabian Sea, quite peacefully and with no loss of life, whilst being towed by her new owners along the coast of Gujarat. Digant has better news of the crew, some of whom, including the captain, are, he thinks, living up in the town of Mandvi in Kutch, the northernmost part of Gujarat. He has information that the captain lives in the Sulaiya district of the town.

'Everyone will know him,' he says confidently.

Which is why we find ourselves at Bandra Terminus to catch the overnight Kutch Express. It sounds romantic but sadly isn't. The windows are tiny and dirty and the heavy metal light covers and roof fans give the odd impression of being in a submarine. Obligingly, they leave the doors at the end of each coach open and I fight off incipient claustrophobia by standing at the doorway as we rumble northwards. An hour out of Mumbai the countryside looks timeless and serene, bathed in the dusty pink glow of the setting sun. Only thirteen more hours to go.

We eventually reach the town of Bhuj, the capital of Kutch and the end of the line, some fifteen hours after leaving Mumbai. On Republic Day, 26 January 2001, a terrible tragedy befell this place. Bhuj was close to the epicentre of an earthquake with a strength of 8.9, and at least 80,000 were killed. Aid and reconstruction came quickly and the central area of town is apparently much improved, with wider streets and better-built, low-rise accommodation. But there are some buildings which still stand as witnesses to the power of the earthquake, including the Jubilee Hospital, once a fine example of the graceful Anglo-Indian style, her strong stone walls now cracked and tottering.

As we drive to Mandvi, forty miles due south, the surroundings become less industrial and the countryside greener. Fields of cows and narrow lanes with their arches of overhanging trees remind me of East Anglia. Mandvi is approached by a bridge over a very dry tidal creek. There has always been a shipbuilding industry here. Its heyday was the 18th century when four hundred ships were moored up in the estuary, including one that went all the way to England. Now, with the pile-up of sediment, it's a shadow of its former self.

We're staying just outside the town, in a 'beach resort' comprising ten colourfully striped tents and a dog that howls like a maniac in the night. The tented camp, beside a long, fine, virtually empty beach, is the property of the Maharao of Kutch. The Maharao, or to give him his full title, HH Maharao Shri Pragmalji Madansinhji III, 19th Maharao of Kutch, apparently owns not just the coast but the sea as well. When I meet him later he clarifies this. He only owns the sea at high tide, when it comes up over *his* beach. He has a very fine palace next door, open to the public, with polite signs everywhere ranging from 'No Firearms' to 'Kindly Remove Footwear And Maintain Decorum'.

Mandvi, Kutch   20 October 2008

This morning we prepare for the climax of our trip, the reunion with Captain Suleyman. Digant Joshi mentioned Salaiya, which turns out to be the district across the river from the main town. So clogged is the estuary that the sea channel at low tide can be waded across, as some do, walking beside, and almost as fast as, the leisurely punted ferry. As I disembark I notice the green flag of Islam fluttering above a cemetery, reminding me that the captain and his crew were all Indian Muslims.

Digant was right. Everyone I speak to knows Hassan Suleyman. Indeed most of them seem to be related to him. But when I find his house its location is almost too good to be true. Outside the front door, between the house and the sea, looms a huge, half-constructed dhow.

This is the moment of truth. The captain knows I'm in town but doesn't know exactly when I'm coming to see him, and the moment when we meet can only be filmed once. Even at this late stage I have misgivings. What if it's the wrong Captain Suleyman? It's a common enough name. And if it isn't, how much will he really want to see me again?

A cat lies stretched across one of the three front-door steps, oblivious to the moment. I'm suddenly aware of how very hot it is. Then Nigel runs the camera and I step up to a pair of white wooden doors, decorated with an abstract shell-like pattern, and knock.

I hear his voice before I see him and I know I've got the right man. The door is pulled open and there he is. The man who welcomed me on *Al Shama* at Dubai now welcomes me, with open arms, to his house in Mandvi. He's put on weight, his face is fuller and his beard well-trimmed and distinguished. As he clasps me in a powerful embrace I sense that this man, a little jumpy on the dhow journey, has matured into someone of substance, a Godfather of the dhow world.

He ushers me into a long thin courtyard, and suddenly from the darkened interior of the house come other faces I recognise. Anwar, the cabin boy with the shock of black curls, is now thirty-six, married to Suleyman's daughter and a captain of a ship in his own right. Ibrahim the Chief Engineer grasps my hand as does Kishore the 2nd Engineer and, long before I'd intended to, I bring out my portable DVD player and put on the episode in which we all starred and everyone squeezes round for a look.

Captain Suleyman keeps up a running commentary as each member of the crew appears on the film. Kasim, the old man who listened to Bruce Springsteen and walked on my back, is dead, so is the cook and Deyji Ramji, the studious-looking navigator. Mahomet, Anwar's father, who had talked on film about his preference for working on dhows for no money, rather than supertankers for a lot of money, is not so well now, the captain says. A couple of minutes later the front door opens behind us and there he is, his skin drawn tight across his face, his figure brittle and thin, but his face wide in a smile.

It's all happened so fast, but I can think of no better way for it to have happened. Mandvi may be over four thousand miles from London, but here beside the dhows of the future with my friends of the past it is a home from home. Twenty years ago I said it was 'almost impossible to accept that I shall never see them again'. Today, here in Mandvi, we celebrate the art of the possible.

Acknowledgements

It's impossible to list all the individuals, companies, organisations and governments who helped me round the world. Most are in the book. Among those who aren't, I would especially like to thank: Romany Helmy, Don Bannerman, Captain Bill Nelson, Shernaz Italia, Bruno Burigana, Ian Markham-Smith, Mark Tozer, Sandy Gall, Alan Whicker, Huw Young-Jones, Dave Thomas, Howard Billingham, Brian Hall, Kitty Anderson, Anne James, Alison Davies and, at BBC Books, Linda Blakemore, Sarah Hoggett and Suzanne Webber.

Acknowledgements for new chapter

Thanks to all those who made our return journey possible. Many are already named in the text, but I should like to add my debt of gratitude to our crew: Roger Mills, director, and Nigel Meakin on camera (companions on the road for over twenty years now), John Pritchard, for sound and photographs, Vanessa Courtney for immaculate planning and organisation – and photographs. To Steve Abbott, Sue Grant, Paul Bird, Lyn Dougherty and Mimi Robinson at Prominent and Richard Klein at the BBC.

And to Clem Vallance, who dreamt up the *Eighty Days* idea all those years ago.

Picture credits